W9-BRD-427

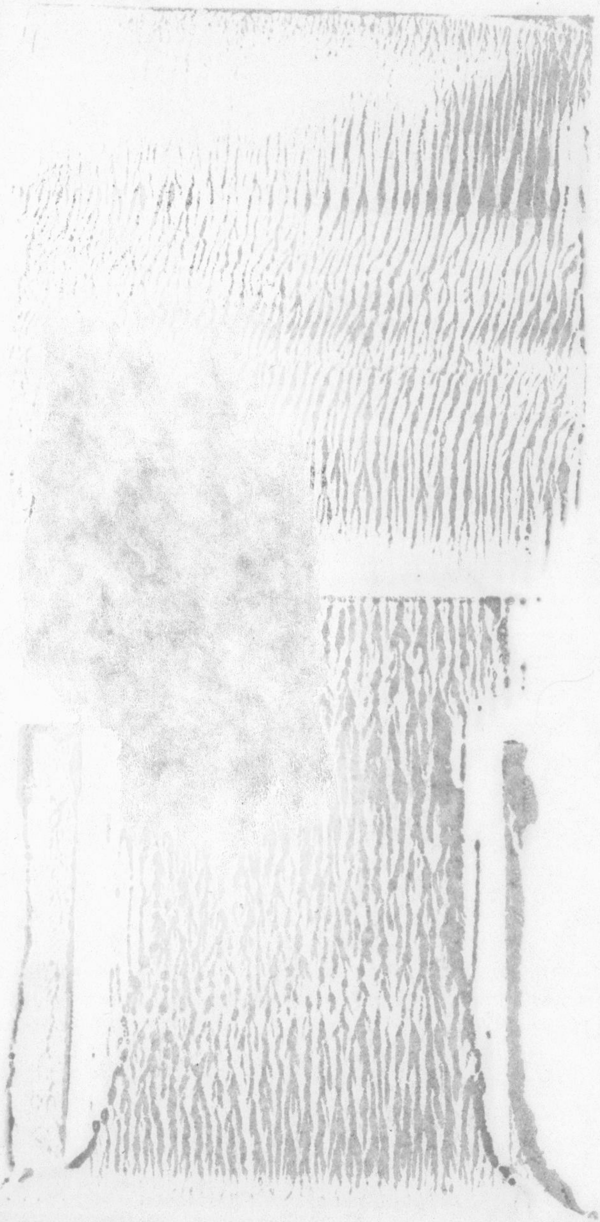

DICTIONARY OF FICTIONAL CHARACTERS

by
WILLIAM FREEMAN

Revised by
FRED URQUHART

With Indexes of Authors and Titles by
E. N. PENNELL

BOSTON

THE WRITER, INC.

PUBLISHERS

Published in Great Britain by J. M. Dent and Sons Ltd.

Published in the United States by THE WRITER, INC.
1974

Reprinted 1977

Library of Congress Cataloging in Publication Data

Freeman, William, 1880–
Dictionary of fictional characters.
1. English literature—Dictionaries. 2. American literature—Dictionaries. 3. Characters and characteristics in literature—Dictionaries. I. Urquhart, Fred, 1912– ed. II. Title.
PR19.F7 1974 820'.3 73–18065
ISBN 0–87116–085–4

Printed in the United States of America

DICTIONARY OF FICTIONAL CHARACTERS

CONTENTS

ACKNOWLEDGMENTS

IN A BOOK that during many months has passed from a mere idea to final materialization, it would be a literal impossibility to thank all the people, in a private capacity or as representatives of public authorities, who have helped so generously. But a few at least may be mentioned. They include the librarian (Mr Awdry) of the National Liberal Club, Mr Frank Easton of the Essex County Library, the head librarian and assistants of Chelmsford Borough Library, the Westminster Public Library, and the publishers' own staff.

The army of 'private suggestors' (to invent a term) must remain anonymous.

And finally, of course, the typist-secretary-collaborator-sternest critic. (But she has had three books dedicated to her already.)

W. F.

INTRODUCTION

ANY dictionary, concise or otherwise, is, from A to Z, handicapped by certain fundamental and inescapable limitations.

The first is that it cannot hope to be wholly up to date. A living language is permanently in a state of development; and English is the most vital of them all. Daily, one might almost say hourly, there are additions and modifications to its vocabulary, already numbering approximately half a million words. While a dead language—Latin is the obvious example—is always vulnerable to changes in pronunciation.

The second handicap, common to all works of reference, from the monumental *Dictionary of National Biography* to the humblest paper-covered crossword guide, is the necessity for a certain degree of selection. And selection, even when tersely and colourlessly recorded, is bound to reflect the likes, prejudices and general make-up of the recorder, however much he may pride himself on his detachment.

This particular work of reference has in addition unique handicaps of its own, principally owing to the fact of its being very much off the beaten track. It includes the names of 20,000 fictitious characters, derived from approximately 2,000 books written by some 500 authors of British, Commonwealth and American nationality during the past six centuries, and covers novels, short stories, poems and plays (the last-named being non-musical, with the exception of Gilbert & Sullivan and John Gay's two operas). Classic but non-human creations such as Black Beauty, the Jabberwock, Bagheera and Winnie-the-Pooh are also there.

This collection involved an almost fantastic number of complications. What authors it was necessary to include, what merely advisable, what definitely worth while; what books our selected authors had written, and eventually which characters in the selected books. (True, there were certain absolutely essential entrants, along with practically all their works: Shakespeare, Dickens, Scott, Hardy, Kipling, Wells, Jane Austen, the Brontës. But even the *élite* of literature included characters who were not worth bothering about.) [1]

There also arose the problem of semi-classics, ranging from one to half a dozen, which have achieved a permanent and universal popularity out of a total output of many readable but undistinguished and now forgotten works by the same authors. Blackmore, Mrs Henry Wood,

[1] The play *Henry VIII* is attributed in the present work to Shakespeare, in accordance with early tradition, though it is now commonly believed to be by Fletcher and Massinger, with passages from Shakespeare's hand.

The author has made no attempt to assign to Beaumont or Fletcher separately certain plays now believed to be by one or other though traditionally attributed to both.—[Publisher's Note.]

Marryat and Mrs Braddon will serve as examples. On the other hand there is a terrifying horde of writers who during the last hundred and fifty years achieved immense popularity, but whose works are now read only by literary explorers, ribald critics and an elderly, diminishing band of admirers. Where now are the reputations of the egregious Samuel Warren, the humourless Dean Farrar or Lady Florence Dixie (daughter of a marquis, who married 'a respectable baker'), of David Christie Murray and of Catherine Sinclair, whose novel *Modern Accomplishments*, fulsomely dedicated 'by permission' to Queen Victoria, ran into eight editions?

Anno Domini is as ruthless with literature as with the merely popular manifestations of the other arts. Nevertheless this phantom host had to be surveyed and considered, and, out of deference to the nostalgically minded reader, some of their works included.

A minor problem of an entirely different type was to determine where the line should be drawn separating fictional from historical characters (as distinct from those who were semi-historical or legendary). Sir Walter Scott provided a headache, inasmuch as he not only introduced real people to give variety and verisimilitude to his narratives, but light-heartedly altered dates and other details, either because it suited his immediate purpose or because he simply decided that it was too much trouble to check his facts. (Shakespeare, for example, appears as a guest of honour in 1575, when the dramatist was a schoolboy of eleven.) Thackeray on the other hand varies this process by entangling his historical characters with fictitious princes and nobles whose preposterously silly titles suggest a mid-Victorian Drury Lane pantomime.

A brief note concerning the general arrangement of the entries. Normally the principal character in a family is placed first, followed by husband or wife, children, parents and other relatives, in that order. But where descendants come into the story they are indented, to prevent confusion about who married whom, e.g.:

Jones, George.
  Barbara, his wife, *née* Brown.
  Emily, their daughter, m. Peter Robinson.
    Arthur, their son.
  Fanny, his aunt.

(Arthur is the child of Emily and Peter, and Fanny the aunt of the original George.)

The names of almost all wives are cross-indexed under their maiden names (except where these are barely mentioned and are of no importance); with them are included their own relations. There is by the way a distinction between 'Barbara, his wife,' which implies that the couple were married when the story began, and 'm. Barbara Brown,' which indicates that they get married in the course of the story (or that there is every prospect of their marrying shortly after the story is finished).

Illegitimate children appear under the surname by which they are known, with a cross-reference if necessary.

A few large and complicated families, whose records straggle on from century to century—the Forsytes, the Herrieses, the Newcomes, the Rakonitzes—refuse to fit in with this general plan, and are dealt with on their own merits by whatever arrangement best makes for clarity.

Quite frequently, surprisingly so in fact, characters are referred to by their authors by their Christian name only. In such cases, if sufficiently important, they are included under that name. In the rare cases where the surname though mentioned is almost unknown to the average reader (e.g. Little Nell) the character is cross-referenced under the Christian name.

De, de la, d'. Here the rule is that if the 'de' is virtually inseparable from the rest of the name, and the character is always alluded to with that prefix, it is indexed under 'D,' e.g. de Lyndesay. But where it is purely territorial, or not used in general conversation, it is ignored. (Cross-indexing in such cases is not practicable.)

The date given after a title is that of its original publication.[1] The absence of a date means that it cannot be traced with any certainty; but such cases are very rare. Generally speaking individual short stories, many of them drawn from anthologies, are undated; where the story appears in a collection under the author's name—e.g. 'William the Conqueror' in Kipling's *The Day's Work*—the date of the book is quoted.

Abbreviations have been reduced to a minimum. All are self-explanatory.

A final note. In the compilation of a dictionary which has occupied most of the waking, not to say sleeping, hours of the compilers for over two years, it is reasonably certain that, while every possible effort has been made to achieve accuracy, inaccuracies, omissions and inconsistencies will occur. Which reduced to commercial English amounts to E. & O. E. And for the benefit of the Carping Critic (I crown him with his inevitable, his unique adjective; no living creature except a critic ever did carp), let me add that he will assuredly discover also variations in style and in the presentation of details. But so long as the general reader finds the book fundamentally useful and interesting, I remain impenitent.

WILLIAM FREEMAN.

[1] Either in serial or in book form. In the case of plays the date is either of first presentation or of first authorized printing for public issue.—[Publisher's Note.]

PREFACE TO NEW EDITION

ALMOST every book of this kind is hallmarked by the idiosyncrasies of its compiler. Very few compilers are so objective that they don't show some quirks of tolerance or intolerance, affection or affectation, dislike, idolatrous adoration or blindness in their choice of authors or literary works to be represented. The late William Freeman was no exception. Neither am I.

One of Mr Freeman's quirks was his overpowering fondness for all the characters, no matter how obscure or unimportant, in the Kipling canon. Another was his devotion to the works of late Victorian novelists.

When the publishers asked me to bring Mr Freeman's *Dictionary* up to date, I wished I could start from scratch; for it isn't entirely satisfactory for any editor to patch up a work of this nature. Mr Freeman's ideas and mine do not exactly coalesce. However, I've done the best I can under the circumstances. Because of the time and costs factors involved in preparing this new edition, I've been unable to do anything about the overwhelming Kipling 'tribe' of 'lesser breeds within [or without] the law.' But I've ruthlessly eliminated about four hundred characters from novels by Madame Albanesi, Walter Besant, Rosa N. Carey, Mary Cholmondeley, F. Marion Crawford, Ellen T. Fowler, Edna Lyall, Lucas Malet and a few other late Victorians who are now unread and forgotten except by a handful of very old readers.

To replace them, and to attempt to bring the *Dictionary* more into keeping with modern ideas, I have added 1,614 new references. These references give the names and details of over 2,000 characters taken from some 360 novels and plays. This includes about 180 works by 90 contemporary authors, works which either had not been published when Mr Freeman made his compilation or which he hadn't considered important enough to mention, and 180 recent works by 88 authors already represented. It also includes characters from the works of about ten great authors of the past, such as Thomas Dekker, John Skelton, John Webster, George Borrow, Stephen Crane, Baron Corvo (Frederick Rolfe), Siegfried Sassoon and Ronald Firbank, who were omitted by some extraordinary oversight from the original edition.

These additions of mine are also, no doubt, open to criticism. I'm well aware of it, but I have tried my best to be objective. I would have liked to include many more contemporary authors who have produced memorable characters, as well as older authors whose work is not properly represented (Compton Mackenzie, for instance), but to have done so would have meant making this a much bigger and more expensive volume.

I wish to thank Mrs Herta Ryder, Miss Anne Carter, Mr Graham Stewart and Mr Peter Wyndham Allen for suggestions made in the compiling of this new edition, and I am most grateful to Mr C. M. Smith and the staff of the Uckfield Public Library for their help in getting the books I wished to consult.

FRED URQUHART.

A

Aaron, a Moor, loved by Tamora. *Titus Andronicus* (play), W. Shakespeare.

Aaron. *See* 'Riah.

Abarak, hunchback magician. *The Shaving of Shagpat,* G. Meredith, 1856.

Abbas, Ismail, sheriff. *Saïd the Fisherman,* M. Pickthall, 1903.

Abbas Bey, Mudir of the Fayoum. 'The Eye of the Needle' (s.s.), *Donovan Pasha,* Gilbert Parker, 1902.

Abbeville, Horace. *Cannery Row,* J. Steinbeck, 1945.

Abbott, Sir Buckstone, Bt.

Alice ('Toots'), *née* Bulpitt, his wife.

Imogen ('Jane'), their daughter, m. Joe Vanringham.

Summer Moonshine, P. G. Wodehouse, 1938.

Abbott, Caroline, with whom Lilia Herriton goes to Italy. *Where Angels Fear To Tread,* E. M. Forster, 1905.

Abbott, Jerusha, 'oldest orphan,' central character, m. Jervis Pendleton. *Daddy-Long-Legs,* Jean Webster, 1912.

Abbott family, the, cousins of the Dodsons. *The Mill on the Floss,* George Eliot, 1860.

Abdael. *Absalom and Achitophel* (poem), J. Dryden, 1681.

Abdalla, Saracen slave. *Ivanhoe,* W. Scott, 1819.

Abdallah, murdered by his brother. *The Bride of Abydos* (poem), Lord Byron, 1820.

Abdallah, Caliph. *Kismet* (play), E. Knoblock, 1911.

Abdallah el Hadgi (The Pilgrim), Saladin's ambassador. *The Talisman,* W. Scott, 1825.

Abderrahman, Emir. *The Tragedy of the Korosko,* A. Conan Doyle, 1898.

Abdiel, a seraph. *Paradise Lost* (poem), J. Milton, 1667.

Abdul Gafur, Gisborne's servant.

His daughter, m. Mowgli.

'In the Rukh' (s.s.), *Many Inventions,* R. Kipling, 1893.

Abdulla, chief of Syed Arab trading-post. *Almayer's Folly,* J. Conrad, 1895.

Abdullah, old Tunisian thief who disappears. *The Tremor of Forgery,* Patricia Highsmith, 1969.

Abdullah Khan, one of the 'Four,' with Dost Akbar, Mahomet Singh and Jonathan Small. *The Sign of Four,* A. Conan Doyle, 1890.

Abdur Rahman, G.C.S.I., Amir of Afghanistan. 'The Amir's Homily' (s.s.), *Life's Handicap,* 1891, and 'Ballad of the King's Mercy' (poem), *Barrack-room Ballads,* 1892, R. Kipling.

Abednego, Moses, clerk to the Independent W. Diddlesex Insurance Co. *The Great Hoggarty Diamond,* W. M. Thackeray, 1841.

Abel, a farmer.

His wife, a housekeeper.

Middlemarch, Geo. Eliot, 1871–2.

Abel, Guevez de Argensola ('Mr Abel'), Venezuelan explorer and traveller, central character and narrator. *Green Mansions,* W. H. Hudson, 1904.

Abellino, central character. *The Bravo of Venice,* M. G. Lewis, 1805.

Aben Ezra, Raphael. *Hypatia,* C. Kingsley, 1853.

Aberfordbury, Lord. *See* Ogilvy Hibberd.

Abergavenny, Lord. *Henry the Eighth* (play), W. Shakespeare.

Aberystwith, Delilah. 'Delilah' (poem), *Departmental Ditties,* R. Kipling, 1886.

Abessa, a damsel. *The Faërie Queene* (poem), E. Spenser, 1590.

Abhorson, executioner. *Measure for Measure* (play), W. Shakespeare.

Abinger, Colonel.

Mary, his daughter, m. Rob Angus.

When a Man's Single, J. M. Barrie, 1888.

Abinger, Mrs Ellie, of the Corner

Stores, Portobello Road; adopts Joy Stretton.
George, her husband.
Phyll, George's sister.
Violet, Phyll's daughter.
Joy and Josephine, Monica Dickens, 1948.

Able, Private Peter. *A Sleep of Prisoners* (play), Christopher Fry, 1951.

Ablett, Mr. *Trelawny of the Wells* (play), A. W. Pinero, 1898.

Ablett, Mark.
Robert, his brother.
The Red House Mystery, A. A. Milne, 1922.

Ablewhite, Godfrey, financier and swindler. *The Moonstone,* W. Collins, 1868.

Abney, Mr. 'Lost Hearts' (s.s.), *Ghost Stories of an Antiquary,* M. R. James, 1910.

Abney, Arnold, proprietor, Stanstead House School. *The Little Nugget,* P. G. Wodehouse, 1913.

Abou Taher Achmed, Emir of Masre.
Ghulendi, his wife.
Vathek, W. Beckford, 1786.

Abram, servant to Montague. *Romeo and Juliet* (play), W. Shakespeare.

Abrams, Moss, money-lender. *Pendennis,* W. M. Thackeray, 1848–50.

Abramson, Jake, 'old, subtle, sensual.' *You Can't Go Home Again,* T. Wolfe, 1947.

Abreskov, Paul, Bolshevik enemy of Saskia. *Huntingtower,* J. Buchan, 1922.

Absalom. *Absalom and Achitophel* (poem), J. Dryden, 1681.

Absolute, Sir Anthony.
Captain Jack, his son, alias Ensign Beverley.
The Rivals (play), R. B. Sheridan, 1775.

Abu Bakr, Wazir. *Kismet* (play), E. Knoblock, 1911.

Acheson, double-crossing solicitor. *Campbell's Kingdom,* Hammond Innes, 1952.

Achillas. *Caesar and Cleopatra* (play), G. B. Shaw, 1900.

Achilles, Grecian commander. *Troilus and Cressida* (play), W. Shakespeare.

Achilles Tatius ('The Follower'), head of the Imperial Bodyguard. *Count Robert of Paris,* W. Scott, 1832.

Achitophel. *Absalom and Achitophel* (poem), J. Dryden, 1681.

Achsah, mad wife of Sadrach. 'A Father in Sion' (s.s.), *My People,* Caradoc Evans, 1915.

Ackerman ('Tacks'), doctor. 'Unprofessional' (s.s.), *Limits and Renewals,* R. Kipling, 1932.

Ackley, Robert, pupil at same school as Holden Caulfield. *The Catcher in the Rye,* J. D. Salinger, 1951.

Acland, Sir Thomas, cavalier. *Woodstock,* W. Scott, 1826.

Acrasia, witch. *The Faërie Queene* (poem), E. Spenser, 1590.

Acres, Bob. *The Rivals* (play), R. B. Sheridan, 1775.

Ada, a girl graduate. *Princess Ida* (comic opera), Gilbert & Sullivan, 1884.

Adair, Azalea, poverty-stricken writer, m. Major Wentworth Caswell. 'A Municipal Report' (s.s.), *Strictly Business,* O. Henry, 1910.

Adair, Hon. Robert. 'The Empty House' (s.s.), *The Return of Sherlock Holmes,* A. Conan Doyle, 1905.

Adair, Sally, m. David Eliot.
John, her father, artist.
The Herb of Grace, Elizabeth Goudge, 1948.

Adam. *Adam's Opera* (play), Clemence Dane, 1928.

Adam, servant to Oliver. *As You Like It* (play), W. Shakespeare.

Adam, Miss, landlady. *Daniel Deronda,* George Eliot, 1876.

Adam, John.
Mary, his wife. Central characters.
Holy Deadlock, A. P. Herbert, 1934.

Adam, Stephen, head gardener, narrator. 'The Gardener' (s.s.), *Here and Hereafter,* Barry Pain, 1911.

Adams, seaman, foster-father of Willy Peters; died in action. *The King's Own,* Captain Marryat, 1830.

Adams, grocer, Whipham Market. *The Adventures of Philip,* W. M. Thackeray, 1861–2.

Adams, Rev. Abraham, curate. *Joseph Andrews,* H. Fielding, 1742.

Adams, Miss Eliza.
Sadie, her niece.
The Tragedy of the Korosko, A. Conan Doyle, 1898.

Adams, Francis J., middle-aged American busy-body visiting Tunisia. *The Tremor of Forgery*, Patricia Highsmith, 1969.

Adams, Jack ('W.P.'), *Dombey and Son*, C. Dickens, 1848.

Adams, Captain Joe. *A Sleep of Prisoners*, Christopher Fry, 1951.

Adams, John, lieutenant and quartermaster. *The Spanish Farm* trilogy, R. H. Mottram, 1927.

Adams, Sam, wealthy business man; m. as 2nd wife Lucy Marling.
- **Amabel Rose,** their daughter.
- **Heather,** his daughter by 1st wife, m. Ted Pilward.

The *Barsetshire* series, Angela Thirkell, 1933 onwards.

Addams, F. Jasmine (Frankie), twelve-year-old girl, central character.
- **Royal Quincy Addams,** her father.
- **Jarvis,** her brother.
  - **Janice Evans,** Jarvis's bride.

The Member of the Wedding, Carson McCullers, 1946.

Addenbrooke, Bennett, lawyer, *Raffles*, E. W. Hornung, 1899–1901.

Addison, Rose. *Landmarks*, E. V. Lucas, 1914.

Addison, Thyra, fashion writer, *Chicago Sentinel*, Paris. *Trial by Terror*, P. Gallico, 1952.

Aderyn, the Bird Queen, mother of Llew. *M.F.*, Anthony Burgess, 1971.

Adhemar, Prior, 'an exemplary prelate.' *The Antiquary*, W. Scott, 1816.

Adie, Mrs, cook to the Minivers. *Mrs Miniver*, Jan Struther, 1939.

Adjutant, The, a crane. 'The Undertakers' (s.s.), *The Second Jungle Book*, R. Kipling, 1895.

Adler, Irene, later Norton. 'A Scandal in Bohemia,' *The Adventures of Sherlock Holmes*, A. Conan Doyle, 1892.

Adlerstein, Freiherr Eberhard von Kunigunde.
- His wife.
- **Lady Ermentrude Eberhard,** their daughter.
- **Eberhard,** their son.
- **Gottfried,** their son, m. Christine Sorel.

The Dove in the Eagle's Nest, Charlotte M. Yonge, 1866.

Adlerstein Wildschloss, Kasimir von. *The Dove in the Eagle's Nest*, Charlotte M. Yonge, 1866.

Adolph, Negro dandy and major-domo to St Clare. *Uncle Tom's Cabin*, Harriet B. Stowe, 1851.

Adolphe, Monsieur, Reception Manager, Imperial Palace Hotel. *Imperial Palace*, Arnold Bennett, 1930.

Adon-ai, spirit of love and beauty. *Zanoni*, Lord Lytton, 1842.

Adrastus, essayist. *Theophrastus Such*, George Eliot, 1879.

Adriana. *See* ANTIPHOLUS.

Adscombe, Richard.
- **Olive,** his wife, later div., m. (2) Shenley.
  - **Stuart,** their son.
- **Julia** , Richard's sister.

Judgment in Suspense, G. Bullett, 1946.

Adverse, Anthony, central character, m. Dolores de la Fuente. *See also* VINCITATA. *Anthony Adverse*, Hervey Allen, 1934.

Aegeon, merchant of Syracuse.
- **Aemilia,** his wife. *See also* ANTIPHOLUS.

A Comedy of Errors (play), W. Shakespeare.

Aelis, girl loved by Harry Talvace the younger. *The Heaven Tree* trilogy, Edith Pargeter, 1961–3.

Aelueva, The Lady. *See* SIR R. DALYNGRIDGE.

Aemilia. *See* AEGEON.

Aemilius, a nobleman. *Titus Andronicus* (play), W. Shakespeare.

Aeneas, Trojan commander. *Troilus and Cressida* (play), W. Shakespeare.

Aesop, hunchback villain. *The Duke's Motto*, J. H. McCarthy, 1908.

Aetion. *Colin Clout's Come Home Again* (poem), E. Spenser, 1595.

Afzal Khan, Pathan. 'At Howli Thana' (s.s.), *Soldiers Three*, R. Kipling, 1888.

Agamemnon, a Grecian general. *Troilus and Cressida* (play), W. Shakespeare.

Aged, The. *See* WEMMICK.

Agelastes, Michael, 'aged and adroit sycophant.' *Count Robert of Paris*, W. Scott, 1832.

Agent-General, The. 'The Puzzler' (s.s.), *Actions and Reactions*, 1909, and 'The Vortex' (s.s.), *A Diversity of Creatures*, 1917, R. Kipling.

Agg, a carrier. 'Steam Tactics' (s.s.), *Traffics and Discoveries,* R. Kipling, 1904.

Agnes, Sister, formerly Lady Laurentini; a penitent nun. *The Mysteries of Udolpho,* Mrs Radcliffe, 1794.

Agnette. 'The Revisitation' (poem), *Time's Laughing Stocks,* T. Hardy, 1909.

Agravaine the Dolorous, Sir, m. Yvonne. 'Sir Agravaine' (s.s.), *The Man Upstairs,* P. G. Wodehouse, 1914.

Agrippa, friend of Octavius Caesar. *Antony and Cleopatra* (play), W. Shakespeare.

Agrippa, Cornelia. 'Army Headquarters' (poem), *Departmental Ditties,* R. Kipling, 1886.

Aguecheek, Sir Andrew. *Twelfth Night* (play), W. Shakespeare.

Agustin. *For Whom the Bell Tolls,* E. Hemingway, 1940.

Agydas, a Median lord. *Tamburlaine* (play), C. Marlowe, 1587.

Ah Fe, Chinese servant. 'An Episode of Fiddletown' (s.s.), *The Luck of Roaring Camp,* Bret Harte, 1868.

Ah Fong. *The Middle Watch* (play), Ian Hay & S. King-Hall, 1929.

Ah Loi, of Penang.
  His wife.
Gallions Reach, H. M. Tomlinson, 1927.

Ah Sin, the 'Heathen Chinee.' *Plain Language from Truthful James* (poem), Bret Harte, 1870.

Ahab, one-legged captain of the *Pequod*; central character, *Moby Dick,* H. Melville, 1851.

Aikwood, Ringan, 'a sable personage.'
  Saunders, his father.
The Antiquary, W. Scott, 1816.

Aimwell, Thomas. *The Beaux' Stratagem* (play), G. Farquhar, 1707.

Ainger, house prefect. *Young Woodley* (play), J. van Druten, 1928.

Ainger, Arnold, m. Judy Corder. *Four Frightened People,* E. Arnot Robertson, 1931.

Ainslie, Dr. *To Have the Honour* (play), A. A. Milne, 1924.

Ainslie, Andrew, robber. *Deacon Brodie* (play), W. E. Henley & R. L. Stevenson, 1892.

Ainslie, Helen, Shiel Carne's governess. *The Brontës went to Woolworth's,* Rachel Ferguson, 1931.

Ainsworth, Dr.
  Marjorie, his wife. Friends of the Maxwells.
'The Brownings' (s.s.), *Louise,* Viola Meynell, 1954.

Ainsworth, Alex, photographer. *The Distant Horns of Summer,* H. E. Bates, 1967.

Aisgill, Alice, mistress of Joe Lampton.
  George, her husband.
Room at the Top, J. Braine, 1957.

Aissa, half-bred Fulani from Kolu, maid to Mrs Carr, and central character. *Aissa Saved,* Joyce Cary, 1932.

Aitken, friend of Tam Dyke. *Prester John,* J. Buchan, 1910.

Ajax, Grecian commander. *Troilus and Cressida* (play), W. Shakespeare.

Akela, the Lone Wolf, leader of the Seonee Pack. 'Mowgli's Brothers' and elsewhere, *The Jungle Books,* R. Kipling, 1894–5.

Akershem, Sophronia, m. Mr Lammle. *Our Mutual Friend,* C. Dickens, 1865.

Akut, ape-man. *Tarzan* series, E. R. Burroughs, 1912 onwards.

Alabama Red, lover of Temple Drake Stevens.
  Pete, his brother, another of Temple's lovers.
Requiem for a Nun, William Faulkner, 1950.

Alabaster, A. W. *The Horse's Mouth,* J. Cary, 1944.

Alan, member of the *Hispaniola*'s crew. *Treasure Island,* R. L. Stevenson, 1883.

Alarbus, Tamora's son. *Titus Andronicus* (play), W. Shakespeare.

Alard, Sir Hugh, head of the house.
  His wife.
  Their children:
    Peter, the heir.
      Vera, his wife.
    George, vicar of Leasan.
      Rose, his wife.
    Gervase.
    Mary.
    Doris.
    Jane.
The End of the House of Alard, Sheila Kaye-Smith, 1923.

Alasi, Prince of Kharezme, central character and narrator. *Vathek,* W. Beckford, 1786.

Albani, music master. 'Mr Gilfil's Love Story,' *Scenes of Clerical Life,* George Eliot, 1857.

Albany, Duke of. *King Lear* (play), W. Shakespeare.

Albany, Joseph, student and practical joker (later referred to as Dr Joseph Rochecliffe). *Woodstock,* W. Scott, 1826.

Alberighi, Count Federigo Degli, m. the Lady Giovanna. *The Falcon* (play), Lord Tennyson, 1879.

Albert, assistant to Raunce, the butler. *Loving,* Henry Green, 1945.

Albert, manservant of Tommy and Tuppence Beresford.
  Milly, his wife.
By The Pricking of My Thumbs, 1968, and others, Agatha Christie.

Albert, page-boy to Lord Marshmoreton. *A Damsel in Distress,* P. G. Wodehouse, 1919.

Albino, Miss Lucretia, liaison officer in Italian hotel. *They Winter Abroad,* T. H. White, 1932.

Albro, James O'Shaughnessy, Irish-Spanish adventurer. *The Lost God* (s.s.), John Russell.

Alcander, lover of Hypatia, victim of his friendship for Septimus. Essay, *The Bee,* O. Goldsmith, 1759–60.

Alcar, Lord Leonard. *The Great Adventure* (play), Arnold Bennett, 1913.

Alce, Arthur, suitor of Joanna Godden, who eventually marries her sister Ellen. *Joanna Godden,* Sheila Kaye-Smith, 1921.

Alcester, Lord, 'The Night of Glory' (s.s.), *Here and Hereafter,* Barry Pain, 1911.

Alcharisi. *See* PRINCESS LEONORA HALM-EBERSTEIN.

Alcibiades, an Athenian general. *Timon of Athens* (play), W. Shakespeare.

Alconleigh, Lord (Matthew). (Family name Radlett.)
  Sadie, his wife.
  Their children:
    Louisa, m. Lord Fort William.
    Linda, m. (1) Anthony Kroesig; (2) Christian Talbot.
    Jassy, m. Cary Goon.
    Robin.
    Matt.
    Victoria.
  David, a relative.
  Emily, David's wife.
The Pursuit of Love, 1945, and elsewhere, Nancy Mitford.

Aldclyffe, Captain (formerly Bradleigh).
  His wife.
  Cytherea, their daughter. *See also* AENEAS MANSTON.
Desperate Remedies, T. Hardy, 1871.

Alden, Mrs 'Billy,' div. wife of Robert Walling, eng. to the Duke of London. *The Metropolis,* Upton Sinclair, 1908.

Alden, John, Standish's deputy wooer, m. Priscilla. *The Courtship of Miles Standish* (poem), H. W. Longfellow.

Alden, Roberta, murdered by Clyde Griffiths.
  Titus, her father.
  Her mother.
  Tom and **Gifford,** her brothers.
  Emily, her sister.
An American Tragedy, T. Dreiser, 1925.

Aldermanbury, young tallow merchant. *The Book of Snobs,* W. M. Thackeray, 1846–7.

Alderney, Mrs and **Master.** *Vanity Fair,* W. M. Thackeray, 1847–8.

Aldiborontiphoscophornio. *Chrononhotonthologos* (play), H. Carey, 1743.

Aldingar, Sir. 'Sir Aldingar' (poem), *Percy's Reliques,* Bishop Thomas Percy, 1765.

Aldred, seneschal. *Unending Crusade,* R. E. Sherwood, 1932.

Aldrich, Harry, partner of Frederic Ide.
  His wife.
  Dorcy, their daughter.
The Heritage of Hatcher Ide, Booth Tarkington, 1941.

Aldrick, the Countess of Derby's Jesuit confessor. *Peveril of the Peak,* W. Scott, 1822.

Aldridge, Forrester's C.O. *The Purple Plain,* H. E. Bates, 1947.

Aldringham, Lord Hubert, uncle of Paul Verdayne. *Three Weeks,* Elinor Glyn, 1907.

Aldrovand, Father, chaplain to Sir R. Berenger. *The Betrothed,* W. Scott, 1825.

Aldwinkle, Mrs Lilian.

Irene, her niece, m. Lord Hovenden.
Those Barren Leaves, A. Huxley, 1925.

Alençon, Duke of. *Henry the Sixth* (play), W. Shakespeare.

Alesandro, Ivy, woman interested in the occult. *A Story That Ends With A Scream,* James Leo Herlihy, 1968.

Alexander. *Alexander and Campaspe* (play), J. Lyly, 1584.

Alexander, a beetle. *Now We Are Six,* A. A. Milne, 1927.

Alexander VI (Pope) (hist.), father of the Borgias.
Vanossa Catanei, his concubine.
The Duke of Gandia (play), A. C. Swinburne, 1908.

Alexandros, Arab antique and curio dealer in Jerusalem, *The Mandelbaum Gate,* Muriel Spark, 1965.

Alexievna, Anna, Russian prostitute. *The Research Magnificent,* H. G. Wells, 1915.

Alexis. *The Faithful Shepherdess* (play), Beaumont & Fletcher, 1609.

Alexis, Prince Paul Howard, central character.
Etta, his wife, formerly Mrs Sydney Bamborough.
The Sowers, H. S. Merriman, 1896.

Alf, Ferdinand, ed. the *Evening Pulpit. The Way We Live Now,* A. Trollope, 1875.

Alfagi, Hamet, relapsed convert. *Ivanhoe,* W. Scott, 1820.

Algardi, Count Freddy, Italian who enchants Mary Anne Gogan. 'Liars' (s.s.), *The Talking Trees,* Sean O'Faolain, 1971.

Alhambra del Bolero, Don, Grand Inquisitor. *The Gondoliers* (comic opera), Gilbert & Sullivan, 1889.

Alibi, Tom, Jonathan Grubbet's solicitor. *Waverley,* W. Scott, 1814.

Alice, central character. *Alice in Wonderland,* 1865, and *Alice Through the Looking-glass,* 1872, Lewis Carroll.

Alice, lady to Katherine. *Henry the Fifth* (play), W. Shakespeare.

Alice, Christopher Robin's nurse. 'Buckingham Palace' (poem), *When We Were Very Young,* A. A. Milne, 1924.

Alice, maid to Countess Czerlaski, m. Edmund Bridmain. 'The Rev. Amos Barton,' *Scenes of Clerical Life,* George Eliot, 1857.

Alice, maid to the Deanes. *The Mill on the Floss,* George Eliot, 1860.

Alice, maid to the Knowles. *The Romantic Age* (play), A. A. Milne, 1920.

Alice of the Hermitage. *The Forest Lovers,* M. Hewlett, 1898.

Alick, shepherd and head man to Martin Poyser. *Adam Bede,* George Eliot, 1859.

Alicompayne, eldest son of the Earl of Brandyball. *The Book of Snobs,* W. M. Thackeray, 1846–7.

Alimony, Agatha, 'dusky and deep-voiced.' *Marriage,* 1912, and elsewhere, H. G. Wells.

Aliris, Sultan of Lower Bucharia, m. Lalla Rookh. *Lalla Rookh* (poem), T. Moore, 1817.

Alison, Lewis, publisher, internee in Holland, central character. *The Fountain,* C. Morgan, 1932.

Allaby, Rev. Mr, rector of Crampsford.
His wife.
Christina, one of his nine children, m. Theobald Pontifex.
The Way of all Flesh, S. Butler, 1903.

Allan, Major, Cavalier 'officer of experience.' *Old Mortality,* W. Scott, 1816.

Allan, Mrs, Colonel Mannering's housekeeper. *Guy Mannering,* W. Scott, 1815.

Allan, Jack. *The House with the Green Shutters,* George Douglas, 1901.

Allan-a-Dale, northern minstrel. *Ivanhoe,* W. Scott, 1820.

Allande, Maria de, Italian cardinal. *Death Comes for the Archbishop,* Willa Cather, 1927.

Allard, Dr, an alienist. *The Accident* (s.s.), Ann Bridge.

Allardyce, Miss, eng. to Lieut. Brandis.
Major Allardyce, her father.
'Wee Willie Winkie' (s.s.), *Wee Willie Winkie,* R. Kipling, 1888.

Allaster, minstrel. *Rob Roy,* W. Scott, 1818.

Allbee, Kirby. *The Victim,* Saul Bellow, 1947.

Allegre, Henry, art connoisseur. *The Arrow of Gold,* J. Conrad, 1919.

Allen, Mr and Mrs, friends of the

Morlands. *Northanger Abbey*, Jane Austen, 1818.

Allen, Mrs, 'Nannie' to the Leslies and others.

Selina, her daughter, m. (1) Crockett; (2) Sgt Hopkins.

The *Barsetshire* series, Angela Thirkell, 1933 onwards.

Allen, Rev. Mr, scoundrelly tutor of Richard Carvel. *Richard Carvel*, W. Churchill, 1899.

Allen, Sister. *Adam Bede*, George Eliot, 1859.

Allen, Arabella, attractive brunette, m. Nathaniel Winkle.

Benjamin, her brother.

Pickwick Papers, C. Dickens, 1837.

Allen, Liddy, Rachel Innes's maid. *The Circular Staircase*, Mary R. Rinehart, 1908.

Allen, Madge, keeper of an animal farm. *The Postman Always Rings Twice*, James M. Cain, 1934.

Allestree, Sir John.

His wife and daughter.

Sir Charles Grandison, S. Richardson, 1754.

Alleyn, Chief Detective Inspector, C.I.D. (later Superintendent), 'Handsome Alleyn,' m. Agatha Troy. *Enter a Murderer*, 1935, and many others, Ngaio Marsh.

Allie-Dolly. *See* JENNICO GRANT.

Allingham, Australian gunnery officer, the *Saltash*. *The Cruel Sea*, N. Monsarrat, 1951.

Alliot, Dr. *A Bill of Divorcement* (play), Clemence Dane, 1921.

Allison, Andrew and **John,** youthful friends of Patrick Heron.

Their mother.

Rab, their cousin.

The Raiders, S. R. Crockett, 1894.

Allitsen, Robert, 'the disagreeable man'; consumptive; in love with Bernardine Holme. *Ships that Pass in the Night*, Beatrice Harraden, 1893.

Allnutt, Charlie. *The African Queen*, C. S. Forester, 1935.

Allo, a Pict. 'On the Great Wall' (s.s.) and 'The Winged Hats' (s.s.), *Puck of Pook's Hill*, R. Kipling, 1906.

Alloa, Lord. *The Thirty-nine Steps*, J. Buchan, 1915.

Allonby, Sir Giles.

Grace, his daughter.

Holmby House, G. Whyte-Melville, 1860.

Allworth. *A New Way to Pay Old Debts* (play), P. Massinger, 1633.

Allworthy, Squire.

Bridget, his sister, m. Captain Blifil; mother of Tom Jones.

Tom Jones, H. Fielding, 1749.

Allwright, William ('Toro').

Caroline, his wife.

Their nephew.

The Dancing Druids, Gladys Mitchell, 1948.

Allyn, Colonel.

Jessie, his daughter, m. John Pescud.

'Best Seller' (s.s.), *Options*, O. Henry, 1909.

Almagro, follower of Pizarro. *Pizarro* (play), R. B. Sheridan, 1799.

Almanzor. *The Conquest of Granada* (play), J. Dryden, 1672.

Almayer, Kaspar.

His wife, adopted Malay daughter of Hudig.

Nina, their daughter.

Almayer's Folly, J. Conrad, 1895.

Almeria, a heroine. *The Mourning Bride* (play), W. Congreve, 1697.

Almond, Mrs, sister of Dr Sloper.

Marian, her daughter, eng. to Arthur Townsend.

Washington Square, Henry James, 1880.

Alonso, King of Naples. *The Tempest* (play), W. Shakespeare.

Alonzo.

Cora, his wife.

Pizarro (play), R. B. Sheridan, 1799.

Alonzo the Brave. *Alonzo the Brave and the Fair Imogene* (poem), M. G. Lewis.

Alp, a renegade. *The Siege of Corinth* (poem), Lord Byron, 1816.

Alphrey, Mr, guest of Milton. *The Maiden and Married Life of Mary Powell*, Anne Manning, 1849.

Alquist, Miss. 'The Pledge' (s.s.), *The Baseless Fabric*, Helen Simpson, 1925.

Alquist, Paula. *Gaslight* (play), Patrick Hamilton, 1939.

Alroy, Lady, widow. *The Sphinx without a Secret* (s.s.), Oscar Wilde, 1888.

Altamont, Colonel Jack, alias Armstrong and Amory; bigamist and

ex-convict; 1st husband of Lady Clavering.
Blanche (Amory), their daughter. *See also* MADAME FRISBY.
Pendennis, W. M. Thackeray, 1848–50.

Alter, Wingfield, O.M., great author. *The Gunroom*, Charles Morgan, 1919.

Alvar, Don, friend of Duke Silva. *The Spanish Gypsy* (poem), George Eliot, 1868.

Alvarao, Captain. *The Bridge of San Luis Rey*, T. Wilder, 1927.

Alvarez, President of Olancho.
Countess Manuelata, his wife, *née* Hernandez.
Soldiers of Fortune, R. H. Davis, 1897.

Alvarito, Barone, friend of Col. Cantrell in Venice. *Across the River and Into the Trees,* Ernest Hemingway, 1950.

Alveric, son of the Lord of Erl, m. Lirazel.
Orion, their son.
The King of Elfland's Daughter, Lord Dunsany, 1924.

Alwyn, Nicholas, foster-brother of Marmaduke Nevile. *The Last of the Barons,* Lord Lytton, 1843.

Alyface, Annot, maiden to Dame Custance. *Ralph Roister Doister,* N. Udall, 1551.

Alyosha, saddlemaker. *Tobit Transplanted,* Stella Benson, 1931.

Amador, Don, master of Duke Silva's retinue. *The Spanish Gypsy* (poem), George Eliot, 1868.

Amal. *Hypatia,* C. Kingsley, 1853.

Amal, a Dane. 'The Winged Hats' (s.s.), *Puck of Pook's Hill,* R. Kipling, 1906.

Amalfi, Giovanna, Duchess of.
Antonio Bologna, her 2nd husband.
Ferdinand, Duke of Calabria, Giovanna's jealous brother.
The Cardinal, another brother.
The Duchess of Malfi (play), John Webster, *c.* 1613.

Amalia, a cook. *Barry Lyndon,* W. M. Thackeray, 1844.

Amarantha. *To Amarantha* (poem), R. Lovelace.

Amarillis. *The Faithful Shepherdess* (play), Beaumont & Fletcher, 1609.

Amaryllis. *Colin Clout's Come Home Again* (poem), E. Spenser, 1595.

Amaury, Giles, Grand Master of the Templars. *The Talisman,* W. Scott, 1825.

Ambassador, the American (Mr Ambassador). *Berkeley Square* (play), J. L. Balderston, 1926.

Amberley, Mary, drug-ridden alcoholic. *Eyeless in Gaza,* Aldous Huxley, 1936.

Ambermere, Lady. *Queen Lucia,* E. F. Benson, 1920.

Amboyne, Dr ('Jack Doubleface'). *Put Yourself in his Place,* C. Reade, 1870.

Ambrose, valet of Sir C. Tregellis. *Rodney Stone,* A. Conan Doyle, 1896.

Ambrose, Mr, the Misses Arthuret's servant; 'half-physician, half-almoner, half-butler and entire governor.' *Redgauntlet,* W. Scott, 1824.

Ambrose, Ianthe, a schoolteacher. *The Widow's Cruise,* Nicholas Blake, 1959.

Ambrosio, Abbot, central character. *The Monk,* M. G. Lewis, 1796.

Ambrosius, monk. *Idylls of the King* (poem), Lord Tennyson, 1859.

Ameera, native girl, mistress of John Holden.
Toto, their son.
'Without Benefit of Clergy' (s.s.), *Life's Handicap,* R. Kipling, 1891.

Amelia. *The Seasons* (poem), J. Thomson, 1730.

Amelot, page to Damian de Lacy. *The Betrothed,* W. Scott, 1825.

Amenartas, wife of Kallikrates, ancestor of Leo Vincey. *She,* H. Rider Haggard, 1887.

Amerigo, Prince, impoverished Italian, m. Maggie Verver. *The Golden Bowl,* Henry James, 1904.

Ames, Anros.
Louisa, his wife.
Mourning becomes Electra (play), E. O'Neill, 1931.

Ames, Cathy, m. Adam Trask. Changes her name to Kate; a prostitute and murderess. *East of Eden,* John Steinbeck, 1952.

Amex, Hon. Rupert, nephew of Lady Elizabeth Carn, m. Bobby Crane.
Antonia, his sister.

The Case for the Defence, Mary Fitt, 1958.

Amherst, John, assistant manager of a mill.

Bessy Westmore, his 1st wife, owner of the mill, *née* Langhope.

Justine Brent, his 2nd wife, nurse.

The Fruit of the Tree, Edith Wharton, 1907.

Amiens, lord attendant on the duke. *As You Like It* (play), W. Shakespeare.

Aminadab, sheriff's officer. *The Great Hoggarty Diamond,* W. M. Thackeray, 1841.

Amintor, noble gentleman, betrothed to Aspatia. *The Maid's Tragedy* (play), Beaumont & Fletcher, 1611.

Amlet, Richard, a gamester. *The Confederacy* (play), J. Vanbrugh, 1705.

Ammersfoort. *The Thirty-nine Steps,* J. Buchan, 1915.

Ammidon, Captain Jeremy.

His children:

William.

Rhoda, his wife.

Sidsall.

Camilla.

Janet.

Laurel.

Captain Gerrit.

Taou Yuen, Manchu widow, his wife.

Java Head, J. Hergesheimer, 1919.

Amoraq. *See* KADLU.

Amoret. *The Faërie Queene* (poem), E. Spenser, 1590.

Amoret. *The Faithful Shepherdess* (play), Beaumont & Fletcher, 1609.

Amoret. *A Hue and Cry after Fair Amoret* (poem), W. Congreve.

Amory, Blanche (christened Betsy), daughter of Lady Clavering by her 1st marriage (*see* ALTAMONT); m. Count Montmorenci de Valentinois. *Pendennis,* W. M. Thackeray, 1848–1850.

Amory, Gertrude (formerly known as Flint), m. William Sullivan.

Philip, her father, m. (1) Lucy, her mother; (2) Emily Graham.

The Lamplighter, Maria S. Cummins, 1854.

Amory, Richard, m. Bertha Herrick.

Their children:

Jane.

Jack.

Meg.

Through One Administration, Frances H. Burnett, 1881.

Amphialus. *Arcadia* (poem), Sir P. Sidney, 1590.

Amrah, slave. *Ben Hur,* L. Wallace, 1880.

Amswell, James Caplon, eng. to Mary Hume.

Reginald, his cousin, blackmailer.

The Judas Window, Carter Dickson, 1938.

Amundeville, The Lady Adeline. *Don Juan* (poem), Lord Byron, 1819–1824.

Amy. *Locksley Hall* (poem), Lord Tennyson.

Amy, old woman in a workhouse. *Oliver Twist,* C. Dickens, 1838.

Amy, Rev. George. *Mary Rose* (play), J. M. Barrie, 1920.

Anacleto, Alison Langdon's Filipino servant. *Reflections in a Golden Eye,* Carson McCullers, 1940.

Anah. *Heaven and Earth* (poem), Lord Byron, 1822.

Anaitis, Dame, Lady of the Lake. *Jurgen,* J. B. Cabell, 1921.

Anatole, valet to Henry Foker. *Pendennis,* W. M. Thackeray, 1848–50.

Ancrum, Tom ('Daddy'), minister, m. Isabella Lomax. *The History of David Grieve,* Mrs Humphry Ward, 1892.

Anderoch, Elizabeth Frieda, Austrian professional pianist; the 'other woman.' *See also* RODERICK STROOD. *The Jury,* G. Bullett, 1935.

Anderson. 'No. 13' (s.s.), *Ghost Stories of an Antiquary,* M. R. James, 1910.

Anderson, Colonel, Chief Constable. *Requiem for Robert,* Mary Fitt, 1942.

Anderson, Mr and Mrs, Ethel Garrard's parents. *Thursday Afternoons,* Monica Dickens, 1945.

Anderson, Rev. Anthony.

Judith, his wife.

The Devil's Disciple (play), G. B. Shaw, 1899.

Anderson, Bridget, pretty maid of the Claytons. *Cricket in Heaven,* G. Bullett, 1949.

Anderson, Carol. *Thank Heaven Fasting,* E. M. Delafield, 1932.

Anderson, Charley, aeroplane manufacturer. *U.S.A.* trilogy, John dos Passos, 1930–6.

Anderson, Donovan, civil servant, first boy-friend of Martha Quest. *Children of Violence* series, Doris Lessing, 1952–69.

Anderson, Eppie, one of Meg Dods's maids. *St Ronan's Well,* W. Scott, 1824.

Anderson, Dr Gilbert, mental specialist. *The Return of the Soldier,* Rebecca West, 1918.

Anderson, Harvey.
Edward, his brother.
Fanny, his sister.
The Daisy Chain, Charlotte M. Yonge, 1856.

Anderson, Henry. *East of Suez* (play), W. S. Maugham, 1922.

Anderson, Job, member of the *Hispaniola*'s crew. *Treasure Island,* R. L. Stevenson, 1883.

Anderson, John. *John Anderson, My Jo John* (poem), R. Burns.

Anderson, Walter, bookshop assistant.
George, his brother.
Jim, their father.
Bella, their mother, *née* Gillespie.
Time Will Knit, Fred Urquhart, 1938.

Andrea, Count. *Across the River and Into the Trees,* Ernest Hemingway, 1950.

Andrews, Nurse. 'The Daughters of the late Colonel' (s.s.), *The Garden Party,* Katherine Mansfield, 1922.

Andrews, John (Andy), soldier from Virginia. *Three Soldiers,* John dos Passos, 1921.

Andrews, Joseph, central character.
Pamela, his sister.
Joseph Andrews, H. Fielding, 1742.

Andrews, Pamela, central character and narrator.
John and **Elizabeth,** her parents.
Pamela, S. Richardson, 1740.

Andrews, Polly, graduate of Vassar. *The Group,* Mary McCarthy, 1963.

Andromache, wife of Hector. *Troilus and Cressida* (play), W. Shakespeare.

Androvsky, Boris (alias **Hadj**), renegade monk, m. Domini Enfilden. *The Garden of Allah,* R. S. Hichens, 1904.

Anemolius, laureate of Utopia. *Utopia,* Sir Thomas More, 1515–16.

Angaray, James. *See* James Ayrton.

'Angel,' m. Freckles O'More. *Freckles,* Gene S. Porter, 1904.

Angel, B.B.C. interviewer. *The Ordeal of Gilbert Pinfold,* Evelyn Waugh, 1957.

Angel, Hosmer. *See* Windibank.

Angel, Lucasta, illegitimate daughter of Sir Claude Mulhammer, m. Barnabas Kaghan. *The Confidential Clerk* (play), T. S. Eliot, 1954.

Angela, blind and aged servant of the Malatesta. *Paolo and Francesca* (play), Stephen Phillips, 1900.

Angela, partner and fiancée of Diabolo. *The Cue* (s.s.), T. Burke.

Angela, Lady, a rapturous maiden, m. Major Murgatroyd. *Patience* (comic opera), Gilbert & Sullivan, 1881.

Angelica. *Love for Love* (play), W. Congreve, 1695.

Angelica, only daughter of King Valoroso. *The Rose and the Ring,* W. M. Thackeray, 1855.

Angelina, heroine of ballad. *See* Edwin.

Angelo, a goldsmith. *A Comedy of Errors* (play), W. Shakespeare.

Angelo, Lord Deputy to the Duke of Vienna, betrothed to Mariana. *Measure for Measure* (play), W. Shakespeare.

Angelo. *On the Spot* (play), Edgar Wallace, 1930.

Angelus, Dr.
Iris, his wife.
Dr Angelus (play), J. Bridie, 1947.

Angereau, General. 'Leipzig,' *Wessex Poems,* T. Hardy, 1898.

Angioletto. 'The Judgment of Borso' (s.s.), *Little Novels of Italy,* M. Hewlett, 1899.

Angiolina. *Marino Faliero* (poem), Lord Byron, 1821.

'Angry Snake,' nickname of enemy Indian. *Settlers in Canada,* Captain Marryat, 1844.

Angstrom, Harry ('Rabbit'), former baseball star, now a salesman.
Janice, his wife.
Nelson, their son.
Rabbit, Run, John Updike, 1960.

Angus, nobleman of Scotland. *Macbeth* (play), W. Shakespeare.

Angus, Rob, saw-miller, late leader-writer, *The Wire*; central character, m. Mary Abinger. *When a Man's Single*, J. M. Barrie, 1888.

Anippe, maid to Zenocrate. *Tamburlaine* (play), C. Marlowe, 1587.

Ann. *Outward Bound* (play), Sutton Vane, 1923.

Ann ('Modest Ann'), waiting-maid, Low Wood Inn. *Starvecrow Farm*, S. J. Weyman, 1905.

Anna, Frau Ebermann's maid. 'Swept and Garnished' (s.s.), *A Diversity of Creatures*, R. Kipling, 1917.

Anna, Burmese nurse, in love with Forrester.

Dorothy, her elder sister.

The Purple Plain, H. E. Bates, 1947.

Anna, a servant, m. Charles Raye. 'On the Western Circuit,' *Life's Little Ironies*, T. Hardy, 1894.

Anna, old friend of Deeley's wife Kate. *Old Times* (play), Harold Pinter, 1971.

Annable, gamekeeper. *The White Peacock*, D. H. Lawrence, 1911.

Anne, Dombey's housemaid. *Dombey and Son*, C. Dickens, 1848.

Anne, maid to the Mardens. *Mr Pim Passes By* (play), A. A. Milne, 1920.

Anne. *See* NICHOLAS. *The Dover Road*, A. A. Milne, 1922.

Anne, Lady, widow of Edward Prince of Wales (later married to Richard III) (hist.). *Richard the Third* (play), W. Shakespeare.

Annerly, Mrs. *Mid-Channel* (play), A. W. Pinero, 1909.

Annette, maid to Emily St Aubert. *The Mysteries of Udolpho*, Mrs Radcliffe, 1794.

Annibale, a gondolier. *The Gondoliers* (comic opera), Gilbert & Sullivan, 1889.

Annina. 'Ippolita in the Hills' (s.s.), *Little Novels of Italy*, M. Hewlett, 1899.

Anselm, Prior, confessor to King Robert. *The Fair Maid of Perth*, W. Scott, 1828.

Ansell, Moses, pious Jew.

Esther, his daughter.

Children of the Ghetto, Israel Zangwill, 1892.

Ansell, Stewart, Cambridge friend of Rickie Elliot. *The Longest Journey*, E. M. Forster, 1907.

Anselmo, old Spaniard. *For Whom the Bell Tolls*, E. Hemingway, 1940.

Anson, Garry, racehorse owner, central character. *The Calendar*, Edgar Wallace.

Anson, Pierre, French peasant and murderer. *Mr Billingham, the Marquis and Madelon*, E. P. Oppenheim.

Anstey, Lord. *Laura's Bishop*, G. A. Birmingham, 1949.

Anstey, Sir John.

His son.

A Modern Tragedy, Phyllis Bentley, 1934.

Anstey, Sybil, m. (1) Charles Herbert, (2) Harry Jardine. *The Ballad and the Source*, Rosamond Lehmann, 1944.

Anstruther, Mr. *The Young in Heart*, I. A. R. Wylie, 1939.

Anstruther, Lilah. *The Fortunes of Christina McNab*, S. Macnaughtan, 1901.

Anstruther, Sir Richard, Bt, friend of Peter Vibart. *The Broad Highway*, J. Farnol, 1910.

Antenor, a Trojan commander. *Troilus and Cressida* (play), W. Shakespeare.

Anteoni, Count, friend of Domini Enfilden. *The Garden of Allah*, R. S. Hichens, 1904.

Anthea. *To Anthea* (poem), R. Herrick.

Anthony, Meg Dods's humpbacked postilion. *St Ronan's Well*, W. Scott, 1824.

Anthony, Brother. 'The Janeites' (s.s.), *Debits and Credits*, R. Kipling, 1926.

Anticant, Dr Pessimist. *The Warden*, A. Trollope, 1855.

Antigonus, a Sicilian lord. *A Winter's Tale* (play), W. Shakespeare.

Antiochus, King of Antioch. *Pericles* (play), W. Shakespeare.

Antiphila, waiting-woman to Aspatia. *The Maid's Tragedy* (play), Beaumont & Fletcher, 1611.

Antipholus of Ephesus.

Adriana, his wife.

Antipholus of Syracuse. Twin sons

of Aegeon. *A Comedy of Errors* (play), W. Shakespeare.

'Antirosa' (Aunt Rosa), unkind temporary guardian of Dick Heldar and Maisie. *The Light that Failed,* R. Kipling, 1890.

Antolini, schoolmaster. *The Catcher in the Rye,* J. D. Salinger, 1951.

Anton, Gregory. *Gaslight* (play), Patrick Hamilton, 1939.

Antonapoulos, Spiros, a dumb man. *The Heart is a Lonely Hunter,* Carson McCullers, 1940.

Antonia, Donna, sister of Ambrosio, m. Don Lorenzo de Medina.
Elvira, her mother.
Leonella, her aunt.
The Monk, M. G. Lewis, 1796.

Antonio, merchant of Venice; defended against Shylock by Portia. *The Merchant of Venice* (play), W. Shakespeare.

Antonio, sea captain. *Twelfth Night* (play), W. Shakespeare.

Antonio, usurping Duke of Milan. *The Tempest* (play), W. Shakespeare.

Antonio, father of Proteus. *Two Gentlemen of Verona* (play), W. Shakespeare.

Antonio, brother of Leonato. *Much Ado about Nothing* (play), W. Shakespeare.

Antonio. *Antonio and Mellida* (play), John Marston, 1602.

Antonio, a gondolier. *The Gondoliers* (comic opera), Gilbert & Sullivan, 1889.

Antonio, guide from the Grison country. *Anne of Geierstein,* W. Scott, 1829.

Antony, Mark, friend of Caesar, triumvir after his death. *Julius Caesar* and *Antony and Cleopatra* (plays), W. Shakespeare.

Antrim, Colonel.
His wife.
Roger, their son.
Violet, their daughter, m. Alec Peacock.
The Well of Loneliness, Radclyffe Hall, 1928.

Antrobus, Mrs.
Her daughters:
Piggy and **Goosie.**
Queen Lucia, E. F. Benson, 1920.

Antrobus, George (Adam).
Maggie, his wife (Eve).
Henry, their son (Cain).
Gladys, their daughter.
The Skin of Our Teeth (play), Thornton Wilder, 1942.

Anville, Evelina. *See* EVELINA.

Aoaecides, a priest; brother of Ione. *The Last Days of Pompeii,* Lord Lytton, 1834.

Ap-Llymry, Mr and Mrs. *Crotchet Castle,* T. L. Peacock, 1831.

Ape, Mrs Melrose, an evangelist. *Vile Bodies,* Evelyn Waugh, 1930.

Apemantus, churlish philosopher. *Timon of Athens* (play), W. Shakespeare.

Apis, a fighting bull. 'The Bull that Thought' (s.s.), *Debits and Credits,* R. Kipling, 1926.

Apley, George, rich Bostonian.
Catherine, his wife.
John, their son.
Eleanor, their daughter.
The Late George Apley, J. P. Marquand, 1937.

Apollodoros. *Firmilian* (poem), W. E. Aytoun, 1854.

Apollodoros. *Caesar and Cleopatra* (play), G. B. Shaw, 1900.

Apollos, Rev. Mr, popular Congregational preacher. *Theophrastus Such,* George Eliot, 1879.

Apollyon, 'the Foul Fiend.' *Pilgrim's Progress,* J. Bunyan, 1678 and 1684.

Appin, Cornelius. *Tobermory* (s.s.), 'Saki' (H. H. Munro).

Appleby, Charles. *Eden End* (play), J. B. Priestley, 1935.

Appleby, George.
His wife.
Caesar's Wife (play), W. S. Maugham, 1919.

Appleby, Detective Inspector John. *Hamlet, Revenge!,* 1937, and many others, M. Innes.

Appledore, Theophilus, tenant of flat above Alfred Thipps.
His wife.
Whose Body?, Dorothy L. Sayers, 1923.

Appleton, Stella, first love of Eugene Witla. *The Genius,* Theodore Dreiser, 1915.

Appleton, Will.
Tom, his father.
His mother.
Fred, his brother.

Kate, his sister.
'The Sad Horn Blowers' (s.s.), *Horses and Men,* Sherwood Anderson, 1924.

Appleyard, Melchisedec, U.S. Secret Service. *No Man's Land,* L. J. Vance, 1910.

Appleyard, Nick. *The Black Arrow,* R. L. Stevenson, 1888.

Apthorpe, fellow officer of Guy Crouchback in Royal Corps of Halberdiers. *Men at Arms,* Evelyn Waugh, 1952.

Aquila, conversational trifler. *Theophrastus Such,* George Eliot, 1879.

Aquila, Rev. John Spencer, m. Lucy Tolefree. 'A Case of Conscience' (s.s.), *Love and Money,* Phyllis Bentley, 1957.

Arabia, King of. *Tamburlaine* (play), C. Marlowe, 1587.

Arabin, Very Rev. Francis, Dean of Barchester, m. as 2nd husband Eleanor Bold, *née* Harding. *Barchester Towers,* A. Trollope, 1857.

Aram, Eugene (hist.). *Eugene Aram,* Lord Lytton, 1832. *The Dream of Eugene Aram* (poem), T. Hood, 1829.

Arane, queen mother. *A King and No King* (play), Beaumont & Fletcher, 1611.

Arb, Mrs, confectioner, m. Henry Earlforward. *Riceyman Steps,* Arnold Bennett, 1923.

Arbaces, King of Iberia. *A King and No King* (play), Beaumont & Fletcher, 1611.

Arbaces, Egyptian priest, supposed possessor of the Evil Eye. *The Last Days of Pompeii,* Lord Lytton, 1834.

Arbaces the Mede. *Sardanapalus* (poem), Lord Byron, 1821.

Arble, Eric, fruit farmer, m. Iseult Smith. *Eva Trout,* Elizabeth Bowen, 1969.

Arbuthnot, Dr. *Secrets* (play), R. Besier & May Edginton, 1922.

Arbuthnot, Mrs, mistress of Deborah Loveday. *The Fallow Land,* H. E. Bates, 1932.

Arbuthnot, Hon. Freddy, friend of Lord Peter Wimsey. *Whose Body?,* 1923, and others, Dorothy L. Sayers.

Arbuthnot, Laurence, cousin of Richard Amory. *Through One Administration,* Frances H. Burnett, 1881.

Arbuthnot, Mrs Patience, grandmother of Henrietta Mountjoy. *The House in Paris,* Elizabeth Bowen, 1935.

Arbuthnot, Mrs Peggy, m. (2) Francis Brandon. The *Barsetshire* series, Angela Thirkell, 1933 onwards.

Arbuthnot, Mrs Rose.
Frederick, her husband, alias Ferdinand Arundel.
The Enchanted April, Countess von Arnim, 1922.

Arbuthnot, Tom. 'A Case of Have To' (s.s.), *Short Stories,* Morley Roberts, 1928.

Arcati, Madame, spiritualist medium. *Blithe Spirit* (play), Noël Coward, 1941.

Archbold, Mrs Edith, 'female rake' reformed, m. Frank Beverley. *Hard Cash,* C. Reade, 1863.

Archdale, Alan. *Porgy,* Du Bose Heyward, 1925.

Archer, 'unworthy friend' of Col. Mannering. *Guy Mannering,* W. Scott, 1815.

Archer, 'literary man' and humbug. *Pendennis,* W. M. Thackeray, 1848–50.

Archer, Mrs, maid to Mrs Latimer. *The Lifted Veil,* George Eliot, 1859.

Archer, Alayne, m. (1) Eden Whiteoak (div.); (2) Renny Whiteoak.
Helen and **Harriet,** her aunts.
The Whiteoak Chronicles, Mazo de la Roche, 1927 onwards.

Archer, Clement, radio producer.
Kitty, his wife.
Jane, their daughter.
The Troubled Air, Irwin Shaw, 1951.

Archer, Francis. *The Beaux' Stratagem* (play), G. Farquhar, 1707.

Archer, Mrs Gloria, *née* Stokes, ex-mistress of James Flitestone. 'The Skeleton' (s.s.), *Blind Love,* V. S. Pritchett, 1969.

Archer, Helen (Mère Marie Hélène, Rev. Mother).
Henry, her father.
The Land of Spices, Kate O'Brien, 1941.

Archer, Isabel, American heiress, m. Gilbert Osmond. *The Portrait of a Lady,* Henry James, 1881.

Archer, Miles, Sam Spade's partner who is killed. *The Maltese Falcon,* Dashiell Hammett, 1930.

Archibald, John, groom of the Chambers to the Duke of Argyll. *The Heart of Midlothian,* W. Scott, 1818.

Archibald, Dr Thomas Thornton. 'No Road' (s.s.), *Love and Money,* Phyllis Bentley, 1957.

Archidamus, a Bohemian lord. *A Winter's Tale* (play), W. Shakespeare.

Archie, Dr Howard, friend and adviser of Thea Kronborg. *The Song of the Lark,* Willa Cather, 1915.

Archimago, enchanter. *The Faërie Queene* (poem), E. Spenser, 1590.

archy, a cockroach, central character and narrator. *archy and mehitabel* (poems), Don Marquis, 1927.

Arcoll, Captain James. *Prester John,* J. Buchan, 1910.

Ardale, Captain Hugh, former lover of Paula Tanqueray, in love with Ellean. *The Second Mrs Tanqueray* (play), A. W. Pinero, 1893.

Arden, Enoch, m. Annie Lee. *Enoch Arden* (poem), Lord Tennyson.

Arden, Julia, schoolmate of Catherine. *Catherine Furze,* M. Rutherford, 1893.

Ardorix of Curdun, Guemoné.
His wife.
Their children.
Caltane, his cousin.
The Conquered, Naomi Mitchison, 1923.

Arena, Mary, eng. to Marcus Macauley. *The Human Comedy,* W. Saroyan, 1943.

Aresby, Captain. *Cecilia,* Fanny Burney, 1782.

Arethusa, daughter of the king. *Philaster* (play), Beaumont & Fletcher, 1611.

Argallo, Felix, 'a genius for Pity.' 'Argallo and Ledgett' (s.s.), *Seven Men,* Max Beerbohm, 1919.

Argante, a giantess. *The Faërie Queene* (poem), E. Spenser, 1590.

Argentine, Lord, victim of Helen Vaughan. *The Great God Pan,* A. Machen, 1894.

Argier (Algiers), King of. *Tamburlaine* (play), C. Marlowe, 1587.

Ariel, an air spirit. *The Tempest* (play), W. Shakespeare.

Aristobulus, High Priest, brother of Mariamne.
His wife.
Herod (play), Stephen Phillips, 1900.

Arkroyd, Murgatroyd.
William, his eldest son.
Judith and **Sybil,** his daughters.
It Never Can Happen Again, W. de Morgan, 1909.

Arkwright, Lieutenant Richard, H.M.S. *Rodney,* m. Penny Hambledon. *Through the Storm,* Philip Gibbs, 1945.

Arlingford, Lady, Sir Henry Rotherham's sister. *I Live Under a Black Sun,* Edith Sitwell, 1937.

Arlow, Henry, first mate, SS. *Jane Vosper. The Loss of the 'Jane Vosper,'* F. Wills Crofts, 1936.

Arlworth, Father, uncle of Domini Enfilden. *The Garden of Allah,* R. S. Hichens, 1904.

Armado, Don Adriano, a fantastical Spaniard. *Love's Labour's Lost* (play), W. Shakespeare.

Armgart, prima donna. *Armgart* (poem), George Eliot, 1871.

Armiger, the Field Bee. *Parliament of Bees* (poem), John Day, 1641.

Armine, Hon. Nigel, m. Ruby Chepstow. *See also* HARWICH. *Bella Donna,* R. S. Hichens, 1909.

Armine, 'Uncle.'
Bella, his wife.
'A Madonna of the Trenches' (s.s.), *Debits and Credits,* R. Kipling, 1926.

Armitage, Major, friend of the Dons. *A Well-remembered Voice* (play), J. M. Barrie, 1918.

Armitage, Mrs. *The Green Hat,* M. Arlen, 1924.

Armitage, Mrs. *Robert's Wife* (play), St John Ervine, 1937.

Armitage, Humphrey.
Ethel, his daughter, m. Ireton.
'A Capitalist' (s.s.), *The House of Cobwebs,* G. Gissing, 1906.

Armitage, Jacob, servant and friend of the Beverleys. *The Children of the New Forest,* Captain Marryat, 1847.

Armitage, Leonard, blind lawyer. 'Blind Love' (s.s.), *Blind Love,* V. S. Pritchett, 1969.

Armsby, Mrs. 'Tea at Mrs Armsby's'

(s.s.), *The Owl in the Attic,* J. Thurber, 1931.

Armstrong, wealthy client of Robert Dempster. 'Janet's Repentance,' *Scenes of Clerical Life,* George Eliot, 1857.

Armstrong, director, Pym's Publicity. *Murder Must Advertise,* Dorothy L. Sayers, 1933.

Armstrong, Archie, court jester. *The Fortunes of Nigel,* W. Scott, 1822.

Armstrong, Grace, m. Hobbie Elliot, her cousin. *The Black Dwarf,* W. Scott, 1816.

Armstrong, Hugh, crippled woodcarver, central character and chief narrator, 'willed' by Si Prindle to Lize Lewis. *The Woodcarver of 'Lympus,* Mary E. Waller, 1909.

Armstrong, Jane, m. as 2nd wife Stephen Monk. *The World in the Evening,* C. Isherwood, 1954.

Armstrong, Paul, defaulting financier.
  Arnold, his son.
  Louise, his daughter, m. Halsey Innes.
The Circular Staircase, Mary R. Rinehart, 1908.

Armstrong, Robert, farming student, m. Rhoda Fleming. *Rhoda Fleming,* G. Meredith, 1865.

Armstrong, Rev. Thomas (later Bishop).
  His grandchildren:
    Harry and Suzette.
  His aunt.
Romance (play), E. Sheldon, 1914.

Armsworth, Mark, banker, solicitor, etc.; lifelong friend and next-door neighbour of Thurnall.
  Mary, his daughter.
Two Years Ago, C. Kingsley, 1857.

Armusia, lover of Quisara. *The Island Princess,* J. Fletcher, 1647.

Armytage, Captain, 'bad hat,' lodger at Mrs Galer's. *Mrs Galer's Business,* W. Pett Ridge, 1905.

Arnheim, Baron and Baroness von, grandparents of Anne.
  Sybilla, their daughter, m. Count Albert of Geierstein.
Anne of Geierstein, W. Scott, 1829.

Arnold, Mr and Mrs, temporary hosts of the Primrose family. *The Vicar of Wakefield,* O. Goldsmith, 1766.

Arnold, Anne, friend of Gertrude Amory.
  Her father.
The Lamplighter, Maria S. Cummins, 1854.

Arnold, Ida.
  Tom, her husband.
Brighton Rock, Graham Greene, 1938.

Arnold, J., trusted servant turned spy. *Pamela,* S. Richardson, 1740.

Arnold, Madeleine. *Strange Interlude* (play), E. O'Neill, 1928.

Arnold, Michael, m. Julie Hempel.
  Eugene, their son.
  Paula, their daughter, m. Theodore Storm.
So Big, Edna Ferber, 1924.

Arnold-Browne, Dr Thomas, elderly lecher.
  His wife.
They Winter Abroad, T. H. White, 1932.

Arnott, Mrs, sister of Mrs May. *The Daisy Chain,* Charlotte M. Yonge, 1856.

Arnott, Eustace, of the Aerial Board of Control. 'As Easy as A B C' (s.s.), *A Diversity of Creatures,* R. Kipling, 1917.

Arnott, Fulke, sidereal chemist, m. Ruby Frew-Gaff. *Landscape with Figures,* R. Fraser, 1925.

Arnott, Priscilla, m. Harrel.
  Her brother, m. Henrietta Belfield.
Cecilia, Fanny Burney, 1782.

Arragon, Prince of, unsuccessful suitor to Portia. *The Merchant of Venice* (play), W. Shakespeare.

Arrifa, Si El Hadj, Moroccan friend of Paul Ravenel. *The Winding Stair,* A. E. W. Mason, 1923.

Arrius Quintus, tribune, adopted Ben Hur. *Ben Hur,* L. Wallace, 1880.

Arrow, Mr, member of the *Hispaniola's* crew. *Treasure Island,* R. L. Stevenson, 1883.

Arrowhead, a Tuscarora Indian. *The Pathfinder,* J. F. Cooper, 1840.

Arrowpoint, 'a perfect gentleman.'
  His wife.
    Catherine, their daughter, m. Klesmer.
Daniel Deronda, George Eliot, 1876.

Arrowsmith, Dr Martin, central character.

m. (1) Leora Tozer, who died of plague.
(2) Joyce Lanyon.
John, their son.
Martin Arrowsmith, Sinclair Lewis, 1925.

Arsenius, a porter. *Hypatia*, C. Kingsley, 1853.

Artavan of Hautlieu. *Count Robert of Paris*, W. Scott, 1832.

Artegal, a knight. *The Faërie Queene* (poem), E. Spenser, 1590.

Artemidorus, a sophist. *Julius Caesar* (play), W. Shakespeare.

Artemis, Melissa, Greek dancer and prostitute. *The Alexandria Quartet*, Lawrence Durrell, 1957–61.

Arthur, King of Britain, m. Guinevere.
Uther, his father.
Ygerne, his mother.
Idylls of the King (poem), Lord Tennyson, 1859.

Arthur, nephew of King John. *King John* (play), W. Shakespeare.

Arthur, George, new boy, protégé of Tom Brown. *Tom Brown's Schooldays*, T. Hughes, 1857.

Arthuret, Misses Seraphina and Angelica, 'the Vestals of Fairladies.' *Redgauntlet*, W. Scott, 1824.

Arundel, Mrs, widow of Captain Arundel, really Desborough.
Rose, their daughter, m. Richard Frere.
Lewis, their son (later recognized as Lewis Desborough), m. Annie Grant.
Lewis Arundel, F. E. Smedley, 1852.

Arundel, Myra. *Hay Fever* (play), N. Coward, 1925.

Arviragus (Cadwal), Cymbeline's son. *Cymbeline* (play), W. Shakespeare.

Asano, Japanese attendant on Graham. *When the Sleeper Awakes*, H. G. Wells, 1899.

Ascot, Lord and Lady.
Adelaide, their adopted daughter.
Ravenshoe, H. Kingsley, 1861.

Ascott, Mrs Alida, m. (2) William Portlaw. *The Firing Line*, R. W. Chambers, 1908.

Ash, Churdles, *The Farmer's Wife* (play), E. Phillpotts, 1924.

Ashburnham, Captain Edward (Teddy), good soldier, magistrate, Hampshire landowner and pursuer of women.
Leonora, his wife, *née* Powys.
The Good Soldier, Ford Madox Ford, 1915.

Ashburton, Dr.
His wife.
Arthur, their son.
The Strange Adventures of a Phaeton, W. Black, 1872.

Ashby, Simon.
Patrick, his dead twin.
Eleanor, his sister, m. Brat Farrar.
Ruth, his sister.
Bee, their aunt.
Brat Farrar, Josephine Tey, 1949.

Ashby, Sir Thomas, m. Rosalie Murray.
His mother.
Agnes Grey, Anne Brontë, 1847.

Ashcroft, Mrs.
Arthur, her grandson.
'The Wish House' (s.s.), *Debits and Credits*, R. Kipling, 1926.

Ashe, Claude. *Thank Heaven Fasting*, E. M. Delafield, 1932.

Ashenden, writer, British secret agent, 1914–18 war. *Ashenden*, 1928 and *Cakes and Ale*, 1930, W. S. Maugham.

Asher, Captain.
Lise, his wife.
High Tor (play), Maxwell Anderson, 1937.

Asher, Helen, chief model of Zizzbaum & Son, m. John Platt. 'The Buyer from Cactus City' (s.s.), *The Trimmed Lamp*, O. Henry, 1907.

Ashford, Rev. Mr. *The Heir of Redclyffe*, Charlotte M. Yonge, 1853.

Ashleigh, Margaret, 'kind lady,' m. Albert-next-door's uncle (Morrison).
John, her 'reverend and surprising brother.'
The Would-be-Goods, E. Nesbit, 1901.

Ashley, Lady (Brett), one of the lost generation. *The Sun Also Rises* (or *Fiesta*), Ernest Hemingway, 1926.

Ashley, Caroline, a schoolmistress. *Sylvia Scarlett*, C. Mackenzie, 1918.

Ashley, Caroline. *Caroline* (play), W. S. Maugham, 1916.

Ashley, The Hon. Fred.
Lady Charlotte, his wife.
The Sky Pilot, R. Connor, 1899.

Ashley, Philip, central character and narrator, cousin and heir of Ambrose Ashley; m. Rachel Coryn, widow of Ambrose. *My Cousin Rachel,* Daphne du Maurier, 1951.

Ashley, Thomas, Mrs Halliburton's landlord. *Mrs Halliburton's Troubles,* Mrs Henry Wood, 1862.

Ashton, Annie, actress, m. Robert Vandiver. 'Rus in Urbe' (s.s.), *Options,* O. Henry, 1909.

Ashton, Sir William, lawyer and politician.
His wife.
Their children:
Colonel Sholto Douglas.
Lucy, m. Frank Hayston.
Henry.
The Bride of Lammermoor, W. Scott, 1819.

Ashurst, Frank, m. Stella Halliday. *The Apple Tree,* J. Galsworthy, 1918.

Ashworth, traveller. *The Good Companions,* J. B. Priestley, 1929.

Askill, friend of Mr Ingleside. *Mr Ingleside,* E. V. Lucas, 1910.

Asmodelius, Brother, Chief of the Brotherhood. 'Secret Worship,' *John Silence,* A. Blackwood, 1908.

Asmund, Asmundson, m. (1) Gudruda the Gentle.
Bjorn, their son.
Gudruda the Fair, their daughter, m. Eric Brighteyes.
(2) **Unna,** daughter of Thorod.
Swanhild, their daughter, m. Atli the Good.
Eric Brighteyes, H. Rider Haggard, 1891.

Asmunsen, quarry owner. *The Iron Heel,* Jack London, 1908.

Asparagus ('Gus'), theatre cat. *Old Possum's Book of Practical Cats* (poems), T. S. Eliot, 1939.

Aspatia, betrothed to Amintor. *The Maid's Tragedy* (play), Beaumont & Fletcher, 1611.

Aspent, Caroline, m. Ned Hipcroft. *See also* WAT OLLAMOOR.
Julia, her sister.
Her father.
'The Fiddler of the Reels,' *Life's Little Ironies,* T. Hardy, 1894.

Aspramonte, Knight of.
Lady of Aspramonte, his wife.
Brenhilda, their daughter, m. Count Robert of Paris.
Count Robert of Paris, W. Scott, 1832.

Assher, Lady, widow of Sir John.
Beatrice, her daughter, beautiful and cold-hearted, eng. to Anthony Wybrow.
'Mr Gilfil's Love Story,' *Scenes of Clerical Life,* George Eliot, 1857.

Assheton, Dr Francis. *The Thing in the Hall* (s.s.), E. F. Benson.

Assingham, Colonel Robert.
Fanny, his wife.
The Golden Bowl, Henry James, 1904.

Astarte. *Manfred* (poem), Lord Byron, 1817.

Astarte, Queen, m. Shehaab Fakredeen. *Tancred,* B. Disraeli, 1847.

Astell, Joe, Socialist councillor. *South Riding,* Winifred Holtby, 1936.

Asterias, Mr, 'the ichthyologist'; friend of Christopher Glowry.
Aquarius, his son.
Nightmare Abbey, T. L. Peacock, 1818.

Aston, slow-witted man who rents a room in his younger brother's house. *The Caretaker* (play), Harold Pinter, 1960.

Astrupp, Lady (Lillian), in love with John Loder. *John Chilcote, M.P.,* Katherine C. Thurston, 1904.

At-All. *The Double Gallant* (play), C. Cibber, 1707.

Ataliba. *Pizarro* (play), R. B. Sheridan, 1799.

Atheist. *Pilgrim's Progress,* J. Bunyan, 1678, 1684.

Athelny, Thorpe, friend of Philip Carey.
Betty, his 'unmarried wife.'
Their children:
Thorpe.
Athelstan.
Harold.
Edward.
Sally, m. Philip Carey.
Mollie.
Connie.
Rosie.
Jane.
Of Human Bondage, W. S. Maugham, 1915.

Athill, Rev. Mr, friend of Frank Gresham. *Doctor Thorne,* A. Trollope, 1858.

Athling, yeoman farmer and poet. *A Glastonbury Romance,* J. C. Powys, 1932.

Athon Daze, High Priest of Dungara. 'The Judgment of Dungara' (s.s.), *Soldiers Three,* R. Kipling, 1888.

Atkins, Group Secretary, Pym's Publicity. *Murder Must Advertise,* Dorothy L. Sayers, 1933.

Atkins, Will, mutineer, subsequently a penitent Christian.
His wife.
Robinson Crusoe, D. Defoe, 1719.

Atkinson, Idris, murderer of Dilys Pritchard. *How Green Was My Valley,* R. Llewellyn, 1939.

Atkinson, Joseph, servant of Jack Meredith. *With Edged Tools,* H. Seton Merriman, 1894.

Atkyns, Sir Thomas. *Pamela,* S. Richardson, 1740.

Atlas, Stanley, Negro actor. *The Troubled Air,* Irwin Shaw, 1951.

Atley. 'The Dog Hervey' (s.s.), *A Diversity of Creatures,* R. Kipling, 1917.

Atli the Good, Earl of the Orkneys, m. Swanhild Asmund. *Eric Brighteyes,* H. Rider Haggard, 1891.

Attentive, Mr, friend of Mr Wiseman. *The Life and Death of Mr Badman,* J. Bunyan, 1680.

Atterbury, Legare, lawyer. *An American Tragedy,* T. Dreiser, 1925.

Attwell, Mrs, matron, Stanstead School. *The Little Nugget,* P. G. Wodehouse, 1913.

Atwood, John de G., consul at Coralie. *Cabbages and Kings,* O. Henry, 1905.

Aubéry, Jean-Benoît, Frenchman and pirate, loved by Donna St Colomb. *Frenchman's Creek,* Daphne du Maurier, 1941.

Aubrac, Colonel Michel.
Emile, his father.
The Other Side, Storm Jameson, 1946.

Aubrey, Rev. Edward, curate of Brook Green. *Alice,* Lord Lytton, 1838.

Aubrey of Yatton, Charles, M.P., m. Agnes St Clair.
His mother.
Catherine, his sister.
Ten Thousand a Year, S. Warren, 1841.

Auclair, Euclide, Parisian apothecary who goes to Canada at end of 17th century.
Cecile, his daughter.
Shadows on the Rock, Willa Cather, 1932.

Audley, Mr. *Judith Paris,* Hugh Walpole, 1931.

Audley, Dr David, Ministry of Defence adviser. Chief character. *The Labyrinth Makers,* Anthony Price, 1970.

Audley, Sir Michael, Bt.
Lady Audley, his supposed wife, legally Mrs George Talboys (originally calling herself Lucy Graham).
Robert, his nephew.
Lady Audley's Secret, Mary E. Braddon, 1862.

Audrey, a country wench, m. Touchstone. *As You Like It* (play), W. Shakespeare.

Aufidius, Tullius, Volscian general. *Coriolanus* (play), W. Shakespeare.

Aufugus, Father. *Hypatia,* C. Kingsley, 1853.

Augustine, Father. *The Duenna* (play), R. B. Sheridan, 1775.

Auldearn, Lord (Ian Stewart), Lord Chancellor; guest at Scamnum. *Hamlet, Revenge!,* M. Innes, 1937.

Aumerle, Duke of, son of Duke of York. *Richard the Second* (play), W. Shakespeare.

Aunt, Mr F.'s, grim and mentally deficient old lady, left by Mr F. in the charge of Flora Finching. *Little Dorrit,* C. Dickens, 1857.

Aurigans, The, strange beings from Outer Space. *The Saliva Tree,* Brian W. Aldiss, 1966.

Austell, Mr and Mrs, a couple at odds with each other.
Toby, their son ('His Majesty').
'His Majesty the King' (s.s.), *Wee Willie Winkie,* R. Kipling, 1888.

Austell, Dowager Countess of (Teresa).
James, Earl of, her son.
Lady Dora West, her daughter, m. Claude Osborne.
The Osbornes, E. F. Benson, 1910.

Austin, club friend of Villiers. *The Great God Pan,* A. Machen, 1894.

Austin, George Fred ('Beau'). *Beau*

Austin (play), W. E. Henley & R. L. Stevenson, 1892.

Austria, Archduke of. *King John* (play), W. Shakespeare.

Autolycus, rogue. *A Winter's Tale* (play), W. Shakespeare.

Auvergne, Countess. *Henry the Sixth* (play), W. Shakespeare.

Avalon, Fay.
  John, K.C., her husband.
 'The Cavalier of the Streets' (s.s.), *These Charming People,* M. Arlen, 1920.

Avenal, Nora and Dick. *My Novel,* Lord Lytton, 1853.

Avenel, Baron of (Walter).
  Alice, his wife.
  Mary, their daughter, m. Halbert Glendenning.
  Julian, Walter's younger brother.
 See also CATHERINE OF NEWPORT. *The Monastery,* W. Scott, 1820.

Averill, Averill.
  Leolin, his father.
 Aylmer's Field (poem), Lord Tennyson.

Avery, Julia (Aunt Juley). *Howard's End,* E. M. Forster, 1910.

Avery, Maurice, school and college friend of Michael Fane. *Sinister Street,* 1913, and elsewhere, Compton Mackenzie.

Avon, a book collector. *Landmarks,* E. V. Lucas, 1914.

Avon, Lord (Edward).
  His wife, formerly Polly Hunter, actress.
  Jim, his son (known as Harrison and brought up as the blacksmith's nephew).
 Rodney Stone, A. Conan Doyle, 1896.

A-Water, John, Mayor of Cork. *Perkin Warbeck,* John Ford, 1634.

Axworthy, Francis.
  Samuel, his nephew and murderer.
 The Trial, Charlotte M. Yonge, 1864.

Ayacanora, Indian maiden, m. Amyas Leigh. *Westward Ho!,* C. Kingsley, 1855.

Ayesha (also addressed as 'Hiýa'), i.e. 'She who must be obeyed'; reincarnation of Amenartas. *She,* H. Rider Haggard, 1887.

Ayesha, the Maid of Kars. *Ayesha,* J. J. Morier, 1834.

Ayliffe, barrister. *Pendennis,* W. M. Thackeray, 1848–50.

Aylmer, prior of Jervaulx Abbey. *Ivanhoe,* W. Scott, 1820.

Aylmer, Mrs. *Woodstock,* W. Scott, 1826.

Aylmer, Alfred, owner of Cherry Hill Colliery. *A Safety Match,* Ian Hay, 1911.

Aylmer, Sir Aylmer.
  Edith, his daughter.
 Aylmer's Field (poem). Lord Tennyson.

Aylmer, Rose. *Rose Aylmer* (poem), W. S. Landor.

Aylward, Sam, an archer. *The White Company,* A. Conan Doyle, 1891.

Aylward, Sybil, friend of the Inglesides. *Mr Ingleside,* E. V. Lucas, 1910.

Aylwin, Henry, central character and narrator, m. Winnie Wynne.
  Philip, his father.
  His mother.
  Frank, his elder brother.
  Cyril, his kinsman, and heir to the Aylwin peerage; Bohemian painter.
 Aylwin, T. Watts-Dunton, 1899.

Ayr and Stirling, Duke of, m. Mabel Crum.
  Lady Elizabeth Randall, his daughter, m. Lord Harpenden.
 While the Sun Shines (play), T. Rattigan, 1943.

Ayresleigh, Mr, shabby middle-aged man under arrest. *Pickwick Papers,* C. Dickens, 1837.

Ayrton, James, John Brodie's junior partner, alias James Angaray, m. Isobel, *née* Easdaile, widow of Ronald McCaskie, alias John Brodie. *God's Prisoner,* J. Oxenham, 1898.

Ayrton, William. *I Live Under a Black Sun,* Edith Sitwell, 1937.

Ayscue, Miss, artist. *Albert Grope,* F. O. Mann, 1931.

Aythorne, Reg, m. Bessy Warbuckle. *South Riding,* Winifred Holtby, 1936.

Aziz, Dr, an Indian doctor. *A Passage to India,* E. M. Forster, 1924.

Azra. *See* JURGEN.

Azuma-zi, Asiatic half-caste attendant at Camberwell power-station. *Lord of the Dynamos* (s.s.), H. G. Wells, 1894.

Azzolati. *The Arrow of Gold,* J. Conrad, 1919.

B

B., Mr, villain-turned-hero, m. Pamela.
  Lady Dakers, his sister.
 Pamela, S. Richardson, 1740.

Baba, friend of Kate Brady.
  Frank, her husband, builder.
 Girls in Their Married Bliss, Edna O'Brien, 1964.

Baba, Hajji, of Ispahan. *Hajji Baba,* J. J. Morier, 1824.

Babalatchi, Mahmat, head of Almayer's household. *Almayer's Folly,* J. Conrad, 1895.

Babberley, Lord Fancourt, undergraduate. *Charley's Aunt* (play), Brandon Thomas, 1892.

Babbie, Lady (The Egyptian), m. Gavin Dishart. *The Little Minister,* J. M. Barrie, 1891.

Babbitt, Bob, reformed drunkard.
  Jessie, his wife.
 'The Rubaiyat of a Scotch Highball' (s.s.), *The Trimmed Lamp,* O. Henry, 1907.

Babbitt, George F., real-estate agent, 'Elk' and 'Booster,' central character.
  Myra, his wife, *née* Thompson.
  Their children:
   Verona, m. Kenneth Escott.
   Theodore Roosevelt (Ted), m. Eunice Littlefield.
   Katherine ('Tinka').
 Babbitt, Sinclair Lewis, 1923.

'Babe,' The, central character. *The Babe, B.A.,* E. F. Benson, 1897.

Babie (Barbara), attendant of Old Alice Gray. *The Bride of Lammermoor,* W. Scott, 1819.

Babington, Spencer, diplomat, in love with Paula Field. *The Great Pandolfo,* W. J. Locke, 1925.

Babraham, Marquess of (Henry), ('The Emir'), m. Jane Palfrey. *Antigua Penny Puce,* R. Graves, 1936.

Baby, Papin, bridge-keeper and keeper of the post office. *The Pomp of the Lavilettes,* Gilbert Parker, 1897.

Bachelor, a police-inspector. *The Mother,* E. Phillpotts, 1908.

Backbite, Sir Benjamin. *The School for Scandal* (play), R. B. Sheridan, 1777.

Backhouse, Arnold, young biologist, m. Elizabeth Fairford. *Late in the Afternoon,* Lettice Cooper, 1971.

Backystopper, coachman to Lady Kew. *Pendennis,* W. M. Thackeray, 1848–50.

Bacon, publisher; partner, later rival, of Bungay.
  His wife.
  His sister.
 Pendennis, W. M. Thackeray, 1848–50.

Bacurius, a lord. *A King and No King* (play), Beaumont & Fletcher, 1611.

Badcock, Mrs Heather, who gets murdered.
  Arthur, her husband.
 The Mirror Crack'd from Side to Side, Agatha Christie, 1962.

Baddeley, Commander, R.N. *The Middle Watch* (play), Ian Hay & S. King-Hall, 1929.

Badge, Miss, daughter of a wealthy soap-boiler. *The Virginians,* W. M. Thackeray, 1857–9.

Badgecumbe, Mr. *Mrs Miniver,* Jan Struther, 1939.

Badger, Captain. *Monsieur Beaucaire* (play), Booth Tarkington, 1902.

Badger, Mr, a badger. *The Wind in the Willows,* K. Grahame, 1908.

Badger, Dr Bayham, Kenge's cousin.
  Laura, his wife, previously twice widowed.
 Bleak House, C. Dickens, 1853.

Badger, Will, huntsman and servant of Sir Hugh Robsart, *Kenilworth,* W. Scott, 1821.

Badgery, Lord (Edmund). 'The Tillotson Banquet' (s.s.), *Mortal Coils,* A. Huxley, 1922.

Badman, Mr, eldest and wickedest of family, central character. *The Life and Death of Mr Badman,* J. Bunyan, 1680.

Baeticus, Spanish sea captain. 'The Manner of Men' (s.s.), *Limits and Renewals,* R. Kipling, 1932.

Bagarag, Shibli, chief barber to the Court of Persia. *The Shaving of Shagpat,* G. Meredith, 1856.

Bagenhall, James, friend of Sir Hargrave Pollexfen. *Sir Charles Grandison,* S. Richardson, 1754.

Bagg, Miss, heiress with whom Towrowski eloped. *Book of Snobs,* W. M. Thackeray, 1846–7.

Baggins, Bilbo, famous hobbit, finder of the One Ring.
Frodo, his young kinsman and heir.
The Lord of the Rings trilogy, 1954–5, J. R. R. Tolkien.

Bagheera, the Black Panther, friend of Mowgli. *The Jungle Books,* R. Kipling, 1894–5.

Baglioni, Pietro, Professor of Medicine at Padua. *Rappaccini's Daughter* (s.s.), N. Hawthorne, 1844.

Bagnet, Matthew, ex-artilleryman and owner of musician's shop.
His wife.
Malta and **Quebec,** their daughters.
Woolwich, their son.
Matthew's father and mother.
Bleak House, C. Dickens, 1853.

Bagot, creature to Richard. *Richard the Second* (play), W. Shakespeare.

Bagot, Jane, Henry Knowle's niece. *The Romantic Age* (play), A. A. Milne, 1920.

Bagot, Rev. John, Vicar of Bilberry. *Berry and Co.,* Dornford Yates, 1920.

Bagot, Myrtle, refreshment-room manageress. *Brief Encounter* (play), N. Coward, 1945.

Bagot, William ('Little Billie'), art student.
His mother, m. Sandy McAllister.
Blanche, his sister.
The Rev. T., his uncle.
Trilby, George du Maurier, 1894.

Bagshaw, employer of Eliza's husband. *Eliza's Husband,* etc., Barry Pain, 1900 onwards.

Bagshaw, Rev. Cyril Boom. *If Winter Comes,* A. S. M. Hutchinson, 1920.

Bagshot, highwayman. *The Beaux' Stratagem* (play), G. Farquhar, 1707.

Bagshot, M.P. for a Norfolk borough. *The Newcomes,* W. M. Thackeray, 1854–5.

Bagster, Whig M.P. for Middlemarch. *Middlemarch,* Geo. Eliot, 1871–2.

Bagster, Florrie. *Hilda Lessways,* Arnold Bennett, 1911.

Bagster, Freddie, in love with Helen Rolt. *The Heart of the Matter,* Graham Greene, 1948.

Bagstock, Major. *Dombey and Son,* C. Dickens, 1848.

Bahadur Khan, Imray's servant and his murderer. 'The Return of Imray' (s.s.), *Life's Handicap,* R. Kipling, 1891.

Bahni, a redeemed Sleepee in a world of the future. *Earthjacket,* Jon Hartridge, 1970.

Bailey. *Through a Window* (s.s.), H. G. Wells, 1894.

Bailey, Captain. *David Copperfield,* C. Dickens, 1850.

Bailey, Master, bailiff. *Gammer Gurton's Needle* (play), Anon. 1575.

Bailey, Agnes, m. Walter Herries. *The Fortress,* Hugh Walpole, 1932.

Bailey, Benjamin, boy at Mrs Todger's boarding-house. *Martin Chuzzlewit,* C. Dickens, 1844.

Bailey, Frank, m. Belinda Pye. *We're Here,* D. Mackail, 1947.

Bailey, Jack, bank cashier, posing as Alex Graham, under-gardener, m. Gertrude Innes. *The Circular Staircase,* Mary R. Rinehart, 1908.

Bailey, Oscar, political journalist, ex-civil servant.
Altiora, his wife.
The New Machiavelli, H. G. Wells, 1911.

Baillie, A.
His wife, son and three daughters.
Pickwick Papers, C. Dickens, 1837.

Baillie, Gabriel (known also as Gabriel Faa, and as Tod, or Hunter Gabbie).
Giles, his father.
Guy Mannering, W. Scott, 1815.

Baines, of Holly & Baines, Col. Newcome's bankers.
His daughters:
Euphemia and **Flora.**
The Newcomes, W. M. Thackeray, 1854–5.

Baines, Mrs. *Major Barbara* (play), G. B. Shaw, 1905.

Baines, Constance, m. Samuel Povey.
Sophia, her sister, m. Gerald Scales. Later known as Mrs Frensham, and keeper of a Parisian boarding-house.

John, their father, draper, Bursley.
His wife.
The Old Wives' Tale, Arnold Bennett, 1908.

Baines, Marjorie, Francie Comper's real mother. *For Us in the Dark,* Naomi Royde-Smith, 1937.

Bains, Lulu, Elmer Gantry's mistress. *Elmer Gantry,* Sinclair Lewis, 1927.

Baird, Rev. Mr. 'The Rev. Amos Barton,' *Scenes of Clerical Life,* George Eliot, 1857.

Baird, Angus, receiver and blackmailer. *Raffles,* E. W. Hornung, 1899–1901.

Baird, Francis Clark. *Counsellor-at-Law* (play), Elmer Rice, 1931.

Baird, Stephanie, Mark Stainer's secretary. *Thursday Afternoons,* Monica Dickens, 1945.

Baiteman, Roger. *A New Departure* (s.s.), R. S. Hichens.

Bajazet. *Tamerlane* (play), N. Rowe, 1701.

Bajazeth, Turkish emperor.
Zabina, his wife.
Tamburlaine (play), C. Marlowe, 1587.

Baker. 'Little Foxes' (s.s.), *Actions and Reactions,* R. Kipling, 1909.

Baker, Lady, widow, mother-in-law of Lovel.
Captain Clarence, her son.
Lovel the Widower, W. M. Thackeray, 1860.

Baker, Mrs, widowed postmistress. *The Postmistress of Laurel Run* (s.s.), Bret Harte, 1892.

Baker, Mrs Cherry, Miss Marple's young charlady. *The Mirror Crack'd from Side to Side,* Agatha Christie, 1962.

Baker, Freddy, m. Alice Hambro.
Dodo, their daughter.
Britannia Mews, Margery Sharp, 1946.

Baker, Henry.
His wife.
'The Blue Carbuncle,' *Adventures of Sherlock Holmes,* A. Conan Doyle, 1892.

Baker, John, scientist. *Other Gods,* Pearl Buck, 1940.

Baker, Jordan, friend of the Buchanans. *The Great Gatsby,* F. Scott Fitzgerald, 1925.

Baker, Steve, actor, m. Julie Dozier. *Show Boat,* Edna Ferber, 1926.

Baker, Lieutenant Tom, of *Compass Rose. The Cruel Sea,* N. Monsarrat, 1951.

Bakewell, Thomas, ploughman accused of arson. *The Ordeal of Richard Feverel,* G. Meredith, 1859.

Bakharoff, opera singer. *Grand Opera,* Vicki Baum, 1942.

Balaam.
His wife.
The Virginian, O. Wister, 1902.

Balakireff, Anton, famous violinist, in love with Lady Mary Wickham.
General Boris, his father.
His mother.
A Bargain with the Kremlin (s.s.), P. Gibbs.

Balan, Sir Balin, the savage.
His brother.
'Balin and Balan,' *Idylls of the King,* Lord Tennyson, 1859.

Balance, Mr.
His wife.
Tom Varnish (s.s.), R. Steele, *c.* 1709.

Balaton, Mme, wife of Percy Bowling. *They Wanted to Live,* Cecil Roberts, 1939.

Balchristie, Mrs Janet, mistress of the Laird of Dumbledikes.
The Heart of Midlothian, W. Scott, 1818.

Balcombe, Lady Caroline, Secretary of State for Foreign Affairs. *But Soft—We Are Observed!,* H. Belloc, 1928.

Baldassare, Sir, m. Giovanna Scarpa. 'Madonna of the Peach Tree' (s.s.), *Little Novels of Italy,* M. Hewlett, 1899.

Balder. *Balder* (poem), S. Dobell, 1853. *Balder Dead* (poem), M. Arnold, 1855.

Balderstone, Caleb, sole male servant of the Ravenswood family. *The Bride of Lammermoor,* W. Scott, 1819.

Balderstone, T. *Sketches by Boz,* C. Dickens, 1836.

Baldmoney, Mr and Mrs, butler and cook to John Sylvester Clayton. *Cricket in Heaven,* G. Bullett, 1949.

Baldock, Lord (George).
His wife.
Phineas Finn, 1869, and elsewhere, A. Trollope.

Baldrick, Saxon hero.
Vanda, his wife.
The Betrothed, W. Scott, 1825.

Baldringham, Lady of (Ermengarde). *The Betrothed,* W. Scott, 1825.

Baldry, Captain Chris.
Kitty, his wife.
Oliver, their dead son.
Jenny, Chris's cousin.
The Return of the Soldier, Rebecca West, 1918.

Baldwin, George, attorney.
Cicely, his wife.
Manhattan Transfer, J. dos Passos, 1925.

Balfour of Kinloch, John, leader in the army of the Covenanters. *Old Mortality,* W. Scott, 1816.

Balfour of Pilrig, cousin of David Balfour. *Catriona,* R. L. Stevenson, 1893.

Balfour of Shaws, David, central character and narrator, m. Catriona Drummond.
Alexander, his father.
Ebenezer, his uncle.
Kidnapped, 1886, and *Catriona,* 1893, R. L. Stevenson.

Bali, Chevalier de (Cornelius Barry), Irish dandy and adventurer, uncle of Barry Lyndon.
Barry Lyndon, W. M. Thackeray, 1844.

Balim, Mr. *Sketches of Young Gentlemen,* C. Dickens, 1838.

Balin. *See* BALAN.

Baliol, Martha Bethune, 'Lady of Quality.' *The Highland Widow,* W. Scott, 1827.

Balkis, Solomon's Queen. 'The Butterfly that Stamped' (s.s.), *Just So Stories,* R. Kipling, 1902.

Ball, evil genius of Dormitory 7. *Eric, or Little by Little,* F. W. Farrar, 1858.

Ball, Cain, boy assistant to Gabriel Oak. *Far from the Madding Crowd,* T. Hardy, 1874.

Ballam, Thomas. 'The Distracted Preacher,' *Wessex Tales,* T. Hardy, 1888.

Ballantrae. *See* DURRISDEER.

Ballard, railwayman. *Mrs Galer's Business,* W. Pett Ridge, 1905.

Ballardaile, Lady Jemima. *The Choice* (play), A. Sutro, 1919.

Ballart, Martin, ex-corporal. 'The Miracle of St Jubanus' (s.s.), *Limits and Renewals,* R. Kipling, 1932.

Ballater, internee in Holland. *The Fountain,* C. Morgan, 1932.

Ballenger, Major. *Jorrocks's Jaunts and Jollities,* R. S. Surtees, 1838.

Ballenkeiroch, clansman of Fergus McIvor. *Waverley,* W. Scott, 1814.

Balliol, The Misses, friends of Clive Newcome. *The Newcomes,* W. M. Thackeray, 1854–5.

Baloo, the brown bear, friend and teacher of Mowgli. *The Jungle Books,* R. Kipling, 1894–5.

Balthasar. *See* PORTIA.

Balthazar, merchant. *A Comedy of Errors* (play), W. Shakespeare.

Balthazar, servant of Romeo. *Romeo and Juliet* (play), W. Shakespeare.

Balthazar, servant to Don Pedro. *Much Ado about Nothing* (play), W. Shakespeare.

Balthazar. *The Spanish Tragedy* (play), T. Kyd, 1594.

Balthazar, S., Jewish doctor and mystic. *The Alexandria Quartet,* 1957–61, Lawrence Durrell.

Balue, John of, Cardinal and Bishop of Auxerre. *Quentin Durward,* W. Scott, 1823.

Balveeny, Lord, kinsman of the Earl of Douglas. *The Fair Maid of Perth,* W. Scott, 1828.

Balwhidder, Rev. Micah, minister at Dalmailing.
Betty Lanshaw, his 1st wife.
Lizy Kibbock, his 2nd wife.
Mrs Nugent, widow, his 3rd wife.
Annals of the Parish, John Galt, 1821.

Bamber, Jack, attorney's clerk. *Pickwick Papers,* C. Dickens, 1837.

Bamboo, Miami Mouth's fisherman lover who gets eaten by a shark. *Prancing Nigger,* Ronald Firbank, 1924.

Bamborough, Lord, 'Descendant of the Hotspurs.' *The Virginians,* W. M. Thackeray, 1857–9.

Bamborough, Mrs Sydney. *See* PRINCE ALEXIS.

Bambridge, a horse-dealer. *Middlemarch,* George Eliot, 1871–2.

Bamforth, Rosina (Rozzie), friend of Sara Monday: one of Gulley Jimson's 'wives'. *Herself Surprised,* 1941, and others, Joyce Cary.

Banbury, Jane.
William, her husband.
Fallen Angels (play), N. Coward, 1925.

Bancroft, Marcy, degenerate young woman. *Lovey Childs,* John O'Hara, 1969.

Bandar-Log, The, the Monkey people, vain and empty-headed. 'Kaa's Hunting' and elsewhere, *The Jungle Books,* R. Kipling, 1894–5.

Bando, Dai, miner and prize-fighter, friend of Huw Morgan. *How Green Was My Valley,* R. Llewellyn, 1939.

Bandon, 'Ally.' *One Day in the Shires* (s.s.), G. Frankau.

Bangham, Mrs, charwoman. *Little Dorrit,* C. Dickens, 1857.

Banghurst, unscrupulous journalist. *Filmer,* 1901, and other s.s., H. G. Wells.

Bangs, Lieutenant-General. 'A Code of Morals' (poem), *Departmental Ditties,* R. Kipling, 1886.

Bangs, Tommy, m. Dora West. *Little Men,* 1871, and *Jo's Boys,* 1886, Louisa M. Alcott.

Bangtext, Captain Salathiel, 'a godly gentleman.' *The Heart of Midlothian,* W. Scott, 1818.

Bankes, William, elderly scientist. *To The Lighthouse,* Virginia Woolf, 1927.

Banks, bailiff to Sir H. Mallinger.
His wife.
Daniel Deronda, George Eliot, 1876.

Banks, miller of Waltham. *The Merry Devil of Edmonton,* Anon.

Banks, Major (alias **Meltham**), old East India director. *Hunted Down,* C. Dickens, 1860.

Banks, George.
His wife.
Their children:
Jane.
Michael.
John.
Barbara.
Annabel.
Mary Poppins Opens The Door, 1944, and others, P. L. Travers.

Banks, Goodloe. 'Buried Treasure' (s.s.), *Options,* O. Henry, 1909.

Banks, Joey, friend of the Corries. *Pilgrimage,* Dorothy M. Richardson, 1915–38.

Banks, Myrtle, m. William Mulliner. *Meet Mr Mulliner,* P. G. Wodehouse, 1927.

Bann, Captain, scoundrel, partner of Denburn. *Rogue Herries,* Hugh Walpole, 1930.

Bannal. *Fanny's First Play* (play), G. B. Shaw, 1905.

Bannerbridge, lawyer.
His wife and daughter.
Adventures of Harry Richmond, G. Meredith, 1871.

Bannerman, Mabel, friend of Sylvia Scarlett. *Sylvia Scarlett,* C. Mackenzie, 1918.

Bannister, actor at Budmouth theatre, *The Trumpet Major,* T. Hardy, 1880.

Bannister, Mr. *Mr Rowl,* D. K. Broster, 1924.

Bannister, 'Young,' sea captain. 'Bread upon the Waters' (s.s.), *The Day's Work,* R. Kipling, 1898.

Bannister-Paget, Mrs Catherine. *Another Year,* R. C. Sherriff, 1948.

Banquo, general of the King's army. *Macbeth* (play), W. Shakespeare.

Bantam, Angelo Cyrus. *Pickwick Papers,* C. Dickens, 1837.

Bantam, Sir Hong Kong. *Theophrastus Such,* George Eliot, 1879.

Bantisor. *Monsieur Beaucaire* (play), Booth Tarkington, 1902.

Bantry, Mrs Dolly, former owner of Gossington Hall, old friend of Miss Marple. *The Mirror Crack'd from Side to Side,* 1962, and others, Agatha Christie.

Baps, dancing-master at Dr Blimber's. *Dombey and Son,* C. Dickens, 1848.

Baptista, rich gentleman of Padua, father of Katharine and Bianca. *The Taming of the Shrew* (play), W. Shakespeare.

Barabas, a wealthy Jew.
Abigail, his daughter.
The Jew of Malta (play), C. Marlowe, 1633.

Barabbas, a swindler. *Theophrastus Such,* George Eliot, 1879.

Baradas, favourite of Louis XIII. *Richelieu* (play), Lord Lytton, 1839.

Barban, Tommy, war hero. *Tender is the Night,* F. Scott Fitzgerald, 1934.

Barbante, Dominic, radio scriptwriter. *The Troubled Air*, Irwin Shaw, 1951.

Barbara, a nurse. *Barbara's Wedding* (play), J. M. Barrie, 1927.

Barbara, the Garlands' maid, m. Kit Nubbles.
Her mother.
The Old Curiosity Shop, C. Dickens, 1841.

Barbary, Miss, aunt and godmother of Esther Summerson. *Bleak House*, C. Dickens, 1853.

Barbason, Claude, Colin March's rival in the army. 'Honours Easy' (s.s.), *Fiery Particles*, C. E. Montague, 1923.

Barber, Nicol, friend of Dorothy Glover. *The Fair Maid of Perth*, W. Scott, 1828.

Barbi, Enrico Ottavio, Marchese. *Bluebeard's Keys*, Anne Thackeray, 1874.

Barbon, 'Nosy,' art student. *The Horse's Mouth*, Joyce Cary, 1944.

Barbree, m. Tranter Sweatley. 'The Fire at Tranter Sweatley's,' *Wessex Poems*, T. Hardy, 1898.

Barchester, Bishop of. *See* PROUDIE.

Barclay, Captain, narrator. 'The Striped Chest' (s.s.), *Tales of Pirates and Blue Water*, A. Conan Doyle.

Barclay, Colonel James. 'The Crooked Man,' *Memoirs of Sherlock Holmes*, A. Conan Doyle, 1894.

Barclay, Captain Tom, m. Lettice Watson, *née* Marling. The *Barsetshire* series, Angela Thirkell, 1933 onwards.

Bardell, Mrs Martha. Pickwick's landlady.
Tommy, her son.
Pickwick Papers, C. Dickens, 1837.

Bardi, Romola de, m. Tito Melema.
Bardo, her blind father.
Bernardino ('Dino'), her brother. *See* FRA LUCA.
Romola, George Eliot, 1863.

Bardolph, follower of Falstaff, later a soldier. *The Merry Wives of Windsor*, *Henry the Fourth* and *Henry the Fifth* (plays), W. Shakespeare.

Bardon, Hugh, scoutmaster to Prince John. *Ivanhoe*, W. Scott, 1820.

Bardshare, Mr and Mrs. 'The Sad Horn Blowers' (s.s.), *Horses and Men*, Sherwood Anderson, 1924.

Bareacres, Earl of (George), impoverished peer. Family name Thistlewood.
His wife.
Lady Blanche, their daughter, m. Lord Gaunt.
Lady Angela, their daughter, m. George Silvertop.
Vanity Fair, 1847–8, and *Pendennis*, 1848–50, W. M. Thackeray.

Barentz, Wilhelm, captain of the *Vrow Katerina*. *The Phantom Ship*, Captain Marryat, 1839.

Barfield, Major. *Tobermory* (s.s.), 'Saki' (H. H. Munro).

Barfield, Arthur.
His father, 'the Gaffer.'
Esther Waters, G. Moore, 1894.

Barfoot, Captain, town councillor.
Ellen, *née* Coppard, his wife.
Jacob's Room, Virginia Woolf, 1922.

Bargrave, Mrs, close friend of Mrs Veal.
Her husband and daughter.
The Apparition of Mrs Veal (s.s.), D. Defoe.

Baring, Martella, actress, charged with murder of Edna Druce. *Enter Sir John*, Clemence Dane & Helen Simpson, 1929.

Barker, artist. *The Newcomes*, W. M. Thackeray, 1854–5.

Barker, publisher. 'Why Billy Went Back' (s.s.), *All the World Wondered*, L. Merrick, 1911.

Barker, school bully. *Eric, or Little by Little*, F. W. Farrar, 1858.

Barker, Nurse, predecessor of Simpson at the Torrents. *Simpson*, E. Sackville-West, 1931.

Barker, Alastair.
His father.
Chosen Country, J. dos Passos, 1951.

Barker, Betty. *Cranford*, Mrs Gaskell, 1853.

Barker, Hon. James, Provost of South Kensington. *The Napoleon of Notting Hill*, G. K. Chesterton, 1904.

Barker, Jeremiah, cab-driver.
Polly, his wife.
Black Beauty, Anna Sewell, 1877.

Barker, Phil. *Oliver Twist*, C. Dickens, 1838.

Barkiarokh, Prince, youngest son of a fisherman.

Homaiouna, his wife, a disguised peri.
Vathek, W. Beckford, 1786.

Barkis, carrier, m. Clara Peggotty. *David Copperfield* C. Dickens, 1850.

Barkley, Nurse Catherine. *A Farewell to Arms,* E. Hemingway, 1939.

Barkston, George. *Dr Nikola,* G. Boothby, 1896.

Barlasch, Sergeant, French veteran, central character. *Barlasch of the Guard,* H. Seton Merriman, 1903.

Barley, Clara.
Old Barley, her father.
Great Expectations, C. Dickens, 1861.

Barley, Daisy (Mrs Fillans), ex-music-hall artist, landlady, Dog and Bell, Dunbury; m. Timmy Tiverton. *Let the People Sing.* J. B. Priestley, 1939.

Barley, Ernest Saunders.
Mary, his wife.
The One Before, Barry Pain, 1902.

Barlow, Captain, self-styled Duke of Shoreditch. *Windsor Castle,* W. H. Ainsworth, 1843.

Barlow, Mr and Mrs. *Love on the Dole,* W. Greenwood, 1933.

Barlow, Rev. Mr, tutor to Tom Merton and Harry Sandford. *Sandford and Merton,* T. Day, 1783–9.

Barlow, Christine, m. Andrew Manson. *The Citadel,* A. J. Cronin, 1937.

Barlow, Edith, a writer. *There Were No Windows,* Norah Hoult, 1944.

Barnabas, Rev. Mr. *Joseph Andrews,* H. Fielding, 1742.

Barnabas, Tom, of Barnabas Ltd, publishers.
Ritchie, his brother.
Sir Alexander, K.C., their cousin.
Flowers for the Judge, Margery Allingham, 1936.

Barnacle Family, The, including, among others:
Lord Decimus Tite-Barnacle.
Mr Tite-Barnacle.
Junior, his son.
Clarence, a genial idiot.
Ferdinand, private secretary to Lord Decimus. All of the Circumlocution Office.
Little Dorrit, C. Dickens, 1857.

Barnaclough, Lady. *The Thinking Reed,* Rebecca West, 1936.

Barnadine, a friar. *The Jew of Malta* (play), C. Marlowe, 1633.

Barnard. C.P.O., *Saltash. The Cruel Sea,* N. Monsarrat, 1951.

Barnard, Henry D., U.S. citizen. *Lost Horizon,* J. Hilton, 1933.

Barnard, Dr Thomas, friend and guardian of Denis Duval.
His wife.
Denis Duval, W. M. Thackeray, 1861.

Barnard, Toby, aircraft engineer and consultant.
Venetia, his wife.
Sebastian, their son.
A Net for Venus, David Garnett, 1959.

Barnes, Inspector. *Requiem for Robert,* Mary Fitt, 1942.

Barnes, Miss, journalist. *The Winslow Boy* (play), T. Rattigan, 1946.

Barnes, Betsy. *Joseph and his Brethren,* H. W. Freeman, 1928.

Barnes, George, brother of the Earl of Kew.
Lady Julia, his sister.
The Newcomes, W. M. Thackeray, 1854–5.

Barnes, Jake, American newspaperman in Europe. *The Sun Also Rises* (or *Fiesta*), Ernest Hemingway, 1926.

Barnes, Jonathan.
His daughters **Belle** and **Maddie.**
Robbery under Arms, R. Boldrewood, 1888.

Barnes, Stevie, m. Dolly Targett. *The Sailor's Return,* David Garnett, 1925.

Barnes, Will, country gallant. *Tom Jones,* H. Fielding, 1749.

Barnet, Mr, nephew of Lady Allestree. *Sir Charles Grandison,* S. Richardson, 1754.

Barnet, Frederick, infantry officer and wireless employer. *The World Set Free,* H. G. Wells, 1914.

Barnet, George, gentleman-burgher.
His wife.
'Fellow Townsmen,' *Wessex Tales,* T. Hardy, 1888.

Barney, a Jew, waiter in a low public-house, friend of Fagin. *Oliver Twist,* C. Dickens, 1838.

Barney, Bill, showman, friend of Paul

Finn. *The Fortunate Youth*, W. J. Locke, 1914.

Barney, Private Peg. 'The Big Drunk Draf' (s.s.), *Soldiers Three*, R. Kipling, 1888.

Barnstaple, Alfred, subeditor, *The Liberal. Men like Gods*, H. G. Wells, 1923.

Barnwell, B. B. *Martin Chuzzlewit*, C. Dickens, 1844.

Barnwell, George. *George Barnwell* (play), G. Lillo, 1731.

Baroni, Eastern servant of Lord Montacute. *Tancred*, B. Disraeli, 1847.

Baroski, Signor Benjamin. 'The Ravenswing,' *Men's Wives*, W. M. Thackeray, 1843.

Baroudi, Mahmoud, wealthy Turco-Egyptian. *Bella Donna*, R. S. Hichens, 1909.

Barr-Saggott, Antony, Commissioner. 'Cupid's Arrows' (s.s.), *Plain Tales from the Hills*, R. Kipling, 1888.

Barrack, Dr Elihu, of Sundering-on-Sea. *The Undying Fire*, H. G. Wells, 1919.

Barraclough, Rev. Amos. 'On Greenhow Hill' (s.s.), *Life's Handicap*, R. Kipling, 1891.

Barracott, Captain James, of the *Bluewing. God's Prisoner*, J. Oxenham, 1898.

Barralonga, Lord. *Men Like Gods*, H. G. Wells, 1923.

Barratter, Counsellor, an old Templar. *The Fortunes of Nigel*, W. Scott, 1822.

Barraway, Miss, nurse-secretary to Sir Henry Harcourt-Reilly. *The Cocktail Party* (play), T. S. Eliot, 1950.

Barrett, Jack and Mrs. 'The Story of Uriah' (poem), *Departmental Ditties*, R. Kipling, 1886.

Barrington, Captain.
His son.
Mr Rowl, D. K. Broster, 1924.

Barrington, Captain, card-sharper, brother of Lord Avon. *Rodney Stone*, A. Conan Doyle, 1896.

Barron, Deacon. *The Heart of Midlothian*, W. Scott, 1818.

Barron, Wilkie, opportunist. *World Enough and Time*, Robert Penn Warren, 1950.

Barrus, Titus Veturius, m. Aemilia.
Caius, their son.
Laelia, their daughter.
Caius, Titus's grandfather.
The Conquered, Naomi Mitchison, 1923.

Barry, Redmond. *See* Barry Lyndon.
Mrs Barry, mother of Barry Lyndon.
Sir Charles, diplomat and *roué*, whose widow m. Barry Lyndon.
Barry Lyndon, W. M. Thackeray, 1852.

Barry, Tom, m. Rosie Phelan. *Without My Cloak*, Kate O'Brien, 1931.

Barrymore, caretaker at Baskerville Hall.
His wife, sister of Selden.
The Hound of the Baskervilles, A. Conan Doyle, 1902.

Barsad, John. *See* Solomon Pross.

Barstow, Captain. *See* Fenwicke.

Bart, Lily, central character.
Hudson, her father.
Her mother.
The House of Mirth, Edith Wharton, 1905.

Bartels, Schoffer, owner of galliot *Johannes*.
Karl, his son.
The Riddle of the Sands, E. Childers, 1903.

Barter, Rev. Hussell, rector at Worsted Skeynes. *The Country House*, John Galsworthy, 1907.

Barter, Timothy, K.C., divorce advocate. *Holy Deadlock*, A. P. Herbert, 1934.

Barter, Tom, Philip Crow's manager. *A Glastonbury Romance*, J. C. Powys, 1932.

Bartholomew, Mark. *Britannia Mews*, Margery Sharp, 1946.

Bartleby, Sydney, American writer living in Suffolk.
Alicia, his English wife, *née* Sneezum, who disappears.
A Suspension of Mercy, Patricia Highsmith, 1965.

Bartlett, Mr and Mrs and Family, Denham Dobie's paternal relations. *Crewe Train*, Rose Macaulay, 1926.

Bartlett, Miss Charlotte. *A Room with a View*, E. M. Forster, 1908.

Bartley, Ned, chemist, scholar and antiquarian, school friend of Derry Middleton. *Both of this Parish*, J. S. Fletcher.

Bartoli, Dr, veterinary surgeon. *The Small Miracle,* P. Gallico, 1951.

Barton, Mr. *Tom Burke of Ours,* C. Lever, 1844.

Barton, Mr, architect.
His wife.
Guy, their son.
Alice, their daughter, m. Roddy Wicklow.
The *Barsetshire* series, Angela Thirkell, 1933 onwards.

Barton, Rev. Amos, curate of Shepperton.
Amelia (Milly), his wife.
Frederick, Patty, Sophy, Walter, and two others, their children.
'The Rev. Amos Barton,' *Scenes of Clerical Life,* George Eliot, 1857.

Barton, Sir Andrew, pirate gun-runner. 'Hal o' the Draft' (s.s.), *Puck of Pook's Hill,* R. Kipling, 1906.

Barton, Arthur, artist.
Anna, his wife.
Olive, their daughter.
Alice, their daughter, m. Dr Reed.
A Drama in Muslin, G. Moore, 1886.

Barton, Herminia, central character. *The Woman who Did,* Grant Allen, 1895.

Barton, Jacob, grocer.
His wife.
Sketches by Boz, C. Dickens, 1836.

Barton, John.
Mary, his wife.
Mary, their daughter, m. Jem Wilson.
Esther, his sister.
Mary Barton, Mrs Gaskell, 1848.

Barton, Ralph, friend of Jeremy Melford. *Humphry Clinker,* T. Smollett, 1771.

Bartram, George, nephew of Andrew Vanstone.
Admiral Arthur Bartram, his uncle.
No Name, W. Collins, 1862.

Barty, Barnabas (alias **Beverley),** central character, m. Lady Cleone Meredith.
John, his father, ex-champion prize-fighter and landlord of the Coursing Hound.
The Amateur Gentleman, J. Farnol, 1913.

Barwick, Mrs. *Berkeley Square* (play), J. L. Balderston, 1926.

Bascom, Sally, masquerading as the Marquis, whom she m. 'The Marquis and Miss Sally' (s.s.), *Rolling Stones,* O. Henry, 1913.

Bascomb, Maury L., brother of Mrs Compson. *The Sound and the Fury,* W. Faulkner, 1931.

Basil, central character and narrator, m. Margaret Sherwin.
Ralph, his elder brother.
Clara, his sister.
His father, an M.P.
Basil, W. Collins, 1852.

Basildon, Lady (Olivia). *An Ideal Husband* (play), O. Wilde, 1895.

Basilios, Prince. *The Gates of Summer* (play), John Whiting, 1956.

Baskerville, Sir Charles, deceased.
Sir Henry, his nephew and successor.
The Hound of the Baskervilles, A. Conan Doyle, 1902.

Baslow, Mr. *Yellow Sands* (play), E. & A. Phillpotts, 1926.

Bass, trapping poacher. *Middlemarch,* George Eliot, 1871–2.

Bassanio, friend of Antonio, m. Portia. *The Merchant of Venice* (play), W. Shakespeare.

Basset, Anthony, attorney.
Nelly, his niece.
Tom Burke of Ours. C. Lever, 1844.

Basset, Sir Reginald, K.C.B., guardian of Muriel Roscoe.
His wife.
The Way of an Eagle, Ethel M. Dell, 1912.

Basset, Simon. *Jerome,* Mary E. Wilkins, 1897.

Basset-Holmer, Captain. 'The Man Who Was' (s.s.), *Life's Handicap,* R. Kipling, 1891.

Bassett, gardener, partner with Paul. *The Rocking Horse Winner* (s.s.), D. H. Lawrence.

Bassianus, in love with Lavinia. *Titus Andronicus* (play), W. Shakespeare.

Bassington, Comus, central character.
Francesca, his mother.
The Unbearable Bassington, 'Saki' (H. H. Munro), 1912.

Bassompierre, Count, father of Paulina Home. *Villette,* Charlotte Brontë, 1853.

Bast, Leonard, clerk, occupant with

Jacky of flat in Camelia Road; lover of Helen Schlegel.

Jacky, his mistress, later his wife.

Howard's End, E. M. Forster, 1910.

Bastable, Sir Raymond, K.C. ('Beefy'), m. Barbara Crowe. *Cocktail Time,* P. G. Wodehouse, 1958.

Bastable, Richard.

His children:

Dora.

Oswald.

Dicky.

Alice and Noel (twins).

Horace Octavius (H.O.).

The Treasure Seekers, 1899, and *The Would-be-Goods,* 1901, E. Nesbit.

Bas-Thornton. *See* FREDERICK BAS THORNTON.

Bastling, Captain. *The Gay Lord Quex* (play), A. W. Pinero, 1899.

Baston, Jenny, central character, m. Sir Humphrey Mallard.

Tom, her father.

Lizzie, her mother.

Timothy, her brother, m. Wing Halnaker.

Iron and Smoke, Sheila Kaye-Smith, 1928.

Bastwick, Engineer Lieutenant Charles, of *Artemis. The Ship,* C. S. Forester, 1943.

Batch, Katie, landlady's daughter.

Her mother.

Clarence, her brother.

Zuleika Dobson, M. Beerbohm, 1911.

Batchelor, Charles, sentimental bachelor with literary tastes, friend of Lovel. *Lovel the Widower,* W. M. Thackeray, 1860.

Batchelor, Clyde, central character, m. Lucy Page, widow. *Steamboat Gothic,* Frances Parkinson Keyes, 1952.

Bates, headmaster of United Services College. *Stalky & Co.,* R. Kipling, 1899.

Bates, gardener to Sir Christopher Cheverel. 'Mr Gilfil's Love Story,' *Scenes of Clerical Life,* George Eliot, 1857.

Bates, Farmer. *The Hampdenshire Wonder,* J. D. Beresford, 1911.

Bates, Mrs, widow of the Vicar of Highbury.

Her daughter.

Emma, Jane Austen, 1816.

Bates, Belinda. 'The Haunted House' (s.s.), *Christmas Stories,* C. Dickens, 1859.

Bates, Bill (alias **Alan Beverley**), m. Annette Brougham. *The Man Upstairs,* P. G. Wodehouse, 1914.

Bates, Charley, one-time pupil of Fagin. *Oliver Twist,* C. Dickens, 1838.

Bates, Ida, stenographer. 'The Enchanted Profile' (s.s.), *Roads of Destiny,* O. Henry, 1909.

Bates, Susan. *The Bachelor's Dream* (poem), T. Hood.

Bates, William, m. Jane Packard. 'Rodney Fails to Qualify' (s.s.). *The Heart of a Goof,* P. G. Wodehouse, 1926.

Bath, Dr, Casterbridge doctor. *The Mayor of Casterbridge,* T. Hardy, 1886.

Batherbolt, Rev. Mr, curate, m. Georgiana Longestaffe. *The Way We Live Now,* A. Trollope, 1875.

Bathgate, Bella, landlady to Pamela Reston. *Penny Plain,* O. Douglas, 1920.

Bathgate, Noel, 'Watson' to Roderick Alleyn. *Enter a Murderer,* 1935, and many others, Ngaio Marsh.

Bathsheba, maid to Herod's wife. *Herod* (play), Stephen Phillips, 1900.

Bathurst, Mrs, hotel-keeper. 'Mrs Bathurst' (s.s.), *Traffics and Discoveries,* R. Kipling, 1904.

Bathwick, Miss, Boon's secretary. *Boon,* H. G. Wells, 1915.

Batney, Bill, of the Foreign Office. *Sunrise in the West,* Bechofer Roberts, 1945.

Batouch, Arab poet and wanderer. *The Garden of Allah,* R. S. Hichens, 1904.

Batt & Cowley, lawyers of the Bycliffes. *Felix Holt,* George Eliot, 1866.

Batt, Mr A. J., Mrs Tuke's ancient deaf lodger. *Miss Gomez and The Brethren,* William Trevor, 1971.

Battchilena, Leon, Spanish musician. *No Other Tiger,* A. E. W. Mason, 1927.

Battersby, officer at Waterloo. 'The Peasant's Confession,' *Wessex Poems,* T. Hardy, 1898.

Battersby, Simon.

Angela, his daughter.

To Have the Honour (play), A. A. Milne, 1924.

Batterson, Maisie. *See* MRS CARGHILL. *The Elder Statesman* (play), T. S. Eliot, 1958.

Battiscombe, Laura, m. Rev. Aloysius Cleary.
  Sir George, her father.
Laura's Bishop, G. A. Birmingham, 1949.

Battle, Ben. *Faithless Nelly Gray* (poem), T. Hood.

Battle, David.
  David, his father, a painter.
  His mother.
The Dancing Druids. Gladys Mitchell, 1948.

Battle, Mrs Sarah, devotee of whist. *Essays of Elia*, Charles Lamb, 1823.

Batts, Captain, adventurer. *The Virginians*, W. M. Thackeray, 1857–9.

Bauche, La Mère.
  Adolphe, her son.
La Mère Bauche (s.s.), A. Trollope.

Baudricourt, Robert de (hist.), *Saint Joan* (play), G. B. Shaw, 1924.

Bauer, servant of von Tarlenheim. *Rupert of Hentzau*, A. Hope, 1898.

Bauer, Karl, A.B., the *Blackgauntlet*. *The Bird of Dawning*, J. Masefield, 1933.

Bauersch, Mr, American book-buyer. *Riceyman Steps*, A. Bennett, 1923.

Bauerstein, Dr, spy. *The Mysterious Affair at Styles*, Agatha Christie, 1920.

Baughton, Sir Curry.
  His wife and daughter.
The Newcomes, W. M. Thackeray, 1854–5.

Bauldie, old shepherd story-teller. *The Black Dwarf*, W. Scott, 1816.

Baum, Carlo (real name Christopher Potter), m. Elvira Vian Cookson.
  Joseph Potter, his son.
The Long Time Growing Up, John Pudney, 1971.

Baumgartner, Karl, alcoholic lawyer.
  Greta, his wife.
Ship of Fools, Katherine Anne Porter, 1962.

Baviaan, a wise baboon. 'How the Leopard got his Spots' (s.s.), *Just So Stories*, R. Kipling, 1902.

Bawne, Myra, mistress of Paul Presset. *We the Accused*, E. Raymond, 1935.

Baxby, Lord and Lady. 'Old Audrey's Experience,' *Life's Little Ironies*, T. Hardy, 1894.

Baxter, Harold. *Belinda* (play), A. A. Milne, 1918.

Baxter, J. M. M., solicitor. 'The House Surgeon' (s.s.), *Actions and Reactions*, R. Kipling, 1909.

Baxter, Jody, central character.
  Ezra Ezekiel, his father.
  Ory, his mother.
The Yearling, Marjorie K. Rawlings, 1938.

Baxter, John, narrator. *The Four Armourers*, 1930, and others, F. Beeding.

Baxter, Samuel, detective. *The Silver King* (play), H. A. Jones, 1882.

Baxter, Timothy, tool of Squire Thornhill, abductor of Olivia Primrose. *The Vicar of Wakefield*, O. Goldsmith, 1766.

Bayer, friend of Arthur Norris. *Mr Norris Changes Trains*, C. Isherwood, 1935.

Bayham, Frederick, eccentric journalist and mimic; friend of Colonel Newcome.
  Squire Bayham, his father.
The Newcomes, W. M. Thackeray, 1854–5.

Bayley, Colonel ('Boy'). 'The Army of a Dream' (s.s.), *Traffics and Discoveries*, R. Kipling, 1904.

Baynard.
  His wife, an extravagant vixen.
Humphry Clinker, T. Smollett, 1771.

Bayne, Foreman of works. *Put Yourself in his Place*, C. Reade, 1870.

Baynes, General Charles, retired Indian officer, henpecked; trustee of Philip Firmin.
  His wife.
  Their children:
    Charlotte, m. Philip Firmin.
    Jany.
    Mary.
    Moira.
    Ochterlong.
    M'Grigor.
    Carrick.
The Adventures of Philip, W. M. Thackeray, 1861–2.

Baynes, Frederick Peak, youthful poetaster. *Love and Mr Lewisham*, H. G. Wells, 1900.

Baynes, Hon. Morison. *Tarzan* series, E. R. Burroughs, 1912 onwards.

Baynet, Patricia, m. Peter Jackson.
Dr Heron, her father, psychiatrist.
John, her brother.
Violet, her sister, m. Hubert Rawlings.
Peter Jackson, Cigar Merchant, G. Frankau, 1919.

Bazalgette, Captain Reginald, of *Vulture*, cousin of Captain Dodd. *Hard Cash,* C. Reade, 1863.

Bazardo, Spanish painter. *The Spanish Tragedy* (play), T. Kyd, 1594.

Bazzard, clerk to Grewgious. *Edwin Drood,* C. Dickens, 1870.

Beach, Esther. *The Trumpet Major,* T. Hardy, 1880.

Beach-Mandarin, Lady, friend of Lady Harman. *The Wife of Sir Isaac Harman,* 1914, and elswhere, H. G. Wells.

Beacon, Tone, groom attached to Tom Chiffinch. *Peveril of the Peak,* W. Scott, 1822.

Beadle, Harriet. *See* TATTYCORAM.

Beagham, Mrs Caroline, blackmailer.
Judy, her daughter.
No Other Tiger, A. E. W. Mason, 1927.

Beagle-Boy, an unpleasant half-witted foxhound in the Gihon Hunt. 'Little Foxes' (s.s.), *Actions and Reactions,* R. Kipling, 1909.

Beaker, Sheila (Sheikie), m. Trevor Artworth, house agent. *The Little Girls,* Elizabeth Bowen, 1964.

Beaksby, magistrate. *Adventures of Philip,* W. M. Thackeray, 1861–2.

Bealby, Arthur, central character, junior servant at Shonts, Sir Peter Laxton's house. *Bealby,* H. G. Wells, 1915.

Beale, 'hired retainer.'
His wife.
Love Among the Chickens, P. G. Wodehouse, 1906.

Beam, Mrs, boarding-house keeper. *At Mrs Beam's* (play), C. K. Munro, 1923.

Beaminster, Lord, once eng. to Jennifer Card. *Judith Paris,* Hugh Walpole, 1931.

Beamish, Mrs, landlady.
Tilly, her daughter, m. (1) Mr Ocock. (2) Purdy Smith.
Jinny, her daughter, m. John Turnham as 2nd wife.
The Fortunes of Richard Mahoney, H. H. Richardson, 1917–30.

Beamish, Alderman Giles. *Harry Lorrequer,* C. Lever, 1839.

Beamish, Victor. *Housemaster* (play), Ian Hay, 1936.

Bean, of Wilson & Bean, solicitors. *Kipps,* H. G. Wells, 1905.

Bean, Jimmy. *Pollyanna,* Eleanor H. Porter, 1913.

Bear, Edward. *See* WINNIE-THE-POOH.

Bearcliff, Deacon. *Guy Mannering,* W. Scott, 1815.

Beardsall, Cyril, central character.
Frank, his father.
Rebecca, his mother.
Lettice, his sister, m. Leslie Tempest.
The White Peacock, D. H. Lawrence, 1911.

Beasley, Miss, companion to Mrs Parkington. *Mrs Parkington,* L. Bromfield, 1944.

Beatrice, niece of Leonato, m. Benedick. *Much Ado about Nothing* (play), W. Shakespeare.

Beaucaire, Monsieur. *Monsieur Beaucaire* (play), Booth Tarkington, 1902.

Beauchamp, Viscount.
Lady Diana Vernon, his sister, m. Francis Osbaldistone. (Both titles conferred by ex-James II.)
Rob Roy, W. Scott, 1818.

Beauchamp, Charles, Conservative candidate.
Lady Edith, his wife.
Fed Up, G. A. Birmingham, 1931.

Beauchamp, Sir Edward, Bt., m. Emily Gervois. *Sir Charles Grandison,* S. Richardson, 1754.

Beauchamp, Henry. *Diary of a Late Physician,* S. Warren, 1832.

Beauchamp, Richard de. *See* WARWICK.

Beaucock, Fred, lawyer's clerk. *The Woodlanders,* T. Hardy, 1887.

Beauffet, butler to Mrs Bethune Baliol. *The Highland Widow,* W. Scott, 1827.

Beaufoy, Philip, of the Playgoers' Club.
Mina, his wife.
Ulysses, James Joyce, 1922.

Beaufrere, Mrs Claudia. *The Human Comedy,* W. Saroyan, 1942.

Beaugard, Captain, soldier of fortune. *The Soldier's Fortune* (play), Thomas Otway, 1681.

Beaujeu, Count de, of the Young Chevalier's bodyguard. *Waverley,* W. Scott, 1814.

Beaujeu, Monsieur de, 'King of the Card-pack, Duke of the Dice-box,' *The Fortunes of Nigel,* W. Scott, 1822.

Beaujolais, Major Henri de. *Beau Geste,* P. C. Wren, 1924.

Beaumanoir, Lucas de, Grand Master of the Templars. *Ivanhoe,* W. Scott, 1820.

Beaumont, Adam. 'Revenge upon Revenge' (s.s.), *Love and Money,* Phyllis Bentley, 1957.

Beaumont, Jeremiah, lawyer and idealist.
    Rachael, his wife, *née* Jordan.
World Enough and Time, Robert Penn Warren, 1950.

Beaumont, Ned, gambler and amateur detective. *The Glass Key,* Dashiell Hammett, 1931.

Beaumont-Green, George. *The Hill,* H. A. Vachell, 1905.

Beaumoris, 'Beau,' 'a sort of Grand Seigneur.' *Vanity Fair,* 1847–1848, and elsewhere, W. M. Thackeray.

Beaupertuys, Marquis of. 'Roads of Destiny' (s.s.), *Roads of Destiny,* O. Henry, 1909.

Beaupré, Madame de. *No Son of Mine,* G. B. Stern, 1948.

Beauseant, rich gentleman. *The Lady of Lyons* (play), Lord Lytton, 1838.

Beautiman, Kate, owner of typewriting agency.
    Ellen and **Sarah,** her sisters.
Mr Ingleside, E. V. Lucas, 1910.

Beaver, Captain of frigate. *Waverley,* W. Scott, 1814.

Beaver, Mrs, interior decorator.
    John, her son.
A Handful of Dust, Evelyn Waugh, 1934.

Beavis, Anthony, modest philosopher. *Eyeless in Gaza,* Aldous Huxley, 1936.

Bebb, Mrs.
    James, her son.
At Mrs Beam's (play), C. K. Munro, 1923.

Beca, wife of Simon. 'The Way of the Earth' (s.s.), *My People,* Caradoc Evans, 1915.

Bechamel, objectionable art critic and Hoopdriver's adversary. *The Wheels of Chance,* H. G. Wells, 1896.

Beck, Mrs, lodging-house keeper. *Middlemarch,* Geo. Eliot, 1871–2.

Beck, Mrs, maid to Lady Rockminster. *Pendennis,* W. M. Thackeray, 1848–50.

Beck, Modeste, schoolmistress; *née* Maria Kent. *Villette,* Charlotte Brontë, 1853.

Becker, Harry and Sarah. *Counsellor-at-Law* (play), Elmer Rice, 1931.

Beckett, Mr and Mrs.
    Lucy, their daughter.
Fanny by Gaslight, M. Sadleir, 1940.

Beckett, Bob, carpenter's mate. *H.M.S. Pinafore* (comic opera), Gilbert & Sullivan, 1878.

Beckett, Sarah, m. Martin Whitelaw as 2nd wife. *Roots,* Naomi Jacob, 1931.

Beckwith, Seth. *Mourning becomes Electra* (play), E. O'Neill, 1931.

Beddoes, Sir John, Bt. *The Pride of Jennico,* A. & E. Castle, 1898.

Beddows, Alderman Mrs Emma.
    Jim, her husband.
    Their children:
        Willie, a widower.
            Wendy, his daughter.
        Chloe.
        Sybil.
South Riding, Winifred Holtby, 1936.

Bede, Adam, carpenter, central character, m. Dinah Morris.
    Mathias, his father.
    Lisbeth, his mother.
    Seth, his brother.
Adam Bede, George Eliot, 1859.

Bedford, playwright and bankrupt, narrator; later alias Blake. *The First Men in the Moon,* H. G. Wells, 1901.

Bedford, Duke of (Prince John of Lancaster). *Henry the Fourth* and *Henry the Fifth* (plays), W. Shakespeare.

Bedford, Duke of, Regent of France. *Henry the Sixth* (play), W. Shakespeare.

Bedford, Dick, butler to Lovel.
    Mary, *née* Pinhorn, his wife.

Lovel the Widower, W. M. Thackeray, 1860.

Bedivere, Sir, last survivor of the Round Table. *Idylls of the King,* Lord Tennyson, 1859.

Bedloe, Augustus. *A Tale of the Ragged Mountains* (s.s.), E. A. Poe.

Bedonebyasyoudid, Mrs. *Water Babies,* C. Kingsley, 1863.

Bedrooket, Lady. *Redgauntlet,* W. Scott, 1824.

Bedwin, Mrs, housekeeper to Brownlow. *Oliver Twist,* C. Dickens, 1838.

Beebe, Rev. Arthur. *A Room with a View,* E. M. Forster, 1908.

Beech, Patty. 'At Casterbridge Fair' (poem), *Time's Laughing Stocks,* T. Hardy, 1909.

Beechcroft, Abel and Trussell, brothers, uncles of Randolph Crew. *The Miser's Daughter,* W. H. Ainsworth, 1842.

Beeder, Sir William and Lady. *The Horse's Mouth,* Joyce Cary, 1944.

Beedle, Mr, station-master at Winter Overcotes.
  Henry, their son.
Growing Up, Angela Thirkell, 1943.

Beefington, Milor. *The Rovers* (play), G. Canning, 1820.

Beekman, Sir Frances.
  His wife.
Gentlemen Prefer Blondes, Anita Loos, 1925.

Beel, friend of Kenn. *Highland River,* N. M. Gunn, 1937.

Beelbrow, Mrs Poulteney.
  Her husband, stockbroker.
'Mrs Beelbrow's Lions' (s.s.), *Miss Bracegirdle and Others,* Stacy Aumonier, 1923.

Beere, John, solicitor.
  Angela, his daughter.
A Glastonbury Romance, J. C. Powys, 1932.

Beesley, friend and fellow lodger of James Dixon. *Lucky Jim,* K. Amis, 1953.

Beetle, one of the 'Stalky' trio. *Stalky & Co.* throughout, 1899, and stories in later books, R. Kipling.

Beetle, Mrs.
  Agony, her husband.
  Meriam, her daughter, hired girl, mother of four.
Cold Comfort Farm, Stella Gibbons, 1932.

Beeton, Dick Helder's landlord.
  His wife.
The Light that Failed, R. Kipling, 1890.

Beevor, Mrs, stepdaughter of Lord Grinsell. *Middlemarch,* George Eliot, 1871–2.

Beevor, William, rival architect and neighbour of Horace Ventimore. *The Brass Bottle,* F. Anstey, 1900.

Begs, Mrs Ridger, *née* Micawber. *David Copperfield,* C. Dickens, 1850.

Beguildy, Jancis.
  Felix, her father (Wizard).
  Hephzibah, her mother.
Precious Bane, Mary Webb, 1924.

Behrens, Oxford don and authority on molecular physics. *Marriage,* H. G. Wells, 1912.

Behrman, old and unsuccessful artist. 'The Last Leaf' (s.s.), *The Trimmed Lamp,* O. Henry, 1907.

Beighton, Kitty. 'Cupid's Arrows' (s.s.), *Plain Tales from the Hills,* R. Kipling, 1888.

Bel Affris. *Caesar and Cleopatra* (play), G. B. Shaw, 1900.

Bel the Harper. 'The Melancholy of Ulad' (s.s.), *Spiritual Tales,* Fiona Macleod, 1903.

Belarius (Morgan), banished lord. *Cymbeline* (play), W. Shakespeare.

Belch, Sir Toby, uncle of Olivia. *Twelfth Night* (play), W. Shakespeare.

Belfield, draper's son posing as a society man.
  Henrietta, his youngest sister, m. Arnott.
Cecilia, Fanny Burney, 1782.

Belfield, Duke of. *Evan Harrington,* G. Meredith, 1861.

Belford. *The Clandestine Marriage* (play), G. Colman the Elder, 1766.

Belford, John, friend of Robert Lovelace. *Clarissa Harlowe,* S. Richardson, 1748.

Belinda. *The Rape of the Lock* (poem), A. Pope, 1714.

Belinda. *Belinda,* Maria Edgeworth, 1801.

Belknap, Alvin, defending counsel for Clyde Griffiths. *An American Tragedy,* T. Dreiser, 1925.

Bell, skipper of the *Kite*. 'Bread upon the Waters' (s.s.), *The Day's Work*, R. Kipling, 1898.

'Bell,' ward and companion of Titania, m. Count van Rosen. *The Strange Adventures of a Phaeton*, W. Black, 1872.

Bell, Adam, godfather and benefactor of Margaret Hale. *North and South*, Mrs Gaskell, 1855.

Bell, Rev. Francis, chaplain, Coventry Island.

Martha, *née* Coacher, his ill-tempered wife.

Helen Laura, their daughter, adopted by Helen Pendennis, m. Arthur Pendennis.

Pendennis, 1848–50, and *The Newcomes*, 1854–5, W. M. Thackeray.

Bell, Gladys, widowed sister of Bob Tallow, eng. to Jim Watts. *The Cruel Sea*, N. Monsarrat, 1951.

Bell, Jane, central character, m. (1) Ernest Higgins; (2) Fred Green.

Albert, her father, cornet player, m. (2) Emily Higgins.

Lily, her sister, mistress of 'Bunny' Moss.

The Water Gipsies, A. P. Herbert, 1930.

Bell, Laura. *A Well-remembered Voice* (play), J. M. Barrie, 1918.

Bell, Natty, prize-fighter, friend of the Bartys. *The Amateur Gentleman*, J. Farnol, 1913.

Bell, Peter. *Peter Bell* (poem), W. Wordsworth, 1819.

Bell, Queenie, protégée of Val Power. *A Deputy was King*, G. B. Stern, 1926.

Bella. *The Dark is Light Enough* (play), Christopher Fry, 1954.

Belladonna, Countess of, mistress of Lord Steyne, superseding Becky Sharp. *Vanity Fair*, W. M. Thackeray, 1847–8.

Bellair. *The Man of Mode* (play), Sir G. Etherege, 1676.

Bellair, Lady. *The Marquis of Lossie*, G. MacDonald, 1877.

Bellairs, Mrs, 'fortune-teller' and spy. *The Ministry of Fear*, Graham Greene, 1943.

Bellairs, Arthur, m. Dorothy Herries.

Timothy, their son.

Violet, Timothy's wife.

Timothy and **Violet,** their children.

The Fortress, 1932, and elsewhere, Hugh Walpole.

Bellairs, Kitty, central character. *The Bath Comedy*, 1900, and *Incomparable Bellairs*, 1904, A. & E. Castle.

Bellamine, courtesan. *The Jew of Malta* (play), C. Marlowe, 1633.

Bellamont, Duke of (George).

Katherine, his wife.

Tancred, Lord Montacute, their son.

Tancred, B. Disraeli, 1847.

Bellamy, ed. of *The Liberal*. *The Street of Adventure*, P. Gibbs, 1909.

Bellamy, a farmer.

His wife.

Catherine Furze, M. Rutherford, 1893.

Bellamy, Mr and Mrs, butler and housekeeper to Sir Charles Cheverel. 'Mr Gilfil's Love Story,' *Scenes of Clerical Life*, George Eliot, 1857.

Bellamy, Mrs, housekeeper to Pomfret Herries. *Rogue Herries*, Hugh Walpole, 1930.

Bellamy, Rev. Ernest, m. Camilla Christy. *Men and Wives*, Ivy Compton-Burnett, 1931.

Bellario. *See* EUPHRASIA.

Bellaroba. 'The Judgment of Borso,' *Little Novels of Italy*, M. Hewlett, 1899.

Bellasis, Lord, father of Richard Devine. *For the Term of his Natural Life*, M. Clarke, 1874.

Bellasis, Viscount (Horatio). *The Amateur Gentleman*, J. Farnol, 1913.

Bellaston, Lady. *Tom Jones*, H. Fielding, 1749.

Bellefield, Lord, gambler and *roué*. (Family name Leicester.) *Lewis Arundel*, F. E. Smedley, 1852.

Bellefontaine, Evangeline.

Benedict, her father.

Evangeline (poem), H. W. Longfellow, 1848.

Bellegarde, Marquis de.

His wife.

Comte Valentin de. Both brothers of Claire de Cintré.

The Dowager Marquise, their mother.

The American, H. James, 1877.

Bellenden, Bessie, of Princes Theatre. (Stage name of Elizabeth Prior.)

Lovel the Widower, W. M. Thackeray, 1860.

Bellenden, Lady Margaret.
Willie, her dead son.
Edith, his daughter.
Sir Arthur, her brother-in-law.
Old Mortality, W. Scott, 1816

Bellew, Mrs Helen, separated from her husband, Captain Bellew. *The Country House*, John Galsworthy, 1907.

Bellew, Louisa, m. Jack Hinton.
Sir Simon, Bt, her father.
Jack Hinton, C. Lever, 1843.

Bellimperia, sister of Lorenzo. *The Spanish Tragedy* (play), T. Kyd, 1594.

Belling, Master, pupil of Squeers. *Nicholas Nickleby*, C. Dickens, 1839.

Bellingham, Governor of Boston. *The Scarlet Letter*, N. Hawthorne, 1850.

Bellingham, Mr. *Mr Ingleside*, E. V. Lucas, 1910.

Bellman, Baptist, Chief Registrar, Calcutta Tape and Sealing Wax Office. *The Newcomes*, W. M. Thackeray, 1854–5.

Bellomont, Sir Richard.
Isabella, his illegitimate daughter.
Thomas, his nephew, m. Isabella.
'Isabella, Isabella' (s.s.), *Love and Money*, Phyllis Bentley, 1957.

Belmaine, Mr and Mrs, friends of the Doncastles. *The Hand of Ethelberta*, T. Hardy, 1876.

Belmann. *The Dark is Light Enough* (play), Christopher Fry, 1954.

Belmont, Mr and Mrs. *The Tragedy of the Korosko*, A. Conan Doyle, 1898.

Belmont, Flora, loved by Digby. *Digby Grand*, G. Whyte-Melville, 1853.

Belmont, Sir John, father of Evelina. *Evelina*, Fanny Burney, 1778.

Belor, Roger, magistrate and Quaker-persecutor. *Sampson Rideout, Quaker*, Una Silberrad, 1911.

Belpher, Lord. *See* MARSHMORETON.

Belphoebe. *The Faërie Queene* (poem), E. Spenser, 1590.

Belrose, Charlie, confectioner.
His wife.
Riceyman Steps, A. Bennett, 1923.

Belsize, Inspector. *Night Must Fall* (play), Emlyn Williams, 1935.

Belsize, Hon. Charles ('Jack'), later Lord Highgate; one of Lord Kew's cronies. *The Newcomes*, W. M. Thackeray, 1854–5.

Beltham, Squire.
Dorothy, his daughter.
Marian, his daughter, m. Augustus F. G. Roy Richmond.
The Adventures of Harry Richmond, G. Meredith, 1871.

Belthorpe, Tom.
Angela, his wife.
A Penniless Millionaire, D. Christie Murray.

Belton, Fred.
Lucy, his wife.
Their children:
Freddy, Commander, R.N.
Susan, his wife.
Elsa, m. Admiral Christopher Hornby.
Charles, m. Clarissa Graham.
The *Barsetshire* series, Angela Thirkell, 1933 onwards.

Belton, Sir James ('Howlieglass'), surgeon. 'Tender Achilles' (s.s.), *Limits and Renewals*, R. Kipling, 1932.

Belturbet, Lady Wilhelmina.
Lady Thomasina.
Lady Noelina.
The Amazons (play), A. W. Pinero, 1893.

Belvawney, Miss, member of Crummles's Theatrical Company. *Nicholas Nickleby*, C. Dickens, 1839.

Belvidera. *Venice Preserved* (play), T. Otway, 1682.

Belvil, Mr. *The Conscious Lovers* (play), R. Steele, 1722.

Belville, Lord Ernest, society swindler. *Raffles*, E. W. Hornung, 1899–1901.

Belworthy, unscrupulous trader. *A Deputy was King*, G. B. Stern, 1926.

Belzanor. *Caesar and Cleopatra* (play), G. B. Shaw, 1900.

Belzebub. *Doctor Faustus* (play), C. Marlowe, 1604.

Bembridge, Christopher, civil servant. *The Porch*, 1937, and *The Stronghold*, 1939, R. Church.

Bemerton, second-hand bookseller. *Over Bemerton's*, E. V. Lucas, 1908.

Ben, Governor of a province in

Ethiopia and *ex officio* master of the Gihon Hunt. 'Little Foxes' (s.s.), *Actions and Reactions*, R. Kipling, 1909.

Ben, 'Young.' *Faithful Sally Brown* (poem), T. Hood.

Ben Hur. *See* HUR.

Benarbuck, Laird of, 'second-sighted.' *The Black Dwarf*, W. Scott, 1816.

Benbow, Albert, m. Clara Clayhanger.
Their children:
Bert.
Flossie.
Amy.
Lucy.
Rupert.
The *Clayhanger* trilogy, Arnold Bennett, 1910–16.

Benbow, Horace, lawyer.
Belle, his wife.
Sanctuary, W. Faulkner, 1931.

Benbow, Professor William.
Joan, his daughter, m. Saturday Keith.
Poet's Pub, E. Linklater, 1929.

Bencombe, Marcia, m. (1) Leverre; (2) Jocelyn Pierston.
Her parents.
The Well Beloved, T. Hardy, 1897.

Bendall, Sarah, old actress. *My Son, My Son*, H. Spring, 1938.

Bendien, Cornelius. *You Can't Go Home Again*, T. Wolfe, 1947.

Bendrix, Maurice, novelist, narrator, lover of Sarah Miles. *The End of the Affair*, Graham Greene, 1951.

Benedetto. Italian conspirator. 'The Wrong Thing' (s.s.), *Rewards and Fairies*, R. Kipling, 1910.

Benedick, a young lord, m. Beatrice. *Much Ado about Nothing* (play), W. Shakespeare.

Benedick. *The Merry Devil of Edmonton* (play), Anon.

Benedictus. *The Immortal Sergeant*, J. Brophy, 1942.

Benfleet, missionary, brother-in-law of Gladys Medwin.
His wife.
Dr Nikola, G. Boothby, 1896.

Benfleet, George, of Paragon Pictures, Hollywood. *Another Year*, R. C. Sheriff, 1948.

Benham, William Porphyry, central character, m. Amanda Morris.
Rev. Harold, his father, 1st husband of Lady Marayne.
His mother.
The Research Magnificent, H. G. Wells, 1915.

Benito, peasant, of Agna Secreta.
Josepha, his daughter.
Salvatore, his son.
José and **Santiago,** his grandsons.
Death Comes for the Archbishop, Willa Cather, 1927.

Benjamin, of Harter & Benjamin, jewellers, friend of Lady Eustace. *The Eustace Diamonds*, A. Trollope, 1873.

Benjamin, Jorrocks's boy. *Jorrocks's Jaunts and Jollities*, R. S. Surtees, 1838.

Benjamin, Herries's manservant.
His wife.
Rogue Herries, Hugh Walpole, 1930.

Benjamin Bunny.
His father.
The Tale of Benjamin Bunny, 1904, and elsewhere, Beatrix Potter.

Benjamin Ram, Mr, harp-playing ram. *Uncle Remus*, J. C. Harris, 1895.

Bennet, Mr and Mrs.
Their daughters:
Jane, m. Charles Bingley.
Elizabeth, m. Fitzwilliam Darcy.
Catherine.
Mary.
Lydia, m. George Wickham.
Pride and Prejudice, Jane Austen, 1813.

Bennet, Neville, cousin of Robert Blair and member of his firm. *The Franchise Affair*, Josephine Tey, 1948.

Bennett, Captain, Master of the *Altair*. *Gallions Reach*, H. M. Tomlinson, 1927.

Bennett, Mr, a Communist. *It's a Battlefield*, Graham Greene, 1935.

Bennett, Mrs. *Amelia*, H. Fielding, 1752.

Bennett, Rev. Arthur, chaplain to the Mavericks. *Kim*, R. Kipling, 1901.

Bennett, 'Bobbie,' niece and heiress of Handcock. *Some Experiences of an Irish R.M.*, Œ. Somerville & Martin Ross, 1899.

Bennett, Sam. *The Virginian*, O. Wister, 1902.

Benoit, Seneschal to Kercadiou. *Scaramouche*, R. Sabatini, 1921.

Bensey, Lou, m. Pearl Lester. *Tobacco Road,* E. Caldwell, 1948.

Benshaw, Farmer, strawberry grower. *Bealby,* H. G. Wells, 1915.

Bensington, F.R.S., joint discoverer of the Food.
Jane, his cousin and housekeeper.
The Food of the Gods, H. G. Wells, 1904.

Benson, Miss, heiress courted by Dr Firmin. *The Adventures of Philip,* W. M. Thackeray, 1861–2.

Benson, Major Anthony.
Alvin, his murdered brother and partner.
The Benson Murder Case, S. S. van Dine, 1926.

Benson, Jan.
His mother.
'The Well' (s.s.), *The Lady of the Barge,* W. W. Jacobs, 1902.

Benson, Molly, m. Colonel Martin Lambert. *The Virginians,* W. M. Thackeray, 1857–9.

Bent, Miss, friend of Miss Hampton. The *Barsetshire* series, Angela Thirkell, 1933 onwards.

Bent, Mr ('The Dancing Master'). 'A Second-rate Woman' (s.s.), *Wee Willie Winkie,* R. Kipling, 1888.

Bent, Bill.
Violet, his wife, aunt of Karen Michaelis.
The House in Paris, Elizabeth Bowen, 1935.

Benteen, Will. *Gone with the Wind,* Margaret Mitchell, 1936.

Bentham, Charlie, school-teacher. *Juno and the Paycock* (play), S. O'Casey, 1925.

Bentinck-Jones, Ivor, a blackmailer. *The Widow's Cruise,* Nicholas Blake, 1959.

Bentinct-Major, Canon, of Polchester Cathedral. *The Cathedral,* Hugh Walpole, 1922.

Bentley, Mr. *Mr Rowl,* D. K. Broster, 1924.

Bentley, Bert, musical director. *Red Peppers* (play), Noël Coward, 1936.

Bentley, Geoffrey, publisher. *Put Out More Flags,* E. Waugh, 1942.

Benton, sailor in the torpedoed *Aurora. The Ocean,* J. Hanley, 1946.

Benton, Miss, housekeeper to Master Humphrey. *Master Humphrey's Clock,* C. Dickens, 1840–1.

Benton, Phyllis. *Bulldog Drummond,* 'Sapper' (H. C. McNeile), 1920.

Benvolio, friend of Romeo. *Romeo and Juliet* (play), W. Shakespeare.

Benvolio, Countess. *Jorrocks's Jaunts and Jollities,* R. S. Surtees, 1838.

Benwell. *Dr Nikola,* G. Boothby, 1896.

Benwick, Captain, guest of the Harvilles at Lyme Regis. *Persuasion,* Jane Austen, 1818.

Benzaguen, Vidal, actress. 'The Village that Voted the Earth was Flat' (s.s.), *A Diversity of Creatures,* 1917.
Her mother. 'Dayspring Mishandled' (s.s.), *Limits and Renewals,* 1932.
R. Kipling.

Berenger, Sir Raymond.
Eveline, his daughter, betrothed to Hugo de Lacy.
The Betrothed, W. Scott, 1825.

Beresford, Lady, passenger, the *Agra. Hard Cash,* C. Reade, 1863.

Beresford, Maurice, cigar merchant.
Charlie, his brother.
Peter Jackson, Cigar Merchant, G. Frankau, 1919.

Beresford, Tommy, and his wife **Tuppence** (*née* Prudence Cowley), once the Young Adventurers, later Blunt's Brilliant Detectives.
Deborah, their daughter.
Derek, their son.
By The Pricking of My Thumbs, 1968, and others, Agatha Christie.

Beret, Max, priest; 'Aumonier' of Amara. *The Garden of Allah,* R. S. Hichens, 1904.

Berg, Howard. *Wickford Point,* J. P. Marquand, 1939.

Berg, Rosa, daughter of Yvonne, herself illegitimate daughter of Robert Raynald's father and companion to Mrs Raynald. *Requiem for Robert,* Mary Fitt, 1942.

Bergfeld, Anna.
Her husband.
The Silver Spoon, J. Galsworthy, 1926.

Bergmann, Clara and Emma. *Pilgrimage,* Dorothy M. Richardson, 1915–38.

Bergson, Alexandra, Swedish homesteader in Nebraska.
Her brothers:
Oscar.
Lou.
Emil.
O Pioneers!, Willa Cather, 1913.

Berinthia, a widow. *A Trip to Scarborough* (play), R. B. Sheridan, 1777.

Berinthia, niece of Mrs Pipchin. *Dombey and Son*, C. Dickens, 1848.

Berkeley, Sir William, Governor of Virginia. *The Old Dominion*, Mary Johnston, 1899.

Berkely, Lady Augusta of. *Castle Dangerous*, W. Scott, 1832.

Berman, O. J., a Hollywood agent. *Breakfast at Tiffany's*, Truman Capote, 1958.

Berman, Rose, m. John Cooper.
Her mother.
Ada, her sister, m. Johnny Hummel.
Magnolia Street, L. Golding, 1932.

Bernac, Charles. *Uncle Bernac*, A. Conan Doyle, 1897.

Bernadin, Noel, advocate defending Alain Carbonec. *Barbe of Grand Bayou*, J. Oxenham, 1903.

Bernadine, poet to Montoni. *The Mysteries of Udolpho*, Mrs Radcliffe, 1794.

Bernadotte, Jean, Crown Prince. 'Leipzig,' *Wessex Poems*, T. Hardy, 1898.

Bernard, Capt., a gluttonous Frenchman. *Pending Heaven*, William Gerhardie, 1930.

Bernard, Fre. *The Small Miracle*, P. Gallico, 1951.

Bernard, Miss.
Her father and mother.
Adventures of Mr Ledbury, Albert Smith, 1844.

Bernard, John, friend of Basil. *Basil*, W. Collins, 1852.

Bernardo, an officer. *Hamlet* (play), W. Shakespeare.

Bernardo. *Bibliomania*, T. F. Dibdin, 1809.

Bernenstein. *The Prisoner of Zenda*, 1894, and *Rupert of Hentzau*, 1898, A. Hope.

Berners, Mrs, cancer patient. 'Unprofessional' (s.s.), *Limits and Renewals*, R. Kipling, 1932.

Berners, Isobel (Belle), woman of the roads, Lavengro's companion. *Lavengro*, George Borrow, 1851.

Bernheim, Bernard, central character, in love with Ethel Stornway.
Baron Bernheim, his father.
David, his uncle.
Sir Moses, his great-grandfather.
A Penniless Millionaire, D. Christie Murray.

Bernier, Edmond, actor, m. Olga Jibinsky. 'The Crime of Olga Jibinsky' (s.s.), *The Little Dog Laughed*, L. Merrick, 1930.

Bernstein, dissolute German baron, ex-valet, m. Beatrix Esmond. *The Virginians*, W. M. Thackeray, 1857–9.

Beroldy, Jeanne, *née* Daubreuil. *Murder on the Links*, Agatha Christie, 1923.

Berolles, Lady Frederick. *Lady Frederick* (play), W. S. Maugham, 1907.

Berrendo, Lieutenant, Fascist officer. *For Whom the Bell Tolls*, E. Hemingway, 1940.

Berridge, Mrs. the narrator's landlady. *The Hampdenshire Wonder*, J. D. Beresford, 1911.

Berry, Mrs. *The Ordeal of Richard Feverel*, G. Meredith, 1859.

Berry, The Misses, friends of Deborah Herries. *Judith Paris*, Hugh Walpole, 1931.

Berry, James H, private inquiry agent. *Mr Billingham, the Marquis and Madelon*, E. P. Oppenheim.

Berryl, Sir John.
Arthur, his son.
The Absentee, Maria Edgeworth, 1812.

Bertha, central character. *Lummox*, Fannie Hurst, 1924.

Bertha, a farm girl. *The Spanish Farm*, R. H. Mottram, 1924.

Berthelini, Léon, strolling player.
Elvira, his wife.
'Providence and the Guitar,' *New Arabian Nights*, R. L. Stevenson, 1882.

Bertie and Bellair, Lady. *Tancred*, B. Disraeli, 1847.

Bertram, faithful minstrel. *Castle Dangerous*, W. Scott, 1832.

Bertram, Count of Rousillon. *All's Well That Ends Well* (play), W. Shakespeare.

Bertram, Mrs, mother of Sarah Miles. *The End of the Affair*, Graham Greene, 1951.

Bertram, Allan, Laird of Ellangowan. Temp. *Charles I.*
- **Dennis,** his son.
- **Donahoe,** son of Dennis.
- **Lewis,** son of Donahoe.
- **Godfrey,** son of Lewis.
  - His wife.
  - **Harry,** their son, kidnapped and taken to Holland, served in India, renamed Vanbeest Brown, finally restored to name and estates; m. Julia Mannering.
  - **Lucy,** their daughter.
- **Commissioner Bertram,** cousin.

Guy Mannering, W. Scott, 1815.

Bertram, Lady (Maria), *née* **Ward.**
- **Sir Thomas,** her husband.
- Their children;
  - **Thomas.**
  - **Rev. Edmund,** m. Fanny Price.
  - **Maria,** m. James Rushworth.
  - **Julia,** m. John Yates.

Mansfield Park, Jane Austen, 1814.

Bertran, French naturalist. 'Bertran and Bimi' (s.s.), *Life's Handicap*, R. Kipling, 1891.

Bertrand, Mme Josephine, Max Tryte's unscrupulous French housekeeper. *Portrait of a Playboy*, W. Deeping, 1947.

Berwick, Duchess of (Arabella). *Lady Windermere's Fan* (play), O. Wilde, 1892.

Beryl, assistant to Myrtle Bagot. *Brief Encounter* (play), N. Coward, 1945.

Besnard, Commissioner of Police. *At the Villa Rose*, A. E. W. Mason, 1910.

Bess, Negro ex-prostitute and drug-taker. *Porgy*, Du Bose Heyward, 1925.

Bessie, nurse to the Reed children, m. Robert Leavens. *Jane Eyre*, Charlotte Brontë, 1847.

Besso, Hillel.
- His wife. Foster-parents of Emir Fakredeen.
- **Eva,** their daughter.
- **Adam,** Hillel's uncle.

Tancred, B. Disraeli, 1847.

Bessus. *A King and No King* (play), Beaumont & Fletcher, 1611.

Beste-Chetwynde, Hon. Mrs Margot, m. (2) Viscount Metroland.
- **Peter,** her son by 1st husband, later the Earl of Pastmaster, m. Lady Mary Meadowes.

Decline and Fall, E. Waugh, 1928.

Bet, Betsy, female thief, accomplice of Fagin. *Oliver Twist*, C. Dickens, 1838.

Bethany, Rev. Mr. *The Return*, Walter de la Mare, 1910.

Bethel, Colonel Otway. *East Lynne*, Mrs H. Wood, 1861.

Bethia, maid to the Edgeworths. *A House and its Head*, Ivy Compton-Burnett, 1935.

Bethune, Sir Richard, father of Martha Baliol. *The Highland Widow*, W. Scott, 1827.

Betsey Jane, Mrs Wickham's uncle's daughter. *Dombey and Son*, C. Dickens, 1848.

Betsy, maid to Bob Sawyer. *Pickwick Papers*, C. Dickens, 1837.

Bettany, Dr, Judith Paris's doctor. *The Fortress*, Hugh Walpole, 1932.

Betteredge, Gabriel, house steward to Lady Verinder.
- **Selena,** his dead wife.
- **Penelope,** their daughter.

The Moonstone, W. Collins, 1868.

Betteridge, schoolboy at Fernhurst. *The Loom of Youth*, A. Waugh, 1917.

Betteson, Joseph.
- His wife. Near neighbours of Paterson.

The Jacaranda Tree, H. E. Bates, 1949.

Bettisher, Tony, close friend of Dick Munt. *The Travelling Grave* (s.s.), L. P. Hartley.

Betts, Mrs, a nurse. 'A Habitation Enforced' (s.s.), *Actions and Reactions*, R. Kipling, 1909.

Betty, Belinda Tremayne's servant. *Belinda* (play), A. A. Milne, 1918.

Bevan, George, song composer, m. Lady Maud Marsh. *A Damsel in Distress*, P. G. Wodehouse, 1919.

Beveridge, Herbert, M.P., m. Mary Hendon.
- **Horace,** their son, central character, m. Ada Herbert.

In Greek Waters, G. A. Henty, 1892.

Beverley. *See* BARNABAS BARTY.

Beverley, Colonel.
- His wife, *née* Villiers.
- Their children:
  - **Edward,** m. Patience Heatherstone.

Humphrey.
Edith.
Alice.
The Children, of the New Forest, Captain Marryat, 1847.

Beverley, Ensign. *See* CAPTAIN ABSOLUTE.

Beverley, Bill, friend of Antony Gillingham, in love with Betty Calladine. *The Red House Mystery,* A. A. Milne, 1922.

Beverley, Cecilia, central character, m. Mortimer Delvile. *Cecilia,* Fanny Burney, 1782.

Beverley, Frank, one-time lunatic, m. Edith Archbold. *Hard Cash,* C. Reade, 1863.

Beverley, Sir Peregrine, Bt. *The Broad Highway,* J. Farnol, 1910.

Beverly, central character.
His wife.
The Gamester (play), E. Moore, 1753.

Bevil. *The Conscious Lovers* (play), R. Steele, 1722.

Bevin, ex-sergeant and chicken-farmer. 'A Friend of the Family' (s.s.), *Debits and Credits,* R. Kipling, 1926.

Bevis, Henry, special correspondent to *The Times. The Gates of Summer* (play), John Whiting, 1956.

Beynon, Butcher.
Bess, his wife.
Gossamer, their daughter, schoolmistress.
Billy, their son.
Under Milk Wood (play), Dylan Thomas, 1954.

Beynon, Mrs, Davy Morgan's landlady.
Evan, her husband.
Tegwen, their daughter.
How Green Was My Valley, R. Llewellyn, 1939.

Beynon, Watt, manager of a coal pit. *Tomorrow To Fresh Woods,* Rhys Davies, 1941.

Bhaer, Friedrich, m. Jo March.
Rob, their son.
Teddy, their son.
Franz, Friedrich's nephew, merchant.
Emil, Friedrich's nephew, sailor, m. Mary Hardy.
Little Men, 1871, and *Jo's Boys,* 1886, Louisa M. Alcott.

Bhakaroff, Sasha, celebrated opera singer. *Grand Opera,* Vicki Baum, 1942.

Bhanavar the Beautiful. *The Shaving of Shagpat,* G. Meredith, 1856.

Bianca, Katharine's sister. *The Taming of the Shrew* (play), W. Shakespeare.

Bianca, Isabella of Vicenza's maid. *The Castle of Otranto,* Horace Walpole, 1765.

Bibbet, secretary to General Harrison. *Woodstock,* W. Scott, 1826.

Bibot, Sergeant. *The Scarlet Pimpernel,* Baroness Orczy, 1905.

Biche, La, Indian mistress of Museau. *The Virginians,* W. M. Thackeray, 1857–9.

Bickerton, Ed., *Pall Mall Gazette*; supercilious snob. *Adventures of Philip,* W. M. Thackeray, 1861–2.

Bickerton, Mrs, of Castle Gate, York.
Moses, her husband.
The Heart of Midlothian, W. Scott, 1818.

Bickerton, Caroline, 1st wife of Adam Lindsell. *God's Stepchildren,* Sarah G. Millin, 1924.

Bicket, Tony, packer at Darby & Winter.
Victorine, his wife.
The White Monkey, 1924, and elsewhere, J. Galsworthy.

Bicknell, Miss, friend of Elfride Swancourt. *A Pair of Blue Eyes,* T. Hardy, 1873.

Bicksett. *Monsieur Beaucaire* (play), Booth Tarkington, 1902.

Bi-coloured Rock Snake, The. 'The Elephant's Child' (s.s.), *Just So Stories,* R. Kipling, 1902.

Bidborough, Lord, Pamela Reston's brother, m. Jean Jardine. *Penny Plain,* O. Douglas, 1920.

Bidderman, a Flemish noble. 'A Flemish Tradition,' *The Bee,* O. Goldsmith, 1759–60.

Biddlecomb, schoolfellow of Bultitude. *Vice Versa,* F. Anstey, 1882.

Biddlecombe, Mrs.
Susan, her daughter, m. Joseph Quinney.
Quinneys', H. A. Vachell, 1914.

Biddulph, villainous husband of Hannah Irwin. *St Ronan's Well,* W. Scott, 1824.

Biddums, Miss, Toby Austell's governess. 'His Majesty the King' (s.s.), *Wee Willie Winkie*, R. Kipling, 1895.

Bide-the-Bent, Peter, minister. *The Bride of Lammermoor*, W. Scott, 1819.

Bideawhile, the Trevelyans' 'ancient family lawyer.' *He Knew He Was Right*, A. Trollope, 1869.

Bidlake, Elinor, m. Philip Quarles.
John, her father.
Her mother.
Walter, her brother.
Point Counter Point, Aldous Huxley, 1928.

Bidmore, Lord.
Augustus, his son.
Augusta, his daughter.
St Ronan's Well, W. Scott, 1824.

Bidwell, George.
His wife.
The Private Life of Mr Bidwell (s.s.), J. Thurber.

Biederman, Arnold, rightfully Count of Geierstein.
Bertha, his wife.
His sons:
Rudiger.
Ernst.
Sigismond.
Ulrick.
Anne of Geierstein, W. Scott, 1829.

Biel. 'The Bronckhorst Divorce Case' (s.s.), *Plain Tales from the Hills*, R. Kipling, 1888.

Big Daddy, wealthy Mississippi landowner.
Big Mama, his wife.
Cooper, their son, sometimes called Brother Man.
Mae, his wife, sometimes called Sister Woman.
Brick, another son, dipsomaniac.
Margaret, his wife, 'the Cat.'
Cat on a Hot Tin Roof (play), Tennessee Williams, 1955.

Biggidy, Dicky Big-Bag (alias **Blue Rabbit**). *Uncle Remus*, J. C. Harris, 1880–95.

Bigglesworth, Air-Detective Inspector, central character in long series of 'Biggles' books, Captain W. E. Johns.

Biggs, bosun, H.M.S. *Harpy*. *Mr Midshipman Easy*, Captain Marryat, 1836.

Biggs, Mrs, widow, m. Mr Blake. 'Lost Mr Blake' (poem), *The Bab Ballads*, W. S. Gilbert, 1869.

Biggs, Arthur J. Jnr. *High Tor* (play), Maxwell Anderson, 1937.

Biggs, Sir Impey, defending counsel for Harriet Vane. *Strong Poison*. Dorothy L. Sayers, 1930.

Biggs, Jno. Horatio, Mayor of Tooting East.
Gladys, his daughter, m. Clarence Mulliner.
Meet Mr Mulliner, P. G. Wodehouse, 1927.

Bighead, Bessie. *Under Milk Wood* (play), Dylan Thomas, 1954.

Bigstaff, John, constable. *Peveril of the Peak*, W. Scott, 1822.

Bilbo. *The Merry Devil of Edmonton* (play), Anon.

Bildad, Captain, retired whaler, Quaker, part-owner of the *Pequod*. *Moby Dick*, H. Melville, 1851.

Biles, Hezekiah. *Two on a Tower*, T. Hardy, 1882.

Biles, John. 'Absent-mindedness in a Parish Choir,' *Life's Little Ironies*, T. Hardy, 1894.

Billali, aged chief and servant of 'She.' *She*, H. Rider Haggard, 1887.

Billig, Gershan, marriage broker.
His wife.
Magnolia Street, L. Golding, 1932.

Billikin, Mrs, lodging-house keeper. *Edwin Drood*, C. Dickens, 1870.

Billingham, Samuel T., of New York, central character, m. (1) Harriet, (2) Madelon de Felan. *Mr Billingham, the Marquis and Madelon*, E. P. Oppenheim.

Billiter, friend of Ephraim Quixtus. *The Glory of Clementina Wing*, W. J. Locke, 1911.

Billson, Wilberforce ('Battling Billson'), prize-fighter. *Ukridge*, P. G. Wodehouse, 1924.

Billy, a battery mule. 'Her Majesty's Servants' (s.s.), *The Jungle Book*, R. Kipling, 1894.

Billy Bluetail (Mr Hawk). *Uncle Remus*, J. C. Harris, 1880–95.

Billy Hedgehog. *The Wind in the Willows*, K. Grahame, 1908.

Billy the Boy. *Robbery under Arms*, R. Boldrewood, 1888.

Bilsiter, Leonard. *The She Wolf* (s.s.), 'Saki' (H. H. Munro).

Bimi, a jealous orang-outang which kills his master and his master's wife. 'Bertran and Bimi' (s.s.), *Life's Handicap*, R. Kipling, 1891.

Binat, French landlord.
His wife.
The Light that Failed, R. Kipling, 1890.

Bindloose, copper-nosed sheriff-clerk. *St Ronan's Well,* W. Scott, 1824.

Bindon-Botting, Mrs, socialite, friend of the Walsinghams. *Kipps,* H. G. Wells, 1905.

Binet, head of theatrical troupe.
Climène, his daughter, seduced by de la Tour d'Azyr.
Scaramouche, R. Sabatini, 1921.

Bingham, ex-bank manager turned thief. 'Mr Ledbetter's Vacation' (s.s.), *Tales of Life and Adventure,* 1923, and elsewhere, H. G. Wells.

Bingham, Rose, m. David Leslie. The *Barsetshire* series, Angela Thirkell, 1933 onwards.

Bingley, actor-manager, Chatteris Theatre.
His wife.
Pendennis, W. M. Thackeray, 1848–50.

Bingley, Mr and Mrs, employers of Esther Waters. *Esther Waters,* G. Moore, 1894.

Bingley, Charles, m. Jane Bennet.
Caroline and **Louisa** (Mrs Hurst), his sisters.
Pride and Prejudice, Jane Austen, 1813.

Binker. *Now We Are Six* (poems), A. A. Milne, 1927.

Binkie, Torpenhow's dog. *The Light that Failed,* R. Kipling, 1890.

Binkie, Lady Grizzel, m. Sir Pitt Crawley. *Vanity Fair,* W. M. Thackeray, 1847–8.

Binks, Sir Bingo.
Rachel, his wife.
St Ronan's Well, W. Scott, 1824.

Binnie, James, civil servant; friend of Colonel Newcome. *The Newcomes,* W. M. Thackeray, 1854–5.

Binns, Noah, gardener. *The Whiteoak Chronicles.* Mazo de la Roche, 1927 onwards.

Binny, Rev. Beilby, curate and keeper of small school, m. Miss Grits.
His sister and housekeeper.
Vanity Fair, W. M. Thackeray, 1847–8.

Birch, Inspector. *The Red House Mystery,* A. A. Milne, 1922.

Birch, Cynthia.
Gerald, her husband.
Tessa, their daughter.
Through the Storm, P. Gibbs, 1945.

Birch, Milly, lady's maid to Paula Power. *A Laodicean,* T. Hardy, 1881.

Birch, Stephen, lover of Isabel Summers, killed in action. *Tom Tiddler's Ground,* E. Shanks, 1934.

Bird, Senator.
His wife. Helpers and friends of Eliza.
Uncle Tom's Cabin, Harriet B. Stowe, 1851.

Bird, Luke. *Mr Weston's Good Wine.* T. F. Powys, 1927.

Bird Woman, The, friend of Freckles. *Freckles,* Gene S. Porter, 1904.

Birdett, P. C. Neville. *We the Accused,* E. Raymond, 1935.

Birdseye, Miss, 'celebrated abolitionist.' *The Bostonians,* H. James, 1886.

Birdseye, Nellie, later Mrs Casey; narrator.
Aunt Lydia.
Her three sisters.
My Mortal Enemy, Willa Cather, 1928.

Birkett, Bill, schoolmaster.
Ann, his wife.
Their daughters:
Rose, m. John Fairweather.
Geraldine, m. Geoff Fairweather.
The *Barsetshire* series, Angela Thirkell, 1933 onwards.

Birkin, Rupert, school inspector, m. Ursula Brangwen. *Women in Love,* D. H. Lawrence, 1921.

Birkinshaw, office boy. *London Wall* (play), J. van Druten, 1931.

Birkland, schoolmaster. *Mr Perrin and Mr Traill,* Hugh Walpole, 1911.

Birnam, Don, an alcoholic, an unsuccessful writer. Chief character.
Wick, his brother.
The Lost Weekend, Charles Jackson, 1944.

Birnbaum, Mr. *Act of God,* F. Tennyson Jesse, 1936.

Birnbaum, Jacob, m. Antonia Sanger. *The Constant Nymph,* Margaret Kennedy, 1924.

Biron, lord attendant on Ferdinand. *Love's Labour's Lost* (play), W. Shakespeare.

Biron. *The Fatal Marriage* (play), T. Southerne, 1694.

Birse, Gavin, m. 'Mag' Lownie. *A Window in Thrums,* J. M. Barrie, 1889.

Birten, Lord. *The Queen's Husband* (play), R. E. Sherwood, 1928.

Birtle, Kit, doctor.
Sir Harry, his father.
'Beauty Spots' (s.s.), *Limits and Renewals,* R. Kipling, 1932.

Bisarre. *The Inconstant* (play), G. Farquhar, 1702.

Biscuit, Edward, butler to Sir Roger de Coverley. Essays in *The Spectator,* J. Addison, 1711–14.

Bisesa, young widow. 'Beyond the Pale' (s.s.), *Plain Tales from the Hills,* R Kipling, 1888.

Bisesa, a beautiful girl. 'The Sacrifice of Er-Heb' (poem), *Barrack-room Ballads,* R Kipling, 1892.

Bishop, Bow Street runner. *Starvecrow Farm,* Stanley Weyman, 1905.

Bishop, Colonel.
Arabella, his niece, m. Peter Blood.
Captain Blood, R. Sabatini, 1922.

Bishop, John, murderer, illegitimate son of Mrs Farmer. *The Protégé* (s.s.), W. B. Maxwell.

Bishop, Luke, countryman, central character, m. Lily Thompson.
Lizzie, their daughter, m. Walter Vine.
Buck Bishop, Luke's father.
The Poacher, H. E. Bates, 1935.

Bishop, Meg, journalist. *The Roman Spring of Mrs Stone,* Tennessee Williams, 1950.

Bite'm, an otter-hound. *Tarka the Otter,* H. Williamson, 1927.

Bittern, Captain of the *Unicorn. Anthony Adverse,* Hervey Allen, 1934.

Bittlebrains, Lord. *The Bride of Lammermoor,* W. Scott, 1819.

Bitzer, pupil at Coketown. *Hard Times,* C. Dickens, 1854.

Bivvins, Henry Albert, sailor swallowed by the whale. 'How the Whale got his Throat' (s.s.), *Just So Stories,* R. Kipling, 1902.

Bixbee, Mrs (Aunt Polly), sister of David Harum. *David Harum,* E. Noyes Westcott, 1898.

Blaber, Nurse. 'In the Same Boat' (s.s.), *A Diversity of Creatures,* R. Kipling, 1917.

Black, Captain, central character. *The Iron Pirate,* M. Pemberton, 1893.

Black, Robert (alias **Merrill, Falcone,** etc.), central character *No Son of Mine,* G. B. Stern, 1948.

Black, Stanford. *The Happy Prisoner,* Monica Dickens, 1946.

Black Beauty ('Darkie'), a horse, central character and narrator. *Black Beauty,* Anna Sewell, 1877.

Black Captain, The, m. Jessamine.
Jackanapes, their son.
Jackanapes, Juliana H. Ewing, 1879.

Black Dog, member of the *Hispaniola*'s crew. *Treasure Island,* R. L. Stevenson, 1883.

Black Dwarf, known also as Elshender the Recluse, Cannie Elshie and The Solitary. *See* SIR EDWARD MAULEY.
The Black Dwarf, W. Scott, 1816.

'Black George,' blacksmith.
Simon the Ancient, his father.
Prudence, his daughter.
The Broad Highway, J. Farnol, 1910.

Black Jack, cobbler. *Under Milk Wood* (play), Dylan Thomas 1954.

Black Wolf, Indian chief. *The Old Dominion,* Mary Johnston, 1899.

Blackacre, The Widow. *The Plain Dealer* (play), W. Wycherley, 1677.

Blackadder, Phyllis, mistress of Max Fisher. *Pending Heaven,* William Gerhardie, 1930.

Blackball, Captain, disreputable friend of the Duchesse d'Ivry. *Pendennis,* 1848–50, and *The Newcomes,* 1854-5, W. M. Thackeray.

Blackborough, Russell. *Waste* (play), H. Granville-Barker, 1907.

Blackchester, Countess of, sister of Lord Dalgarno. *The Fortunes of Nigel,* W. Scott, 1822.

Blackett, Herbert.
Bertha, his wife.
His daughters:
Flora.
Rhoda.
Mary.
Chatterton Square, E. H. Young, 1947.

Blackett, Nancy (Ruth) and Peggy. *Swallows and Amazons*, A. Ransome, 1930.

Blackhall, victim of Allan, Lord Ravenswood *The Bride of Lammermoor*, W. Scott, 1819.

Blacking, Alfred, professional golfer at James Bond's club. *Goldfinger*, Ian Fleming, 1959.

Blackland, gambling friend of Colonel **Altamont**. *Pendennis*, W. M. Thackeray, 1848–50.

Blacklees, Tomalin, warder. *The Talisman*, W. Scott, 1825.

Blackless, Jesse, 'Red' artist, uncle of Lanny Budd. *Dragon's Teeth*, Upton Sinclair, 1942.

Blackmore, London manager, Bundelcund Bank. *The Newcomes*, W. M. Thackeray, 1854–5.

Blackmore, Honour (known as Mrs Honour), maid to Sophia Western. *Tom Jones*, H. Fielding, 1749.

Blackpool, Stephen, millhand, wrongly accused of theft. *Hard Times*, C. Dickens, 1854

Blackstick, Fairy. *The Rose and the Ring*, W. M. Thackeray, 1855.

Blackstock, Douglas, smuggler and murderer, m. Katherine Thaxter. *No Man's Land*, L. J. Vance, 1910.

Blackwater, Lord (Wilfrid Pargeter), in love with Fancy Fawkes. *See also* MARK WOODROFE. *Trumpeter Sound!*, D. L. Murray, 1933.

Bladamour, friend of Paridel. *The Faërie Queene* (poem), E. Spenser, 1590.

Bladderskate, Lord, judge. *Redgauntlet*, W. Scott, 1824.

Bladen, 'Boy.' *Campbell's Kingdom*, Hammond Innes, 1952.

Blades, Ensign. *Quality Street* (play), J. M. Barrie, 1902.

Blague, innkeeper. *The Merry Devil of Edmonton*, Anon.

Blaine, Amory, rich playboy. *This Side of Paradise*, F. Scott Fitzgerald, 1920.

Blaine, Elizabeth (Fanny), m. Nicholas Forsyte. The *Forsyte* series, J. Galsworthy, 1906–33.

Blair, minister ('predikant'). *The City of Gold*, F. Brett Young, 1939.

Blair, stage doorkeeper. *Enter a Murderer*, Ngaio Marsh, 1935.

Blair, Mrs Medwin, central character, *née* Fosdick.
  Jervis, her dead husband.
  Susan, her daughter.
The Prodigal Heart, Susan Ertz, 1950.

Blair, Montgomery, of Lincoln's cabinet (hist.). *Abraham Lincoln* (play), J. Drinkwater, 1918.

Blair, Robert, solicitor, m. Marion Sharpe. *The Franchise Affair*, Josephine Tey, 1948.

Blaise, friend and servant of Lord Castlewood. *Henry Esmond*, W. M. Thackeray, 1852.

Blaith, Sibyl. *The Young Idea* (play), N. Coward, 1923.

Blaize, Lucy, m. Richard Feverel.
  Tom, her father.
  Young Tom, her brother.
The Ordeal of Richard Feverel, G. Meredith, 1859.

Blake, m. Widow Biggs, 'Lost Mr Blake' (poem), *The Bab Ballads*, W. S. Gilbert, 1869.

Blake, alias of Bedford after return to earth. *The First Men in the Moon*, H. G. Wells, 1901.

Blake, 'wild Irishman.' *The Sky Pilot*, R. Connor, 1899.

Blake, Captain.
  Neddy, his son.
Rambles of a Rat, A.L.O.E., 1854.

Blake, Miss, governess to Dan and Una. *Puck of Pook's Hill*, R. Kipling, 1906.

Blake, Mr, elderly widower.
  Margaret, his daughter.
'Silver Trumpets' (s.s.), *Louise*, Viola Meynell, 1954.

Blake, Mr ('A. V. Laider'). *Seven Men*, Max Beerbohm, 1919.

Blake, Archie, of Astwick, fiancé of Joy Stretton. *Joy and Josephine*, Monica Dickens, 1948.

Blake, Audrey, governess to Ogden Ford, m. (1) Sheridan, (2) Peter Burns. *The Little Nugget*, P. G. Wodehouse, 1913.

Blake, Darrell. *The Moon in the Yellow River* (play), D. Johnston, 1932.

Blake, Franklin, central character and part narrator, m. Rachel Verinder. *The Moonstone*, W. Collins, 1868.

Blake, Fred, young Australian in Far East. *The Narrow Corner*, W. S. Maugham, 1932.

Blake, Honor. *The Playboy of the*

Western World (play), J. M. Synge, 1907.

Blake, Dr Joseph. *Mourning becomes Electra* (play), E. O'Neill, 1931.

Blake, Rev. Joseph, formerly lieutenant in English army in America.
Joseph Clinton, his son, m. Theodosia Warrington.
The Virginians, W. M. Thackeray, 1857–9.

Blake, Ken, narrator.
Evelyn, his wife.
The Judas Window, 1938, and others, Carter Dickson.

Blake, Lydia. *Yellow Sands* (play), E. & A. Phillpotts, 1926.

Blake, Mary. *David Harum*, E. Noyes Westcott, 1891.

Blake, Nat, violinist, m. Daisy Brooke. *Little Men*, 1871, and *Jo's Boys*, 1886, Louisa M. Alcott.

Blake, Philip.
His wife.
Nora, their daughter.
Matthew, their son.
Charles O'Malley, C. Lever, 1841.

Blake, Sandy, boat-owner. *Sun on the Water*, L. A. G. Strong, 1940.

Blake, Sexton, famous detective in long series of anonymous novelettes for boys.

Blake, Simon, husband of Mary Rose Morland.
Harry, their son.
Mary Rose (play), J. M. Barrie, 1920.

Blakeley, Denis, a socialist.
Kathleen, his daughter.
Radcliffe, David Storey, 1963.

Blakeney, Felicia, m. Chester Meredith.
Crispin, her brother.
'Chester Forgets Himself' (s.s.), *The Heart of a Goof*, P. G. Wodehouse, 1926.

Blakeney, Sir Percy, 'the Scarlet Pimpernel.'
Marguerite, *née* St Just, his wife.
The Scarlet Pimpernel, Baroness Orczy, 1905, and elsewhere.

Blakeston, Jim, lover of Liza Kemp.
His wife.
Liza of Lambeth, W. S. Maugham, 1897.

Blampied, Rev. John Sylvester. *Random Harvest*, J. Hilton, 1941.

Blanc. *Beau Geste*, P. C. Wren, 1924.

Blanc, Pierre, of La Mouette. *Frenchman's Creek*, Daphne du Maurier, 1941.

Blanchard, Miss Augusta, artist. *Roderick Hudson*, H. James, 1875.

Blanchard, Jenny.
Emmy, her sister.
'Pa,' their father.
Nocturne, F. Swinnerton, 1917.

Blanche, Lady, Professor of Abstract Science.
Melissa, her daughter, m. Florian.
The Princess (poem), Lord Tennyson, 1847. *Princess Ida* (comic opera), Gilbert & Sullivan, 1884.

Blanche, Anthony, 'aesthete.' *Brideshead Revisited*, E. Waugh, 1945.

Blancove, Sir William, Bt., m. (2) Mrs Lovell.
Edward, his son, law student.
Algernon, his nephew, in love with Mrs Lovell.
Rhoda Fleming, G. Meredith, 1865.

Bland, Dr, Lady Tiptoff's physician. *The Great Hoggarty Diamond*, W. M. Thackeray, 1841.

Bland, Mrs. *Shall We Join the Ladies?* (play), J. M. Barrie, 1921.

Bland, Pigling.
His brothers:
Alexander.
Chinchin.
Stumpy.
The Tale of Pigling Bland, Beatrix Potter, 1913.

Blandeville, Lady Emily, m. Colonel Talbot. *Waverley*, W. Scott, 1814.

Blandish, central character, 'Spoils of Mr Blandish,' story read by Boon. *Boon*, H. G. Wells, 1915.

Blandish, Lady, friend of the Feverels. *The Ordeal of Richard Feverel*, G. Meredith, 1859.

Blandsbury, Sir Cyril and Lady. *The Hand of Ethelberta*, T. Hardy, 1876.

Blandy, Sir Peregrine, Governor, Coventry Island, successor to Rawdon Crawley. *The Newcomes*, W. M. Thackeray, 1854–5.

Blane, Niel, town piper.
Jenny, his daughter.
Old Mortality, W. Scott, 1816.

Blaney. *The Borough* (poem), G. Crabbe, 1810.

Blanquart, schoolmaster and secretary to the Mairie.
  Cécile, his daughter.
  His sister.
The Spanish Farm trilogy, R. H. Mottram, 1924–6.

Blaquart, Monsieur Auguste. *The Adventures of Mr Ledbury,* Albert Smith, 1844.

Blastel, Dick. *Other Gods,* Pearl Buck, 1940.

Blathers, Bow Street officer. *Oliver Twist,* C. Dickens, 1838.

Blatherwick, attorney. *The Great Hoggarty Diamond,* W. M. Thackeray, 1841.

Blattergowl, Dr, dull and prosy minister of Trotcosey. *The Antiquary,* W. Scott, 1816.

Blaydon, Melissa, a wealthy widow. *The Widow's Cruise,* Nicholas Blake, 1959.

Blayds, Oliver.
  Isobel, his younger daughter. *See* BLAYDS-CONWAY.
The Truth about Blayds (play), A. A. Milne, 1921.

Blayds-Conway, Mrs Marion, elder daughter of Oliver Blayds.
  William, her husband.
    Oliver, their son.
    Septima, their daughter.
The Truth about Blayds (play), A. A. Milne, 1921.

Blazer, The, slum woman. *Britannia Mews,* Margery Sharp, 1946.

Blazey, Reuben, government agent. *The American Prisoner,* E. Phillpotts, 1904.

Bleane, Lord. *Our Betters* (play), W. S. Maugham, 1923.

Blejo, Jesus, head of police, Havana. *Anthony Adverse,* Hervey Allen, 1934.

Blemley, Lady.
  Sir Wilfrid, her husband.
Tobermory (s.s.), 'Saki' (H. H. Munro).

Blend, Miss, poetess, mistress of Arthur Stubland. *Joan and Peter,* H. G. Wells, 1918.

Blenkensop, Lady, close confederate of Sarah, Duchess of Marlborough. *The Bride of Lammermoor,* W. Scott, 1819.

Blenkins, Bonaparte, rascally Englishman. *The Story of an African Farm,* Olive Schreiner, 1883.

Blenkinsop, grocer, Leyminster. *Both of this Parish,* J. S. Fletcher.

Blenkinsop, Dr. *The Doctor's Dilemma* (play), G. B. Shaw, 1906.

Blenkinsop, Miss, 'actress of high comedy.' *Pendennis,* W. M. Thackeray, 1848–50.

Blenkinsop, Mrs.
  Barbara, her daughter, m. Crosbie Carruthers.
  Maud, a cousin.
Diary of a Provincial Lady, E. M. Delafield, 1930.

Blenkinsop, Samuel, bank clerk, m. Hannah Mole. *Miss Mole,* E. H. Young, 1930.

Blent, Major. *The Queen's Husband* (play), R. E. Sherwood, 1928.

Bless, Christopher. 'The Melancholy Hussar,' *Life's Little Ironies,* T. Hardy, 1894.

Blessington, Robert, John Chilcote's secretary. *John Chilcote, M.P.,* Katherine C. Thurston, 1904.

Bletson, Joshua, Parliamentary commissioner. *Woodstock,* W. Scott, 1826.

Blewett, Richard, partner with Deuceace in swindling Dawkins. 'The Amours of Mr Deuceace,' *Yellowplush Papers,* Thackeray, 1852.

Blifil, Dr.
  His brother, the captain, m. Bridget Allworthy.
  Their son.
Tom Jones, H. Fielding, 1749.

Bligh, family name of LORD ROCKAGE.

Bligh, Miss Gertrude (Nellie), church worker. *By The Pricking of My Thumbs,* Agatha Christie, 1968.

Blimber, Dr, schoolmaster.
  His wife and daughter.
Dombey and Son, C. Dickens, 1848.

Blinkhoolie. *See* BONIFACE.

Blinkhorn, housemaster at Dr Grimstone's. *Vice Versa,* F. Anstey, 1882.

Blinkinsop, Colonel, old officer. *The Virginians,* W. M. Thackeray, 1857–9.

Bliss, schoolboy. *St Winifred's,* F. W. Farrar, 1862.

Bliss, Detective Inspector. *The Ringer* (play), E. Wallace, 1926.

Bliss, Judith.
  David, her husband.

Sorel, their daughter.
Simon, their son.
Hay Fever (play), N. Coward, 1925.

Bliss, Reginald, friend and literary executor of George Boon. *Boon,* H. G. Wells, 1915.

Blitch, Mabel, school friend of Undine Spragg, m. Henry Lipscombe. *The Custom of the Country,* Edith Wharton, 1913.

Blitzen, Boanerges. 'The Man who could Write' (poem), *Departmental Ditties,* R. Kipling, 1886.

Block, Martin, butcher of Dijon. *Anne of Geierstein,* W. Scott, 1829.

Bloeckman, Joseph, vice-president of film company. *The Beautiful and the Damned,* F. Scott Fitzgerald, 1922.

Blofeld, Ernst Stavro, founder and chairman of SPECTRE. *Thunderball,* Ian Fleming, 1961.

Blogg, William, late Master of Boniface. *Pendennis,* W.M. Thackeray, 1848–50.

Blois, Chevalier de, aristocratic *émigré,* Thomas Newcome's French master. *The Newcomes,* W. M. Thackeray, 1853–5.

Blok, Nikkel, of Liège, butcher. *Quentin Durward,* W. Scott, 1823.

Blomefield, Rev. Mr, Vicar of Birtwick. *Black Beauty,* Anna Sewell, 1877.

Blood, Captain, 'The Old Ancient Ship' (s.s.), *Short Stories,* Morley Roberts, 1928.

Blood, Captain Peter, central character (semi-hist.), m. Arabella Bishop. *Captain Blood,* 1922, and elsewhere, R. Sabatini.

Bloodenough, General Victor, V.C., Chairman of Governors, Harchester College. *Meet Mr Mulliner,* P. G. Wodehouse, 1927.

Bloom, Leopold, journalist, m. Marion Tweedy.
Milly, their daughter.
Ulysses, James Joyce, 1922.

Bloomfield, Mr.
His wife, *née* Robson.
Their children, Agnes Grey's pupils:
Tom.
Mary.
Ann.
Fanny.
Mrs Bloomfield, their grandmother.
Agnes Grey, Anne Brontë, 1847.

Bloomfield, Edward Hugh, uncle of Gideon Forsyth. *The Wrong Box,* R. L. Stevenson & L. Osbourne, 1889.

Bloor, wealthy American dilettante. *Landmarks,* E. V. Lucas, 1914.

Blore, the Monts' butler, The *Forsyte* series, J. Galsworthy, 1906–1933.

Blore, colleague of Forrester. *The Purple Plain,* H. E. Bates, 1947.

Blore, Sammy, farm labourer. *Two on a Tower,* T. Hardy, 1882.

Blotton, member of the Pickwick Club. *Pickwick Papers,* C. Dickens, 1837.

Bloundel, Stephen, grocer.
Amabel, his daughter.
Old St Paul's, W. H. Ainsworth, 1841.

Bloundell (also called Bloundell-Bloundell), gambler. *Pendennis,* W. M. Thackeray, 1848–50.

Blount, Sir Frederick. *Money* (play), Lord Lytton, 1840.

Blount, Jake, a frustrated idealist. *The Heart is a Lonely Hunter,* Carson McCullers, 1940.

Blount, Joyce, grand-niece of Mrs Caroline Faraday. *Police at the Funeral,* Margery Allingham, 1931.

Blount, Sir Nicholas, Master of the Horse to the Earl of Sussex. *Kenilworth,* W. Scott, 1821.

Blount, Nina, fiancée of Adam Fenwick-Symes.
Colonel Blount, her father.
Vile Bodies, Evelyn Waugh, 1930.

Blount, Thomas, unscrupulous page of Ralf Isambard. *The Heaven Tree* trilogy, Edith Pargeter, 1961–1963.

Blow, Adeline Maud, of Leeds, fiancée of Dr O'Grady. *The Search Party,* G. A. Birmingham, 1913.

Blow, Mrs Goliath. *Abraham Lincoln* (play), J. Drinkwater, 1918.

Blow, Sam, cousin of the Campions.
m. (1) **Lizzie.**
(2) **Daisy.**
The Perennial Bachelor, Anne Parrish, 1925.

Blowberry, bookseller, employer of Grope.

His wife.
Albert, their son.
Ted, their son.
Albert Grope, F. O. Mann, 1931.

Blower, Mrs Peggy.
John, her dead husband.
St Ronan's Well, W. Scott, 1824.

Blowsalinda, chambermaid at the Red Lion. *The House with the Green Shutters,* G. Douglas, 1901.

Blowselinda (or Bonstrops), landlady of Nigel. *The Fortunes of Nigel,* W. Scott, 1822.

Bloxham, John, friend of Brodie. *God's Prisoner,* J. Oxenham, 1898.

Bludgeon, Mrs, of the Church of Ancient Truth. *Albert Grope,* F. O. Mann, 1931.

Bludso, Jim. *Jim Bludso* (poem), John Hay.

Bludyer, writer and critic. *Pendennis,* 1848–50, and elsewhere, W. M. Thackeray.

Bludyer, Colonel.
The Hon. Mrs, his wife.
Vanity Fair, 1847–8, and elsewhere, W. M. Thackeray.

Bludyer, Lady, wife of General Sir Roger. *Vanity Fair,* 1847–8, W. M. Thackeray.

Blue, Angela, schoolteacher, m. Eugene Witla. *The Genius,* Theodore Dreiser, 1915.

Blueskin, Jack Sheppard's devoted friend. *Jack Sheppard,* W. H. Ainsworth, 1839.

Bluff, Sylvanus.
Rosamund, his wife.
Hawbuck Grange, R. S. Surtees, 1847.

Blum, Walther, sculptor, central character.
Karen, his wife.
The Smile of Karen (s.s.), O. Onions.

Blundel, Senator Sam. *Through One Administration,* Frances H. Burnett, 1881.

Blundell, Theodore.
Zoe, his wife.
Mid-Channel (play), A. W. Pinero, 1909.

Blunt, captain of the *Pretty Mary,* 'a jovial coarse fellow.' *For the Term of his Natural Life,* M. Clarke, 1874.

Blunt, Inspector. *The Stolen White Elephant,* Mark Twain, 1882.

Blunt, Rev. Godfrey, m. Cecilia Vereker. *A Safety Match,* Ian Hay, 1911.

Blunt, Captain J. K. *The Arrow of Gold,* J. Conrad, 1919.

Blunt, Sir Thomas.
Julia, his wife. Uncle and aunt of Lord Dreever.
A Gentleman of Leisure, P. G. Wodehouse, 1910.

Blunt, Sir Walter, friend of Henry. *Henry the Fourth* (play), W. Shakespeare.

Bluntschli, Captain ('The Chocolate Soldier'). *Arms and the Man* (play), G. B. Shaw, 1894.

Blushington, elderly dandy who uses rouge. *Pendennis,* W. M. Thackeray, 1848–50.

Bly, Chief. *Tracy's Tiger,* W. Saroyan, 1951.

Bly, Mr. *Britannia Mews,* Margery Sharp, 1946.

Bly, Nelly. *See* HELEN BLYESDALE.

Blyesdale, Helen (alias Nelly Bly), journalist posing as maid, m. Quentin Cotton. *Poet's Pub,* E. Linklater, 1929.

Blythe, Pevensey, Ed. the *Outpost.* The *Forsyte* series, J. Galsworthy, 1906–33.

Boabdil, Saracen ruler. *Ivanhoe,* W. Scott, 1820.

Boaler, Paul Bultitude's butler. *Vice Versa,* F. Anstey, 1882.

Boam, cockney constable, Gartumna. 'Another Temple Gone' (s.s.), *Fiery Particles,* C. E. Montague, 1923.

Boanerges. *The Apple Cart* (play), G. B. Shaw, 1929.

Bobadil, Captain, braggart and coward. *Every Man in his Humour* (play), B. Jonson, 1598.

Bobbe, socialist friend of George Winterbourne. *Death of a Hero,* R. Aldington, 1929.

Bobsborough, Bishop of. *See* EUSTACE and GREYSTOCK.

Bobstay, Bill, bosun's mate. *H.M.S. Pinafore* (comic opera), Gilbert & Sullivan, 1878.

Bobster, Mr.
Cecilia, his daughter.
Nicholas Nickleby, C. Dickens, 1839.

Boddy, Lewis, innkeeper and coal merchant.
Vittoria, his Italian wife.

'Three Ladies' (s.s.), *Last Recollections of My Uncle Charles*, N. Balchin, 1954.

Bode, Mr and Mrs.
Almeric, their son.
Dulcia, their daughter.
A House and its Head, Ivy Compton-Burnett, 1935.

Bodfish, Martin, ex-policeman, uncle of Mrs Negget. 'Cupboard Love' (s.s.), *The Lady of the Barge*, W. W. Jacobs, 1902.

Bodie, Mr Dick, artist.
Nellie, his sister.
A Kiss for Cinderella (play), J. M. Barrie, 1916.

Bodkin, Dr Elias, Dr Finn's partner. *Phineas Finn*, A. Trollope, 1869.

Boffin, Nicodemus, originally servant of John Harmon, senior.
Henrietta, his wife.
Our Mutual Friend, C. Dickens, 1865.

Boffkin, Judge.
His wife.
Minnie, their daughter.
'The Post that Fitted' (poem), *Departmental Ditties*, R. Kipling, 1886.

Boh da Thone, rebel chief. 'The Ballad of Boh da Thone' (poem), *Barrack-room Ballads*, R. Kipling, 1892.

Bohemia, King of. 'A Scandal in Bohemia' (s.s.), *The Adventures of Sherlock Holmes*, A. Conan Doyle, 1892.

Bohemond of Tarentum, son of Robert Guiscard; leader in the First Crusade. *Count Robert of Paris*, W. Scott, 1832.

Bohm, Ortrud, German school friend of Margaret Roundelay. *A Footman for the Peacock*, Rachel Ferguson, 1940.

Bohun, Colonel the Hon. Norman.
Rev. and Hon. Wilfred, his brother.
'The Hammer of God' (s.s.), *The Innocence of Father Brown*, G. K. Chesterton, 1911.

Bohun, Walter, son of Walter Boon ('William'). *You Never Can Tell* (play), G. B. Shaw, 1894.

Boielle, Paul, waiter and artist. 'Rough-hew them how we Will' (s.s.), *The Man Upstairs*, P. G. Wodehouse, 1914.

Boileau, 'Tick,' subaltern. 'A Conference of the Powers' (s.s.), *Many Inventions*, R. Kipling, 1893.

Bois-Guilbert, Brian de, Commander of the Knights Templars. *Ivanhoe*, W. Scott, 1820.

Boisgelin, Comtesse de. *Anne of Geierstein*, W. Scott, 1829.

Bojanus, tailor. *Antic Hay*, A. Huxley, 1923.

Boland, Con, dentist.
Mary, his daughter, and other children.
The Citadel, A. J. Cronin, 1937.

Bold, John, surgeon, m. Eleanor Harding.
Mary, his sister.
The Warden, 1855, and elsewhere, A. Trollope.

Boldero, Hon. Mrs, adventuress.
Brenda and **Minna,** her school-age daughters.
The Adventures of Philip, W. M. Thackeray, 1861–2.

Boldero, Herbert, capitalist. *Antic Hay*, A. Huxley, 1923.

Boldini. *Beau Geste*, P. C. Wren, 1924.

Boldwig, Captain. *Pickwick Papers*, C. Dickens, 1837.

Boldwood, creditor of Michael Henchard. *The Mayor of Casterbridge*, T. Hardy, 1886.

Boldwood, William, in love with Bathsheba Everdene; murders her husband, Sergeant Troy. *Far from the Madding Crowd*, T. Hardy, 1874.

Bolfry, 'Duke and General of Legions' summoned from Hell. *Mr Bolfry* (play), James Bridie, 1943.

Bolgolam, a courtier in Lilliput. *Gulliver's Travels*, J. Swift, 1726.

Bolidar. *Beau Geste*, P. C. Wren, 1924.

Bolingbroke, later Henry IV (hist.). *Richard the Second* and *Henry the Fourth* (plays), W. Shakespeare.

Bollen, Mr, farmer, m. Adelaide Hinton. *Desperate Remedies*, T. Hardy, 1871.

Boller, Jacob ('Pennsylvania'), preacher, and later seaman on the *We're Here*. *Captains Courageous*, R. Kipling, 1897.

Bologna, Antonio, second husband of the Duchess. *The Duchess of Malfi* (play), John Webster, *c.* 1613.

Bolt, Henry Little's partner. *Put Yourself in his Place,* C. Reade, 1870.

Bolt, Rachel, m. (1) Samuel.
Samuel, their son.
(2) Peter Toop.
The Mother, E. Phillpotts, 1908.

Bolt, Tom.
His wife.
Their children:
Charlie.
Jack.
Annie, eng. to Jim Maynard.
Polly.
All Our Yesterdays H. M. Tomlinson, 1930.

Boltby, clerk to Hobson Bros. *The Newcomes,* W. M. Thackeray, 1853–5.

Bolter. *See* NOAH CLAYPOLE.

Bolter, Jack, friend of Barry Lyndon, *Barry Lyndon,* W. M. Thackeray, 1844.

Boltomy, ship's captain. *Unending Crusade,* R. E. Sherwood, 1932.

Bolton, Lieutenant, of the *Indefatigable.* The *Hornblower* series, C. S. Forester, 1937 onwards.

Bolton, Mrs, 'portress' of Shepherds Inn.
Her children:
Barney.
Amelia.
Betsy.
Fanny (with whom Pendennis is temporarily in love), m. Sam Huxter.
Pendennis, W. M. Thackeray, 1848–50.

Bolton, Harry, young English prodigal. *Redburn,* Herman Melville, 1849.

Bolton, Detective-Sergeant Leonard. *The Jury,* G. Bullett, 1935.

Bolton, Captain Stawarth. *The Monastery,* W. Scott, 1820.

Boltro, Chief Inspector Jack.
Sam, his father.
We the Accused, E. Raymond, 1935.

Bolverson, Mrs, worker of charms. *The Delectable Duchy,* A. Quiller-Couch, 1893.

Bompard, estate agent.
Valentine, his daughter, m. (1) Victor Dutripon; (2) Zambra.
'The Vengeance of Monsieur Dutripon' (s.s.), *The Little Dog Laughed* L. Merrick, 1930.

Bonaccord of Outremer, Friar. *The Forest Lovers,* M. Hewlett, 1898.

Bonapart, Joe, young boxer.
His father.
Golden Boy (play), Clifford Odets, 1937.

Bonaventura, Friar, Giovanni's tutor and confessor. *'Tis Pity She's A Whore* (play), John Ford, *c.* 1624.

Bond, James, secret service agent 007, *Dr No* and others, Ian Fleming.

Bond, Lord (Alured).
Lucasta, his wife.
Their sons: **Cedric,** m. Daphne Stonor.
Weyland.
The *Barsetshire* series, Angela Thirkell, 1933 onwards.

Bond, May, revue actress. *Prisoner of Grace,* Joyce Cary, 1952.

Bond, Sebastian, M.A., headmaster. *Twelve Horses and the Hangman's Noose,* Gladys Mitchell, 1956.

Bonduca (Boadicea) (hist.). *Bonduca* (play), Beaumont & Fletcher, 1614.

Bone, Malachi, Canadian guide. *Settlers in Canada,* Captain Marryat, 1844.

Bonelli, Baron, Prime Minister, shot by Roma Volonna, his mistress. *The Eternal City,* Hall Caine, 1901.

Bones, Captain Billy, of the *Hispaniola. Treasure Island,* R. L. Stevenson, 1883.

Boney, a yellow horse preaching sedition. 'A Walking Delegate' (s.s.), *The Day's Work,* R. Kipling, 1898.

Bonfante, Arturo, old revolutionary in Paris. *Birds of America,* Mary McCarthy, 1971.

Bongwan. *See* COMMANDER GOOD.

Bonham-Hervey, Mrs, a dog-fancier.
Major Renton Bonham-Hervey, her husband.
Mr Ingleside, E. V. Lucas, 1910.

Boniface, Lord Abbot of St Mary's. *The Monastery,* 1820. Later as Blinkhoolie, gardener, of Kinross. *The Abbot,* 1820, W. Scott.

Boniface, a landlord.
Cherry, his daughter.
The Beaux' Stratagem (play), G. Farquhar, 1707.

Bonington, Sir Ralph Bloomfield. *The Doctor's Dilemma* (play), G. B. Shaw, 1906.

Bonner, Mrs.
Her daughters: **Lady Jocelyn.**
Juliana.
Evan Harrington, G. Meredith, 1861.

Bonner, Edmund, wealthy Sydney draper, one of Johann Voss's sponsors.
His wife.
Voss, Patrick White, 1957.

Bonner, Susan, maid to Lady Clavering, m. Lightfoot, Sir F. Clavering's valet. *Pendennis*, W. M. Thackeray, 1848–50.

Bonnet, Madame, *pensionnaire.*
Leontine, her niece.
Fanny by Gaslight, M. Sadleir, 1940.

Bonney, company promoter. *Nicholas Nickleby*, C. Dickens, 1839.

Bonnington, Rev. Mr, second husband of Mrs Lovel. *Lovel the Widower*, W. M. Thackeray, 1860.

Bonnycastle, a schoolmaster. *Mr Midshipman Easy*, Captain Marryat, 1836.

Bonnyface, Mrs, pretty landlady of the Swan, Exeter. *Barry Lyndon*, W. M. Thackeray, 1844.

Bonnyfeather, merchant, benefactor and first master of Anthony Adverse. *Anthony Adverse*, Hervey Allen, 1934.

Bonover, George, headmaster, Whortley Proprietary School. *Love and Mr Lewisham*, H. G. Wells, 1900.

Bonteen, Mr, Liberal M.P.
His wife.
Phineas Finn, 1869, and elsewhere, A. Trollope.

Bonthron, Antony, Sir J. Ramorny's 'dark satellite.' *The Fair Maid of Perth*, W. Scott, 1828.

Bonville, Lady Katherine. *The Last of the Barons*, Lord Lytton, 1843.

Bonzig (Le Grand Bonzig), head of boys' school in Paris. *The Martian*, George du Maurier, 1897.

Booby, Sir Thomas.
His wife. One-time employers of Joseph Andrews.
Joseph Andrews, H. Fielding, 1742.

Booch, Mrs, pensioner of Lady Drew. *Tono Bungay*, H. G. Wells, 1909.

Boocock, Michael.
Rosa, his wife, later m. **Eli,** his brother.
'No Road' (s.s.), *Love and Money*, Phyllis Bentley, 1957.

Boody, Mrs, housekeeper to Mr Ingleside.
Horace (alias Timbs), her husband.
Mr Ingleside, E. V. Lucas, 1910.

Booker, Alfred, publisher. *The Way We Live Now*, A. Trollope, 1875.

Boom, Lord, newspaper proprietor, opponent of Ponderevo. *Tono Bungay*, H. G. Wells, 1909.

Boom, Hilary, divorce solicitor for John Adam. *Holy Deadlock*, A. P. Herbert, 1934.

Boomer, the kangaroo. 'The Sing-song of Old Man Kangaroo' (s.s.), *Just So Stories*, R. Kipling, 1902.

Boomer, Captain of the Fishbourne Fire Brigade. *The History of Mr Polly*, H. G. Wells, 1910.

Booms, of *The Rocket*. *Reginald Cruden*, T. Baines Reed, 1894.

Boon, George, central character, popular playwright and novelist. *Boon*, H. G. Wells, 1915.

Boon, Percy.
Clarice, his mother.
London Belongs to Me, N. Collins, 1945.

Boon, Walter. *See* William.

Boondi Queen, The. 'The Last Suttee' (poem), *Barrack-room Ballads*, R. Kipling, 1892.

Boorman, Alice, friend of Laura Menzies. The *Mrs Bradley* detective stories, Gladys Mitchell, 1929 onwards.

Booth, John Wilkes (hist.). *Abraham Lincoln* (play), J. Drinkwater, 1918.

Bootham, Harry, nephew of Ted Goold, private secretary to Chester Nimmo. *Prisoner of Grace*, Joyce Cary, 1952.

Booty, Fred, friend of John Ransome.
Maudie, his girl-friend.
The Combined Maze, May Sinclair, 1913.

Borden, Josiah.
Emma, his wife.
Mourning becomes Electra (play), E. O'Neill, 1931.

Boreas, Nicholas, a film producer. *Barefoot in the Head*, Brian W. Aldiss, 1969.

Borel, Monsieur, pastor of French Church, Winchelsea. *Denis Duval*, W. M. Thackeray, 1864.

Borg, Isabelle. *This Side of Paradise*, F. Scott Fitzgerald, 1920.

Borgia, Francesco, Duke of Gandia (hist.).
Caesar, his brother.
Lucretia, his sister. *See* POPE ALEXANDER VI and VANOZZA CATANEI.
The Duke of Gandia (play), A. C. Swinburne, 1908.

Boris, 'a square man and honest.' *Idylls of the King* (poems), Lord Tennyson, 1859.

Borkin, Mr, photographer. *The One Before,* Barry Pain, 1902.

Bornewell, Sir Thomas.
Aretina, his wife.
The Lady of Pleasure (play), J. Shirley, 1635.

Borodale, Marquis of, calling himself 'Miss Sally,' m. Sally Bascom. 'The Marquis and Miss Sally' (s.s.), *Rolling Stones,* O. Henry, 1913.

Borodino, Countess de, keeper of a *pension* at Brussels. *Vanity Fair,* W. M. Thackeray, 1847–8.

Borring, Augustus. *Loyalties* (play), J. Galsworthy, 1922.

Borso, Duke. 'The Judgment of Borso' (s.s.), *Little Novels of Italy,* M. Hewlett, 1899.

Borth, Sergeant, Joppolo's assistant. *A Bell for Adano,* John Hersey, 1944.

Borvitch, Vaclav. *Trial by Terror,* P. Gallico, 1952.

Bosambo, Krooman; adventurer-at-large. *Sanders of the River,* E. Wallace, 1911.

Bose, Hindu guest at Scamnum. *Hamlet, Revenge!,* M. Innes, 1937.

Boselli, Gian-Luca, central character; illegitimate son of **Olga,** illegitimate daughter of **Teresa,** wife of **Fabio Boselli,** naturalized English *restaurateur;* m. Maddalena Trevi. *Adam's Breed,* Radclyffe Hall, 1926.

Bosmaun, Afrikander prospector. *The City of Gold,* F. Brett Young, 1939.

Bosola, Daniel de, master of horse, spy of the Duchess's brothers. *The Duchess of Malfi* (play), John Webster, *c.* 1613.

Bossnowl, Lord, Earl of Foolincourt, friend of MacCrotchet.
Lady Clarinda, his sister.
Crotchet Castle, T. L. Peacock, 1831.

Bostock, John, inventor.
Mary, his wife.
Bob, their son, aged 13.
Jennifer, their daughter.
Michael, youngest son.
The French Lieutenant, Richard Church, 1971.

Bosville, Cornet, later Sir Humphrey, m. Mary Cave. *Holmby House,* G. Whyte-Melville, 1860.

Boswell, Joe, handsome gipsy. *The Virgin and The Gipsy,* D. H. Lawrence, 1930.

Botany, Sir Brian. 'Bad Sir Brian Botany' (poem), *When We Were Very Young,* A. A. Milne, 1924.

Boteler, Adam, foster-brother of Harry Talvace, who marries Talvace's widow, Gilleis Otley. *The Heaven Tree* trilogy, Edith Pargeter, 1961–3.

Bothwell, Sergeant Francis Stewart. *Old Mortality,* W. Scott, 1816.

Bott, Gladstone. 'High Stakes' (s.s.), *The Heart of a Goof,* P. G. Wodehouse, 1926.

Bott, Rev. Samuel, vicar. *The Feast,* Margaret Kennedy, 1950.

Bottell, Captain, master of cargo ship *Oroya. Captain Bottell,* James Hanley, 1933.

Bottinius, Johannes-Baptista, Doctor of Law, Apostolic Advocate. *The Ring and the Book,* R. Browning, 1868–9.

Bottle, Sam, of Bottle's Hooks and Eyes. *Flamingo,* Mary Borden, 1927.

Bottleby, friend of Talbot Twysden. *The Adventures of Philip,* W. M. Thackeray, 1861–2.

Bottom, a weaver. *A Midsummer Night's Dream* (play) W. Shakespeare.

Bottsford, John, thresher; employer of Tom Edwards. 'An Ohio Pagan' (s.s.), *Horses and Men,* Sherwood Anderson, 1924.

Boucher, Colonel, m. Mrs Weston. *Queen Lucia,* E. F. Benson.

Boucher, François (hist.). *The Story of Rosina* (poem), A. Dobson, 1895.

Bouchier, Captain, Vice-chamberlain, Windsor Castle. *Windsor Castle,* W. H. Ainsworth, 1843.

Boulby, Mrs, innkeeper, the Pilot. *Rhoda Fleming,* G. Meredith, 1865.

Boulte, engineer.
Emma, his wife.
'A Wayside Comedy' (s.s.), *Wee Willie Winkie*, R. Kipling, 1888.

Boulter, Hon, George, son of Lord Levant.
His wife, *née* Mango.
Vanity Fair, W. M. Thackeray, 1847–8.

Bouncer, a landlord. *Box and Cox* (play), J. M. Morton, 1847.

Bouncer, Henry, undergraduate friend of Verdant Green, m. Fanny Green.
His sister.
The Adventures of Mr Verdant Green, Cuthbert Bede, 1853.

Bounderby, Josiah, banker, m. Louisa Gradgrind. *Hard Times*, C. Dickens, 1854.

Bountiful, Lady, mother of Squire Sullen.
Dorinda, her daughter.
The Beaux' Stratagem, G. Farquhar, 1707.

Bourbon, Duke of. *Henry the Fifth* (play), W. Shakespeare.

Bourchier, Cardinal, Archbishop of Canterbury. *Richard the Third* (play), W. Shakespeare.

Bourne, Miss. *The Ghost Train* (play), A. Ridley, 1925.

Bowee, valet to Lord Scoutbush. *Two Years Ago*, C. Kingsley, 1857.

Bowen, Agatha, m. Nathanael Locke Harper. *Agatha's Husband*, Mrs Craik, 1853.

Bowen, Garnet, author.
Barbara, his wife.
Their children:
Sandra.
David.
Mark.
I Like It Here, Kingsley Amis, 1958.

Bowen, Mrs Laura.
Charles, her husband.
The Custom of the Country, Edith Wharton, 1913.

Bowen, Roderick, a family grocer.
Hannah, his wife.
Their children:
Dilys.
Madoc.
Susan.
Penry, chief character.
Tomorrow To Fresh Woods, Rhys Davies, 1941.

Boweri, Bernard, film producer. *Fergus*, Brian Moore, 1971.

Bowers, Captain, uncle of Prudence Drewitt. *Dialstone Lane*, W. W. Jacobs, 1904.

Bowlby, James St George Bernard.
His wife.
The Buick Saloon (s.s.), Ann Bridge.

Bowles, Corcoran's landlord. *Ukridge*, P. G. Wodehouse, 1924.

Bowles, a missionary.
His wife.
The Heart of the Matter, Graham Greene, 1948.

Bowles, Master, the *Justinian*. The *Hornblower* series, C. S. Forester, 1950.

Bowles, Beppo. *Eyeless in Gaza*, Aldous Huxley, 1936.

Bowles, Martin, barrister. *The Bachelors*, Muriel Spark, 1961.

Bowles, Sally, would-be demi-mondaine: actress and singer in night clubs. *Goodbye to Berlin*, Christopher Isherwood, 1939.

Bowling, Lieutenant, uncle of Roderick Random. *Roderick Random*, T. Smollett, 1748.

Bowling, Percy.
His wife, **Madame Balaton.**
Pension keepers.
They Wanted to Live, Cecil Roberts, 1939.

Bowling, Tom. *Tom Bowling* (poem), C. Dibdin.

Bowls, butler to Miss Crawley, m. Mrs Firkin, her maid. *Vanity Fair*, W. M. Thackeray, 1847–8.

Bowman, Mrs, Mary Mahony's servant. *The Fortunes of Richard Mahony*, H. H. Richardson, 1917–30.

Bowman, Stella. *No News from Helen*, L. Golding, 1943.

Bowntance, Bryan, innkeeper. *Windsor Castle*, W. H. Ainsworth, 1843.

Bows, crippled fiddler and teacher of acting and singing. *Pendennis*, W. M. Thackeray, 1848–50.

Bowser, Ben, alias of Benjamin Middleton. *The Dark Horse*, Nat Gould.

Bowyer, one of Queen Elizabeth's ushers. *Kenilworth*, W. Scott, 1821.

Bowyer, 'Honest,' money-lender.
Alice, his daughter.

Master Humphrey's Clock, C. Dickens, 1840–1.

Box, journeyman printer. *Box and Cox* (play), J. M. Morton, 1847.

Box, Joe ('Chunks'), of the *Jolly Bargee*. *Fanny by Gaslight*, M. Sadleir, 1940.

Box-Bender, Arthur, Member of Parliament, m. Angela Crouchback.
 Tony, their son.
 Men at Arms, Evelyn Waugh, 1952.

Boxe, Lady. *Diary of a Provincial Lady*, E. M. Delafield, 1930.

Boxton, Dorothy, m. 'Young' Nicholas Forsyte. The *Forsyte* series, J. Galsworthy, 1906–33.

'Boy,' narrator, brother of Daphne Pleydell, m. Adele Feste. *Berry and Co.*, D. Yates, 1920.

Boy, The, a subaltern. 'Thrown Away' (s.s.), *Plain Tales from the Hills*, R. Kipling, 1888.

Boyce, Marcella, central character; social worker, m. Aldous Raeburn.
 Richard, her father.
 Evelyn, her mother.
 Marcella, Mrs Humphry Ward, 1894.

Boyd, Peter, Labour candidate. *Fed Up*, G. A. Birmingham, 1931.

Boyes, Philip, novelist, murdered by his cousin, Norman Urquhart.
 Rev. Arthur, his father.
 Strong Poison, Dorothy L. Sayers, 1930.

Boylan, Hugh (Blazes), Molly Bloom's lover. *Ulysses*, James Joyce, 1922.

Boylan, Teddy, rich man who wants Gretchen Jordache to be his mistress. *Rich Man, Poor Man*, Irwin Shaw, 1970.

Boyle, Rev. Dr, parson at Oakhurst. *The Virginians*, W. M. Thackeray, 1857–9.

Boyle, 'Captain' Jack.
 Juno, his wife.
 Johnny, their son.
 Mary, their daughter.
 Juno and the Paycock (play), S. O'Casey, 1925.

Boyne, Dr, 'Protestant champion.' *Pendennis*, W. M. Thackeray, 1848–50.

Boythorn, Lawrence, friend of Mr Jarndyce. *Bleak House*. C. Dickens, 1853.

Bozzle, S., retired policeman, employed by Louis Trevelyan.
 Maryanne, his wife.
 He Knew He Was Right, A. Trollope, 1869.

Brabantio, a senator. *Othello* (play), W. Shakespeare.

Brace, Colonel, escort of Lord Montacute to Palestine. *Tancred*, B. Disraeli, 1847.

Brace, Detective Sergeant. *Ten Minute Alibi* (play), A. Armstrong, 1933.

Brace, Willie, one of Angelica Deverell's publishers.
 Elspeth, his wife.
 Angel, Elizabeth Taylor, 1957.

Bracebridge, Squire.
 His sons: **Frank.**
 Guy, m. Julia Templeton.
 Simon (Master Simon), his bachelor cousin.
 The Sketch Book, 1819, and *Bracebridge Hall*, 1822, W. Irving.

Bracebridge, Stephen, farmer. *Joseph and his Brethren*, H. W. Freeman, 1928.

Bracegirdle, Mary, repressed young woman. *Crome Yellow*, Aldous Huxley, 1922.

Bracegirdle, Millicent. *Miss Bracegirdle does her Duty* (s.s.), Stacy Aumonier, 1923.

Bracely, Olga, prima donna, wife of George Shuttleworth. *Queen Lucia*, E. F. Benson, 1920.

Braceweight, Samuel, chocolate manufacturer.
 Walter, his son.
 Hurry on Down, John Wain, 1953.

Brack, Madame Coralie, a horserider.
 Her daughter. Friends of Henry Foker.
 Pendennis, W. M. Thackeray, 1848–50.

Brackett, prison jailer, Boston. *The Scarlet Letter*, N. Hawthorne, 1850.

Brackley, Lord, fop and scoundrel. *Sampson Rideout, Quaker*. Una Silberrad, 1911.

Brackley, Sir Daniel. *The Black Arrow*, R. L. Stevenson, 1888.

Bracknel, Mr, wealthy self-made businessman.
 His wife.
 Alfred, their sports-loving son.

Denis, their neurotic younger son.
May and **Amy,** their daughters.
The Bracknels, Forrest Reid, 1911.

Bracknell, Lady (Aunt Augusta), Jack Worthing's aunt. *The Importance of Being Earnest* (play), O. Wilde, 1895.

Bracy, Miss, governess to the Mays. *The Daisy Chain,* 1856, and elsewhere, Charlotte M. Yonge.

Bracy, Maurice de, leader of a band of mercenaries. *Ivanhoe,* W. Scott, 1820.

Bracy, Tom, friend of Lewis Arundel. *Lewis Arundel,* F. E. Smedley, 1852.

Bradbourne, Lilias, handmaiden of Lady Mary Avenal. *The Abbot,* W. Scott, 1820.

Bradbourne, Paul, aged gentleman-jockey. *Before the Bombardment,* O. Sitwell, 1926.

Bradford, Eliot Story.
Elizabeth, his mother.
Chosen Country, J. dos Passos, 1951.

Bradgate, assistant officer, Yanrin. *Aissa Saved,* Joyce Cary, 1932.

Bradgate, of Bradgate, Smith & Barrow, Lord Ringwood's lawyers. *The Adventures of Philip,* W. M. Thackeray, 1861–2.

Bradleigh, Captain. *See* ALDCLYFFE.

Bradley, Mrs (later **Dame**) **Beatrice Adela Lestrange,** psychiatrist and detective. *See also* LESTRANGE.
Her nephews: **Denis.**
Jonathan.
Deborah, his wife.
Many books by Gladys Mitchell, 1929 onwards.

Bradley, Dolores, m. John Gordon.
Tessa, m. Peter Jackson, sen.
Peter Jackson, Cigar Merchant, G. Frankau, 1919.

Bradman, Dr George.
Violet, his wife.
Blithe Spirit (play), Noël Coward, 1941.

Bradshaw, Sir William, Harley Street specialist. *Mrs Dalloway,* Virginia Woolf, 1925.

Bradshaw, William, friend of Arthur Norris, narrator. *Mr Norris Changes Trains,* C. Isherwood, 1935.

Bradwardine, Baron Cosmo of Comyne.
Rose, his daughter.
Malcolm of Inchgrabbit, heir to the title.
Waverley, W. Scott, 1814.

Brady, Cecilia, narrator, daughter of film producer. *The Last Tycoon,* F. Scott Fitzgerald, 1941.

Brady, Kate, m. Eugene Gaillard.
Cash, their small son.
Girls in Their Married Bliss, Edna O'Brien, 1964.

Brady, Kid, ex-member of the Stovepipe Gang, eng. to Molly McKeever. 'Vanity and some Sables' (s.s.), *The Trimmed Lamp,* O. Henry, 1907.

Brady, Michael, Barry Lyndon's uncle.
His wife.
Honoria, his daughter, 'country flirt,' m. Captain Quin; and other children.
Barry Lyndon, W. M. Thackeray, 1844.

Brady, Sam.
Ruth, his wife. Assistants of Archie Goodwin.
The Second Confession, R. Stout, 1950.

Brady, Susan. *The Playboy of the Western World* (play), J. M. Synge, 1907.

Braggadochio. *The Faërie Queene* (poem), E. Spenser, 1590.

Bragin, Colour-Sergeant.
Annie, his wife.
'The Solid Muldoon' (s.s.), *Soldiers Three,* 1888, and elsewhere, R. Kipling.

Braiding, Mr and Mrs, servants of G. J. Hoape. *The Pretty Lady,* Arnold Bennett, 1918.

Brailsford, Madge. *Love Among the Artists,* G. B. Shaw, 1900.

Brain, Major. *The Jacaranda Tree,* H. E. Bates, 1949 .

Brainworm. *Every Man in his Humour* (play), B. Jonson, 1598.

Braithewaite, Maurice, rugby player. *This Sporting Life,* David Storey, 1960.

Bramber, Miss.
Sally, her sister.
Sir Charles Grandison, S. Richardson, 1754.

Bramble, Lord, employer of John

Julip. *The Dream*, H. G. Wells, 1924.

Bramble, Matthew, travelling in search of health, father of Humphry Clinker.

Tabitha, his sister, 'starched, vain, ridiculous,' m. Lismahago, soldier.

Humphry Clinker, T. Smollett, 1771.

Bramble, Sir Robert. *The Poor Gentleman* (play), G. Colman the Younger, 1802.

Brame, Roger, Bert Holm's publicity agent. *Other Gods*, Pearl Buck, 1940.

Bramley, Miss Teresa ('Tibbits'), central character; companion to Miss Collier-Floodgaye. *Before the Bombardment*, O. Sitwell, 1926.

Bramsley, family name of LORD HENGRAVE.

Bramson, Mrs. *Night Must Fall* (play), Emlyn Williams, 1935.

Bramson, Sam ('Pretty').

Marcus, his cousin.

Peter Jackson, Cigar Merchant, G. Frankau, 1919.

Brand, Sir Deryck, eminent doctor.

Flower, his wife.

The Rosary, Florence Barclay, 1909.

Brand, Fanny, John Shaynor's sweetheart. 'Wireless' (s.s.), *Traffics and Discoveries*, R. Kipling, 1904.

Brand, Rev. Robert, m. Stella Carter.

Rebecca, his sister.

Pink Sugar, O. Douglas, 1924.

Brand, Robert, motor mechanic and socialist, m. Lily Jennings. *A Knight on Wheels*, Ian Hay, 1914.

Brande, Paul R., of Barnabas Ltd, publishers.

Gina, his wife, m. (2) Mike Wedgwood.

Flowers for the Judge, Margery Allingham, 1936.

Brander, Captain. 'His Private Honour' (s.s.), *Many Inventions*, R. Kipling, 1893.

Brander, Senator, Jennie's first lover. *Jennie Gerhardt*, Theodore Dreiser, 1911.

Brandis ('Coppy'), subaltern, eng. to Miss Allardyce. 'Wee Willie Winkie' (s.s.). *Wee Willie Winkie*, R. Kipling, 1888.

Brandon. *Henry the Eighth* (play), W. Shakespeare.

Brandon, crime expert, *The Liberal*. *The Street of Adventure*, P. Gibbs, 1909.

Brandon, Colonel, friend of Sir John Middleton, m. Marianne Dashwood. *Sense and Sensibility*, Jane Austen, 1811.

Brandon, Dr, American alias of Dr Firmin.

Mrs Brandon (The Little Sister), his long-suffering wife, tricked into marrying him. *See* CAROLINE GANN.

The Adventures of Philip, 1861–2, and *A Shabby Genteel Story*, 1840, W. M. Thackeray.

Brandon, Adam, Archdeacon of Polchester.

Amy, his wife.

Falk, their son.

Joan, their daughter.

The Cathedral, Hugh Walpole, 1927.

Brandon, Lady Augustus. *Beau Geste*, P. C. Wren, 1924.

Brandon, David, in love with Hannah Jacobs. *Children of the Ghetto*, Israel Zangwill, 1892.

Brandon, Lady Elizabeth.

Emma, her daughter, m. Mark Gardner.

Heartsease, Charlotte M. Yonge, 1854.

Brandon, Joseph.

Lucy, his daughter, m. Paul Clifford.

Sir William, his brother, father of Paul.

Paul Clifford, Lord Lytton, 1830.

Brandon, Mrs Lavinia, widow, m. Bishop Joram.

Francis, her son, m. Mrs Peggy Arbuthnot.

Delia, her daughter, m. Hilary Grant.

Amelia (Aunt Sissie), her sister-in-law.

The *Barsetshire* series, Angela Thirkell, 1933 onwards.

Brandon, Rev. Stanley, Vicar of Lower Briskett-in-the-Midden.

Jane, his daughter, m. Rev. Augustine Mulliner.

Meet Mr Mulliner, P. G. Wodehouse, 1927.

Brandt, Dr. 'Music' (s.s.), *A Beginning*, W. de la Mare, 1955.

Brandt, Peter (Peter the Magician). *The Cloister and the Hearth*, C. Reade, 1861.

Brandybuck, Meriadoc (Merry), cousin of Frodo Baggins. *The Lord of the Ring* trilogy, 1954–5, J. R. R. Tolkien.

Brangwen, Tom, Nottinghamshire farmer.
Lydia Lensky, his wife, widow of a Pole.
Anna, Lydia's daughter by 1st husband.
Brangwen, Will, handicrafts instructor, Tom's nephew, m. Anna Lensky.
Their daughters:
Ursula, schoolteacher, m. Rupert Birkin.
Gudrun, art student.
The Rainbow, 1915, and *Women in Love,* 1921, D. H. Lawrence.

Brannon, Biff, café proprietor. *The Heart is a Lonely Hunter,* Carson McCullers, 1940.

Branston, butler to Austin Ruthyn. *Uncle Silas,* Sheridan le Fanu, 1864.

Brant, Captain Adam, lover of Christine Mannon, murdered by her son, Orin. *Mourning becomes Electra* (play), E. O'Neill, 1931.

Brantés, Duc de, first husband of Alice Parkington. *Mrs Parkington,* L. Bromfield, 1944.

Braose, Gunnora, foster-mother to the Duke of Somerset. *The Tower of London,* W. H. Ainsworth, 1840.

Brash, Albert.
His wife.
A Safety Match, Ian Hay, 1911.

Brasher, Phil, founder of a new religion.
Angeline, his wife.
Barefoot in the Head, Brian W. Aldiss, 1969.

Brass, Sampson, Quilp's lawyer.
Sally, his sister.
The Old Curiosity Shop, C. Dickens, 1849.

Brassbound, Captain. *Captain Brassbound's Conversion* (play), G. B. Shaw, 1900.

Brassett, college scout. *Charley's Aunt* (play), Brandon Thomas, 1892.

Bravassa, Miss, member of Crummles's Theatrical Company. *Nicholas Nickleby,* C. Dickens, 1839.

Braxton, Stephen, author; rival of Hilary Maltby. 'Maltby and Braxton,' *Seven Men,* Max Beerbohm, 1919.

Bray, Colonel (Evelyn) James, central character.
Olivia, his wife.
Rebecca Edwards, his mistress.
A Guest of Honour, Nadine Gordimer, 1971.

Bray, Sir Ingoldsby. 'The Ingoldsby Penance' (poem). *The Ingoldsby Legends,* R. H. Barham, 1837.

Bray, Madeline, m. Nicholas Nickleby.
Walter, her father.
Nicholas Nickleby, C. Dickens, 1839.

Brayton, Harker. 'The Man and the Snake' (s.s.), *In the Midst of Life,* A. Bierce, 1898.

Brazen, Molly. *Polly* (comic opera), J. Gay, 1729.

Brazenose, Lieutenant. 'The Taking of Lungtungpen' (s.s.), *Plain Tales from the Hills,* R. Kipling, 1888.

Bread, Mrs. *The American,* H. James, 1877.

Bread, Dai.
His two wives.
Under Milk Wood, Dylan Thomas, 1954.

Break, Dr. 'Marklake Witches' (s.s.), *Rewards and Fairies,* R. Kipling, 1910.

Bream, Horace, an American. *Sweet Lavender,* A. W. Pinero, 1888.

Breck, Alan (Stewart) (alias Thomson), close friend of David Balfour. *Kidnapped,* 1886, and elsewhere, R. L. Stevenson.

Breck, Alison, fishwife. *The Antiquary,* W. Scott, 1816.

Breckinridge, poultry-dealer. 'The Blue Carbuncle' (s.s.), *The Adventures of Sherlock Holmes,* A. Conan Doyle, 1892.

Breckinridge, Myra (formerly Myron) who has had a sex operation. *Myra Breckinridge,* Gore Vidal, 1968.

Bredon, Miles, detective, Indescribable Insurance Co.
Angela, his wife.
Francis, their son.
The Three Taps, R. A. Knox, 1927.

Breeve, Dr, chief organist, Melchester Cathedral. *The Hand of Ethelberta,* T. Hardy, 1876.

Breitman, Hans, narrator of 'Bertran and Bimi' and 'Reingelder and the

German Flag' (s.ss.), *Life's Handicap*, R. Kipling, 1891.

Breitner, Hans, in love with Freya Roth and father of her child.
His mother.
Her other children.
Karl.
Anna.
Michel.
The Mortal Storm, Phyllis Bottome, 1937.

Breitslein, Johann. *Counsellor-at-Law* (play), Elmer Rice, 1931.

Bremmil, Tom Cusack.
His wife.
'Three and an Extra' (s.s.), *Plain Tales from the Hills*, R. Kipling, 1888.

Brengwain, childless wife of Gwenwyn. *The Betrothed*, W. Scott, 1825.

Brennan, owner of waxwork show. 'À propos des bottes' (s.s.), *Fiery Particles*, C. E. Montague, 1923.

Brennan, Captain, Irish Citizen Army. *The Plough and the Stars* (play), S. O'Casey, 1926.

Brennan, Father Malachi. *Harry Lorrequer*, C. Lever, 1839.

Brennan, Matthew. *The Porch*, 1937, and *The Stronghold*, 1939, R. Church.

Brent, Carradine, American student. *A Daughter of Time*, Josephine Tey, 1951.

Brent, George.
Jennifer, his 1st wife.
Gerda, their daughter.
Sholto, their son.
Cicely, his 2nd wife.
The Young Idea (play), N. Coward, 1923.

Brent, Justine, nurse, 2nd wife of John Amherst. *The Fruit of the Tree*, Edith Wharton, 1907.

Brentford, Earl of, father of Lord Chiltern and Lady Laura Standish. *Phineas Finn*, 1869, and elsewhere, A. Trollope.

Brentmoor, Lord. *No. 5 John Street*, R. Whiteing, 1902.

Bresnihan, Father. *The Private Wound*, Nicholas Blake, 1968.

Bret, Alexander, Captain of London Trained Bands. *The Tower of London*, W. H. Ainsworth, 1840.

Breton, Captain. *The Wonder* (play), Mrs S. Centlivre, 1714.

Brett, Mrs, maid to Mme Bernstein. *The Virginians*, W. M. Thackeray, 1857–9.

Brett, Percy, Negro trumpeter and partner of Jeremy Coleman. *Strike the Father Dead*, John Wain, 1962.

Brett, Sergeant-Master-Tailor, comrade of John Loveday. *The Trumpet Major*, T. Hardy, 1880.

Bretton, Harry, C.B.E., famous painter and devotee of the simple life.
Rachel, his wife.
Rose, their daughter, m. Joe MacPhail.
Cressida, their grand-daughter, m. David Little.
The Wedding Group, Elizabeth Taylor, 1968.

Bretton, Sir Lionel.
Jane, Lady Bretton, his mother.
Dance of the Years, Margery Allingham, 1943.

Bretton, Mrs Maria, widow.
John Graham, her godson, later Dr John.
Villette, Charlotte Brontë, 1853.

Breuer, veterinary surgeon, m. Maria Heiss. *The Heart of a Child*, Phyllis Bottome, 1940.

Brevard, Roger, marine insurance agent. *Java Head*, J. Hergesheimer, 1919.

Brewer, member of Pinkie's gang. *Brighton Rock*, Graham Greene, 1938.

Brewer, Eric, clerk. *London Wall* (play), J. van Druten, 1931.

Brewer, Francis. *Other Gods*, Pearl Buck, 1940.

Brewer, Mary, district nurse, in love with Oliver North. *The Happy Prisoner*, Monica Dickens, 1946.

Brewster, Sergeant Gregory.
Norah, his great-niece.
'A Straggler of '15,' *Round the Red Lamp*, A. Conan Doyle, 1894.

Brewster, Maud, authoress, m. Humphrey van Weyden. *The Sea Wolf*, Jack London, 1904.

Brian. *The Merry Devil of Edmonton* (play), Anon.

Brice, butler to Dr Firmin. *The Adventures of Philip*, W. M. Thackeray, 1861–2.

Brick, Jefferson, war correspondent. *Martin Chuzzlewit*, C. Dickens, 1844.

Brickett, Joe, landlord of the George.
His wife.
Mary, his niece.
Letty, her coloured child. *See* SAMUELSON.
'The Tinfield Mascot' (s.s.), *Last Recollections of My Uncle Charles,* N. Balchin, 1954.

Bricknell, Naomi, bigamously m. William Geake.
Abe, her husband, sailor.
The Delectable Duchy, A. Quiller-Couch, 1893.

Bridehead, Susanna Florence Mary (Sue), cousin and lover of Jude Fawley, m. Richard Phillotson. *Jude the Obscure,* T. Hardy, 1896.

Brideshead, Earl of. *See* MARCHMAIN.

Bridgenorth, Major Ralph.
Alice Christian, his dead wife.
Alice, his daughter.
Peveril of the Peak, W. Scott, 1822.

Bridges, Ronald, assistant curator in a museum. *The Bachelors,* Muriel Spark, 1961.

Bridget, Mother, Abbess of St Catherine. *The Abbot,* W. Scott, 1820.

Bridget, Mrs, servant to the Widow Wadman, m. Corporal Trim. *Tristram Shandy,* L. Sterne, 1767.

Bridgett, William, tramp and thief. *Bealby,* H. G. Wells, 1915.

Bridmain, Edmund, Countess Czerlaski's half-brother, m. her maid Alice. 'The Rev. Amos Barton,' *Scenes of Clerical Life,* George Eliot, 1857.

Bridson, Nelly, adopted daughter of Captain Erle Brooker.
Jack, her father, brother officer of Brooker.
If Sinners Entice Thee, W. le Queux, 1898.

Brierly, Captain. *Lord Jim,* J. Conrad, 1900.

Briggs, fellow shop assistant of Hoopdriver. *The Wheels of Chance,* H. G. Wells, 1896.

Briggs, a miserly trustee.
His wife.
Cecilia, Fanny Burney, 1782.

Briggs, pupil of Dr Blimber. *Dombey and Son,* C. Dickens, 1848.

Briggs, odd-job man.
His wife.
Tony, their son.
Magnolia Street, L. Golding, 1932.

Briggs, Arabella, companion to Miss Crawley, *Vanity Fair,* W. M. Thackeray, 1847–8.

Briggs, Hortense, temporary girl-friend of Clyde Griffiths. *An American Tragedy,* T. Dreiser, 1925.

Briggs, Joe, ex-heavyweight, innkeeper. *Another Year,* R. C. Sherriff, 1948.

Briggs, Thomas, owner of San Salvatore, m. Lady Caroline Dester. *The Enchanted April,* Countess von Arnim, 1922.

Briggs, Sir William, M.P. *The Water Gipsies,* A. P. Herbert, 1930.

Bright, Effie. *If Winter Comes,* A. S. M. Hutchinson, 1920.

Bright, Flossie, draper assistant and girl-friend of Grubb. *War in the Air,* H. G. Wells, 1908.

Brigson, 'an ulcer to the school,' who incited other boys to throw crusts. *Eric, or Little by Little,* F. W. Farrar, 1858.

Brill, Hugh (decd.), 1st husband of Clothilde Wright.
Their children: **Sidney.**
Bella, m. Joe Stowe.
Mary.
Harry, Hugh's father.
Wickford Point, J. P. Marquand, 1939.

Brill-Oudener, Commander Keith. *The Snow Goose,* P. Gallico, 1941.

Brimber, Mr, civil servant. *Tom Tiddler's Ground,* E. Shanks, 1934.

Brimblecombe, Vindex, schoolmaster, later curate. *Westward Ho!,* C. Kingsley, 1855.

Brimsley, Mrs Jessy, smallholder, m., as 2nd wife, Barnabas Holly.
George and **Nat,** her sons.
South Riding, Winifred Holtby, 1936.

Brimstone, Mrs (Brinnie), nurse to the Bramsleys. *C.,* M. Baring, 1924.

Brindle, Mrs, village charlady. *The Wedding Group,* Elizabeth Taylor, 1968.

Brine, Dr, organic chemist. *The Small Back Room,* N. Balchin, 1943.

Brine, Ellen. *Ellen Brine of Allenburn* (poem), W. Barnes.

Bringier, Dr. *Steamboat Gothic,* Frances Parkinson Keyes, 1952.

Brinkley, one-time manservant to Bertie Wooster. *Thank You, Jeeves,* P. G. Wodehouse, 1934.

Brinklow, Miss Roberta, 'Eastern Mission.' *Lost Horizon,* J. Hilton, 1933.

Brinkman, secretary to Jephthah Mottram. *The Three Taps,* R. A. Knox, 1927.

Briones, Don Caesar, Mexican rancho.
  Donna Anna, his sister.
A Ward of the Golden Gate, Bret Harte.

Briscoe, Lily, artist. *To The Lighthouse,* Virginia Woolf, 1927.

Briscoll, Mrs, the Pressets' charwoman.
  Alfred, her husband.
We the Accused, E. Raymond, 1935.

Brisher, Mr.
  Jane, his one-time fiancée.
'Mr Brisher's Treasure,' *Tales of Life and Adventure,* 1923, and elsewhere, H. G. Wells.

Brisk, Mr, suitor of Mercy. *Pilgrim's Progress,* J. Bunyan, 1678, 1684.

Brisk, Fastidious. *Every Man out of his Humour* (play), B. Jonson, 1599.

Brisket, Captain. *Dialstone Lane,* W. W. Jacobs, 1904.

Bristol, Duke of. *On Approval* (play), F. Lonsdale, 1927.

Bristow, Hon. Reggie, son of Lord Grantchester. *The Babe, B.A.,* E. F. Benson, 1897.

Britannus. *Caesar and Cleopatra* (play), G. B. Shaw, 1900.

Brithwood, Richard, rich young snob, m. Lady Caroline Ravenel. *John Halifax, Gentleman,* Mrs Craik, 1856.

Britling, Hugh, art critic and author, central character.
  m. (1) **Mary.**
    Hugh, their son.
  (2) **Edith.**
    Gilbert, and another boy, their sons.
Mr Britling Sees It Through, H. G. Wells, 1916.

Briton, Jules, Communist. *It's a Battlefield,* Graham Greene, 1935.

Britt, Miss, over-strict matron of children's home. *Children of the Archbishop,* N. Collins, 1951.

Britten-Close, friend of Remington. *The New Machiavelli,* H. G. Wells, 1911.

Brixham, Mrs, landlady of Major Pendennis. *Pendennis,* W. M. Thackeray, 1848–50.

Broadback, Esau, innkeeper. *Hawbuck Grange,* R. S. Surtees, 1847.

Broadbent, Jack, R.N.
  Lady Lilian, his wife.
One Day in the Shires (s.s.), G. Frankau.

Broadbent, Thomas, civil engineer. *John Bull's Other Island* (play), G. B. Shaw, 1904.

Broadhurst, Lady. *A Knight on Wheels,* Ian Hay, 1914.

Broadwheel, Joe, wagoner. *The Heart of Midlothian,* W. Scott, 1818.

Brocken, Henry, central character and narrator. *The Diary of Henry Brocken,* W. de la Mare, 1904.

Brockett, Jonathan, playwright. *The Well of Loneliness,* Radclyffe Hall, 1928.

Brockett, Mrs Sarah, 2nd wife of Martin Whitelaw.
  Eleanor, her daughter, m. James Crowther.
Roots, Naomi Jacob, 1931.

Brocklebank, Fanny, hostess. *Miss Tarrant's Temperament* (s.s.), May Sinclair.

Brocklehurst, treasurer of Lowood School. *Jane Eyre,* Charlotte Brontë, 1847.

Brocklehurst, Earl of.
  Emily, his wife.
The Admirable Crichton, J. M. Barrie, 1902.

Brockway, Inspector, Ipswich C.I.D. *A Suspension of Mercy,* Patricia Highsmith, 1965.

Broddle, Constance. *Esmé* (s.s.), 'Saki' (H. H. Munro).

Brodie, Bennett, m. Sarah Henderson. *Pilgrimage,* Dorothy M. Richardson, 1915–38.

Brodie, James.
  Margaret, his wife.
  Their children:
    Matthew.
    Mary. *See* DENIS FOYLE
    Nessie.
  Mary, James's mother.
Hatter's Castle, A. J. Cronin, 1931.

Brodie, Jean, schoolteacher in Edinburgh. *The Prime of Miss Jean Brodie,* Muriel Spark, 1961.

Brodie, John, export merchant. *God's Prisoner,* J. Oxenham, 1898.

Brodie, William.
Old Brodie, his father.
Mary, his sister.
Deacon Brodie (play), W. E. Henley & R. L. Stevenson, 1892.

Brodrick, Sir George, eminent doctor. *The Notorious Mrs Ebbsmith* (play), A. W. Pinero, 1895.

Brogan, John, M.B. ('Ruby'), tycoon. *The Weak and the Strong,* G. Kersh, 1945.

Brogley, broker and valuer. *Dombey and Son,* C. Dickens, 1848.

Broke, Bessie, Dick Helder's model, who destroys his picture through spite. *The Light that Failed,* R. Kipling, 1890.

Bromley, Harold, army friend of Peter Jackson. *Peter Jackson, Cigar Merchant,* G. Frankau, 1919.

Bronckhorst, Edward.
His wife.
'The Bronckhorst Divorce Case' (s.s.), *Plain Tales from the Hills,* R. Kipling, 1888.

Bronsden, Shadwell shopkeeper.
Hetty, his wife.
The Yellow Scarf (s.s.), T. Burke.

Bronson, Captain Scott.
Aubrey, his wife.
Chosen Country, J. dos Passos, 1951.

Bronwen, wife of Ivor Morgan; chief female character. *How Green Was My Valley,* R. Llewellyn, 1939.

Brook, Ben.
Ruth, his wife.
Thunder on the Left, C. Morley, 1925.

Brook, Rhoda, milkmaid. 'The Withered Arm,' *Wessex Tales,* T. Hardy, 1888.

Brooke, head boy at Rugby. *Tom Brown's Schooldays,* T. Hughes, 1857.

Brooke, Dorothea, m. (1) Edward Casaubon; (2) Will Ladislaw.
Celia, her sister, m. Sir James Chettam.
Middlemarch, Geo. Eliot, 1871–2.

Brooke, Helen, m. Rudd Sergison. *Landmarks,* E. V. Lucas, 1914.

Brooke, John, m. Meg March.
Their children:
John (Denis), journalist, m. Alice.
Daisy, m. Nat Blake.
Josie.
Little Women, 1868, *Little Men,* 1871, and *Jo's Boys,* 1886, Louisa M. Alcott.

Brooke, Stanley, central character.
His mother and sisters.
Harry, his cousin (later succeeds to the earldom), m. Agnes, Stanley's sister.
On the Irrawaddy, G. A. Henty, 1897.

Brooker, employed by Ralph Nickleby. *Nicholas Nickleby,* C. Dickens, 1839.

Brooker, Captain Erle.
Liane, his daughter, m. George Stratfield.
If Sinners Entice Thee, W. le Queux, 1898.

Brookes, Nathaniel, uncle of James Havern. *The One Before,* Barry Pain, 1902.

Brooks, Mrs, owner of The Herons. *Tess of the D'Urbervilles,* T. Hardy, 1891.

Broom, Grace.
Florrie, her sister. Pupils of the Misses Perne.
Pilgrimage, Dorothy M. Richardson, 1915–38.

Broome, Nanny, old nurse of Kinnit family. *The China Governess,* Margery Allingham, 1963.

Brosnan, Donough, eng. to Jane Geoghegan. *The White-headed Boy* (play), L. Robinson, 1920.

Broster, Reggie, tutor to Ogden Ford. *The Little Nugget,* P. G. Wodehouse, 1913.

Brotherton, gas inspector and murderer. 'The Footsteps that Ran,' *Lord Peter Views the Body,* Dorothy L. Sayers, 1928.

Brouette, Suzanne, actress, m. Quinquart. 'The Judgment of Paris' (s.s.), *All the World Wondered,* L. Merrick, 1911.

Brough, John, promoter of swindling companies.
Isabella, his wife.
Belinda, their ill-bred daughter.
The Great Hoggarty Diamond, W. M. Thackeray, 1841.

Brougham, Annette (alias Brown), m. Bill Bates. 'The Man Upstairs' (s.s.), *The Man Upstairs,* P. G. Wodehouse, 1914.

Broun, Jessie, one-time mistress of James Durie. *The Master of Ballantrae,* R. L. Stevenson, 1889.

Broune, Elizabeth, m. Robert Rogers.
  Rev. Arthur, her father.
  Her mother.
    Jane, her sister.
  Northwest Passage, Kenneth Roberts, 1938.

Broune, Nicholas, Ed. *The Morning Breakfast Table,* m. Lady Carbury. *The Way We Live Now,* A. Trollope, 1875.

Broussard, Monsieur.
  Louis, his son.
  Gentlemen Prefer Blondes, Anita Loos, 1925.

Browdie, John, Yorkshire farmer, m. 'Tilda Price. *Nicholas Nickleby,* C. Dickens, 1839.

Browell, Bishop.
  Clare, his daughter, in love with Willan.
  Right Off the Map, C. E. Montague, 1927.

Brower, Dierich. *The Cloister and the Hearth,* C. Reade, 1861.

Brown. 'The Folly of Brown' (poem), *The Bab Ballads,* W. S. Gilbert, 1869.

Brown, hotel owner, the narrator. *The Comedians,* Graham Greene, 1966.

Brown, coxswain and confidential servant of Hornblower, m. Annette. The *Hornblower* series, C. S. Forester, 1937 onwards.

Brown ('Gentleman' Brown). *Lord Jim,* J. Conrad, 1900.

Brown.
  Midge, his wife.
    Susan and **Felicity,** their daughters.
  Utility Baby and *A Sister for Susan,* Dale Collins.

Brown, of Calaveras.
  Kate, his wife.
  'Brown of Calaveras' (s.s.), *The Luck of Roaring Camp,* Bret Harte, 1868.

Brown, Captain.
  Miss Brown, his daughter.
  Miss Jessie, his daughter, m. Major Gordon.
  Cranford, Mrs Gaskell, 1853.

Brown, Father, priest-detective, central character of series. *The Innocence of Father Brown,* etc., G. K. Chesterton, 1911 onwards.

Brown, Mr.
  His wife.
  His children: **Reggie.**
    Maggie.
    Amy.
    Sid.
  An Englishman's Home (play), Guy du Maurier, 1909.

Brown, Mrs, disreputable rag-and-bone merchant.
  Alice, her daughter.
  Dombey and Son, C. Dickens, 1848.

Brown, Abraham, old lodging-house keeper. *Desperate Remedies,* T. Hardy, 1871.

Brown, Alistair. *Call it a Day* (play), Dodie Smith, 1935.

Brown, Arthur, village schoolmaster, m. Aviza Pomeroy. *The Mother,* E. Phillpotts, 1908.

Brown, Berenice Sadie, Negress cook with a glass eye, married four times.
  Big Mama, her mother who tells fortunes.
  Honey Camden Brown, her brother.
  The Member of the Wedding, Carson McCullers, 1946.

Brown, Bill, foreign agent. *A Sort of Traitors,* N. Balchin, 1949.

Brown, 'Bo-Jo,' head boy, St Swithins, later President, Paisley Mills. *H. M. Pulham, Esq.,* J. P. Marquand, 1941.

Brown, Cecil, diplomatist. *The Tragedy of the Korosko,* A. Conan Doyle, 1898.

Brown, Charmian. *See* LADY SOPHIA SEFTON.

Brown, Danny (Cinnamon), sailor. *Time Will Knit,* Fred Urquhart, 1938.

Brown, Dolores, farmer. *Hawbuck Grange,* R. S. Surtees, 1847.

Brown, George, Paymaster-commander. *The Ship,* C. S. Forester, 1943.

Brown, Henrietta. 'The Clerk's Quest' (s.s.), *The Untilled Field,* G. Moore, 1903.

Brown, Jenny, mistress of David Scott. *Ship of Fools,* Katherine Anne Porter, 1962.

Brown, Jim, central character, m. Lizzie Parrish.
  His mother.
  Nellie, his sister.

They Wanted to Live, Cecil Roberts, 1939.

Brown, Joe, alias Lucas Burch, bootlegger, partner of Joe Christmas. *Light in August*, William Faulkner, 1932.

Brown, Ladbroke, author of *Savonarola*. 'Savonarola Brown' (s.s.), *Seven Men*, Max Beerbohm, 1919.

Brown, Lovell, young reporter. *South Riding*, Winifred Holtby, 1936.

Brown, Mrs Maggie, millionaire and miser. 'The Enchanted Profile' (s.s.), *Roads of Destiny*, O. Henry, 1909.

Brown, Martha, central character and narrator.
Her husband.
Mrs Brown in Paris, and others, A. Sketchley.

Brown, Meredith. *Comrade, O Comrade*, Ethel Mannin, 1946.

Brown, Michael. *See* PRINCE MICHAEL ROBOLSKI.

Brown, Pete.
His mother.
Another Year, R. C. Sherriff, 1948.

Brown, Phil, m. Julia Pellagrin, *née* Springster.
Vivien, their daughter, ward of Judge Gaskony, m. Henry Lerrick.
The Judge's Story, C. Morgan, 1947.

Brown, Puggy, head of unorthodox religious sect, m. Lucy Wilcher.
Robert, their son, m. cousin Ann Wilcher.
To Be A Pilgrim, Joyce Cary, 1942.

Brown, Rosamund, harpsichordist. Mother of Peter Levi. *Birds of America*, Mary McCarthy, 1971.

Brown, Sally. *Faithful Sally Brown* (poem), T. Hood.

Brown, Silas, trainer to Lord Backwater, 'Silver Blaze' (s.s.), *Memoirs of Sherlock Holmes*, A. Conan Doyle, 1894.

Brown, Susan, m. Joe Lampton.
Her father and mother.
Room at the Top, J. Braine, 1957.

Brown, Thomas, central character.
Squire Brown, his father.
Tom Brown's Schooldays, T. Hughes, 1857.

Brown, Valentine, m. Phoebe Throssel. *Quality Street* (play), J. M. Barrie, 1902.

Brown, Vanbeest. *See* ALLAN BERTRAM.

Brown, Velvet, winner of the Grand National.
William, her father, a butcher.
Araminta, her mother, former Channel swimmer.
Velvet's sisters:
Edwina.
Malvolia (Mally).
Meredith (Merry).
Donald, her brother.
National Velvet, Enid Bagnold, 1935.

Brown, Victor Arthur, young engineering draughtsman, central character.
Arthur, his father.
Lucy, his mother, 'the Old Lady'.
Chris, his sister, schoolteacher, m. David Lester.
Jim, his young brother.
A Kind of Loving, Stan Barstow, 1960.

Browne, Mrs, widow.
Edward, her son.
Maggie, her daughter, m. Frank Buxton.
The Moorland Cottage, Mrs. Gaskell, 1850.

Browne, 'Nosey,' retired cockney. *Jorrocks's Jaunts and Jollities*, R. S. Surtees, 1838.

Browne, General Richard, friend of Lord Woodville. *The Tapestried Chamber*, W. Scott, 1828.

Brownell, 'Mister,' schoolmaster. 'The United Idolaters' (s.s.), *Debits and Credits*, R. Kipling, 1926.

Browner, James. 'The Cardboard Box' (s.s.), *His Last Bow*, A. Conan Doyle, 1917.

Browning, Miss.
Phoebe, her sister.
Wives and Daughters, Mrs Gaskell, 1866.

Brownlow. *Bulldog Drummond*, 'Sapper' (H. C. McNeile), 1920.

Brownlow, Mr. *Oliver Twist*, C. Dickens, 1838.

Bruce, Nannie, Johnny Pearce's housekeeper, m. Constable McMurdo. *Cocktail Time*, P. G. Wodehouse, 1958.

Bruce, Wilfred, narrator; employed by Dr Nikola, m. Gladys Medwin. *Dr Nikola*, G. Boothby, 1896.

Brudenell, Rev. Mr (hist.), chaplain.

The Devil's Disciple (play), G. B. Shaw, 1899.

Bruff, family solicitor to the Herncastle family and part narrator. *The Moonstone,* W. Collins, 1868.

Brugglesmith (corruption of Brook Street, Hammersmith, and the only name by which the drunken man could be identified). 'Brugglesmith' (s.s.), *Many Inventions,* R. Kipling, 1893.

Brugh, Ronald. *Other Gods,* Pearl Buck, 1940.

Brumby, Mrs, wealthy widow. *The Newcomes,* W. M. Thackeray, 1853–1855.

Brumfit, Dr Norman, 'wild man' of the medical school. *Martin Arrowsmith,* Sinclair Lewis, 1925.

Brumley, George, essayist and traveller. *The Wife of Sir Isaac Harman,* H. G. Wells, 1914.

Brundit, Courtenay (Joe), baritone of the Dinky Doos Concert Party.
 Stella Cavendish, his wife, actress.
The Good Companions, J. B. Priestley, 1929.

Brune, Anton (Anthony Brown), artist. *Shabby Tiger,* H. Spring, 1934.

Brunger, David, private detective. *Once Aboard the Lugger,* A. S. M. Hutchinson, 1908.

Brunner, Max, Napoleonic spy. *Barlasch of the Guard,* H. Seton Merriman, 1903.

Bruno.
 Elena, his wife, with whom Rossi lodges.
The Eternal City, Hall Caine, 1901.

Brunoni, Signor, conjuror. *Cranford,* Mrs Gaskell, 1853.

Brunt, jockey. 'The Broken Link Handicap' (s.s.), *Plain Tales from the Hills,* R. Kipling, 1888.

Brunton, Mollie, friend of Sylvia Robson.
 Her father and mother.
 Bessie, her sister.
Sylvia's Lovers, Mrs Gaskell, 1863.

Brush, valet to Joe Sedley. *Vanity Fair,* W. M. Thackeray, 1847–8.

Brush. *The Clandestine Marriage* (play), G. Colman the Elder, 1766.

Brush, George Marvin, travelling salesman, chief character. *Heaven's My Destination,* Thornton Wilder, 1935.

Brush, Milly. *Mrs Dalloway,* Virginia Woolf, 1925.

Brute, Sir John. *The Provok'd Wife* (play), J. Vanbrugh, 1697.

Brutt, Major, retired officer. *The Death of the Heart,* Elizabeth Bowen, 1938.

brutus, Australian 'bad hat.' *See also* MEPHISTOPHELES. *It Is Never Too Late to Mend,* C. Reade, 1856.

Brutus, Junius, tribune. *Coriolanus* (play), W. Shakespeare.

Brutus, Marcus, conspirator against Caesar. *Julius Caesar* (play), W. Shakespeare.

Bryan, Irish employee of the fur traders. *Ungava,* R. M. Ballantyne, 1857.

Bryan, Viscount. *See* BARRY LYNDON.

Bryan, Hon. Gordon, artist. *The Water Gipsies,* A. P. Herbert, 1930.

Bryan, Terry. *South Riding,* Winifred Holtby, 1936.

Bryerly, Dr, Swedenborgian priest, friend of Austin Ruthyn. *Uncle Silas,* Sheridan le Fanu, 1864.

Brygandine, Bob, clerk. 'The Wrong Thing' (s.s.), *Rewards and Fairies,* R. Kipling, 1910.

Bubb, Mrs, Kennington landlady. *The Town Traveller,* G. Gissing, 1898.

Bubble, Madame, witch, and temptress of Standfast. *Pilgrim's Progress,* J. Bunyan, 1678, 1684.

Bubbleton, Captain George Frederick Augustus, later Lieutenant-General.
 Anna Maria, his sister.
Tom Burke of Ours, C. Lever, 1844.

Bubenberg, Adrian de, knight, of Berne. *Anne of Geierstein,* W. Scott, 1829.

Buchanan, Colonel. *Captain Desmond, V.C.,* Maud Diver, 1906.

Buchanan, Mr, chief engineer of the *Dimbula.* 'The Ship that Found Herself' (s.s.), *The Day's Work,* R. Kipling, 1898.

Buchanan, Tom. *See also* MYRTLE WILSON.
 Daisy, his wife, cousin of Nick Carraway.
The Great Gatsby, F. Scott Fitzgerald, 1925.

Buck, half-owner of ranch.
 'French Rose,' his wife.
Tex of Bar-20, C. E. Mulford, 1922.

Buck, provost of North Kensington. *The Napoleon of Notting Hill,* G. K. Chesterton, 1904.

Buck, trumpeter, comrade of John Loveday. *The Trumpet Major,* T. Hardy, 1880.

Buck, tutor to Pendennis at Oxbridge. *Pendennis,* W. M. Thackeray, 1848–50.

Buck, ex-sergeant, first porter, the Pelican. *Sorrell and Son,* W. Deeping, 1925.

Buck, Joe, a lonesome Texan who tries to be a hustler in New York. *Midnight Cowboy,* James Leo Herlihy, 1966.

Bucket, Inspector, detective.
  His wife.
Bleak House, C. Dickens, 1853.

Buckhurst, Sir Charles, close friend of Coningsby. *Coningsby,* B. Disraeli, 1844.

Buckhurst, John, criminal and traitor. *The Maids of Paradise,* R. W. Chambers, 1903.

Buckie, Miss, resident doctor, Denbury Hospital. *Let the People Sing,* J. B. Priestley, 1939.

Buckingham, Duke of (hist.), *Richard the Third, Henry the Sixth, Henry the Eighth* (plays), W. Shakespeare.

Buckland, Widow Aglaura. 'Piffingcap' (s.s.), *Adam and Eve and Pinch Me,* A. E. Coppard, 1921.

Bucklaw, Laird of. *See* FRANK HAYSTON.

Buckler, Morrice, central character and narrator, m. Ilga, Countess Luxstein. *The Courtship of Morrice Buckler,* A. E. W. Mason, 1896.

Buckley. *The Christian,* Hall Caine, 1897.

Buckley, Lady, *née* Augusta Whiteoak. *The Whiteoak Chronicles,* Mazo de la Roche, 1927 onwards.

Buckley, Bob, bank president. 'Friends in San Rosario' (s.s.), *Roads of Destiny,* O. Henry, 1909.

Buckmaster. *See* STRETHER.

Bucknell, Mrs Leila, child playmate and later lover of Caryl Bramsley.
  Terence, her husband.
C., M. Baring, 1924.

Buckram, Lord, son of the Marquess of Bagwig. *The Book of Snobs,* W. M. Thackeray, 1846–7.

Bucksteed, Philadelphia.
  Squire Bucksteed, her father.
'Marklake Witches' (s.s.), *Rewards and Fairies,* R. Kipling, 1910.

Bucktrout, Mr. *All Passion Spent,* V. Sackville-West, 1931.

Bud, Rosa, betrothed as a child to Edwin Drood. *Edwin Drood,* C. Dickens, 1870.

Budd, Billy, young British sailor. *Billy Budd,* Herman Melville, 1924.

Budd, Sir Button. *Right Royal* (poem), J. Masefield, 1920.

Budd, Lanny, central character, dealer in old masters.
  Irma, his wife, *née* Barnes.
  Robert, his father, munitions manufacturer.
  Mabel ('Beauty'), widow of Detaze, artist, his mother.
Dragon's Teeth, 1942, *Dragon Harvest,* 1945, and others, Upton Sinclair.

Budden, Octavius.
  Amelia, his wife.
  Alexander Augustus, their son.
Sketches by Boz, C. Dickens, 1836.

Buddy, Nanuet bank robber. *High Tor* (play), Maxwell Anderson, 1937.

Buddy. *Beau Geste,* P. C. Wren, 1924.

Bude, Duke of (Gilbert).
  Maud, his wife. Parents of Lady Emily Winter-Willoughby.
The General, C. S. Forester, 1936.

Budgie and Toddie. *See* TOM LAWRENCE.

Buena, Yerba, daughter of Mrs Kate Howard and José de Arguello, m. Paul Hathaway. *A Ward of the Golden Gate,* Bret Harte.

Buffers, fellow tenant of Philip Firmin in Parchment Buildings. *The Adventures of Philip,* W. M. Thackeray, 1861–2.

Buford, Chadwick, central character, captain, Federal army, m. Margaret Dean.
  Chadwick, his father.
  Mary, his mother.
  Major Calvin, distant relative.
    Lucy, his sister.
The Little Shepherd of Kingdom Come, J. Fox, Jnr, 1903.

Bufton, Miss, typist. *London Wall* (play), J. van Druten, 1931.

Buggins, assistant at the Folkestone Drapery Bazaar, friend of Kipps. *Kipps,* H. G. Wells, 1905.

Bugsby, Mrs, lodging-house keeper. *The Newcomes*, W. M. Thackeray, 1853–5.

Bukaty, Prince Michael, in love with Netty Cahere.
Prince Michael, his father.
Princess Wanda, his sister, in love with Cartoner.
The Vultures, H. Seton Merriman, 1902.

Bukta, native officer. 'The Tomb of his Ancestors' (s.s.), *The Day's Work*, R. Kipling, 1898.

Bulbo, Prince, heir of Padella. *The Rose and the Ring*, W. M. Thackeray, 1855.

Bulby, a cathedral chorister. *Pendennis*, W. M. Thackeray, 1848–1850

Buldeo, village hunter. 'Tiger Tiger' and elsewhere, *The Jungle Books*, R. Kipling, 1894–5.

Bulders, Dr, friend of Rev. Lawrence Veal. *Vanity Fair*, W. M. Thackeray, 1847–8.

Bule, Hon. William ('Honbill'), lover of Jill Manning. *A Way through the Wood*, N. Balchin, 1951.

Bulfinch, Mrs Grace, barmaid. *Strong Poison*, Dorothy L. Sayers, 1930.

Bulger, hairdresser and wigmaker. *Sweet Lavender*, A. W. Pinero, 1888.

Bulger, Mrs Jennifer, alias of Mrs Michael Brown. *See* Robolski. *To Have the Honour* (play), A. A. Milne, 1924.

Bulgruddery, Dennis.
His wife.
John Bull (play), G. Colman the Younger, 1805.

Bull, Captain. *The Book of Snobs*, W. M. Thackeray, 1846–7.

Bull, Dr (Saturday). *The Man who was Thursday*, G. K. Chesterton, 1908.

Bull, Mrs. *Love on the Dole*, W. Greenwood, 1933.

Bull, James, dead climber. *The Accident* (s.s.), Ann Bridge.

Bull, Johnny, one of the Famous Five at Greyfriars. The *Billy Bunter* series, Frank Richards.

Bullamy, porter in Loan and Life Assurance Office. *Martin Chuzzlewit*, C. Dickens, 1844.

Bullar, Dame Mary, Prime Minister, 1979. *But Soft—We Are Observed!*, H. Belloc, 1928.

Bullard, J. T., advertising agent. *H. M. Pulham, Esq.*, J. P. Marquand, 1944.

Bullen, Anne (hist.). *Henry the Eighth* (play), W. Shakespeare.

Buller, games- and house-master at Fernhurst. *The Loom of Youth*, A. Waugh, 1917.

Bulleshorn, Sir Oliver. *The White Company*, A. Conan Doyle, 1891.

Bullington, Viscount, inheritor of his mother's titles, and a bitter enemy of Barry Lyndon, his stepfather, whom he horsewhips. *Barry Lyndon*, W. M. Thackeray, 1844.

Bullivant, butler in the Lamb household. *Manservant and Maidservant*, Ivy Compton-Burnett, 1947.

Bullivant, Sir Walter. *The Thirty-nine Steps*, J. Buchan, 1915.

Bullock, master's mate. *The King's Own*, Captain Marryat, 1830.

Bullock, 'gouty, bald-headed, bottle-nosed banker.'
Francis, his son, m. Maria Osborne.
Vanity Fair, W. M. Thackeray, 1847–8.

Bullocksmithy, Bishop of. *The Newcomes* and elsewhere, W. M. Thackeray, 1853–5.

Bullsegg, Laird of Killancursit, 'cowardly half-bred swine.' *Waverley*, W. Scott, 1814.

Bulmer, Valentine, m. Clara Mowbray. *St Ronan's Well*, W. Scott, 1824.

Bulminster, Sir John.
His wife.
Vanity Fair, W. M. Thackeray, 1847–8.

Bulpitt, Samuel, ex-waiter, multi-millionaire, brother of Lady Abbot. *Summer Moonshine*, P. G. Wodehouse, 1938.

Bulsted, Captain William, R.N., of *Polyphemus*.
Squire Gregory, his brother.
Adventures of Harry Richmond, G. Meredith, 1871.

Bulstrode, Nicholas, banker, of Middlemarch.
Harriet, his wife, formerly Mrs Dunkirk.
Ellen and **Kate,** their daughters.
Middlemarch, George Eliot, 1871–2.

Bultitude, Paul, colonial produce merchant.
Richard (Dick), his son.
Barbara, his daughter.
'Roly,' his son.
Vice Versa, F. Anstey, 1882.

Bumble, workhouse beadle, m. Mrs Corney. *Oliver Twist,* C. Dickens, 1838.

Bummel, Rev. Joshua, minister of Chapel of Ancient Truth.
Jacob and **Gladstone,** his sons.
Albert Grope, F. O. Mann, 1931.

Bumpas, Dickie, don who wrote novel which Nicholas Herrick tries to claim as his own. *Pastors and Masters,* Ivy Compton-Burnett, 1925.

Bumper, Sir Harry. *The School for Scandal* (play), R. B. Sheridan, 1777.

Bumphrey, C. P., defaulting bank manager. 'Arthur in Avalon' (s.s.), *Last Recollections of My Uncle Charles,* N. Balchin, 1954.

Bumppo, Natty, the deerslayer, central character of the *Leatherstocking Tales,* J. F. Cooper, 1823–46.

Bumpsher, George, M.P., wealthy wholesale stationer.
His wife, 'an overdressed woman three times the size of her husband.'
Bryanstone, their son.
Our Street, W. M. Thackeray, 1848.

Bumptious, Sergeant. *Jorrocks's Jaunts and Jollities,* R. S. Surtees, 1838.

Bumpus, Beatrice, woman's suffrage worker. *The Dream,* H. G. Wells, 1924.

Bunce, M.P. for Newcome. *The Newcomes,* W. M. Thackeray, 1853–1855.

Bunce, inmate of Hiram's Hospital. *The Warden,* A. Trollope, 1855.

Bunce, Jack, lieutenant, *Fortune's Favourite. The Pirate,* W. Scott, 1822.

Bunce, Jacob, copying journeyman.
Jane, his wife, Finn's landlady.
Phineas Finn, 1869, and elsewhere, A. Trollope.

Bunce, Thomas, innkeeper.
Bessy, his wife.
Jenny, their daughter.
Mr Weston's Good Wine. T. F. Powys, 1927.

Buncle, servant and secret messenger of Sir J. Ramorny. *The Fair Maid of Perth,* W. Scott, 1828.

Bunder, Teddy, drug distributor. *Hurry on Down,* John Wain, 1953.

Bunfit, eminent detective employed in search for the missing diamonds. *The Eustace Diamonds,* A. Trollope, 1872.

Bung, wine merchant and member of the Sarcophagus Club. *The Book of Snobs,* W. M. Thackeray, 1846–1847.

Bungay, publisher of the *Pall Mall Gazette,* formerly in partnership with his brother-in-law Bacon, now his enemy.
His kind-hearted wife.
Pendennis, W. M. Thackeray, 1848–50.

Bunion, Miss, writer of sentimental love poems. *Pendennis,* W. M. Thackeray, 1848–50.

Bunker, Minetta, m. Dr Tibbitt. 'Zenobia's Infidelity' (s.s.), *Short Sixes,* H. C. Bunner, 1890.

Bunn, Avonia, of Bagnigge Wells Theatre. *Trelawny of the Wells,* A. W. Pinero, 1898.

Bunner, Calvin C., American secretary to Sigsbee Manderson. *Trent's Last Case,* E. C. Bentley, 1912.

Bunney, Dr, of Oswego, phonetics expert; guest at Scamnum. *Hamlet, Revenge!,* M. Innes, 1937.

'Bunny,' close friend and intimate of Raffles; narrator. *Raffles* series, E. W. Hornung, 1899–1909.

'Bunny.' 'Aunt Ellen' (s.s.), *Limits and Renewals,* R. Kipling, 1932.

Bunny Bushtail, a squirrel. *Uncle Remus,* J. C. Harris, 1880–1906.

Bunsby, Captain.
His wife, formerly Mrs MacStinger.
Dombey and Son, C. Dickens, 1848.

Bunster, B.B.C. expert. *Sunrise in the West,* Bechofer Roberts, 1945.

Bunter, Mervyn, manservant, colleague and close friend of Lord Peter Wimsey. The *Lord Peter* stories throughout, Dorothy L. Sayers, 1923–37.

Bunter, William George (Billy), the Owl of the Remove at Greyfriars. *Billy Bunter* series, Frank Richards.

Bunthorne, Edna, m. Bert Smallways. *The War in the Air*, H. G. Wells, 1908.

Bunthorne, Reginald, a fleshly poet. *Patience* (comic opera), Gilbert & Sullivan, 1881.

Bunting, Miss (Bunny), governess to David Leslie and later to Anne Fielding. The *Barsetshire* series, Angela Thirkell, 1933 onwards.

Bunting, Mr and Mrs.
Their children:
Fred, Betty and **Netty.**
The Sea Lady, H. G. Wells, 1902.

Bunting, Rev. Mr, Vicar of Iping. *The Invisible Man*, H. G. Wells, 1897.

Buonaventure, Father, alias of Prince Charles Edward. *Redgauntlet*, W. Scott, 1824.

Burbidge, Mrs, sister of Josiah Hambling. *Joseph and his Brethren*, H. W. Freeman, 1928.

Burbo, wine seller and retired gladiator.
Stratonice, his wife.
The Last Days of Pompeii, Lord Lytton, 1834.

Burchell, alias of Sir William Thornhill. *The Vicar of Wakefield*, O. Goldsmith, 1766.

Burden. *Beau Geste*, P. C. Wren, 1924.

Burden, Jack, journalist and political lackey. *All The King's Men*, Robert Penn Warren, 1946.

Burden, Jim, narrator. *My Antonia*, Willa Cather, 1918.

Burden, Joanna, benefactress and lover of Joe Christmas, who murders her. *Light in August*, William Faulkner, 1932.

Burden, Simon, pensioner. *The Trumpet Major*, T. Hardy, 1880.

Burdock, Miss, manageress of the Rimini Hotel. *The Old Boys*, William Trevor, 1964.

Burdock, Haviland.
Martin, his elder brother.
'The Bone of Contention' (s.s.), *Lord Peter Views the Body*, Dorothy L. Sayers, 1928.

Burdock, James, country servant of Ernest Vane. *Peg Woffington*, C. Reade, 1853.

Burge, Jonathan, employer of Adam and Seth Bede. *Adam Bede*, George Eliot, 1859.

Burges, Lewis Holroyd, tobacconist and freemason.
His wife.
'In the Interests of the Brethren' (s.s.), *Debits and Credits*, 1926, and elsewhere, R. Kipling.

Burgess, headmaster of Melton School. *Sonia*, S. McKenna, 1917.

Burgess, Candida Morell's father. *Candida* (play), G. B. Shaw, 1894.

Burgess, Bessie, street fruit-vendor. *The Plough and the Stars* (play), S. O'Casey, 1926.

Burgess, Brooke, employed at Somerset House.
Rev. Barty, his father.
He Knew He Was Right, A. Trollope, 1869.

Burgess, Ted, farmer, Marian Maudsley's lover. *The Go-Between*, L. P. Hartley, 1953.

Burghley, Rev. Mr.
Minnie, his wife.
Lighten our Darkness, R. Keable, 1927.

Burgoyne, General (hist.). *The Devil's Disciple*, G. B. Shaw, 1899.

Burgrave, Tommy, nephew of Ephraim Quixtus, m. Etta Concannon. *The Glory of Clementina Wing*, W. J. Locke, 1911.

Burgundy, Duke of. *Henry the Fifth* and *Henry the Sixth* (plays), W. Shakespeare.

Burgundy, Duke of. *King Lear* (play), W. Shakespeare.

Burjoyce, printer.
His wife.
Vanity Fair, W. M. Thackeray, 1847–8.

Burke, nursing sister. *The Purple Plain*, H. E. Bates, 1947.

Burke, driver of taxi in which Philip Boyes was discovered dying. *Strong Poison*, Dorothy L. Sayers, 1930.

Burke, Captain, 'professional promoter of revolutions,' *Soldiers of Fortune*, R. H. Davis, 1897.

Burke, Miss, Emma Greatheart's companion. *Mother and Son*, Ivy Compton-Burnett, 1954.

Burke, Aileen, m. Tony Grace.
Owen, her grandfather.
'General Burton's Ghost (s.s.), *Countrymen All*, Katherine Tynan, 1915.

Burke, Dan.
Nora, his wife.

Shadow of the Glen (play), J. M. Synge, 1903.

Burke, Chevalier de (Francis), Irish colonel in the service of the Pretender. *The Master of Ballantrae,* R. L. Stevenson, 1889.

Burke, Mat. *Anna Christie* (play), E. O'Neill, 1922.

Burke, Pat, horse thief. *Robbery under Arms,* R. Boldrewood, 1888.

Burke, Reginald, bank manager. 'A Bank Fraud' (s.s.), *Plain Tales from the Hills,* R. Kipling, 1888.

Burke, Sadie, Willie Stark's mistress. *All The King's Men,* Robert Penn Warren, 1946.

Burke, Tom, central character and narrator, m. Marie d'Auvergne, *née* de Meudon.
Matthew, his father.
George, his elder brother.
Tom Burke of Ours, C. Lever, 1844.

Burke, Ulick, gentleman jockey and spy. *Jack Hinton,* C. Lever, 1843.

Burke, Woodrow, news commentator. *The Troubled Air,* Irwin Shaw, 1951.

Burkett, Dinah Dorothea, m. Jo Hermann.
Madeleine, her sister, m. Rickie Masters.
The Echoing Grove, Rosamond Lehmann, 1953.

Burkin, George, peeping Tom. *Heaven's My Destination,* Thornton Wilder, 1935.

Burkin-Jones, Clare (Mumbo), who is also Mopsie Pye, owner of chain of gift shops. *The Little Girls,* Elizabeth Bowen, 1964.

Burlap, editor. *Point Counter Point,* Aldous Huxley, 1928.

Burleigh, Burton, police-officer. *An American Tragedy,* T. Dreiser, 1925.

Burleigh, Cecil. *Men Like Gods,* H. G. Wells, 1923.

Burleigh, Trayton, murderer. 'In the Library' (s.s.), *The Lady of the Barge,* W. W. Jacobs, 1902.

Burley, John. *My Novel,* Lord Lytton, 1853.

Burnaby, Mrs (Nanny), nurse to the Lampreys. *Surfeit of Lampreys,* Ngaio Marsh, 1941.

Burnage, Cyril, Ed., *The Voice.*
Rose, his wife.
Right Off the Map, C. E. Montague, 1927.

Burnea, cockney. 'The Woman in his Life' (s.s.), *Limits and Renewals,* R. Kipling, 1932.

Burnell, Linda, *née* Fairfield.
Stanley, her husband.
Their daughters:
Isabel.
Lottie.
Kezia.
Prelude (s.s.), Katherine Mansfield.

Burnet, Susan, furniture renovator. *The Wife of Sir Isaac Harman,* H. G. Wells, 1914.

Burnet, Vincent.
Dr and Mrs, his father and mother.
Cormorant Crag, G. Manville Fenn, 1895.

Burnett, Hon. Arabella ('Balmy Jane'). *But Soft—We Are Observed!,* H. Belloc, 1928.

Burnett, Belle. *Britannia Mews,* Margery Sharp, 1946.

Burnett, James, Australian Naval Reserve, first lieutenant, *Compass Rose. The Cruel Sea,* N. Monsarrat, 1951.

Burnham, Dr Leicester, Jeremiah Beaumont's teacher. *World Enough and Time,* Robert Penn Warren, 1950.

Burns, Police-captain. *The Stolen White Elephant* (s.s.), Mark Twain, 1882.

Burns, Gerald ('Shifty'), a scaler in the Liverpool docks. *Ebb and Flood,* James Hanley, 1932.

Burns, Peter, central character and (after Part I) narrator, m. Audrey Sheridan, *née* Blake. *The Little Nugget,* P. G. Wodehouse, 1913.

Burnside, Captain Dakers's batman. *Sixty-four, Ninety-four,* R. H. Mottram, 1925.

Burnside, Reggie. *Death of a Hero,* R. Aldington, 1929.

Burnwell, Sir George. 'The Beryl Coronet' (s.s.), *The Adventures of Sherlock Holmes,* A. Conan Doyle, 1892.

Burrage, Mrs, socialite.
Henry, her husband.
The Bostonians, H. James, 1886.

Burrows, Dr, sub-dean, Helstonleigh. *The Channings,* Mrs Henry Wood, 1862.

Burrows, 'Battling,' prize-fighter. *The Chink and the Child* (s.s.), T. Burke.

Burrows, Sir Eliphaz, Governor of Woldingstanton School. *The Undying Fire,* H. G. Wells, 1919.

Burstall, Andrew Michael. *C.,* M. Baring, 1924.

Burt, Negro. 'I'm a Fool' (s.s.), and elsewhere, *Horses and Men,* Sherwood Anderson, 1924.

Burtenshaw, Alexander.
 Rosamund, his daughter.
A House and its Head, Ivy Compton-Burnett, 1935.

Burton, Banjo, leader of a pop group.
 Army, his brother, guitarist.
Barefoot in the Head, Brian W. Aldiss, 1969.

Burton, General and Mrs. 'General Burton's Ghost' (s.s.), *Countrymen All,* Katherine Tynan, 1915.

Burton, Hannah, maid to Clarissa Harlowe. *Clarissa Harlowe,* S. Richardson, 1748.

Burton, Harry, narrator, m. Alice Mayton.
 Helen, his sister, m. Colonel Tom Lawrence.
Helen's Babies, J. Habberton, 1876.

Burton, Lady (Millicent). *Mrs Dalloway,* Virginia Woolf, 1925.

Burton, Sarah, M.A., central character, headmistress of Kiplington High School.
 Pattie, her married sister.
South Riding, Winifred Holtby, 1936.

Burton, Ted. *Pilgrimage,* Dorothy M. Richardson, 1915–38.

Burtt, Ivy, waitress, eng. to Syd. *Shining and Free,* G. B. Stern, 1935.

Burtwell, Rev. Thomas. *God's Stepchildren,* Sarah G. Millin, 1924.

Burwen-Fossilton, actor. *Diary of a Nobody,* G. & W. Grossmith, 1892.

Bury, Mrs Caroline. *It's a Battlefield,* Graham Greene, 1935.

Buryan, John Thomas, Cornish farmer. *Kangaroo,* D. H. Lawrence, 1923.

Busby, Mortimer, shady publisher. *Summer Moonshine,* P. G. Wodehouse, 1938.

Bush, Lieutenant, later Captain. The *Hornblower* series, C. S. Forester, 1937 onwards.

Bushy, creature to Richard. *Richard the Second* (play), W. Shakespeare.

Bushy-Jones, Rev. Powell. *The Weak and the Strong,* G. Kersh, 1945.

Buskbody, Martha, mantua-maker of Gandercleugh. *Old Mortality,* W. Scott, 1816.

Bustington, Lord. *The Newcomes,* W. M. Thackeray, 1853–5.

Bustopher Jones, St James's Street cat. *Old Possum's Book of Practical Cats,* T. S. Eliot, 1939.

Butcher, orchid collector. *Aepyornis Island* (s.s.), H. G. Wells, 1905.

Bute, war correspondent. 'Two or Three Witnesses' (s.s.), *Fiery Particles,* C. E. Montague, 1923.

Butler, Mr, speculative builder. *Badger's Green* (play), R. C. Sherriff, 1930.

Butler, Edward, contractor and politician.
 Aileen, his daughter.
The Financier, Theodore Dreiser, 1912.

Butler, Lieutenant (later **Captain**) **Julius.** *Waverley,* W. Scott, 1814.

Butler, Major Jack, of Ministry of Defence. *The Labyrinth Makers,* Anthony Price, 1970.

Butler, Rhett, blockader, m. as her 3rd husband Scarlett O'Hara.
 Bonnie, their daughter, killed by a fall from a pony.
Gone with the Wind, Margaret Mitchell, 1936.

Butler, Stephen, corporal in Cromwell's dragoons.
 Judith, his wife.
 Benjamin, their son.
  Reuben, his son, m. Jeanie Deans.
 Their children:
  David, Reuben and **Femie.**
The Heart of Midlothian, W. Scott, 1818.

Butt, Sir Gregory. *Dr Angelus* (play), J. Bridie, 1947.

Butterby, detective. *The Channings,* Mrs Henry Wood, 1862.

Buttercup, bumboat woman (Mrs Cripps), m. Captain Corcoran. *H.M.S. Pinafore* (comic opera), Gilbert & Sullivan, 1878.

Butteridge, Alfred, loud-voiced and fraudulent claimant to be an airship inventor. *The War in the Air,* H. G. Wells, 1908.

Buttermere, family retainer and confidant. *Men and Wives,* Ivy Compton-Burnett, 1931.

Butters, Mrs, missionary's wife, Manchuria. *Tobit Transplanted,* Stella Benson, 1931.

Butterworth, Mrs Gertie, housekeeper. *The Sleepless Moon,* H. E. Bates, 1956.

Butterworth, Clara, m. Hugh McVey.
  Tom Butterworth, her father.
Poor White, Sherwood Anderson, 1920.

Buttock, Tessie, owner of private hotel. *The Rich Pay Late,* 1964, and others in the *Alms for Oblivion* sequence, Simon Raven.

Button, late research dynamiter (Monday). *The Man who was Thursday,* G. K. Chesterton, 1908.

Button, drunkard and thief, m. Mrs Kegworthy.
  Their six children.
The Fortunate Youth, W. J. Locke, 1914.

Button, Pabuck, sailor, survivor from the *Ohio* with Dick and Emmeline Lestrange. *The Blue Lagoon,* H. de Vere Stacpoole, 1909.

Butts, Dr, physician to the King. *Henry the Eighth* (play), W. Shakespeare.

Butts, Ronald.
  His wife.
    Ronald, their son.
'Lucky Boy' (s.s.), *Louise,* Viola Meynell, 1954.

Buxton, Frank, m. Maggie Browne.
  Lawrence, his father.
  His mother.
  Ermina (Minnie), his cousin.
The Moorland Cottage, Mrs Gaskell, 1850.

Buzfuz, Sergeant, barrister for Mrs Bardell. *Pickwick Papers,* C. Dickens, 1837.

Buzzford, general dealer at Casterbridge. *The Mayor of Casterbridge,* T. Hardy, 1886.

Bycliffe, Maurice Christian, claimant to the Transome Estates.
  Annette, *née* Ledru, his wife.
    Esther, their daughter adopted by Rev. Rufus Lyon.
Felix Holt, George Eliot, 1866.

Byers, Jessie. *The Story of Ragged Robyn,* O. Onions, 1943.

Byfield, Professor, balloonist. *St Ives,* R. L. Stevenson, 1897.

Bygrave, alias of Mrs Wragge. *No Name,* W. Collins, 1862.

Byles, Sir Cockle, of the Bengal Service. *The Book of Snobs,* W. M. Thackeray, 1846–7.

Byng, Alexander.
  Sarah and **Jane,** his sisters.
  Bill, his brother.
Cautionary Tales, H. Belloc, 1907.

Byng, Lady Caroline, sister of Lord Marshmoreton.
  Clifford, her dead husband.
  Reginald, her stepson, m. Alice Faraday.
A Damsel in Distress, P. G. Wodehouse, 1919.

Byrne, steward to Lord Manton. *The Search Party,* G. A. Birmingham, 1913.

Byrne, Lucy, formerly eng. to Ivor Gates. *A Sort of Traitors,* N. Balchin, 1949.

Byrne, Michael, tinker.
  Mary, his mother.
The Tinker's Wedding (play), J. M. Synge, 1909.

Byron, Harriet, central character and chief letter-writer, m. Sir Charles Grandison. *Sir Charles Grandison,* S. Richardson, 1754.

Bywater, Stephen, schoolboy. *The Channings,* Mrs Henry Wood, 1862.

C

Cabadens, Charles-Marie, *curé* of Fraxinet. *Act of God,* F. Tennyson Jesse, 1936.

Cabestainy, William, troubadour. *Anne of Geierstein,* W. Scott, 1829.

Cable, Captain, of the *Minnie. The Vultures,* H. Seton Merriman, 1902.

Cabot, Ephraim, farmer.
Simeon, Peter and **Eben,** his sons.
Abbie, his 3rd wife, who seduces Eben.
Desire Under The Elms (play), Eugene O'Neill, 1924.

Cabot, Lionel, close friend of Ulysses Macaulay. *The Human Comedy,* W. Saroyan, 1943.

Cacafogo, Dr. *A Citizen of the World,* O. Goldsmith, 1762.

Cackle, assistant surgeon in George Osborne's regiment. *Vanity Fair,* W. M. Thackeray, 1847–8.

Caddles, Albert Edward, giant child, grandson of Mrs Skinner. *The Food of the Gods,* H. G. Wells, 1904.

Cade, Jack (hist.), rebel. *Henry the Fourth* and *Henry the Sixth* (plays), W. Shakespeare.

Cadogan, Mrs, Yeates's housekeeper.
Peter, her nephew.
Some Experiences of an Irish R.M., Œ. Somerville & Martin Ross, 1899.

Cadoual, George, partner, later rival, of Alain Carbonec.
His mother.
Barbe of Grand Bayou, J. Oxenham, 1903.

Cadwal. *See* Arviragus.

Cadwallon, Gwenwyn's bard. *The Betrothed,* W. Scott, 1825.

Caerleon, Lady Clarissa. *The Choice* (play), A. Sutro, 1919.

Caerlyon, Lady Mary, m. the Marquess of Steyne. *Pendennis,* W. M. Thackeray, 1848–50.

Caesar ('Uncle'), Negro cab-driver and descendant of Congo kings. 'A Municipal Report' (s.s.), *Strictly Business,* O. Henry, 1910.

Caesar, Julius (hist.).
Calphurnia, his wife.
Julius Caesar (play), W. Shakespeare. *Caesar and Cleopatra* (play), G. B. Shaw, 1900.

Cahel, Delia. *Kathleen ni Houlihan* (play), W. B. Yeats, 1902.

Cahere, Netty, niece of Joseph P. Mangles. *The Vultures,* H. Seton Merriman, 1902.

Cainge, Amos. 'You See—' (s.s.), *Love and Money,* Phyllis Bentley, 1957.

Cairns. *Wandering Stars,* Clemence Dane, 1924.

Cairns, Kitty. *Fanny by Gaslight,* M. Sadleir, 1940.

Cairo, Joel, former agent of Casper Gutman. *The Maltese Falcon,* Dashiell Hammett, 1930.

Caitlin, daughter of MacMurrachu; a shepherd girl. *The Crock of Gold,* James Stephens, 1912.

Caius, Dr, French physician. *The Merry Wives of Windsor* (play), W. Shakespeare.

Caius Lucius, Roman general. *Cymbeline* (play), W. Shakespeare.

Caius Marcius. *See* Coriolanus.

Calabria, Ferdinand, Duke of.
The Cardinal, his brother.
The Duchess of Malfi (play), John Webster, *c.* 1613.

Calamy. *Those Barren Leaves,* A. Huxley, 1925.

Calbraith, Miss Clinton, English school-teacher. *Sanders of the River,* E. Wallace, 1911.

Calchas, Trojan priest.
Cressida, his daughter.
Troilus and Cressida (play), W. Shakespeare.

Calcraft, Leonard ('Lenny'), central character.
His father.
Sarah, his sister, m. Holway.
Jane, his sister, m. Kent.
In Cotton Wool, W. B. Maxwell, 1912.

Caldecott, Rev. Augustan, rector of Royal.
Bessie, his wife.
It Never Can Happen Again, W. de Morgan, 1909.

Calder, James, narrator, m. Pat Leighton. *Wickford Point,* J. P. Marquand, 1939.

Caldwell, George, science teacher, who is also Chiron, noblest of the centaurs.
Cassie, his wife, *née* Kramer.
Peter, their teenage son.
The Centaur, John Updike, 1963.

Calenus, priest. *The Last Days of Pompeii*, Lord Lytton, 1834.

Caley, treacherous maid to 'Lady Florimel Colonsay.' *The Marquis of Lossie*, G. MacDonald, 1877.

Calhoun, Freddy, friend of Caryl Bramsley.
His father and mother.
C., M. Baring, 1924.

Calianax, father of Aspatia. *The Maid's Tragedy* (play), Beaumont & Fletcher, 1611.

Caliban, a savage and deformed slave. *The Tempest* (play), W. Shakespeare.

Calidore, Mrs R., with a passion for private theatricals. *Our Street*, W. M. Thackeray, 1848.

Calipolis. *The Battle of Alcazar* (play), G. Peele, 1594.

Calista. *The Fair Penitent* (play), N. Rowe, 1703.

Calista of Montfaucon, chief 'bower woman' of Queen Berengaria. *The Talisman*, W. Scott, 1825.

Calkin, Agatha. *Men and Wives*, Ivy Compton-Burnett, 1931.

Calladine, Betty.
Her mother.
The Red House Mystery, A. A. Milne, 1922.

Callaghan, Captain. *The Bay*, L. A. G. Strong, 1941.

Callaghan, Bat.
His mother.
Some Experiences of an Irish R.M., Œ. Somerville & Martin Ross, 1899.

Callaghan, Christine, student; one-time 'girl' of Bertrand Welch. *Lucky Jim*, K. Amis, 1953.

Callander, Miss Daisy, matron, colleague of Inigo Jollifant. *The Good Companions*, J. B. Priestley, 1929.

Callard, Mr. *Precious Bane*, Mary Webb, 1924.

Callard, Mrs. *The Lie* (play), H. A. Jones, 1923.

Callcome, Nat, best man at Dick Dewy's wedding. *Under the Greenwood Tree*, T. Hardy, 1872.

Callcott, Jack, Australian neighbour of R. L. Somers.
Victoria, his wife.
Kangaroo, D. H. Lawrence, 1923.

Callendar, Major.
His wife.
A Passage to India, E. M. Forster, 1924.

Callendar, James, friend of Cleg Kelly. *Cleg Kelly*, S. R. Crockett, 1896.

Callender, Mrs. *The Christian*, Hall Caine, 1897.

Callender, George B., dramatist, m. Mary Vaughan. 'Deep Waters' (s.s.), *The Man Upstairs*, P. G. Wodehouse, 1914.

Callender, Wilfred. *The Clever Ones* (play), A. Sutro, 1914.

Callonby, Earl of.
Lord Kilkee, his son.
Lady Catherine, his daughter.
Lady Jane, his daughter, m. Harry Lorrequer.
Harry Lorrequer, C. Lever, 1839.

Calloway, Bert. *Other Gods*, Pearl Buck, 1940.

Calloway, H. B., news reporter, *The Enterprise*. 'Calloway's Code' (s.s.), *Whirligigs*, O. Henry, 1910.

Calmady, school friend of Caryl Bramsley. *C.*, M. Baring, 1924.

Caloveglia, Count.
His daughter.
South Wind, N. Douglas, 1917.

Calphurnia, wife of Caesar. *Julius Caesar* (play), W. Shakespeare.

Calsabigi, lottery contractor. *Barry Lyndon*, W. M. Thackeray, 1844.

Calton, boarder at Mrs Tibbs's. *Sketches by Boz*, C. Dickens, 1836.

Calton, Duncan, lawyer. *The Mystery of a Hansom Cab*, F. Hume, 1886.

Calverley, Colonel, Dragoon Guards, m. Lady Saphir. *Patience* (comic opera), Gilbert & Sullivan, 1881.

Calverley, Sir Hugh. *The White Company*, A. Conan Doyle, 1891.

Calvert, Cathleen.
Cade, her brother.
Their parents.
Gone with the Wind, Margaret Mitchell, 1936.

Calvert, Herbert, commission agent and property owner. *The Card*, Arnold Bennett, 1911.

Calvert, Roy, closest friend of Lewis Eliot. *Strangers and Brothers* sequence, 1949 onwards, C. P. Snow.

Calvo, Baldassarre, adoptive father of Tito Melema. *Romola,* George Eliot, 1863.

Calymath, Selim, son of the Grand Seignior. *The Jew of Malta* (play), C. Marlowe, 1633.

Camberhurst, Duchess of, friend of Barnabas Barty, godmother of Lady Cleone Meredith. *The Amateur Gentleman,* J. Farnol, 1913.

Camel, The. 'How the Camel got his Hump,' *Just So Stories,* R. Kipling, 1902.

Cameron, Highland boatman, later minister. *Mary Rose* (play), J. M. Barrie, 1920.

Cameron, Dr, Finlay's colleague. *Beyond This Place,* A. J. Cronin, 1953, later adapted into a popular television series, *Dr Finlay's Casebook.*

Cameron, Alister, m. Lilian Stonor. The *Barsetshire* series, Angela Thirkell, 1933 onwards.

Cameron, Brian. *Gaslight* (play), Patrick Hamilton, 1939.

Cameron, Evelyn. *See* VARGRAVE.

Cameron, Kenneth, m. Kim Ravenal, *Show Boat,* Edna Ferber, 1926.

Cameron, Rachel, spinster schoolteacher in Canadian prairie town.
Her mother, widow of an undertaker.
A Jest of God, Margaret Laurence, 1966.

Cameron, Simon, of Lincoln's cabinet (hist.). *Abraham Lincoln* (play), J. Drinkwater, 1918.

Camillo, Sicilian lord, m. Perdita. *A Winter's Tale* (play), W. Shakespeare.

Cammysole, Mrs, Titmarsh's unpleasant and extortionate landlady. *Our Street,* W. M. Thackeray, 1848.

Campan, Theodore ('Le Capitaine'), m. Marie Clavert. *La Mère Bauche* (s.s.), A. Trollope.

Campaspe. *Alexander and Campaspe* (play), J. Lyly, 1584.

Campbell, landscape painter. *The Five Red Herrings,* Dorothy L. Sayers, 1931.

Campbell, bullying schoolboy. 'The Moral Reformers,' *Stalky & Co.,* R. Kipling, 1899.

Campbell ('Barcaldine'), commander of troop. *The Highland Widow,* W. Scott, 1827.

Campbell, Colonel.
His wife.
Jane, their daughter, m. Mr Dixon.
Emma, Jane Austen, 1816.

Campbell, Corporal, friend of Lilyworth. *The Progress of Private Lilyworth,* Russell Braddon, 1971.

Campbell, Alan. *The Picture of Dorian Gray,* O. Wilde, 1891.

Campbell, Sir Duncan, Knight of Ardenvohr.
His wife.
Annot Lyle, his daughter.
The Legend of Montrose, W. Scott, 1819.

Campbell, Elsie, m. McAndrew. 'McAndrew's Hymn' (poem), *The Seven Seas,* R. Kipling, 1896.

Campbell, Helen, m. Robert MacGregor (Rob Roy). Name annexed by him when the name MacGregor was abolished by Act of Parliament. *Rob Roy,* W. Scott, 1818.

Campbell, Henry, surgeon.
Emily, his wife.
His sons:
Henry, Jnr.
Alfred.
Percival.
John.
Emma and **Mary,** his adopted nieces.
Douglas, successful claimant to his estate.
The Settlers in Canada, Captain Marryat, 1844.

Campbell, Lachlan, Free Church minister.
Flora, his daughter.
Beside the Bonnie Brier Bush, I. Maclaren, 1894.

Campbell, Mike, Brett Ashley's fiancé. *The Sun Also Rises* (or *Fiesta*), Ernest Hemingway, 1926.

Campbell, Peter, architect and central character.
Adelaide, *née* Jamieson, his wife.
Amanda, his mother.
Christopher, his half-wit brother.
Flamingo, Mary Borden, 1927.

Campbell, Stuart, grandfather of

Bruce Wetheral and founder of 'Campbell's Kingdom.' *Campbell's Kingdom,* Hammond Innes, 1952.

Campeius, Cardinal. *Henry the Eighth* (play), W. Shakespeare.

Camperdine, Mr, squire's son.
Dollabella, his sister.
Precious Bane, Mary Webb, 1924.

Camperdown, Sir Florian Eustace's family lawyer and determined opposer of Lady Eustace.
John, his son and partner.
The Eustace Diamonds, A. Trollope, 1873.

Camperton, Major.
His wife.
A Laodicean, T. Hardy, 1881.

Campian, Jesuit priest. *Westward Ho!,* C. Kingsley, 1855.

Campion, Mrs, friend of Mr Ingleside.
John, her son.
Mr Ingleside, E. V. Lucas, 1910.

Campion, Albert, amateur detective, m. Lady Amanda Fitton. Many detective stories, Margery Allingham, 1929 onwards.

Campion, Lieutenant-General Lord Edward, V.C., etc., godfather of Mark Tietjens. *Last Post,* Ford Madox Ford, 1928.

Campion, Mrs Gladys, mistress of Major Knott, elderly neighbour of Christine Cornwell. *The Widow,* Francis King, 1957.

Campion, Maggie.
Victor, her father.
Margaret, her mother.
May, her sister.
Lily, her sister.
Victor, her brother.
Uncle Willie.
Aunt Priscilla.
The Perennial Bachelor, Anne Parrish, 1925.

Campo-Gasso, Count. *Quentin Durward,* 1823, and *Anne of Geierstein,* 1829, W. Scott.

Canby, saloon keeper. *The Ox-Bow Incident,* Walter Van Tilburg Clark, 1940.

Cancellarius, Chancellor of Grunewald. *Prince Otto,* R. L. Stevenson, 1885.

Candour, Mrs. *The School for Scandal* (play), R. B. Sheridan, 1777.

Candover, handyman. *Let the People Sing,* J. B. Priestley, 1939.

Candy, Dr. *The Moonstone,* W. Collins, 1868.

Cann, Miss, ex-governess, 'brisk, honest, cheerful.' *The Newcomes,* W. M. Thackeray, 1853–5.

Cannel.
Aline, his wife.
'Revenge upon Revenge' (s.s.), *Love and Money,* Phyllis Bentley, 1957.

Canning, family name of Earl of Manton.

Cannister, Gilbert (alias Jaffa Codling).
Mildred, his wife.
Their children: **Adam.**
Eve.
Gabriel.
'Adam and Eve and Pinch Me' (s.s.), *Adam and Eve and Pinch Me,* A. E. Coppard, 1921.

Cannister, Martin, sexton at Endelstow, m. Unity. *A Pair of Blue Eyes,* T. Hardy, 1873.

Cannon, George, bigamous husband of Hilda Lessways.
Charlotte, his real wife.
The *Clayhanger* trilogy, Arnold Bennett, 1910–16.

Cannot, Janet. *The Great Adventure* (play), Arnold Bennett, 1913.

Canonbury, Lady Fanny, daughter of 'old Lady Kew.' *The Newcomes,* W. M Thackeray, 1853–5.

Cantacute, Verity, one-time fiancée of Lionel de Lyndesay. *Crump Folk Going Home,* Constance Holme, 1913.

Canteloupe, the Marquis. *The Rich Pay Late,* 1964, and others in the *Alms for Oblivion* sequence, Simon Raven.

Cantelupe, Lord Charles. *Waste* (play), H. Granville-Barker, 1907.

Canter, Simon, alibi assumed by Edward Christian when travelling with Peveril. *Peveril of the Peak,* W. Scott, 1822.

Canterbury, Archbishop of. *Henry the Fifth* (play), W. Shakespeare.

Canterville, Lord, owner of Canterville Chase. *The Canterville Ghost* (s.s.), O. Wilde, 1887.

Cantle, Christian, a simpleton.
Grandfer Cantle, his father.
The Return of the Native, T. Hardy, 1878.

Cantlop, William.
Amelia, his wife, *née* Darke.

The House in Dormer Forest, Mary Webb, 1920.

Canton, valet to Lord Ogleby. *The Clandestine Marriage*, G. Colman the Elder, 1766.

Cantourne, Lady. *With Edged Tools*, H. Seton Merriman, 1894.

Cantrell, Col. Richard, of U.S. Army. Central character. *Across The River and Into The Trees*, Ernest Hemingway, 1950.

Cantrip, Earl of, Colonial Secretary.
His wife.
Phineas Finn, 1869, and elsewhere, A. Trollope.

Cantrips, Jess, street-walker and pickpocket. *Redgauntlet*, W. Scott, 1824.

Cantwell, Dr. *The Hypocrite*, I. Bickerstaffe, 1768.

Canty, Albert, multi-millionaire. *Other Gods*, Pearl Buck, 1940.

Canty, James, farmer.
His wife.
Some Experiences of an Irish R.M., Œ. Somerville & Martin Ross, 1899.

Canty, Tom, central character.
John, thief and drunkard, his father.
His mother, a professional beggar.
His sisters: **Bet.**
Nan.
The Prince and the Pauper, Mark Twain, 1882.

Canynge, General. *Loyalties* (play), J. Galsworthy, 1922.

Capes, Godwin, demonstrator in biology, later dramatist, as 'Thomas More,' m. Ann Veronica Stanley. *Ann Veronica*, H. G. Wells, 1909.

Caplan, Robert.
Freda, his wife, sister of Gordon Whitehouse.
Martin, his dead brother.
Dangerous Corner (play), J. B. Priestley, 1932.

Capolin, Egyptian captain. *Tamburlaine*, C. Marlowe, 1587.

Caponsacchi, Canon Giuseppe, friend of Pompilia Comparini. *The Ring and the Book* (poem), R. Browning, 1868–9.

Capsas, Sophia, 'The Capsina' of Hydra, central character.
Christos, her cousin.
The Capsina, E. F. Benson, 1899.

Capstan. *Polly* (comic opera), J. Gay, 1729.

Capstern, Captain. *The Surgeon's Daughter*, W. Scott, 1827.

Capstick, Rev. Benaiah. *Joseph Vance*, W. de Morgan, 1906.

Captain, otter-hound. *Tarka the Otter*, H. Williamson, 1927.

Captax, Fredric, poses as psychiatrist and seduces Janet Links. *A Travelling Woman*, John Wain, 1959.

Caption, Mr, W. S., m. Jenny Pawkie. *The Provost*, J. Galt, 1822.

Capucius, ambassador of Charles V. *Henry the Eighth* (play), W. Shakespeare.

Capulet, head of his House.
Lady Capulet, his wife.
Juliet, their daughter.
Romeo and Juliet (play), W. Shakespeare.

Cara, mistress of Lord Marchmain. *Brideshead Revisited*, E. Waugh, 1945.

Carabas, Marquess of.
His wife. Bankrupt super-snobs. *The Book of Snobs*, W. M. Thackeray, 1846–7.

Carabine, James, ex-prize-fighter, valet and close friend of Sir Valentine Macfarlane. *Destiny Bay*, Donn Byrne, 1928.

Caradoc. Family name of EARL OF VALLEYS.

Caramel, Richard, novelist, cousin of Gloria Gilbert Patch. *The Beautiful and the Damned*, F. Scott Fitzgerald, 1922.

Caratach, cousin of Bonduca. *Bonduca* (play), Beaumont & Fletcher, 1614.

Caraway, Miss. *We're Here*, D. Mackail, 1947.

Caraway, Earle. *Wickford Point*, J. P. Marquand, 1939.

Carbonec, Alain, m. Barbe Carcassone. *Barbe of Grand Bayou*, J. Oxenham, 1903.

Carbuncle, Mrs Jane, 'a wonderful woman.' *The Eustace Diamonds*, A. Trollope, 1873.

Carbury, Roger, in love with Henrietta.
Sir Felix, his second cousin.
Henrietta, Sir Felix's sister, m. Paul Montagu.
Matilda, Lady Carbury, mother of Henrietta, m. Nicholas Broune.

The Way We Live Now, A. Trollope, 1875.

Carcassone, Pierre, master mariner.
  Barbe, his daughter, m. Alain Carbonec.
  Barbe of Grand Bayou, J. Oxenham, 1903.

Carcow, Ezra, antique dealer.
  Rebecca, his wife (Mme Fortunata).
  The One Before, Barry Pain, 1902.

Cardan, Tom ('one of the obscure great'). *Those Barren Leaves*, A. Huxley, 1935.

Carden, Lieutenant-Colonel, commanding Lorrequer's regiment. *Harry Lorrequer*, C. Lever, 1839.

Carden, Grace, m. Henry Little.
  Walter, her father.
  Put Yourself in his Place, C. Reade, 1870.

Cardew, Flight-Lieutenant. *The Green Goddess* (play), W. Archer, 1921.

Cardew, Cecily, ward of Jack Worthing, m. Algernon Moncrieff, *The Importance of Being Earnest* (play), O. Wilde, 1895.

Cardew, Rev. Theophilus.
  Jane, his wife.
  Catherine Furze, M. Rutherford, 1893.

Cardigan, Lord (hist.). *Trumpeter, Sound !*, D. L. Murray, 1933.

Cardigan, Jack, m. Imogen Dartie.
  Their two sons.
  The *Forsyte* series, J. Galsworthy, 1906–33.

Cardross, Neville.
  His wife.
  Their children:
    Shiela (adopted), m. (1) Louis Malcourt; (2) Garret Hamil.
    Jessie, m. Carrick.
    Cecile.
    Gray.
  The Firing Line, R. W. Chambers, 1908.

Cards, Humphrey.
  Charlotte, his wife.
    Dorothy, their daughter. *See* WARREN FORSTER.
    Jeremy, their son.
  Maurice, brother of Humphrey.
  Jennifer, great-grand-daughter of Humphrey, m. Francis Herries.
  Adrian, great-nephew of Jennifer.
The *Herries* Chronicles, Hugh Walpole, 1930–3.

Careless. *The School for Scandal* (play), R. B. Sheridan, 1777.

Carella, Gino, dentist's son, 2nd husband of Lilia Herriton. *Where Angels Fear To Tread*, E. M. Forster, 1905.

Carew, Allan, central character, m. Suzette Vincent.
  George, his father.
  Lady Emily, *née* Darnleigh, his mother.
  Sons of Fire, Mary E. Braddon, 1896.

Carew, Lady (Ann), mistress of Richard Thurstan. *Lighten our Darkness*, R. Keable, 1927.

Carew, Baines. 'Baines Carew, Gentleman' (poem), *The Bab Ballads*, W. S. Gilbert, 1869.

Carew, Beau, friend of Captain Jennico. *The Pride of Jennico*, A. & E. Castle, 1898.

Carew, Sir Charles, Bt. *The Old Dominion*, Mary Johnston, 1899.

Carew, Sir Danvers, M.P., murdered by Hyde. *Dr Jekyll and Mr Hyde*, R. L. Stevenson, 1886.

Carey, Dr.
  His wife.
  The Harvester, Gene S. Porter, 1911.

Carey, Widow. *Sybil*, B. Disraeli, 1845.

Carey, Philip, central character, m. Sally Athelny.
  Stephen, his dead father.
  Helen, his dead mother.
  William and **Louisa,** his uncle and aunt and his guardians.
  Of Human Bondage, W. S. Maugham, 1915.

Carey, Rupert, m. Viola, Lady Holme. *The Woman with the Fan*, R. S. Hichens, 1904.

Carfax, Lady Frances. 'The Disappearance of Lady Frances Carfax,' *His Last Bow*, A. Conan Doyle, 1917.

Carford, Earl of. *Simon Dale*, A. Hope, 1898.

Carfrae, Mrs, elderly friend of Sir Johnson Carr. *A Safety Match*, Ian Hay, 1911.

Cargill, Rev. Josiah, minister of St Ronan's. *St Ronan's Well*, W. Scott, 1824.

Carghill, Mrs (Maisie Batterson, alias Maisie Montjoy), woman out of Lord Claverton's past. *The Elder Statesman* (play), T. S. Eliot, 1958.

Cargreen, assessor of dilapidations. *In the Roar of the Sea,* S. Baring Gould, 1892.

Cariola, servant girl. *The Duchess of Malfi* (play), John Webster, *c.* 1613.

Carisbrooke, Mr. *See* EARL OF ILBURY.

Carker, James, office manager of Paul Dombey.
Harriet, his sister, m. Morfin.
John, his brother.
Dombey and Son, C. Dickens, 1848.

Carleon, Patricia and Morris. *Magic* (play), G. K. Chesterton, 1913.

Carleton, lover of Fleda Ringgan. *Queechy,* Elizabeth Wetherell, 1852.

Carling, Marjorie, mistress of Walter Bidlake. *Point Counter Point,* Aldous Huxley, 1928.

Carlisle, Admiral. *Lady Frederick* (play), W. S. Maugham, 1907.

Carlisle, Lady Agatha, daughter of the Duke of Berwick. *Lady Windermere's Fan,* O. Wilde, 1892.

Carlisle, Gordon ('Oily').
Gertie, his wife. Crooks.
Cocktail Time, P. G. Wodehouse, 1958.

Carlo, servant to Giovanni Malatesta. *Paolo and Francesca,* S. Phillips, 1900.

Carlos, Don. *The Duenna* (play), R. B. Sheridan, 1775.

Carlton, John (later **Sir**), m. Mary Marlowe.
Their children:
Blanche, later Lady Lessington.
Audrey.
John.
Robert.
Secrets (play), R. Besier & May Edginton, 1922.

Carlton, Mary. *The Middle Watch* (play), Ian Hay & S. King-Hall, 1929.

Carlyle, lawyer to Ballantrae. *The Master of Ballantrae,* R. L. Stevenson, 1889.

Carlyle, Archibald, m. (1) Lady Isabel Vane.
Their children: **Isabel.**
William.
Archibald.
(2) Barbara Hare.
Cornelia, his half-sister.
East Lynne, Mrs Henry Wood, 1861.

Carlyle, Aubrey, author.
Gloria, his wife.
'The Hunter after Wild Beasts' (s.s.), *These Charming People,* M. Arlen, 1920.

Carlyle, Lady Mary. *Monsieur Beaucaire* (play), Booth Tarkington, 1902.

Carlyle, Poppy. *Sinister Street,* C. Mackenzie, 1913.

Carlyon, Captain Seymour ('Sahib').
His wife (**'Marmy'**).
George-Ann, their daughter.
Richard (Ricky), their son.
The Young in Heart, I. A. R. Wylie, 1939.

Carmichael, Augustus, poet. *To The Lighthouse,* Virginia Woolf, 1927.

Carmichael, Christabel, m. Will Herries. *Judith Paris,* Hugh Walpole, 1931.

Carmichael, Miss Louise, aunt of Medwin Blair. *The Prodigal Heart,* Susan Ertz, 1950.

Carmichael, William David, an alcoholic solicitor.
Edna, his wife.
Madge, their daughter.
Norman, their son.
Time, Gentlemen! Time!, Norah Hoult, 1930.

Carmine, Captain Lawrence, authority on the Orient and friend of Britling. *Mr Britling Sees It Through,* H. G. Wells, 1916.

Carn, Lady Elizabeth.
Percival, her husband who deserted her.
Her two dead children.
The Case for the Defence, Mary Fitt, 1958.

Carnaby, Earl of, brilliant *roué.* *Tono Bungay,* H. G. Wells, 1909.

Carnaby, Sir Mortimer, friend of the Regent and a scoundrel. *The Amateur Gentleman,* J. Farnol, 1913.

Carnach, Jimmy.
Jimmy, Sen., his father, lobster fisher.
Cormorant Crag, G. Manville Fenn, 1895.

Carnal, Lord, in love with Jocelyn Leigh. *By Order of the Company,* Mary Johnston, 1900.

Carne, Clinton, Californian artist, in love with Tiphany Lane. *The Face of Clay,* H. A. Vachell, 1906.

Carne, Robert, central character, sporting farmer.
Muriel, his wife, daughter of Lord Sedgmire, in an asylum.
Midge, their daughter.
William, his brother, architect.
Mavis, his wife.
South Riding, Winifred Holtby, 1936.

Carnehan, Peachey Taliaferro. 'The Man who would be King' (s.s.), *Wee Willie Winkie,* R. Kipling, 1888.

Caro, Avice.
Her mother.
Jim, her cousin, whom she marries.
Ann Avice, their daughter, m. Isaac Pierston.
The Well Beloved, T. Hardy, 1897.

Carr, missioner, Yanrin.
His wife.
Aissa Saved, Joyce Cary, 1932.

Carr, Hugo. 'When the Nightingale Sang in Berkeley Square' (s.s.), *These Charming People,* M. Arlen, 1920.

Carr, Sir Johnson ('Juggernaut'), one-time fag to Rev. Brian Vereker, m. Daphne Vereker. *A Safety Match,* Ian Hay, 1911.

Carr, Katherine, central character of series.
Dr Phillip, her father.
Her sisters:
Elsie.
Clover.
Dorry.
Phil, her brother.
Helen, her cousin.
What Katy Did and others, Susan Coolidge, 1872–86.

Carr, Wilfred. 'The Well' (s.s.), *The Lady of the Barge,* W. W. Jacobs, 1902.

Carrasco, Don Ramon. *The Plumed Serpent,* D. H. Lawrence, 1926.

Carraway, Nick, narrator. *The Great Gatsby,* F. Scott Fitzgerald, 1925.

Carraze, Delphine (Mme Delphine).
Olive, her daughter.
'Madame Delphine' (s.s.), *Old Creole Days,* G. W. Cable, 1879.

Carrel, Monsieur, artist and head of an art school, *Trilby,* George du Maurier, 1894.

Carrera, Felipe, 'Admiral.' *Cabbages and Kings,* O. Henry, 1905.

Carrick, m. Jessie Cardross. *The Firing Line,* R. W. Chambers, 1908.

Carrick, Earl of, brother of Lady Augusta Yorke. *The Channings,* Mrs Henry Wood, 1862.

Carrickfergus, Mrs Marianne Caroline Matilda, rich, vulgar and good-hearted widow, m. Andrew Montfitchet. *A Shabby Genteel Story,* 1840, and, as Mrs Montfitchet, *The Adventures of Philip,* 1861–2. W. M. Thackeray.

Carrickson, Mrs, employer of Violet Ustis. *A New Departure* (s.s.), R. S. Hichens.

Carrington, young airman. *The Purple Plain,* H. E. Bates, 1947.

Carrington, Sir Henry (Rico), Australian artist, m. Lou Witt. *St Mawr,* D. H. Lawrence, 1925.

Carrington, Lukey, science teacher. *The Food of the Gods,* H. G. Wells, 1904.

Carrington, Major Miles, surveyor-general, Virginia.
Betty, his daughter, friend of Pat Verney.
The Old Dominion, Mary Johnston, 1899.

Carroll, Charles. *See Naples and Die,* Elmer Rice, 1932.

Carroll, Sir William (later Lord), head of shipping line.
Diana, his wife.
All Our Yesterdays, H. M. Tomlinson, 1930.

Carruthers, central character and narrator. *The Riddle of the Sands,* E. Childers, 1903.

Carruthers, Dame, housekeeper to the Tower of London, m. Sergeant Meryll, *The Yeomen of the Guard* (comic opera), Gilbert & Sullivan, 1888.

Carruthers, Lady Alice. *Miss Esperance and Mr Wycherley,* L. Allen Harker, 1908.

Carruthers, Sir Andrew, K.B.E.
Maggie, his wife.
Pink Sugar, O. Douglas, 1924.

Carruthers, Crosbie, m. Barbara Blenkinsop. *The Diary of a Provincial Lady,* E. M. Delafield, 1930.

Carruthers, Gordon, schoolboy at Fernhurst, central character. *The Loom of Youth,* A. Waugh, 1917.

Carruthers, Mabel.
Her mother.
Sinister Street, C. Mackenzie, 1913.

Carsley, Professor Sir George, eminent scientist. *Sanders of the River,* E. Wallace, 1911.

Carslogie, Laird of. *The Abbot,* W. Scott, 1820.

Carson, head of the school. 'The Last Term,' *Stalky & Co.,* R. Kipling, 1899.

Carson, Harry, rival of Jem Wilson.
His sisters:
Sophia.
Helen.
Amy.
Mary Barton, Mrs Gaskell, 1848.

Carson, Kit (hist.), American hunter. *Death Comes for the Archbishop,* Willa Cather, 1927.

Carson, Louis. *The Villa Desirée* (s.s.), May Sinclair.

Carson, Rev. Robert.
Sanchia, his wife.
Bob, his son by his first wife.
Robert's Wife (play), St John Ervine, 1937.

Carson, Thelma, with whom Eddie Ryan falls in love. *The Silence of History,* James T. Farrell, 1963.

Carstairs, Colonel.
Christabel, his daughter.
'The Head of Caesar' (s.s.), *The Wisdom of Father Brown,* G. K. Chesterton, 1914.

Carstairs, Johnnie, horse dealer and 'packer.' *Campbell's Kingdom,* Hammond Innes, 1952.

Carstone, Richard, ward in Chancery, m. his cousin, Ada Clare. *Bleak House,* C. Dickens, 1853.

Cartaret, Colonel, ('Cold-steel Cartaret'), Rose Maynard's guardian. *Meet Mr Mulliner,* P. G. Wodehouse, 1927.

Cartaret, Julian, friend of Harry Somerford. *Fanny by Gaslight,* M. Sadleir, 1940.

Carter, Lieutenant. 'The Lost Legion' (s.s.), *Many Inventions,* R. Kipling, 1893.

Carter, Bill, night-watchman.
Sally, his wife.
Magnolia Street, L. Golding, 1932.

Carter, Edward. *The Fourth Wall,* A. A. Milne, 1928.

Carter, Everard, schoolmaster, m. Kate Keith.
Bobbie, Angela and **Philip,** their children.
The Barsetshire series, Angela Thirkell, 1933 onwards.

Carter, Gil., a ranch hand. *The Ox-Bow Incident,* Walter Van Tilburg Clark, 1940.

Carter, Henry.
Mabel, his daughter.
Grand Opera, Vicki Baum, 1942.

Carter, Philip, engineer, wrongly imprisoned for embezzlement.
Hazel, his wife.
Timmie, their young son.
The Glass Cell, Patricia Highsmith, 1965.

Carter, Stella, governess to the Crawford children, m. Rev. Robert Brand. *Pink Sugar,* O. Douglas, 1924.

Carteret, Sir Gabriel.
Lady Elizabeth, his wife.
C., M. Baring, 1924.

Carthew, Jim, Sir Johnson Carr's secretary, m. Nina Tallentyre. *A Safety Match,* Ian Hay, 1911.

Carthew, Maud, governess to the Fanes, m. Kenneth Ross.
Enid, her mother.
Her sisters:
Joan.
May.
Nancy.
Sinister Street, 1913, and elsewhere, C. Mackenzie.

Cartledge, James, ruthless business tycoon, schoolboy friend of Ned Bartley, m. Lisette Courtaud. *Both of this Parish,* J. S. Fletcher.

Cartlett, Mr, hotel keeper, Sydney, m. Arabella Fawley, *née* Donn (first bigamously). *Jude the Obscure,* T. Hardy, 1896.

Cartney, Muriel, victim of Philip Sevilla. *Ten Minute Alibi,* A. Armstrong, 1933.

Carton, Sidney, m. Madeleine Sparling. The *Barsetshire* series, Angela Thirkell, 1933 onwards.

Carton, Sydney, guillotined to save Charles Darnay. *A Tale of Two Cities,* C. Dickens, 1859.

Cartoner, Reginald, diplomat, in love with Wanda Bukaty. *The Vultures,* H. Seton Merriman, 1902.

Cartouch, Colonel, Digby's commanding officer. *Digby Grand,* G. Whyte-Melville, 1853.

Cartwright, Oliver, medical attendant to Mrs Strood. *The Jury,* G. Bullett, 1935.

Carve, Ilam.
Cyrus, his brother.
The Great Adventure (play), Arnold Bennett, 1913.

Carvel, Richard, central character and narrator, m. Dorothy Manners.
John, his father.
Elizabeth, his mother.
Lionel, his grandfather.
Grafton, his uncle.
Caroline, his wife, *née* Flaven.
Philip, their son.
Richard Carvel, W. Churchill, 1899.

Carver, Captain, retired. *The Kicklebury's on the Rhine,* W. M. Thackeray, 1850.

Carver, Captain Jonathan. *Northwest Passage,* Kenneth Roberts, 1938.

Carver, Sir Robin, m. Phoebe Thorpe. *Dance of the Years,* Margery Allingham, 1943.

Carvil, Josiah, blind boat-builder.
Bessie, his daughter.
'Tomorrow' (s.s.), *Typhoon,* J. Conrad, 1903.

Cary, Mr, of Clovelly Court.
Will, his son.
Westward Ho!, C. Kingsley, 1855.

Cary, Mrs Sophia, mother of Lucy Batchelor. *Steamboat Gothic,* Frances Parkinson Keyes, 1952.

Caryll, Sir Leslie.
His wife.
The Voice from the Minaret (play), R. S. Hichens, 1919.

Carysbrooke, distant relative of the Earl of Ilbury. *Uncle Silas,* Sheridan le Fanu, 1864.

Casamassina, Prince, m. Christina Light. *Roderick Hudson,* H. James, 1875.

Casaubon, Rev. Edward, m. Dorothea Brooke. *Middlemarch,* George Eliot, 1871–2.

Casby, Christopher, landlord, of Bleeding Heart Yard, father of Flora Finching. *Little Dorrit,* C. Dickens, 1857.

Casca, conspirator against Caesar. *Julius Casear* (play), W. Shakespeare.

Case, island trader, villain, enemy of Wiltshire. 'The Beach of Falesa' (s.s.), *Island Nights' Entertainments,* R. L. Stevenson, 1893.

Casey, Jack, 1st husband of Emma Newcome. *The Newcomes,* W. M. Thackeray, 1853–5.

Casey, James, m. Matty Dwyer. *Handy Andy,* S. Lover, 1842.

Casey, Mrs Nellie, *née* Birdseye. *My Mortal Enemy,* Willa Cather, 1928.

Casey, Sarah, young tinker woman. *The Tinker's Wedding* (play), J. M. Synge, 1909.

Cashel, Roland, central character, m. Mary Leicester.
Godfrey, his father.
Roland Cashel, C. Lever, 1850.

Cashell, Young Mr, wireless enthusiast. 'Wireless' (s.s.), *Traffics and Discoveries,* R. Kipling, 1904.

Cass, Miss, personal secretary to Evelyn Orcham. *Imperial Palace,* Arnold Bennett, 1930.

Cass, Squire.
His sons:
Godfrey
m. (1) Molly Farren.
Eppie, their daughter adopted by Silas Marner, m. Aaron Winthrop;
(2) Nancy Lammeter.
Dunstan, thief and wastrel.
Bob.
Silas Marner, George Eliot, 1861.

Cassandra, prophetess. *Troilus and Cressida* (play), W. Shakespeare.

Cassands, Minnie, *née* Miranda Straw, celebrated artist, owner of 'The Beckoning Lady.'
Tonker, her husband, friend of Albert Campion.
The Beckoning Lady, Margery Allingham, 1955.

Casse-une-Croute, quadroon courtesan. *Moths,* Ouida, 1880.

Cassidy, Hopalong, cowboy hero of many novels, Clarence E. Mulford.

Cassidy, Mame.
Jack, her wife-beating husband.
'A Harlem Tragedy' (s.s.), *The Trimmed Lamp,* O. Henry, 1907.

Cassilis, Frank, central character and narrator, m. Clara Huddlestone. 'The Pavilion on the Links' (s.s.), *New Arabian Nights,* R. L. Stevenson, 1882.

Cassilis, George. *Tancred,* B. Disraeli, 1847.

Cassini, Dr Stephen, prison doctor

who gives drugs to Philip Carter. *The Glass Cell*, Patricia Highsmith, 1965.

Cassio, Othello's lieutenant. *Othello* (play), W. Shakespeare.

Cassius, conspirator against Caesar. *Julius Caesar* (play), W. Shakespeare.

Cassius. *See* CONCAVERTY.

Cassy, slave of Legree. *Uncle Tom's Cabin*, Harriet B. Stowe, 1851.

Casterley, Countess of.
Lady Gertrude Semmering, her daughter, m. Lord Valleys.
The Patrician, J. Galsworthy, 1911.

Castillonnes, Victor de (*né* Cabasse), snobbish and blustering poet. *The Newcomes*, W. M. Thackeray, 1853–5.

Castine, Vanne, scoundrel, friend of Shangois. *The Pomp of the Lavilettes*, Gilbert Parker, 1897.

Castle, Captain. *Sixty-four, Ninety-four*, R. H. Mottram, 1925.

Castle-Cuddy, Lord, friend of Captain Craigengelt. *The Bride of Lammermoor*, W. Scott, 1819.

Castlejordan, Marchioness of (Miriam). *The Amazons* (play), A. W. Pinero, 1893.

Castleton, college friend of Michael Fane. *Sinister Street*, C. Mackenzie, 1913.

Castlewood, Sir Francis Edward, Bt., 1st Viscount.
His children:
George, 2nd Viscount.
Eustace, his son.
Isabel, his daughter.
Thomas.
Rev. Francis.
Thomas, 3rd Viscount, m. (1) Gertrude Maes. *See also* HENRY ESMOND; (2) Isabel, his cousin.
Francis, wrongful successor as 4th Viscount.
Rachel, his wife, *née* Armstrong.
Francis, their son, 5th Viscount (*see below*).
Beatrix, their daughter.
Francis, 1st Earl and 5th Viscount.
m. (1) **Clotilda de Wertheim.**
Eugene, their son, 2nd Earl (*see below*).
Maia, their daughter.
(2) **Anna.**
William, their son.
Fanny, their daughter.
Eugene, 2nd Earl, m. Lydia van den Bosch.
Henry Esmond, 1852, and *The Virginians*, 1857–9, W. M. Thackeray.

Caston, degenerate American artist, shot for cowardice. *The Secret Places of the Heart*, H. G. Wells, 1922.

Castor, Judge Edwin, friend of James Galantry, 'a sad, cold man.'
Frank, his son. *See also* ELIZABETH GALANTRY.
Dance of the Years, Margery Allingham, 1943.

Castorley, Alured. 'Dayspring Mishandled' (s.s.), *Limits and Renewals*, R. Kipling, 1932.

Castracane, Pilade. 'Ippolita in the Hills' (s.s.), *Little Novels of Italy*, M. Hewlett, 1899.

Castries, Miss. 'Kidnapped' (s.s.), *Plain Tales from the Hills*, R. Kipling, 1888.

Castro, Mrs, mysterious widow. *Shall We Join the Ladies?* (play), J. M. Barrie, 1921.

Caswell, Major Wentworth, drunken good-for-nothing.
Azalea Adair, his wife.
'A Municipal Report' (s.s.), *Strictly Business*, O. Henry, 1910.

Casy, Rev. Jim, ex-preacher. *The Grapes of Wrath*, J. Steinbeck, 1939.

Cat, Captain Jack. *Under Milk Wood* (play), Dylan Thomas, 1954.

Catanach, Mrs, midwife. *The Marquis of Lossie*, G. Macdonald, 1877.

Catanei, Vannozza (La Rosa), concubine to Pope Alexander VI; mother of the Borgias. *The Duke of Gandia* (play), A. C. Swinburne, 1908.

Catchpole, Harold, 'greasy and sententious.' *Portrait of a Playboy*, W. Deeping, 1947.

Catchpole, Tom, assistant to Furze.
Mike, his father.
Catherine Furze, M. Rutherford, 1893.

Caterham, John, prominent politician. *The Food of the Gods*, H. G. Wells, 1904.

Cathardis, Dr Gabriel. *Cricket in Heaven*, G. Bullett, 1949.

Catherick, Mrs, sister of Mrs Kempe; part narrator.
Anne, her daughter.
The Woman in White, W. Collins, 1860.

Catherine, wife of Elias, mother of Gerard. *The Cloister and the Hearth*, C. Reade, 1861.

Catherine of Newport, mistress of Julian Avenel and mother of his son. *See* ROLAND GRAEME. *The Monastery*, W. Scott, 1820.

Cathro, Dominie. *Sentimental Tommy*, J. M. Barrie, 1896.

Cato. *Cato* (play), J. Addison, 1713.

Cator, Eddie, local policeman, brother of Elsie Pearce. *A Way through the Wood*, N. Balchin, 1951.

Catskill, Rupert, Secretary of State for War. *Men Like Gods*, H. G. Wells, 1923.

Catt-Wilkins, Rev. Mr.
His wife.
Mr Ingleside, E. V. Lucas, 1910.

Cauchon, Peter, Bishop of Beauvais (hist.). *Saint Joan*, G. B. Shaw, 1924.

Caulfield, Holden, sixteen-year-old schoolboy, central character.
Phoebe, his small sister.
The Catcher in The Rye, J. D. Salinger, 1951.

Caution, Lemmy, 'G' man, alias Perry C. Rice, central character and narrator. *Poison Ivy*, 1937, and others, P. Cheyney.

Cavallini, Madame Margherita. *Romance* (play), E. Sheldon, 1914.

Cavanagh, Eustace, League of Nations official.
Felicity, his wife.
Ronald, their son.
Sheila, their daughter.
The Pied Piper, N. Shute, 1942.

Cave, Mary, close friend of Grace Allonby, m. Sir Humphrey Bosville. *Holmby House*, G. Whyte-Melville, 1860.

Cavendish, John.
Mary, his wife.
Lawrence, his brother. *See also* EMILY INGLETHORP.
The Mysterious Affair at Styles, Agatha Christie, 1920.

Cavendish, Stella. *See* COURTENAY BRUNDIT.

Caversham, The Earl of, K.G., father of Lord Goring. *An Ideal Husband* (play), O. Wilde, 1895.

Cavor, inventor of cavorite, 'opaque to gravity.' *The First Men in the Moon*, H. G. Wells, 1901.

Cawker, William ('Moleskin'), poaching expert.
Mary, his daughter.
The Mother, E. Phillpotts, 1908.

Cawtree, farmer, Little Hintock. *The Woodlanders*, T. Hardy, 1887.

Cawwawkee. *Polly* (comic opera), J. Gay, 1729.

Caxon, Jacob, barber.
Jenny, his daughter.
The Antiquary, W. Scott, 1816.

Cayenne, Mr, industrialist. *Annals of the Parish*, John Galt, 1821.

Cayley, Matthew, cousin and secretary of Mark Abblett. *The Red House Mystery*, A. A. Milne, 1922.

Caylus, Gabrielle de, m. (1) Louis Duke de Nevers; (2) Louis de Gonzague.
Her father.
The Duke's Motto, J. H. McCarthy, 1908.

Cecco, pirate. *Peter Pan* (play), J. M. Barrie, 1904.

Cecil, Mr, of Warborne, Lady Constantine's solicitor. *Two on a Tower*, T. Hardy, 1882.

Cecil, Hon. Bertie, 1st Life Guards.
Viscount Royallieu, his father.
Berkeley, his brother.
Under Two Flags, Ouida, 1867.

Cecile, wife of Valerian. 'The Second Nun's Tale' (poem), *Canterbury Tales*, G. Chaucer, 1373 onwards.

Cecilia, artist. 'The Third Ingredient' (s.s.), *Options*, O. Henry, 1909.

Cedric of Rotherwood, 'proud, fierce, jealous and irritable.' *Ivanhoe*, W. Scott, 1820.

Celestine, maid to Mrs Manderson. *Trent's Last Case*, E. C. Bentley, 1912.

Celia, daughter of Duke Frederick, m. Oliver. *As You Like It* (play), W. Shakespeare.

Celia, a fairy. *Iolanthe* (comic opera), Gilbert & Sullivan, 1882.

Cellini, Mr, leaves Velvet Brown five horses. *National Velvet*, Enid Bagnold, 1935.

Cenci, Beatrice.
Her father.
The Cenci (play), P. B. Shelley, 1819.
Ceneus, a Persian lord. *Tamburlaine,* C. Marlowe, 1587.
Ceres, a spirit. *The Tempest* (play), W. Shakespeare.
Ceria, in charge of hotel grill-room. *Imperial Palace,* Arnold Bennett, 1930.
Cerr-Nore, Charlie.
Rev. Mr Cerr-Nore, Vicar of Rookhurst, his father.
The Beautiful Years, H. Williamson, 1921.
Cesario. *See* VIOLA.
Chaddesley-Corbett, Mrs Veronica. *Love in a Cold Climate,* Nancy Mitford, 1949.
Chadwick, Mr. *The Warden,* A. Trollope, 1855.
Chadwick, Bernard William, commercial traveller.
Frances, his wife.
The Franchise Affair, Josephine Tey, 1948.
Chadwick, Jocelyn, land agent. *Famine,* L. O'Flaherty, 1937.
Chadwick, Leonard. 'Humplebee' (s.s.), *The House of Cobwebs,* G. Gissing, 1906.
Chaffery, James, fraudulent medium and embezzler, stepfather of Ethel Henderson. *Love and Mr Lewisham,* H. G. Wells, 1900.
Chainmail, 'fond of poetry; a poet himself,' *Crotchet Castle,* T. L. Peacock, 1831.
Chakchek, a Greenland falcon. *Tarka the Otter,* H. Williamson, 1927.
Chalk.
His wife.
Dialstone Lane, W. W. Jacobs, 1904.
Chalk, Lieutenant, of the *Goliath.* The *Hornblower* series, C. S. Forester, 1937 onwards.
Chalkfield, Mayor of Casterbridge. *The Mayor of Casterbridge,* T. Hardy, 1886.
Challard, Jan, m. Donald Graeme.
Her sisters: **Helen.**
Barney.
Still She Wished for Company, Margaret Irwin, 1924.
Challenger, Professor G. E., scientist and explorer.
His wife.
The Lost World, 1912, and *The Poison Belt,* 1913, Conan Doyle.
Challis, Alfred Titus (later Sir) ('Titus Scroop,' the well-known novelist), friend of the Arkroyds.
Marianne, his dead wife's sister, whom he marries.
It Never Can Happen Again, W. de Morgan, 1909.
Challis, Henry, anthropologist and local magnate. *The Hampdenshire Wonder,* J. D. Beresford, 1911.
Challoner, Blanche.
Lydia (Mrs Waring).
Alice, m. Sir Francis Levison.
East Lynne, Mrs Henry Wood, 1861.
Challoner, Kitty, m. Charles Crane.
Her father and mother.
The Case for the Defence, Mary Fitt, 1958.
Challong, an Orang-laut. 'A Disturber of Traffic' (s.s.), *Many Inventions,* R. Kipling, 1893.
Chalmers, Carson, wealthy solicitor.
His wife.
'A Madison Square Arabian Night' (s.s.), *The Trimmed Lamp,* O. Henry, 1907.
Chalmers, Primrose, child too interested in psychology for her own good. *The Widow's Cruise,* Nicholas Blake, 1959.
Chamberlayne, Edward.
Lavinia, his wife.
The Cocktail Party, T. S. Eliot, 1950.
Chambers, Frank, a young drifter. *The Postman Always Rings Twice,* James M. Cain, 1934.
Chamont. *The Orphan* (play), T. Otway, 1680.
Champagne, Earl of (Henry), vassal of King Philip. *The Talisman,* W. Scott, 1825.
Champignac, Monsieur de, attaché, French Embassy, London. *Vanity Fair,* W. M. Thackeray, 1847–8.
Champion, Brenda, mistress of Rex Mottram. *Brideshead Revisited,* E. Waugh, 1945.
Champion, Hon. Jane, central character, m. Garth Dalmain. *The Rosary,* Florence Barclay, 1909.
Chan Hung, mandarin of the eighth grade. *The Wallet of Kai Lung,* E. Bramah, 1900.
Chance, Miss Elizabeth, sister of

murderess, m. Tenbruggen. *The Legacy of Cain*, W. Collins, 1889.

Chancellor, the Lord, husband of Iolanthe and father of Strephon. *Iolanthe* (comic opera), Gilbert & Sullivan, 1882.

Chancellor, Olive.
  Adeline, her sister (Mrs Luna).
The Bostonians, H. James, 1886.

Chandler, carrier. *The Wrong Box*, R. L. Stevenson & Lloyd Osbourne, 1889.

Chandler, Robin.
  Henry, his younger brother, temporarily eng. to Iris Pinsent.
Bachelors (s.s.), Hugh Walpole.

Chandler, Tommy, friend of Ignatius Gallagher.
  Annie, his wife.
'A Little Cloud' (s.s.), *The Dubliners*, James Joyce, 1914.

Chang, lama, Shangri-la. *Lost Horizon*, J. Hilton, 1933.

Chang-Ch'un, 'one of the wealthiest men in Canton.' *The Wallet of Kai Lung*, E. Bramah, 1900.

Channing, Elizabeth. *Secrets* (play), R. Besier & May Edginton, 1922.

Channing, James.
  His wife.
  Their children:
    Hamish, m. Ellen Huntly.
    Arthur.
    Constance, m. William Yorke.
    Tom.
    Annabel.
    Charlie.
The Channings, Mrs Henry Wood, 1862.

Chant, Mercy.
  Dr Chant, her father.
Tess of the D'Urbervilles, T. Hardy, 1891.

Chantry-Pigg, Rev. the Hon. Father Hugh, 'an ancient bigot.' *The Towers of Trebizond*, Rose Macaulay, 1956.

Chapel, Arnold, partner of Peter Gresham, m. Denham Dobie. *Crewe Train*, Rose Macaulay, 1926.

Chapin, George, American millionaire.
  Sophie, his wife.
'A Habitation Enforced' (s.s.), *Actions and Reactions*, R. Kipling, 1909.

Chapin, Joe, politician.
  Edith, his ambitious wife.
  Ann, their daughter.
  Joby, their son.
Ten North Frederick, John O'Hara, 1956.

Chapman, Labour M.P., friend of Thomas Doloreine. *The Power House*, J. Buchan, 1916.

Chapman, Dr, school doctor, Kensingtowe. *Tell England*, E. Raymond, 1922.

Chapman, Zedorah. *Counsellor-at-Law* (play), Elmer Rice, 1931.

Charegite, a religious fanatic. *The Talisman*, W. Scott, 1825.

Charisi, Daniel.
  Ephraim, his son, father of Daniel Deronda.
Daniel Deronda, George Eliot, 1876.

Charity. *See* PRUDENCE.

Charles, Dauphin, later **Charles VII** (hist.). *Henry the Sixth* (play), W. Shakespeare. *Saint Joan* (play), G. B. Shaw, 1924.

Charles, butler. *The Last of Mrs Cheyney* (play), F. Lonsdale, 1925.

Charles. *The Skin Game* (play), J. Galsworthy, 1920.

Charles, wrestler. *As You Like It*, W. Shakespeare.

Charles VI, King of France (hist.). *Henry the Fifth* (play), W. Shakespeare.

Charles, Uncle, central character and narrator. *Last Recollections of My Uncle Charles*, N. Balchin, 1954.

Charles, Helena, friend of Alison Porter and temporary mistress of Jimmy. *Look Back in Anger*, J. Osborne, 1956.

Charles, Nick, private investigator, central character and narrator.
  Nora, his wife.
The Thin Man, 1932, and others, D. Hammett.

Charley, marine store dealer. *David Copperfield*, C. Dickens, 1850.

Charlie, Egdon youth attached to Eustacia Vye. *The Return of the Native*, T. Hardy, 1878.

Charlotte, maid to Mrs Sowerberry. *Oliver Twist*, C. Dickens, 1838.

Charlotte, Lady, probationer nurse. *A Kiss for Cinderella* (play), J. M. Barrie, 1916.

Charlson, Dr, Port Breedy. 'Fellow Townsmen,' *Wessex Tales*, T. Hardy, 1888.

Charlton, Mr (Charley), Income Tax official, m. Mariette Larkin. *The Darling Buds of May*, H. E. Bates, 1958.

Charlton, Conker (Charley), strong-arm man, a fixer. *Thin Air*, John Pudney, 1961.

Charmazel. *See* PRINCESS ZISKA.

Charmian, attendant to Cleopatra. *Antony and Cleopatra* (play), W. Shakespeare. *Caesar and Cleopatra* (play), G. B. Shaw, 1900.

Charmond, Felice, widow. *The Woodlanders*, T. Hardy, 1887.

Charney, Ed, big shot gangster. *Appointment in Samarra*, John O'Hara, 1935.

Charolois. *The Fatal Dowry* (play), P. Massinger, 1632.

Charpot, Suzanne, maid to Domini Enfilden. *The Garden of Allah*, R. S. Hichens, 1904.

Charrington, Mr, antique dealer and member of Thought Police. *1984*, G. Orwell, 1949.

Charron, Pierre, fur trader. *Shadows on the Rock*, Willa Cather, 1932.

Charteris, Colin, a Serbian 'saint' who leads a hippy crusade. *Barefoot in the Head*, Brian W. Aldiss, 1969.

Charteris, Leonard. *The Philanderer* (play), G. B. Shaw, 1893.

Charteris, Sir Patrick, baron of Kinfauns, Provost of Perth. *The Fair Maid of Perth*, W. Scott, 1828.

Charteris, Winifred ('Winsome'), owner of the lilac sunbonnet, central character, m. Ralph Peden. *The Lilac Sunbonnet*, S. R. Crockett, 1894.

Charters, Sir Eldon, K.C., chancellor. *Laura's Bishop*, G. A. Birmingham, 1949.

Charters, Lord Magnus, college friend of Arthur Pendennis. *Pendennis*, W. M. Thackeray, 1848–50.

Chartersea, Duke of, dissolute rake. *Richard Carvel*, W. Churchill, 1899.

Chartley, farmer.
His wife.
The Prodigal Heart, Susan Ertz, 1950.

Chartres, Sir John, nerve specialist. 'In the Same Boat' (s.s.), *A Diversity of Creatures*, R. Kipling, 1917.

Charwell, Rt Rev. Cuthbert, Bishop of Porthminster.
Elizabeth, his wife.
His children:
Gen. Sir Conway, K.C.B., C.M.G.
Hubert, D.S.O., his son, m. Jean Tasbrugh.
Dinny, his daughter (central character of the last three volumes), m. Eustace Dornford, K.C.
Clare, his daughter, m. Sir Gerald Corven; later mistress of Tony Croom.
Adrian, m. as 2nd husband, Diana Ferse.
Two children.
Lionel, judge.
Lady Alison, his wife.
Wilmet.
Rev. Hilary.
Mary, his wife.
The *Forsyte* series, J. Galsworthy, 1906–33.

Chase, Elyot.
Sibyl, his wife.
Private Lives (play), N. Coward, 1930.

Chase, Jack, petty officer. *White-Jacket*, Herman Melville, 1850.

Chase, Peregrine, central character.
Phillida, his aunt.
The Heir, V. Sackville-West, 1922.

Chase, Solomon, of Lincoln's Cabinet (hist.). *Abraham Lincoln*, J. Drinkwater, 1918.

Chase, Tom, lieutenant, R.N. *Love Among the Chickens*, P. G. Wodehouse, 1906.

Chasuble, Canon Frederick, D.D., m. Lætitia Prism. *The Importance of Being Earnest* (play), O. Wilde, 1895.

Chat, Dame, alehouse keeper. *Gammer Gurton's Needle* (play), Anonymous, 1575.

Chateaucloux, chamberlain to Princess Clementina Sobieska. *Clementina*, A. E. W. Mason, 1901.

Chater, Mr and Mrs, Mary Humfray's employers. *Once Aboard the Lugger*, A. S. M. Hutchinson, 1908.

Chatillon, French Ambassador. *King John* (play), W. Shakespeare.

Chator, Rev. Mark, friend of Michael Fane. *Sinister Street*, C. Mackenzie, 1913.

Chatteris, Brookfield headmaster. *Goodbye, Mr Chips,* J. Hilton, 1934.

Chatteris, Harry, one-time fiancé of Adeline Glendower. *The Sea Lady,* H. G. Wells, 1902.

Chatterley, Sir Clifford, baronet paralysed from waist down, Nottinghamshire landowner.
  Constance, his wife.
Lady Chatterley's Lover, D. H. Lawrence, 1928.

Chatterly, Simon, 'man of religion.' *St Ronan's Well,* W. Scott, 1824.

Chattersworth, Emily, friend of Lanny Budd. *Dragon's Teeth,* Upton Sinclair, 1942.

Chauncey, Ellen.
  Her father and mother.
The Wide, Wide World, Elizabeth Wetherell, 1850.

Chauvelin, French agent. *The Scarlet Pimpernel,* Baroness Orczy, 1905.

Chavenay, Marquis de. *The Duke's Motto,* J. H. McCarthy, 1908.

Chaver, Manuel, Kit Carson's wealthy rival. *Death Comes for the Archbishop,* Willa Cather, 1927.

Chawk, grocer.
  Gladys, his wife.
    George, their son.
Tom Tiddler's Ground, E. Shanks, 1934.

'Chawley' (alias Cove, Covey, Low Covey). *No. 5 John Street,* R. Whiteing, 1902.

Chawner, wholesale stationer, Bursley. *The Old Wives' Tale,* Arnold Bennett, 1908.

Chawner, schoolfellow of Dick Bultitude. *Vice Versa,* F. Anstey, 1882.

Chayse, Harberry, arch-criminal.
  Charles, his son, alias Charles Frene, Willie the Goop.
Poison Ivy, P. Cheyney, 1937.

Cheadle, Sir Albert, K.B.E.
  His wife.
  Dudley, their son.
We're Here, D. Mackail, 1947.

Chedglow, Percy, apprentice, *Blackgauntlet. The Bird of Dawning,* J. Masefield, 1933.

Cheeryble, the brothers, Ned and Charles.
  Frank, their nephew, m. Kate Nickleby.
Nicholas Nickleby, C. Dickens, 1839.

Cheesewright, Mr, dentist and churchwarden. *Another Year,* R. C. Sherriff, 1948.

Cheetham, John, wood-carver. *Put Yourself in his Place,* C. Reade, 1870.

Cheezle, Miss. *At Mrs Beam's* (play), C. K. Munro, 1923.

Cheggs, Alick, m. Sophia Wackles. *The Old Curiosity Shop,* C. Dickens, 1841.

Chelifer, Francis, Ed. of a livestock paper.
  His mother.
Those Barren Leaves, A. Huxley, 1925.

Chell, Countess of.
  The Earl, her husband, 'ornamental' mayor of Bursley.
The Card, Arnold Bennett, 1911.

Chell, John.
  His wife.
  Jacky, their son.
  Emily and **Dorothy,** their daughters.
Pip, Ian Hay, 1907.

Chelles, Marquis of (Raymond), 3rd husband of Undine Spragg. *The Custom of the Country,* Edith Wharton, 1913.

Cheney, Mrs Malvina, nosey neighbour. 'The Astral Body of a U.S. Mail Truck' (s.s.), *A Story That Ends With A Scream,* James Leo Herlihy, 1968.

Cheng, Brander, orchestra conductor. *The Cue* (s.s.), T. Burke.

Cheng Huan. *The Chink and the Child* (s.s.), T. Burke.

Chepstow, Mrs Ruby (Bella Donna), social outcast, widow of Wodehouse Chepstow, m. (2), Hon. Nigel Armine. *Bella Donna,* R. S. Hichens, 1909.

Cheron, Madame, sister of St Aubert, m. (2) Montoni. *The Mysteries of Udolpho,* Mrs Radcliffe, 1790.

Cherrington, Hilda, central character.
  Eustace, her brother.
  Barbara, her sister.
  Alfred, their father.
  Sarah, their aunt.
The Shrimp and the Anemone, etc., L. P. Hartley, 1944 onwards.

Cherry, Bob, one of the Famous Five at Greyfriars. The *Billy Bunter* series, Frank Richards.

Chervil, Lord and Lady. *Mrs Miniver,* Jan Struther, 1939.

Cheshire, Anne (Anne Raven), m. Gerard le Faber. *The Five Sons of Le Faber,* E. Raymond, 1945.

Cheshire, Duke of (Cecil), m. Virginia Otis. *The Canterville Ghost* (s.s.), O. Wilde, 1887.

Cheshire Cat, The. *Alice in Wonderland,* L. Carroll, 1865.

Chesney, Colonel Sir Francis, Bt, late Indian Service.
Jack, his son, undergraduate.
Charley's Aunt (play), Brandon Thomas, 1892.

Chesney, Marcus.
Joe, his brother. *See also* MARJORIE WILLS.
The Black Spectacles, J. Dickson Carr, 1948.

Chesney, Stella, wife of Augie March. *The Adventures of Augie March,* Saul Bellow, 1953.

Chester, pearler, wrecker, whaler. *Lord Jim,* J. Conrad, 1900.

Chester, Sir John.
Edward, his son, m. Emma Haredale.
Barnaby Rudge, C. Dickens, 1841.

Chesterton, Arthur, bailiff. *The City of Beautiful Nonsense,* E. T. Thurston, 1909.

Cheswardine, Stephen.
Vera, his wife.
These Twain, Arnold Bennett, 1916.

Chettam, Sir James, m. Celia Brooke. *Middlemarch,* Geo. Eliot, 1871–2.

Chetwynd, Miss Aline, schoolmistress.
Elizabeth, her sister.
The Old Wives' Tale, Arnold Bennett, 1908.

Cheveley, Mrs Laura. *An Ideal Husband* (play), O. Wilde, 1895.

Chevenix, Major. *St Ives,* R. L. Stevenson, 1897.

Cheveral, Sir Edward. *Incomparable Bellairs,* A. & E. Castle, 1904.

Cheverel, Sir Christopher.
Henrietta, his wife.
'Mr Gilfil's Love Story,' *Scenes of Clerical Life,* George Eliot, 1857.

Cheviot, Rev. Charles, m. Mary May. *The Trial,* Charlotte M. Yonge, 1864.

Chew, Wilfred (Chu-wei-fu), Chinese barrister. *Tobit Transplanted,* Stella Benson, 1931.

Cheyne, Harvey, central character, spoilt boy reformed by life on a fishing-boat.
Harvey, his father.
Constance, his mother.
Captains Courageous, R. Kipling, 1897.

Cheyne, Reginald, servant of Lord Glenallan.
Elspeth, his daughter, m. Mucklebackit.
The Antiquary, W. Scott, 1816.

Cheyney, Mrs. *The Last of Mrs Cheyney* (play), F. Lonsdale, 1925.

Cheyneys, Simon, shipbuilder. 'Simple Simon' (s.s.), *Rewards and Fairies,* R. Kipling, 1910.

Chibiabos, musician, friend of Hiawatha. *The Song of Hiawatha* (poem), H. W. Longfellow, 1855.

Chichely, coroner. *Middlemarch,* George Eliot, 1871–2.

Chichester, enemy of Barnabas Barty. *The Amateur Gentleman,* J. Farnol, 1913.

Chichester, James, ex-lover of Marion Lane. *The Cotillon* (s.s.), L. P. Hartley.

Chick, John.
Louisa, his wife, *née* Dombey.
Dombey and Son, C. Dickens, 1848.

Chickenstalker, Anne, shopkeeper. *A Christmas Carol,* C. Dickens, 1843.

Chickerell, Mr and Mrs, Ethelberta Petherwin's parents.
Their other children:
Georgina.
Gwendoline.
Cornelia.
Myrtle.
Picotee, m. Christopher Julian.
Joey.
Dan.
The Hand of Ethelberta, T. Hardy, 1876.

Chickney, Lord. *Bealby,* H. G. Wells, 1915.

Chickweed, Conkey, burglar. *Oliver Twist,* C. Dickens, 1838.

Chidleigh, Lady (Harriet). (Family name Clare.)
Her children:
Lucian, Lord Chidleigh.
Fanny, m. Daunt.
George.
Vesey.
Juliana, central character, m. R. E. Daintree.
The Dowager Lady Chidleigh.
Emily, her daugher.
Still She Wished for Company, Margaret Irwin, 1924.

Chiffinch, Sister. The *Barsetshire* series, Angela Thirkell, 1933 onwards.

Chiffinch, Tom, 'prime master of the King's pleasures.'
Kate, his mistress, given wifely status.
Peveril of the Peak, W. Scott, 1822.

Chil, the kite, to whom all things come in the end. 'How Fear Came' and elsewhere, *The Jungle Books,* R. Kipling, 1894–5.

Chilcote, John, M.P., drug addict.
Eve, his wife.
John Chilcote, M.P., Katherine C. Thurston, 1904.

Chilcox, Parliamentary candidate. *The Patrician,* J. Galsworthy, 1911.

Child, Bob, landlord, the Honour Bound. 'Mine Host,' *Last Recollections of My Uncle Charles,* N. Balchin, 1954.

Child, Sir Joshua, merchant and fortune-hunter. *Henry Esmond,* W. M. Thackeray, 1852.

Childe, Josephine. *Berry and Co.,* Dornford Yates, 1920.

Childs, John.
Susan, his daughter, m. Jake Cram.
Evelyn, his daughter, m. Roger Western.
A Lamp for Nightfall, E. Caldwell, 1952.

Childs, Schuyler (Sky), millionaire playboy, m. Charlotte (Lovey) Lewis. *Lovey Childs,* John O'Hara, 1969.

Chiles, John. 'The Superstitious Man's Story,' *Life's Little Ironies,* T. Hardy, 1894.

Chillingford, Rev. Thomas.
His wife.
Dorothy, their daughter, friend of Elizabeth Trant.
The Good Companions, J. B. Priestley, 1929.

Chillingworth, Dr. *The Scarlet Letter,* N. Hawthorne, 1850.

Chillip, Dr, the Copperfield family doctor. *David Copperfield,* C. Dickens, 1850.

Chilson, Hetty, keeper of brothel in Chicago. *Show Boat,* Edna Ferber, 1926.

Chilt, J. Ruskin, M.P. *Mr Fortune Finds a Pig,* H. C. Bailey, 1943.

Chiltern, Lord (Oswald Standish), son of the Earl of Brentford, m. Violet Effingham. *Phineas Finn,* 1869, and elsewhere, A. Trollope.

Chiltern, Sir Robert.
Gertrude, his wife.
Mabel, his sister.
An Ideal Husband (play), O. Wilde, 1895.

Chilton, Dr. *Polyanna,* Eleanor H. Porter, 1913.

Chilvers, Daisy, shoemaker's daughter, m. Joseph Geaiter. *Joseph and his Brethren,* H. W. Freeman, 1928.

Chin Mao Shu. *Ming Yellow,* J. P. Marquand, 1935.

Ching, Wang-Lung's steward. *The Good Earth,* Pearl Buck, 1931.

Chingachgook, Mohican chief. The *Leatherstocking* series, J. Fenimore Cooper, 1823–46.

Chinn, John (the Second), grandson of John Chinn the First.
Lionel, his father.
'The Tomb of his Ancestors' (s.s.), *The Day's Work,* R. Kipling, 1898.

Chinnery, Elmer. *Summer Moonshine,* P G. Wodehouse, 1938.

Chinnery, Joseph, porter. *Desperate Remedies,* T. Hardy, 1871.

Chinnock, Bet, a madwoman. *A Glastonbury Romance,* J. C. Powys, 1932.

Chinston, Dr. *The Mystery of a Hansom Cab,* F. Hume, 1886.

Chipley, Elly, actress known as Lenore La Verne, m. Harold Westbrook. *Show Boat,* Edna Ferber, 1926.

Chipping, Mr (Mr Chips).
Katherine, his dead wife.
Goodbye, Mr Chips, J. Hilton, 1934.

Chirac, Father, friend of Gerald Scales. *The Old Wives' Tale,* Arnold Bennett, 1908.

Chirnside, Quartermaster. *The Crime at Vanderlyndens,* R. H. Mottram, 1920.

Chiron, Tamora's son. *Titus Andronicus* (play), W. Shakespeare.

Chisholm, Canon Diccon, relative of the Penriddockes.
Adela, his sister, m. George Norrington.
For Us in the Dark, Naomi Royde-Smith, 1937.

Chisholm, Eustace ('Ace'), narrative poet in Chicago.
Carla, his wife.
Eustace Chisholm and the Works, James Purdy, 1968.

Chitterlow, Harry, playwright, friend of Kipps, whose fortune he makes.
His wife.
Kipps, H. G. Wells, 1905.

Chivery, John.
His father, turnkey at the Marshalsea.
His mother, tobacconist.
Little Dorrit, C. Dickens, 1857.

Chloe, a girl graduate. *Princess Ida* (comic opera), Gilbert & Sullivan, 1884.

Chloe, Martin Lillywhite's 'girl-friend.' *Lise Lillywhite*, Margery Sharp, 1951.

Chloe. *The Skin Game*, J. Galsworthy, 1920.

Chloris, a hamadryad. *Jurgen*, J. B. Cabell, 1921.

Chollop, Hannibal. *Martin Chuzzlewit*, C. Dickens, 1844.

Cholmondeley, of Vale Royal. *Peveril of the Peak*, W. Scott, 1822.

Cholmondeley, Cuthbert, squire to Lord Dudley Guilford. *The Tower of London*, W. H. Ainsworth, 1840.

Cholmondeley, Sir Richard, Lieutenant of the Tower. *The Yeomen of the Guard* (comic opera), Gilbert & Sullivan, 1888.

Chowbok (Kahabuka), native chief. *Erewhon*, S. Butler, 1872.

Chowne, Farmer.
His wife.
Adam Bede, George Eliot, 1859.

Choyse, Rev. Mr, m. Miss Merriman. The *Barsetshire* series, Angela Thirkell, 1933 onwards.

Chremes, learned Greek. *The Wonderful History of Titus and Gisippus* (s.s.), Sir T. Elyot, *c.* 1540.

Chrestoff, Madame, prima donna. *No Other Tiger*, A. E. W. Mason, 1927.

Christabel. *Christabel* (poem), S. T. Coleridge, 1816.

Christal, Martin, 'broker and apraiser.' *Peveril of the Peak*, W. Scott, 1823.

Christfield, soldier from Indiana. *Three Soldiers*, John dos Passos, 1921.

Christian (formerly Graceless), central character.
Christiana, his penitent wife.
Pilgrim's Progress, J. Bunyan, 1678, 1684.

Christian, Mr, neighbour and friend of Percy Munn. *Night Rider*, Robert Penn Warren, 1939.

Christian, Edward, 'demon of vengeance,' all-round villain; also called Dick Gaulesse and Simon Canter.
William, his brother.
Dame Christian, William's widow.
Fenella, daughter of Edward, but brought up believing she was William's daughter; posed for years as a deaf mute.
Peveril of the Peak, W. Scott, 1822.

Christian, Lady Mary, m. Justin.
Philip, her brother.
The Passionate Friends, H. G. Wells, 1913.

Christian, Maurice (real name Henry Scaddon), adventurer. *Felix Holt*, George Eliot, 1866.

Christie, Anna, *see* ANNA CHRISTOPHERSON.

Christie, Christine (Kirsty), m. Rev. Andrew Hamilton. *The Setons*, O. Douglas, 1917.

Christie, Jack, subeditor; friend of Mr Ingleside. *Mr Ingleside*, E. V. Lucas, 1910.

Christie, John, ship's chandler.
Nelly, his jolly wife.
Sandie, his father.
The Fortunes of Nigel, W. Scott, 1822.

Christie of Clinthill, 'henchman' of Julian Avenel. *The Monastery*, W. Scott, 1820.

Christily, Adam Yestreen's servant. *Farewell, Miss Julie Logan*, J. M. Barrie, 1932.

Christine (The Pretty Lady), 'accidental daughter of a prostitute.' *The Pretty Lady*, Arnold Bennett, 1918.

Christmas, Joe, white Negro, central character.
Doc Hines, his grandfather.
Light in August, William Faulkner, 1932.

Christophe, herdsman. 'The Bull that Thought' (s.s.), *Debits and Credits*, R. Kipling, 1926.

Christopher Robin, central character. *When We Were Very Young* (poems), 1924, *Winnie the Pooh*, 1926, etc., A. A. Milne.

Christopherson, book collector. *Christopherson* (s.s.), G. Gissing.

Christopherson, Chris.
Anna, his daughter.
Anna Christie (play), E. O'Neill, 1922.

Christy, Camilla, m. (1) Rev. Ernest Bellamy; (2) Matthew Haslam; (3) Dominic Spong.
Her mother.
Men and Wives, Ivy Compton-Burnett, 1931.

Chubb, William, landlord of the Sugar Loaf, Sprexton. *Felix Holt,* George Eliot, 1866.

Chubinov, Vassili Iulievitch, revolutionary son of a lawyer. *The Birds Fall Down,* Rebecca West, 1966.

Chuckster, clerk to Mr Witherden. *The Old Curiosity Shop,* C. Dickens, 1841.

Chuffey, clerk to Anthony Chuzzlewit. *Martin Chuzzlewit,* C. Dickens, 1844.

Chuffnell, Lord (Marmaduke), m. Pauline Stoker.
The Dowager Lady Chuffnell, his Aunt Myrtle.
Seabury, her son by 1st husband.
Thank You, Jeeves, P. G. Wodehouse, 1934.

Chumly, Captain John, ex-commander of the *Bully-Sawyer*; guardian of Lady Cleone Meredith. *The Amateur Gentleman,* J. Farnol, 1913.

Chung Hi. *The Letter* (play), W. S. Maugham, 1927.

Churchill, Ethel. *Ethel Churchill,* L. E. Landon, 1837.

Churchill, Florence, m. Lewis Dodd.
Charles, her father.
The Constant Nymph, Margaret Kennedy, 1924.

Churchill, Frank, son of Mr Weston by 1st wife, assumed his uncle's name, m. Jane Fairfax.
His uncle and aunt.
Emma, Jane Austen, 1816.

Churton. 'The Bisara of Pooree' (s.s.), *Plain Tales from the Hills,* R. Kipling, 1888.

Chuzzlewit, Martin the Younger, central character, m. Mary Graham.
Martin, his grandfather, cousin to Pecksniff.
Anthony, brother of old Martin.
Jonas, his son, m. Mercy Pecksniff.
Toby (decd.).
Diggory.
George, bachelor cousin of Martin.
Mrs Ned, widow of another brother of old Martin.
Martin Chuzzlewit, C. Dickens, 1844.

Chyne, Millicent, fiancée of both Jack and Guy Oscard. *With Edged Tools,* H. Seton Merriman, 1894.

Cicero, senator. *Julius Caesar* (play), W. Shakespeare.

'Cigarette,' a *vivandière. Under Two Flags,* Ouida, 1867.

Cignolesi, Marietta, servant to Peter Marchdale. *The Cardinal's Snuff-box,* H. Harland, 1900.

Cimon, Greek engineer. *Unending Crusade,* R. E. Sherwood, 1932.

Cinderella. *See* MISS THING.

Cinna, conspirator against Caesar. *Julius Caesar* (play), W. Shakespeare.

Cino, poet. 'Messer Cino and the Live Coal' (s.s.), *Little Novels of Italy,* M. Hewlett, 1899.

Cinqbars, Viscount, 2nd Earl of Ringwood; young, dissipated and despicable. *A Shabby Genteel Story,* 1840, and elsewhere, W. M. Thackeray.

Cintré, Claire de. *The American,* H. James, 1877.

Cissie, nurse to Philadelphia Buckstead. 'Marklake Witches' (s.s.), *Rewards and Fairies,* R. Kipling, 1910.

Civility. *See* LEGALITY.

Clack, Miss Drusilla, niece of the late Sir J. Verinder, and part narrator. *The Moonstone,* W. Collins, 1868.

Claelia, Princess, patroness of Gerard Eliasson. *The Cloister and the Hearth,* C. Reade, 1861.

Clagett, Wyseman, King's Attorney. *Northwest Passage,* K. Roberts, 1938.

Claggart, John, master-at-arms on H.M.S. *Indomitable. Billy Budd,* Herman Melville, 1924.

Clairval, Madame, aunt of Valancourt. *The Mysteries of Udolpho,* Mrs Radcliffe, 1794.

Clairveaux, Toussaint, philosopher and instructor of Anthony in French. *Anthony Adverse,* Hervey Allen, 1934.

Clall, Mrs Eglantine, cook. *The Sailor's Return,* David Garnett, 1925.

Clancy, Jamesy.
Archibald, his brother, grocer.
'A Stroke of Business' (s.s.), *Sun on the Water,* L. A. G. Strong, 1940.

Clandon, Mrs Lanerey, wife of Fergus Crampton.
Gloria and **Dorothy,** her daughters.
Philip, her son.
You Never Can Tell (play), G. B. Shaw, 1895.

Clane, Fox, a fat, senile old Judge in Georgia.
Johnny, his dead son.
(John) Jester, his teenage grandson.
Clock Without Hands, Carson McCullers, 1961.

Clanronald, Highland chief. *Waverley,* W. Scott, 1814.

Clapp, faithful old clerk with whom the Sedleys sheltered after their downfall.
His wife.
Mary, their daughter, devoted to Amelia.
Vanity Fair, W. M. Thackeray, 1847–8.

Clapperclaw, Miss, Mrs Cammysole's first-floor lodger. *Our Street,* W. M. Thackeray, 1848.

Clapsaddle, Captain John. *Richard Carvel,* W. Churchill, 1899.

Clara, beloved by Captain Breton. *The Wonder* (play), Mrs Susanna Centlivre, 1714.

Clara, companion to Lady Franklin. *Money* (play), Lord Lytton, 1840.

Clara, Lady. *Lady Clara Vere de Vere* (poem), Lord Tennyson.

Clare. Family name of Lord Chidleigh.
Charlotte, cousin of the Clares, m. Ramshall.
Sophia, another cousin.
Still She Wished for Company, Margaret Irwin, 1924.

Clare, Mother, abbess of Imber Abbey. *The Bell,* Iris Murdoch, 1958.

Clare, Ada, ward of Mr Jarndyce, m. Richard Carstone. *Bleak House,* C. Dickens, 1853.

Clare, Angel, central character.
Rev. James, his father.
His mother.
Rev. Cuthbert, his brother.
Rev. Felix, his brother.
Tess of the D'Urbervilles, T. Hardy, 1891.

Clare, Sir Arthur.
Lady Dorcas, his wife.
Millicent, their daughter.
Harry, their son.
The Merry Devil of Edmonton (play), Anon.

Clare, Francis, neighbour of the Vanstones.
His sons:
Frank, a weak fortune-hunter, ex-fiancé of Magdalen Vanstone.
Cecil.
Arthur.
No Name, W. Collins, 1862.

clarence, the ghost. *archy and mehitabel* (poems), D. Marquis, 1927.

Clarence, Duke of. *Henry the Fourth, Henry the Sixth* and *Richard the Third* (plays), W. Shakespeare.

Clarendon, Antony, company director.
Margaret, his wife.
All Men Are Enemies, Richard Aldington, 1933.

Clarenton, Anglo-French, shot by the Germans as a spy. *The Pied Piper,* N. Shute, 1942.

Claret, Captain, commander of U.S.S. *Neversink. White-Jacket,* Herman Melville, 1850.

Clarinda. *To Clarinda* (four poems), R. Burns.

Clark, employee of Dombey. *Dombey and Son,* C. Dickens, 1848.

Clark, Bernard, 'sinister son of Queen Victoria,' m. Ethel Monticue. *The Young Visiters,* Daisy Ashford, 1919.

Clark, Charlotte Anne (Mrs Robinson), college servant. *Gaudy Night,* Dorothy L. Sayers, 1935.

Clark, George, octogenarian art collector. 'The Skeleton' (s.s.), *Blind Love,* V. S. Pritchett, 1969.

Clark, Mark, employed on the farm at Weatherbury. *Far from the Madding Crowd,* T. Hardy, 1874.

Clark, Oriana, actress, *née* Sarah Grocott, mistress of Hawkesworth. *Sophia,* Stanley Weyman, 1900.

Clarke, 1st husband of Mrs Weller. *Pickwick Papers,* C. Dickens, 1837.

Clarke, friend of Dr Raymond. *The Great God Pan*, A. Machen, 1894.

Clarke, Jim, smuggler. 'The Distracted Preacher,' *Wessex Tales*, T. Hardy, 1888.

Clarke, Thomas, attorney, nephew of Sam Crowe, m. Dorothy Greaves.
Will, his father.
Sir Lancelot Greaves, T. Smollett, 1762.

Clarkson, bailiff's man. *Phineas Finn*, A. Trollope, 1869.

Clarsdale, Lord. *Roots*, Naomi Jacob, 1931.

Claude. *Amours de Voyage* (poem), A. H. Clough.

Claude, Madame. *Lady Frederick* (play), W. S. Maugham, 1907.

Claudio, a young gentleman. *Measure for Measure* (play), W. Shakespeare.

Claudio, a young lord. *Much Ado about Nothing* (play), W. Shakespeare.

Claudius, King of Denmark. *Hamlet* (play), W. Shakespeare.

Clavering, Sir Francis, Bt, impoverished and unscrupulous gambler.
His wife ('The Begum'), rich and uneducated widow of Colonel John Altamont.
Francis, his son.
His wife.
Pendennis, W. M. Thackeray, 1848–50.

Clavering, Admiral Sir Richard.
General Sir Ralph, his brother.
Mrs Anthea Singleton, Sir Ralph's daughter.
Harvey Singleton, her husband.
A Pride of Heroes, Peter Dickinson, 1969.

Clavert, Marie, orphan adopted by Mère Bauche, m. 'Captain' Theodore Campan. *La Mère Bauche* (s.s.), A. Trollope.

Claverton, Lord.
Michael Claverton-Ferry, his son.
Monica Claverton-Ferry, his daughter.
The Elder Statesman (play), T. S. Eliot, 1958.

Clawson, Clif, doctor. *Martin Arrowsmith*, Sinclair Lewis, 1925.

Clay, Mrs, housekeeper to Canon Ronder. *The Cathedral*, Hugh Walpole, 1922.

Clay, Mrs, widowed daughter of John Shepherd, friend of Anne Elliot. *Persuasion*, Jane Austen, 1818.

Clay, John (alias Vincent Spaulding), criminal. 'The Red-headed League' (s.s.), *Adventures of Sherlock Holmes*, A. Conan Doyle, 1892.

Clay, Melville, celebrated actor, guest at Scamnum. *Hamlet, Revenge!*, M. Innes, 1937.

Clay, Parry, coloured boy.
Minerva, his mother.
Abel, his father.
In this our Life, Ellen Glasgow, 1942.

Clay, Robert, engineering expert, central character, m. Hope Langham. *Soldiers of Fortune*, R. H. Davis, 1897.

Clay, Thornton. *Our Betters* (play), W. S. Maugham, 1923.

Clay, Sir Wilfrid. *C.*, M. Baring, 1924.

Clayhanger, Edwin, central character, m. Hilda Lessways.
Darius, his father, printer.
Maggie, his sister.
Clara, his sister, m. Albert Benbow.
The *Clayhanger* trilogy, Arnold Bennett, 1910–16.

Claypole, Noah (alias Bolter), charity boy and thief under Fagin. *Oliver Twist*, C. Dickens, 1838.

Claypole, Tom, dull son of a baronet.
Flora, his wife, *née* Warrington.
The Virginians, W. M. Thackeray, 1857–9.

Clayton, John. *See* Lord Greystoke.

Clayton, John Sylvester.
Anthea, his wife, *née* Winterfield.
Basil, their son.
Priscilla, their daughter.
Sir Ferris, his father.
Cricket in Heaven, G. Bullett, 1949.

Cleary, Rev. Aloysius, m. Laura Battiscombe. *Laura's Bishop*, G. A. Birmingham, 1949.

Cleaver, Fanny (Jenny Wren), dolls' dressmaker.
Her father.
Our Mutual Friend, C. Dickens, 1865.

Cleeve, Lucas.
Sybil, his wife.
Sir Sandford, his brother.
The Notorious Mrs Ebbsmith (play), A. W. Pinero, 1895.

Cleever, Eustace, novelist. 'A Conference of the Powers' (s.s.), *Many Inventions*, R. Kipling, 1893.

Clegg, Harry, archaeologist, fiancé of Barbara Vaughan. *The Mandelbaum Gate,* Muriel Spark, 1965.

Clegg, Jane.
Henry, her husband.
Her mother-in-law.
Johnnie, their son.
Jenny, their daughter.
Jane Clegg (play), St John Ervine, 1913.

Cleishbotham, Jedediah, schoolmaster and parish clerk, Gandercleugh, nominal recorder of the tales. *Tales of my Landlord,* W. Scott, 1816–32.

Clelia, a vain coquette. *The Borough* (poem), G. Crabbe, 1810.

Clemanthe. *Ion* (play), T. N. Talfourd, 1835.

Clemency, maid of Dr Jeddler. *The Battle of Life,* C. Dickens, 1846.

Clemens, Mrs, landlady.
James, her husband.
Farewell to Youth, Storm Jameson, 1928.

Clement, Brother. *The Cloister and the Hearth,* C. Reade, 1861.

Clement, Father, accused of 'seven rank heresies.' *The Fair Maid of Perth,* W. Scott, 1828.

Clement, Father. *The Marquise* (play), N. Coward, 1927.

Clement, Sir Joseph, Bt, Parliamentary candidate, North Loamshire. *Felix Holt,* George Eliot, 1866.

Clementina, Paula Power's French maid. *A Laodicean,* T. Hardy, 1881.

Clementine, Clayton Claw Cleaver, of the Three Glands, young American visiting his ancestral Irish home. *The Onion Eaters,* J. P. Donleavy, 1971.

Clements, Mrs, friend of Anne Catherick. *The Woman in White,* W. Collins, 1860.

Clemmens, solicitor. *Middlemarch,* George Eliot, 1871–2.

Clennam, Arthur, m. Little Dorrit.
His widowed stepmother, a brilliant business woman, though crippled.
Little Dorrit, C. Dickens, 1857.

Cleomenes, Sicilian lord. *A Winter's Tale* (play), W. Shakespeare.

Cleon. *The Maid's Tragedy* (play), Beaumont & Fletcher, 1611.

Cleon, Governor of Tharsus. *Pericles* (play), W. Shakespeare.

Cleopatra, Queen of Egypt. *Antony and Cleopatra* (play), W. Shakespeare. *Caesar and Cleopatra* (play), G. B. Shaw, 1900.

Cleremont. *Philaster* (play), Beaumont & Fletcher, 1611.

Clerval, Henry, close friend of Victor Frankenstein. *Frankenstein,* Mary W. Shelley, 1818.

Cleveland, Captain Clement, pirate, son of Basil Mertoun and Ulla Troil. *The Pirate,* W. Scott, 1822.

Cleveland, Myra, *née* Richards, sister of Effie Conford. *The Second Mrs Conford,* Beatrice K. Seymour, 1951.

Cleves, Prince of (Adolf).
Helen, his daughter.
A Legend of the Rhine, W. M. Thackeray, 1845.

Cleves, Rev. Martin, Rector of Tripplegate, friend of Amos Barton. 'The Rev. Amos Barton,' *Scenes of Clerical Life,* George Eliot, 1857.

Clewer, a bullied fag. 'The Moral Reformers' (s.s.), *Stalky & Co.,* R. Kipling, 1899.

Cliff, retired tailor. *Silas Marner,* George Eliot, 1861.

Cliff, Jasper, m. Netty Sargent. 'Netty Sargent's Copyhold,' *Life's Little Ironies,* T. Hardy, 1894.

Clifford, Lord. *Henry the Sixth* (play), W. Shakespeare.

Clifford, Madra. *Java Head,* J. Hergesheimer, 1919.

Clifford, Paul, central character, illegitimate son of Sir William Brandon, m. his cousin, Lucy Brandon.
Judith, his mother.
Paul Clifford, Lord Lytton, 1830.

Clifford, Sir Robert. *Perkin Warbeck* (play), John Ford, 1634.

Climpson, Katherine, protégée of Lord Peter Wimsey and member of jury at trial of Harriet Vane. *Strong Poison,* Dorothy L. Sayers, 1930.

Clincham, Earl of. *The Young Visiters,* Daisy Ashford, 1919.

Clink, Corporal. *Vanity Fair,* W. M. Thackeray, 1847–8.

Clink, Jem, turnkey at Newgate. *Peveril of the Peak,* W. Scott, 1822.

Clinker, Humphry, central character, illegitimate son of Matthew Bramble. *Humphry Clinker,* T. Smollett, 1771.

Clint, family solicitor. *Lost Sir Massingberd*, James Payn, 1864.

Clint, Roger. *Brat Farrar*, Josephine Tey, 1949.

Clintock, Archdeacon. *Daniel Deronda*, George Eliot, 1876.

Clinton, schoolmaster. *Mr Perrin and Mr Traill*, Hugh Walpole, 1911.

Clinton, Mrs, aunt of Hilda Scarve. *The Miser's Daughter*, W. H. Ainsworth, 1842.

Clinton, Ben.
Fanny and **Isabel,** his sisters.
The Lamplighter, Maria S. Cummins, 1854.

Clintup, nurseryman. *Middlemarch*, George Eliot, 1871–2.

Clippurse, the Waverleys' lawyer. *Waverley*, W. Scott, 1814.

Clitheroe, Arnold, friend of Elizabeth Grey. *The Happy Prisoner*, Monica Dickens, 1946.

Clitheroe, Jack, bricklayer.
Nora, his wife.
The Plough and the Stars (play), S. O'Casey, 1926.

Clive, clerk in Circumlocution Office. *Little Dorrit*, C. Dickens, 1857.

Clive, Lady Harriet. *C.*, M. Baring, 1924.

Cliveden, Sir Roger.
His wife.
Roger, their son.
'Teigne' (s.s.), *The Baseless Fabric*, Helen Simpson, 1925.

Cliveden-Banks, Mrs. *Outward Bound* (play), S. Vane, 1923.

Clodius, effeminate dandy. *The Last Days of Pompeii*, Lord Lytton, 1834.

Cloe. *The Faithful Shepherdess* (play), Beaumont & Fletcher, 1609.

Cloke, Mr, farmer.
His wife.
Mary, their daughter.
'A Habitation Enforced' (s.s.), *Actions and Reactions*, R. Kipling, 1909.

Clon, dumb servant of de Cocheforet. *Under the Red Robe*, Stanley Weyman, 1894.

Clonbrony, Lord and Lady.
Lord Colambre, their son.
The Absentee, Maria Edgeworth, 1812.

Cloncurry, Lady. 'The Fête Champêtre' (poem), *Collected Poems*, John Betjeman, 1958.

Clootz, Baron de, student and successful gambler. *Barry Lyndon*, W. M. Thackeray, 1844.

Clorin. *The Faithful Shepherdess* (play), Beaumont & Fletcher, 1609.

Cloten, son of Cymbeline's Queen. *Cymbeline* (play), W. Shakespeare.

Cloudesley, Angela, younger sister of Evelyn Roundelay. *A Footman for the Peacock*, Rachel Ferguson, 1940.

Clouston, Janet, reputed witch. *Kidnapped*, R. L. Stevenson, 1886.

Clout, Colin, a wanderer. *Colin Clout* (poem), John Skelton, 1521.

Clout, Colin. *The Faërie Queene* (poem), 1590. *Colin Clout's Come Home Again* (poem), 1595, E. Spenser.

Clover, Aubrey, actor-manager, m. Jessica Dean. The *Barsetshire* series, Angela Thirkell, 1933 onwards.

Clover, Charles, m. Sally Pickle. *Peregrine Pickle*, T. Smollett, 1751.

Clover, Mrs Louisa, 'china and glass for hire.'
Minnie, her daughter.
The Town Traveller, G. Gissing, 1898.

Clubber, Bob, Virginian with whom Warrington quarrels. *The Virginians*, W. M. Thackeray, 1857–9.

Clubber, Sir Thomas.
His wife and daughter.
Pickwick Papers, C. Dickens, 1837.

Clues, Alexander, deacon; cousin of James Pawkie. *The Provost*, J. Galt, 1822.

Clumber, Duke and Duchess of.
Henry Sydney, their son, school friend of Coningsby.
Coningsby, B. Disraeli, 1844.

Clump, apothecary to Miss Crawley. *Vanity Fair*, W. M. Thackeray, 1847–8.

Clumsy, Sir Tunbelly. *The Relapse* (play), J. Vanbrugh, 1696. *A Trip to Scarborough* (play), R. B. Sheridan, 1777.

Cluppins, friend of Mrs Bardell. *Pickwick Papers*, C. Dickens, 1837.

Clutter, Archie, convict escaped from Cayenne.
Elizabeth, his wife, one-time friend of Corinne.

No Other Tiger, A. E. W. Mason, 1927.

Clutterbuck, Lady Ann.
 Clementina, her daughter, cadaverous red-haired poetess, author of 'The Death Shriek,' etc.
The Book of Snobs, W. M. Thackeray, 1846–7.

Clutterbuck, Cuthbert, imaginary editor of *The Abbot. The Fortunes of Nigel,* W. Scott, 1822.

Cly, servant to Charles Darnay. *A Tale of Two Cities,* C. Dickens, 1859.

Clyde, Alaric. *Cross Currents* (s.s.), 'Saki' (H. H. Munro).

Clyde, Joyce, designer, friend of the Granvilles. *Thunder on the Left,* C. Morley, 1925.

Clyde, Toby. *The Fanatics* (play), M. Malleson, 1924.

Clyne, Captain Anthony, late R.N., m. Henrietta Mary Damer. *Starvecrow Farm,* Stanley Weyman, 1905.

Coacher, private secretary to Rev. F. Bell.
 Martha, his coarse and bad-tempered daughter, who held Bell to a youthful promise to marry her.
Pendennis, W. M. Thackeray, 1848–50.

Coade (Coady).
 Emma, his wife (also Coady).
Dear Brutus (play), J. M. Barrie, 1917.

Coaker, Richard Henry. *The Farmer's Wife* (play), E. Phillpotts, 1924.

Coan, Jock. 'The Lang Men o' Larut' (s.s.), *Life's Handicap,* R. Kipling, 1891.

Coast, Garrett (alias Handyside), central character. *No Man's Land,* L. J. Vance, 1920.

Coates, Adrian, Mrs Morland's publisher, m. Sybil Knox. The *Barsetshire* series, Angela Thirkell, 1933 onwards.

Coates, Bob, m. Milly. *Mrs Galer's Business,* W. Pett Ridge, 1905.

Coavinses. *See* NECKETT.

Coaxer, Mrs. *Polly* (comic opera), J. Gay, 1729.

Cob, Oliver. *Every Man in his Humour* (play), B. Jonson, 1598.

Cobb, Jeremiah (Uncle Jerry), mail-coach driver. *Rebecca of Sunnybrook Farm,* Kate D. Wiggin, 1903.

Cobbett, cathedral verger, Polchester. *The Cathedral,* Hugh Walpole, 1922.

Cobham, Kitty. *See* WHARFEDALE.

Coburn, Rev. Arthur, Protestant minister.
 His wife.
Famine, L. O'Flaherty, 1937.

Cocardasse, Gascon swashbuckler. *The Duke's Motto,* J. H. McCarthy, 1908.

Cochrane, Beatrice, m. Francis Gordon. *Peter Jackson, Cigar Merchant,* G. Frankau, 1919.

Cochrane, Lady Betty, m. Sir Thomas Maitland. *Sophia,* Stanley Weyman, 1900.

Cochrane, Colonel Cochrane. *The Tragedy of the Korosko,* A. Conan Doyle, 1898.

Cock, Gammer Gurton's boy. *Gammer Gurton's Needle* (play), Anonymous, 1575.

Cockburn, landlord of the George, near Bristoport. *Guy Mannering,* W. Scott, 1815.

'Cockney,' ordinary seaman, the *Berinthia. Tom Fool,* F. Tennyson Jesse, 1926.

Cockton, draughtsman. *A Laodicean,* T. Hardy, 1881.

Codd, Emanuel, 'soured and suspicious' worker at Vixen Tor Farm. *The Mother,* E. Phillpotts, 1908.

Codger, tutor at Trinity. *The New Machiavelli,* H. G. Wells, 1911.

Codger, Miss, 'literary lady.' *Martin Chuzzlewit,* C. Dickens, 1844.

Codleyn, Mrs, wealthy widow and owner of seventy cottages, whose rent-collector Denry Machin becomes. *The Card,* Arnold Bennett, 1911.

Codlin, Thomas, proprietor of Punch and Judy show. *The Old Curiosity Shop,* C. Dickens, 1841.

Codling, Jaffa. *See* GILBERT CANNISTER.

Codones, Mitzos ('Little Mitzos'), captain, the *Revenge. The Capsina,* E. F. Benson, 1899.

Codrington, Christopher, of *The Liberal. The Street of Adventure,* P. Gibbs, 1909.

Cœur-de-Lion, Duke of. *The Book*

of Snobs, W. M. Thackeray, 1846–1847.

Coffey, Mary. 'The Nice Cup o' Tea' (s.s.), *Sun on the Water*, L. A. G. Strong, 1940.

Coffin, Mr. *Westward Ho!*, C. Kingsley, 1855.

Coffin, Peter, landlord of the Spouter Inn. *Moby Dick*, H. Melville, 1851.

Coffinkey, Captain, specialist in punch-making. *Rob Roy*, W. Scott, 1818.

Coggan, Jan, employed at Weatherbury.
His wife.
Far from the Madding Crowd, T. Hardy, 1874.

Cogglesby, Andrew, m. Harriet Harrington.
Tom, his brother.
Evan Harrington, G. Meredith, 1861.

Coggs, schoolfellow of Dick Bultitude. *Vice Versa*, F. Anstey, 1882.

Coghgan, Dr David, of Chicago, close friend of Daniel Howitt. *The Shepherd of the Hills*, H. B. Wright, 1907.

Cogweiler, Len, of Paragon Films. *Another Year*, R. C. Sherriff, 1948.

Cohen, Mrs Bella. *Ulysses*, James Joyce, 1922.

Cohen, Ezra, pawnbroker.
Addy, his wife.
His mother.
Daniel Deronda, George Eliot, 1876.

Cohen, Gordon, Jewish cockney shopkeeper, now a soldier. *Mr Bolfry* (play), James Bridie, 1943.

Cohen, Isaac, Jewish money-lender. *Tents of Israel*, G. B. Stern, 1924.

Cohen, Isadore. *Juan in America*, E. Linklater, 1931.

Cohen, Mirah, m. Daniel Deronda.
Cohen, alias Lapidoth, her father, a villainous actor.
Sara, her mother.
Mordecai, her brother, close friend of Daniel Deronda.
Daniel Deronda, George Eliot, 1876.

Cohn, Robert, American writer in Spain. *The Sun Also Rises* (or *Fiesta*), Ernest Hemingway, 1926.

Coiler, Mrs, widow. *Silas Marner*, George Eliot, 1861.

Cokane, William de Burgh, *Widowers' Houses* (play), G. B. Shaw, 1892.

Coke, Connie, broken-down old actress. *London Belongs to Me*, N. Collins, 1945.

Coke, Sir Hervey, m. Sophia Maitland. *Sophia*, Stanley Weyman, 1900.

Coker, D., barmaid.
Her mother.
The Horse's Mouth, Joyce Cary, 1944.

Cokeson, Robert, managing clerk to the Hows. *Justice* (play), J. Galsworthy, 1910.

Colambre. See LORD CLONBRONY.

Colander, supercilious London servant of Ernest Vane. *Peg Woffington*, C. Reade, 1853.

Colbert, Lieutenant. *While the Sun Shines* (play), T. Rattigan, 1943.

Colbrand, Monsieur, Swiss servant. *Pamela*, S. Richardson, 1740.

Colchicum, Viscount, elderly and dissipated friend of Pendennis. *Pendennis*, 1848–50, and elsewhere, W. M. Thackeray.

Coldfoot, Sir Harry, Liberal Home Secretary. *Phineas Finn*, 1869, and elsewhere, A. Trollope.

Cole, Mr Justice, divorce judge. *Holy Deadlock*, A. P. Herbert, 1934.

Cole, Mrs. *The Minor* (play), S. Foote, 1760.

Cole, Jeremy, central character.
Rev. Herbert Cole, Rector of St James's, Polchester, his father.
His mother, *née* Trefusis.
His sisters:
Mary and **Helen.**
Jeremy, 1919, and elsewhere, Hugh Walpole.

Cole, Julia, m. William Galantry. *Dance of the Years*, Margery Allingham, 1943.

Cole, Kate, aunt of General Curzon. *The General*, C. S. Forester, 1936.

Cole, Sam, tool of Frederick Coventry. *Put Yourself in his Place*, C. Reade, 1870.

Coleman.
Zoe, his wife.
Antic Hay, A. Huxley, 1923.

Coleman, Fred, friend of Fairlegh, m. Lucy Markham.
His father and mother.
Frank Fairlegh, F. E. Smedley, 1850.

Coleman, Jeremy, jazz pianist.

Professor Alfred Coleman, his father.
Eleanor, his aunt.
Strike the Father Dead, John Wain, 1962.

Colenso, Reuben, of the *Lady Nepean. St Ives,* R. L. Stevenson, 1897.

Colepepper, Captain, yachtsman. *Phineas Finn,* 1869, and elsewhere, A. Trollope.

Colepepper, Captain Jack, 'cowardly rascal.' *The Fortunes of Nigel,* W. Scott, 1822.

Coles, Barney, cousin of Jesse Piggot. *The Oriel Window,* Mrs Molesworth, 1896.

Colet, James, staff manager at Perriani's, later purser, the *Altair,* central character. *Gallions Reach,* H. M. Tomlinson, 1927.

Colford, Major. *Loyalties* (play), J. Galsworthy, 1922.

Colin. *Colin and Lucy* (poem), T. Ticknell, 1720.

Colin. *Colin and Phoebe* (poem), J. Byrom.

Colin. *At Mrs Beam's* (play), C. K. Munro, 1923.

Colin, Dr, atheist serving at leprosarium in Belgian Congo. *A Burnt-Out Case,* Graham Greene, 1961.

Colin, Pierre, orchestra conductor.
Margot, his wife.
Grand Opera, Vicki Baum, 1942.

Colin of Glenure ('The Red Fox'), King's Factor of Appin (hist.). *Kidnapped,* R. L. Stevenson, 1886.

Colladine, Sir Hector, Bt, D.S.O.
Lady Marjorie, his wife.
The Laughing Lady, A. Sutro, 1922.

Collen, Fay. *Spring Cleaning* (play), F. Lonsdale, 1925.

Colleoni, gang leader. *Brighton Rock,* Graham Greene, 1938.

Colles, Mr. *Prester John,* J. Buchan, 1910.

Collet, Mary. *John Inglesant,* J. H. Shorthouse, 1881.

Collett, Joan. *Call it a Day* (play), Dodie Smith, 1935.

Colley-Mahoney, Father, Mrs Hurstpierpoint's chaplain. *Valmouth,* Ronald Firbank, 1919.

Collier-Floodgaye, Miss Cecilia. *Before the Bombardment,* O. Sitwell, 1926.

Collins, Jeb, ex-privateersman of the *Wampanoag. Anthony Adverse,* Hervey Allen, 1934.

Collins, Master John, gunsmith. 'Hal o' the Draft' (s.s.), *Puck of Pook's Hill,* R. Kipling, 1906.

Collins, Prudence (Pruie), housekeeper to Sir Borlase St Aubyn. 'The Young Men are Coming' (s.s.), *The Young Men are Coming,* M. P. Shiel, 1937.

Collins, Rev. William, m. Charlotte Lucas. *Pride and Prejudice,* Jane Austen, 1813.

Collinson, unsuccessful lawyer.
His wife and child.
The One Hundred Dollar Bill (s.s.) Booth Tarkington, 1923.

Collinson, General, K.C.B., school governor. 'The Flag of their Country' (s.s.), *Stalky & Co.,* R. Kipling, 1899.

Collyer, Hester, mistress of Freddie Page.
Sir William, her husband.
The Deep Blue Sea (play), T. Rattigan, 1952.

Colocynth, Dr. *Peregrine Pickle,* T. Smollett, 1751.

Colonna, Madame.
Prince Colonna, her husband.
Princess Lucretia, her stepdaughter, m. Lord Monmouth.
Coningsby, B. Disraeli, 1844.

'Colonsay, Lady Florimel,' wrongly installed as successor to the Marquisate of Lossie; *de facto* Miss Gordon, illegitimate daughter of the old Marquis, m. Raoul Lenorme. *The Marquis of Lossie,* G. MacDonald, 1877.

Colpoys, Augustus, of Bagnigge Wells Theatre. *Trelawny of the Wells,* A. W. Pinero, 1898.

Colquhoun, A.B., *Artemis. The Ship,* C. S. Forester, 1943.

Colquhoun, Rev. Robert, 2nd husband of Chris Guthrie. *A Scots Quair* trilogy, 1932–4, Lewis Grassic Gibbon.

Colston, Mrs, brewer's wife.
Charlie, her son.
Catherine Furze, M. Rutherford, 1893.

Colston, Godfrey, rich active octogenarian.
Charmian Piper Colston, his wife.
Dame Lettie Colston, his sister.
Memento Mori, Muriel Spark, 1959.

Colston, Leo (Lionel), boy who acts

as messenger for the lovers. *The Go-Between*, L. P. Hartley, 1953.

Coltherd, Benjie, 'impudent urchin.' *Redgauntlet*, W. Scott, 1824.

Colvin, Henry, Master of Artillery. *Anne of Geierstein*, W. Scott, 1829.

Colwood, Stephen, George Sherston's schoolmaster. *Memoirs of a Fox-Hunting Man*, Siegfried Sassoon, 1929.

Comandine, Lord. *Our Street*, W. M. Thackeray, 1848.

Comber, Freddie, schoolmaster.
His wife.
Mr Perrin and Mr Traill, Hugh Walpole, 1911.

Combermere, Mrs. *The Cathedral*, Hugh Walpole, 1922.

Comfort, James, blacksmith.
His wife.
The Trumpet Major, T. Hardy, 1880.

Cominius, Roman general. *Coriolanus* (play), W. Shakespeare.

Commissioner of Police, The. *It's a Battlefield*, Graham Greene, 1935.

Comnenus, Isaac. *Isaac Comnenus* (play), H. Taylor, 1827.

Comparini, Pietro.
Violante, his wife.
Pompilia, their adopted daughter, m. Guido Franceschini.
The Ring and the Book, R. Browning, 1868–9.

Comper, Violet.
Peter, her husband.
Francie, her supposed daughter, m. Lord Trehick. *See* MARJORIE BAINES.
For Us in the Dark, Naomi Royde-Smith, 1937.

Compeyson, false lover of Miss Havisham. *Great Expectations*, C. Dickens, 1861.

Comport, Jane, sweetheart of Dowgate. *The Uncommercial Traveller*, C. Dickens, 1860.

Compson, Jason.
Caroline, his wife, *née* Bascomb.
Their children:
Jason.
Candace (Caddy).
Quentin, her illegitimate son.
Quentin.
Benjy, congenital idiot.
The Sound and the Fury, W. Faulkner, 1931.

Compton, Benny, Jewish radical. *U.S.A.* trilogy, John dos Passos, 1930–6.

Comyn, Viscount (John), friend of Richard Carvel. *Richard Carvel*, W. Churchill, 1899.

Conant, Melancthon, general jobber. *Anthony Adverse*, Hervey Allen, 1934.

Conant, Sir Walter, landowner.
His wife.
'A Habitation Enforced' (s.s.), *Actions and Reactions*, R. Kipling, 1909.

Concannon, Etta, m. Tommy Burgrave.
Her father, admiral.
The Glory of Clementina Wing, W. J. Locke, 1911.

Concannon, Superintendent, Irish constabulary. *The Private Wound*, Nicholas Blake, 1968.

Concasseur, Captain, member of the Tontons Macoute in Haiti. *The Comedians*, Graham Greene, 1966.

Concaverty, Rufus (alias Cassius).
Ivor Sisyphus, his son.
The Dancing Druids, Gladys Mitchell, 1948.

Conder, journalist. *It's a Battlefield*, Graham Greene, 1935.

Condiddle, Sir Coolie. *The Bride of Lammermoor*, W. Scott, 1819.

Condomine, Charles, author.
Ruth, his 2nd wife.
Elvira, ghost of his 1st wife.
Blithe Spirit (play), Noël Coward, 1941.

Condon, Mrs, mother of Maud Murphy. *The Land of Spices*, Kate O'Brien, 1941.

Condon, Linda, central character, m. Arnaud Hallet.
Stella, her mother, m. (2) Moses Feldt. *See also* BARTRAM LOWRIE.
Linda Condon, J. Hergesheimer, 1918.

Condor, Charley, auditor, Bundecund Bank. *The Newcomes*, W. M. Thackeray, 1853–5.

Condron, Michael, scaler and riveter in the Liverpool docks.
Mrs Condron, his old deaf and dumb mother.
Ebb and Flood, James Hanley, 1932.

Coney, Christopher, dissipated workman. *The Mayor of Casterbridge*, T. Hardy, 1886.

Conford, Howard Ruan, barrister and landowner, m.
(1) Effie Richards of U.S.A.
Pauline ('Lina'), their daughter.
(2) Lucia Frensham.
Geoffrey Ruan, Captain, their son.
Tresilla Ann, their daughter.
The Second Mrs Conford, Beatrice K. Seymour, 1951.

Congrigo, cook to Diomed. *The Last Days of Pompeii,* Lord Lytton, 1834.

Coningsburgh, Lord (Athelstane), descendant of the Saxon king. *Ivanhoe,* W. Scott, 1820.

Coningsby, Harry, central character, m. Edith Millbank. *Coningsby,* 1844, and elswhere, B. Disraeli.

Conington, Donald, barrister.
Tom, his brother.
Death of a Hero, R. Aldington, 1929.

Conklin, Jim, a veteran soldier. *The Red Badge of Courage,* Stephen Crane, 1895.

Conmee, Very Rev. John, S.J., *Ulysses,* James Joyce, 1922.

Connage, Rosalind, with whom Amory Blaine falls in love. *This Side of Paradise,* F. Scott Fitzgerald, 1920.

Conneau, Georges, murderer. *See* PAUL RENAULD.

Conner, Mr, superintendent of home for the aged.
Buddy, his assistant.
The Poorhouse Fair, John Updike, 1959.

Connolly, Mr. *Love Among the Artists,* G. B. Shaw, 1900.

Connolly, Doris, Micky and Marlene, evacuee children. *Put Out More Flags,* E. Waugh, 1942.

Connor, Bartle, wholesale book dealer, in love with Louise. *Louise,* Viola Meynell, 1954.

Connor, Ralph, schoolmaster and narrator. *The Sky Pilot,* R. Connor, 1899.

Connor, Tommy. *The Informer,* L. O'Flaherty, 1925.

Conolly, Mrs Jim. *Captain Desmond, V.C.,* Maud Diver, 1906.

Conrad. *The Saint's Tragedy* (poem), C. Kingsley, 1848.

Conrad. *The Corsair* (poem), Lord Byron, 1814.

Conrad, Sir Martin, explorer, nominal compiler of the story; in love with Mary O'Neill. *The Woman Thou Gavest Me,* Hall Caine, 1913.

Conroy. 'In the Same Boat' (s.s.), *A Diversity of Creatures,* R. Kipling, 1917.

Conroy, city missionary. *No. 5 John Street,* R. Whiteing, 1902.

Conroy, Albert, engineering draughtsman. *A Kind of Loving,* Stan Barstow, 1960.

Considine, Anthony, central character.
Molly, his wife.
Their children:
Denis, m. Anna Hennessy.
Joey.
Jack.
Mary.
Paddy.
Tess.
Floss.
Jim.
John, his father, founder of Considines.
Sophia, *née* Quillihey, his mother.
His brothers and sisters:
Joe.
Victor.
Millicent, m. Gerard Hennessy.
Agnes.
Tom, priest.
Mary, nun.
Caroline, m. Jim Lanigan.
Teresa, m. Danny Mulqueen.
Eddy.
Without My Cloak, Kate O'Brien, 1931.

Considine, Count (Billy). *Charles O'Malley,* C. Lever, 1841.

Constable, Robert, tutor of Lancester College, Cambridge. *The Rich Pay Late,* 1964, and others in the *Alms for Oblivion* sequence, Simon Raven.

Constable, Yvonne, divorced wife of Geoffrey Firmin. *Under the Volcano,* Malcolm Lowry, 1947.

Constance, mother of Arthur. *King John* (play), W. Shakespeare.

Constantine, Jennifer, m. Tom Fould. *Tom Fool,* F. Tennyson Jesse, 1926.

Constantine, Lady (Viviette), central character.
Sir Blount, her husband. She later m. Swithin St Cleeve bigamously.
Two on a Tower, T. Hardy, 1882.

Contessina, portress at convent. *Anthony Adverse,* Hervey Allen, 1934.

Conti, Mademoiselle Aspasie, ex-mistress of Gus Parkington. *Mrs Parkington,* L. Bromfield, 1944.

Conway, General. *Barnaby Rudge,* C. Dickens, 1841.

Conway, George. *East of Suez* (play), W. S. Maugham, 1922.

Conway, Hugh ('Glory'), H.M. Consul. *Lost Horizon,* J. Hilton, 1933.

Conway, Kitty, Haymarket actress. *The Miser's Daughter,* W. H. Ainsworth, 1842.

Conway, Maggie. 'The Count and the Wedding Guest' (s.s.), *The Trimmed Lamp,* O. Henry, 1907.

Conyers, Dr, cancer research expert. 'The Dragon's Head,' *Lord Peter Views the Body,* Dorothy L. Sayers, 1928.

Cookson, pirate. *Peter Pan* (play), J. M. Barrie, 1904.

Cookson, Elvira Vian. *See* VIAN and BAUM.

'Cooky,' cook of the *Seamew. The Skipper's Wooing,* W. W. Jacobs, 1897.

Cooley, Benjamin (Kangaroo), leader of political organization in Sydney, N.S.W. *Kangaroo,* D. H. Lawrence, 1923.

Coombe, Eliah, marine store dealer. *The Silver King* (play), H. A. Jones, 1882.

Coombes, Harden. *Other Gods,* Pearl Buck, 1940.

Cooper, sexton, father of Mrs Sullivan. *The Lamplighter,* Maria S. Cummins, 1854.

Cooper, Birmingham merchant, uncle of Edgar Halliburton. *Mrs Halliburton's Troubles,* Mrs Henry Wood, 1862.

Cooper, Miss, boarding-house proprietor. *Separate Tables* (play), T. Rattigan, 1955.

Cooper, Augustus.
His mother.
Sketches by Boz, C. Dickens, 1836.

Cooper, John, gentile husband of Rose Berman.
Mary and **Enid,** his sisters.
Dick, his brother.
Magnolia Street, L. Golding, 1932.

Cooper, Mrs Marlene, a patron. *The Bachelors,* Muriel Spark, 1961.

Cooper, Sally, friend of Liza Kemp.
Her mother.
Liza of Lambeth, W. S. Maugham, 1897.

Coote, Bobby. *The Romantic Age* (play), A. A. Milne, 1920.

Coote, Chester, house agent and social aspirant.
His son.
Kipps, H. G. Wells, 1905.

Coote, J. G. (Looney Coote), friend of Corcoran and Ukridge. *Ukridge,* P. G. Wodehouse, 1924.

Cope, small schoolboy. *Young Woodley,* J. van Druten, 1928.

Cope, Madeline, cousin of Hugh Armstrong, m. Philip Vanever. *The Woodcarver of 'Lympus,* Mary E. Waller, 1909.

Cope, Rev. Percival, eng. to Frances Frankland. 'For Conscience' Sake,' *Life's Little Ironies,* T. Hardy, 1894.

Cope, Sir Richard T., Minister of Re-education of Germany, m. Diavolina Krutch. *Sunrise in the West,* Bechofer Roberts, 1945.

Cope, Sir Rodney, Bt, uncle of Joy Stretton. *Joy and Josephine,* Monica Dickens, 1948.

Copeland, Benedict, a Negro doctor.
Willie, his son.
Portia, his daughter.
The Heart is a Lonely Hunter, Carson McCullers, 1940.

Copleigh, Maud and Edith. 'False Dawn' (s.s.), *Plain Tales from the Hills,* R. Kipling, 1888.

Coplestone, Celia. *The Cocktail Party* (play), T. S. Eliot, 1950.

Copley, of Pym's Publicity. *Murder Must Advertise,* Dorothy L. Sayers, 1933.

Copley, John Singleton, artist (hist.). *Northwest Passage,* Kenneth Roberts, 1938.

Coppard, George.
Gertrude, his daughter, m. Walter Morel.
Sons and Lovers, D. H. Lawrence, 1913.

Coppard, James, mayor and local bigwig, father of Ellen Barfoot. *Jacob's Room,* Virginia Woolf, 1922.

Copper, Private Alf. 'The Comprehension of Private Copper' (s.s.), *Traffics and Discoveries,* R. Kipling, 1904.

Copperfield, David, central character and narrator, m. (1) Dora Spenlow, (2) Agnes Wickfield.
Clara, his mother, m. (2) Edward Murdstone.
David Copperfield, C. Dickens, 1850.

Coppinger, Major-General Brown. *The General*, C. S. Forester, 1936.

Coppinger, Captain Curll ('Cruel Coppinger'), smuggler, m. Judith Trevisa. *In the Roar of the Sea*, S. Baring-Gould, 1892.

Copshrews, Lenda.
Laurence ('Lonny'), artist, her father.
Aline, her mother.
Melloney Holtspur (play), J. Masefield, 1922.

Coraglia, Don Michele (Michelotto), agent of Caesar Borgia. *The Duke of Gandia* (play), A. C. Swinburne, 1908.

Corah. *Absalom and Achitophel* (poem), J. Dryden, 1681.

Coral, Mrs. *The Little Girls*, Elizabeth Bowen, 1964.

Coralie, premier *danseuse*, Ludwiglust Court Theatre. *Barry Lyndon*, W. M. Thackeray, 1844.

Coralie, Mademoiselle, horse-rider at Franconi's. *Pendennis*, W. M. Thackeray, 1848–50.

Coram, Jane, theatrical star. *Adam's Breed*, Radclyffe Hall, 1926.

Corbet, lawyer. *Henry Esmond*, W. M. Thackeray, 1852.

Corby, Mary, survivor from wreck of *Warren Hastings*. *Ravenshoe*, H. Kingsley, 1861.

Corbyn, Walter Decies (Kurban Sahib). 'A Sahib's War' (s.s.), *Traffics and Discoveries*, R. Kipling, 1904.

Corcoran, narrator, close friend of Ukridge. *Ukridge*, 1924, and elsewhere, P. G. Wodehouse.

Corcoran, Captain, m. Buttercup.
Josephine, his daughter, m. Ralph Rackstraw.
H.M.S. Pinafore (comic opera), Gilbert & Sullivan, 1878.

Corcoran, Mrs. *Dr Angelus* (play), J. Bridie, 1947.

Corcoran, Phoebe, innkeeper's daughter. *The Sleepless Moon*, H. E. Bates, 1956.

Cordelia, daughter of Lear. *King Lear* (play), W. Shakespeare.

Corder, Judy Muriel, central character and narrator, m. Arnold Ainger. *Four Frightened People*, E. Arnot Robertson, 1931.

Corder, Marjorie, air hostess, m. Theodore Honey. *No Highway*, N. Shute, 1948.

Corder, Robert, minister.
His children: **Howard.**
Ethel.
Ruth.
Wilfred, his nephew.
Miss Mole, E. H. Young, 1930.

Corderey, Dr. *Thank Heaven Fasting*, E. M. Delafield, 1932.

Cordier. *Beau Geste*, P. C. Wren, 1924.

Cordover, Adolphus ('Doll').
Pilar ('Pill'), his sister.
Act of God, F. Tennyson Jesse, 1936.

Cordways, Rt. Hon. John Ingleby.
His wife.
Timothy, his brother.
The Choice (play), A. Sutro, 1919.

Coreb, a spirit. *The Merry Devil of Edmonton*, Anon.

Corey, Bromfield, artist.
Anna, his wife.
Their children:
Tom, m. Penelope Lapham.
Lily.
Nanny.
The Rise of Silas Lapham, W. D. Howells, 1885.

Corin, a shepherd. *As You Like It* (play), W. Shakespeare.

Corinna. *Corinna's Gone A-maying* (poem), R. Herrick.

Corinne, dancer, mistress of Leon Battchilena. *No Other Tiger*, A. E. W. Mason, 1927.

Corinthian Tom, a man of fashion.
Corinthian Kate (Catherine), his mistress.
Life in London (or *Tom and Jerry*), Pierce Egan, 1821.

Coriolanus (Caius Marcius), a noble Roman. *Coriolanus* (play), W. Shakespeare.

Corisande, Lady. *Lothair*, B. Disraeli, 1870.

Corkery, Phil, friend of Ida Arnold. *Brighton Rock*, Graham Greene, 1938.

Corkett, Henry, clerk to Geoffrey Ware. *The Silver King* (play), H. A. Jones, 1882.

Corkran, Arthur (Stalky), central character throughout *Stalky & Co.*, 1899, and several stories in later volumes. R. Kipling.
Corley, Mr. 'Two Gallants' (s.s.), *The Dubliners*, James Joyce, 1914.
Cornelius, friend of Faustus. *Doctor Faustus* (play), C. Marlowe, 1604.
Corner, Cicely, remote cousin of Direck.
  Letty, her sister, wife of 'Teddy.'
Mr Britling Sees It Through, H. G. Wells, 1916.
Corney, Mrs, widow, matron of workhouse, m. Bumble. *Oliver Twist*, C. Dickens, 1838.
Corney, Molly.
  Nelly, her mother.
  Bessie, her sister.
Sylvia's Lovers, Mrs Gaskell, 1863.
Cornichon, Madame, calling herself Valentinois, keeper of *pension* in Paris. *The Adventures of Philip*, W. M. Thackeray, 1861–2.
Cornichon, Monsieur, French architect. *Barry Lyndon*, W. M. Thackeray, 1844.
Cornish, Councillor, father of Tim Kinnit. *The China Governess*, Margery Allingham, 1963.
Cornish, Dr. *Caroline* (play), W. S. Maugham, 1916.
Cornplanter, American Indian. 'Brother Square Toes' (s.s.), *Rewards and Fairies*, R. Kipling, 1910.
Cornu, Madame, widow, with 'dropsy and 200,000 livres a year,' whom Barry almost marries. *Barry Lyndon*, W. M. Thackeray, 1844.
Cornwall, Duke of. *King Lear* (play), W. Shakespeare.
Cornwell, Mrs Christine, widow of Adrian, Indian Civil Servant.
  Gwyneth, her daughter, a doctor.
  Tim, her son, R.A.F. pilot, m. Maureen Phillibrand.
  Larry, her stepson, Indian Army officer, m. Louise, Eurasian.
The Widow, Francis King, 1957.
Corodale, Col of.
  His mother.
  Duncan, his half-brother, m. Anna MacNeil.
Children of the Tempest, N. Munro, 1903.
Corombona, Vittoria, Venetian lady.
  Camillo, her husband.
  Flamineo, her brother.
  Marcello, another brother.
The White Devil (play), John Webster, *c.* 1612.
Corrado, officer of Paolo's company. *Paolo and Francesca*, S. Phillips, 1900.
Correze, Raphael de, famous singer and devoted friend of Vere Herbert. *Moths*, Ouida, 1880.
Corrie, Mrs Rollo, employer of Miriam Henderson.
  Felix, her husband.
  Their two children.
Pilgrimage, Dorothy M. Richardson, 1915-38.
Corrigan, Cornelius.
  Miles, his grandfather.
Roland Cashel, C. Lever, 1850.
Cortelyon, Mrs Alice. *The Second Mrs Tanqueray*, A. W. Pinero, 1893.
Corthell, Sheldon, artist, in love with Laura Dearborn. *The Pit*, F. Norris, 1903.
Cortright, Edith, widow with whom Sam Dodsworth falls in love in Venice. *Dodsworth*, Sinclair Lewis, 1929.
Corven, Sir Gerald, husband of Clare Charwell. *Over the River*, J. Galsworthy, 1933.
Corydon, Jackie. *Hay Fever* (play), N. Coward, 1925.
Coryn, Rachel, central character, m. (1) Count Sangaletti; (2) Ambrose Ashley; (3) Philip Ashley.
  Alex, her relation and friend.
My Cousin Rachel, Daphne du Maurier, 1951.
Cosens, Dr. *The Professor's Love Story* (play) J. M. Barrie, 1894.
Cosroe, brother of Mycetes. *Tamburlaine* (play), C. Marlowe, 1587.
Cosser, civil engineer. *The Food of the Gods*, H. G. Wells, 1904.
Cost (alias Travers), member of spy ring. *The Ministry of Fear*, Graham Greene, 1943.
Costanza, cook at San Salvatore. *The Enchanted April*, Countess von Arnim, 1922.
Costanza, kinswoman of Francesca. *Paolo and Francesca*, S. Phillips, 1900.
Costard, a clown. *Love's Labour's Lost* (play), W. Shakespeare.
Costello, m. Enid Howard. *The Pied Piper*, N. Shute, 1942.

Costigan, Captain J. Chesterfield ('Cos'), disreputable jolly Irishman.
Emily, his daughter. *See* FOTHERINGAY.
Pendennis, W. M. Thackeray, 1848–50.

Costlett, Captain, Cavalier turncoat. *Rob Roy,* W. Scott, 1818.

Cosway, Antoinette, Creole who marries Mr Rochester.
Her mother.
Pierre, her brother.
Wide Sargasso Sea, Jean Rhys, 1966.

Coth. *See* JURGEN.

Cothill, Charles, central character, m. Emily Crowthorne. *Right Royal* (poem), J. Masefield, 1920.

Cothorpe. *Tono Bungay,* H. G. Wells, 1909.

Cottar, Major George, D.S.O. ('The Brushwood Boy'), m. Miriam Lacy.
His father and mother.
'The Brushwood Boy' (s.s.), *The Day's Work,* R. Kipling, 1898.

Cotterill, Nellie, ex-pupil of Ruth Earp, m. Denry Machin.
Councillor Cotterill, her father.
The Card, Arnold Bennett, 1911.

Cotton. *The Sin of David* (play), S. Phillips, 1914.

Cotton, Quentin, friend of Saturday Keith, m. Helen Blyesdale.
Sewald, his father.
Lady Mercy, his sister.
Poet's Pub, E. Linklater, 1929.

Coulson, Mr, m. Mrs Widdup.
Constantia, their daughter.
'The Merry Month of May' (s.s.), *Whirligigs,* O. Henry, 1910.

Coulson, William, friend of Philip Hepburn. *Sylvia's Lovers,* Mrs Gaskell, 1863.

Coupland, Eliza Ann ('Lizarann').
James, her father, match-seller.
Dolly, her mother.
It Never Can Happen Again, W. de Morgan, 1909.

Coupler, Mrs. *A Trip to Scarborough* (play), R. B. Sheridan, 1777.

Courage, butler to Canon Chisholm. *For Us in the Dark,* Naomi Royde-Smith, 1937.

Courcelles, de, Canon of Paris. *Saint Joan* (play), G. B. Shaw, 1921.

Court, Adeline, m. Philip Whiteoak.
Sarah, a distant relative, m (1) Arthur Leigh, (2) Finch Whiteoak.
Dermot, a cousin.
Malahide, uncle of Sarah.
His wife.
Paris, their son.
The Whiteoak Chronicles, Mazo de la Roche, 1927 onwards.

Court, Landry, m. Page Dearborn. *The Pit,* F. Norris, 1903.

Courtaud, Monsieur. French drawing master, Leyminster.
Lisette, his daughter, m. James Cartledge.
Both of this Parish, J. S. Fletcher.

Courtier, freelance politician. *The Patrician,* J. Galsworthy, 1911.

Courtine, friend of Captain Beaugard. *The Soldier's Fortune* (play), Thomas Otway, 1681.

Courtney, Harry, wealthy Australian, who adopts Hurtle Duffield by buying him from his parents for £500.
Alfreda, his wife.
Rhoda, their hunchback daughter.
The Vivisector, Patrick White, 1970.

Courtney, Ross. *Ziska,* Marie Corelli, 1897.

Coutell, Lane, boy-friend of Franny Glass. *Franny and Zooey,* J. D. Salinger, 1961.

Cove. *See* CHAWLEY.

Cove, Mrs.
Her daughters:
Blanche.
Beatrix.
Maud.
The Feast, Margaret Kennedy, 1950.

Coventry, Frederick, 'villain.' *Put Yourself in his Place,* C. Reade, 1870.

Coventry, Jane. *Sampson Rideout, Quaker,* Una Silberrad, 1911.

Coverdale, Mr and Mrs.
Mary, their daughter, m. Howat Freemantle.
Lavinia (Aunt Viney).
And Now Goodbye, J. Hilton, 1931.

Covey, The Young, fitter, cousin of Jack Clitheroe. *The Plough and the Stars,* S. O'Casey, 1926.

Cowan, Sir Benjamin, famous lawyer.
His wife.
For Us in the Dark, Naomi Royde-Smith, 1937.

Cowcher, George, butler to Lord Culalla. *No Other Tiger,* A. E. W. Mason, 1927.

Cowdray, Sir Walter. 'The Man in the Passage,' *The Wisdom of Father Brown,* G. K. Chesterton, 1914.

Cowland, Linda, mistress of the late Sanger. *The Constant Nymph,* Margaret Kennedy, 1924.

Cowley, cashier. *Justice* (play), J. Galsworthy, 1910.

Cowley, Father, Roman Catholic priest. *Requiem for Robert,* Mary Fitt, 1942.

Cowley, Edward, author.
Ruth, his wife.
A Travelling Woman, John Wain, 1959.

Cowper-Cowper, Mrs. *Lady Windermere's Fan* (play), O. Wilde, 1892.

Cowperwood, Frank Algernon, central character.
Lilian, his wife.
Henry, his father.
The Financier, Theodore Dreiser, 1912.

Cowslip, Dolly (real name Dorothy Greaves). *Sir Lancelot Greaves,* T. Smollett, 1762.

Cox, journeyman hatter. *Box and Cox* (play), J. M. Morton, 1847.

Cox, Mr ('Coxy'), cook to Sir Gulliver Deniston. *The World My Wilderness,* Rose Macaulay, 1950.

Cox, Mr, an astrologer. *Malcolm,* James Purdy, 1959.

Cox, John, suicide. *The Life and Death of Mr Badman,* J. Bunyan, 1680.

Cox, Sam, barber, jolly, good-natured, happy, until his wife temporarily inherits money.
Jemima, his wife, a vulgar snob.
Jemima Ann, their pretty daughter, m. Orlando Crump.
Barber Cox, W. M. Thackeray, 1847.

Coxe, Captain, Director of Pageants, Kenilworth Castle. *Kenilworth,* W. Scott, 1821.

Coxe, Mr. *Wives and Daughters,* Mrs Gaskell, 1866.

Cozens, Mrs Norma, friend of Fanny Logan. *Love in a Cold Climate,* Nancy Mitford, 1949.

Crab, Launcelot, surgeon, rival of Roger Potion. *Roderick Random,* T. Smollett, 1748.

Crabb, Mrs, mother of Juliana Gann. *A Shabby Genteel Story,* W. M. Thackeray, 1840.

Crabbe, Cissie. *Diary of a Provincial Lady,* E. M. Delafield, 1930.

Crabble, Inspector. *The Last Revolution,* Lord Dunsany, 1951.

Crablove. *The Sin of David* (play), Stephen Phillips, 1914.

Crabs, 13th Earl of (Gustavus Adolphus), scoundrel in high favour with the king. *Barry Lyndon,* W. M. Thackeray, 1844.

Crabs, Earl of (John A. A. P.), dissipated elderly scoundrel, m. Lady Griffin.
Hon. A. P. Deuceace, his son, card-sharper, m. Matilda Griffin, Lady Griffin's stepdaughter.
The Great Hoggarty Diamond, 1841, and elsewhere, W. M. Thackeray.

Crabshaw, Timothy, squire to Lancelot Greaves. *Sir Lancelot Greaves,* T. Smollett, 1762.

Crabtree, uncle of Sir Benjamin Backbite. *The School for Scandal* (play), R. B. Sheridan, 1777.

Crabtree, lawyer. *The Amateur Gentleman,* J. Farnol, 1913.

Crabtree, Antony. *Sonia,* S. McKenna, 1917.

Crabtree, Cadwallader, deaf and elderly. *Peregrine Pickle,* T. Smollett, 1751.

Crabtree, Lady Constance, aunt of Lord Hemstitch. *We're Here,* D. Mackail, 1947.

Crabtree, Lavinia, m. Walter Egmont.
Her father and mother.
Love and Money, Phyllis Bentley, 1957.

Crackenbury, Lady, possessor of a shabby reputation. *Vanity Fair,* W. M. Thackeray, 1847–8.

Crackenthorp, Rev. Mr, Rector of Raveloe.
His wife.
Silas Marner, George Eliot, 1861.

Crackenthorp, Joe, landlord of inn on the Cumberland coast.
His wife.
Redgauntlet, W. Scott, 1824.

Crackenthorpe, Miss. *Sinister Street,* C. Mackenzie, 1913.

Crackit, Toby, housebreaker and partner of Fagin. *Oliver Twist,* C. Dickens, 1838.

Crackner, Mrs, fraudulent medium.
Kathy, her daughter.
'Mrs Sludge' (s.s.), *Last Recollections of My Uncle Charles,* N. Balchin, 1954.

Crackthorpe, Captain, friend of Clive Newcome. *The Newcomes,* W. M. Thackeray, 1853–5.

Craddock, Mrs, landlady, Bath. *Pickwick Papers,* C. Dickens, 1837.

Craddock, Chief Inspector Dermot, of Scotland Yard. *The Mirror Crack'd from Side to Side,* Agatha Christie, 1962.

Craddock, Eric, bookshop assistant.
Celia, his mother.
Hemlock and After, Angus Wilson, 1952.

Cradock, Jack, meat-buyer to Imperial Palace Hotel. *Imperial Palace,* Arnold Bennett, 1930.

Cradson, lawyer. *Both of this Parish,* J. S. Fletcher.

Cragg, Maria, housekeeper to Ben Geaiter. *Joseph and his Brethren,* H. W. Freeman, 1928.

Cragg, Tom, prize-fighter. *The Broad Highway,* J. Farnol, 1910.

Craggs, lawyer. *The Battle of Life,* C. Dickens, 1846.

Cragstone, Lady, gambler. *Daniel Deronda,* George Eliot, 1876.

Cragworthy, Julia. *The Young Idea,* N. Coward, 1923.

Craig, Scotch gardener, in love with Hetty Sorrel. *Adam Bede,* George Eliot, 1859.

Craig, Charles Butcher, surgeon. *My Brother Jonathan,* F. Brett Young, 1928.

Craigdallie, Bailie Adam. *The Fair Maid of Perth,* W. Scott, 1828.

Craigengelt, Captain, gambler and informer. *The Bride of Lammermoor,* W. Scott, 1819.

Craigie, Captain Nicholas. 'The Captain of the *Polestar*' (s.s.), *Tales of Pirates and Blue Water,* A. Conan Doyle.

Crail, Captain. *The Master of Ballantrae,* R. L. Stevenson, 1889.

Cram, Jake, m. Susan Childs.
Fred, his brother.
A Lamp for Nightfall, E. Caldwell, 1952.

Crambagge, Sir Paul, 'a sour fanatic knight.' *The Fortunes of Nigel,* W. Scott, 1822.

Cramchild, Cousin. *The Water Babies,* C. Kingsley, 1863.

Cramp, cabinet maker. *Last Post,* Ford Madox Ford, 1928.

Crampton, Fergus, husband of Mrs Clandon. *You Never Can Tell,* G. B. Shaw, 1895.

Crampton, Jack. *Famine,* L. O'Flaherty, 1937.

Crampton, Josiah, politician, uncle of John Perkins. *The Bedford Row Conspiracy,* W. M. Thackeray, 1840.

Cranage, Ben ('Wiry Ben'), carpenter and rustic dancer.
Chad, blacksmith.
Bessie, his daughter ('Chad's Bess').
Adam Bede, George Eliot, 1859.

Cranbourne, Sir Jasper, old cavalier. *Peveril of the Peak,* W. Scott, 1822.

Cranch, Mrs Matilda.
Tom, her son.
Middlemarch, Geo. Eliot, 1871–2.

Crandall, Lieutenant R. ('Toffee'), an old boy. 'A Little Prep' (s.s.), *Stalky & Co.,* R. Kipling, 1899.

Crane, of the Surrey Hunt. *Jorrocks's Jaunts and Jollities,* R. S. Surtees, 1838.

Crane, Dame Alison, of the Crane Inn, Marlborough. *Kenilworth,* W. Scott, 1821.

Crane, Mrs Biddy, old servant of Maddison. *The Beautiful Years,* H. Williamson, 1921.

Crane, Harvey, m. Gail Tallant. *Other Gods,* Pearl Buck, 1940.

Crane, Ichabod, schoolteacher. *The Legend of Sleepy Hollow,* Washington Irving, 1819–20.

Crane, John, m. Janie Sykes.
Yolande (Yolly), their daughter.
Charles, his brother, m. (1) Kitty Challoner.
Roberta (Bobby), their daughter, m. Rupert Amex.
(2) Maire Robotham.
Rev. Henry, their father.
Their mother.
The Case for the Defence, Mary Fitt, 1958.

Cranmer, Emile, grocer's boy, Melissa's lover. *The Wapshot Scandal,* John Cheever, 1963.

Cranmer, J. Barclay, character actor. *Enter a Murderer,* Ngaio Marsh, 1935.

Cranmer, Thomas, Archbishop of Canterbury (hist.). *Henry the Eighth* (play), W. Shakespeare.

Cranston, Bertine, friend of Sandra Finchley. *An American Tragedy,* T. Dreiser, 1925.

Crashaw, Rev. Percy. *The Hampdenshire Wonder,* J. D. Beresford, 1911.

Crashaw, Sidney, victim of Helen Vaughan. *The Great God Pan,* A. Machen, 1894.

Crasher, the Honourable, friend of John Standish Sawyer. *Market Harborough,* G. Whyte-Melville, 1861.

Cratchit, Bob, clerk to Scrooge.
His wife.
Tiny Tim, his crippled son.
Belinda, his daughter.
Other children.
A Christmas Carol, C. Dickens, 1843.

Craven, Colonel Daniel.
Julia and **Sylvia,** his daughters.
The Philanderer (play), G. B. Shaw, 1893.

Craven, Louis, journalist. *Marcella,* Mrs Humphry Ward, 1894.

Crawford, Earl of.
His wife.
Perkin Warbeck (play), J. Ford, 1634.

Crawford, Alan, brother of Blanche Cunningham.
Ilsa, his dead wife.
Barbara, Specky and **Bill,** their children.
Pink Sugar, O. Douglas, 1924.

Crawford, Henry.
Mary, his sister.
Admiral Crawford, their uncle and guardian.
Mansfield Park, Jane Austen, 1814.

Crawford, Miles, journalist. *Ulysses,* James Joyce, 1922.

Crawford, Redvers, biologist, Paul Jago's main opponent for the Mastership. *The Masters,* 1951, part of the *Strangers and Brothers* sequence, C. P. Snow.

Crawfurd, David, central character and narrator.
His father and mother.
Prester John, J. Buchan, 1910.

Crawley, Dr, Dean.
His wife.
Octavia, his daughter, m. Rev. Tommy Needham.
The *Barsetshire* series, Angela Thirkell, 1933 onwards.

Crawley, General.
Flora, his wife.
Ian, their son.
Jane, their daughter.
Spears Against Us, Cecil Roberts, 1932.

Crawley, Young Mr, visitor at the Assembly Rooms, Bath. *Pickwick Papers,* C. Dickens, 1837.

Crawley, Frank, Maxim de Winter's agent. *Rebecca,* Daphne du Maurier, 1938.

Crawley, Rev. Josiah, incumbent of Hogglestock.
Kate, his wife.
Their children.
Framley Parsonage, A. Trollope, 1861.

Crawley, Sir Pitt, Bt, M.P., cunning, mean, selfish, disreputable.
m. (1) Lady Grizzel Binkie.
Their children:
Pitt, m. Lady Jane Sheepshanks.
Pitt Binkie.
Matilda, m. Rawdon Jnr.
Rawdon, m. Rebecca (Becky) Sharp.
Rawdon Jnr, their son, m. Matilda.
m. (2) Rose Dawson.
Bute, Sir Pitt's brother.
His wife, *née* McTavish.
Their children: **James, Frank, Emma, Fanny, Kate, Louisa** and **Martha.**
Matilda, his half-sister.
Vanity Fair, W. M. Thackeray, 1847–8.

Crawley, Sir Wilmot, neighbour of the Castlewoods.
Wilmot, his son.
Henry Esmond, W. M. Thackeray, 1852.

Cray, Colonel. 'The Salad of Colonel Cray,' *The Wisdom of Father Brown,* G. K. Chesterton, 1914.

Cray, Ailie, schoolmistress, m. Ivie McLean.
Kitty, her sister.
Sentimental Tommy, J. M. Barrie, 1896.

Cray, Captain Raymond, fiancé of Josephine Foster. *Mr Fortune Finds a Pig,* H. C. Bailey, 1943.

Craye, prefect. 'The Impressionists,'

and elsewhere, *Stalky & Co.*, R. Kipling, 1899.

Crayle, Lord. *The High Road* (play), F. Lonsdale, 1927.

Crazy Ivar, hired man. *O Pioneers!*, Willa Cather, 1913.

Crazy, Sheila, girl loved by Max Fisher. *Pending Heaven*, William Gerhardie, 1930.

Creakle, schoolmaster, Salem House.
His wife and daughter.
David Copperfield, C. Dickens, 1850.

Credulous, Justice.
Bridget, his wife.
Lauretta, their daughter.
St Patrick's Day (play), R. B. Sheridan, 1775.

Creed, landlord, White Hart, Margate. *Jorrocks's Jaunts and Jollities*, R. S. Surtees, 1838.

Creedle, Robert, old man working for Giles Winterbourne. *The Woodlanders*, T. Hardy, 1887.

Creedy, Samuel, inquiry agent. *Mr Rowl*, D. K. Broster, 1924.

Cregeen, owner of old lifeboat. *The Card*, Arnold Bennett, 1911.

Creighton, Colonel William, Secret Service. *Kim*, R. Kipling, 1901.

Crespigny, Mrs Genevieve, Brighton landlady. *The Truth* (play), Clyde Fitch, 1907.

Crespin, Major Antony.
Lucilla, his wife.
The Green Goddess (play), W. Archer, 1921.

Cresset, Salathiel.
His father and mother. *See also* KOHNSTAMM.
Simpson, E. Sackville-West, 1931.

Cressida, daughter of Calchas. *Troilus and Cressida* (play), W. Shakespeare.

Cressler, Charles, speculator in wheat. *The Pit*, F. Norris, 1903.

Cresswell, Oscar, uncle of Paul. *The Rocking Horse Winner* (s.s.), D. H. Lawrence.

Creston, Laurel (alias Elvirita Jones). *Dragon Harvest*, Upton Sinclair, 1946.

Crestwell, Fred, the Countess of Marshwood's butler. *Relative Values* (play), Noël Coward, 1951.

Crèvecœur de Cordés, Count Philip, celebrated French counsellor and knight. *Quentin Durward*, W. Scott, 1823.

Crew, Randolph, nephew of Abel and Trussell Beechcroft. *The Miser's Daughter*, W. H. Ainsworth, 1842.

Crewe, Rev. Mr, curate of Milby.
His wife.
'Janet's Repentance,' *Scenes of Clerical Life*, George Eliot, 1857.

Crewe, Humphrey, financier. *Mr Crewe's Career*, W. Churchill, 1908.

Crewler, Sophy, m. Traddles.
Rev. Horace and Mrs, her parents.
David Copperfield, C. Dickens, 1850.

Cribbens, gold miner. *McTeague*, F. Norris, 1899.

Crich, Gerald, owner of a coal-mine.
Thomas, his father.
Winifred, his sister.
Women in Love, D. H. Lawrence, 1921.

Crichley, Rev. Mr, Rector of Cumbermoor. 'Mr Gilfil's Love Story,' *Scenes of Clerical Life*, George Eliot, 1857.

Crichton, Bill, butler to Lord Loam, central character. *The Admirable Crichton* (play), J. M. Barrrie 1902.

Crick, Richard, dairy farmer, employer of Tess.
Christiana, his wife.
Tess of the D'Urbervilles, T. Hardy, 1891.

Crickett, Richard, parish clerk of Carriford.
His wife.
Desperate Remedies, T. Hardy, 1871.

Cridley, ex-public schoolboy. *The Old Boys*, William Trevor, 1964.

Crimple, David, of a loan and life assurance company. *Martin Chuzzlewit*, C. Dickens, 1844.

Crimplesham, Thomas. *Whose Body?*, Dorothy L. Sayers, 1923.

Crimsworth, William (The Professor), central character, m. Frances Evans Henri.
Victor, their son.
Edward, William's elder brother.
His wife.
The Professor, Charlotte Brontë, 1857.

Cringer, Mr, *Roderick Random*, T. Smollett, 1748.

Cringle, Thomas, R.N., Captain. *Tom Cringle's Log*, M. Scott, 1836.

Cripples, Mr, owner of academy.
His son.
Little Dorrit, C. Dickens, 1857.

Cripplestraw, Anthony, Mr Derriman's odd man. *The Trumpet Major,* T. Hardy, 1880.

Cripps, locksmith. *The Silver King* (play), H. A. Jones, 1882.

Cripps, Mrs. *See* BUTTERCUP.

Cripps, Ben, villainous innkeeper.
Jeff, his father.
The Fifth Form at St Dominic's, T. Baines Reed, 1887.

Cripps, Crackenthorpe, hired by Jukes to spy on Randolph Crew. *The Miser's Daughter,* W. H. Ainsworth, 1842.

Crisp, 'commercial editor,' *The Voice,* Ria. *Right Off the Map,* C. E. Montague, 1927.

Crisp, Rev. Mr, curate of Chiswick.
His mother.
Vanity Fair, W. M. Thackeray, 1847–8.

Crisp, James, solicitor. *A Safety Match,* Ian Hay, 1911.

Crisparkle, Rev. Septimus, minor canon. *Edwin Drood,* C. Dickens, 1870.

Crispin, Lady Elizabeth. *See* DUKE OF HORTON.
Gervase, the Duke's cousin.
Hamlet, Revenge!, M. Innes, 1937.

Crisson, Frances, 1st wife of Young Jolyon Forsyte. The *Forsyte* series, J. Galsworthy, 1906–33.

Cristoforo, Fra, Franciscan priest. *Romola,* George Eliot, 1863.

Critchlow, chemist, Bursley. *The Old Wives' Tale,* Arnold Bennett, 1908.

Croaker, Miss. *Little Women,* 1868, and elsewhere, Louisa M. Alcott.

Crocker-Harris, Andrew, housemaster.
Millie, his wife.
The Browning Version (play), T. Rattigan, 1948.

Crockett, Selina, daughter of Nannie Allen; maid to the Warings, m. Sergeant Hopkins. The *Barsetshire* series, Angela Thirkell. 1933 onwards.

Crocus, Dr, phrenologist. *American Notes,* C. Dickens, 1842.

Croft, Admiral of the White.
His wife, *née* Wentworth.
Tenants of Kellynch Hall.
Persuasion, Jane Austen, 1818.

Croft, Art, narrator. *The Ox-Bow Incident,* Walter Van Tilburg Clark, 1940.

Croft, Denman, m. Stanley Garden. *Told by an Idiot,* Rose Macaulay, 1923.

Croft, Elisha, lawyer.
Elsie, his wife.
Chosen Country, J. dos Passos, 1951.

Croftangry, Chrystal, fictitious editor of the *Chronicles of the Canongate,* W. Scott, 1827–8.

Crofts, solicitor for the defence at trial of Harriet Vane. *Strong Poison,* Dorothy L. Sayers, 1930.

Crofts, Sir George. *Mrs Warren's Profession* (play), G. B. Shaw, 1902.

Crofts, Captain Montague. *Tom Burke of Ours,* C. Lever, 1844.

Crombie, Susan, friend and secretary of the Isambards. *The Whistling Chambermaid,* Naomi Royde-Smith, 1957.

Crome, Rev. Mr.
His grandson.
'The Ash-tree' (s.s.), *Ghost Stories of an Antiquary,* M. R. James, 1910.

Cromlech, David, friend of George Sherston. *Memoirs of an Infantry Officer,* Siegfried Sassoon, 1930.

Cromwell, servant to Wolsey (hist.), *Henry the Eighth* (play), W. Shakespeare.

Cronk, Rev. Adrian. *The Sailor's Return,* David Garnett, 1925.

Cronshaw, J., poet. *Of Human Bondage,* W. S. Maugham, 1915.

Crookey, attendant. *Pickwick Papers,* C. Dickens, 1837.

Crookhill, George. 'An Incident in the Life of Mr George Crookhill,' *Life's Little Ironies,* T. Hardy, 1894.

Crooklyn, Professor. *The Egoist,* G. Meredith, 1879.

Croom, James Bernard (Tony), lover of Clare Corven. *Over the River,* J. Galsworthy, 1933.

Croop, shoemaker. *Daniel Deronda,* George Eliot, 1876.

Crosbie. *See* SWAYNE.

Crosbie, journalist, friend of George Hillier. *All the World Wondered,* L. Merrick, 1911.

Crosbie, Robert.
Leslie, his wife.
The Letter (play), W. S. Maugham, 1927.

Crosbie, William, Provost of Dumfries.
Jenny, his wife.
Redgauntlet, W. Scott, 1824.

Crosby, maid in Pargiter household. *The Years,* Virginia Woolf, 1937.

Crosby, Mr and Mrs, employers of Lady Isabel Vane.
Helena, their daughter.
East Lynne, Mrs Henry Wood, 1861.

Crosby, Morton. *The Romancers* (s.s.), 'Saki' (H. H. Munro).

Crosland, Henry Clay, head of textile family.
Richard, his dead son.
Elaine, his grand-daughter, m. Walter Haigh.
Ralph, his grandson.
A Modern Tragedy, Phyllis Bentley, 1934.

Cross, Sir Henry, lawyer. *The General,* C. S. Forester, 1936.

Crossby, Angela.
Ralph, her husband.
The Well of Loneliness, Radclyffe Hall, 1928.

Crossfield, Mrs Ursula, sister of Jim Beddows.
Her husband.
Rose, their daughter.
South Riding, Winifred Holtby, 1936.

Crossland, Jem, thatcher, hedger, poacher and violinist, in love with Patty Verity. *High Meadows,* Alison Uttley, 1938.

Crossley, judge at first trial of Harriet Vane. *Strong Poison,* Dorothy L. Sayers, 1930.

Crossthwaite, Mr, friend of Jill Dealtry. *The City of Beautiful Nonsense,* E. T. Thurston, 1909.

Crotchet. *See* MACCROTCHET.

Crouch, Toby. *If Four Walls Told* (play), E. Percy, 1922.

Crouchback, Guy, romantic who goes to war, central character.
Mr Crouchback, his father.
Angela, his sister, m. Arthur Box-Bender, M.P.
Men at Arms, Evelyn Waugh, 1952.

Crow, High Constable of Treby. *Felix Holt,* George Eliot, 1866.

Crow, steward to Chris Glowry. *Nightmare Abbey,* T. L. Peacock, 1818.

Crow, Jem, the canonized jackdaw. 'The Jackdaw of Rheims' (poem), *The Ingoldsby Legends,* R. H. Barham, 1837.

Crow, Philip, industrialist, owner of dye works.
Tilly, his wife.
John and **Mary,** his cousins.
A Glastonbury Romance, J. C. Powys, 1932.

Crowborough, Lady Thisbe. 'Maltby and Braxton,' *Seven Men,* M. Beerbohm, 1919.

Crowder, Thomas, artist. 'The Man with no Face,' *Lord Peter Views the Body,* Dorothy L. Sayers, 1928.

Crowe, Mrs, in love with Pope Hadrian. *Hadrian the Seventh,* Baron Corvo (F. W. Rolfe), 1904.

Crowe, Barbara, assistant to Howard Saxby, m. Sir Raymond Bastable. *Cocktail Time,* P. G. Wodehouse, 1958.

Crowe, Polly, barmaid at the Jolly Bargee. *Fanny by Gaslight,* M. Sadleir, 1940.

Crowe, Captain Sam, seaman, uncle of Thomas Clarke. *Sir Lancelot Greaves,* T. Smollett, 1762.

Crowhurst, Phoebe, maid to the Furzes. *Catherine Furze,* M. Rutherford, 1893.

Crowl, fellow lodger of Newman Noggs. *Nicholas Nickleby,* C. Dickens, 1839.

Crown, stevedore, murderer. *Porgy,* Du Bose Heyward, 1925.

Crowne, Lenina, an Alpha worker. *Brave New World,* Aldous Huxley, 1932.

Crowse, Rev. Mr, curate. *Middlemarch,* George Eliot, 1871–2.

Crowther, sick-berth attendant, *Compass Rose. The Cruel Sea,* N. Monsarrat, 1951.

Crowther, blackmailer. *Young Emmanuel,* Naomi Jacobs, 1932.

Crowther, James, m. Eleanor Brockett.
Joan, their daughter, m. Charles Whitelaw.
Roots, Naomi Jacob, 1931.

Crowthorne, Emily, m. Charles Cothill. *Right Royal* (poem), J. Masefield, 1920.

Croy, Kate, a young Englishwoman.
Mrs Lowder, her aunt.
Merton Densher, her fiancé.
The Wings of the Dove, Henry James, 1902.

Croye, Countesse de (Isabelle).
Reinold, her father.
Hameline, her aunt.
Quentin Durward, W. Scott, 1823.

Cruchecassée, Baroness de la, of dubious reputation. *Vanity Fair,* 1847–8, and elsewhere, W. M. Thackeray.

Cruden, Reginald, central character.
Horace, his younger brother.
His mother.
Reginald Cruden, T. Baines Reed, 1894.

Cruger, Gerald.
Camilla, his wife.
'Horsie' (s.s.), *Here Lies,* Dorothy Parker, 1939.

Cruickshanks, Ebenezer, landlord of the Seven-branched Golden Candlesticks.
His wife.
Waverley, W. Scott, 1814.

Cruikshanks, Joe. *The Little Minister,* J. M. Barrie, 1891.

Cruler, Captain, insane murderer. *All in a Month,* A. Raine, 1908.

Crum, tutor of Val Dartie. *In Chancery,* J. Galsworthy, 1920.

Crum, Jenny, witch of Kinder Scout. *The History of David Grieve,* Mrs Humphry Ward, 1892.

Crum, Mabel, m. the Duke of Ayr and Stirling. *While the Sun Shines* (play), T. Rattigan, 1943.

Crumb, John, m. Ruby Ruggles. *The Way We Live Now,* A. Trollope, 1875.

Crummles, Vincent, manager of travelling theatre.
His wife.
Ninetta, his daughter, the Infant Phenomenon.
His two sons.
Nicholas Nickleby, C. Dickens, 1839.

Crump, President of St Boniface's, and super-snob. *The Book of Snobs,* W. M. Thackeray, 1846–7.

Crump, landlord of the Bootjack Hotel.
His wife, ex-dancer.
Morgiana, their daughter, 'the Ravenswing,' m. Howard Walker.
'The Ravenswing,' *Men's Wives,* W. M. Thackeray, 1843.

Crump, Dr, of Siddermorton. *The Wonderful Visit,* H. G. Wells, 1895.

Crump, Mrs, head cleaner, Pym's Publicity. *Murder Must Advertise,* Dorothy L. Sayers, 1933.

Crump, Lottie, hotel proprietress. *Vile Bodies,* Evelyn Waugh, 1930.

Crump, 'Old.' *Housemaster* (play), Ian Hay, 1936.

Crump, Orlando, m. Jemima Ann Cox. *Barber Cox,* W. M. Thackeray, 1847.

Crumpton, Misses Amelia and Maria, proprietors of boarding school. *Sketches by Boz,* C. Dickens, 1836.

Cruncher, Jeremiah, messenger, Telson's Bank, by day, resurrectionist by night.
His wife.
Young **Jerry,** his son.
A Tale of Two Cities, C. Dickens, 1859.

Crupp, Mrs, landlady, the Adelphi. *David Copperfield,* C. Dickens, 1850.

Crushton, Hon. Mr, friend of Lord Mutanhed. *Pickwick Papers,* C. Dickens, 1837.

Crusoe, Robinson, central character and narrator. *Robinson Crusoe,* Daniel Defoe, 1719.

Crutchley, Frank, murderer of Noakes. *Busman's Honeymoon,* Dorothy L. Sayers, 1937.

Cruttenden (alias Rice), swindler and murderer. *The Loss of the 'Jane Vosper,'* F. Wills Crofts, 1936.

Cryspyn, Tony. *Windsor Castle,* W. H. Ainsworth, 1843.

Crystal, a Utopian youth. *Men Like Gods,* H. G. Wells, 1923.

Cubbon, an army officer. 'Cupid's Arrows' (s.s.), *Plain Tales from the Hills,* R. Kipling, 1888.

Cubitt, member of Pinkie's gang. *Brighton Rock,* Graham Greene, 1938.

Cubitt, Hilton.
Elsie, his wife.
'The Dancing Men,' *The Return of Sherlock Holmes,* A. Conan Doyle, 1905.

Cuckoo, keeper of bad house. *The Good Earth,* Pearl Buck, 1931.

Cucq, André, veteran star, Theatre Duphot. 'The Crime of Olga Jibinsky' (s.s.), *The Little Dog Laughed,* L. Merrick, 1930.

Cudjoe, slave of Senator Bird. *Uncle Tom's Cabin,* Harriet B. Stowe, 1851.

Cudmore, Garret. *Harry Lorrequer,* C. Lever, 1839.

Cuff, Sergeant, detective and part narrator. *The Moonstone,* W. Collins, 1868.

Cuff, Jacob, 'charity man.' *Felix Holt,* George Eliot, 1866.

Cuff, Reginald, school bully, thrashed by William Dobbin. *Vanity Fair,* W. M. Thackeray, 1847–8.

Cuffney, Mr, neighbour of Abraham Lincoln. *Abraham Lincoln* (play), J. Drinkwater, 1918.

Culalla, Lord (Gideon Bramber), financial magnate. *No Other Tiger,* A. E. W. Mason, 1927.

Cullen. Family name of EARL OF DUNGORY.

Cullen, Sir Patrick. *The Doctor's Dilemma* (play), G. B. Shaw, 1906.

Cullen, Philly, farmer. *The Playboy of the Western World* (play), J. M. Synge, 1907.

Culloden, Lord, guardian of Lothair. *Lothair,* B. Disraeli, 1870.

Cully, Tom, intellectual soldier. *Mr Bolfry* (play), James Bridie, 1943.

Cullyngham, Rupert. *Pip,* Ian Hay, 1907.

Culver.
His wife.
John, his son.
Hildegarde, his daughter.
The Title (play), Arnold Bennett, 1918.

Culver, Mr.
His wife.
Adelaide, their daughter, m. Henry Lambert.
Treff, their son.
Britannia Mews, Margery Sharp, 1946.

Culverin. *Polly* (comic opera), J. Gay, 1729.

Culverton, John, head of engineering firm. *The French Lieutenant,* Richard Church, 1971.

Culverwell, Fred, alias Federico Gomez. *The Elder Statesman,* T. S. Eliot (play), 1958.

Cumberland, bad hat. *Frank Fairlegh,* F. E. Smedley, 1850.

Cumberland, Rev. Edwin S. ('Duke').
Primrose, his daughter, m. (1) Rossiter, (2) Justin le Faber.
The Five Sons of Le Faber, E. Raymond, 1945.

Cumberlege, John, corn-dealer.
His wife.
Hetty, their daughter.
Rogue Herries, Hugh Walpole, 1930.

Cuming, John, narrator. *The Prescription* (s.s.), Marjorie Bowen.

Cummings, friend of the Pooters. *Diary of a Nobody,* G. & W. Grossmith, 1892.

Cummings, John, innkeeper, Friars Oak. *Rodney Stone,* A. Conan Doyle, 1896.

Cummings, John, Sir Julian Freke's manservant. *Whose Body?,* Dorothy L. Sayers, 1923.

Cummins, Avilda, of White Farm.
Martha, her dead and disgraced sister.
Timothy's Quest, Kate D. Wiggin, 1896.

Cumnor, Lord.
His wife.
Lady Harriet, his daughter.
Wives and Daughters, Mrs Gaskell, 1866.

Cunningham, Avis, narrator, m. Ernest Everhard.
Professor John, her father.
The Iron Heel, Jack London, 1908.

Cunningham, Blanche.
Tim, her husband.
Pink Sugar, O. Douglas, 1924.

Cunningham, Rex. *Caroline* (play), W. S. Maugham, 1916.

Cunningham, Susan. *The Fourth Wall* (play), A. A. Milne, 1928.

Cupples, Nathaniel Burton, uncle by marriage of Mabel Manderson. *Trent's Last Case,* E. C. Bentley, 1912.

Cuppy, Mrs, Clyde Griffiths's landlady. *An American Tragedy,* T. Dreiser, 1925.

Curdle, 'literary man.'
His wife, patroness of Crummles.
Nicholas Nickleby, C. Dickens, 1839.

Curfew, Bertie, lover of Marjorie Ferrar.
Norah, his sister.
The Silver Spoon, J. Galsworthy, 1926.

Curley.
His wife.
Of Mice and Men, J. Steinbeck, 1937.

Curley, Florence, of Barnabas Ltd. *Flowers for the Judge,* Margery Allingham, 1936.

Curly, one of Peter's band. *Peter Pan* (play), J. M. Barrie, 1904.
Current, Isabella (Aunt Bel). *Evan Harrington*, G. Meredith, 1861.
Curry, Mrs, lady of many interests. *Hemlock and After*, Angus Wilson, 1952.
Curry, Desmond, family friend of the Winslows, in love with Catherine. *The Winslow Boy* (play), T. Rattigan, 1946.
Curtain, Michael, sailor torpedoed on the *Aurora*, central character. *The Ocean*, J. Hanley, 1946.
Curtenty, Jos. *Clayhanger*, Arnold Bennett, 1910.
Curtis, Dr, police surgeon. *Surfeit of Lampreys*, Ngaio Marsh, 1941.
Curtis, Brian. *French without Tears* (play), T. Rattigan, 1936.
Curtis, Charles.
Ethel, his wife.
Their children: **Kate.**
Olivia.
James.
Uncle Oswald.
Invitation to the Waltz, Rosamond Lehmann, 1932.
Curtis, Don.
Helen, his wife.
A Town like Alice, N. Shute, 1950.
Curtis, Sir Henry, Bt (native name Incubu), one of the three explorers, with Quatermain and Good.
Neville, his missing brother.
King Solomon's Mines, H. Rider Haggard, 1885.
Curtis, Hugh. *The Travelling Grave* (s.s.), L. P. Hartley.
Curzon, Charles, adjutant, Lorrequer's regiment. *Harry Lorrequer*, C. Lever, 1839.
Curzon, Lieutenant-General Sir Herbert, K.C.M.G., m. Lady Emily Winter-Willoughby. *The General*, C. S. Forester, 1936.
Cushing, Sarah. 'The Cardboard Box' (s.s.), *His Last Bow*, A. Conan Doyle, 1917.
Cusins, Adolphus. *Major Barbara* (play), G. B. Shaw, 1905.
Cuspard, 'Bunny,' friend of Joan and Peter, killed in Irish Rebellion. *Joan and Peter*, H. G. Wells, 1918.
Cuss, Dr, of Iping. *The Invisible Man*, H. G. Wells, 1897.
Custance, Dame Christian, widow, affianced to Gawyn Goodluck. *Ralph Roister Doister*, N. Udall, 1551.
Custer, Lily, a suffragette. *Mr Ingleside*, E. V. Lucas, 1910.
Cut-Glass, Lord. *Under Milk Wood*, Dylan Thomas, 1954.
Cuthbertson, Joseph, father of Grace Tranfield.
Molly, his wife.
The Philanderer, G. B. Shaw, 1893.
Cutlace. *Polly* (comic opera), J. Gay, 1729.
Cutler, Dr, regimental surgeon. *Vanity Fair*, W. M. Thackeray, 1847–8.
Cutler, Mr and Mrs. *Nicholas Nickleby*, C. Dickens, 1839.
Cutler, Mrs, Dixon's landlady. *Lucky Jim*, K. Amis, 1953.
Cutpurse, Moll (Mary Frith), a notorious thief, fortune-teller and forger. *The Roaring Girle* (play), Thomas Dekker and Thomas Middleton, 1611.
Cutter. *Cutter of Coleman Street* (play), A. Cowley, 1663.
Cuttle, Captain Ned. *Dombey and Son*, C. Dickens, 1848.
Cuvering, Matilda. *The Boar Pig* (s.s.), 'Saki' (H. H. Munro).
Cuxsom, Mother, a low workwoman. *The Mayor of Casterbridge*, T. Hardy, 1886.
Cydalia. *See* NELL GWYNN.
Cymbeline, King of Britain.
His wife.
Cymbeline (play), W. Shakespeare.
Cynara. *Cynara* (poem), E. Dowson.
Cypress, Major Hugo, fiancé of Shirley St George. 'Major Cypress goes off the Deep End' (s.s.), *These Charming People*, M. Arlen, 1920.
Cypress, Mr, friend of Chris Glowry. *Nightmare Abbey*, T. L. Peacock, 1818.
Cypros, Herod's mother. *Herod* (play), S. Phillips, 1900.
Cyril, friend of Hilarion, m. Psyche. *The Princess* (poem), Lord Tennyson, 1847, *Princess Ida* (comic opera), Gilbert & Sullivan, 1884.
Cyril ('St Firebrand'). *Hypatia*, C. Kingsley, 1853.
Czelovar, Karl.
m. (1) **Simone Rakonitz.**
Their children:
Haidée, m. Francis Power.
Raoul, m. Constance Wyatt.

Their children: **Neil, Sylvia** and **Helen.**
(2) **Gustava.**
Leon, Karl's brother.
His children:
Elsa, m. Albrecht Rakonitz.
Konrad, m. Berthe Michel (Aunt Berthe).
Anatol, m. Armgard Ehrensberger.
Rudi, their son, composer, m. Millie Wyman.
Harriet and **Hans,** their children.

Tents of Israel and others, G. B. Stern, 1924 onwards.

Czerlaski, Countess, husband-hunting widow. 'The Rev. Amos Barton,' *Scenes of Clerical Life,* George Eliot, 1857.

D

Dabbit, Eustace. *The Young Idea* (play), N. Coward, 1923.

Dabis, Geraldine, sister of Agatha Calkin.
Kate, their half-sister.
Men and Wives, Ivy Compton-Burnett, 1931.

Dabney, of 'The Balance,' friend of Kent Falconer. *Over Bemerton's,* E. V. Lucas, 1908.

Dabney, Colonel G. M., J.P. 'In Ambush,' *Stalky & Co.,* R. Kipling, 1899.

Dacey, Lord.
His wife.
Adam Bede, George Eliot, 1859.

Dacier, Sir Percy, young politician in love with Diana Warwick. *Diana of the Crossways,* George Meredith, 1885.

Da Costa, Manasseh.
Deborah, his daughter, m. Yankele ben Yitzchok.
The King of Schnorrers, I. Zangwill, 1894.

Dacre, Hugh. *Windsor Castle,* W. H. Ainsworth, 1843.

Dacres, Sim, head hind.
Gillian, his wife.
Polly, their daughter.
The Story of Ragged Robyn, O. Onions, 1945.

D'Acunha, Teresa, accomplice of E. G. Neville. *The Antiquary,* W. Scott, 1816.

Dad, William, a governor of Woldingstanton School. *The Undying Fire,* H. G. Wells, 1919.

Dadson, writing master, Minerva House.
His wife.
Sketches by Boz, C. Dickens, 1836.

Dagenham, Charles, writer killed by shark. *The Towers of Trebizond,* Rose Macaulay, 1956.

Dagge, Joel, blacksmith's son. *Daniel Deronda,* George Eliot, 1876.

Dagley, Farmer.
His wife.
Jacob, their son.
Middlemarch, Geo. Eliot, 1871–2.

Dagonet, mock knight, Arthur's fool. *Idylls of the King* (poem), Lord Tennyson, 1859.

Dagonet, Clare, m. Peter van Degen. *The Custom of the Country,* Edith Wharton, 1913.

Dahfu, chief of the Wariri tribe. *Henderson The Rain King,* Saul Bellow, 1959.

Dain, Oliver, barber to Louis XI. *Quentin Durward,* W. Scott, 1823.

Dain, Waris, chief of Patusan. *Lord Jim,* J. Conrad, 1900.

Dainton, Sir Roger, Bt.
His wife.
Tom and **Sam,** their sons.
Sonia, their daughter, central character, m. David O'Rane.
Sonia, S. McKenna, 1917.

Daintree, R. F., m. Juliana Clare. *Still She Wished for Company,* Margaret Irwin, 1924.

Dainty, Lady. *The Double Gallant* (play), C. Cibber, 1707.

Daisy, Solomon, parish clerk. *Barnaby Rudge,* C. Dickens, 1841.

Dakers, Captain (Uncle). *Sixty-four, Ninety-four,* 1925, and *The Winner* (s.s.). R. H. Mottram.

Dakers, Lady, sister of Mr B. *Pamela,* S. Richardson, 1740.

Dakers, Joan, student at Leys College. *Miss Pym Disposes,* Josephine Tey, 1946.

Dakers, Dr Jonathan, central character, m. Edith Martyn.
Eugene, his father.
Lavinia, his mother.
Harold, his brother.
My Brother Jonathan, F. Brett Young, 1928.

Dale, Dr, Congregational minister. *South Riding,* Winifred Holtby, 1936.

Dale, Dr. *The Soul of a Bishop,* H. G. Wells, 1917.

Dale, Lady.
Bella, her daughter.
The Story of Ivy, Mrs Belloc Lowndes, 1927.

Dale, Mr. *My Novel,* Lord Lytton, 1853.

Dale, Andrew ('Black Andie'), shepherd and gamekeeper of the Bass. *Catriona*, R. L. Stevenson, 1893.

Dale, Edward, stockbroker.
 Louisa, *née* Cutts, his wife.
 Vanity Fair, W. M. Thackeray, 1847–8.

Dale, Isabel, secretary to Mrs Marling, m. Lord Silverbridge; novelist *Lisa Bedale*. The *Barsetshire* series, Angela Thirkell, 1933 onwards.

Dale, Jack, cousin of Connor. *The Sky Pilot*, R. Connor, 1899.

Dale, Jack, a horse trader. *Romany Rye*, George Borrow, 1857.

Dale, Laetitia, m. Sir Willoughby Patterne.
 Doctor Dale, her father.
 The Egoist, G. Meredith, 1879.

Dale, Reuben, gravedigger. *The Mighty Atom*, Marie Corelli, 1896.

Dale, Richard, tutor in charge of Saxe. *The Crystal Hunters*, G. Manville Fenn.

Dale, Robin, schoolmaster, m. Anne Fielding.
 Their twin daughters.
 The Rev. Dr, his father.
 The *Barsetshire* series, Angela Thirkell, 1933 onwards.

Dale, Simon, central character and narrator. *Simon Dale*, A. Hope, 1898.

Dale, Suzanne, loved by Eugene Witla.
 Emily, her mother, wealthy socialite.
 The Genius, Theodore Dreiser, 1915.

Dale-Carrington, Hon. Brenda. *No Son of Mine*, G. B. Stern, 1948.

Dalgarno, Lord, raffish and scoundrelly son of the Earl of Huntinglen. *The Fortunes of Nigel*, W. Scott, 1822.

Dalgetty, Dugald, captain in Montrose's army. *The Legend of Montrose*, W. Scott, 1819.

Dallington, Lady Ralph (Maud). *C.*, M. Baring, 1924.

Dallow, member of Pinkie's gang. *Brighton Rock*, Graham Greene, 1938.

Dalloway, Mrs Clarissa.
 Richard, her husband.
 Elizabeth, their daughter.
 Mrs Dalloway, Virginia Woolf, 1925.

Dalmain, Garth, central character, m. Jane Champion. *The Rosary*, Florence Barclay, 1909.

Dalman, Robert. *The Choice* (play), A. Sutro, 1919.

D'Almanza, Donna Clara. *The Duenna* (play), R. B. Sheridan, 1775.

Dalmellington, Mrs, social climber and false friend of Violet Comper. *For Us in the Dark*, Naomi Royde-Smith, 1937.

D'Alperoussa, Madame.
 Her husband.
 The Thinking Reed, Rebecca West, 1936.

Dalrymple, Major, regimental paymaster.
 His wife.
 Matilda and **Fanny,** their daughters.
 Charles O'Malley, C. Lever, 1841.

D'Alvadorez, Donna Lucia (from Brazil). *Charley's Aunt* (play), Brandon Thomas, 1892.

Daly, Dr, D.D., Vicar of Ploverleigh, m. Constance Partlet. *The Sorcerer* (comic opera), Gilbert & Sullivan, 1877.

Daly, 'Joxer.' *Juno and the Paycock* (play), S. O'Casey, 1925.

Daly, Patsey, horse thief. *Robbery under Arms*, R. Boldrewood, 1888.

Dalyell, Lord. *Perkin Warbeck* (play), J. Ford, 1634.

Dalyngridge, Sir Richard, Norman knight.
 Lady Aelueva, his wife.
 'Young Men at the Manor' and others (s.ss.), *Puck of Pook's Hill*, 1906, and *Rewards and Fairies*, 1910, R. Kipling.

Damague, Princess Cornoa. *Under Two Flags*, Ouida, 1867.

Damascus, Governor of. *Tamburlaine* (play), C. Marlowe, 1587.

Damer, Henrietta Mary, m. Captain Clyne.
 Sir Charles, her brother.
 Starvecrow Farm, Stanley Weyman, 1905.

Damico, Father. *The Small Miracle*, P. Gallico, 1951.

Damon. *The Seasons* (poem), J. Thomson, 1730.

Damson, Suke, 'a hoydenish maiden,' m. Tim Tangs. *The Woodlanders*, T. Hardy, 1887.

Dan.
Una, his sister. Central characters, visited by Puck and others.
Puck of Pook's Hill, 1906, and *Rewards and Fairies*, 1910, R. Kipling.

Dan, son of Samson and Mali. 'As it is Written' (s.s.), *My People*, Caradoc Evans, 1915.

Dan, house-boy to Mrs Bramson, and murderer. *Night Must Fall* (play), Emlyn Williams, 1935.

Dana Da. 'The Sending of Dana Da' (s.s.), *Soldiers Three*, R. Kipling, 1888.

Danagher, Mrs Bridget, aunt and guardian of Christian Roche.
John, one of her sons.
Without My Cloak, Kate O'Brien, 1931.

Danby, Philip Norman, head of Danby & Winter, Michael Mont's firm of publishers; 'always right.' The *Forsyte* series, J. Galsworthy, 1906–33.

Dancey, Rev. Mr and Mrs.
Catrina and **Louise,** their daughters.
Andrew, their son.
Henry, their son, friend of Eva.
Eva Trout, Elizabeth Bowen, 1969.

Dancy, Captain Ronald, D.S.O.
Mabel, his wife.
Loyalties (play), J. Galsworthy, 1922.

Dando, Roland, Welsh Attorney-General of a newly independent African state. *A Guest of Honour*, Nadine Gordimer, 1971.

Dandolo, self-styled count, Professor of Dancing; has a love-affair with Adeliza Grampus. *The Professor*, W. M. Thackeray, 1837.

Dandy, Mick, Trade Unionist leader. *Sybil*, B. Disraeli, 1845.

Dane, William, treacherous friend of Silas Marner. *Silas Marner*, George Eliot, 1861.

Dangerfield, Captain, spy and informer. *Peveril of the Peak*, W. Scott, 1822.

Dangerfield, Monte, shady financier. *The Great Pandolfo*, W. J. Locke, 1925.

Dangerfield, Stanard, cousin of Lucy Batchelor. *Steamboat Gothic*, Frances Parkinson Keyes, 1952.

Dangle.
His wife.
The Critic (play), R. B. Sheridan, 1779.

Dangle, Mr, friend of Mrs Hetty Milton. *The Wheels of Chance*, H. G. Wells, 1896.

Daniels, group manager, Pym's Publicity. *Murder Must Advertise*, Dorothy L. Sayers, 1933.

Dannisburgh, Lord, friend of Diana Warwick. *Diana of the Crossways*, George Meredith, 1885.

Danvers, Mrs, housekeeper at Manderley. *Rebecca*, Daphne du Maurier, 1938.

Daoud Shah. 'Dray Wara Yow Dee' (s.s.), *Soldiers Three*, R. Kipling, 1888.

Daphnis. *The Faithful Shepherdess* (play), Beaumont & Fletcher, 1610.

Dara, Michael. *The Shadow of the Glen* (play), J. M. Synge, 1903.

Darch, Car, mistress of Alec D'Urberville.
Nancy, her sister.
Tess of the D'Urbervilles, T. Hardy, 1891.

D'Archeville, Baron, landed proprietor, owner of the Spanish Farm.
Eugénie, his wife.
Georges, their son, loved by Madeleine Vanderlynden.
The Spanish Farm, 1924, and *D'Archeville, a Portrait* (s.s.), R. H. Mottram.

Darcy, Dennis, 'thriftless, witless wastrel.' *The Bay*, L. A. G. Strong, 1941.

Darcy, Fitzwilliam, friend of Charles Bingley, m. Elizabeth Bennet.
Lady Anne, his mother.
Georgiana, his sister.
Pride and Prejudice, Jane Austen, 1813.

D'Arcy, John, cousin of Dermot McDermot, m. (1) Maeve Hogan, (2) Connaught O'Brien. *Hangman's House*, Donn Byrne, 1926.

D'Arcy, T., artist and picture dealer, friend of Henry Aylwin. *Aylwin*, T. Watts-Dunton, 1899.

Dare, Anthony.
Julia, his wife, cousin of Edgar Halliburton.
Anthony, jnr, their eldest son.
Mrs Halliburton's Troubles, Mrs Henry Wood, 1862.

Dare, William, illegitimate son of Captain de Stancy. *A Laodicean,* T. Hardy, 1881.

D'Argens, Marquis. *Barry Lyndon,* W. M. Thackeray, 1844.

D'Argent, Louise Eugénie, French *émigrée* (alias Louise Silver), governess, m. Edwin Halifax. *John Halifax, Gentleman,* Mrs Craik, 1856.

Da Rimini. *See* FRANCESCA.

'Dark John,' saved from drowning by Col of Corodale. *Children of the Tempest,* N. Munro, 1903.

Darke, Solomon.
  Rachel, *née* Velindre, his wife.
  Their children:
    Peter.
    Jasper.
    Ruby, m. Rev. E. Swyndle.
    Amber, m. Michael Hallowes.
  Amelia, Solomon's sister, m. William Cantlop.
The House in Dormer Forest, Mary Webb, 1920.

Darley, Helen, schoolmistress. *Elsie Venner,* O. W. Holmes, 1861.

Darley, L. G., Anglo-Irish schoolteacher and would-be writer. *The Alexandria Quartet,* 1957–61, Lawrence Durrell.

Darling, Mr and Mrs.
  Their children: **Wendy Moira Angela, John** and **Michael.**
Peter Pan (play), J. M. Barrie, 1904.

Darling, Dora. *Fanny's First Play* (play), G. B. Shaw, 1905.

Darlington, Lord. *Lady Windermere's Fan* (play), O. Wilde, 1892.

Darnas, Colonel, French officer. *The Lady of Lyons,* Lord Lytton, 1838.

Darnay, Rev. Mr, curate. *Portrait of Clare,* F. Brett Young, 1927.

Darnay, Charles, French *émigré,* m. Lucie Manette. *See* ST EVREMONDE. *A Tale of Two Cities,* C. Dickens, 1859.

Darnel, Aurelia, m. Lancelot Greaves.
  Her father.
  Anthony, her uncle.
Sir Lancelot Greaves, T. Smollett, 1762.

Darnford, Lady, daughter of Lady Jones. *Pamela,* S. Richardson, 1740.

Darnleigh, Admiral the Hon. George.
  Lady Emily, his sister, m. George Carew.
Sons of Fire, M. E. Braddon, 1896.

Darragh, Sir Piers.
  Lacy, his twin brother, m. Nuala McMurrough.
  His mother.
'The Fox Hunter' (s.s.), *Countrymen All,* Katherine Tynan, 1945.

D'Arragon, Charles, French captain, Napoleonic spy and traitor, m. Desirée Sebastian.
  Louis Darragon (Anglicized), captain in the British Navy, his cousin, in love with Desirée.
Barlasch of the Guard, H. Seton Merriman, 1903.

Darrell, Dr Edmund, lover of Nina Leeds. *Strange Interlude,* E. O'Neill, 1928.

Darrell, Peter. *Bulldog Drummond,* 'Sapper' (H. C. McNeile), 1920.

Darrell, Thames. *Jack Sheppard,* W. H. Ainsworth, 1839.

Darroll, Nurse ('The Amazon'). *A Daughter of Time,* Josephine Tey, 1951.

Darth, Emily, m. (1) Steve Hardcome, (2) James Hardcome. 'The History of the Hardcomes,' *Life's Little Ironies,* T. Hardy, 1894.

Dartie, Montague, m. Winifred Forsyte, sister of Soames.
  Their children:
    Publius Valerius (Val), m. Holly Forsyte.
    Imogen, m. Jack Cardigan.
    Maud.
    Benedict.
The *Forsyte* series, J. Galsworthy, 1906–33.

Dartle, Rosa, companion to Mrs Steerforth. *David Copperfield,* C. Dickens, 1850.

Darton, Charles. 'Interlopers at the Knap,' *Wessex Tales,* T. Hardy, 1888.

Darvell, Thomas ('Corney'), killed in air-raid. *The Flower Girls,* Clemence Dane, 1954.

Darvil, Alice. *See* LADY VARGRAVE.

Darwin, Roy. *Counsellor-at-Law* (play), Elmer Rice, 1931.

Darzee, the tailor-bird.
  His wife.
'Rikki Tikki Tavi' (s.s.), *The Jungle Book,* R. Kipling, 1894.

Dashfort, Lady. *The Absentee,* Maria Edgeworth, 1812.

Dashwood, General Sir George.
  Captain Dashwood, his son.

Lucy, his daughter, m. Charles O'Malley.
Charles O'Malley, C. Lever, 1841.

Dashwood, Henry, of Norland Park.
His wife.
Their children:
John, his son by a former wife.
Fanny, his wife, *née* Ferrars.
Harry, their son.
Elinor, m. Edward Ferrars.
Marianne, m. Colonel Brandon.
Margaret.
Sense and Sensibility, Jane Austen, 1811.

Dass, Durga and Ram, twins. 'Gemini' (s.s.), *Soldiers Three,* R. Kipling, 1888.

Dass, Secundra, Indian friend of James Ballantrae (Mr Bally). *The Master of Ballantrae,* R. L. Stevenson, 1889.

Datchery, Dick. *Edwin Drood,* C. Dickens, 1870.

Daubeny ('Dubby'), Tory leader. *Phineas Finn,* 1869, and elsewhere, A. Trollope.

Daubeny, John (Dubbs), schoolboy. *St Winifred's,* F. W. Farrar, 1862.

Daubreuil, Madame, formerly Jeanne Beroldy, murderess and blackmailer.
Marthe, her daughter.
Murder on the Links, Agatha Christie, 1923.

D'Aulnais, maiden name of Charles Darnay's mother, from which he takes the name he adopts in England. *A Tale of Two Cities,* C. Dickens, 1859.

Daunt, Mr, m. Fanny Clare. *Still She Wished for Company,* Margaret Irwin, 1924.

Dauntless, Richard, foster-brother of Sir Ruthven Murgatroyd, m. Rose Maybud. *Ruddigore* (comic opera), Gilbert & Sullivan, 1887.

Dauphin, The (Prince Louis). *Henry the Fifth* (play), W. Shakespeare.

D'Auvergne, General, m. Marie de Meudon as 1st husband. *Tom Burke of Ours,* C. Lever, 1844.

Dauvray, Madame, wealthy widow, murderer. *At the Villa Rose,* A. E. W. Mason, 1910.

D'Auzac, Prince Zertho, blackmailer and murderer. *If Sinners Entice Thee,* W. le Queux, 1898.

Davenant, Lord and Lady (pseudo). *See* TIMOTHY and CLARA CLITHEROE.

Davenport, Lady Lucy. *Waste* (play), H. Granville-Barker, 1907.

Davenport, Mrs Olivia. *See* HOLLINGRAKE.

Davers, Lady, sister of 'Mr B.'
Her husband.
Pamela, S. Richardson, 1740.

Davey, Francis, John Fane's solicitor. *Going their own Ways,* A. Waugh, 1938.

David, servant of Bob Acres. *The Rivals* (play), R. B. Sheridan, 1775.

David, old butler of Cheeryble Brothers. *Nicholas Nickleby,* C. Dickens, 1839.

David, policeman. *A Kiss for Cinderella* (play), J. M. Barrie, 1916.

David, employed by Miller Loveday. *The Trumpet Major,* T. Hardy, 1880.

David. *Absalom and Achitophel* (poem), J. Dryden, 1681.

David, Megan, in love with Frank Ashurst. *The Apple Tree,* J. Galsworthy, 1918.

Davidge, Lucia (Loo), Coventry girl on holiday in Stockholm. *England Made Me,* Graham Greene, 1935.

Davidson, Sergeant. *The Little Minister,* J. M. Barrie, 1891.

Davidson, Rev. Alfred, missionary.
His wife.
'Miss Thompson' (s.s.), *The Trembling of a Leaf,* W. S. Maugham, 1921: also *Rain* (play).

Davidson, Captain. *Victory,* Joseph Conrad, 1915.

Davies, an old storekeeper. *The Ox-Bow Incident,* Walter Van Tilburg Clark, 1940.

Davies, an old tramp. *The Caretaker* (play), Harold Pinter, 1960.

Davies, Mr, ship's engineer. 'Judson and the Empire' (s.s.), *Many Inventions,* R. Kipling, 1893.

Davies, Mrs, aunt of Winnie Wynne. *Aylwin,* T. Watts-Dunton, 1899.

Davies, Andrew ('Dago'), scaler in the Liverpool docks. *Ebb and Flood,* James Hanley, 1932.

Davies, Arthur H., college friend of Carruthers, owner of yacht *Dulcibella.* *The Riddle of the Sands,* E. Childers, 1903.

Davies, Evan.
 Cherry, his wife, *née* Martyn.
 September Tide, Daphne du Maurier, 1948.

Davies, John, superintendent of the Tidenet Fishing Co.'s station. *Redgauntlet,* W. Scott, 1824.

Davies, Ken, amateur actor. *That Uncertain Feeling,* Kingsley Amis, 1955.

Davilla, follower of Pizarro. *Pizarro* (play), R. B. Sheridan, 1799.

Davilow, Captain, stepfather of Gwen Harleth.
 Fanny, his wife.
 Their daughters:
  Alice.
  Bertha.
  Fanny.
  Isobel.
 Daniel Deronda, George Eliot, 1876.

Davis, Mrs, landlady, the Load of Mischief. *The Three Taps,* R. Knox, 1927.

Davis, Ben ('The Welsher'), racing man. *Under Two Flags,* Ouida, 1867.

Davis, Bill, fiancé of Phyllis Lee. *Mr Fortune Finds a Pig,* H. C. Bailey, 1943.

Davis, Lavender. *The Pursuit of Love,* Nancy Mitford, 1945.

Davis, Meg, who 'lived, loved and lost.' *A Voyage to Purilia,* Elmer Rice, 1930.

Davison, Helena, graduate of Vassar. Ex-room-mate of Kay Strong. *The Group,* Mary McCarthy, 1963.

Davray, Edmund, artist. *The Cathedral,* Hugh Walpole, 1922.

Daw, Ikey, Jewish financier. *Flamingo,* Mary Borden, 1927.

Daw, Susan, eng. to Jim Noon, m. Hans Orthoven. *I Live Under a Black Sun,* Edith Sitwell, 1937.

Dawbeney, Lord. *Perkin Warbeck* (play), J. Ford, 1634.

Dawe, Sir Harry. 'Hal o' the Draft' and elsewhere, *Puck of Pook's Hill,* R. Kipling, 1906.

Dawes, Mrs, cook to the Barleys. *The One Before,* Barry Pain, 1902.

Dawes, Alice, waitress, mistress of Patrick Seton. *The Bachelors,* Muriel Spark, 1961.

Dawes, Baxter, m. Clara Radford. *Sons and Lovers,* D. H. Lawrence, 1913.

Dawes, Gerald, engaged to Agnes Pembroke, dies from injury playing football. *The Longest Journey,* E. M. Forster, 1907.

Dawes, Mary, kitchenmaid. *Dombey and Son,* C. Dickens, 1848.

Dawes, Rufus. *See* RICHARD DEVINE.

Dawkbell, Rev. James, headmaster, Leyminster Grammar School. *Both of this Parish,* J. S. Fletcher.

Dawkins, Jack, thief, trainee of Fagin. *Oliver Twist,* C. Dickens, 1838.

Dawkins, Thomas Smith, swindled by Deuceace and Blewett. 'The Amours of Mr Deuceace,' *Yellowplush Papers,* W. M. Thackeray, 1838.

Dawlish, assistant to Dr Trump. *Children of the Archbishop,* N. Collins, 1951.

Dawson, Lady Shuttleworth's agent. *Princess Priscilla's Fortnight,* Countess von Arnim, 1905.

Dawson, Dr. *The Woman in White,* W. Collins, 1860.

Dawson, Major.
 Dick ('The Divil'), his son.
 Fanny, his daughter, m. Edward O'Connor.
 Handy Andy, S. Lover, 1842.

Dawson, Dave, albino. *God's Little Acre,* E. Caldwell, 1933.

Dawson (Brown), **Dinah and Hannah,** pastry-cooks. *Cousin Phillis,* Mrs Gaskell, 1864.

Dawson, Elias (Lias), schoolmaster.
 Margaret, his wife.
 The History of David Grieve, Mrs Humphry Ward, 1892.

Dawson, Emilie, friend of Margaret Owen. *The Whistling Chambermaid,* Naomi Royde-Smith, 1957.

Dawson, Jemmy. *Jemmy Dawson* (poem), W. Shenstone, 1745.

Dawson, Louise, *High Wind in Jamaica,* R. Hughes, 1929.

Dawson, Rose, m. as 2nd wife, Sir Pitt Crawley. *Vanity Fair,* W. M. Thackeray, 1847–8.

Dawtry, Sir Oliver, a banker and financier. *Caprice,* Ronald Firbank, 1917.

Day, Fancy, school-teacher, m. Dick Dewy.
 Geoffrey, her father.
 Jane, her stepmother.
 Under the Greenwood Tree, T. Hardy, 1872.

Day, Ferquhard, of the Clan Chattan. *The Fair Maid of Perth,* W. Scott, 1828.

Day, Halcyon, central character, m. Eden Herring.
  Captain Robert, her father.
  Eveline, *née* Wincott, her dead mother.
Little Red Horses, G. B. Stern, 1932.

Daygo, Joe, old fisherman. *Cormorant Crag,* G. Manville Fenn, 1895.

Dayson, Arthur. *Hilda Lessways,* Arnold Bennett, 1911.

De, Grish Chunder, M.A. 'The Head of the District' (s.s.), *Life's Handicap,* R. Kipling, 1891.

Deacon, The, horse which, with others, executes judgment on Boney, an agitator. 'A Walking Delegate' (s.s.), *The Day's Work,* R. Kipling, 1898.

Deadeye, Dick, seaman. *H.M.S. Pinafore* (comic opera), Gilbert & Sullivan, 1878.

Deadlock, 'great pied' otter-hound. *Tarka the Otter,* H. Williamson, 1927.

Deakin, Teddie (Detective-Inspector Morrison). *The Ghost Train* (play), A. Ridley, 1925.

Dealtry, Jill, m. John Grey.
  Ronald, her brother.
The City of Beautiful Nonsense, E. T. Thurston, 1909.

Deamer, Dulcie, actress. *Enter a Murderer,* Ngaio Marsh, 1935.

Dean, Mr.
  Rachel, his wife.
  Their children:
    Laurence, m. Margaret Tebben.
    Helen.
    Betty.
    Susan, m. Richard Tebben.
    Jessica, actress, m. Aubrey Clover.
    And others.
The *Barsetshire* series, Angela Thirkell, 1933 onwards.

Dean, Mrs Ellen, housekeeper to Lockwood and principal narrator. *Wuthering Heights,* Emily Brontë 1847.

Dean, Margaret, m. Chad Buford.
  Harry and **Dan,** her brothers.
  General and Mrs Dean, her parents.
The Little Shepherd of Kingdom Come, John Fox, Jnr, 1903.

Dean, Dr Maxwell. *Ziska,* Marie Corelli, 1897.

Dean, Susie, comedienne of the Dinky Doos Concert Party, later Good Companions, m. Inigo Jollifant. *The Good Companions,* J. B. Priestley, 1929.

Dean, Victor, killed on staircase, Pym's Publicity. *Murder Must Advertise,* Dorothy L. Sayers, 1933.

Deane, tutor to Vincent Burnet. *Cormorant Crag,* G. Manville Fenn, 1895.

Deane, junior partner in Guest & Co.
  Susan, his wife, *née* Dodson.
  Lucy, their daughter, m. Stephen Guest.
The Mill on the Floss, George Eliot, 1860.

Deans, David.
  Christian, his 1st wife.
    Jeanie, their daughter, m. Reuben Butler.
  Rebecca, his 2nd wife.
    Effie, their daughter, m. George Staunton.
The Heart of Midlothian, W. Scott, 1818.

De Aquila, Gilbert, Lord of Pevensey. 'Young Men at the Manor' and others, *Puck of Pook's Hill,* R. Kipling, 1906.

Dearborn, Miss, schoolmistress. *Rebecca of Sunnybrook Farm,* Kate D. Wiggin, 1903.

Dearborn, Laura, central character, m. Curtis Jadwin.
  Page, her sister, m. Landry Court.
The Pit, F. Norris, 1903.

De Arguello, José, father of Yerba Buena, m. Kate Howard. *A Ward of the Golden Gate,* Bret Harte.

Dearsley, Sahib. 'The Incarnation of Krishna Mulvaney' (s.s.), *Life's Handicap,* R. Kipling, 1891.

Dearth, Will.
  Mabel, his wife.
  Margaret, his dream-daughter.
Dear Brutus (play), J. M. Barrie, 1917.

Deasy, schoolmaster. *Ulysses,* James Joyce, 1922.

De Avila, Pedro, Spaniard. 'Gloriana' (s.s.), *Rewards and Fairies,* R. Kipling, 1910.

Debarry, Sir Maximus.
His wife.
Their children: **Philip, Harriet** and **Selina.**
Augustus, Rector of Treby Magna, his brother.
Felix Holt, George Eliot, 1866.

Debbitch, Deborah, nurse and guardian of Alice Bridgenorth. *Peveril of the Peak,* W. Scott, 1822.

De Beaulieu, Denis, m. Blanche de Malétroit.
Guichard, his brother.
'The Sire de Malétroit's Door' (s.s.), *New Arabian Nights,* R. L. Stevenson, 1882.

De Beauvais, Henry. *Tom Burke of Ours,* C. Lever, 1844.

Debenham, Joan, central character, illegitimate daughter of Will Sydenham, adopted by the Stublands, m. Peter Stubland. *Joan and Peter,* H. G. Wells, 1918.

De Berault, m. de Cocheforet's sister. *Under the Red Robe,* Stanley Weyman, 1894.

De Beringham, Sieur. *Richelieu* (play), Lord Lytton, 1839.

Debingham, Henry, friend of Becky Mintley. *I Live Under a Black Sun,* Edith Sitwell, 1937.

De Bourgh, Lady Catherine, *patronne* of William Collins, aunt of Darcy.
Her daughter.
Pride and Prejudice, Jane Austen, 1813.

De Bréville, Nesta, adventuress, widow of Count de Bréville, m. Sir Victor Pandolfo. *The Great Pandolfo,* W. J. Locke, 1925.

Debriseau, Captain, of the *Sainte Vierge,* smuggler. *The King's Own,* Captain Marryat, 1830.

De Carlos ('Old Charlie'). 'Belles Demoiselles Plantation' (s.s.), *Old Creole Days,* G. W. Cable, 1879.

De Casimir, Colonel, spy and traitor. *Barlasch of the Guard,* H. Seton Merriman, 1903.

De Castro, Señor Raoul. *The Four Armourers,* F. Beeding, 1930.

De Centeville, Sir Eric.
Osmond, his son.
Dame Astrida, his mother. Guardians of Richard, Duke of Normandy.
The Little Duke, Charlotte M. Yonge, 1854.

De Chabrillanne, Chevalier, cousin of de la Tour d'Azyr, killed in duel with Scaramouche. *Scaramouche,* R. Sabatini, 1921.

De Chanet, Marquise. *See* Labouisse.
Pierre, her son, m. Armande Vincent.
Steamboat Gothic, Frances Parkinson Keyes, 1952.

De Charleu, Colonel Jean Albert.
His seven daughters.
'Belles Demoiselles Plantation' (s.s.), *Old Creole Days,* G. W. Cable, 1879.

De Chatellan, Count Armand, guardian of Patrick Mahon. *Drums of War,* H. de Vere Stacpoole, 1910.

De Chaurellon, Claude, Colonel of Chasseurs, Foreign Legion. *Under Two Flags,* Ouida, 1867.

De Chauxville, Baron Claude, evil genius. *The Sowers,* H. Seton Merriman, 1896.

Decius Brutus, conspirator against Caesar. *Julius Caesar* (play), W. Shakespeare.

De Clancy, Phelim (*né* Clancy). *The Book of Snobs,* W. M. Thackeray, 1846–7.

De Cocheforet.
His wife, posing as his sister.
His sister, posing as his wife, m. de Berault.
Under the Red Robe, Stanley Weyman, 1894.

De Coigny, Count. *Drums of War,* H. de Vere Stacpoole, 1910.

De Courcy. *See* Kilcoran.

De Courcy, Admiral, capricious and violent.
William, his son.
Edward, his son, enlisted in navy as E. Peters.
The King's Own, Captain Marryat, 1830.

De Courcy, Countess.
Her children:
Lord Porlock.
George.
John.
Amelia, m. Mortimer Gazebee.
Rosina.
Margaretta.
Alexandrina.
Doctor Thorne, A. Trollope, 1858.

De Coverley, Sir Roger, J.P., Bt, bachelor. Essays in *The Spectator,* J. Addison, 1711–14.

De Craye, Colonel Horace. *The Egoist*, G. Meredith, 1879.

De Cretien, Raymond, French P.O.W. in 18th century. *The French Lieutenant*, Richard Church, 1971.

De Croissy, Colbert (Charles II). *Simon Dale*, A. Hope, 1898.

D'Cruze, Michele. 'His Chance in Life' (s.s.), *Plain Tales from the Hills*, R. Kipling, 1888.

Dedalus, Stephen (Kinch), schoolmaster. *Ulysses*, James Joyce, 1922.

Dede, Inspector. *Loyalties* (play), J. Galsworthy, 1922.

Dedlock, Sir Leicester, Bt.
His wife; mother, before her marriage, of Esther Summerson, by Captain Hawdon.
Volumnia, his cousin.
Bleak House, C. Dickens, 1853.

De Duvarney, elder brother of Count of Valancourt. *The Mysteries of Udolpho*, Mrs Radcliffe, 1794.

Deeley, film man.
Kate, his wife.
Old Times (play), Harold Pinter, 1971.

Deemes, Mrs. 'A Friend's Friend' (s.s.), *Plain Tales from the Hills*, R. Kipling, 1888.

Deepmere, Lord. *The American*, H. James, 1877.

Deercourt, Emma, bosom friend of Minnie Gadsby (wife of Capt. Philip Gadsby). *The Story of the Gadsbys*, R. Kipling, 1888.

Deesa, mahout. 'Moti Guj—Mutineer' (s.s.), *Life's Handicap*, R. Kipling, 1891.

De Espinosa, Captain Don Diego. *Captain Blood*, R. Sabatini, 1922.

Deever, Danny. 'Danny Deever' (poem), *Barrack-room Ballads*, R. Kipling, 1892.

Defarge, proprietor of wine-shop.
Madame, his wife.
A Tale of Two Cities, C. Dickens, 1859.

De Félan, Marquis, French adventurer and gambler.
Madelon, his niece, m. Sam Billingham.
Mr Billingham, the Marquis and Madelon, E. P. Oppenheim.

De Ferrars, Lord (Compton). *Cecilia*, Fanny Burney, 1782.

De Ferrières, Sir Rainulf. *The Little Duke*, Charlotte M. Yonge, 1854.

De Flouncy, Mr and Mrs, dancing instructors. *Before the Bombardment*, O. Sitwell, 1926.

De Fœnix, Clare.
Her husband.
Trelawny of the Wells, A. W. Pinero, 1898.

De Foley, Dame Alicia, prioress of the Benedictine convent at Oby (1351–60).
Thomas, her cousin, prior of Etchingdon.
The Corner That Held Them, Sylvia Townsend Warner, 1948.

De Fontelles. *Simon Dale*, A. Hope, 1898.

De Forest, of the Aerial Board of Control. 'As Easy as A B C' (s.s.), *A Diversity of Creatures*, R. Kipling, 1917.

De Freville, Max, gambler. *The Rich Pay Late*, 1964, and others in the *Alms for Oblivion* sequence, Simon Raven.

De Frey, Elaine, heiress. *The Unbearable Bassington*, 'Saki' (H. H. Munro), 1912.

De Frontenac, Count, Governor-General of Canada at end of 17th century. *Shadows on the Rock*, Willa Cather, 1932.

De Graçay, Viscountess (Marie), mistress of Hornblower. The *Hornblower* series, C. S. Forester, 1937 onwards.

De Grival, Count André. *The Amazons* (play), A. W. Pinero, 1893.

De Grouchy, card-sharper, ally of Colonel Tracey. 'Patience' (s.s.), *Last Recollections of My Uncle Charles*, N. Balchin, 1954.

De Ham, Miss, millionaire laundry proprietress. *The Weak and the Strong*, G. Kersh, 1945.

De Hamal, Count, m. Ginevra Fanshawe. *Villette*, Charlotte Brontë, 1853.

De Horter, Monsieur, consul, Boulogne. *Jorrocks's Jaunts and Jollities*, R. S. Surtees, 1838.

Deipholus, son of Priam. *Troilus and Cressida* (play), W. Shakespeare.

De Jong, Amelie (Aunt Amelie), of the Rakonitz clan.

Nathan, her husband.
Camille, her daughter, m. Étienne Levine.
Jeanne-Marie, her daughter, eng. to Orlo Vassiloff.
Tents of Israel, etc., G. B. Stern, 1924 onwards.

De Jong, Dirk ('So Big'), central character.
Selina, his mother, *née* Peake.
His father.
So Big, Edna Ferber, 1924.

De Jongh, keeper of grog-shop. *Lord Jim*, J. Conrad, 1900.

De Kercadiou, Quintin, Lord of Gavrillac, godfather of Scaramouche.
Aline, his niece, in love with Scaramouche.
Scaramouche, R. Sabatini, 1921.

Dekker, Rev. Mathew, Vicar of Glastonbury. *A Glastonbury Romance*, J. C. Powys, 1932.

De La Brière, Contesse. *What Every Woman Knows* (play), J. M. Barrie, 1908.

De La Casas, Carmen, m. John Foster.
Antonio, her father.
'John O' Dreams' (s.s.), *Countrymen All*, Katherine Tynan, 1915.

De La Casternas, Marquis (Raymond) (alias d'Averada), m. Agnes de Medina. *The Monk*, M. G. Lewis, 1796.

De Lacey.
Agatha, his daughter.
Felix, his son.
Frankenstein, Mary W. Shelley, 1818.

Delacour, Maurice, old Englishman living in Italy. *Late in the Afternoon*, Lettice Cooper, 1971.

Delacourt, Laura.
Roger, her husband.
David, their son.
The Duenna, Mrs Belloc Lowndes.

Delacroix, Mrs Dinah, formerly Diana Piggott (Dicey).
William and **Roland,** her sons.
The Little Girls, Elizabeth Bowen, 1964.

De La Croye. *See* QUENTIN DURWARD.

Delafield, Maggie, central character. *The Sowers*, H. Seton Merriman, 1896.

Delagrange, Madame, proprietor of Villa Iris, Casablanca. *The Winding Stair*, A. E. W. Mason, 1923.

Delahay, Ela, an orphan. *Charley's Aunt*, Brandon Thomas, 1892.

De Laine, Miss. *The Aspiring Miss De Laine* (poem), Bret Harte.

Delamere, Hon. Geoffrey L., in love with Catherine Aubrey. *Ten Thousand a Year*, S. Warren, 1839.

Delaney, Dr, fashionable physician. *Sweet Lavender* (play), A. W. Pinero, 1888.

Delaney, Delina, central character, m. Lord Gifford. *Delina Delaney*, Amanda Ros.

Delany, Cornelius ('Corny'), Philip O'Grady's manservant. *Jack Hinton*, C. Lever, 1843.

De La Pole, Sir Arthur.
Jane, his wife.
Barbara and **Ursula,** their daughters.
The Land of Spices, Kate O'Brien, 1941.

Delarey, General, conqueror of the Rians. *Right Off the Map*, C. E. Montague, 1927.

Delaroche, Madeline, in love with Kit Hardy. *Through the Storm*, P. Gibbs, 1945.

De La Rue, Charlotte. *Poison Ivy*, P. Cheyney, 1937.

De La Scaze, wealthy Frenchman.
Olivia, his Spanish wife.
The Seven Who Fled, Frederic Prokosch, 1937.

De La Touche, Mehée (Leon Guichard). *Tom Burke of Ours*, C. Lever, 1844.

De La Tour d'Azyr. *See* ANDRÉ-LOUIS MOREAU.

De Lauzun, Claude. *Tom Burke of Ours*, C. Lever, 1844.

De Laval, Bishop. *Shadows on the Rock*. Willa Cather, 1932.

Delaval, Frederick (or Frank), cousin of the Honeywoods, m. Kitty Honeywood. *The Adventures of Mr Verdant Green*, C. Bede, 1853.

Delaval, Lady Lucy, sister of Lord St Erme. *Heartsease*, Charlotte M. Yonge, 1854.

De Lavardens, General.
Captain George, his son, m. Jeanne Laurent.
'The Doll in the Pink Silk Dress' (s.s.), *All the World Wondered*, L. Merrick, 1911.

De Lavel, Louis, central character. *Uncle Bernac*, A. Conan Doyle, 1897.

Delavere, William, private secretary to the Prime Minister. *But Soft—We Are Observed!,* H. Belloc, 1928.

De La Zouch, Lord, friend of C. Aubrey. *Ten Thousand a Year,* S. Warren, 1839.

Del Bosco, Martin, Vice-Admiral of Spain. *The Jew of Malta* (play), C. Marlowe, 1633.

De Levis, Ferdinand. *Loyalties* (play), J. Galsworthy, 1922.

De Leyva, Miguel, hidalgo.
 Carlotta, his youngest daughter, eng. to Don Manuel.
 Emilia, his sister, m. Piranha.
Odtaa, J. Masefield, 1926.

Delia, m. Freeman. *A House of Children,* Joyce Cary, 1941.

Delisport, 1st Marquess of (George Goodge), Captain of Industry. *But Soft—We Are Observed!,* H. Belloc, 1928.

Dell, Cynthia. *The Laughing Lady* (play), A. Sutro, 1922.

Dell, Teddie, mistress of Paul Brande, *Flowers for the Judge,* Margery Allingham, 1936.

Della Arcola, principesse. *Our Betters* (play), W. S. Maugham, 1923.

Del Lago, Alexandra, alcoholic ex-movie star. *Sweet Bird of Youth* (play), Tennessee Williams, 1959.

De Lorme, Marion. *Richelieu* (play), Lord Lytton, 1839.

Delphine, a Belgian child. *A Kiss for Cinderella* (play), J. M. Barrie, 1916.

Delves, Sergeant. *Mrs Halliburton's Troubles,* Mrs Henry Wood, 1862.

Delvile, trustee.
 His wife.
 Mortimer, their son, m. Cecilia Beverley.
Cecilia, Fanny Burney, 1782.

Delville, Mrs ('The Dowd'). 'A Second-rate Woman' (s.s.), *Wee Willie Winkie,* R. Kipling, 1888.

De Lyndesay, Alicia.
 m. (1) **Egbert** (of another branch).
  Stanley ('Slinker'), their son, m. Nettie Stone.
 (2) **William,** Egbert's cousin.
  Christian, their son, m. Deborah.
 Deborah (of another branch), m. Christian.
 Roger, her father.
 Lionel ('Larrupper'), a cousin.
Crump Folk Going Home, Constance Holme, 1913.

De Maine, Madam. *Delina Delaney,* Amanda Ros.

Demas, 'son of Judas.' *Pilgrim's Progress,* J. Bunyan, 1678 and 1684.

De Mauprat, chevalier. *Richelieu* (play), Lord Lytton, 1839.

De Mendez, Portuguese captain of the ship that rescued Gulliver. *Gulliver's Travels,* J. Swift, 1726.

Demeter, Lady (Clara).
 Frank, Lord Demeter, her husband.
The Great Pandolfo, W. J. Locke, 1925.

Demetri. *Phroso,* A. Hope, 1897.

Demetrius, Tamora's son. *Titus Andronicus* (play), W. Shakespeare.

Demetrius, in love with Hermia. *A Midsummer Night's Dream* (play), W. Shakespeare.

De Meudon, Charles Gustave.
 Marie, his sister (de Rochefort), m. (1) General d'Auvergne, (2) Tom Burke.
Tom Burke of Ours, C. Lever, 1844.

De Momerie, Dian. *Murder Must Advertise,* Dorothy L. Sayers, 1933.

De Montémar, Baron Alberic. *The Little Duke,* Charlotte M. Yonge, 1854.

De Montignac, Captain Gerard, friend of Paul Ravenel. *The Winding Stair,* A. E. W. Mason, 1923.

De Mortemar, Julie, ward of Richelieu. *Richelieu* (play), Lord Lytton, 1839.

Dempsey, Constable. 'Brugglesmith' (s.s.), *Many Inventions,* R. Kipling, 1893.

Dempsey, Corporal. 'The Courtship of Dinah Shadd' (s.s.), *Life's Handicap,* R. Kipling, 1891.

Dempsey, Father. *John Bull's Other Island* (play), G. B. Shaw, 1904.

Dempsey, Edward, clerk. 'The Clerk's Quest' (s.s.), *The Untilled Field,* G. Moore, 1903.

Dempster, village schoolmaster. *The Woman in White,* W. Collins, 1860.

Dempster, Robert, lawyer.
 Janet, his ill-used wife.
 Old Mrs Dempster, his mother.
'Janet's Repentance,' *Scenes of Clerical Life,* George Eliot, 1857.

De Nanjec, Vicomte de, young attaché. *An Ideal Husband,* O. Wilde, 1895.

Denberry-Baxter, Sir George.
His nephew.
Let the People Sing, J. B. Priestley, 1939.

Denburn, Mr, scoundrelly farmer killed by David Herries.
Sarah, his niece, m. David Herries.
Rogue Herries, Hugh Walpole, 1930.

Dence, Jael, maid of Grace Carden, m. Guy Raby.
Martha, her sister.
Her father.
Put Yourself in His Place, C. Reade, 1870.

Dench, Araminta. *The Farmer's Wife* (play), E. Phillpotts, 1924.

Denevale, John, French shoemaker. 'Sir Simon Eyer' (s.s.), *The Gentle Craft,* T. Deloney, 1598.

Denison, Mrs. *Caleb Williams,* W. Godwin, 1794.

Deniston, Sir Gulliver, K.C.
m. (1) **Helen** (div.), later Michel.
Richmond, their son.
Barbary, their daughter, central character.
(2) **Pamela.**
David, their son.
The World My Wilderness, Rose Macaulay, 1950.

Denner, maid to Mrs Transome. *Felix Holt,* George Eliot, 1866.

Dennis, civil servant. 'A Conference of the Powers' (s.s.), *Many Inventions,* R. Kipling, 1893.

Dennis, orderly to General Grant. *Abraham Lincoln,* J. Drinkwater, 1918.

Dennis, chaplain. 'The Mutiny of the Mavericks' (s.s.), *Life's Handicap,* R. Kipling, 1891.

Dennis, solicitor. *Porgy,* Du Bose Heyward, 1925.

Dennis, young undertaker, accomplice of Hal McLeavy. *Loot* (play), Joe Orton, 1966.

Dennis, Ned, hangman. *Barnaby Rudge,* C. Dickens, 1841.

Dennison, Charles, Oxford friend of Matthew Bramble.
His son, alias Wilson, actor, m. Lydia Melford.
Humphry Clinker, T. Smollett, 1771.

Dennison, Jenny, maid to Edith Bellenden, m. Cuddie Headrigg. *Old Mortality,* W. Scott, 1816.

Dennison, Virginia, undergraduate, later nurse. *The Dark Tide,* Vera Brittain, 1923.

Dennistoun, Mr, 'Canon Alberic's Scrapbook' (s.s.), *Ghost Stories of an Antiquary,* M. R. James, 1910.

Denny. *Bulldog Drummond,* 'Sapper' (H. C. McNeile), 1920.

Denny, Sir Anthony. *Henry the Eighth* (play), W. Shakespeare.

Denny, Helen. *Gallions Reach,* H. M. Tomlinson, 1927.

Denny, William, young chemical engineer from Texas. *Ship of Fools,* Katherine Anne Porter, 1962.

Denny, Dr Philip. *The Citadel,* A. J. Cronin, 1937.

De Noailles, French ambassador. *The Tower of London,* W. H. Ainsworth, 1840.

Densher, Merton, engaged to Kate Croy. *The Wings of the Dove,* Henry James, 1902.

Dent, Enid. *The Story of Ivy,* Mrs Belloc Lowndes, 1927.

Denton, flying-stage attendant, m. Elizabeth Mwres. *Story of the Days to Come* (s.s.), H. G. Wells.

Denver, Duke of (Gerald).
His wife.
Viscount St George, their son ('Gherkins').
The Dowager Duchess, Honoria, his mother.
Lord Peter Wimsey, his brother. *See* WIMSEY.
Lady Mary, his sister, m. Inspector Charles Parker.
Dorothy L. Sayers's detective stories, throughout, 1923–37.

Denver, Wilfred. *The Silver King* (play), H. A. Jones, 1882.

Denvers, Olive, sister of Joan Desborough. *The Shulamite,* A. & C. Askew, 1904.

Denvil, Harry ('Boy'), subaltern. *Captain Desmond, V.C.,* Maud Diver, 1906.

Denys, a soldier. *The Cloister and the Hearth,* C. Reade, 1861.

Denzil, Somers, poet, betrayer of Lady Feverel. *The Ordeal of Richard Feverel,* G. Meredith, 1859.

Deo Gratias, Querry's native servant, a burnt-out leper case. *A Burnt-Out Case,* Graham Greene, 1961.

Deotlan, a Malay.
  Wan Lan, his wife.
  Four Frightened People, E. Arnot Robertson, 1931.

Depecarde, Sir Archibald, 'celebrated gambler.' *Handley Cross,* R. S. Surtees, 1843.

De Perrencourt (the King of France). *Simon Dale,* A. Hope, 1898.

Depignerolles, Mademoiselle Adele (alias Dessin).
  Marquis Depignerolles, her father.
  The Cornet of Horse, G. A. Henty, 1888.

Deplis, Henri. *The Background* (s.s.), 'Saki' (H. H. Munro).

Derbyshire. *Bulldog Drummond,* 'Sapper' (H. C. McNeile), 1920.

D'Ercilla, Don Antonio. *The Duenna* (play), R. B. Sheridan, 1775.

De Retteville, Dame Adela, half-witted nun at Oby, who runs away with a whore and a valuable tapestry. *The Corner That Held Them,* Sylvia Townsend Warner, 1948.

De Ribera, Don Andres, Viceroy of Peru.
  Don Jaime, his son by Camila Perichole.
  The Bridge of San Luis Rey, T. Wilder, 1927.

Dering, Captain, late the Colonel's gardener. *Barbara's Wedding* (play), J. M. Barrie, 1927.

Dering, Rolf.
  Martha, his wife.
  The Villa Desirée (s.s.), May Sinclair.

Deriot, Agatha. *Berry and Co.,* Dornford Yates, 1920.

De Rivolte, Coralie, famous dancer. *Digby Grand,* G. Whyte-Melville, 1853.

Dermott, Jonah. *At Mrs Beam's* (play), C. K. Munro, 1923.

De Robinson, Mr, Mrs and Miss, *nouveau riche* family. *The Adventures of Mr Ledbury,* Albert Smith, 1844.

De Rochefort, Marie. *See* DE MEUDON.

De Rohault, Duc, French ambassador. 'The Mystery of Lady Arabella Ware' (s.s.), *Old Patch's Medley,* Marjorie Bowen, 1930.

Deronda, Daniel, a Jew, central character, ward of Sir Hugo Mallinger, m. Mirah Cohen. *See also* CHARISI. *Daniel Deronda,* George Eliot, 1876.

Déroulède, Paul (hist.). Rich parvenu, m. Juliette de Marny.
  His mother.
  I Will Repay, Baroness Orczy, 1906.

Deroulett. *See* TOMMY DODD.

De Rouse, Jane Austen Beecher Stowe. 'The Mare's Nest' (poem), *Departmental Ditties,* R. Kipling, 1886.

Derrick, Phyllis.
  Patrick, her father.
  Love Among the Chickens, P. G. Wodehouse, 1906.

Derrick, Tom, quartermaster of the *Fortune's Favourite. The Pirate,* W. Scott, 1822.

Derricks, Henry.
  Bridget, his wife.
  Their children:
    George.
    Wilfred, 'the Longton nightingale.'
  Magnolia Street, L. Golding, 1932.

Derriford, Hilda.
  Her father and mother. Friends of the Barleys.
  The One Before, Barry Pain, 1902.

Derriman, Benjamin, owner of Oxwell Hall.
  Festus, his nephew, m. Matilda Johnson.
  The Trumpet Major, T. Hardy, 1880.

Dersingham, Mr. *Angel Pavement,* J. B. Priestley, 1930.

De Ruell, Count. 'A Matter of Taste,' *Lord Peter Views the Body,* Dorothy L. Sayers, 1928.

D'Ervan, Abbé. *Tom Burke of Ours,* C. Lever, 1844.

Derwen, Nellie, Ned and Cissie. *The Silver King* (play), H. A. Jones, 1882.

Derwent, Colin, m. Betty Findon. *Ten Minute Alibi* (play), A. Armstrong, 1933.

Derwent, George.
  His sister, m. Adam Silvercross.
  The Old Bank, W. Westall, 1902.

De St Foix, Françoise Auguste. 'The Black Mosquetaire,' *The Ingoldsby Legends,* R. H. Barham, 1837.

De St Gonval, Mme Léocadie, great-aunt of Sophia Willoughby in Paris. *Summer Will Show,* Sylvia Townsend Warner, 1936.

De St Saphorin, Vicomte Blaise, m. as 2nd husband Marie-Gilberte Penriddocke. *For Us in the Dark,* Naomi Royde-Smith, 1937.

De St Vallier, Bishop. *Shadows on the Rock,* Willa Cather, 1932.

De Saldar, Conde Silva Diaz, m. Louise Harrington. *Evan Harrington,* G. Meredith, 1861.

Des Amis, Bertrand, killed during Revolution. *Scaramouche,* R. Sabatini, 1921.

Desart, Fabian ('Carrots').
  Captain Desart, his father.
  Lucy, his mother.
  His brothers and sisters:
    Jack.
    Cecil.
    Louise.
    Maurice.
    Floss.
  Florence, his aunt.
    Sybil, her daughter.
Carrots, Mrs Molesworth, 1876.

Desart, Isabel, m. Archie Traill. *Mr Perrin and Mr Traill,* Hugh Walpole, 1911.

De Sautron, Madame, sister of Quintin de Kercadiou. *Scaramouche,* R. Sabatini, 1921.

Desborough, Colonel, Parliamentary commissioner. *Woodstock,* W. Scott, 1826.

Desborough, Joan, m. Robert Waring. *The Shulamite,* A. & C. Askew, 1904.

Desborough, Walter, imbecile pupil of Lewis. *Lewis Arundel,* F. E. Smedley, 1852.

Deschapelles, Madame.
  Her husband.
  Pauline, her daughter.
The Lady of Lyons (play), Lord Lytton, 1838.

Desdemona, wife of Othello. *Othello* (play), W. Shakespeare.

Desert, Hon. Wilfrid, once in love with Fleur Mont, later eng. to Dinny Cherwell. The *Forsyte* series, J. Galsworthy, 1906–33.

Desmond, close friend of John Verney.
  Charles, his father.
The Hill, H. A. Vachell, 1905.

Desmond, Lady Flora. *The Story of Ivy,* Mrs Belloc Lowndes, 1927.

Desmond, Captain Theo, V.C., central character.
  Evelyn, his wife.
  m. (2) Honor Meredith.
Captain Desmond, V.C., Maud Diver, 1906.

Desormeaux, Marcel. *The One Before,* Barry Pain, 1902.

Despain, Bernie, gambler. *The Glass Key,* Dashiell Hammett, 1931.

Despair, Giant. *Pilgrim's Progress,* J. Bunyan, 1678, 1684.

Desprez, Dr. 'The Treasure of Franchard' (s.s.), *The Merry Men,* R. L. Stevenson, 1887.

Desprez, General Sir Hugh, m. Lucilla (Lossie) Thorpe.
  Their children.
Joseph Vance, W. de Morgan, 1906.

Des Sablières, Raoul ('Mr Rowl'), central character, French prisoner in England, m. Juliana Forrest. *Mr Rowl,* D. K. Broster, 1924.

De Stancy, Captain, father of William Dare.
  Sir William, his father.
  Charlotte, his sister.
A Laodicean, T. Hardy, 1881.

De Stapledon, Dame Matilda, prioress of the Benedictine convent at Oby (1368–80).
  Dame Lovisa, her illegitimate relation, an ambitious nun.
The Corner That Held Them, Sylvia Townsend Warner, 1948.

D'Este, Isotta, m. Duke of Verona.
  Impolito, her father.
The Viper of Milan, Marjorie Bowen, 1905.

Dester, Lady Caroline ('Scrap'), m. Thomas Briggs. *The Enchanted April,* Countess von Arnim, 1922.

Desterro, Teresa, student at Leys College, m. Richard Gillespie. *Miss Pym Disposes,* Josephine Tey, 1946.

De Sussa, Mrs. 'Private Learoyd's Story' (s.s.), *Soldiers Three,* R. Kipling, 1888.

Detaze, Marcelline, dancer, half-sister of Lanny Budd.
  Marcel, her son.
Dragon's Teeth, 1942, and others, Upton Sinclair.

Detchard. *The Prisoner of Zenda,* A. Hope, 1894.

De Terrier, Lord, Tory Prime Minister. *Phineas Finn,* 1869, and elsewhere, A. Trollope.

De Thoux, Madame, long-lost sister of George. *Uncle Tom's Cabin,* Harriet B. Stowe, 1851.

De Travers. Family name of LORD TORTILLION.

De Travest, Lord. *The Green Hat,* M. Arlen, 1924.

Detterling, Captain. *The Rich Pay Late,* 1964, and others in the *Alms for Oblivion* sequence, Simon Raven.

Deuceace, Hon. A. P. *See* EARL OF CRABS.

Deulin, Paul, French diplomat. *The Vultures,* H. Seton Merriman, 1902.

Deuteronomy, Old. *Old Possum's Book of Practical Cats,* T. S. Eliot, 1939.

De Varenne, Paul, dramatist, narrator. 'The Doll in the Pink Silk Dress' (s.s.), *All the World Wondered,* L. Merrick, 1911.

De Varennes, Lucie. 'Roads of Destiny' (s.s.), *Roads of Destiny,* O. Henry, 1909.

De Vassart, Countess Eline, French revolutionary, m. Scarlett. *The Maids of Paradise,* R. W. Chambers, 1903.

Devenish, Claude. *Belinda* (play), A. A. Milne, 1918.

De Ventadour, Madame Valerie, old-time friend of Ernest Maltravers.
Her husband.
Alice, Lord Lytton, 1838.

De Vere, Lord Dudley, society adventurer. *Jack Hinton,* C. Lever, 1843.

Deverell, Angelica, romantic novelist, m. Esmé Howe-Nevinson, artist.
Mrs Emmie Deverell, her mother, provincial grocer.
Lottie, her aunt, lady's maid.
Angel, Elizabeth Taylor, 1957.

De Vernier, Marie-Gilberte, m. (1) Lord Penriddocke, (2) Vicomte Blaize de St Saphorin. *For Us in the Dark,* Naomi Royde-Smith, 1937.

De Verviers, André. *The Thinking Reed,* Rebecca West, 1936.

De Villeroi, Marquis.
Lady Blanche, his daughter.
The Mysteries of Udolpho, Mrs Radcliffe, 1790.

De Vilmorin, Philippe, student of divinity, killed by de la Tour d'Azyr. *Scaramouche,* R. Sabatini, 1921.

Devilsdust, Trade Unionist. *Sybil,* B. Disraeli, 1845.

De Vine, Miss, research fellow. *Gaudy Night,* Dorothy L. Sayers, 1935.

Devine, Jerry. *Juno and the Paycock,* S. O'Casey, 1925.

Devine, Richard (alias Rufus Dawes), central character, illegitimate son of Lady Devine, *née* Eleanor Wade, and her cousin, Lord Bellasis.
Sir Richard, his nominal father.
For the Term of his Natural Life, M. Clarke, 1874.

De Vionnet, Comtesse, in love with Chadwick Newsome. *The Ambassadors,* Henry James, 1903.

Devizes, Simon, solicitor.
Robert, his son.
The Will (play), J. M. Barrie, 1913.

Devizes, Wilfred, mental specialist, father of Christina Alberta (*see* PREEMBY). *Christina Alberta's Father,* H. G. Wells, 1925.

Devon, Mrs, multi-millionairess. *The Metropolis,* Upton Sinclair, 1908.

Devoy, Martin, Jesuit master at Denis Considine's school. *Without My Cloak,* Kate O'Brien, 1931.

De Vriaac, Compte Raoul, m. Elvise de Kestournel.
Adrienne, their daughter, m. Jacques Rijar.
The Marquise (play), N. Coward, 1927.

Dewcy, Major. 'My Lord the Elephant' (s.s.), *Many Inventions,* R. Kipling, 1893.

Dewey, Colonel. *The Shepherd of the Hills,* H. B. Wright, 1907.

Dewhurst, Lord Anthony. *The Scarlet Pimpernel,* Baroness Orczy, 1905.

De Winter, Maximilian, m. (1) Rebecca, (2) the anonymous heroine and narrator.
Beatrice, his sister, m. Giles Lacy.
His grandmother.
Rebecca, Daphne du Maurier, 1938.

Dewitt, in love with Lise Asher. *High Tor* (play), Maxwell Anderson, 1937.

Dewitt, George, in love with Mehalah Sharland.
His mother.
Mehalah, S. Baring-Gould, 1880.

Dewlap, Florrie, barmaid, m. Griggs. *Albert Grope,* F. O. Mann, 1931.

Dewlin, Brigadier-General. *Sixty-four, Ninety-four,* R. H. Mottram, 1925.

De Worms, Professor (Friday). *See* WILKS. *The Man who was Thursday,* G. K. Chesterton, 1908.

Dewsbury, Anastasia, actress, mother of Augustus Richmond. *Adventures of Harry Richmond,* G. Meredith, 1871.

Dewsey, James, Galantry's solicitor. *Dance of the Years,* Margery Allingham, 1943.

Dewy, Dick, central character, m. Fancy Day.
 Reuben, his father.
 Ann, his mother.
 His brothers and sisters:
  Susan.
  Jimmy.
  Bob.
  Bessy.
  Charley.
 William, his grandfather. *See also* GRANDFATHER JAMES.
Under the Greenwood Tree, T. Hardy, 1872.

Dexter, Andy, cricketer, m. Nellie Tawnie. *Magnolia Street,* L. Golding, 1932.

D'Hemecourt, refugee café owner.
 Pauline, his daughter, m. Major Shaughnessy.
'Café des Exiles' (s.s.), *Old Creole Days,* G. W. Cable, 1879.

Diabolo, trapezist. *The Case* (s.s.), T. Burke.

Diabologh (or Diavolo), Georges Hamlet Alexander, young White Russian.
 Connie, his father.
 Lucy, his uncle.
 Molly, his aunt, Lucy's wife.
 Teresa, his aunt, m. Emmanuel Vanderflint.
The Polyglots, William Gerhardie, 1925.

Diagoras, servant to Calianax. *The Maid's Tragedy* (play), Beaumont & Fletcher, 1611.

Diakonov, Count Nikolai, Russian in exile in Paris.
 Sofia Andreievna, his wife.
  Tania, their daughter, m. Edward Rowan, English gentleman.
  Laura Rowan, their granddaughter.
The Birds Fall Down, Rebecca West, 1966.

Diana. *All's Well That Ends Well* (play), W. Shakespeare.

Diana, elderly English waitress, 2nd wife of Scripps O'Neil. *The Torrents of Spring,* Ernest Hemingway, 1933.

Dibabs, Mrs. *Nicholas Nickleby.* C. Dickens, 1839.

Dibbitts, chemist. *Middlemarch,* George Eliot, 1871-2.

Dibble, Ferdinand, m. Barbara Medway. 'The Heart of a Goof' (s.s.), *The Heart of a Goof,* P. G. Wodehouse, 1926.

Dibdin, Noll. *The Lie* (play), H. A. Jones, 1923.

Diccon, the bedlam. *Gammer Gurton's Needle* (play), Anon., 1575.

Diccon. Ralph Percy's servant. *By Order of the Company,* Mary Johnston, 1900.

Dick, boyhood friend of Oliver Twist. *Oliver Twist,* C. Dickens, 1838.

Dick, mate of the *Seamew.* *The Skipper's Wooing,* W. W. Jacobs, 1897.

Dick, Mary, schoolmistress.
 Her mother.
For Us in the Dark, Naomi Royde-Smith, 1937.

Dick, Richard, M.P.
 His wife. Prisoners of Guy Red.
The Search Party, G. A. Birmingham, 1913.

Dickens, Martha, housekeeper to Major Bridgenorth. *Peveril of the Peak,* W. Scott, 1822.

Dickerman, Rita. *An American Tragedy,* T. Dreiser, 1925.

Dickerson, Seth, American multimillionaire. *Mr Billingham, the Marquis and Madelon,* E. P. Oppenheim.

Dickinson, Roger, of the *Morning Record.* *The Pied Piper,* N. Shute, 1942.

Dickison, landlord. *The Mill on the Floss,* George Eliot, 1860.

Dickson, wagonette owner. *Pink Sugar,* O. Douglas, 1924.

Dickson Quartus ('Dick Four'). 'Slaves of the Lamp,' *Stalky & Co.,* 1899, and elsewhere in later books, R. Kipling.

Diddler, Jeremy. *Raising the Wind,* J. Kenney, 1803.

Diddler, Jeremy. *The Kickleburys on the Rhine,* W. M. Thackeray, 1850.

Digby, Hamilton, 'greenroom free-lance.' *Going their own Ways,* A. Waugh, 1938.

Digby, Lt-Col. M.A., *The Progress of Private Lilyworth,* Russell Braddon, 1971.

Diggs, friend of Scarve. *The Miser's Daughter,* W. H. Ainsworth, 1842.

Diggs, school friend of Tom Brown. *Tom Brown's Schooldays,* T. Hughes, 1857.

Dilcey.
  Prissy, her daughter. Slaves of the O'Haras.
Gone with the Wind, Margaret Mitchell, 1936.

Di Leo, Count Paolo, young Italian gigolo. *The Roman Spring of Mrs Stone,* Tennessee Williams, 1950.

Dilke, Dr. *The Prescription* (s.s.), Marjorie Bowen.

Dill, barber. *Middlemarch,* George Eliot, 1871–2.

Dill, John, Archibald Carlyle's clerk. *East Lynne,* Mrs Henry Wood, 1861.

Dilling, Lord. *The Last of Mrs Cheyney* (play), F. Lonsdale, 1925.

Dillon, Daws.
  Tad, his son.
  Nancy, his daughter.
  Old Tad, his father.
The Little Shepherd of Kingdom Come, J. Fox, Jnr, 1903.

Dillon, Lionel, artist.
  Anne, his daughter, m. the Duke of Horton.
Hamlet, Revenge!, M. Innes, 1937.

Dilnott, Dr. *His House in Order* (play), A. W. Pinero, 1906.

Dilsey, Negro servant of the Compsons. *The Sound and the Fury,* W. Faulkner, 1931.

Dimbula, The. S.S. 'The Ship that Found Herself' (s.s.), *The Day's Work,* R. Kipling, 1898.

Dimmesdale, Arthur, Pastor of Boston. *The Scarlet Letter,* N. Hawthorne, 1850.

'Di'monds and Pearls,' loved by Larry Tighe. 'Love o' Women' (s.s.), *Many Inventions,* R. Kipling, 1893.

Dimple, Rev. Mr, Vicar of Matchings Easy. *Mr Britling Sees It Through,* H. G. Wells, 1916.

Din, Imam.
  Muhammed, his little son.
'The Story of Muhammed Din' (s.s.), *Plain Tales from the Hills,* R. Kipling, 1888.

Din, Iman, Strickland's servant. 'A Deal in Cotton' (s.s.), *Actions and Reactions,* R. Kipling, 1909.

Dinah, head cook to St Clare. *Uncle Tom's Cabin,* Harriet B. Stowe, 1851.

Dinah, John Marden's dog. 'The Woman in his Life' (s.s.), *Limits and Renewals,* R. Kipling, 1932.

Dinent, Abbé, friend of Helen Michel. *The World My Wilderness,* Rose Macaulay, 1950.

Dingo, Professor, second husband of Mrs Badger. *Bleak House,* C. Dickens, 1840.

Dingo, Yellow Dog. 'The Sing-song of Old Man Kangaroo' (s.s.), *Just So Stories,* R. Kipling, 1902.

Dingwall, M.P. *Sketches by Boz,* C. Dickens, 1836.

Dingwall, David, 'a sly, dry, shrewd attorney.' *The Bride of Lammermoor,* W. Scott, 1819.

Dinmont, Andrew ('Dandy'), 'store-farmer.'
  Ailie, his wife.
    Jenny, their daughter.
Guy Mannering, W. Scott, 1815.

Diogenes, slave to Agelastes. *Count Robert of Paris,* W. Scott, 1832.

Diomed, middle-aged man of fashion.
  Julia, his daughter.
The Last Days of Pompeii, Lord Lytton, 1834.

Diomedes, Grecian commander. *Troilus and Cressida* (play), W. Shakespeare.

Dion, a Sicilian lord. *A Winter's Tale* (play), W. Shakespeare.

Dion, a lord.
  Euphrasia, his daughter.
Philaster (play), Beaumont & Fletcher, 1611.

Dionyza, wife of Cleon. *Pericles* (play), W. Shakespeare.

Diphilus, brother of Evadne. *The Maid's Tragedy* (play), Beaumont & Fletcher, 1611.

Dippy, Nell, simple-minded semi-prostitute.
  Maggie, her mother.
  Truth, her brother.
Time Will Knit, Fred Urquhart, 1938.

Direck, Mr, secretary of a Massachusetts cultural society. *Mr Britling Sees It Through,* H. G. Wells, 1916.

Dirkovitch, Cossack officer. 'The Man Who Was' (s.s.), *Life's Handicap,* R. Kipling, 1891.

Di Santangiolo, Duchess (Beatrice), m. Peter Marchdale.
Emilia, her sister, m. Manfredi.
The Cardinal's Snuffbox, H. Harland, 1900.

Discontent and Shame, encountered by Faithful. *Pilgrim's Progress,* J. Bunyan, 1678 and 1684.

Dishart, Rev. Gavin, m. Lady Babbie.
Gavin, their son.
Gavinia, their daughter.
Margaret, his mother.
The Little Minister, 1891, and elsewhere, J. M. Barrie.

'Dismal Jimmy,' story-teller. *Pickwick Papers,* C. Dickens, 1837.

Disthal, Countess Irmgard von, lady-in-waiting to Princess Priscilla of Lotten-Kunitz, m. Dr Kraus. *Princess Priscilla's Fortnight,* Countess von Arnim, 1905.

Dith, Gallic slave of Titus Barrus. *The Conquered,* Naomi Mitchison, 1923.

Ditta Mull. 'Tods' Amendment' (s.s.), *Plain Tales from the Hills,* R. Kipling, 1888.

Diver, Colonel, Editor, *New York Journal. Martin Chuzzlewit,* C. Dickens, 1844.

Diver, Dick, psychologist addicted to alcohol.
Nicole, his wife.
Tender is the Night, F. Scott Fitzgerald, 1934.

Diver, Jenny. *The Beggar's Opera,* 1728, and *Polly,* 1729 (comic operas), J. Gay.

D'Ivry, Duc.
His wife.
Antoinette, his daughter.
The Newcomes, W. M. Thackeray, 1853–5.

Dixon, servant of the Hales. *North and South,* Mrs Gaskell, 1855.

Dixon, Mr, m. Jane Campbell. *Emma,* Jane Austen, 1816.

Dixon, Mrs, farmer's wife. *Swallows and Amazons,* A. Ransome, 1930.

Dixon, Anthony, m. as 2nd husband Nettie de Lyndesay. *Crump Folk Going Home,* Constance Holme, 1913.

Dixon, Danby, ex-guardsman and director of swindling public company.
Fanny, his wife.
Our Street, W. M. Thackeray, 1848.

Dixon, James, central character. *Lucky Jim,* K. Amis, 1953.

Dixon, Tom, Aunt Evelyn's groom. *Memoirs of a Fox-Hunting Man,* Siegfried Sassoon, 1929.

Djinn, The, in Charge of All Deserts. 'How the Camel got his Hump' (s.s.), *Just So Stories,* R. Kipling, 1902.

Djuna, boy-of-all-work in the Queen household. *The Chinese Orange Mystery,* 1934, and many others, Ellery Queen.

Dmitry, servant of Madame Zalenska. *Three Weeks,* Elinor Glyn, 1907.

Doane, Seneca. *Babbitt,* Sinclair Lewis, 1923.

Doasyouwouldbedoneby, Mrs. *The Water Babies,* C. Kingsley, 1863.

Dobbin, Major William, awkward, gallant, m. as 2nd husband Amelia Osborne, *née* Sedley.
Sir William, rich grocer, his father.
Vanity Fair, W. M. Thackeray, 1847–8.

Dobbins, Humphrey, Sir Robert Bramble's servant. *The Poor Gentleman* (play), G. Colman the Younger, 1802.

Dobbs, companion-maid to Mrs Reece. *Mrs Halliburton's Troubles,* Mrs Henry Wood, 1862.

Dobelle, Mr.
Blanaid, his daughter.
Columba, his son.
The Moon in the Yellow River (play), D. Johnston, 1932.

Dobie, Denham, central character, m. Arnold Chapel.
Her father, retired clergyman.
Sylvia, her dead mother.
Her Andorran stepmother, with four children.
Crewe Train, Rose Macaulay, 1926.

Doboobie, Dr Demetrius, 'bold, adventurous practitioner.' *Kenilworth,* W. Scott, 1821.

Dobrinton. *Cross Currents* (s.s.), 'Saki' (H. H. Munro).

Dobson, farmer. *The Promise of May* (play), Lord Tennyson, 1882.

Dobson, rascally innkeeper. *Huntingtower*, J. Buchan, 1922.

Dobson, Constable, nephew of Sergeant Voules. *Thank You, Jeeves*, P. G. Wodehouse, 1934.

Dobson, Zuleika, central character. *Zuleika Dobson*, Max Beerbohm, 1911.

Dodd, Captain David, of the *Agra* (alias William Thompson of the *Vulture*).
 Lucy, his wife, *née* Fountain.
 Edward, their son.
 Julia, their daughter, m. Alfred Hardie.
Hard Cash, C. Reade, 1863.

Dodd, Edwin, 'militant agnostic.' *Boon*, H. G. Wells, 1915.

Dodd, Lewis, m. Florence Churchill, later elopes with Tessa Sanger. *The Constant Nymph*, Margaret Kennedy, 1924.

Dodd, Tommy (Deroulett). 'The Head of the District' (s.s.), *Life's Handicap*, R. Kipling, 1891.

Doddington, Susan, maid to Lincoln. *Abraham Lincoln* (play), J. Drinkwater, 1918.

Dodds, Charles Beauchamp's election agent. *Fed Up*, G. A. Birmingham, 1931.

Dodge, owner of the great ruby. *No Other Tiger*, A. E. W. Mason 1927.

Dodge, William, guest at the pageant. *Between The Acts*, Virginia Woolf, 1941.

Dods, Meg, landlady of the Cleikum Inn, St Ronan's. *St Ronan's Well*, W. Scott, 1824.

Dodson, of Dodson & Fogg, shady attorneys acting for Mrs Bardell. *Pickwick Papers*, C. Dickens, 1837.

Dodson, Jane, m. Glegg.
 Sophy, m. Pullet.
 Susan, m. Deane.
 Elizabeth, m. Edward Tulliver.
The Mill on the Floss, George Eliot, 1860.

Dodsworth, Sam, American car manufacturer.
 Fran, his wife, *née* Voelker.
 Emily, their daughter.
 Brent, their son.
Dodsworth, Sinclair Lewis, 1929.

Doe, Edgar Gray. *Tell England*, E. Raymond, 1922.

Doeg. *Absalom and Achitophel* (poem), J. Dryden, 1681.

Doffield, Julian, illegitimate cousin of Jacy Florister. *The Flower Girls*, Clemence Dane, 1954.

Dogberry, a foolish officer. *Much Ado about Nothing* (play), W. Shakespeare.

Dogget, prison warder. *The Betrothed*, W. Scott, 1825.

Doherty, Eileen, a novice.
 Her father and mother.
The Land of Spices, Kate O'Brien, 1941.

Dol Common. *The Alchemist* (play), B. Jonson, 1610.

Dolabella, friend of Octavius Caesar. *Antony and Cleopatra* (play), W. Shakespeare.

Dolan, Irish-American bookie and scoundrel. *A Penniless Millionaire*, D. Christie Murray, 1907.

Dolbie, Rhoda, maid.
 Charlie, her illegitimate son.
'My Son's Wife' (s.s.), *A Diversity of Creatures*, R. Kipling, 1917.

Doleful, Miserrimus, half-pay captain. *Handley Cross*, R. S. Surtees, 1843.

Doleman, Thomas, friend of Robert Lovelace. *Clarissa Harlowe*, S. Richardson, 1748.

Dolfin, Peter, a pedlar. *Rogue Herries*, Hugh Walpole, 1930.

Dollery, Mrs, carrier. *The Woodlanders*, T. Hardy, 1887.

Dollmann, ex-English officer, spy, owner of yacht *Medusa*.
 Clara, his daughter.
The Riddle of the Sands, E. Childers, 1903.

Dolloby, second-hand-clothes dealer. *David Copperfield*, C. Dickens, 1850.

Dollop, Jack. *Tess of the D'Urbervilles*, T. Hardy, 1891.

Dolly, maid of the Temperleys, in love with Jim Hollman. *The Beautiful Years*, H. Williamson, 1921.

Doloreine, Thomas. *The Power House*, J. Buchan, 1916.

Dolour, Mark, farm hand.
 Nancy, his daughter.
Cold Comfort Farm, Stella Gibbons, 1932.

Dolphin, theatre manager. *Pen-*

dennis, 1848–50, and *Lovel the Widower*, 1860, W. M. Thackeray.

Dolphin, Sam Smith's butler. *Shall We Join the Ladies?* (play), J. M. Barrie, 1921.

Dolphin, Mrs, wardrobe mistress, Flower Theatre.
Fred, her husband.
The Flower Girls, Clemence Dane, 1954.

Doltimore, Lord. *Alice*, Lord Lytton, 1838.

Dombey, Paul, merchant.
m. (1) **Fanny.**
Florence, their daughter, m. Walter Gay.
Paul, their son.
(2) **Edith Granger,** widow, daughter of Mrs Skewton.
Louisa, his sister, m. John Chick.
Dombey and Son, C. Dickens, 1848.

Dombrowski, Count Stanislas, Polish 'spiv.'
His aunt.
Lise Lillywhite, Margery Sharp, 1951.

Domenico, gardener at San Salvatore. *The Enchanted April*, Countess von Arnim, 1922.

Dominguez, assistant to Thomas Fowler. *The Quiet American*, Graham Greene, 1955.

Dominic, Mr Latimer's butler. *The Dover Road* (play), A. A. Milne, 1922.

Dominic, valet and cook to Harold Transome. *Felix Holt*, George Eliot, 1866.

Don, Robert, artist.
Grace, his wife.
Dick, his dead son.
A Well-remembered Voice (play), J. M. Barrie, 1918.

Donado, citizen of Parma.
Bergetto, his foolish nephew.
'Tis Pity She's A Whore (play), John Ford, *c.* 1624.

Donalbain, son of Duncan. *Macbeth* (play), W. Shakespeare.

Donald, Mrs.
Peggy, her dying daughter.
The Setons, O. Douglas, 1917.

Donald, Nan Ord (of the Hammer), Highland captain. *The Abbot*, W. Scott, 1820.

Doncastle, Mr and Mrs. *The Hand of Ethelberta*, T. Hardy, 1876.

Donkin, Charles, housemaster, guardian of the Faringdon children. *Housemaster* (play), Ian Hay, 1936.

Donn, Arabella, false wife of Jude Fawley.
Her father and mother.
Jude the Obscure, T. Hardy, 1896.

Donne, Rev. Joseph, curate of Whinbury. *Shirley*, Charlotte Brontë, 1849.

Donnelly, Kevin, Sinn Feiner.
Maggie, his daughter, m. Rory O'Riordan.
My Son, My Son, H. Spring, 1938.

Donnerhugel, Rudolph of, Swiss deputy.
Stephen, his father.
Theodore, his uncle.
Anne of Geierstein, W. Scott, 1829.

Donnithorne, Squire, penurious owner of Donnithorne Chase.
Lydia, his tyrannical daughter.
Arthur, his grandson. *See also* HESTER SORREL.
Adam Bede, George Eliot, 1859.

Donny, Mrs, boarding-school mistress. *Bleak House*, C. Dickens, 1853.

Donovan, Andy, in love with Maggie Conway. 'The Count and the Wedding Guest' (s.s.), *The Trimmed Lamp*, O. Henry, 1907.

Donovan, Father Dan, parish priest. *The Woman Thou Gavest Me*, Hall Caine, 1913.

Donovan, 'Dicky,' central character, in the service of the Khedive of Egypt. *Donovan Pasha*, Gilbert Parker, 1902.

Donovan, Larry, who deceives Antonia. *My Antonia*, Willa Cather, 1918.

Doolan, journalist on staff of *Tom and Jerry*. *Pendennis*, W. M. Thackeray, 1848–50.

Doolan, Patsy. *See* NAMGAY DOOLA.

Doolittle, half-pay captain. *The Monastery*, W. Scott, 1820.

Doolittle, Eliza.
Alfred, her father.
Pygmalion (play), G. B. Shaw, 1914.

Doom, Aunt Ada. *See* STARKADDER.

Doon, Lieutenant Jimmy. *Tell England*, E. Raymond, 1922.

Doone, Lorna (really **Lady Lorna Dugal,** daughter of the Earl of Dugal), central character, m. John Ridd.

Sir Ensor, her supposed grandfather.
His sons:
Charleworth.
Counsellor.
And others.
Carver, Counsellor's son.
Lorna Doone, R. D. Blackmore, 1869.

Doorm, Earl. 'Geraint and Enid' (poem), *Idylls of the King,* Lord Tennyson, 1859.

Dope, Nanuet bank robber. *High Tor* (play), Maxwell Anderson, 1937.

Doramin, 'big pot' and murderer of Jim. *Lord Jim,* J. Conrad, 1900.

Doran, Barney. *John Bull's Other Island* (play), G. B. Shaw, 1904.

Doran, Bob, lover of Polly Mooney. 'The Boarding-house' (s.s.), *The Dubliners,* James Joyce, 1914.

Doran, Hatty, fiancée of Lord R. St Simon, m. Francis Moulton.
Aloysius, her father.
'The Noble Bachelor,' *Adventures of Sherlock Holmes,* A. Conan Doyle, 1892.

Doran, Robert.
His wife.
Landmarks, E. V. Lucas, 1914.

Dorax, a noble Portuguese. *Don Sebastian* (play), J. Dryden, 1690.

Dorbell, Mrs. *Love on the Dole,* W. Greenwood, 1933.

Dordan, counsellor to Ferrex, son of Gorboduc. *Gorboduc* (play), T. Sackville & T. Norton, 1562.

Dore, Billie, actress and secretary, m. Lord Marshmoreton. *A Damsel in Distress,* P. G. Wodehouse, 1919.

Doreen, maid. *Separate Tables* (play), T. Rattigan, 1955.

Doria, Clare, m. John Todhunter. *The Ordeal of Richard Feverel,* G. Meredith, 1859.

Doria, Ugo, rebel poet. *Adam's Breed,* Radclyffe Hall, 1926.

Doricourt. *The Belle's Stratagem* (play), Mrs Hannah Cowley, 1780.

Dorimant. *The Man of Mode* (play), Sir G. Etherege, 1676.

Dorincourt, Earl of (Molyneux), grim aristocrat with a heart of gold. *Little Lord Fauntleroy,* Frances H. Burnett, 1886.

Dorker, deceased pupil of Squeers. *Nicholas Nickleby,* C. Dickens, 1839.

Dorking, Earl of, impoverished peer (Family name Pulleyn).
His wife.
Viscount Rooster, their son.
Their daughters:
Lady Clara, m. Barnes Newcome.
Lady Henrietta, m. Lord Kew.
Lady Belinda.
Lady Adelaide.
The Newcomes, W. M. Thackeray, 1853–5.

Dorm, Earl, father of Yvonne. 'Sir Agravaine' (s.s.), *The Man Upstairs,* P. G. Wodehouse, 1914.

Dormer, attendant, National Portrait Gallery.
Harold, his son, m. Adelaide Moon.
Antigua Penny Puce, R. Graves, 1936.

Dormer, schoolmaster.
His wife.
Mr Perrin and Mr Traill, Hugh Walpole, 1911.

Dormer, Private. 'Only a Subaltern' (s.s.), *Wee Willie Winkie,* R. Kipling, 1888.

Dormer, Captain Stephen Doughty, central character. *The Crime at Vanderlynden's,* R. H. Mottram, 1926.

Dormouse, The. *Alice in Wonderland,* L. Carroll, 1865.

Dornberg, Graf. *Armgart* (poem), George Eliot, 1871.

Dornford, Eustace, K.C., M.P., m. Dinny Charwell. *Over the River,* J. Galsworthy, 1924.

Dorothy, friend and companion of Lorelei Lee. *Gentlemen Prefer Blondes,* Anita Loos, 1925.

Dorrit, Amy (Little Dorrit), central character, m. Arthur Clennam.
William, her father.
Her mother.
Edward, her brother.
Fanny, her spoilt elder sister, m. Edward Sparkler.
Frederick, her uncle, clarionet player.
Little Dorrit, C. Dickens, 1857.

Dorset, Duke of, undergraduate. *Zuleika Dobson,* Max Beerbohm, 1911.

Dorset, Marquis of, son of Queen Elizabeth. *Richard the Third* (play), W. Shakespeare.

Dorset, Mrs Bertha.

George, her husband.
The House of Mirth, Edith Wharton, 1905.

Dorset, Ebenezer.
'Johnny Red Chief,' his son.
'The Ransom of Red Chief' (s.s.), *Whirligigs,* O. Henry, 1910.

Dorward, Rev. Mr. *Sylvia Scarlett,* C. Mackenzie, 1918.

Dory, John, bookmaker. *The Calendar,* E. Wallace.

D'Ossorio, Don Christoval Condé, nephew of the Duke of Medina. *The Monk,* M. G. Lewis, 1796.

Dost Akbar, one of the 'Four.' *See* ABDULLAH KHAN. *The Sign of Four,* A. Conan Doyle, 1890.

Doto. *A Phoenix too Frequent* (play), Christopher Fry, 1946.

Dottrell, Joe. *Memoirs of an Infantry Officer,* Siegfried Sassoon, 1930.

Doubledick, Richard. *Seven Poor Travellers,* C. Dickens, 1854.

Doublefee, Jacob, agent of the Duke of Buckingham. *Peveril of the Peak,* W. Scott, 1822.

Dougal, Chief of the Gorbals Diehards. *Huntingtower,* J. Buchan, 1922.

Dougdale, Harvey ('Boy'), m. (1) Lady Patricia, (2) Polly Hampton. *Love in a Cold Climate,* Nancy Mitford, 1949.

Dougherty, Mrs, widow.
Katie, her daughter.
'The Mother' (s.s.), *Countrymen All,* Katherine Tynan, 1915.

Doughtie, Dobinet, 'boy' to Roister Doister. *Ralph Roister Doister* (play), N. Udall, 1551.

Douglas, narrator, owner of the MS. *The Turn of the Screw,* H. James, 1898.

Douglas, Captain, cousin of Lady Laxton, eng. to Madeleine Philips. *Bealby,* H. G. Wells, 1915.

Douglas, Widow. *Tom Sawyer,* 1876, and *Huckleberry Finn,* 1884, Mark Twain.

Douglas, James (alias James Greyman), ex-officer and jockey.
Zora, his native wife.
On the Face of the Waters, Flora A. Steel, 1896.

Douglas, Jane, Lady Katherine Gordon's attendant. *Perkin Warbeck* (play), John Ford, 1634.

Douglas, Monica, schoolgirl, member of 'the Brodie set.' *The Prime of Miss Jean Brodie,* Muriel Spark, 1961.

Douglas, Timmy, blinded soldier.
Molly, his wife.
Invitation to the Waltz, Rosamond Lehmann, 1932.

Douglas-Stuart, Wilhelmina ('Williamina, Meenie'), m. Ronald Strang.
Dr Douglas-Stuart, her father.
White Heather, W. Black, 1885.

Douglass, Frederic, Negro. *Abraham Lincoln* (play), J. Drinkwater, 1918.

Dousterswivel, Hermaun, impudent and fraudulent agent for the Glen Withershins mining works. *The Antiquary,* W. Scott, 1816.

D'Outreville, Duchess. *The American,* H. James, 1877.

Dove, Parson, fox-hunting clergyman.
Cecilia, his daughter, with whom John Standish Sawyer falls in love.
Market Harborough, G. Whyte-Melville, 1861.

Dove, Q.C. ('Turtle Dove'), Camperdown's consultant concerning the diamonds. *The Eustace Diamonds,* A. Trollope, 1873.

Dove, Sir Benjamin. *The Brothers* (play), R. Cumberland, 1769.

Dovedale, Lord, fleeced at cards by Rawdon Crawley. *Vanity Fair,* W. M. Thackeray, 1847–8.

Dover, silversmith, chief creditor of Tertius Lydgate. *Middlemarch,* George Eliot, 1871–2.

Dover, Dennis, Chairman of Directors, Imperial Palace Hotel. *Imperial Palace,* Arnold Bennett, 1930.

Dow. *Dow's Flat* (poem), Bret Harte, 1856.

Dow, Rob.
Micah, his son.
The Little Minister, J. M. Barrie, 1891.

Dowden, Olly, maker of heath brooms. *The Return of the Native,* T. Hardy, 1878.

Dowdeswell, Seraphina, servant and later 2nd wife of Christopher Vance. *Joseph Vance,* W. de Morgan, 1906.

Dowdle, Robert, clarionet player. 'Absent-mindedness in a Parish Choir,' *Life's Little Ironies,* T. Hardy, 1894.

Dowell, John, millionaire from Philadelphia, narrator.
Florence, his wife, *née* Hurlbird, who has a weak heart; mistress of Edward Ashburnham.
The Good Soldier, Ford Madox Ford, 1915.

Dowey, Mrs Sarah Ann, charwoman.
Kenneth, private, Black Watch, adopted by her.
The Old Lady Shows Her Medals (play), J. M. Barrie, 1917.

Dowgate, sweetheart of Jane Comport. *The Uncommercial Traveller,* C. Dickens, 1860.

Dowlas, farrier. *Silas Marner,* George Eliot, 1861.

Dowlas, Dick.
Daniel, his father.
The Heir at Law (play), G. Colman the Younger, 1797.

Dowler, Captain. *Pickwick Papers,* C. Dickens, 1837.

Dowler, Mrs Hettie, one of Elmer Gantry's mistresses. *Elmer Gantry,* Sinclair Lewis, 1927.

Dowling, attorney. *Tom Jones,* H. Fielding, 1749.

Dowling, Margo, film star. *U.S.A.* trilogy, John dos Passos, 1930–6.

Downe, Charles, lawyer.
His wife.
'Fellow Townsmen,' *Wessex Tales,* T. Hardy, 1888.

Downes, Captain, neighbour of the Middletons. *Both of this Parish,* J. S. Fletcher.

Downing, Lord Monchensey's servant. *The Family Reunion* (play), T. S. Eliot, 1939.

Downing, Jim. *Dr Nikola,* G. Boothby, 1896.

Dowse, lighthouse keeper. 'A Disturber of Traffic' (s.s.), *Many Inventions,* R. Kipling, 1893.

Dowse, H. L., housemaster at public school. *The Old Boys,* William Trevor, 1964.

Dowsing, Abraham, shepherd. *Mehalah,* S. Baring-Gould, 1880.

Dowton, Sir Clement, Bt. *When a Man's Single,* J. M. Barrie, 1888.

Doxy, Betty. *Polly* (comic opera), J. Gay, 1729.

Doyce, Daniel, smith and engineer. *Little Dorrit,* C. Dickens, 1857.

Doye, Basil, wounded officer, in love with Evie Tucker. *Non-Combatants and Others,* Rose Macaulay, 1916.

Doyle, Laurence, civil engineer.
Cornelius, his father.
Judy, his aunt.
John Bull's Other Island (play), G. B. Shaw, 1904.

Doyle, Minta, in love with Paul Rayley. *To The Lighthouse,* Virginia Woolf, 1927.

Doyle, Phil, an Inspector of Irish schools.
Abby, his wife.
Molly, Abby's sister, m. Fairley Quigley, a Cabinet Minister.
'Hymeneal' (s.s.), *The Talking Trees,* Sean O'Faolain, 1971.

Dozier, Julie, half-caste actress, m. Steve Baker. *Show Boat,* Edna Ferber, 1926.

Drabble, Archie. *Cleg Kelly,* S. R. Crockett, 1896.

Dracula, Count, *Dracula,* Bram Stoker, 1897.

Dragomiroff, Ivan, of the Aerial Board of Control. 'As Easy as A B C' (s.s.,) *A Diversity of Creatures,* R. Kipling, 1917.

Drake. *The Christian,* Hall Caine, 1897.

Drake, Dr, Pinfold's physician. *The Ordeal of Gilbert Pinfold,* Evelyn Waugh, 1957.

Drake, Mrs, landlady of the Admiral Benbow. *Admiral Guinea* (play), W. E. Henley & R. L. Stevenson, 1892.

Drake, Alexander.
His father and mother.
Joy and Josephine, Monica Dickens, 1948.

Drake, Arthur, friend of Michael Fane, *Sinister Street,* C. Mackenzie, 1913.

Drake, Fergus. 'The Enthusiast' (s.s.), *Last Recollections of My Uncle Charles,* N. Balchin, 1954.

Drake, Temple, central character, m. Gowan Stevens. *Requiem for a Nun,* William Faulkner, 1950.

Dramm, Tobias, hangman. 'The Gallowsmith' (s.s.), *From Place to Place,* Irvin S. Cobb, 1920.

Draper, London lawyer and agent. *The Virginians,* W. M. Thackeray, 1857–9.

Drassilis, Cynthia, one-time fiancée of Peter Burns, m. Lord Mountry.
Hon. Hugo, her father.

The Little Nugget, P. G. Wodehouse, 1913.

Dravot, Daniel. 'The Man who would be King' (s.s.), *Wee Willie Winkie*, R. Kipling, 1888.

Drebber, Enoch. *A Study in Scarlet*, A. Conan Doyle, 1887.

Dreddlington, Earl of.
Lady Cecilia, his daughter, m. Tittlebat Titmouse.
Ten Thousand a Year, S. Warren, 1839.

Drede, poet-narrator. *The Bowge of Court*, John Skelton, 1498.

Dredge, Mabel, Quinney's typist. *Quinneys'*, H. A. Vachell, 1914.

Dreever, Earl of. *A Gentleman of Leisure*, P. G. Wodehouse, 1910.

Drencher, Lovel's family doctor. *Lovel the Widower*, W. M. Thackeray, 1860.

Drew, Lady, of Bladesover House. *Tono Bungay*, H. G. Wells, 1909.

Drew, Euphemia, elderly spinster, Mary Crow's employer. *A Glastonbury Romance*, J. C. Powys, 1932.

Drewer, Sir Hayman, prosecuting counsel. *We the Accused*, E. Raymond, 1935.

Drewett, Andrew, college friend of Miles Wallingford. *Afloat and Ashore*, J. Fenimore Cooper, 1844.

Drewett, Nic, amateur jockey. *The Dark Horse*, Nat Gould.

Drewitt, Mr. *Brighton Rock*, Graham Greene, 1938.

Drewitt, Miss Prudence. *Dialstone Lane*, W. W. Jacobs, 1904.

Drewitt, Tom, comedian, repertory company. *Enter Sir John*, Clemence Dane & Helen Simpson, 1929.

Driffield, Edward, great Victorian writer.
Rosie, his 1st wife, *née* Gann.
Amy, his 2nd wife.
Cakes and Ale, W. S. Maugham, 1930.

Drifting Crane, Indian chief. 'Drifting Crane' (s.s.), *Prairie Folk*, H. Garland, 1892.

Drinkwater, Felix. *Captain Brassbound's Conversion* (play), G. B. Shaw, 1900.

Driscoll, Eily, m. Patrick Sullivan.
Her mother.
Bill, her brother.
Min, his wife.
'The Whistling Thief' (s.s.), *Countrymen All*, Katherine Tynan, 1915.

Driscoll, Myra, m. Oswald Henshawe.
John, her great-uncle.
My Mortal Enemy, Willa Cather, 1928.

Driver, clerk to Lawyer Pleydell. *Guy Mannering*, W. Scott, 1815.

Driver, Mrs, widow. 'Cupboard Love' (s.s.), *The Lady of the Barge*, W. W. Jacobs, 1902.

Drizzle, Mrs Caroline, an English busybody. *The Black Venus*, Rhys Davies, 1944.

Dromio of Ephesus.

Dromio of Syracuse. Twin brothers. *A Comedy of Errors* (play), W. Shakespeare.

Drood, Edwin, central character, who mysteriously disappears; betrothed to Rosa Bud. *Edwin Drood*, C. Dickens, 1870.

Drouet, Charles, Carrie's first lover. *Sister Carrie*, Theodore Dreiser, 1900.

Drover, Jim, condemned to death.
Milly, his wife, *née* Rimmer.
Conrad, his brother.
It's a Battlefield, Graham Greene, 1935.

Druce, Gordon, manager of repertory company.
Edna, his wife (Edna Warwick).
Enter Sir John, Clemence Dane & Helen Simpson, 1929.

Drudgeit, Saunders (or Peter), clerk to Lord Bladderskate. *Redgauntlet*, W. Scott, 1824.

Drum, Countess of, wizen-faced dowager who alleges relationship with S. Titmarsh. *The Great Hoggarty Diamond*, W. M. Thackeray, 1841.

Drummle, Bentley (The Spider), m. Estella. *Great Expectations*, C. Dickens, 1864.

Drummle, Cayley, friend of Aubrey Tanqueray. *The Second Mrs Tanqueray*, A. W. Pinero, 1893.

Drummond, Lady Anne.
Dick, her husband.
Joan, their daughter.
The Fortunes of Christina McNab, S. Macnaughtan, 1901.

Drummond, Catriona, central character, m. David Balfour.
James, alias Macgregor and More, her father.
Catriona, R. L. Stevenson, 1893.

Drummond, Captain Hugh (Bulldog Drummond), central character. *Bulldog Drummond,* 'Sapper' (H. C. McNeile), 1920.

Drummond, Hugh, nephew of Sir W. Swanney, m. Molly West. *The Winds of Chance,* S. K. Hocking.

Drummond, Kate, girl with whom Joe Chapin finds brief happiness. *Ten North Frederick,* John O'Hara, 1956.

Dryasdust, Dr, literary friend of the Antiquary. *The Antiquary,* 1816, and (as an editor, etc.) in others, W. Scott.

Dryden, Gerald, hero of shipwreck, m. Alma Reed. *In Cotton Wool,* W. B. Maxwell, 1912.

Dryfesdale, Jasper, steward of Lochleven Castle. *The Abbot,* W. Scott, 1820.

Dubbley, police officer. *Pickwick Papers,* C. Dickens, 1837.

Dubbo, Alf, aborigine artist. *Riders in the Chariot,* Patrick White, 1961.

Dubedat, Louis.
Jennifer, his wife. *See also* MINNIE TINWELL.
The Doctor's Dilemma (play), G. B. Shaw, 1906.

Du Bois, Monsieur. *Evelina,* Fanny Burney, 1778.

Du Bois, Blanche, Stella Kowalski's sister. *A Streetcar Named Desire* (play), Tennessee Williams, 1949.

Dubourg, French merchant.
Clement, his nephew.
Rob Roy, W. Scott, 1818.

Ducane, Sir Harold, husband of Marjorie Bramsley. *C.,* M. Baring, 1924.

Ducat, Mr.
His wife.
Polly (comic opera), J. Gay, 1729.

Ducayne, Gerald, m. Harriett Henderson. *Pilgrimage,* Dorothy M. Richardson, 1915–38.

Duchesne, Mademoiselle, aunt of Armand and Lucile Rollencourt. *Through the Storm,* P. Gibbs, 1945.

Duchess, a dog. *The Pie and the Patty Pan,* Beatrix Potter, 1905.

Duchess, The. *Alice in Wonderland,* L. Carroll, 1865.

Duchess, The. 'Outcasts of Poker Flat' (s.s.), *The Luck of Roaring Camp,* etc., Bret Harte, 1868.

Duchot, Pierre, one of the children taken to England by John Howard. *The Pied Piper,* N. Shute, 1942.

Ducie, Hon. Mrs. *East Lynne,* Mrs Henry Wood, 1861.

Duckett, Corporal, Royal Marines. *The Middle Watch* (play), Ian Hay & S. King-Hall, 1929.

Duckie, waiter.
His wife, landlady.
Their children:
Herbert (Alf Pinto), music-hall artist, m. Birdie Twist.
Beatrice.
Ern.
Over Bemerton's, E. V. Lucas, 1908.

Duclos, Marina. *Fallen Angels,* N. Coward, 1925.

Ducrosne. *The Thirty-nine Steps,* J. Buchan, 1915.

Duddon, Lady, sister of Dr Joseph Foster. *Mr Fortune Finds a Pig,* H. C. Bailey, 1943.

Dudeney, Mr, shepherd. 'The Knife and Naked Chalk,' *Rewards and Fairies,* R. Kipling, 1910.

Dudeney, Mrs, employer of Judith Paris. *Judith Paris,* Hugh Walpole, 1930.

Dudgeon, Mrs Annie.
Timothy, her husband, recently decd.
Richard and **Christy,** their sons.
William and **Titus,** brothers of Timothy.
The Devil's Disciple (play), G. B. Shaw, 1899.

Dudgeon, Thomas, clerk to Daniel Romaine. *St Ives,* R. L. Stevenson, 1897.

Dudleigh, Henry, ruined shipowner.
His wife, son and daughter.
Diary of a Late Physician, S. Warren, 1832.

Dudley, Mrs.
Maudie, her daughter by her 1st husband.
Reuben, her 2nd husband.
Joan, his daughter by 1st wife.
The Top of the Stairs (s.s.), T. Burke.

Dudley, Bruce (real name John Stockton), Chicago reporter in search of adventure. *Dark Laughter,* Sherwood Anderson, 1925.

Dudley, Herman, narrator. 'The Man Who Became a Woman' (s.s.), *Horses and Men,* Sherwood Anderson, 1924.

Dudu. *Don Juan* (poem), Lord Byron, 1819-24.

Duenna, The (Margaret), central character. *The Duenna* (play), R. B. Sheridan, 1775.

Duer, Angus, doctor. *Martin Arrowsmith,* Sinclair Lewis, 1925.

Duessa, an enchantress. *The Faërie Queene* (poem), E. Spenser, 1590.

Duff, Bow Street officer. *Oliver Twist,* C. Dickens, 1838.

Duff, Mrs, housekeeper. *The Last and the First,* Ivy Compton-Burnett, 1971.

Duff, Colin, schoolmaster, m. Lise Lillywhite. *Lise Lillywhite,* Margery Sharp, 1951.

Duffield, Hurtle, Australian artist, genius, central character. *The Vivisector,* Patrick White, 1970.

Duff-Whalley, Mrs Agnes.
Her children:
Minnie, Gordon and **Muriel.**
Penny Plain, 1920, and elsewhere, O. Douglas.

Dufferin, Dr Anthony. *Men and Wives,* Ivy Compton-Burnett, 1931.

Duffy, James, bank cashier. 'A Painful Case' (s.s.), *The Dubliners,* James Joyce, 1914.

Duffy, John, chairman, R.D.C.
Delia, his daughter, eng. to Denis Geoghegan.
The White-headed Boy (play), L. Robinson, 1920.

Dugal, Lady Lorna. *See* LORNA DOONE.

Dugan, Mame, m. Jeff Peters. 'Cupid à la Carte' (s.s.), *Heart of the West,* O. Henry, 1907.

Dugdale, Marmaduke, m. Harriet Harper. *Agatha's Husband,* Mrs Craik, 1853.

Duggan, Danny, convalescent soldier. *A Kiss for Cinderella,* J. M. Barrie, 1916.

Duggan, Dora, ex-wife of Steve Sorrel, mother of Kit. *Sorrell and Son,* W. Deeping, 1925.

Du Guesclin, Bertrand, knight (hist).
Lady Tiphaine, his wife.
The White Company, A. Conan Doyle, 1891.

Duhamel, Canadian seigneur. *The Pomp of the Lavilettes,* Gilbert Parker, 1897.

Duhamel, Sylvenne (alias Sylvia Elven), actress. *The Maids of Paradise,* R. W. Chambers, 1903.

Duigan, Mr and Mrs, lodging-house keepers. *The Bay,* L. A. G. Strong, 1941.

Duke, The, living in exile. *As You Like It* (play), W. Shakespeare.

Duke, Rev. Archibald. 'The Rev. Amos Barton,' *Scenes of Clerical Life,* George Eliot, 1857.

Duke, Diana.
Her aunt, boarding-house keeper.
Manalive, G. K. Chesterton, 1912.

Duke, Rev. William. *Outward Bound* (play), S. Vane, 1923.

Dula, waiting-woman to Evadne. *The Maid's Tragedy* (play), Beaumont & Fletcher, 1611.

Dulver, Herbert, m. Elsie Longstaff. *The Good Companions,* J. B. Priestley, 1929.

Dumain, lord attending on Ferdinand. *Love's Labour's Lost* (play), W. Shakespeare.

Dumbello, Lord, later Lord Hartletop, m. Griselda Grantly. *Framley Parsonage,* A. Trollope, 1861.

Dumbiedikes, Lord of, mean and grasping landlord.
Jock, his gawky son.
The Heart of Midlothian, W. Scott, 1818.

Dumby, Mr. *Lady Windermere's Fan* (play), O. Wilde, 1892.

Dumetrius, art dealer. The *Forsyte* series, J. Galsworthy, 1906–33.

Dummerar, Rev. Mr, Vicar of Martindale-cum-Moultrassie. *Peveril of the Peak,* W. Scott, 1822.

Dumoise, civil surgeon.
His wife.
'By Word of Mouth' (s.s.), *Plain Tales from the Hills,* R. Kipling, 1888.

Dumps, Nicodemus, bank clerk. *Sketches by Boz,* 1836, and *Pickwick Papers,* 1837, C. Dickens.

Dumtoustie, Daniel, lawyer, nephew of Lord Bladderskate. *Redgauntlet,* W. Scott, 1824.

Dun, Hughie, body-servant of the Archbishop of St Andrews. *The Fair Maid of Perth,* W. Scott, 1828.

Dunbar, Ginevra, friend of Amy Grey. *Alice-sit-by-the-Fire* (play), J. M. Barrie, 1905.

Dunboyne, Philip, m. Eunice Gracedieu.
His father.
The Legacy of Cain, W. Collins, 1889.

Duncalf, town clerk of Bursley, solicitor, Henry Machin's first employer. *The Card,* Arnold Bennett, 1911.

Duncan, King of Scotland. *Macbeth* (play), W. Shakespeare.

Duncan, head teamster to McLean.
His wife.
Freckles, Gene S. Porter, 1904.

Duncan ('Fat Sow'). 'A Little Prep,' *Stalky & Co.,* R. Kipling, 1899.

Duncan, Major. *The Pathfinder,* J. Fenimore Cooper, 1840.

Duncan, Archibald. *Middlemarch,* George Eliot, 1871–2.

Duncan, Myra (alias Harvest V. Mellander). *Poison Ivy,* P. Cheyney, 1937.

Duncan, Long Rob, a miller. *A Scots Quair,* trilogy, 1932–4, Lewis Grassic Gibbon.

Duncannon, Gregor, landlord of the Highlander and the Hawick Gill. *Waverley,* W. Scott, 1814.

Duncansby, Lieutenant Hector. *Catriona,* R. L. Stevenson, 1893.

Duncanson, Neil. *Catriona,* R. L. Stevenson, 1893.

Dunce, Lady, in love with Captain Beaugard.
Sir Davy, her elderly husband.
Sylvia, Sir Davy's niece.
The Soldier's Fortune (play), Thomas Otway, 1681.

Duncombe, Humphrey, central character.
Sir Everard, his father.
His dead mother.
Miles, his brother.
Misunderstood, Florence Montgomery, 1869.

Dundas, journalist. *No Man's Land,* L. J. Vance, 1910.

Dunford, Bishop Walter.
Dame Sibilla, his niece, nun at the convent of Oby.
The Corner That Held Them, Sylvia Townsend Warner, 1948.

Dungory, Earl of (Family name Cullen).
His sisters:
Cecilia, a cripple.
Jane.
Sarah.
A Drama in Muslin, G. Moore, 1886.

Dunham, Mabel, m. Jasper Western.
Sergeant Dunham, her father.
'Cap,' her uncle.
The Pathfinder, J. Fenimore Cooper, 1840.

Dunkerley, senior assistant at Bonover School. *Love and Mr Lewisham,* H. G. Wells, 1900.

Dunkerley, Martin, schoolmaster who jilts Patty Verity. *High Meadows,* Alison Uttley, 1938.

Dunkirk, rich pawnbroker with a disreputable past.
Harriet, his wife, later Mrs Bulstrode.
Sarah, their daughter, m. Will Ladislaw.
Middlemarch, Geo. Eliot, 1871–2.

Dunmaya, a hillwoman. 'Yoked with an Unbeliever' (s.s.), *Plain Tales from the Hills,* R. Kipling, 1888.

Dunn, Mr, draper in Milby.
His wife.
Mary, their daughter.
'Janet's Repentance,' *Scenes from Clerical Life,* George Eliot, 1857.

Dunn, Ann, household help and nurse to Luke Mangan, m. Walters, seaman. *The Bay,* L. A. G. Strong, 1941.

Dunn, Ellie, Mazzini and Billy. *Heartbreak House,* G. B. Shaw, 1917.

Dunn, John. *The Skipper's Wooing,* W. W. Jacobs, 1897.

Dunne, Mrs (*née* Grace Hogan), grandmother of Eddie Ryan. *The Silence of History,* J. T. Farrell, 1963.

Dunne, Michael. 'The Fisherman' (s.s.), *Sir Pompey and Madame Juno,* M. Armstrong, 1927.

Dunne, Molly, m. Richard Marcus. *Tents of Israel,* G. B. Stern, 1924.

Dunne, Susan, central character and narrator, m. Johnnie. *See* LADY JEAN. *The White Cliffs* (poem), Alice D. Miller, 1941.

Dunning, Sir Giles Piercey's servant. *The Cuckoo in the Nest,* Mrs Oliphant, 1894.

Dunnock, Rev. Charles, widower.
Anne, his daughter, m. Gerald Grandison.
Go She Must!, David Garnett, 1927.

Dunnybrig, Valiant. *The Farmer's Wife* (play), E. Phillpotts, 1924.

Dunois, Bastard of Orleans. *Saint Joan* (play), G. B. Shaw, 1924.

Dunsack, Barzil, ship's captain, friend of Jeremy Ammidon.
Edward, his son.

Kate, his daughter.
Java Head, J. Hergesheimer, 1919.

Dunscombe, Captain.
His wife.
Margaret, their daughter.
The Wide, Wide World, E. Wetherell, 1850.

Dunstable, Lieutenant, The Duke of, Dragoon Guards, m. Lady Jane. *Patience* (comic opera), Gilbert & Sullivan, 1881.

Dunstable, Miss, heiress. *Doctor Thorne,* 1858, and elsewhere, A. Trollope.

Dunstan, Lady Helen, loved by Sir Peregrine Beverley. *The Broad Highway,* J. Farnol, 1910.

Dunstane, Lady Emma, friend of Diana Warwick. *Diana of the Crossways,* George Meredith, 1885.

Dunston, Major Maxwell, cousin-in-law to the Roundelays, m. Crystal Roundelay. *A Footman for the Peacock,* Rachel Ferguson, 1940.

Dunstone.
His wife.
'Dunstone's Dear Lady' (s.s.), *Certain Personal Matters,* H. G. Wells, 1901.

Dunthorne, Major. *The Woman in White,* W. Collins, 1860.

Duntisbourne, Captain Icelin, of the *Blackgauntlet. The Bird of Dawning,* J. Masefield, 1933.

Duphot, Mademoiselle, governess and faithful friend of Stephen Gordon.
Julie, her blind sister.
The Well of Loneliness, Radclyffe Hall, 1928.

Dupin, C. Auguste, French super-sleuth. *The Mystery of Marie Roget* and other stories, E. A. Poe.

Dupont, Mademoiselle ('Dewy'), governess. *Spears Against Us,* Cecil Roberts, 1932.

Dupont, Monsieur, cat with white spats. *The Loving Eye,* William Sansom, 1956.

Dupont, Emil, French journalist. *Men Like Gods,* H. G. Wells, 1923.

Duport, Bob, ex-husband of Jean Templer. *A Question of Upbringing,* 1951, and others in *The Music of Time* series, Anthony Powell.

Dupree, James James Morrison Morrison Weatherby George. 'Disobedience' (poem), *When We Were Very Young,* A. A. Milne, 1924.

Durango, Bishop, of Santa Fé. *Death Comes for the Archbishop,* Willa Cather, 1927.

Durant, Mr, assistant manager, rubber company; seducer. 'Mr Durant' (s.s.), *Here Lies,* Dorothy Parker, 1939.

Durant, Alfred, m. Louise Lindley.
His father and mother.
Daughters of the Vicar (s.s.), D. H. Lawrence.

D'Urberville, Sir Pagan, ancestor of the D'Urberville and Durbeyfield family.
Also Stoke-D'Urberville.
Alexander (Alec), seduced and later m. Tess.
His mother.
John Stoke, his father.

Durbeyfield, Tess, central character, see above.
John, her father.
Joan, her mother.
Eliza-Louisa ('Liza-Lu), her sister.
Other sisters and brothers.
Tess of the D'Urbervilles, T. Hardy, 1891.

Durbin, Mrs, barber.
Albert, her blind husband.
Arthur, Albert's brother.
Magnolia Street, L. Golding, 1932.

Durden, Dame. *See* ESTHER SUMMERSON.

Durden, Tabitha. *The Silver King* (play), H. A. Jones, 1882.

Durdles, stonemason in Cloisterham. *Edwin Drood,* C. Dickens, 1870.

Durette, Mademoiselle Clemence, companion of Countess Luxstein. *The Courtship of Morrice Buckler,* A. E. W. Mason, 1896.

Durfey-Transome, relations of earlier Transomes, to whom their estates passed. *Felix Holt,* George Eliot, 1866.

Durfy, of the *Rocket. Reginald Cruden,* T. Baines Reed, 1894.

Durfy, Tom, m. Kitty Flanagan, *née* Riley. *Handy Andy,* S. Lover, 1842.

Durgan, Miss, postmistress, Hickleybrow. *The Food of the Gods,* H. G. Wells, 1904.

Durham, Clive, owner of Penge, barrister and country gentleman; platonic lover of Maurice Hall. *Maurice,* E. M. Forster, 1971.

Durham, Constantia.
Sir John, her father.
The Egoist, G. Meredith, 1879.

Durham, Katzerl, daughter of Kati Lanik.
Cyril, her husband.
Grand Opera, Vicki Baum, 1942.

Durham, Regina, mistress of Philip Warren.
Rex, her husband, American politician.
The Judgment of Paris, Gore Vidal, 1952.

Durie. Family name of LORD DURRISDEER AND BALLANTRAE.

Durley, Julian. *Memoirs of an Infantry Officer,* Siegfried Sassoon, 1930.

Durnovo, Victor, villain. *With Edged Tools,* H. S. Merriman, 1894.

Duroch, Duncan, leader under Donald Lean. *Waverley,* W. Scott, 1814.

Durrant, Timothy, college friend of Jacob Flanders.
Clara, his sister.
His mother.
Jacob's Room, Virginia Woolf, 1922.

Durrisdeer and Ballantrae, Lord (Family name Durie).
James, Marquis of Ballantrae, presumed killed at Culloden.
Henry, Marquis of Ballantrae, later Lord Durrisdeer, m. Alison Graeme.
Alexander, their son.
Katherine, their daughter.
The Master of Ballantrae, R. L. Stevenson, 1889.

Durrows, Mr. *At Mrs Beam's,* C. K. Munro, 1923.

Durward, Quentin, of Louis XI's Scottish Guard, central character. *Quentin Durward,* 1823, and (as M. de la Croye) *Anne of Geierstein,* 1829, W. Scott.

Dusack, Kate. *See* VOLLAR.

Duthie, Jimsy, poet and master printer and brewer.
Jess, his sister, m. Hendry McQumpha.
A Window in Thrums, J. M. Barrie, 1889.

Dutripon, Victor, of the Chariot d'Or, m. (1) Valentine Bompard, (2) Mme Lemoine, widow. 'The Vengeance of Monsieur Dutripon' (s.s.), *The Little Dog Laughed,* L. Merrick, 1930.

Dutton, seaman on the *Sarah.* *The Master of Ballantrae,* R. L. Stevenson, 1889.

Dutton, Dolly, dairymaid to the Duke of Argyll. *The Heart of Midlothian,* W. Scott, 1818.

Duvach, herdsman-prince.
Conn, his son.
Bride, his daughter.
'St Bride of the Isles' (s.s.), *Spiritual Tales,* Fiona Macleod, 1903.

Duval, Denis, smuggler and *perruquier.*
Peter, his grandfather, from whom he learned the trade.
Ursule, his mother.
Denis Duval, W. M. Thackeray, 1864.

Duval, Winnie.
Charles, her husband.
The Metropolis, Upton Sinclair, 1908.

Duvallet. *Fanny's First Play* (play), G. B. Shaw, 1905.

Duveen, Dulcie, acrobat, m. Arthur Hastings.
Bella, her sister and partner, m. Jack Renauld.
Murder on the Links, Agatha Christie, 1923.

Dwining, Henbane, 'a sneaking varlet.' *The Fair Maid of Perth,* W. Scott, 1828.

Dwornitzchek, Princess Heloise von and zu, ex Mrs Franklin, *née* Bulpitt, m. (3) Adrian Peake. *Summer Moonshine,* P. G. Wodehouse, 1938.

Dwyer, Matty, m. James Casey. *Handy Andy,* S. Lover, 1842.

Dyer, Mormon bishop, kidnapper of Bess Erne. *Riders of the Purple Sage,* Zane Grey, 1912.

Dyer, Mr and Mrs, occupants of flat above Philip Boyes. *Strong Poison,* Dorothy L. Sayers, 1930.

Dyke, Tam, boyhood friend of David Crawfurd. *Prester John,* J. Buchan, 1910.

Dykes, gamekeeper to Austin Ruthyn. *Uncle Silas,* Sheridan le Fanu, 1864.

Dymoke, Sergeant, Puritan. *Holmby House,* G. Whyte-Melville, 1860.

Dymond, Winny ('Winky'), in love with John Ransome. *The Combined Maze,* May Sinclair.

Dynamene. *A Phoenix too Frequent* (play), Christopher Fry, 1946.

Dyson, itinerant preacher *The History of David Grieve,* Mrs Humphry Ward, 1892.

E

E.23, a Mahratta in the Secret Service. *Kim,* R. Kipling, 1901.

Eager, Rev. Cuthbert, English chaplain, Florence. *A Room with a View,* E. M. Forster, 1908.

Eagles, Mrs Hook, at first patronizing, then cold-shouldering, Becky Sharp. *Vanity Fair,* W. M. Thackeray, 1847–8.

Eaglesham, Lord, friend and patron of Rev. Micah Balwhidder. *Annals of the Parish,* John Galt, 1821.

Ealing, undergraduate, friend of the Babe. *The Babe, B.A.,* E. F. Benson, 1897.

Eames, ex Church of England rector, Bishop of Pullford's secretary. *The Three Taps,* R. A. Knox, 1927.

Eames, subaltern. 'The Honours of War' (s.s.), *A Diversity of Creatures,* R. Kipling, 1917.

Eames, Ernest, bibliographer. *South Wind,* N. Douglas, 1917.

Eames, Wilfred Emerson, Warden, Brakespeare College, *Manalive,* G. K. Chesterton, 1912.

Earlforward, Henry, bookseller.
His wife, formerly Mrs Arb.
Rev. Augustus, his brother.
Riceyman Steps, Arnold Bennett, 1923.

Earnscliff, Patrick, m. Isabel Vere. *The Black Dwarf,* W. Scott, 1816.

Earnshaw, Lieutenant. *Sixty-four, Ninety-four,* R. H. Mottram, 1925.

Earnshaw, Catherine, central character, m. Edgar Linton.
Hindley, her brother.
His wife.
Hareton, their son, m. Cathy Heathcliff, *née* Linton.
Wuthering Heights, Emily Brontë, 1847.

Earp, Ruth, teacher of dancing, onetime fiancée of Denry Machin, later Mrs Capron-Smith. *The Card,* Arnold Bennett, 1911.

Earwhicker, Humphrey Chimpden, also called Haveth Childer Everywhere, a publican.
Ann, his wife, called Anna Livia Plurabelle.
Isobel, their daughter.
Their twin sons:
Kevin, also Shaun the Postman, Chuff, Jaun and Yawn.
Jerry, also Shem the Penman, Dolph and Glugg.
Finnegans Wake, James Joyce, 1939.

Easdaile, friend of John Bloxham.
Isobel, his sister, m. (1) Ronald McCaskie (posing as Brodie), (2) James Ayrton, alias Angeray.
God's Prisoner, J. Oxenham, 1898.

East, schoolfellow and close friend of Tom Brown. *Tom Brown's Schooldays,* T. Hughes, 1857.

Easthupp, bosun, purser's steward. *Mr Midshipman Easy,* Captain Marryat, 1836.

Eastlake, Lord, governor-designate, Bombay. The *Hornblower* series, C. S. Forester, 1937 onwards.

Eastlake, Elinor (Lakey), graduate of Vassar. *The Group,* Mary McCarthy, 1963.

Easton, Sir Lewis, Chairman, National Council. *The Small Back Room,* N. Balchin, 1943.

Easton, Sir Philip, lover of Amanda Morris. *The Research Magnificent,* H. G. Wells, 1915.

Eastwood, Major Charles, lover of Mrs Fawcett. *The Virgin and The Gipsy,* D. H. Lawrence, 1930.

Easy, Lady. *The Careless Husband* (play), C. Cibber, 1705.

Easy, John, midshipman, central character.
Nicodemus, his father.
Mr Midshipman Easy, Captain Marryat, 1836.

Eathorne, William, Washington Bank President. *Babbitt,* Sinclair Lewis, 1923.

Eaton, Fay. *The Middle Watch* (play), Ian Hay & S. King-Hall, 1929.

Eaves, Tom, club gossip. *Vanity Fair,* 1847–8, and elsewhere, W. M. Thackeray.

Eavesdrop, Mr, a social climber. *Crotchet Castle,* T. L. Peacock, 1831.

Ebag. *The Great Adventure* (play), Arnold Bennett, 1913.

Ebbsmith, Mrs Agnes, *née* Thorold. *The Notorious Mrs Ebbsmith* (play), A. W. Pinero, 1895.

Ebbsworth, Norah, mistress of Gus Parkington. *Mrs Parkington,* L. Bromfield, 1944.

Ebea, maid to Zabina. *Tamburlaine,* C. Marlowe, 1587.

Eben, son of Hannah. 'The Talent Thou Gavest' (s.s.), *My People,* Caradoc Evans, 1915.

Ebermann, Frau. 'Swept and Garnished' (s.s.), *A Diversity of Creatures,* R. Kipling, 1917.

Eberson, Carl, illegitimate son of William de la Marck. *Quentin Durward,* W. Scott, 1823.

Ebhart, Max, eng. to Naomi Fisher.

Leopold, their illegitimate son, lover of Karen Michaelis.

The House in Paris, Elizabeth Bowen, 1935.

Ebley, Lord Dilling's cousin. *The Last of Mrs Cheyney* (play), F. Lonsdale, 1925.

Ebsworthy, renegade sailor turned Indian. *Westward Ho!,* C. Kingsley, 1855.

Eccles, tutor and scoundrel. *Diary of a Late Physician,* S. Warren, 1832.

Eccles, First Lieutenant, of the *Indefatigable.* The *Hornblower* series, C. S. Forester, 1937 onwards.

Eccles, Claud. *The Young Idea* (play), N. Coward, 1923.

Eccles, James, shady lawyer. *By The Pricking of My Thumbs,* Agatha Christie, 1968.

Eccles, John Scott. 'Wisteria Lodge,' *His Last Bow,* A. Conan Doyle, 1917.

Eccles, Robert.

Jonathan, his father.

Rhoda Fleming, G. Meredith, 1865.

Eckdorf, Ivy, a photographer. *Mrs Eckdorf in O'Neill's Hotel,* William Trevor, 1969.

Eddi, St Wilfrid's priest. 'The Conversion of St Wilfrid' (s.s.), *Rewards and Fairies,* R. Kipling, 1910.

Eddie, works in Tom Quayne's advertising agency. *The Death of the Heart,* Elizabeth Bowen, 1938.

Eddy, Sir Kenneth, defending counsel. *We the Accused,* E. Raymond, 1935.

Ede, Thomas, farmer, former owner of Grand National 'Piebald.' *National Velvet,* Enid Bagnold, 1935.

Edelman, Mrs.

Benny, her son, elopes with Jessie Wright.

Norman, her son, m. Fanny Gustav.

Jacky, their son.

Old Mrs Edelman, her mother-in-law.

Magnolia Street, L. Golding, 1932.

Edelmann, Mr, Lithuanian refugee. 'You See—' (s.s.), *Love and Money,* Phyllis Bentley, 1957.

Edelstein, Count Franz von.

Katharina, *née* von Ahm, his wife.

Their children:

Karl.

Paul.

Anna and Hugh (twins).

Spears Against Us, Cecil Roberts, 1932.

Eden, Arthur, protégé of Walter Evson. *St Winifred's,* F. W. Farrar, 1862.

Eden, Rev. Frank, humanitarian jail chaplain. *It Is Never Too Late to Mend,* C. Reade, 1856.

Eden, Mrs Jack.

Muriel, her sister-in-law.

The Gay Lord Quex, A. W. Pinero, 1899.

Ederic the Forester, Saxon leader against the Normans. *Count Robert of Paris,* W. Scott, 1832.

Edgar, Gloster's son. *King Lear* (play), W. Shakespeare.

Edge, Halsey.

Leda, his wife.

The Thin Man, D. Hammett, 1934.

Edgehill. *Dr Nikola,* G. Boothby, 1896.

Edgeworth, Duncan.

Ellen, his 1st wife.

Their daughters:

Nance, m. Oscar Jekyll.

Sybil, m. Grant.

Alison, his 2nd wife.

Cassie, *née* Jekyll, his 3rd wife.

Grant, his nephew, m. Sybil.

A House and its Head, Ivy Compton-Burnett, 1935.

Edgeworth, Harold, friend of Henry Maitland. *The Private Life of Henry Maitland,* Morley Roberts, 1912.

Edith, maid in love with Raunce, the butler. *Loving*, Henry Green, 1945.
Edlin, Mrs. *Jude the Obscure*, T. Hardy, 1896.
Edmonstone, Edward.
His wife.
Their children:
Charles.
Laura, m. Philip Morville.
Amy, m. Sir Guy Morville.
Charlotte.
The Heir of Redclyffe, Charlotte M. Yonge, 1853.
Edmund, bastard son of Gloster. *King Lear* (play), W. Shakespeare.
Edmunds, John, central character. 'The Convict's Return,' *Pickwick Papers*, C. Dickens, 1837.
Edricson, Alleyne. *The White Company*, A. Conan Doyle, 1891.
Edward, Prince of Wales, son of Henry (hist.), *Henry the Sixth* (play), W. Shakespeare.
Edward, Prince of Wales, later Edward VI (hist.). *The Prince and the Pauper*, Mark Twain, 1882.
Edward the Fourth (hist.). *Richard the Third* (play), W. Shakespeare.
Edward the Fifth (hist.). *Richard the Third* (play), W. Shakespeare.
Edwards, Mr, theatre manager. *Red Peppers* (play), Noël Coward, 1936.
Edwards, Eleanor ('Magdalen'). *Diary of a Late Physician*, S. Warren, 1832.
Edwards, Eurydice, companion of Mme Ruiz. *Prancing Nigger*, Ronald Firbank, 1924.
Edwards, Foxhall, publisher's editor. *You Can't Go Home Again*, T. Wolfe, 1947.
Edwards, Jerome, central character, m. Lucina Merritt.
Elmira, his sister, m. Lawrence Prescott.
Abel, his father.
Ann, his mother, *née* Lamb.
Jerome, Mary E. Wilkins, 1897.
Edwards, Mr Mog, in love with Myfanwy Price. *Under Milk Wood*, Dylan Thomas, 1954.
Edwards, Morris.
Kate, his wife.
A Lamp for Nightfall, E. Caldwell, 1952.
Edwards, Rebecca, mistress of James Bray.
Gordon Edwards, her husband.
A Guest of Honour, Nadine Gordimer, 1971.
Edwards, Tom. 'An Ohio Pagan' (s.s.), *Horses and Men*, Sherwood Anderson, 1924.
Edwin, hermit. 'Edwin and Angelina,' ballad, read by Burchell. *The Vicar of Wakefield*, O. Goldsmith, 1766.
Edwin of the Green. *A Fairy Tale* (poem), T. Parnell, *c.* 1710.
Eeles, Julie, actress, mistress of Thomas and Edward Wilcher. *To Be A Pilgrim*, Joyce Cary, 1942.
Eerith, Samuel, oiler to the Monster. *The Last Revolution*, Lord Dunsany, 1951.
Eeyore, an old grey donkey. *Winnie the Pooh*, 1926, and others, A. A. Milne.
Efans, Llewellyn, Welsh seaman, *Blackgauntlet*. *The Bird of Dawning*, J. Masefield, 1933.
Effick, David and Rose. *The Clever Ones* (play), A. Sutro, 1914.
Effingham, Major, of the 60th Loyal American Regiment (alias Hawkeye). *The Last of the Mohicans*, J. Fenimore Cooper, 1826.
Effingham, Violet, Lady Baldock's niece, m. Lord Chiltern. *Phineas Finn*, 1869, and elsewhere, A. Trollope.
Egan, Edward, squire of Merryvale. *Handy Andy*, S. Lover, 1842.
Egan, 'Horse,' Irish private. 'The Mutiny of the Mavericks' (s.s.), *Life's Handicap*, R. Kipling, 1891.
Egerton, Audley. *My Novel*, Lord Lytton, 1853.
Egerton, Lady Julia, cousin of Jack Hinton, m. Colonel Philip O'Grady. *Jack Hinton*, C. Lever, 1843.
Egeus, father of Hermia. *A Midsummer Night's Dream* (play), W. Shakespeare.
Eggerson, confidential clerk to Sir Claude Mulhammer. *The Confidential Clerk* (play), T. S. Eliot, 1954.
Eglantine, barber and perfumer. 'The Ravenswing,' *Men's Wives*, W. M. Thackeray, 1843.
Egmont, Walter, m. Lavinia Crabtree.
May, their daughter.
His mother.
Love and Money, Phyllis Bentley, 1957.

Ego, Pomponius. *Handley Cross,* R. S. Surtees, 1843.

Egremont. Family name of EARL OF MARNEY.

Egstrom & Blake, ships' chandlers, employers of Jim. *Lord Jim,* J. Conrad, 1900.

Egypt, Soldan of. *Tamburlaine,* C. Marlowe, 1587.

Ehrenberger, Armgard, m. Anatol Czelovar. *Tents of Israel,* G. B. Stern, 1924.

Eichorn, Mrs. *Mrs Wiggs of the Cabbage Patch,* Alice H. Rice, 1901.

Einhorn, William, Augie's friend and employer. *The Adventures of Augie March,* Saul Bellow, 1953.

Einion, Father, chaplain to Gwenwyn. *The Betrothed,* W. Scott, 1825.

Eisman, Mr. *Gentlemen Prefer Blondes,* Anita Loos, 1925.

Ek, Oscar, athletics coach. *The Human Comedy,* W. Saroyan, 1943.

Elaine, 'the lily maid of Astolat,' in love with Lancelot.
Her father and brother.
'Lancelot and Elaine' (poem). *Idylls of the King,* Lord Tennyson, 1859.

Elbourne, Colonel and Mrs. 'A. V. Laider,' *Seven Men,* M. Beerbohm, 1919.

Elderson, Robert, defaulting insurance broker. *The White Monkey,* J. Galsworthy, 1924.

Eldest Magician, The. 'The Crab that Played with the Sea,' *Just So Stories,* R. Kipling, 1902.

Eldridge, John.
His wife, cook to Marianne Challis.
It Never Can Happen Again, W. de Morgan, 1909.

Elena, central character. *Philip van Artevelde* (play), H. Taylor, 1834.

Elena, George and William. *Odtaa,* J. Masefield, 1926.

Elephant's Child, The. 'The Elephant's Child,' *Just So Stories,* R. Kipling, 1902.

Elfrida, a lady of the English court. *Eric Brighteyes,* H. Rider Haggard, 1891.

Elias of Bury.
Adah, his wife.
'The Treasure and the Law,' *Puck of Pook's Hill,* R. Kipling, 1906.

Elias of Tergon, father of Gerard Eliasson.
Catherine, his wife.
The Cloister and the Hearth, C. Reade, 1861.

Elias the Shop, Abishai. *How Green Was My Valley,* R. Llewellyn, 1939.

Eliasson, Gerard, central character. *The Cloister and the Hearth,* C. Reade, 1861.

Elinor, Queen, mother of King John. *King John* (play), W. Shakespeare.

Eliot, Helen. *The Human Comedy,* W. Saroyan, 1943.

Eliot, Kenneth, cabinet-maker, m. Mabel Pinkney. 'Death of a Dog,' *Louise,* Viola Meynell, 1954.

Eliot, Lewis, barrister, narrator and chief character. *Time of Hope,* 1949, part of the *Strangers and Brothers* sequence, C. P. Snow.

Eliot, Lady (Lucilla), grandmother.
Rev. Hilary, her son.
George, her son.
Nadine, his wife.
Their children:
Ben.
Tommy.
Caroline.
José.
Jerry.
Margaret, her daughter.
David, her grandson, m. Sally Adair.
The Herb of Grace, Elizabeth Goudge, 1948.

Elisa, German servant of Miss Collier-Floodgaye. *Before the Bombardment,* O. Sitwell, 1926.

Elissa, step-sister of Medina and Perissa. *The Faërie Queene* (poem), E. Spenser, 1590.

Eliza, central character.
Her husband and mother.
Eliza, 1900, and others, Barry Pain.

Eliza, housemaid to Mrs Ingle. *The Last Revolution,* Lord Dunsany, 1951.

Elizabeth, Queen (hist.) (Gloriana). 'Gloriana,' *Rewards and Fairies,* R. Kipling, 1910.

Elizabeth, Queen, widow of Edward IV. *Richard the Third* (play), W. Shakespeare.

El Khalil, Ibrahim, mufti. *Saïd the Fisherman,* M. Pickthall, 1903.

Elkus, Nanuet bank robber. *High Tor* (play), Maxwell Anderson, 1937.

Ella, Lady, a rapturous maiden. *Patience* (comic opera), Gilbert & Sullivan, 1881.

Elland, Sir John. 'Revenge upon Revenge' (s.s.), *Love and Money,* Phyllis Bentley, 1957.

Ellangowan. *See* BERTRAM.

Ellen, erring servant of Theobald Pontifex, m. John the coachman, later bigamously m. Ernest Pontifex.
 Georgie, their son.
 Alice, their daughter.
The Way of all Flesh, S. Butler, 1903.

Ellen, Aunt. *The White-headed Boy* (play), L. Robinson, 1920.

Ellen, Burd. 'Childe Waters' (poem), *Percy's Reliques,* Bishop Thomas Percy, 1765.

Ellen-Maudie, maid of the Barleys. *See also* JANE. *The One Before,* Barry Pain, 1902.

Ellesmere, Mistress, housekeeper at Martindale Castle. *Peveril of the Peak,* W. Scott, 1822.

Ellieslaw. *See* RICHARD VERE.

Ellinger, Frank, bachelor who has affair with Mrs Marian Forrester. *A Lost Lady,* Willa Cather, 1923.

Elliot, Detective Inspector Andrew. *The Black Spectacles,* J. Dickson Carr, 1948.

Elliot, Frederick (Rickie), lame schoolmaster, m. Agnes Pembroke.
 Stephen Wonham, his half-brother.
The Longest Journey, E. M. Forster, 1907.

Elliot, Halbert ('Hobbie of the Heughfoot'), m. Grace Armstrong.
 John and **Harry,** his brothers.
 Lilias, Joan and **Annot,** his sisters, 'rustic coquettes.'
The Black Dwarf, W. Scott, 1816.

Elliot, Lewis, m. Pamela Reston. *Penny Plain,* O. Douglas, 1920.

Elliot, Ralph (alias Richard Frampton), close friend of Frank Fairlegh. *Frank Fairlegh,* F. E. Smedley, 1850.

Elliot, Sir Walter, Bt, of Kellynch Hall, widower.
 His daughters:
 Elizabeth Mary, m. Charles Musgrove.
 Anne, m. Captain Wentworth.
 Walter, heir presumptive to the baronetcy.
 His wife.
Persuasion, Jane Austen, 1818.

Elliott, Christina (Kirstie), housekeeper to Lord Weir.
 Gilbert, her brother.
 His sons (The Four Black Brothers): **Robert, Gilbert, Clement** and **Andrew.**
 Christina (Kirstie), his daughter.
Weir of Hermiston, R. L. Stevenson, 1896.

Elliott, Henry, merchant's clerk.
 Mary, *née* Hillary, his wife.
Diary of a Late Physician, S. Warren, 1832.

Elliott, Stephen, orphan cousin of Mr Abney. 'Lost Hearts' (s.s.), *Ghost Stories of an Antiquary,* M. R. James, 1910.

Ellis, Judge. *The Metropolis,* Upton Sinclair, 1908.

Ellis, Dai (the stable).
 Mervyn, his son.
How Green Was My Valley, R. Llewellyn, 1939.

Ellis, Dorothy, hotel employee. *The Feast,* Margaret Kennedy, 1950.

Ellis, Mrs Edie, Middleton's mother-in-law. *The Restoration of Arnold Middleton* (play), David Storey, 1967.

Ellis, Mrs Sarah, housekeeper. *The Lamplighter,* Maria S. Cummins, 1854.

Ellis, Sophy. 'The Wish House' (s.s.), *Debits and Credits,* R. Kipling, 1926.

Ellison, John, J.P., manufacturer, partner of John Manning.
 Margaret, his daughter, m. Paul Manning.
Cousin Phillis, Mrs Gaskell, 1864.

Elmham, Bishop of.
 Mrs Yeld, his wife.
The Way We Live Now, A. Trollope, 1875.

Elmore, Sir Henry, Bt, midshipman saved from drowning by Billy Freeborn. *True Blue,* W. H. G. Kingston.

Elmscott, Lord, cousin of Morrice Buckler. *The Courtship of Morrice Buckler,* A. E. W. Mason, 1896.

Eloi, The, frail and exquisite inhabitants of the upper world. *The Time Machine,* H. G. Wells, 1895.

Elphinstone, a butler. *It Never Can Happen Again,* W. de Morgan, 1909.
Elphinstone, Mr and Mrs. *The War of the Worlds,* H. G. Wells, 1898.
Elshender. *See* BLACK DWARF.
Elsie, central character.
Gottlieb, her father.
Ursula, her mother.
The Golden Legend (poem), H. W. Longfellow, 1851.
Elsing, Mrs.
Hugh, her son.
Fanny, her daughter, m. Tommy Wellburn.
Gone with the Wind, Margaret Mitchell, 1936.
Elsinore, Eva's room-mate at school. *Eva Trout,* Elizabeth Bowen, 1969.
Elspie. *The Bothie of Tober-na-Vuolich* (poem), A. H. Clough, 1848.
Elsworthy, Father. *The Voice from the Minaret* (play), R. S. Hichens, 1919.
Elton, eligible bachelor, unsuccessful suitor of Emma Woodhouse.
Augusta, his wife.
Emma, Jane Austen, 1816.
Elton, Lord. *The Last of Mrs Cheyney,* F. Lonsdale, 1925.
Elton, Mrs. *The Deep Blue Sea* (play), T. Rattigan, 1952.
Elver.
Grace, his sister.
Those Barren Leaves, A. Huxley, 1925.
Elvery, Dr and Mrs, friends of Ralph Hingston. *Portrait of Clare,* F. Brett Young, 1927.
Elvira, Pizarro's lover. *Pizarro* (play), R. B. Sheridan, 1799.
Elwood, Cherry. *The Daisy Chain,* Charlotte M. Yonge, 1856.
Ely, Bishop of, *Henry the Fifth* (play), W. Shakespeare.
Ely, Rev. Mr, of Milby. 'The Rev. Amos Barton,' *Scenes of Clerical Life,* George Eliot, 1857.
Elya, lame refugee, m. Evan Gwyddr. *The Whistling Chambermaid,* Naomi Royde-Smith, 1957.
Em, stepdaughter of Tant Sannie. *The Story of an African Farm,* Olive Schreiner, 1883.
Emanuel, Don.
Inez, his daughter, m. Frederick Powy.
Charles O'Malley, C. Lever, 1841.
Emanuel, Isaac, clerk to Jewish Board of Guardians.
Slatta, his wife.
Their sons:
Max.
David.
Moisheh.
Magnolia Street, L. Golding, 1932.
Emanuel, Professor Paul Carl David. *Villette,* Charlotte Brontë, 1853.
Emerson, Miss Fortune, aunt and godmother of Ellen Montgomery, m. Abraham van Brunt. *The Wide, Wide World,* E. Wetherell, 1850.
Emerson, George, m. Lucy Honeychurch. *A Room with a View,* E. M. Forster, 1908.
Emerson, Paul, news sponsor for James Sperling.
Connie, his wife.
The Second Confession, R. Stout, 1950.
Emerson, Thede.
Rosa, his wife.
Jean, their daughter, m. Frank Gervais.
Howard, their son.
A Lamp for Nightfall, E. Caldwell, 1952.
Emery, attorney. *Manhattan Transfer,* J. dos Passos, 1925.
Emery, Enoch, zoo attendant. *Wise Blood,* Flannery O'Connor, 1952.
Emilia, Iago's wife. *Othello* (play), W. Shakespeare.
Emilie, Grand Duchess of Zalgar, aunt of Keri. *The Queen was in the Parlour,* N. Coward, 1926.
Emilius, 'The Rev.,' Jewish adventurer and blackmailer, m. Lady Eustace. *The Eustace Diamonds,* A. Trollope, 1873.
Emmeline, quadroon sold with Uncle Tom to Legree. *Uncle Tom's Cabin,* Harriet B. Stowe, 1851.
Emmerick, Count.
Countess Dorothy, his sister.
Jurgen, J. B. Cabell, 1921.
Emmersen, English engineer and emigrant. *Settlers in Canada,* Captain Marryat, 1844.
Emmett, Miss, Catherine Faber's guardian. *M.F.,* Anthony Burgess, 1971.
Emmet, Wilbur. *The Black Spectacles,* J. Dickson Carr, 1948.
Emmy, serving-woman. *The Doctor's Dilemma* (play), G. B. Shaw, 1906.

Emmy, Aunt. *Lolly Willowes*, Sylvia Townsend Warner, 1926.

Emory, Julian B., American doctor. 'My Sunday at Home' (s.s.), *The Day's Work*, R. Kipling, 1898.

Endena, mate of Ugh-lomi. 'Story of the Stone Age,' *Tales of Space and Time*, H. G. Wells, 1899.

Endicott, George.
Anthony, his brother. Uncles of Mirabell Starr.
Thomas.
George, his son.
Robert, his son. Descendants of George.
Rogue Herries, 1930, and *Vanessa*, 1933, Hugh Walpole.

Endorfield, Elizabeth, 'a deep body,' a witch. *Under the Greenwood Tree*, T. Hardy, 1872.

Enfield, Richard, kinsman and friend of Utterson. *Dr Jekyll and Mr Hyde*, R. L. Stevenson, 1886.

Enfilden, Hon. Domini, central character, m. Boris Androvsky.
Her father.
The Garden of Allah, R. S. Hichens, 1904.

Engelred, one of the leaders of the Foresters, who fought against Rufus.
Bertha, his daughter.
Count Robert of Paris, W. Scott, 1832.

English, Julian, garage proprietor in Gibbsville.
Caroline Walker English, his wife.
Dr William Dilworth English, his father.
Appointment in Samarra, John O'Hara, 1935.

Enid, daughter of Earl of Yniol, m. Geraint. 'Geraint and Enid' (poem), *Idylls of the King*, Lord Tennyson, 1859.

Enobarbus (Domitius), friend of Antony. *Antony and Cleopatra* (play), W Shakespeare.

Entwhistle, Rev. Trevor, headmaster, Harchester College, friend of the Bishop of Stortford. *Meet Mr Mulliner*, P. G. Wodehouse, 1927.

Entwistle, Amos, collier.
Jacob, his father.
A Safety Match, Ian Hay, 1911.

Envy, Superstition and Pickthank, witnesses against Christian and Faithful. *Pilgrim's Progress*, J. Bunyan, 1678 and 1684.

Ephraim Yahudi.
Miriam, his wife.
'Jews in Shushan' (s.s.), *Life's Handicap*, R. Kipling, 1891.

Epicene, wife of Morose. *Epicene* (play), B. Jonson, 1609.

Eppenwelzen-Sarkeld, Princess Ottilia, W. F. H., m. Prince Hermann.
The Margrave and Margravine, her parents.
Prince Otto, her cousin.
Adventures of Harry Richmond, G. Meredith, 1871.

Eppie, servant of Rev. Josiah Cargill. *St Ronan's Well*, W. Scott, 1824.

Eppington, Earl of, father of Lady Edith Beauchamp. *Fed Up*, G. A. Birmingham, 1931.

Erceldoun, Thomas of ('The Rhymer'). *Castle Dangerous*, W. Scott, 1832.

Erckmann, Sir Adolf. *Sonia*, S. McKenna, 1917.

Ercole, Italian prince and scoundrel. *Destiny Bay*, Donn Byrne, 1928.

Erconwald, leader of an experimenting band. *The Onion Eaters*, J. P. Donleavy, 1971.

Eric VIII, King.
Martha, his queen.
Princess Anne, their daughter.
The Queen's Husband (play), R. E. Sherwood, 1928.

Eric Brighteyes, central character.
Thorgrimur, his father.
Saevina, his mother.
Eric Brighteyes, H. Rider Haggard, 1891.

Ericson, Lieutenant - Commander George E., Captain of *Compass Rose*.
Grace, his wife.
John, their son.
The Cruel Sea, N. Monsarrat, 1951.

Ericsson, mate of the *Bluewing*. *God's Prisoner*, J. Oxenham, 1898.

Erif Der, the Spring Queen.
Tarrik, the Corn King, her husband.
Berris Der, her brother.
The Corn King and The Spring Queen, Naomi Mitchison, 1931.

Erl, The Lord of.
Alveric, his son.
The King of Elfland's Daughter, Lord Dunsany, 1924.

Erle, Barrington, nephew of William Mildmay. *Phineas Finn,* 1869, and elsewhere, A. Trollope.

Erley, James, brother-in-law of Robert Corder. *Miss Mole,* E. H. Young, 1930.

Erlin, Frau Professor.
Thekla and **Anna,** her daughters.
Of Human Bondage, W. S. Maugham, 1915.

Erlton, Major Herbert.
Kate, his wife.
On the Face of the Waters, Flora A. Steel, 1896.

Erlynne, Mrs Margaret, mother of Lady Windermere. *Lady Windermere's Fan* (play), O. Wilde, 1892.

Ern, a small boy. *The Romantic Age,* A. A. Milne, 1920.

Erne, Elizabeth ('Bess'), the Masked Rider, m. Bern Venters.
Milly, her mother.
Riders of the Purple Sage, Zane Grey, 1912.

Ernescliffe, Alan, eng. to Margaret May, but died abroad.
Hector, his brother, m. Blanche May.
The Daisy Chain, 1856, and elsewhere, Charlotte M. Yonge.

Ernestus, Abbot. *The Golden Legend* (poem), H. W. Longfellow, 1851.

Eros, friend of Antony. *Antony and Cleopatra* (play), W. Shakespeare.

Errol, Hon. Mrs ('Dearest'), mother of Lord Fauntleroy. *Little Lord Fauntleroy,* Frances H. Burnett, 1886.

Erskine, Matthew, of Dumfries, Patrick Heron's lawyer. *The Raiders,* S. R. Crockett, 1894.

Erskine, Colonel Toby, central character.
Claire, his dead wife.
Act of God, F. Tennyson Jesse, 1936.

Esa, mother of Imhotep; grandmother of Yahmose, by whom she is murdered, and of Sobek, Ipy and Renisenb. *Death Comes as the End,* Agatha Christie, 1945.

Escalus, Prince of Verona. *Romeo and Juliet* (play), W. Shakespeare.

Escalus, an ancient lord. *Measure for Measure* (play), W. Shakespeare.

Escanes, a lord of Tyre. *Pericles* (play), W. Shakespeare.

Esclairmonde, Lady. *See* SIR HUON.

Escott, Kenneth, m. Verona Babbitt. *Babbitt,* Sinclair Lewis, 1923.

Esdale, friend of Adam Hartley. *The Surgeon's Daughter,* W. Scott, 1827.

Eskdale, Lord. *Coningsby,* B. Disraeli, 1844.

Esmond, Colonel Harry, central character, believed illegitimate, but rightfully Viscount Castlewood, m. Isabel, widow of Lord Castlewood. *See also* WARRINGTON.
His daughter and grandsons.
Beatrix, his second cousin, m. (1) Bishop Tusher, (2) Baron Bernstein.
Lady Maria, sister of the Earl of Castlewood, aged beauty, m. Geohegan Hagan.
Henry Esmond, 1852, and *The Virginians,* 1857–8, W. M. Thackeray.

Esperance, Miss.
Archie, her nephew.
Montagu and **Edmund,** her great-nephews.
Miss Esperance and Mr Wycherley, L. Allen Harker, 1908.

Espinel, Thérèse, mistress of Henry Maitland.
Her mother.
The Private Life of Henry Maitland, Morley Roberts, 1912.

Essex, Earl of (Geffrey Fitz-Peter), Chief Justice. *King John* (play), W. Shakespeare.

Essex, William, central character and narrator.
Nellie, his wife, *née* Moscrop.
Oliver, their son.
My Son, My Son, H. Spring, 1938.

Essie, illegitimate daughter of Peter Dudgeon, who was hanged as a rebel. *The Devil's Disciple* (play), G. B Shaw, 1899.

Estabrook, stockbroker, school friend of Kent Falconer.
His family.
Over Bemerton's, E. V. Lucas, 1908.

Esteban, foundling, twin brother of Manuel. *The Bridge of San Luis Rey,* T. Wilder, 1927.

Estella, daughter of Magwitch, adopted by Miss Havisham, m. Bentley Drummle. *Great Expectations,* C. Dickens, 1861.

Estivat, d', Canon of Bayeux. *Saint Joan* (play), G. B. Shaw, 1924.

Estrella, Trock. *Winterset* (play), Maxwell Anderson, 1935.

Etches, Harold, 'wealthiest manufacturer of his years.' *The Card,* Arnold Bennett, 1911.

Ethelwyn ('Wyn'), m. Davy Morgan. *How Green Was My Valley,* R. Llewellyn, 1939.

Etheridge, Mrs. *Caesar's Wife* (play), W. S. Maugham, 1919.

Etherington, Francis, 5th Earl of. m. (1) Countess de Martigny (secretly).
Francis Tyrrel, their son.
(2) Ann Bulmer.
Valentine Bulmer Tyrrel, their son, subsequently 6th Earl.
St Ronan's Well, W. Scott, 1824.

Ethiopian, The (Sambo). 'How the Leopard got his Spots,' *Just So Stories,* R. Kipling, 1902.

Ettarre. 'Pelleas and Ettarre' (poem), *Idylls of the King,* Lord Tennyson, 1859.

Eubulus, Gorboduc's secretary. *Gorboduc* (play), T. Sackville & T. Norton, 1562.

Eugene, Monsieur Charles Adolphe. *Jorrocks's Jaunts and Jollities,* R. S. Surtees, 1838.

Eumolphus, a gladiator. *The Last Days of Pompeii,* Lord Lytton, 1834.

Euphrasia, daughter of Dion, disguised as a page, Bellario. *Philaster* (play), Beaumont & Fletcher, 1611.

Eurgain, Miss, a piano teacher. *The Black Venus,* Rhys Davies, 1944.

Eusabio, Navajo Indian, chief friend of Vaillant. *Death Comes for the Archbishop,* Willa Cather, 1927.

Eustace, Father (formerly known as William Allan), sub-prior and later prior of St Mary's, Kennaquhair. *The Monastery* and *The Abbot,* W. Scott, 1820.

Eustace, Lady (Elizabeth), *née* Greystock, m. (2) Emilius.
Sir Florian, her dead 1st husband.
John, M.P., his brother.
The Bishop of Bobsborough, his uncle.
The Eustace Diamonds, A. Trollope, 1873.

Eustasia. *See* LEONARD.

Eustick, Thomas, neighbour of the St Colombs. *Frenchman's Creek,* Daphne du Maurier, 1941.

Eva, Little. *See* ST CLARE.

Eva, Sister. 'The Record of Badalia Herodsfoot' (s.s.), *Many Inventions,* R. Kipling, 1893.

Evadne, sister of Melantius and Diphilus. *The Maid's Tragedy* (play), Beaumont & Fletcher, 1611.

Evan Dhu of Lochiel, Highland chief. *The Legend of Montrose,* W. Scott, 1819.

Evandale, Lord (William Maxwell), young and gallant fighter. *Old Mortality,* W. Scott, 1816.

Evangeline, central character. *Evangeline* (poem), H. W. Longfellow, 1847.

Evangelist, Christian's first guide. *Pilgrim's Progress,* J. Bunyan, 1678 and 1684.

Evans, rescuer of Jose da Silvestre. *King Solomon's Mines,* H. Rider Haggard, 1885.

Evans, humanitarian warder. *It Is Never Too Late to Mend,* C. Reade, 1856.

Evans, Chris, journalist. *H. M. Pulham, Esq.,* J. P. Marquand, 1941.

Evans, Dafydd, Welsh land-grabber. *Blind Raftery,* Donn Byrne, 1924.

Evans, Dick, Rhodes scholar. *The Secret Vanguard,* M. Innes, 1940.

Evans, Sir Hugh, Welsh parson. *The Merry Wives of Windsor* (play), W. Shakespeare.

Evans, Iestyn, m. Angharad Morgan.
Christmas, his father.
Blodwen, his sister, m. Owen Morgan.
How Green Was My Valley, R. Llewellyn, 1939.

Evans, Jemima, 'shoe - binder.' *Sketches by Boz,* C. Dickens, 1836.

Evans, Lucy. *See Naples and Die* (play), Elmer Rice, 1932.

Evans, Marged, sweetheart of Owen Morgan, later m. Gwilym Morgan.
Sion, her father.
How Green Was My Valley, R. Llewellyn, 1939.

Evans, Mary, sister of Ned Talbot.
Charlie, her husband.
Mrs Parkington, L. Bromfield, 1944.

Evans, Morgan. *The Corn is Green* (play), Emlyn Williams, 1938.

Evans, Owen, Welsh antiquary. *A Glastonbury Romance,* J. C. Powys, 1932.

Evans, Sam, m. Nina Leeds.
His mother.
Strange Interlude, E. O'Neill, 1928.

Evans, Sir Stephen. *Colonel Jack*, D. Defoe, 1722.

Evans the Death. *Under Milk Wood*, Dylan Thomas, 1954.

Evarra. 'Evarra and his Gods' (poem), *Barrack-room Ballads*, R. Kipling, 1892.

Eve, Mildred. *The Villa Desirée* (s.s.), May Sinclair.

Evelina, central character, known as Miss Anville, actually daughter of Sir John Belmont; m. Lord Orville. *Evelina*, Fanny Burney, 1778.

Evelyn. *Money* (play), Lord Lytton, 1840.

Evelyn, Mrs Alice. *C.*, M. Baring, 1924.

Evenson, John, boarder of Mrs Tibbs. *Sketches by Boz*, C. Dickens, 1836.

Everard, Markham, distinguished soldier. *Woodstock*, W. Scott, 1826.

Everdene, Bathsheba, central character, m. (1) Sergeant Troy, (2) Gabriel Oak.
Levi, her father.
Farmer James, her uncle.
Far from the Madding Crowd, T. Hardy, 1874.

Everett, subordinate informer under Titus Oates. *Peveril of the Peak*, W. Scott, 1822.

Everhard, Ernest, m. Avis Cunningham. *The Iron Heel*, Jack London, 1908.

Eves, Jessie. *Joseph and his Brethren*, H. W. Freeman, 1928.

Evesham, eminent politician. *The New Machiavelli*, 1911, *Marriage*, 1912, and elsewhere, H. G. Wells.

Eviot, page to Sir John Ramorny. *The Fair Maid of Perth*, W. Scott, 1828.

Evson, Walter, central character.
His parents.
Charles, his brother.
St Winifred's, F. W. Farrar, 1862.

Ewart, 'monumental artist,' schoolfellow of George Ponderevo.
Millie, his mistress.
Tono Bungay, H. G. Wells, 1909.

Ewart, Anthony ('Nanty'), captain of the *Jumping Jenny*. *Redgauntlet*, W. Scott, 1824.

Ewbank, tent contractor. *Radcliffe*, David Storey, 1963.

Exeter, Duke of, uncle to the king. *Henry the Fifth* (play), W. Shakespeare.

Exeter, Duke of. *Henry the Sixth* (play), W. Shakespeare.

Exmoor, Duke of. 'The Purple Wig,' *The Wisdom of Father Brown*, G. K. Chesterton, 1914.

Experience. *See* KNOWLEDGE.

Eybe, William, one of John Howard's protégés. *The Pied Piper*, N. Shute, 1942.

Eyer, Sir Simon, shoemaker and sheriff.
His wife.
'Sir Simon Eyer' (s.s.), *The Gentle Craft*, T. Deloney, *c.* 1600.

Eynsford-Hill, Freddy.
His mother and sister.
Pygmalion (play), G. B. Shaw, 1914.

Eyre, Dominic, a novelist. *The Private Wound*, Nicholas Blake, 1968.

Eyre, Jane, governess, central character and narrator, m. Edward Rochester. *Jane Eyre*, Charlotte Brontë, 1847.

Eyre, Kelly, balloonist, m. Jacqueline. *The Maids of Paradise*, R. W. Chambers, 1903.

Eyre, Simon, a London shoemaker.
Margery, his wife.
The Shoemaker's Holiday (play), Thomas Dekker, 1599.

F

Faa, Gabriel. *See* GABRIEL BAILLIE.

Faa, Hector, outlaw. *The Raiders,* S. R. Crockett, 1894.

Fabell, Peter ('The Merry Devil'). *The Merry Devil of Edmonton* (play), Anon.

Faber, Mrs, neighbour of Britling; food-hoarder. *Mr Britling Sees It Through,* H. G. Wells, 1916.

Faber, Miles, a college throw-out, heir to a fortune

Catherine, his sister.

Llew, his double.

M.F., Anthony Burgess, 1971.

Fabian, servant of Olivia. *Twelfth Night* (play), W. Shakespeare.

Fabian, Andrew.

His wife.

The Voice from the Minaret (play), R. S. Hichens, 1919.

Fadden, Fergus, an Irish novelist writing a film script in Hollywood.

Dr and Mrs Fadden, his dead parents, who reappear and talk to him.

Fergus, Brian Moore, 1971.

Faenza, Italian swashbuckler. *The Duke's Motto,* J. H. McCarthy, 1908.

Fag, servant of Captain Absolute. *The Rivals* (play), R. B. Sheridan, 1775.

Fagan, Augustus, schoolmaster.

Flossie, his daughter.

Diana ('Dingy'), his daughter.

Decline and Fall, E. Waugh, 1928.

Faggus, Tom, highwayman, cousin of John Ridd. *Lorna Doone,* R. D. Blackmore, 1869.

Fagin, thief, receiver and unmitigated villain. *Oliver Twist,* C. Dickens, 1838.

Fagoni, Baron, overseer of diamond mine. *Martin Rattler,* R. M. Ballantyne, 1858.

Fainall.

His wife, daughter of Lady Wishfort.

The Way of the World (play), W. Congreve, 1700.

Fairbairn, Otho, friend of Herbert Rayne. *The Actor Manager,* L. Merrick, 1898.

Fairbrother, Effie Deans's counsel. *The Heart of Midlothian,* W. Scott, 1818.

Fairchild, Mr.

His wife.

Their children: **Henry.**

Lucy.

Emily.

The History of the Fairchild Family, Mrs Sherwood, 1818.

Fairchild, Dabney, bride, m. Troy Flavin.

Ellen, her mother.

Battle, her father.

Shelley, her sister.

George, her uncle.

Robbie, George's wife.

Delta Wedding, Eudora Welty, 1946.

Fairfax, Colonel, m. Elsie Maynard. *The Yeomen of the Guard* (comic opera), Gilbert & Sullivan, 1888.

Fairfax, Mrs, housekeeper and relative of Edward Rochester. *Jane Eyre,* Charlotte Brontë, 1847.

Fairfax, Hon. Gwendolen, daughter of Lady Bracknell, m. Jack Worthing. *The Importance of Being Earnest* (play), O. Wilde, 1895.

Fairfax, Jane, orphan, foster-daughter of the Bateses and protégée of Colonel Campbell, m. Frank Churchill. *Emma,* Jane Austen, 1816.

Fairfield, Mrs, Linda Burnell's mother.

Beryl, her daughter.

Prelude (s.s.), Katherine Mansfield.

Fairfield, Leonard, celebrated author. *My Novel,* Lord Lytton, 1853.

Fairfield, Margaret.

Hilary, her husband.

Sydney, her daughter.

Hester, Hilary's sister.

A Bill of Divorcement (play), Clemence Dane, 1921.

Fairford, Alan, close friend of Darsie Latimer.

Saunders, his father.

Redgauntlet, W. Scott, 1824.

Fairford, Charles, second cousin of Flora Poste, whom he marries.

His mother, cousin **Helen.**

Cold Comfort Farm, Stella Gibbons, 1932.

Fairford, Henley, m. Clare Marvell. *The Custom of the Country,* Edith Wharton, 1913.

Fairford, James, mate, *Blackgauntlet. The Bird of Dawning,* J. Masefield, 1933.

Fairford, Sybil, English widow living in Italy.
Richard, her dead husband.
Geoffrey, their son, m. (1) Antonia, (2) Clare.
Elizabeth, daughter of Geoffrey and Clare, m. Arnold Backhouse.
Late in the Afternoon, Lettice Cooper, 1971.

Fairies, Queen of the, m. Private Willis. *Iolanthe* (comic opera), Gilbert & Sullivan, 1882.

Fairlegh, Frank, central character and narrator, m. Clara Saville.
Fanny, his sister, m. Harry Oaklands.
Frank Fairlegh, F. E. Smedley, 1850.

Fairlie, Frederick, of Limmeredge House, part narrator.
Laura, his niece.
Marian (Holcombe), his foster-daughter.
Philip, his brother.
Eleanor, his sister, m. Count Fosco.
Woman in White, W. Collins, 1860.

Fairlight, Bruce. *The Vortex* (play), N. Coward, 1924.

Fairscribe, solicitor.
James, his son.
The Surgeon's Daughter, W. Scott, 1827.

Fairservice, Andrew, gardener at Osbaldistone Hall. *Rob Roy,* W. Scott, 1818.

Fairway, Timothy, turf-cutter. *The Return of the Native,* T. Hardy, 1878.

Fairweather, Rev. Dr. *Elsie Venner,* O. W. Holmes, 1861.

Fairweather, John, m. Rose Birkett.
Geoffrey, his brother, m. Geraldine Birkett.
The *Barsetshire* series, Angela Thirkell, 1933 onwards.

Faithful, Christian's neighbour and fellow pilgrim, martyred at Vanity Fair. *Pilgrim's Progress,* J. Bunyan, 1678 and 1684.

Faithful, Mrs.
Imogen, her daughter.
To Have the Honour (play), A. A. Milne, 1924.

Faiz Ullah, Scott's servant. 'William the Conqueror' (s.s.), *The Day's Work,* R. Kipling, 1898.

Faizanne, Henry Augustus Ramsay ('The Worm'), subaltern. 'His Wedded Wife' (s.s.), *Plain Tales from the Hills,* R. Kipling, 1888.

Fakrash-el-Aamash, the jinnee of the Bottle. *The Brass Bottle,* F. Anstey, 1900.

Fakredeen, Shehaab, Emir of Canobia, m. Queen Astarte of the Ansarey. *See also* HILLEL BESSO. *Tancred,* B. Disraeli, 1847.

Falconer, Laird of Balmawhopple.
Cornet, his brother.
Waverley, W. Scott, 1814.

Falconer, Kent, central character and narrator, m. Naomi Wynne. *Over Bemerton's,* E. V. Lucas, 1908.

Falconer, Marguerite Evelyn ('Pegs'), central character, m. Philip Meldrum.
Montague, her father, artist, A.R.A.
A Knight on Wheels, Ian Hay, 1914.

Falconer, Sharon, an evangelist. *Elmer Gantry,* Sinclair Lewis, 1927.

Falder, William, central character. *Justice* (play), J. Galsworthy, 1910.

Falk, Scandinavian pilot. 'Falk' (s.s.), *Typhoon,* J. Conrad, 1903.

Falkiner, Sir Frederick, Recorder of Dublin. *Ulysses,* James Joyce, 1922.

Falkirk, Lady (Delia), widow, m. Sampson Rideout. *Sampson Rideout, Quaker,* Una Silberrad, 1911.

Falkland, central character. *Caleb Williams,* W. Godwin, 1794.

Falkland, Herbert, 'big squatter.'
Fanny, his daughter.
Robbery under Arms, R. Boldrewood, 1888.

Fall, Conjurer, weather prophet. *The Mayor of Casterbridge,* 1886, and *Tess of the D'Urbervilles,* 1891, T. Hardy.

Fallik, theatrical agent. *Manhattan Transfer,* J. dos Passos, 1925.

Falloux, atheist schoolmaster. 'The Miracle of St Jubanus' (s.s.), *Limits and Renewals,* R. Kipling, 1932.

Falstaff, Sir John. *The Merry Wives*

of Windsor and *Henry the Fourth* (plays), W. Shakespeare.

Falve, charcoal-burner. *The Forest Lovers,* M. Hewlett, 1898.

Falx, Labour leader, ex-engine driver. *Those Barren Leaves,* A. Huxley, 1925.

Famish, Robert, ensign, lieutenant and captain; a raffish and detestable snob. *The Book of Snobs,* 1846–7, and elsewhere, W. M. Thackeray.

Fan Ko, manager of opium den. *A Penniless Millionaire,* D. Christie Murray, 1907.

Fancourt, Lord. *The Scarlet Pimpernel,* Baroness Orczy, 1905.

Fancy, Sir Patient. *Sir Patient Fancy,* Mrs Aphra Behn, 1678.

Fane, 'raw-hand' war correspondent. 'Two or Three Witnesses' (s.s.), *Fiery Particles,* C. E. Montague, 1923.

Fane, Barbara. *Housemaster* (play), Ian Hay, 1936.

Fane, Handell, Eurasian actor. *Enter Sir John,* Clemence Dane & Helen Simpson, 1929.

Fane, John, publisher.
Mary, his 1st wife.
Their children:
Basil, m. Julia Norman.
Barbara, m. Hugh Forrest.
Muriel, m. Henry Morton.
Joyce, m. Hope Thurston.
Mabel, formerly Walmsley, his 2nd wife.
Going their own Ways, A. Waugh, 1938.

Fane, Michael.
Stella, his sister, m. Alan Merivale. Illegitimate children of Valerie Fane and Lord Saxby.
Sinister Street, 1913, and elsewhere, C. Mackenzie.

Fane-Herbert, Hugh, midshipman.
Margaret, his sister with whom John Lynwood is in love.
The Gunroom, Charles Morgan, 1919.

Fang, overbearing and blustering police magistrate. *Oliver Twist,* C. Dickens, 1838.

Fanning, Else. 'The Mother' (s.s.), *Countrymen All,* Katherine Tynan, 1915.

Fanny. *Fanny's First Play* (play), G. B. Shaw, 1905.

Fanny, maid to Lady Glyde. *The Woman in White,* W. Collins, 1860.

Fanny, sweetheart of Joseph Andrews. *Joseph Andrews,* H. Fielding, 1742.

Fanny, the Greys' maid. *Alice-sit-by-the-Fire* (play), J. M. Barrie, 1905.

Fansharpe, Miss, Teresa Bramley's first employer. *Before the Bombardment,* O. Sitwell, 1926.

Fanshawe, Miss Ada, Tommy Beresford's great-aunt. *By The Pricking of My Thumbs,* Agatha Christie, 1968.

Fanshawe, Charles. The *Barsetshire* series, Angela Thirkell, 1933 onwards.

Fanshawe, Ginevra, m. Count de Hamal. *Villette,* Charlotte Brontë, 1853.

Fanshawe, Mrs Vera, cousin of Toby Erskine. *Act of God,* F. Tennyson Jesse, 1936.

Faraday, Alice, Lord Marshmoreton's secretary, m. Reggie Byng. *A Damsel in Distress,* P. G. Wodehouse, 1919.

Faraday, Mrs Caroline (Great-aunt Caroline), *née* Seeley, widow of Dr John Faraday.
Julia, her daughter.
Catherine, her daughter (Aunt Kitty).
William, her son (Uncle William).
Joyce Blount, her grand-niece.
Andrew Seeley, her nephew.
George Makepeace Faraday, disreputable cousin.
Police at the Funeral, Margery Allingham, 1931.

Farag, 'the Fatherless,' native kennel-boy to the Gihon Hunt. 'Little Foxes' (s.s.), *Actions and Reactions,* R. Kipling, 1909.

Faramond, Sophie.
Selwyn, her husband, archaeologist.
Caroline Traherne, Selwyn's daughter.
The Gates of Summer (play), John Whiting, 1956.

Farcinelle, Magou, farrier, farmer and member of provincial legislature, m. Sophie Lavilette. *The Pomp of the Lavilettes,* Gilbert Parker, 1897.

Fardarougha, miser. *Fardarougha the Miser,* W. Carleton, 1839.

Fardet, Monsieur. *The Tragedy of the Korosko*, A. Conan Doyle, 1898.

Farebrother, solicitor. *The Heir*, V. Sackville-West, 1922.

Farebrother, Rev. Camden, Vicar of St Botolph's, Middlemarch.
His wife.
Winifred, his sister.
Middlemarch, Geo. Eliot, 1871–2.

Farfrae, Donald, m. (1) Lucetta le Sueur, (2) Elizabeth Jane Henchard. *The Mayor of Casterbridge*, T. Hardy, 1886.

Fargus and family. *If Winter Comes*, A. S. M. Hutchinson, 1920.

Faringdon, Bimbo, schoolboy.
His sisters:
Rosemary.
Chris.
Button.
Housemaster (play), Ian Hay, 1936.

Farintosh, Marquess of, wealthy brainless dandy, one-time eng. to Ethel Newcome. *The Newcomes*, 1853–5, and elsewhere, W. M. Thackeray.

Farish, Gertrude, cousin of Lawrence Selden. *The House of Mirth*, Edith Wharton, 1905.

Farkhoonda, widowed princess. *On the Face of the Waters*, Flora A. Steel, 1896.

Farley, Mrs.
Nathan, her husband.
Rollo, their son, seduces Bertha.
Felix, Rollo's and Bertha's son.
Lummox, Fannie Hurst, 1924.

Farmer, Mrs.
Her husband.
Their children: **Millicent, Hugh, Dick** and **Ethel.**
The Protégé (s.s.). W. B. Maxwell.

Farquar, Lois, central character. *The Last September*, Elizabeth Bowen, 1929.

Farquhar, secondary squire, Shepperton.
His wife.
Arabella and **Julia,** their daughters.
'The Rev. Amos Barton,' *Scenes of Clerical Life*, George Eliot, 1857.

Farquhar, Peyton, Confederate soldier. 'An Occurrence at Owl Creek Bridge' (s.s.), *In the Midst of Life*, A. Bierce, 1898.

Farquharson, Colonel, uncle of Sheila Grant. *The Secret Vanguard*, M. Innes, 1940.

Farquharson, Alison, m. Sarita Spencer. *Joseph Vance*, W. de Morgan, 1906.

Farr, Daniel, K.C.
Esmee, his wife.
The Laughing Lady (play), A. Sutro, 1922.

Farr, Joseph, head of technical staff, Woldingstanton. *The Undying Fire*, H. G. Wells, 1919.

Farrant, Anthony, drifter in Stockholm.
Kate, his twin sister.
England Made Me, Graham Greene, 1935.

Farrant, Geoffrey. *Eden End* (play), J. B. Priestley, 1935.

Farrant, George.
His wife.
Waste (play), H. Granville-Barker, 1907.

Farrar, Brat, impostor, m. Eleanor Ashby. *Brat Farrar*, Josephine Tey, 1949.

Farrel, Jimmy, farmer. *The Playboy of the Western World* (play), J. M. Synge, 1907.

Farrell, Patsy. *John Bull's Other Island* (play), G. B. Shaw, 1904.

Farrell, Peter, chief accountant, Considines. *Without My Cloak*, Kate O'Brien, 1931.

Farrell, Lady Selina. *Marcella*, Mrs Humphry Ward, 1894.

Farrell, Tom, farmer, and owner of illicit still. 'Another Temple Gone' (s.s.), *Fiery Particles*, C. E. Montague, 1923.

Farrelly, sergeant in charge of police barracks, R.I.C. *The Search Party*, G. A. Birmingham, 1913.

Farrelly, Paul, actor. 'The Soldier's Song' (s.s.), *The Sun on the Water*, L. A. G. Strong, 1940.

Farren, Hugh, figure and landscape painter. *The Five Red Herrings*, Dorothy L. Sayers, 1931.

Farren, Molly, m. Godfrey Cass. *Silas Marner*, George Eliot, 1861.

Farretti, Lucia, opera singer and mistress of Raymond Sylvester. *The Dark Tide*, Vera Brittain, 1923.

Farrinder, Mrs. *The Bostonians*, H. James, 1886.

Fashion, Tom, brother of Lord Foppington. *A Trip to Scarborough* (play), R. B. Sheridan, 1777.

Fashions, Sir Novelty, central character. *Love's Last Shift* (play), C. Cibber, 1696.

Fastolfe, Sir John. *Henry the Sixth* (play), W. Shakespeare.

Fat Boy, The. *See* JOE.

Faulconbridge, Robert.
Philip, bastard son of Richard I.
Lady Faulconbridge, their mother.
King John (play), W. Shakespeare.

Faulkland, friend of Captain Absolute. *The Rivals* (play), R. B. Sheridan, 1775.

Faunt, Nick, m. (1) Jenny Kepple, (2) Anna Fitzgerald.
Sir George, his father.
Shabby Tiger, H. Spring, 1934.

Fauntleroy, Lord (Cedric Errol), central character, grandson of Lord Dorincourt. *See also* ERROL. *Little Lord Fauntleroy*, Frances H. Burnett, 1886.

Fauntley, Robert, schoolmaster, colleague of Inigo Jollifant. *The Good Companions*, J. B. Priestley, 1929.

Faustus. *The History of Dr Faustus* (play), C. Marlowe, 1604.

Faux, David, confectioner and thief (alias Edward Freely).
Jonathan, his father.
His mother.
Jonathan, Jnr, his brother.
Jacob, his idiot brother, who exposes him.
Brother Jacob, George Eliot, 1864.

Favell, Jack, cousin and lover of Rebecca de Winter. *Rebecca*, Daphne du Maurier, 1938.

Fawcett, Mrs.
Mildred, her daughter.
The Doves' Nest, Katherine Mansfield, 1923.

Fawcett, Mrs, lover of Charles Eastwood. *The Virgin and The Gipsy*, D. H. Lawrence, 1930.

Fawcett, Rev. Oswald, mentor of Wilfred Chew. *Tobit Transplanted*, Stella Benson, 1931.

Fawkes, Fancy, central character, m. Mark Woodrofe.
Oliver, her father.
Trumpeter, Sound!, D. L. Murray, 1933.

Fawley, Catherine, about to become a nun.
Dick, her drunken, malicious brother.
The Bell, Iris Murdoch, 1958.

Fawley, Jude, orphan, m. Arabella Donn.
Little Father Time, their son. *See also* SUE BRIDEHEAD.
Drusilla, his great-aunt.
Jude the Obscure, T. Hardy, 1896.

Fawn, Lord (Frederic), rich peer, one-time fiancé of Lady Eustace.
His sisters:
Clara, m. Hittaway.
Amelia.
Georgiana.
Lydia.
Cecilia.
Nina.
Lady Fawn, their mother, 'a miracle of Virtue, Benevolence and Persistency.'
Phineas Finn, 1869, and others, A. Trollope.

Fawnia, central character. *Pandosto* (play), Robert Greene, 1588.

Fearnleigh, Mrs, Eden Herring's grandmother. *Little Red Horses*, G. B. Stern, 1932.

Featherstone, Lady, escorted incognito to Bologna by Charles Wogan. *Clementina*, A. E. W. Mason, 1901.

Featherstone, Peter, of Stone Court, rich and miserly widower.
Joshua Rigg, his illegitimate son.
Solomon, his rich and greedy brother.
Jonah, his poor brother.
Jane, his rich sister, widow of Waule.
Middlemarch, Geo. Eliot, 1871–2.

Fedalma, beautiful gypsy daughter of Zarca, betrothed to Duke Silva. *The Spanish Gypsy* (poem), George Eliot, 1868.

Feeble-Mind. *Pilgrim's Progress*, J. Bunyan, 1678, 1684.

Feeder, assistant to Dr Blimber. *Dombey and Son*, C. Dickens, 1848.

Feeley, Father Innocent. *Adam of Dublin*, C. O'Riordan, 1920.

Feeney, Mike. *On the Spot* (play), E. Wallace, 1930.

Feenix, cousin of Edith Granger. *Dombey and Son*, C. Dickens, 1848.

Feivel, Reb, Mrs Seipel's grandfather. *Magnolia Street*, L. Golding, 1932.

Feldt, Moses, m. Mrs Stella Condon.

Judith and **Pansy,** his daughters by his 1st wife.
Linda Condon, J. Hergesheimer, 1918.

Felena, shepherd's wife. *Precious Bane,* Mary Webb, 1924.

Felice, maid to Roma Volonna. *The Eternal City,* Hall Caine, 1901.

Felician, Father. *Evangeline* (poem), H. W. Longfellow, 1848.

Feliciani, Count, banker.
His wife.
Eloise, his daughter, m. (1) Franzius, (2) Count P. Mahon.
Drums of War, H. de Vere Stacpoole, 1910.

Felix, Don, central character. *The Wonder* (play), Mrs Susanna Centlivre, 1714.

Felix, Monsieur (pseudonym), friend of Leithen. *The Power House,* J. Buchan, 1916.

Felixthorpe, Lord ('Scipio'), college friend of William Arkroyd. *It Never Can Happen Again,* W. de Morgan, 1909.

Fell, Dr Charles M.
Barbara, his sister.
A Glastonbury Romance, J. C. Powys, 1932.

Fell, Dr Gideon, amateur detective. *The Black Spectacles,* 1948, and many others, J. Dickson Carr.

Fell, Sir Matthew, deputy sheriff.
Sir Matthew, his son.
Sir Richard, his grandson.
'The Ash-tree' (s.s.), *Ghost Stories of an Antiquary,* M. R. James, 1910.

Fellamar, Lord. *Tom Jones,* H. Fielding, 1749.

Fellbright, Jack, solicitor, m. Aldrith O'Murry. *A Georgian Love Story,* Ernest Raymond, 1971.

Fellman, Dr. *The Queen's Husband* (play), R. E. Sherwood, 1928.

Fellmer, Albert, m. Rosa Halborough.
His mother.
'A Tragedy of Two Ambitions,' *Life's Little Ironies,* T. Hardy, 1894.

Fellowes, Rev. Mr, J.P. 'The Rev. Amos Barton,' *Scenes of Clerical Life,* George Eliot, 1857.

Fellows, Beatrice, niece of Alexander Burtenshaw. *A House and Its Head,* Ivy Compton-Burnett, 1935.

Feltham, undergraduate. *The Babe, B.A.,* E. F. Benson, 1897.

Felton, Harold, schoolmaster, colleague of Inigo Jollifant. *The Good Companions,* J. B. Priestley, 1929.

Fenchel, Thea, mistress of Augie. *The Adventures of Augie March,* Saul Bellow, 1953.

Fenerator, the Usuring Bee. *Parliament of Bees* (play), J. Day, 1641.

Fenmore, Jack, of the *Courier. Master Jim Probity,* F. Swinnerton, 1952.

Fenn, M.P. for West Orchards.
Juliet, his daughter.
Daniel Deronda, George Eliot, 1876.

Fenn, Burchell, 'luscious rogue.' *St Ives,* R. L. Stevenson, 1897.

Fennel, George, friend of Finch Whiteoak. *Finch's Fortune,* Mazo de la Roche, 1931.

Fenner, Martin, consumptive friend of Owen Kettle. *Captain Kettle* series, J. Cutcliffe Hyne, 1898–1932.

Fenny, companion of Dora Randolph. *Dear Octopus* (play), Dodie Smith, 1939.

Fenton. *The Merry Wives of Windsor* (play), W. Shakespeare.

Fenton, Garry Anson's lawyer. *The Calendar,* E. Wallace.

Fenwick, lighthouse keeper. 'A Disturber of Traffic' (s.s.), *Many Inventions,* R. Kipling, 1893.

Fenwick, Arthur. *Our Betters* (play), W. S. Maugham, 1923.

Fenwick, Charlie, farmer.
Isa and **Nellie,** his sisters.
No Son of Mine, G. B. Stern, 1948.

Fenwick, Iris, central character. *The Green Hat,* M. Arlen, 1924.

Fenwick, John. *Beau Austin* (play), W. E. Henley & R. L. Stevenson, 1892.

Fenwicke (alias Captain Barstow), Jesuit. *Peveril of the Peak,* W. Scott, 1822.

Fenwick-Symes, Adam, young writer. *Vile Bodies,* Evelyn Waugh, 1930.

Fenwolf, Morgan, keeper of Windsor Forest. *Windsor Castle,* W. H. Ainsworth, 1843.

Ferdinand, King of Navarre. *Love's Labour's Lost* (play), W. Shakespeare.

Ferdinand, son of Alonso. *The Tempest* (play), W. Shakespeare.

Ferdinand, Don. *The Duenna* (play), R. B. Sheridan, 1775.

Ferguson, Helen, nurse. *A Farewell to Arms,* E. Hemingway, 1929.

Ferguson, Robert. 'The Miasma' (s.s.), *The Man Upstairs,* P. G. Wodehouse, 1914.

Ferideh, mistress of Saïd.
Suleyman, their son.
Yuhanna, her mother.
Saïd the Fisherman, M. Pickthall, 1903.

Fermor, Lord (George), uncle of Lord Henry Wotton. *The Picture of Dorian Gray,* O. Wilde, 1891.

Fernandez, Margaret.
Jimmie and **Harry,** her brothers.
High Wind in Jamaica, R. Hughes, 1929.

Fernando. *For Whom the Bell Tolls,* E. Hemingway, 1940.

Ferndale, Captain, gambler and bad hat. *Not so Bad after All,* Nat Gould.

Ferne, Lady Ariadne, daughter of the Earl of Browden, central character, m. John Strickland. *No Other Tiger,* A. E. W. Mason, 1927.

Ferneze, Governor of Malta.
Lodowick, his son.
The Jew of Malta (play), C. Marlowe, 1633.

Fernyhurst, Edward, lover of Jennifer Herries. *Judith Paris,* Hugh Walpole, 1931.

Ferraby, Gordon, sub-lieutenant, *Compass Rose.*
Mavis, his wife.
Ursula, their baby.
The Cruel Sea, N. Monsarrat, 1951.

Ferraby, Sir William. *Fanny by Gaslight,* M. Sadleir, 1940.

Ferrand, Bishop, missionary. *Death Comes for the Archbishop,* Willa Cather, 1927.

Ferranti, Gabriel, poet. *A City of Bells,* Elizabeth Goudge, 1936.

Ferrar, Bobbie, of the Foreign Office. *Maid in Waiting,* J. Galsworthy, 1931.

Ferrar, Marjorie, rival of Fleur Forsyte.
Lord Charles, her father. *See also* SHROPSHIRE.
The Silver Spoon, 1926, and elsewhere, J. Galsworthy.

Ferrar, Nicholas, *John Inglesant,* J. H. Shorthouse, 1881.

Ferrars, Edward, brother of Fanny Dashwood, m. Elinor Dashwood.
Robert, his brother, m. Lucy Steele.
His mother.
Sense and Sensibility, Jane Austen, 1811.

Ferret.
Bridget, his wife, *née* Maple.
Sir Lancelot Greaves, T. Smollett, 1762.

Ferrex, son of Gorboduc. *Gorboduc* (play), T. Sackville & T. Norton, 1562.

Ferris, Leonard. *Mid-Channel* (play), A. W. Pinero, 1909.

Ferrol, Hon. Thomas. *The Pomp of the Lavilettes,* Gilbert Parker, 1897.

Ferrybridge, Lord.
His wife.
Gretna, his son, friend of Pendennis.
Pendennis, W. M. Thackeray, 1848–50.

Ferse, Diana, *née* Montjoy.
Ronald, her 1st husband.
Sheila, their daughter.
Ronald, their son.
m. as 2nd husband Adrian Charwell.
Maid in Waiting, J. Galsworthy, 1931.

Feshnavat, Vizier, father of Noorna. *The Shaving of Shagpat,* G. Meredith, 1856.

Fessaday, Sir Alfred, leader of mountaineering expedition. *Other Gods,* Pearl Buck, 1940.

Feste, a clown. *Twelfth Night* (play), W. Shakespeare.

Feste, Adèle, m. 'Boy.' *Berry and Co.,* Dornford Yates, 1920.

Fettes, drunken old Scots medical student. 'The Body Snatcher' (s.s.), *The Wrong Box,* R. L. Stevenson & L. Osbourne, 1889.

Fettley, Mrs (Liz). 'The Wish House' (s.s.), *Debits and Credits,* R. Kipling, 1926.

Feuillée, Enguerrand de la, Seigneur de Brisetout. 'A Lodging for the Night' (s.s.), *New Arabian Nights,* R. L. Stevenson, 1882.

Fever, Jesus, old Negro pygmy.
Missouri (Zoo), his grand-daughter.
Other Voices, Other Rooms, Truman Capote, 1948.

Feverel, Richard, central character, m. Lucy Blaize. *See also* FOREY, HARLEY and WENTWORTH.
Sir Austin, Bt, his father.
His uncles: **Algernon, Hippias,** and **Richard.**
The Ordeal of Richard Feverel, G. Meredith, 1859.

Fez, King of. *Tamburlaine* (play), C. Marlowe, 1587.

Ffolliot, bookseller. 'The Dragon's Head,' *Lord Peter Views the Body,* Dorothy L. Sayers, 1928.

Ffolrigg, Felicia, daughter of Frau Kohnstamm.
Piers, her brother.
Simpson, E. Sackville-West, 1931.

Ffoulkes, Sir Andrew. *The Scarlet Pimpernel,* Baroness Orczy, 1905.

ffoulkes-Corbett, Mrs Dorothea (Aunt Dot), Anglican missionary in Turkey. *The Towers of Trebizond,* Rose Macaulay, 1956.

Fiametta. *The Gondoliers* (comic opera), Gilbert & Sullivan, 1889.

Fibbitson, Mrs, almshouse inmate. *David Copperfield,* C. Dickens, 1850.

Fiche, confidential servant of Lord Steyne. *Vanity Fair,* W. M. Thackeray, 1847–8.

Fiddler, Tom, twin of Tom Tiddler. *Adam's Opera* (play), Clemence Dane, 1928.

Fidelia, Manly's page, heiress in disguise. *The Plain Dealer,* W. Wycherley, 1677.

Fidenza, Gian Battista, nicknamed 'Nostromo,' central character, *Nostromo,* J. Conrad, 1904.

Field, Mrs Paula, *née* Veresy, central character, m. Sir Victor Pandolfo. *The Great Pandolfo,* W. J. Locke, 1925.

Fielder, George, m. Lady Eveleen de Courcy. *The Heir of Redclyffe,* Charlotte M. Yonge, 1853.

Fielder, Louis. *The Thing in the Hall* (s.s.), E. F. Benson.

Fielding, Alan. *The Thinking Reed,* Rebecca West, 1936.

Fielding, Cyril, principal of Government College, m. Stella Moore. *A Passage to India,* E. M. Forster, 1924.

Fielding, George, farmer turned goldminer, m. Susan Merton.
Wilhelm, his father.
It Is Never Too Late to Mend, C. Reade, 1856.

Fielding, May, m. Edward Plummer.
Her mother.
The Cricket on the Hearth, Christmas Books, C. Dickens, 1845.

Fielding, Sir Robert.
Dora, his wife.
Anne, their daughter, m. Robin Dale.
The *Barsetshire* series, Angela Thirkell, 1933 onwards.

Fielding Bey. *Donovan Pasha,* Gilbert Parker, 1902.

Figg, Roger, theatrical manager, friend of Mary Adam. *Holy Deadlock,* A. P. Herbert, 1934.

Filby, friend of the Time Traveller. *The Time Machine,* H. G. Wells, 1895.

Filch. *The Beggar's Opera* (comic opera), J. Gay, 1728.

Filcher, Robert, Verdant Green's 'scout.' *The Adventures of Mr Verdant Green,* C. Bede, 1853.

Filippo, foster-brother of Count Alberighi. *The Falcon* (play), Lord Tennyson, 1879.

Fillans, Mrs Daisy. *See* DAISY BARLEY.

Fillet, Dr. *Sir Lancelot Greaves,* T. Smollett, 1766.

Fillet, Mr, housemaster. *Tell England,* E. Raymond, 1922.

Fillgrave, Dr, professional rival of Dr Thorne. *Doctor Thorne,* A. Trollope, 1858.

Fillimore, Mrs Letitia, widow.
Julian, her son.
'The Contessa' (s.s.), *Sir Pompey and Madame Juno,* M. Armstrong, 1927.

Filmer, flying-machine inventor. *Twelve Stories and a Dream,* H. G. Wells, 1901.

Finch. *The Sin of David* (play), S. Phillips, 1914.

Finch, m. Georgina Gardner. *Heartsease,* Charlotte M. Yonge, 1854.

Finch, Captain. *An Englishman's Home* (play), Guy du Maurier, 1909.

Finch, Robert, itinerant parson. *Rogue Herries,* Hugh Walpole, 1930.

Finch, Robin.
Mary, his wife, *née* Sinnier.
The Porch, 1937, and *The Stronghold,* 1939, R. Church.

Finch, Valentine. *The Immortal Sergeant,* J. Brophy, 1942.

Finching, Mrs Flora, former sweetheart of Arthur Clennam, daughter of Christopher Casby. *See also* AUNT, MR F'S. *Little Dorrit,* C. Dickens, 1857.

Finchley, Sandra ('Miss X' of Clyde Griffiths's trial).
Stuart, her brother.
Her parents.
An American Tragedy, T. Dreiser, 1925.

Finck, von, fashionable German doctor. *The Newcomes,* W. M. Thackeray, 1853–5.

Findlater, Mrs Edna, woman Fergus was in love with when he was a boy, *Fergus,* Brian Moore, 1971.

Findlayson, civil engineer. 'The Bridge Builders' (s.s.), *The Day's Work,* R. Kipling, 1898.

Findon, Betty, m. Colin Derwent. *Ten Minute Alibi* (play), A. Armstrong, 1933.

Fink, Maggie.
Mart, her insufferably meek husband.
'A Harlem Tragedy' (s.s.), *The Trimmed Lamp,* O. Henry, 1907.

Finlay, Dr, central character. *Beyond This Place,* A. J. Cronin, 1953, later adapted into a popular television series, *Dr Finlay's Casebook.*

Finley, Heavenly.
'Boss' Finley, her father, politician.
Thomas J. Finley, Jr, her brother.
Sweet Bird of Youth, (play), Tennessee Williams, 1959.

Finn, Huckleberry, central character and narrator, friend of Tom Sawyer.
His father, village drunkard.
Huckleberry Finn, 1884 (and *Tom Sawyer*), Mark Twain.

Finn, Phineas, central character, m. Mary Flood-Jones.
Malachi, his father, doctor.
His mother.
Matilda and **Barbara,** two of his sisters.
Phineas Finn, A. Trollope, 1869.

Finn, Silas, fish-dealer and Parliamentary candidate.
Paul, his son, known as Kegworthy, later as P. Savelli, central character, m. Princess Sophie Zobraska.
The Fortunate Youth, W. J. Locke, 1911.

Finnerty, Dr. *Tom Burke of Ours,* C. Lever, 1844.

Finnis, The Misses Pansy and Penelope. *Before the Bombardment,* O. Sitwell, 1926.

Finsberry, Odo. *Tobermory* (s.s.), 'Saki' (H. H. Munro), 1911.

Finsbury, Joseph.
Masterman, his brother, popular writer. Two last survivors of the tontine.
Jacob, their brother.
Michael, Masterman's son.
Morris and **John,** sons of Jacob, adopted by Joseph. *See also* HAZELTINE.
The Wrong Box, R. L. Stevenson & L. Osbourne, 1889.

Finucane, Dr. *Harry Lorrequer,* C. Lever, 1839.

Finucane, The Misses, heads of girls' school. *Pendennis,* W. M. Thackeray, 1848–50.

Finucane, Jack, Irish subeditor, *Pall Mall Gazette,* later editor, devoted friend of Captain Shandon, whose widow he m. *Pendennis,* 1848–50, and *Adventures of Philip,* 1861–2, W. M. Thackeray.

Fionnguisa, Michael. 'Marching to Zion' (s.s.), *Adam and Eve and Pinch Me,* A. E. Coppard, 1921.

Fips, Mr. *Martin Chuzzlewit,* C. Dickens, 1844.

Firanz, Prince of Shirvan. *Vathek,* W. Beckford, 1786.

Firebird, Leonora Penderton's stallion. *Reflections in a Golden Eye,* Carson McCullers, 1940.

Firebrace, Jack, young Virginian. *The Virginians,* W. M. Thackeray, 1857–9.

Firebrace, Sir Vavasour, Bt.
His wife, 'great Tory stateswoman.'
Sybil, B. Disraeli, 1845.

Firebras, Cordwell. *The Miser's Daughter,* W. H. Ainsworth, 1842.

Firedamp, meteorologist, friend of MacCrotchet. *Crotchet Castle,* T. L. Peacock, 1831.

Firkin, Mrs, Miss Crawley's maid, jealous of Becky Sharp, m. Bowls, butler. *Vanity Fair,* W. M. Thackeray, 1847–8.

Firman. *The Dancing Druids,* Gladys Mitchell, 1948.

Firmin, Geoffrey, British consul in Mexico.
Yvonne Constable, his divorced wife.
Hugh, his half-brother.
Under the Volcano, Malcolm Lowry, 1947.

Firmin, Philip, central character, m. Charlotte Baynes.
Laura, their daughter.
Dr George Brand, his father.
His mother, *née* Ringwood. *See also* BRANDON.
Dr Brand, his grandfather.
Adventures of Philip, W. M. Thackeray, 1861–2.

Firminger, Colonel.
Elizabeth, his daughter, in love with Robyn Skyrme.
The Story of Ragged Robyn, O. Onions, 1945.

Firmly, Lord. *A Citizen of the World,* O. Goldsmith, 1762.

Firniss, Miss, mistress of boarding-school of Maggie Tulliver and Lucy Deane. *The Mill on the Floss,* George Eliot, 1860.

Fish, Billy. 'The Man who would be King' (s.s.), *Wee Willie Winkie,* R. Kipling, 1888.

Fish, Paisley. 'Telemachus, Friend' (s.s.), *Heart of the West,* O. Henry, 1907.

Fisher, Miss, Lady Mary Lazenby's maid. *The Admirable Crichton* (play), J. M. Barrie, 1902.

Fisher, Mrs, widow. *The Enchanted April,* Countess von Arnim, 1922.

Fisher, Bradbury.
Evangeline, his wife, *née* Maplebury.
'High Stakes' (s.s.), *The Heart of a Goof,* P. G. Wodehouse, 1926.

Fisher, Jeremy, a frog. *The Tale of Jeremy Fisher,* Beatrix Potter, 1906.

Fisher, Mark, author who considers becoming a Mohammedan. *Pending Heaven,* William Gerhardie, 1930.

Fisher, Miss Naomi, mistress of Max Ebhart and mother of his children.
Her mother.
The House in Paris, Elizabeth Bowen, 1935.

Fisher, 'Smooth' Sam (alias White), detective posing as butler. *The Little Nugget,* P. G. Wodehouse, 1913.

Fiske, Mrs Ann, niece of Mrs Harrington. *Evan Harrington,* G. Meredith, 1861.

Fiske, John. 'An Anniversary' (s.s.), *A Beginning,* W. de la Mare, 1955.

Fisker, Hamilton K., m. Marie Melmotte. *The Way We Live Now,* A. Trollope, 1875.

Fitch, Andrea, cockney artist, m. Mrs Carrickfergus. *See* MONTFICHET. *A Shabby Genteel Story,* W. M. Thackeray, 1840.

Fittleworth, Earl of.
His wife.
Last Post, F. M. Ford, 1928.

Fitton, Lady Amanda, m. Albert Campion. Margery Allingham's detective stories.

Fitzadam, Mrs Mary (*née* Hoggins), widow. *Cranford,* Mrs Gaskell, 1853.

Fitzague, Lady Blanche, snob with 'a medical turn.'
Lady Rose, her sister, snob with 'a literary turn.'
The Book of Snobs, W. M. Thackeray, 1846–7.

Fitzaquitane, Duke of. *Sybil,* B. Disraeli, 1845.

Fitzbattleaxe, Duchess of.
The Duke, her husband.
The Book of Snobs, 1846–7, and elsewhere, W. M. Thackeray.

Fitz-Boodle, central character and narrator of *Fitz-Boodle Papers,* and narrator of *Men's Wives*; younger son of country baronet.
Tom, his elder brother, heir to the title.
Maria, Tom's wife.
W. M. Thackeray, 1842–3.

Fitzbrown, Dr, close friend of Superintendent Mallett. *Requiem for Robert,* 1942, and others, Mary Fitt.

Fitzchrome, Captain. *Crotchet Castle,* T. L. Peacock, 1831.

Fitzclare, Beatrice, *née* Lord.
Vincent, her husband.
Mary, Vincent's sister.
C., M. Baring, 1924.

Fitzgeorge, Mr. *All Passion Spent,* V. Sackville-West, 1931.

Fitzgerald, Anna, m. Nick Faunt.
Brian, her illegitimate son.
Shabby Tiger, H. Spring, 1934.

Fitzgerald, Brian, m. Madge Frettleby. *The Mystery of a Hansom Cab,* F. Hume, 1886.

Fitzgibbon, Hon. Laurence.
Aspasia, his sister.
Phineas Finn, 1869, and elsewhere, A. Trollope.

Fitzharold, Lord Dennis, brother of Lady Casterley. *The Patrician,* J. Galsworthy, 1911.

Fitzmarshall, Charles. Alias of JINGLE.

Fitzmichael, Lady Eugenia (Mother Eugénie). *The Land of Spices,* Kate O'Brien, 1941.

Fitznorton, Hon. Reginald. *Pip,* Ian Hay, 1907.

Fitzpatrick, Brian.
Harriet, his wife, Squire Western's niece.
Tom Jones, H. Fielding, 1749.

Fitzpatrick, Mrs Dorothy, widow interested in spiritualism. 'The Astral Body of a U.S. Mail Truck' (s.s.), *A Story That Ends With A Scream,* James Leo Herlihy, 1968.

Fitzpiers, Dr Edred, m. Grace Melbury. *The Woodlanders,* T. Hardy, 1887.

Fitzroy, William.
Charlotte, his wife.
Lavinia, his niece, m. Asa Timberlake.
In this our Life, Ellen Glasgow, 1942.

Fitzsimons, Mrs Fitzgerald.
Her husband.
Barry Lyndon, W. M. Thackeray, 1844.

Fitzurse, Waldmar, devotee of King John.
Alicia, his daughter.
Ivanhoe, W. Scott, 1820.

Fitzwilliam, Colonel, uncle of Fitzwilliam Darcy. *Pride and Prejudice,* Jane Austen, 1813.

Fizgig, Captain Francis, penniless dandy. *The Great Hoggarty Diamond,* W. M. Thackeray, 1841.

Fizkin, Horatio, of Fizkin Hall. *Pickwick Papers,* C. Dickens, 1837.

Flack, Mrs, malevolent gossip.
Blue, her illegitimate son.
Riders in the Chariot, Patrick White, 1961.

Flaherty, Michael James, publican.
Margaret (Pegeen Mike), his daughter.
The Playboy of the Western World, J. M. Synge, 1907.

Flahy, Corporal. 'The Solid Muldoon' (s.s.), *Soldiers Three,* R. Kipling, 1888.

Flambeau, ex-criminal, close friend of Father Brown. *The Innocence of Father Brown,* etc., G. K. Chesterton, 1911 onwards.

Flamborough, Solomon.
His two daughters; the younger m. Moses Primrose. Next-door neighbours of the Primroses.
The Vicar of Wakefield, O. Goldsmith, 1766.

Flamingo, dancer and entertainer. *The Weak and the Strong,* G. Kersh, 1945.

Flamm the Second ('Flammchen'), secretary.
Flamm the First, her sister.
Grand Hotel, Vicki Baum, 1931.

Flammock, Wilkin, Flemish weaver.
Rose, his daughter.
The Betrothed, W. Scott, 1825.

Flamwell, Mr. *Sketches by Boz,* C. Dickens, 1836.

Flanagan, m. Kitty Riley. *Handy Andy,* S. Lover, 1842.

Flanagan, Mrs, laundress and caretaker. *Pendennis,* 1848–50, and elsewhere, W. M. Thackeray.

Flanagan, Betty, servant to Mrs Clapp. *Vanity Fair,* W. M. Thackeray, 1847–8.

Flanders, Elizabeth (Betty), widow.
Her sons: **Archer.**
Jacob, central character.
Jacob's Room, Virginia Woolf, 1922.

Flanders, Moll (Betty), central character and narrator. *Moll Flanders,* D. Defoe, 1722.

Flanders, Sally, old nurse. *The Uncommercial Traveller,* C. Dickens, 1860.

Flannery, clerk to Considine. *Without My Cloak,* Kate O'Brien, 1931.

Flare, Colonel. 'Lieutenant-Colonel Flare' (poem), *Bab Ballads,* W. S. Gilbert, 1869.

Flashman, school bully. *Tom Brown's Schooldays,* T. Hughes, 1857.

Flask, third mate, the *Pequod*. *Moby Dick*, H. Melville, 1851.

Flather, Rev. Marcus, friend of Charles Honeyman. *The Newcomes*, W. M. Thackeray, 1853–5.

Flavell, Methodist preacher. *Middlemarch*, George Eliot, 1871–2.

Flavia. *When First I Dared* (poem), W. Mason.

Flavia, Princess. *The Prisoner of Zenda*, etc., A. Hope, 1894–8.

Flavin, Troy, plantation manager, m. Dabney Fairchild. *Delta Wedding*, Eudora Welty, 1946.

Flavio, little yellow cat belonging to the Pope. *Hadrian the Seventh*, Baron Corvo (F. W. Rolfe), 1904.

Flavius, steward to Timon. *Timon of Athens* (play), W. Shakespeare.

Fleance, Banquo's son. *Macbeth* (play), W. Shakespeare.

Fledgeby, Old, ex-money-lender.
  Young Fledgeby ('Fascination'), his son, also money-lender as Pubsey & Co.
Our Mutual Friend, C. Dickens, 1865.

Fleecebumpkin, John, bailiff. *The Two Drovers*, W. Scott, 1827.

Fleete, victim of the 'beast.' 'The Mark of the Beast' (s.s.), *Life's Handicap*, R. Kipling, 1891.

Fleming, Agnes, mother of Oliver.
  Rose, her sister. *See* MAYLIE.
Oliver Twist, C. Dickens, 1838.

Fleming, Craig. *In this our Life*, Ellen Glasgow, 1942.

Fleming, Henry, young recruit in American Civil War. *The Red Badge of Courage*, Stephen Crane, 1895.

Fleming, Sir Malcolm, lover of Margaret Hautlieu. *Castle Dangerous*, W. Scott, 1832.

Fleming, Randolph, friend of Avory Hume. *The Judas Window*, Carter Dickson, 1938.

Fleming, William John, farmer.
  His wife, *née* Hackbut.
  Their daughters:
    Dahlia.
    Rhoda, m. Robert Armstrong.
Rhoda Fleming, G. Meredith, 1865.

Fleta, a fairy. *Iolanthe* (comic opera), Gilbert & Sullivan, 1882.

Fletcher, gardener to Chris Marrapit.
  Frederick, his son.
Once Aboard the Lugger, A. S. M. Hutchinson, 1908.

Fletcher, Archie, schoolboy at Fernhurst. *The Loom of Youth*, A. Waugh, 1917.

Fletcher, Dick, seaman, of *Fortune's Favourite*. *The Pirate*, W. Scott, 1822.

Fletcher, Fletcher, Quaker friend of Simeon Halliday. *Uncle Tom's Cabin*, Harriet B. Stowe, 1851.

Fletcher, Mrs Helen. *In Cotton Wool*, W. B. Maxwell, 1912.

Fletcher, James. 'In the Library' (s.s.), *The Lady of the Barge*, W. W. Jacobs, 1902.

Fletcher, Jed, innkeeper.
  Joan, his daughter.
  Whippy, his son.
Dance of the Years, Margery Allingham, 1943.

Fletcher, Phineas, narrator.
  Abel, his father, a tanner.
John Halifax, Gentleman, Mrs Craik, 1856.

Fletcher, Sam.
  Eppie, *née* Lownie, his wife.
A Window in Thrums, J. M. Barrie, 1889.

Fleury, Mademoiselle, French governess. *The Education of Uncle Paul*, A. Blackwood, 1909.

Fleury, Monsieur, chef. *The Admirable Crichton* (play), J. M. Barrie, 1902.

Fleury, Carl, Nazi agent. *Mr Fortune Finds a Pig*, H. C. Bailey, 1943.

Fliegler, Luther, car salesman.
  Irma, his wife.
Appointment in Samarra, John O'Hara, 1935.

Flimnap, Lord High Treasurer, Lilliput. *Gulliver's Travels*, J. Swift, 1726.

Flimsy, Sir George.
  His wife.
  Emily, his 7th daughter.
Jeames's Diary, W. M. Thackeray, 1846.

Flint, prefect. 'A Little Prep,' *Stalky & Co.*, R. Kipling, 1899.

Flint, Corporal. *St Patrick's Day* (play), R. B. Sheridan, 1775.

Flint, Augustus, railroad president.
  Victoria, his daughter, m. Austen Vane.
Mr Crewe's Career, W. Churchill, 1908.

Flint, Trueman, lamplighter.
Gertrude, his adopted daughter (*see* AMORY), m. William Sullivan.
The Lamplighter, Maria S. Cummins, 1854.

Flint, William ('Wull'), servant and 'fool' to Squire Gauntry. *Judith Paris,* Hugh Walpole, 1931.

Flintwinch, Jeremiah.
Affery, his wife.
Ephraim, his twin brother.
Little Dorrit, C. Dickens, 1857.

Flite, Miss, 'ancient' ward in Chancery. *Bleak House,* C. Dickens, 1848.

Flitestone, James, dead artist. 'The Skeleton' (s.s.), *Blind Love,* V. S. Pritchett, 1969.

Flitter, Wyndham, man-about-town. *The Pottleton Legacy,* Albert Smith, 1849.

Flitton, Pamela, a troublemaker, m. Kenneth Widmerpool. *Books Do Furnish A Room,* 1971, and others in *The Music of Time* series, Anthony Powell.

Flo, Aunt, plump landlady of the Potwell Inn. *The History of Mr Polly,* H. G. Wells, 1910.

Flokes, Lady. *The Pottleton Legacy,* Albert Smith, 1854.

Flood, Mrs, Hazel Motes's landlady. *Wise Blood,* Flannery O'Connor, 1952.

Flood, Rev. Andrew, m. Silla.
Isaac, their son.
Deborah, their daughter. *See* KLEINHANS.
God's Stepchildren, Sarah G. Millin, 1924.

Flood, Dora, brothel-keeper. *Cannery Row,* J. Steinbeck, 1945.

Flood, Tomsy. *Some Experiences of an Irish R.M.,* Œ. Somerville & Martin Ross, 1899.

Flood-Jones, Mary, m. Phineas Finn.
Her mother.
Phineas Finn, A. Trollope, 1869.

Floodgay, Mrs.
Her husband, a Canon.
Cécile, their daughter.
Before the Bombardment, O. Sitwell, 1926.

Flopsy Bunnies, The (six of them). *The Tale of the Flopsy Bunnies,* 1909, and elsewhere, Beatrix Potter.

Flora, sister of Miles. *The Turn of the Screw,* H. James, 1898.

Florac, Comte de, distinguished French officer.
Léonore, his wife, daughter of the Chevalier de Blois.
Paul, their son, later Prince de Moncontour.
His wife.
Abbé Florac, their son.
The Newcomes. W. M. Thackeray, 1853–5.

Florence, Duke of. *All's Well That Ends Well* (play), W. Shakespeare.

Florence, Miss, blind woman. 'They' (s.s.), *Traffics and Discoveries,* R. Kipling, 1904.

Florence, Mrs, headmistress. *What Katy Did at School,* Susan Coolidge, 1873.

Florey, Tom, central character, m. Isabel Summers.
Albert, his father.
His mother.
Tom Tiddler's Ground, E. Shanks, 1934.

Florian, friend of Hilarion and brother of Lady Psyche, m. Melissa. *The Princess* (poem), Lord Tennyson, 1847. *Princess Ida* (comic opera), Gilbert & Sullivan, 1884.

Florian, Mrs Sarah, *née* Lash. *The Heritage of Hatcher Ide,* Booth Tarkington, 1941.

Floribel, heroine, murdered by her husband, Hesperus. *The Bride's Tragedy,* T. L. Beddoes, 1822.

Florimel, a vampire. *Jurgen,* J. B. Cabell, 1921.

Florio, citizen of Parma.
Giovanni, his son.
Annabella, his daughter.
Putana, Annabella's duenna.
'Tis Pity She's A Whore (play), John Ford, *c.* 1624.

Florise, assistant in beauty salon. *For Us in the Dark,* Naomi Royde-Smith, 1937.

Florister, Jacy Picken, ultimate manager Flower Theatre, central character. *See also* JULIAN DOFFIELD.
Ernest, his father.
Isabel, *née* Picken, his mother.
Sir Paxton, his uncle, owner Flower Theatre.
Julius, his uncle.
Gina, his wife.

Their daughters:
Carmen.
Bell.
Olive.
His aunts:
Lily.
May.
Myrtle.
The Flower Girls, Clemence Dane, 1954.

Florizel, son of Polixenes. *A Winter's Tale* (play), W. Shakespeare.

Florizel, Prince of Bohemia (alias Theophilus Godall). 'The Suicide Club,' *New Arabian Nights*, R. L. Stevenson, 1882.

Flosky, friend of Chris Glowry, m. Celinda Toobad. *Nightmare Abbey*, T. L. Peacock, 1818.

Floss, Dr, physician attending Miss Pinkerton's Academy. *Vanity Fair*, W. M. Thackeray, 1847–8.

Flouncey, Mrs Guy. *Tancred*, B. Disraeli, 1847.

Flower, Captain. *The Hand of Ethelberta*, T. Hardy, 1876.

Flower, Sergeant. *The Clandestine Marriage* (play), G. Colman the Elder, 1766.

Flower, Mrs Freda, rich widow interested in spiritualism. *The Bachelors*, Muriel Spark, 1961.

Flowerdale, Sir John.
Clarissa, his daughter.
Lionel and Clarissa (play), I. Bickerstaffe, 1768.

Flowers, maid to the Rosses. *The Oriel Window*, Mrs Molesworth, 1896.

Floyd, Rev. Andrew, principal of Maresfield House. *Jacob's Room*, Virginia Woolf, 1922.

Floyer, Sir Robert, Bt. *Cecilia*, Fanny Burney, 1782.

Fluellen, an officer. *Henry the Fifth* (play), W. Shakespeare.

Flute, bellows-mender. *A Midsummer Night's Dream*, W. Shakespeare.

Flutter, Sir Fopling. *The Man of Mode* (play), Sir G. Etherege, 1676.

Flynn, Atlas, young Irish labourer who fancies Mrs Tuke. *Miss Gomez and The Brethren*, William Trevor, 1971.

Flynn, Father James.
Eliza, his sister.
The Dubliners, James Joyce, 1914.

Flynn, Michael, Sinn Feiner. *My, Son, My Son*, H. Spring, 1938.

Flynn, Oweny, lawyer. 'A Dead Cert' (s.s.), *The Talking Trees*, Sean O'Faolain, 1971.

Flynn, Peter, labourer, uncle of Nora Clitheroe. *The Plough and the Stars* (play), S. O'Casey, 1926.

Flynn, Tom, of Virginia. *In the Tunnel* (poem), Bret Harte.

Flyte. Family name of MARQUIS OF MARCHMAIN.

Fogg, of Dodson & Fogg. *Pickwick Papers*, C. Dickens, 1837.

Fogle, Sir Horace, member of Barnes Newcome's club. *The Newcomes*, 1853–5, and *Vanity Fair*, 1847–8, W. M. Thackeray.

Foible, woman to Lady Wishfort. *The Way of the World*, W. Congreve, 1700.

Foker, Hermann (originally Voelker), rich and kindly brewer.
Henry, his great-grandson, gay and eccentric friend of Pendennis.
The Virginians, W. M. Thackeray, 1857–9.

Foliar, pantomimist in Crummles's company. *Nicholas Nickleby*, C. Dickens, 1839.

Folliott, Rev. Dr, friend of MacCrotchet. *Crotchet Castle*, T. L. Peacock, 1831.

Fondlewife, banker. *The Old Bachelor* (play), W. Congreve, 1693.

Fontaine, Dr.
His parents.
Alex, Tony and **Sally**, his children.
Gone with the Wind, Margaret Mitchell, 1936.

Fontaine, Mrs Lena. *The Glory of Clementina Wing*, W. J. Locke, 1911.

Fontover, Miss, employer of Sue Bridehead. *Jude the Obscure*, T. Hardy, 1896.

Fontwell, Dick, m. Julia Rainier. *Random Harvest*, J. Hilton, 1941.

Fool. *King Lear* (play), W. Shakespeare.

Foppington, Lord. *The Relapse* (play), J. Vanbrugh, 1696.

Foppington, Lord. *A Trip to Scarborough* (play), R. B. Sheridan, 1777.

Forbes, Mr and Mrs, hotel keepers. *The Wide, Wide World*, E. Wetherell, 1850.

Forbes, Georgie, enemy of Chad Buford. *The Little Shepherd of Kingdom Come,* J. Fox, Jnr, 1903.

Forbes, Jean, daughter of Mrs Tommy Mandeville by 1st husband. *Poet's Pub,* E. Linklater, 1929.

Forbes, Juliet, singer, in love with Emmanuel Gollantz. *Young Emmanuel,* Naomi Jacob, 1932.

Ford, Mr, a Windsor gentleman.
His wife.
The Merry Wives of Windsor (play), W. Shakespeare.

Ford, Bob, first and only great love of Jim Willard. *The City and The Pillar,* Gore Vidal, 1948.

Ford, Elmer, American millionaire.
Nesta, his wife.
Ogden, their son.
The Little Nugget, P. G. Wodehouse, 1913.

Ford, Dr James. The *Barsetshire* series, Angela Thirkell, 1933 onwards.

Fordyce, Mrs, aunt of Herbert Beveridge. *In Greek Waters,* G. A. Henty, 1892.

Fordyce, Stephen, witness at trial of Harriet Vane. *Strong Poison,* Dorothy L. Sayers, 1930.

Fordyce, Canon Theobald, grandfather of Jocelyn Irvin.
Jane, his wife.
Hugh Anthony, their grandson.
Henrietta, their adopted grandchild.
A City of Bells, Elizabeth Goudge, 1936.

Foresight, Professor of Astrology. *Love for Love,* W. Congreve, 1695.

Forest, Joe, property man. *Grand Opera,* Vicki Baum, 1942.

Forester, Dr, member of spy gang. *The Ministry of Fear,* Graham Greene, 1943.

Forester, Mr. *Caleb Williams,* W. Godwin, 1794.

Forester, Sir Philip.
Jemima, *née* Falconer, his wife.
My Aunt Margaret's Mirror, W. Scott, 1827.

Forey, Helen Doria, sister of Sir Austin Feverel.
Clare, her daughter, m. John Todhunter.
The Ordeal of Richard Feverel, G. Meredith, 1859.

Forlingham, Lord, a steward of the Jockey Club. *The Calendar,* E. Wallace.

Formalist and Hypocrisy. *Pilgrim's Progress,* J. Bunyan, 1678 and 1684.

Forrest, Elsie. *The Bachelors,* Muriel Spark, 1961.

Forrest, Hugh, m. Barbara Fane. *Going their own Ways,* A. Waugh, 1938.

Forrest, Juliana, daughter of Lord Fulgrave, m. Raoul des Sablières. *Mr Rowl,* D. K. Broster, 1924.

Forrester, Major.
His wife.
Badger's Green (play), R. C. Sherriff, 1930.

Forrester, Mrs, friend of Mary Morstan. *The Sign of Four,* A. Conan Doyle, 1890.

Forrester, Pa and Ma.
Their sons:
Lem.
Mill-Wheel.
Buck.
Gabby.
Fodder-Wing.
The Yearling, Marjorie Rawlings, 1938.

Forrester, Squadron-Leader, central character, in love with Anna. *The Purple Plain,* H. E. Bates, 1947.

Forrester, Letitia, god-daughter of Dr Honeywood. *Elsie Venner,* O. W. Holmes, 1861.

Forrester, Mrs Marian, 'the lost lady'.
Captain Forrester, her husband, railway constructor.
A Lost Lady, Willa Cather, 1923.

Forrestier, Ray, m. Karen Michaelis.
Angela, his sister.
The House in Paris, Elizabeth Bowen, 1935.

Forster, Colonel. *Settlers in Canada,* Marryat, 1844.

Forster, Colonel.
Harriet, his wife.
Pride and Prejudice, Jane Austen, 1813.

Forster, Cacalie. *Of Human Bondage,* W. S. Maugham, 1915.

Forster, Gerald. *The Lie* (play), H. A. Jones, 1923.

Forster, Rupert. *Marching Song,* J. Whiting, 1954.

Forster, Warren, father of Adam Paris by Judith.

Will, his father, son of Dorothy Cards.
Judith Paris, Hugh Walpole, 1931.

Forsyte Family, The. Children and descendants of **Jolyon** ('Superior Dosset') **Forsyte,** son of **Jolyon,** farmer, *b.* 1741.
Ann.
Jolyon ('Old'), tea merchant, Stanhope Gate, m. Edith Moor.
Jolyon ('Young'), their son, underwriter and artist, St John's Wood and Robin Hill.
m. (1) Frances Crisson.
June, their daughter.
(2) Hélène Hilmer.
Jolly, their son.
Holly, their daughter, m. Val Dartie.
(3) Irene, *née* Heron, div. wife of Soames Forsyte.
Jolyon ('Jon'), their son, m. Anne Wilmot.
James, solicitor, founder of Forsyte, Bustard & Forsyte, Park Lane, m. Emily Golding.
Their children:
Soames, solicitor and connoisseur, Montpelier Sq. and Mapledurham.
m. (1) Irene Heron, see above.
(2) Annette Lamotte.
Fleur, their daughter, m. Michael Mont.
Winifred, m. Montague Dartie.
Rachel.
Cicely.
Swithin, estate and land agent ('Four-in-Hand Forsyte'), Hyde Park Mansions.
Roger, collector of house property, Princes Gardens, m. Mary Monk.
Their children:
Roger ('Young'), m. Muriel Wake.
Roger ('Very Young'), their son.
George.
Francie, composer, poetess.
Eustace.
Thomas.
Julia, m. Septimus Small, reverted after his death to Bayswater Road.
Hester, Bayswater Road.
Nicholas, mines, railways and house property, Ladbroke Grove, m. Elizabeth Blaine ('Fanny').
Their children:
Nicholas ('Young'), m. Dorothy Boxton.
Their children: **Nicholas** ('Very Young'), **Blanche, Christopher, Violet, Gladys** and **Patrick.**
Ernest.
Archibald.
Marian.
Florence.
Euphemia.
Timothy, publisher, Bayswater Road.
Susan, m. Hayman.
The Forsyte Saga, 1906-22, and other Forsyte tales, John Galsworthy.

Forsyth, Colonel. 'In the Presence' (s.s.), *A Diversity of Creatures*, R. Kipling, 1917.

Forsyth, Gideon, m. Julia Hazeltine. *The Wrong Box*, R. L. Stevenson & Lloyd Osbourne, 1889.

Fort, Colonel Cassius, frontier politician. *World Enough and Time*, Robert Penn Warren, 1950.

Fort William, Lord (John), m. Louisa Radlett.
Their children.
The Pursuit of Love, Nancy Mitford, 1945.

Fortescue, Charles Augustus. *Cautionary Tales*, H. Belloc.

Forth, Peter, policeman. 'Peter the Wag' (poem), *Bab Ballads*, W. S. Gilbert, 1869.

Fortinbras, Prince of Norway. *Hamlet* (play), W. Shakespeare.

Fortinbras, Lord. *Felix Holt*, George Eliot, 1866.

Fortis, Stephen, m. Lady Sarah Pryde.
James, M.P., his brother.
'The Mystery of Hannah Power' (s.s.), *Old Patch's Medley*, Marjorie Bowen, 1930.

Fortunata, Madame, palmist. *See* REBECCA CARCOW.

Fortunato. *The Cask of Amontillado* (s.s.), E. A. Poe.

Fortuné, manservant. *The Notorious Mrs Ebbsmith* (play), A. W. Pinero, 1895.

Fortune, Miss Ellen, lovable old lady. *The Young in Heart,* I. A. R. Wylie, 1939.

Fortune, Reginald, central character.
  Joan, his wife.
Mr Fortune series of detective stories, H. C. Bailey.

Fortune, Rev. Sebastian, partner in East & Sabre. *If Winter Comes,* A. S. M. Hutchinson, 1920.

Fortune, Rev. Timothy, missionary. *Mr Fortune's Maggot,* Sylvia Townsend Warner, 1927.

Foscari, Benedetta, Venetian courtesan, mistress of Ralf Isambard: later known as the Holy Woman of Aber. *The Heaven Tree* trilogy, Edith Pargeter, 1961–3.

Fosco, Count, first fat villain in English literature.
  Eleanor, his wife, sister of Frederick Fairlie.
The Woman in White, W. Collins, 1860.

Fosdick, Mr and Mrs, parents of Medwin Blair. *The Prodigal Heart,* Susan Ertz, 1950.

Fosdyke, Sir Hugh, uncle of Matthew Ligne. *The Loving Eye,* William Sansom, 1956.

Foss, Corporal, attendant on Lieutenant Worthington. *The Poor Gentleman* (play), G. Colman the Younger, 1802.

Fossett, Rev. Augustus, Vicar of St Vulgate.
  Adeline, his sister, schoolmistress of Lizarann Coupland.
It Never Can Happen Again, W. de Morgan, 1909.

Foster. Family name of LORD POMFRET.

Foster, Diocesan Missioner, Polchester. *The Cathedral,* Hugh Walpole, 1922.

Foster, Captain, of the *Dreadnought.* The *Hornblower* series, C. S. Forester, 1937 onwards.

Foster, Amy, m. Yanko Goorall.
  Isaac, her father.
'Amy Foster' (s.s.), *Typhoon,* J. Conrad, 1903.

Foster, Anthony, jailer of Amy Robsart.
  Janet, his daughter.
Kenilworth, W. Scott, 1821.

Foster, Evelina, aunt of Dorothy Musgrave. *Beau Austin* (play), W. E. Henley & R. L. Stevenson, 1892.

Foster, Jacqueline. *Comrade, O Comrade,* Ethel Mannin, 1946.

Foster, Sir John, Warden of the Marches. *The Monastery,* W. Scott, 1820.

Foster, John, m. Carmen de las Casas.
  Alice, his mother.
  His father.
'John O' Dreams' (s.s.), *Countrymen All,* Katherine Tynan, 1915.

Foster, John and **Jeremiah,** brother shopkeepers, Monkshaven. *Sylvia's Lovers,* Mrs Gaskell, 1863.

Foster, Dr Joseph, formerly Joachim Pfleger, expert chemist.
  Josephine, his daughter, fiancée of Raymond Cray.
Mr Fortune Finds a Pig, H. C. Bailey, 1943.

Fothergill, J.P., agent to the Duke of Omnium. *Framley Parsonage,* 1861, and elsewhere, A. Trollope.

Fothergill, Major. *The Fourth Wall* (play), A. A. Milne, 1928.

Fothergill, Miss. *The Shrimp and the Anemone,* L. P. Hartley, 1944.

Fotheringay, stage name of Emily Costigan, beautiful but stupid actress, daughter of Captain Costigan, m. Sir Charles Mirabel. *Pendennis,* W. M. Thackeray, 1848–50.

Fotheringham, Percival, m. Theodora Martindale.
  Sir Anthony, his uncle.
  Lady Fotheringham, his aunt.
    Pelham, their son, m. Jane Gardner.
Heartsease, Charlotte M. Yonge, 1854.

Foucault, Madame, Sophia Scales's fraudulent French landlady. *The Old Wives' Tale,* Arnold Bennett, 1908.

Fouchard, Madame.
  Her husband.
Dragon's Teeth, Upton Sinclair, 1942.

Foulata, native girl, victim of Gagool. *King Solomon's Mines,* H. Rider Haggard, 1885.

Fould, Thomas Henry, central character, m. Jennifer Constantine.
  Reuben, his father.
  His mother.

Jennie, his sister.
Reuben, his brother. Twins.
Tom Fool, F. Tennyson Jesse, 1926.

Fouldes, Paradine. *Lady Frederick* (play), W. S. Maugham, 1907.

Foulkes, Mr, friend of Mr Bastable.
Denny, his son.
Daisy, his daughter.
The Treasure Seekers, 1899, and *The Would-be-Goods*, 1901, E. Nesbit.

Fowler, former tenant of Squire Cass. *Silas Marner*, George Eliot, 1861.

Fowler, Miss, Mary Postgate's employer.
Wyndham, her nephew.
'Mary Postgate' (s.s.), *A Diversity of Creatures*, R. Kipling, 1917.

Fowler, Mr, one of Harriet Byron's suitors. *Sir Charles Grandison*, S. Richardson, 1754.

Fowler, Mr. *Separate Tables* (play), T. Rattigan, 1955.

Fowler, Thomas, journalist, narrator. *The Quiet American*, Graham Greene, 1955.

Fox, Bishop of Durham. *Perkin Warbeck* (play), John Ford, 1634.

Fox, 'Brer.' *Uncle Remus*, J. C. Harris, 1880–95.

Fox, Sergeant, later Inspector, subordinate and friend of Roderick Alleyn. *Enter a Murderer*, Ngaio Marsh, 1935, and many others.

Fox, Kate, a prostitute. *The Informer*, L. O'Flaherty, 1925.

Fox, Madeline, one-time fiancée of Martin Arrowsmith. *Martin Arrowsmith*, Sinclair Lewis, 1925.

Fox, Ninian, theatre manager. *Wakefield's Course*, Mazo de la Roche, 1942.

Foxe, Brian. *Eyeless in Gaza*, Aldous Huxley, 1936.

Foxe-Donnell, Leo, Irish patriot.
Judith, his mother.
Julie, his wife.
Johno, his son.
A Nest of Simple Folk, Sean O'Faolain, 1933.

Foxfield, Sir Reginald, Bt.
His mother.
Let the People Sing, J. B. Priestley, 1939.

Foxley, squire and magistrate. *Redgauntlet*, W. Scott, 1824.

'Foxy,' drill sergeant. *Stalky & Co.*, R. Kipling, 1899.

Foxy-Whiskered Gentleman, The. *The Tale of Jemima Puddleduck*, Beatrix Potter, 1908.

Foyle, Denis, father of Mary Brodie's child. *Hatter's Castle*, A. J. Cronin, 1931.

Fradubio. *The Faërie Queene* (poem), E. Spenser, 1590.

Fraide, Herbert, M.P., leader of the Opposition.
Lady Sarah, his wife.
John Chilcote, M.P., Katherine C. Thurston, 1904.

Frame, Miss, John Adam's secretary. *Holy Deadlock*, A. P. Herbert, 1934.

Frampton, Emily, cousin of Alix Sandomir.
Laurence, her dead 2nd husband. *See also* TUCKER.
Non-Combatants and Others, Rose Macaulay, 1916.

Frampton, James, mate, *Blackgauntlet*. *The Bird of Dawning*, J. Masefield, 1933.

Frampton, Richard. *See* RALPH ELLIOT.

France, King of. *King Lear* (play), W. Shakespeare.

France, King of. *All's Well That Ends Well* (play), W. Shakespeare.

France, Princess of. *Love's Labour's Lost* (play), W. Shakespeare.

Francesca, parlour-maid at San Salvatore. *The Enchanted April*, Countess von Arnim, 1922.

Francesca da Rimini, bride of Giovanni Malatesta, loves Paolo. *Paolo and Francesca*, S. Phillips, 1900.

Francesco, a gondolier. *The Gondoliers* (comic opera), Gilbert & Sullivan, 1889.

Francesco, Don, Roman Catholic priest. *South Wind*, N. Douglas, 1917.

Francheschini, Count Guido, mercenary scoundrel, m. Pompilia Comparini. *The Ring and the Book* (poem), R. Browning, 1868–9.

Franching, of Peckham, friend of the Pooters. *The Diary of a Nobody*, G. & W. Grossmith, 1892.

Francis, manager of J. Fane's publishing firm. *Going their own Ways*, A. Waugh, 1938.

Francis, Maltese houseboy. *The Little Girls*, Elizabeth Bowen, 1964.

Francis, Father. *The Duenna* (play), R. B. Sheridan, 1775.

Francis, Paul and **Ethel.** *Call it a Day* (play), Dodie Smith, 1935.

Francisca, a nun. *Measure for Measure* (play), W. Shakespeare.

Francisco, a soldier. *Hamlet* (play), W. Shakespeare.

François, French half-breed fur-hunter. *Ungava,* R. M. Ballantyne, 1857.

François, page to Richelieu. *Richelieu* (play), Lord Lytton, 1839.

Françoise, servant at *pension* of Madame Smolensk. *The Adventures of Philip,* W. M. Thackeray, 1861–2.

Frankenstein, Victor, central character and part narrator, creator of the monster, m. Elizabeth Lavenza.
 Alphonse, his father.
 Caroline, his mother.
 William and **Ernest,** his brothers.
Frankenstein, Mary W. Shelley, 1818.

Frankland, Leonora, seduced by Millborne.
 Frances, their daughter, eng. to Rev. Percival Cope.
'For Conscience' Sake,' *Life's Little Ironies,* T. Hardy, 1894.

Franklin, schoolboy. *St Winifred's,* F. W. Farrar, 1862.

Franklin, Lady, half-sister of Sir J. Vesey. *Money* (play), Lord Lytton, 1840.

Franklin, Mrs. *See* HELOISE DWORNITZCHEK.

Franklin, Desmond, killer of three sharks with a boy-scout's knife, unsuccessful rival of William Mulliner. *Meet Mr Mulliner,* P. G. Wodehouse, 1927.

Franklin, Henry, m. Lady May Thurston. *The Osbornes,* E. F. Benson, 1910.

Franks, Edward, Captain of the *Young Rachel. The Virginians,* W. M. Thackeray, 1857–9.

Frant, Marjorie, eng. to Peter Standish. *Berkeley Square* (play), J. L. Balderston, 1926.

Franzius, 1st husband of Eloise Feliciani. *Drums of War,* H. de Vere Stacpoole, 1910.

Franzy, Paul, close friend of Richard Adscombe. *Judgment in Suspense,* G. Bullett, 1946.

Frapp, Nicodemus, baker, Chatham, cousin of Ponderevo (referred to as 'Uncle'). *Tono Bungay,* H. G. Wells, 1909.

Fraser, tutor of Daniel Deronda. *Daniel Deronda,* George Eliot, 1876.

Fraser, Lieutenant Bobbie. *The Way of an Eagle,* Ethel M. Dell, 1912.

Fraser, James.
 Janet, his 1st wife.
  Murdo, their son.
   Alice, his wife.
  Ninian, their son.
 Elsie, Fraser's 2nd wife.
The First Mrs Fraser (play), St John Ervine, 1929.

Fraser, Laura. *The Truth* (play), Clyde Fitch, 1907.

Fraser, Rosamund.
 Fergus, her husband, living apart.
 Their children:
  Felix.
  James.
  Chloe, m. Mr Stephens.
  Sandra.
  Paul.
Chatterton Square, E. H. Young, 1947.

Fraser, Simon, Master of Lovat, chief of the clan. *Catriona,* R. L. Stevenson, 1893.

Frasier, Negro attorney. *Porgy,* Du Bose Heyward, 1925.

Fray, Henry, farm-hand at Weatherbury. *Far from the Madding Crowd,* T. Hardy, 1874.

Frayle, Miranda, film star. *Relative Values* (play), Noël Coward, 1951.

Frayne, Sir Chichester. *The Gay Lord Quex* (play), A. W. Pinero, 1899.

Frazier, Miss, daughter of 'the owner.' 'The Ship that Found Herself' (s.s.). *The Day's Work,* R. Kipling, 1898.

Freckles. *See* TERENCE O'MORE.

freddy, the rat. *archy and mehitabel,* D. Marquis, 1927.

Frederic, pirate apprentice, m. Mabel Stanley. *The Pirates of Penzance* (comic opera), W. S. Gilbert, 1880.

Frederick, Count, eng. to Bellafront Worldly. *A Woman is a Weathercock* (play), N. Field, 1612.

Frederick, Duke, usurper. *As You Like It* (play), W. Shakespeare.

Free, Micky, O'Malley's Irish servant. *Charles O'Malley*, C. Lever, 1841.

Freebody, David, divorce solicitor for Mary Adam. *Holy Deadlock*, A. P. Herbert, 1934.

Freeborn, Billy ('True Blue'), central character, orphan, m. Mary Ogle. *True Blue*, W. H. G. Kingston.

Freely, Edward. *See* David Faux.

Freeman ('Pinto'), holiday tutor and dramatist, m. Delia. *A House of Children*, Joyce Cary, 1941.

Freeman, Captain of the *Porta Coeli*. The *Hornblower* series, C. S Forester, 1937 onwards.

Freeman, Mr.
His wife.
John, their son.
Gwen, their daughter.
The Fanatics (play), M. Malleson, 1924.

Freeman, Sir Charles, Mrs Sullen's brother, *The Beaux' Stratagem* (play), G. Farquhar, 1707.

Freemantle, Rev. Howat, central character.
Mary, his wife, *née* Coverdale.
Mary, their daughter.
And Now Goodbye, J. Hilton, 1931.

Freen, platoon commander. 'On Patrol' (s.s.), *Sir Pompey and Madame Juno*, M. Armstrong, 1927.

Freeport, Sir Andrew, London merchant. Essays in *The Spectator*, J. Addison, 1711–14.

Freer, Captain, of the *Berinthia*. *Tom Fool*, F. Tennyson Jesse, 1926.

Freke, Sir Julian, eminent neurologist. *Whose Body?*, Dorothy L. Sayers, 1923.

Fremisson, Dr, friend of the Stublands and family doctor. *Joan and Peter*, H. G. Wells, 1918.

French, Chief Detective Inspector. *The Loss of the 'Jane Vosper,'* 1936, and many others, F. Wills Crofts.

French, Mrs, housekeeper to Sir Hugo Mallinger. *Daniel Deronda*, George Eliot, 1876.

French, Mrs.
Camilla and **Arabella,** her daughters.
He Knew He Was Right, A. Trollope, 1869.

French, Bob, racehorse trainer. 'I'm a Fool' (s.s.), *Horses and Men*, Sherwood Anderson, 1924.

French, Kit, privateersman. *Admiral Guinea* (play), W. E. Henley & R. L. Stevenson, 1892.

French, Mary, political worker. *U.S.A.* trilogy, John dos Passos, 1930–6.

Frensham, Countess of. *Mr Britling Sees It Through*, H. G. Wells, 1916.

Frensham, Mrs. *See* Sophia Baines.

Frensham, Lucia (alias Mary Barton), central character, governess to Lina Conford, m. as 2nd wife Howard Conford.
Henry, her father.
Hester, *née* Winchford, her mother.
The Second Mrs Conford, Beatrice K. Seymour, 1951.

Frenton, Mrs, Mildred Sinclair's mother. *Lighten our Darkness*, R. Keable, 1927.

Frere, Lieutenant Maurice, of the *Malabar*, m. Sylvia Vickers.
Anthony, his father, m. Sir R. Devine's sister.
For the Term of his Natural Life, M. Clarke, 1874.

Frere, Richard, close friend of Lewis, m. Rose Arundel. *Lewis Arundel*, F. E. Smedley, 1852.

Frettleby, Mark. *See also* Sal Rawlins.
Rosanne, his 1st wife, daughter of Ma Guttersnipe.
Madge, their daughter, m. Brian Fitzgerald.
The Mystery of a Hansom Cab, F. Hume, 1886.

Frew-Gaff, Sir Richard, scientific adviser to Lord Sombremere.
Vera, his wife.
Ruby, their daughter, m. Fulke Arnott.
Landscape with Figures, R. Fraser, 1925.

Frewen, Doc.
His wife.
A Way through the Wood, N. Balchin, 1951.

Frewin, Philip, cousin of Hilda Scarve, rival of Randolph Crew. *The Miser's Daughter*, W. H. Ainsworth, 1842.

Freytag, William, young German engineer. *Ship of Fools*, Katherine Anne Porter, 1962.

Fribble, a coxcomb. *Miss in her Teens* (play), D. Garrick, 1747.

'Friday,' native friend and servant

of Robinson Crusoe. *Robinson Crusoe*, D. Defoe, 1719.

Friedlander, Fanny, accompanist to Skratch. 'Mrs Beelbrow's Lions' (s.s.), *Miss Bracegirdle and Others*, Stacy Aumonier, 1923.

Frink, T. Cholmondeley, poet. *Babbitt*, Sinclair Lewis, 1923.

Frinton, Lady. *The Last of Mrs Cheyney* (play), F. Lonsdale, 1925.

Frion, Stephen, Perkin Warbeck's secretary. *Perkin Warbeck* (play), J. Ford, 1634.

Frisby, Madame, milliner, m. Colonel Altamont, who deserted her. *Pendennis*, W. M. Thackeray, 1848–50.

Frisk, James, journalist. *Other Gods*, Pearl Buck, 1940.

Frith, Anne, ex-mistress of Oliver North. *The Happy Prisoner*, Monica Dickens, 1946.

Frith, Mary. *See* CUTPURSE.

Fritha. *The Snow Goose*, P. Gallico, 1941.

'Frithiof,' boatswain. 'A Matter of Fact' (s.s.), *Many Inventions*, R. Kipling, 1893.

Fritz, lover of Ottila Gottesheim. *Prince Otto*, R. L. Stevenson, 1885.

Fritzing, Herr Geheimarchvrath, librarian, fellow conspirator of Princess Priscilla of Lotten-Künitz. *Princess Priscilla's Fortnight*, Countess von Arnim, 1905.

Frobisher, Dr, headmaster. *The Browning Version* (play), T. Rattigan, 1948.

Frobisher, Sir William.
His wife.
Diary of a Provincial Lady, E. M. Delafield, 1930.

Frome, Ethan, central character.
Zeena, his wife.
Ethan Frome, Edith Wharton, 1911.

Front-de-Bœuf, Reginald, Norman knight. *Ivanhoe*, W. Scott, 1820.

Frosch, Morton, lawyer and friend of Stephen Monk. *The World in the Evening*, C. Isherwood, 1954.

Frost, American millionaire. *Mr Billingham, the Marquis and Madelon*, E. P. Oppenheim.

Frost, ex-navy valet. 'Unprofessional' (s.s.), *Limits and Renewals*, R. Kipling, 1932.

Frost, Miss, Alvina Houghton's governess. *The Lost Girl*, D. H. Lawrence, 1920.

Frost, Sir Percival, King's Proctor. *Holy Deadlock*, A. P. Herbert, 1934.

Froth, Lord.
His wife.
The Double Dealer (play), W. Congreve, 1693.

Froud, Richard, friend of Eddy Considine. *Without My Cloak*, Kate O'Brien, 1931.

Frusk, Indiana, m. James Rolliver, *The Custom of the Country*, Edith Wharton, 1913.

Fry, principal warder in Hawes's jail. *It Is Never Too Late to Mend*, C. Reade, 1856.

Fry, Amos ('Haymoss'). *Two on a Tower*, T. Hardy, 1882.

Fry, John, servant to John Ridd. *Lorna Doone*, R. D. Blackmore, 1869.

Fryern, Sir Montague, salvage officer. *The Spanish Farm*, R. H. Mottram, 1924.

Ftatateeta, Cleopatra's chief nurse. *Caesar and Cleopatra* (play), G. B. Shaw, 1900.

Fudge, Poll, one-eyed rebel in Shepperton workhouse. 'The Rev. Amos Barton,' *Scenes of Clerical Life*, George Eliot, 1857.

Fuego, Juan del, President of Nicaragua. *The Napoleon of Notting Hill*, G. K. Chesterton, 1904.

Fuente, Dolores de la, m. Anthony Adverse. *Anthony Adverse*, Hervey Allen, 1934.

Fugger, Melpomene, ex Sister Agatha.
Professor Fugger, her father.
'Nuns at Luncheon' (s.s.), *Mortal Coils*, A. Huxley, 1922.

Fulgrave, Lord, Juliana Forrest's father, *Mr Rowl*, D. K. Broster, 1924.

Fulke, Norman baron. 'Old Men at Pevensey,' *Puck of Pook's Hill*, R. Kipling, 1906.

Fuller, Joe, a wealthy Philadelphian. *Lovey Childs*, John O'Hara, 1969.

Fullerton, Archie, solicitor. *The Prodigal Heart*, Susan Ertz, 1950.

Fullgarney, Sophie, manicurist. *The Gay Lord Quex* (play), A. W. Pinero, 1899.

Fullilove, timber merchant, Grimeworth.
His daughter.
Brother Jacob, George Eliot, 1864.

Fulton, Maude. *Caroline* (play), W. S. Maugham, 1916.

Fulton, Pearl, friend of Bertha Young. 'Bliss' (s.s.), *Bliss and Other Stories*, Katherine Mansfield, 1920.

Fulverton-Fane, Mrs. *The Fourth Wall*, A. A. Milne, 1928.

Fuma, native girl. *Mr Fortune's Maggot*, Sylvia Townsend Warner, 1927.

Fun. *The Alchemist* (play), B. Jonson, 1610.

Fung-Tching. 'The Gate of a Hundred Sorrows' (s.s.), *Plain Tales from the Hills*, R. Kipling, 1888.

Fungoso. *Every Man in his Humour*, B. Jonson, 1598.

Furic, art dealer. *The Face of Clay*, H. A. Vachell, 1906.

Furle, Mrs Bessie, friend of Elinor Presset. *We the Accused*, E. Raymond, 1935.

Furlong, Dublin fop. *Handy Andy*, S. Lover, 1842.

Furnival, Lawrence ('Lorry'), m. Molly Milner. *Miss Tarrant's Temperament* (s.s.), May Sinclair.

Furor, son of Occasion. *The Faërie Queene* (poem), E. Spencer, 1590.

Furry, an old blind rat. *Rambles of a Rat*, A.L.O.E.

Furst, Marie, mistress of Count von Edelstein.
  Maximilian, their son.
Spears Against Us, Cecil Roberts, 1932.

Furze, Catherine, central character.
  Her father.
  Amelia, her mother.
Catherine Furze, M. Rutherford, 1893.

Furze, Mrs Emma, ex-actress (Miss Pomeroy), cook and mistress to Squire Gauntry. *Judith Paris*, Hugh Walpole, 1931.

Fuseli, artist. *Lolly Willowes*, Sylvia Townsend Warner, 1926.

Fuseli, Eddie, a gunman. *Golden Boy* (play), Clifford Odets, 1937.

Fuselli, Dan, soldier from San Francisco. *Three Soldiers*, John dos Passos, 1921.

Futvoye, Inspector. *Robert's Wife* (play), St John Ervine, 1937.

Futvoye, Sylvia, m. Horace Ventimore.
  Professor Anthony, her father, archaeologist.
  Her mother.
The Brass Bottle, F. Anstey, 1900.

Fyfe, 'Moggy,' dwarf. *See also* WITHERNSEA.
  Hobley, her brother, landlord of inn.
The Story of Ragged Robyn, O. Onions, 1945.

Fynes, Mrs, widow, *née* Caryll. *See also* LACKLAND.
  Ida, her adopted daughter, m. Julian Silvercross.
The Old Bank, W. Westall, 1902.

Fytton, Mark, butcher hanged for lese-majesty. *Windsor Castle*, W. H. Ainsworth, 1843.

G

Gabbadeo, Maestro, 'wise doctor.' *Romola,* George Eliot, 1863.

Gabbett, leader of mutiny. *For the Term of his Natural Life,* M. Clarke, 1874.

Gabelle, Theophile, postmaster and local taxmaster. *A Tale of Two Cities,* C. Dickens, 1859.

Gabriel, of the *Jeroboam.* *Moby Dick,* H. Melville, 1851.

Gabriel, farm labourer, in love with Patty Verity. *High Meadows,* Alison Uttley, 1938.

Gadd, Ferdinand, of Bagnigge Wells Theatre. *Trelawny of the Wells* (play), A. W. Pinero, 1898.

Gaddi, Luca, owner of silk-mills.
Ottima, his wife.
Pippa Passes (poem), R. Browning, 1841.

Gadias. *Herod* (play), S. Phillips, 1900.

Gadow, Madame, the Lewishams' first landlady. *Love and Mr Lewisham,* H. G. Wells, 1900.

Gadsby, Mrs, widow of Captain Gadsby; formerly kitchen-maid. *Daniel Deronda,* George Eliot, 1876.

Gadsby, Captain Philip, m. Minnie Threegan (friend of Emma Deercourt). *The Story of the Gadsbys,* R. Kipling, 1888.

Gage, Mrs, postmistress. *The Tree of Man,* Patrick White, 1955.

Gage, Henry, who is murdered in Harlem. *Lovey Childs,* John O'Hara, 1969.

Gagool, witch-doctor. *King Solomon's Mines,* H. Rider Haggard, 1885.

Gahagan, Major Goliah, Irish adventurer.
Gregory and
Count Godfrey, his brothers.
The Adventures of Major Gahagan, W. M. Thackeray, 1838–9.

Gaige, Mr and Mrs.
Dolly, their daughter.
My Brother Jonathan, F. Brett Young, 1928.

Gaigern, Baron Felix von. *Grand Hotel,* Vicki Baum, 1931.

Gailey, Sarah, George Cannon's half-sister. *Hilda Lessways,* Arnold Bennett, 1911.

Gaillard, Eugene, m. Kate Brady. *Girls in Their Married Bliss,* Edna O'Brien, 1964.

Gaius. *Pilgrim's Progress,* J. Bunyan, 1678, 1684.

Gajere, ex-convict, lover of Aissa. *Aissa Saved,* Joyce Cary, 1932.

Galadriel, Elf Queen of Lothlorien. *The Lord of the Rings* trilogy, 1954–1955, J. R. R. Tolkien.

Galahad, the stainless knight. 'The Holy Grail' (poem), *Idylls of the King,* Lord Tennyson, 1859.

Galantry, Old Will (Squire).
His children by 1st wife:
William.
Libby.
Lucius, M.P.
Septimus, his son.
Shulie, the gipsy, his 2nd wife.
Their children:
James, central character, m. Elizabeth Timson.
William, Elizabeth's son by Frank Castor, m. Julia Cole.
Deborah, and other children.
Dance of the Years, Margery Allingham, 1943.

Galatea, Arethusa's lady. *Philaster* (play), Beaumont & Fletcher, *c.* 1611.

Galathea. *Galathea* (play), J. Lyly, 1592.

Galbraith, Mrs, breeder of Persian cats. *A Footman for the Peacock,* Rachel Ferguson, 1940.

Gale, John, small clothier.
His wife.
Shirley, Charlotte Brontë, 1849.

Gale, Tom, narrator, 'The Old Ancient Ship,' and others, *Short Stories,* Morley Roberts, 1928.

Galer, Mrs, washerwoman and landlady, central character.
Sid, her son, m. Miss Carthew.
Mrs Galer's Business, W. Pett Ridge, 1905.

Galgenstein, Count G. A. M. von,

depraved and dissipated German officer in an English regiment. *Catherine,* W. M. Thackeray, 1839–1840.

Gallagher, Commandant Dan. *The Informer,* L. O'Flaherty, 1925.

Gallaher, Ignatius, London journallist. 'A Little Cloud' (s.s.), *The Dubliners,* James Joyce, 1914.

Gallegher, Johnny, mill manager. *Gone with the Wind,* Margaret Mitchell, 1936.

Galloway, Richard, proctor.
Robert, his cousin.
Mark, his nephew.
The Channings, Mrs Henry Wood, 1862.

Gallowglass, Viscount, Bishop of Ballyshannon, son-in-law of Lord Dorking. *The Newcomes,* W. M. Thackeray, 1853–5.

Galopin, dramatist, m. Leslie, his ex-mistress. 'The Elevation of Lulu' (s.s.), *The Little Dog Laughed,* L. Merrick, 1930.

Galore, Mr, 'Indian nabob.'
Nelly, his sister.
The Provost, J. Galt, 1822.

Galore, Miss Pussy, head of lesbian gang, 'The Cement Mixers', in Harlem. *Goldfinger,* Ian Fleming, 1959.

Galors, Dom, villainous almoner to the Abbot of St Thorn. *The Forest Lovers,* M. Hewlett, 1898.

Gam, Mrs, widow, *née* Molloy.
Jemima Amelia, her daughter, m. Dionysius Haggarty.
Men's Wives, W. M. Thackeray, 1843.

Gama, King.
Ida, his daughter, m. Hilarion.
His sons:
Arac.
Guron.
Scynthius.
The Princess (poem), Lord Tennyson, 1847. *Princess Ida* (comic opera), Gilbert & Sullivan, 1884.

Gambit, Dr. *Middlemarch,* George Eliot, 1871–2.

'Game Chicken,' The, prize-fighter. *Dombey and Son,* C. Dickens, 1848.

Gamgee, Samwise, hobbit, Frodo Baggins's servant. *The Lord of the Rings* trilogy, 1954–5, J. R. R. Tolkien.

Gamm, Jerry, witchmaster. 'Marklake Witches,' *Rewards and Fairies,* R. Kipling, 1910.

Gammon, rascally solicitor, of Gammon, Quirk & Co. *Ten Thousand a Year,* S. Warren, 1839.

Gammon, 'town-traveller' and dog-fancier, central character. *The Town Traveller,* G. Gissing, 1898.

Gamp, Mrs Sarah, drunken old midwife and nurse.
Her late husband.
Martin Chuzzlewit, C. Dickens, 1844.

Gandalf the Grey, a wizard. *The Lord of the Rings* trilogy, 1954–5, J. R. R. Tolkien.

Gandish, Professor, head of Gandish's Drawing Academy.
His wife and daughters.
Charles, his son.
The Newcomes, W. M. Thackeray, 1853–5.

Gandoc the Briton. *The Conquered,* Naomi Mitchison, 1923.

Gann, James, head of Gann & Blubbery, oil merchants.
Juliana, his wife, *née* Crabb, formerly Mrs Wellesley Macarty.
Caroline, their daughter (same as Mrs Brandon, *Adventures of Philip*).
A Shabby Genteel Story, W. M. Thackeray, 1840.

Gann, Rosie, 1st wife of Edward Driffield. *Cakes and Ale,* W. S. Maugham, 1930.

Gant, Oliver.
m. (1) Cynthia.
(2) Eliza Pentland.
Their children: **Steve, Daisy, Helen, Grover, Ben, Luke** and **Eugene.**
Look Homeward, Angel, T. Wolfe, 1929.

Gantry, Elmer, minister.
Cleo, his wife, *née* Benham.
Elmer Gantry, Sinclair Lewis, 1927.

Gantz, Norman, American G.I., 2nd husband of Bessie Hipkiss. *Jezebel's Dust,* Fred Urquhart, 1951.

Garbets, tragic actor, friend of Captain Costigan. *Pendennis,* W. M. Thackeray, 1848–50.

Garcia. 'Wistaria Lodge,' *His Last Bow,* A. Conan Doyle, 1917.

Garcia, Maurice, leader of the Carlist movement. *The Four Just Men,* E. Wallace, 1905.

Garden, Rev. Aubrey, 'in search of a creed.'
Anne, his wife.
Their children:
Victoria, m. Charles.
Maurice, Ed. *The Gadfly,* m. Amy Wilbur.
Rome, in love with Frank Jayne (also appears in *Crewe Train*).
Stanley, m. and div. Denman Croft.
Irving.
Una, m. Ted.
Told by an Idiot, Rose Macaulay, 1923.

Garden Minimus, a schoolboy. *Mr Perrin and Mr Traill,* Hugh Walpole, 1911.

Gardener, Felix, leading actor. *Enter a Murderer,* Ngaio Marsh, 1935.

Gardiner, Bishop of Winchester. *Henry the Eighth* (play), W. Shakespeare.

Gardiner, Colonel, commanding officer at Dundee. *Waverley,* W. Scott, 1814.

Gardiner, Edward, brother of Mrs Bennet.
His wife.
Pride and Prejudice, Jane Austen, 1813.

Gardiner, Eunice, schoolgirl, member of 'the Brodie Set'. *The Prime of Miss Jean Brodie,* Muriel Spark, 1961.

Gardner, Georgina, m. Finch.
Jane, her sister, m. Pelham Fotheringham.
Mark, their cousin, m. Emma Brandon.
Heartsease, Charlotte M. Yonge, 1854.

Gardner, Rev. Samuel.
Frank, his son.
Mrs Warren's Profession (play), G. B. Shaw, 1902.

Garenne, Robert ('The Lizard'), poacher. *The Maids of Paradise,* R. W. Chambers, 1903.

Gargery, Joe, blacksmith.
His 1st wife, sister of Philip Pirrip.
Biddy, his 2nd wife.
Pip, their son.
Great Expectations, C. Dickens, 1861.

Gargrave, Sir Thomas. *Henry the Sixth* (play), W. Shakespeare.

Garland, Mr and Mrs.
Abel, their son.
The Old Curiosity Shop, C. Dickens, 1841.

Garland, Anne, m. Robert Loveday.
Martha, her mother, m. Miller Loveday, Robert's father.
The Trumpet Major, T. Hardy, 1880.

Garland, Elizabeth.
Her father and mother.
And Now Goodbye, J. Hilton, 1931.

Garland, Fanny, head waitress, the Pelican, m. Steve Sorrell.
Her mother, Sorrell's landlady.
Sorrell and Son, W. Deeping, 1925.

Garland, Mary, distant cousin of the Hudsons, eng. to Roderick Hudson. *Roderick Hudson,* H. James, 1875.

Garm, Private Ortheris' bulldog. 'Garm—a Hostage' (s.s.), *Actions and Reactions,* R. Kipling, 1909.

Garnet, Jeremy, central character and narrator. *Love Among the Chickens,* P. G. Wodehouse, 1906.

Garnett, Proserpine, typist. *Candida* (play), G. B. Shaw, 1894.

Garrard, Ethel.
Arthur, her husband.
Tom, their son.
Thursday Afternoons, Monica Dickens, 1945.

Garret, Miss Ruth.
Sarah, her sister.
Campbell's Kingdom, Hammond Innes, 1952.

Garron, Phil. 'Yoked with an Unbeliever' (s.s.), *Plain Tales from the Hills,* R. Kipling, 1888.

Garstin, Peter, mine owner and party candidate. *Felix Holt,* George Eliot, 1866.

Garter, Polly. *Under Milk Wood* (play), Dylan Thomas, 1954.

Garth, Dr, partner to Dr Goodricke. *The Woman in White,* W. Collins, 1860.

Garth, Miss, governess to and good genius of the Vanstone family. *No Name,* W. Collins, 1862.

Garth, Miss, secretary who turns out to be more than she appears. *Thin Air,* John Pudney, 1961.

Garth, Mrs, companion to Theodora

Martindale. *Heartsease,* Charlotte M. Yonge, 1854.

Garth, Sergeant. *An Englishman's Home* (play), Guy du Maurier, 1909.

Garth, Caleb, land agent and builder.
  Susan, his wife.
  Their children:
    Christy.
    Alfred.
    Mary, m. Fred Vincy.
    Jim.
    Ben.
    Letty.
  Middlemarch, Geo. Eliot, 1871–2.

Garth, Duncan. 'The Feast and the Reckoning' (s.s.), *Here and Hereafter,* Barry Pain, 1911.

Garth, Sir John, senior steward, Jockey Club. *The Calendar,* E. Wallace.

Garton, Robert, college friend of Frank Ashurst. *The Apple Tree,* J. Galsworthy, 1918.

Garvace, proprietor of Port Burdock Bazaar. *The History of Mr Polly,* H. G. Wells, 1910.

Garvell, Archie, half-brother to Beatrice Normandy, childhood enemy of George Ponderevo. *Tono Bungay,* H. G. Wells, 1909.

Gascoigne, Gerald. *The Dancing Druids,* Gladys Mitchell, 1948.

Gascoigne, Rev. Henry (formerly Gaskin), Rector of Pennicote.
  Nancy, his wife.
  Their children:
    Rex.
    Edwy.
    Warham.
    Anna.
    Lotta.
  Daniel Deronda, George Eliot, 1876.

Gascoigne, Joe, friend of Sam Billingham. *Mr Billingham, the Marquis and Madelon,* E. P. Oppenheim.

Gashe, Toby, student. *The Bell,* Iris Murdoch, 1958.

Gashford, secretary to Lord George Gordon. *Barnaby Rudge,* C. Dickens, 1841.

Gashleigh, Mrs.
  Eliza and **Emily,** her daughters.
  A Little Dinner at Timmins, W. M. Thackeray, 1852.

Gaskony, Sir William, retired judge. *See* JULIA SPRINGSTER and PHIL BROWN.

  Dick, his brother, Provost of St Peter's, Oxford.
  The Judge's Story, C. Morgan, 1947.

Gaspar. *The Lady of Lyons* (play), Lord Lytton, 1838.

Gaspard, murderer of the Marquis de St Evremonde. *A Tale of Two Cities,* C. Dickens, 1859.

Gates, Ivor, badly disabled ex-soldier, cared for by Lucy Byrne. *A Sort of Traitors,* N. Balchin, 1949.

Gates, Martin, friend of Stephen Monk. *The World in the Evening,* C. Isherwood, 1954.

Gates, Robert, lodge porter. *The Great Hoggarty Diamond,* W. M. Thackeray, 1841.

Gatsby, Major Jay, tycoon, central character. *The Great Gatsby,* F. Scott Fitzgerald, 1925.

Gauberon, Cissie, assistant to John Mapsted. *Twelve Horses and the Hangman's Noose,* Gladys Mitchell, 1956.

Gaudriol, Sergeant, *gendarme. Barbe of Grand Bayou,* J. Oxenham, 1903.

Gaulesse, Dick, alias of Edward Christian. *Peveril of the Peak,* W. Scott, 1822.

Gault, Selena, mistress of Wolf's father. *Wolf Solent,* J. C. Powys, 1929.

Gaunt. Family name of MARQUESS OF STEYNE.

Gaunt, sailor in the torpedoed *Aurora. The Ocean,* J. Hanley, 1946.

Gaunt, Judge. *Winterset* (play), Maxwell Anderson, 1935.

Gaunt, Jasper, villainous moneylender. *The Amateur Gentleman,* J. Farnol, 1913.

Gaunt, John ('Admiral Guinea').
  Arethusa, his daughter.
  Admiral Guinea (play), W. E. Henley & R. L. Stevenson, 1892.

Gaunt, John of, Duke of Lancaster. *Richard the Second* (play), W. Shakespeare.

Gaunt, William, senior choirboy. *The Channings,* Mrs H. Wood, 1862.

Gauntlet, Emilia, loved by Peregrine.
  Godfrey, her brother.
  Sophy, her cousin.
  Peregrine Pickle, T. Smollett, 1751.

Gauntry, Squire Tom. *Judith Paris,* Hugh Walpole, 1931.

Gauss, Richard, m. Lotte von Leyde.

The Other Side, Storm Jameson, 1946.

Gaux, Antoinette, light woman.
  Jacques, her small son.
Shadows on the Rock, Willa Cather, 1932.

Gavin, David, detective, m. Laura Menzies. Gladys Mitchell's *Mrs Bradley* detective stories.

Gawill, Gregory, a crooked businessman. *The Glass Cell*, Patricia Highsmith, 1965.

Gawky, Lieutenant. *Roderick Random*, T. Smollett, 1748.

Gawler, coal merchant and lodging-house keeper. *The Newcomes*, W. M. Thackeray, 1853–5.

Gay, Walter, employee of Paul Dombey, m. Florence Dombey. *Dombey and Son*, C. Dickens, 1848.

Gayerson ('Very young').
  'Young' Gayerson, his father.
'Venus Annodomini' (s.s.), *Plain Tales from the Hills*, R. Kipling, 1888.

Gayford, Mirabelle. *Poison Ivy*, P. Cheyney, 1937.

Gaylord, Tom, senator.
  Tom ('Young'), his son.
Mr Crewe's Career, W. Churchill, 1908.

Gayson, Major, in Dillon's regiment, friend of Charles Wogan. *Clementina*, A. E. W. Mason, 1901.

Gaze-oh, King, father of Tulip Targett.
  Geleley, his son.
The Sailor's Return, David Garnett, 1925.

Gazebee, Mortimer, m. Lady Amelia de Courcy. *Doctor Thorne*, A. Trollope, 1858.

Gazingi, Miss, member of Crummles's Company. *Nicholas Nickleby*, C. Dickens, 1839.

Geaiter, Benjamin, farmer.
  m. (1) **Emily.**
    Their sons: **Ben jnr, Hiram, Bob, Ernest** and **Harry.**
  (2) **Nancy,** *née* Hambling.
    Joseph, their son, m. Daisy Chilvers.
Joseph and his Brethren, H. W. Freeman, 1928.

Geake, William, m. Naomi Bricknell bigamously. *The Delectable Duchy*, A. Quiller-Couch, 1893.

Geard, John, Mayor of Glastonbury.
  Megan, his wife.
  Cordelia and **Crummie,** his daughters.
A Glastonbury Romance, J. C. Powys, 1932.

Geary, L. L. 'With the Night Mail' (s.s.), *Actions and Reactions*, R. Kipling, 1909.

Geary, Thomas. 'Bill's Paper Chase' (s.s.), *The Lady of the Barge*, W. W. Jacobs, 1902.

Gebbie, Mrs, Catriona's escort to Holland.
  Her husband.
Catriona, R. L. Stevenson, 1893.

Gecko, fiddler, companion of Svengali. *Trilby*, George du Maurier, 1894.

Geddes, Joshua, Quaker, friend of Darsie Latimer.
  Rachel, his sister.
Redgauntlet, W. Scott, 1824.

Gedge, friend of Cruden. *Reginald Cruden*, T. Baines Reed, 1894.

Gedge, landlord of the Royal Oak, Shepperton. *Adam Bede*, George Eliot, 1859.

Gedye, Miss Sarah Ann. *The Delectable Duchy*, A. Quiller-Couch, 1893.

Geelan, Father Thomas, curate. *Famine*, L. O'Flaherty, 1937.

Gehenna, Red-Eye Rod, Chicago gangster.
  Lalage, his daughter.
Juan in America, Eric Linklater, 1931.

Geierstein, Anne of.
  Count Albert, her father, wrongful holder of the title. *See also* ARNOLD BIEDERMAN.
  Sybilla, her mother, *née* Arnheim.
  Williewald, father of Arnold and Albert.
  Heinrich, their grandfather.
Anne of Geierstein, W. Scott, 1829.

Geiger, Warren, college friend of Stephen Monk. *The World in the Evening*, C. Isherwood, 1954.

Gellatley, Davie, 'a crack-brained knave.'
  Jamie, his brother.
  Janet, his mother.
Waverley, W. Scott, 1814.

Gemmill, Agatha.
  Her husband. Sister and brother-in-law of Meenie Douglas-Stuart.
White Heather, W. Black, 1885.

General, Mrs, chaperon to Dorrit's

daughters. *Little Dorrit*, C. Dickens, 1857.

Genevieve, Mademoiselle. French maid to Mrs Rawdon Crawley. *Vanity Fair*, W. M. Thackeray, 1847–8.

Genoux, faithful maid of Lady Slane. *All Passion Spent*, V. Sackville-West, 1931.

Geoghegan, Mrs.
Her children: **George, Peter, Kate, Jane, Baby** and **Denis.**
The White-headed Boy (play), L. Robinson, 1920.

George, one of the 'three.' *Three Men in a Boat*, J. K. Jerome, 1889.

George, fiancé of Jane. *The One Before*, Barry Pain, 1902.

George, mulatto slave of Harris.
Eliza, his wife.
Harry ('Jim Crow'), their son.
Uncle Tom's Cabin, Harriet B. Stowe, 1851.

George, servant and later husband of Mrs Jarley. *The Old Curiosity Shop*, C. Dickens, 1841.

George, insolvent friend of Weller senior. *Pickwick Papers*, C. Dickens, 1837.

George ('Gentleman George'), host of the Jolly Angler. *Paul Clifford*, Lord Lytton, 1830.

George, friend and guardian of Lennie. *Of Mice and Men*, J. Steinbeck, 1937.

George, almost criminal assistant of Bullivant the butler. *Manservant and Maidservant*, Ivy Compton-Burnett, 1947.

George, a footman. *The Last of Mrs Cheyney* (play), F. Lonsdale, 1925.

George, Mrs Bradley's chauffeur. The *Mrs Bradley* detective stories, Gladys Mitchell.

George, Mr, proprietor of a shooting-gallery. *Bleak House*, C. Dickens, 1853.

George, Monsieur, narrator. *The Arrow of Gold*, J. Conrad, 1919.

George, Tobey, army friend of Marcus Macauley, m. Bess Macauley. *The Human Comedy*, W. Saroyan, 1943.

Georgette, a dancing club hostess. *Nobody Answered the Bell*, Rhys Davies, 1971.

Georgi, hall porter's assistant. *Grand Hotel*, Vicki Baum, 1931.

Georgiano, Black. 'The Red Circle,' *His Last Bow*, A. Conan Doyle, 1917.

Georgie Porgie.
Georgina, his native 'wife.'
Grace, his real wife.
'Georgie Porgie' (s.s.), *Life's Handicap*, R. Kipling, 1891.

Geraint, m. Enid. 'Geraint and Enid' (poem), *Idylls of the King*, Lord Tennyson, 1859.

Gerald, Mrs Letty Pace, widow who marries Lester Kane. *Jennie Gerhardt*, Theodore Dreiser, 1911.

Geraldin, Lord William. *See* LOVEL.

Geraldine, Colonel, Master of the Horse to Prince Florizel; alias Major Alfred Hammersmith. 'The Suicide Club,' *New Arabian Nights*, R. L. Stevenson, 1882.

Gerard. *See* ELIASSON.

Gerard, Lieutenant. The *Hornblower* series, C. S. Forester, 1937 onwards.

Gerard, Etienne, lieutenant, later brigadier. *The Exploits of Brigadier Gerard*, 1899, and elsewhere, A. Conan Doyle.

Gerard, Lucy, m. Marmaduke Heath.
Harvey, her father.
Lost Sir Massingberd, James Payn, 1864.

Gerard, Walter, 'overlooker' at Trafford's Mill.
Sybil, his daughter, m. Hon. Charles Egremont.
Sybil, B. Disraeli, 1845.

Gerhardt, Jennie, central character.
Vesta, her daughter.
William, her father, a glass blower.
Sebastian, her brother.
Jennie Gerhardt, Theodore Dreiser, 1911.

Gertrude, mother of Hamlet. *Hamlet* (play), W. Shakespeare.

Gertrude, a witch. *Christabel* (poem), S. T. Coleridge, 1816.

Gervais, Frank, m. Jean Emerson. *A Lamp for Nightfall*, E. Caldwell, 1952.

Gervas, old monk and tutor to Martin of Elchester. *Unending Crusade*, R. E. Sherwood, 1932.

Gervase, Armand, French artist. *Ziska*, Marie Corelli, 1897.

Gervois, Emily, m. Sir Edward Beauchamp. *Sir Charles Grandison*, S. Richardson, 1754.

Geste, Beau, central character.
Digby and **John,** his brothers.
Beau Geste, P. C. Wren, 1924.

Gething, Annis.
Captain Gething, her father.
Her mother.
The Skipper's Wooing, W. W. Jacobs, 1897.

Getliffe, Francis, Cambridge physicist, m. Katherine March.
Herbert, his elder half-brother, lawyer.
The Conscience of the Rich, 1958, part of the *Strangers and Brothers* sequence, C. P. Snow.

Gettner, Richard, 1st husband of Gelda Rosmarin. *The Dark is Light Enough* (play), C. Fry, 1954.

Ghost (of Hamlet's father). *Hamlet* (play), W. Shakespeare.

Ghulendi. *See* ABOU TAHER ACHMED.

Giacosa, Cavaliere, possibly father of Christina Light. *Roderick Hudson,* H. James, 1875.

Gianetta, a *contadina,* m. Marco Palmieri. *The Gondoliers* (comic opera), Gilbert & Sullivan, 1889.

Gianotto, secretary to the Duke of Milan.
Filippo and **Matteo,** his brothers.
The Viper of Milan, Marjorie Bowen, 1905.

Gibbet, a highwayman. *The Beaux' Stratagem* (play), G. Farquhar, 1707.

Gibbon, Martin Lynch. *A Severed Head,* Iris Murdoch, 1961.

Gibbons, theatrical dresser. 'A Curious Story' (s.s.), *The Baseless Fabric,* Helen Simpson, 1925.

Gibbs. 'The Haughty Actor' (poem), *Bab Ballads,* W. S. Gilbert, 1869.

Gibbs, Alexander Maccolgie. *The Cocktail Party* (play), T. S. Eliot, 1950.

Gibbs, Dr, family physician.
His wife.
Rebecca, their daughter.
George, their son, m. Emily Webb.
Our Town (play), Thornton Wilder, 1938.

Gibbs, Janet, spinster. 'The Rev. Amos Barton,' *Scenes of Clerical Life,* George Eliot, 1857.

Gibbs, John, captain and owner of the *Arabella.*
Louisa, his wife.
The Lady of the Barge, W. W. Jacobs, 1902.

Gibbs, Wash. *The Shepherd of the Hills,* H. B. Wright, 1907.

Gibby, servant of Captain Breton. *The Wonder* (play), Mrs Susanna Centlivre, 1714.

Gibley Gobbler, leader of the turkeys. *Uncle Remus,* J. C. Harris, 1880–1895.

Gibson, builder. *The House with the Green Shutters,* G. Douglas, 1901.

Gibson, Dr.
His wife, formerly Mrs Kirkpatrick.
Molly, their daughter.
Wives and Daughters, Mrs Gaskell, 1866.

Gibson, Mrs, landlady. *Miss Mole,* E. H. Young, 1930.

Gibson, Jane, bookseller. *No Son of Mine,* G. B. Stern, 1948.

Gibson, Leah, fiancée of Barty Josselin. *The Martian,* George du Maurier, 1897.

Gibson, Lewis.
Marise, his sister.
Friends and Relations, Elizabeth Bowen, 1931.

Gibson, Thomas, jilts Camilla French. *He Knew He Was Right,* A. Trollope, 1869.

Giddens, Regina, *née* Hubbard, central character.
Horace, her husband.
Alexandra, their daughter.
The Little Foxes (play), Lillian Hellman, 1939.

Gidding, rich American. *The Passionate Friends,* H. G. Wells, 1913.

Giddy, Miss Patricia, discoverer of gold ore in Anglesea. *War in the Air,* H. G. Wells, 1908.

Gideon, Arthur, eng. to Jane Potter. *Potterism,* Rose Macaulay, 1920.

Giffen, 'Giffen's Debt' (poem), *Departmental Ditties,* R. Kipling, 1886.

Gifford, Lord, m. Delina Delaney.
His mother.
Delina Delaney, Amanda Ros.

Gifford, Avery.
Betty, his wife.
Wickford Point, J. P. Marquand, 1939.

Gifford, Sir Henry.
Eirene, his wife.
Caroline, their daughter.

Hebe, Michael and **Luke,** their adopted children.
The Feast, Margaret Kennedy, 1950.

Giggle, William, Lord Wutherwood's chauffeur. *Surfeit of Lampreys,* Ngaio Marsh, 1941.

Giglio, Prince, legitimate King of Paflagonia, m. Rosalba. *The Rose and the Ring,* W. M. Thackeray, 1855.

Gilbert, a clerk. 'Old Men at Pevensey,' *Puck of Pook's Hill,* R. Kipling, 1906.

Gilbert, Mark, hosier's apprentice. *Barnaby Rudge,* C. Dickens, 1841.

Gilbert, Peter.
His wife.
The Browning Version (play), T. Rattigan, 1948.

Gilbert of Cranberry Moor, landowner. *The Monastery,* W. Scott, 1820.

Gilbey.
His wife.
Bobby, their son.
Fanny's First Play (play), G. B. Shaw, 1905.

Gilbright, Theo, one of Angelica Deverell's publishers.
Hermione, his wife.
Angel, Elizabeth Taylor, 1957.

Gilchrist, Flora, m. Vicomte de Kéroual de St Yves.
Miss Gilchrist, her aunt.
Ronald, her brother.
St Ives, R. L. Stevenson, 1897.

Gildersleeve, Lucian, m. Hon. Adela Trefoyle. *The Town Traveller,* G. Gissing, 1898.

Gilding, Sir George.
His wife.
The Professor's Love Story (play), J. M. Barrie, 1894.

Gildoy, Lord. *Captain Blood,* R. Sabatini, 1922.

Giles, central character. *The Farmer's Boy* (poem), R. Bloomfield, 1800.

Giles, unsuccessful party candidate. *Middlemarch,* Geo. Eliot, 1871–2.

Giles, butler to Mrs Maylie. *Oliver Twist,* C. Dickens, 1838.

Giles, Henry, coroner. 'A Tragedy of Two Ambitions,' *Life's Little Ironies,* T. Hardy, 1894.

Giles, N. A., author, friend of Basil Fane.
Tania, his mistress.
Going their own Ways, A. Waugh, 1938.

Giles, Oliver. 'The Three Strangers,' *Wessex Tales,* T. Hardy, 1888.

Gilfil, Rev. Maynard, Vicar of Shepperton and Knebley, m. Caterina Sarti.
Lucy, his sister, m. Arthur Heron.
'Mr Gilfil's Love Story,' *Scenes of Clerical Life,* George Eliot, 1857.

Gilfillan, Habakkuk ('Gifted Gilfillan'), leader of the Cameronians. *Waverley,* W. Scott, 1814.

Gilfillian, Mrs, Geoffrey Wedderburn's widowed sister.
Minnie, her daughter.
Sweet Lavender (play), A. W. Pinero, 1888.

Gilford, Colonel. *Sixty-four, Ninety-four,* R. H. Mottram, 1925.

Gillane, Peter.
Bridget, his wife.
Patrick and **Michael,** their sons.
Kathleen ni Houlihan (play), W. B. Yeats, 1903.

Gillespie, Jack. 'The Fall of Jack Gillespie' (poem), *Departmental Ditties,* R. Kipling, 1886.

Gillespie, Richard, m. Teresa Desterro, his cousin. *Miss Pym Disposes,* Josephine Tey, 1946.

Gillespie, Wattie, old retired sawmill worker, an idealist.
Mirren, his wife.
Tom, Arnold and **Walter,** their sons.
Their daughters:
Meg, m. Bernard Ashe.
Grace, m. George Wilson.
Bella, m. Jim Anderson.
Kate, spinster.
Time Will Knit, Fred Urquhart, 1938.

Gillett, Rev. John, school chaplain. *Stalky & Co.,* 1899, and elsewhere, R. Kipling.

Gillian, Dame, Eveline Berenger's tire-woman. *The Betrothed,* W. Scott, 1825.

Gillian, Robert.
Septimus, his uncle.
'One Thousand Dollars' (s.s.), *The Voice of the City,* O. Henry, 1908.

Gillies, prisoner in Hawes's jail. *It Is Never Too Late to Mend,* C. Reade, 1856.

Gillies, Connie. *Spring Cleaning* (play), F. Lonsdale, 1925.

Gilliewhackit, 'Young,' victim of smallpox and kidnapping. *Waverley*, W. Scott, 1814.

Gillingham, Antony, amateur detective, central character. *The Red House Mystery*, A. A. Milne, 1922.

Gillingham, George, schoolmaster at Leddenton, friend of Richard Phillotson. *Jude the Obscure*, T. Hardy, 1896.

Gillon, Miss Ellen. 'Aunt Ellen' (s.s.), *Limits and Renewals*, R. Kipling, 1932.

Gills, Solomon, nautical instrument maker, uncle of Walter Gay. *Dombey and Son*, C. Dickens, 1848.

Gilly, teenage girl who looks after James Sampson. *The Distant Horns of Summer*, H. E. Bates, 1967.

Gilmore, Richard, valet to Sir Massingberd Heath. *Lost Sir Massingberd*, James Payn, 1864.

Gilmore, Vincent, family solicitor of the Fairlies, part narrator. *The Woman in White*, W. Collins, 1860.

Gilmour, Kirsty, central character, m. Archibald Home.

Fanny, her aunt.

Lady Gilmour, her stepmother.

Pink Sugar, O. Douglas, 1924.

Gilpin, John.

His wife and family.

John Gilpin (poem), W. Cowper.

Gilray. *My Lady Nicotine*, J. M. Barrie, 1890.

Gilray, Beatrice, Burlap's mistress. *Point Counter Point*, Aldous Huxley, 1928.

Gilson, Thomas ('Long Tom'), landlord, Low Wood Inn.

His wife.

Starvecrow Farm, Stanley Weyman, 1905.

Gines. *Caleb Williams*, W. Godwin, 1794.

Ginger, a bad-tempered chestnut mare. *Black Beauty*, Anna Sewell, 1877.

Ginger. *See* Woods.

Ginger Dick. *Captains All* (s.s.), and elsewhere, W. W. Jacobs.

Ginger Ted, beachcomber, lecher and drunkard. 'The Vessel of Wrath' (s.s.), *Ah King*, W. S. Maugham, 1933.

Ginright, Nellie. *The Yearling*, Marjorie K. Rawlings, 1938.

Giorgio, a gondolier. *The Gondoliers* (comic opera), Gilbert & Sullivan, 1889.

Giovanelli, Daisy Miller's Italian suitor. *Daisy Miller*, Henry James, 1878.

Giovanna, Lady, m. Count Alberighi.

Her brother.

The Falcon (play), Lord Tennyson, 1879.

Gippings, Mrs, landlady of the George. *Three Men in a Boat*, J. K. Jerome, 1889.

Gipples, coward and bully. *True Blue*, W. H. G. Kingston.

Gipps, Nancy, school-teacher. *Mr Weston's Good Wine*, T. F. Powys, 1927.

Girard, Girard, magnate.

Mme Girard, his wife, an alcoholic.

Malcolm, James Purdy, 1959.

Giraud, Monsieur, famous French detective. *Murder on the Links*, Agatha Christie, 1923.

Girder, Gibbie Cooper.

Jean, *née* Lightbody, his wife.

The Bride of Lammermoor, W. Scott, 1819.

Girouette, Emily, society beauty who jilted Scythrop Glowry. *Nightmare Abbey*, T. L. Peacock, 1818.

Girvan, grocer. 'A Stroke of Business' (s.s.), *Sun on the Water*, L. A. G. Strong, 1940.

Gisborne, of Woods and Forests. 'In the Rukh' (a Mowgli story), *Many Inventions*, R. Kipling, 1893.

Gisippus, rich friend of Titus Fulvius. *The Wonderful History of Titus and Gisippus* (s.s.), Sir Thomas Elyot (16th century).

Gisquet, Minister of Police.

Henri, his son.

Tom Burke of Ours, C. Lever, 1844.

Gissing, Mrs Alice, formerly Mrs Saumarez. *On the Face of the Waters*, Flora A. Steel, 1896.

Giulia, a *contadina*. *The Gondoliers* (comic opera), Gilbert & Sullivan, 1889.

Gladwin, Major, uncle of Captain Sinclair, in charge of Fort Detroit. *Settlers in Canada*, Captain Marryat, 1844.

Gladwin, John. *John Gladwin Says—* (s.s.), O. Onions.

Gladys, a servant. *The Admirable Crichton* (play), J. M. Barrie, 1902.

Glamber, Mrs Helen.
John, her husband.
'Hubert and Minnie' (s.s.), *The Little Mexican*, A. Huxley, 1924.

Glanders, Captain, 50th Dragoon Guards.
His wife.
Anglesea, his son.
Pendennis, W. M. Thackeray, 1848–50.

Glansdale, Sir William. *Henry the Sixth* (play), W. Shakespeare.

Glasby, Harry, pirate and traitor. *The Pirate*, W. Scott, 1822.

Glascock, Hon. Charles, eldest son of Lord Peterborough. *He Knew He Was Right*, A. Trollope, 1869.

Glasher, Colonel.
Lydia, his wife.
Her children by Henleigh Grandcourt:
Henleigh.
Antonia.
Josephine.
Daniel Deronda, George Eliot, 1876.

Glass, Edward, a marine. 'The Bonds of Discipline' (s.s.), *Traffics and Discoveries*, R. Kipling, 1904.

Glass, Franny, an actress.
Zooey, her brother, television actor.
Buddy, another brother, a writer.
Seymour, eldest brother, who commits suicide.
Bessie, their mother.
Franny and Zooey, J. D. Salinger, 1961.

Glass, Mistress Margaret, tobacconist. *The Heart of Midlothian*, W. Scott, 1818.

Glaucus, voluptuary and gambler. *The Last Days of Pompeii*, Lord Lytton, 1834.

Glavis, friend of Beauseant. *The Lady of Lyons* (play), Lord Lytton, 1838.

Gleave, Carey, Jim Manning's solicitor. *A Way through the Wood*, N. Balchin, 1951.

Gleeson, Barney.
Ellen, his wife.
Their children:
Mary, m. Martin Kilmartin.
Ellie.
Patrick.
Famine, L. O'Flaherty, 1937.

Glegg, retired wool-stapler.
Jane, his wife, *née* Dodson.
The Mill on the Floss, George Eliot, 1860.

Glen, Mrs, proprietress of an hotel. *The Virginian*, O. Wister, 1902.

Glenallan, Earl of (William).
'Mr Lovel,' his son.
The Antiquary, W. Scott, 1816.

Glenalmond, Lord (David Keith), friend of Archie Weir. *Weir of Hermiston*, R. L. Stevenson, 1896.

Glendale, Sir Richard, loyal supporter of the Pretender. *Redgauntlet*, W. Scott, 1824.

Glendinning, Pierre, wealthy, cultured young man.
His mother.
Isabel, his illegitimate sister.
Lucy Tartan, his fiancée.
Pierre, Herman Melville, 1852.

Glendinning, Simon.
Elspeth, his wife.
Their sons:
Halbert, m. Mary Avenel.
Edward, later Father Ambrose.
The Monastery and *The Abbot*, W. Scott, 1820.

Glendower, Adeline, heiress, paying guest living with the Buntings, one-time fiancée of Chatteris. *The Sea Lady*, H. G. Wells, 1902.

Glendower, Owen (hist.). *Henry the Fourth* (play), W. Shakespeare.

Glenellen, Lord, eccentric homosexual English peer exiled in Rome. *The Judgment of Paris*, Gore Vidal, 1952.

Glenmaline, Lord (James O'Brien, L.C.J., 'Jimmy the Hangman').
Connaught O'Brien, his daughter, m. (1) John d'Arcy, (2) Dermot McDermot.
Hangman's House, Donn Byrne, 1926.

Glenmire, Lady, sister-in-law of the Hon. Mrs Jamieson. *Cranford*, Mrs Gaskell, 1853.

Glenvarlock, Lord. *See* NIGEL OLIFAUNT.

Glim, Rev. Mr, curate at Endelstow. *A Pair of Blue Eyes*, T. Hardy, 1873.

Glitters, Lucy, actress and sportswoman, m. Soapey Sponge. *Mr Sponge's Sporting Tour*, 1853, and *Mr Facey Romford's Hounds*, 1865, R. S. Surtees.

Glock. *Beau Geste*, P. C. Wren, 1924.

Gloriana. *The Faërie Queene* (poem), E. Spenser, 1590.

Glorieux, le, jester to Charles the Bold. *Quentin Durward*, W. Scott, 1823.

Glossin, Gilbert, Ellangowan's agent, a 'wily scoundrel.' *Guy Mannering*, W. Scott, 1815.

Glossmore, Lord. *Money* (play), Lord Lytton, 1840.

Glossop, assistant master, Stanstead School. *The Little Nugget*, P. G. Wodehouse, 1913.

Glossop, Sir Roderick, nerve specialist.
 Honoria, his daughter.
Thank You, Jeeves, P. G. Wodehouse, 1934.

Gloster, Duchess of (hist.). *Richard the Second* (play), W. Shakespeare.

Gloster, Duke of, Prince Humphrey (hist.). *Henry the Fourth* and *Henry the Fifth* (plays), W. Shakespeare.

Gloster, Duke of, Protector (hist.).
 His wife.
Henry the Sixth (play), W. Shakespeare.

Gloster, Earl of. *King Lear* (play), W. Shakespeare.

Gloster, Sir Anthony, Bt, merchant prince.
 Dick, his son.
'The Mary Gloster' (poem), *The Seven Seas*, R. Kipling, 1896.

Gloucester, forger. *Diary of a Late Physician*, S. Warren, 1832.

Glover, rival of Captain Wilson. *The Skipper's Wooing*, W. W. Jacobs, 1897.

Glover, Catherine ('The Fair Maid').
 Simon, her father.
 Dorothy, his housekeeper.
The Fair Maid of Perth, W. Scott, 1828.

Glowry, Scotch surgeon, fellow club member with Major Pendennis. *Pendennis*, W. M. Thackeray, 1848–50.

Glowry, Christopher, owner of the abbey.
 Scythrop, his son.
Nightmare Abbey, T. L. Peacock, 1818.

Glumboso, Prime Minister to King Valoroso. *The Rose and the Ring*, W. M. Thackeray, 1855.

Glumdalitch, Gulliver's child nurse in Brobdingnag. *Gulliver's Travels*, J. Swift, 1726.

Glyde, Sir Percival, Bt.
 Laura, his wife.
The Woman in White, W. Collins, 1860.

Glyn, Horace. *The Prisoner of Zenda*, A. Hope, 1894.

Gnatho. *Parliament of Bees* (play), J. Day, 1641.

Goate, Silas, mate of the *Dusky Bride*. *Tom Fool*, F. Tennyson Jesse, 1926.

Gobble, Justice.
 His wife and daughter.
Sir Lancelot Greaves, T. Smollett, 1762.

Gobbo, Launcelot, clown.
 Old Gobbo, his father.
The Merchant of Venice (play), W. Shakespeare.

Gobin, Marthe. *At the Villa Rose*, A. E. W. Mason, 1910.

Gobind, a holy man. 'The Finances of the Gods' (s.s.), and Preface, *Life's Handicap*, R. Kipling, 1891.

Gobrias, father of Arbaces. *A King and No King* (play), Beaumont & Fletcher, 1611.

Goby, saddler, of Treddlestone. *Adam Bede*, George Eliot, 1859.

Goby, Captain, friend of Mrs Mackenzie, middle-aged and kindly. *The Newcomes*, W. M. Thackeray, 1853–5.

Godall, Theophilus. *See* FLORIZEL.

Godalming, Lord. *Dracula*, Bram Stoker, 1897.

Godbold, Mrs Ruth, laundress, a simple, kind woman. *Riders in the Chariot*, Patrick White, 1961.

Godby, Albert, ticket collector. *Brief Encounter* (play), N. Coward, 1945.

Goddard, District Inspector, R.I.C. *The Search Party*, G. A. Birmingham, 1913.

Goddard, Mrs, mistress of a Highbury boarding-school. *Emma*, Jane Austen, 1816.

Goddard, Giles, m. Toni Rakonitz.
 Babs, Paul and **Anthony,** their children.
 Jimmy, Giles's father.
 Nancy, his dead mother.
 Reginald and **Fred,** his brothers.
A Deputy was King, G. B. Stern, 1926.

Godden, Joanna, wealthy landowner.
Ellen, her sister.
Joanna Godden, Sheila Kaye-Smith, 1921.

Godesberg, Margrave of (Karl).
Theodora, his wife.
A Legend of the Rhine, W. M. Thackeray, 1845.

Godfrey, Ben, of Fourhouses Farm. *The End of the House of Alard,* Sheila Kaye-Smith, 1923.

Godfrey, Mrs Ella.
Her two daughters.
'The Dog Hervey' (s.s.), *A Diversity of Creatures,* R. Kipling, 1917.

Godmer, British giant. *The Faërie Queene* (poem), E. Spenser, 1590.

Godowsky, Rusty, youth with sex appeal. *Myra Breckinridge,* Gore Vidal, 1968.

Godsoe, Sergeant John. 'A Madonna of the Trenches' (s.s.), *Debits and Credits,* R. Kipling, 1926.

Godwin, Dr. *Adam Bede,* George Eliot, 1859.

Godwyn, Robert, 'mender of nets,' rebel. *The Old Dominion,* Mary Johnston, 1899.

Goesler, Marie Max. *Phineas Finn,* 1869, and elsewhere, A. Trollope.

Goffe, captain of the *Fortune's Favourite. The Pirate,* W. Scott, 1822.

Goffe, tenant farmer, Rabbits' End. *Felix Holt,* George Eliot, 1866.

Gog, with Magog and Og, three Tower giants. *The Tower of London,* W. H. Ainsworth, 1840.

Gogan, Mrs, charwoman.
Mollser, her daughter.
The Plough and the Stars (play), S. O'Casey, 1926.

Gogan, Mary Anne, Irish spinster on holiday in Italy. 'Liars' (s.s.), *The Talking Trees,* Sean O'Faolain, 1971.

Gogol (Tuesday). *The Man who was Thursday,* G. K. Chesterton, 1908.

Goguelat, French prisoner of war, killed in duel with St Ives. *St Ives,* R. L. Stevenson, 1897.

Golbusto, Emperor of Lilliput. *Gulliver's Travels,* J. Swift, 1726.

Gold, Agnes, invalid friend of Kent Falconer. *Over Bemerton's,* E. V. Lucas, 1908.

Goldfinger, Auric, richest man in the world. *Goldfinger,* Ian Fleming, 1959.

Golding, Emily, m. James Forsyte. The *Forsyte* series, J. Galsworthy, 1906–33.

Goldmore, Colonel, from India. *The Book of Snobs,* W. M. Thackeray, 1846–7.

Goldner, Mrs, cleaner at the hospital. *Joy and Josephine,* Monica Dickens, 1948.

Goldring, Gertrude, Australian. *Pilgrimage,* Dorothy M. Richardson, 1915–38.

Goldsmith, Cecil, college tutor.
Carol, his wife.
Lucky Jim, K. Amis, 1953.

Goldsmith, Mrs Henry, Esther Ansell's benefactress. *Children of the Ghetto,* Israel Zangwill, 1892.

Goldstein, Emmanuel, Enemy of the People. *1984,* G. Orwell, 1949.

Goldthorpe, young writer. *The House of Cobwebs* (s.s.), G. Gissing, 1906.

Goldthred, Laurence, mercer, of Abingdon. *Kenilworth,* W. Scott, 1821.

'Goldy-Hair, Miss,' m. Geoffrey Gower. *The Boys and I,* Mrs Molesworth.

Golightly, Lieutenant. 'The Arrest of Lieutenant Golightly' (s.s.), *Plain Tales from the Hills,* R. Kipling, 1888.

Golightly, Mrs, employer of Elizabeth Herries. *The Fortress,* Hugh Walpole, 1932.

Golightly, Holiday (Holly), a gay girl travelling. *Breakfast at Tiffany's,* Truman Capote, 1958.

Gollaby, Lady (Augusta). *Albert Grope,* F. O. Mann, 1931.

Gollantz, Emmanuel.
His sons:
Max Algernon.
Angela, his wife.
Their children.
Emmanuel.
Julian.
Bill.
Young Emmanuel, 1932, and elsewhere, Naomi Jacob.

Gollo.
Tessa, his wife.
Romola, George Eliot, 1863.

Gollop, Joe Sedley's London doctor. *Vanity Fair,* W. M. Thackeray, 1847–8.

Golloper, Sir George.
His wife.
The Book of Snobs, W. M. Thackeray, 1846–7.

Gollwitzer, Herr, famous conductor.
Friedl, his adopted baby.
They Wanted to Live, Cecil Roberts, 1939.

Golp, Mrs, of the Church of Ancient Truth.
Her dead husband.
Albert Grope, F. O. Mann, 1931.

Golspie, Mr Lena. *Angel Pavement,* J. B. Priestley, 1930.

Golubchik, H.H. Prince, masquerading as Papkov, his valet. *The Weak and the Strong,* G. Kersh, 1945.

Gombauld, artist. *Crome Yellow,* Aldous Huxley, 1922.

Gombold, hero-pilgrim, chief character. *Head to Toe,* Joe Orton, 1971.

Gomez. *Pizarro* (play), R. B. Sheridan, 1799.

Gomez, Miss, Jamaican orphan, office cleaner, striptease club performer and prostitute, saved by Church of Brethren of the Way, causing havoc in London suburb. Central character. *Miss Gomez and The Brethren,* William Trevor, 1971.

Gomez, Federico, formerly Fred Culverwell. *The Elder Statesman* (play), T. S. Eliot, 1958.

Goneril, daughter of Lear. *King Lear* (play), W. Shakespeare.

Gonsalez, Leon, one of the four just men sworn to execute justice on evildoers who escaped the law, with Thery, Poiccart and George Manfred. *The Four Just Men,* E. Wallace, 1905.

Gonzague, Louis de, Prince, m. as 2nd husband Gabrielle de Nevers, *née* de Caylus, *The Duke's Motto,* J. H. McCarthy, 1908.

Gonzago, Louisa. *See* BASIL MERTOUN.

Gonzales, Colonel don Elias, commandant, El Paso. *Anthony Adverse,* Hervey Allen, 1934.

Gonzales, Pablo. *A Streetcar Named Desire* (play), Tennessee Williams, 1949.

Gonzalo, an honest counsellor. *The Tempest* (play), W. Shakespeare.

Gonzalo, follower of Pizarro. *Pizarro* (play), R. B. Sheridan, 1799.

Gooch, Mr, solicitor. *The Good Companions,* J. B. Priestley, 1929.

Good, Fluther, carpenter. *The Plough and the Stars* (play), S. O'Casey, 1926.

Good, Commander John, R.N. (retd) (native name Bongwan), one of the three explorers. *See* ALAN QUATERMAIN. *King Solomon's Mines,* H. Rider Haggard, 1885.

Good. Matilda, kindly boarding-house keeper. *The Dream,* H. G. Wells, 1924.

Goodacre, Rev. Simon, Vicar of Pagglesham. *Busman's Honeymoon,* Dorothy L. Sayers, 1937.

Goodall, Walter, a consumptive. 'A Fog in Santone' (s.s.), *Rolling Stones,* O. Henry, 1913.

Goodenough, naturalist and explorer, employer of Frank Hargate. *By Sheer Pluck,* G. A. Henty, 1883.

Goodenough, Mrs. *Wives and Daughters,* Mrs Gaskell, 1866.

Goodenough, Mrs. *The Mayor of Casterbridge,* T. Hardy, 1886.

Goodenough, Dr John, generous and kindly friend. *Pendennis,* 1848–1850, and elsewhere, W. M. Thackeray.

Goodfellow, Charles. *Thou Art the Man* (s.s.), E. A. Poe.

Goodfellow, Robin, 'Puck' of the Shaws Dramaticals. *St Ronan's Well,* W. Scott, 1824.

Goodhay, J. C., militant rural evangelist. *The Snopes* trilogy, William Faulkner, 1940–59.

Goodheart, Adam, Sir Ruthven Murgatroyd's manservant. *Ruddigore* (comic opera), Gilbert & Sullivan, 1887.

Goodluck, Gawyn, affianced to Dame Custance. *Ralph Roister Doister,* N. Udall, 1551.

Goodman, Mrs, chaperon to Paula Power. *A Laodicean,* T. Hardy, 1881.

Goodman, Rev. Timothy. *Hawbuck Grange,* R. S. Surtees, 1847.

Goodnight, Gracie, Kang Foo Ah's shop assistant. *Gracie Goodnight* (s.s.), T. Burke.

Goodpenny, Janet, librarian, *Chicago Sentinel,* Paris. *Trial by Terror,* P. Gallico, 1952.

Goodrich, drawing master. *The Mill on the Floss,* George Eliot, 1860.

Goodricke, Dr. *The Woman in White,* W. Collins, 1860.

Goodstock the Host (alias Lord Frampul), innkeeper. *The New Inn* (play), B. Jonson, 1630.
Goodwill, keeper of the wicket-gate. *Pilgrim's Progress,* J. Bunyan, 1678, 1684.
Goodwillie, Professor.
His sister.
The Professor's Love Story (play), J. M. Barrie, 1894.
Goodwin, wood inlayer, member of the Philosophers' Club. *Daniel Deronda,* George Eliot, 1859.
Goodwin, Archie (alias Andrew), chief assistant to Nero Wolfe, central character and narrator, in love with Madeline Sperling. *The Second Confession,* Rex Stout, 1950.
Goodwin, Clara.
Colonel Goodwin, her father.
Adventures of Harry Richmond, G. Meredith, 1871.
Goodwin, Frank, American speculator, m. Isabel Wahrfield. *Cabbages and Kings,* O. Henry, 1905.
Goodwin, Lee. *Sanctuary,* W. Faulkner, 1931.
Goodwood, Caspar, Isabel Archer's American suitor. *The Portrait of a Lady,* Henry James, 1881.
Goold, Ted, grocer who receives a knighthood.
Daisy, his wife, farm girl.
Prisoner of Grace, Joyce Cary, 1952.
Goole, Peter. *Cautionary Tales,* H. Belloc, 1907.
Goon, Cary, m. Jassy Radlett. *The Pursuit of Love,* Nancy Mitford, 1945.
Goorall, Yanko, castaway, m. Amy Foster.
Little Johnnie, their son.
'Amy Foster' (s.s.), *Typhoon,* J. Conrad, 1903.
Goose, Gibbie, a small half-witted lad. *Old Mortality,* W. Scott, 1816.
Gooseberry, Lord (Hugo). *We're Here,* D. Mackail, 1947.
Gopak, ex-friend of Nameless. *The Hollow Man* (s.s.), T. Burke.
Gorboduc, King of Britain.
Videna, his queen.
Ferrex and **Porrex,** their sons.
Gorboduc (play), T. Sackville & T. Norton, 1562.
Gorby, Sam, detective. *The Mystery of a Hansom Cab,* F. Hume, 1886.
Gordon, mate of the *Mohock*. *The Good Ship 'Mohock,'* W. Clark Russell, 1894.
Gordon, Colonel. *Prince Otto,* R. L. Stevenson, 1885.
Gordon, Major, friend of Captain Brown, m. Jessie Brown. *Cranford,* Mrs Gaskell, 1853.
Gordon, Miss. *See* LADY FLORIMEL COLONSAY.
Gordon, Squire.
George, his son, killed hare-coursing.
Black Beauty, Anna Sewell, 1877.
Gordon, Lord George (hist.). *Barnaby Rudge,* C. Dickens, 1841.
Gordon, Captain Hugh Montgomery. *Non-Combatants and Others,* Rose Macaulay, 1916.
Gordon, Jocelyn, central character.
Maurice, her brother.
With Edged Tools, H. Seton Merriman, 1894.
Gordon, John, m. Dolores Bradley.
Francis, their son, m. Beatrice Cochrane.
Peter Jackson, Cigar Merchant, G. Frankau, 1919.
Gordon, Lady Katherine. *Perkin Warbeck* (play), John Ford, 1634.
Gordon, Regina. *Counsellor-at-Law* (play), Elmer Rice, 1931.
Gordon, Stephen Mary Olivia Gertrude, central character.
Sir Philip, her father.
Lady Anne, her mother.
The Well of Loneliness, Radclyffe Hall, 1928.
Gordon-Nasmyth, explorer and exploiter of 'quap.' *Tono Bungay,* H. G. Wells, 1909.
Gore, 'Lawyer.' *The Mill on the Floss,* George Eliot, 1860.
Gore, Bill, gang-leader and bully, shot by Smallways. *The War in the Air,* H. G. Wells, 1908.
Gore-Urquhart, Julius, rich devotee of the arts. *Lucky Jim,* K. Amis, 1953.
Goren, tailor. *Evan Harrington,* G. Meredith, 1861.
Gorgon, Major-General Sir George.
His wife, brewer's daughter.
George Augustus, their son.
Henrietta, their daughter.
Other children.
Lucy, his niece.
Her mother.

The Bedford Row Conspiracy, W. M. Thackeray, 1840.

Goring, senior constable. *Robbery under Arms,* R. Boldrewood, 1888.

Goring, Viscount (Arthur), son of the Earl of Caversham. *An Ideal Husband* (play), O. Wilde, 1895.

Goro. *Romola,* George Eliot, 1863.

Gorsand, Mrs. *The Judge's Story,* C. Morgan, 1947.

Gorton, Bill, friend of Jake Barnes. *The Sun Also Rises* (or *Fiesta*), Ernest Hemingway, 1926.

Gosford, farmer.
His wife.
Catherine Furze, M. Rutherford, 1893.

Gosheron, builder. *All Passion Spent,* V. Sackville-West, 1931.

Gosling, Giles, landlord of the Black Bear, Cumnor.
Cicely, his daughter.
Kenilworth, W. Scott, 1821.

Gostrey, Maria, friend of Lambert Strether. *The Ambassadors,* Henry James, 1903.

Gotch, Sir John, landowner, Siddermorton. *The Wonderful Visit,* H. G. Wells, 1895.

Gott, Giles, tutor to Noel Gylby, eminent Elizabethan scholar. *Hamlet, Revenge!,* M. Innes, 1937.

Gottesheim, Killian, of the River Farm.
Ottila, his daughter.
Prince Otto, R. L. Stevenson, 1885.

Gottfried, Sir, traitor. *A Legend of the Rhine,* W. M. Thackeray, 1845.

Gottlieb, August. *The Human Comedy,* W. Saroyan, 1943.

Gottlieb, Professor Max.
His wife.
Miriam, his daughter.
Robert, his son.
Martin Arrowsmith, Sinclair Lewis, 1925.

Gottschalk, Mrs, Grope's landlady.
Her husband.
Albert Grope, F. O. Mann, 1931.

Goudremark, Baron Heinrich von. *Prince Otto,* R. L. Stevenson, 1885.

Gould, Humphrey, idle bachelor. 'The Melancholy Hussar' (s.s.), *Life's Little Ironies,* T. Hardy, 1894.

Gould, May, school friend of the Bartons. *A Drama in Muslin,* C. Moore, 1886.

Gould, Moses. *Manalive,* G. K. Chesterton, 1912.

Goumont, Hougomont. 'The Peasant's Confession,' *Wessex Poems,* T. Hardy, 1898.

Goupilliere, Belgian criminal. *The Seven Who Fled,* Frederic Prokosch, 1937.

Gourlay, Mr. *Shall We Join the Ladies?* (play), J. M. Barrie, 1921.

Gourlay, Ailshire, jester to Sir Anthony Wardour. *The Antiquary,* W. Scott, 1816.

Gourlay, John, corn-broker and carter.
His wife.
John, his son.
The House with the Green Shutters, G. Douglas, 1901.

Governor, Jack, sailor. *The Haunted House,* C. Dickens, 1859.

Gow, Harmon, 'village oracle.' *Ethan Frome,* Edith Wharton, 1911.

Gow (Smith), Henry ('Hal of the Wynd'). *The Fair Maid of Perth,* W. Scott, 1828.

Gowan, Harry, artist, m. 'Pet' Meagles. *Little Dorrit,* C. Dickens, 1857.

Gower, an officer. *Henry the Fourth* and *Henry the Fifth* (plays), W. Shakespeare.

Gower, as chorus. *Pericles* (play), W. Shakespeare.

Gower, Arthur, vice-chancellor.
Sir William, his father.
Trafalgar, his aunt.
Trelawny of the Wells (play), A. W. Pinero, 1898.

Gower, Horace.
Marie, his wife.
Audrey, Tom and **Racey,** their children.
Geoffrey, his brother, m. 'Miss Goldy-hair.'
The Boys and I, Mrs Molesworth.

Gowing, friend of the Pooters. *The Diary of a Nobody,* G. & W. Grossmith, 1892.

Gowran, 'Andy,' steward and bailiff of Portray Castle. *The Eustace Diamonds,* A. Trollope, 1873.

Grace, Captain, drunken officer in Virginia. *The Virginians,* W. M. Thackeray, 1857–9.

Grace, Mabel, actress. *Red Peppers* (play), Noël Coward, 1936.

Grace, Tony, cousin and heir of General Burton, m. Aileen Burke.

'General Burton's Ghost' (s.s.), *Countrymen All*, Katherine Tynan, 1915.

Gracedieu, Rev. Abel.
Eunice, his daughter, m. Philip Dunboyne.
Helena, his adopted daughter.
The Legacy of Cain, W. Collins, 1889.

Graceless. *See* CHRISTIAN.

Gradfield, Mr, Budmouth architect. *Desperate Remedies*, T. Hardy, 1871.

Gradgrind, Thomas, retired millowner.
His wife.
Thomas jnr, his son, embezzling bank clerk.
Louisa, his daughter, m. Josiah Bounderby.
Hard Times, C. Dickens, 1854.

Gradka, Mixo-Lydian maid of the Fieldings. *Miss Bunting*, Angela Thirkell, 1945.

Gradman, Thomas, clerk to Soames Forsyte. The *Forsyte* series, J. Galsworthy, 1906–33.

Gradus, Jacob, an assassin. *Pale Fire*, Vladimir Nabokov, 1962.

Grady, 'common mariner,' of the *Sarah*. *The Master of Ballantrae*, R. L. Stevenson, 1889.

Grady, servant of Captain Strong and Colonel Altamont. *Pendennis*, W. M. Thackeray, 1848–50.

Grady, Dan, Irish soldier. 'The Mutiny of the Mavericks' (s.s.), *Life's Handicap*, R. Kipling, 1891.

Graem, Margery, faithful nurse of Garth Dalmain. *The Rosary*, Florence Barclay, 1909.

Graeme, Alison, kinswoman and heiress of Ballantrae, m. Henry, Lord Ballantrae. *The Master of Ballantrae*, R. L. Stevenson, 1889.

Graeme, Donald, m. Jan Challard. *Still She Wished for Company*, Margaret Irwin, 1924.

Graeme, Roland, son of Julian Avenel and Catherine of Newport.
Magdalen, his grandmother.
The Abbot, W. Scott, 1820.

Graff, Stanley, salesman. *Babbitt*, Sinclair Lewis, 1923.

Grafinski, treasurer, Gottesheim. *Prince Otto*, R. L. Stevenson, 1885.

Grafton. 'Piffingcap' (s.s.), *Adam and Eve and Pinch Me*, A. E. Coppard, 1921.

Grafton, John.
Lisbet, *née* Prinsloo, his wife.
Their children:
Adrian, m. Suzanna Strijdom.
Andries.
Piet, m. Lavinia Haskard.
James, their son.
Janse.
Maria, m. Carel Strijdom.
Sarie, m. Hans Oosthuizen.
The City of Gold, F. Brett Young, 1939.

Graham, discovered by Isbister in an apparent cataleptic trance for over two hundred years. *When the Sleeper Awakes*, H. G. Wells, 1899.

Graham, Alexander. *See* JACK BAILEY.

Graham, Alexander, schoolmaster to Lossie, and preacher. *The Marquis of Lossie*, G. Macdonald, 1877.

Graham, Cecil. *Lady Windermere's Fan* (play), O. Wilde, 1892.

Graham, Mrs Helen, m. (2) Arthur Huntingdon, (3) Gilbert Markham.
Arthur, her son by 1st husband.
The Tenant of Wildfell Hall, Anne Brontë, 1848.

Graham, J. H., m. (2) Mrs Holbrook.
Emily, his blind daughter, m. Philip Amory.
The Lamplighter, Maria S. Cummins, 1854.

Graham, John, head of Graham & Co., pork-packers, Chicago.
Pierrepont, his son, at Harvard.
Letters from a Self-made Merchant to his Son, G. H. Lorimer, 1903.

Graham, Lucy. *See* LADY AUDLEY.

Graham, Mary, m. Martin Chuzzlewit. *Martin Chuzzlewit*, C. Dickens, 1844.

Graham, Sir Robert.
Agnes, his wife, *née* Leslie.
Their children:
James.
John.
Robert.
Emmy, m. Tom Grantly.
Clarissa, m. Charles Belton.
Edith, m. Rev. Lord William Harcourt.
The *Barsetshire* series, Angela Thirkell, 1933 onwards.

Grahn, Dr. *Armgart* (poem), George Eliot, 1871.

Grainger, family lawyer to the Vibart family. *The Broad Highway*, J. Farnol, 1910.

Grainger, Dr, called when P. Boyes was found dying. *Strong Poison,* Dorothy L. Sayers, 1930.

Grammont, V. V., daughter of American oil millionaire. *The Secret Places of the Heart,* H. G. Wells, 1922.

Grampus, Alderman.
His wife.
Adeliza, their daughter.
The Professor, W. M. Thackeray, 1837.

Grampus, Greenland. *Theophrastus Such,* George Eliot, 1879.

Granby, Lieutenant-Colonel Alistair, central character, m. Julia Hazelrigg. *The Four Armourers,* 1930, and others, F. Beeding.

Grand, Digby, young Guards' officer.
Sir Peregrine, his father.
Digby Grand, G. Whyte-Melville, 1853.

Grand Lunar, Ruler of the Moon. *The First Men in the Moon,* H. G. Wells, 1901.

Grandamour. *The Pastyme of Pleasure* (poem), S. Hawes, 1509.

Grandcourt, Henleigh Mallinger, m. Gwen Harleth.
Henleigh, his father, formerly Mallinger, m. Miss Grandcourt and took her name. *See also* COLONEL GLASHER.
Daniel Deronda, George Eliot, 1876.

Grandier, Urbain. *The Devils,* J. Whiting, 1961.

Grandison, Cardinal. *Lothair,* B. Disraeli, 1870.

Grandison, Hon. Sir Charles, 'faultily faultless' English aristocrat, central character, m. Harriet Byron.
Caroline, his sister, m. Lord L.
Charlotte, his sister.
Sir Thomas, his father.
Charles, his cousin.
Sir Charles Grandison, S. Richardson, 1754.

Grandison, Gerald, artist in Paris, m. Anne Dunnock. *Go She Must!,* David Garnett, 1927.

Grandoni, Madame. *Roderick Hudson,* H. James, 1875.

Graneangowl, chaplain to the Marquis of Argyll. *The Legend of Montrose,* W. Scott, 1819.

Grange, Captain Blake, V.C., cousin of Daisy Musgrave. *The Way of an Eagle,* Ethel M. Dell, 1912.

Granger, Bill. *The Quiet American,* Graham Greene, 1955.

Granger, Edith, m. as 2nd wife Paul Dombey Snr. *Dombey and Son,* C. Dickens, 1848.

Grangerford, Colonel.
His wife.
Their children: **Bob, Tom, Charlotte** and **Sophia.**
The Adventures of Huckleberry Finn, Mark Twain, 1884.

Grant, of Loranogie, farmer. *The House with the Green Shutters,* G. Douglas, 1901.

Grant, Dr.
Susan and **Enid,** his daughters.
In Cotton Wool, W. B. Maxwell, 1912.

Grant, Mrs, daughter of Mr Skellorn. *Hilda Lessways,* Arnold Bennett, 1911.

Grant, Rev. Dr.
His wife.
Mansfield Park, Jane Austen, 1814.

Grant, Rev. Mr, in love with Verity Cantacute. *Crump Folk Going Home,* Constance Holme, 1913.

Grant, Detective Inspector Alan, of Scotland Yard. *The Franchise Affair,* 1948, and others, Josephine Tey.

Grant, General Archibald.
Annie, his daughter, m. Lewis Arundel.
Lewis Arundel, F E. Smedley, 1852.

Grant, Bertha, m. Latimer. *The Lifted Veil,* George Eliot, 1859.

Grant, Donovan ('Red'), who becomes Krassno Granitski, chief executioner of SMERSH, the official murder organization of the Soviet Union. *From Russia, With Love,* Ian Fleming, 1957.

Grant, Hilary, cousin of the Brandons, m. Delia Brandon. The *Barsetshire* series, Angela Thirkell, 1933 onwards.

Grant, Jennico, cousin of Kerry Macfarlane.
Alleyne, his wife ('Allie-Dolly').
Destiny Bay, Donn Byrne, 1928.

Grant, Nan.
Ben, her husband, carpenter and seaman.
The Lamplighter, Maria S. Cummins, 1854.

Grant, Sheila. *The Secret Vanguard,* M. Innes, 1940.

Grant, General Ulysses S. (hist.). *Abraham Lincoln* (play), J. Drinkwater, 1918.

Grant, William, of Prestongrange, Lord Advocate of Scotland.
His three daughters.
Miss Grant, his sister and housekeeper.
Catriona, R. L. Stevenson, 1893.

Grantchester, Lord, father of Reggie Bristow. *The Babe, B.A.*, E. F. Benson, 1897.

Grantly, Bishop of Barchester.
Theophilus, his son, archdeacon, m. Susan Harding.
Their children:
Charles.
Henry.
Samuel.
Florinda.
Griselda, m. Lord Dumbello.
The Warden, 1855, *Barchester Towers*, 1857, and others, A. Trollope.

Grantly, Rev. Septimus.
His wife.
Their children:
Tom, m. Emmy Graham.
Eleanor, m. Colin Keith.
Grace, m. Lord Lufton.
The *Barsetshire* series, Angela Thirkell, 1933 onwards.

Grant-Menzies, Jock, friend of Tony Last. *A Handful of Dust*, Evelyn Waugh, 1934.

Granton, Frederick. *The Queen's Husband* (play), R. E. Sherwood, 1928.

Granvile, George, grown-up incarnation of Martin Richmond.
Phyllis, his wife.
Their daughters:
Janet.
Sylvia.
Rose.
Thunder on the Left, C. Morley, 1925.

Granville, Juliet. *The Wanderer*, Fanny Burney, 1814.

Grapnell & Co., firm whose failure ruins Mrs Davilow. *Daniel Deronda*, George Eliot, 1876.

Gratiano, friend of Antonio. *The Merchant of Venice*, W. Shakespeare.

Grattan. Edmund, of *The Liberal*, m. Margaret Hubbard. *The Street of Adventure*, P. Gibbs, 1909.

Gravell, Walter.
James ('Jerry'), his son.
'Beauty Spots' (s.s.), *Limits and Renewals*, R. Kipling, 1932.

Graves. *Money* (play), Lord Lytton, 1840.

Graves, Sir Reuben Levy's valet. *Whose Body?*, Dorothy L. Sayers, 1923.

Graves, Josiah, bank manager.
His son.
Of Human Bondage, W. S. Maugham, 1915.

Graves, Muley. *Grapes of Wrath*, J. Steinbeck, 1939.

Graves family, the, English emigrants. *Settlers in Canada*, Captain Marryat, 1844.

Graviter, Edward. *Loyalties* (play), J. Galsworthy, 1922.

Gray, disreputable fellow conspirator of Wolfe Macfarlane. 'The Body Snatcher' (s.s.), *The Wrong Box*, R. L. Stevenson & L. Osbourne, 1889.

Gray, Captain, of the *Polynia*.
His wife.
Born to be a Sailor, G. Stables.

Gray, Lady, aunt of Edgar Doe. *Tell England*, E. Raymond, 1922.

Gray, Mrs, milliner. *The Mill on the Floss*, George Eliot, 1860.

Gray, Abe, of the *Hispaniola*. *Treasure Island*, R. L. Stevenson, 1883.

Gray, Alice, 'ancient domestic' of the Ravenswoods.
Habbie, her husband.
The Bride of Lammermoor, W. Scott, 1819.

Gray, Dorian, central character. *The Picture of Dorian Gray*, O. Wilde, 1891.

Gray, Edward. *Edward Gray* (poem), Lord Tennyson.

Gray, Elizabeth, nurse, m. Oliver North. *The Happy Prisoner*, Monica Dickens, 1946.

Gray, Ewan, in love with Esther Sinclair. *My Mortal Enemy*, Willa Cather, 1928.

Gray, Fielding, novelist, formerly regular officer of the Light Dragoons. *The Sabre Squadron*, 1966, and others in the *Alms for Oblivion* sequence, Simon Raven.

Gray, Gideon, surgeon, of Middlemas.
Jean, his wife.
Menie, their daughter.
The Surgeon's Daughter, W. Scott, 1827.

Gray, Jenny, schoolgirl, member of

'the Brodie Set'. *The Prime of Miss Jean Brodie,* Muriel Spark, 1961.

Gray, Lucy. *Lucy Gray* (poem), W. Wordsworth.

Gray, Nelly. *Faithless Nelly Gray* (poem), T. Hood.

Gray, Pauline, school friend of Joy Stretton. *Joy and Josephine,* Monica Dickens, 1948.

Gray, Raymond, barrister, 'an ingenuous youth without the least practice.'
His wife.
Polly, their daughter.
The Book of Snobs, W. M. Thackeray, 1846–7.

Gray, Robin. *Auld Robin Gray* (poem), Lady Anne Lyndsay.

Gray, Nurse Rosemary, alias of Jane Champion. *The Rosary,* Florence Barclay, 1909.

Gray, Walter.
Jock, his brother.
Madeleine and **Tishy,** his sisters.
Desolate Splendour, M. Sadleir, 1923.

Graye, Amos, architect.
His wife.
Cytherea, their daughter, m. Edward Springrove.
Owen, their son.
Desperate Remedies, T. Hardy, 1871.

Grayne, Olivia, niece of Mrs Bramson. *Night Must Fall* (play), Emlyn Williams, 1935.

Grayston, Lady George. *Our Betters* (play), W. S. Maugham, 1923.

Greatham, Richard. *Hay Fever* (play), N. Coward, 1925.

Greatheart, servant of the Interpreter. *Pilgrim's Progress,* J. Bunyan, 1678, 1684.

Greatheart, Emma, middle-aged gentlewoman. *Mother and Son,* Ivy Compton-Burnett, 1954.

Greatorix, Lady Elizabeth.
Agnew, her son, m. Jess Kissock.
The Lilac Sunbonnet, S. R. Crockett, 1894.

Greaves, Sir Lancelot, central character, m. Aurelia Darnel.
Sir Everhard, his father.
Jonathan, his uncle.
Dorothy, illegitimate daughter of Jonathan (*see* Cowslip), m. Thomas Clarke.
Sir Lancelot Greaves, T. Smollett, 1762.

Grecco, Al, a bootlegger (real name Tony Murascho). *Appointment in Samarra,* John O'Hara, 1935.

Greech, Henry, Bassington's uncle. *The Unbearable Bassington,* 'Saki' (H. H. Munro), 1912.

Greedy, Justice. *A New Way to Pay Old Debts* (play), P. Massinger, 1633.

Green, creature to Richard. *Richard the Second* (play), W. Shakespeare.

Green, Anthony, servant of Lady Constantine.
His wife, her maid.
Two on a Tower, T. Hardy, 1882.

Green, Bessie. *Counsellor-at-Law* (play), Elmer Rice, 1931.

Green, Edward, solicitor and unofficial guardian of Lucia Frensham.
Lottie, his daughter.
The Second Mrs Conford, Beatrice K. Seymour, 1951.

Green, Fred, m. Jane Higgins, *née* Bell.
Tom, his father.
His mother.
Arthur, his brother.
The Water Gipsies, A. P. Herbert, 1930.

Green, 'Goodhearted', sharp horse-trader. *Mr Facey Romford's Hounds,* R. S. Surtees, 1865.

Green, James, friend of Jorrocks. *Jorrocks's Jaunts and Jollities,* R. S. Surtees, 1838.

Green, Joe, stable boy. *Black Beauty,* Anna Sewell, 1877.

Green, John, boatman. 'Fellow Townsmen,' *Wessex Tales,* T. Hardy, 1888.

Green, Mrs Kate, countrywoman. *The French Lieutenant,* Richard Church, 1971.

Green, 'Poppet,' mistress of Basil Seal. *Put Out More Flags,* E. Waugh, 1942.

Green, Tom, one-armed ex-soldier. *Barnaby Rudge,* C. Dickens, 1841.

Green, Verdant, central character, undergraduate of Brazenface College, Oxford, m. Patty Honeywood.
Verdant, his father.
Mary, his mother.
His sisters:
Mary, m. Charles Larkyns.
Helen, m. Rev. Josiah Meek.

Fanny, m. Henry Bouncer.
The Adventures of Mr Verdant Green, C. Bede, 1853.

Greenacre, friend of Gammon. *The Town Traveller,* G. Gissing, 1898.

Greenbury, Countess of. *Monsieur Beaucaire* (play), Booth Tarkington, 1902.

Greene, Aubrey, artist. *The White Monkey,* J. Galsworthy, 1924.

Greene, Nicholas, poet pensioned by Orlando. *Orlando,* Virginia Woolf, 1928.

Greenfield, Oliver, central character.
Stephen, his brother.
The Fifth Form at St Dominic's, T. Baines Reed, 1887.

Greenfield, Paul, art historian.
Dora, his wife.
The Bell, Iris Murdoch, 1958.

Greengoose, George. *The Knight of the Burning Pestle* (play), Beaumont & Fletcher, 1609.

Greenhorn, Girnigo, Sir A. Wardour's man of business.
Gilbert, his son.
The Antiquary, W. Scott, 1816.

Greening, agent for Sir H. Alard. *The End of the House of Alard,* Sheila Kaye-Smith, 1923.

Greenleaf, Gilbert, old archer. *Castle Dangerous,* W. Scott, 1832.

Greensleeves, Dorothy. *St Ives,* R. L. Stevenson, 1897.

Greenway, Norah. 'Blind Man's Holiday' (s.s.), *Whirligigs,* O. Henry, 1910.

Greenways, Stephen, m. Val Power.
Giles, their son.
A Deputy was King, G. B. Stern, 1926 onwards.

Gregan, Desmond, m. Enid Mary Sinnott. *Mrs Eckdorf in O'Neill's Hotel,* William Trevor, 1969.

Gregarina, Miss. *Theophrastus Such,* George Eliot, 1879.

Gregg, A. B., *Compass Rose.*
Edith, his wife.
The Cruel Sea, N. Monsarrat, 1951.

Gregg, Billy, inmate of home for the aged. *The Poorhouse Fair,* John Updike, 1959.

Gregg, Marina, film star.
Jason Rudd, her 5th husband.
The Mirror Crack'd from Side to Side, Agatha Christie, 1962.

Gregory, celebrated doctor. *Weir of Hermiston,* R. L. Stevenson, 1896.

Gregory, Father, Roman Catholic priest. *Requiem for Robert,* Mary Fitt, 1942.

Gregory, Rev. Mr. 'The Treasure of Abbot Thomas' (s.s.), *Ghost Stories of an Antiquary,* M. R. James, 1910.

Gregory, Lucian, red-haired anarchic poet.
Rosamond, his sister.
The Man who was Thursday, G. K. Chesterton, 1908.

Gregory, Millicent, sister of Lewis Dodd. *The Constant Nymph,* Margaret Kennedy, 1924.

Gregsbury, pompous M.P. to whom Nicholas unsuccessfully applies for a post. *Nicholas Nickleby,* C. Dickens, 1839.

Gregson, Tobias, of Scotland Yard. *A Study in Scarlet,* 1887, and other Sherlock Holmes adventures, A. Conan Doyle.

Greme, Mrs, Lord M.'s housekeeper. *Clarissa Harlowe,* S. Richardson, 1748.

Gremio, suitor of Bianca. *The Taming of the Shrew* (play), W. Shakespeare.

Grendall, Lord Alfred. *The Way We Live Now,* A. Trollope, 1875.

Grendon, Joseph, a Norfolk farmer.
Marjorie, his wife.
Nancy, their daughter.
The Saliva Tree, Brian W. Aldiss, 1966.

Gresham, Prime Minister. *Phineas Finn,* 1869, and elsewhere, A. Trollope.

Gresham, Edith, widow.
Ernest, her dead husband.
David, her son.
The Prodigal Heart, Susan Ertz, 1950.

Gresham, Francis, m. Jane Palliser. *Miss Bunting,* Angela Thirkell, 1945.

Gresham, Frank, M.P., m. Lady Arabella de Courcy.
Their children:
Francis Newbold, m. Mary Thorne.
Augusta.
Beatrice, m. Rev. Caleb Oriel.
Nina.
Doctor Thorne, A. Trollope, 1858.

Gresham, Peter, publisher.
Evelyn, his wife, aunt of Denham Dobie.

Their children:
Catherine.
Tim, her husband.
Audrey.
Guy.
Humphrey.
Noel.
Crewe Train, Rose Macaulay, 1926.

Gresley, Harry.
His father.
Pip, Ian Hay, 1907.

Gretchen, German child. *A Kiss for Cinderella* (play), J. M. Barrie, 1916.

Gretry, Samuel, wheat broker. *The Pit*, F. Norris, 1903.

Grewgious, guardian of Rosa Bud. *Edwin Drood*, C. Dickens, 1870.

Grey, Lady, later Edward IV's queen. *Henry the Sixth* (play), W. Shakespeare.

Grey, Lord, son of Elizabeth. *Richard the Third* (play), W. Shakespeare.

Grey, Agnes, central character and narrator, m. Rev. Edward Weston.
Mary, her sister.
Richard, her father.
Her mother.
Agnes Grey, Anne Brontë, 1847.

Grey, Lady Caroline, aunt of Barty Josselin. *The Martian*, George du Maurier, 1897.

Grey, Fred, owner of motor-car wheel company.
Aline, his wife, in love with Bruce Dudley.
Dark Laughter, Sherwood Anderson, 1925.

Grey, John, central character, m. Jill Dealtry. *The City of Beautiful Nonsense*, E. T. Thurston, 1909.

Grey, Matt, smuggler. 'The Distracted Preacher,' *Wessex Tales*, T. Hardy, 1888.

Grey, Colonel Robert.
Alice, his wife.
Cosmo, their son.
Amy, their daughter.
Alice-sit-by-the-Fire (play), J. M. Barrie, 1905.

Grey, Una ('The Incubus'), George Knox's secretary. The *Barsetshire* series, Angela Thirkell, 1933 onwards.

Grey Brother, wolf friend of Mowgli. *The Jungle Books*, R. Kipling, 1894–5.

Greyman, James. *See* JAMES DOUGLAS.

Greymuzzle, a female otter. *Tarka the Otter*, H. Williamson, 1927.

Greystock, Frank, cousin of Lady Eustace and only son of the Bishop of Bobsborough. *The Eustace Diamonds*, A. Trollope, 1873.

Greystoke, Lord (John Clayton, Tarzan of the Apes).
Jane, his wife.
Jack (Korak), his son, m. Meriem (Jeanne Jacot).
The *Tarzan* series, E. R. Burroughs, 1912–32.

Gribling, Mr. 'Tea at Mrs Armsby's' (s.s.), *The Owl in the Attic*, J. Thurber, 1931.

Grice, Albert, handyman.
His wife, housekeeper to Philip Meldrum.
A Knight on Wheels, Ian Hay, 1916.

Grice, Superintendent Bill, C.I.D. Series of 'The Toff' detective novels, John Creasey, 1938 on.

Grice, Compson, Wilfrid Desert's publisher. *Flowering Wilderness*, 1932, and elsewhere, J. Galsworthy.

Gride, Arthur, miserly money-lender, eventually murdered. *Nicholas Nickleby*, C. Dickens, 1839.

Gridley, ruined Shropshire litigant in Court of Chancery. *Bleak House*, C. Dickens, 1853.

Grierson, John. *Hatter's Castle*, A. J. Cronin, 1931.

Grieve, Lady (Belinda).
Sir Algernon, her husband.
Daniel, their son, in love with Viola Marvell.
Desolate Splendour, M. Sadleir, 1923.

Grieve, David Suveret, central character, m. Lucy Purcell.
Sandy, their son.
Cecile, their daughter.
Alexander (Sandy), his father, cabinet-maker.
Louise, his mother.
Louie, his sister.
James, his grandfather.
Jenny, formerly Pierson, his grandmother.
Reuben, his uncle.
The History of David Grieve, Mrs Humphry Ward, 1892.

Griffin, scientific demonstrator, central character. *The Invisible Man*, H. G. Wells, 1897.

Griffin, next-door neighbour of the Pooters. *The Diary of a Nobody,* G. & W. Grossmith, 1892.

Griffin, Lady, widow of General Sir George Griffin, young, rich, m. Earl of Crabs.
Matilda, her stepdaughter, m. Hon. A. P. Deuceace.
'The Amours of Mr Deuceace,' *Yellowplush Papers,* 1852, and elsewhere, W. M. Thackeray.

Griffin, Mr and Mrs, parishioners of Rev. Mr Tyke. *Middlemarch,* George Eliot, 1871–2.

Griffin, Mrs, neighbour of the Longstaffes. 'Lucky Boy' (s.s.), *Louise,* Viola Meynell, 1954.

Griffin, Ray, ex-lover of Jane Monk. *The World in the Evening,* C. Isherwood, 1954.

Griffith, gentleman usher to Queen Catherine. *Henry the Eighth* (play), W. Shakespeare.

Griffith, Molly, illegitimate daughter of Renny Whiteoak.
Her supposed father.
Christopher, Althea, Gemmel and **Garda,** her half-brothers and half-sisters.
Wakefield's Course, Mazo de la Roche, 1942.

Griffiths, Clyde, central character.
Asa, his father.
Elvira, his mother.
Hester (Esta), his sister.
Julia, his sister.
Frank, his brother.
Samuel, his uncle.
Elizabeth, Samuel's wife.
Gilbert, Myra and **Bella,** their children.
An American Tragedy, T. Dreiser, 1925.

Griffiths, Dai, miner. *How Green Was My Valley,* R. Llewellyn, 1939.

Griffiths, Harry, friend of Philip Carey. *Of Human Bondage,* W. S. Maugham, 1915.

Griffiths, Samuel, London banker. *Redgauntlet,* W. Scott, 1824.

Grifone. 'The Duchess of Nono' (s.s.), *Little Novels of Italy,* M. Hewlett, 1899.

Grig, Lieutenant, ultimately **Colonel,** 'without two ideas.'
Lord Grig, his rich father.
Mrs Perkins's Ball, W. M. Thackeray, 1847.

Grigg, Captain, Life Guards.
Sir Joshua, his father.
Tom, his younger brother.
Vanity Fair, W. M. Thackeray, 1847–8.

Griggs, assistant in Grope's bookshop, m. Florrie Dewlap. *Albert Grope,* F. O. Mann, 1931.

Grigsby, Captain Mark. *Three Weeks,* Elinor Glyn, 1907.

Grildrig, Gulliver's name in Brobdingnag. *Gulliver's Travels,* J. Swift, 1726.

Grimaldi, Roman gentleman. *'Tis Pity She's A Whore* (play), John Ford, *c.* 1624.

Grimble, Mr. *Precious Bane,* Mary Webb, 1924.

Grimes, chimney sweep, employer of Tom. *The Water Babies,* C. Kingsley, 1863.

Grimes, lawyer. *Agatha's Husband,* Mrs Craik, 1853.

Grimes, Lady Charlotte Sydenham's lawyer. *Joan and Peter,* H. G. Wells, 1918.

Grimes, Mrs, housekeeper.
Henry, wharfinger, her brother-in-law.
The Hole in the Wall, A. Morrison, 1902.

Grimes, Edgar, bigamous crook. *Decline and Fall,* E. Waugh, 1928.

Grimes, John, an illegitimate boy.
Elizabeth, his mother.
Gabriel Grimes, a deacon, his stepfather.
Deborah, Gabriel's 1st wife.
Esther, Gabriel's mistress.
Royal, son of Gabriel and Esther.
Go Tell It On The Mountain, James Baldwin, 1953.

Grimes, Peter, drunkard, thief and murderer. *The Borough* (poem), G. Crabbe, 1810.

Grimley, Miss Jane.
Her father, friend of the Ledburys.
Horatio, her brother.
The Adventures of Mr Ledbury, Albert Smith, 1844.

Grimsby & Cole, publishers of Philip Boyes's books. *Strong Poison,* Dorothy L. Sayers, 1930.

Grimshaw, Helen, Miss Fothergill's companion. *The Shrimp and the Anemone,* L. P. Hartley, 1944.

Grimshaw, Nathaniel, central character, m. (1) Denny Sadgrove, (2) Ann, his cousin.
Sir James, his father.
Emily, his mother.
Daniel, Lord Grimshaw, his uncle.
Fanny, Daniel's wife.
Farewell to Youth, Storm Jameson, 1928.

Grimston, Austin Ruthyn's attorney. *Uncle Silas,* Sheridan le Fanu, 1864.

Grimstone, Dr, schoolmaster.
His wife.
Tom, their son.
Dulcie, their daughter, one-time sweetheart of Dick Bultitude.
Vice Versa, F. Anstey, 1882.

Grimstone, Mrs Jocasta, an old despot.
Hamilton, her son.
Osbert, Erica and **Amy,** children of a dead son.
The Last and the First, Ivy Compton-Burnett, 1971.

Grimthorpe, Dr. *Magic* (play), G. K. Chesterton, 1913.

Grimwig, lawyer friend of Brownlow. *Oliver Twist,* C. Dickens, 1838.

Grinderson, Gabriel, clerk, later partner of Gilbert Greenhorn. *The Antiquary,* W. Scott, 1816.

Grindley of Corpus, tutor to Clive Newcome. *The Newcomes,* W. M. Thackeray, 1853–5.

Grinny Granny, Brer Wolf's mother. *Uncle Remus,* J. C. Harris, 1880–1895.

Grinsell, Lord. *Middlemarch,* George Eliot, 1871–2.

Grinton, Lord, amateur jockey. 'The County Wench' (s.s.), *Last Recollections of My Uncle Charles,* N. Balchin, 1954.

Grip, Barnaby's raven. *Barnaby Rudge,* C. Dickens, 1841.

Gripp & Co., publishers. *Middlemarch,* George Eliot, 1871–2.

Grippy, Leddy, central character. *The Entail,* J. Galt, 1823.

Griselda, central character.
Grizzel and **Tabitha,** her great-aunts.
The Cuckoo Clock, Mrs Molesworth, 1877.

Grish Chunder, law student. 'The Finest Story in the World' (s.s.), *Many Inventions,* R. Kipling, 1893.

Grisha. *See* LAJOS.

Grits, Miss, plain but wealthy, m. Rev. Beilby Binny. *Vanity Fair,* W. M. Thackeray, 1847–8.

Grizel.
'The Painted Lady,' her mother.
Sentimental Tommy, J. M. Barrie, 1896.

Grizzle, Captain, half-pay officer. *The Book of Snobs,* W. M. Thackeray, 1846–7.

Grizzle, Mrs, sister of Gamaliel Pickle, m. Commodore Trunnion. *Peregrine Pickle,* T. Smollett, 1751.

Grobe, Rev. Nicholas.
Alice, his dead wife.
Tamar, their daughter.
Mr Weston's Good Wine, T. F. Powys, 1927.

Grobstock, Joseph, 'pillar of the Synagogue.'
His wife.
The King of Schnorrers, I. Zangwill, 1894.

Groby, Farmer, employer of Tess. *Tess of the D'Urbervilles,* T. Hardy, 1891.

Grocott, grocer.
Sarah, his daughter. *See* ORIANA CLARK.
Sophia, Stanley Weyman, 1900

Groder, Michael, villainous servant of Countess Luxstein. *The Courtship of Morrice Buckler,* A. E. W. Mason, 1896.

Grofina, a whore in a world of the future. *Earthjacket,* Jon Hartridge, 1970.

Grogan, William, telegraph operator. *The Human Comedy,* W. Saroyan, 1943.

Groombride, Lethabie, M.P. 'Little Foxes' (s.s.), *Actions and Reactions,* R. Kipling, 1909.

Groosens, Madame. *Mr Billingham, the Marquis and Madelon,* E. P. Oppenheim.

Grope, Albert Edward, central character and narrator, jilted by Rosalind Malley, m. Laurette Taube.
His mother.
Albert Grope, F. O. Mann, 1931.

Grose, Mrs, housekeeper at Bly, in charge of Miles and Flora. *The Turn of the Screw,* H. James, 1898.

Grosvenor, Archibald, an idyllic poet, m. Patience. *Patience* (comic opera), Gilbert & Sullivan, 1881.

Grotait, George, innkeeper. *Put Yourself in his Place,* C. Reade, 1870.

Grove, Mrs, widow, companion to Blake. 'Silver Trumpets' (s.s.), *Louise,* Viola Meynell, 1954.

Grove, Phyllis.
Her father.
'The Melancholy Hussar,' *Life's Little Ironies,* T. Hardy, 1894.

Grovelgrub, Dr. *Melincourt,* T. L. Peacock, 1817.

Groves, Sergeant. *A Way through the Wood,* N. Balchin, 1951.

Groves, 'Honest' James, publican and gambler. *The Old Curiosity Shop,* C. Dickens, 1841.

Grower, Mr, J.P. *The Mayor of Casterbridge,* T. Hardy, 1886.

Growltiger, bravo cat. *Old Possum's Book of Practical Cats,* T. S. Eliot, 1939.

Grubb, pal and partner of Bert Smallways. *The War in the Air,* H. G. Wells, 1908.

Grubbet, Jonathan, bookseller. *Waverley,* W. Scott, 1814.

Grudden, Mrs, member of Crummles's company. *Nicholas Nickleby,* C. Dickens, 1839.

Gruffanuff, Jenkins, ill-mannered porter turned into a brass knocker.
Countess Barbara Griselda, his hideous wife.
The Rose and the Ring, W. M. Thackeray, 1855.

Gruffydd, Rev. Merddyn, minister of the Morgans' chapel, in love with Angharad Morgan. *How Green Was My Valley,* R. Llewellyn, 1939.

Gruffydd-Williams, Vernon, wealthy citizen of Welsh town.
Elizabeth, his wife.
That Uncertain Feeling, Kingsley Amis, 1955.

Grumball, Dr. *Redgauntlet.* W. Scott, 1824.

Grumbit, Mrs Dorothy, aunt of Martin Rattler. *Martin Rattler,* R. M. Ballantyne, 1858.

Grumby, Major, bushwhacker Southerner, killer of Rosa Millard. *The Unvanquished,* William Faulkner, 1938.

Grundt, Philip.
Regina, his wife.
The Dove in the Eagle's Nest, Charlotte M. Yonge, 1866.

Grundy, Mrs, symbol of social convention. *Speed the Plough* (play), T. Morton, 1800.

Grundy, Sam. *Love on the Dole,* W. Greenwood, 1933.

Grundy, Solomon, court official.
His wife.
Adam's Opera (play), Clemence Dane, 1928.

Grunter, parish clerk.
His wife.
Mr Weston's Good Wine, T. F. Powvs, 1927.

Grusinskaya, Elisabeta, dancer. *Grand Hotel,* Vicki Baum, 1931.

Gryce, Percy. *The House of Mirth,* Edith Wharton, 1905.

Gryphon, The. *Alice in Wonderland,* L. Carroll, 1865.

Gryseworth, Dr.
His wife.
Netta and **Ellen,** their daughters.
The Lamplighter, Maria S. Cummins, 1854.

Guarine, Philip, squire to Hugo de Lacy. *The Betrothed,* W. Scott, 1825.

Guasconti, Giovanni, student of Padua. *Rappaccini's Daughter* (s.s.), N. Hawthorne, 1844.

Gubbins, Potiphar. 'Study of an Elevation in Indian Ink' (poem), *Departmental Ditties,* R. Kipling, 1886.

Gudruda the Fair. *See* ASMUNDSON ASMUND.

Gudyill, John, drunken butler. *Old Mortality,* W. Scott, 1816.

Guest, head clerk to Utterson. *Dr Jekyll and Mr Hyde.* R. L. Stevenson, 1886.

Guest, Stephen, in love with Maggie Tulliver, m. Lucy Deane.
Miss Guest and **Laura,** his sisters.
His father.
The Mill on the Floss, George Eliot, 1860.

Guichard, Leon. *See* MEHÉE DE LA TOUCHE.

Guiderius (Polydore), Cymbeline's son. *Cymbeline* (play), W. Shakespeare.

Guildenstern, a courtier. *Hamlet* (play), W. Shakespeare.

Guildford, Sir Henry. *Henry the Eighth* (play), W. Shakespeare.

Guildford, Ripley.
His mother.

The Saving Grace (play), C. Haddon Chambers, 1917.

Guilford, Lord Dudley. *The Tower of London.* W. H. Ainsworth, 1840.

Guinevere, wife of King Arthur.
Leodogran, her father.
Idylls of the King (poem), Lord Tennyson, 1859.

Guinness, Nurse. *Heartbreak House* (play), G. B. Shaw, 1917.

Guiscard, Robert, father of Bohemond.
Gaita, his wife.
Count Robert of Paris, W. Scott, 1832.

Gules, Lord, grandson of Lord Saltire. *The Book of Snobs,* W. M. Thackeray, 1846–7.

Gulla Kuttah Mullah, The, bandit chief. 'The Lost Legion' (s.s.), *Many Inventions,* R. Kipling, 1893.

Gulliver, Lemuel, central character and narrator.
His wife.
John, his son.
Betty, his daughter.
Gulliver's Travels, J. Swift, 1726.

Gulnare, 'The Harem Queen.' *The Corsair* (poem), Lord Byron, 1814.

Gumbiecat. *See* JENNYANYDOTS.

Gumbo, Negro slave and valet of Henry Warrington, m. Molly. *The Virginians,* W. M. Thackeray, 1857–9.

Gumbril, Theodore, central character.
His father.
Antic Hay, A. Huxley, 1923.

Gunby, Ned, New York detective. *Mr Billingham, the Marquis and Madelon,* E. P. Oppenheim.

Gunch, Vergil, coal-dealer. *Babbitt,* Sinclair Lewis, 1923.

Gunga Din. 'Gunga Din' (poem), *Barrack-room Ballads,* R. Kipling, 1892.

Gungas Dass. 'The Strange Ride of Morrowbie Jukes' (s.s.), *Wee Willie Winkie,* R. Kipling, 1888.

Gunn. *Fanny's First Play* (play), G. B. Shaw, 1905.

Gunn, The Misses. *Silas Marner,* George Eliot, 1861.

Gunn, Mrs, South African landlady. *Children of Violence* series, Doris Lessing, 1952–69.

Gunn, Ben, a castaway. *Treasure Island,* R. L. Stevenson, 1883.

Gunn, Nick, blackmailer. 'Captain Rogers' (s.s.), *The Lady of the Barge,* W. W. Jacobs, 1902.

Gunn, Peter, sweep, first employer of Joseph Vance. *Joseph Vance,* W. de Morgan, 1906.

Gunne, Ulysses. 'Delilah' (poem), *Departmental Ditties,* R. Kipling, 1886.

Gunning, 'heavy, elderly, pleasant.' *Last Post,* Ford Madox Ford, 1928.

Gunpowder, horse borrowed by Ichabod Crane. *The Legend of Sleepy Hollow,* Washington Irving, 1819–1820.

Gunter, visitor to Bob Sawyer. *Pickwick Papers,* C. Dickens, 1837.

Guntry, bully and drunkard. *The Bay,* L. A. G. Strong, 1941.

Guppy, William, clerk to Kenge & Carboy. *Bleak House,* C. Dickens, 1853.

Gurth, 'son of Beowulph.' *Ivanhoe,* W. Scott, 1820.

Gurton, Gammer. *Gammer Gurton's Needle* (play), Anonymous, 1575.

Gustav, Fanny, m. Norman Edelman. *Magnolia Street,* L. Golding, 1932.

Gustavsen, Fröken Sigrid, gym mistress at Leys College.
Her mother.
Miss Pym Disposes, Josephine Tey, 1946.

Guthrie, Miss, enthusiastic gardener. 'Neighbours' (s.s.), *A Beginning,* W. de la Mare, 1955.

Guthrie, Chris, heroine, m. (1) Ewan Tavendale, farmer, (2) Rev. Robert Colquhoun, (3) Ake Ogilvie, a peasant-poet.
Ewan Tavendale, junior, her son.
John Guthrie, her father, a crofter.
Jean Guthrie, her mother, a drudge.
Will, her brother.
A Scots Quair, a trilogy, 1932–4, Lewis Grassic Gibbon.

Gutman, Casper, Brigid O'Shaughnessy's employer. *The Maltese Falcon,* Dashiell Hammett, 1930.

Guttersnipe, Ma, mother of Rosanna Frettleby. *The Mystery of a Hansom Cab,* F. Hume, 1886.

Guttlebury, Lord, epicure. *The Book of Snobs,* 1846–7, and elsewhere, W. M. Thackeray.

Guttleton, professional diner-out. *The Book of Snobs*, 1846–7, and elsewhere, W. M. Thackeray.

Guy, Octavius ('Gooseberry'). *The Moonstone*, W. Collins, 1868.

Guzzard, Mrs Sarah, mother of Colby Simpkins. *The Confidential Clerk* (play), T. S. Eliot, 1954.

Gwenwyn (or **Gwenwynwen**), Prince of Powys.

Brengwain, his wife.

The Betrothed, W. Scott, 1825.

Gwyddr, Evan, singing genius, m. Elya, refugee. *The Whistling Chambermaid*, Naomi Royde-Smith, 1957.

Gwyllin, Mrs, housekeeper to the Brambles. *Humphry Clinker*, T. Smollett, 1771.

Gwynn, Nell (hist.) (alias Cydaria). *Simon Dale*, A. Hope, 1898.

Gwynne, Beatrice. *Call it a Day* (play), Dodie Smith, 1935.

Gybbon, Mrs. *The Way of an Eagle*, Ethel M. Dell, 1912.

Gylby, Noel, nephew of the Duchess of Horton. *Hamlet, Revenge!*, M. Innes, 1937.

H

H., Mr, a minister. *Farewell, Miss Julie Logan*, J. M. Barrie, 1932.

Hableton, Mrs. *The Mystery of a Hansom Cab*, F. Hume, 1886.

Hack, Bacon's reader and editorial manager. *Pendennis*, W. M. Thackeray, 1848–50.

Hackabury, Ezra, of 'Bluebird' soap. *Dragon Harvest*, Upton Sinclair, 1946.

Hackbut, Anthony.
His sister, m. William Fleming.
Rhoda Fleming, G. Meredith, 1865.

Hackbutt, Tarver.
Fanny, his daughter.
Middlemarch, Geo. Eliot, 1871–2.

Hacker. *Polly* (comic opera), J. Gay, 1729.

Hacker, a schoolboy. The *Barsetshire* series, Angela Thirkell, 1933 onwards.

Hackitt, farmer and churchwarden.
His wife.
'The Rev. Amos Barton' and 'Mr Gilfil's Love Story,' *Scenes of Clerical Life*, George Eliot, 1857.

Hackitt, Samuel, ex-convict.
His wife.
The Ringer (play), E. Wallace, 1926.

Haddocriss, Mrs.
Her husband, archdeacon.
Before the Bombardment, O. Sitwell, 1926

Haden, Lily.
Her mother.
Doris, her sister.
Sinister Street, 1913, and elsewhere, C. Mackenzie.

Hadgi, Swiss valet to Peregrine. *Peregrine Pickle*, T. Smollett, 1751.

Haffen, Mrs, blackmailer. *The House of Mirth*, Edith Wharton, 1905.

Hafter, Harvey, confidence trickster. *The Bowge of Court*, John Skelton, 1498.

Hagan, Geohegan, Irish actor, later parson, m. Lady Maria Esmond.
His mother.
The Virginians. W. M. Thackeray, 1857–9.

Hagberd, Captain. 'Tomorrow' (s.s.), *Typhoon*, J. Conrad, 1903.

Hagedorn, Captain Carl. firearms expert. *The Benson Murder Case*, S. S. van Dine, 1926.

Hagenbach, Archibald von, robber-knight. *Anne of Geierstein*, W. Scott, 1829.

Hagg, Mrs Louisa, widow, ex-governess of Vivien Brown.
William, her son.
The Judge's Story, C. Morgan, 1947.

Haggage, Dr, Marshalsea inmate. *Little Dorrit*, C. Dickens, 1857.

Haggard, Sally, John Reddin's mistress. *Gone to Earth*, Mary Webb, 1917.

Haggart, Tammas, stone-breaker. *When a Man's Single*, J. M. Barrie, 1888.

Haggarty, Dionysius (Dennis), Irish army surgeon.
Jemima Amelia, *née* Gann, his slatternly and disfigured wife,
Molloy and **Jemima,** their children.
His father, a doctor.
His mother, *née* Burke.
Charles, his brother.
Men's Wives, W. M. Thackeray, 1843.

Haggerston, tutor to Dudley Cheadle. *We're Here*, D. Mackail, 1947.

Haggerty, Paulie, friend of Studs Lonigan. *Studs Lonigan*, a trilogy, James T. Farrell, 1935.

Haggistoun, Mrs, chaperon to Rhoda Swartz. *Vanity Fair*, W. M. Thackeray, 1847–8.

Hagthorne, Gabriel. *Windsor Castle*, W. H. Ainsworth, 1843.

Hagthorpe, Nathaniel, ex-naval officer, *Captain Blood*, R. Sabatini, 1922.

Haigh, a Yorkshireman. *The Porch*, 1937, and *The Stronghold*, 1939, R. Church.

Haigh, Walter, central character, m. Elaine Crosland.
Dyson, his father.
Emily, his mother.
Rosamund, his sister, in love with Leonard Tasker.
A Modern Tragedy, Phyllis Bentley, 1934.

Haigha and Hatta, messengers. *Alice Through the Looking-glass,* L. Carroll, 1872.

Hailworthy, Sir Henry. 'A Pirate of the Land' (s.s.), *Tales of Pirates and Blue Water,* A. Conan Doyle.

Haines. *Ulysses,* James Joyce, 1922.

Haines, 'Bud,' 'natural killer.' *Tex of Bar-20,* C. E. Mulford, 1922.

Haines, Frank. *Call it a Day* (play), Dodie Smith, 1935.

Hairun, 'Bearward.' *The Tower of London,* W. H. Ainsworth, 1840.

Hajj, central character.
  Marsinah, his daughter.
Kismet (play), E. Knoblock, 1911.

Hajji Baba. *Hajji Baba and the Stolen Money* (s.s.), 1824, and elsewhere, J. Morier.

Halberton, Lord, cousin of James Martyn. *My Brother Jonathan,* F. Brett Young, 1928.

Halborough, Joshua, Snr, master-millwright.
  Joshua and **Cornelius,** his sons.
  Rosa, his daughter, m. Albert Fellmer.
  Selina, his 2nd wife.
'A Tragedy of Two Ambitions,' *Life's Little Ironies,* T. Hardy, 1894.

Halcro, Claud, Zetland poet. *The Pirate,* W. Scott, 1822.

Halcyon, a kingfisher. *Tarka the Otter,* H. Williamson, 1927.

Haldimund, Sir Ewes, friend of Lord Dalgarno. *The Fortunes of Nigel,* W. Scott, 1822.

Haldin, Victor, student in St Petersburg, a revolutionary.
  Natalia Victorovna, his sister.
  His mother.
Under Western Eyes, Joseph Conrad, 1911.

Hale, captain of the *Altair. Gallions Reach,* H. M. Tomlinson, 1927.

Hale, Charles (Fred), murdered by Pinkie's gang. *Brighton Rock,* Graham Greene, 1938.

Hale, Clement, adopted son of Geoffrey Wedderburn. *Sweet Lavender* (play), A. W. Pinero, 1888.

Hale, Margaret, central character, m. John Thornton.
  Rev. Richard, her father.
  Maria, her mother.
  Frederick, her brother.
North and South, Mrs Gaskell, 1855.

Hale, Mrs Ruth, widow, *née* Varnum, landlady. *Ethan Frome,* Edith Wharton, 1911.

Hales, fellow traveller with Judy Corder on cholera ship. *Four Frightened People,* E. Arnot Robertson, 1931.

Haley, slave trader. *Uncle Tom's Cabin,* Harriet B. Stowe, 1851.

Halifax, Mrs. *The Heart of the Matter,* Graham Greene, 1948.

Halifax, John, central character, m. Ursula March.
  Their children:
    Muriel, born blind.
    Guy.
    Walter.
    Ralph.
    Edwin, m. Louise d'Argent.
    Maud, m. Lord Ravenel.
John Halifax, Gentleman, Mrs Craik, 1856.

Hall, 'the Perfect Fool.' *The Iron Pirate,* M. Pemberton, 1893.

Hall, Christopher, lover of Leo Proudhammer. *Tell Me How Long The Train's Been Gone,* James Baldwin, 1968.

Hall, Fred, Krogh's agent and oldest friend. *England Made Me,* Graham Greene, 1935.

Hall, Mrs Jenny, proprietor of the Coach and Horses, Iping. *The Invisible Man,* H. G. Wells, 1897.

Hall, Maurice Christopher, central character, homosexual stockbroker in love with (1) Clive Durham, (2) Alec Scudder. *Maurice,* E. M. Forster, 1971.

Hall, Philip.
  Helena, his wife.
  His mother.
  Sarah, his sister.
'Interlopers at the Knap,' *Wessex Tales,* T. Hardy, 1888.

Hall, Tom, ship's captain. 'The Rhyme of the Three Sealers' (poem), *The Seven Seas,* R. Kipling, 1896.

Hall of Lithdale, mate on Eric's sea-stag. *Eric Brighteyes,* H. Rider Haggard, 1891.

Hallam, Inspector. *The Franchise Affair,* Josephine Tey, 1948.

Hallam, Sir Howard. *Captain Brassbound's Conversion* (play), G. B. Shaw, 1900.

Hallam, Second Officer Julie, W.R.N.S., in love with Keith

Lockhart. *The Cruel Sea,* N. Monsarrat, 1951.

Hallam, Martin, m. Mary Llewellyn. *The Well of Loneliness,* Radclyffe Hall, 1928.

Hallard, Marta, actress, friend of Alan Grant. *A Daughter of Time,* Josephine Tey, 1951.

Hallet, Arnaud, m. Linda Condon.
Vigne, their daughter.
Lowrie, their son.
Linda Condon, J. Hergesheimer, 1918.

Halley, Lieutenant. 'The Lost Legion' (s.s.), *Many Inventions,* R. Kipling, 1895.

Halliburton, Edgar, maths master, later curate.
Jane, his wife, *née* Tait.
Mrs Halliburton's Troubles, Mrs Henry Wood, 1862.

Halliday, Mrs, Benjie Herries's landlady.
Marion, her daughter, m. Benjie.
Vanessa, Hugh Walpole, 1933.

Halliday, Philip, school friend of Frank Ashurst.
His sisters:
Stella, m. Frank Ashurst.
Sabina.
Freda.
The Apple Tree, J. Galsworthy, 1918.

Halliday, Simeon, Quaker.
Rachel, his daughter. Friends to Eliza and George.
Uncle Tom's Cabin, Harriet B. Stowe, 1851.

Hallijohn, George, murdered by Francis Levison.
Aphrodite, his daughter, m. Joe Jiffin.
Joyce, her half-sister, servant of Lady Isabel Carlyle.
East Lynne, Mrs Henry Wood, 1861.

Hallin, Edward, lecturer on economics, college friend of Aldous Raeburn. *Marcella,* Mrs Humphry Ward, 1894.

Halliwell, Captain. *The Little Minister,* J. M. Barrie, 1891.

Hallorsen, Professor Edward, American archaeologist. *Maid in Waiting,* J. Galsworthy, 1931.

Hallowes, Michael, friend of Jasper Darke, m. Amber Darke. *The House in Dormer Forest,* Mary Webb, 1920.

Hallward, Basil, artist. *The Picture of Dorian Gray,* O. Wilde, 1891.

Halm-Eberstein, Leonora Princess (Alcharisi, prima donna), mother of Daniel Deronda. *Daniel Deronda,* George Eliot, 1876.

Halnaker, Isabel, former mistress of Humphrey Mallard and friend of Jenny Mallard.
Claude, her husband.
Their children:
Wilfred.
Lance.
Wingfield, m. Timothy Baston.
Iron and Smoke, Sheila Kaye-Smith, 1928.

Halstead, Charlotte, sister of Medwin Blair.
Harold, her husband.
Their children: **Richard, Louise, Tony** and **Karen.**
Joan, her sister-in-law.
The Prodigal Heart, Susan Ertz, 1950.

Halstead, Katherine, fashion correspondent, *The Liberal,* in love with Frank Luttrell. *The Street of Adventure,* P. Gibbs, 1909.

Halton, Richard. *On Approval* (play), F. Lonsdale, 1927.

Hamard, auctioneer. *The Drums of War,* H. de Vere Stacpoole, 1910.

Hamble, Priscilla, childhood sweetheart of George Winterbourne. *Death of a Hero,* R. Aldington, 1929.

Hambledon, Edward, artist, of Boston.
Anthony, his brother.
Penelope, his sister, m. Richard Arkwright.
His father.
Through the Storm, P. Gibbs, 1945.

Hambling, Josiah, saddler.
Nancy, his daughter, 2nd wife of Ben Geaiter, m. as 2nd husband Ted Willett.
Joseph and his Brethren, H. W. Freeman, 1928.

Hambro, Mrs, sister of Mrs Culver.
Alice, her daughter, m. Freddy Baker.
Jimmy, her son.
Britannia Mews, Margery Sharp, 1946.

Hamil, Garret, landscape architect, central character, m. Shiela Cardross. *The Firing Line,* R. W. Chambers, 1908.

Hamilton, Rev. Andrew, m. Kirsty Christie. *The Setons,* O. Douglas, 1917.

Hamilton, Freddy, official in British Legation in Jerusalem. *The Mandelbaum Gate,* Muriel Spark, 1965.

Hamilton, Melanie, m. Ashley Wilkes.
Charles, her brother, Scarlett O'Hara's 1st husband.
Wade, their son.
Sarah Jane (Miss Pittypat), their aunt.
Uncle Henry.
Gone with the Wind, Margaret Mitchell, 1936.

Hamilton, Samuel, neighbour of the Trask family. *East of Eden,* John Steinbeck, 1952.

Hamlet, Prince of Denmark. *Hamlet* (play), W. Shakespeare.

Hamley, Squire.
His wife.
Roger and **Osborne,** their sons.
Wives and Daughters, Mrs Gaskell, 1866.

Hamlin, John ('Comanche Jack'), card-sharper. 'Brown of Calaveras' (s.s.), *The Luck of Roaring Camp,* Bret Harte, 1868.

Hammerfield, Dr. *The Iron Heel,* Jack London, 1908.

Hammergallow, Lady, of Siddermorton. *The Wonderful Visit,* H. G. Wells, 1895.

Hammersley, Jack, Mayor of San Francisco, guardian of Yerba Buena. *A Ward of the Golden Gate,* Bret Harte.

Hammersley, Will.
Sheila, his daughter.
The Glory of Clementina Wing, W. J. Locke, 1911.

Hammerton, Mrs, aunt of Andrea Fitch.
Her husband, auctioneer.
Vanity Fair, W. M. Thackeray, 1847–8.

Hammerton, William. *The Knight of the Burning Pestle* (play), Beaumont & Fletcher, 1609.

Hammond, Captain ('Black Charlie'), of the *Calypso.* The *Hornblower* series, C. S. Forester, 1937 onwards.

Hammond, Dr.
Rachel, his daughter.
Hilda, his dead wife, *née* Higgins.
My Brother Jonathan, F. Brett Young, 1928.

Hammond, Mrs, Arthur Machin's landlady.
Her children:
Lynda and **Ian.**
This Sporting Life, David Storey, 1960.

Hammond, Geoffrey, *The Letter* (play), W. S. Maugham, 1927.

Hammond, Hec, fiancé of Miss Milligan. *London Wall* (play), J. van Druten, 1931.

Hammond, John.
Jane, his wife.
'The Stranger' (s.s.), *The Garden Party,* Katherine Mansfield, 1922.

Hammond, Philip, nephew of old Mrs Maitland. *The Pottleton Legacy,* Albert Smith, 1849.

Hamps, Mrs Clara, aunt of the Clayhangers. The *Clayhanger* trilogy, Arnold Bennett, 1910–16.

Hampton. Family name of EARL OF MONTDORE.

Hampton, Miss, friend of Miss Bent. The *Barsetshire* series, Angela Thirkell, 1933 onwards.

Hampton, Cedric, heir presumptive to Lord Montdore. *Love in a Cold Climate,* Nancy Mitford, 1949.

Hamson, Mrs Chris. *These Twain,* Arnold Bennett, 1916.

Hamson, Dr Freddie, fake specialist. *The Citadel,* A. J. Cronin, 1937.

Hamud, a one-eyed Arab shepherd. *Smith's Gazelle,* Lionel Davidson, 1971.

Hamza, donkey-boy. *Bella Donna,* R. S. Hichens, 1909.

Hanaud, famous French detective. *At the Villa Rose,* 1910, and many others, A. E. W. Mason.

Hanbury, Mr. *Pip,* Ian Hay, 1907.

Hance, T. W. 'Thomas Winterbottom Hance' (poem), *Bab Ballads,* W. S. Gilbert, 1869.

Hand, Robert, newspaper editor. *Exiles* (play), James Joyce, 1918.

Handcock. *Some Experiences of an Irish R.M.,* E. Œ. Somerville & Martin Ross, 1899.

Handford, Julius. See JOHN HARMON.

Handley, James. *Bulldog Drummond,* 'Sapper' (H. C. McNeile), 1920.

Hands, Israel, of the *Hispaniola. Treasure Island,* R. L. Stevenson, 1883.

Handy, Abel, inmate of Hiram's Hospital. *The Warden,* A. Trollope, 1855.

Handyman, Captain F., m. Hester Warrington. *The Virginians,* W.M. Thackeray, 1857–9.

Handyside. *See* GARRETT COAST.

Hank. *Beau Geste,* P. C. Wren, 1924.

Hankin, director of Pym's Publicity. *Murder Must Advertise,* Dorothy L. Sayers, 1933.

Hanks, Rev. Mr.
Emma, his wife.
Millie, their daughter. Befrienders of Myra Bawne.
We the Accused, E. Raymond, 1935.

Hanmer, engineer. *Middlemarch,* George Eliot, 1871–2.

Hanna, Rev. Eustace. 'The Record of Badalia Herodsfoot' (s.s.), *Many Inventions,* R. Kipling, 1893.

Hannah, servant to the Marches. *Little Women,* 1868, and sequels, Louisa M. Alcott.

Hannah, old retainer of Mrs Martin. *Two on a Tower,* T. Hardy, 1882.

Hannah, Dame, m. Sir Roderic Murgatroyd. *Ruddigore* (comic opera), Gilbert & Sullivan, 1887.

Hannasyde. 'On the Strength of a Likeness' (s.s.), *Plain Tales from the Hills,* R. Kipling, 1888.

Hannay, Richard, central character and narrator. *The Thirty-nine Steps,* 1915, and others, J. Buchan.

Hannigan, Bessie. *The Crock of Gold,* J. Stephens, 1912.

Hanning, Emily, m. Mr Lester. 'To Please his Wife,' *Life's Little Ironies,* T. Hardy, 1894.

Hanslett, Helen. *See* RAINIER.

Hanson, Jeffrey, friend of Middleton. *The Restoration of Arnold Middleton* (play), David Storey, 1967.

Hanvey, June. *Robert's Wife* (play), St John Ervine, 1937.

Hapfel, Dr Otto, German spy. *London Belongs to Me,* N. Collins, 1945.

Hapgood, solicitor, friend of Mark Sabre. *If Winter Comes,* A. S. M. Hutchinson, 1920.

Hapgood, Nurse. *The Shrimp and the Anemone,* L. P. Hartley, 1944.

Haphazard, Sir Abraham, eminent lawyer. *The Warden,* A. Trollope, 1855.

Hapless, Miss M., secretary to Jane Palfry. *Antigua Penny Puce,* R. Graves, 1936.

Happer, Mysie.
'Hob Miller,' her father.
Kate, her aunt.
The Monastery, W. Scott, 1820.

Harbinger, Viscount (Claud Fresnay), m. Lady Barbara Caradoc. *The Patrician,* J. Galsworthy, 1911.

Harborough, Mrs. *Select Conversations with an Uncle,* H. G. Wells, 1895.

Harbottle, General. *Bracebridge Hall,* W. Irving, 1823.

Harcombe, Anthony, K.C., counsel for the defence. *The Jury,* G. Bullett, 1935.

Harcourt. Family name of the DUKE OF TOWERS.

Harcourt, gallant in love with Alithea Pinchwife. *The Country Wife* (play), William Wycherley, 1673.

Harcourt, Count Bernard of. *The Little Duke,* Charlotte M. Yonge, 1854.

Harcourt-Reilly, Sir Henry. *The Cocktail Party* (play), T. S. Eliot, 1950.

Hardacre, publican. *No News from Helen,* L. Golding, 1943.

Hardcastle, Mr, a country squire.
Dorothy, his wife.
Kate, their daughter.
Tony Lumpkin, Mrs Hardcastle's son by her first marriage.
She Stoops to Conquer (play), Oliver Goldsmith, 1773.

Hardcastle, Lord (Michael) ('Barnabas'). *The Fortunes of Christina McNab,* S. Macnaughtan, 1901.

Hardcastle, Sally.
Her mother and father.
Harry, her brother.
Love on the Dole, W. Greenwood, 1933.

Hardcome, James, m. (1) Olive Pawle, (2) Emily Hardcome, *née* Darth.
Steve, his cousin, Emily Darth's 1st husband.
'The History of the Hardcomes,' *Life's Little Ironies,* T. Hardy, 1894.

Harden, Rev. Charles.
Mary, his sister.
Marcella, Mrs Humphry Ward, 1894.

Harden, Margaret, m. 'Rogue'

Herries. *Rogue Herries,* Hugh Walpole, 1930.

Hardey, Michael. one-time M.F.H. *Handley Cross,* R. S. Surtees, 1843.

Hardie, Mr, Edinburgh advocate. *The Heart of Midlothian,* W. Scott, 1818.

Hardie, Richard, banker.
Julia, *née* Dodd, his wife.
Alfred, his son.
Jane, his daughter.
Hard Cash, C. Reade, 1863.

Harding, Colonel, J.P. *Lorna Doone,* R. D. Blackmore, 1869.

Harding, Charles, central character and part narrator.
Dick, his brother.
Lost Endeavour, J. Masefield, 1910.

Harding, Dickon, shoeing-smith. *The Story of Ragged Robyn,* O. Onions, 1945.

Harding, George, m. Marjorie Wills. *The Black Spectacles,* J. Dickson Carr, 1948.

Harding, John, trainer. *Right Royal* (poem), J. Masefield, 1920.

Harding, Nan, medical student. *Little Men* and *Jo's Boys,* Louisa M. Alcott, 1871–86.

Harding, Rev. Septimus.
His daughters:
Susan, m. Theophilus Grantly.
Eleanor, m. (1) John Bold, (2) Francis Arabin.
The Warden, 1855, and elsewhere, A. Trollope.

Hardinge, Rev. Mr, Miles Wallingford's guardian.
Rupert, his son.
Lucy, his daughter.
Afloat and Ashore, J. Fenimore Cooper, 1844.

Hardisty, Sir Percy, 'gentleman of the old order.'
Rachel, his wife.
Mellicent and **Polly,** their daughters.
Men and Wives, Ivy Compton-Burnett, 1931.

Hardross, John. 'The Quiet Woman' (s.s.), *Adam and Eve and Pinch Me,* A. E. Coppard, 1921.

Hardwick, Stanley.
Irene, his wife.
The Second Mrs Conford, Beatrice K. Seymour, 1951.

Hardy, Captain. *Journey's End,* R. C. Sherriff, 1928.

Hardy, Major. *Tell England,* E. Raymond, 1922.

Hardy, Mr, humorist and amateur entertainer. *Sketches by Boz,* C. Dickens, 1836.

Hardy, Captain Christopher, in love with Madeline Delaroche. *Through the Storm,* P. Gibbs, 1945.

Hardy, Letitia. *The Belle's Stratagem* (play), Hannah Cowley, 1780.

Hardy, Mary, m. Emil Bhaer. *Jo's Boys,* Louisa M. Alcott, 1886.

Hardy, Sir Richmond.
His wife.
The Secret Places of the Heart, H. G. Wells, 1922.

Hardy, Salcombe, reporter. 'The Man with no Face,' *Lord Peter Views the Body,* 1928, and elsewhere, Dorothy L. Sayers.

Hardy, Captain Thomas (hist.), Lord Nelson's post-captain. *The Trumpet Major,* T. Hardy, 1880.

Hare, Jonathan, central character (Jonathan Swift), m. Anne Marton. *I Live Under a Black Sun,* Edith Sitwell, 1937.

Hare, Mary, elderly spinster who lives in Xanadu. *Riders in the Chariot,* Patrick White, 1961.

Hare, Mr Justice Richard.
Anne, his wife.
Their children:
Richard.
Anne.
Barbara, m. Archie Carlyle.
East Lynne, Mrs Henry Wood, 1861.

Haredale, Geoffrey.
Reuben, his elder brother.
Emma, his niece, m. Edward Chester.
Barnaby Rudge, C. Dickens, 1841.

Harendra Mukerjee. 'The Ballad of Boh da Thone' (poem), *Barrack-room Ballads,* R. Kipling, 1892.

Harewood, Tom. *The Heir of Redclyffe,* Charlotte M. Yonge, 1853.

Hargate, Frank, central character.
Lucy, his sister.
Captain Hargate, his father.
By Sheer Pluck, G. A. Henty, 1883.

Hargrave. *Self-Control,* Mrs Brunton, 1811.

Hargrave, Ralph.
His mother.
His sisters:
Milicent, m. Hattersley.

Esther, m. Frederick Lawrence.
The Tenant of Wildfell Hall, Anne Brontë, 1848.

Harkaway, Lord Harry. *Hawbuck Grange,* R. S. Surtees, 1847.

Harker, Jonathan.
Minna, his wife.
Dracula, Bram Stoker, 1897.

Harland, Celia, companion to Mme Dauvray. *At the Villa Rose,* A. E. W. Mason, 1910.

Harland, Joe. *Manhattan Transfer,* J. dos Passos, 1925.

Harleigh, Sir Henry, Bt. *Diary of a Late Physician,* S. Warren, 1832.

Harleth, Gwendolen, daughter of Mrs Davilow, m. Henleigh Mallinger Grandcourt. *Daniel Deronda,* George Eliot, 1876.

Harley, central character. *The Man of Feeling,* H. Mackenzie, 1771.

Harley, Adrian, tutor to his cousin, Richard Feverel.
Mr Justice Harley, his father.
His mother, *née* Feverel.
The Ordeal of Richard Feverel, G. Meredith, 1859.

Harlin, friend of Maria Schoning. *Maria Schoning* (s.s.), S. T. Coleridge.

Harlowe, Clarissa, central character.
James, her father.
Her mother.
Uncle Anthony.
Uncle John.
Clarissa Harlowe, S. Richardson, 1748.

Harman, in love with Diana Oldboy. *Lionel and Clarissa* (play), I. Bickerstaffe, 1768.

Harman, Sir Isaac.
Ellen, his wife, *née* Sawbridge.
The Wife of Sir Isaac Harman, H. G. Wells, 1914.

Harman, Joe, Australian stockman, m. Jean Paget.
Their children.
A Town like Alice, N. Shute, 1950.

Harmer, Phyllis, friend of Ariadne Ferne. *No Other Tiger,* A. E. W. Mason, 1927.

Harmon, Dr. *The Harvester,* Gene S. Porter, 1911.

Harmon, Dick. *Je ne parle pas Français* (s.s.), Katherine Mansfield.

Harmon, John (alias Julius Handford and John Rokesmith), central character, m. Bella Wilfer.
His father, decd, a dust-contractor.
Our Mutual Friend, C. Dickens, 1865.

Harms, Clayton, electric-sign salesman. 'Ace' Chisholm's lodger. *Eustace Chisholm and the Works,* James Purdy, 1968.

Harness, Simeon, pastor and schoolmaster. *Rogue Herries,* Hugh Walpole, 1930.

Harnham, Mr.
Edith, his wife.
'On the Western Circuit,' *Life's Little Ironies,* T. Hardy, 1894.

Harnwood, Sir Julian, close friend of Morrice Buckler. *The Courtship of Morrice Buckler,* A. E. W. Mason, 1896.

Harold, Childe. *Childe Harold's Pilgrimage* (poem), Lord Byron, 1812–1818.

Haroun al Raschid, caliph. *Hassan* (play), J. E. Flecker, 1923.

Harpax, centurion. *Count Robert of Paris,* W. Scott, 1832.

Harpax. *Ralph Roister Doister* (play), N. Udall, 1551.

Harpenden, Earl of, m. Lady Elizabeth Randall. *While the Sun Shines* (play), T. Rattigan, 1943.

Harpenden, Napier.
His father, baronet.
The Green Hat, M. Arlen, 1924.

Harper, Sir Bodley, later **Lord Harper,** employer of Tom Florey. *Tom Tiddler's Ground,* E. Shanks, 1934.

Harper, Joe, close friend of Tom, *The Adventures of Tom Sawyer,* Mark Twain, 1876.

Harper, Nathanael.
His children:
Major Frederick.
Nathanael Locke, m. Agatha Bowen.
Eulalie.
Mary.
Harriet, m. Marmaduke Dugdale.
Agatha's Husband, Mrs Craik, 1853.

Harpour, bully. *St Winifred's,* F. W. Farrar, 1862.

Harrel, a trustee of Cecilia's fortune.
Priscilla, his wife, *née* Arnott.
Cecilia, Fanny Burney, 1782.

Harries ('Bull'), astronomer. 'Unprofessional' (s.s.), *Limits and Renewals,* R. Kipling, 1932.

Harriet, Archduchess of Roumania, admirer of Orlando. *Orlando*, Virginia Woolf, 1928.

Harrigan, Captain. *On the Spot* (play), E. Wallace, 1930.

Harrington, Catherine, girlhood friend of Marietta Lyddon. *The Prodigal Heart*, Susan Ertz, 1950.

Harrington, Evan, central character, m. Rose Jocelyn.
  Melchisedek, his father, tailor.
  His mother.
  His sisters:
    Caroline, m. Major Strike.
    Harriet, m. Andrew Cogglesby.
    Louise, m. Comte de Saldar.
  Evan Harrington, G. Meredith, 1861.

Harrington, Lulie, central character, m. Jay Pignatelli.
  Ezekiel, her father.
  Lucy, her mother, *née* Waring.
  Ben, her brother.
  Zeke, her brother, m. Mugsie.
  Chosen Country, J. dos Passos, 1951.

Harrington, Polly, Pollyanna Whittier's aunt. *Pollyanna*. Eleanor H. Porter, 1913.

Harris, brutal owner of George, ruins his career. *Uncle Tom's Cabin*, Harriet B. Stowe, 1851.

Harris, squadron doctor. *The Purple Plain*, H. E. Bates, 1947.

Harris, silk merchant. 'Secret Worship' (s.s.), *John Silence*, A. Blackwood, 1908.

Harris, Miss, fiancée of Ted. *The Lady of the Barge*, W. W. Jacobs, 1902.

Harris, Mr, alias of Lord Highgate. *The Newcomes*, W. M. Thackeray, 1853–5.

Harris, Mrs, mythical but extensively quoted friend of Mrs Gamp. *Martin Chuzzlewit*, C. Dickens, 1844.

Harris, William Samuel, one of the 'three.' *Three Men in a Boat*, J. K. Jerome, 1889.

Harrison, narrator, secretary to Charles Rainier. *Random Harvest*, J. Hilton, 1941.

Harrison, gardener, m. Miss Piper. *Heartsease*, Charlotte M. Yonge, 1854.

Harrison, sailor on *Ghost*. *The Sea Wolf*, Jack London, 1904.

Harrison, British Intelligence agent. *The Heat of the Day*, Elizabeth Bowen, 1949.

Harrison ('Champion'), blacksmith.
  Jim, his so-called nephew (later Lord Avon).
  Rodney Stone, A. Conan Doyle, 1896.

Harrison, a prefect. 'The Impressionists' and elsewhere. *Stalky & Co.*, R. Kipling, 1899.

Harrison, Joseph. 'The Naval Treaty,' *Memoirs of Sherlock Holmes*, A. Conan Doyle, 1894.

Harrison, Mary, m. Arthur Jarvis.
  John, her brother.
  Their parents.
  Cry, the Beloved Country, A. Paton, 1948.

Harrowdean, Mrs, friend of Mr Britling.
  Oliver, her husband.
  Mr Britling Sees It Through, H. G. Wells, 1916.

Harry. *See* UNCLEHARRI.

Harry, of the *Hispaniola*. *Treasure Island*. R. L. Stevenson, 1883.

Harsanyi, Andor, concert pianist. *The Song of the Lark*, Willa Cather, 1915.

Hart, Dr. 'Mr Gilfil's Love Story,' *Scenes of Clerical Life*, George Eliot, 1857.

Hart, George Greydon (George Greydon, playwright). *Wandering Stars*, Clemence Dane, 1924.

Hart, Jeff. *Campbell's Kingdom*, Hammond Innes, 1952.

Hart, Margaret, companion to Dame Eleanor Pryke.
  Sweetie, her illegitimate daughter by Derek Pryke. m. Ginger Woods.
  Children of the Archbishop, N. Collins, 1951.

Hart, Miranda, m. Steven Hingston.
  Colonel Robert, her father.
  Portrait of Clare, F. Brett Young, 1927.

Hart-Harris, Claud, friend of Flora Poste. *Cold Comfort Farm*. Stella Gibbons, 1932.

Harthouse, James, political agent of Gradgrind. *Hard Times*, C. Dickens, 1854.

Harthover, Sir John.
  Ellie, his daughter.
  Water Babies, C. Kingsley, 1863.

Hartington, Sub-Lieut., R.N., who befriends John Lynwood *The Gunroom,* Charles Morgan, 1919.

Hartleberry, Priscilla. *The Young Idea* (play), N. Coward, 1923.

Hartletop, Marchioness of, *née* Griselda Grantly.
  The Dowager Marchioness.
  Phineas Finn, 1869, and elsewhere, A. Trollope.

Hartley, Adam, surgeon. *The Surgeon's Daughter,* W. Scott, 1827.

Hartley, Dr Baring. *Bella Donna,* R. S. Hichens, 1909.

Hartley, Harry, secretary to Sir Thomas Vandeleur. 'The Rajah's Diamond' (s.s.), *New Arabian Nights,* R. L. Stevenson, 1882.

Hartley, Mary Agnes, prostitute. *Magnolia Street,* L. Golding, 1932.

Hartman, Dr. 'The Footsteps that Ran,' *Lord Peter Views the Body,* Dorothy L. Sayers, 1928.

Hartman, Rev. Curtis, admirer of Kate Swift. *Winesburg, Ohio,* Sherwood Anderson, 1919.

Hartmore, Lord and Lady. *The Cuckoo in the Nest.* Mrs Oliphant, 1894.

Harton, lawyer. *The Circular Staircase,* Mary R. Rinehart, 1908.

Hartopp, Rev. Mr, housemaster. *Stalky & Co.,* R. Kipling, 1899.

Hartright, Walter, drawing master, part narrator.
  His mother.
  Sarah, his sister.
  The Woman in White, W. Collins, 1860.

Hartshorn, Priss, graduate of Vassar. *The Group,* Mary McCarthy, 1963.

Harum, David, central character. *David Harum.* E. Noyes Westcott, 1898.

Harvey, Dr Alec. *Brief Encounter* (play), N. Coward, 1945.

Harvey, Fleming. *Our Betters* (play), W. S. Maugham, 1923.

Harvey, Geoffrey, of the Red Tape and Sealing Wax Dept.
  Frances, his sister.
  The *Barsetshire* series, Angela Thirkell, 1933 onwards.

Harvey, Grace, schoolmistress, centra character, in love with Tom Thurnall.
  Her widowed mother.
  Two Years Ago, C. Kingsley, 1857.

Harvey family, English emigrants. *Settlers in Canada,* Captain Marryat, 1844.

Harville, Captain.
  His wife. Friends of Captain Wentworth.
  Persuasion, Jane Austen, 1818.

Harwen, Mr and Mrs, ostler and housekeeper at the Fortress. *Vanessa,* Hugh Walpole, 1933.

Harwich, Earl of, elder brother of Nigel Armine.
  Zoe, his wife.
  Bella Donna, R. S. Hichens, 1909.

Hasbrook, client of Allan Montague. *The Metropolis,* Upton Sinclair, 1908.

Haskard, Major, English farmer.
  His wife.
  Edward, their son.
  Lavinia, their daughter, m. Piet Grafton.
  The City of Gold, F. Brett Young, 1939.

Haslam, Sir Godfrey.
  Harriet, his wife.
  Their children:
    Matthew, m. as 2nd husband. Camilla Christy.
    Jermyn.
    Griselda.
    Gregory.
  Men and Wives, Ivy Compton-Burnett, 1931.

Hassan, a confectioner. *Hassan* (play), J. E. Flecker, 1923.

Hassan, a porter. *Captain Brassbound's Conversion* (play), G. B. Shaw, 1900.

Hassell, Captain James, of S.S. *Jane Vosper. The Loss of the 'Jane Vosper,'* F. Wills Crofts, 1936.

Hassock, Fred, distant cousin of Hope Ollerton, entertainer and auctioneer. *Let the People Sing,* J. B. Priestley, 1939.

Hastings, Lord. *Richard the Third* (play), W. Shakespeare.

Hastings, Arthur, 'Watson' to Hercule Poirot, m. Dulcie Duveen. *The Mysterious Affair at Styles,* 1920, and many others, Agatha Christie.

Hastings, Frank. *Housemaster* (play), Ian Hay, 1936.

Hastings, George, friend of Marlow, suitor of Constance Neville. *She Stoops to Conquer* (play), Oliver Goldsmith, 1773.

Hatch, Bennet. *The Black Arrow,* R. L. Stevenson, 1888.

Hatch, Hutchinson, newspaper reporter and confidant of Prof. van Duren. *The Professor in the Case* (series), J. Futrelle.

Hatchway, Lieutenant Jack, friend of Trunnion. *Peregrine Pickle,* T. Smollett, 1751.

Hatfield, Rev. Mr. *Agnes Grey,* Anne Brontë, 1847.

Hathaway, Paul, co-guardian of Yerba Buena, whom he marries. *A Ward of the Golden Gate,* Bret Harte.

Hatherleigh, Ted, fellow undergraduate of Remington at Trinity. *The New Machiavelli,* H. G. Wells, 1911.

Hatherley, ex-officer of the Buffs, rescued by Donovan. *Donovan Pasha,* Gilbert Parker, 1902.

Hathi, the Wild Elephant. 'Kaa's Hunting' and elsewhere, *The Jungle Books,* R. Kipling, 1894–5.

Hatt, Dicky. 'In the Pride of his Youth' (s.s.), *Plain Tales from the Hills,* R. Kipling, 1888.

Hatta. *See* HAIGHA.

Hattersley, rich banker, m. Milicent Hargrave. *The Tenant of Wildfell Hall,* Anne Brontë, 1848.

Hatton, 'Bishop of Woodgate,' nailmaker.
  His virago wife and two sons.
Sybil, B. Disraeli, 1845.

Hauksbee, Mrs Lucy, fast but goodhearted woman. 'Three and an Extra' and elsewhere, *Plain Tales from the Hills,* R. Kipling, 1888.

Hauser, Otto, publisher's reader. *You Can't Go Home Again,* T. Wolfe, 1947.

Hautet, Monsieur, examining magistrate. *Murder on the Links,* Agatha Christie, 1923.

Hautia, dark Polynesian queen, symbolizing Evil. *Mardi,* Herman Melville, 1849.

Hautlieu, Margaret (Sister Ursula). *See also* SIR MALCOLM FLEMING. *Castle Dangerous,* W. Scott, 1832.

Havelock, Edward.
  Leila, his wife.
Mrs Miniver, Jan Struther, 1939.

Haverford, Giles, once eng. to Marietta Lyddon. *The Prodigal Heart,* Susan Ertz, 1950.

Haverley, Miss. 'Only a Subaltern' (s.s.), *Wee Willie Winkie,* R. Kipling, 1895.

Havern, James, artist, related by marriage to Mrs Barley. *The One Before,* Barry Pain, 1902.

Haversham, Lord Dorincourt's family lawyer. *Little Lord Fauntleroy,* Frances H. Burnett, 1886.

Haversham, Walter, one-time fiancé of Kitty. *See* RAINIER. *Random Harvest,* J. Hilton, 1941.

Havill, Mr, dishonest architect and builder.
  His wife.
A Laodicean, T. Hardy, 1881.

Havisham, Miss, embittered spinster, benefactor of Philip Pirrip. *See also* COMPEYSON. *Great Expectations,* C. Dickens, 1861.

Hawbuck, Sir John.
  His wife.
  Hugh, his son.
  Lucy, his daughter.
The Book of Snobs, W. M. Thackeray, 1846–7.

Hawdon, Captain (alias Nemo), lover of Lady Dedlock and father of Esther Summerson. *Bleak House,* C. Dickens, 1853.

Hawes, ex-lieutenant, brutal governor of jail *It Is Never Too Late to Mend,* C. Reade, 1856.

Hawk, Harry, boatman. *Love Among the Chickens,* P. G. Wodehouse, 1906.

Hawk, Sir Mulberry, middle-aged adventurer, scoundrel, and client of Ralph Nickleby. *Nicholas Nickleby,* C. Dickens, 1839.

Hawk-Eye, 'The Pathfinder.' *See* EFFINGHAM. *The Pathfinder* and others, J. Fenimore Cooper, 1823–46.

Hawk-Monitor, Richard, m. Elfine Starkadder.
  His mother.
  Joan, his sister.
Cold Comfort Farm, Stella Gibbons, 1932.

Hawke, Dixon, famous detective, central character in series of novelettes for boys: anonymous authors.

Hawke, Rev. Gideon, Ernest Pontifex's first vicar. *The Way of all Flesh,* S. Butler, 1903.

Hawkes, Dickon ('Pegtop'), miller.
  Meg ('Beauty'), his daughter.
Uncle Silas, Sheridan le Fanu, 1864.

Hawkesley, Viscount, friend of Anthony Dare Jnr. *Mrs Halliburton's Troubles,* Mrs Henry Wood, 1862.

Hawkesworth (alias Count Plomer), adventurer. *Sophia,* Stanley Weyman, 1900.

Hawkins, bo'sn of *Fortune's Favourite. The Pirate,* W. Scott, 1822.

Hawkins, lawyer. *The Devil's Disciple* (play), G. B. Shaw, 1899.

Hawkins, Captain, illegitimate son of Lord Privilege. *Peter Simple,* Captain Marryat, 1834.

Hawkins, Helen. *Love on the Dole,* W. Greenwood, 1933.

Hawkins, Sir James.
 'Mrs Jim,' his wife.
 'William the Conqueror' (s.s.), *The Day's Work,* R. Kipling, 1898.

Hawkins, Jim, central character.
 His mother.
 Treasure Island, R. L. Stevenson, 1883.

Hawks, Capt. Andy, of the Cotton Blossom Floating Palace Theatre.
 Parthenia Ann, his wife.
 Magnolia, their daughter, m. Gaylord Ravenal.
 Show Boat, Edna Ferber, 1926.

Hawks, Asa, blind preacher.
 Sabbath Lily, his daughter.
 Wise Blood, Flannery O'Connor, 1952.

Hawkshaw, Bryan, schoolfellow of Henry Esmond. *Henry Esmond,* W. M. Thackeray, 1852.

Hawley, Frank, lawyer and town clerk, Middlemarch.
 'Young Hawley,' his son, law student.
 Middlemarch, Geo. Eliot, 1871–2.

Haws, Daniel, part-Cherokee landlord in Chicago. *Eustace Chisholm and the Works,* James Purdy, 1968.

Hawthorn, Jerry, cousin of Corinthian Tom. *Life in London* (or *Tom and Jerry*), Pierce Egan, 1821.

Hawthorn, Lucy, eng. to Victor Campion, m. Comte de la Villeblanche. *The Perennial Bachelor,* Anne Parrish, 1925.

Hay, John. 'The Wandering Jew' (s.s.), *Life's Handicap,* R. Kipling, 1891.

Hayden, Irish doctor. *Captain Kettle* series, C. Hyne, 1898–1932.

Hayden, Miss, ward of Septimus Gillian. 'One Thousand Dollars' (s.s.), *The Voice of the City,* O. Henry, 1908.

Haydon, Robert.
 Ethel, his wife, *née* Ormiston.
 The Delectable Duchy, A. Quiller-Couch, 1893.

Hayes, Laura, narrator, stepdaughter of Captain Sinclair, m. Frank Jervis. *The Good Ship 'Mohock,'* W. Clark Russell, 1894.

Hayes, Sally, teenage girl, friend of Holden Caulfield. *The Catcher* in *The Rye,* J. D. Salinger, 1951.

Hayle, Helen. *On Approval* (play), F. Lonsdale, 1927.

Haylock, Morrison, caterer. 'The Tie' (s.s.), *Limits and Renewals,* R. Kipling, 1932.

Hayman, m. Susan Forsyte.
 Five children, including 'The Dromios,' Giles and Jesse.
 The *Forsyte* series, J. Galsworthy, 1906–33.

Hayne, Marty, landgirl. 'Invasion Exercise on the Poultry Farm,' *Collected Poems,* John Betjeman, 1958.

Haynes, Rev. Gerald. *Lighten our Darkness,* R. Keable, 1927.

Hayraddin, Maugrabin, Quentin's guide to Liège. *Quentin Durward,* W. Scott, 1823.

Hayston, Frank, Laird of Bucklaw, m. Lucy Ashton. *The Bride of Lammermoor,* W. Scott, 1819.

Hayter, Mrs, sister of Mrs Musgrove Snr. *Persuasion,* Jane Austen, 1818.

Hayter, Max. *Comrade, O Comrade,* Ethel Mannin, 1946.

Hayward, Etheridge, friend of Philip Carey. *Of Human Bondage,* W. S. Maugham, 1915.

Hazard. *The Gamester* (play), J. Shirley, 1637.

Haze, Mrs Charlotte, widow who marries Humbert Humbert.
 Dolores, or **Dolly,** or **Lolita Haze,** her daughter, m. Richard F. Schiller.
 Lolita, Vladimir Nabokov, 1955.

Haze, Cunningham, chief constable. *A Laodicean,* T. Hardy, 1881.

Hazel, Mrs Amy. *The Benefactor,* J. D. Beresford.

Hazel, Caleb, schoolmaster. *The Little Shepherd of Kingdom Come,* J. Fox, Jnr, 1903.

Hazeldean, Squire. *My Novel,* Lord Lytton, 1853.

Hazelow, Tom. *Adam Bede,* George Eliot, 1859.

Hazelrigg, Julia, m. Colonel Granby.
Julius P., her father, inventor of Hazelrigg machine-gun.
The Four Armourers, F. Beeding, 1930.

Hazeltine, Julia, niece adopted by Joseph Finsbury, m. Gideon Forsyth. *The Wrong Box,* R. L. Stevenson & L. Osbourne, 1889.

Hazey, Mr, Master of the Hard and Sharp Hunt.
His wife.
Anna Maria, their daughter.
Bill, their son.
Mr Facey Romford's Hounds, R. S. Surtees, 1865.

Hazlewood, Charles, lover of Lucy Bertram.
Sir Robert, his father.
Guy Mannering, W. Scott, 1815.

Hazlewood, Guy, college friend of Michael Fane. *Sinister Street,* 1913, and others, C. Mackenzie.

Hazy, Miss Chris. *Mrs Wiggs of the Cabbage Patch,* Alice H. Rice, 1901.

Headingley, John N., of Boston. *The Tragedy of the Korosko,* A. Conan Doyle, 1898.

Headrigg, Judden.
Mause, his wife, *née* Middlemas.
Cuddie, their son, m. Jenny Dennison.
Jennie, their daughter.
Old Mortality, W. Scott, 1816.

Headstone, Bradley, schoolmaster, blackmailed by Rogue Riderhood. *Our Mutual Friend,* C. Dickens, 1865.

Headthelot, Lord. *East Lynne,* Mrs Henry Wood, 1861.

Heal, Margaret, eng. to Colin Mackenzie. *The Fanatics* (play), M. Malleson, 1924.

Heale, drunken and incompetent doctor. *Two Years Ago,* C. Kingsley, 1857.

Heard, Michael, cousin of Salvation Yeo. *Westward Ho!,* C. Kingsley, 1855.

Heard, Thomas, ex-Bishop of Bampopo. *South Wind,* N. Douglas, 1917.

Hearn, Jim, fiancé of Martha, maid to Miss Matty. *Cranford,* Mrs Gaskell, 1853.

Hearn, Mary. *The Farmer's Wife* (play), E. Phillpotts, 1924.

Hearne, Bryan, ship's officer, m. Alison Ingleside. *Mr Ingleside,* E. V. Lucas, 1910.

Heartfree, good man.
His good wife.
Jonathan Wild, Henry Fielding, 1743.

Hearts, King, Queen and Knave of. *Alice in Wonderland,* L. Carroll, 1865.

Heaslop, Ronald, city magistrate, son of Mrs Moore. *A Passage to India,* E. M. Forster, 1924.

Heasman, A., schoolmaster.
Winifred, his wife.
We the Accused, E. Raymond, 1935.

Heat, Chief Inspector. *The Secret Agent,* Joseph Conrad, 1907.

Heath, Sergeant. *The Benson Murder Case,* S. S. van Dine, 1926.

Heath, Charles, m. (1) Lavinia Straker, (2) Alicia Kavanagh.
Andrew, his father, silk merchant.
His mother.
His brothers and sisters:
Robert.
Ellen.
Archie.
Margaret, m. Sir Rupert Johnson.
Joan.
Alice-for-Short, W. de Morgan, 1907.

Heath, Sir Massingberd, Bt.
Sinnamenta, his wife, *née* Liversedge, married by gipsy rites.
Sir Wentworth, his father.
Marmaduke, his nephew and heir, m. Lucy Gerard.
Lost Sir Massingberd, James Payn, 1864.

Heathcliff, farmer, central character, m. Isabella Linton.
Linton, their son, m. Cathy Linton. *See also* EARNSHAW.
Wuthering Heights, Emily Brontë, 1847.

Heathcote, Adolphus, friend of the Wynnes. *Over Bemerton's,* E. V. Lucas, 1908.

Heatherlegh, Dr. 'The Phantom Rickshaw' (s.s.), *Wee Willie Winkie,* R. Kipling, 1888.

Heatherstone, Patience, m. Edward Beverley.
Her father.
Children of the New Forest, Captain Marryat, 1847.

Heathfield, Alfred, m. Grace Jeddler. *The Battle of Life,* C. Dickens, 1846.

Heatleigh, Lord. 'A Naval Mutiny' (s.s.), *Limits and Renewals,* R. Kipling, 1932.

Heaviside, Mrs ('Nannie'), housekeeper to the Seymores. *Fanny by Gaslight,* M. Sadleir, 1940.

Heavistone, Brander, American tourist. 'Patience' (s.s.), *Last Recollections of My Uncle Charles,* N. Balchin, 1954.

Heavyside, Captain Charles, member of Barnes Newcome's club. *The Newcomes,* W. M. Thackeray, 1853–1855.

Heavytop, Colonel.
His wife.
Vanity Fair, W. M. Thackeray, 1847–8.

Heccomb, Mrs, Anna Quayne's ex-governess.
Daphne, her stepdaughter.
The Death of the Heart, Elizabeth Bowen, 1938.

Hector, son of Priam. *Troilus and Cressida* (play), W. Shakespeare.

Hector of the Mist, an outlaw. *The Legend of Montrose,* W. Scott, 1819.

Hedzoff, Count K., captain of King Valoroso's guard. *The Rose and the Ring,* W. M. Thackeray, 1855.

Heeny, Mrs, society masseuse. *The Custom of the Country,* Edith Wharton, 1913.

Heep, Uriah, hypocritical and fawning clerk to Mr Wickfield.
His father and mother.
David Copperfield, C. Dickens, 1850.

Hegan, Jim, railway magnate.
Laura, his daughter.
The Metropolis, Upton Sinclair, 1908.

Hegarty, Simon, bailiff.
Louisa, his sister, m. John Hynes.
Famine, L. O'Flaherty, 1937.

Hei, Miss, sister of Phuong. *The Quiet American,* Graham Greene, 1955.

Heidelberg, Mrs. *The Clandestine Marriage* (play), G. Colman the Elder, 1766.

Heilig, Franz, librarian. *You Can't Go Home Again,* T. Wolfe, 1947.

Heineman, Elizabeth, inmate of home for aged. *The Poorhouse Fair,* John Updike, 1959.

Heinrich, Herr, tutor to the Britling boys. *Mr Britling Sees It Through,* H. G. Wells, 1916.

Heiss, Maria, friend of Karl Spiel, m. Breuer.
Her father and mother.
Franz, her brother.
The Heart of a Child, Phyllis Bottome, 1940.

Heit, Colonel, coroner. *An American Tragedy,* T. Dreiser, 1925.

Heldar, Dick, war correspondent and artist, central character, in love with Maisie. *The Light that Failed,* R. Kipling, 1890.

Helen, wife of Menelaus. *Troilus and Cressida* (play), W. Shakespeare.

Helen. *When the Sleeper Awakes,* H. G. Wells, 1899.

Helen, friend of Don Birnam. *The Lost Weekend,* Charles Jackson, 1944.

Helen, loved by Modus. *The Hunchback* (play), J. S. Knowles, 1832.

Helena, in love with Demetrius. *A Midsummer Night's Dream* (play), W. Shakespeare.

Helena, a gentlewoman. *All's Well That Ends Well* (play), W. Shakespeare.

Helenus, son of Priam. *Troilus and Cressida* (play), W. Shakespeare.

Helicanus, a lord of Tyre. *Pericles* (play), W. Shakespeare.

Hellstern, Emil, Jewish financier.
Marie Thérèse, his wife.
'Portrait of a Gentleman' (s.s.), *These Charming People,* M. Arlen, 1920.

Helm, Charlotte ('Aunt Sharley'), aged Negro servant. 'Quality Folk' (s.s.), *From Place to Place,* Irvin S. Cobb, 1920.

Helmont, Rose, blackmailing nurse. *God's Prisoner,* J. Oxenham, 1898.

Helmsdale, Cuthbert. *See* MELCHESTER.

Helotius, Mrs Zoe, vulgar, wealthy international hostess. *The Judgment of Paris,* Gore Vidal, 1952.

Help, rescuer of Christian from the Slough of Despond. *Pilgrim's Progress,* J. Bunyan, 1678 and 1684.

Helsing, chancellor.
His wife and daughter.
Rupert of Hentzau, A. Hope, 1898.

Helsing, Abraham van. *Dracula*, Bram Stoker, 1897.

Helstone, Rev. Matthewson.
Caroline, his niece, m. Robert Moore.
Shirley, Charlotte Brontë, 1849.

Helstonleigh, Bishop of.

Helstonleigh, Dean of.
The Channings, Mrs Henry Wood, 1862.

Helvellyn, Lord. *See* JOHN JOHNES.

Hely, Walsingham, attaché at the British Embassy, Paris, in love with Charlotte Baynes.
His mother and sister.
The Adventures of Philip, W. M. Thackeray, 1861–2.

Hemington, Charles, fiancé of Monica Claverton-Ferry. *The Elder Statesman* (play), T. S. Eliot, 1958.

Hemingway, mining engineer. 'The Lost Generation' (s.s.), *These Charming People*, M. Arlen, 1920.

Hempel, m. Sarah Turnham. *The Fortunes of Richard Mahony*, H. H. Richardson, 1917–30

Hempel, Julie, friend of Selina Peake, m. Michael Arnold.
August, her father.
So Big, Edna Ferber, 1924.

Hemstitch, Lord. *We're Here*, D. Mackail, 1947.

Hemworth, Mabel.
Natty, her husband.
Distinguished Villa (play), Kate O'Brien, 1926.

Henchard, Michael, hay-trusser.
Susan, his wife, whom he sells at a fair.
Elizabeth Jane, Susan's daughter by Richard Newson, m. Donald Farfrae as 2nd wife.
The Mayor of Casterbridge, T. Hardy, 1886.

Henderland, travelling preacher. *Kidnapped*, R. L. Stevenson, 1886.

Henderson, 'creator' of Caxton school. *Joan and Peter*, H. G. Wells, 1918.

Henderson, schoolboy. *St Winifred's*, F. W. Farrar, 1862.

Henderson, hunter on board *Ghost*. *The Sea Wolf*, Jack London, 1904.

Henderson, Elias, the Lady of Lochleven's chaplain. *The Abbot*, W. Scott, 1820.

Henderson, Ethel, stepdaughter of James Chaffery, and his assistant at séances, m. George Lewisham. *Love and Mr Lewisham*, H. G. Wells, 1900.

Henderson, Eugene, an American millionaire travelling in Africa. *Henderson The Rain King*, Saul Bellow, 1959.

Henderson, Miriam, central character.
Her mother and father.
Her sisters:
Sarah, m. Bennett Brodie.
Eve.
Harriet, m. Gerald Ducayne.
Pilgrimage, Dorothy M. Richardson, 1915–38.

Henderson, Olaf, architect, central character, m. Hedda Maning.
His father, bank manager.
His mother.
The Benefactor, J. D. Beresford.

Hendie, musical critic, *The Voice*, Ria. *Right Off the Map*, C. E. Montague, 1927.

Hendon, Mary, m. Herbert Beveridge. *In Greek Waters*, G. A. Henty, 1892.

Hendon, Miles, later Earl of Kent, rescuer and friend of the Prince of Wales, m. widow of Hugh, his villainous brother. *The Prince and the Pauper*, Mark Twain, 1882.

Henet, a widow, old and mischief-making chief servant in Imhotep's household, murdered by Yahmose. *Death Comes as the End*, Agatha Christie, 1945.

Hengo, nephew to Caratach. *Bonduca* (play), Beaumont & Fletcher, 1614.

Hengrave, Lord (Charles) (Family name Bramsley).
His wife.
Their children:
Caryl ('C'), centra character.
Edward, m. Marie.
Gilbert.
Harry.
Julia, m. Tommy Holden.
Marjorie, m. Sir Harold Ducane.
C., M. Baring, 1924.

Henley, Dr, m. Margaret Mozville. *The Heir of Redclyffe*, Charlotte M. Yonge, 1853.

Hennessy, John Aloysius.
His children:
Gerard, m. Millicent Considine.

Anna, m. Denis Considine.
Dominic, m. Louise.
Without My Cloak, Kate O'Brien, 1931.

Henny-Penny, Sally. *The Tale of Mrs Tiggy-Winkle,* Beatrix Potter, 1905.

Henri, Frances Evans, pupil and later wife of W. Crimsworth. *The Professor,* Charlotte Brontë, 1857.

Henriques, 'poor white' Portuguese. *Prester John,* J. Buchan, 1910.

Henry. *Outward Bound* (play), S. Vane, 1923.

Henry, boy on the *Seamew.* *The Skipper's Wooing,* W. W. Jacobs, 1897.

Henry IV (Bolingbroke). *Richard the Second* (play), W. Shakespeare.

Henry VII (Richmond). *Richard the Third* (play), W. Shakespeare. *Perkin Warbeck* (play), John Ford, 1634.

Henry, Judge.
His wife.
The Virginian, O. Wister, 1902.

Henry, Mr, agent to Lawrence Buxton. *The Moorland Cottage,* Mrs Gaskell, 1850.

Henry, Prince, later Henry III. *King John* (play), W. Shakespeare.

Henry, Prince. *The Golden Legend* (poem), H. W. Longfellow, 1851.

Henry, Senator, protégé of Paul Madvig.
Janet, his daughter.
The Glass Key, Dashiell Hammett, 1931.

Henry, Frederick, American, *Tenente* in the Italian Army, central character and narrator. *A Farewell to Arms,* E. Hemingway, 1929.

Henschil, Miss. 'In the Same Boat' (s.s.), *A Diversity of Creatures,* R. Kipling, 1917.

Henshaw, Kitt, Tay boatman. *The Fair Maid of Perth,* W. Scott, 1828.

Henshawe, Myra, *née* Driscoll.
Oswald, her husband.
My Mortal Enemy, Willa Cather, 1928.

Henty. *See* SNOW.

Hentzau, Rupert of. *The Prisoner of Zenda* and *Rupert of Hentzau,* A. Hope, 1894–8.

Hepburn, Philip, shop assistant, cousin of Sylvia Robson, whom he marries.
Bella, their daughter.
Sylvia's Lovers, Mrs Gaskell, 1863.

Hephzibah, Gertrude Thorpe's maid. *The Notorious Mrs Ebbsmith* (play), A. W. Pinero, 1895.

Herb, newspaper reporter.
Elizabeth, his daughter.
Heaven's My Destination, Thornton Wilder, 1935.

Herbert, Ada, m. Horace Beveridge, taken prisoner, with her mother, by the Turks. *In Greek Waters,* G. A. Henty, 1892.

Herbert, Adrian. *Love Among the Artists,* G. B. Shaw, 1900.

Herbert, Ambrose, diarist to Lord Sombremere, m. Lychnis Sombremere. *Landscape with Figures,* R. Fraser, 1925.

Herbert, Charles, lover and victim of Helen Vaughan. *The Great God Pan,* A. Machen, 1894.

Herbert, Major Charles, m. Sybil Anstey.
Ianthe, their daughter, m. Thomson.
The Ballad and the Source, Rosamond Lehmann, 1944.

Herbert, Eliza. *Diary of a Late Physician,* S. Warren, 1832.

Herbert, Herbert, bookish recluse.
Grisel, his sister.
The Return, Walter de la Mare, 1910.

Herbert, Niel, nephew of Judge Pommeroy. *A Lost Lady,* Willa Cather, 1923.

Herbert, Tom. *East Lynne,* Mrs Henry Wood, 1861.

Herbert, Vere, daughter of Dolly Vanderdecken by her 1st husband, Vere, son of Duchess of Mull; m. Prince Sergius Zouroff. *Moths,* Ouida, 1880.

Herd, Eli, Samuel Billingham's lawyer, m. Harriet, Billingham's 1st wife. *Mr Billingham, the Marquis and Madelon,* E. P. Oppenheim.

Hereward, of Hampton. *Count Robert of Paris,* W. Scott, 1832.

Herf, Jimmy, cub reporter.
Lily, his mother.
Manhattan Transfer, J. dos Passos, 1925.

Heriot, Eliza, Lady, an autocrat.
Sir Robert, her husband.
Roberta, her daughter.
Angus, her son.
Hermia, her stepdaughter.
Madeline, her stepdaughter.

The Last and the First, Ivy Compton-Burnett, 1971.

Heriot, George, goldsmith to James I (hist.).
Judith, his sister.
The Fortunes of Nigel, W. Scott, 1822.

Heriot, Tony.
David and **Bill,** his twin brothers.
Invitation to the Waltz, Rosamond Lehmann, 1932.

Heriot, Sir Walter, cousin of Angela Gollantz.
Beatrice, his wife.
Viva, their daugher, in love with Emmanuel Gollantz.
Walter, their son.
Young Emmanuel, Naomi Jacob, 1932.

Heriot, Walter, head boy and friend of Harry Richmond. *The Adventures of Harry Richmond,* G. Meredith, 1871.

Heritage, John, paper maker and poet. *Huntingtower,* J. Buchan, 1922.

Herman, shoe salesman. *Winterset* (play), Maxwell Anderson, 1935.

Herman of Goodalricke, a Preceptor of the Order of the Temple. *Ivanhoe,* W. Scott, 1820.

Hermann, King Rudolf's majordomo. *Rupert of Hentzau,* A. Hope, 1898.

Hermia, in love with Lysander. *A Midsummer Night's Dream* (play), W. Shakespeare.

Hermione, Leontes's Queen. *A Winter's Tale* (play), W. Shakespeare.

Hermione, Lady, exposer of Lord Dalgarno's villainy. *The Fortunes of Nigel,* W. Scott, 1822.

Hermon, a parasite. *Gorboduc* (play), T. Sackville & T. Norton, 1562.

Hernandez, Countess Manuelata, m. President Alvarez. *Soldiers of Fortune,* R. H. Davis, 1897.

Herncastle, Colonel John, uncle of Franklin Blake.
Julia, his sister, m. Sir John Verinder.
The Moonstone, W. Collins, 1868.

Herne, Mrs, an old crone. *Lavengro,* George Borrow, 1851.

Herne, Patrick. *Destiny Bay,* Donn Byrne, 1928.

Herne the Hunter, spectre haunting Windsor Forest. *Windsor Castle,* W. H. Ainsworth, 1843.

Hernon, Patch.
Kitty, his wife, *née* Kilmartin.
Their seven children.
Kate, his aunt, 'wise woman.'
Famine, L. O'Flaherty, 1937.

Hero, Leonato's daughter. *Much Ado about Nothing* (play), W. Shakespeare.

Herod.
Marianne, his wife.
Cypros, his mother.
Salome, his sister.
Herod (play), S. Phillips, 1900.

Herodsfoot, Badalia, flower girl.
Tom, her husband.
'The Record of Badalia Herodsfoot' (s.s.), *Many Inventions,* R. Kipling, 1893.

Heron, Rev. Arthur.
Lucy, his wife, *née* Gilfil.
Oswald, their son.
'Mr Gilfil's Love Story,' *Scenes of Clerical Life,* George Eliot, 1857.

Heron, Irene, m. (1) Soames Forsyte (div.), (2) Young Jolyon Forsyte. The *Forsyte* series, J. Galsworthy, 1906–33.

Heron, Patrick, Laird of Rathan, central character and narrator.
John, his father.
The Raiders, S. R. Crockett, 1894.

Herres, Victor, actor.
Nancy, his wife.
Clement, their small son.
The Troubled Air, Irwin Shaw, 1951.

Herrick, Chief Detective Inspector John, of Scotland Yard. *Poison Ivy,* P. Cheyney, 1937.

Herrick, Professor Nathan.
Catherine, his wife.
Bertha, their daughter, m. Richard Amory.
Through One Administration, Frances H. Burnett, 1881.

Herrick, Nicholas, owner of a school.
Emily, his half-sister.
Pastors and Masters, Ivy Compton-Burnett, 1925.

The Herries Family

Herries, Francis ('Rogue'), central character.
m. (1) Margaret Harden.
Their children:
David, m. Sarah Denburn (see below).
Mary, m. Raisley Herries.
Deborah, m. Gordon Sunwood.
m. (2) Mirabell Starr.

Judith, their daughter. *See* PARIS.
Pomfret, Francis's elder brother.
Janice, his wife.
Their children:
Anabel.
Raisley, m. Mary Herries.
Judith, m. Ernest Bligh (Lord Rockage).
Harcourt, Francis's younger brother.
Robert, his cousin.
Pelham, Helen and **Grandison,** his children.
'Great-Aunt Maria.'
Rogue Herries, Hugh Walpole, 1930.

Herries, David (see above).
Sarah, his wife.
Their children:
Francis, m. Jennifer Cards.
Their children:
John, m. Elizabeth Herries.
Dorothy, m. Arthur Bellairs.
Deborah, m. Squire Withering.
Sir William.
m. (1) Christabel Carmichael.
Walter, their son.
m. (2) Valerie Morgan.
Ellis, their son.
Judith Paris, Hugh Walpole, 1931.

Herries, Walter (see above), m. Agnes Bailey.
Their children:
Uhland, murders his cousin John and shoots himself.
Elizabeth, m. John Herries.
John, son of Francis and Jennifer (see above), m. Elizabeth Herries; murdered.
Benjamin, their son.
The Fortress, Hugh Walpole, 1932.

Herries, Benjamin (see above), son of John and Elizabeth, m. Marion Halliday.
Tom, their son.
Ellis (Sir), son of William, m. Vanessa Paris.
Sally, Vanessa's daughter by Benjie.
Alfred, also of the clan.
Maurice, his son.
Vanessa, Hugh Walpole, 1933.

Herries of Birrenswork, alias of Redgauntlet. *Redgauntlet,* W. Scott, 1824.

Herring, Eden, boy actor, central character, m. Halcyon Day.
Will, his father.
Lilian, his dead mother.
Rhoda, his sister.
Melissa, his half-sister.
Joe and **Charlie,** his uncles.
Little Red Horses, G. B. Stern, 1932.

Herriot, pilot, interned in Holland. *The Fountain,* C. Morgan, 1932.

Herriot, Mrs. *The Story of the Gadsbys,* R. Kipling, 1888.

Herriton, Mrs Lilia, widow of Charles Herriton.
Irma, her daughter.
Philip, her brother-in-law.
Harriet, her intolerant spinster sister-in-law.
Where Angels Fear To Tread, E. M. Forster, 1905.

Hertford, Duke and Duchess of. 'Maltby and Braxton,' *Seven Men,* Max Beerbohm, 1919.

Hervey, a dog. 'The Dog Hervey' (s.s.), *A Diversity of Creatures,* R. Kipling, 1917.

Hervey, Mrs Dorothy, Clarissa's aunt.
Dolly, her daughter.
Clarissa Harlowe, S. Richardson, 1748.

Herzenberg, Graf. *Dragon Harvest,* Upton Sinclair, 1946.

Heseltine, Joan. *C.,* M. Baring, 1924.

Hesketh, Harry, m. Alicia Orgreave. The *Clayhanger* trilogy, Arnold Bennett, 1910–16.

Hesperus, murderer of his wife, Floribel. *The Bride's Tragedy,* T. L. Beddoes, 1822.

Hesselius, Dr, narrator, *Green Tea* (s.s.), Sheridan le Fanu.

Hetherton, Ambrose. *The Secret Vanguard,* M. Innes, 1940.

Hetty, Aunt. 'Aunt Hetty' (s.s.), *Sir Pompey and Madame Juno,* M. Armstrong, 1927.

Heve, Dr.
His brother, the vicar.
Clayhanger, Arnold Bennett, 1910.

Heveland, William, A.D.C. *Handley Cross,* R. S. Surtees, 1843.

Hewby, Mr, London architect. *A Pair of Blue Eyes,* T. Hardy, 1873.

Hewer, David, playwright.
Josephine, his wife.
'Among Friends' (s.s.), *Last Recollections of My Uncle Charles,* N. Balchin, 1954.

Hewit, Beau. *The Man of Mode* (play), Sir G. Etherege, 1676.

Hewitt, Admiral Sir Hercules, K.C.B.
His wife.
Nancy, their daughter.
The Middle Watch (play), Ian Hay & S. King-Hall, 1929.

Hewitt, Patience ('Patty'), m. (1) Gervase Piercey, (2) Roger Pearson.
Richard, her father.
Patience, her aunt.
The Cuckoo in the Nest, Mrs Oliphant, 1894.

Hexam, Jesse ('Gaffer'), 'night-bird' (robber of bodies found floating in the Thames).
Lizzie, his daughter, m. Eugene Wrayburn.
Charlie, his son, a boorish snob.
Our Mutual Friend, C. Dickens, 1865.

Heybrook, Lord. *French without Tears* (play), T. Rattigan, 1936.

Heydinger, Alice, student at School of Science, in love with Lewisham. *Love and Mr Lewisham,* H. G. Wells, 1900.

Heyduke, Lady Mary. *Green Tea* (s.s.), Sheridan le Fanu.

Heyer, Bill, smallholder. *South Riding,* Winifred Holtby, 1936.

Heyford. *The Last of the Barons,* Lord Lytton, 1843.

Heyling, George. *Pickwick Papers,* C. Dickens, 1837.

Heyst, Axel, idealist. *Victory,* Joseph Conrad, 1915.

Heythorp, Sylvanus, shipowner. *See also* ROSAMUND LARNE.
Ernest, his son.
Adela, his daughter.
A Stoic, J. Galsworthy, 1918.

Heyward, Major Duncan. *The Last of the Mohicans,* J. Fenimore Cooper, 1826.

Heywood, Charles, schoolmaster.
Clare, his dead wife.
Judgment in Suspense, G. Bullett, 1946.

Hialas, Spanish agent. *Perkin Warbeck* (play), John Ford, 1634.

Hiawatha, central character.
Minnehaha, his wife.
Mudjekeewis, his father.
Wenonah, his mother.
The Song of Hiawatha (poem), H. W. Longfellow, 1855.

Hibberd, Sir Ogilvy, later Lord Aberfordbury. The *Barsetshire* series, Angela Thirkell, 1933 on.

Hibbert. *Journey's End* (play), R. C. Sherriff, 1928.

Hibbert, Clara. *The Vortex* (play), N. Coward, 1924.

Hibbins, Mrs, reputed witch, sister of Governor Bellingham. *The Scarlet Letter,* N. Hawthorne, 1850.

Hibou, Mademoiselle, French governess. *The Virginians,* W. M. Thackeray, 1857–9.

Hickey, Dr Jerome. *Some Experiences of an Irish R.M.,* Œ. Somerville & Martin Ross, 1899.

Hickman, Mr, fiancé of Anne Howe. *Clarissa Harlowe,* S. Richardson, 1748.

Hickmot (or **Hickmer),** Australian soldier. 'Friend of the Family' (s.s.), *Debits and Credits,* R. Kipling, 1926.

Hicks, gardener to the Derrifords. *The One Before,* Barry Pain, 1902.

Hicks, George, Robert Carne's groom. *South Riding,* Winifred Holtby, 1936.

Hicks, Hannah, Martha Honeyman's maid. *The Newcomes,* W. M. Thackeray, 1853–5.

Hicks, Telemachus. 'Telemachus, Friend' (s.s.), *Heart of the West,* O. Henry, 1907.

Hicksey, of the Indian Police. 'A Conference of the Powers' (a 'Stalky' story), *Many Inventions,* R. Kipling, 1893.

Hicksey, Bill. 'Bill's Paperchase' (s.s.), *The Lady of the Barge,* W. W. Jacobs, 1902.

Hickson, Albert, property master. *Enter a Murderer,* Ngaio Marsh, 1935.

Hickson, George.
Philip, his nephew.
The Horse's Mouth, Joyce Cary, 1944.

Hieronimo, Marshal of Spain.
Isabella, his wife.
Horatio, their son.
The Spanish Tragedy (play), T. Kyd, 1594.

Higden, Betty, old woman who keeps a 'minding' school at Brentford. *Our Mutual Friend,* C. Dickens, 1865.

Higgins, Mrs, elderly widow. 'Mr Gilfil's Love Story,' *Scenes of Clerical Life,* George Eliot, 1857.

Higgins, Ernest, m. Jane Bell.
Emily, his mother, m. Albert Bell.
The Water Gipsies, A. P. Herbert, 1930.

Higgins, Henry.
His mother.
Pygmalion (play), G. B. Shaw, 1914.

Higgins, Josiah.
Hilda, his daughter, m. John Hammond.
George, Hilda's nephew.
My Brother Jonathan, F. Brett Young, 1928.

Higgins, Nicholas.
Bessy and **Mary,** his daughters.
North and South, Mrs Gaskell, 1855.

Higgs, solicitor. *Vanity Fair,* W. M. Thackeray, 1847–8.

Higgs, central character and narrator. *Erewhon,* 1872, and *Erewhon Revisited,* 1901, S. Butler.

Higgs, Captain Lucius (alias Luke Settle, alias Mr X). *The Splendid Spur,* A. Quiller-Couch, 1889.

Highgate, Lord, father of Jack Belsize, who succeeds him. *The Newcomes,* W. M. Thackeray, 1853–5.

Hignett, Lieutenant-Commander A. L. 'Their Lawful Occasions' (s.s.), *Traffics and Discoveries,* R. Kipling, 1904.

Hilaion. *See* HILDEBRAND.

Hilary, uncle to Scythrop Glowry. *See also* MARIONETTA O'CARROLL.
His wife.
Nightmare Abbey, T. L. Peacock, 1818.

Hilary, Elsie.
James, her husband.
The High Road (play), F. Lonsdale, 1927.

Hilary, King. *Now We Are Six* (poems), A. A. Milne, 1926.

Hildebrand, King.
Hilarion, his son, m. Princess Ida.
Princess Ida (comic opera), Gilbert & Sullivan, 1884. Not named in *The Princess* (poem), Lord Tennyson.

Hildebrandt, Sir, half-brother of Theodora, Margravine of Godesberg. *A Legend of the Rhine,* W. M. Thackeray, 1845.

Hildebrod, Duke Jacob, Grand Protector of the Liberties of Alsatia. *The Fortunes of Nigel,* W. Scott, 1822.

Hildersham, Friar. *The Merry Devil of Edmonton* (play), Anon.

Hilfe, Anna, refugee, m. Arthur Rowe.
Willi, her brother, spy.
The Ministry of Fear, Graham Greene, 1943.

Hill, an N.C.O. training R.A.F. recruits. *Chips With Everything* (play), Arnold Wesker, 1962.

Hill, Albert, Joanna's betrayer. *Joanna Godden,* Sheila Kaye-Smith, 1921.

Hill, Eveline.
Harry, her brother.
Frank, her lover.
'Eveline' (s.s.), *The Dubliners,* James Joyce, 1914.

Hill, Humphrey.
Bertie, his brother.
The Sky Pilot, R. Connor, 1899.

Hill, Jenny. *Major Barbara* (play), G. B. Shaw, 1905.

Hill, Mary, m. Joe Rendal. 'Three from Dunsterville' (s.s.), *The Man Upstairs,* P. G. Wodehouse, 1914.

Hill, Tom, huntsman. *Jorrocks's Jaunts and Jollities,* R. S. Surtees, 1838.

Hillary, wealthy merchant.
Mary, his daughter, m. Henry Elliott.
Diary of a Late Physician, S. Warren, 1832.

Hillcot, ex-burglar, valet, butler and friend of Garry Anson. *The Calendar,* E. Wallace.

Hillcrist.
His wife.
Jill, their daughter.
The Skin Game, J. Galsworthy, 1920.

Hillel, a patriarch. *Ben Hur,* L. Wallace, 1880.

Hillier, George, playwright and journalist, m. Peggy Marsden. *All the World Wondered,* L. Merrick, 1911.

Hills, Everett, D.D., Congregational minister.
His wife.
Mourning becomes Electra (play), E. O'Neill, 1931.

Hilmer, Hélène, 2nd wife of Young Jolyon Forsyte. The *Forsyte* series, J. Galsworthy, 1906–33.

Hilton, Marion, prostitute and drunkard, Henry Maitland's 1st wife.

The Private Life of Henry Maitland, Morley Roberts, 1912.

Hilton, Roger.
  Dorothy, his wife.
    Catherine, Martin and **Anne,** their children.
  Call it a Day (play), Dodie Smith, 1935.

Hilyard, Captain Raymond, one-time fiancé of Etta Concannon. *The Glory of Clementina Wing*, W. J. Locke, 1911.

Hilyard, Robert, friend of Adam Warner. *The Last of the Barons*, Lord Lytton, 1843.

Hilyer, Rev. K., Vicar of Siddermorton. *The Wonderful Visit*, H. G. Wells, 1895.

Himmelfarb, Mordecai, ex-Professor of English, Jewish immigrant in Australia. *Riders in the Chariot*, Patrick White, 1961.

Hinchcliffe, assistant master. *The Apple* (s.s.), H. G. Wells, 1896.

Hinchcliffe, Henry Salt, chief engineer. 'Their Lawful Occasions' and elsewhere, *Traffics and Discoveries*, R. Kipling, 1904.

Hind, Henry, attorney. *Abraham Lincoln* (play), J. Drinkwater, 1918.

Hines, Cosmo, bookseller, m. Dorothy Merlin. *The Unspeakable Skipton*, Pamela Hansford Johnson, 1959.

Hingston, Sir Joseph, Bt, later Lord Wolverbury.
  Margaret, his wife.
  Their children:
    George, m. Eleanor Pomfret.
    Vivien.
    Edward.
    Steven, m. Miranda Hart.
    Ralph, m. Clare Lydiatt.
  Portrait of Clare, 1927, and *My Brother Jonathan*, 1928, F. Brett Young.

Hinkley, Rev. Ira, medical student. *Martin Arrowsmith*, Sinclair Lewis, 1925.

Hinks, saddler, neighbour of Polly at Fishbourne. *The History of Mr Polly*, H. G. Wells, 1910.

Hinkson, Bess, mistress of Tyson.
  Her father and mother.
  Starvecrow Farm, Stanley Weyman, 1905.

Hinton, Adelaide, eng. to Edward Springrove, m. Farmer Bollens. *Desperate Remedies*, T. Hardy, 1871.

Hinton, Jack, central character and narrator, m. Louisa Bellew.
  General Sir George, his father.
  Lady Charlotte, his mother.
  Jack Hinton, C. Lever, 1843.

Hinze, 'superlatively deferential' man. *Theophrastus Such*, George Eliot, 1879.

Hipcroft, Ned, m. Caroline Aspent. 'The Fiddler of the Reels,' *Life's Little Ironies*, T. Hardy, 1894.

Hipgrave, Mrs (Kennett).
  Beatrice, her daughter.
  Phroso, A. Hope, 1897.

Hipkiss, Bessie, central character who changes her name to Campbell, m. (1) Josef Rolewicz, (2) Norman Gantz.
  Bert Hipkiss, her father.
  Jenny, her sister.
  Billy, her brother.
  Mabel Stevens, her stepmother.
  Jezebel's Dust, Fred Urquhart, 1951.

Hipper, Blanche, m. Loftus Wilcher.
  Clarissa, her sister.
  Herself Surprised, Joyce Cary, 1941.

Hipplewayne, Philip, 'warned-off' racing owner. *The Calendar*, E. Wallace.

Hippolita, wife of Manfred, false Prince of Otranto. *The Castle of Otranto*, Horace Walpole, 1765.

Hippolyta, Queen of the Amazons, betrothed to Theseus. *A Midsummer Night's Dream* (play), W. Shakespeare.

Hipsley, Sir John, Bt. *The Book of Snobs*, W. M. Thackeray, 1846–7.

Hira Singh Ressaldar. 'The Man Who Was' (s.s.), *Life's Handicap*, R. Kipling, 1891.

Hire, Captain la. *Saint Joan* (play), G. B. Shaw, 1924.

Hiren, central character. *The Turkish Mahomet* (play), G. Peele, 1584.

Hirnam Singh. 'In Flood Time' (s.s.), *Soldiers Three*, R. Kipling, 1888.

Hirsch, Dr. 'The Duel of Doctor Hirsch,' *The Wisdom of Father Brown*, G. K. Chesterton, 1914.

Hirsch, Lorenzo, clerk to Moses Löwe

of Bonn, traitorous friend of Fitz-Boodle. *The Fitz-Boodle Papers*, W. M. Thackeray, 1842–3.

Hirte, Toby, apothecary. 'Brother Square Toes,' and elsewhere, *Rewards and Fairies*, R. Kipling, 1910.

His Majesty the King. *See* AUSTELL.

Hist (Hist-oh-Hist), Indian maiden. *The Deerslayer*, J. Fenimore Cooper, 1841.

Hitchcock, engineer. 'The Bridge Builders' (s.s.), *The Day's Work*, R. Kipling, 1898.

Hitchcock, Tommy. *Britannia Mews*, Margery Sharp, 1946.

Hittaway, Mrs Clara, daughter of Lady Fawn.

Her husband, Chairman of Court of Criminal Appeals.

The Eustace Diamonds, A. Trollope, 1873.

Hoang, Chinese beachcomber. *Shanghaied*, F. Norris, 1904.

Hoape, G. J., American tycoon. *The Pretty Lady*, Arnold Bennett, 1918.

Hoare, Captain Philip, m. Elisa Minden. 'The Orford Mystery' (s.s.), *Old Patch's Medley*, Marjorie Bowen, 1930.

Hobanob, Lord. *Pendennis*, 1848–1850, and elsewhere, W. M. Thackeray.

Hobart, Miss, friend of Miss Horne. *Sylvia Scarlett*, C. Mackenzie, 1918.

Hobart, Oliver, m. Jane Potter. *Potterism*, Rose Macaulay, 1920.

Hobart, Lieutenant Rian. *An Englishman's Home* (play), Guy du Maurier, 1909.

Hobart, Snecky. *The Little Minister*, J. M. Barrie, 1891.

Hobbs, New York store-keeper with strong Republican views. *Little Lord Fauntleroy*, Frances H. Burnett, 1886.

Hobbs, Elsie, former secretary of Charles Rainier. *Random Harvest*, J. Hilton, 1941.

Hobby, John, servant of Roger Belor. *Sampson Rideout, Quaker*, Una Silberrad, 1911.

Hobden, Ralph, an old countryman, friend of Dan and Una. *Puck of Pook's Hill*, 1906, and *Rewards and Fairies*, 1910, R. Kipling.

Hobson, Rev. Mr, chaplain to Lord Rosherville, m. Lady Ann Milton, Lord Rosherville's daughter. *Pendennis*, W. M. Thackeray, 1848–50.

Hobson, Clarence, Editor, *Fiz. Mr Fortune Finds a Pig*, H. C. Bailey, 1943.

Hobson, Mrs Esther, mistress of Amory Stilham. *Mrs Parkington*, L. Bromfield, 1944.

Hobson, Sam. 'The Son's Veto,' *Life's Little Ironies*, T. Hardy, 1894.

Hobson, Zachariah, of Hobson Bros, cloth factors.

Sophia Alethea, his niece, m. as 2nd wife Thomas Newcome.

The Newcomes, W. M. Thackeray, 1853–5.

Hodge, Gammer Gurton's servant. *Gammer Gurton's Needle* (play), Anonymous, 1575.

Hodge, Henrietta, Principal of Leys College. *Miss Pym Disposes*, Josephine Tey, 1946.

Hodge & Smithers, Liberal solicitors. *The Great Hoggarty Diamond*, W. M. Thackeray, 1841.

Hodgem, public-house vocalist. *Pendennis*, W. M. Thackeray, 1848–50.

Hodges, Mrs, midwife. *Liza of Lambeth*, W. S. Maugham, 1897.

Hodgkin, Saul, station-master. *The Ghost Train* (play), A. Ridley, 1925.

Hodgkins, chauffeur to Charles Beauchamp. *Fed Up*, G. A. Birmingham, 1931.

Hodgson, Captain. 'With the Night Mail' (s.s.), *Actions and Reactions*, R. Kipling, 1909.

Hodson, Mr, rich American.

Carry, his daughter, in love with Jack Huysen.

White Heather, W. Black, 1885.

Hoffman, Mr. *Britannia Mews*, Margery Sharp, 1946.

Hogan, Bill. 'The Nice Cup o' Tea' (s.s.), *Sun on the Water*, L. A. G. Strong, 1940.

Hogan, Dinny.

Patrice ('Citizen'), his son.

Maeve, his daughter, m. John d'Arcy.

Hangman's House, Donn Byrne, 1926.

Hogan-Yale, Irish officer. 'The Rout of the White Hussars' (s.s.), *Plain Tales from the Hills*, R. Kipling, 1888.

Hogarth, John, M.P. *The Gates of Summer* (play), John Whiting, 1956.

Hogbary, social leader, Beckenham. *Tono Bungay*, H. G. Wells, 1909.

Hogg, Sam, landlord of the Dog and Pilchard.
  Annie, his daughter, barmaid.
The Cathedral, Hugh Walpole, 1922.

Hoggarty, Mrs Susan, rich aunt of Samuel Titmarsh, m. Rev. Grimes Wapshot.
  Her thirteen sisters-in-law.
The Great Hoggarty Diamond, W. M. Thackeray, 1841.

Hoggett, Miss Grace, housekeeper to Sam Adams. The *Barsetshire* series, Angela Thirkell, 1933 onwards.

Hogginarmo, Count, of Crim Tartary. *The Rose and the Ring*, W. M. Thackeray, 1855.

Hoggins, Dr. *Cranford*, Mrs Gaskell, 1853.

Hoggins, Mary Ann, m. Jeames de la Pluché. *Jeames's Diary*, W. M. Thackeray, 1846.

Hogsflesh (Mr H.). *Mr H.* (play), C. Lamb, 1813.

Hohenstockwitz, Dr Gotthold, cousin of, and librarian to, Prince Otto. *Prince Otto*, R. L. Stevenson, 1885.

Hokey, Nurse. *The Newcomes*, W. M. Thackeray, 1853–5.

Holabird, Rippleton, of McGurk Institute. *Martin Arrowsmith*, Sinclair Lewis, 1925.

Holbrook, Mrs, J. H. Graham's 2nd wife, *The Lamplighter*, Maria S. Cummins, 1854.

Holbrook, Thomas, yeoman, cousin of Miss Pole. *Cranford*, Mrs Gaskell, 1853.

Holcombe, Mrs Marian, sister of Laura Fairlie and part narrator. *The Woman in White*, W. Collins, 1860.

Holden, Bailie, later Lord Provost. *Cleg Kelly*, S. R. Crockett, 1896.

Holden, John, lover of Ameera. 'Without Benefit of Clergy' (s.s.), *Life's Handicap*, R. Kipling, 1891.

Holden, Tommy, m. Julia Bramsley. *C.*, M. Baring, 1924.

Holdenhurst, Reverdy J.
  Lizbeth, his daughter.
Dragon Harvest, Upton Sinclair, 1946.

Holdenough, Nehemiah, Presbyterian minister. *Woodstock*, W. Scott, 1826.

Holder, Alexander, of Holder & Stevenson, bankers.
  Arthur, his son.
  Mary, his niece.
'The Beryl Coronet,' *The Adventures of Sherlock Holmes*, A. Conan Doyle, 1892.

Holderness, Lucas, author and swindler. *Love and Mr Lewisham*, H. G. Wells, 1900.

Holdernesse, Duke of. 'The Adventure of the Priory School,' *The Return of Sherlock Holmes*, A. Conan Doyle, 1905.

Holdfast, Aminadab. *A Bold Stroke for a Wife* (play), Mrs Susanna Centlivre, 1718.

Holdhurst, Lord. 'The Naval Treaty,' *Memoirs of Sherlock Holmes*, A. Conan Doyle, 1894.

Holding, Dorothy, devoted servant of the Galantrys. *Dance of the Years*, Margery Allingham, 1943.

Holdsworth, railway engineer, employer and friend of Phyllis Holman. *Cousin Phillis*, Mrs Gaskell, 1864.

Holdsworth, Michael, an inefficient farmer.
  Young Mike, his son.
Adam Bede, George Eliot, 1859.

Holford, Maria, widow, stepdaughter of Captain Sinclair. *The Good Ship 'Mohock,'* W. Clark Russell, 1894.

Holgrave, 'daguerreotypist,' revolutionary fellow tenant with Hephzibah Pyncheon, m. Phoebe Pyncheon. *The House of the Seven Gables*, N. Hawthorne, 1851.

Holiday, Burne, Amory Blaine's friend at Princeton. *This Side of Paradise*, F. Scott Fitzgerald, 1920.

Holkar, Indian commander. *The Adventures of Major Gahagan*, W. M. Thackeray, 1838–9.

Holl, Lily, m. Dick Povey. *The Old Wives' Tale*, Arnold Bennett, 1908.

Holland. Family name of LORD SLANE.

Holland, Colonel. *The Small Back Room*, N. Balchin, 1943.

Holland, Bill.
  Eileen, his wife.
    Freddy, Jane and **Robin,** their children.
A Town like Alice, N. Shute, 1950.

Holland, Jed. *The Shepherd of the Hills*, H. B. Wright, 1907.

Hollander, a butler. *The Last and the First,* Ivy Compton-Burnett, 1971.

Holliday, Arthur. *The Dead Hand* (s.s.), W. Collins, 1857.

Holliday, Rupert, central character.
  Dorothy, his mother.
  The Cornet of Horse, G. A. Henty, 1888.

Hollingford, Lord. *Wives and Daughters,* Mrs Gaskell, 1866.

Hollingrake, Boo (Mrs Olivia Davenport), sugar heiress, Hurtle Duffield's first patron. *The Vivisector,* Patrick White, 1970.

Hollins, Irish fish-hawker and drunkard, m. Maggie. *The Old Wives' Tale,* Arnold Bennett, 1908.

Hollis, Miss. 'The Bisara of Pooree' (s.s.), *Plain Tales from the Hills,* R. Kipling, 1888.

Hollis, Mr.
  Lady Flora, his wife.
  Daniel Deronda, George Eliot, 1876.

Holloman, Jim, farm-hand, 'origin unknown.' *The Beautiful Years,* H. Williamson, 1921.

Holly, barman. *Poet's Pub,* E. Linklater, 1929.

Holly, Miss, mistress, Hosiers' School. The *Barsetshire* series, Angela Thirkell, 1933 onwards.

Holly, Barnabas, builder's labourer.
  Annie, his 1st wife.
  Their children: **Bert, Lydia, Daisy, Alice, Gertie, Kitty, Lennie.**
  m. (2) Jessy Brimsley.
  South Riding, Winifred Holtby, 1936.

Holly, Ludwig Horace ('The Baboon'), central character and narrator. *She,* H. Rider Haggard, 1887.

Holm, Bert, mountain climber, central character, m. (1) Lily Roos (div.), (2) Kit Tallant.
  Jake, his father.
  Kitty, his mother.
  Other Gods, Pearl Buck, 1940.

Holman, Helene, torch singer. *Appointment in Samarra,* John O'Hara, 1935.

Holman, Phyllis, central character.
  Rev. Ebenezer, minister and farmer, her father.
  Her mother.
  Cousin Phillis, Mrs Gaskell, 1864.

Holme, Bernadine, central character, consumptive.
  Zerviah, her uncle.
  Malvina, his dead wife.
  Ships that Pass in the Night, Beatrice Harraden, 1893.

Holme, Lord (Fritz).
  Viola, his wife (div.), who later m. Rupert Carey.
  The Woman with a Fan, R. S. Hichens, 1904.

Holmes, Dr. *Mrs Dalloway,* Virginia Woolf, 1925.

Holmes, Sherlock, detective. *A Study in Scarlet, The Sign of Four,* etc., and about fifty 'Adventures.'
  Mycroft, his brother. 'The Empty House,' *The Return of Sherlock Holmes,* and elsewhere.
  A. Conan Doyle.

Holofernes, a schoolmaster. *Love's Labour's Lost* (play), W. Shakespeare.

Holohan, assistant secretary. 'A Mother' (s.s.), *The Dubliners,* James Joyce, 1914.

Holroyd, James, Yorkshire bully in charge of Camberwell power-station, killed by Azuma-Zi. *The Lord of the Dynamos* (s.s.), H. G. Wells, 1894.

Holsten, mathematician and chemist. *The World Set Free,* H. G. Wells, 1914.

Holt, Mother.
  Rosa, her daughter.
  Rupert of Hentzau, A. Hope, 1898.

Holt, Felix, watchmaker and radical, central character, m. Esther Lyon.
  Mary, his mother.
  Felix Holt, George Eliot, 1866.

Holt, Gavin, midshipman, *Saltash. The Cruel Sea,* N. Monsarrat, 1951.

Holt, Father Henry (alias Captain von Holtz and Holton), Jesuit priest and conspirator. *Henry Esmond,* W. M. Thackeray, 1852.

Holt, Jack, tobacco smuggler. *Pendennis,* W. M. Thackeray, 1848–50.

Holt, Leonard, apprentice to Stephen Bloundel. *Old St Paul's,* W. H. Ainsworth, 1841.

Holt, Captain Robert.
  Ethel, his wife.

To Have the Honour (play), A. A. Milne, 1924.

Holton, Captain. *See* HENRY HOLT.

Holway, Mrs Sarah, sister of Lenny Calcraft. *In Cotton Wool*, W. B. Maxwell, 1912.

Holy Joe ('Old '48'), bill-poster. *No. 5 John Street*, R. Whiteing, 1902.

Holyday, Erasmus, learned dominie. *Kenilworth*, W. Scott, 1821.

Homartyn, Lady, friend of Mr Britling. *Mr Britling Sees It Through*, H. G. Wells, 1916.

Home, Colonel Archibald, m. Kirsty Gilmour. *Pink Sugar*, O. Douglas, 1924.

Home, Harry, of San Francisco, P.O. agent. *The Postmistress of Laurel Run* (s.s.), Bret Harte, 1892.

Home, Paulina Mary (Bassompierre), left in care of Mrs Bretton. *Villette*, Charlotte Brontë, 1853.

Hominy, Major.
His wife and daughter.
Martin Chuzzlewit, C. Dickens, 1844.

Honest, Mr, an old pilgrim. *Pilgrim's Progress*, J. Bunyan, 1678, 1684.

Honey, Theodore, 'boffin.'
Mary, his dead wife.
Elspeth, their daughter.
m. (2) Marjorie Corder.
No Highway, N. Shute, 1948.

Honeybun, 'ubiquitous socialist.'
His wife.
Quinneys', H. A. Vachell, 1914.

Honeychurch, Lucy, cousin of Charlotte Bartlett, m. George Emerson.
Freddy, her brother.
Her mother.
A Room with a View, E. M. Forster, 1908.

Honeycomb, Will, 'well-bred fine gentleman.' Essays in *The Spectator*, J. Addison, 1711–14.

Honeyman, Charles, vain and hypocritical incumbent of Lady Whittlesea's chapel, brother-in-law of Colonel Newcome, m. Julia Sherrick.
Martha, his sister.
The Newcomes, W. M. Thackeray, 1853–5.

Honeythunder, Luke, chairman of philanthropic committee. *Edwin Drood*, C. Dickens, 1870.

Honeywill, Ruth. *Justice* (play), J. Galsworthy, 1910.

Honeywood, m. Miss Richland. *The Good Natured Man* (play), O. Goldsmith, 1768.

Honeywood, Rev. Dr. *Elsie Venner*, O. W. Holmes, 1861.

Honeywood, Patty, m. Verdant Green.
Kitty, her sister, m. Fred (or Frank) Delaval.
The Adventures of Mr Verdant Green, C. Bede, 1853.

Honnetong, Jacques, farmer. *Anthony Adverse*, Hervey Allen, 1934.

Honour, Mrs. *See* HONOUR BLACKMORE.

Hood, cattle owner. *Robbery under Arms*, R. Boldrewood, 1888.

Hook, Burnet, of Lincoln's cabinet (hist.). *Abraham Lincoln* (play), J. Drinkwater, 1918.

Hook, Ebie, steersman of the *Van Hoorn*. *The Raiders*, S. R. Crockett, 1894.

Hook, Captain James, one-armed pirate captain. *Peter Pan* (play), J. M. Barrie, 1904.

Hook, John, inmate of home for aged. *The Poorhouse Fair*, John Updike, 1959.

Hookham, John, improvident sailor.
Tom, his son, friend of Denis Duval.
Denis Duval, W. M. Thackeray, 1864.

Hookhorn, Philip. 'The Superstitious Man's Story,' *Life's Little Ironies*, T. Hardy, 1894.

Hoolan, journalist. *Pendennis*, W. M. Thackeray, 1848–50.

Hooley, Mrs Percival de (The Snob). *The Passing of the Third Floor Back*, J. K. Jerome, 1907.

Hoopdriver, J. E., central character, juvenile draper's assistant with ambitions. *The Wheels of Chance*, H. G. Wells, 1896.

Hooper, Inspector. 'Mrs Bathurst' (s.s.), *Traffics and Discoveries*, R. Kipling, 1904.

Hooper, Miss, typist. *London Wall* (play), J. van Druten, 1931.

Hooper, Mrs, nurse to the Desarts. *Carrots*, Mrs Molesworth, 1876.

Hooper, Rev. Clayton. 'The Rival Curates,' *Bab Ballads*, W. S. Gilbert, 1869.

Hooper, Fanny ('Vandra'), illegitimate daughter of Mary Hopwood (*née* Hooper) and Clive Seymore.

Evelyn, her daughter by Harry Somerford.
Fanny by Gaslight, M. Sadleir, 1940.

Hop ('Op), yeoman of signals. 'The Bonds of Discipline' (s.s.), *Traffics and Discoveries*, R. Kipling, 1904.

Hop Sing, Chinese merchant. 'Wan Lee the Pagan' (s.s.), *The Luck of Roaring Camp*, Bret Harte, 1868.

Hope, Mrs Augusta.
Archie, Jack and **Sandy,** her dead sons.
Penny Plain, O. Douglas, 1920.

Hope, Jefferson. *A Study in Scarlet*, A. Conan Doyle, 1887.

Hope, Trelawney. 'The Second Stain,' *The Return of Sherlock Holmes*, A. Conan Doyle, 1905.

Hope-Ashburn, Myra Lady, wealthy friend of Gwyneth Cornwell.
Sir Noël, her husband, gynaecologist.
The Widow, Francis King, 1957.

Hopeful, companion to Christian. *Pilgrim's Progress*, J. Bunyan, 1678 and 1684.

Hophead, Sue.
Benny the Stump, her father.
A Voyage to Purilia, Elmer Rice, 1930.

Hopkins, draper. *Middlemarch*, George Eliot, 1871–2.

Hopkins, ex-Sergeant, m. Selina Crockett. The *Barsetshire* series, Angela Thirkell, 1933 onwards.

Hopkins, Inspector Stanley. *The Return of Sherlock Holmes* (various stories), A. Conan Doyle, 1905.

Hopkinson, housemaster at Grey Friars. *The Newcomes*, W. M. Thackeray, 1853–5.

Hopkinson, Charlotte. *The Middle Watch* (play), Ian Hay & S. King-Hall, 1929.

Hopper, James. *Lady Windermere's Fan* (play), O. Wilde, 1892.

Hopper, Nora, eng. to George Trimmins.
Her father and mother.
Emma, her aunt.
Ben, her uncle.
'The Face' (s.s.), *A Beginning*, W. de la Mare, 1955.

Hopwood, William, supposed father of Fanny Hooper.
Mary, his wife, Fanny's mother.
Fanny by Gaslight, M. Sadleir, 1940.

Horatio, friend of Hamlet. *Hamlet* (play), W. Shakespeare.

Horatio, Don. *The Spanish Tragedy* (play), T. Kyd, 1603.

Hori, manager of Imhotep's estate, m. Renisenb. *Death Comes as the End*, Agatha Christie, 1945.

Horn, Miss, cousin and companion to Lossie's mother. *The Marquis of Lossie*, G. MacDonald, 1877.

Hornbeck.
His wife, of whom he is intensely jealous.
Peregrine Pickle, T. Smollett, 1751.

Hornblow, ex-smuggler.
Susan, his daughter, m. Captain M'Elvina.
The King's Own, Captain Marryat, 1830.

Hornblower. *The Skin Game*, J. Galsworthy, 1920.

Hornblower, Horatio, midshipman to admiral, K.C.B., and Lord Hornblower of Smallbridge, central character, m. Lady Barbara Leighton, *née* Wellesley. The *Hornblower* series, C. S. Forester, 1937 onwards.

Hornblower, Rev. Silas, much-tattooed missionary, m. Lady Emily Sheepshanks. *Vanity Fair*, W. M. Thackeray, 1847–8.

Hornby, Captain, finally **Admiral Christopher,** m. Elsa Belton. The *Barsetshire* series, Angela Thirkell, 1933 onwards.

Hornby, Reginald. *The Land of Promise* (play), W. S. Maugham, 1914.

Horne, Miss, friend of Miss Hobart. *Sylvia Scarlett*, C. Mackenzie, 1918.

Horner, Mr, gallant alleged to be impotent. *The Country Wife* (play), William Wycherley, 1673.

Horner, Rev. Mr, 'independent' minister and quarrelsome drunkard. 'Janet's Repentance,' *Scenes of Clerical Life*, George Eliot, 1857.

Horner, John, plumber. 'The Blue Carbuncle,' *Adventures of Sherlock Holmes*, A Conan Doyle, 1892.

Hornhead, Dan'l, serpent-player. 'Absent-mindedness in a Parish Choir,' *Life's Little Ironies*, T. Hardy, 1894.

Horniman, Miss, ex-schoolmistress.

The *Barsetshire* series, Angela Thirkell, 1933 onwards.

Horning, Edward Peter. *The Great Adventure* (play), Arnold Bennett, 1913.

Hornyold, rector and magistrate. *Starvecrow Farm,* Stanley Weyman, 1905.

Horringe, Sir Thomas, K.C.B. ('Scree'), surgeon. 'Tender Achilles' (s.s.), *Limits and Renewals,* R. Kipling, 1932.

Horrock, veterinary surgeon. *Middlemarch,* Geo. Eliot, 1871–2.

Horrocks, butler with whom Sir Pitt Crawley becomes friends.

His vulgar and ambitious daughter. *Vanity Fair,* W. M. Thackeray, 1847–8.

Horrocks, Gladys, servant to Mr Thipps. *Whose Body?,* Dorothy L. Sayers, 1923.

Horse, Alexandre, French horse-dealer. *Pending Heaven,* William Gerhardie, 1930.

Horseman, The Headless, ghost of Sleepy Hollow. *The Legend of Sleepy Hollow,* Washington Irving, 1819–20.

Horseman, Miss. *Men's Wives,* W. M. Thackeray, 1843.

Horsham, Earl of. *Waste* (play), H. Granville-Barker, 1907.

Hortense, maid to Lady Dedlock. *Bleak House,* C. Dickens, 1853.

Hortensio, suitor to Bianca. *The Taming of the Shrew* (play), W. Shakespeare.

Horton, Lord Harpenden's man-servant. *While the Sun Shines* (play), T. Rattigan, 1943.

Horton, Duke of, m. Anne Dillon.

The Marquis of Kincrae, his son.

Lady Elizabeth Crispin, his daughter.

The Dowager Duchess.

Hamlet, Revenge!, M. Innes, 1937.

Horvendile. *Jurgen,* J. B. Cabell, 1921.

Hoseason, Elias, Captain of the brig *Covenant.* *Kidnapped,* R. L. Stevenson, 1886.

Hoskins, Gus, fellow clerk and close friend of Samuel Titmarsh.

His father, leather-seller.

His sisters.

The Great Hoggarty Diamond. W. M. Thackeray, 1841.

Hosnani, Nessim, Coptic banker and conspirator.

Justine, his Jewish wife.

Falthaus Hosnani, his father.

Leila, his intellectual mother, who loves Mountolive.

Nabouz, his young hare-lipped brother.

Justine and others in *The Alexandria Quartet,* 1957–61, Lawrence Durrell.

Hossett, Christina, owner of Limpid Steam Laundry, m. Albert Edward Preemby.

Christina, her daughter by Wilfred Devizes.

Christina Alberta's Father, H. G. Wells, 1925.

Hotspur (Henry Percy). *Henry the Fourth* (play), W. Shakespeare.

Houghton, Alvina, central character, m. Francesco Marasca.

James, her father, draper who becomes owner of a cinema.

Clariss, her mother.

The Lost Girl, D. H. Lawrence, 1920.

Hounslow, highwayman. *The Beaux' Stratagem* (play), G. Farquhar, 1707.

House, Oscar H., barman, witness for the Crown. *The Jury,* G. Bullett, 1935.

Houston, Charles Duguid, hero who goes to Tibet on a bicycle. *The Rose of Tibet,* Lionel Davidson, 1962.

Hovenden, Lord, m. Irene Aldwinkle. *Those Barren Leaves,* A. Huxley, 1925.

How, James.

Walter, his son. Solicitors.

Justice (play), J. Galsworthy, 1910.

Howard, 'short, fat and thickset,' Graham's guardian during his trance. *When the Sleeper Awakes,* H. G. Wells, 1899.

Howard, Professor, entomologist. *The Weak and the Strong,* G. Kersh, 1945.

Howard, Hon. Alan. *French without Tears* (play), T. Rattigan, 1936.

Howard, Donald, young Research Fellow accused of fraud.

Laura, his wife.

The Affair, 1960, part of the *Strangers and Brothers* sequence, C. P. Snow.

Howard, Evelyn, companion to Mrs Inglethorp, cousin of Alfred. *The Mysterious Affair at Styles,* Agatha Christie, 1920.

Howard, John Sidney, central character.
John, his son, killed over Heligoland.
Enid, his daughter, m. Costello-
Martin, their son.
The Pied Piper, N. Shute, 1942.

Howard, Kate, m. José de Arguello-
Yerba Buena, their daughter.
A Ward of the Golden Gate, Bret Harte.

Howard, Vivian, famous author and cat-lover. *Once Aboard the Lugger,* A. S. M. Hutchinson, 1908.

Howden, widow, auctioneerl *The Heart of Midlothian,* W. Scott, 1818.

Howe, Miss Anne, confidante of Clarissa, eng. to Mr Hickman.
Anabella, her mother.
Clarissa Harlowe, S. Richardson, 1748.

Howe, George, M.A.
William, his father.
Marget, his mother.
Beside the Bonnie Brier Bush, I. Maclaren, 1894.

Howell, 'Taffy.' 'The Propagation of Knowledge' (a 'Stalky' story), *Debits and Credits,* R. Kipling, 1926.

Howe-Nevinson, Esmé, artist, m. Angelica Deverell, romantic novelist.
Nora, his sister, Angelica's companion for thirty years.
Lord Norley, their uncle.
Angel, Elizabeth Taylor, 1957.

Howie, Willie. *The Antiquary,* W. Scott, 1816.

Howittat, Daniel.
Howard, his son, father of Pete Matthews.
The Shepherd of the Hills, H. B. Wright, 1907.

Howler, Rev. M., ranting nonconformist minister. *Dombey and Son,* C. Dickens, 1848.

Hoxton, headmaster. *The Daisy Chain,* Charlotte M. Yonge, 1856.

Hoyden, Miss. *A Trip to Scarborough* (play), R. B. Sheridan, 1777.

Hoyland, Algernon. *Antigua Penny Puce,* R. Graves, 1936.

Hoyle, Priscilla. *Dragon Harvest,* Upton Sinclair, 1946.

Hoyser, Dan, Irish poet and monk. *Hangman's House,* Donn Byrne, 1926.

Hoyt, Rosemary, film actress. *Tender is the Night,* F. Scott Fitzgerald, 1934.

Hromka, Stepan, famous composer. *The Weak and the Strong,* G. Kersh, 1945.

Hubbard, alias of the narrator as secretary to Silence. 'The Nemesis of Fate,' (s.s.), *John Silence,* A. Blackwood, 1908.

Hubbard, Madame.
Her husband.
Gladys, their daughter.
South Riding, Winifred Holtby, 1936.

Hubbard, Bartley, journalist.
Marcia, his wife.
The Rise of Silas Lapham, 1885, and elsewhere, W. D. Howells.

Hubbard, Benjamin,
Hubbard, Oscar, brothers of Regina Giddens.
Birdie, Oscar's wife.
The Little Foxes (play), Lillian Hellman, 1939.

Hubbard, Margaret, of *The Liberal,* m. Edmund Grattan. *The Street of Adventure,* P. Gibbs, 1909.

Hubbard, Walter, tram conductor. *Magnolia Street,* L. Golding, 1932.

Hubbel, Steve.
Eunice, his wife.
A Streetcar Named Desire (play), Tennessee Williams, 1949.

Hubert (de Burgh), chamberlain to King John. *King John* (play), W. Shakespeare.

Huckaback, Reuben, great-uncle of John Ridd.
Ruth, his daughter.
Lorna Doone, R. D. Blackmore, 1869.

Huckaback, Robert, shopman, friend of Titmouse. *Ten Thousand a Year,* S. Warren, 1839.

Huckaby, Eustace, friend of Ephraim Quixtus. *The Glory of Clementina Wing,* W. J. Locke, 1911.

Huddle, J.P.
His sister.
The Unrest Cure (s.s.), 'Saki' (H. H. Munro).

Huddlestone, Bernard, defaulting banker.

Clara, his daughter, m. Frank Cassilis.
'The Pavilion on the Links,' *New Arabian Nights,* R. L. Stevenson, 1882.

Hudig, Dutch merchant, father-in-law of Almayer. *Almayer's Folly,* J. Conrad, 1895.

Hudson, Mrs, Holmes's landlady at Baker Street. *The Adventures of Sherlock Holmes,* 1892, and elsewhere, A. Conan Doyle.

Hudson, Augusta, *née* Drake, lifelong friend of Sarah Burling Ward.
Thomas, her husband, magazine editor.
Angle of Repose, Wallace Stegner, 1971.

Hudson, Roderick, central character, eng. to Mary Garland.
His mother.
Roderick Hudson, H. James, 1875.

Huett, Izz, fellow dairymaid with Tess. *Tess of the D'Urbervilles,* T. Hardy, 1891.

Huff, Captain. *Northwest Passage,* Kenneth Roberts, 1938.

Huff, Dr, Rector of Hackton. *Barry Lyndon,* W. M. Thackeray, 1844.

Hugby, Rev. F., of St Boniface College, Varsity snob.
His father, haberdasher.
Betsy, his sister.
The Book of Snobs, W. M. Thackeray, 1846–7.

Huggins, Mr. *Incomparable Bellairs,* A. & E. Castle, 1904.

Huggins, Councillor Alfred Ezekiel, haulage contractor and Methodist preacher.
Nell, his wife.
South Riding, Winifred Holtby, 1936.

Hugh, ostler at the Maypole. *Barnaby Rudge,* C. Dickens, 1840.

Hugh of Dallington (The Novice). 'Weland's Sword' and others, *Puck of Pook's Hill,* 1906, and *Rewards and Fairies,* 1910, R. Kipling.

Hughes, Rhisiart, one of Olwen Powell's many suitors. *The Black Venus,* Rhys Davies, 1944.

Hughes, Will. *The Corn is Green* (play), Emlyn Williams, 1938.

Huglet, farmer. *Precious Bane,* Mary Webb, 1924.

Hugo, Father, Redgauntlet's pseudonym when entering the monastery. *Redgauntlet,* W. Scott, 1824.

Huguet, spy. *Richelieu* (play), Lord Lytton, 1839.

Hulker, banker.
His daughter, m. Prince Ragamoffski.
Vanity Fair, 1847–8, *Pendennis,* 1848–50, and elsewhere, W. M. Thackeray.

Hullington, Lord. *The Weak and the Strong,* G. Kersh, 1945.

Humberstall, R.G.A. 'The Janeites' (s.s.), *Debits and Credits,* R. Kipling, 1926.

Humbert, Humbert, a moral leper.
Valeria, his 1st wife.
Mrs Charlotte Haze, his 2nd wife, a widow.
Dolores (Dolly) or **Lolita Haze,** his stepdaughter.
Lolita, Vladimir Nabokov, 1955.

Humbey, James, half-brother of Charles Ravenshoe. *Ravenshoe,* H. Kingsley, 1861.

Humbie, Mistress, aged maid to Lady Elizabeth Greatorix. *The Lilac Sunbonnet,* S. R. Crockett, 1894.

Humbold, Toni, Virginian, neighbour of the Esmonds. *Henry Esmond,* W. M. Thackeray, 1852.

Hume, Sir Lothian, Bt, evil genius. *Rodney Stone,* A. Conan Doyle, 1896.

Hume, Mary, eng. to James Amswell.
Avory, her father, bank director.
Dr Spencer, her uncle.
The Judas Window, Carter Dickson, 1938.

Hume, Miranda, domestic tyrant.
Julius, her husband.
Rosebery, Miranda's son.
Mother and Son, Ivy Compton-Burnett, 1954.

Humfray, Mary, nursery governess, m. George Marrapit. *Once Aboard the Lugger,* A. S. M. Hutchinson, 1908.

Humgudgeon, Corporal. *Woodstock,* W. Scott, 1826.

Hummel, Johnnie, photographer, m. Ada Berman. *Magnolia Street,* L. Golding, 1932.

Hummil, engineer. 'At the End of the Passage' (s.s.), *Life's Handicap,* R. Kipling, 1891.

Humphrey, furze-cutter. *The Return of the Native,* T. Hardy, 1878.

Humphrey. *The Knight of the Burning Pestle* (play), Beaumont & Fletcher, 1609.

Humphreys, Alice, close friend of Ellen Montgomery.
Rev. John, her brother.
The Wide, Wide World, Elizabeth Wetherell, 1850.

Humplebee, Harry. 'Humplebee' (s.s.), *The House of Cobwebs,* G. Gissing, 1906.

Humpty-Dumpty. *Alice Through the Looking-glass,* L. Carroll, 1872.

Huneefa, blind native woman. *Kim,* R. Kipling, 1901.

Hungerford, M.P. *Tancred,* B. Disraeli, 1847.

Hunker, American cinema magnate. *Men Like Gods,* H. G. Wells, 1923.

Hunsaker, Cyrus P., American art collector. *Quinneys',* H. A. Vachell, 1914.

Hunsden, Hunsden Yorke, benefactor of William Crimsworth. *The Professor,* Charlotte Brontë, 1857.

Hunt, Bow Street runner. *Deacon Brodie,* W. E. Henley & R. L. Stevenson, 1892.

Hunt, Mrs Arabella. *Tom Jones,* H. Fielding, 1749.

Hunt, Charles, American journalist *Through the Storm,* P. Gibbs, 1945.

Hunt, Rosamund, heiress. *Manalive,* G. K. Chesterton, 1912.

Hunt, Rev. Thomas Tufton, blackguardly parson. *The Adventures of Philip,* 1861–2, and, as Tufthunt, *A Shabby Genteel Story,* 1840, W. M. Thackeray.

Hunter, Sevilla's manservant. *Ten Minute Alibi,* A. Armstrong, 1933.

Hunter, of the *Hispaniola. Treasure Island,* R. L. Stevenson, 1883.

Hunter, Captain. *Sixty-four, Ninety-four,* R. H. Mottram, 1925.

Hunter, Frank. *The Browning Version,* T. Rattigan, 1948.

Hunter, Polly, actress, m. Lord Avon. *Rodney Stone,* A. Conan Doyle, 1896.

Hunter, Steve, Hugh McVey's partner. *Poor White,* Sherwood Anderson, 1920.

Hunter, Violet. 'The Copper Beeches,' *The Adventures of Sherlock Holmes,* A. Conan Doyle, 1892.

Hunter-Dunn, Joan. *A Subaltern's Love Song* (poem), J. Betjeman.

Hunter-Oakleigh, Violet, cousin of George Oakleigh, m. Jim Loring.
Greville, Alan and **Laurence,** her brothers.
Sonia, S. McKenna, 1917.

Huntingdon, Arthur, 2nd husband of Helen Graham. *The Tenant of Wildfell Hall,* Anne Brontë, 1848.

Huntinglen, Earl of.
His wife.
Lord Dalgarno, their son.
The Fortunes of Nigel, W Scott, 1822.

Huntley, Earl of. *Perkin Warbeck* (play), John Ford, 1634.

Huntley, Gavan, sex-ridden novelist and dramatic critic. *Joan and Peter,* H. G. Wells, 1918.

Huntly, Mr.
Harry, his son.
Ellen, his daughter, m. Hamish Channing.
The Channings, Mrs Henry Wood, 1862.

Hunziker, Dawson T. *Martin Arrowsmith,* Sinclair Lewis, 1925.

Huon, Sir, of Bordeaux.
Lady Esclairmonde, his wife.
'Weland's Sword,' *Puck of Pook's Hill,* 1906, and elsewhere, R. Kipling.

Hur, Judah (Ben Hur), son of Ithamar, m. Esther Simonides.
His mother.
Tirzah, his sister.
Ben Hur, L. Wallace, 1880.

Hurd, Jim, poacher charged with murder.
Minta, his wife.
Marcella, Mrs Humphry Ward, 1894.

Hurlbird, Florence, m. John Dowell. *The Good Soldier,* Ford Madox Ford, 1915.

Hurree, Chunder Mookerjee, Babu (R.17) in the Secret Service. *Kim,* R. Kipling, 1901.

Hurst.
Louisa, his wife, sister of Charles Bingley.
Pride and Prejudice, Jane Austen, 1813.

Hurst, a schoolboy. *The Channings,* Mrs Henry Wood, 1862.

Hurst, Mrs, Bathsheba Everdene's aunt. *Far from the Madding Crowd,* T. Hardy, 1874.

Hurst, Lady Gloria, who runs The Marigold Club. Aunt of 'The

Toff' (Hon. Richard Rollison) in series of detective novels by John Creasey, 1938 on.

Hurst, Jack, Peter Boyd's election agent. *Fed Up,* G. A. Birmingham, 1931.

Hurstpierpoint, Mrs Eulalia, a wealthy old woman, a flagellant. *Valmouth,* Ronald Firbank, 1919.

Hurstwood, G. W., Carrie's second lover. *Sister Carrie,* Theodore Dreiser, 1900.

Hurtle, a reviewer. *Pendennis,* W. M. Thackeray, 1848–50.

Hurtle, Winifred, widow, ex-fiancée of Paul Montagu. *The Way We Live Now,* A. Trollope, 1875.

Hushabye, Hesione and **Hector.** *Heartbreak House* (play), G. B. Shaw, 1917.

Hushai. *Absalom and Achitophel* (poem), J. Dryden, 1681.

Huskisson, Miss Harriet, C.B.E., school headmistress. *Elsie and the Child,* Arnold Bennett, 1924.

Huss, Job, Headmaster, Woldingstanton School.
  Gilbert, his son.
The Undying Fire, H. G. Wells, 1919.

Hussey, Johnny, a policeman.
  Bid, his wife.
    Denis, their son.
A Nest of Simple Folk, Sean O'Faolain, 1933.

Hustler, Sir George, Commander-in-chief, India. *The Newcomes,* W. M. Thackeray, 1853–5.

Hutt, Lloyd, head of radio agency. *The Troubled Air,* Irwin Shaw, 1951.

Hutter, Tom.
  Judith and **Hetty,** his daughters.
The Deerslayer, J. Fenimore Cooper, 1841.

Hutto, Grandma.
  Oliver, her grandson, friend of Jody Baxter.
The Yearling, Marjorie K. Rawlings, 1938.

Hutton, Henry.
  Emily, his 1st wife.
  Doris, his mistress, later his 2nd wife.
'The Gioconda Smile' (s.s.), *Mortal Coils,* A. Huxley, 1922.

Huxtable, theatrical agent. *No Name,* W. Collins, 1862.

Huxtable, boat builder. *No Man's Land,* L. J. Vance, 1910.

Huxtable, Dr Thorneycroft. 'The Adventure of the Priory School,' *The Return of Sherlock Holmes,* A. Conan Doyle, 1905.

Huxter, surgeon and apothecary.
  Samuel, his son, medical student, m. Fanny Bolton.
Pendennis, W. M. Thackeray, 1848–50.

Huysen, Jack, of the *New York Sun,* in love with Carry Hodson. *White Heather,* W. Black, 1885.

Huzinga, Captain. *Tracy's Tiger,* W. Saroyan, 1951.

Hyam, David, Quaker missionary.
  Faith, his wife, *née* Marlowe.
'All the World's Mad,' *Donovan Pasha,* Gilbert Parker, 1902.

Hyde, Edward, evil materializing intermittently in the body of Jekyll. *Dr Jekyll and Mr Hyde,* R. L. Stevenson, 1886.

Hyde, Jim, assistant in Melford Turner's grocery. *The Sleepless Moon,* H. E. Bates, 1956.

Hyman, Benny, publisher. *I Like It Here,* Kingsley Amis, 1958.

Hynde, Rev. Mr, vicar.
  His wife.
Lise Lillywhite, Margery Sharp, 1951.

Hyndmarsh, grocer, St Oggs. *The Mill on the Floss,* George Eliot, 1860.

Hynes, John.
  Louisa, his wife, *née* Hegarty.
  Their children:
    Dr Hynes.
    Tony, m. Mary Anne Rabbit.
    Bridget.
  Julie, his sister.
Famine, L. O'Flaherty, 1937.

Hynes, Thomsy, brother of Maggie Kilmartin. *Famine,* L. O'Flaherty, 1937.

Hypatia, the Gentile, central character *Hypatia,* C. Kingsley, 1853. Also *The Bee,* O. Goldsmith, 1759–60.

Hypocrisy. *See* FORMALIST.

Hypolito, student. *The Spanish Student* (poem), H. W. Longfellow, 1858.

Hythloday, Ralph, Portuguese traveller and narrator. *Utopia,* Sir Thomas More, 1551.

I

Iachimo, friend of Philario. *Cymbeline* (play), W. Shakespeare.

Iago, Othello's ancient.
  Emilia, his wife.
  Othello (play), W. Shakespeare.

Ianson, Dr.
  His wife and family.
  Agatha's Husband, Mrs. Craik, 1853.

Ianto.
  Dinah, his daughter.
  'The Devil in Eden' (s.s.), *My People,* Caradoc Evans, 1915.

Ibn Mararreh (The Hajji), chieftain. 'A Deal in Cotton' (s.s.), *Actions and Reactions,* R. Kipling, 1909.

Ibrahim, Mahommed, orderly. 'Fielding had an Orderly,' *Donovan Pasha,* Gilbert Parker, 1902.

Ickenham, Earl of (Frederick Altamont Cornwallis Twistleton).
  Jane, his wife, half-sister of Sir Raymond Bastable.
  Pongo, his nephew.
  Cocktail Time, P. G. Wodehouse, 1958.

Ida, Countess, German heiress whom Lyndon wants to marry. *Barry Lyndon,* W. M. Thackeray, 1844.

Ida, Princess. *See* GAMA.

Iddleston, a policeman. *The Last Revolution,* Lord Dunsany, 1951.

Ide, Frederick, m. Harriet Linley.
  Hatcher, their son, central character.
  Frances, their daughter.
  Ada, Frederick's sister.
  The Heritage of Hatcher Ide, Booth Tarkington, 1941.

Iden, Alexander, Kentish gentleman. *Henry the Sixth* (play), W. Shakespeare.

Iggiwick ('vuz-pig'), a hedgehog. *Tarka the Otter,* H. Williamson, 1927.

Iggulden, countryman.
  His son.
  'A Habitation Enforced' (s.s.), *Actions and Reactions,* R. Kipling, 1909.

Iggulsden, Tom.
  His wife.
  Ivy, their daughter.
  His mother.
  Mrs Miniver, Jan Struther, 1939.

Ignorance, 'a brisk lad.' *Pilgrim's Progress,* J. Bunyan, 1678 and 1684.

Ignosi. *See* UMPOPA.

Ikki, the Porcupine. 'Mowgli's Brothers' and elsewhere, *The Jungle Books,* R. Kipling, 1894–5.

Ilbury, Earl of (calling himself Mr Carisbrooke), tenant of the Grange.
  Lady Mary, his daughter.
  Uncle Silas, Sheridan le Fanu, 1864.

Ilchester, Bishop of. *Mr Ingleside,* E. V. Lucas, 1910.

Ilchester, Janet, m. Harry Richmond, her cousin.
  Sir Roderick, Bt, her father.
  Her mother.
  Charles, her brother.
  The Adventures of Harry Richmond, G. Meredith, 1871.

Ilderim, Sheik, benefactor of Ben Hur. *Ben Hur,* L. Wallace, 1880.

Ilderton, Lucy, confidante of Isabel Vere.
  Nancy, her cousin.
  The Black Dwarf, W. Scott, 1816.

Imgani, Sandi. *See* SANDERS.

Imhotep, head of the family, father of Yahmose, etc. *Death Comes as the End,* Agatha Christie, 1945.

Imogen, Cymbeline's daughter, wife of Posthumus. *Cymbeline* (play), W. Shakespeare.

Imogene, The Fair. *Alonzo the Brave and the Fair Imogene* (poem), M. G. Lewis.

Imoinda, central character. *Oroonoko,* Mrs Aphra Behn, 1688.

Imray, murdered by his servant. 'The Return of Imray' (s.s.), *Life's Handicap,* R. Kipling, 1891.

Inamorato, the Passionate Bee. *Parliament of Bees* (play), J. Day, 1641.

Inchcape, Professor, in charge of British propaganda in Bucharest during 1939–45 war. *The Great Fortune,* Olivia Manning, 1960.

Incubu. *See* Sir H. Curtis.

Indian Joe, murders Dr Robinson. *The Adventures of Tom Sawyer,* Mark Twain, 1876.

Indiana. *The Conscious Lovers* (play), R. Steele, 1722.

Ines. *Fair Ines* (poem), T. Hood.

Inez, the King of Barataria's foster-mother. *The Gondoliers* (comic opera), Gilbert & Sullivan, 1889.

Infadoos, son of Kafa, King of the Kukuana tribe; uncle of Twala. *King Solomon's Mines,* H. Rider Haggard, 1885.

Infant, The, a subaltern, ater Sir George. 'A Conference of the Powers' (a 'Stalky' story), *Many Inventions,* 1893, and elsewhere, R. Kipling.

Infant Phenomenon, The. *See* Crummles.

Ingelbrecht, Josquin, revolutionary in Paris in 1848. *Summer Will Show,* Sylvia Townsend Warner, 1936.

Ingell, Sir Thomas, Bt, M.P., magistrate. 'The Village that Voted the Earth was Flat' (s.s.), *A Diversity of Creatures,* R. Kipling, 1917.

Ingham, Nurse ('The Midget'). *A Daughter of Time,* Josephine Tey, 1951.

Ingham, Howard, American novelist visiting Tunisia. *The Tremor of Forgery,* Patricia Highsmith, 1969.

Ingle, Mrs Mary, aunt of Ablard Pender. *The Last Revolution,* Lord Dunsany, 1951.

Ingleblad, Miss Agnes, patient of Martin Arrowsmith. *Martin Arrowsmith,* Sinclair Lewis, 1925.

Ingleby, Alfred H. *No Son of Mine,* G. B. Stern, 1948.

Inglesant, John, central character.
- **Eustace,** his father.
- **Richard,** servant of the Earl of Essex, his grandfather.
- **Eustace,** his brother.

John Inglesant, J. H. Shorthouse, 1881.

Ingleside, Mr (later knighted), central character.
- His wife.
- Their daughters:
  - **Alison,** m. Bryan Hearne.
  - **Ann.**
- His mother.

Mr Ingleside, E. V. Lucas, 1910.

Inglethorp, Mrs Emily, stepmother of John and Laurence Cavendish.
- **Alfred,** her husband.

The Mysterious Affair at Styles, Agatha Christie, 1920.

Inglewood, Squire, 'a whitewashed Jacobite.' *Rob Roy,* W. Scott, 1818.

Inglewood, Arthur. *Manalive,* G. K. Chesterton, 1912.

Inglewood, Leonard, schoolmaster. *We the Accused,* E. Raymond, 1935.

Ingoldsby, Squire, Cumberland alias of Redgauntlet. *Redgauntlet,* W. Scott, 1824.

Ingoldsby, Caroline, m. Charles Seaforth.
- **Tom,** her brother.

'The Spectre of Tappington' (s.s.), *The Ingoldsby Legends,* R. H. Barham, 1837.

Ingpen, Tertius, factory inspector. *These Twain,* Arnold Bennett, 1916.

Ingram, Colonel. *The Iron Heel,* Jack London, 1908.

Ingram, Professor. *The Black Spectacles,* J. Dickson Carr, 1948.

Ingram, Monica, central character, m. Herbert Pelham.
- **Vernon,** her father.
- **Imogen,** her mother.

Thank Heaven Fasting, E. M. Delafield, 1932.

Iniquity. *The Devil Is an Ass* (play), B. Jonson, 1616.

Innes, Elsie, m. Pip Wilmot.
- **Raven,** her brother.

Pip, Ian Hay, 1907.

Innes, Frank, one-time friend of Archie Weir, later his enemy. *Weir of Hermiston,* R. L. Stevenson, 1896.

Innes, Mary, close friend of Pamela Nash.
- **Dr Gervase,** her father.
- Her mother.

Miss Pym Disposes, Josephine Tey, 1946.

Innes, Rachel, middle-aged spinster, central character and narrator.
- Her wards:
  - **Halsey,** her nephew, m. Louise Armstrong.
  - **Gertrude,** her niece, m. Jack Bailey.

The Circular Staircase, Mary R. Rinehart, 1908.

Innsbrook, Lord, steward, Jockey Club. *The Calendar*, E. Wallace.

Interpreter, The. *Pilgrim's Progress*, J. Bunyan, 1678, 1684.

Inverarity Sahib. 'Baa Baa Black Sheep' (s.s.), *Wee Willie Winkie*, R. Kipling, 1888.

Iolande. *St Clement's Eve* (poem), H. Taylor, 1862.

Iolanthe, a fairy, wife of the Lord Chancellor and mother of Strephon, *Iolanthe* (comic opera), Gilbert & Sullivan, 1882.

Ione, recent rich and beautiful arrival in Pompeii from Naples. *The Last Days of Pompeii*, Lord Lytton, 1834.

Ippolita. 'Ippolita in the Hills' (s.s.), *Little Novels of Italy*, M. Hewlett, 1899.

Ipps. 'The Infant's' butler. 'The Honours of War' (a 'Stalky' story), *Diversity of Creatures*, 1917 and elsewhere, R. Kipling.

Iras, attendant on Cleopatra *Antony and Cleopatra* (play), W. Shakepeare. *Caesar and Cleopatra* (play), G. B. Shaw, 1900.

Iras, daughter of Balthazar, one of the Wise Men. *Ben Hur*, L. Wallace, 1880.

Iredale, Philip, m. Sylvia Scarlett. *Sylvia Scarlett*, C. Mackenzie, 1918.

Ireton, capitalist and snob, m. Ethel Armitage. 'A Capitalist' (s.s.). *The House of Cobwebs*, G. Gissing, 1906.

Iris, a spirit. *The Tempest* (play). W. Shakespeare.

Iron. *The Sin of David* (play), S. Phillips, 1914.

Irons, Rev. Bartholomew, 'an awakening man.' *Vanity Fair*. W. M. Thackeray, 1847–8.

Irvin, Jocelyn, bookseller in Torminster, chief character.

Canon Theobald Fordyce, his grandfather. *See* FORDYCE.

A City of Bells, Elizabeth Goudge, 1936.

Irvine, Mrs, landlady who befriends Bessie Hipkiss. *Jezebel's Dust*, Fred Urquhart, 1951.

Irwin, Judge. *All The King's Men*, Robert Penn Warren, 1946.

Irwin, Ellen. *Ellen Irwin* (poem), W. Wordsworth, 1803.

Irwin, Hannah, companion to Clara Mowbray, m. Biddulph. *St Ronan's Well*, W. Scott, 1824.

Irwine, Rev. Adolphus, Rector of Broxton and Vicar of Blythe and Hayslope.

His mother.

Anne and **Kate,** his sisters.

Adam Bede, George Eliot, 1859.

Isaac, African Freedom Fighter, m. Tselane (Agnes) Mookodi, cousin of Chief Letlotse.

Amos, their small son.

When We Become Men, Naomi Mitchison, 1965.

Isaac, Sawyer's groom. *Market Harborough*, G. Whyte-Melville, 1861.

Isaac of York, father of Rebecca. *Ivanhoe*, W. Scott, 1820.

Isaacs, Sol, J.P., cockney-bred farmer. *The Beautiful Years*, H. Williamson, 1921.

Isaacson, Dr Meyer. *Bella Donna*, R. S. Hichens, 1909.

Isabel, Queen of France. *Henry the Fifth* (play), W. Shakespeare.

Isabella, sister of Claudio. *Measure for Measure* (play), W. Shakespeare.

Isabella, a schoolgirl. *Quality Street* (play), J. M. Barrie, 1902.

Isador, Father, prior of San Domingo, uncle of Duke Silva. *The Spanish Gypsy* (poem), George Eliot, 1868.

Isaev, Piotr Gavrilovitch ('Petya'), rejected lover of Tatiana Ostapenko.

Olga, his mother.

Tobit Transplanted, Stella Benson, 1931.

Isambard, Sir Isodore.

Beulah, his wife.

Sir Elias, his father.

The Whistling Chambermaid, Naomi Royde-Smith, 1957.

Isambard, Ralf, Lord of Parfois.

William, his son.

The Heaven Tree trilogy, Edith Pargeter, 1961–3.

Isbister, artist friend of Graham, to whom he leaves his fortune. *When the Sleeper Awakes*, H. G. Wells, 1899.

Iscott, Jude ('Captain Judas'), harmless lunatic.

Mary, his daughter, m. George Latter.

My Son, My Son, H. Spring, 1938.

Ishak, the Caliph's minstrel. *Hassan* (play), J. E. Fletcher, 1923.

Isham, Kathryn, *née* Jay, mistress of Jim Pignatelli and mother of Jay Pignatelli.
Randy, her husband.
Rob, her brother.
Chosen Country, J. dos Passos, 1951.

Ishbosheth. *Absalom and Achitophel* (poem), J. Dryden, 1681.

'Ishmael,' narrator, sole survivor of *Pequod.* *Moby Dick,* H. Melville, 1851

Isidor, Joe Sedley's Belgian servant. *Vanity Fair,* W. M. Thackeray, 1847–8.

Isinglass, Peter. *Comrade, O Comrade,* Ethel Mannin, 1946.

Isit, Miss. *Shall We Join the Ladies?* (play), J. M. Barrie, 1921.

Isolt the White, of Brittany. 'The Last Tournament' (poem), *Idylls of the King,* Lord Tennyson, 1859.

Isoult La Desirous (and La Desirée). *See* PIETOSA DE BRÉAUTÉ.

Issyvoo, Herr, or **Christoph,** 'camera-eye' narrator. *Goodbye to Berlin,* Christopher Isherwood, 1939.

Itelo, the prince-champion of the Arnewi tribe. *Henderson The Rain King,* Saul Bellow, 1959.

Ithamore, Barabas's slave. *The Jew of Malta* (play), C. Marlowe, 1633.

Ivanhoe, Wilfred, Knight of, m. Lady Rowena. *Ivanhoe,* W. Scott, 1820.

Iverach, Donald, junior partner, Iverach & Co., m. Cecilia Tennant. *Cleg Kelly,* S. R. Crockett, 1896.

Ivory, Charles, fake specialist. *The Citadel,* A. J. Cronin, 1937.

Ivory, Margaret, singing teacher, m. Rev. Richard Owen.
Lettice and **Julia,** her aunts.
The Whistling Chambermaid, Naomi Royde-Smith, 1957.

Ivy, Dick, friend of Jeremy Melford. *Humphry Clinker,* T. Smollett, 1771.

J

'J,' one of the 'three,' narrator. *Three Men in a Boat,* J. K. Jerome, 1889.

Jabberwocky. *Alice Through the Looking-glass,* L. Carroll, 1872.

Jabez, a woodman. 'Friendly Brook' (s.s.), *A Diversity of Creatures,* R. Kipling, 1917.

Jabos, Jack, Guy Mannering's guide to Ellangowan, later postilion. *Guy Mannering,* W. Scott, 1815.

Jabotière, Chevalier de la, officer with whom Warrington fought a duel. *The Virginians,* W. M. Thackeray, 1857–9.

Jaccottet, theatrical manager.
Yvette, his mistress.
'The Elevation of Lulu' (s.s.), *The Little Dog Laughed,* L. Merrick, 1930.

Jacintha, landlady. *The Monk,* M. G. Lewis, 1796.

Jacinto, servant to Bishop Latour. *Death Comes for the Archbishop,* Willa Cather, 1927.

Jack, 'Captain,' companion of Colonel Jack. *Colonel Jack,* D. Defoe, 1722.

Jack, 'Colonel,' central character and narrator; pickpocket and pirate.
'Moggy,' his faithful wife.
Colonel Jack, D. Defoe, 1722.

Jack, Daddy. *Uncle Remus,* J. C. Harris, 1880–95.

Jack, 'Major,' companion of Colonel Jack. *Colonel Jack,* D. Defoe, 1722.

Jack, Esther, mistress of George Webber.
Frederick, her husband.
Edith, her sister.
You Can't Go Home Again, T. Wolfe, 1947.

Jack, Owen. *Love Among the Artists,* G. B. Shaw, 1900.

Jackanapes, central character, son of the Black Captain and Jessamine. *Jackanapes,* Juliana H. Ewing, 1879.

Jackie, aborigine guide who stabs and decapitates Voss. *Voss,* Patrick White, 1957.

Jackman, Mr and Mrs. *The Skin Game* (play), J. Galsworthy, 1920.

Jackson. *The Ghost Train* (play), A Ridley, 1925.

Jackson, soldier from Wyoming, Col. Cantrell's driver in Italy. *Across the River and Into the Trees,* Ernest Hemingway, 1950.

Jackson, Miss, aunt of Mrs Barton. 'The Rev. Amos Barton,' *Scenes of Clerical Life,* George Eliot, 1857.

Jackson, Mr and Mrs, landlords of Lenny Calcraft. *In Cotton Wool,* W. B. Maxwell, 1912.

Jackson, Mrs, farmer's wife. *Swallows and Amazons,* A. Ransome, 1930.

Jackson, Jackie. *The Deep Blue Sea* (play), T. Rattigan, 1952.

Jackson, Joby, fairground showman. *The Good Companions,* J. B. Priestley, 1929.

Jackson, Peter, central character, m. Patricia Baynet.
Their children: **Evelyn, Peter** and **Primula.**
His father.
Tessa, his mother, *née* Bradley.
His grandfather, Peter the First.
Arthur, his brother.
Peter Jackson, Cigar Merchant, G. Frankau, 1919.

Jackson, Samuel, solicitor. *The Great Hoggarty Diamond,* W. M. Thackeray, 1841.

Jackson family, The. English emigrants. *Settlers in Canada,* Captain Marryat, 1844.

Jacky, Australian aboriginal, rescued by George Fielding. *It Is Never Too Late to Mend,* C. Reade, 1856.

Jacob (Yacubu), cook to the Company's agent, Shibi. *Aissa Saved,* Joyce Cary, 1932.

Jacobs, Tom Tulliver's schoolmaster. *The Mill on the Floss,* George Eliot, 1860.

Jacobs, Miss, pupil at the Misses Pidge's Academy. *The Professor,* Charlotte Brontë, 1837.

Jacobs, Hannah, beautiful young girl.
Reb Shemuel, her father, rabbi.

Children of the Ghetto, Israel Zangwill, 1892.

Jacobson, Johan, seaman, *Blackgauntlet. The Bird of Dawning,* J. Masefield, 1933.

Jacomo, a friar. *The Jew of Malta* (play), C. Marlowe, 1633.

Jacot, Captain Armand, of the Foreign Legion.
Jeanne, his daughter (Meriem), m. Jack Clayton (son of Tarzan).
The *Tarzan* series, E. R. Burroughs, 1912–32.

Jacqueline, German spy, m. Kelly Eyre. *The Maids of Paradise,* R. W. Chambers, 1903.

Jadwin, Curtis, central character, speculator in wheat, m. Laura Dearborn. *The Pit,* F. Norris, 1903.

Jael, servant of Abel Fletcher. *John Halifax, Gentleman,* Mrs Craik, 1856.

Jafar, the Caliph's Vizier. *Hassan* (play), J. E. Flecker, 1923.

Jaggers, legal adviser to Miss Havisham. *Great Expectations,* C. Dickens, 1861.

Jago, Paul, Senior Tutor, Professor of Literature. *The Masters,* 1951, part of the *Strangers and Brothers* sequence, C. P. Snow.

Jaikes, Daniel. *The Silver King* (play), H. A. Jones, 1882.

Jakin, drummer boy. 'The Drums of the Fore and Aft' (s.s.), *Wee Willie Winkie,* R. Kipling, 1888.

Jakin, Bob, holiday friend of Tom Tulliver.
Prissy, his wife.
The Mill on the Floss, George Eliot, 1860.

Jakob. *The Dark is Light Enough* (play), Christopher Fry, 1954.

James, coachman to the 3rd Viscount Castlewood. *Henry Esmond,* W. M. Thackeray, 1852.

James, Rudolf Rassendyll's servant. *Rupert of Hentzau,* A. Hope, 1898.

James IV, King of Scotland. *Perkin Warbeck* (play), John Ford, 1634.

James, Grandfather, maternal grandfather of the Dewys. *Under the Greenwood Tree,* T. Hardy, 1872.

James, Mr and Mrs, friends of the Pooters. *The Diary of a Nobody,* G. & W. Grossmith, 1892.

James, Ebenezer. *East Lynne,* Mrs Henry Wood, 1861.

James, Laura. *Look Homeward, Angel,* T. Wolfe, 1929.

Jameson, Bet, nurse to Richard Middlemas. *The Surgeon's Daughter,* W. Scott, 1827.

Jameson, Dolores, schoolmistress. *South Riding,* Winifred Holtby, 1936.

Jameson, 'Domsie,' village schoolmaster. *Beside the Bonnie Brier Bush,* I. Maclaren, 1894.

Jameson, Ruth, m. David Langston.
Her grandparents.
Henry, her villainous uncle.
The Harvester, Gene S. Porter, 1911.

Jamieson, detective. *The Circular Staircase,* Mary R. Rinehart, 1908.

Jamieson, Hon. Mrs. *Cranford,* Mrs Gaskell, 1853.

Jamieson, J. J., steel king, father of Adelaide Campbell.
Adele, his wife.
Flamingo, Mary Borden, 1927.

Jamieson, Sir Maxwell, Chief Constable. *The Five Red Herrings,* Dorothy L. Sayers, 1931.

Jan Byl, Mrs, m. Henry Squales. *London Belongs to Me,* N. Collins, 1945.

Jane. *Now We Are Six,* A. A. Milne, 1924.

Jane, servant. *The Admirable Crichton* (play), J. M. Barrie, 1902.

Jane, maid of the Barleys, with Ellen-Maudie. *The One Before,* Barry Pain, 1902.

Jane, 'domestic' employed by the narrator; jilted by William Piddingquirk. 'The Jilting of Jane' (s.s.), *The Plattner Story,* H. G. Wells, 1897.

Jane, Lady, a rapturous maiden, m. the Duke of Dunstable. *Patience* (comic opera), Gilbert & Sullivan, 1881.

Janet, maid to Betsey Trotwood. *David Copperfield,* C. Dickens, 1850.

Janet, housekeeper to Drs Cameron and Finlay at Tannochbrae. *Beyond This Place,* A. J. Cronin, 1953, later adapted into a popular television series, *Dr Finlay's Casebook.*

Janet, innkeeper's daughter.
Her father.

The Lady of Lyons (play), Lord Lytton, 1838.

Janey, Mrs. *The Prescription* (s.s.), Marjorie Bowen.

Janik, Colonel. *The Dark is Light Enough* (play), Christopher Fry, 1954.

Janki Meah.
Unda, his wife.
'At Twenty-two' (s.s.), *Soldiers Three*, R. Kipling, 1888.

Janoo. 'In the House of Suddhoo' (s.s.), *Plain Tales from the Hills*, R. Kipling, 1888.

Janos, servant of Captain Jennico. *The Pride of Jennico*, A. & E. Castle, 1898.

Jansen, Captain, Danish sailor. *My Son, My Son*, H. Spring, 1938.

Jansen, Sigurd, restaurant keeper. 'Nocturne in Nyaskov' (s.s.), *Sun on the Water*, L. A. G. Strong, 1940.

Janus, Miss, typist. *London Wall* (play), J. van Druten, 1931.

Japp, Detective Inspector James, of Scotland Yard. *The Mysterious Affair at Styles*, 1920, and elsewhere, Agatha Christie.

Japp, Peter, drunken store-keeper. *Prester John*, J. Buchan, 1910.

Jaquenetta, a country wench. *Love's Labour's Lost* (play), W. Shakespeare.

Jaques, 'melancholy,' lord attendant on the banished Duke. *As You Like It* (play), W. Shakespeare.

Jaques, French servant of Sir Deakin Killigrew. *The Splendid Spur*, A. Quiller-Couch, 1889.

Jaraby, Mr, old ex-public schoolboy.
His wife.
Basil, their son, a bird fancier.
The Old Boys, William Trevor, 1964.

Jardine, Jean, central character, m. Lord Bidborough.
Francis, her dead father.
David and **Jock,** her brothers.
Mhor. *See* GERVASE TAUNTON.
Great-Aunt Alison.
Penny Plain, O. Douglas, 1920.

Jardine, Mrs Sybil, formerly Herbert, *née* Anstey.
Harry, her 2nd husband.
Her grandchildren. *See* IANTHE THOMSON.
The Ballad and the Source, Rosamond Lehmann, 1944.

Jaresky, Countess Sophie, employer of John and Alice Mundy. *Farewell Victoria*, T. H. White, 1933.

Jarl, sailor companion of Taji. *Mardi*, Herman Melville, 1849.

Jarley, Mrs, owner of waxworks, m. George. *The Old Curiosity Shop*, C. Dickens, 1841.

Jarman, miniature painter. *The Adventures of Philip*, W. M. Thackeray, 1861–2.

Jarndyce, John, guardian of Richard Carstone and Ada Clare. *Bleak House*, C. Dickens, 1853.

Jarrett, village carpenter. *Daniel Deronda*, George Eliot, 1876.

Jarrk, the seal. *Tarka the Otter*, H. Williamson, 1927.

Jarvis, James.
Margaret, his wife.
Arthur, their son.
Mary, his wife, *née* Harrison.
Their children.
Cry, the Beloved Country, A. Paton, 1948.

Jarvis, Jeremiah. 'Jerry Jarvis's Wig' (s.s.), *The Ingoldsby Legends*, R. H. Barham, 1837.

Jason, Dick, estate servant. *Dance of the Years*, Margery Allingham, 1943.

Jasper, Jack, uncle of Edwin Drood. *Edwin Drood*, C. Dickens, 1870.

Jawan, Sheikh. *Kismet* (play), E. Knoblock, 1911.

Jawleyford, a sportsman. *Mr. Sponge's Sporting Tour*, R. S. Surtees, 1853.

Jay, Kathryn. *See* ISHAM.

Jayne, Frank, elegant essayist, in love with Rome Garden.
Olga, his Russian wife, *née* Naryshkin.
Told by an Idiot, Rose Macaulay, 1923.

Jayne, Gordon, M.D., friend of Aubrey Tanqueray. *The Second Mrs Tanqueray* (play), A. W. Pinero, 1893.

Jeames, footman to Lady Clavering. *Pendennis*, W. M. Thackeray, 1848–50.

Jean, servant to Gavin Dishart. *The Little Minister*, J. M. Barrie, 1891.

Jean, Lady.
Her sons:
Percy.
Johnnie, m. Susan Dunne.
Their son.

The White Cliffs (poem), Alice D. Miller, 1941.

Jeanne, Mademoiselle, Lady Agatha Lasenby's maid. *The Admirable Crichton* (play), J. M. Barrie, 1902.

Jeavons, Lady Molly, society hostess (formerly Lady Sleaford).
Ted Jeavons, her 2nd husband.
At Lady Molly's, 1958, and others in *The Music of Time* series, Anthony Powell.

Jedburgh, Lady. *Lady Windermere's Fan* (play), O. Wilde, 1892.

Jeddler, Dr.
His daughters:
Marion, m. Michael Warden.
Grace, m. Alfred Heathfield.
The Battle of Life, C. Dickens, 1846.

Jedwell, Colonel, internee in Holland. *The Fountain,* C. Morgan, 1932.

Jeeves, Bertie Wooster's manservant. *Thank You, Jeeves,* 1934, and many others. P. G. Wodehouse.

Jefferson, Rev. Arthur. *Robert's Wife* (play), St John Ervine, 1937.

Jeffrey, Miss, neighbour and gossip. *Mrs Galer's Business,* W. Pett Ridge, 1905.

Jeffrey, Arnold, manager, Land and Sea Insurance Co. *The Loss of the 'Jane Vosper,'* F. Wills Crofts, 1936.

Jehan the Crab, man-at-arms. 'Old Men at Pevensey,' *Puck of Pook's Hill,* R. Kipling, 1906.

Jehoram, Jessica, 'arty' widow. *The Wonderful Visit,* H. G. Wells, 1895.

Jekyll, Cassie, m. Duncan Edgeworth.
Gretchen, her mother.
Rev. Oscar, her brother, rector, m. Nance Edgeworth.
A House and its Head, Ivy Compton-Burnett, 1935.

Jekyll, Henry, distinguished doctor, intermittent victim of Hyde's personality. *Dr Jekyll and Mr Hyde,* R. L. Stevenson, 1886.

Jelaluddin, Mir, Cambridge undergraduate in love with Joan Debenham. *Joan and Peter,* H. G. Wells, 1918.

Jellaludin, Mcintosh.
His wife, a native woman.
'To be Filed for Reference' (s.s.), *Plain Tales from the Hills,* R. Kipling, 1888.

Jellicle Cats. *Old Possum's Book of Practical Cats,* T. S. Eliot, 1939.

Jellicot, Joan, senile, blind and deaf. *Woodstock,* W. Scott, 1826.

Jellicott, Mr, fifth-form master. *The Fifth Form at St Dominic's,* T. Baines Reed, 1887.

Jellyband, landlord, the Fisherman's Rest, Dover. *The Scarlet Pimpernel,* Baroness Orczy, 1905.

Jellybrand, Rev. William, senior curate, St. James's. *Jeremy,* Hugh Walpole, 1919.

Jellyby, Mrs, devoted to the improvement of African natives, and neglectful of her home.
Her husband.
Their children:
Caddy, m. Prince Turveydrop.
Peepy, and others.
Bleak House, C. Dickens, 1853.

Jemima, Queen. *The Apple Cart* (play), G. B. Shaw, 1929.

Jenkins, steward to Sir John Flowerdale. *Lionel and Clarissa* (play), I. Bickerstaffe, 1768.

Jenkins, Dr ('Buffer'), headmaster of Tom Florey's school. *Tom Tiddler's Ground,* E. Shanks, 1924.

Jenkins, Ahasuerus. 'Army Headquarters' (poem), *Departmental Ditties,* R. Kipling, 1886.

Jenkins, Rev. Eli. *Under Milk Wood,* Dylan Thomas, 1954.

Jenkins, Jones. *Hawbuck Grange,* R. S. Surtees, 1847.

Jenkins, Joseph, Richard Galloway's clerk.
His wife.
The Channings, Mrs Henry Wood, 1862.

Jenkins, Nicholas, novelist, central character, m. Isobel Tolland. *A Question of Upbringing,* 1951, and others in *The Music of Time* series, Anthony Powell.

Jenkins, Mrs Tom, keeper of a school.
Tom, her husband.
Eunice and **Eiluned,** their daughters.
How Green Was My Valley, R. Llewellyn, 1939.

Jenkins, Winifred, servant to Tabitha Bramble. *Humphry Clinker,* T. Smollett, 1771.

Jenkinson, fellow prisoner and friend of the Vicar. *The Vicar of Wakefield,* O. Goldsmith, 1766.

Jenkinson, Alice, Bursar, Drayton

College, Oxford. *The Dark Tide*, Vera Brittain, 1923.

Jenkinson, Alice, church-going spinster.
Minnie, her sister.
Poor Women, Norah Hoult, 1929.

Jenkinson, Richard, groom to John Mapsted. *Twelve Horses and the Hangman's Noose*, Gladys Mitchell, 1956.

Jenkyns, Deborah.
Matilda, her sister.
Peter Marmaduke, her brother.
Cranford, Mrs Gaskell, 1853.

Jennett, Mrs. *The Light that Failed*, R. Kipling, 1890.

Jennico, Captain Basil. *The Pride of Jennico*, A. & E. Castle, 1898.

Jennings, tutor at Peregrine's boarding-school. *Peregrine Pickle*, T. Smollett, 1751.

Jennings, Miss. 'Mr Gilfil's Love Story,' *Scenes of Clerical Life*, George Eliot, 1857.

Jennings, Mr, eng. to Lady Jane Raye. *Shall We Join the Ladies?* (play), J. M. Barrie, 1921.

Jennings, Mr. *A Kiss for Cinderella* (play), J. M. Barrie, 1916.

Jennings, Mrs, mother of Lady Middleton and Charlotte Palmer. *Sense and Sensibility*, Jane Austen, 1811.

Jennings, Rev. Mr, Vicar of Kenlis. *Green Tea* (s.s.), Sheridan le Fanu.

Jennings, Alice (alias Lydia Protheroe).
Bertie, her brother.
His wife.
Emily, her sister.
'The Christmas Party' (s.s.), *The Heir*, V. Sackville-West, 1922.

Jennings, Caleb. *Abraham Lincoln* (play), J. Drinkwater, 1918.

Jennings, Ezra, hypnotist, part narrator. *The Moonstone*, W. Collins, 1868.

Jennings, Lily, typist at the Britannia Motor Co., m. Robert Brand. *A Knight on Wheels*, Ian Hay, 1916.

Jennings, Rev. Oswald. *Laura's Bishop*, G. A. Birmingham, 1949.

Jenny, Clarissa Flowerdale's maid. *Lionel and Clarissa* (play), I. Bickerstaffe, 1768.

Jenny, maid to the Misses Jenkyns. *Cranford*, Mrs Gaskell, 1853.

Jenny Wren. *See* CLEAVER.

Jennyanydots, Gumbiecat. *Old Possum's Book of Practical Cats*, T. S. Eliot, 1939.

Jensen, Herr. 'No 13' (s.s.), *Ghost Stories of an Antiquary*, M. R. James, 1910.

Jensen, Anders, a Danish artist in Tunisia. *The Tremor of Forgery*, Patricia Highsmith, 1969.

Jensen, Tony, friend of Pete Brown. *Another Year*, R. C. Sherriff, 1948.

Jenssen, Carl. The *Tarzan* series, E. R. Burroughs, 1912–32.

Jephson, partner of Belknap. *An American Tragedy*, T. Dreiser, 1925.

Jeremy, Dr.
His wife.
The Lamplighter, Maria S. Cummins, 1854.

Jerkin, Bishop, religious director, Mirage. *Sunrise in the West*, Bechofer Roberts, 1945.

Jermyn (Jerry), private, batman to Geoffrey Skene. *Sixty-four, Ninety-four*, R. H. Mottram, 1925.

Jermyn, Mr, M.P. *Sybil*, B. Disraeli, 1845.

Jermyn, Matthew, lawyer. *See also* TRANSOME.
His elder daughter, 'vulgarity personified.'
Louisa, his younger daughter.
Felix Holt, George Eliot, 1866.

Jerningham, Marquess of. *The Amateur Gentleman*, J. Farnol, 1913.

Jerningham, James, paymaster, sub-lieutenant, Captain's secretary, *Artemis*. *The Ship*, C. S. Forester, 1943.

Jerningham, Jerry, light comedian of Dinky Doos concert party, later Good Companions, m. Lady Partlit. *The Good Companions*, J. B. Priestley, 1929.

Jerningham, Sir Ralph.
Frank, his son.
The Merry Devil of Edmonton, Anon.

Jerningham, Tom, confidential servant of the Duke of Buckingham. *Peveril of the Peak*, W. Scott, 1822.

Jerningham of Costessy, Julian. *Incomparable Bellairs*, A. & E. Castle, 1904.

Jerome, Don.
Don Ferdinand, his son.
Donna Louisa, his daughter.

The Duenna (play), R. B. Sheridan, 1775.

Jerome, Father, legally Count of Falconara. *The Castle of Otranto,* Horace Walpole, 1765.

Jerome, Père, Creole priest. 'Madame Delphine' (s.s.), *Old Creole Days,* G. W. Cable, 1879.

Jerome, Thomas, retired corn-factor.
Susan, his wife.
'Janet's Repentance,' *Scenes of Clerical Life,* George Eliot, 1857.

Jerrythought, Jeffery, close friend of Charles Heath, m. Dorothea Prynne.
Lucy, their daughter.
Alice-for-Short, W. de Morgan, 1907.

Jerton, Kenelm. *A Holiday Task* (s.s.), 'Saki' (H. H. Munro).

Jervis, Mrs, housekeeper. *Pamela,* S. Richardson, 1740.

Jervis, Lieutenant Frank, R.N., m. Laura Hayes. *The Good Ship 'Mohock,'* W. Clark Russell, 1894.

Jessamine, Miss.
Jessamine, her niece, m. the Black Captain.
Jackanapes, Juliana H. Ewing, 1879.

Jessamy, Mr. *See* Oldboy.

Jesse, a woodman. 'Friendly Brook' (s.s.), *A Diversity of Creatures,* R. Kipling, 1917.

Jessel, Miss, ex-governess to Miles and Flora. *The Turn of the Screw,* H. James, 1898.

Jessica, daughter of Shylock. *The Merchant of Venice* (play), W. Shakespeare.

Jesson, Hilary.
Filmer, M.P., his brother.
m. (1) Annabel Mary Ridgeley.
Derek, their son.
(2) Nina.
His House in Order (play), A. W. Pinero, 1906.

Jesson, Laura, central character.
Fred, her husband.
Their two children.
Brief Encounter (play), N. Coward, 1945.

Jessop, Mrs, matron at Bolt House Children's Home. *Joy and Josephine,* Monica Dickens, 1948.

Jessop, Dr Thomas.
His wife.
His brother, a banker.
John Halifax, Gentleman, Mrs Craik, 1856.

Jessup, Widow. 'Telemachus, Friend' (s.s.), *Heart of the West,* O. Henry, 1907.

Jessup, Timothy, central character.
Gabrielle (Gay), his sister, with whom he sets out in search of foster-parents.
Timothy's Quest, Kate D. Wiggin, 1896.

Jethway, Mrs Gertrude, a 'crazed forlorn woman.'
Felix, her dead son, who had loved Elfride Swancourt.
A Pair of Blue Eyes, T. Hardy, 1873.

Jetsome, worthless protégé of Lawyer Wakem. *The Mill on the Floss,* George Eliot, 1860.

Jevons. 'A Friend's Friend' (s.s.), *Plain Tales from the Hills,* R. Kipling, 1888.

Jewell, Arthur, amateur soldier. *Mr Britling Sees It Through,* H. G. Wells, 1916.

Jewett, Mary, programme seller, the Pelargonium. *Sorrell and Son,* W. Deeping, 1925.

Jewkes, Mrs, villainous housekeeper. *Pamela,* S. Richardson, 1740.

'Jezebel, Lady,' nickname of Lady Castlewood. *Henry Esmond,* W. M. Thackeray, 1852.

Jibinsky, Olga, m. Edmond Bernier. 'The Crime of Olga Jibinsky' (s.s.), *The Little Dog Laughed,* L. Merrick, 1930.

Jiffin, Joe, m. Afy Hallijohn. *East Lynne,* Mrs Henry Wood, 1861.

Jike, Mrs. *Love on the Dole,* W. Greenwood, 1933.

Jilks, Sir Danby, apothecary. *The Newcomes,* W. M. Thackeray, 1853–1855.

Jillgall, Miss Selina, cousin of Abel Gracedieu. *The Legacy of Cain,* W. Collins, 1889.

Jim, Miss Watson's coloured boy, close friend of Tom Sawyer. *Tom Sawyer,* 1876, and *Huckleberry Finn,* 1884, Mark Twain.

Jim, 'Lord' (Tuan), water-clerk, formerly ship's officer, central character. *Lord Jim,* J. Conrad, 1900.

Jim, Uncle, nephew of 'Aunt Flo,' wastrel. *The History of Mr Polly,* H. G. Wells, 1910.

Jimson, Gulley, artist, central character.

His 'wives.'
Sara Monday.
Rozzie.
Tommy, their son.
Liz.
Two children.
Jenny Mud, his sister, m. Robert Ranken.
The Horse's Mouth, Joyce Cary, 1944.

Jingle, Alfred (alias Charles Fitzmarshall), strolling player. *Pickwick Papers*, C. Dickens, 1837.

Jinkins, boarder at Mrs Todger's. *Martin Chuzzlewit*, C. Dickens, 1844.

Jinks, Rebecca ('High').
Sarah, her sister ('Low'). Maids of the Sabres.
If Winter Comes, A. S. M. Hutchinson, 1920.

Jinkson, Giles ('The Bantam'). *The Ordeal of Richard Feverel*, G. Meredith, 1859.

Jo, crossing sweeper.
Bleak House, C. Dickens, 1853.

Joad, Tom, ex-criminal on parole.
His brothers and sister:
Noah, a simpleton.
Winfield.
Alfred.
Rose of Sharon ('Rosasharn'), m. Connie Rivers.
Ruthie.
'Old' Tom, his father.
'Ma,' his mother.
John, his uncle.
Grampa.
Granma.
The Grapes of Wrath, J. Steinbeck, 1939.

Joan, country girl who saves the life of John Marvel. *The Splendid Spur*, A. Quiller-Couch, 1889.

Joan of Arc (hist.), *Saint Joan* (play), G. B. Shaw, 1924. *Henry the Sixth* (play), W. Shakespeare.

Joanna ('Johnsy'), artist friend of Sue. 'The Last Leaf' (s.s.), *The Trimmed Lamp*, O. Henry, 1907.

Joaquim of Siena. *Unending Crusade*, R. E. Sherwood, 1932.

Job, manservant to Ludwig Holly. *She*, H. Rider Haggard, 1887.

Jobley, George, racing man. *The Good Companions*, J. B. Priestley, 1929.

Jobling, Dr John, M.O. of the Bengalee Disinterested Loan Co. *Martin Chuzzlewit*, C. Dickens, 1844.

Jobling, Tony ('Weevle'), friend of Guppy. *Bleak House*, C. Dickens, 1853.

Jobson, Joseph, clerk to Squire Inglewood. *Rob Roy*, W. Scott, 1818.

Jobson, Sam, secretary, Edge-tool Forgers Union. *Put Yourself in his Place*, C. Reade, 1870.

Jocelyn, Baron (decd), father of Baron Malise and Prosper le Gai. *The Forest Lovers*, M. Hewlett, 1898.

Jocelyn, Mrs, landlady to Benjie and Vanessa Herries.
Hester, her daughter.
Vanessa, Hugh Walpole, 1933.

Jocelyn, Elizabeth Mary. *Poor Women*, Norah Hoult, 1929.

Jocelyn, Sir Franks and Lady.
Their children:
Rose, m. Evan Harrington.
Hamilton.
Seymour.
Harry.
Hon. Melville, Sir Franks's brother, diplomat.
Evan Harrington, G. Meredith, 1861.

Joe, husband of Elsie, formerly Sprickett. *Riceyman Steps*, 1923, and *Elsie and the Child*, 1924, Arnold Bennett.

Joe, the Fat Boy, servant of Wardle. *Pickwick Papers*, C. Dickens, 1837.

Joe, Uncle, stonemason. *Jude the Obscure*, T. Hardy, 1896.

Jogglebury, carver of canes. *Mr. Sponge's Sporting Tour.* R. S. Surtees, 1853.

Johansen, mate of *Ghost*. *The Sea Wolf*, Jack London, 1904.

John, butler to the Pendennis family. *Pendennis*, W. M. Thackeray, 1848–50.

John, coachman to Theobald Pontifex, m. Ellen. *The Way of all Flesh*, S. Butler, 1903.

John, second footman. *The Admirable Crichton* (play), J. M. Barrie, 1902.

John ('Hordle'). *The White Company*, A. Conan Doyle, 1891.

John (the Colonel).
Ellen, his wife.
Billy, their dead son.

Barbara's Wedding (play), J. M. Barrie, 1927.

John, a savage. *Brave New World,* Aldous Huxley, 1932.

John, Dr. *See* JOHN GRAHAM BRETTON.

John, Dr. *Farewell, Miss Julie Logan,* J. M. Barrie, 1932.

John, Don, bastard brother of Don Pedro. *Much Ado about Nothing* (play), W. Shakespeare.

John the Fletcher, bowman of Madonna Benedetta Foscari. *The Heaven Tree* trilogy, Edith Pargeter, 1961–3.

John, Sir, priest. *The Merry Devil of Edmonton,* Anon.

Johnes, John, 1st Baron Helvellyn, father of Lady George Gaunt. *Vanity Fair,* W. M. Thackeray, 1847–8.

Johnny, of the *Hispaniola. Treasure Island,* R. L. Stevenson, 1883.

Johnny-the-Priest. *Anna Christie* (play), E. O'Neill, 1922.

Johns, assistant to Dr Forester. *The Ministry of Fear,* Graham Greene, 1943.

Johns, Rev. Abel, m. Augusta O'Murry. *A Georgian Love Story,* Ernest Raymond, 1971.

Johns, Ellen, girl friend of young Ewan Tavendale. *A Scots Quair,* trilogy, 1932–4, Lewis Grassic Gibbon.

Johnson, sailor on *Ghost. The Sea Wolf,* Jack London, 1904.

Johnson, nursing sister. *The Purple Plain,* H. E. Bates, 1947.

Johnson. *Anna Christie* (play), E. O'Neill, 1922.

Johnson. *Captain Brassbound's Conversion* (play), G. B. Shaw, 1900.

Johnson, friend of Arthur Machin. *This Sporting Life,* David Storey, 1960.

Johnson, Lieutenant, of *Saltash. The Cruel Sea,* N. Monsarrat, 1951.

Johnson, Mr, name given by Noggs to Nickleby. *Nicholas Nickleby,* C. Dickens, 1839.

Johnson, De Witt, air pilot, friend of the anonymous narrator. *A Voyage to Purilia,* Elmer Rice, 1930.

Johnson, Mrs Emily. *Poor Women,* Norah Hoult, 1929.

Johnson, Frankie, pianist in cinema, lover of Constance Turner. *The Sleepless Moon,* H. E. Bates, 1956.

Johnson, Harold, ticket clerk, cousin of Mr Polly.

Grace, his wife.

The History of Mr Polly, H. G. Wells, 1910.

Johnson, Mrs Helen, secretary-housekeeper. 'Blind Love' (s.s.), *Blind Love,* V. S. Pritchett, 1969.

Johnson, Jack, close friend of Titus Ledbury, m. Emma Ledbury. *The Adventures of Mr Ledbury,* Albert Smith, 1844.

Johnson, John, election agent. *Felix Holt,* George Eliot, 1866.

Johnson, Matilda, actress, eng. to Bob Loveday, m. Festus Derriman. *The Trumpet Major,* T Hardy, 1880.

Johnson, Norman, an Internal Revenue agent. *The Wapshot Scandal,* John Cheever, 1963.

Johnson, Peter.

His mother.

Peter, his son.

Grand Opera, Vicki Baum, 1942.

Johnson, Rupert, junior 'hind,' Vixen Tor Farm, m. Jill Wickett. *The Mother,* E. Phillpotts, 1908.

Johnson, Sir Rupert, brain specialist m. Margaret Heath. *Alice-for-Short,* W. de Morgan, 1907.

Johnson, Tony, friend of Jackanapes.

Jane, his sister.

Their parents.

Jackanapes, Juliana H. Ewing, 1879.

Johnson, Yogi, worker in pump factory. *The Torrents of Spring,* Ernest Hemingway, 1933.

Johnstone, Willie, boat-owner. *Guy Mannering,* W. Scott, 1815.

Joiner, John, a dog. *The Tale of Samuel Whiskers,* Beatrix Potter.

Jo-Jo, illegitimate son of Antonia, 1st wife of Geoffrey Fairford *Late in the Afternoon,* Lettice Cooper, 1971.

Joliffe, master's mate, H.M.S. *Harpy. Mr Midshipman Easy,* Captain Marryat, 1836.

Joliffe, Miss, mistress at Leys College. *Miss Pym Disposes,* Josephine Tey, 1946.

Joliffe, Jocelin, under-keeper at Woodstock Lodge. *Woodstock,* W. Scott, 1826.

Jolland, schoolfellow of Dick Bultitude. *Vice Versa,* F. Anstey, 1882.

Jolley, Mrs, housekeeper. *Riders in the Chariot,* Patrick White, 1961.

Jollice, Farmer. 'An Incident in the Life of Mr George Crookhill,' *Life's Little Ironies,* T. Hardy, 1894.

Jollifant, Inigo, ex-schoolmaster, pianist and song writer to the Good Companions, m. Susie Dean. *The Good Companions,* J. B. Priestley, 1929.

Jollife, Jack, diner-out. *Sketches and Travels,* W. M. Thackeray, 1847–1850.

Jolliffe, Captain Shadrach.
  Joanna, his wife, *née* Phippard.
    George and **Jim,** their sons.
'To Please his Wife,' *Life's Little Ironies,* T. Hardy, 1894.

Jolliver, Hannah.
  Her father.
'Tony Kytes, the Arch-Deceiver,' *Life's Little Ironies,* T. Hardy, 1894.

Jolly, manservant of 'The Toff' (Hon. Richard Rollison) in series of detective novels by John Creasey, 1938 on.

Jolly & Baines, bankers and agents. *The Newcomes,* W. M. Thackeray, 1853–5.

Jolter, tutor at Peregrine's school at Winchester, and his companion abroad. *Peregrine Pickle,* T. Smollett, 1751.

Jonas. *Absalom and Achitophel* (poem), J. Dryden, 1681.

Jonas Sessions, Elijah, Huw Morgan's schoolmaster. *How Green Was My Valley,* R. Llewellyn, 1939.

Jonathan, nine-year-old Jewish boy. *Smith's Gazelle,* Lionel Davidson, 1971.

Jones, private detective. *The Ministry of Fear,* Graham Greene, 1943.

Jones, bully and evil influence. *St Winifred's,* F. W. Farrar, 1862.

Jones. 'A Code of Morals' (poem), *Departmental Ditties,* R. Kipling, 1886.

Jones, Captain, commanding the *Chesterfield* packet. *True Blue,* W. H. G. Kingston.

Jones, Dr, attends Grace Fitzpiers. *The Woodlanders,* T. Hardy, 1887.

Jones, Lady, 'a woman of virtue,' mother of Lady Darnford. *Pamela,* S. Richardson, 1740.

Jones, Miss, governess to the Cole children. *Jeremy,* Hugh Walpole, 1919.

Jones, Miss, companion to Claire Temple. *There Were No Windows,* Norah Hoult, 1944.

Jones, Mrs, of Ostcott Manor. 'Disturbing Experience of an Elderly Lady' (s.s.), *The Baseless Fabric,* Helen Simpson, 1925.

Jones, Saddle-Sergeant, comrade of John Loveday. *The Trumpet Major,* T. Hardy, 1880.

Jones, Ada. *An Englishman's Home* (play), Guy du Maurier, 1909.

Jones, Andrew, architect. 'Fellow-Townsmen,' *Wessex Tales,* T. Hardy, 1888.

Jones, Aristotle, a herbalist. *Tomorrow To Fresh Woods,* Rhys Davies, 1941.

Jones, Athelney, official detective. *The Sign of Four,* 1890, and elsewhere, A. Conan Doyle.

Jones, Master Augustus. *Sketches and Travels,* W. M. Thackeray, 1847–50.

Jones, Bob. *The Newcomes,* W. M. Thackeray, 1853–5.

Jones, Clare, lawyer, confederate of Tom Linton. *Roland Cashel,* C. Lever, 1850.

Jones, Gwen, former secretary to Mrs Gresham and Miss Lyddon. *The Prodigal Heart,* Susan Ertz, 1950.

Jones, Major H. J., English adventurer in Haiti. *The Comedians,* Grahame Greene, 1966.

Jones, Jenny. *See* MRS WATERS.

Jones, John Goronwy. *The Corn is Green* (play), Emlyn Williams, 1938.

Jones, Martha, missionary in South Seas.
  Rev. Owen, her brother.
'The Vessel of Wrath' (s.s.), *Ah King,* W. S. Maugham, 1933.

Jones, Mary, hanged at Tyburn for theft. *Barnaby Rudge,* C. Dickens, 1841.

Jones, Mrs Mildred, of mysterious social eminence. *The Unspeakable Skipton,* Pamela Hansford Johnson, 1959.

Jones, Orville.
  His wife.
Babbitt, Sinclair Lewis, 1923.

Jones, Captain Paul (alias John Paul) (hist.). *Richard Carvel,* W. Churchill, 1899.

Jones, Rodney, central character, m. Mel Newall. *Ming Yellow,* J. P. Marquand, 1935.

Jones, Tex (alias Ewalt), cowpuncher and rover, central character. *Tex of Bar-20,* 1922, and others, C. E. Mulford.

Jones, Tom, foundling, central character, son of Bridget Allworthy. *Tom Jones,* H. Fielding, 1749.

Jonsen, Captain of the pirates. *High Wind in Jamaica,* R. Hughes, 1929.

Jonson, Louisa, fiancée of Charles Curzon.

 Sir Alfred, her father.

Harry Lorrequer, C. Lever, 1839.

Jopley, Marmaduke. *The Thirty-nine Steps,* J. Buchan, 1915.

Jopp, Duncan, executed criminal. *Weir of Hermiston,* R. L. Stevenson, 1896.

Jopp, Joshua, one-time manager to Henchard. *The Mayor of Casterbridge,* T. Hardy, 1886.

Joppolo, Major Victor, American Military Governor of Adano, 2nd World War. *A Bell for Adano,* John Hersey, 1944.

Joram, Bishop, m. Mrs Lavinia Brandon. The *Barsetshire* series, Angela Thirkell, 1933 onwards.

Jordache, Axel, German baker in small American town.

 Mary Pease Jordache, his wife.

  Gretchen, their daughter, a journalist.

  Rudolph, their ambitious eldest son who makes a fortune before he is thirty.

  Thomas, their youngest son who runs away from home, becoming a boxer and a sailor.

Rich Man, Poor Man, Irwin Shaw, 1970.

Jordan, Amelia. *The Judas Window,* Carter Dickson, 1938.

Jordan, Dupont, collector and expert. *Quinneys',* H. A. Vachell, 1914.

Jordan, Father Malachy, P.P., pilgrim to Lourdes. 'Feed My Lambs' (s.s.), *The Talking Trees,* Sean O'Faolain, 1971.

Jordan, Robert, American fighting in Spain, central character. *For Whom the Bell Tolls,* E. Hemingway, 1940.

Jordan, Thomas, of Jordan's Appliances. *Sons and Lovers,* D. H. Lawrence, 1913.

Jorgan, Captain. 'A Message from the Sea,' *Christmas Stories,* C. Dickens, 1860.

Jorgensen, Mrs, Mimi, formerly Wynant.

 Christian, a gigolo, her 2nd husband.

The Thin Man, D. Hammett, 1934.

Jorham, Captain Elisha, of the *Wampanoag.*

 Jane, his wife, *née* Putnam.

Anthony Adverse, Hervey Allen, 1934.

Jorkins, partner of Spenlow. *David Copperfield,* C. Dickens, 1850.

Jorrocks, John, M.F.H., grocer and natural sportsman, central character.

 Julia, his wife.

 Joe, his brother.

  Belinda, Joe's daughter, m. Charley Stobbs.

Jorrocks's Jaunts and Jollities, 1838, and many others, R. S. Surtees.

Jorworth, Ap Jevan, messenger dispatched by Gwenwyn to Sir R. Berenger. *The Betrothed,* W. Scott, 1825.

Jose, member of Jonsen's crew. *High Wind in Jamaica,* R. Hughes, 1929.

Josef. *The Prisoner of Zenda,* A. Hope, 1894.

Joseph, a Capucin, *Richelieu* (play), Lord Lytton, 1839.

Joseph, servant of Heathcliff. *Wuthering Heights,* Emily Brontë, 1847.

Joseph, boy prisoner, tortured to death by Hawes. *It Is Never Too Late to Mend,* C. Reade, 1856.

Joseph, Colonel ('Uncle'), guardian of Philip Meldrum. *A Knight on Wheels,* Ian Hay, 1914.

Joseph, Sergeant. *The Mystery of a Hansom Cab,* F. Hume, 1886.

Josephine, foundling at Bolt House. *Joy and Josephine,* Monica Dickens, 1948.

Josephs, barber, posing as Sir Clement Dowton. *When a Man's Single,* J. M. Barrie, 1888.

Josh, African Freedom Fighter,

When We Become Men, Naomi Mitchison, 1965.

Josselin, Bartholomew ('Barty'), illegitimate son of Antoinette Josselin and Lord Runswick, adopted by his uncle, Lord Archibald Rohan; central character, eng. to Leah Gibson. *The Martian*, George du Maurier, 1897.

Josser, Frederick.
Carrie, his wife.
Their children:
Ted, m. Cynthia.
Cynthia, their daughter.
Doris, m. Bill.
London Belongs to Me, N. Collins, 1945.

Josserant, Norman knight. *Unending Crusade*, R. E. Sherwood, 1932.

Jourdain, Margery, a witch. *Henry the Sixth* (play), W. Shakespeare.

Jourdemayne, Jennet, chief character, said to be a witch. *The Lady's Not For Burning* (play), Christopher Fry, 1948.

Jouvenet, Marie, m. Johann von Leyde.
Suzanne, her sister.
Her father.
The Other Side, Storm Jameson, 1946.

Jowl, Mat, gambler in partnership with Isaac List. *The Old Curiosity Shop*, C. Dickens, 1840.

Jowler, Lieutenant-Colonel Julius, of the Bundelcund Invincibles.
His ugly half-caste wife.
Julia, their daughter m. Chowder Loll.
Adventures of Major Gahagan, W. M. Thackeray, 1838–9.

Jowls, Rev. Giles. *Vanity Fair*, W. M. Thackeray, 1847–8.

Joy, Sylvia, dancer. *The Quest of the Golden Girl*, R. le Gallienne, 1896.

Joyce, of the *Hispaniola*. *Treasure Island*, R. L. Stevenson, 1883.

Joyce, Lieutenant. *The Sin of David* (play), S. Phillips, 1914.

Joyce, Howard.
His wife.
The Letter (play), W. S. Maugham, 1927.

Joyce, Rt. Hon. Victor, M.P., Under-Secretary for the Colonies.
Frederika, his wife.
Flamingo, Mary Borden, 1927.

Joyner, Lafayette, grandfather of George Webber.
His children:
Mark. ironmonger, m. Mag.
Maw.
Amelia, m. John Webber.
You Can't Go Home Again, T. Wolfe, 1947.

Juan, poet and minstrel, friend of Duke Silva, in love with Fedalma. *The Spanish Gypsy* (poem), George Eliot, 1868.

Jubal, youngest son of Lamech. *The Legend of Jubal* (poem), George Eliot, 1874.

Jubberknowl, Samuel. *Hawbuck Grange*, R. S. Surtees, 1847.

Judas, corporal, a cowardly, hungry knave. *Bonduca* (play), Beaumont & Fletcher, 1614.

Judd, member of Voss's expedition. *Voss*, Patrick White, 1957.

Judique, Mrs Tanis. *Babbitt*, Sinclair Lewis, 1923.

Judith, typist, m. Van Dorn. *High Tor* (play), Maxwell Anderson, 1937.

Judkin, manager, Anglo-Patagonian Bank. *The Wrong Box*, R. L. Stevenson & L. Osbourne, 1889.

Judson, head gamekeeper to Robert Raynald.
Paul, his son, playmate of Robert, later hotel manager.
Requiem for Robert, Mary Fitt, 1942.

Judson, Lieutenant Harrison ('Bai-Jove Judson'). 'Judson and the Empire' (s.s.), *Many Inventions*, R. Kipling, 1893.

Judy, Punch's small sister. 'Baa Baa Black Sheep' (s.s.), *Wee Willie Winkie*, R. Kipling, 1888.

Juffles, Rev. Mr.
Dora, his wife, *née* Warrington.
The Virginians, W. M. Thackeray, 1857–9.

Juggernaut, Duke of. *Vivian Grey*, B. Disraeli, 1827.

Juggins. *Fanny's First Play* (play), G. B. Shaw, 1905.

Juke, Hon. and Rev. Laurence, son of Lord Aylesbury. *Potterism*, Rose Macaulay, 1920.

Jukes, chief mate, the *Nan Shan*. *Typhoon*, J. Conrad, 1903.

Jukes, Bill, pirate. *Peter Pan* (play), J. M. Barrie, 1904.

Jukes, Josiah, butler to the Beechcrofts. *The Miser's Daughter,* W. H. Ainsworth, 1842.

Jukes, Morrowbie. 'The Strange Ride of Morrowbie Jukes' (s.s.), *Wee Willie Winkie,* R. Kipling, 1888.

Jules, French sailor. 'The Horse Marines' (s.s.), *A Diversity of Creatures,* R. Kipling, 1917.

Julia, a lady of Verona. *Two Gentlemen of Verona* (play), W. Shakespeare.

Julia. *The Philanderer* (play), G. B. Shaw, 1893.

Julia, central character. *The Hunchback* (play), J. S. Knowles, 1832.

Julian, Christopher, music teacher, loves Ethelberta Petherwin, m. Picotee Chickerell, her sister.
His father, a doctor.
Faith, his sister.
The Hand of Ethelberta, T. Hardy, 1876.

Juliana, wife of Virolet. *The Double Marriage* (play), J Fletcher, 1647.

Juliet, daughter of Capulet, loves Romeo. *Romeo and Juliet* (play), W. Shakespeare.

Juliet, loved by Claudio. *Measure for Measure* (play), W. Shakespeare.

Julip, John, gardener to Lord Bramble. *The Dream,* H. G. Wells, 1924.

Julius Caesar. *See* CAESAR.

Julyan, Colonel, J.P. *Rebecca,* Daphne du Maurier, 1938.

Jumble, Sir Jolly, old rake turned pimp. *The Soldier's Fortune* (play), Thomas Otway, 1681.

Juniper, Brother, priest; narrator. *The Bridge of San Luis Rey,* T. Wilder, 1927.

Juniper, Sarah, maid to the Sergisons. *Landmarks,* E. V. Lucas, 1914.

Junius, Roman captain in love with Bonduca's daughter. *Bonduca* (play), Beaumont & Fletcher, 1614.

Juno, Negro servant of the Seagraves. *Masterman Ready,* Captain Marryat, 1841–2.

Juno, Madame. 'On Patrol' (s.s.), *Sir Pompey and Madame Juno* (s.s.), M. Armstrong, 1927.

Jupe, Cecilia, strolling player's daughter. *Hard Times,* C. Dickens, 1854.

Jupp, Mrs, Ernest Pontifex's landlady. *The Way of all Flesh,* S. Butler, 1903.

Jura, Lord (Jack), one-time lover of Dolly Vanderdecken. *Moths,* Ouida, 1880.

Jurgan, Joel de, Breton swashbuckler. *The Duke's Motto,* J. H. McCarthy, 1908.

Jurgen, pawnbroker.
Adelais, his wife.
Azra, his mother.
Coth, his father.
Jurgen, J. B. Cabell, 1921.

Justice, a roan cob. *Black Beauty,* Anna Sewell, 1877.

Justice, Beatrice, music teacher. *Exiles* (play), James Joyce, 1918.

Justin, wealthy financier, m. Lady Mary Christian. *The Passionate Friends,* H. G. Wells, 1913.

Justine, maid and friend of the Frankensteins, falsely charged with murder and executed. *Frankenstein,* Mary W. Shelley, 1818.

Justine, wife of Nessim Hosnani. *Justine* and others in *The Alexandria Quartet,* 1957–61, Lawrence Durrell.

Justis, steward to Ernest Maltravers. *Alice,* Lord Lytton, 1838.

K

Kaa, the rock python. 'Kaa's Hunting' and elsewhere, *The Jungle Books*, R. Kipling, 1894–5.

Kadir Baksh. 'My own True Ghost Story' (s.s.), *Wee Willie Winkie*, R. Kipling, 1888.

Kadlu, an Eskimo.
  Amoraq, his wife.
   Kotuko, their son.
  Kotuko, their dog.
 'Quiquern,' *The Second Jungle Book*, R. Kipling, 1895.

Kadmiel, a Jew. 'The Treasure and the Law,' *Puck of Pook's Hill*, R. Kipling, 1906.

Kaghan, Barnabas, illegitimate son of Lady Elizabeth Mulhammer, m. Lucasta Angel. *The Confidential Clerk* (play), T. S. Eliot, 1954.

Kags, returned transported convict, friend of Fagin. *Oliver Twist*, C. Dickens, 1838.

Kahtan, Sultan's son. *Unending Crusade*, R. E. Sherwood, 1932.

Kai Lung, central character and narrator. *The Wallet of Kai Lung*, 1900, and many others, E. Bramah.

Kail, Jonathan, farm-hand. *Tess of the D'Urbervilles*, T. Hardy, 1891.

Kaile, commissioned gunner, *Artemis*. *The Ship*, C. S. Forester, 1943.

Kait, wife of Sobek. *Death Comes as the End*, Agatha Christie, 1945.

Kala Nag, the elephant. 'Toomai of the Elephants,' *The Jungle Book*, 1894.

Kalish, Papa and Mamma.
  Olga, their daughter, eng. to Mike Stern.
  Cora, their married daughter.
 Grand Opera, Vicki Baum, 1942.

Kalkman, Brother. 'Secret Worship,' *John Silence*, A. Blackwood, 1908.

Kallikrates, priest of Isis, reincarnated in Leo Vincey. *She*, H. Rider Haggard, 1887.

Kalon, priest of the Sun-God. 'The Eye of Apollo,' *The Innocence of Father Brown*, G. K. Chesterton, 1911.

Kalonymos, Joseph, Jewish merchant, friend of Charisi. *Daniel Deronda*, George Eliot, 1876.

Kamel. 'A Ballad of East and West,' *Barrack-room Ballads*, R. Kipling, 1892.

Kameni, handsome young scribe, in love with Renisenb, loved by Nofret. *Death Comes as the End*, Agatha Christie, 1945.

Kamensky, Alexander, Russian official who follows Count Nikolai Diakonov into exile. *The Birds Fall Down*, Rebecca West, 1966.

Kamworth, Colonel.
  Mary, his daughter.
 Harry Lorrequer, C. Lever, 1839.

Kanaris, Constantine, sea captain. *The Capsina*, E. F. Benson, 1899.

Kane, Elizabeth (Betty, Liz), juvenile delinquent.
  Bert, her father.
  Her mother.
 The Franchise Affair, Josephine Tey, 1948.

Kane, Lester, Jennie's 2nd lover.
  Robert, his brother.
 Jennie Gerhardt, Theodore Dreiser, 1911.

Kane, Webster (alias William Reynolds), economist and Communist. *The Second Confession*, Rex Stout, 1950.

Kang Foo Ah, Limehouse store-keeper. *Gracie Goodnight* (s.s.), T. Burke.

Kanga, a kangaroo.
  Roo, her baby.
 Winnie the Pooh and others, A. A. Milne, 1926.

Kantripp, Dr. *Surfeit of Lampreys*, Ngaio Marsh, 1941.

Karenin, Marcus, advanced educationalist. *The World Set Free*, H. G. Wells, 1914.

Karkeek, Q., solicitor. *Hilda Lessways*, Arnold Bennett, 1911.

Karl, friend of Billy, son of Colonel John. *Barbara's Wedding* (play), J. M. Barrie, 1927.

Karl Albert, Prince, commanding German air fleet, shot by Bert Smallways. *The War in the Air*, H. G. Wells, 1908.

Karnscheit, old watchmaker.
Sepp, his son.
Simpson, E. Sackville-West, 1931.

Karolides, Constantine. *The Thirty-nine Steps,* J. Buchan, 1915.

Kasim, a beggar. *Kismet* (play), E. Knoblock, 1911.

Kaspar.
Wilhelmine, his grand-daughter.
Peterkin, his grandson.
After Blenheim (poem), R. Southey.

Kassel, Dr. *The Dark is Light Enough* (play), Christopher Fry, 1954.

Kate, niece of Dame Carruthers. *The Yeomen of the Guard* (comic opera), Gilbert & Sullivan, 1888.

Kate. *See* SIR HARRY SIMS.

Katharina, the shrew, daughter of Baptista. *The Taming of the Shrew* (play), W. Shakespeare.

Katharine of Aragon (hist.). *Henry the Eighth* (play), W. Shakespeare.

Katherine, attending on the princess. *Love's Labour's Lost* (play), W. Shakespeare.

Katherine, daughter of the French king (hist.). *Henry the Fifth* (play), W. Shakespeare.

Kathleen, Claire Temple's fiery Irish cook. *There Were No Windows,* Norah Hoult, 1944.

Katisha, elderly lady, m. Ko-Ko. *The Mikado* (comic opera), Gilbert & Sullivan, 1885.

Katy. *See* CARR.

Katya, Tatiana Ostapenko's servant. *Tobit Transplanted,* Stella Benson, 1931.

Katz, a lawyer. *The Postman Always Rings Twice,* James M. Cain, 1934.

Kavanagh, colleague of Stephen Dormer. *The Crime at Vanderlynden's,* R. H. Mottram, 1926.

Kavanagh, Alicia ('Alice-for-Short'), central character, m. Charles Heath as 2nd wife.
Samuel, her father.
Hannah, her mother.
Her brothers.
Alice-for-Short, W. de Morgan, 1907.

Kavanagh, Mat, schoolmaster. *The Hedge School,* W. Carleton, 1830.

Kavannah, Vara, m. Cleg Kelly. *Cleg Kelly,* S. R. Crockett, 1896.

Kawdle, Dr and Mrs. *Sir Lancelot Greaves,* T. Smollett, 1762.

Kazlik, Nick, milkman's son, now a teacher in Winnipeg. *A Jest of God,* Margaret Laurence, 1966.

Kean, Dan, 'Firebrand.' *Little Men,* 1871, and *Jo's Boys,* 1886, Louisa M. Alcott.

Keane, Tom, 'caretaker.'
Cathleen, his daughter.
Roland Cashel, C. Lever, 1850.

Kear, Alroy, popular novelist. *Cakes and Ale,* W. S. Maugham, 1930.

Kearney, Captain. *Captain Brassbound's Conversion* (play), G. B. Shaw, 1900.

Kearney, Mrs.
Kathleen, her daughter.
'A Mother' (s.s.), *The Dubliners,* James Joyce, 1914.

Keats, John, an English journalist. *The Alexandria Quartet,* 1957–61, Lawrence Durrell.

Keats, Johnnie, a Californian. *The Face of Clay,* H. A. Vachell, 1906.

Keawe, purchaser of the bottle, m. Kokua. 'The Bottle Imp' (s.s.), *Island Nights' Entertainments,* R. L. Stevenson, 1893.

Keck, Ed. *Middlemarch Trumpet. Middlemarch,* George Eliot, 1871–2.

Kedgick, Captain, landlord of National Hotel. *Martin Chuzzlewit,* C. Dickens, 1844.

Keede, Dr Robin, freemason. 'In the Interests of the Brethren' (s.s.), *Debits and Credits,* 1926, and elsewhere, R. Kipling.

Keegan, Father. *John Bull's Other Island* (play), G. B. Shaw, 1904.

Keeldar, Shirley, cousin of Robert Moore, m. Louis Moore. *Shirley,* Charlotte Brontë, 1849.

Keene, fellow criminal of Cruttenden. *The Loss of the 'Jane Vosper,'* F. Wills Crofts, 1936.

Keene, Captain, of the *Justinian.* The *Hornblower* series, C. S. Forester, 1937 onwards.

Keezer, Bill. *Chosen Country,* J. dos Passos, 1951.

Keggs, butler to Lord Marshmoreton. *A Damsel in Distress,* P. G. Wodehouse, 1919.

Kegworthy, Mrs Polly, widow, m. Button.
Paul, nominally her son. *See* SILAS FINN.
The Fortunate Youth, W. J. Locke, 1914.

Keith, Mr. *South Wind,* N. Douglas, 1917.

Keith, Lady (Catherine), daughter of Mrs Lindsay and aunt of Ellen Montgomery. *The Wide, Wide World,* E. Wetherell, 1850.

Keith, Colin, m. Eleanor Grantly.
His father.
Helen, his mother.
His brothers and sisters:
Robert.
Edith, his wife.
Kate, m. Everard Carter.
Lydia, m. Noel Merton.
The *Barsetshire* series, Angela Thirkell, 1933 onwards.

Keith, Saturday, youngest of seven sons, m. Joan Benbow.
Sir Colin, his father.
His mother.
Poet's Pub, E. Linklater, 1929.

Keith-Wessington, Mrs Agnes. 'The Phantom Rickshaw' (s.s.), *Wee Willie Winkie,* R. Kipling, 1888.

Keller, journalist. 'A Matter of Fact' (s.s.), *Many Inventions,* R. Kipling, 1893.

Kello, Sir Ralph, false priest who ministers to the nuns of the convent at Oby (1349–80). *The Corner That Held Them,* Sylvia Townsend Warner, 1948.

Kelly, Sergeant. *The Immortal Sergeant,* J. Brophy, 1942.

Kelly, Cleg, central character, m. Vara Kavannah.
Tim, his father, burglar.
Isbel ('Beattie'), his mother.
Cleg Kelly, S. R. Crockett, 1896.

Kelly, Detective John. *On the Spot* (play), E. Wallace, 1930.

Kelly, Lizzie Timms, 3rd wife of John Turnham. *The Fortunes of Richard Mahony,* H. H. Richardson, 1917–30.

Kelly, Mick, a fourteen-year-old girl, chief character. *The Heart is a Lonely Hunter,* Carson McCullers, 1940.

Kelway, Hon. Basil Leigh, 'earnest young Radical.' *Some Experiences of an Irish R.M.,* Œ. Somerville & Martin Ross, 1899.

Kelway, Robert, in love with Stella Rodney. *The Heat of the Day,* Elizabeth Bowen, 1949.

Kemble, William ('Doc'), A.B., *Blackgauntlet. The Bird of Dawning,* J. Masefield, 1933.

Kemp, Dr, scientific research worker. *The Invisible Man,* H. G. Wells, 1897.

Kemp, Dadda, gaga old man.
Kath, his daughter.
Ed, his son.
Entertaining Mr. Sloane (play), Joe Orton, 1964.

Kemp, George, Rosie Driffield's lover. *Cakes and Ale,* W. S. Maugham, 1930.

Kemp, Liza, central character.
Her mother.
Liza of Lambeth, W. S. Maugham, 1897.

Kemp, Stephen, central character and narrator.
Nathaniel, his father, chief mate, brig *Juno.*
Ellen, his mother.
Nathaniel, his grandfather, 'Cap'n' Kemp, landlord of The Hole in the Wall, Wapping.
The Hole in the Wall, A. Morrison, 1902.

Kempe, Mrs, village store-keeper. *The Woman in White,* W. Collins, 1860.

Kendal, 'Hi.' *The Sky Pilot,* R. Connor, 1899.

Kendall, Nicholas, godfather of Philip Ashley.
Louise, his daughter.
My Cousin Rachel, Daphne du Maurier, 1951.

Kendrew, Mrs. *In Cotton Wool,* W. B. Maxwell, 1912.

Kendrick, Lieutenant-Commander. *The African Queen,* C. S. Forester, 1935.

Kenealy, Colonel. *Hard Cash,* C. Reade, 1863.

Kenealy, Katherine, in love with Con Lantry.
Her father.
'The Lost Blend' (s.s.), *The Trimmed Lamp,* O. Henry, 1907.

Kenge, of Kenge & Carboy, solicitors. *Bleak House,* C. Dickens, 1853.

Kenn, central character.
Davy, his father, seaman.
His mother.
Joe, his elder brother.
Highland River, N. M. Gunn, 1937.

Kenn, Rev. Dr, Vicar of St Oggs, good friend to Maggie Tulliver.
His invalid wife.
The Mill on the Floss, George Eliot, 1860.

Kennedy, country doctor, narrator. *Amy Foster* (s.s.), J. Conrad, 1903.
Kennedy, Dr Charles, friend of Steve Monk. *The World in the Evening,* C. Isherwood, 1954.
Kennedy, Frank, supervisor. *Guy Mannering,* W. Scott, 1815.
Kennedy, Frank, Scarlett O'Hara's 2nd husband.
Ella, their daughter.
Gone with the Wind, Margaret Mitchell, 1936.
Kennedy, Kit. *Cleg Kelly,* 1896, and elsewhere, S. R. Crockett.
Kennedy, Quentin, late owner of Huntingtower. *Huntingtower,* J. Buchan, 1922.
Kennedy, Robert, m. Lady Laura Standish. *Phineas Finn.* A. Trollope, 1869.
Kenny, a lesbian. *Nobody Answered the Bell,* Rhys Davies, 1971.
Kennyfeck, Mountjoy, Dublin solicitor.
Matilda, his wife.
Their daughters:
Miss Kennyfeck, the elder.
Olivia, m. Rev. Knox Softly.
Roland Cashel, C. Lever, 1850.
Kenrick, Harry, school friend of Walter Evson.
His father, a curate.
His mother.
St Winifred's, F. W. Farrar, 1862.
Kent, Earl of. *King Lear* (play), W. Shakespeare.
Kent, Mrs Jane, sister of Lenny Calcraft. *In Cotton Wool,* W. B, Maxwell, 1912.
Kent, Mary, m. Rollo Podmarsh, 'The Awakening of Podmarsh' (s.s.), *The Heart of a Goof,* P. G. Wodehouse, 1926.
Kent, Walter. *Waste* (play), H. Granville-Barker, 1907.
Kentuck, gold-miner. *The Luck of Roaring Camp,* Bret Harte. 1868.
Kenwigs, turner in ivory.
His wife.
Morleena, their eldest daughter.
Nicholas Nickleby, C. Dickens, 1839.
Keogh, Billy. *Cabbages and Kings,* O. Henry, 1905.
Keogh, Shawn, young farmer. *The Playboy of the Western World* (play), J. M. Synge, 1907.
Keola.
Lehua, his wife, daughter of Kalamake.
'The Isle of Voices' (s.s.), *Island Nights' Entertainments,* R. L. Stevenson, 1893.
Keon, Denis. 'The Daisy' (s.s.), *Countrymen All,* Katherine Tynan, 1915.
Keppet, 'wireless applauder.' *Sunrise in the West,* Bechofer Roberts, 1945.
Kepple, Jenny, m. Nick Faunt.
Joe, her father.
Shabby Tiger, H. Spring, 1934.
Kerfoot, sailor on *Ghost.* *The Sea Wolf,* Jack London, 1904.
Keri, Prince of Zalgar, m. Nadya. *The Queen was in the Parlour* (play), N. Coward, 1926.
Kerick Booterin, seal hunter.
Patalamon, his son.
'The White Seal,' *The Jungle Book,* R. Kipling, 1894.
Kernahans, Hannah, aunt of Angele Maury.
Tom and **Martin,** her sons.
The Last of Summer, Kate O'Brien, 1943.
Kernan, drunken commercial traveller.
His wife.
'Grace' (s.s.), *The Dubliners,* James Joyce, 1914.
Kernan, Johnny, one-time friend of Barney Woods. 'The Clarion Call' (s.s.), *The Voice of the City,* O. Henry, 1908.
Kerner, Johann, valet to Baron de Magny; government spy. *Barry Lyndon,* W. M. Thackeray. 1844.
Kerrigan, Toby, publican. 'Mr Kerrigan and the Tinkers' (s.s.), *Sun on the Water,* L. A. G. Strong, 1940.
Kershaw, Reginald. *Invitation to the Waltz,* Rosamond Lehmann, 1932.
Kester, farm manager. *Sylvia's Lovers,* Mrs Gaskell, 1863.
Kestournel, Elvise de, marquise, m. Raoul de Vriaac. *The Marquise* (play), N. Coward, 1927.
Ketch, Jack, cloister porter. *The Channings,* Mrs Henry Wood, 1862.
Ketel, Jorian, servant of van Swieten. *The Cloister and the Hearth,* C. Reade, 1861.

Ketley, Sir G. Denberry-Baxter's butler. *Let the People Sing,* J. B, Priestley, 1939.

Kettle, La Fayette. *Martin Chuzzlewit,* C. Dickens, 1844.

Kettle, Captain Owen, later the Rev. Sir Owen, central character.
His wife and daughter.
Captain Kettle series, C. J. Cutcliffe Hyne, 1898–1932.

Kettledrummle, Gabriel, fiery preacher, member of the Council of Covenanters. *Old Mortality,* W. Scott, 1816.

Kew, Dowager Countess of (Louisa Joanna) (Old Lady Kew) (Family name Barnes), mother of Lady Ann Newcome and Lady Fanny Canonbury.
Lady Julia, her unmarried daughter.
Frank, Lord Kew, her grandson, m. Lady Henrietta Pulleyn.
George, his brother.
The Newcomes, W. M. Thackeray, 1853–5.

Kewsy, eminent Q.C.
His wife and daughters.
The Book of Snobs, Pendennis and elsewhere, W. M. Thackeray.

Keyhole, Dr Tomlinson, reviewer. *Boon,* H. G. Wells, 1915.

Keys, journalist, friend of Keith Lockhart. *The Cruel Sea,* N. Monsarrat, 1951.

Keyte, ex-army tuckshop keeper. 'The Flag of their Country,' *Stalky & Co.,* R. Kipling, 1899.

Kezia, housemaid to Mrs Tulliver. *The Mill on the Floss,* George Eliot, 1860.

Khiva, Zulu servant. *King Solomon's Mines,* H. Rider Haggard, 1885.

Khoda Dad Khan. 'The Head of the District' (s.s.), *Life's Handicap,* R. Kipling, 1891.

Kicklebury, Sir Thomas, Bt.
His wife, gambler and snob.
Their children:
Clarence.
Fanny.
Lavinia, m. Horace Milliken.
The Kickleburys on the Rhine, W. M. Thackeray, 1850.

Kicksey, Jemima, poverty-stricken sister of Lady Griffin. 'The Amours of Mr Deuceace,' *Yellow-plush Papers,* W. M. Thackeray, 1852.

Kiddle, Joseph.
His wife.
Phoebe, Ada and **Ann,** their daughters.
Mr Weston's Good Wine, T. F. Powys, 1927.

Kiernan, Bridget, Irish maid. *Poor Women,* Norah Hoult, 1929.

Kiffin, new boy at Dr Grimstone's. *Vice Versa,* F. Anstey, 1882.

Kilbarry, Lord, friend and alleged relation of Barry Lyndon. *Barry Lyndon,* W. M. Thackeray, 1844.

Kilcarney, Marquess of, m. Violet Scully. *A Drama In Muslin,* G. Moore, 1886.

Kilcoran, Earl of (Family name De Courcy), cousin of Mr Edmonstone.
His wife:
Their children;
Maurice.
Eveleen, m. George Fielder.
The Heir of Redclyffe, Charlotte M. Yonge, 1853.

Kiljoy, Amelia, Irish heiress. *Barry Lyndon,* W. M. Thackeray, 1844.

Kilkee, Lord. *See* EARL OF CALLONBY.

Killick, James, socialist. *A Safety Match,* Ian Hay, 1911.

Killigrew, Anthony.
Sir Deakin, his father.
Delia, his sister.
The Splendid Spur, A Quiller-Couch, 1889.

Killigrew, H. P.
His wife.
The Young Men are Coming, M. P. Shiel, 1937.

Kilman, Doris. *Mrs Dalloway,* Virginia Woolf, 1925.

Kilmartin, Brian.
Maggie, his wife, *née* Hynes.
Their children:
Kitty, m. Patch Hermon.
Martin, m. Mary Gleeson.
Michael, their son.
Napp, m. Dan Toomey.
Michael.
Famine, L. O'Flaherty, 1937.

Kilmeny. *Kilmeny* (poem), J. Hogg.

Kim. *See* O'HARA.

Kimble, doctor at Raveloe.
His wife.
Silas Marner, George Eliot, 1861.

Kimpton, Milly, m. Harry Smith. *The Dream,* H. G. Wells, 1924.

Kin Yen, picture maker. *The Wallet of Kai Lung,* E. Bramah, 1900.

Kinbote, Dr Charles, a Zemblan scholar. *Pale Fire,* Vladimir Nabokov, 1962.

Kincrae, Marquess of, heir of the Duke of Horton; eccentric colonial governor. *Hamlet, Revenge!,* M. Innes, 1937.

Kinfauns, Baron. *See* SIR PATRICK CHARTERIS.

King, a housemaster. *Stalky & Co.,* R. Kipling, 1899.

King, Adolph, Martha Quest's 1st lover. *Children of Violence* series, Doris Lessing, 1952–69.

King, Alma, actress. *The Actor Manager,* L. Merrick, 1898.

King, Barbara, actress. *Tell Me How Long The Train's Been Gone,* James Baldwin, 1968.

King, Bill, friend of Pulham. *H. M. Pulham, Esq.,* J. P. Marquand, 1941.

King, Private David. *A Sleep of Prisoners* (play), Christopher Fry, 1951.

King, Reginald, close friend of the Langhams, especially Alice. *Soldiers of Fortune,* R. H. Davis, 1897.

Kingman, Major Tom, bank president.
  Alice, his wife.
'Friends in San Rosario' (s.s.), *Roads of Destiny,* O. Henry, 1909.

Kingsley Bey, slave owner. 'A Tyrant and a Lady,' *Donovan Pasha,* Gilbert Parker, 1902.

Kingsmill, Peter, m. Roy Timberlake.
  John, his brother.
In this our Life, Ellen Glasgow, 1942.

Kingsmore, Arthur, actor, m. Lady Elfride Luxellian; grandfather of Elfride Swancourt. *A Pair of Blue Eyes,* T. Hardy, 1873.

Kinloch, Lord Esmé, son of the Duke of Trent. *The Hill,* H. A. Vachell, 1905.

Kinnit, Eustace, of an old county family, wealthy owner of antique salerooms in London.
  Timothy, his adopted son, in love with Julia Laurell.
The China Governess, Margery Allingham, 1963.

Kinraid, Charlie, officer, R.N. *Sylvia's Lovers,* Mrs Gaskell, 1863.

Kinzey, Miss, Harvey Cheyne's typist. *Captains Courageous,* R. Kipling, 1897.

Kiomi, gipsy girl. *The Adventures of Harry Richmond,* G. Meredith, 1871.

Kipps, Arthur, illegitimate son of Margaret Euphemia Kipps and Waddy; eng. to Helen Walsingham, m. Ann Pornick.
  Edward George, his uncle.
    Molly, his wife. Kipps's guardians during childhood.
Kipps, H. G. Wells, 1905.

Kirby, Dr.
  Wilfrid, Lilian and **Stella,** his children.
Eden End (play), J. B. Priestley, 1935.

Kiriki. *On the Spot* (play), E. Wallace, 1930.

Kirk, Mrs.
  Captain Kirk, her husband.
Vanity Fair, W. M. Thackeray, 1848.

Kirk, Superintendent. *Busman's Honeymoon,* Dorothy L. Sayers, 1937.

Kirkby, head gardener.
  Mattie, Luke, Joe, Maggie and **Ellen,** their children.
The Things which Belong, Constance Holme, 1925.

Kirke, Captain of the *Deliverance*; m. as 2nd husband Magdalen Vanstone. *No Name,* W. Collins, 1862.

Kirke, Dr. *The Notorious Mrs Ebbsmith* (play), A. W. Pinero, 1895.

Kirker, chief reporter, the *Silchester Mirror. When a Man's Single,* J. M. Barrie, 1888.

Kirkley, Lord. *A Safety Match,* Ian Hay, 1911.

Kirkpatrick, Mrs Clare, m. Dr Gibson.
  Cynthia, her daughter.
Wives and Daughters, Mrs Gaskell, 1865.

Kirsch, Joseph Sedley's courier. *Vanity Fair,* W. M. Thackeray, 1847–8.

Kishwegin, Mme, head of the music hall act, the Natcha-Kee-Tawara Troupe. *The Lost Girl,* D. H. Lawrence, 1920.

Kissock, Meg.
  Jess, her sister, m. Agnew Greatorix.
  Andrew, her brother.
The Lilac Sunbonnet, S. R. Crockett, 1894.

Kitchell, Captain Alvinza, of the *Bertha Millner*. *Shanghaied*, F. Norris, 1904.

Kitchener, Tom, m. Sally Preston. 'Something to Worry About' (s.s.), *The Man Upstairs*, P. G. Wodehouse, 1914.

Kite, Miss (the Painted Lady). *The Passing of the Third Floor Back* (play), J. K. Jerome, 1910.

Kite, Sergeant. *The Recruiting Officer* (play), G. Farquhar, 1706.

Kitely, City merchant. *Every Man in his Humour* (play), B. Jonson, 1598.

Kitterbell, Charles, nephew of Nicodemus Dumps. *Sketches by Boz*, C. Dickens, 1836.

Kittiwake, Colonel and **Mrs.** 'Camberley,' *Collected Poems*, John Betjeman, 1958.

Kittle, Jacob, schoolmaster and sessions clerk, Dallarg. *The Lilac Sunbonnet*, S. R. Crockett, 1894.

Kittridge, Dr. *Elsie Venner*, O. W. Holmes, 1861.

Klaus, Hugo von. *See Naples and Die* (play), Elmer Rice, 1932.

Klebb, Rosa, head of the Operation Department of SMERSH. *From Russia, With Love*, Ian Fleming, 1957.

Klein, Honor. *A Severed Head*, Iris Murdoch, 1961.

Kleinhans, Hans.
Kleinhans, his son by Deborah Flood, m. Lena Smith.
Elmira, their daughter, m. Adam Lindsell.
Other children.
God's Stepchildren, Sarah G. Millin, 1924.

Kleomenes III, King of Sparta.
Agiatis, his wife.
The Corn King and The Spring Queen, Naomi Mitchison, 1931.

Klesmer, Julius, German-Slav musician, m. Catherine Arrowpoint. *Daniel Deronda*, Geo. Eliot, 1876.

Klingenspohr, Stiefel von.
Dorothea, his wife, *née* von Speck.
The Fitz-Boodle Papers, W. M. Thackeray, 1842–3.

Kloots, Captain, of the *Ter Schilling*. *The Phantom Ship*, Captain Marryat, 1839.

Knag, Miss, forewoman at Mme Mantalini's.
Her uncle.
Nicholas Nickleby, C. Dickens, 1839.

Knapp, Misses Amalia and Ysabelle, great-aunts of Janie Sykes. *The Case for the Defence*, Mary Fitt, 1958.

Knapp, Ann. *The Choice* (play), A. Sutro, 1919.

Kneebreeches, Mr, tutor to Griselda. *The Cuckoo Clock*, Mrs Molesworth, 1877.

Knibbs, Beck, helper at Talbothays Farm. *Tess of the D'Urbervilles*, T. Hardy, 1891.

Knight, Miss, nurse-attendant whom Miss Marple does not like. *The Mirror Crack'd from Side to Side*, Agatha Christie, 1962.

Knight, Henry, barrister, reviewer and essayist, loves Elfride Swancourt. *A Pair of Blue Eyes*, T. Hardy, 1873.

Knight, Norman.
His wife.
Bliss (s.s.), Katherine Mansfield, 1920.

Knightley, gold-fields commissioner.
His wife.
Robbery under Arms, R. Boldrewood, 1888.

Knightley, George, m. Emma Woodhouse.
John, his brother.
Isabella, his wife, *née* Woodhouse.
Emma, Jane Austen, 1816.

Knightsbridge, Countess of. *The Kickleburys on the Rhine*, W. M. Thackeray, 1850.

Kniveat, Major. 'Beauty Spots' (s.s.), *Limits and Renewals*, R. Kipling, 1932.

Knockell, Henry, brother of Mrs Josser. *London Belongs to Me*, N. Collins, 1945.

Knollys, of the Arctic Research Laboratory. *The Small Back Room*, N. Balchin, 1943.

Knollys, Duncan, Laird of Knocktarlitie; the Duke of Argyle's bailie. *The Heart of Midlothian*, W. Scott, 1818.

Knollys, Lady (Monica), cousin of Austin and Silas Ruthyn. *Uncle Silas*, Sheridan le Fanu, 1864.

Knott, Dorcas, one-time maid, friend of Caterina Sarti. 'Mr Gilfil's Love Story,' *Scenes of Clerical Life*, George Eliot, 1857.

Knott, Major Terry, elderly man who lives with Mrs Campion, neighbour of Christine Cornwell. *The Widow,* Francis King, 1957.

Knowell, Douglas, m. Martha Quest. *Children of Violence* series, Doris Lessing, 1952–69.

Knowle, Henry.
Mary, his wife.
Melisande, their daughter.
The Romantic Age (play), A. A. Milne, 1920.

Knowledge, Experience, Watchful and Sincere, shepherds on the Delectable Mountains. *Pilgrim's Progress,* J. Bunyan, 1678, 1684.

Knowles, London draughtsman. *A Laodicean,* T. Hardy, 1881.

Knowles, Floyd. *The Grapes of Wrath,* J. Steinbeck, 1939.

Knowles, Sylvia, Pulham's cousin. *H. M. Pulham, Esq.,* J. P. Marquand, 1941.

Knox, Mr and Mrs.
Margaret, their daughter.
Fanny's First Play (play), G. B. Shaw, 1905.

Knox, Mr Florence McCarthy ('Flurry'), Yeates's landlord, m. Sally Knox.
His grandmother.
Sir Valentine Knox.
Lady Knox.
Sally, their daughter, m. Flurry.
Some Experiences of an Irish R.M., Œ. Somerville & Martin Ross, 1899

Knox, George, author.
Anne, his second wife.
Sibyl, his daughter by first marriage, m. Adrian Coates.
His mother.
The *Barsetshire* series, Angela Thirkell, 1933 onwards.

Knox, Harold.
Sylvia, his wife.
East of Suez (play), W. S. Maugham, 1922.

Knox, Joel Harrison, a boy, central character.
Edward R. Sansom, his paralysed father.
Miss Amy Skully, his stepmother.
Randolph, Amy's cousin, a transvestite.
Other Voices, Other Rooms, Truman Capote, 1948.

Koch, Peter, shoemaker. *Barlasch of the Guard,* H. Seton Merriman, 1903.

Kohnstamm, Frau, mother of Mrs Cresset.
Childeric, her step-grandson.
Anton, his father.
Karin, his mother.
Simpson, E. Sackville-West, 1931.

Ko-Ko, Lord High Executioner, m. Katisha. *The Mikado* (comic opera), Gilbert & Sullivan, 1885.

Kokua, wife of Keawe.
Kiano, her father.
'The Bottle Imp' (s.s.), *Island Nights' Entertainments,* R. L. Stevenson, 1893.

Konkapot, John, American Indian. *Northwest Passage,* Kenneth Roberts, 1938.

Koppig, Kristian, 'rosy-faced Dutchman,' m. 'Tite Poulette. ''Tite Poulette' (s.s.), *Old Creole Days,* G. W. Cable, 1879.

Korak. *See* GREYSTOKE.

Korischelski, Zillah, protégée of Anastasia Rakonitz. *Tents of Israel,* G. B. Stern, 1924.

Korpenning, Bud. *Manhattan Transfer,* J. dos Passos, 1925.

Kortes. *Phroso,* A. Hope, 1897.

Koschei the Deathless. *Jurgen,* J. B. Cabell, 1921.

Kosmaroff, Polish patriot. *The Vultures,* H. Seton Merriman, 1902.

Kotick, the White Seal. 'The White Seal,' *The Jungle Book,* R. Kipling, 1894.

Kotuko. *See* KADLU.

Kowalski, Stanley.
Stella, his wife.
A Streetcar Named Desire (play), Tennessee Williams, 1949.

Kraft, Caesar, Chartist.
Margaret, his daughter, m. Adam Paris.
The Fortress, Hugh Walpole, 1932.

Krame, Peter, senior midshipman, a bully. *The Gunroom,* Charles Morgan, 1919.

Kramer, Pop, father of Cassie Caldwell. *The Centaur,* John Updike, 1963.

Krant, Nicholas, deputy sheriff. *An American Tragedy,* T. Dreiser, 1925.

Krantz, second captain. *The Phantom Ship,* Captain Marryat, 1839.

Krasinsky, Julia, dumb orphan. 'The Quiet Woman' (s.s.), *Adam and Eve and Pinch Me,* A. E. Coppard, 1921.

Kraus, Dr, m. Countess Irmgard von Disthal. *Princess Priscilla's Fortnight,* Countess von Arnim, 1905.

Krax, Otto, servant of Countess Luxstein. *The Courtship of Morrice Buckler,* A. E. W. Mason, 1896.

Kreisler, Otto, an artist in Paris. *Tarr,* Wyndham Lewis, 1918.

Krempe, Professor. *Frankenstein,* Mary W. Shelley, 1818.

Krenk, Rev. Justus.
 Lotta, his wife. Missionaries.
'The Judgment of Dungara' (s.s.), *Soldiers Three,* R. Kipling, 1888.

Kresney, Owen, District Superintendent of Police, of mixed blood.
 Linda, his sister.
Captain Desmond, V.C., Maud Diver, 1906.

Kreymborg, Alfred. 'The Man Who Became a Woman' (s.s.), *Horses and Men,* Sherwood Anderson, 1924.

Krillet, Simeon, Boer farmer.
 Deborah, his 2nd wife.
 Trante and **Annie,** his sisters.
The Shulamite, A. & C. Askew, 1904.

Kringelein, book-keeper.
 Anna, his wife.
Grand Hotel, Vicki Baum.

Krish, General. *The Queen was in the Parlour* (play), N. Coward, 1926.

Kroesig, Anthony.
 m (1) Linda Radlett.
 Moira, their daughter.
 (2) Pixie Townsend.
 Sir Leicester, his father.
 His mother.
 Marjorie, his sister.
The Pursuit of Love, 1945, and elsewhere, Nancy Mitford.

Krogh, Erik, great Swedish financier. *England Made Me,* Graham Greene, 1935.

Kronak, Professor Ernest, Czech refugee (alias Jeremy Bentham). *Let the People Sing,* J. B. Priestley, 1939.

Kronborg, Thea, young singer.
 Tilly, her aunt.
The Song of the Lark, Willa Cather, 1915.

Krook, rag and bone dealer, brother of Mrs Smallweed. *Bleak House,* C. Dickens, 1853.

Krutch, Diavolina, m. Sir Richard Cope.
 Abaddon, her father.
Sunrise in the West, Bechofer Roberts, 1945.

Kubs and Koibs, children of Brer Rabbit. *Uncle Remus,* J. C. Harris, 1880–95.

Kulu, The Old Woman of. *Kim,* R. Kipling, 1901.

Kumalo, Rev. Stephen, African priest.
 His wife.
 Abraham, their son.
 Gertrude, Stephen's sister.
 John, his brother.
 Matthew, his son.
Cry, the Beloved Country, A. Paton, 1948.

Kundoo. 'At Twenty-two' (s.s.), *Soldiers Three,* R. Kipling, 1895.

Kuno, 'ignorant and intemperate' hunt servant. *Prince Otto,* R. L. Stevenson, 1885.

Kuno, thief. 'Nuns at Luncheon' (s.s.), *Mortal Coils,* A. Huxley, 1922.

Kurban Sahib. *See* WALTER CORBYN.

Kurrell, Captain Ted. 'A Wayside Comedy' (s.s.), *Wee Willie Winkie,* R. Kipling, 1888.

Kurt, Luft-Lieutenant, of the *Vaterland*; Anglo-German killed in action. *The War in the Air,* H. G. Wells, 1908.

Kurtz, manager of Inner Station, Belgian Congo. *Heart of Darkness,* Joseph Conrad, 1902.

Kyle, David, landlord of the George Inn, Kennaquhair. *The Monastery,* W. Scott, 1820.

Kyrle, William, solicitor, partner of Gilmore. *The Woman in White,* W. Collins, 1860.

Kysh, friend of the narrator. 'Steam Tactics' (s.s.), *Traffics and Discoveries,* R. Kipling, 1904.

Kytes, Tony, m. Milly Richards. 'Tony Kytes, the Arch-Deceiver,' *Life's Little Ironies,* T. Hardy, 1894.

L

L., Lord, m. Caroline Grandison. *Sir Charles Grandison,* S. Richardson, 1754.

Labouisse, Madame Dorothée, widow, later Marquise de Labouisse Chanet. *Steamboat Gothic,* Frances Parkinson Keyes, 1952.

Labron, lawyer, agent for the Debarry family. *Felix Holt,* George Eliot, 1866.

Lacey, The Misses. *The Whiteoak Chronicles,* Mazo de la Roche, 1927 onwards.

Lacey, Alfred, suitor of Mrs Campion. *The Perennial Bachelor,* Anne Parrish, 1925.

Lacey, Madge. *Berry and Co.,* Dornford Yates, 1920.

Lackland, ex-criminal made good, father of Ida Fynes. *The Old Bank,* W. Westall, 1902.

La Cordifiamma, Marie, actress Marie Lavington, m. Stangrave. *Two Years Ago,* C. Kingsley, 1857.

Lacostellerie, Count de.
His wife.
Pauline, their daughter.
Tom Burke of Ours, C. Lever, 1844.

La Creevy, Miss, miniature painter. *Nicholas Nickleby,* C. Dickens, 1839.

Lacy, Mr, Home Office jail inspector. *It Is Never Too Late to Mend,* C. Reade, 1856.

Lacy, Beatrice, Max de Winter's sister.
Giles, her husband.
Roger, their son.
Rebecca, Daphne du Maurier, 1938.

Lacy, Sir Hugh, Earl of Lincoln.
Rowland Lacy, his nephew.
The Shoemaker's Holiday, Thomas Dekker (play), 1599.

Lacy, Hugo de, Constable of Chester, Lord of the Marches, betrothed to Eveline Berenger.
Damian, his nephew.
Randal, a distant and disreputable kinsman.
The Betrothed, W. Scott, 1825.

Lacy, Miriam ('The Brushwood Girl'), m. George Cottar.
Her mother.
'The Brushwood Boy' (s.s.), *The Day's Work,* R. Kipling, 1898.

Ladd, Adam. *Rebecca of Sunny brook Farm,* Kate D. Wiggin, 1903.

Ladelle, Mike ('Ladle'), son of Sir Francis Ladelle and close friend of Vince Burnet. *Cormorant Crag,* G. Manville Fenn, 1895.

Ladislaw, William, cousin of Edward Casaubon, whose widow, Dorothea, he marries.
Will, his father.
Sarah, his mother, *née* Dunkirk.
Middlemarch, Geo. Eliot, 1871–2.

Ladvenu, Brother Martin. *Saint Joan* (play), G. B. Shaw, 1924.

Ladywell, Eustace, artist, suitor of Ethelberta Petherwin. *The Hand of Ethelberta,* T. Hardy, 1876.

Laertes, son of Polonius. *Hamlet* (play), W. Shakespeare.

Lafen, an old lord. *All's Well That Ends Well* (play), W. Shakespeare.

Laferte, retired ironmaster. *The Martian,* George du Maurier, 1897.

Lagardere, Henri de, m. Gabrielle de Nevers. *The Duke's Motto,* J. H. McCarthy, 1908.

Lagrange, Madame, *pension*-keeper. *The Adventures of Mr Ledbury,* Albert Smith, 1844.

Laguerre. *Polly* (comic opera), J. Gay, 1729.

Lagune, rich and gullible student of spiritualism, swindled by Chaffery. *Love and Mr Lewisham,* H. G. Wells, 1900.

Lahmann, Pastor. *Pilgrimage,* Dorothy M. Richardson, 1915–38.

Laider, A. V., 'A. V. Laider.' *Seven Men,* Max Beerbohm, 1919.

'Laird, The.' *See* SANDY MCALLISTER.

Laiter, Agnes. 'Yoked with an Unbeliever' (s.s.), *Plain Tales from the Hills,* R. Kipling, 1888.

Lajeunesse, Basil, blacksmith.
Gabriel, his son, betrothed to Evangeline.
Evangeline (poem), H. W. Longfellow, 1847.

Lajos, Gabor (alias Grisha).
  Maria, his wife.
    Ilya, their daughter.
  Trial by Terror, P. Gallico, 1952.

Lakamba, Rajah and gunpowder smuggler. *Almayer's Folly,* J. Conrad, 1895.

Lake, Nurse Audrey, in love with Steven Sheppard. *Thursday Afternoons,* Monica Dickens, 1945.

Lake, Gunter, rich American banker, in love with V. V. Grammont. *The Secret Places of the Heart,* H. G. Wells, 1922.

Lake, Hannah, mother of Susan Rakonitz. *Tents of Israel,* G. B. Stern, 1924.

Lake, Kenneth ('Babe').
  Diana.
  French without Tears (play), T. Rattigan, 1936.

Lakeley, editor. *John Chilcote, M.P.,* Katherine C. Thurston, 1904.

Lakely, Lettice Parker's confidential maid. *A New Departure* (s.s.), R. S. Hichens.

Lakenheath, Lady (Elizabeth), aunt of Millie Ukridge. *Love Among the Chickens,* 1906, and elsewhere, P. G. Wodehouse.

Lakington, Dr Henry. *Bulldog Drummond,* 'Sapper' (H. C. McNeile), 1920.

Lal, Chowder, servant of Major Sholto. *The Sign of Four,* A. Conan Doyle, 1890.

Lalla Rookh, m. Aliris. *Lalla Rookh* (poem), T. Moore, 1817.

Lalun. 'On the City Wall' (s.s.), *Soldiers Three,* R. Kipling, 1888.

Lamar, Ruby. *Sanctuary,* W. Faulkner, 1931.

Lamb, retired butcher.
  His wife and daughters.
  The Sketch Book, W. Irving, 1820.

Lamb, Ann, m. Abel Edwards.
  Ozias, her brother, shoemaker.
  Jerome, Mary E. Wilkins, 1897.

Lamb, Charity, Tom Brown's nurse. *Tom Brown's Schooldays,* T. Hughes, 1857.

Lamb, Horace, master of household.
  Charlotte, wife whom he has married for her money.
  Mortimer, his cousin, Charlotte's lover.
  Emma, Horace's aunt.
  Manservant and Maidservant, Ivy Compton-Burnett, 1947.

Lamb, Jerry, farmer, m. Rita Lyons. 'Feed My Lambs' (s.s.), *The Talking Trees,* Sean O'Faolain, 1971.

Lamb, Leonard ('Baa-lamb'). *Middlemarch,* George Eliot, 1871–2.

Lamb, Richard, English adventurer in South America.
  Paquita, his wife.
  Dona Isadora, her aunt.
  The Purple Land, W. H. Hudson, 1885.

Lambert, Adelaide, *née* Culver, central character.
  Henry, her husband. *See also* LAUDERDALE.
  Britannia Mews, Margery Sharp, 1946.

Lambert, Marguerite, m. Paul Ravenel. *The Winding Stair,* A. E. W. Mason, 1923.

Lambert, Colonel Martin, friend of Warrington.
  Molly, his wife, *née* Benson.
  Their children:
    Jack, priggish parson.
    Charles.
    Theodosia, m. George Warrington.
    Hester.
    Lucy.
  The Virginians, W. M. Thackeray, 1857–9.

Lambert, Terence, stage designer. *Hemlock and After,* Angus Wilson, 1952.

Lambert, Major Thomas. *Reginald Cruden,* T. Baines Reed, 1894.

Lambert, Wilfred. *The Napoleon of Notting Hill,* G. K. Chesterton, 1904.

Lambone, Paul, novelist, friend of Christina Alberta. *Christina Alberta's Father,* H. G. Wells, 1925.

Lambourne, Michael, tapster's boy and general 'bad hat.'
  Benedict, his father.
  Kenilworth, W. Scott, 1821.

Lambsbreath, Adam, dairyman. *Cold Comfort Farm,* Stella Gibbons, 1932.

Lambskin, Mrs Alice, attendant of Mrs Bethune Balliol. *The Highland Widow,* W. Scott, 1827.

Lamech. *The Legend of Jubal* (poem), George Eliot, 1874.

La Mentera, Duke of, Spanish nobleman.
Antonia Dorotea, his granddaughter, the duchess; travels with him as a boy, 'Don Anthony.'
Destiny Bay, Donn Byrne, 1928.

Lammers, 'Chuck,' General in U.S. Army, attached to NATO in Paris.
Letitia, his wife.
Jean, their daughter.
Birds of America, Mary McCarthy, 1971.

Lammeter, Nancy, m. Godfrey Cass as 2nd wife.
Priscilla, her plain sister.
Her father.
Silas Marner, George Eliot, 1861.

Lammie, Andrew. *The Haunted Ships* (s.s.), Allan Cunningham.

Lammiter. 'The Lang Men o' Larut' (s.s.), *Life's Handicap,* R. Kipling, 1891.

Lammle, Alfred, unscrupulous adventurer, friend of Veneering, m. Sophronia Akershem. *Our Mutual Friend,* C. Dickens, 1865.

Lamotte, Captain. *Mr Rowl,* D. K. Broster, 1924.

Lamotte, Annette, m. Soames Forsyte as 2nd wife.
Madame Lamotte, her mother.
The *Forsyte* series, J. Galsworthy, 1906–33.

Lamplugh, Father. *The Christian,* Hall Caine, 1897.

Lamprey, Lord Charles, later Lord Wutherwood.
Imogen, his wife.
Their children:
Henry, later Lord Rune.
Frieda ('Frid').
Colin } Twins.
Stephen }
Patricia ('Patch').
Michael.
Surfeit of Lampreys, Ngaio Marsh, 1941.

Lampton, Joe, central character, m. Susan Brown. *See also* ALICE AISGILL. *Room at the Top,* J. Braine, 1957.

Lamson, Colonel Jack, close friend of Squire Merritt. *Jerome,* Mary Wilkins, 1897.

Lanaghan, Larry, central character, m. Norah Sheehy.
Seamus, his father.
Comrade, O Comrade, Ethel Mannin, 1946.

Lancaster, Florence.
David, her husband.
Nicky, their son, eng. to Bunty Mainwaring.
The Vortex (play), N. Coward, 1924.

Lance, army surgeon, later in London. *Vanity Fair,* 1847–8, and *The Virginians,* 1857–9, W. M. Thackeray.

Lancelot, Sir, of the Lake, favourite of King Arthur, lover of Guinevere. *Idylls of the King* (poem), Lord Tennyson, 1859.

Lancester, Mrs Julia, inmate of Home for Elderly Ladies. *By The Pricking of My Thumbs,* Agatha Christie, 1968.

Lancoch, Betti.
Joshua, her brother.
'The Woman who Sowed Iniquity' (s.s.), *My People,* Caradoc Evans, 1915.

Landauer, Herr, Jewish head of great department store.
His wife.
Natalie, their pretty teenage daughter.
Bernhard, his nephew and co-director of the store, liquidated by the Nazis.
Goodbye to Berlin, Christopher Isherwood, 1939.

Landless, Godfrey, Roundhead sent as convict to Virginia, later secretary to Colonel Verney; central character. *The Old Dominion,* Mary Johnston, 1899.

Landless, Helena, ward of Honeythunder.
Neville, her brother, also his ward.
Edwin Drood, C. Dickens, 1870.

Landon, Edward, M.P.
Mary, his wife.
Their children:
Jess.
Rebecca, central character.
Sylvia.
Boy.
The Ballad and the Source, Rosamond Lehmann, 1944.

Landor, banker of Milby.
Eustace, his son.
'Belle of Milby,' his daughter.
Benjamin, his son, lawyer (also in 'Amos Barton').

'Janet's Repentance,' *Scenes of Clerical Life,* George Eliot, 1857.

Landsman, Itzik, Mrs Seipel's cousin. *Magnolia Street,* L. Golding, 1932.

Landys-Haggart, Mrs. 'On the Strength of a Likeness' (s.s.), *Plain Tales from the Hills,* R. Kipling, 1888.

Lane, Algernon Moncreiff's man-servant. *The Importance of Being Earnest* (play), O. Wilde, 1895.

Lane, would-be man of fashion (alias Fanshaw). *Sophia,* Stanley Weyman, 1900.

Lane, Dr, Headmaster, St Winifred's. *St Winifred's,* F. W. Farrar, 1862.

Lane, Captain Christopher.
Alice, his sister.
Thank Heaven Fasting, E. M. Delafield, 1932.

Lane, Marion. *The Cotillon* (s.s.), L. P. Hartley.

Lane, Sammy.
Jim, her father.
The Shepherd of the Hills, H. B. Wright, 1907.

Lane, Stephen, friend of Alec Harvey. *Brief Encounter* (play), N. Coward, 1945.

Lane, Tiphany, artist and opera singer, m. Michael Ossory.
Harry, her father.
Marie, her mother.
The Face of Clay, H. A. Vachell, 1906.

Laney, Lady Caroline. *Dear Brutus* (play), J. M. Barrie, 1917.

Langdale, vintner of Holborn. *Barnaby Rudge,* C. Dickens, 1840.

Langdale, Countess of. *Castle Rackrent, The Absentee,* etc., Maria Edgeworth, 1801–12.

Langden, Sam, bushranger and murderer. *The Dark Horse,* Nat Gould.

Langdon, Bernard O. *Elsie Venner,* O. W. Holmes, 1861.

Langdon, Major Morris, lover of Leonora Penderton.
Alison, his wife.
Reflections in a Golden Eye, Carson McCullers, 1940.

Lange, landlord of the Red Shoes, Copenhagen. *The Franchise Affair,* Josephine Tey, 1948.

Langham, financier, and owner of the Valencia Mining Company.
His children:
Theodore.
Alice.
Hope, m. Robert Clay.
Soldiers of Fortune, R. H. Davis, 1897.

Langley, David, writer who uses dead friend's material, passing it off as his own. *The Towers of Trebizond,* Rose Macaulay, 1956.

Langley, Sir Frederick, proud, dark, ambitious. *The Black Dwarf,* W. Scott, 1816.

Langon, Lieutenant, of the Irish Volunteers. *The Plough and the Stars* (play), S. O'Casey, 1926.

Langston, David, 'The Harvester,' central character, m. Ruth Jameson. *The Harvester,* Gene S. Porter, 1911.

Languish, Lydia. *The Rivals* (play), R. B. Sheridan, 1775.

Lanier, Mrs. 'The Custard Heart' (s.s.), *Here Lies,* Dorothy Parker, 1939.

Lanigan, Commandant. *The Moon in the Yellow River* (play), D. Johnston, 1932.

Lanigan, James, m. Caroline Considine.
Peter, John, Tony, Lucie and **Nonie,** their children.
Without My Cloak, Kate O'Brien, 1931.

Laniger, 'a man with a temper.' *Theophrastus Such,* George Eliot, 1879.

Lanik, Kati, prima donna.
Katzerl, her daughter, m. Cyril Durham.
Grand Opera, Vicki Baum, 1942.

Lanovitch, Count Stepan.
His wife.
Caterina, their daughter.
The Sowers, H. Seton Merriman, 1896.

Lanster, Monsieur Emile, waiter. *Manhattan Transfer,* J. dos Passos, 1925.

Lant, Mary, school friend of Marcella Boyce. *Marcella,* Mrs Humphry Ward, 1894.

Lantry, Con, bar-tender, in love with Katie Kenealy. 'The Lost Blend' (s.s.), *The Trimmed Lamp,* O. Henry, 1907.

Lanyon, Dr Hastie, eminent physician and friend of Jekyll and Utterson. *Dr Jekyll and Mr Hyde,* R. L. Stevenson, 1886.

Lanyon, Mrs Joyce, m. Martin Arrowsmith as 2nd wife.
 Roger, her dead husband.
 Martin Arrowsmith, Sinclair Lewis, 1925.

Laohwan. *Dr Nikola,* G. Boothby, 1896.

Laoyeh, Yoo. *Dr Nikola,* G. Boothby, 1896.

Lapell, Hubert, temporarily in ove with Minnie. 'Hubert and Minnie' (s.s.), *The Little Mexican,* A. Huxley, 1924.

Lapham, 'Dad,' managing editor, *Chicago Sentinel,* Paris. *Trial by Terror,* P. Gallico, 1952.

Lapham, Colonel Silas, paint merchant.
 Persis, his wife.
 Their daughters:
  Irene.
  Penelope, m. Tom Corey.
 His five brothers.
 The Rise of Silas Lapham, W. D. Howells, 1885.

Lapidoth. *See* MIRAH COHEN.

Lapp, Gabriel, keeper, Windsor Forest. *Windsor Castle,* W. H. Ainsworth, 1843.

Laputa, Rev. John, renegade Negro priest. *Prester John,* J. Buchan, 1910.

Lara, Count of, nobleman of Madrid. *The Spanish Student* (poem), H. W. Longfellow, 1858.

Lara, Louis, cousin and partner of Emmanuel Gollantz. *Young Emmanuel,* Naomi Jacob, 1932.

Larch, servant of J. Galantry. *Dance of the Years,* Margery Allingham, 1943.

Larch, Miss Freda, a 'Second Resurrectionist.' *The Good Companions,* J. B. Priestley, 1929.

Largo, Emilio, modern pirate. *Thunderball,* Ian Fleming, 1961.

Larivaudière, Lise, friend of Christie. *The Pretty Lady,* Arnold Bennett, 1918.

Lark, Gustavus, art dealer. *Quinneys',* H. A. Vachell, 1914.

Lark, Tabitha. *Two on a Tower,* T. Hardy, 1882.

Larkcom, Harry (The Cad). *The Passing of the Third Floor Back* (play), J. K. Jerome, 1910.

Larke, Jack, fellow student at Leyden of Morrice Buckler. *The Courtship of Morrice Buckler,* A. E. W. Mason, 1896.

Larkin. *See* MARSHALL.

Larkin, Fay, adopted child of Jane Withersteen. *Riders of the Purple Sage,* Zane Grey, 1912.

Larkin, Sidney Charles (Pop), gay-hearted spiv, dealer and farmer.
 Ma, his wife.
 Their children:
  Zinnia.
  Petunia.
  Primrose.
  Victoria.
  Montgomery.
  Mariette, m. Mr Charlton.
 The Darling Buds of May, 1958, and others, H. E. Bates.

Larkins, Mr.
 His eldest daughter.
 David Copperfield, C. Dickens, 1850.

Larkins, Amelia, pupil of Baroski. 'The Ravenswing,' *Men's Wives,* W. M. Thackeray, 1843.

Larkins, George.
 His father.
 The Daisy Chain, Charlotte M. Yonge, 1856.

Larkins, Mrs Grace, widow.
 Her daughters:
  Annie.
  Miriam, m. Mr Polly.
  Minnie.
 The History of Mr Polly, H. G. Wells, 1910.

Larkyn, Mrs. 'Watches of the Night' (s.s.), *Plain Tales from the Hills,* R. Kipling, 1888.

Larkyns, Rev. Mr.
 Charley, his son, m. Mary Green.
 The Adventures of Mr Verdant Green, C. Bede, 1853.

Larne, Rosamund, daughter-in-law of Sylvanus Heythorp.
 Phyllis, her daughter.
 Jock, her son.
 A Stoic, J. Galsworthy, 1918.

La Roche, French employee of the fur-traders. *Ungava,* R. M. Ballantyne, 1857.

Larolle, Captain. *Under the Red Robe,* Stanley Weyman, 1894.

Larolles, Miss. *Cecilia,* Fanny Burney, 1782.

Larpent, Miss. *Mr Ingleside,* E. V. Lucas, 1910.

Larpent, Mrs. *The Daisy Chain,* Charlotte M. Yonge, 1856.

Larry. *Anna Christie* (play), E. O'Neill, 1922.

Larsen, 'Wolf,' Captain of *Ghost*. *The Sea Wolf*, Jack London, 1904.

Lartius, Titus, Roman general. *Coriolanus* (play), W. Shakespeare.

Larue, Lillian. *Counsellor-at-Law* (play), Elmer Rice, 1931.

Laruelle, Jacques, a film director. *Under the Volcano*, Malcolm Lowry, 1947.

La Ruse, Count, knave. *Jonathan Wild*, Henry Fielding, 1743.

Larynx, Rev. Mr, Vicar of Claydyke; 'an accommodating divine.' *Nightmare Abbey*, T. L. Peacock, 1818.

Lascar Loo's Mother. 'The Record of Badalia Herodsfoot' (s.s.), *Many Inventions*, R. Kipling, 1893.

Las Casas, follower of Pizarro. *Pizarro* (play), R. B. Sheridan, 1799.

Las Casas, General, Spanish governor. *Anthony Adverse*, Hervey Allen, 1934.

Lascelles, tutor to Guy Morville. *The Heir of Redclyffe*, Charlotte M. Yonge, 1853.

Lasenby. Family name of EARL OF LOAM.

Lash, Sarah, m. Florian. *The Heritage of Hatcher Ide*, Booth Tarkington, 1941.

Lashbrooke, Olive. *The Voice of the Turtle* (play), J. van Druten, 1943.

Lashmars, The, maternal relatives of Sophie Chapin. 'A Habitation Enforced' (s.s.), *Actions and Reactions*, R. Kipling, 1909.

Lasker, Eva, a *poseuse*. *Landmarks*. E. V. Lucas, 1914.

Lassiter, uncle of Bess Erne, central character, m. Jane Withersteen. *Riders of the Purple Sage*, Zane Grey, 1912.

Lassman, speculator who ruins Grapnell & Co. *Daniel Deronda*, George Eliot, 1876.

Lasswade, Kitty, Lady, cousin of the Pargiters. *The Years*, Virginia Woolf, 1937.

Last, Tony, owner of Hetton Abbey, chief character.
  Brenda, his wife.
    John, their son.
  A Handful of Dust, Evelyn Waugh, 1934.

Latch, William, Esther's lover, father of her illegitimate child; later her husband. *Esther Waters*, G. Moore, 1894.

La Testolina. 'Madonna of the Peach Tree' (s.s.), *Little Novels of Italy*, M. Hewlett, 1899.

Latimer, poet with second sight, m. Bertha Grant.
  Alfred, his half-brother.
  The Lifted Veil, George Eliot, 1859.

Latimer, Mr. *The Dover Road* (play), A. A. Milne, 1922.

Latimer, Mrs. *East Lynne*, Mrs Henry Wood, 1861.

Latimer, Darsie. *See* SIR ARTHUR REDGAUNTLET.

Latimer, Joan, loved by John Adam. *Holy Deadlock*, A. P. Herbert, 1934.

Latimer, Will. 'The Distracted Preacher,' *Wessex Tales*, T. Hardy, 1888.

Latour, 'the Old Timer.'
  Gwen, his daughter.
  The Sky Pilot, R. Connor, 1899.

Latour, Jean Marie, Bishop of Agathonica, later Archbishop, central character. *Death Comes for the Archbishop*, Willa Cather, 1927.

La Trobe, Miss, writer and director of the pageant. *Between The Acts*, Virginia Woolf, 1941.

Latta, Aaron, one-time lover of Jean Myles. *Sentimental Tommy*, J. M. Barrie, 1896.

Latta, Sir James. *Hatter's Castle*, A. J. Cronin, 1931.

Latter, Captain Jim, Devonshire gentleman.
  Sir Robert, his eldest brother.
    Aunt Latter, who brings them up.
    Nina Woodville, their cousin, who loves Jim but marries Chester Nimmo.
      Tom Nimmo, Nina's son by Jim Latter.
      Sally Nimmo, Nina's daughter by Jim.
  Prisoner of Grace, Joyce Cary, 1952.

Latter, Mary, actress, daughter of Jude Iscott.
  George, her husband.
  My Son, My Son, H. Spring, 1938.

Latude-Fernay, pensioner of Lady Drew. *Tono Bungay*, H. G. Wells, 1909.

Lauderdale, Gilbert, lived for many years as Adelaide Lambert's husband, under the name of Lambert. *Britannia Mews,* Margery Sharp, 1946.

Launce, servant to Proteus. *Two Gentlemen of Verona* (play), W. Shakespeare.

Laura. *Laura* (poem), T. Campion.

Laura. *Self-Control,* Mrs Brunton, 1811.

Laura, Jocelyn Pierston's 'Well Beloved.' *The Well Beloved,* T. Hardy, 1897.

Laure, Madame, French actress who stabbed her husband on the stage. *Middlemarch,* Geo. Eliot, 1871–2.

Laurell, Sir Anthony, great industrialist.

Julia, his daughter, in love with Timothy Kinnit.

The China Governess, Margery Allingham, 1963.

Laurence, Friar, Franciscan. *Romeo and Juliet* (play), W. Shakespeare.

Laurence, Madame, friend of Mme Foucault. *The Old Wives' Tale,* Arnold Bennett, 1908.

Laurence, Theodore ('Laurie'), m. Amy March.

Bess, their daughter.

His grandfather.

Little Women, 1868, and sequels, Louisa M. Alcott.

Laurent, Jeanne, actress, m. Captain de Lavardens. 'The Doll in the Pink Silk Dress' (s.s.), *All the World Wondered,* L. Merrick, 1911.

Laurentini, Lady. *See* Sister Agnes.

Laurie, central character and narrator.

Dot, her aunt. (*See* ffoulkes-Corbett.)

The Towers of Trebizond, Rose Macaulay, 1956.

Laurie, Annie. *Annie Laurie* (poem), Douglass.

Laurie, Hubert. *Night Must Fall,* Emlyn Williams, 1935.

Laurier, wealthy young American. *The War in the Air,* H. G. Wells, 1908.

Lavaine, Sir. 'Lancelot and Elaine' (poem), *Idylls of the King,* Lord Tennyson, 1859.

Lavander, Lady, Griselda's godmother. *The Cuckoo Clock,* Mrs Molesworth, 1877.

La Varole, servant to Lord Foppington. *A Trip to Scarborough* (play), R. B. Sheridan, 1777.

Lavement, French apothecary, employer of Roderick. *Roderick Random,* T. Smollett, 1748.

Lavender, Rev. Edmund, tutor to Bryan Lyndon. *Barry Lyndon,* W. M. Thackeray, 1844.

Lavengro, a scholar gipsy. *Lavengro,* 1851, and *Romany Rye,* 1857, George Borrow.

Lavenza, Elizabeth, adopted daughter of Alphonse Frankenstein, m. Victor Frankenstein. *Frankenstein,* Mary W. Shelley, 1818.

Laverick, Edward. *The Fourth Wall* (play), A. A. Milne, 1928.

Lavery, Inspector. 'The Burglar' (s.s.), *Cops 'n' Robbers,* J. Russell, 1913.

La Vie, Mr, antiquarian expert. 'Teigne' (s.s.), *The Baseless Fabric,* Helen Simpson, 1925.

Lavilette, Louis, of Bonaventure.

His wife.

Their daughters:

Sophie, m. Magou Farcinelle.

Christine.

The Pomp of the Lavilettes, G. Parker, 1897.

Lavinia, Titus's daughter. *Titus Andronicus* (play), W. Shakespeare.

Lavis, friend of Rudd Sergison. *Landmarks,* E. V. Lucas, 1914.

Lavish, Miss, authoress known as J. E. Prank. *A Room with a View,* E. M. Forster, 1908.

Law, Major, American naval attaché. *The Plumed Serpent,* D. H. Lawrence, 1926.

Lawford, Town Clerk, Middlemas. *The Surgeon's Daughter,* W. Scott, 1827.

Lawford, Arthur, middle-aged man who changes into personality of man who committed suicide 200 years ago.

Sheila, his wife.

Alice, their daughter.

The Return, Walter de la Mare, 1910.

Lawless, outlaw. *The Black Arrow,* R. L. Stevenson, 1888.

Lawless, Hon. George, friend of Fairlegh. *Frank Fairlegh,* F. E. Smedley, 1850.

Lawless, Sir Hedworth.
His wife.
C., M. Baring, 1924.

Lawley, Eric's first master, 'a little wrong in the head.' *Eric, or Little by Little*, F. W. Farrar, 1858.

Lawrance, Lady Betty, aunt of Lovelace. *Clarissa Harlowe*, S. Richardson, 1748.

Lawrence, head of Verney's house. *The Hill*, H. A. Vachell, 1905.

Lawrence, Mrs Frances. *The Citadel*, A. J. Cronin, 1937.

Lawrence, Frederick, m. Esther Hargrave. *The Tenant of Wildfell Hall*, Anne Brontë, 1848.

Lawrence, Colonel Tom, m. Helen Burton.
Budgie and **Toddie,** their children.
Helen's Babies, J. Habberton, 1876.

Laws, Virginian judge.
His wife.
The Virginians, W. M. Thackeray, 1857–9.

Lawson, Bob, 'a precious small man.' *The Wide, Wide World*, Elizabeth Wetherell, 1850.

Lawson, Clarence, of the British Council in Bucharest. *The Great Fortune*, Olivia Manning, 1960.

Lawson, William, Procurator-fiscal, uncle of Brodie. *Deacon Brodie* (play), W. E. Henley & R. L. Stevenson, 1892.

Laxley, Lord.
Ferdinand, his son.
Evan Harrington, G. Meredith, 1861.

Laxton, Sir Peter, Bt.
Lucy, his wife.
Bealby, H. G. Wells, 1915.

Layeville, English explorer. *The Seven Who Fled*, Frederic Prokosch, 1937.

Laylock, Chester Kirby, salesman in Babbitt's firm. *Babbitt*, Sinclair Lewis, 1923.

Lazarus, spunging-house keeper. *The Newcomes*, W. M. Thackeray, 1853–1855.

Lazytongs, Lord Lionel, son of the Marquis of Fender and Fireirons.
His wife.
Hawbuck Grange, R. S. Surtees, 1847.

Leach, Sergeant, V.C., clerk-in-charge, *The Liberal*. *The Street of Adventure*, P. Gibbs, 1909.

Leach, Fuchsia, m. Duke of Mull and Cantire. *Moths*, Ouida, 1880.

Leach, George, cabin-boy on *Ghost*. *The Sea Wolf*, Jack London, 1904.

Leadbetter, lodger at Mrs Galer's.
Johnnie. his son.
Mrs Galer's Business, W. Pett Ridge, 1905.

Leadbitter, Sally, friend of Mary Barton. *Mary Barton*, Mrs Gaskell, 1848.

Leadford, William, socialist clerk in Staffordshire office, narrator, m. Anna Reeves. *In the Days of the Comet*, H. G. Wells, 1906.

Leaf, Robert.
Fanny, his sister, m. Prentice Page.
The Perennial Bachelor, Anne Parrish, 1925.

Leaf, Thomas, simple-minded villager. *Under the Greenwood Tree*, T. Hardy, 1872.

Leake, Freddy, blacksmith. *The Sailor's Return*, David Garnett, 1925.

Lean, Donald Beau, Highland robber.
Alice, his daughter.
Waverley, W. Scott, 1814.

Lear, King of Britain.
His daughters:
Goneril.
Regan.
Cordelia.
King Lear (play), W. Shakespeare.

Lear, Miss Marty. *The Delectable Duchy*, A. Quiller-Couch, 1893.

Learoyd, Jock, one of the 'Soldiers Three.' *See also* ORTHERIS and MULVANEY. 'The Three Musketeers' (s.s.), *Plain Tales from the Hills*, 1888, and many others, R. Kipling.

Leary, barman. *The Bay*, L. A. G. Strong, 1941.

Leat, Elizabeth, postmistress at Carriford.
Her son.
Desperate Remedies, T. Hardy, 1871.

Leathwaite, Will, servant of Judith Paris. *The Fortress*, Hugh Walpole, 1932.

Leavens, Robert, m. Bessie. *Jane Eyre*, Charlotte Brontë, 1847.

Le Bailey, Dame Lilias, nun at the convent of Oby, who wishes to become an anchoress. *The Corner*

That Held Them, Sylvia Townsend Warner, 1948.

Lebas, Lady Violet, Editor, the *Spring Annual*. *Pendennis*, W. M. Thackeray, 1848–50.

Leblanc, French ambassador, Washington. *The World Set Free*, H. G. Wells, 1914.

Leblanc, Baptiste. *Evangeline* (poem), H. W. Longfellow, 1848.

Lebraux, Antoine, fox-farmer.
Clara, his wife.
Pauline, their daughter.
Finch's Fortune, 1931, and elsewhere, Mazo de la Roche.

Le Brocq, Jeanne, waitress. 'Roughhew them how we Will' (s.s.), *The Man Upstairs*, P. G. Wodehouse, 1914.

Le Brun, Baron, French emissary. The *Hornblower* series, C. S. Forester, 1937 onwards.

Lebrun, Mademoiselle, French governess. *The Newcomes*, W. M. Thackeray, 1853–5.

Lebrun, Jaques, Captain of the *Belle Marie*, French smuggler. *Cormorant Crag*, G. Manville Fenn, 1895.

Le Chapelier, lawyer, of Rennes. *Scaramouche*, R. Sabatini, 1921.

Lecherie, Anne, novelist. *The Feast*, Margaret Kennedy, 1950.

Lecount, Mrs Virginie, housekeeper of Michael and Noel Vanstone. *No Name*, W. Collins, 1862.

Ledbetter, F. W., schoolmaster, later vicar. 'Mr Ledbetter's Vacation' (s.s.), *Tales of Life and Adventure*, 1923, and elsewhere, H. G. Wells.

Ledbury, Titus, central character.
His father.
Emma, his sister, m. Jack Johnson.
Adventures of Mr Ledbury, Albert Smith, 1844.

Ledgett, Walter, 'popular' biographer and novelist. 'Argallo and Ledgett,' *Seven Men*, Max Beerbohm, 1919.

Ledru, Annette, mother of Esther Lyon, m (1) Maurice Bycliffe, (2) Rufus Lyon. *Felix Holt*, George Eliot, 1866.

Ledwich, Mrs. *The Daisy Chain*, Charlotte M. Yonge, 1856.

Ledwidge, Helen. *Eyeless in Gaza*, Aldous Huxley, 1936.

Lee, William Bule's chauffeur. *A Way through the Wood*, N. Balchin, 1951.

Lee, Company Colour Sergeant. 'Gentle Counsels' (s.s.), *Last Recollections of My Uncle Charles*, N. Balchin, 1954.

Lee, Annabel. *Annabel Lee* (poem), E. A. Poe.

Lee, Annie, m. (1) Enoch Arden, (2) Philip Ray. *Enoch Arden* (poem), Lord Tennyson.

Lee, Sir Henry, of Ditchley, ranger of Woodstock Park.
Alice, his daughter.
Woodstock, W. Scott, 1826.

Lee, Lorelei, central character. *Gentlemen Prefer Blondes*, Anita Loos, 1925.

Lee, Lovey, miserly old servant of the Malherbs.
John, her grandson, illegitimate son of Jane Lee and Norrington Malherb; in love with Grace Malherb.
The American Prisoner, E. Phillpotts, 1904.

Lee, Mehitabel. 'Study of an Elevation' (poem), *Departmental Ditties*, R. Kipling, 1886.

Lee, Minn. *On the Spot* (play), E. Wallace, 1930.

Lee, Pharaoh ('Brother Square Toes'), smuggler. 'Brother Square Toes' and elsewhere, *Rewards and Fairies*, R. Kipling, 1910.

Lee, Phyllis, eng. to Bill Davis. *Mr Fortune Finds a Pig*, H. C. Bailey, 1943.

Lee, General Robert E. (hist.). *Abraham Lincoln* (play), J. Drinkwater, 1918.

Lee, Sir Simon (Lockhart of Lee). *The Talisman*, W. Scott, 1825.

Lee Chong, Chinese grocer. *Cannery Row*, J. Steinbeck, 1945.

Lee-Johnson, Henrietta, m. Sir Aubrey Mallard. *Iron and Smoke*. Sheila Kaye-Smith, 1928.

Lee Tai Cheng. *East of Suez* (play), W. S. Maugham, 1922.

Leeds, Martin, artist, mistress of Sir Richmond Hardy. *The Secret Places of the Heart*, H. G. Wells, 1922.

Leeds, Nina, central character, m Sam Evans.
Professor Leeds, her father.
Strange Interlude (play), E. O'Neill, 1928.

Leeford, Edward (alias Monks), confederate of Fagin. *Oliver Twist*, C. Dickens, 1838.

Lees-Noel, Mrs Aubrey. *The Patrician*, J. Galsworthy, 1911.

Leeson, church organist, narrator. 'The Parasite' (s.s.), *Sir Pompey and Madame Juno*, M. Armstrong, 1927.

Leeson, Flurry, an Irish landowner.
  Harriet, his wife.
  Kevin, his brother.
    Maire, Kevin's wife.
The Private Wound, Nicholas Blake, 1969.

Leet, Guy, crippled critic. *Memento Mori*, Muriel Spark, 1959.

Le Faber, Augustus, chief cashier.
  Beatrice, his wife.
  Their sons:
    Justin, headmaster, m. Primrose Rossiter, *née* Cumberland.
    Gerard (later Sir), actor, m. Anne Cheshire.
      Constantine, their son.
      Rosemary, their daughter.
    Hector.
    Robin, m. Lady Jessica Seldom.
      Denys, their son.
      Esther, their daughter.
    Arthur Bossuet ('Bozzy').
The Five Sons of Le Faber, E. Raymond, 1945.

Le Farge, Captain of the wrecked *Ohio*. *The Blue Lagoon*, H. de Vere Stacpoole, 1909.

Le Fever, Lieutenant.
  His son.
Tristram Shandy, L. Sterne, 1767.

Lefevre, Madame Marie, mistress at Leys College. *Miss Pym Disposes*, Josephine Tey, 1946.

Lefferts, Jim, Elmer Gantry's companion at college. *Elmer Gantry*, Sinclair Lewis, 1927.

Le Gai. *See* PROSPER LE GAI.

Legality, Mr.
  Civility, his son.
Pilgrim's Progress, J. Bunyan, 1678 and 1684.

Legard, George, m. Evelyn Cameron. *Alice*, Lord Lytton, 1838.

Legaré, Mrs.
  Sally, her sister-in-law. Great-aunts of Juan Motley.
Juan in America, E. Linklater, 1931.

Legeru, Sib, a dead poet and painter. *M.F.*, Anthony Burgess, 1971.

Legg, Captain, son of Lord Levant. *The Book of Snobs*, W. M. Thackeray, 1846–7.

Leggatt, the narrator's chauffeur. 'The Horse Marines' (s.s.), *A Diversity of Creatures*, 1917, and elsewhere, R. Kipling.

Legge, 'Mother,' procuress. *A Glastonbury Romance*, J. C. Powys, 1932.

Legge-Wilson, M.P. *Phineas Finn*, 1869, and elsewhere, A. Trollope.

Le Grand, Sir Narcissus. *See* XIT.

Legrand, William. *The Gold Bug* (s.s.), E. A. Poe.

Legree, Simon, brutal owner of cotton plantation, purchaser of Uncle Tom and Emmeline. *Uncle Tom's Cabin*, Harriet B. Stowe, 1851.

Legson, Maria ('Missy'), devoted governess and companion of Francie Comper. *For Us in the Dark*, Naomi Royde-Smith, 1937.

Leicester, original name of Don Petro Rica.
  Mary, known as Leicester, living with her grandfather, Cornelius Corrigan. *See* RICA.
Roland Cashel, C. Lever, 1850.

Leicester, Earl of, m. Amy Robsart. *Kenilworth*, W. Scott, 1821.

Leicester, Hon. Charles, brother of Lord Bellefield, m. Laura Peyton. *Lewis Arundel*, F. E. Smedley, 1852.

Leigh, Captain Sir Amyas, central character, m. Ayacanora.
  His father.
  His mother, *née* Foljambe.
  Frank, his brother, victim of the Inquisition.
  Thomas, his uncle.
    Eustace, Thomas's son, papist plotter.
Westward Ho!, C. Kingsley, 1855.

Leigh, Arthur, friend of Finch Whiteoak; Sarah Court's 1st husband.
  Ada, his sister.
  His mother.
The Whiteoak Chronicles, Mazo de la Roche, 1927 onwards.

Leigh, Aurora. *Aurora Leigh* (poem), Elizabeth B. Browning, 1856.

Leigh, Harriott, central character, mistress of Oscar Wade. *Where their Fire is not Quenched* (s.s.), May Sinclair.

Leigh, Lady Jocelyn, m. Ralph Percy. *By Order of the Company,* Mary Johnston, 1900.

Leighton, Patricia, m. James Calder. *Wickford Point,* J. Marquand, 1939.

Leighton, Admiral Sir Percy, m. Lady Barbara Wellesley. The *Hornblower* series, C. S. Forester, 1937 onwards.

Leila, a fairy. *Iolanthe* (comic opera), Gilbert & Sullivan, 1882.

Leiter, Felix, Texan with iron hook instead of right hand, member of C.I.A. *Goldfinger,* 1959, and others, Ian Fleming.

Leithen, M.P., central character and narrator. *The Power House,* J. Buchan, 1916.

Leivers, farmer.
His wife.
Miriam, Edgar and **Maurice,** their children.
Sons and Lovers, D. H. Lawrence, 1913.

Lejaune, Sergeant-Major. *Beau Geste,* P. C. Wren, 1924.

Lemaitre, Brother John, Inquisitor. *Saint Joan* (play), G. B. Shaw, 1924.

Lemaitre, Jules. *The Four Armourers,* F. Beeding, 1930.

Lemaitre-Vignevielle, Captain Ursin, one-time pirate, later banker. 'Madame Delphine' (s.s.), *Old Creole Days,* G. W. Cable, 1879.

Leman, Joseph. *Clarissa Harlowe,* S. Richardson, 1748.

Lemerre, Chef de la Sûreté. *At the Villa Rose,* A. E. W. Mason, 1910.

Lemesurier. *The Four Armourers,* F. Beeding, 1930.

Lemming, Brother, freemason. 'In the Interests of the Brethren' (s.s.), *Debits and Credits,* 1926, and elsewhere, R. Kipling.

Lemoine, Widow, 2nd wife of Victor Dutripon. 'The Vengeance of Monsieur Dutripon' (s.s.), *The Little Dog Laughed,* L. Merrick, 1930.

Lemon, Mrs, schoolmistress. *Middlemarch,* George Eliot, 1871–2.

Le Moyne, Scipio, friend of Trampas. *The Virginian,* O. Wister, 1902.

Lemuel, Minna, Jewish actress and revolutionary, loved by Sophia and Frederick Willoughby. *Summer Will Show,* Sylvia Townsend Warner, 1936.

Lena, heroine, an entertainer. *Victory,* Joseph Conrad, 1915.

Leneham, friend of Corley. 'Two Gallants' (s.s.), *The Dubliners,* James Joyce, 1914.

Lenley, Mary and **John.** *The Ringer* (play), E. Wallace, 1926.

'Lennie,' 'dumb as hell.' *Of Mice and Men,* J. Steinbeck, 1937.

Lennox, a nobleman of Scotland. *Macbeth* (play), W. Shakespeare.

Lennox, Captain, m. Edith Shaw.
Henry, his brother.
Janet, his sister.
North and South, Mrs Gaskell, 1855.

Lennox, Miss Lucy.
Agnes, her companion.
'The Count's Courtship' (s.s.), *The Riddle,* W. de la Mare, 1923.

Lenoir, 'gambling prince' at Rougetnoirburg.
His younger brother.
The Kickleburys on the Rhine, W. M. Thackeray, 1850.

Lenorme, Raoul, French portrait-painter, m. 'Lady Florimel Colonsay.' *The Marquis of Lossie,* G. Macdonald, 1877.

Lenox, John Knox. *David Harum,* E. N. Westcott, 1898.

Lensky, Lydia, widow, m. Tom Brangwen.
Anna, her daughter, m. Will Brangwen.
The Rainbow, D. H. Lawrence, 1915.

Lentulus, a man 'surprised at his own originality.' *Theophrastus Such,* George Eliot, 1879.

Lenville, tragedian in Crummles's theatre company.
His wife.
Nicholas Nickleby, C. Dickens, 1839.

Leo, Armgart's music master. *Armgart* (poem), George Eliot, 1871.

Leo, Joseph, Mirah Cohen's music master. *Daniel Deronda,* George Eliot, 1876.

Leodagran, King of Cameliard. *Idylls of the King* (poem), Lord Tennyson, 1859.

Leon, rascally Belgian ex-valet. *Huntingtower,* J. Buchan, 1922.

Leon, Raphael, journalist. *Children of the Ghetto,* Israel Zangwill, 1892.

Leonard, child hero.
His father and mother.
The Story of a Short Life, Juliana H. Ewing, 1885.

Leonard.
Eustasia, his wife.
The Dover Road, A. A. Milne, 1922.

Leonard, Mr, school principal.
Margaret, his wife.
Their two children.
Look Homeward, Angel, T. Wolfe, 1929.

Leonard, Ruth, mistress of Harry Angstrom. *Rabbit, Run,* John Updike, 1960.

Leonardo, servant of Bassanio. *The Merchant of Venice* (play), W. Shakespeare.

Leonato, Governor of Messina. *Much Ado about Nothing* (play), W. Shakespeare.

Leone, David. *See* Rossi.

Leonidas. *Marriage à la Mode* (play), J. Dryden, 1671.

Leonora, a jilt. *Joseph Andrews,* H. Fielding, 1742.

Leontes, King of Sicilia.
Hermione, his Queen.
A Winter's Tale (play), W. Shakespeare.

Le Page, Charlotte.
Her mother.
Jeremy, Hugh Walpole, 1919.

Lepage, Mariette (alias Marie Blanc), 'the Golden Hand,' m. Max Richards. *If Sinners Entice Thee,* W. le Queux, 1898.

Lepel, visiting justice, Hawes's jail. *It Is Never Too Late to Mend,* C. Reade, 1856.

Lepidus. *The Last Days of Pompeii,* Lord Lytton, 1834.

Lepidus, M. Aemilius, triumvir after the death of Caesar. *Julius Caesar* (play), W. Shakespeare.

Lequesne, Aimée, buyer at 'Toni's.' *A Deputy was King,* G. B. Stern, 1926.

Lerouge, Jacques (alias Célestine Berger). 'The Article in Question,' *Lord Peter Views the Body,* Dorothy L. Sayers, 1928.

Leroux, Tata, a Zouave. *Under Two Flags,* Ouida, 1867.

Le Roy, Toppy.
Joseph, her husband.
The Citadel, A. J. Cronin, 1937.

Lerrick, Henry, m. Vivien Brown.
Tom, his father.
The Judge's Story, C. Morgan, 1947.

Lerrys, Colchian friend and fellow slave of Meromic.
Coisha, his wife.
The Conquered, Naomi Mitchison, 1923.

Lesley. *Bonnie Lesley* (poem), R. Burns.

Leslie, Mrs, widow, close friend of Lady Vargrave. *Alice,* Lord Lytton, 1838.

Leslie, Mrs, poetess. *The Treasure Seekers,* E. Nesbit, 1899.

Leslie, Archie, boyhood friend of David Crawfurd. *Prester John,* J. Buchan, 1910.

Leslie, Lady Emily.
Her children:
John.
Mary, his wife.
David, m. Rose Bingham.
Agnes, m. Robert Graham.
Martin, her nephew.
Sylvia, his wife.
Their children.
Leslie Major, Minor and Minimus, young relatives.
The *Barsetshire* series, Angela Thirkell, 1933 onwards.

Leslie, Jean, artist, m. Montague Falconer. *A Knight on Wheels,* Ian Hay, 1916.

Leslie, Kate, twice widowed, m. General Viedima. *The Plumed Serpent,* D. H. Lawrence, 1926.

Leslie, Sandars, architect, friend of Mr Ingleside. *Mr Ingleside,* E. V. Lucas, 1910.

Leslie, Walter. *Deacon Brodie* (play), W. E. Henley & R. L. Stevenson, 1892.

Lesly, Ludovic le Balafré, of Louis's Scottish guard. *Quentin Durward,* W. Scott, 1823.

L'Espanaye, Madame.
Camille, her daughter.
The Murders in the Rue Morgue (s.s.), E. A. Poe.

Lessington, Lady, *née* Blanche Carlton. *Secrets* (play), R. Besier & May Edginton, 1922.

Lessways, Hilda.
m. (1) (bigamously) George Cannon.
George, their son.
(2) Edwin Clayhanger.
Her mother.
The *Clayhanger* trilogy, Arnold Bennett, 1910–16.

Lester, Mr, m. Emily Hanning.
Their two sons.
'To Please his Wife,' *Life's Little Ironies,* T. Hardy, 1894.

Lester, Mrs, housekeeper to Conford. *The Second Mrs Conford,* Beatrice K. Seymour, 1951.

Lester, David, schoolteacher, m. Chris Brown. *A Kind of Loving,* Stan Barstow, 1960.

Lester, Elsie. *Call it a Day* (play), Dodie Smith, 1935.

Lester, Jeeter.
Ada, his wife.
Some of their children:
Tom.
Lizzie Belle.
Clara.
Ellie May.
Dude, m. Bessie Rice.
Pearl, m. Lou Bensey.
His mother.
Tobacco Road, E. Caldwell, 1948.

Lestrade, of Scotland Yard. *A Study in Scarlet,* 1887, and many others, A. Conan Doyle.

Lestrange, Dick.
Emmeline, his cousin, wrecked with him.
The Blue Lagoon, H. de Vere Stacpoole, 1909.

Lestrange, Ferdinand, K.C., son of Mrs Bradley. *The Dancing Druids,* 1948, and elsewhere, Gladys Mitchell.

L'Estrange, Harley. *My Novel,* Lord Lytton, 1853.

Le Sueur, Lucetta, m. Donald Farfrae. *The Mayor of Casterbridge,* T. Hardy, 1886.

Lesworth, Gerald, English subaltern in Ireland. *The Last September,* Elizabeth Bowen, 1929.

Letcombe-Bassett. *Odtaa,* J. Masefield, 1926.

Letford, Angela, m. Frederick Mather.
Her sisters: **Susan, Bertha, Lavinia, Mona** and **Edie.**
No News from Helen, L. Golding, 1943.

Lethbridge, Daphne, undergraduate, central character, m. Raymond Sylvester.
Her father and mother.
The Dark Tide, Vera Brittain, 1923.

Letlotse (the leopard), chief of the Bamatsienge people in Bechuanaland; educated in England.
Seneo, his sister, a nurse in London.
When We Become Men, Naomi Mitchison, 1965.

Lettcombe, Henry Brankes, O.B.E. 'Aunt Ellen' (s.s.), *Limits and Renewals,* R. Kipling, 1932.

Leuknor, Stephen, unscrupulous fortune-hunter.
His sisters:
Amelia.
Lydia, m. Verdley.
The Old Bank, W. Westall, 1902.

Levant, Lord, impecunious exile.
Captain Legg, his son.
The Book of Snobs, 1846–7, and elsewhere, W M. Thackeray.

Levasseur, rascally pirate. *Captain Blood,* R. Sabatini, 1922.

Leven, Darry, friend of Sampson Rideout. *Sampson Rideout, Quaker,* Una Silberrad, 1911.

Leven, Sir Felix.
Henry, his eldest son.
Mr Ingleside, E. V. Lucas, 1910.

Leven, Frank. *Marcella,* Mrs Humphry Ward, 1894.

Leventhal, Asa, chief character.
Mary, his wife.
Max, his brother.
Elena, Max's wife.
The Victim, Saul Bellow, 1947.

Leverett, Foxy, British diplomat. *The Great Fortune,* Olivia Manning, 1960.

Leverre, Mr, m. Marcia Bencombe.
Henri, his son by 1st wife.
The Well Beloved, T. Hardy, 1897.

Levi, Isaac, 'Oriental Jew.' *It Is Never Too Late to Mend,* C. Reade, 1856.

Levi, Peter, American student in Paris, chief character.
Paolo, his father, a lecturer.
Rosamund Brown, his mother, a famous harpsichordist.
Hans and **Bob,** his stepfathers.
Millie, his aunt.
Birds of America, Mary McCarthy, 1971.

Levine, Adrien, m. Letti Michel.
Etienne, their son, m. Camille de Jong.
Nine children.
Mosaic, 1930, and elsewhere, G. B. Stern.

Levinsohn, solicitor to the Imperial Palace Hotel. *Imperial Palace,* Arnold Bennett, 1930.

Levison, Francis, later **Sir** (alias Thorn), lover of Lady Isabel Carlyle and murderer of Hallijohn, m. Alice Challoner.
His grandmother.
Sir Peter, his great-uncle.
East Lynne, Mrs Henry Wood, 1861.

Levitt, Frank, footpad. *The Heart of Midlothian,* W. Scott, 1818.

Levy, Sir Reuben, financier. *Whose Body?,* Dorothy L. Sayers, 1923.

Levy, Walter, poet. *Tom Tiddler's Ground,* E. Shanks, 1934.

Lew, 'Piggy,' drummer boy. 'The Drums of the Fore and Aft' (s.s.), *Wee Willie Winkie,* R. Kipling, 1888.

Lewes, Gregory, Henry Challis's secretary. *The Hampdenshire Wonder,* J. D. Beresford, 1911.

Lewis, doctor and close friend of Matthew Bramble. *Humphry Clinker,* T. Smollett, 1771.

Lewis, Charlotte (Lovey), central character, m. Schuyler (Sky) Childs, millionaire playboy.
Dorothy Lewis, her mother.
F. Willingham (Billy) Lewis, her dead father.
Lovey Childs, John O'Hara, 1969.

Lewis, Cliff, friend of Jimmy Porter. *Look Back in Anger* (play), J. Osborne, 1956.

Lewis, Cyfartha, miner and prize-fighter. *How Green Was My Valley,* R. Llewellyn, 1939.

Lewis, John Aneurin, librarian.
Jean, his wife.
That Uncertain Feeling, Kingsley Amis, 1955.

Lewis, Morgan, St Mawr's groom. *St Mawr,* D. H. Lawrence, 1925.

Lewis, 'Shim,' Si Prindle's hired man.
Lize, his wife. Uncle and aunt of 'Twiddie,' and her guardians.
The Woodcarver of 'Lympus, Mary E. Waller, 1909.

Lewisham, George E., student and schoolmaster, central character, m. Ethel Henderson. *Love and Mr Lewisham,* H. G. Wells, 1900.

Lewsome, medical assistant. *Martin Chuzzlewit,* C. Dickens, 1844.

Lexton, Ivy, central character.
Jervis, her husband, whom she poisons.
The Story of Ivy, Mrs Belloc Lowndes, 1927.

Ley, Beulah, widow. 'The Lost Generation' (s.s.), *These Charming People,* M. Arlen, 1920.

Leyburn, M.P., St Oggs. *The Mill on the Floss,* George Eliot, 1860.

Leyburn, Peveril.
Erda, his wife.
The Constant Nymph, Margaret Kennedy, 1924.

Leyden, Baron Pieter von.
Ella, his 2nd wife, formerly Mrs Quinlan, governess.
His children by 1st wife:
Allard, Sophie, Jan and **Govert** ('Goof').
The Fountain, C. Morgan, 1932.

Leyland, Police Inspector. *The Three Taps,* R. A. Knox, 1927.

Liang, Chinese servant. *Ming Yellow,* J. P. Marquand, 1935.

Libbard, Dr. 'The Gioconda Smile' (s.s.), *Mortal Coils,* A. Huxley, 1922.

Libby, Nurse. *Night Must Fall* (play), Emlyn Williams, 1935.

Lickcheese, rent collector. *Widowers' Houses* (play), G. B. Shaw, 1892.

Lickpan, Robert, Endelstow carrier.
Joseph, his son.
A Pair of Blue Eyes, T. Hardy, 1873.

Licquorish, George Frederick, Editor and proprietor, the *Silchester Mirror. When a Man's Single,* J. M. Barrie, 1888.

Liebman, Colonel Warren, friend of Christine Cornwell. *The Widow,* Francis King, 1957.

Lien Chi Altangi, central character, writer of letters concerning his experiences in England. *A Citizen of the World,* O. Goldsmith, 1762.

Liftore, Earl of, formerly Lord Meikleham. *The Marquis of Lossie,* G. MacDonald, 1877.

Light, Christina, m. Prince Casamassina.
Mary, her mother, *née* Savage.
Roderick Hudson, H. James, 1875.

Lightfoot, Frederick, valet to Sir F. Clavering.
His wife, formerly Mrs Bonner, Lady Clavering's maid.
Pendennis, W. M. Thackeray, 1848–50.

Lightfoot, Martin. *Martin Lightfoot's Song* (poem), C. Kingsley.

Lightfoot, Nance, prostitute who becomes Hurtle Duffield's mistress and the inspiration for many of his paintings. *The Vivisector*, Patrick White, 1970.

Lightwood, Mortimer, barrister, friend of Eugene Wrayburn. *Our Mutual Friend*, C. Dickens, 1865.

Ligne, Matthew, central character, bachelor in love with Lily McGhee. *The Loving Eye*, William Sansom, 1956.

Ligozzi, Tomaso.
  Georgio, his dead father.
  Vittore, his cousin.
The Viper of Milan, Marjorie Bowen, 1905.

Liliengarten, Countess of (Rosina). *Barry Lyndon*, W. M. Thackeray, 1844.

Lilly, copying clerk and member of the Philosophers' Club. *Daniel Deronda*, George Eliot, 1876.

Lilly, Eva, governess to the Rosses, m. Rev. Mr Mayhew.
  Dr Lilly, her grandfather.
The Oriel Window, Mrs Molesworth, 1896.

Lillycraft, Lady, widowed sister of Squire Bracebridge. *Bracebridge Hall*, W. Irving, 1823.

Lillyvick, uncle of the Kenwigses. *Nicholas Nickleby*, C. Dickens, 1839.

Lillywhite, Lise, central character, m. Colin Duff.
  Charles, her grandfather.
  'Tante Amelie,' her aunt.
  Martin, her cousin.
  Luke, her cousin.
    Kate, his wife.
    Their children.
Lise Lillywhite, Margery Sharp, 1951.

Lilybanks, Mrs Grace, an elderly widow. *A Suspension of Mercy*, Patricia Highsmith, 1965.

Lilyworth, young English soldier in Ulster. *The Progress of Private Lilyworth*, Russell Braddon, 1971.

Limmason, Lieutenant Austin. 'The Man Who Was' (s.s.), *Life's Handicap*, R. Kipling, 1891.

Limp, shoemaker. *Middlemarch*, George Eliot, 1871–2.

Lin, aunt of Robert Blair. *The Franchise Affair*, Josephine Tey, 1948.

Lin Yi, noted brigand. *The Wallet of Kai Lung*, E. Bramah, 1900.

Lincoln, half-brother of Ostrog. *When the Sleeper Awakes*, H. G. Wells, 1899.

Lincoln, Abraham (hist.).
  His wife.
Abraham Lincoln (play), J. Drinkwater, 1918.

Linden, Lucy, early love of Jonathan Hare.
  Her mother.
  Penelope, her younger sister.
I Live Under a Black Sun, Edith Sitwell, 1937.

Lindinnock, Mistress, Julie Logan's great-aunt. *Farewell, Miss Julie Logan*, J. M. Barrie, 1932.

Lindley, Rev. Ernest.
  His wife.
  Their daughters:
    Mary, m. Edward Massey.
    Louisa, m. Alfred Durant.
Daughters of the Vicar (s.s.), D. H. Lawrence.

Lindon, Frederick.
  Eve, his wife.
The Truth (play), Clyde Fitch, 1907.

Lindsay, Captain. *An Englishman's Home* (play), Guy du Maurier, 1900.

Lindsay, Mrs, grandmother of Ellen Montgomery.
  Lady Keith (Catherine), her daughter.
  Her son.
The Wide, Wide World, E. Wetherell, 1850.

Lindsay, Leezie. *Will ye go to the Hielands?* (poem), R. Burns.

Lindsell, Adam.
  m. (1) Caroline Bickerton.
    Their daughters:
    Edith.
    May, m. Darrell Tibbitts.
  (2) Elmira Kleinhans.
    Barry, their son, m. Nora.
God's Stepchildren, Sarah G. Millin, 1924.

Lindsey, Chief Inspector John. *Robert's Wife* (play), St John Ervine, 1937.

Lindsey, Piers, cousin of Bertha Blackett, loves Rosamund Fraser. *Chatterton Square*, E. H. Young, 1947.

Lindstrum, Carl, neighbour of the Bergsons. *O Pioneers!*, Willa Cather, 1913.

Linford, last boy to see Mr Chips. *Goodbye, Mr Chips,* J. Hilton, 1934.

Ling. *The Wallet of Kai Lung,* E. Bramah, 1900.

Ling Tan, Chinese farmer.
Ling Sao, his wife.
Their children:
Lao Ta, m. Orchid.
Lao Er, m. Jade.
Pansiao, m. Wu Lien.
Lao San.
Dragon Seed, Pearl Buck, 1942.

Lingard, Adelaide, partner with Miss Muirhead. *Mr Ingleside,* E. V. Lucas, 1910.

Lingard, Tom, 'Rajah-laut.' *Almayer's Folly,* J. Conrad, 1895.

Lingley, Mr (Feltman). *Outward Bound* (play), S. Vane, 1923.

Lingnam, Mr. 'The Vortex' (s.s.), *A Diversity of Creatures,* R. Kipling, 1917.

Lingon, Rev. John, Rector of Little Treby, brother of Arabella Transome. *Felix Holt,* George Eliot, 1866.

Linklater, Laurie, yeoman of the King's Kitchen. *The Fortunes of Nigel,* W. Scott, 1822.

Links, George, young country solicitor.
Janet, his wife.
A Travelling Woman, John Wain, 1959.

Linlay, Norman, ex-fiancé of Kit Tallant. *Other Gods,* Pearl Buck, 1940.

Linley, Harriet, m. Frederick Ide.
Victor, her brother, architect.
Nancy and **Alice,** her sisters.
The Heritage of Hatcher Ide, Booth Tarkington, 1941.

Linlithgow, Countess of (Penelope), aunt of Lady Eustace. *The Eustace Diamonds,* A. Trollope, 1873.

Linnet, Mrs, widow.
Mary and **Rebecca,** her daughters.
'Janet's Repentance,' *Scenes of Clerical Life,* George Eliot, 1857.

Linscott, Aubrey, friend of Richard Thurstan. *Lighten our Darkness,* R. Keable, 1927.

Linton, assistant to Pestler, apothecary. *Vanity Fair,* W. M. Thackeray, 1847–8.

Linton, Anne. *See* GARDNER COOLIDGE.

Linton, Edgar, m. Catherine Earnshaw.
Cathie, their daughter, m. (1) Linton Heathcliff, (2) Hareton Earnshaw.
Isabella, his sister, m. Heathcliff.
Wuthering Heights, Emily Brontë, 1847.

Linton, Tom, a murderer. *Roland Cashel,* C. Lever, 1850.

Lionel, in love with Clarissa Flowerdale. *Lionel and Clarissa* (play), I. Bickerstaffe, 1768.

Lionel, the Senior Subaltern. 'His Wedded Wife' (s.s.), *Plain Tales from the Hills,* R. Kipling, 1888.

Lionel, Ivor, in love with Bella Winberg. *Magnolia Street,* L. Golding, 1932.

Lippe, Count, agent of SPECTRE. *Thunderball,* Ian Fleming, 1961.

Lippett, Mrs, matron of John Grier Home for Orphans. *Daddy-Long-Legs,* Jean Webster, 1912.

Lipscombe, Henry, m. Mabel Blitch. *The Custom of the Country,* Edith Wharton, 1913.

Lirazel, m. Alveric.
Orion, their son.
The King of Elfland's Daughter, Lord Dunsany, 1924.

Liret, Monsieur, Vaudois clergyman living in Lausanne. *Middlemarch,* George Eliot, 1871–2.

Lirriper Family, The. *Mrs Lirriper's Lodgings,* C. Dickens, 1863.

Lisa, m. Perdicone. *How Lisa Loved the King* (poem), George Eliot, 1869.

Lisa, Monna, deaf old woman who befriends Tessa. *Romola,* George Eliot, 1863.

Lisetta. *The Question to Lisetta* (poem), M. Prior.

Lisle, Sir Hubert, m. Miriam, widow of Colonel Mardyke.
Hubert, their son.
The Sin of David (play), S. Phillips, 1914.

Lismahago, Scottish soldier, m. (1) an Indian virago, (2) Tabitha Bramble. *Humphry Clinker,* T. Smollett, 1771.

Lispeth, a hill girl. 'Lispeth' (s.s.), *Plain Tales from the Hills,* R. Kipling, 1888.

Liss, Roger, Hope Ollerton's fiancé. *Let the People Sing,* J. B. Priestley, 1939.

List, Isaac, fellow gambler of Jowl. *The Old Curiosity Shop*, C. Dickens, 1841.

Listless, Hon. Mr, college friend of Scythrop Glowry. *Nightmare Abbey*, T. L. Peacock, 1818.

Lithebe, Mrs, landlady to Stephen Kumalo in Johannesburg. *Cry, the Beloved Country*, A. Paton, 1948.

Litterley, Viscount (Barrington). *The Amazons* (play), A. W. Pinero, 1893.

Littimer, Steerforth's servant. *David Copperfield*, C. Dickens, 1850.

Little, Sir Arthur. *Caesar's Wife* (play), W. S. Maugham, 1919.

Little, James, m. Edith Raby.
  Henry, their son, central character, m. Grace Carden.
  Joseph, their son.
Put Yourself in his Place, C. Reade, 1870.

Little, Midge, warm-hearted woman.
  Archie, husband who deserted her.
    David, their son, journalist, m. Cressida MacPhail.
The Wedding Group, Elizabeth Taylor, 1968.

Little Billie. *See* WILLIAM BAGOT.

Little Nell. *See* TRENT, NELLIE.

Littlefield, Dr Howard.
  Eunice, his daughter, m. Ted Babbitt.
Babbitt, Sinclair Lewis, 1923.

Littlejohn, Captain Eddy (Ginger), in love with Nina Blount. *Vile Bodies*, Evelyn Waugh, 1930.

Liu, Dr, Chinese merchant. *The Seven Who Fled*, Frederic Prokosch, 1937.

Liu, Philip, scheming 'college' Chinese. *Ming Yellow*, J. P. Marquand, 1935.

Livermore, Sam. *Northwest Passage*, Kenneth Roberts, 1938.

Liversedge, Sinnamenta, m. secretly Sir Massingberd Heath.
  Rachel, her mother.
Lost Sir Massingberd, James Payn, 1864.

Livesey, Dr. *Treasure Island*, R. L. Stevenson, 1883.

Livingstone, Harriette. *Mrs Parkington*, L. Bromfield, 1944.

Livingstone, John, sailor and 'judicious Christian.' *The Heart of Midlothian*, W. Scott, 1818.

Liza, the Darlings' maid. *Peter Pan* (play), J. M. Barrie, 1904.

Llano Kid, The, pretended Don Francisco Urique. 'A Double-dyed Deceiver' (s.s.), *Roads of Destiny*, O. Henry, 1909.

Llewellyn, Francis. *Distinguished Villa* (play), Kate O'Brien, 1926.

Llewellyn, Mary, m. Martin Hallam. *The Well of Loneliness*, Radclyffe Hall, 1928.

Llewyllyn, Tom, author and journalist, m. Patricia Turbot. *The Rich Pay Late*, 1964, and others in the *Alms for Oblivion* sequence, Simon Raven.

Lloyd, Dr. *Jane Eyre*, Charlotte Brontë, 1847.

Lloyd, Teddy, art teacher. *The Prime of Miss Jean Brodie*, Muriel Spark, 1961.

Lloyd-James, Somerset, an editor. *The Rich Pay Late*, 1964, and others in the *Alms for Oblivion* sequence, Simon Raven.

Llywarch, Blethyn, m. Ceridwen Morgan. *How Green Was My Valley*, R. Llewellyn, 1939.

Lo Tsen, Manchu maiden. *Lost Horizon*, J. Hilton, 1933.

Loam, Earl of (Henry) (family name Lasenby).
  His daughters:
    Lady Mary.
    Lady Catherine.
    Lady Agatha.
The Admirable Crichton (play), J. M. Barrie, 1902.

Lob. *Dear Brutus* (play), J. M. Barrie, 1917.

Lobbs, 'Old,' saddler.
  Maria, his pretty daughter.
Pickwick Papers, C. Dickens, 1837.

Lobe, Lady Katharine, aunt of Lord Charles Lamprey. *Surfeit of Lampreys*, Ngaio Marsh, 1941.

Lobkins, Mrs Margery ('Piggy Lob'), hostess of the Mug. *Paul Clifford*, Lord Lytton, 1830.

Lobley, servant of Tartar. *Edwin Drood*, C. Dickens, 1870.

Lockaby, Reuben, friend and companion of Micah Clarke. *Micah Clarke*, A. Conan Doyle, 1889.

Locke, Roger, Lucinda Raydon's foster-brother. *An Affair of Dishonour*, W. de Morgan, 1910.

Locke, Townsend P. (Towny), a paper manufacturer from Chicago. *Midnight Cowboy*, James Leo Herlihy, 1966.

Lockert, Clyde, admirer of Fran Dodsworth. *Dodsworth,* Sinclair Lewis, 1929.

Lockhart, Keith, Sub-Lieutenant, later Lieutenant-Commander, *Compass Rose,* later *Saltash,* in love with Julie Hallam. *The Cruel Sea,* N. Monsarrat, 1951.

Lockit.
  Lucy, his daughter.
 The Beggar's Opera (comic opera), J. Gay, 1728.

Locksley ('Diccon bend the Bow'), leader of a band of outlaws. *Ivanhoe,* W Scott, 1820.

Locksley-Jones, Lieutenant. *Peter Jackson, Cigar Merchant,* G. Frankau, 1919.

Lockwood, narrator, tenant of Heathcliff. *Wuthering Heights,* Emily Brontë, 1847.

Lockwood, porter at Castlewood.
  Esmond, John and **Molly,** his children.
 Henry Esmond, 1852, and *The Virginians,* 1857–9, W. M. Thackeray.

Lockwood, William de. 'Revenge upon Revenge' (s.s.), *Love and Money,* Phyllis Bentley, 1957.

Loder, artist and murderer. 'The Man with Copper Fingers,' *Lord Peter Views the Body,* Dorothy L. Sayers, 1928.

Loder, Major, gambler and scoundrel. *Vanity Fair, The Newcomes* and *Pendennis,* W. M. Thackeray, 1847–50.

Loder, John, impersonator of John Chilcote. *John Chilcote, M.P.,* Katherine C. Thurston, 1904.

Lodge, Farmer.
  Gertrude, his wife.
 'The Withered Arm,' *Wessex Tales,* T. Hardy, 1888.

Loding, Alec, former friend of the Ashbys. *Brat Farrar,* Josephine Tey, 1949.

Lodovico, Count, banished nobleman. *The White Devil* (play), John Webster, *c.* 1612.

Loftie, pathologist. 'Unprofessional' (s.s.), *Limits and Renewals,* R. Kipling, 1932.

Logan, Cuthbert, reporter on morning paper at trial of Harriet Vane. *Strong Poison,* Dorothy L. Sayers, 1930.

Logan, Hon. Frances (Fanny), central character and narrator, cousin of the Radletts, m. Alfred Wincham.
  Her father, m. five times.
  Her mother, 'The Bolter.'
 The Pursuit of Love, 1945, and elsewhere, Nancy Mitford.

Logan, Julie. *Farewell Miss Julie Logan,* J. M. Barrie, 1932.

Logan, Philip. *The First Mrs Fraser* (play), St John Ervine, 1929.

Logan, 'Piggy,' owner of puppet circus. *You Can't Go Home Again,* T. Wolfe, 1947.

Loggerheads, Mrs Louise, landlady, the Dragon. *Clayhanger,* Arnold Bennett, 1910.

Logic, Bob, a merry prankster. *Life in London* (or *Tom and Jerry*), Pierce Egan, 1821.

Loker, Tom, friend of Haley. *Uncle Tom's Cabin.* Harriet B. Stowe, 1851.

Lolita, a nymphet. *See* Haze *and* Humbert. *Lolita,* Vladimir Nabokov, 1955.

Loll, Chowder, m. Julia Jowler. *Adventures of Major Gahagan,* W. M. Thackeray, 1838–9.

Loll, Jewab, Indian servant of Joseph Sedley. *Vanity Fair,* W. M. Thackeray, 1847–8.

Loll Mahommed, General of cavalry. *Adventures of Major Gahagan,* W. M. Thackeray, 1838–9.

Lollipop, Lord Claud, younger son of the Marquis of Sillabub. *The Book of Snobs,* Thackeray, 1846–7.

Lollo, conjurer's assistant. *Romola,* George Eliot, 1862.

Loman, 'bad boy' of the school. *The Fifth Form at St Dominic's,* T. Baines Reed, 1887.

Loman, James, R.A. 'The Puzzler' (s.s.), *Actions and Reactions,* R. Kipling, 1909.

Loman, Willie. *Death of a Salesman,* A. Miller, 1949.

Lomas, Superintendent. *Mr Fortune Finds a Pig,* H. C. Bailey, 1943.

Lomas, Willy, mate of Vic Brown, *A Kind of Loving,* Stan Barstow, 1960.

Lomax, restaurant keeper.
  Dora, his daughter.
   Isabella, his sister, m. Tom Ancrum.
 The History of David Grieve. Mrs Humphry Ward, 1892.

Lomax, Charles. *Major Barbara* (play), G. B. Shaw, 1905.

Lombard, Lady (Sarah), *nouveau riche. Lewis Arundel,* F. E. Smedley, 1852.

Lomond, Dr, divisional surgeon. *The Ringer* (play), E. Wallace, 1926.

Lone Hand Kid, train bandit. 'The Gallowsmith' (s.s.), *From Place to Place,* Irvin S. Cobb, 1920.

Lone Sahib. 'The Sending of Dana Da' (s.s.), *Soldiers Three,* R. Kipling, 1888.

Loner, Buck, uncle of Myra/Myron. *Myra Breckinridge,* Gore Vidal, 1968.

Long, Mrs. *Pride and Prejudice,* Jane Austen, 1813.

Long, Rev. Mr, rector and tutor. *Lost Sir Massingberd,* James Payn, 1864.

Long, Captain Adrian, friend of Colonel Aubrac. *The Other Side,* Storm Jameson, 1946.

Long Jack, one of the crew of the *We're Here. Captains Courageous,* R. Kipling, 1897.

Longaville, lord attendant on Ferdinand. *Love's Labour's Lost* (play), W. Shakespeare.

Longer, Esdras B. 'The Lang Men o' Larut' (s.s.), *Life's Handicap,* R. Kipling, 1891.

Longestaffe, Lady Pomona, widow.
Her children:
Adolphus ('Dolly').
Sophia, m. George Whitstable.
Georgiana, m. Rev. Mr. Batherbolt, curate.
The Way We Live Now, A. Trollope, 1875.

Longman, bailiff. *Pamela,* S. Richardson, 1740.

Longridge, Dean of the college. *The Babe, B.A.,* E. F. Benson, 1897.

Longstaff, Elsie, member of the Dinky Doos concert party, later Good Companions, m. Herbert Dulver.
Effie, her sister.
The Good Companions, J. B. Priestley, 1939.

Longstaffe, bank manager, friend of the Butts. 'Lucky Boy' (s.s.), *Louise,* Viola Meynell, 1954.

Longueville, Lady. *The Last of the Barons,* Lord Lytton, 1843.

Longueville, Thomas de, 'The Red Rover.' *The Fair Maid of Perth,* W. Scott, 1828.

Longways, Solomon, an old man employed by Michael Henchard. *The Mayor of Casterbridge,* T. Hardy, 1886.

Longworth, Algy. *Bulldog Drummond,* 'Sapper' (H. C. McNeile), 1920.

Lonigan, William ('Studs'), young Irish-American native of Chicago.
His mother.
Frances, his sister.
Catherine Banahan, his mistress.
Studs Lonigan, a trilogy, James T. Farrell, 1935.

Lonnergan, Lovetin, suitor of Miss Betsy Shannon. *Mr Facey Romford's Hounds,* R. S. Surtees, 1865.

Looe, Honoria.
Her father.
The Great Adventure (play), Arnold Bennett, 1913.

Loomis, Charlie. *The One Hundred Dollar Bill* (s.s.), Booth Tarkington, 1923.

Lopez. *The Duenna* (play), R. B. Sheridan, 1775.

Lopez. *The Power and the Glory,* Graham Greene, 1940.

Lopez, Andres. *For Whom the Bell Tolls,* E. Hemingway, 1940.

Loraine, distant cousin of the Rakonitzes. *A Deputy was King,* G. B. Stern, 1926.

Lord, Cuthbert.
His wife.
Beatrice, their daughter, m. Vincent FitzClare.
C., M. Baring, 1924.

Lorenzo. *The Merchant of Venice* (play), W. Shakespeare.

Lorenzo. *The Spanish Tragedy* (play), T. Kyd, 1594.

Lorenzo, Sir Tomaso, court painter, Crim Tartary. *The Rose and the Ring,* W. M. Thackeray, 1855.

L'Orge, Chevalier de. 'The Amours of Mr Deuceace,' *Yellowplush Papers,* W. M. Thackeray, 1852.

Lorimer, schoolmaster. *Summer Half,* Angela Thirkell, 1934.

Lorimer, Rose, senior lecturer in medieval history. *Anglo-Saxon Attitudes,* Angus Wilson, 1956.

Loring, Jim, Earl of Chepstow, later Lord Loring, m. Violet Hunter-Oakleigh.
Sandy, their son.

The Marquess of Loring, his father.
His mother.
Amy, his sister.
Sonia, S. McKenna, 1917.

Loring, Sir Nigel.
Mary, his wife.
Maude, his daughter.
The White Company, 1890, and *Sir Nigel,* 1906, A. Conan Doyle.

Lorison. 'Blind Man's Holiday' (s.s.), *Whirligigs,* O. Henry, 1910.

Lorraine, Mrs Felix. *Vivian Grey,* B. Disraeli, 1826–7.

Lorrequer, Harry, central character and narrator, m. Lady Jane Callonby.
Sir Guy, his uncle.
Guy, his son.
Harry Lorrequer, C. Lever, 1839.

Lorriedaile, Lady Constantia, sister of Lord Dorincourt, great-aunt of Lord Fauntleroy.
Sir Henry, her husband.
Little Lord Fauntleroy, Frances H. Burnett, 1886.

Lorry, Jarvis, confidential clerk, Tellson's Bank. *A Tale of Two Cities,* C. Dickens, 1859.

Lortat, Pierre.
Syringa, his wife.
Mosaic, G. B. Stern, 1930.

Lorton, Lord Augustus, brother of the Duke of Berwick. *Lady Windermere's Fan* (play), O. Wilde, 1892.

Lory, Tom Fashion's servant. *A Trip to Scarborough* (play), R. B. Sheridan, 1777.

Losberne, surgeon. *Oliver Twist,* C. Dickens, 1838.

Lossie, Marquis of (Malcolm) (wrongly known as Malcolm MacPhail), central character, m. Lady Clementina Thornicroft. *The Marquis of Lossie,* G. MacDonald, 1877.

Losson, Private. 'In the Matter of a Private' (s.s.), *Soldiers Three,* R. Kipling, 1888.

Lot, King of Orkney.
Bellicent, his wife.
Gawain, Modred and **Garth,** their sons.
'The Coming of Arthur' (poem), *Idylls of the King,* Lord Tennyson, 1859.

Lothair, Lord, central character, m. Lady Corisande. *Lothair,* B. Disraeli, 1870.

Lotten-Kunitz, Princess Priscilla of, m. her cousin, a prince.
Her father.
Princess Priscilla's Fortnight, Countess von Arnim, 1905.

Lottingar, 'Captain' Cuthbert, adventurer.
Lottie, his daughter.
Pip, Ian Hay, 1907.

Lotus, Father, conjurer. *The Tragedy of the Till* (s.s.), D. Jerrold.

Loudon, London factor of Quentin Kennedy's estate. *Huntingtower,* J. Buchan, 1922.

Louis, the Dauphin (hist.). *King John* (play), W. Shakespeare.

Louis, sailor on *Ghost.* *The Sea Wolf,* Jack London, 1904.

Louis IV, King of France (hist.).
Lothaire and **Carloman,** his sons.
The Little Duke, Charlotte M. Yonge, 1854.

Louis XI, King of France (hist.). *Henry the Sixth* (play), W. Shakespeare.

Louis XIII, King of France (hist.). *Richelieu* (play), Lord Lytton, 1839.

Louise, in love with Bartle Connor. *Louise,* Viola Meynell, 1954.

Louka, a servant. *Arms and the Man* (play), G. B. Shaw, 1894.

Lousada, Maria, m. Rudolph Whitelaw. *Roots,* Naomi Jacob, 1931.

Love, Rev. Paul.
Polly, his sister.
The Christian, Hall Caine, 1897.

Loveday, Mrs, mistress of Harold Halstead. *The Prodigal Heart,* Susan Ertz, 1950.

Loveday, Deborah, maidservant, central character, m. Jess Mortimer, farmer's son.
Their sons:
Benjamin, m. Ada.
David, killed 1914–18 war.
The Fallow Land, H. E. Bates, 1932.

Loveday, John, central character.
Robert, his brother, m. Anne Garland.
His father, a miller, m. (2) Martha Garland.
The Trumpet Major, T. Hardy, 1880.

Lovegood, manager to Sir J. Chettam. *Middlemarch,* George Eliot, 1871–2.

Lovel, Mr, 'a youth of genteel appearance,' actually Lord William Geraldin; m. Isabella Wardour.

See also GLENALLAN. *The Antiquary*, W. Scott, 1816.

Lovel, Adolphus Frederick (Fred).
 Cecilia, his 1st wife, *née* Baker.
  Frederick Popham, their son.
  Cissy, their daughter.
 Elizabeth, his 2nd wife, *née* Prior (Bessie Bellenden, actress).
 Emma, his mother, m. (2) Rev. Mr Bonnington.
Lovel the Widower, 1860, and elsewhere, W. M. Thackeray.

Lovelace, Major, house captain of Fernhurst.
 His brother.
The Loom of Youth, A. Waugh, 1917.

Lovelace, Leslie, out-of-work actor playing at being Matthew Ligne's manservant. *The Loving Eye*, William Sansom, 1956.

Lovelace, Robert, in love with Clarissa Harlowe. *Clarissa Harlowe*, S. Richardson, 1748.

Loveless.
 Amanda, his wife.
A Trip to Scarborough (play), R. B. Sheridan, 1777.

Lovell, Chips, nephew of Lord Sleaford, m. Priscilla Tolland. *A Question of Upbringing*, 1951, and others in *The Music of Time* series, Anthony Powell.

Lovell, Margaret, widow, m. Sir William Blancove. *Rhoda Fleming*, G. Meredith, 1865.

Lovell, Sinfi, gipsy girl.
 Panuel, her father.
Aylwin, T. Watts-Dunton, 1899.

Lovell, Sir Thomas. *Henry the Eighth* (play), W. Shakespeare.

Lovely, Anne. *A Bold Stroke for a Wife* (play), Mrs Susanna Centlivre, 1718.

Lovewell, m. Fanny Sterling. *The Clandestine Marriage* (play), G. Colman the Elder, 1766.

Lovey Mary. *Mrs Wiggs of the Cabbage Patch*, 1901, and elsewhere, Alice H. Rice.

Lovick, Mrs, guardian of Clarissa Harlowe in captivity. *Clarissa Harlowe*, S. Richardson, 1748.

Loviebond, Dr. *Portrait of a Playboy*, W. Deeping, 1947.

Low, Mr, barrister.
 His wife.
Phineas Finn, 1869, and elsewhere, A. Trollope.

Lowborough, Lord, m. Annabella Wilmot. *The Tenant of Wildfell Hall*, Anne Brontë, 1848.

Lowder, Mrs, aunt of Kate Croy. *The Wings of the Dove*, Henry James, 1902.

Lowe, Moses, banker and unscrupulous money-lender.
 Solomon, his son and partner.
  His wife.
 Emma } His pretty daughters.
 Minna }
The Fitz-Boodle Papers, W. M. Thackeray, 1852.

Lowenstein, Marie (Princess Popoffski), fraudulent medium. *Queen Lucia*, E. F. Benson, 1920.

Lowestoffe, Reginald, young Templar. *The Fortunes of Nigel*, W. Scott, 1822.

Lowme, elderly aristocrat.
 His wife.
 Robert, their son.
 Their daughters.
'Janet's Repentance,' *Scenes of Clerical Life*, George Eliot, 1857.

Lowndes, of the Indian Civil Service, 'At the End of the Passage' (s.s.). *Life's Handicap*, R. Kipling, 1891.

Lownie, Janet, *née* Ogilvy.
 Margaret, her daughter, m. Gavin Birse.
A Window in Thrums, J. M. Barrie, 1889.

Lowrie, Bartram, father of Linda Condon (her mother reassumed her maiden name after his desertion).
 Amelia and **Eloise,** his sisters.
Linda Condon, J. Hergesheimer, 1918.

Lowther, Bryn, dead fiancée of Robin Le Faber. *The Five Sons of Le Faber*, E. Raymond, 1945.

Lowther, Gordon, music teacher. *The Prime of Miss Jean Brodie*, Muriel Spark, 1961.

Lowton, Jack, law student. *Pendennis*, W. M. Thackeray, 1848–50.

Loyalty, Ralph.
 Joan, his wife.
'When the Nightingale Sang in Berkeley Square' (s.s.), *These Charming People*, M. Arlen, 1920.

Luard, editor of the *Post Meridian*. *Landmarks*, E. V. Lucas, 1914.

Luard, Monsignor, French priest. *The Good Ship 'Mohock,'* W. Clark Russell, 1894.

Luba, Russian *émigrée*. *The Thinking Reed*, Rebecca West, 1936.

Lubbock, Sir James, Crown witness at trial of Harriet Vane. *Strong Poison*, Dorothy L. Sayers, 1930.

Luca, Fra (Bernadino di Bardi), Dominican monk, brother of Romola. *Romola*, George Eliot, 1863.

Lucard, Madame, *estaminet* keeper. *The Pied Piper*, N. Shute, 1942.

Lucas, Mrs Emmeline (Lucia).
Philip (Peppino), her husband.
Queen Lucia, E. F. Benson, 1920.

Lucas, George.
Martha, his wife.
Inmates of home for the aged.
The Poorhouse Fair, John Updike, 1959.

Lucas, Jean, m. Bruce Wetheral. *Campbell's Kingdom*, Hammond Innes, 1952.

Lucas, Solomon, fancy-dress dealer. *Pickwick Papers*, C. Dickens, 1837.

Lucas, Sir William.
His wife.
Their daughters:
Charlotte, m. Rev. William Collins.
Marie.
Pride and Prejudice, Jane Austen, 1813.

Lucas-Dockery, Sir Wilfred, Governor of Egdon Heath prison. *Decline and Fall*, E. Waugh, 1928.

Luce, solicitor, employed by the Newcomes. *The Newcomes*, W. M. Thackeray, 1853–5.

Luce, Rev. Mr, Vicar of Vinehall. *The End of the House of Alard*, Sheila Kaye-Smith, 1923.

Lucentio, Vincentio's son. *The Taming of the Shrew* (play), W. Shakespeare.

Lucero, horse tamer. *The Purple Land*, W. H. Hudson, 1885.

Lucero, Father, miser, unfrocked priest. *Death Comes for the Archbishop*, Willa Cather, 1927.

Lucetta, servant to Julia. *Two Gentlemen of Verona* (play), W. Shakespeare.

Lucia, 'street-piano man.' *Winterset* (play), Maxwell Anderson, 1935.

Luciana, sister of Adriana. *A Comedy of Errors* (play), W. Shakespeare.

Lucifer. *Doctor Faustus* (play), C. Marlowe, 1604.

Lucio, a fantastick. *Measure for Measure* (play), W. Shakespeare.

Lucius, Titus Andronicus' son.
Young Lucius, his son.
Titus Andronicus (play), W. Shakespeare.

Lucius, a lord. *Timon of Athens* (play), W. Shakespeare.

Lucius Septimius. *Caesar and Cleopatra* (play), G. B. Shaw, 1900.

Luck, Anne. *Iron and Smoke*, Sheila Kaye-Smith, 1928.

Lucky. *Waiting for Godot*, S. Beckett, 1952.

Lucrezia Degl' Onesti, cousin of Giovanni. *Paolo and Francesca* (play), S. Phillips, 1900.

Lucullus, a lord. *Timon of Athens* (play), W. Shakespeare.

Lucy. *Colin and Lucy* (poem), T. Tickell, 1720.

Lucy, Lydia Languish's maid. *The Rivals* (play), R. B. Sheridan, 1775.

Lucy, maid to Beatrix Esmond, fiancée of John Lockwood. *Henry Esmond*, W. M. Thackeray, 1852.

Ludgrove, Jimmy and **Arthur.** *The Fourth Wall* (play), A. A. Milne, 1928.

Ludovico, servant and friend of Emily St Aubert. *The Mysteries of Udolpho*, Mrs Radcliffe, 1794.

Ludwig of Hombourg, Sir, old Crusader. *A Legend of the Rhine*, W. M. Thackeray, 1845.

Lueli, Mr Fortune's only convert.
His mother.
Mr Fortune's Maggot, Sylvia Townsend Warner, 1927.

Luff, draper, Grimsworth. *Brother Jacob*, George Eliot, 1864.

Lufford, Charles, friend of Joe Lampton. *Room at the Top*, J. Braine, 1957.

Lufton, Lady, patroness of Mark Robarts.
Lord Lufton (Ludovic), her son, m. Lucy Robarts.
Justina, her daughter, Lady Meredith.
Framley Parsonage, A. Trollope, 1861.

Lufton, Lady.
Her children:
Lord Lufton, m. Grace Grantly.
Maria, m. Oliver Marling.
Justina, m. Eric Swan.
The *Barsetshire* series, Angela Thirkell, 1933 onwards.

Lugg, Magersfontein, ex-criminal and manservant of Albert Campion. Margery Allingham's series of 'Albert Campion' detective stories.

Lui Hei Ch'I. *Ming Yellow,* J. P. Marquand, 1935.

Luigi, officer of Paolo's company. *Paolo and Francesca* (play), S. Phillips, 1900.

Luisa. *See Naples and Die* (play), Elmer Rice, 1932.

Luiz, rightful king of Barataria, attendant on the Duke of Plaza Toro; m. Casilda. *The Gondoliers* (comic opera), Gilbert & Sullivan, 1889.

Lujon, Manuel, rich Mexican ranch-owner. *Death Comes for the Archbishop,* Willa Cather, 1927.

Luke, Superintendent Charles, C.I.D. *The China Governess,* 1963 and others, Margery Allingham.

Luke, Walter. *The Masters,* 1951, part of the *Strangers and Brothers* sequence, C. P. Snow.

Luker, Septimus, dealer in antiques. *The Moonstone,* W. Collins, 1868.

Lull, Ramon, Captain of the *Ariostatica. Anthony Adverse,* Hervey Allen, 1934.

Lumb, Arnold, head of textile firm.
  Reetha, his daughter.
  William Henry, his father.
  His mother.
A Modern Tragedy, Phyllis Bentley, 1934.

Lumley, Captain, R.N., friend of Alfred Campbell. *Settlers in Canada,* Captain Marryat, 1844.

Lumley, Dr. *Nicholas Nickleby,* C. Dickens, 1839.

Lumley, Andrew, art collector, friend of Charles Pitt-Heron. *The Power House,* J. Buchan, 1916.

Lumley, Charles, varsity man who breaks with his middle-class upbringing. *Hurry on Down,* John Wain, 1953.

Lumpkin, Tony. *She Stoops to Conquer* (play), Oliver Goldsmith, 1773.

Luna, Mrs Adeline, *née* Chancellor. *The Bostonians,* H. James, 1886.

Lundie, Lord, law lord. 'The Puzzler' (s.s.), *Actions and Reactions,* 1909, and elsewhere, R. Kipling.

Lundin, Sir Louis, town clerk of Perth. *The Fair Maid of Perth,* W. Scott, 1828.

Lundin, Dr Luke, chamberlain to the Lady of Lochleven. *The Abbot,* W. Scott, 1820.

Lung, Wang, farmer, central character.
  O-Lan, his wife.
  Their children:
    Nung-En, Nung-Wen, and three others.
  Lotus, Lung's concubine.
The Good Earth, Pearl Buck, 1931.

Lunken, Bertha, German art student, Tarr's fiancée. *Tarr,* Wyndham Lewis, 1918.

Lunsby, Bob, butcher, Raveloe. *Silas Marner,* George Eliot, 1861.

Lunt, Henry, fanatical chartist. *The Fortress,* Hugh Walpole, 1932.

Lupin, Mrs, landlady of the Blue Dragon, m. Mark Tapley. *Martin Chuzzlewit,* C. Dickens, 1844.

Lurell, Miss. 'Mr and Mrs Monroe' (s.s.), *The Owl in the Attic,* J. Thurber, 1931.

Lurgan Sahib, jewel dealer. *Kim,* R. Kipling, 1901.

Lurulu, a troll. *The King of Elfland's Daughter,* Lord Dunsany, 1924.

Luscombe, solicitor. *No Name,* W. Collins, 1862.

Lush, Mr. *Lise Lillywhite,* Margery Sharp, 1951.

Lush, Thomas Cranmer, companion and general factotum to Grandcourt. *Daniel Deronda,* George Eliot, 1876.

Luster, Negro servant of the Compsons. *The Sound and the Fury,* W. Faulkner, 1931.

Luthy, Laura.
  Her father and mother.
Tracy's Tiger, W. Saroyan, 1951.

Luttrell, Francis, of *The Liberal,* central character, in love with Katherine Halstead.
  His father.
The Street of Adventure, P. Gibbs, 1909.

Lutyens, Captain, captain of the polo team. 'The Maltese Cat' (s.s.), *The Day's Work,* R. Kipling, 1898.

Lux, Catherine, mistress at Leys College. *Miss Pym Disposes,* Josephine Tey, 1946.

Luxellian, Lord (Spenser Hugo), m. (2) Elfride Swancourt.
  His two daughters by 1st wife.

A Pair of Blue Eyes, T. Hardy, 1873.

Luxmore, Earl of (Family name Ravenel).

William, Viscount Ravenel, his son, m. Maud Halifax.

Lady Caroline, his daughter, m. Richard Brithwood.

John Halifax, Gentleman, Mrs Craik, 1856.

Luxstein, Count.

Ilga, his wife, m. (2) Morrice Buckler.

The Courtship of Morrice Buckler, A. E. W. Mason, 1896.

Luzau-Luzau Rischenheim, Count of. *Rupert of Hentzau*, A. Hope, 1898.

Lyall, Miss, Lady Ambermere's companion. *Queen Lucia*, E. F. Benson, 1920.

Lychnis, in charge of the earthlings when they arrive in Utopia. *Men Like Gods*, H. G. Wells, 1923.

Lyddon, Miss Marietta.

Her brothers:

Lord Lyddon.

Fanny, his wife.

Luke.

Mark.

Robert, her nephew, son of Mark.

Sybil, his wife.

The Prodigal Heart, Susan Ertz, 1950.

Lyddy, Old, servant of Rufus Lyon. *Felix Holt*, George Eliot, 1866.

Lydgate, Miss, tutor, Shrewsbury College. *Gaudy Night*, Dorothy L. Sayers, 1935.

Lydgate, Sir Godwin.

Captain Lydgate, his son. *See also* MRS MENGAN.

Tertius, doctor, his nephew, m. Rosamund Vincy.

Middlemarch, Geo. Eliot, 1871–2.

Lydia, maid to Kitty Bellairs. *The Bath Comedy*, 1899, and *Incomparable Bellairs*, 1904, A. & E. Castle.

Lydiatt, Claerwn (Clare), central character, m. (1) Ralph Hingston, (2) Dudley Wilburn.

Ambrose, her father.

Sylvia, her mother, *née* Weir.

Portrait of Clare, F. Brett Young, 1927.

Lydon, gladiator, conqueror of Tetraides, slain by Eumolphus. *The Last Days of Pompeii*, Lord Lytton, 1834.

Lygones, father of Spaconia. *A King and No King* (play), Beaumont & Fletcher, 1611.

Lyle, Annot, daughter of Sir Duncan Campbell. *The Legend of Montrose*, W. Scott, 1819.

Lyle, Sir Chetwynd.

His wife.

Ziska, Marie Corelli, 1897.

Lymes, Geoffrey.

Anne, his wife.

Canaries Sometimes Sing (play), F. Lonsdale, 1929.

Lyndall, cousin of Em. *The Story of an African Farm*, Olive Schreiner, 1883.

Lyndesay. *See* DE LYNDESAY.

Lyndon, Barry, central character and narrator, also Redmond Barry and Chevalier de Barry, m. Lady Lyndon, countess in her own right, widow of Sir C. Barry.

Bryan, Viscount Castle Lyndon, their son.

Barry Lyndon, W. M. Thackeray, 1844.

Lyndwood, Mabel.

Tristram, her grandfather.

Windsor Castle, W. H. Ainsworth, 1843.

Lyne, Mrs Angela.

Cedric, her 1st husband.

She m. (2) Basil Seal.

Put Out More Flags, E. Waugh, 1942.

Lynn, Samuel, Quaker, widower, manager of glove factory.

Anna, his daughter.

Mrs Halliburton's Troubles, Mrs Henry Wood, 1862.

Lynton, Mary, ex-governess, m. Tom Trellick. *The Second Mrs Conford*, Beatrice K. Seymour, 1951.

Lynwood, John, midshipman in the Royal Navy, central character. *The Gunroom*, Charles Morgan, 1919.

Lyon, Esther, actually Esther Bycliffe, heiress, m. Felix Holt.

Rev. Rufus, her supposed father, m. Annette Ledru, her mother.

Felix Holt, George Eliot, 1866.

Lyons, Laura. *The Hound of the Baskervilles*, A. Conan Doyle, 1902.

Lyons, Rita, schoolteacher, m. Jerry Lamb. 'Feed My Lambs' (s.s.),

The Talking Trees, Sean O'Faolain, 1971.

Lypiatt, Casimir, artist. *Antic Hay*, A. Huxley, 1923.

Lysander, in love with Hermia. *A Midsummer Night's Dream* (play), W. Shakespeare.

Lysimachus, governor of Mitylene. *Pericles* (play), W. Shakespeare.

Lysimachus, designer. *Count Robert of Paris*, W. Scott, 1832.

Lysippus, the king's brother. *The Maid's Tragedy* (play), Beaumont & Fletcher, 1611.

Lysirra, Sultan's daughter, loved by Martin of Elchester. *Unending Crusade*, R. E. Sherwood, 1932.

M

M., James Bond's boss in the Secret Service. *Goldfinger,* 1959, and others, Ian Fleming.

M., Lord, uncle of Lovelace. *Clarissa Harlowe,* S. Richardson, 1748.

Maartens, Professor and Mrs. *C.,* M. Baring, 1924.

Maas, Hendryk, Dutch churchmason, Mixton, to whom Robyn Skyrme is apprenticed. *The Story of Ragged Robyn,* O. Onions, 1945.

Mabel, a maid. *Separate Tables* (play), T. Rattigan, 1955.

Maberg, Graf von (Ulrich).
His wife.
Their children:
Fritz, in love with Freya Roth.
Sophia, m. Olaf von Rohn.
The Mortal Storm, Phyllis Bottome, 1937.

Maberley, Jim. *In this our Life,* Ellen Glasgow, 1942.

Mablethorpe, Julius, novelist, who adopts Philip Meldrum.
Sylvia ('Dumps'), his daughter.
A Knight on Wheels, Ian Hay, 1916.

Mabsley, Mrs. *Monsieur Beaucaire,* Booth Tarkington, 1902.

MacAdam, Lady, high-spirited old woman. *Annals of the Parish,* John Galt, 1821.

MacAindra, Stacey, *née* Cameron, a Canadian housewife.
Mac, her husband, a salesman.
Their children:
Kate.
Ian.
Duncan.
Jen.
The Fire-Dwellers, Margaret Laurence, 1969.

McAlister, Colonel, widower.
Mary, his daughter.
The Fitz-Boodle Papers, W. M. Thackeray, 1852.

Macallan, Mr. *Brat Farrar,* Josephine Tey, 1949.

Macallister, Archie ('Bony'), friend of Joseph Vance, m. Jeannie McGaskin. *Joseph Vance,* W. de Morgan, 1906.

McAllister, Sandy, 'Laird of Cockpen,' art student, friend of Bagot and Wynne, m. Mrs Bagot. *Trilby,* George du Maurier, 1894.

McAlpin, Sergeant.
Janet, his sister.
The Legend of Montrose, W. Scott, 1819.

MacAlpine, Jeanie, landlady of inn at Aberfoil. *Rob Roy,* W. Scott, 1818.

McAndrew, narrator.
Elsie, his dead wife, *née* Campbell.
'McAndrew's Hymn' (poem), *The Seven Seas,* 1896, and elsewhere, R. Kipling.

McAndrew, Alexander. *Dr Nikola,* G. Boothby, 1896.

Macane, Katey, Irish cook, adopts Marian. *Marian,* Mrs S. C. Hall, 1840.

Macapa, Maria, Mexican housecleaner, m. Zerkow. *McTeague,* F. Norris, 1899.

McArthur, Willie, central character, m. Mavis, his cousin.
Alister, his father.
Dr John, 'black sheep,' his uncle.
Born to be a Sailor, G. Stables.

Macarty, Mrs Wellesley, widow, *née* Juliana Crabb, m. (2) James Gann.
Isabella.
Rosalind. Her twin daughters.
A Shabby Genteel Story, W. M. Thackeray, 1840.

Macascree, Nizza, beggar's daughter. *Old St Paul's,* W. H. Ainsworth, 1841.

McAuden, Mrs, friend of Winifred Dartie. The *Forsyte* series, J. Galsworthy, 1906–33.

McAulay, Angus, Laird of Darnlin-Varach.
Allan, his brother.
The Legend of Montrose, W. Scott, 1819.

Macaulay, Herbert (alias George Foley), attorney, murderer. *The Thin Man,* D. Hammett, 1934.

Macauley, Mrs, widow.
Her children:
Marcus, eng. to Mary Arena.

Homer, telegraph boy.
Ulysses.
Bess, m. Tobey George.
The Human Comedy, W. Saroyan, 1943.

MacAusland, Libby, graduate of Vassar. *The Group*, Mary McCarthy, 1963.

Macavity ('Hidden Paw'). *Old Possum's Book of Practical Cats*, T. S. Eliot, 1939.

Macbeth, general of the King's army.
His wife.
Macbeth (play), W. Shakespeare.

MacBeth, Hugh, boy of fourteen, central character.
His mother.
John, his father, fisherman.
Alan, his brother, shepherd and fisherman.
Kirsty, his sister, dairymaid.
Grace, his sister.
Morning Tide, Neil M. Gunn, 1931.

MacBride, Captain. 'The Knight and the Lady' (poem), *The Ingoldsby Legends*, R. H. Barham, 1837.

Macbride, Rev. Mr.
His wife.
The Good Ship 'Mohock,' W. Clark Russell, 1894.

Macbride, Rev. Alexander. *The Virginian*, O. Wister, 1902.

McBryde, District Superintendent of Police. *A Passage to India*, E. M. Forster, 1924.

McCall, Larry. 'The Angel and the Sweep' (s.s.), *Adam and Eve and Pinch Me*, A. E. Coppard, 1921.

MacCandlish, Mrs, widowed landlady of the Gordon Arms. *Guy Mannering*, W. Scott, 1815.

Candlish, Rev. Norman.
Agnes, his wife.
Pink Sugar, O. Douglas, 1924.

McCarthy, Charles.
James, his son.
'The Boscombe Valley Mystery,' *The Adventures of Sherlock Holmes*, A. Conan Doyle, 1892.

McCarthy, Great-Uncle Denis, ghost haunting Yeates's house. *Some Experiences of an Irish R.M.*, Œ. Somerville & Martin Ross, 1899.

McCaskie, Ronald, cashier, posing as John Brodie, m. (as Brodie) Isobel Easdaile.
Ranald, their son.
God's Prisoner, J. Oxenham, 1898.

McClellan.
Florence, his sister.
James, his son, m. Pauline.
Two children.
Campbell's Kingdom, Hammond Innes, 1952.

M'Clour, Janet, housekeeper to Murdoch Soulis; witch wife. 'Thrawn Janet' (s.s.), *The Merry Men*, R. L. Stevenson, 1887.

McClure, Andrew, sensitive young member of R.A.F. *Chips With Everything* (play), Arnold Wesker, 1962.

McClure, Mary Ellen, a neurotic woman.
Matt, her husband, cinema manager.
A Story That Ends With A Scream, James Leo Herlihy, 1968.

M'Collop, Sandy, fellow student of Newcome at Gandish's Drawing Academy. *The Newcomes*, W. M. Thackeray, 1853–5.

McComas, Finch, solicitor. *You Never Can Tell* (play), G. B. Shaw, 1895.

Maccombich, Even Dhu, foster-brother of Fergus MacIvor. *Waverley*, W. Scott, 1814.

McCombich, Robin 'Oig,' drover.
Lachlan, his father.
Janet, his aunt.
The Two Drovers, W. Scott, 1827.

Macconochie, 'old, ill-spoken, drunken dog,' serving man. *The Master of Ballantrae*, R. L. Stevenson, 1889.

McCosh, Mrs Maggie, servant of the Jardines.
Andrew, her dead husband.
Penny Plain, O. Douglas, 1920.

M'Crae, Colin, m. Christina McNab. *The Fortunes of Christina McNab*, S. Macnaughtan, 1901.

McCrathie, estate factor.
His wife.
The Marquis of Lossie, G. MacDonald, 1877.

M'Craw, Dr, Scotch minister.
Josey, his 3rd wife, *née* Mackenzie.
The Newcomes. W. M. Thackeray, 1853–5.

McCreary, Fainy, labour organizer. *U.S.A.* trilogy, John dos Passos, 1930–6.

McCrimmon, Rev. Mr, Free Church minister.
His wife.
Mr Bolfry (play), James Bridie, 1943.

MacCrotchet (abbreviated to Crotchet).
MacCrotchet jnr, his son, financier and company promoter.
Lemma, his daughter.
Crotchet Castle, T. L. Peacock, 1831.

McCunn, Dickson, retired grocer.
Robina, his wife, *née* Dickson.
Huntingtower, J. Buchan, 1922.

McDermot, Dermot, central character, last surviving child of Anne and Michael, m. Connaught d'Arcy. *Hangman's House,* Donn Byrne, 1926.

Macdermott, Levin, barrister friend of Robert Blair. *The Franchise Affair,* Josephine Tey, 1948.

McDolan, Rev. Kenneth, Negro missioner. *Sanders of the River,* E. Wallace, 1911.

Macdonald, Marshal. 'Leipzig,' *Wessex Poems,* T. Hardy, 1898.

Macdonald, Sergeant Archie. 'A Straggler of '15' (s.s.), *Round the Red Lamp,* A. Conan Doyle, 1894.

Macdonald, Rev. John.
Anne, his wife.
Duncan, their dead son.
Penny Plain, O. Douglas, 1920.

Macdonnell, Alaster, 'young Colkitto.' *The Legend of Montrose,* W. Scott, 1819.

McDruggy, 'fresh from Canton.' *Sybil,* B. Disraeli, 1845.

Macduff, nobleman of Scotland. *Macbeth* (play), W. Shakespeare.

McEachern, Mr, farmer, Joe Christmas's foster father. *Light in August,* William Faulkner, 1932.

McEachern, Molly, m. Jimmy Pitt.
Her father, ex-New York police chief.
A Gentleman of Leisure, P. G. Wodehouse, 1910.

MacEagh, Ranald, Highland freebooter.
Kenneth, his grandson.
The Legend of Montrose, W. Scott, 1819.

M'Elvina, Captain.
Susan, his wife, *née* Hornblow.
The King's Own, Captain Marryat, 1830.

Macer, Major, friend of Captain Legg. *The Book of Snobs,* W. M. Thackeray, 1846–7.

MacEvoy, Janet, Highland landlady, later housekeeper. *The Highland Widow,* W. Scott, 1827.

Macey, parish clerk and tailor, Raveloe.
Solomon, his father, fiddler.
Silas Marner, George Eliot, 1861.

MacFadden, Adam, central character.
Malachy, his father.
Adam of Dublin, C. O'Riordan, 1920.

McFadden, Charles. *Counsellor-at-Law* (play), Elmer Rice, 1931.

MacFadden, Douglas, uncle and benefactor of Jean Paget. *A Town like Alice,* N. Shute, 1950.

McFarish, Willie.
Angus, his father. Fishers.
The Brothers, L. A. G. Strong, 1932.

Macfarlane, Dr, ship's surgeon. *In Greek Waters,* G. A. Henty, 1892.

McFarlane, Dr Hugh, m. Elizabeth Trant. *The Good Companions,* J. B. Priestley, 1929.

Macfarlane, John Hector. 'The Norwood Builder,' *The Return of Sherlock Holmes,* A. Conan Doyle, 1905.

Macfarlane, Kerry (later Sir Garrett) ('Kerry of the Horses'), narrator.
Sir Valentine, his uncle.
Cossimo, Bishop of Borneo, Sir Valentine's brother.
Destiny Bay, Donn Byrne, 1928.

Macfarlane, Wolfe ('Toddy'), celebrated London doctor. 'The Body Snatcher' (s.s.), *The Wrong Box,* R. L. Stevenson & L. Osbourne, 1889.

Macfie, Mr Sergeant, M.P. *Adam of Dublin,* C. O'Riordan, 1920.

MacFugger, Lady Gail Allouise Trudy, a rich woman.
Major Jeffrey MacFugger, her husband, a sporting Irishman.
The Onion Eaters, J. P. Donleavy, 1971.

McGarth, Jimmy. *On the Spot* (play), E. Wallace, 1930.

McGaskin, Mr ('Ferret').
Jeannie, his daughter, m. Archie Macallister.
Joseph Vance, W. de Morgan, 1906.

McGhee, Dawn, night club hostess.
Lily (Liliane), her kid sister, with

whom Matthew Ligne falls in love.
The Loving Eye, William Sansom, 1956.

MacGillie, Chattanach, 'high-mettled' Highland chief. *The Fair Maid of Perth,* W. Scott, 1828.

Macgillivray, of the C.I.D., friend of Leithen. *The Thirty-nine Steps,* 1915, and *The Power House,* 1916, J. Buchan.

McGillivray, Lily, Edinburgh good-time girl, pal of Bessie Hipkiss. *Jezebel's Dust,* Fred Urquhart, 1951.

Macginnis, Buck, professional kidnapper. *The Little Nugget,* P. G. Wodehouse, 1913.

McGoggin, Aurelian. 'The Conversion of Aurelian McGoggin' (s.s.), *Plain Tales from the Hills,* R. Kipling, 1888.

McGoun, Teresa, Babbitt's secretary. *Babbitt,* Sinclair Lewis, 1923.

McGovern, Dr. *Secrets* (play), R. Besier & May Edginton, 1922.

MacGown, Sir Alexander, eng. to Marjorie Ferrar. *The Silver Spoon,* J. Galsworthy, 1926.

M'Grath, Captain Aeneas. *The Brothers,* L. A. G. Strong, 1932.

Mcgrath, Duncan.
His father, a general.
The Young in Heart, I. A. R. Wylie, 1939.

MacGrawler, Peter, Editor of the *Asinaeum. Paul Clifford,* Lord Lytton, 1830.

Macgregor ('Wee Macgregor'), small Scots boy, central character in series of sketches, J. J. Bell.

Macgregor (alias James More). *Catriona,* R. L. Stevenson, 1893.

McGregor, Mr.
His wife.
The Tale of Peter Rabbit, 1902, and elsewhere, Beatrix Potter.

Macgregor, Mary, schoolgirl, member of 'the Brodie set'. *The Prime of Miss Jean Brodie,* Muriel Spark, 1961.

MacGregor, Robert or **Robin** (Rob Roy), central character.
Helen, his wife, *née* Campbell.
Robert, one of their sons.
Rob Roy, W. Scott, 1818.

McGregor, Stumpy, old man. *Time Will Knit,* Fred Urquhart, 1938.

MacGuffog, *pension*-keeper at Portanferry, later under-turnkey.
His wife.
Guy Mannering, W. Scott, 1815.

McGuffog, gamekeeper. *Huntingtower,* J. Buchan, 1922.

McGurk, Ross, head of the Gurk Institute.
Capitola, his wife.
Martin Arrowsmith, Sinclair Lewis, 1925.

Macharg, Alex, laird.
His wife.
The Haunted Ships (s.s.), A. Cunningham.

McHarg, Lloyd, author of best seller. *You Can't Go Home Again,* T. Wolfe, 1947.

MacHeath, central character, m. Polly Peachum. *The Beggar's Opera,* 1728, and *Polly,* 1729 (comic operas), J. Gay.

Machell, Len, second gardener under Kirkby.
Dolly, his wife.
The Things which Belong, Constance Holme, 1925.

Machin, Arthur, professional rugby player, central character. *This Sporting Life,* David Storey, 1960.

Machin, Edward Henry ('Denry'), central character.
His widowed mother.
The Card, 1911, and elsewhere, Arnold Bennett.

Machin, Mary, companion to Tiphany Lane. *The Face of Clay,* H. A. Vachell, 1906.

Machir Ben Azariah. *Unending Crusade,* R. E. Sherwood, 1932.

M'Intyre, overseer. *Robbery under Arms,* R. Boldrewood, 1888.

MacIvor, Inspector. *Doctor Angelus* (play), J. Bridie, 1947.

MacIvor, Fergus, Highland chieftain. *Waverley,* W. Scott, 1814.

Mackay, Miss, headmistress of school. *The Prime of Miss Jean Brodie,* Muriel Spark, 1961.

McKee, Mr and Mrs. *The Great Gatsby,* F. Scott Fitzgerald, 1925.

McKeever, Molly, fiancée of Kid Brady. 'Vanity and some Sables' (s.s.), *The Trimmed Lamp,* O. Henry, 1907.

Mackel, Ira. *Mourning becomes Electra* (play), E. O'Neill, 1931.

MacKellar, friend of Father Buonaventure. *Redgauntlet,* W. Scott, 1824.

Mackellar, Ephraim, servant and friend of the family, narrator. *The Master of Ballantrae,* R. L. Stevenson, 1889.

M'Kellop, butler to Lord Weir. *Weir of Hermiston,* R. L. Stevenson, 1896.

McKelvey, Charlie.
 Lucile, his wife.
 Babbitt, Sinclair Lewis, 1923.

McKenna, Jhansi, m. Corporal Slane.
 Bridget, her mother.
 'Old Pummaloe,' sergeant, her father.
 'A Daughter of the Regiment' (s.s.), *Plain Tales from the Hills,* 1888, and elsewhere, R. Kipling.

Mackenzie, Scotch detective. *Raffles,* E. W. Hornung, 1899–1901.

Mackenzie, Mrs ('The Campaigner'), widow, *née* Binnie.
 Her daughters:
 Rosey, m. Clive Newcome.
 Josey, m. Dr M'Craw.
 The Newcomes, W. M. Thackeray, 1853–5.

Mackenzie, Angusina, m. John Macrae.
 Alexander, her father.
 The Brothers, L. A. G. Strong, 1932.

Mackenzie, Colin, eng. to Margaret Heal. *The Fanatics* (play), M. Malleson, 1924.

Mackenzie, Flora ('Auntie Mack'), relative of the Thomsons. *The Ballad and the Source,* Rosamond Lehmann, 1944.

MacKenzie, Major-General G., born intriguer. *The General,* C. S. Forester, 1936.

Mackenzie, Dr Robert. *The Rosary,* Florence Barclay, 1909.

McKeown, Darby ('The Blast'), piper. *Tom Burke of Ours,* C. Lever, 1844.

Mackie, Corporal. 'Love o' Women' (s.s.), *Many Inventions,* R. Kipling, 1893.

Mackintosh, assistant administrator of South Sea island. 'Mackintosh' (s.s.), *The Trembling of a Leaf,* W. S. Maugham, 1921.

Mackintosh, seamen's leader. *Masterman Ready,* Capt. Marryat, 1841–2.

Mackintosh, friend of Dickson McCunn. *Huntingtower,* J. Buchan, 1922.

Mackintosh, Alaster, nephew of Belamy Mannering. *The Secret Vanguard,* M. Innes, 1940.

Mackintosh, James, editor. *Abraham Lincoln* (play), J. Drinkwater, 1918.

McInvert, Mr, bachelor in search of love in Italy. *They Winter Abroad,* T. H. White, 1932.

Macklin, gentleman ranker. 'The Janeites' (s.s.), *Debits and Credits,* R. Kipling, 1926.

Mackness, Ada, cashier in Melford Turner's grocery. *The Sleepless Moon,* H. E. Bates, 1956.

Mackridge, Mrs, pensioner of Lady Drew. *Tono Bungay,* H. G. Wells, 1909.

Mackworth. 'The Tie' (s.s.), *Limits and Renewals,* R. Kipling, 1932.

Mackworth, a bully. *St Winifred's,* F. W. Farrar, 1862.

Mackworth, Father John. *Ravenshoe,* H. Kingsley, 1861.

MacLain, King, wandering patriarch.
 Snowdie Hudson, his wife, albino.
 Eugene and **Randall,** their twin sons.
 The Golden Apples, Eudora Welty, 1949.

Maclaren, Miss, head housekeeper. *Imperial Palace,* Arnold Bennett, 1930.

McLean, field manager of lumber camp. *Freckles,* Gene S. Porter, 1904.

McLean, Ivie, m. Ailie Cray. *Sentimental Tommy,* J. M. Barrie, 1896.

Macleary, John, Irish-Australian sheep farmer. 'A propos des Bottes' (s.s.), *Fiery Particles,* C. E. Montague, 1923.

Macleary, 'Luckie,' mistress of inn at Tully-Veolan. *Waverley,* W. Scott, 1814.

McLeavy, a newly widowed man.
 Harold (Hal), his son, a crook.
 Loot (play), Joe Orton, 1966.

Macleod, Dugald. *The Brothers,* L. A. G. Strong, 1932.

M'Leod, L. Maxwell.
 His wife.
 Thea, their daughter.
 'The House Surgeon' (s.s.), *Actions and Reactions,* R. Kipling, 1909.

M'Lucre, Bailie Andrew.
 Gabriel, his son.
 The Provost, J. Galt, 1822.

Maclure, Bessie, old widow.
Ninian and **Johnnie,** her sons.
Peggy, her grand-daughter.
Old Mortality, W. Scott, 1816.

Maclure, Nonie, art student.
Peggy, her sister.
Non-Combatants and Others, Rose Macaulay, 1916.

MacLure, William, village doctor. *Beside the Bonnie Brier Bush,* I. Maclaren, 1894.

McMahon, Fay Jean (otherwise Phyllis Jean), nurse who has had seven husbands. *Loot* (play), Joe Orton, 1966.

Macmanus, Mrs Hoggarty's Irish agent. *The Great Hoggarty Diamond,* W. M. Thackeray, 1841.

McMillan, Rev. Duncan. *An American Tragedy,* T. Dreiser, 1925.

Macmoran.
Barbara, his grand-daughter.
The Haunted Ships (s.s.), A. Cunningham.

McMull, Hon. James.
Rhoda, his wife, *née* Swartz.
Macduff, their son.
Vanity Fair, W. M. Thackeray, 1847–8.

McMurdo, servant of Bartholomew Sholto. *The Sign of Four,* A. Conan Doyle, 1890.

MacMurdo, Captain, friend of Rawdon Crawley. *Vanity Fair,* W. M. Thackeray, 1847–8.

McMurdo, Constable Cyril, m. Nannie Bruce. *Cocktail Time,* P. G. Wodehouse, 1958.

Macmurrachu, Meehawl, farmer.
Caitlin, his daughter.
The Crock of Gold, J. Stephens, 1912.

M'Murrough, Nuala, m. Lacy Darragh. 'The Fox Hunter' (s.s.), *Countrymen All,* Katherine Tynan, 1915.

McMurrough, O'Reilly, Irish chieftain. *Hangman's House,* Donn Byrne, 1926.

McNab, Miss, missionary. *The Purple Plain,* H. E. Bates, 1947.

McNab, Christina, heiress, m. Colin M'Crae. *The Fortunes of Christina McNab,* S. Macnaughtan, 1901.

McNab, Sandy, chief clerk to Bonnyfeather. *Anthony Adverse,* Hervey Allen, 1934.

McNairn, Mrs.
Connie, her daughter.
The Jacaranda Tree, H. E. Bates, 1949.

MacNeil, Father Ludovick.
Anna, his sister and housekeeper, m. Duncan Corodale.
Dermosary, his uncle.
Children of the Tempest, N. Munro, 1903.

McNiel, milkman.
Nellie, his wife.
Manhattan Transfer, J. dos Passos, 1925.

McNott, Sergeant Robert.
His Indian wife.
Northwest Passage, Kenneth Roberts, 1938.

Macnulty, Julia, poverty-stricken hanger-on of Lady Eustace. *The Eustace Diamonds,* A. Trollope, 1873.

MacPhadraick, Miles, 'a cautious man.' *The Highland Widow,* W. Scott, 1827.

MacPhail. *See* MARQUIS OF LOSSIE.

Macphail, Dr Alec.
His wife.
'Miss Thompson' (s.s.), *The Trembling of a Leaf,* W. S. Maugham, 1921: also *Rain* (play).

MacPhail, Cressida Mary (Cressy), heroine, m. David Little.
Joe and **Rose,** her parents.
Harry and **Rachel Bretton,** her grandparents.
The Wedding Group, Elizabeth Taylor, 1968.

McPhee, ship's engineer.
Janet, his wife.
'Bread upon the Waters' (s.s.), *The Day's Work,* 1898, and elsewhere, R. Kipling.

Macpherson, agent at Rushwater, faithful devotee of Lady Emily Leslie. The *Barsetshire* series, Angela Thirkell, 1933 onwards.

Macpherson, Inspector. *The Five Red Herrings,* Dorothy L. Sayers, 1931.

Macpherson, Miss, secretary to Peter Jackson. *Peter Jackson, Cigar Merchant,* G. Frankau, 1919.

Macpherson, Cluny, chief of Clan Vourich (hist.). *Kidnapped,* R. L. Stevenson, 1886.

Mcphillip, Francis Joseph.
Jack, his father, bricklayer.

His mother.
Mary, his sister.
The Informer, L. O'Flaherty, 1929.

MacQuarry, Master Douglas, son of local sporting tenant of estate. *Highland River,* N. M. Gunn, 1937.

MacQuedy, economist, friend of MacCrotchet. *Crotchet Castle,* T. L. Peacock, 1831.

MacQuern, The, of Balliol. *Zuleika Dobson,* Max Beerbohm, 1911.

McQuern, Archie.
Susan, his wife, *née* Miniver.
Alison, their daughter.
Mrs Miniver, Jan Struther, 1939.

McQumpha, Hendry.
Jass, his wife, *née* Duthie.
Janie, Joey and **Leeby,** their children.
A Window in Thrums, J. M. Barrie, 1889.

Macrae, Hector.
John, his brother, m. Angusina Mackenzie.
Fergus, his brother.
The Brothers, L. A. G. Strong, 1932.

McRaven, Laura, child cousin of the Fairchilds. *Delta Wedding,* Eudora Welty, 1946.

Macrea, housemaster. *Stalky & Co.,* R. Kipling, 1899.

McRimmon, shipowner. 'Bread upon the Waters' (s.s.), *The Day's Work,* R. Kipling, 1898.

Macrob, Neil Ray, skipper of ferryboat. *Kidnapped,* R. L. Stevenson, 1886.

MacSarcasm, Sir Archie. *Love à la Mode* (play), C. Macklin, 1759.

Macshane, ship's surgeon, the *Thunder. Roderick Random,* T. Smollett, 1748.

McSpurt, Alexander, advertising expert. *Albert Grope,* F. O. Mann, 1931.

MacStinger, Mrs, widowed landlady of Captain Cuttle, m. Captain Bunsby.
The Little MacStingers, her family.
Dombey and Son, C. Dickens, 1848.

Macsweeney, Sergeant Aloysius, of the Irish police. *Destiny Bay,* Donn Byrne, 1928.

MacSycophant, Sir Pertinax. *The Man of the World* (play), C. Macklin, 1781.

MacTab, Hon. Lucretia. *The Poor Gentleman* (play), G. Colman the Younger, 1802.

MacTavish, Elspat, 'The Woman of the Tree.'
Hamish, her husband.
Hamish Bean, their son.
The Highland Widow, W. Scott, 1827.

McTavish, Lieutenant-Colonel Hector.
His daughter, m. Bute Crawley.
Vanity Fair, W. M. Thackeray, 1847–8.

McTeague, dentist and miner, central character, m. Trina Sieppe. *McTeague,* F. Norris, 1899.

McTodd, Neil Angus, ship's engineer. The *Captain Kettle* series, C. J. Cutcliffe Hyne, 1898–1932.

MacTurk, Bell. *The Raiders,* S. R. Crockett, 1894.

MacTurk, Captain Mungo (or **Hector**), 'Man of Peace.' *St Ronan's Well,* W. Scott, 1824.

M'Turk, William ('Turkey'), one of the Stalky trio. *Stalky & Co.,* 1899, and other stories in later books, R. Kipling.

Macumazahn. *See* ALLAN QUATERMAIN.

McVey, Hugh, inventor and manufacturer of a crop-setting machine.
Clara Butterworth, his wife.
Poor White, Sherwood Anderson, 1920.

MacVittie, Ephraim, partner in MacVittie & Co.
His wife.
Alison, their daughter.
Rob Roy, W. Scott, 1818.

MacWhirr, Captain Tom, of the *Nan-Shan. Typhoon,* J. Conrad, 1903.

MacWhirter, Major, late Bengal Cavalry.
His wife, sister of Mrs Baynes.
The Adventures of Philip, W. M. Thackeray, 1861–2.

MacWhirter, Jerry, boyhood friend of Patrick Heron. *The Raiders,* S. R. Crockett, 1894.

MacWilliams, in charge of mining railroad. *Soldiers of Fortune,* R. H. Davis, 1897.

McWilliams, Mortimer.
Evangeline, his wife.
Mrs McWilliams and the Lightning (s.s.), Mark Twain.

Maddack, Harriet, aunt of the Baines

sisters. *The Old Wives' Tale*, Arnold Bennett, 1908.

Madden, Mr and Mrs, butler and housekeeper to Miss Florence. 'They' (s.s.), *Traffics and Discoveries*, R. Kipling, 1904.

Madden, Arthur. *Sylvia Scarlett*, C. Mackenzie, 1918.

Madder, butler to Emilie Dawson.
His wife.
The Whistling Chambermaid, Naomi Royde-Smith, 1957.

Maddingham, Lieutenant-Commander, R.N.V.R. 'Sea Constables' (s.s.), *Debits and Credits*, R. Kipling, 1926.

Maddison, William, central character.
John, barrister and farmer, his father.
The Beautiful Years, H. Williamson, 1921.

Madeley, Dr. 'Amos Barton,' *Scenes of Clerical Life*, George Eliot, 1857.

Madeline, m. Porphyro. 'The Eve of St Agnes' (poem), *Lamia and other Poems*, J. Keats, 1820.

Madgwick, Tom, potman. *The Sailor's Return*, David Garnett, 1925.

Madigan, Mrs Maisie. *Juno and the Paycock* (play), S. O'Casey, 1925.

Madrigal, Miss, companion/governess with a past. *The Chalk Garden* (play), Enid Bagnold, 1955.

Madu, charcoal burner.
Athira, his wife.
'Through the Fire' (s.s.), *Life's Handicap*, R. Kipling, 1891.

Madvig, Paul, political boss of an American city. Friend of Ned Beaumont.
Opal, his daughter.
The Glass Key, Dashiell Hammett, 1931.

Maes, Gertrude, mother of Henry Esmond, m. Viscount Castlewood; later enters a convent as Sœur Marie-Madeleine. *Henry Esmond*, W. M. Thackeray, 1852.

Maffin, Captain Jack, Philip Gadsby's close friend.
The Story of the Gadsbys, R. Kipling, 1888.

Maginnis, Damaris Payne's manager. *Wandering Stars*, Clemence Dane, 1924.

Magiot, Dr, Communist. *The Comedians*, Graham Greene, 1966.

Magnet, Will, humorous writer, m. Daphne Pope. *Marriage*, H. G. Wells, 1912.

Magnetes, a Median lord. *Tamburlaine* (play), C. Marlowe, 1587.

Magnon, a privileged Texec in a world of the future. *Earthjacket*, Jon Hartridge, 1970.

Magnus, King. *The Apple Cart* (play), G. B. Shaw, 1929.

Magnus, Peter, traveller with Pickwick to Ipswich. *Pickwick Papers*, C. Dickens, 1837.

Magny, General Baron Chevalier de.
His scapegrace grandson.
Barry Lyndon, W. M. Thackeray, 1844.

Magog. *See* GOG.

Magua ('le Renard subtil'), traitorous Huron chief. *The Last of the Mohicans*, J. Fenimore Cooper, 1826.

Maguire, police sergeant, Gartumna. 'Another Temple Gone' (s.s.), *Fiery Particles*, C. E. Montague, 1923.

Maguire, Barney, Lieutenant Seaforth's 'man.' 'The Spectre of Tappington' (s.s.), *The Ingoldsby Legends*, R. H. Barham, 1837.

Magwitch, Abel (alias Provis), escaped convict, father of Estella. *Great Expectations*, C. Dickens, 1861.

Mahaina, dipsomaniac friend of the Nosnibors. *Erewhon*, S. Butler, 1872.

Mahboob Ali, chief eunuch, prime minister. *On the Face of the Waters*, Flora A. Steel, 1896.

Mahbub Ali, horse-trader, secret service C.25 1B. *Kim*, R. Kipling, 1901.

Mahmud Ali, sewing man. 'The Debt' (s.s.), *Limits and Renewals*, R. Kipling, 1932.

Mahogany, Mrs, medium. *The Prescription* (s.s.), Marjorie Bowen.

Mahomet Singh, one of the 'four.' *See* ABDULLAH KHAN. *The Sign of Four*, A. Conan Doyle, 1890.

Mahon, Christopher.
His father, a squatter.
The Playboy of the Western World (play), J. M. Synge, 1907.

Mahon, Count P., m. as 2nd husband Eloise Franzius, *née* Feliciani.
Patrick, his son, narrator.
The Drums of War, H. de Vere Stacpoole, 1910.

Mahony, Richard Townshend, central character.
 Mary ('Polly'), his wife, *née* Turnham.
 Cuthbert, Lallie and **Luce,** their children.
The Fortunes of Richard Mahony, H. H. Richardson, 1917–30.

Maidan, Mrs Maisie, *née* Flaherty, young woman whom Edward Ashburnham follows from India to Nauheim, spa in Germany. *The Good Soldier,* Ford Madox Ford, 1915.

Maidston, Alicia, m. Ablard Pender.
 Her mother.
The Last Revolution, Lord Dunsany, 1951.

Mail, Michael, villager of Mellstock. *Under the Greenwood Tree,* T. Hardy, 1872.

Mailsetter, postmaster, Fairport.
 His wife.
 Davie, their son.
The Antiquary, W. Scott, 1816.

Main, Miss, proprietor, girls' school. *Madcap Violet,* W. Black, 1876.

Maine, Sackville, coal merchant, ruined by the Sarcophagus Club.
 His wife.
The Book of Snobs, W. M. Thackeray, 1846–7.

Maine, Susan. *The Farmer's Wife* (play), E. Phillpotts, 1924.

Maingot, Monsieur.
 Jacqueline, his daughter.
French without Tears (play), T. Rattigan, 1936.

Mainward, English waster. *Sanders of the River,* E. Wallace, 1911.

Mainwaring, Colonel, Sir Oliver Raydon's friend. *An Affair of Dishonour,* W. de Morgan, 1910.

Mainwaring, Lieutenant, in charge of prisoners of war. *The American Prisoner,* E. Phillpots, 1904.

Mainwaring, Bunty, eng. to Nicky Lancaster. *The Vortex* (play), N. Coward, 1924.

Mainwaring, Clifford, boy actor. *Little Red Horses,* G. B. Stern, 1932.

Mainwaring, Mrs Eustace. *Secrets* (play), R. Besier & May Edginton, 1922.

Mainwaring, Sir Joseph. *Put Out More Flags,* E. Waugh, 1942.

Mainwaring, Mrs Lydia. *The Constant Nymph,* Margaret Kennedy, 1924.

Mainwearing, Head of High Cross School. *Joan and Peter,* H. G. Wells, 1918.

Mair, Professor, head of section employing Sammy Rice. *The Small Back Room,* N. Balchin, 1943.

Mair, Joseph, boatman.
 Anne, his wife.
The Marquis of Lossie, G. MacDonald, 1877.

Maisie. *Proud Maisie* (poem), W. Scott.

Maisie, chief female character, loved by Dick Heldar. *The Light that Failed,* R. Kipling, 1890.

Maisie, a whore. *The Rich Pay Late,* 1964, and others in the *Alms for Oblivion* sequence, Simon Raven.

Maitland, officer at Waterloo. 'The Peasant's Confession,' *Wessex Poems,* T. Hardy, 1898.

Maitland, manservant. *The Chalk Garden,* Enid Bagnold, 1955.

Maitland, Captain, R.N. *The Middle Watch* (play), Ian Hay & S. King-Hall, 1929.

Maitland, Annie. *The Pottleton Legacy,* Albert Smith, 1849.

Maitland, Arthur, friend of Jim Manning. *A Way through the Wood,* N. Balchin, 1951.

Maitland, Henry, man of letters, central character, m. (1) Marion Hilton, (2) an uneducated shrew. *See also* Thérèse Espinel. *The Private Life of Henry Maitland,* Morley Roberts, 1912.

Maitland, John, manager, Bernheim's. *A Penniless Millionaire,* D. C. Murray, 1907.

Maitland, Oliver.
 Sophie, his wife, *née* Rakonitz.
 Danny, their supposed son, really illegitimate son of Oliver and his mistress.
Tents of Israel, G. B. Stern, 1924.

Maitland, Sophia, central character, m. Sir Hervey Coke.
 Sir Thomas, her brother, m. Lady Betty Cochrane.
 Their sister, m. Northey.
Sophia, Stanley Weyman, 1900.

Major, Emma.
 Thomas, her husband.
Yellow Sands (play), E. Phillpotts, 1926.

Major, Lucy, widow, m. Chris Marrapit. *Once Aboard the Lugger,* A. S. M. Hutchinson, 1908.

Makebody, actor. 'A Curious Story' (s.s.), *The Baseless Fabric,* Helen Simpson, 1925.

Makepeace, Julia, 1st wife of Martin Whitelaw. *Roots,* Naomi Jacob, 1931.

Mala, wife of Tarn. 'Mala' (s.s.), *Here and Hereafter,* Barry Pain, 1911.

Malagrowther, Sir Mungo, of Girnigo Castle. *The Fortunes of Nigel,* W. Scott, 1822.

Malakite, Christie, Wolf's spiritual mate.
Her father, a bookseller.
Wolf Solent, J. C. Powys, 1929.

Malam, J.P. *Silas Marner,* George Eliot, 1861.

Malaprop, Mrs. *The Rivals* (play), R. B. Sheridan, 1775.

Malatesta, revolutionary who fights a duel with Rossi. *The Eternal City,* Hall Caine, 1901.

Malatesta, Giovanni (Lo Scantiato), tyrant of Rimini, m. Francesca da Rimini.
Paolo (Il Bello), his elder brother, loves Francesca.
Paolo and Francesca (play), S. Phillips, 1900.

Malbihn, Sven. The *Tarzan* series, E. R. Burroughs, 1912–32.

Malcolm, son of Duncan. *Macbeth* (play), W. Shakespeare.

Malcolm, fifteen-year-old boy waiting for his lost father, central character. *Malcolm,* James Purdy, 1959.

Malcolm, John, ex-husband of Mrs Shankland. *Separate Tables* (play), T. Rattigan, 1955.

Malcourt, Louis, superintendent of Portlaw's estate, m. Shiela Cardross.
Helen, his sister, m. (1) James Wayward, (2) Lord Tressilvain.
The Firing Line, R. W. Chambers, 1908.

Malden, Jack, waster cousin of Mrs Strong. *David Copperfield,* C. Dickens, 1850.

Malderton, Mr, and family. *Sketches by Boz,* C. Dickens, 1836.

Malétroit, Sire de (Alain).
Blanche, his niece, m. Denis de Beaulieu.
'The Sire de Malétroit's Door' (s.s.), *New Arabian Nights,* R. L. Stevenson, 1882.

Malherb, Maurice, m. Annabel.
Grace, their daughter, m. Cecil Stark.
Sir Nicholas, his father.
Norrington, his brother. *See also* Lovey Lee.
The American Prisoner, E. Phillpotts, 1904.

Malinin, Sergei.
Anna, his wife. White Russian refugees.
Seryozha, their son, m. Tatiana Ostapenko.
Tobit Transplanted, Stella Benson, 1931.

Malins. *See* William Walterson.

Malins, Captain. *Abraham Lincoln* (play), J. Drinkwater, 1918.

Malise, Baron, of Starning & Parrox, elder brother of Prosper le Gai. *The Forest Lovers,* M. Hewlett, 1898.

Mallard, clerk to Sergeant Snubbin. *Pickwick Papers,* C. Dickens, 1837.

Mallard, Chief Inspector of police. *The Patriots,* James Barlow, 1960.

Mallard, Sir Humphrey, m. Jenny Baston. *See also* Isabel Halnaker.
Aubrey, their son, m. Henrietta Lee-Johnson.
Iron and Smoke, Sheila Kaye-Smith, 1928.

Mallard, Jason, congressman. 'The Thunders of Silence' (s.s.), *From Place to Place,* Irvin S. Cobb, 1920.

Mallard, Richard, migrant to Europe. *But Soft—We Are Observed!,* H. Belloc, 1928.

Mallet, 'Serjeant,' P.C. *The Fourth Wall* (play), A. A. Milne, 1928.

Mallet, Rowland.
Jonas, his father.
Cecilia, his cousin.
Bessie, her daughter.
Roderick Hudson, H. James, 1875.

Mallett, Superintendent. *Requiem for Robert,* 1942, and many others, Mary Fitt.

Malley, Rosalind, music-shop assistant, jilts Albert Grope and m. Thorold Progers. *Albert Grope,* F. O. Mann, 1931.

Mallinger, Sir Hugo.
Louisa, his wife.
Theresa, one of their three daughters.
Henleigh, his nephew and heir. *See* Grandcourt.

Daniel Deronda, George Eliot, 1876.

Mallison, Captain Charles, Vice-consul. *Lost Horizon,* J. Hilton, 1933.

Mallison, Charles ('Chick'), nephew of Gavin Stevens. *The Snopes* trilogy, William Faulkner, 1940–1959.

Mallinson, Edith, governess to the Clayton children. *Cricket in Heaven,* G. Bullett, 1949.

Mallory, Gervase. *The Romantic Age* (play), A. A. Milne, 1920.

Mallow, Canon, late warden of orphan home. *Children of the Archbishop,* N. Collins, 1951.

Mallowe, Mrs Polly, friend of Mrs Hauksbee. 'The Education of Otis Yeere' (s.s.), *Wee Willie Winkie,* R. Kipling, 1888.

Malloy, Sam.
His wife.
Cannery Row, J. Steinbeck, 1945.

Malluch, Simonides's servant. *Ben Hur,* L. Wallace, 1880.

Malmayne, Judith, wicked nurse. *Old St Paul's,* W. H. Ainsworth, 1841.

Malone, Billy (Brer Rabbit). *Uncle Remus,* J. C. Harris, 1880–95.

Malone, E. D., journalist, accompanying Prof. Challenger. *The Lost World,* 1912, and *The Poison Belt,* 1913, A. Conan Doyle.

Malone, Gerald, friend of Caryl Bramsley, and collector of his papers. *C.,* M. Baring, 1924.

Malone, Hector, American, m. Violet Robinson. *Man and Superman* (play), G. B. Shaw, 1903.

Malone, J. T., a pharmacist who has leukemia.
Martha, his wife, *née* Greenlove.
Ellen and **Tommy,** their young children.
Clock Without Hands, Carson McCullers, 1961.

Malone, Ned. *Tom Burke of Ours,* C. Lever, 1844.

Malone, Pansy.
Her mother.
Charlie, her brother.
A Voyage to Purilia, Elmer Rice, 1930.

Malone, Rev. Peter, curate of Briarfield. *Shirley,* Charlotte Brontë, 1849.

Malone, Peter J. *Counsellor-at-Law* (play), Elmer Rice, 1931.

Malone, Tom, murderer. *For Us in the Dark,* Naomi Royde-Smith, 1937.

Maloney, Mrs. *A Kiss for Cinderella* (play), J. M. Barrie, 1916.

Maloney, Dicky. *Cabbages and Kings,* O. Henry, 1905.

Maloney, Rosita, convent schoolgirl. *The Land of Spices,* Kate O'Brien, 1941.

Maloney, Rev. Timothy.
His wife.
Joan, their daughter.
'The Camp of the Dog,' *John Silence,* A. Blackwood, 1908.

Malony, Jim, comedian, mistakenly m. Annie-Laurie Redmayne bigamously.
Midge, their daughter.
The Herb of Grace, Elizabeth Goudge, 1948.

Malory, Richard. *The Woodcarver of 'Lympus,* Mary E. Waller, 1909.

Malouet, Louis de, portrait-painter, cousin of Lisette Courtaud. *Both of this Parish,* J. S. Fletcher.

Malpractice, Miles, bright young thing. *Vile Bodies,* Evelyn Waugh, 1930.

Maltby, Hilary, author, rival of Braxton. 'Maltby and Braxton,' *Seven Men,* Max Beerbohm, 1919.

Maltese Cat, The, polo pony. 'Past, Pluperfect, Prestissimo Player of the Game.' 'The Maltese Cat' (s.s.), *The Day's Work,* R. Kipling, 1898.

Malthus, Bartholomew, honorary member of the Suicide Club. 'The Suicide Club,' *New Arabian Nights,* R. L. Stevenson, 1882.

Maltravers, Ernest, of Burleigh, mystic and poet, central character. *Ernest Maltravers,* 1837, and *Alice,* 1838, Lord Lytton.

Maltravers, Sir Humphrey, Minister of Transportation, later Lord Metroland; m. Margot Beste-Chetwynde, *Decline and Fall,* 1928, and elsewhere, E. Waugh.

Malvoisin, Philip de, Norman noble.
Albert, his brother, Preceptor.
Ivanhoe, W. Scott, 1820.

Malvolio, steward to Olivia. *Twelfth Night* (play), W. Shakespeare.

Mameena, m. (1) Saduko, (2) Masapo.
Umbesi, her father.
Child of Storm, H. Rider Haggard, 1913.

Mamillius, Leontes's son. *A Winter's Tale* (play), W. Shakespeare.

Mammon, Sir Epicure. *The Alchemist* (play), B. Jonson, 1610.

Mammy, the O'Haras' faithful slave. *Gone with the Wind,* Margaret Mitchell, 1936.

Mammy-Bammy, Big Money witch-rabbit. *Uncle Remus,* J. C. Harris, 1880–95.

Man in Black, The, guide and friend of Lien chi Altangi. *A Citizen of the World,* O. Goldsmith, 1762.

Manallace, James Andrew. 'Dayspring Mishandled' (s.s.), *Limits and Renewals,* R. Kipling, 1932.

Manasseh, chief creditor of Rawdon Crawley. *Vanity Fair,* W. M. Thackeray, 1847–8.

Manby, Flora, friend of Henry (Rico) Carrington. *St Mawr,* D. H. Lawrence, 1925.

Mandane, a waiting woman. *A King and No King* (play), Beaumont & Fletcher, 1611.

Manders Minor, a fag. 'Slaves of the Lamp,' *Stalky & Co.,* R. Kipling, 1899.

Manderson, Sigsbee, American financier.
  Mabel, his wife, *née* Domecq.
Trent's Last Case, E. C. Bentley, 1912.

Manderstroke, Lord (Gerry), killer of Harry Somerford. *Fanny by Gaslight,* M. Sadleir, 1940.

Mandes, Señora Chiquita. *Little Red Horses,* G. B. Stern, 1932.

Mandeville, Earl of, m. Rachel Peace. *Incomparable Bellairs,* A. & E. Castle, 1904.

Mandeville, Mrs 'Tommy,' mother of Jean Forbes. *Poet's Pub,* E. Linklater, 1929.

Mandy, waitress. *The Torrents of Spring,* Ernest Hemingway, 1933.

Manette, Dr, prisoner in the Bastille, later escapes to England.
  Lucie, his daughter, m. Charles Darnay.
A Tale of Two Cities, C. Dickens, 1859.

Manetti, Sibilla. *Romola,* George Eliot, 1863.

Manfred, (usurping) Prince of Otranto.
  Hippolita, his wife.
    Conrad, their sickly son.
    Matilda, their daughter.
The Castle of Otranto, Horace Walpole, 1765.

Manfred, George, one of the Four Just Men. *See* GONSALEZ. *The Four Just Men,* E. Wallace, 1905.

Manfredi, m. Emilia di Santangiolo. *The Cardinal's Snuffbox,* H. Harland, 1900.

Mang, the bat. 'Kaa's Hunting' and elsewhere, *The Jungle Books,* R. Kipling, 1894–5.

Mangan, Boss. *Heartbreak House* (play), G. B. Shaw, 1917.

Mangan, Luke, central character and narrator, m. (1) Muriel Travers, (2) Kathleen.
  John, his uncle, auctioneer and furniture expert.
  His wife.
  George, his uncle, master of tramp steamer.
The Bay, 1941, and elsewhere, L. A. G. Strong.

Manger, executioner. *The Tower of London,* W. H. Ainsworth, 1840.

Mangles, Joseph P., American diplomat.
  Julie, his sister.
The Vultures, H. Seton Merriman, 1902.

Mangles, Sarah, m. Dudley Ruthyn. *Uncle Silas,* Sheridan le Fanu, 1864.

Mango, of Mango Plantain & Co. *Vanity Fair,* 1847–8, and *Our Street,* 1848, W. M. Thackeray.

Mangum, May Martha, m. Jim, narrator.
  Her father, entomologist.
'Buried Treasure' (s.s.), *Options,* O. Henry, 1909.

Maning, Andrew.
  Eric, his grandson.
  Hedda, his grand-daughter, m. Olaf Henderson.
The Benefactor, J. D. Beresford.

Mankeltow, Captain, later Lord Marshalton. 'The Captive' (s.s.), *Traffics and Discoveries,* 1904, and elsewhere, R. Kipling.

Manly, central character. *The Plain Dealer* (play), W. Wycherley, 1677.

Manly, John, coachman. *Black Beauty,* Anna Sewell, 1877.

Mann, Miss, 'crabbed old maid,' friend of Caroline Helstone. *Shirley,* Charlotte Brontë, 1849.

Mann, Mrs, workhouse matron. *Oliver Twist,* C. Dickens, 1838.

Mannering, junior porter. *Savoir Faire* (s.s.), W. Pett Ridge.

Mannering, Belamy, uncle of Alaster Mackintosh. *The Secret Vanguard,* M. Innes, 1940.

Mannering, Colonel Guy, central character.
  Sophia, his wife, *née* Wellwood.
    Julia, their daughter, m. Harry Bertram.
  Sir Paul and **Bishop Mannering,** his uncles.
Guy Mannering, W. Scott, 1815.

Mannering, Kitty. 'The Phantom Rickshaw' (s.s.), *Wee Willie Winkie,* R. Kipling, 1888.

Mannering, Percy, poet. *Memento Mori,* Muriel Spark, 1959.

Manners, Dom Cuthbert. *Sinister Street,* C. Mackenzie, 1913.

Manners, Dorothy, m. Richard Carvel.
  Her father and mother.
Richard Carvel, W. Churchill, 1899.

Mannheim, Gerda, German refugee.
  Peter, her husband.
The World in the Evening, C. Isherwood, 1954.

Mannigoe, Nancy, Negress condemned to death for murder. *Requiem for a Nun,* William Faulkner, 1950.

Manning, London journalist, neighbour of Britling. *Mr Britling Sees It Through,* H. G. Wells, 1916.

Manning, Hubert, civil servant and poet, one-time fiancé of Ann Veronica Stanley. *Ann Veronica,* H. G. Wells, 1909.

Manning, Jane.
  John, her husband.
The Cotillon (s.s.), L. P. Hartley.

Manning, Jim, central character.
  Jill, his wife.
A Way through the Wood, N. Balchin, 1951.

Manning, Paul, central character and narrator, m. Margaret Ellison.
  John, his father.
  Margaret, his mother.
Cousin Phillis, Mrs Gaskell, 1864.

Mannion, Robert, managing clerk to Sherwin. *Basil,* W. Collins, 1852.

Mannon, Brigadier-General Ezra, murdered by his wife.
  Christine, his wife; kills herself.
  Lavinia, their daughter.
  Orin, their son. *See also* ADAM BRANT.
Mourning becomes Electra (play), E. O'Neill, 1931.

Manolin, young boy. *The Old Man and The Sea,* Ernest Hemingway, 1952.

Manon, girl at the thieves' tavern. *The Cloister and the Hearth,* C. Reade, 1861.

Manresa, Mrs, wealthy, vulgar guest at the pageant. *Between The Acts,* Virginia Woolf, 1941.

Mansel, Sir Edward, Lieutenant of the Tower.
  His wife.
The Fortunes of Nigel, W. Scott, 1822.

Mansel, Captain Jonathan. *Berry and Co.,* D. Yates, 1920.

Mansell, C. J., schoolboy at Fernhurst. *The Loom of Youth,* A. Waugh, 1917.

Mansfield, Lieutenant. *Sixty-four, Ninety-four,* R. H. Mottram, 1925.

Manson, Dr Andrew, central character, m. Christine Barlow. *The Citadel,* A. J. Cronin, 1937.

Manston, Aeneas, son of Cytherea Aldclyffe.
  Eunice, his wife.
  His foster-mother.
Desperate Remedies, T. Hardy, 1871.

Mansur, Wazir.
  Lut-al-Kubub, his 1st wife.
Kismet (play), E. Knoblock, 1911.

Mant, May (*née* Rene Iris), a child actress. *Caprice,* Ronald Firbank, 1917.

Mantalini, Mr (originally Muntle), worthless man-about-town.
  His wife, dressmaker.
Nicholas Nickleby, C. Dickens, 1839.

Manton, Earl of.
  Lady Flavia Canning, his daughter.
The Search Party, G. A. Birmingham, 1913.

Mantrap, Sir Gavial, swindler. *Theophrastus Such,* George Eliot, 1879.

Manuel, sailor on the *We're Here. Captains Courageous,* R. Kipling, 1897.

Manuel, foundling, twin brother of Esteban. *The Bridge of San Luis Rey,* T. Wilder, 1927.

Manuel, Don, of Encinitas, eng. to Carlotta de Leyva. *Odtaa,* J. Masefield, 1926.

Manuma, chief's son on island of Talua. 'Mackintosh' (s.s.), *The Trembling of a Leaf,* W. S. Maugham, 1921.

Mao (Mor), the peacock. 'Mowgli's Brothers' and elsewhere, *The Jungle Books,* Rudyard Kipling, 1894.

Mapen, Rose. *The Ox-Bow Incident,* Walter Van Tilburg Clark, 1940.

Maple, Bridget, aunt of Sam Crowe and wife of Ferret. *Sir Lancelot Greaves,* T. Smollett, 1762.

Mapsted, John, owner of riding stables.
His mother.
Twelve Horses and the Hangman's Noose, Gladys Mitchell, 1956.

Maputa, Zulu friend of Allan Quatermain. *Child of Storm,* H. Rider Haggard, 1913.

Marasca, Francesco (Cicio), m. Alvina Houghton. *The Lost Girl,* D. H. Lawrence, 1920.

Marayne, Lady, m. (1) Rev. Harold Benham.
Sir Godfrey, celebrated surgeon, her 2nd husband.
The Research Magnificent, H. G. Wells, 1915.

Marble, Moses, mate of the *John. Afloat and Ashore,* J. Fenimore Cooper, 1844.

Marcella, central character. *The Duke of Milan* (play), P. Massinger, 1623.

Marcella. *Gorboduc* (play), T. Sackville & T. Norton, 1562.

Marcellus, an officer. *Hamlet* (play), W. Shakespeare.

March, gardener to James Probity Snr. *Master Jim Probity,* F. Swinnerton, 1952.

March, Lord. *The Virginians,* W. M. Thackeray, 1857–9.

March, Mr, philosopher and teacher.
His wife ('Marmee').
Their daughters:
Meg, m. John Brooke.
Josephine (Jo), m. Friedrich Bhaer.
Beth.
Amy, m. Theodore Laurence.
Aunt March, his sister.
Little Women and sequels, Louisa M. Alcott, 1868–86.

March, Augie, illegitimate son of a Chicago charwoman.
Stella Chesney, his wife.
Simon, his older brother.
Charlotte, Simon's wife.
Georgie, Augie's feeble-minded young brother.
The Adventures of Augie March, Saul Bellow, 1953.

March, Charles, member of an Anglo-Jewish banking family.
Ann, his wife, active Communist.
Leonard, his father.
Katherine, his sister, m. Francis Getliffe.
Sir Philip March, his uncle, head of the family.
The Conscience of the Rich, 1958, part of the *Strangers and Brothers* sequence, C. P. Snow.

March, Colin, rival in the army to C. Barbason. 'Honours Easy' (s.s.), *Fiery Particles,* C. E. Montague, 1923.

March, Gerald Haveleur. *The Green Hat,* M. Arlen, 1924.

March, Henry ('Hurry Harry'). *The Deerslayer,* J. Fenimore Cooper, 1841.

March, Henry.
Ursula, his daughter, m. John Halifax.
John Halifax, Gentleman, Mrs Craik, 1856.

March, Juan, 'financier of kings.' *Dragon Harvest,* Upton Sinclair, 1946.

March, Robin, boy actor. *Little Red Horses,* G. B. Stern, 1932.

March Hare, The. *Alice in Wonderland,* L. Carroll, 1865.

Marchbanks, Eugene. *Candida* (play), G. B. Shaw, 1894.

Marchdale, Peter (pseudonym Felix Mildmay), m. Beatrice di Santangiolo. *The Cardinal's Snuff-box,* H. Harland, 1900.

'Marchioness, The,' maid-of-all-work to the Brass family, m. Dick Swiveller. *The Old Curiosity Shop,* C. Dickens, 1841.

Marchmain, Marquis of (Family name Flyte).
Teresa, his wife.
Their children:
The Earl of Brideshead, m. Mrs Beryl Muspratt.
Lord Sebastian.
Lady Julia, m. Rex Mottram.
Lady Cordelia.

Brideshead Revisited, E. Waugh, 1945.

Marchmill, William.
Ella, his wife.
'An Imaginative Woman,' *Wessex Tales,* T. Hardy, 1888.

Marchmont, a herald. *Perkin Warbeck* (play), John Ford, 1634.

Marchmont, rich cripple, employer of Lucy Snowe. *Villette,* Charlotte Brontë, 1853.

Marchmont, Mrs Margaret. *An Ideal Husband* (play), O. Wilde, 1895.

Marck, William de la, 'Wild Boar of Ardennes,' father of Carl Eberson. *Quentin Durward,* W. Scott, 1823.

Marco, soldier. *Paolo and Francesca,* S. Phillips, 1900.

Marcovitch. *Bulldog Drummond,* 'Sapper' (H. C. McNeile), 1920.

Marcus, central character. *The Sign of the Cross,* W. Barrett, 1896.

Marcus, Hetty, m. (1) Harry Smith, (2) Fred Sumner, father of her children. *The Dream,* H. G. Wells, 1924.

Marcus, Hugo. *Going their own Ways,* A. Waugh, 1938.

Marcus, Richard, of the Rakonitz clan, m. Molly Dunne.
Deborah, his sister.
Tents of Israel, G. B. Stern, 1924.

Marcus Andronicus, brother of Titus. *Titus Andronicus* (play), W. Shakespeare.

Marden, Agatha. *The Parasite,* A. Conan Doyle, 1894.

Marden, George, M.P.
Olivia, his wife, formerly Mrs Jacob Telworthy.
Dinah, his niece.
Lady Marden (Aunt Julia), his aunt.
Mr Pim Passes By (play), A. A. Milne, 1920.

Marden, John. 'The Woman in his Life' (s.s.), *Limits and Renewals,* R. Kipling, 1932.

Mardick, Mrs, fellow traveller who escapes from cholera ship with Judy Corder. *Four Frightened People,* E. Arnot Robertson, 1931.

Mardley, James, co-respondent in the Adscombe case. *Judgment in Suspense,* G. Bullett, 1946.

Mardon, purchaser of Sophia Scales's French boarding-house. *The Old Wives' Tale,* Arnold Bennett, 1908.

Mardonius. *A King and No King* (play), Beaumont & Fletcher, 1611.

Mardyke, Colonel.
Miriam, his wife, later m. Hubert Lisle.
Martha, his sister.
The Sin of David (play), S. Phillips, 1914.

Margaret, daughter of Reignier, later wife of Henry (hist.). *Henry the Sixth* and *Richard the Third* (plays), W. Shakespeare.

Margaret. *The Forsaken Merman* (poem), M. Arnold, 1853.

Margaret, young workwoman, m. Will Wilson. *Mary Barton,* Mrs Gaskell, 1848.

Margaret, Dame, prioress of the Benedictine convent at Oby (1381–2). *The Corner That Held Them,* Sylvia Townsend Warner, 1948.

Margaret, Mad, m. Sir Despard Murgatroyd. *Ruddigore* (comic opera), Gilbert & Sullivan, 1887.

Margery, Dame, nurse to Eveline Berenger. *The Betrothed,* W. Scott, 1825.

Marget, Jack, priest. 'A Doctor of Medicine,' *Rewards and Fairies,* R. Kipling, 1910.

Margetts, market gardener.
His wife and son.
'A Friend of the Family' (s.s.), *Debits and Credits,* R. Kipling, 1926.

Margureite, wife of St Leon. *St Leon,* W. Godwin, 1799.

Marguerite, Clare Lydiatt's maid. *Portrait of Clare,* F. Brett Young, 1927.

Maria, mistress of Robert Jordan. *For Whom the Bell Tolls,* E. Hemingway, 1940.

Maria.
Brigette, her daughter.
The Power and the Glory, Graham Greene, 1940.

Maria, Olivia's servant. *Twelfth Night* (play), W. Shakespeare.

Maria, attending on the Princess. *Love's Labour's Lost* (play), W. Shakespeare.

Maria, ward of Sir Peter Teazle. *The School for Scandal* (play), R. B. Sheridan, 1777.

Marian, maid to Pauline des Chappelles. *The Lady of Lyons* (play), Lord Lytton, 1838.

Marian, dairymaid at Talbothays Farm. *Tess of the D'Urbervilles,* T. Hardy, 1891.

Marian, a foundling. *Marian,* Mrs S. C. Hall, 1840.

Mariana. *Mariana* (poem), Lord Tennyson.

Mariana, betrothed to Angelo. *Measure for Measure* (play), W. Shakespeare.

Mariani, keeper of grog-shop and 'unspeakable scoundrel.' *Lord Jim,* J. Conrad, 1900.

Marianne. *See* HEROD.

Marie-Madeleine. *See* GERTRUDE MAES.

Marie-Thérèse, stray child. *A Kiss for Cinderella* (play), J. M. Barrie, 1916.

Marigny. *Beau Geste,* P. C. Wren, 1924.

Marigold, 'Dr,' cheapjack.
His wife.
'Willum,' his father.
'Dr Marigold's Prescription,' *Christmas Stories,* C. Dickens, 1865.

Marion. *A Kiss for Cinderella* (play), J. M. Barrie, 1916.

Marion, landlady of the Three Fish. *The Cloister and the Hearth,* C. Reade, 1861.

Maris. *Beau Geste,* P. C. Wren, 1924.

Marjan, Polish prisoner. *The Pied Piper,* N. Shute, 1942.

Mark, Cornish king.
Isolt of Brittany, his false Queen.
'The Last Tournament' (poem), *Idylls of the King,* Lord Tennyson, 1859.

Mark, Lord, suitor of Kate Croy. *The Wings of the Dove,* Henry James, 1902.

Mark Antony. *See* ANTONY.

Markby, Lady. *An Ideal Husband* (play), O. Wilde, 1895.

Marker, Captain, shot in a quarrel by Rawdon Crawley. *Vanity Fair,* W. M. Thackeray, 1847–8.

Markham, Gilbert, central character and part narrator, m. as 3rd husband Helen Huntingdon.
Fergus, his brother.
Rose, his sister.
The Tenant of Wildfell Hall, Anne Brontë, 1848.

Markham, John F. X., district attorney. *The Benson Murder Case,* S. S. van Dine, 1926.

Markham, Lucy, m. Fred Coleman. *Frank Fairlegh,* F. E. Smedley, 1850.

Markham, Novello, stage manager, repertory company.
'Doucebell Dear,' his wife.
Enter Sir John, Clemence Dane & Helen Simpson, 1924.

Markland, Mr and Mrs. *The Woman in White,* W. Collins, 1860.

Marks, partner of Tom Loker. *Uncle Tom's Cabin.* Harriet B. Stowe, 1851.

Marks, Miss, a publisher's secretary. *The Rose of Tibet,* Lionel Davidson, 1962.

Marks, Billy, criminal and informer. *The Four Just Men,* E. Wallace, 1905.

Marks, Luke. *Lady Audley's Secret,* M. E. Braddon, 1862.

Marks, Mary, housekeeper, the Pelican. *Sorrell and Son,* W. Deeping, 1925.

Marling, William.
Annabel, his wife.
Their children:
Bill,
His wife and four children.
Oliver, m. Maria Lufton.
Lettice, m. (1) Roger Watson, (2) Tom Barclay.
Lucy, m. Sam Adams.
The *Barsetshire* series, Angela Thirkell, 1933 onwards.

Marlow, Charles, suitor of Kate Hardcastle.
Sir Charles, his father.
She Stoops to Conquer (play), Oliver Goldsmith, 1773.

Marlow, Charlie, narrator, and friend of Jim. *Lord Jim,* J. Conrad, 1900, and others.

Marlowe, Lady, twice widowed.
Frederica and **Cecily,** her daughters.
Thank Heaven Fasting, E. M. Delafield, 1932.

Marlowe, John, secretary to Sigsbee Manderson. *Trent's Last Case,* E. C. Bentley, 1912.

Marlowe, Mary, m. John Carlton.
William, her father.
Her mother.
Secrets (play), R. Besier & May Edginton, 1922.

Marlowe, Philip, private investigator, chief character. *The Big Sleep,* 1939, and other detective novels, Raymond Chandler.

Marner, Silas, linen-weaver of Raveloe, central character. *See also* EPPIE CASS. *Silas Marner,* George Eliot, 1861.

Marney, Earl of (George) (Family name Egremont).
  Arabella, his wife.
  The Dowager Countess, his mother.
  Hon. Charles, M.P., his brother, who succeeds him, m. Sybil Gerard.
Sybil, B. Disraeli, 1845.

Marnier, servant to Charles Wogan. *Clementina,* A. E. W. Mason, 1901.

Marny, Juliette de, m. Paul Déroulède.
  Duc de Marny, her father.
  Vicomte de Marny, her brother.
I Will Repay, Baroness Orczy, 1906.

Maroola, Dain, in love with Nina Almayer. *Almayer's Folly,* J. Conrad, 1895.

Marple, Miss Jane, spinster lady who lives in village of St Mary Mead and solves many murders. *The Mirror Crack'd from Side to Side,* 1962, and others, Agatha Christie.

Marpole, James, Captain of *Clorinda.*
  Henry, his son.
High Wind in Jamaica, R. Hughes, 1929.

Marrable, defaulting partner of Ephraim Quixtus. *The Glory of Clementina Wing,* W. J. Locke, 1911.

Marrable, Mr and Mrs, friends of the Vanstones. *No Name,* W. Collins, 1862.

Marrable, Peter, Harold, Doris and **Irene.** *The Clever Ones* (play), A. Sutro, 1914.

Marraby, Sir John, of Brasenose. *Zuleika Dobson,* Max Beerbohm, 1911.

Marrapit, Christopher, cat-lover, m. (2) Mrs Lucy Major.
  Margaret, his daughter, m. William Wyvern.
  George, his nephew and ward, medical student, m. Mary Humfray.
Once Aboard the Lugger, A. S. M. Hutchinson, 1908.

Marriner, Hunking.
  Anne, his mother.
  Lady, his sister.
Northwest Passage, Kenneth Roberts, 1938.

Marriott, Bob, scientist. *A Sort of Traitors,* N. Balchin, 1949.

Marriott, Sybil, friend of Harriet Vane. *Strong Poison,* Dorothy L. Sayers, 1930.

Marrowfat, Dr. *A Citizen of the World,* O. Goldsmith, 1762.

Marryat, Hannah. 'Uncle Meleager's Will,' *Lord Peter Views the Body,* Dorothy L. Sayers, 1928.

Marsden, passenger on the *Mary Prosper. Tom Fool,* F. Tennyson Jesse, 1926.

Marsden, undergraduate, friend of the Babe. *The Babe, B.A.,* E. F. Benson, 1897.

Marsden, Arthur, m. Bella Woodward.
  Peggy, his niece, m. George Hillier.
All the World Wondered, L. Merrick, 1911.

Marsden, Charles. *Strange Interlude* (play), E. O'Neill, 1928.

Marses, overseer of Caius Barrus's slaves. *The Conquered,* Naomi Mitchison, 1923.

Marsh. Family name of LORD MARSHMORETON.

Marsh, Norah, m. Frank Taylor.
  Edward, her brother.
    Gertrude, his wife.
The Land of Promise (play), W. S. Maugham, 1914.

Marsh, Robert, opera singer. *Grand Opera,* Vicki Baum, 1942.

Marshall, Major. *The Way of an Eagle,* Ethel M. Dell, 1912.

Marshall, Nurse Emma. *A House and its Head,* Ivy Compton-Burnett, 1935.

Marshall, George and **Marian,** friends of the Sheppards.
  Rupert, their son.
  Gillian, their daughter.
Thursday Afternoons, Monica Dickens, 1945.

Marshall, Robert C., American multi-millionaire. *Both of this Parish,* J. S. Fletcher.

Marshman, George and **Howard.** *The Wide, Wide World,* E. Wetherell, 1850.

Marshmoreton, Earl of (John) (Family name Marsh), m. Billie Dore.
  Lord Belpher, his son.
  Lady Maud, his daughter, m. George Bevan.

A Damsel in Distress, P. G. Wodehouse, 1919.

Marshwood, Felicity, Countess of.
Nigel, Earl of Marshwood, her son.
Relative Values (play), Noël Coward, 1951.

Marsinah. *See* HAJJ.

Marston, Dick, narrator, m. Grace Storefield.
Jim, his brother, m. Jeanie Morrison.
Ben, their father.
Norah, their mother.
Aileen, their sister.
Robbery under Arms, R. Boldrewood, 1888.

Marston, Rev. Edward, m. Hazel Woodus. *Gone to Earth*, Mary Webb, 1917.

Marston, Hugh.
Betty, his sister, one-time fiancée of Sir Julian Harnwood, later Lady Tracy.
The Courtship of Morrice Buckler, A. E. W. Mason, 1896.

Marston, John. *Ravenshoe*, H. Kingsley, 1861.

Marstone, Sarah Theresa.
Her sister.
Heartsease, Charlotte M. Yonge, 1854.

Marten, Edgar, Jewish geologist. *South Wind*, N. Douglas, 1917.

Martext, Sir Oliver, a vicar. *As You Like It* (play), W. Shakespeare.

Martha, maid to Miss Matty Jenkyns, eng. to Jim Hearn. *Cranford*, Mrs Gaskell, 1853.

Martha, Abbess of Elcho. *The Fair Maid of Perth*, W. Scott, 1828.

Martha, aged housekeeper at Osbaldistone Hall. *Rob Roy*, W. Scott, 1818.

Martha, servant to Mrs Pendennis and Laura Bell. *Pendennis*, 1848–1850, and *The Newcomes*, 1853–5, W. M. Thackeray.

Martha Sarah, village girl. 'The Distracted Preacher,' *Wessex Tales*, T. Hardy, 1888.

Marthon, traitorous waiting-woman. *Quentin Durward*, W. Scott, 1824.

Martia, Barty Josselin's spirit guide and lover. *The Martian*, George du Maurier, 1897.

Martial, Colin, playwright. *A Deputy was King*, G. B. Stern, 1926.

Martigny, Countess de, m. Earl of Etherington. *St Ronan's Well*, W. Scott, 1824.

Martin, Charles Beauchamp's butler. *Fed Up*, G. A. Birmingham, 1931.

Martin, servant of O'Brien. *1984*, G. Orwell, 1949.

Martin, servant of the Castlewoods. *Henry Esmond*, W. M. Thackeray, 1852.

Martin ('Madman'), good-natured, muddle-headed experimenter, schoolfellow of Tom Brown. *Tom Brown's Schooldays*, T. Hughes, 1857.

Martin, butler to Sigsbee Manderson. *Trent's Last Case*, E. C. Bentley, 1912.

Martin, a young milkman. *Nobody Answered the Bell*, Rhys Davies, 1971.

Martin, Brother, of St Illods. 'The Eye of Allah' (s.s.), *Debits and Credits*, R. Kipling, 1926.

Martin, Dame, 'Queen of the Revels.' *Redgauntlet*, W. Scott, 1824.

Martin, Dr, doctor to the Pontifexes. *The Way of all Flesh*, S. Butler, 1903.

Martin, Earl of Elchester, Crusader.
The Old Earl, his grandfather.
Unending Crusade, R. E. Sherwood, 1932.

Martin, Miss, George Smith's secretary. *A Singular Man*, J. P. Donleavy, 1964.

Martin, Mrs.
Henry, her son.
'Her Son' (s.s.), *The Heir*, V. Sackville-West, 1922.

Martin, Mrs, landlady. *Northwest Passage*, Kenneth Roberts, 1938.

Martin, Mrs, grandmother of Swithin St Cleeve.
Giles, her late husband.
Two on a Tower, T. Hardy, 1882.

Martin, Agatha, Shiel Carne's governess.
Mabel, Flossie and **Violet,** her sisters.
The Brontës went to Woolworth's, Rachel Ferguson, 1931.

Martin, Donald, a young rancher. *The Ox-Bow Incident*, Walter Van Tilburg Clark, 1940.

Martin, Don Guillermo, Fascist tradesman. *For Whom the Bell Tolls,* E. Hemingway, 1940.

Martin, Phyl and **Dolly.**
  Maurice, their cousin.
  Invitation to the Waltz, Rosamond Lehmann, 1932.

Martin, Raymond, M.P. ('jelly-bellied flag-flapper'). 'The Flag of their Country,' *Stalky & Co.,* R. Kipling, 1899.

Martin, Richard ('Shifty Dick'). *Put Yourself in his Place,* C. Reade, 1870.

Martin, Robert, owner of Abbey Mill Farm, m. Harriet Smith.
  His mother.
  Emma, Jane Austen, 1816.

Martin, Sally, deformed girl. 'Janet's Repentance,' *Scenes of Clerical Life,* George Eliot, 1857.

Martin, Sponge, workman. *Dark Laughter,* Sherwood Anderson, 1925.

Martindale, Lord and Lady.
  Their children:
    John.
    Arthur, m. Violet Moss.
      Johnnie, Helen and **Arthur,** their children.
    Theodora, m. Percy Fotheringham.
  Heartsease, Charlotte M. Yonge, 1854.

Martindale, Dorcas, attendant on Clarissa Harlowe in her captivity. *Clarissa Harlowe,* S. Richardson, 1748.

Martineau, Dr, Harley Street specialist. *The Secret Places of the Heart,* H. G. Wells, 1922.

Martinez, Antonio Joseph, renegade priest and landowner. *Death Comes for the Archbishop,* Willa Cather, 1927.

Martingale, Major Bob, friend of Rawdon Crawley. *Vanity Fair,* W. M. Thackeray, 1847–8.

Martius, son of Titus Andronicus. *Titus Andronicus* (play), W. Shakespeare.

Martock, Dr and Mrs.
  Arthur, their son.
  My Brother Jonathan, F. Brett Young, 1928.

Marton, kindly old schoolmaster and parish clerk. *The Old Curiosity Shop,* C. Dickens, 1840.

Marton, Anne, m. Jonathan Hare. *I Live Under a Black Sun,* Edith Sitwell, 1937.

Martyn. 'The Rout of the White Hussars' (s.s.), *Plain Tales from the Hills,* R. Kipling, 1888.

Martyn, James.
  His children:
    Alec.
    Sheila.
    Honor.
    Edith, m. Jonathan Dakers.
  My Brother Jonathan, F. Brett Young, 1928.

Martyn, John, doctor. *Landscape with Figures,* R. Fraser, 1925.

Martyn, Stella, mother of Cherry Davies. *September Tide,* Daphne du Maurier, 1948.

Martyn, William, master's mate, later captain. *In Greek Waters,* G. A. Henty, 1892.

Martyn, William ('William the Conqueror'), m. Scott.
  Her brother, in the police.
  'William the Conqueror' (s.s.), *The Day's Work,* R. Kipling, 1898.

Marvel, John, central character and narrator. *The Splendid Spur,* A. Quiller-Couch, 1889.

Marvell, Ralph ('The Little Fellow'), 2nd husband of Undine Spragg.
    Paul, their son.
  Ralph's mother, *née* Dagonet.
  Urban, his grandfather.
  Clare, his sister, m. Henley Fairford.
  The Custom of the Country, Edith Wharton, 1913.

Marvell, Viola, daughter of college friend of Charles Plethern, whom she m. *Desolate Splendour,* M. Sadleir, 1923.

Marvin, General, in command of American invasion troops in Italy. *A Bell for Adano,* John Hersey, 1944.

Marwood, Mrs, mistress of the 4th Lord Castlewood. *Henry Esmond,* W. M. Thackeray, 1852.

Marwood, Mrs, friend of Fainall. *The Way of the World* (play), W. Congreve, 1700.

Marx, Bernard, citizen of the future. *Brave New World,* Aldous Huxley, 1932.

Marx, Carlo, animal trainer in circus, lover of Venetia Barnard. *A Net for Venus,* David Garnett, 1959.

Marxse, Madame, lodging - house keeper. *The Constant Nymph*, Margaret Kennedy, 1924.

Mary, orphan, maid of the Macraes, mistress of Fergus Macrae. *The Brothers*, L. A. G. Strong, 1932.

Mary. 'Marching to Zion' (s.s.), *Adam and Eve and Pinch Me*, A. E. Coppard, 1921.

Mary, maid to Mrs Brandon. *The Adventures of Philip*, W. M. Thackeray, 1861–2.

Mary, victim of operation by Dr Raymond. *The Great God Pan*, A. Machen, 1894.

Mary, housemaid to Nupkins, m. Sam Weller. *Pickwick Papers*, C. Dickens, 1837.

Mary, Mrs, an eminent actress. *Caprice*, Ronald Firbank, 1917.

Mary Andrew, Mother Scholastic. *The Land of Spices*, Kate O'Brien, 1941.

Mary Anne, maid to the Copperfields. *David Copperfield*, C. Dickens, 1850.

Mary Jane, who wouldn't eat rice pudding. 'Rice Pudding' (poem), *When We Were Very Young*, A. A. Milne, 1924.

Marzo. *Captain Brassbound's Conversion* (play), G. B. Shaw, 1900.

Masapo, Zulu chief, m. Mameena. *Child of Storm*, H. Rider Haggard, 1913.

Maske, Lord. *The Story of Ragged Robyn*, O. Onions, 1945.

Maskelyne, a British intelligence officer. *Justine* and others in *The Alexandria Quartet*, 1957–61, Lawrence Durrell.

Maskery, Will, wheelwright and converted drunkard. *Adam Bede*, George Eliot, 1859.

Maso, aged servitor of the Bardi family. *Romola*, George Eliot, 1863.

Mason, Sir Robert Chilton's butler. *An Ideal Husband* (play), O. Wilde, 1895.

Mason, maths master. *Stalky & Co.*, R. Kipling, 1899.

Mason. *Journey's End* (play), R. C. Sherriff, 1928.

Mason, Archdeacon. *Mr Fortune's Maggot*, Sylvia Townsend Warner, 1927.

Mason, Sergeant. *Hamlet, Revenge!*, M. Innes, 1937.

Mason, Bertha, m. Mr Rochester.
Richard, her brother.
Jane Eyre, Charlotte Brontë, 1847.

Mason, Sir Frank.
His wife.
Emma ('Ritzi'), their daughter.
The Benefactor, J. D. Beresford.

Mason, Ned. *If Four Walls Told* (play), E. Percy, 1922.

Mason, Orville W., district attorney. *An American Tragedy*, T. Dreiser, 1925.

Mason, Perry, detective-lawyer, chief character in *The Case of the Blonde Bonanza*, 1962 and many others, Erle Stanley Gardner.

Mason, Roland, murderer. 'Aunt Hetty' (s.s.), *Sir Pompey and Madame Juno*, M. Armstrong, 1927.

Mason, Sarah, old nurse to Colonel Newcome. *The Newcomes*, W. M. Thackeray, 1853–5.

Masquerier, Bat, impresario. 'The Village that Voted the Earth was Flat' (s.s.), *A Diversity of Creatures*, R. Kipling, 1917.

Masrur, Caliph's executioner. *Hassan* (play), J. E. Flecker, 1923.

Massan, chief assistant to the furhunters. *Ungava*, R. M. Ballantyne, 1857.

Massey, Rev. Edward, m. Mary Lindley.
Their son.
Daughters of the Vicar (s.s.), D. H. Lawrence.

Massinger, Clare, sculptress, m. Nigel Strangeways. *The Widow's Cruise*, 1959 and others, Nicholas Blake.

Massinghay, Weston, Conservative politician. *The New Machiavelli*, 1911, and elsewhere, H. G. Wells.

Masson, Dorothy, secretary to Francis Chelifer. *Those Barren Leaves*, A. Huxley, 1925.

Masterman, consumptive socialist, friend of Sid Pornick. *Kipps*, H. G. Wells, 1905.

Masters, Lieutenant, of the *Justinian*. The *Hornblower* series, C. S. Forester, 1937 onwards.

Masters, Dr Conrad. *The Green Hat*, M. Arlen, 1924.

Masters, John, close friend of Tom Fould. *Tom Fool*, F. Tennyson Jesse, 1926.

Masters, Madeleine, *née* Burkett, central character.
Rickie, her husband.
Anthony, their son.
Colin, their son.
Clarissa, their daughter.
Dinah Dorothea Burkett, Madeleine's sister, m. Jo Hermann.
The Echoing Grove, Rosamond Lehmann, 1953.

Masters, Minnie and **Nelly.** *Yellow Sands* (play), E. Phillpotts, 1926.

Masters, Rodney. *The Young Idea* (play), N. Coward, 1923.

Masterson, Reuben, love-sick heir to a Chicago department store. *Eustace Chisholm and the Works,* James Purdy, 1968.

Masterton, Jill, Goldfinger's girl friend, whom he murders.
Tilly, her sister, who seeks to kill Goldfinger.
Goldfinger, Ian Fleming, 1959.

Mat, Malay guide. *Gallions Reach,* H. M. Tomlinson, 1927.

Matany, Count Tibor.
His mother.
Fritzi, his niece.
Mihaly, his nephew.
They Wanted to Live, Cecil Roberts, 1939.

Matanza, Ruiz de la, Captain of *La Fortuna. Anthony Adverse,* Hervey Allen, 1934.

Matcham, Mrs, friend of Mrs Twysden.
Rosa, her daughter.
The Adventures of Philip, W. M. Thackeray, 1861–2.

Matcham, Sergeant Gervase. 'The Dead Drummer' (poem), *The Ingoldsby Legends,* R. H. Barham, 1837.

Matcham, John. *See* JOANNA SEDLEY.

Matchett, old family servant. *The Death of the Heart,* Elizabeth Bowen, 1938.

Mately, Dorothy, thief, killed by miraculous act of God. *The Life and Death of Mr Badman,* J. Bunyan, 1680.

Matey, Jim, Lob's butler. *Dear Brutus* (play), J. M. Barrie, 1917.

Matfield, Miss. *Angel Pavement,* J. B. Priestley, 1930.

Mather, Danny, central character.
Helen, his wife.
Edward, their son.
Angela, his mother, *née* Letford.
Frederick, his dead father.
No News from Helen, L. Golding, 1943.

Mathers, Walter, racehorse owner. 'I'm a Fool' (s.s.), *Horses and Men,* Sherwood Anderson, 1924.

Matheson, Lady. *Separate Tables* (play), T. Rattigan, 1955.

Mathews, Andrew and **Stella,** friends of Martha Quest. *Children of Violence* series, Doris Lessing, 1952–69.

Mathias, lawyer. *High Wind in Jamaica,* R. Hughes, 1929.

Mathias.
Katharine, his mother.
The Jew of Malta (play), C. Marlowe, 1633.

Mathias, Father. *The Phantom Ship,* Captain Marryat, 1839.

Mathias, Gethin, a collier interested in literature.
John, his son, friend of Penry Bowen.
Shan, his daughter.
Tomorrow To Fresh Woods, Rhys Davies, 1941.

Matilda, emissary of the Devil, posing as Rosario, young novice; seducer of Ambrosio. *The Monk,* M. G. Lewis, 1795.

Matilda, bawdy Negress housekeeper. *A Singular Man,* J. P. Donleavy, 1964.

Matkah. *See* SEA CATCH.

Matthew, chief clerk and partner of Adam Silvercross. *The Old Bank,* W. Westall, 1902.

Matthew of Doncaster, bowyer. *Anne of Geierstein,* W. Scott, 1829.

Matthews, servant to Gregsbury, M.P. *Nicholas Nickleby,* C. Dickens, 1839.

Matthews, Grant.
Mollie, his wife.
Young Grant, their son, eldest of six boys.
Maggie, their daughter.
Pete, her illegitimate son by Howard Howittat.
The Shepherd of the Hills, H. B. Wright, 1907.

Matthews, Rev. Roger, central character.
Ruth, his wife.
Rosemary, their daughter.
Another Year, R. C. Sherriff, 1948.

Mattie, Mrs Parkington's maid. *Mrs Parkington,* L. Bromfield, 1944.

Matuchevitz, Prince, Russian ambassador. *Jorrocks's Jaunts and Jollities,* R. S. Surtees, 1838.

Matun, blind beggar. 'The Truce of the Bear' (poem), *The Five Nations,* R. Kipling, 1903.

Mauban, Antoinette de. *The Prisoner of Zenda,* A. Hope, 1894.

Maudsley, Marian, m. Viscount Trimingham.
  W. H. Maudsley, her father, a landowner.
  Madeleine, her mother.
  Marcus and **Denys,** her brothers.
The Go-Between, L. P. Hartley, 1953.

Maule, Matthew, carpenter.
  Matthew, his grandfather, executed as a wizard.
The House of the Seven Gables, N. Hawthorne, 1851.

Mauleverer, Earl of. *Paul Clifford,* Lord Lytton, 1830.

Mauleverer, Lord. *Cranford,* Mrs Gaskell, 1853.

Mauleverer, Lord, schoolboy at Greyfriars. The *Billy Bunter* series, Frank Richards.

Mauleverer, Lucinda, m. Sir Oliver Raydon.
  Colonel Mauleverer, her father, killed in duel with Sir Oliver.
  Vincent, her brother.
An Affair of Dishonour, W. de Morgan, 1910.

Mauley, Sir Edward, The Black Dwarf, wealthy victim of his treacherous friend Richard Vere. *The Black Dwarf,* W. Scott, 1816.

Maulfry, woman ally of Galors. *The Forest Lovers,* M. Hewlett, 1898.

Maulnier, Colonel. *The Other Side,* Storm Jameson, 1946.

Maundrell, Viscount (Cecil), only son of the Earl of Barnstaple. *American Wives and English Husbands,* Gertrude Atherton, 1898.

Maung, H'La, native ex-servant of Elizabeth Clutter. *No Other Tiger,* A. E. W. Mason, 1927.

Maurewarde, Major. *His House in Order* (play), A. W. Pinero, 1906.

Maurice, Sir Robert, Bt, M.P., narrator. *The Martian,* George du Maurier, 1897.

Maury, Angele, actress.
  Hannah Kernahans, her aunt.
    Tom and **Martin,** Hannah's sons.
The Last of Summer, Kate O'Brien, 1943.

Mavis, member of gang living in bomb sites. *The World My Wilderness,* Rose Macaulay, 1950.

Mavis, Annie, maid of the Pressets. *We the Accused,* E. Raymond, 1935.

Mavromichales, Yanni.
  Dramali, his father.
The Capsina, E. F. Benson, 1899.

Maw, solicitor. *Sweet Lavender* (play), A. W. Pinero, 1888.

Maw-worm, a vulgar knave. *The Hypocrite,* I. Bickerstaffe, 1768.

Mawmsey, grocer.
  His wife.
Middlemarch, Geo. Eliot, 1871–2.

Mawson, Winifred, Pamela Reston's maid. *Penny Plain,* O. Douglas, 1920.

Max, German student in love with Becky Sharp. *Vanity Fair,* W. M. Thackeray, 1847–8.

Max, Susan, elderly actress. *Enter a Murderer,* Ngaio Marsh, 1935.

Maxey, Maisie, m. Oliver Thorpe.
  Prentice, her father.
  Lady Sarah, her mother.
Joseph Vance, W. de Morgan, 1906.

Maximus, Emperor of Britain (hist.). 'A Centurion of the Thirtieth,' *Puck of Pook's Hill,* R. Kipling, 1906.

Maxley, James, villainous miser.
  His wife.
Hard Cash, C. Reade, 1863.

Maxwell. Family name of LORD EVANDALE.

Maxwell, Lord, grandfather of Aldous Raeburn.
  His daughter.
Marcella, Mrs Humphry Ward, 1894.

Maxwell, Mrs, aunt of Helen Graham.
  Her husband.
The Tenant of Wildfell Hall, Anne Brontë, 1848.

Maxwell, Sir Angus, brother-in-law of Sir Gulliver Deniston.
  Cynthia, his wife.
The World My Wilderness, Rose Macaulay, 1950.

Maxwell, Gilbert.
Delia, his wife.
'The Brownings' (s.s.), *Louise,* Viola Meynell, 1954.

Maxwell, Mary ('May Mischief'), central character.
Richard, her father.
Her brothers:
Will.
Peter ('Patie').
Richard.
David.
Kennedy.
Steenie.
Lady Grizel, her cousin.
The Raiders, S. R. Crockett, 1894.

Maxwell of Summertrees ('Pate-in-Peril'), old Jacobite. *Redgauntlet,* W. Scott, 1824.

May, 'a Scottish treasure', James Bond's housekeeper. *Thunderball,* 1961, and others, Ian Fleming.

May, Dr and Mrs.
Their children:
Richard, clergyman.
Margaret, eng. to Alan Ernescliffe, who died.
Flora, m. George Rivers.
Norman, m. Meta Rivers.
Richard, their son.
Ethelred.
Harry.
Mary, m. Rev. Charles Cheviot.
Tom, m. Averil Ward.
Blanche, m. Hector Ernescliffe.
Aubrey.
Gertrude ('Daisy').
The Daisy Chain, 1856, and elsewhere, Charlotte M. Yonge.

May, Mr, manager of James Houghton's cinema. *The Lost Girl,* D. H. Lawrence, 1920.

Maybold, Rev. Arthur, incumbent of Mellstock.
His mother.
Under the Greenwood Tree, T. Hardy, 1872.

Maybud, Rose, village maiden, m. Dick Dauntless. *Ruddigore* (comic opera), Gilbert & Sullivan, 1887.

Mayer, Dr, stage manager, Metropolitan Opera House. *Grand Opera,* Vicki Baum, 1942.

Mayflower, Phoebe, Alice Lee's maid. *Woodstock,* W. Scott, 1826.

Mayhew, Rev. Mr, m. Eva Lilly. *The Oriel Window,* Mrs Molesworth, 1896.

Mayhew, Lincoln. *Other Gods,* Pearl Buck, 1940.

Mayli, mission teacher. *Dragon Seed,* Pearl Buck, 1942.

Maylie, Mrs, befriends Oliver.
Harrie, her son.
Rose, her adopted daughter (*see* FLEMING), m. Harrie.
Oliver Twist, C. Dickens, 1838.

Maynard, college friend of Philip Firmin. *The Adventures of Philip,* W. M. Thackeray, 1861–2.

Maynard, Mr, South African magistrate.
Binkie, his son, leader of a gang of 'hearties'.
Children of Violence series, Doris Lessing, 1952–69.

Maynard, Elsie, strolling player, m. Colonel Fairfax. *The Yeomen of the Guard* (comic opera), Gilbert & Sullivan, 1888.

Maynard, Jim, eng. to Annie Bolt. *All Our Yesterdays,* H. M. Tomlinson, 1930.

Maynard, Roger.
His wife.
Non-Combatants and Others, Rose Macaulay, 1916.

Maynard, Rose, 'elfin child,' materialized heroine of the Pinckney novels. *Meet Mr Mulliner,* P. G. Wodehouse, 1927.

Mayne, Farmer.
His wife.
Peter, their son.
Laura's Bishop, G. A. Birmingham, 1949.

Mayton, Alice, m. Harry Burton.
Her mother.
Helen's Babies, J. Habberton, 1876.

Mazaro, Manuel, Cuban traitor. 'Café des Exiles' (s.s.), *Old Creole Days,* G. W. Cable, 1879.

Mazey, seafaring friend of Admiral Bartram. *No Name,* W. Collins, 1862.

M. de C. ('Antonio'), French spy. 'The Bonds of Discipline' (s.s.), *Traffics and Discoveries,* R. Kipling, 1904.

Meacham, Miss. *Separate Tables* (play), T. Rattigan, 1955.

Meade, Dr.
His wife.
Darcy and **Phil,** their sons.
Gone with the Wind, Margaret Mitchell, 1936.

Meade, General. *Abraham Lincoln* (play), J. Drinkwater, 1918.

Meade, Michael, owner of Imber Court. *The Bell,* Iris Murdoch, 1958.

Meader, Zeb. *Mr Crewe's Career,* W. Churchill, 1908.

Meadow, James B., super-crook. 'The Burglar' (s.s.), *Cops 'n' Robbers,* J. Russell, 1913.

Meadowes, Lady Mary, m. the Earl of Pastmaster. *Put Out More Flags,* E. Waugh, 1942.

Meadows, Miss. 'The Singing Lesson' (s.s.), *The Garden Party,* Katherine Mansfield, 1922.

Meadows, Mrs, formerly Retlow, cousin of Thomas Heard. *South Wind,* N. Douglas, 1917.

Meadows, Fay, friend of Gordon Bryan. *The Water Gipsies,* A. P. Herbert, 1930.

Meadows, John, farmer, owner of the Black Horse; in love with Susan Merton.
His mother.
It Is Never Too Late to Mend, C. Reade, 1856.

Meadows, Miss Sally. *Uncle Remus,* J. C. Harris, 1880–95.

Meadows, Private Tim. *A Sleep of Prisoners* (play), Christopher Fry, 1951.

Meagles, retired banker.
His wife.
'Pet,' their daughter, m. Harry Gowan.
Little Dorrit, C. Dickens, 1857.

Mealmaker, Andrew. *The Little Minister,* J. M. Barrie, 1891.

Mealmaker, Tibbie.
David, her husband.
A Window in Thrums, J. M. Barrie, 1889.

Meander, a Persian lord. *Tamburlaine* (play), C. Marlowe, 1587.

Means, Eliphalet, lawyer. *Jerome,* Mary E. Wilkins, 1897.

Means, Tom. The Man Who Became a Woman' (s.s.), *Horses and Men,* Sherwood Anderson, 1924.

Meares, Mrs. *Sylvia Scarlett,* C. Mackenzie, 1918.

Mears, Charlie, bank clerk who remembers his former lives. 'The Finest Story in the World' (s.s.), *Many Inventions,* R. Kipling, 1893.

Meath, Larry. *Love on the Dole,* W. Greenwood, 1933.

Meats, Henry (alias Barnes, alias Brother Aloysius), bad hat and murderer. *Sinister Street,* C. Mackenzie, 1913.

Mecaenas, friend of Octavius Caesar. *Antony and Cleopatra* (play), W. Shakespeare.

Meda, Indian medicine-man. *The Song of Hiawatha* (poem), H. W. Longfellow, 1855.

Media, native king. *Mardi,* Herman Melville, 1849.

Medici, Angelo de and **Hjordis de.** *See Naples and Die* (play), Elmer Rice, 1932.

Medici, Francisco de, Duke of Florence.
Cardinal Monticelso, his brother.
The White Devil (play), John Webster, *c.* 1612.

Medina, stepsister of Elissa. *The Faërie Queene* (poem), E. Spenser, 1590.

Medina, Duke of.
Agnes, his daughter, m. Raymond de la Casternas.
Don Lorenzo, his nephew, m. (1) Antonia, (2) Virginia.
The Monk, M. G. Lewis, 1796.

Medina Saroté, with whom Nunez falls in love.
Yacob, her father.
The Country of the Blind (s.s.), H. G. Wells, 1911.

Medlicote, Lord, patron of hospital, *Middlemarch,* Geo. Eliot, 1871–2.

Medlock, Moses, Jewish swindler. *Reginald Cruden,* T. Baines Reed, 1894.

Medon, old slave. *The Last Days of Pompeii,* Lord Lytton, 1834.

Medora. *The Corsair* (poem), Lord Byron, 1814.

Medway, Duchess of. 'The Article in Question,' *Lord Peter Views the Body,* Dorothy L. Sayers, 1928.

Medway, Barbara, m. Ferdinand Dibble. *The Heart of a Goof,* P. G. Wodehouse, 1926.

Medwin, Gladys, m. Wilfred Bruce. *Dr Nikola,* G. Boothby, 1896.

Meeber, Carrie, girl from small town in Wisconsin. *Sister Carrie,* Theodore Dreiser, 1900.

Meek, Mr and Mrs. *Mr Weston's Good Wine,* T. F. Powys, 1927.

Meek, Rev. Josiah, m. Helen Green. *The Adventures of Mr Verdant Green,* C. Bede, 1853.

Meekin, Rev. Mr, chaplain to convicts. *For the Term of his Natural Life*, M. Clarke, 1874.

Meeks, copperflue salesman. *The Violent Bear It Away*, Flannery O'Connor, 1960.

Meg, of The Ramme, m. George Saxton. *The White Peacock*, D. H. Lawrence, 1911.

Megatherium, Lord, gouty and aged. *Middlemarch*, Geo. Eliot, 1871–2.

Megea, court lady. *Philaster* (play), Beaumont & Fletcher, *c.* 1609.

Meggatt, Rodney, m. Janet Studdard.
 Hermione, their daughter.
 Considine, his uncle.
 Friends and Relations, Elizabeth Bowen, 1931.

Meggot, Mrs Betsy.
 Jane and **Nancy,** her daughters.
 Mrs Perkins's Ball, W. M. Thackeray, 1847.

Meggs, a volunteer. 'The Alarm,' *Wessex Poems*, T. Hardy, 1898.

mehitabel, the cat. *archy and mehitabel* (poems), D. Marquis, 1927.

Mei-Hua, the Chinese rose, abbess of a Tibetan monastery, also known as the Good Mother. *The Rose of Tibet*, Lionel Davidson, 1962.

Meikleham, Lord. *See* Earl of Liftore.

Meiklejohn, Giles, clerk.
 Eleanor, his wife.
 The Brown Wallet (s.s.), Stacy Aumonier.

Meiklewham, Saunders, 'the man of law.' *St Ronan's Well*, W. Scott, 1824.

Meinev, Burman guide and servant of Stanley Brooke. *On the Irrawaddy*, G. A. Henty, 1897.

Meininger, Lili, m. Max Schmalz. *Tom Tiddler's Ground*, E. Shanks, 1934.

Meisner, Emil, friend of Lanny Budd.
 Kurt, his brother.
 Dragon Harvest, Upton Sinclair, 1946.

Meister, Maurice, solicitor. *The Ringer* (play), E. Wallace, 1926.

Mel, Marquess of. *Quinneys'*, H. A. Vachell, 1914.

Melantius, brother of Evadne. *The Maid's Tragedy* (play), Beaumont & Fletcher, 1611.

Melba, popular singer who marries Malcolm. *Malcolm*, James Purdy, 1959.

Melbury, George.
 Lucy, his 2nd wife.
 Grace, his daughter by 1st wife, m. Edred Fitzpiers.
 The Woodlanders, T. Hardy, 1887.

Melchester, Bishop of (Cuthbert Helmsdale). *Two on a Tower*, T. Hardy, 1882.

Melchitsekek, Pinchas, poor poet and scholar. *Children of the Ghetto*, Israel Zangwill, 1892.

Meldrum, Brookfield headmaster. *Goodbye, Mr Chips*, J. Hilton, 1934.

Meldrum, Duchess of (Georgina), aunt of Jane Champion. *The Rosary*, Florence Barclay, 1909.

Meldrum, Philip, central character, m. Marguerite Falconer. *A Knight on Wheels*, Ian Hay, 1914.

Meleager, Uncle. 'Uncle Meleager's Will,' *Lord Peter Views the Body*, Dorothy L. Sayers, 1928.

Melema, Tito, Greek scholar, adopted son of Baldassarre Calvo, m. Romola de Bardi. *See also* Tessa. *Romola*, George Eliot, 1863.

Melesinda. *Mr H.* (play), C. Lamb, 1806.

Melford, Jeremy, nephew of the Brambles.
 Lydia, his romantic sister, m. Dennison.
 Humphry Clinker, T. Smollett, 1771.

Melhuish, Mr, friend of Andrew Maning. *The Benefactor*, J. D. Beresford.

'Melia, housemaid to Dr Blimber. *Dombey and Son*, C. Dickens, 1848.

Meliboeus.
 Prudence, his wife.
 Sophia, their daughter.
 'The Tale of Meliboeus' (poem), *Canterbury Tales*, G. Chaucer, 1373 onwards.

Melicent, Dame. *Jurgen*, J. B. Cabell, 1921.

Melisande, Zuleika's maid. *Zuleika Dobson*, Max Beerbohm, 1911.

Melissa. *See* Lady Blanche.

Melissa, a bee. 'The Mother Hive' (s.s.), *Actions and Reactions*, R. Kipling, 1909.

Mell, Charles, assistant master to Creakle. *David Copperfield*, C. Dickens, 1850.

Mellaby, publisher, and friend of John Tryte. *Portrait of a Playboy*, W. Deeping, 1947.

Mellida. *Antonio and Mellida* (play), J. Marston, 1602.

Mellings, Lord. *See* POMFRET.

Mellish, E. S. 'A Germ Destroyer' (s.s.), *Plain Tales from the Hills*, R. Kipling, 1888.

Mello, Dr Sebastian. *Handley Cross*, R. S. Surtees, 1843.

Mellon, Mrs, housekeeper to Lord Dorincourt. *Little Lord Fauntleroy*, Frances H. Burnett, 1886.

Mellors, Oliver, gamekeeper in love with Connie Chatterley. *Lady Chatterley's Lover*, D. H. Lawrence, 1928.

Mellot, Claude, artist.
Sabina, his wife.
Two Years Ago, C. Kingsley, 1857.

Melmoth, John, young Irishman.
Melmoth the Wanderer, his ill-starred ancestor.
Melmoth the Wanderer, Charles Robert Maturin, 1820.

Melmotte, Marie, m. Hamilton K. Fisker.
Augustus, her father, swindling financier.
The Way We Live Now, A. Trollope, 1875.

Melnotte, Claude.
His mother.
The Lady of Lyons (play), Lord Lytton, 1838.

Melopoyn, poet. *Roderick Random*, T. Smollett, 1748.

Melos. *The Sign of the Cross*, W. Barrett, 1896.

Melrose, Rev. Mr. 'Fellow Townsmen,' *Wessex Tales*, T. Hardy, 1888.

Meltham. *See* MAJOR BANKS.

Melton, Ernest.
Elma, his wife.
Canaries Sometimes Sing (play), F. Lonsdale, 1929.

Melvil, Sir John. *The Clandestine Marriage* (play), G. Colman the Elder, 1766.

Melville, friend of Harry Chatteris. *The Sea Lady*, H. G. Wells, 1902.

Melville, Captain, blackmailer. 'The Practical Joker,' *Lord Peter Views the Body*, Dorothy L. Sayers, 1925.

Melville, Henry, m. Anne de Travers. *Bluebeard's Keys*, Anne Thackeray, 1874.

Melville, Howard, actor. *Enter a Murderer*, Ngaio Marsh, 1935.

Melville, Julia. *The Rivals* (play), R. B. Sheridan, 1775.

Melville, Major William, Laird of Calnvreckan. *Waverley*, W. Scott, 1814.

Members, Mark, literary critic. *A Question of Upbringing*, 1951, and others in *The Music of Time* series, Anthony Powell.

Memsworth, Mr. *The Good Companions*, J. B. Priestley, 1929.

Menaida, Zachary, taxidermist.
Oliver, his son.
In the Roar of the Sea, S. Baring-Gould, 1892.

Menaphon, a Persian lord. *Tamburlaine* (play), C. Marlowe, 1587.

Menas, friend of Pompey. *Antony and Cleopatra* (play), W. Shakespeare.

Mendel, friend of Stephen Trink. *The Bloomsbury Wonder* (s.s.), T. Burke.

Mendham, Rev. George, curate, later Vicar of Siddermorton.
Minnie, his wife.
The Wonderful Visit, H. G. Wells, 1895.

Mendip, Thomas, soldier discharged from the Flanders wars about year 1400. *The Lady's Not For Burning* (play), Christopher Fry, 1948.

Mendoza. *Man and Superman* (play), G. B. Shaw, 1903.

Mendoza, Duke of, court chamberlain. *The Four Armourers*, F. Beeding, 1930.

Mendoza, General, villainous leader of revolution. *Soldiers of Fortune*, R. H. Davis, 1897.

Mendoza, Isaac. *The Duenna* (play), R. B. Sheridan, 1775.

Menecrates, friend of Pompey. *Antony and Cleopatra* (play), W. Shakespeare.

Menelaus, brother of Agamemnon, m. Helen. *Troilus and Cressida* (play), W. Shakespeare.

Menenius Agrippa, friend of Coriolanus. *Coriolanus* (play), W. Shakespeare.

Mengan, Mrs, sister of Captain Lydgate. *Middlemarch*, George Eliot, 1871.

Mengo, Sir Alpheus, distinguished surgeon. *The Undying Fire,* H. G. Wells, 1919.

Mengs, Ian, landlord of the Golden Fleece. *Anne of Geierstein,* W. Scott, 1829.

Meninsky, a Jew, Peruvian trader. *The City of Gold,* F. Brett Young, 1939.

Menlove, Louisa, lady's maid. *The Hand of Ethelberta,* T. Hardy, 1876.

Mennick, secretary to Elmer Ford. *The Little Nugget,* P. G. Wodehouse, 1913.

Menou, Monsieur, landlord of the Hotel Poussin.
His wife.
The Adventures of Philip, W. M. Thackeray, 1861–2.

Menteith, Beau Austin's valet. *Beau Austin* (play), W. E. Henley & R. L. Stevenson, 1892.

Mento, Lady (Julia).
Bunny, her son.
Melloney Holtspur (play), J. Masefield, 1922.

Menzies, Anne, young Scottish hussy, *They Winter Abroad,* T. H. White. 1932.

Menzies, Donald, Free Church minister. *Beside the Bonnie Brier Bush,* I. Maclaren, 1894.

Menzies, Kate, widow, *née* Burnside, wealthy distant connection of Ronald Strang. *White Heather,* W. Black, 1885.

Menzies, Laura, secretary to Mrs Bradley, m. David Gavin. Gladys Mitchell's *Mrs Bradley* detective stories.

Meon, Saxon chief. 'The Conversion of St Wilfrid,' *Rewards and Fairies,* R. Kipling, 1910.

mephistopheles, Australian 'bad hat.' *See* BRUTUS. *It Is Never Too Late to Mend,* C. Reade, 1856.

Mephistopheles. *Doctor Faustus* (play), C. Marlowe, 1604.

Mercadet, 'Old,' interpreter. *Sixty-four, Ninety-four,* R. H. Mottram, 1925.

Mercaptan, writer, friend of Theodore Gumbril. *Antic Hay,* A. Huxley, 1923.

Mercia, Christian martyr. *The Sign of the Cross,* W. Barrett, 1896.

Mercier, Leonard, lover of Vi Ransome. *The Combined Maze,* May Sinclair, 1913.

Mercutio, friend of Romeo. *Romeo and Juliet* (play), W. Shakespeare.

Mercy, companion of Christian. *Pilgrim's Progress,* J. Bunyan, 1678, 1684.

Merdle, Mr, M.P. and swindling financier.
His wife.
Little Dorrit, C. Dickens, 1857.

Meredith, governess to Dorothy Bellairs's children. *The Fortress,* Hugh Walpole, 1932.

Meredith, schoolboy at Fernhurst. *The Loom of Youth,* A. Waugh, 1917.

Meredith, Chester, m. Felicia Blakeney. 'Chester Forgets Himself' (s.s.), *The Heart of a Goof,* P. G. Wodehouse, 1926.

Meredith, Lady Cleone, central character, m. Barnabas Barty. *The Amateur Gentleman,* J. Farnol, 1913.

Meredith, Gray, in love with Margaret Fairfield. *A Bill of Divorcement* (play), Clemence Dane, 1921.

Meredith, Honor, m. Theo Desmond as 2nd wife.
John, her brother.
General Sir John, K.C.B., her father.
Captain Desmond, V.C., Maud Diver, 1906.

Meredith, Jack.
Sir John, Bt, his father.
With Edged Tools, H. Seton Merriman, 1894.

Meredith, Lady (Justinia), *née* Lufton. *Framley Parsonage,* A. Trollope, 1861.

Meredith, Peter, central character and narrator. *Lost Sir Massingberd,* James Payn, 1864.

Meredith, Sir Rowland, matchmaking Welsh uncle of Fowler. *Sir Charles Grandison,* S. Richardson, 1754.

Meredith, William, ex-mayor of Silchester.
Nell, his daughter.
When a Man's Single, J. M. Barrie, 1888.

Meres, Fred, m. Dorothy Simpson.
Rosie, their daughter.
Simpson, E. Sackville-West, 1931.

Mereston, Lord and Lady. *Lady Frederick* (play), W. S. Maugham, 1907.

Mergle, Miss, schoolmistress. *The Wheels of Chance,* H. G. Wells, 1896.

Mergleson, Sir Peter Laxton's butler. *Bealby,* H. G. Wells, 1915.

Merivale, Dr. *Goodbye, Mr Chips,* J. Hilton 1934.

Merivale, Alan, school friend of Michael Fane, m. Stella Fane. *Sinister Street,* 1913, etc., C. Mackenzie.

Merivale, Maisie.
 James, her son.
Manhattan Transfer, J. dos Passos, 1925.

Merkalova, Russian spy, guest at Scamnum. *Hamlet, Revenge!,* M. Innes, 1937.

Merle, Mme, Isabel Archer's friend, ex-mistress of Gilbert Osmond. *The Portrait of a Lady,* Henry James, 1881.

Merlin, guardian of King Arthur. *Idylls of the King* (poem), Lord Tennyson, 1859.

Merlin, Lord. *The Pursuit of Love,* Nancy Mitford, 1945.

Merlin, Anthony, K.C., counsel for Jane Palfrey. *Antigua Penny Puce,* R. Graves, 1936.

Merlin, Dorothy, Australian verse-dramatist, m. Cosmo Hines. *The Unspeakable Skipton,* Pamela Hansford Johnson, 1959.

Merman, Proteus.
 Julia, his wife.
Theophrastus Such, George Eliot, 1879.

Meromic, Gallic patriot, central character.
 Kormiac the Wolf, his father.
 Fiommar, his sister.
The Conquered, Naomi Mitchison, 1923.

Merrick, cousin of Clare Browell. *Right Off the Map,* C. E. Montague, 1927.

Merrick, Alan.
 Sir Arthur, his father.
The Woman who Did, Grant Allen, 1895.

Merridew, Mrs, widowed sister of Sir John Verinder. *The Moonstone,* W. Collins, 1868.

Merridew, Mrs Alice, friend of Mary Adam. *Holy Deadlock,* A. P. Herbert, 1934.

Merrilies, Meg, gipsy queen. *Guy Mannering,* W. Scott, 1815.

Merrill, Mr and Mrs, employers of Robert Black. *No Son of Mine,* G. B. Stern, 1948.

Merriman, solicitor to Sir Percival Glyde. *The Woman in White,* W. Collins, 1860.

Merriman, John Worthing's butler. *The Importance of being Earnest* (play), O. Wilde, 1895.

Merriman, American journalist. *But Soft—We Are Observed!,* H. Belloc, 1928.

Merriman, Miss ('Merry'), companion to Lady Emily Leslie, later to Lady Pomfret; m. Rev. Mr Choyce. The *Barsetshire* series, Angela Thirkell, 1933 onwards.

Merritt, Squire Eben.
 Lucina, his daughter, m. Jerome Edwards.
 Camilla, his sister.
Jerome, Mary E. Wilkins, 1897.

Merrivale, Sir Henry, K.C., amateur sleuth. *The Judas Window,* 1938, and many others, C. Dickson.

Merriwether, Mrs Dolly.
 Maybelle, her daughter.
Gone with the Wind, Margaret Mitchell, 1936.

Merry, of the *Hispaniola. Treasure Island,* R. L. Stevenson, 1882.

Merry, Charles, Latin teacher.
 His wife.
Pastors and Masters, Ivy Compton-Burnett, 1925.

Merrythought.
 His wife.
 Jasper and **Michael,** their sons.
The Knight of the Burning Pestle (play), Beaumont & Fletcher, 1609.

Merton, 'in the wine trade.' *The Diary of a Nobody,* G. & W. Grossmith, 1892.

Merton, Rev. Mr.
 His wife.
 Caroline, their eldest daughter.
Alice, Lord Lytton, 1838.

Merton, Emily.
 General Merton, her father.
Afloat and Ashore, J. Fenimore Cooper, 1844.

Merton, Hetty. *The Picture of Dorian Gray,* O. Wilde, 1891.

Merton, Noel (later **Sir**), barrister, m. Lydia Keith.
 Their children:
  Lavinia, m. Lord Mellings.
  Harry.
  Jessica.
The *Barsetshire* series, Angela Thirkell, 1933 onwards.

Merton, Susan, m. George Fielding, loved by Wilhem Fielding.
Her father.
It Is Never Too Late to Mend, C. Reade, 1856.

Merton, Sybil, m. Lord Arthur Savile. *Lord Arthur Savile's Crime,* O. Wilde, 1891.

Merton, Tommy.
His father and mother.
Sandford and Merton, T. Day, 1783–9.

Mertoun, Basil (formerly Vaughan).
Mordaunt, his son by Louisa Gonzago. *See also* CAPTAIN CLEMENT CLEVELAND.
The Pirate, W. Scott, 1822.

Mertoun, Earl, Henry, suitor of Mildred Tresham. *A Blot in the 'Scutcheon* (play), Robert Browning, 1843.

Mervyn, Lieutenant Christopher, schoolmaster. 'The Tie' (s.s.), *Limits and Renewals,* R. Kipling, 1932.

Merygreeke, Matthew. *Ralph Roister Doister* (play), N. Udall, 1551.

Meryll, sergeant of yeomen, m. Dame Carruthers.
Phoebe, his daughter, m. Wilfred Shadbolt.
Leonard, his son.
The Yeomen of the Guard (comic opera), Gilbert & Sullivan, 1888.

Meshach, Jewish owner of sealing-wax factory. *The Great Hoggarty Diamond,* W. M. Thackeray, 1841.

Messala, Roman enemy of Ben Hur. *Ben Hur,* L. Wallace, 1880.

Messenger, Margaret, *née* Rivers.
Richard, her dead husband.
Their children:
Margaret Christina ('Nixie').
Arabella Lucy ('Toby').
Richard Jonathan ('Jonah').
The Education of Uncle Paul, A. Blackwood, 1909.

Messinger, Dr, explorer. *A Handful of Dust,* Evelyn Waugh, 1934.

Messiter, Mrs Dolly, friend of Laura Jesson. *Brief Encounter* (play), N. Coward, 1945.

Messua, Mowgli's foster- (or real) mother.
Her husband.
'Tiger Tiger' and others, *The Jungle Books,* R. Kipling, 1894–5.

Mesty, Negro servant. *Mr Midshipman Easy,* Captain Marryat, 1836.

Metellus Cimber, conspirator against Caesar. *Julius Caesar* (play), W. Shakespeare.

Meteyard, Miss, copywriter, Pym's Publicity. *Murder Must Advertise,* Dorothy L. Sayers, 1933.

Methusaleh, Lord, m. Emma Trotter. *Mrs Perkins's Ball,* 1847, and elsewhere, W. M. Thackeray.

Metroland, Viscount. *See* SIR HUMPHREY MALTRAVERS.

Meunier, Charles, physician, school friend of Latimer. *The Lifted Veil,* George Eliot, 1859.

Meunier, Jean, *concierge.*
His wife.
Yvonne, their daughter.
Through the Storm, P. Gibbs, 1945.

Meyerbogen, baker, and family, Bertha's last employer. *Lummox,* Fannie Hurst, 1924.

Meyrick, artist, victim of Helen Vaughan. *The Great God Pan,* A. Machen, 1894.

Meyrick, Mrs, half French, half Scottish.
Her children:
Hans, artist.
Amy, school-teacher.
Kate, artist.
Mabel, musical.
Daniel Deronda, George Eliot, 1876.

Micawber, Wilkins, agent for Murdstone & Grinby.
His wife.
Their four children.
David Copperfield, C. Dickens, 1850.

Michael, Mr Weston's junior partner. *Mr Weston's Good Wine,* T. F. Powys, 1927.

Michael. 'The Rash Bride' and 'The Dead Quire' (poems), *Time's Laughing Stocks,* T. Hardy, 1909.

Michael, Duke of Strelsau ('Black Michael'). *The Prisoner of Zenda,* A. Hope, 1894.

Michaelis, 'ticket-of-leave apostle', anarchist. *The Secret Agent,* Joseph Conrad, 1907.

Michaelis, young Irish playwright who has brief affair with Connie Chatterley. *Lady Chatterley's Lover,* D. H. Lawrence, 1928.

Michaelis, Karen, central character, m. Ray Forrestier. *See also* MAX EBHART. *The House in Paris,* Elizabeth Bowen, 1935.

Michaels, Father, priest on the torpedoed *Aurora*. *The Ocean,* J. Hanley, 1946.

Michailos, Eugene.
  Rachel, his wife.
  Tom Tiddler's Ground, E. Shanks, 1934.

Michel, a volunteer. 'The Alarm,' *Wessex Poems,* T. Hardy, 1898.

Michel, officer at Waterloo. 'The Peasant's Confession,' *Wessex Poems,* T. Hardy, 1898.

Michel, Berthe, m. Konrad Czelovar.
  Violette ('Letti'), her sister, m. Adrian Levine.
  Jules, their father.
  Their mother.
  Mosaic, 1930, and elsewhere, G. B. Stern.

Michel, Helen, artist, English widow of Maurice Michel. *See also* Sir Gulliver Deniston.
  Raoul, her stepson.
  Roland, her son.
  Her mother-in-law.
  Armand, brother of Maurice.
    His wife.
  The World My Wilderness, Rose Macaulay, 1950.

Michele, Fra, Carthusian brother. *Romola,* George Eliot, 1863.

Michelson, Eliza, housekeeper to Sir Percival Glyde. *The Woman in White,* W. Collins, 1860.

Michie, student, ex-service corporal. *Lucky Jim,* K. Amis, 1953.

Mick, owner of a house.
  Aston, his older, slow-witted brother who rents a room.
  The Caretaker (play), Harold Pinter, 1960.

Mickle, Mrs, Aubrey Linscott's housekeeper. *Lighten our Darkness,* R. Keable, 1927.

Mickleham, Mrs Emma, charwoman. *The Old Lady Shows Her Medals* (play), J. M. Barrie, 1917.

Middleburgh, Mr, Edinburgh magistrate. *The Heart of Midlothian,* W. Scott, 1818.

Middlemas, Richard, son of Richard Tresham and Zilia de Moncada. *The Surgeon's Daughter,* W. Scott, 1827.

Middleton, Dr. *Mr Midshipman Easy,* Captain Marryat, 1836.

Middleton, Rev. Mr, curate at Pennicote. *Daniel Deronda,* George Eliot, 1876.

Middleton, Arnold, schoolteacher.
  Joan, his wife.
  The Restoration of Arnold Middleton (play), David Storey, 1967.

Middleton, Benjamin (alias Ben Bowser), m. Matilda Seldon.
  Harry, his nephew, m. Dolly Muncaster.
  The Dark Horse, Nat Gould.

Middleton, Clara, ex-fiancée of Sir Willoughby Patterne, m. Vernon Whitford. *The Egoist,* G. Meredith, 1879.

Middleton, Derry, cripple, narrator.
  His mother.
  Both of this Parish, J. S. Fletcher.

Middleton, Gerald, Professor Emeritus of early medieval history.
  Ingeborg, his wife.
    Robin, their elder son, company director.
    John, their younger son, radio celebrity.
  Anglo-Saxon Attitudes, Angus Wilson, 1956.

Middleton, John, farmer.
  Catherine, his wife.
  The *Barsetshire* series, Angela Thirkell, 1933 onwards.

Middleton, Sir John.
  His wife.
  Sense and Sensibility, Jane Austen, 1811

Middleton, Sally. *The Voice of the Turtle* (play), J. van Druten, 1943.

Midget, Mrs. *Outward Bound* (play), S. Vane, 1923.

Midmore, Frankwell, m. Connie Sperrit.
  His mother.
  'My Son's Wife' (s.s.), *A Diversity of Creatures,* R. Kipling, 1917.

Mie, Anne, crippled cousin of Paul Déroulède. *I Will Repay,* Baroness Orczy, 1906.

Miff, Mrs, pew opener. *Dombey and Son,* C. Dickens, 1848.

Mifflin, Arthur, juvenile lead. 'Deep Waters' (s.s.), *The Man Upstairs,* P. G. Wodehouse, 1914.

'Miggles,' central character. 'Miggles' (s.s.), *The Luck of Roaring Camp,* Bret Harte, 1868.

Miggott, James, Quinneys' foreman. *Quinneys'*, H. A. Vachell, 1914.

Miggs, Miss, servant of the Vardens. *Barnaby Rudge,* C. Dickens, 1841.

Mignot, David, ill-starred shepherd and poet. *Roads of Destiny* (s.s.), O. Henry, 1909.

Miguel. *The Power and the Glory,* Graham Greene, 1940.

Mikado of Japan, The.
Nanki-Poo, his son and heir, m. Yum-yum.
The Mikado (comic opera), Gilbert & Sullivan, 1885.

Mike, John Brogan's personal thug. *The Weak and the Strong,* G. Kersh, 1945.

Mikulin, chief of police in St Petersburg. *Under Western Eyes,* Joseph Conrad, 1911.

Milan, Duke of. *See* PROSPERO.

Milan, Duke of. *See* VISCONTI.

Milborough, Countess of, friend of Louis Trevelyan's mother. *He Knew He Was Right,* A. Trollope, 1869.

Milbran, Mr, representing a music publishing firm. *The Good Companions,* J. B. Priestley, 1929.

Mild, Lieutenant. *A Laodicean,* T. Hardy, 1881.

Milden, Denis, friend of George Sherston. *Memoirs of a Fox-Hunting Man,* Siegfried Sassoon, 1929.

Mildman, Dr Samuel, tutor. *Frank Fairlegh,* F. E. Smedley, 1850.

Mildmay, William, great Whig Prime Minister. *Phineas Finn,* 1869, and elsewhere, A. Trollope.

'Mildred, Little,' a subaltern. 'The Man Who Was' (s.s.), *Life's Handicap,* R. Kipling, 1891.

Miles, a small boy. *See also* FLORA. *The Turn of the Screw,* H. James, 1898.

Miles, retd member of Master Humphrey's Club. *Master Humphrey's Clock,* C. Dickens, 1840–1.

Miles, Major, Lady Margaret Bellenden's brother-in-law. *Old Mortality,* W. Scott, 1816.

Miles, Henry, assistant secretary in Ministry of Home Security.
Sarah, his wife, lover of Maurice Bendrix.
Mrs Bertram, her mother.
The End of the Affair, Graham Greene, 1951.

Milford, Webley Alexander. *We're Here,* D. Mackail, 1947.

Mill, Rev. Alexander, curate. *Candida* (play), G. B. Shaw, 1894.

Millamant, Mrs, niece of Lady Wishfort, m. Mirabell. *The Way of the World* (play), W. Congreve, 1700.

Milland, Lottie, governess to Tresilla Conford. *The Second Mrs Conford,* Beatrice K. Seymour, 1951.

Millar, Flora, *danseuse.* 'The Noble Bachelor,' *The Adventures of Sherlock Holmes,* A. Conan Doyle, 1892.

Millard, Miss Rosa, grandmother of old Bayard Sartoris. *The Unvanquished,* William Faulkner, 1938.

Millbank, industrialist.
His wife.
Edith, his daughter, m. Harry Coningsby.
Oswald, his son.
Coningsby, B. Disraeli, 1844.

Millborne, retired gentleman, seducer of Leonora Frankland. 'For Conscience' Sake,' *Life's Little Ironies,* T. Hardy, 1894.

Miller, second-hand bookseller and member of the Philosophers' Club. *Daniel Deronda,* George Eliot, 1876.

Miller, officer, general staff. *The General,* C. S. Forester, 1936.

Miller, Commodore, prisoner of war. *The American Prisoner,* E. Phillpotts, 1904.

Miller, Miss, mistress at Lowood. *Jane Eyre,* Charlotte Brontë, 1847.

Miller, Mr, guest of John Milton. *The Maiden and Married Life of Mary Powell,* Anne Manning, 1849.

Miller, Mr. *The Deep Blue Sea* (play), T. Rattigan, 1952.

Miller, Mrs, landlady.
Nancy and **Betty,** her daughters.
Tom Jones, H. Fielding, 1749.

Miller, Rev. Mr, m. Ella Morris. The *Barsetshire* series, Angela Thirkell, 1933 onwards.

Miller, Daisy, American girl touring Italy. *Daisy Miller,* Henry James, 1878.

Miller, Emil, one-time lover of Mildred Rogers. *Of Human Bondage,* W. S. Maugham, 1915.

Miller, George, in love with Violet North. *Madcap Violet,* W. Black, 1876.

Miller, Greta. *An American Tragedy,* T. Dreiser, 1925.

Miller, Joseph, factory owner. *The Benefactor,* J. D. Beresford.

Miller, St Quentin, author. *The Death of the Heart,* Elizabeth Bowen, 1938.

Millet, Major ('Hopscotch'). *If Winter Comes,* A. S. M. Hutchinson, 1920.

Milligan, Miss, young typist, eng. to Hec Hammond. *London Wall* (play), J. van Druten, 1931.

Milligan, John P., American business man. *Whose Body?,* Dorothy L. Sayers, 1923.

Milliken, David, m. Samantha Ripley. *Timothy's Quest,* Kate D. Wiggin, 1896.

Milliken, Horace.
His wife, *née* Kicklebury.
George, their son.
Arabella, their daughter.
The Wolves and the Lamb, W. M. Thackeray, 1869. (Characters duplicated in *Lovel the Widower.*)

Millington, William.
Margaret, his wife.
Louis, his brother.
'The Cartouche' (s.s.), *A Beginning,* W. de la Mare, 1955.

Millo, patron of the Capo di Monte. *Adam's Breed,* Radclyffe Hall, 1926.

Mills, of the Carlist cavalry. *The Arrow of Gold,* J. Conrad, 1919.

Mills, teacher at Joan and Peter's school. *Joan and Peter,* H. G. Wells, 1918.

Mills, Julia, friend of Dora Copperfield. *David Copperfield,* C. Dickens, 1850.

Mills, Reg, tough ex-paratrooper who turns to crime.
Celia, his wife.
Daphne, their daughter.
The Patriots, James Barlow, 1960.

Millward, Rev. Michael.
Mary and **Eliza,** his daughters.
The Tenant of Wildfell Hall, Anne Brontë, 1848.

Millwood, wealthy and unscrupulous villain. *A Voyage to Purilia,* Elmer Rice, 1930.

Milly, married woman who has an affair with Remington. *The New Machiavelli,* H. G. Wells, 1911.

Miln, General, commanding the defeated Rians. *Right Off the Map,* C. E. Montague, 1927.

Milner, house prefect. *Young Woodley* (play), J. van Druten, 1928.

Milner, Molly, m. Lawrence Furnival. *Miss Tarrant's Temperament* (s.s.), May Sinclair.

Milsom, Harvey Cheyne's secretary. *Captains Courageous,* R. Kipling, 1897.

Milsom, Mrs. *Call it a Day* (play), Dodie Smith, 1935.

Milton, Miss, librarian. *The Cathedral,* Hugh Walpole, 1922.

Milton, Lady Ann. See EARL OF ROSHERVILLE.

Milton, Cora Ann. *The Ringer* (play), E. Wallace, 1926.

Milton, Mrs Hetty (pseudonym Thomas Plantagenet).
Jessie, her stepdaughter, Hoopdriver's inspiration.
The Wheels of Chance, H. G. Wells, 1896.

Milton, John (hist.). *The Maiden and Married Life of Mary Powell,* Anne Manning, 1849.

Miltoun, Lord. See VALLEYS.

Milvain, Jasper, writer.
Dora and **Maud,** his sisters.
The New Grub Street, George Gissing, 1891.

Milverton, Charles Augustus. 'The Adventure of Charles Augustus Milverton,' *The Return of Sherlock Holmes,* A. Conan Doyle, 1905.

Milvey, Rev. Frank. *Our Mutual Friend,* C. Dickens, 1865.

Mimms-Welwyn, Archbishop. *A Footman for the Peacock,* Rachel Ferguson, 1940.

Minchin, Dr. *Middlemarch,* George Eliot, 1871–2.

Minchin, Rev. Roger. *The Amazons* (play), A. W. Pinero, 1893.

Mincing, woman to Mrs Millamant. *The Way of the World* (play), W. Congreve, 1700.

Minden, Elisa, fiancée of Humphrey Orford, m. Captain Philip Hoare.
Dr Minden, her father.
'The Orford Mystery,' *Old Patch's Medley,* Marjorie Bowen, 1930.

Minette, Mademoiselle, *vivandière. Tom Burke of Ours,* C. Lever, 1844.

Ming, Miss, curio dealer, friend of Dr Staminer. *Mr Ingleside,* E. V. Lucas, 1910.

Ming Hi, 'versifier of irregular intellect.' *The Wallet of Kai Lung,* E. Bramah, 1900.

Minghelli, Charles, government spy sent to London by Bonelli. *The Eternal City,* Hall Caine, 1901.

Minho, Gurdon, novelist. The *Forsyte* series, J. Galsworthy, 1906–33.

Miniver, Mistress, a wealthy widow. *Satiromastix* (play), Thomas Dekker, 1601.

Miniver, Mrs Caroline.
  Clem, her husband.
    Vin, Judy and **Toby,** their children.
  Susan, Clem's sister, m. Archie McQuern.
  Mrs Miniver, Jan Struther, 1939.

Minnehaha ('Laughing Water'), wife of Hiawatha. *The Song of Hiawatha* (poem), H. W. Longfellow, 1855.

Minnie, in love with Hubert Lapell. 'Hubert and Minnie' (s.s.), *The Little Mexican,* A. Huxley, 1924.

Minnie, cousin of Louisa Ames. *Mourning becomes Electra* (play), E. O'Neill, 1931.

Minster, Lady. *The High Road* (play), F. Lonsdale, 1927.

Minter, pottery manufacturer, uncle of Remington.
  Gertrude and **Sybil,** his daughters.
  The New Machiavelli, H. G. Wells, 1911.

Mintley, Miss Becky, cousin and housekeeper of Sir Henry Rotherham. *I Live Under a Black Sun,* Edith Sitwell, 1937.

Minty, Ferdinand, seedy Old Harrovian living on his wits in Stockholm. *England Made Me,* Graham Greene, 1935.

Minus, clerk in Somerset House. *Sketches by Boz,* C. Dickens, 1836.

Mirabel, Sir Charles, aged ex-diplomat.
  Emily Fotheringay, his wife, actress.
  Pendennis, W. M. Thackeray, 1848–50.

Mirabell, m. Mrs Millamant. *The Way of the World* (play), W. Congreve, 1700.

Miraflores, decamping President of Anchuria. *Cabbages and Kings,* O. Henry, 1905.

Miranda, daughter of Prospero. *The Tempest* (play), W. Shakespeare.

Miranda. *Tarantella* (poem), H. Belloc.

Mirander, maid to Lady Falkirk. *Sampson Rideout, Quaker,* Una Silberrad, 1911.

Mirepoix, Marquis de. *Monsieur Beaucaire,* Booth Tarkington, 1902.

Miriam, an old Jewess. *Hypatia,* C. Kingsley, 1853.

Mirobolant, Monsieur Alcide, celebrated chef. *Pendennis,* W. M. Thackeray, 1848–50.

Mirra, a peasant girl. *Paolo and Francesca,* S. Phillips, 1900.

Mirrenden, Lola, niece of Dora Duggan. *Sorrell and Son,* W. Deeping, 1925.

Mirvan, Captain.
  His wife.
  Evelina, Fanny Burney, 1778.

Miserden, Captain R., of the *Bird of Dawning. The Bird of Dawning,* J. Masefield, 1933.

Misquita, Gabral. 'The Gate of a Hundred Sorrows' (s.s.), *Plain Tales from the Hills,* R. Kipling, 1888.

Misquith, Frank, Q.C., M.P., friend of Aubrey Tanqueray. *The Second Mrs Tanqueray* (play), A. W. Pinero, 1893.

Misset, Captain, officer in Dillon's regiment, friend of Charles Wogan. *Clementina,* A. E. W. Mason, 1901.

Mistoffelees, the original Conjuring Cat. *Old Possum's Book of Practical Cats,* T. S. Eliot, 1939.

Mistrust. *See* TIMOROUS.

Mitcham, Morton, of the Good Companions concert party. *The Good Companions,* J. B. Priestley, 1929.

Mitchell, cunning fifteen-year-old slum boy with the physique of a man. *Term of Trial,* James Barlow, 1961.

Mitchell, Fred, insurance agent.
  Nancy, his wife. Neighbours of the Hollys.
  Peggy, their baby.
  South Riding, Winifred Holtby, 1936.

Mitchell, Harold. *A Streetcar Named Desire* (play), Tennessee Williams, 1949.

Mitchell, Job. *The Trumpet Major,* T. Hardy, 1880.

Mitchell, Violet, chambermaid. *Holy Deadlock,* A. P. Herbert, 1934.

Mitchens, Rummy. *Major Barbara* (play), G. B. Shaw, 1905.

Mitford, Colonel Dick, friend of Sir Geoffrey Peveril. *Peveril of the Peak,* W. Scott, 1822.

Mitterley, Mrs, landlady.
Raymond, her son.
Fern, her daughter.
Let the People Sing, J. B. Priestley, 1939.

Mitty, Fred.
His wife.
Angel Pavement, J. B. Priestley, 1930.

Mitty, Walter.
His wife.
The Secret Life of Walter Mitty (s.s.), J. Thurber.

Mivins, prisoner in the Fleet. *Pickwick Papers,* C. Dickens, 1837.

Mixet, Joe, friend of John Crumb. *The Way We Live Now,* A. Trollope, 1875.

Mixtus, half-breed business tycoon.
Scintilla, his wife.
Theophrastus Such, George Eliot, 1879.

M'Ling, black-faced humanized beast. *The Island of Dr Moreau,* H. G. Wells, 1896.

M'Lino, native beauty and enchantress. *Sanders of the River,* E. Wallace, 1911.

Mnason, owner of house where Christiana lodged. *Pilgrim's Progress,* J. Bunyan, 1678, 1684.

Mock Turtle, The. *Alice in Wonderland,* L. Carroll, 1865.

Mockler, Harry. 'The Wish House' (s.s.), *Debits and Credits,* R. Kipling, 1926.

Mockridge, Miss. *Dangerous Corner* (play), J. B. Priestley, 1932.

Mockridge, Nance. *The Mayor of Casterbridge,* T. Hardy, 1886.

Moddle, Augustus, young boarder at Todgers's. *Martin Chuzzlewit,* C. Dickens, 1844.

Modred, Sir, traitor, killed by Arthur.
Lot, his father.
'The Passing of Arthur' (poem), *Idylls of the King,* Lord Tennyson, 1859.

Modus, lover of Helen. *The Hunchback* (play), J. S. Knowles, 1832.

Moffat, Parliamentary candidate. *Doctor Thorne,* A. Trollope, 1858.

Moffat, a don. *The Babe, B.A.,* E. F. Benson, 1897.

Moffat, Miss. *The Corn is Green* (play), Emlyn Williams, 1938.

Moffat, Mr and Mrs.
Annie, Belle and **Ned,** their children.
Little Women, 1868, and sequels, Louisa M. Alcott.

Moffat, Elmer, secretary, later railway king, 1st and 4th husband of Undine Spragg. *The Custom of the Country,* Edith Wharton, 1913.

Moffat, Mrs Sallie, friend of Meg Brooke.
Ned, her husband.
Little Women, Louisa M. Alcott, 1868.

Moggeridge, Lord, Lord Chancellor. *Bealby,* H. G. Wells, 1915.

Moggeridge, Rev. Mr, aged, out-of-work curate. *The Dream,* H. G. Wells, 1924.

Moggridge, James. *My Lady Nicotine,* J. M. Barrie, 1890.

Moggs, proprietor of Moggs' Domestic Soap. *Tono Bungay,* H. G. Wells, 1909.

Moggs, Luke, head miller of Dorlcote Mill.
His wife.
The Mill on the Floss, George Eliot, 1860.

Moggy, old Indian woman. *Ungava,* R. M. Ballantyne, 1857.

Mogyns, Sir Alfred de, *né* A. S. Muggins.
Marian, his wife.
Alured Caradoc, his eldest son.
The Book of Snobs, W. M. Thackeray, 1846–7.

Moir, Agnes, in love with Matthew Brodie.
Her mother.
Hatter's Castle, A. J. Cronin, 1931.

Moldan, Luli, mistress of Graf Herzenberg. *Dragon Harvest,* Upton Sinclair, 1946.

Mole, Lady de la, society acquaintance of Becky Sharp. *Vanity Fair,* W. M. Thackeray, 1847–8.

Mole, Mr. *The Wind in the Willows,* K. Grahame, 1908.

Mole, Hannah, central character, m. Samuel Blenkinsop. *Miss Mole,* E. H. Young, 1930.

Molhir, of the Carnutes. *The Conquered,* Naomi Mitchison, 1923.

Mollet, Miss, village gossip. *Iron and Smoke,* Sheila Kaye-Smith, 1928.

Molloy, Sir James, newspaper proprietor and editor-in-chief. *Trent's Last Case,* E. C. Bentley, 1912.

Molly, housekeeper to Jaggers. *Great Expectations,* C. Dickens, 1861.

Molly, housemaid to Mr Poyser. *Adam Bede,* George Eliot, 1859.

Molly, Miller Loveday's servant. *The Trumpet Major,* T. Hardy, 1880.

Molly, servant to the Lambert family, m. Gumbo. *The Virginians,* W. M. Thackeray, 1857–8.

Molten, Farmer. *The Sailor's Return,* David Garnett, 1925.

Molyneux, Major. *Monsieur Beaucaire,* Booth Tarkington, 1902.

Momeby, Mr and Mrs.
  Erik, their son.
The Quest (s.s.), 'Saki' (H. H. Munro).

Mompert, Dr, D.D., bishop.
  His wife and daughters.
Daniel Deronda, George Eliot, 1876.

Monakatocka, Susquehannock Indian, friend of Godfrey Landless. *The Old Dominion,* Mary Johnston, 1899.

Moncada, Alonzo, Spaniard shipwrecked in Ireland. *Melmoth the Wanderer,* Charles Robert Maturin, 1820.

Moncada, Zilia de, m. Richard Tresham.
  Matthias, her father.
The Surgeon's Daughter, W. Scott, 1827.

Monchensey, Dowager Lady (Amy).
  Henry, Lord Monchensey, her son.
  Ivy, Violet and **Agatha,** her sisters.
  Mary, her cousin.
The Family Reunion (play), T. S. Eliot, 1939.

Monck, Bernhardt (alias Herzog, alias Branting), fellow conspirator of Lanny Budd, m. Trudi Schutz. *Dragon's Teeth,* 1942, and elsewhere, Upton Sinclair.

Monckton, plausible society scoundrel.
  Lady Margaret, his wife.
Cecilia, Fanny Burney, 1782.

Moncrieff, Algernon, m. Cecily Cardew. *The Importance of Being Earnest* (play), O. Wilde. 1895.

Mond, Mustapha, a world controller. *Brave New World,* Aldous Huxley, 1932.

Monday, Mr, imaginary friend of James Sampson. *The Distant Horns of Summer,* H. E. Bates, 1967.

Monday, Sara, ex-'wife' of Gulley Jimson. *The Horse's Mouth,* Joyce Cary, 1944, and others.

Money, Mary Ann, charwoman. *Far from the Madding Crowd,* T. Hardy, 1874.

Moneygawl, Isabella, m. Sir Condy Rackrent.
  Her father.
Castle Rackrent, Maria Edgeworth, 1800.

Moneypenny, Miss, private secretary to M. *Thunderball,* 1961, and others, Ian Fleming.

Moniplies, Richie, serving man of Nigel Olifaunt. *The Fortunes of Nigel,* W. Scott, 1822.

Monk, Mr. 'Marching to Zion' (s.s.), *Adam and Eve and Pinch Me,* A. E. Coppard, 1921.

Monk, Hillary, artist. 'Grey Sand and White Sand' (s.s.), *The Baseless Fabric,* Helen Simpson, 1925.

Monk, Joshua, Radical M.P. *Phineas Finn,* A. Trollope, 1869.

Monk, Mary, m. Roger Forsyte. The *Forsyte* series, J. Galsworthy, 1906–1933.

Monk, Stephen, central character and narrator, m. (1) Elizabeth Wrydale, (2) Jane Armstrong. *The World in the Evening,* C. Isherwood, 1954.

Monkbarns, Laird of. *See* JONATHAN OLDBUCK. *The Antiquary,* W. Scott, 1816.

Monkhurst, Lord. *See* NED PYM.

Monkley, James. *Sylvia Scarlett,* C. Mackenzie, 1918.

Monks. *See* EDWARD LEEFORD.

Monks, Miss Letitia, rich old lady. *And Now Goodbye,* J. Hilton, 1931.

Monmouth, Lord, grandfather of Harry Coningsby, m. Princess Lucretia Colonna. *See also* VILLEBECQUE. *Coningsby,* B. Disraeli, 1844.

Monmouth, Duchess of (Gladys). *The Picture of Dorian Gray,* O. Wilde, 1891.

Monmouth, Mr Jaraby's cat. *The Old Boys,* William Trevor, 1964.

Monnasett, Mrs, nurse to David Herries's children. *Rogue Herries,* Hugh Walpole, 1930.

Monofuelli, Professor of Civil Law, Padua. *Anthony Adverse,* Hervey Allen, 1934.

Monogram, Sir Damask, Bt, m. Julia Triplex. *The Way We Live Now,* A. Trollope, 1875.

Monroe, John.
His wife.
'Mr and Mrs Monroe' (s.s.), *The Owl in the Attic,* J. Thurber, 1931.

Monsell, Fanny, m. Mark Robarts. *Framley Parsonage,* A. Trollope, 1861.

Monson, millionaire experimenter with flying machines. *Argonauts of the Air* (s.s.), H. G. Wells, 1895.

Mont, Sir Lawrence.
Emily, his wife.
Michael, their son, m. Fleur Forsyte.
Kit and **Kat,** their children.
The *Forsyte* series, J. Galsworthy, 1906–33.

Montacute, Lord. *See* DUKE OF BELLAMONT.

Montagu, close friend whom Eric rescued from drowning. *Eric, or Little by Little,* F. W. Farrar, 1858.

Montagu, Lord (hist.). *The Last of the Barons,* Lord Lytton, 1843.

Montagu, Paul, m. Henrietta Carbury. *The Way We Live Now,* A. Trollope, 1875.

Montague, head of his house.
Lady Montague, his wife.
Romeo, their son.
Romeo and Juliet (play), W. Shakespeare.

Montague, Mr. *A Safety Match,* Ian Hay, 1911.

Montague, Allan, country lawyer and planter, central character.
Oliver, his younger brother.
Alice, their cousin.
The Metropolis, Upton Sinclair, 1908.

Montague, Charlotte. *Clarissa Harlowe,* S. Richardson, 1748.

Montairy, Lord.
Victoria, his wife.
Lothair, B. Disraeli, 1870.

Montdore, Earl of (Family name Hampton).
Sonia, his wife.
Leopoldina (Polly), their daughter, m. as 2nd wife Harvey Dougdale.
See also CEDRIC HAMPTON.
Love in a Cold Climate, Nancy Mitford, 1949.

Montemayor, Marquesa de. *The Bridge of San Luis Rey,* T. Wilder, 1928.

Montfitchet, Andrew, eccentric kind-hearted artist, m. Mrs Carrickfergus. (Same as ANDREA FITCH.) *The Adventures of Philip,* W. M. Thackeray, 1861–2.

Montford, Mr. *An Ideal Husband* (play), O. Wilde, 1895.

Montgomery, medical student, assistant to Moreau. *The Island of Dr Moreau,* H. G. Wells, 1896.

Montgomery, Captain. *Lady Frederick* (play), W. S. Maugham, 1907.

Montgomery, Mr, tutor to Raisley Herries. *Rogue Herries,* Hugh Walpole, 1920.

Montgomery, Mrs, aunt of Morris Townsend. *Washington Square,* H. James, 1880.

Montgomery, Mrs, aunt of Lee Tarlton.
Randolph, her son.
Tiny, her daughter.
American Wives and English Husbands, Gertrude Atherton, 1898.

Montgomery, Ellen, central character.
Captain Morgan Montgomery, her father.
Her mother.
The Wide, Wide World, E. Wetherell, 1850.

Monticue, Ethel, central character, m. Bernard Clark. *The Young Visiters,* Daisy Ashford, 1919.

Montis, Clea, a blonde painter. *Justine* and others in *The Alexandria Quartet,* 1957–61, Lawrence Durrell.

Montjoie, French sculptor. *The History of David Grieve,* Mrs Humphry Ward, 1892.

Montjoy, French herald. *Henry the Fifth* (play), W. Shakespeare.

Montjoy, Diana, m. (1) Ronald Ferse, (2) Adrian Charwell. *Maid in Waiting,* J. Galsworthy, 1931.

Montjoy, Maisie. *See* MRS CARGHILL. *The Elder Statesman* (play), T. S. Eliot, 1958.

Montmorenci de Valentinois, Countess of (Blanche), *née* Amory. *Pendennis,* W. M. Thackeray, 1848–1850.

Montmorency, 'the dog.' *Three Men in a Boat,* J. K. Jerome, 1889.

Montmorency, Hugo.
Francie, his wife.
The Last September, Elizabeth Bowen, 1929.

Montoni, villain-in-chief, 2nd husband of Mme Cheron, *The Mysteries of Udolpho,* Mrs Radcliffe, 1794.

Montreville, Madame Adela. *The Surgeon's Daughter,* W. Scott, 1827.

Montroya, Friar Baltazar, priest at Acoma, executed for murder by Indians. *Death Comes for the Archbishop,* Willa Cather, 1927.

Monty, Padre. *Tell England,* E. Raymond, 1922.

Moody, Marian Grant.
'Uncle Dee,' her husband.
Leopold, their adopted son.
The House in Paris, Elizabeth Bowen, 1935.

Moody, Tom, a boxing manager. *Golden Boy* (play), Clifford Odets, 1937.

Mookami, James, cousin of Chief Letlotse. *When We Become Men,* Naomi Mitchison, 1965.

Mookerjee, Hurree Chunder. 'What Happened' (poem), *Departmental Ditties,* R. Kipling, 1886.

Moon, Adelaide, m. Harold Dormer. *Antigua Penny Puce,* R. Graves, 1936.

Moon, Lorna, mistress of Tom Moody. *Golden Boy* (play), Clifford Odets, 1937.

Moon, Matthew, farm-hand. *Far from the Madding Crowd,* T. Hardy, 1874.

Moon, Michael, journalist. *Manalive,* G. K. Chesterton, 1912.

Mooney, Mrs, landlady.
Jack, her son.
Polly, her daughter.
'The Boarding-house' (s.s.), *The Dubliners,* James Joyce, 1914.

Moonshine, Saunders, zealous elder and smuggler. *The Bride of Lammermoor,* W. Scott, 1819.

Moor, Edith, m. old Jolyon Forsyte. The *Forsyte* series, J. Galsworthy, 1906–33.

Moore, Commander.
Margery, his wife.
Billy, Wilfrid and **Tessa,** their children.
Joy and Josephine, Monica Dickens, 1948.

Moore, Mrs.
Ronald (Heaslop), her son by 1st husband.
Ralph, her son.
Stella, her daughter, m. Cyril Fielding.
A Passage to India, E. M. Forster, 1924.

Moore, Arthur Wellington, missionary, Swan Creek, central character. *The Sky Pilot,* R. Connor, 1899.

Moore, Denis, father of Anthony Adverse. *See also* VINCITATA.

Moore, Eddy. 'Three from Dunsterville' (s.s.), *The Man Upstairs,* P. G. Wodehouse, 1914.

Moore, Frederick. *Judith Paris,* Hugh Walpole, 1931.

Moore, Harold, tutor to Jack Clayton. The *Tarzan* series, E. R. Burroughs, 1912–32.

Moore, Humphrey, robber. *Deacon Brodie* (play), W. E. Henley & R. L. Stevenson, 1892.

Moore, Kathleen, with whom Monroe Starr falls in love. *The Last Tycoon,* F. Scott Fitzgerald, 1941.

Moore, Lloyd, surgeon. *My Brother Jonathan,* F. Brett Young, 1928.

Moore, Peter, great friend of Eddie Ryan. *The Silence of History,* James T. Farrell, 1963.

Moore, Robert Gerard, Anglo-French cloth-weaver, tenant of Hollow Mill; m. Caroline Helstone.
Hortense, his sister.
Louis, his brother, tutor to the Sympsons, m. Shirley Keeldar.
Shirley, Charlotte Brontë, 1849.

Moore, Sir Stewart. *Harry Lorrequer,* C. Lever, 1839.

Moore, Teresa, schoolgirl who witnesses a robbery. *The Patriots,* James Barlow, 1960.

Moorehouse, J. Ward, public relations executive. *U.S.A.* trilogy, John dos Passos, 1930–6.

Mopus, of Mowbray & Mopus, legal advisers to Lady Eustace. *The Eustace Diamonds,* A. Trollope, 1873.

Mopworth, Peter.
His wife.
Eliza, 1900, and elsewhere, Barry Pain.

Mora, Teodoro ('Little Theo'), language master, central character. *Lost Endeavour,* J. Masefield, 1910.

Moran, police inspector, ex-bank president. *The Benson Murder Case,* S. S. van Dine, 1926.

Moran, Dan, horse thief. *Robbery under Arms,* R. Boldrewood, 1888.

Moran, Colonel Sebastian, chief assistant to Moriarty. 'The Empty House,' *The Return of Sherlock Holmes,* A. Conan Doyle, 1905.

Morano, Count, in love with Emily St Aubert. *The Mysteries of Udolpho,* Mrs Radcliffe, 1794.

Morbific, 'non-believer in any form of contagion.' *Crotchet Castle,* T. L. Peacock, 1831.

Morcombe, close friend of Gordon Carruthers. *The Loom of Youth,* A. Waugh, 1917.

Mordaunt, Rev. Mr, rector. *Little Lord Fauntleroy,* Frances H. Burnett, 1886.

Mordax, 'an intellectual worker.' *Theophrastus Such,* George Eliot, 1879.

Mordecai, Mr. *The Absentee,* Maria Edgeworth, 1812.

Morden, Colonel William, cousin and trustee of Clarissa Harlowe. *Clarissa Harlowe,* S. Richardson, 1748.

More, James. *See* MACGREGOR.

More, Shan.
Bridget, his deserted wife.
Handy Andy, S. Lover, 1842.

More, Thomas, pseudonym of Godwin Capes as dramatist. *Ann Veronica,* H. G. Wells, 1909.

Moreau, Dr, biological experimenter. *The Island of Dr Moreau,* H. G. Wells, 1896.

Moreau, André-Louis ('Scaramouche'), actor, fencer, revolutionary; illegitimate son of de la Tour d'Azyr and the Comtesse de Plougastel; in love with Aline de Kercadiou. *Scaramouche,* R. Sabatini, 1921.

Morecombe, Captain. *On the Face of the Waters,* Flora A. Steel, 1896.

Morecombe, Sir Marmaduke, Liberal M.P. *Phineas Finn,* A. Trollope, 1869.

Morehouse, Bishop. *The Iron Heel,* Jack London, 1908.

Morel, Walter, miner, m. Gertrude Coppard.
Their children:
William.
Annie, m. Leonard.
Paul, clerk and artist, central character.
Arthur.
Sons and Lovers, D. H. Lawrence, 1913.

Moreland, 'Granny.' *The Harvester,* Gene S. Porter, 1911.

Moreland, Emma. *Edward Gray* (poem), Lord Tennyson.

Moreland, Roger. *The Mystery of a Hansom Cab,* F. Hume, 1886.

Morell, Rev. James Mavor.
Candida, his wife, *née* Burgess.
Candida (play), G. B. Shaw, 1894.

Morell, Sub-Lieutenant John, of *Compass Rose.*
Elaine, his wife.
The Cruel Sea, N. Monsarrat, 1957.

Morelli, Shep, gangster. *The Thin Man,* D. Hammett, 1934.

Moreton, Joe. *Robbery under Arms,* R. Boldrewood, 1888.

Morfin, head clerk to Dombey, m. Harriet Carker. *Dombey and Son,* C. Dickens, 1848.

Morgan, departmental chief. *The Porch,* 1937, and *The Stronghold,* 1939, R. Church.

Morgan, Miss, on staff of Sir James Molloy. *Trent's Last Case,* E. C. Bentley, 1912.

Morgan, Miss, governess to the Vincy children. *Middlemarch,* George Eliot, 1871–2.

Morgan, Evan, Welsh apprentice, the *Berinthia. Tom Fool,* F. Tennyson Jesse, 1926.

Morgan, Gwilym, miner.
Beth, his wife.
Their children:
Ivor, m. Bronwen.
Ianto.
Davy, m. Ethelwyn.
Owen, m. Blodwen Evans.
Gwilym, m. Marged Evans.
Ceridwen, m. Blethyn Llywarch.
Angharad, m. Iestyn Evans.
Olwen.
Huw, central character and narrator.
How Green Was My Valley, R. Llewellyn, 1939.

Morgan, James, valet to Major Pendennis, and society spy. *Pendennis,* W. M. Thackeray, 1848–1850.

Morgan, Jenny, mistress of Philip Crow.
'Morgan Nelly,' their daughter. *A Glastonbury Romance,* J. C. Powys, 1932.

Morgan, Organ, grocer. *Under Milk Wood* (play), Dylan Thomas, 1954.

Morgan, Tom, of the *Hispaniola. Treasure Island,* R. L. Stevenson, 1883.

Morgan, Valerie, m. as 2nd wife William Herries. *Judith Paris,* Hugh Walpole, 1931.

Morgari, Domenico Mario, neighbour of the Le Fabers. *The Five Sons of Le Faber,* E. Raymond, 1945.

Moriarty. 'In Error' (s.s.), *Plain Tales from the Hills,* R. Kipling, 1888.

Moriarty, Constable, R.I.C., Rosivera. *The Search Party,* G. A. Birmingham, 1913.

Moriarty, Professor James, arch-criminal. 'The Final Problem,' *Memoirs of Sherlock Holmes,* 1894, and elsewhere, A. Conan Doyle.

Morison, invalid. *Sun on the Water,* L. A. G. Strong, 1940.

Morkan, Misses Kate and **Julia,** proprietors of musical academy. 'The Dead' (s.s.), *The Dubliners,* James Joyce, 1914.

Morland, Catherine, m. Henry Tilney.
Her father and mother.
Her brothers and sisters:
James, Sarah, George, Harriet and others.
Northanger Abbey, Jane Austen, 1818.

Morland, James.
Fanny, his wife.
Mary Rose, their daughter, m. Simon Blake.
Mary Rose (play), J. M. Barrie, 1920.

Morland, Mrs Laura, widow, authoress.
Tony, Dick, Gerald and **John,** her sons.
The *Barsetshire* series, Angela Thirkell, 1933 onwards.

Morlocks, lower world inhabitants, A.D. 802,701. *The Time Machine,* H. G Wells 1895.

Mornac, head of the Imperial Military Police. *The Maids of Paradise,* R. W. Chambers, 1903.

Mornington, Molly, *née* Vincent. *Sons of Fire,* M. E. Braddon, 1896.

Morocco, King of. *Tamburlaine* (play), C. Marlowe, 1587.

Morocco, Prince of, unsuccessful suitor to Portia. *The Merchant of Venice* (play), W. Shakespeare.

Morolt, Dennis, favourite squire of Sir Raymond Berenger. *The Betrothed,* W. Scott, 1825.

Morose, husband of Epicene. *Epicene* (play), B. Jonson, 1609.

Morran, Mrs, landlady of Dickson McCunn and John Heritage. *Huntingtower,* J. Buchan, 1922.

Morringer, Sir Ferdinand, Inspector of Police. *Robbery under Arms,* R. Boldrewood, 1888.

Morris, Mrs, housekeeper to the Aldclyffes. *Desperate Remedies,* T. Hardy, 1871.

Morris, Rev. Mr, Rector of St James's, Polchester. *The Cathedral,* Hugh Walpole, 1922.

Morris, Sergeant-Major. 'The Monkey's Paw' (s.s.), *The Lady of the Barge,* W. W. Jacobs, 1902.

Morris, Amanda, m. William Benham; later mistress of Sir Philip Easton. *The Research Magnificent,* H. G. Wells, 1915.

Morris, Anna, one of Philip Warren's lovers. *The Judgment of Paris,* Gore Vidal, 1952.

Morris, Dinah, niece of Mrs Poyser, m. Adam Bede. *Adam Bede,* George Eliot, 1859.

Morris, Edward, defaulting bank clerk, former friend of Jack Johnson. *The Adventures of Mr Ledbury,* Albert Smith, 1844.

Morris, Ella, m. Rev. Mr Miller. The *Barsetshire* series, Angela Thirkell, 1933 onwards.

Morris, Hon. George, brother of Lord Tulla; Tory M.P.
Rev. Richard, his cousin.
Phineas Finn, A. Trollope, 1869.

Morris, Idwal. *The Corn is Green* (play), Emlyn Williams, 1938.

Morris, Jack, friend of Lord March. *The Virginians,* W. M. Thackeray, 1857–9.

Morris, Jed.
June, his wife.
Chosen Country, J. dos Passos, 1951.

Morris, John. *Distinguished Villa* (play), Kate O'Brien, 1926.

Morris, Lucy, orphan, governess at home of Lady Fawn; childhood friend of Lady Eustace. *The Eustace Diamonds,* A. Trollope, 1873.

Morris, Quincy P. *Dracula,* Bram Stoker, 1897.

Morrison, senior assistant, Port Burdock Bazaar. *The History of Mr Polly,* H. G. Wells, 1910.

Morrison, clerk. *Jane Clegg* (play), St John Ervine, 1913.

Morrison, Detective Inspector. *See* TEDDIE DEAKIN.

Morrison, Albert ('Albert-next-door').
His uncle, m. Margaret Ashleigh.
The Treasure Seekers, 1899, and *The Would-be-Goods,* 1901, E. Nesbit.

Morrison, Rev. Edward.
His wife.
Robin and **Netta,** their children.
Princess Priscilla's Fortnight, Countess von Arnim, 1905.

Morrison, Kate (later Mullockson).
Jeanie, her sister, m. Jim Marston.
Robbery under Arms, R. Boldrewood, 1888.

Morrison, Loch, a boy.
Cassie, his sister.
The Golden Apples, Eudora Welty, 1949.

Morrison, Peter, Norfolk squire and Member of Parliament.
Helen, his wife.
The Rich Pay Late, 1964, and others in the *Alms for Oblivion* sequence, Simon Raven.

Morrissey, friendless pimp. *Mrs Eckdorf in O'Neill's Hotel,* William Trevor, 1969.

Morrissy, Michael.
Patsy and **Jemmy,** his grandsons.
'The Forge' (s.s.), *Countrymen All,* Katherine Tynan, 1915.

Morse, Aubrey Tanqueray's butler. *The Second Mrs Tanqueray* (play), A. W. Pinero, 1893.

Morse, Hazel.
Herbert, her husband.
'Big Blonde' (s.s.), *Here Lies,* Dorothy Parker, 1939.

Morse, John. *My Brother Jonathan,* F. Brett Young, 1928.

Morshed, Mr, midshipman. 'The Bonds of Discipline' (s.s.), *Traffic and Discoveries,* 1904, and 'The Horse Marines' (s.s.), *A Diversity of Creatures,* 1917, R. Kipling.

Morstan, Mary, m. Dr Watson.
Arthur, her father.
The Sign of Four, A. Conan Doyle, 1890.

Mortimer. Alias of MICAWBER.

Mortimer, Miss, of typewriting bureau with 'other activities.' *Holy Deadlock,* A. P. Herbert, 1934.

Mortimer, Abraham, farmer.
Jess, his son, m. Deborah Loveday.
Benjamin and **David,** their sons.
The Fallow Land, H. E. Bates, 1932.

Mortimer, Edmund, Earl of March (hist.). *Henry the Fourth* and *Henry the Sixth* (plays), W. Shakespeare.

Mortimer, Sir George, distinguished surgeon. *The Porch,* 1937, and *The Stronghold,* 1939, R. Church.

Mortimer, Sir Harry, friend of Sir Maurice Vibart. *The Broad Highway,* J. Farnol, 1910.

Mortimer, Chief Inspector Henry.
Emmeline, his wife.
Memento Mori, Muriel Spark, 1959.

Mortimer, Dr James. *The Hound of the Baskervilles,* A. Conan Doyle, 1902.

Mortimer, Monte, impresario. *The Good Companions,* J. B. Priestley, 1929.

Mortis, Mrs, inmate of home for the aged. *The Poorhouse Fair,* John Updike, 1959.

Mortlake, Joe, lawyer. *Chosen Country,* J. dos Passos, 1951.

Morton, Alex ('Sandy'), drunkard and waster. 'The Idyll of Red Gulch' (s.s.), *The Luck of Roaring Camp,* Bret Harte, 1868.

Morton, Cyril. 'The Solitary Cyclist,' *The Return of Sherlock Holmes,* A. Conan Doyle, 1905.

Morton, Frank, fur-trader. *Ungava,* R. M. Ballantyne, 1857.

Morton, Harry, 'a lad of fire, zeal and education.'
Colonel Silas, his father.
Morton of Milnwood, his uncle.
Old Mortality, W. Scott, 1816.

Morton, Henry, m. Muriel Fane. *Going their own Ways,* A. Waugh, 1938.

Morton, James, young engineer who changes his name to Pog Proctor. *Thin Air,* John Pudney, 1961.

Morton, Richard, young farmer, m. Nellie Verity. *High Meadows,* Alison Uttley, 1938.

Morton, Sir Robert, counsel for Ronnie Winslow. *The Winslow Boy* (play), T. Rattigan, 1946.

Mortsheugh, Johnnie, sexton. *The Bride of Lammermoor,* W. Scott, 1819.

Morville, Sir Guy, central character, m. Amy Edmonstone.
  Archdeacon Morville, his uncle.
  His children:
    Philip, m. Laura Edmonstone.
    Mary Verena, poetress.
    Margaret, m. Dr Henley.
    Fanny, died young.
The Heir of Redclyffe, Charlotte M. Yonge, 1853.

Mosca, parasite of Volpone. *Volpone, or the Fox* (play), B. Jonson, 1605.

Moscrop, Nellie, m. William Essex.
  Her father and mother.
My Son, My Son, H. Spring, 1938.

Moses. *The School for Scandal* (play), R. B. Sheridan, 1777.

Mosgrove, Dr Alwyn. *Lady Audley's Secret,* M. E. Braddon, 1862.

Mosher, Mark, city editor, *Chicago Sentinel,* Paris. *Trial by Terror,* P. Gallico, 1952.

Moss, unsuccessful farmer.
  'Gritty,' his wife, sister of Edward Tulliver.
  George, Willie and **Lizzy,** their children.
The Mill on the Floss, George Eliot, 1860.

Moss, spunging-house keeper.
  His wife and daughter.
Vanity Fair, W. M. Thackeray, 1847–8.

Moss, Bobby, Jewish fellow student of Clive Newcome at Gandish's Drawing Academy. *The Newcomes,* W. M. Thackeray, 1853–5.

Moss, 'Bunny,' 'boy-friend' of Lily Bell. *The Water Gipsies,* A. P. Herbert, 1930.

Moss, Duncan, photographer. *The Unspeakable Skipton,* Pamela Hansford Johnson, 1959.

Moss, Violet, m. Arthur Martindale.
  Her father and mother.
  Albert, her brother.
  Matilda, Caroline, Annette, etc., her sisters.
Heartsease, Charlotte M. Yonge, 1854.

Mossop, Mrs. *Trelawny of the Wells* (play), A. W. Pinero, 1898.

Mossrose, Jewish employee of Eglantine and agent for his creditors. 'The Ravenswing,' *Men's Wives,* W. M. Thackeray, 1843.

Motes, Hazel, young preacher. *Wise Blood,* Flannery O'Connor, 1952.

Motford, Cornelia ('Kay'), m. H. M. Pulham.
  Guy, her brother.
H. M. Pulham, Esq., J. P. Marquand, 1941.

Moth, page of Armado. *Love's Labour's Lost* (play), W. Shakespeare.

Moth, Miss, typist at Miss Beautiman's. *Mr Ingleside,* E. V. Lucas, 1910.

Mothersole, Mrs, hanged as a witch. 'The Ash-tree,' *Ghost Stories of an Antiquary,* M. R. James, 1910.

Motherwell, Frances, actress, a Communist. *The Troubled Air,* Irwin Shaw, 1951.

Moti Guj, an elephant. 'Moti Guj—Mutineer' (s.s.), *Life's Handicap,* R. Kipling, 1891.

Motley, Juan, direct descendant of Don Juan, central character.
  Noel, his brother.
  Rhea, his sister.
  Sir Hildebrand, his father.
  Charlotte, his mother.
  'Young Jack,' the original Don Juan.
  Rev. Abel, his guardian, whose name he assumed.
Juan in America, E. Linklater, 1931.

Motshill, Mr, schoolmaster. *How Green Was My Valley,* R. Llewellyn, 1939.

Motswasele, cousin of Chief Letlotse, appointed Regent. *When We Become Men,* Naomi Mitchison, 1965.

Mottleville. *The Mysteries of Udolpho,* Mrs Radcliffe, 1794.

Mottram, of the Indian Survey. 'At the End of the Passage,' *Life's Handicap,* R. Kipling, 1891.

Mottram, Jephthah. *The Three Taps,* R. A. Knox, 1927.

Mottram, Hon. Peter. *Mid-Channel* (play), A. W. Pinero, 1909.

Mottram, Rex, m. Lady Julia Flyte. *See also* BRENDA CHAMPION. *Brideshead Revisited,* E. Waugh, 1945.

Motts, Miss. *Uncle Remus,* J. C. Harris, 1880–95.

Mouchy, Madame de, Quebec acquaintance of Warrington. *The Virginians,* W. M. Thackeray, 1857–9.

Mould, undertaker.
His wife and daughters.
Martin Chuzzlewit, C. Dickens, 1844.

Moulin, Mrs Charlotte, Ethelberta Petherwin's aunt. *The Hand of Ethelberta,* T. Hardy, 1876.

Moulton, Francis D., m. Hatty Doran. 'The Noble Bachelor,' *The Adventures of Sherlock Holmes,* A. Conan Doyle, 1892.

Moultrie, Ag, the Roarer and Greeter. *A Scots Quair,* trilogy, 1932–4, Lewis Grassic Gibbon.

Moultrie, Misses Mary, Elizabeth and **Agnes.** 'The House Surgeon' (s.s.) *Actions and Reactions,* R. Kipling, 1909.

Mouncer.
His mother.
The Porch, 1937, and *The Stronghold,* 1939, R. Church.

Mounchensey, Sir Richard.
Raymond, his son.
The Merry Devil of Edmonton. (play), Anon.

Mounsey, Mrs, old harridan, blackmailer of Adelaide Lambert. *Britannia Mews,* Margery Sharp, 1946.

Mount, Dr.
Stella, his daughter.
The End of the House of Alard, Sheila Kaye-Smith, 1923.

Mount, Mrs Bella, 'enchantress' of Richard Feverel. *The Ordeal of Richard Feverel,* G. Meredith, 1859.

Mount Severn. *See* VANE.

Mountain, Mrs, companion to Mme Esmond.
Fanny, her daughter, m. Henry Warrington.
The Virginians, W. M. Thackeray, 1857–8.

Mountararat, Earl of. *Iolanthe* (comic opera), Gilbert & Sullivan, 1882.

Mountclere, Lord, m. Ethelberta Petherwin.
Hon. Edgar, his brother.
The Hand of Ethelberta, T. Hardy, 1876.

Mountjoy, Angela. *See* CICELY TRUSBUT.

Mountjoy, Henrietta.
Colonel Mountjoy, her father.
The House in Paris, Elizabeth Bowen, 1935.

Mountolive, David, a British diplomat. *Justine* and others in *The Alexandria Quartet,* 1957–61, Lawrence Durrell.

Mountry, Lord, m. Cynthia Drassilis. *The Little Nugget,* P. G. Wodehouse, 1913.

Mouraki Pasha, Turkish governor. *Phroso,* A. Hope, 1897.

Mouth, Mr Ahmadou, the prancing nigger.
His ambitious wife.
Miami, their daughter.
Edna, their youngest daughter, who becomes a harlot.
Charlie, their son.
Prancing Nigger, Ronald Firbank, 1924.

Mowbray, Earl of.
Lady Joan and **Lady Maud,** his daughters.
Sybil, B. Disraeli, 1845.

Mowbray, Miss, factotum to Jessica Dean. The *Barsetshire* series, Angela Thirkell, 1933 onwards.

Mowbray, John, Laird of St Ronan's.
Clara, his sister, m. Valentine Bulmer.
St Ronan's Well, W. Scott, 1824.

Mowcher, Miss, masseuse, a dwarf. *David Copperfield,* C. Dickens, 1850.

Mowdiewort, Saunders (Alexander), minister's man and gravedigger. *The Lilac Sunbonnet,* S. R. Crockett, 1894.

Mowgli (Nathoo among people), boy brought up by wolves, central character, m. Abdul Gafur's daughter. *The Jungle Books,* 1894–5, and 'In the Rukh' (s.s.), *Many Inventions,* 1893, R. Kipling.

Moxton, Mrs, housekeeper to Oswald

Sydenham. *Joan and Peter,* H. G. Wells, 1918.

Moxton, Mrs Dora (Moxie), lady's maid. *Relative Values* (play), Noël Coward, 1951.

Moy-Thompson, Rev. Mr, headmaster.
His wife.
Mr Perrin and Mr Traill, Hugh Walpole, 1911.

Msimangu, Rev. Theophilus, native priest. *Cry, the Beloved Country,* A. Paton, 1948.

Mucklebackit, Saunders.
Maggie, his dominating wife.
Steenie, Patie and **Jennie,** their children.
Simon, his father.
Elspeth, his mother, *née* Cheyne.
The Antiquary, W. Scott, 1816.

Mucklewrath, Habakkuk, insane preacher. *Old Mortality,* W. Scott, 1816.

Mucksweat, Gunner. *Peter Jackson, Cigar Merchant,* G. Frankau, 1919.

Mudel, Dr Adolf, psycho-analyst. *Cold Comfort Farm,* Stella Gibbons, 1932.

Mudjekewis, father of Hiawatha. *The Song of Hiawatha* (poem), H. W. Longfellow, 1855.

Muff, Tarquinius.
Blatheremskite, his brother.
Hawbuck Grange, R. S. Surtees, 1847.

Mufferson, Willie, 'a model boy.' *The Adventures of Tom Sawyer,* Mark Twain, 1876.

Mugford, Frederick, owner of the *Pall Mall Gazette.*
His wife.
The Adventures of Philip, W. M. Thackeray, 1861–2.

Mugger, The, a crocodile. 'The Undertakers,' *The Second Jungle Book,* R. Kipling, 1895.

Muggleton, Mrs. *Fanny by Gaslight,* M. Sadleir, 1940.

Mugridge, Thomas, cook on *Ghost. The Sea Wolf,* Jack London, 1904.

Mugsie, m. Zeke Harrington. *Chosen Country,* J. dos Passos, 1951.

Muhlen, Mr. *See* RETLOW.

Muir, Lieutenant. *The Pathfinder,* J. Fenimore Cooper, 1840.

Muir, Robert.
His wife.
The Sky Pilot, R. Connor, 1899.

Muirhead, Miss, landscape gardener, cousin of Mr Ingleside. *Mr Ingleside,* E. V. Lucas, 1910.

Mulcahy, Corporal, paid agitator. 'The Mutiny of the Mavericks' (s.s.), *Life's Handicap,* R. Kipling, 1891.

Mulcare, Michael, fireman on board the cargo ship *Oroya. Captain Bottell,* James Hanley, 1933.

Mulcaster, Lord ('Boy').
Celia, his sister, m. Charles Ryder.
Brideshead Revisited, E. Waugh, 1945.

Mules, Rev. Mr, new Rector of St Enedoc. *In the Roar of the Sea,* S. Baring-Gould, 1892.

Muleygrubs, Marmaduke, staymaker of Ludgate Hill.
His wife and family.
Handley Cross, R. S. Surtees, 1843.

Mulhammer, Sir Claude.
Lady Elizabeth, his wife. *See also* LUCASTA ANGEL and BARNABAS KAGHAN.
The Confidential Clerk (play), T. S. Eliot, 1954.

Mulholland, a sailor. 'Mulholland's Contract' (poem), *The Seven Seas,* R. Kipling, 1896.

Mulholland, Bartly. *The Informer,* L. O'Flaherty, 1925.

Mulholland, Sir Francis. *Mr Rowl,* D. K. Broster, 1924.

Mull, Lord. *Lise Lillywhite,* Margery Sharp, 1951.

Mull and Cantire, Sarah, Duchess of, grandmother of Vere Herbert.
Frank, the duke, her grandson, m. Fuchsia Leach.
Moths, Ouida, 1880.

Muller, head ranger. 'In the Rukh' (s.s.), *Many Inventions,* R. Kipling, 1893.

Muller, Cora.
Rufus, her father.
The Trial, Charlotte M. Yonge, 1864.

Mullet, Professor. *Martin Chuzzlewit,* C. Dickens, 1844.

Mulligan, Desmond, poet and journalist. *Men's Wives,* W. M. Thackeray, 1843.

Mulligan, Malachi ('Buck'), medical student. *Ulysses,* James Joyce, 1922.

Mulligan, Peter. *The Informer*, L. O'Flaherty, 1925.

Mulligan, Spike, ex-burglar, friend of Jimmy Pitt. *A Gentleman of Leisure*, P. G. Wodehouse, 1910.

Mulliner, butler to Mrs Jamieson. *Cranford*, Mrs Gaskell, 1853.

Mulliner, Mr, central character and narrator.
  Rev. Augustine, his nephew, curate to Rev. Stanley Brandon, later chaplain to the Bishop of Stortford, m. Jane Brandon.
  Clarence, his cousin, m. Gladys Biggs.
  Frederick, his nephew, m. Jane Oliphant.
    George, a doctor, Frederick's brother, a stutterer.
  Lancelot, his nephew, poet and film-star.
  Wilfred, his brother, scientist, inventor of Mulliner's Magic Marvels, m. Angela Purdue.
  William, his uncle, m. Myrtle Banks.
    John San Francisco Earthquake, their son.
  And other relations.
Meet Mr Mulliner, 1927, and elsewhere, P. G. Wodehouse.

Mullinix, detective. 'Hoodwinked' (s.s.), *From Place to Place*, Irvin S. Cobb, 1920.

Mullins, a pirate. *Peter Pan* (play), J. M. Barrie, 1904.

Mullins, games captain. 'Regulus' (s.s.), *A Diversity of Creatures*, 1917, and elsewhere, R. Kipling.

Mullins, Sergeant. 'Black Jack' (s.s.), *Soldiers Three*, R. Kipling, 1888.

Mullion, Jenny, deaf observer. *Crome Yellow*, Aldous Huxley, 1922.

Mullockson. See KATE MORRISON.

Mulqueen, Danny, m. Teresa Considine.
  Ignatius, Reggie, Marie-Rose and **Aggie,** their children.
Without my Cloak, Kate O'Brien, 1931.

Mulvaney, Lieutenant, U.S. Army. *While the Sun Shines* (play), T. Rattigan, 1943.

Mulvaney, Terence, one of the 'Soldiers Three' with Learoyd and Ortheris, m. Dinah Shadd. 'The Three Musketeers' (s.s.), *Plain Tales from the Hills*, 1888, and many others, R. Kipling.

Mumblazen, Michael, heraldic expert. *Kenilworth*, W. Scott, 1821.

Mumblecourt, Margerie, nurse to Dame Custance. *Ralph Roister Doister* (play), N. Udall, 1551.

Mumby, Squire.
  John and **Martin,** his sons.
Mr Weston's Good Wine, T. F. Powys, 1927.

Muncaster, Mrs. 'The Matchmaker' (s.s.), *Sir Pompey and Madame Juno*, M. Armstrong, 1927.

Muncaster, Fred, owner of Wammerawa Station.
  Dolly, his daughter, m. Harry Middleton.
The Dark Horse, Nat Gould.

Munce, bookmaker. *Jane Clegg* (play), St John Ervine, 1913.

Munday, Mrs, shopkeeper, Whortley; Lewisham's landlady. *Love and Mr Lewisham*, H. G. Wells, 1900.

Munday, John, groom, central character.
  m. (1) Ellen.
    Their two sons.
    (2) Alice.
  His mother.
  Nellie, his sister.
Farewell Victoria, T. H. White, 1933.

Munden, Harvey. 'A Lodger in Maze Pond' (s.s.), *The House of Cobwebs*, G. Gissing, 1906.

Mungo, Jock, subeditor, the *Courier*. *Master Jim Probity*, F. Swinnerton, 1952.

Mungojerrie and **Rumpelteazer,** 'a notorious couple.' *Old Possum's Book of Practical Cats*, T. S. Eliot, 1939.

Munn, Mrs, a diabetic. *Thursday Afternoons*, Monica Dickens, 1945.

Munn, Percy, young Kentucky lawyer and farmer.
  May, his wife.
Night Rider, Robert Penn Warren, 1939.

Munnings, Mrs, aunt of Jim Lanigan.
  Thady, her husband.
Without my Cloak, Kate O'Brien, 1931.

Munodi, court noble. *Gulliver's Travels*, J. Swift, 1726.

Munro, Colonel.
Alice and **Cora,** his daughters.
The Last of the Mohicans, J. Fenimore Cooper, 1826.

Munro, Grant. 'The Yellow Face,' *Memoirs of Sherlock Holmes,* A. Conan Doyle, 1894.

Munson, Buford, Negro farmer. *The Violent Bear It Away,* Flannery O'Connor, 1960.

Munt, Dick, collector of coffins. *The Travelling Grave* (s.s.), L. P. Hartley.

Munt, Mrs Julia, aunt of Helen and Margaret Schlegel. *Howards End,* E. M. Forster, 1910.

Murascho, Tony, real name of Al Grecco. *Appointment in Samarra,* John O'Hara, 1935.

Murch, Inspector. *Trent's Last Case,* E. C. Bentley, 1912.

Murchison, Lord (Gerald). *The Sphinx without a Secret* (s.s.), O. Wilde, 1888.

Murchison, Henry, Editor of *The Flame,* friend of John Strickland. *No Other Tiger,* A. E. W. Mason, 1927.

Murchison, Joan, typist and assistant to Lord Peter Wimsey. *Strong Poison,* Dorothy L. Sayers, 1930.

Murcraft. *The Devil Is an Ass* (play), B. Jonson, 1616.

Murdoch, William, landlord, the McClellan Arms. *The Five Red Herrings,* Dorothy L. Sayers, 1931.

Murdock, Charles.
Peggy, his wife.
The Ghost Train (play), A. Ridley, 1925.

Murdock, Cynthia, V.A.D. *The Mysterious Affair at Styles,* Agatha Christie, 1920.

Murdock, Jim. 'Glory in the Day-time' (s.s.), *Here Lies,* Dorothy Parker, 1919.

Murdockson, Madge ('Madge Wild-fire').
Donald, her father.
Meg, her mother.
The Heart of Midlothian, W. Scott, 1818.

Murdstone, Edward, of Murdstone & Grinby, wine merchants; 2nd husband of Mrs Copperfield and step-father of David.
Jane, his sister.
David Copperfield, C. Dickens, 1850.

Murgatroyd, Major, Dragoon Guards, m. Lady Angela. *Patience* (comic opera), Gilbert & Sullivan, 1881.

Murgatroyd, Miss, founder and head of Joan and Peter's first school. *Joan and Peter,* H. G. Wells, 1918.

Murgatroyd, Sir Ruthven, disguised as Robin Oakapple.
Sir Despard, his younger brother, a wicked baronet, m. Mad Margaret.
Sir Roderic, an ancestor, m. Dame Hannah.
Ruddigore (comic opera), Gilbert & Sullivan, 1887.

Murphy, Anna.
Henry, her father.
Maud, her mother, *née* Condon.
Harry, Tom and **Charlie,** her brothers.
The Land of Spices, Kate O'Brien, 1941.

Murray, Mr and Mrs.
Their children:
Rosalie, m. Sir Thomas Ashby.
Matilda.
John.
Charles.
Agnes Grey, Anne Brontë, 1847.

Murray, Denzil, 'pure-blooded High-lander.' *Ziska,* Marie Corelli, 1897.

Murray, Gilpin, boyhood friend of Frederick Ide. *The Heritage of Hatcher Ide,* Booth Tarkington, 1941.

Murray, Nora. *Mixed Marriage* (play), St John Ervine, 1911.

Murray-Forbes, Vice-Admiral Sir Vincent. *The Cruel Sea,* N. Mon-sarrat, 1951.

Murtagh, Lavengro's childhood friend. *Romany Rye,* George Borrow, 1857.

Murtha, detective. 'The Luck Piece' (s.s.), *From Place to Place,* Irvin S. Cobb, 1920.

Murthwaite, Indian traveller and part narrator. *The Moonstone,* W. Col-lins, 1868.

Musallem, a Bedouin boy.
His great-grandfather of the same name.
Smith's Gazelle, Lionel Davidson, 1971.

Muscari, poet. 'The Paradise of Thieves,' *The Wisdom of Father Brown,* G. K. Chesterton, 1914.

Muschat, Nicol, 'debauched and profligate wretch.' *The Heart of Midlothian,* W. Scott, 1818.

Museau, Monsieur, governor of Fort Duquesne. *The Virginians,* W. M. Thackeray, 1857–9.

Musgrave, butler to Sir Edmund Roundelay. *A Footman for the Peacock,* Rachel Ferguson, 1940.

Musgrave, Anthony.
  Dorothy, his sister.
 Beau Austin (play), W. E. Henley & R. L. Stevenson, 1892.

Musgrave, Daisy.
  William, her husband. Friends of Nick Ratcliffe.
 The Way of an Eagle, Ethel M. Dell, 1912.

Musgrave, Reginald. 'The Musgrave Ritual,' *Memoirs of Sherlock Holmes,* A. Conan Doyle, 1894.

Musgrove, of the Great House, Uppercross.
  Mary, his wife.
  Their children:
   Richard.
   Charles, m. Mary Elliot.
   Henrietta.
   Laura, and others.
 Persuasion, Jane Austen, 1818.

Mush, Freddy, secretary to Rupert Catskill. *Men Like Gods,* H. G. Wells, 1923.

Musidora. *The Seasons* (Summer) (poem), J. Thomson, 1730.

Muskham, Jack, horse breeder. *Flowering Wilderness,* J. Galsworthy, 1932.

Musliner, Mr and Mrs. *Lummox,* Fannie Hurst, 1924.

Muspratt, Mrs Beryl, admiral's widow with three children, m. Lord Brideshead. *Brideshead Revisited,* E. Waugh, 1945.

Musset, Phoebe, village coquette. *Mehalah,* S. Baring-Gould, 1880.

Mustapha, Baba, uncle of Shibli Bagarag; later King of Oolb. *The Shaving of Shagpat,* G. Meredith, 1856.

Mutanhed, Lord. *Pickwick Papers,* C. Dickens, 1837.

Mutimer, 'early Georgian' butler of Mr Blandish. 'The Spoils of Mr Blandish,' story read by Boon. *Boon,* H. G. Wells, 1915.

Mutius, son of Titus Andronicus. *Titus Andronicus* (play), W. Shakespeare.

Mutlar, Daisy, one-time fiancée of Lupin Pooter, m. Murray Posh. *The Diary of a Nobody,* G. & W. Grossmith, 1892.

Mutrie, Mrs, widow of railway tycoon. *The Naulakha,* R. Kipling & W. Balestier, 1892.

Mweta, Adamson, President of a newly independent African state. *A Guest of Honour,* Nadine Gordimer, 1971.

Mwres, Elizabeth, m. Denton. *A Story of the Days to Come* (s.s.), H. G. Wells, 1899.

Mybug, author, m. Rennett Starkadder. *Cold Comfort Farm,* Stella Gibbons, 1932.

Mycates, King of Persia. *Tamburlaine* (play), C. Marlowe, 1587.

Myers, racing tipster. *A Farewell to Arms,* E. Hemingway, 1929.

Myles, Jean, m. Tommy Sandys. *Sentimental Tommy,* J. M. Barrie, 1896.

Myles, Marvin, one-time fiancée of H. M. Pulham, m. John Ransome. *H. M. Pulham, Esq.,* J. P. Marquand, 1941.

Mynors, Henry, suitor of Anna Tellwright. *Anna of the Five Towns,* Arnold Bennett, 1902.

Myrrha, female slave. *Sardanapalus* (poem), Lord Byron, 1821.

Myrtle, Mr. *The Conscious Lovers* (play), R. Steele, 1722.

Myrtle, Mrs, housekeeper to Sir Massingberd Heath. *Lost Sir Massingberd,* James Payn, 1864.

Myrtle, May, professional co-respondent. *Holy Deadlock,* A. P. Herbert, 1934.

Mysa, the buffalo. 'How Fear Came' and elsewhere, *The Second Jungle Book,* R. Kipling, 1895.

N

Naboth. 'Naboth' (s.s.), *Life's Handicap*, R. Kipling, 1891.

Nadgett, secret agent of the Anglo-Bengalee Disinterested Loan Life Assurance Co. *Martin Chuzzlewit*, C. Dickens, 1844.

Nadin, Joseph, Deputy Constable of Manchester. *Starvecrow Farm*, Stanley Weyman, 1905.

Nadya, Queen, m. Keri, Prince of Zalgar. *The Queen was in the Parlour* (play), N. Coward, 1926.

Nafferton. 'Pig' (s.s.), *Plain Tales from the Hills*, R. Kipling, 1888.

Nag, a snake.
  Nagaina, his wife.
'Rikki Tikki Tavi,' *The Jungle Book*, R. Kipling, 1894.

Nagel, Undine. *Tom Tiddler's Ground*, E. Shanks, 1934.

Nameless, Limehouse restaurant keeper.
  His wife and daughter.
The Hollow Man (s.s.), T. Burke.

Namgay Doola (corruption of Patsy Doolan), red-haired native of Irish descent. 'Namgay Doola' (s.s.), *Life's Handicap*, R. Kipling, 1891.

Nana, Newfoundland dog, nurse to the Darling children. *Peter Pan* (play), J. M. Barrie, 1904.

Nancarrow, Roderick, solicitor, m. Milly Treloar. *The Winds of Chance*, S. K. Hocking.

Nance, friend of 'Tilda. *No. 5 John Street*, R. Whiteing, 1902.

Nancy, member of Fagin's gang. *Oliver Twist*, C. Dickens, 1838.

Nandie, daughter of King Panda, m. Saduko. *Child of Storm*, H. Rider Haggard, 1913.

Nandy, John Edward, father of Mrs Plornish. *Little Dorrit*, C. Dickens, 1857.

Nanki-Poo. *See* THE MIKADO.

Nanni. 'Be this her Memorial' (s.s.), *My People*, Caradoc Evans, 1915.

Nantauquas, Indian war chief. *By Order of the Company*, Mary Johnston, 1900.

Narcissus. 'The Princess of Kingdom Gone' (s.s.), *Adam and Eve and Pinch Me*, A. E. Coppard, 1921.

Narjis, nurse to Marsinah. *Kismet* (play), E. Knoblock, 1911.

Narracombe, Mrs, aunt of Megan David. *The Apple Tree*, J. Galsworthy, 1918.

Narwitz, Graf von (Rupert), German officer.
  Julie, his wife, *née* Quinlan.
The Fountain, C. Morgan, 1932.

Nash, Anthony. *The Old Dominion*, Mary Johnston, 1899.

Nash, Bunny, an actress. *Tell Me How Long The Train's Been Gone*, James Baldwin, 1968.

Nash, Richard ('Beau') (hist.). *Monsieur Beaucaire* (play), Booth Tarkington, 1902.

Nash, Nancy, charwoman cured by Dr Lydgate. *Middlemarch*, George Eliot, 1871–2.

Nash, Pamela ('Beau'), close friend of Mary Innes. *Miss Pym Disposes*, Josephine Tey, 1946.

Nathan, majordomo at Castlewood. *The Virginians*, W. M. Thackeray, 1857–9.

Nathaniel, Sir, curate. *Love's Labour's Lost* (play), W. Shakespeare.

Nathoo. *See* MOWGLI.

Nawab Bahadur. *A Passage to India*, E. M. Forster, 1924.

Naylor, Sir Richard, Irish landowner, uncle of Lois Farquar.
  Myra, his wife.
  Laurence, Lady Naylor's nephew.
The Last September, Elizabeth Bowen, 1929.

Nazing, Walter.
  Annabel, his wife.
The Silver Spoon, J. Galsworthy, 1926.

Neb, Negro servant of Miles Wallingford. *Afloat and Ashore*, J. Fenimore Cooper, 1844.

Neckett ('Coavinses'), **'a follower'** (sheriff's officer).
  Charlotte, Emma and **Tom,** his children.
Bleak House, C. Dickens, 1853.

Neckland, Bert, farm labourer. *The Saliva Tree,* Brian W. Aldiss, 1966.

Needham, Rev. Tommy, m. Octavia Crawley. The *Barsetshire* series, Angela Thirkell, 1933 onwards.

Negget, George, farmer.
  Lizzie, his wife.
'Cupboard Love' (s.s.), *The Lady of the Barge,* W. W. Jacobs, 1902.

Neigh, Alfred, Mr Doncastle's nephew. *The Hand of Ethelberta,* T. Hardy, 1876.

Neil of the Tom, red-headed son of Duncan. *Catriona,* R. L. Stevenson, 1893.

Neilan, Kit. *French without Tears* (play), T. Rattigan, 1936.

Neilson, Swedish philosopher on South Sea island.
  Sally, his native wife.
'Red' (s.s.), *The Trembling of a Leaf,* W. S. Maugham, 1921.

Nelaguine, Madame Nadine, sister of Sergius Zouroff. *Moths,* Ouida, 1880.

Neleta, half-breed mistress of Anthony. *Anthony Adverse,* Hervey Allen, 1934.

Nella, Venetian servant. *The Notorious Mrs Ebbsmith* (play), A. W. Pinero, 1895.

Nello, Florentine barber. *Romola,* George Eliot, 1863.

Nennius, British commander. *Bonduca* (play), Beaumont & Fletcher, 1614.

Nerissa, waiting-maid to Portia. *The Merchant of Venice* (play), W. Shakespeare.

Nerone, friend of Marie Varese. *Adam's Breed,* Radclyffe Hall, 1926.

Neroni, Signora Madeleine (Vesey Neroni, Vicinironi) (*née* Stanhope), crippled beauty. *Barchester Towers,* A. Trollope, 1857.

Nesbit, Mrs, aunt of Lady Martindale. *Heartsease,* Charlotte M. Yonge, 1854.

Nesbit, Mrs Norah. *Of Human Bondage,* W. S. Maugham, 1915.

Nessus, a centaur. *Jurgen,* J. B. Cabell, 1921.

Nestor, a Grecian commander. *Troilus and Cressida* (play), W. Shakespeare.

Netley, Dora Phyllis, employee of Barnabas Ltd. *Flowers for the Judge,* Margery Allingham, 1936.

Nettlewick, J. F. C., bank examiner. 'Friends in San Rosario' (s.s.), *Roads of Destiny,* O. Henry, 1909.

Neuner, Johann Seppel, friend of Hans Breitner. *The Mortal Storm,* Phyllis Bottome, 1937.

Nevers, Duc de (Louis), m. Gabrielle de Caylus.
  Gabrielle, their daughter, m. Henri de Lagardere.
The Duke's Motto, J. H. McCarthy, 1908.

Nevile, Marmaduke. *The Last of the Barons,* Lord Lytton, 1843.

Nevill, friend of Scudmore. *A Woman is a Weathercock* (play), N. Field, 1612.

Neville, Mr. *Hawbuck Grange,* R. S. Surtees, 1847.

Neville, Constance. *She Stoops to Conquer* (play), Oliver Goldsmith, 1773.

Neville, Edward Geraldin, son of the Countess of Glenallan.
  Eveline, cousin of the Earl of Glenallan, mother of Lovel.
The Antiquary, W. Scott, 1816.

Nevin, subaltern. 'A Conference of the Powers' (s.s.), *Many Inventions,* R. Kipling, 1893.

Nevin, Duncan, of Nimrod Mews. *Handley Cross,* R. S. Surtees, 1843.

New, Elijah. 'The Three Strangers,' *Wessex Tales,* T. Hardy, 1888.

Newall, Edwin, American tycoon.
  Mel, his daughter, m. Rodney Jones.
Ming Yellow, J. P. Marquand, 1935.

Newberry, Lizzy, farmer's widow engaged in smuggling, m. Richard Stockdale. 'The Distracted Preacher,' *Wessex Tales,* T. Hardy, 1888.

Newberry, Richard, Director of Crane & Newberry. *The Dream,* H. G. Wells, 1924.

Newbiggin, Dennis, shady partner of Oliver Essex. *My Son, My Son,* H. Spring, 1938.

Newcome, Thomas, weaver.
  m. (1) Susan.
    Colonel Thomas Newcome, their son, m. Emma, widow of Jack Casey.
    Clive, their son.
      m. (1) Rosey Mackenzie.
        Tommy, their son.

(2) Ethel Newcome, his cousin.
(2) Sophia Alethea Hobson.
Their twin sons:
Brian (later Sir), m. Lady Ann Gaunt.
Their children:
Barnes, m. Lady Clara Pullcyn.
Ethel, m. Clive Newcombe, her cousin.
And others.
Hobson, twin of Brian, m. Maria.
Sammie, Maria, Louisa and others, their children.
The Newcomes, W. M. Thackeray, 1853–5.

Newcomer, Joe (Decent Respectable), in love with Lulie Harrington. *Chosen Country,* J. dos Passos, 1951.

Newent, Mrs Hilda, sister of Elizabeth Trant. *The Good Companions,* J. B. Priestley, 1929.

Newland, Miss, poison pen victim. *Gaudy Night,* Dorothy L. Sayers, 1935.

Newman, Christopher. *The American,* H. James, 1877.

Newman, Miss Lena. *At Mrs Beam's* (play), C. K. Munro, 1923.

Newmark, Stephen, m. Phyllis Bligh.
Barney, their son.
Phyllis, their daughter, m. Clarence Rochester.
Judith Paris, 1931, and *The Fortress,* 1932, Hugh Walpole.

Newsom, Mr and Mrs, servants of Vanessa Herries. *Vanessa,* Hugh Walpole, 1933.

Newsome, Chadwick, American expatriate.
Mrs Pocock, his sister.
The Ambassadors, Henry James, 1903.

Newson, Captain Richard, buys Henchard's wife at a fair. *The Mayor of Casterbridge,* T. Hardy, 1886.

Newton, Sir Isaac, a newt. *The Tale of Jeremy Fisher,* Beatrix Potter, 1906.

Newton, 'Waffles,' reporter. *Strong Poison,* Dorothy L. Sayers, 1930.

Nibby, traveller in Gillingwater burners, m. Carrie Waghorn. *The Town Traveller,* G. Gissing, 1898.

Nibs, one of Peter's band. *Peter Pan* (play), J. M. Barrie, 1904.

Nic Leoid, Sheen. 'The Fisher of Men' (s.s.), *Spiritual Tales,* Fiona Macleod, 1903.

Nicholas ('The Count'), central character. 'The Almond Tree' (s.s.) and others, *The Riddle,* W. de la Mare, 1923.

Nicholas.
Anne, his wife.
The Dover Road (play), A. A. Milne, 1922.

Nicholas, Mrs, housekeeper to Christmas Evans. *How Green Was My Valley,* R. Llewellyn, 1939.

Nicholas, George. *The Mystery of a Hansom Cab,* F. Hume, 1886.

Nichols, Captain, skipper of s.s. *Fenton,* who has chronic dyspepsia. *The Narrow Corner,* W. S. Maugham, 1932.

Nicholson, Joan, niece of Richard Messenger. *The Education of Uncle Paul,* A. Blackwood, 1909.

Nickleby, Nicholas, central character, m. Madeline Bray.
Nicholas, his father.
His mother.
Kate, his sister, m. Frank Cheeryble.
Godfrey, his grandfather.
His wife.
Ralph, his great-uncle.
Ralph jnr, his villainous uncle.
See also SMIKE.
Nicholas Nickleby, C. Dickens, 1839.

Nicola, manservant. *Arms and the Man* (play), G. B. Shaw, 1894.

Nicolaivitch, H.H. Prince Alexis. *Huntingtower,* J. Buchan, 1922.

Nicolas, Dom, fat Picardy monk. 'A Lodging for the Night' (s.s.), *New Arabian Nights,* R. L. Stevenson, 1882.

Nicolo, Lord Carnal's Italian doctor. *By Order of the Company,* Mary Johnston, 1900.

Nicolo, bar-keeper, lover of Karen Blum. *The Smile of Karen* (s.s.), O. Onions.

Niculescu, Bella, English girl married to a Rumanian. *The Great Fortune,* Olivia Manning, 1960.

Nidderdale, Lord.
The Marquis of Auld Reekie, his father.

The Way We Live Now, A. Trollope, 1875.

Nightgall, Lawrence. *The Tower of London*, W. H. Ainsworth, 1840.

Nightingale, 'Flossie.'
 Sir Berkeley, his father.
 Housemaster (play), Ian Hay, 1936.

Nightingale, Jack.
 His father.
 His uncle.
 Tom Jones, H. Fielding, 1749.

Nightingale, Ronald. *The Masters*, 1951, part of the *Strangers and Brothers* sequence, C. P. Snow.

Nikola, Dr, central character. *Dr Nikola*, G. Boothby, 1896.

Nikola, Father, renegade priest, enemy of the Capsina. *The Capsina*, E. F. Benson, 1899.

Niles, Captain Peter, U.S. Artillery.
 Hazel, his sister.
 Mourning becomes Electra (play), E. O'Neill, 1931.

Nilghai, The, war correspondent. *The Light that Failed*, R. Kipling, 1890.

Nimmo. *Tracy's Tiger*, W. Saroyan, 1951.

Nimmo, Chester, radical politician, later Lord Nimmo, m. Nina Woodville.
 Tom, cabaret entertainer, Nina's son by her cousin Jim Latter.
 Sally, Nina's daughter by Latter.
 Prisoner of Grace, Joyce Cary, 1952.

Nimmo, James, servant of the colonel (Uncle Joseph). *A Knight on Wheels*, Ian Hay, 1914.

Nimrod, Apperley, sporting author. *Jorrocks's Jaunts and Jollities*, R. S. Surtees, 1838.

Ninny, Sir Innocent.
 His wife.
 Sir Abraham, their son.
 A Woman is a Weathercock (play), N. Field, 1612.

Nioche, Monsieur.
 Néonie, his daughter.
 The American, H. James, 1877.

Nipper, Susan, Florence Dombey's nurse, m. Toots. *Dombey and Son*, C. Dickens, 1848.

Nipson, Mrs, assistant headmistress. *What Katy Did at School*, Susan Coolidge, 1873.

Nita, maid to Francesca da Rimini. *Paolo and Francesca*, Stephen Phillips, 1900.

Niv, a witless lad. *The King of Elfland's Daughter*, Lord Dunsany, 1924.

Nix, Ernest, private detective. *The Jury*, G. Bullett, 1935.

Nixon, Mrs, servant of the Clayhangers. The *Clayhanger* trilogy, Arnold Bennett, 1910–16.

Nixon, Cristal, confidential servant of Redgauntlet. *Redgauntlet*, W. Scott, 1824.

Nixon, Ralph, half-brother of Myra Winchmore. *Not so Bad after All*, Nat Gould.

Noader, Colonel. 'Cards for the Colonel' (s.s.), *Last Recollections of My Uncle Charles*, N. Balchin, 1954.

Noakes, bicycle dealer. *Busman's Honeymoon*, Dorothy L. Sayers, 1937.

Noakes, Jacob, friend of Festus Derriman. *The Trumpet Major*, T. Hardy, 1880.

Noakes, Percy, law student. *Sketches by Boz*, C. Dickens, 1836.

Noaks, undergraduate. *Zuleika Dobson*, Max Beerbohm, 1911.

Noble, Sir Charles.
 His wife, 'mocker at religion.'
 Augusta, their daughter.
 The History of the Fairchild Family, Mrs Sherwood, 1818.

Noble, Mrs Henrietta, sister of Mrs Farebrother. *Middlemarch*, George Eliot, 1871–2.

Noble, Maury, young man about town. *The Beautiful and the Damned*, F. Scott Fitzgerald, 1922.

Nocentini, Gasparo, Italian vice-admiral, Legnano. *The Ship*, C. S. Forester, 1943.

Noel, Dr. 'The Suicide Club' (s.s.), *New Arabian Nights*, R. L. Stevenson, 1882.

Noel, Mr, housemaster. *St Winifred's*, F. W. Farrar, 1862.

Nofret, young concubine of Imhotep, murdered by Yahmose. *Death Comes as the End*, Agatha Christie, 1945.

Nog, Old, the heron. *Tarka the Otter*, H. Williamson, 1927.

Noggs, Newman, clerk to Ralph Nickleby. *Nicholas Nickleby*, C. Dickens, 1839.

Nogood Boyo. *Under Milk Wood* (play), Dylan Thomas, 1954.

Nokomis, mother of Wenonah. *The Song of Hiawatha* (poem), H. W. Longfellow, 1855.

Nolan, wealthy young man with whom Mrs Benham elopes. *The Research Magnificent,* H. G. Wells, 1915.

Nolan, Baruch, London hosier, retired to Treby. *Felix Holt,* George Eliot, 1866.

Nolan, Gypo, informer, central character. *The Informer,* L. O'Flaherty, 1925.

Nolan, Sheila, m. Dermot O'Riorden. *My Son, My Son,* H. Spring, 1938.

Nolte, Vincent, German friend of Anthony. *Anthony Adverse,* Hervey Allen, 1934.

Nonentity, Dr, metaphysician. *A Citizen of the World,* O. Goldsmith, 1762.

Nonsuch, Susan.
  Johnny, her son.
The Return of the Native, T. Hardy, 1878.

Noodler, a pirate. *Peter Pan* (play), J. M. Barrie, 1904.

Noon, Jim, eng. to Susan Daw, but killed in the war.
  His father and mother.
I Live Under a Black Sun, Edith Sitwell, 1937.

Noorna Bin Noorka, daughter of Vizier Feshnavat. *The Shaving of Shagpat,* G. Meredith, 1856.

Norbert, Father. *The Dove in the Eagle's Nest,* Charlotte M. Yonge, 1866.

Norcot, Peter, in love with Grace Malherb. *The American Prisoner,* E. Phillpotts, 1904.

Norfolk, Duke of (hist.). *Richard the Third* (play), W. Shakespeare.

Norfolk, Duke of (hist.). *Henry the Eighth* (play), W. Shakespeare.

Norley, Lord, patron of the arts. *Angel,* Elizabeth Taylor, 1957.

Norman, Clyde, old British queen in Rome. *The Judgment of Paris,* Gore Vidal, 1952.

Norman, Elsie.
  Her father.
The Beautiful Years, H. Williamson, 1921.

Norman, Julia, m. Basil Fane. *Going their own Ways,* A. Waugh, 1938.

Normandy, Beatrice, cousin of Lady Drew, mistress of Lord Carnaby, in love with George Ponderevo. *Tono Bungay,* H. G. Wells, 1909.

Norrie, prospector. *Gallions Reach,* H. M. Tomlinson, 1927.

Norrington, George, m. Lady Adela Chisholm.
  Jan, their son, eng. to Gilberte Penriddocke.
For Us in the Dark, Naomi Royde-Smith, 1937.

Norris, Mrs, *née* Ward, sister of Lady Bertram.
  Rev. Mr Norris, her husband.
Mansfield Park, Jane Austen, 1814.

Norris, Arthur, 'gent,' central character. *Mr Norris Changes Trains,* C. Isherwood, 1935.

Norris, Ruth, actress. *The Red House Mystery,* A. A. Milne, 1922.

North, Inspector, C.I.D., Bodmin, colleague of Rampion Savage. *The Nettle Shade,* 1963 and others, James Turner.

North, Rev. Mr, scholar and drunkard. *For the Term of his Natural Life,* M. Clarke, 1874.

North, Major Oliver, central character, m. Elizabeth Gray.
  Hattie, his mother.
  His sisters:
    Violet, m. Fred Williams.
    Heather, m. John Sandys.
The Happy Prisoner, Monica Dickens, 1946.

North, Violet, central character.
  Sir Acton, her father.
  Her stepmother.
  Anatolia, her half-sister.
Madcap Violet, W. Black, 1876.

Northerton, Ensign. *Tom Jones,* H. Fielding, 1749.

Northey, Hon. Mr, M.P.
  His wife, sister of Sophia and Tom Maitland.
Sophia, Stanley Weyman, 1900.

Northmore, Matthew, in love with Ruth Rendle. *The Mother,* E. Phillpotts, 1908.

Northmour, R., of Graden Easter. 'The Pavilion on the Links' (s.s.), *New Arabian Nights,* R. L. Stevenson, 1882.

Northrup, General. *The Queen's Husband* (play), R. E. Sherwood, 1928.

Northumberland, Earl of (Henry Percy) (hist.).
  His wife.
Richard the Second and *Henry the Fourth* (plays), W. Shakespeare.

Norton, Lady (the Dreadful Dowager).
Lord Norton, her son.
Eleanor, his wife.
The *Barsetshire* series, Angela Thirkell, 1933 onwards.

Norton, Irene. *See* ADLER.

Norton, Marda, house guest at Danielstown. *The Last September*, Elizabeth Bowen, 1929.

Norton, Mrs Mary, friend of Laura Jesson. *Brief Encounter* (play), N. Coward, 1945.

Norton, Mary Elizabeth Dodge. *See Naples and Die* (play), Elmer Rice, 1932.

Nosnibor, Senoj, eminent inhabitant of Erewhon.
His wife.
Their daughters:
Zulora.
Arowhena, m. the Narrator.
Erewhon, S. Butler, 1872.

Nottingham, Jed. *Twelve Horses and the Hangman's Noose*, Gladys Mitchell, 1956.

Nougher, John, headmaster. *Delina Delaney*, Amanda Ros.

Novak, Henry.
Mary, his daughter. Patients of Martin.
Martin Arrowsmith, Sinclair Lewis, 1925.

Novotny, Sidney.
His wife.
The World in the Evening, C. Isherwood, 1954.

Nowak, Otto, amoral youth keen on physical culture, a gigolo.
His mother, consumptive charlady.
His father, furniture remover.
Lothar, his brother.
Grete, his sister.
Goodbye to Berlin, Christopher Isherwood, 1939.

Nowell, Patricia, novelist, mistress of Tim Cornwell. *The Widow*, Francis King, 1957.

Nox, George, ex-public schoolboy, enemy of Mr Jaraby. *The Old Boys*, William Trevor, 1964.

Nubbles, Christopher, shop-boy to Trent, later employed by Garland; m. Barbara.
His mother.
The Old Curiosity Shop, C. Dickens, 1841.

Nuflo, grandfather of Rima. *Green Mansions*, W. H. Hudson, 1904.

Nugent. *See* GRACE REYNOLDS.

Nugent, Frank, one of the Famous Five at Greyfriars. The *Billy Bunter* series, Frank Richards.

Nugent, 'Needle,' tailor. *Juno and the Paycock* (play), S. O'Casey, 1925.

Nuñez, Ecuadoran mountaineer, central character. *The Country of the Blind* (s.s.), H. G. Wells, 1911.

Nunheim, Arthur, racketeer. *The Thin Man*, D. Hammett, 1934.

Nunn, Jimmy, comedian of Dinky Doos concert party, later Good Companions.
His wife.
The Good Companions, J. B. Priestley, 1929.

Nunsuch, Susan. *The Return of the Native*, T. Hardy, 1878.

Nupkins, George, senior magistrate, Ipswich.
His wife and daughter.
Pickwick Papers, C. Dickens, 1837.

Nupton, T. K., writer. 'Enoch Soames,' *Seven Men*, Max Beerbohm, 1919.

Nur, a harlot. *Saïd the Fisherman*, M. Pickthall, 1903.

Nurkeed, stoker. 'The Limitations of Pambé Serang' (s.s.), *Life's Handicap*, R. Kipling, 1891.

Nurse, to Juliet. *Romeo and Juliet* (play), W. Shakespeare.

Nusthwaite, Rev. Mr, Vicar of Bruisyard.
His wife.
Joseph and his Brethren, H. W. Freeman, 1928.

Nutkin, Squirrel, *The Tale of Squirrel Nutkin*, Beatrix Potter, 1903.

Nutley, solicitor. *The Heir*, V. Sackville-West, 1922.

Nuttel, Framton. *The Open Window* (s.s.), 'Saki' (H. H. Munro).

Nydia, blind flower girl and street singer. *The Last Days of Pompeii*, Lord Lytton, 1834.

Nym, follower of Falstaff, later soldier. *The Merry Wives of Windsor* and *Henry the Fifth* (plays), W. Shakespeare.

O

Oak, Gabriel, small farmer, then bailiff to Bathsheba Everdene, whom he m. as 2nd husband. *Far from the Madding Crowd,* T. Hardy, 1874.

Oakapple, Robin. *See* RUTHVEN MURGATROYD.

Oakhurst, John, gambler and 'bad man.' 'The Outcasts of Poker Flat' (s.s.), *The Luck of Roaring Camp,* Bret Harte, 1868.

Oaklands, Harry, friend of Frank Fairlegh, m. Fanny Fairlegh.
  Sir John and Lady Oaklands, his father and mother.
  Frank Fairlegh, F. E. Smedley, 1850.

Oakleigh, George, narrator.
  Bertrand, his uncle and guardian.
  Beryl, his sister.
  Sonia, S. McKenna, 1917.

Oakley.
  Edward, his son.
  'My Son Edward' (s.s.), *Louise,* Viola Meynell, 1954.

Oakley, Captain Charles, friend of Austin Ruthyn. *Uncle Silas,* Sheridan le Fanu, 1864.

Oakley, Mrs Dorothy.
  Greaves, her son, m. Susan Sedgemoor.
  Sir Lancelot Greaves, T. Smollett, 1762.

Oakroyd, Jess, joiner and carpenter, handyman to the Good Companions.
  His wife.
  Leonard, their son.
  Lily, their daughter.
  The Good Companions, J. B. Priestley, 1929.

Oaks, Lieutenant Sir Derby, in love with Miss Fotheringay. *Pendennis,* W. M. Thackeray, 1848–50.

Oakshott, Charles, tutor to Willie McArthur. *Born to be a Sailor,* G. Stables.

Oakum, brutal captain of the *Thunder. Roderick Random,* T. Smollett, 1748.

Oast, Richard, Labour M.P., friend of Mr Ingleside. *Mr Ingleside,* E. V. Lucas, 1910.

Oates, Sir Oliver, a parson. *The Black Arrow,* R. L. Stevenson, 1888.

Oates, Sally, wife of Raveloe cobbler.
  Jinny, her daughter.
  Silas Marner, George Eliot, 1861.

Oates, Superintendent Stanislaus. *Dancers in Mourning,* 1937, and elsewhere, Margery Allingham.

Obadiah, servant of Walter Shandy. *Tristram Shandy,* L. Sterne, 1767.

Oberon, King of the Fairies. *A Midsummer Night's Dream* (play), W. Shakespeare.

Obersdorf, Kurt, lover of Fran Dodsworth. *Dodsworth,* Sinclair Lewis, 1929.

Oberstein, Hugo, foreign agent. 'The Bruce-Partington Plans,' *His Last Bow,* A. Conan Doyle, 1917.

Oberwaltzer, Justice, judge trying Clyde Griffiths. *An American Tragedy,* T. Dreiser, 1925.

O'Bleary, boarder at Mrs Tibbs's. *Sketches by Boz,* C. Dickens, 1836.

Obregon.
  His wife.
  The Power and the Glory, Graham Greene, 1940.

O'Brien. Family name of LORD GLENMALINE.

O'Brien, Inner Party member. *1984,* G. Orwell, 1949.

O'Brien, Celeste, in love with Peter Simple.
  Colonel O'Brien, her father, French army officer.
  Peter Simple, Captain Marryat, 1834.

O'Brien, Echo, girl loved by Clinton Williams. *All Fall Down,* James Leo Herlihy, 1960.

Obstinate and **Pliable,** neighbours of Christian, who for a time accompany him. *Pilgrim's Progress,* J. Bunyan, 1678 and 1684.

O'Byrne, Norrie, in love with Tom Kernahans. *The Last of Summer,* Kate O'Brien, 1943.

O'Carroll, Marionetta, orphan niece of the Hilarys. *Nightmare Abbey,* T. L. Peacock, 1818.

Occasion, old hag, mother of Furor. *The Faërie Queene* (poem), E. Spenser, 1590.

Ochiltree, Edie, traveller, beggar and 'king's bedesman.' *The Antiquary,* W. Scott, 1816.

Ochs, servant of Stepan Hromka. *The Weak and the Strong,* G. Kersh, 1945.

Ocky Milkman. *Under Milk Wood* (play), Dylan Thomas, 1954.

Ocock, Henry, attorney.
Agnes, his wife.
His father, m. Tilly Beamish.
Tom and **Johnny,** his brothers.
The Fortunes of Richard Mahony, H. H. Richardson, 1917–30.

O'Connell, Justin.
His wife.
Waste (play), H. Granville-Barker, 1907.

O'Connor, former governor of jail. *It Is Never Too Late to Mend,* C. Reade, 1856.

O'Connor, Lieutenant. *St Patrick's Day* (play), R. B. Sheridan, 1775.

O'Connor, Edward, m. Fanny Dawson. *Handy Andy,* S. Lover, 1842.

O'Connor, Feargus, Chartist agitator. *The Fortress,* Hugh Walpole, 1932.

O'Connor, Jim, 'gentleman caller.' *The Glass Menagerie* (play), Tennessee Williams, 1948.

O'Connor, Sheila, schoolgirl. *The Restoration of Arnold Middleton* (play), David Storey, 1967.

Octavia, wife of Antony. *Antony and Cleopatra* (play), W. Shakespeare.

Octavius Caesar, triumvir after the death of Caesar. *Julius Caesar* and *Antony and Cleopatra* (plays), W. Shakespeare.

O'Day, Peep, a legatee. 'Boys will be Boys' (s.s.), *From Place to Place,* Irvin Cobb, 1920.

Oddjob, Goldfinger's Korean bodyguard, a killer. *Goldfinger,* Ian Fleming, 1959.

Oddman, Enoch, employee of Solomon Darke. *The House in Dormer Forest,* Mary Webb, 1920.

O'Dell, Maureen, a painter. *Eustace Chisholm and the Works,* James Purdy, 1968.

O'Donnell, Eileen, student at Leys College. *Miss Pym Disposes,* Josephine Tey, 1946.

O'Donnell, Shaun. *On the Spot* (play), E. Wallace, 1930.

O'Donovan, Seamus, a bailiff. *The Private Wound,* Nicholas Blake, 1968.

O'Dowd, Mrs, hearty Irishwoman.
Her drunken husband.
The Tree of Man, Patrick White, 1955.

O'Dowd, Major (later **General**) **Sir Michael.**
Margaretta ('Peggy'), his wife.
Aurelia, their daughter.
His aged mother.
Glorvina, his sister, m. Captain Posky.
Vanity Fair, W. M. Thackeray, 1847–8.

O'Dowd, Miss Betty. *Harry Lorrequer,* C. Lever, 1839.

O'Dowda, Count. *Fanny's First Play* (play), G. B. Shaw, 1905.

O'Dwyer. *Trelawny of the Wells* (play), A. W. Pinero, 1898.

Oessetrich, Mathilde.
Paula, Ermangarde and **Olga,** her daughters.
Lummox, Fannie Hurst, 1924.

O'Ferrall, Trilby, artist's model, central character.
Patrick, her father.
Trilby, George du Maurier, 1894.

O'Flaherty, Father, chaplain to the Bavarian envoy. *Catherine,* W. M. Thackeray, 1839–40.

O'Flaherty, Tom, army friend of Lorrequer. *Harry Lorrequer,* C. Lever, 1839.

O'Flannagan, Barney, sailor, friend of Martin. *Martin Rattler,* R. M. Ballantyne, 1858.

Og. *See* GOG.

Og, Alasdair Mor, son of Leord Nic sheen. 'The Fisher of Men' (s.s.), *Spiritual Tales,* Fiona Macleod, 1903.

Og, Angus. *The Crock of Gold,* James Stephens, 1912.

Ogg, Marine. *The Middle Watch* (play), Ian Hay & S. King-Hall, 1929.

Ogilvie, Ake, third husband of Chris Guthrie. *A Scots Quair,* trilogy, 1932–4, Lewis Grassic Gibbon.

Ogilvie, Jean, niece of Rev. Mr McCrimmon. *Mr Bolfry* (play), James Bridie, 1943.

Ogilvy, Lawyer.
His wife.
Janet, their daughter, m. Lownie.
A Window in Thrums, J. M. Barrie, 1889.

Ogilvy, Mrs Allardyce. *Catriona,* R. L. Stevenson, 1893.

Ogle, Dan, bad hat. *The Hole in the Wall,* A. Morrison, 1902.

Ogle, Peter, godfather of Billy Freeborn.
Mary, his daughter, m. Billy.
True Blue, W. H. G. Kingston.

Ogleby, Lord. *The Clandestine Marriage* (play), G. Colman the Elder, 1766.

Oglethorpe, Sam, friend of Jess Oakroyd.
Ted, his nephew.
The Good Companions, J. B. Priestley, 1929.

Ogmore, Mrs Ogmore-Pritchard's 1st husband. *Under Milk Wood* (play), Dylan Thomas, 1954.

Ogmore-Pritchard, Mrs. *See* PRITCHARD.

O'Grady, Miss, governess to the daughter of the Duchesse d'Ivry. *The Newcomes,* W. M. Thackeray, 1853–5.

O'Grady, Gustavus Granby.
Gustavus Horatio ('Ratty'), his son.
Augusta, his daughter.
Handy Andy, S. Lover. 1842.

O'Grady, Dr Lucius, M.O. for Clonmore, imprisoned by Guy Red. *The Search Party,* G. A. Birmingham, 1913.

O'Grady, Captain (later **Colonel**) **Philip,** m. Lady Julia Egerton. *Jack Hinton,* C. Lever, 1843.

O'Hagan, inventor. *Captain Kettle* series, C. J. Cutcliffe Hyne, 1898–1932.

O'Halloran, Count. *The Absentee,* Maria Edgeworth, 1812.

O'Halloran, May, servant of Jocelyn Chadwick. *Famine,* L. O'Flaherty, 1937.

O'Hanlon, Patsy.
Sally, his wife.
Their three children.
Famine, L. O'Flaherty, 1937.

O'Hara, Con. *On the Spot* (play), E. Wallace, 1930.

O'Hara, Hon. Denis. *The Bath Comedy,* 1899, and *Incomparable Bellairs,* 1904, A. & E. Castle.

O'Hara, Colour Sergeant Dennis. 'Black Jack' (s.s.), *Soldiers Three,* R. Kipling, 1888.

O'Hara, Kimball (Kim), central character.
Kimball, his father.
Annie, his mother. Both dead.
Kim, R. Kipling, 1901.

O'Hara, Michael. *The Dancing Druids,* Gladys Mitchell, 1948.

O'Hara, Michael. *Mixed Marriage* (play), St John Ervine, 1911.

O'Hara, Scarlett, central character, m. (1) Charles Hamilton.
(2) Frank Kennedy.
(3) Rhett Butler.
Gerald, her father.
Ellen, her mother.
Careen and **Suellen,** her sisters.
Gone with the Wind, Margaret Mitchell, 1936.

Oig, Robert, son of Robert Macgregor (Rob Roy). *Kidnapped,* R. L. Stevenson, 1886.

Ojo, one-time thief and pagan, turned mission leader. *Aissa Saved,* Joyce Cary, 1932.

Oke, common-room butler. 'An Unsavoury Interlude,' *Stalky & Co.,* R. Kipling, 1899.

O'Keefe, Iris, actress. *Britannia Mews,* Margery Sharp, 1946.

O'Kelly. 'Shillin' a Day' (poem), *Barrack-room Ballads,* R. Kipling, 1892.

O'Killigain, foreman stonemason. *Purple Dust* (play), Sean O'Casey, 1940.

Oldacre, Jonas (alias Cornelius), rascally builder. 'The Norwood Builder,' *The Return of Sherlock Holmes,* A. Conan Doyle, 1905.

Oldboy, Colonel.
Lady Mary, his wife.
Diana, their daughter.
Mr Jessamy, their son.
Lionel and Clarissa (play), I. Bickerstaffe, 1768.

Oldbuck, Jonathan, Laird of Monkbarns.
Willie-Wald, his elder brother.
Griselda, his sister.
The Antiquary, W. Scott, 1816.

Oldham, Robert. *Caroline* (play), W. S. Maugham, 1916.

Olding, John, labourer, of Tadd's

Hole. *Adam Bede,* George Eliot, 1859.

Oldinport, Squire of Knebley.
  Lady Felicia, his wife.
  Squire Oldinport, his cousin and successor.
'Mr Gilfil's Love Story' and 'The Rev. Amos Barton,' *Scenes of Clerical Life,* George Eliot, 1857.

Oldring, chief of the Masked Raider Gang. *Riders of the Purple Sage,* Zane Grey, 1912.

Oldtower, Sir Ralph, Bt, honest Tory squire.
  His son.
  Grace, his daughter.
John Halifax, Gentleman, Mrs Craik, 1856.

O'Leary, blackmailing publisher's clerk. 'Why Billy went Back' (s.s.), *All the World Wondered,* L. Merrick, 1911.

Olga, m. Paul Simon. *Through the Storm,* P. Gibbs, 1945.

Olifaunt, Nigel, Lord Glenvarloch, central character, m. Margaret Ramsay.
  Randal, his father.
The Fortunes of Nigel, W. Scott, 1822.

Olinthus, a Nazarene jeweller. *The Last Days of Pompeii,* Lord Lytton, 1834.

Oliphant, F. Neil, a Latin teacher. *The Rose of Tibet,* Lionel Davidson, 1962.

Oliphant, George, suicide who returns to life. *See* STAUNAS. *Thin Air,* John Pudney, 1961.

Oliphant, Jane, m. Frederick Mulliner. *Meet Mr Mulliner,* P. G. Wodehouse, 1927.

Oliphant, Royce, actor. *The Actor Manager,* L. Merrick, 1898.

Olivares, Antonio, wealthy Mexican ranch-owner.
  Isabella, his American 2nd wife.
  Inez, his daughter.
Death Comes for the Archbishop, Willa Cather, 1927.

Oliver, eldest son of Sir Rowland de Bois, m. Celia. *As You Like It* (play), W. Shakespeare.

Oliver, M.P. for Middlemarch. *Middlemarch,* George Eliot, 1871–2.

Oliver, Q.C., Lady Clara's counsel in the Newcome divorce. *The Newcomes,* 1853–5, and elsewhere, W. M. Thackeray.

Oliver, Mr, dull government official. *Mr Britling Sees It Through,* H. G. Wells, 1916.

Oliver, Bartholomew, owner of Pointz Hall.
  Giles, his son.
  Isa, his daughter-in-law.
  Mrs Lucy Swithin, his widowed sister.
Between The Acts, Virginia Woolf, 1941.

Oliver, Doris, friend of James Colet. *Gallions Reach,* H. M. Tomlinson, 1927.

Oliver, Rev. Eustace, early benefactor of William Essex. *My Son, My Son,* H. Spring, 1938.

Oliver, Grammer. *The Woodlanders,* T. Hardy, 1887.

Oliver, Jack.
  Kate, his wife. Friends of Asa Timberlake.
In this our Life, Ellen Glasgow, 1942.

Oliver, James. *To Have the Honour* (play), A. A. Milne, 1924.

Oliver, Sophia, philosopher travelling in Egypt. *The Judgment of Paris,* Gore Vidal, 1952.

Olivia, Manly's mistress. *The Plain Dealer,* W. Wycherley, 1677.

Olivia, rich countess. *Twelfth Night* (play), W. Shakespeare.

Olivia, Princess, wife of Prince Victor of X; infatuated by the Chevalier de Magny, and finally executed. *Barry Lyndon,* W. M. Thackeray, 1844

Olivier, President. 'The Sign of the Broken Sword,' *The Innocence of Father Brown,* G. K. Chesterton, 1911.

Olivier, Sybil, opera singer. *Grand Opera,* Vicki Baum, 1942.

Ollamoor, Wat ('Mop'), musician and dandy, father of Caroline Aspent's child. 'The Fiddler of the Reels,' *Life's Little Ironies,* T. Hardy, 1894.

Ollerton, Hope, rolling stone, Roger Liss's fiancée. *Let the People Sing,* J. B. Priestley, 1939.

Ollier, Walter, postman. *The Horse's Mouth,* Joyce Cary, 1944.

Olliver, Frank.
  Geoff, her husband.
Captain Desmond, V.C., Maud Diver, 1906.

Ollyett, journalist. 'The Village that Voted the Earth was Flat' (s.s.),

A Diversity of Creatures, R. Kipling, 1917.

O'Loughlin, Jimmy, general dealer. *The Search Party*, G. A. Birmingham, 1913.

Olympia, music-hall artist. *Juan in America*, E. Linklater, 1931.

Olympias, waiting-woman to Aspatia. *The Maid's Tragedy* (play), Beaumont & Fletcher, 1611.

O'Maera, Comfort, an American fan who proposes marriage to Max Fisher. *Pending Heaven*, William Gerhardie, 1930.

O'Malley, Charles, Irish Dragoons, central character and narrator, m. Lucy Dashwood.
 Godfrey, his uncle.
Charles O'Malley, C. Lever, 1841.

O'Malley, James, canal-boat owner. *The Bay*, L. A. G. Strong, 1941.

O'Malley, Terence.
 Judy, his cousin.
 Clodagh, her niece.
'An O'Malley comes Home' (s.s.), *Countrymen All*, Katherine Tynan, 1915.

O'Mara, Dallas, commercial artist. *So Big*, Edna Ferber, 1924.

O'Mara, Sir Gerald. *Lady Frederick* (play), W. S. Maugham, 1907.

O'Meagher, Josephine.
 Timothy, her brother, Jesuit instructor.
Adam of Dublin, C. O'Riordan, 1920.

Omer, draper, undertaker, etc. *David Copperfield*, C. Dickens, 1850.

Omnium, Duke of. *Doctor Thorne*, 1858, and elsewhere, A. Trollope.

Omnium, Duke of (Family name Palliser).
 His children:
 Lady Cora, m. Cecil Waring.
 Gerald, killed on D-day.
 Lord Silverbridge, m. Isabel Dale.
The *Barsetshire* series, Angela Thirkell, 1933 onwards.

O'More, Terence ('Freckles'), central character, m. Angel. *Freckles*, Gene S. Porter, 1904.

Omri. *Absalom and Achitophel* (poem), J. Dryden, 1681.

O'Murry, Stewart, journalist, the hero, in love with Irene Wayburn.
 Augustus Aylmer O'Murry, his father, publisher's editor.
 Douglas, his uncle, journalist.
 His sisters:
 Augusta, m. Rev. Abel Johns.
 Aldrith, m. Jack Fellbright.
A Georgian Love Story, Ernest Raymond, 1971.

O'Neil, Captain. 'With the Main Guard' (s.s.), *Soldiers Three*, 1888, and 'The Ballad of Boh da Thone' (poem), *Barrack-room Ballads*, 1892, R. Kipling.

O'Neil, Scripps, worker in pump factory.
 Lucy, his 1st wife.
 Lucy (Lousy), their daughter.
 Diana, his 2nd wife.
The Torrents of Spring, Ernest Hemingway, 1933.

O'Neill, Emmet, executive in a radio agency. *The Troubled Air*, Irwin Shaw, 1951.

O'Neill, Mary, central character, m. and div. Lord Raa, her cousin; in love with Martin Conrad.
 Daniel, originally Neale, her father.
 Isobel, her mother.
 Bridget, her aunt.
 O'Neill, bankrupt heir of Lord Raa.
The Woman Thou Gavest Me, Hall Caine, 1913.

O'Neill, Patricia, history tutor, Drayton College, Oxford, m. Alexis Stepanoff *The Dark Tide*, Vera Brittain, 1923.

Ong Chi Seng. *The Letter* (play), W. S. Maugham, 1927.

Oofty-Oofty, a Kanaka on *Ghost*. *The Sea Wolf*, Jack London, 1904.

Oosthuizen, Hans, m. Sarie Grafton. *The City of Gold*, F. Brett Young, 1939.

Oover, Abimelech V., Rhodes scholar. *Zuleika Dobson*, Max Beerbohm, 1911.

Opechancanough, king of Indian tribe. *By Order of the Company*, Mary Johnston, 1900.

Openshaw, John.
 Joseph, his father.
 Elias, his uncle.
'The Five Orange Pips,' *Adventures of Sherlock Holmes*, A. Conan Doyle, 1892.

Ophelia, daughter of Polonius. *Hamlet* (play), W. Shakespeare.

Opiniam, Dr. *Gryll Grange*, T. L. Peacock, 1860.

O'Quilligan, Major. *The Legend of Montrose*, W. Scott, 1819.

Oram, solicitor. *The Story of Ivy*, Mrs Belloc Lowndes, 1927.

O'Rane, David, central character, illegitimate son of Lord O'Rane, m. Sonia Dainton. *Sonia*, 1917, and elsewhere, S. McKenna.

Orange, Simon, house surgeon. *Sorrell and Son*, W. Deeping, 1925.

Orano. *Pizarro* (play), R. B. Sheridan, 1799.

Orcham, Evelyn, director, Imperial Palace Hotel, m. Violet Powler. *Imperial Palace*, Arnold Bennett, 1930.

Orchard, Rodney, chemist. *The Secret Vanguard*, M. Innes, 1940.

Ordith, Gunnery Lieut. Nicholas, R.N. *The Gunroom*, Charles Morgan, 1919.

Ordy, Andreas, Minister of Affairs, Hungary. *Trial by Terror*, P. Gallico, 1952.

O'Reilly, Boyd, Irish lawyer in charge of Olivares's estate. *Death Comes for the Archbishop*, Willa Cather, 1927.

Oresanu, Sophie, Rumanian girl who pursues Guy Pringle. *The Great Fortune*, Olivia Manning, 1960.

Orestes, a prefect. *Hypatia*, C. Kingsley, 1853.

Orford, Humphrey.
  Flora, his dead wife.
'The Orford Mystery' (s.s.), *Old Patch's Medley*, Marjorie Bowen, 1930.

Orgreave, Osmond.
  His wife.
  Their children:
    Tom.
      Edie, his wife.
    Marian.
    Janet.
    Charlie.
    Johnnie.
    Jimmie.
    Alicia, m. Harry Hesketh.
The *Clayhanger* trilogy, Arnold Bennett, 1910–16.

Ori, native chief.
  Vaili, his daughter.
Mr Fortune's Maggot, Sylvia Townsend Warner, 1927.

Oriana. *The Inconstant* (play), G. Farquhar, 1702.

Oriana. *The Ballad of Oriana* (poem), Lord Tennyson.

Oriel, Rev. Caleb, vicar, m. Gwendolin Harcourt. The *Barsetshire* series, Angela Thirkell, 1933 onwards.

Oriel, Rev. Caleb, Rector of Greshamsbury, m. Beatrice Gresham.
  Patience, his sister.
Doctor Thorne, A. Trollope, 1858.

Oriel, Rev. L., aesthetic young curate. *Pendennis*, 1848–50, and elsewhere, W. M. Thackeray.

Orinthia. *The Apple Cart* (play), G. B. Shaw, 1929.

Orion, son of Alveric and Lirazel. *The King of Elfland's Daughter*, Lord Dunsany, 1924.

O'Riordan, Mrs, Irish widow, head housekeeper. *Imperial Palace*, Arnold Bennett, 1930.

O'Riorden, Dermot, Irish patriot, m. Sheila Nolan.
  Their children:
    Maeve, actress.
    Eileen.
    Rory, m. Maggie Donnelly.
  His father and mother.
  Fergus, his brother.
  Con, his uncle.
My Son, My Son, H. Spring, 1938.

Orlando, youngest son of Sir Rowland de Bois, m. Rosalind. *As You Like It* (play), W. Shakespeare.

Orlando, first a man, then a woman.
  Marmaduke Bonthrop Shelmerdine, her husband.
Orlando, Virginia Woolf, 1928.

Orlay, Lord and Lady. *The Vultures*, H. Seton Merriman, 1902.

Orleans, Bastard of (hist.). *Henry the Sixth* (play), W. Shakespeare.

Orleans, Duke of (Gaston), brother of Louis XIII (hist.). *Richelieu* (play), Lord Lytton, 1839.

Orley, Miss. *Robert's Wife* (play), St John Ervine, 1937.

Orme, Dr, head of Coed Alyth Asylum. *All in a Month*, A. Raine, 1908.

Orme, Mrs, charlady. *The Loving Eye*, William Sansom, 1956.

Orme, Gerald.
  Eleanor, his wife. Uncle and aunt of Alix Sandomir.
    John, Margot, Dorothy, Betty and **Terry,** their children.
Non-Combatants and Others, Rose Macaulay, 1916.

Orme, Margaret. *Loyalties* (play), J. Galsworthy, 1922.

Ormeau, Constantine, friend of Willy r out, Eva's guardian. *Eva Trout,* Elizabeth Bowen, 1969.

Ormerod, Percival.
Maria, his sister.
Sophia, his sister, m. Schofield Priestley.
'West Riding Love Story' (s.s.), *Love and Money,* Phyllis Bentley, 1957.

Ormerod, Rose.
Horace, her brother. Connections of the Herrieses.
Vanessa, Hugh Walpole, 1933.

Ormiston, Ethel, m. Robert Haydon. *The Delectable Duchy,* A. Quiller-Couch, 1893.

Ormsby, Mr. *Tancred,* B. Disraeli, 1847.

O'Roon, mounted policeman, alias of son of the Earl of Ardsley.
Lady Angela, his sister.
'The Badge of Policeman O'Roon' (s.s.), *The Trimmed Lamp,* O. Henry, 1907.

O'Rory, Shad, political rival of Paul Madvig. *The Glass Key,* Dashiell Hammett, 1931.

O'Rourke, Father. 'The Sisters' (s.s.), *The Dubliners,* James Joyce, 1914.

Orozembo. *Pizarro* (play), R. B. Sheridan, 1799.

Orphoot, Mrs Easie, cook to Kirsty Gilmour. *Pink Sugar,* O. Douglas, 1924.

Orreyed, Sir George, Bt.
Mabel, his wife.
The Second Mrs Tanqueray (play), A. W. Pinero, 1893.

Orrin, a schoolboy. 'An Unsavoury Interlude' and others, *Stalky & Co.,* R. Kipling, 1899.

Orsino, Duke of Illyria, m. Viola. *Twelfth Night* (play), W. Shakespeare.

Orsino, murderer by proxy. *The Mysteries of Udolpho,* Mrs Radcliffe, 1794.

Ortheris, Stanley, cockney, one of the 'Soldiers Three.' 'Garm—a Hostage' (s.s.), *Actions and Reactions,* and many others, R. Kipling.

Orthoven, Hans.
Hans, his son by 1st wife.
m. (2) Susan Daw.
I Live Under a Black Sun, Edith Sitwell, 1937.

Ortiz, Rafael, Mexican desperado. 'One Dollar's Worth' (s.s.), *Whirligigs,* O. Henry, 1910.

Orton, 'Aussie.' 'A Friend of the Family' (s.s.), *Debits and Credits,* R. Kipling, 1926.

Orton, Mrs. *Britannia Mews,* Margery Sharp, 1946.

Ortygius, Persian lord. *Tamburlaine* (play), C. Marlowe, 1587.

Orville, Lord, m. Evelina Anville. *Evelina,* Fanny Burney, 1778.

Osbaldistone, Frank, central character and narrator, m. Diana Vernon.
His father.
Sir Hildebrand, his uncle.
His wife.
Their sons: **Archie, Percy, Thorncliffe, John, Dick, Wilfred** and **Rashleigh.**
Sir Henry, his father.
William, his brother.
Rob Roy, W. Scott, 1818.

Osbaldistone, Richard. *Rogue Herries,* Hugh Walpole, 1930.

Osbart, ship's doctor. *The Iron Pirate,* M. Pemberton, 1893.

Osborn, captain, the *Pacific. Masterman Ready,* Captain Marryat, 1841–2.

Osborne, rich and ignorant merchant.
Captain George, his son, m. Amelia Sedley.
Georgy, their son.
Jane, his daughter.
Maria, his daughter, m. Francis Bullock.
Vanity Fair, W. M. Thackeray, 1847–8.

Osborne, Lieutenant, ex-schoolmaster. *Journey's End* (play), R. C. Sherriff, 1928.

Osborne, Edward, M.P., later Lord Osborne, *nouveau riche* Sheffield manufacturer.
Maria, his wife, *née* Parkins.
Their sons:
Percy.
Claude, m. Lady Dora West.
Alfred, his elder brother.
The Osbornes, E. F. Benson, 1910.

Osborne, Colonel Frederic, M.P., old friend of the Rowley family. *He Knew He Was Right,* A. Trollope, 1869.

Osborne, Margaret, *née* Piercey, widow, m. (2) Gerald Piercey.
  Osy, her son by 1st husband.
  The Cuckoo in the Nest, Mrs Oliphant, 1894.

Oscard, Guy. *With Edged Tools,* H. Seton Merriman, 1894.

Osgood, of Raveloe, brother-in-law of Lammeter.
  His wife.
  Gilbert, their son.
  Silas Marner, George Eliot, 1861.

O'Shaughlin. *See* RACKRENT.

O'Shaughnessy, Brigid, client of Sam Spade. *The Maltese Falcon,* Dashiell Hammett, 1930.

O'Shea, hotel porter. *Mrs Eckdorf in O'Neill's Hotel,* William Trevor, 1969.

O'Sheary, Terence. *Landscape with Figures,* R. Fraser, 1925.

Osman. *Captain Brassbound's Conversion* (play), G. B. Shaw, 1900.

Osman Pasha. *Caesar's Wife* (play), W. S. Maugham, 1919.

Osmaston, Mrs Alicia. *Rogue Herries,* 1930, and *The Fortress,* 1932, Hugh Walpole.

Osmond, consulting surgeon. *Hard Cash,* C. Reade, 1863.

Osmond, Gilbert, m. Isabel Archer.
  Pansy, his daughter by previous marriage.
  The Portrait of a Lady, Henry James, 1881.

Osmund, soldier.
  Vexhelia, his wife.
  Count Robert of Paris, W. Scott, 1832.

Ospakar, Blacktooth.
  Gizur the Lawman and **Mord,** his sons.
  Eric Brighteyes, H. Rider Haggard, 1891.

Osprey, Lady, neighbour of Ponderevo. *Tono Bungay,* H. G. Wells, 1909.

Osseo, 'Son of the Evening Star.'
  Oweenee, his wife.
  The Song of Hiawatha (poem), H. W. Longfellow, 1855.

Ossipon, Alexander (Tom), ex-medical student, anarchist. *The Secret Agent,* Joseph Conrad, 1907.

Ossory, Michael, artist, m. Tiphany Lane. *The Face of Clay,* H. A. Vachell, 1906.

Ostapenko, Tatiana Pavlovna ('Tanya'), m. Seryozha Malinin.
  Pavel, her father.
  Varvara, her mother.
  Tobit Transplanted, Stella Benson, 1931.

Ostenburg, Countess Rosmarin.
  Gelda, her daughter, m. (1) Richard Gettner, (2) Count Peter Zichy.
  Stefan, her son.
  The Dark is Light Enough (play), Christopher Fry, 1954.

Ostik, African guide and interpreter. *By Sheer Pluck,* G. A. Henty, 1883.

Ostrog, 'The Boss.' *When the Sleeper Awakes,* H. G. Wells, 1899.

Ostrop, Valentine. *The Travelling Grave* (s.s.), L. P. Hartley.

O'Sullivan, Dr. *The Woman Thou Gavest Me,* Hall Caine, 1913.

Otery, Mrs, caretaker. *Mary Rose* (play), J. M. Barrie, 1920.

Oth, hunter. *The King of Elfland's Daughter,* Lord Dunsany, 1924.

Othello, a Moor.
  Desdemona, his wife.
  Othello (play), W. Shakespeare.

Otherley, Mrs. *Abraham Lincoln* (play), J. Drinkwater, 1918.

Otho, John ('John of Burgos'). 'The Eye of Allah' (s.s.), *Debits and Credits,* R. Kipling, 1926.

Otis, Hiram B., American ambassador.
  His wife.
  Virginia, his daughter, m. the Duke of Cheshire.
  The Canterville Ghost (s.s.), O. Wilde, 1887.

Otley, Gilleis, m. (1) Harry Talvace, (2) Adam Boteler. *The Heaven Tree* trilogy, Edith Pargeter, 1961–1963.

Otley, Sir Roger, Lord Mayor of London.
  Rose, his daughter.
  The Shoemaker's Holiday (play), Thomas Dekker, 1599.

O'Toole, Byron, godfather of Adam Macfadden. *Adam of Dublin,* C. O'Riordan, 1920.

O'Toole, Captain Lucius, officer of Dillon's Regiment and friend of Charles Wogan. *Clementina,* A. E. W. Mason, 1901.

O'Trigger, Sir Lucius. *The Rivals* (play), R. B. Sheridan, 1775.

Ottavia, aunt of Maddalena Trevi. *Adam's Breed,* Radclyffe Hall, 1926.

Ottenburg, Frederick, wealthy patron of the arts. *The Song of the Lark,* Willa Cather, 1915.

Otter, Mr.
Portly, his son.
The Wind in the Willows, K. Grahame, 1908.

Otter, Darnley, Wolf's friend.
Jason, his brother, a poet.
Wolf Solent, J. C. Powys, 1929.

Otter, Mrs Lucy, art student. *Of Human Bondage,* W. S. Maugham, 1915.

Otternschlag, Dr. *Grand Hotel,* Vicki Baum, 1931.

Otto, member of Jonsen's ship's crew. *High Wind in Jamaica,* R. Hughes, 1929.

Otto, Frederic, Prince of Grunewald (alias Transome).
Amalia Seraphina, his wife.
Prince Otto, R. L. Stevenson, 1885.

Otto of Godesberg ('Otto the Archer'). *A Legend of the Rhine,* W. M. Thackeray, 1845.

Otway, Sir Harry. *A Room with a View,* E. M. Forster, 1908.

Ouless, Lieutenant. 'His Private Honour' (s.s.), *Many Inventions,* R. Kipling, 1893.

Outhouse, Rev. Oliphant, of St Diddulph-in-the-East, brother-in-law of Sir M. Rowley. *He Knew He Was Right,* A. Trollope, 1869.

Outram, Lance, park-keeper, Martindale Castle. *Peveril of the Peak,* W. Scott, 1822.

Overdo, Adam. *Bartholomew Fair* (play), B. Jonson, 1614.

Overdone, Mistress, a bawd. *Measure for Measure* (play), W. Shakespeare.

Overreach, Sir Giles. *A New Way to Pay Old Debts* (play), P. Massinger, 1633.

Overstreet, Madeleine, an actress. *Tell Me How Long The Train's Been Gone,* James Baldwin, 1968.

Overton, narrator. *The Way of all Flesh,* S. Butler, 1903.

Ovington, Rev. Edmund, headmaster. *Housemaster* (play), Ian Hay, 1936.

Ovington, Sir James, J.P. *Rodney Stone,* A. Conan Doyle, 1896.

Owbridge, Lady (Julia). *The Gay Lord Quex* (play), A. W. Pinero, 1899.

Oweenee, wife of Osseo. *The Song of Hiawatha* (poem), H. W. Longfellow, 1855.

Owen, Cherry.
His wife.
Under Milk Wood (play), Dylan Thomas, 1954.

Owen, John. *The Corn is Green* (play), Emlyn Williams, 1938.

Owen, Marthy. *Anna Christie* (play). E. O'Neill, 1922.

Owen, Rhys, American socialist. *The Plumed Serpent,* D. H. Lawrence, 1926.

Owen, Rev. Richard.
Delia, his 1st wife.
Melyn, their daughter, killed by a car.
Margaret Ivory, his 2nd wife.
The Whistling Chambermaid, Naomi Royde-Smith, 1957.

Owen, William, chief mate, leader of pirate gang. *The Good Ship 'Mohock,'* W. Clark Russell, 1894.

Owl. *Winnie the Pooh,* 1926, and elsewhere, A. A. Milne.

Owlett, Jim, cousin of Lizzie Newberry; smuggler. 'The Distracted Preacher,' *Wessex Tales,* T. Hardy, 1888.

Owule, old priest of Ketemfe. *Aissa Saved,* Joyce Cary,

Oxbelly, Lieutenant, H.M.S. *Rebiera.*
His wife.
Mr Midshipman Easy, Captain Marryat, 1836.

Oxenham, John, seaman adventurer. *Westward Ho!,* C. Kingsley, 1855.

Oxford, Earl of. *Perkin Warbeck* (play), John Ford, 1634.

Ozell, Easy, employed by Grandma Hutto. *The Yearling,* Marjorie K. Rawlings, 1938.

P

Paarlenberg, Widow, m. Klaas Pool. *So Big*, Edna Ferber, 1924.

Pablo, a gipsy. *The Children of the New Forest*, Captain Marryat, 1847.

Pablo.
 Pilar, his wife.
For Whom the Bell Tolls, E. Hemingway, 1940.

Pace, James Tayper, settlement worker. *The Bell*, Iris Murdoch, 1958.

Pack, 'Grubby,' officer. 'The Bisara of Pooree' (s.s.), *Plain Tales from the Hills*, R. Kipling, 1888.

Packard, Jane, m. William Bates. 'Rodney Fails to Qualify' (s.s.), *The Heart of a Goof*, P. G. Wodehouse, 1926.

Packard, Millicent, matron of Home for Elderly Ladies. *By The Pricking of My Thumbs*, Agatha Christie, 1968.

Packles & Son, theatrical agents. *Let the People Sing*, J. B. Priestley, 1939.

Padda, Meon's seal. 'The Conversion of St Wilfrid,' *Rewards and Fairies*, R. Kipling, 1910.

Paddock, servant of Richard Hannay. *The Thirty-nine Steps*, J. Buchan, 1919.

Padella, usurping King of Crim Tartary. *The Rose and the Ring*, W. M. Thackeray, 1855.

Padge, friend of the Pooters. *The Diary of a Nobody*, G. & W. Grossmith, 1892.

Page, Windsor gentleman.
 Mistress Page, his wife.
  Mistress Anne, their daughter.
  William, their son.
The Merry Wives of Windsor (play), W. Shakespeare.

Page, Mrs Beatrice, Dame Quickly's lodger. *Rosalind* (play), J. M. Barrie, 1912.

Page, Bill. *The Voice of the Turtle* (play), J. van Druten, 1943.

Page, Clara, young widow. *This Side of Paradise*, F. Scott Fitzgerald, 1920.

Page, Dr Edward.
 Blodwen, his sister, m. Aneurin Rees.
The Citadel, A. J. Cronin, 1937.

Page, Freddie, central character, lover of Hester Collyer. *The Deep Blue Sea* (play), T. Rattigan, 1952.

Page, Lucy.
 Forrest, her 1st husband.
 Their sons:
  Bushrod, m. Mabel Stoddard.
  Cary, m. Savoie Vincent.
 m. (2) Clyde Batchelor.
Steamboat Gothic, Frances Parkinson Keyes, 1952.

Page, Mrs Olivia, cousin of the Carrs. *What Katy Did at School*, Susan Coolidge, 1873.

Page, Prentice, m. Fanny Leaf.
 Margery, their youngest daughter.
The Perennial Bachelor, Anne Parrish, 1925.

Paget, Jean, central character, m. Joe Harman.
 Arthur, her father.
 Jean, her mother.
 Donald, her brother.
 Agatha, her aunt.
A Town like Alice, N. Shute, 1950.

Pagett, M.P. (a liar). 'Pagett, M.P.' (poem), *Departmental Ditties*, R. Kipling, 1886.

Pagram, fellow clerk of Eliza's husband. *Eliza*, 1900, and others, Barry Pain.

Pahren, Emil, employer, later husband, of Christina Roche. *Without My Cloak*, Kate O'Brien, 1931.

Paine, Reuben, ship's captain. 'The Rhyme of the Three Sealers' (poem), *The Seven Seas*, R. Kipling, 1896.

Painted Jaguar ('Doffles'). 'The Beginning of the Armadillos,' *Just So Stories*, R. Kipling, 1902.

Painter, Hon. Angela. *Judith Paris*, Hugh Walpole, 1931.

Paish, Mrs.
 Her husband.
 Harriet and **Henrietta,** their daughters.
Albert Grope, F. O. Mann, 1931.

Paisley, Duchess of. *Lord Arthur Savile's Crime,* O. Wilde, 1891.

Paitelot, Miss. *Monsieur Beaucaire* (play), Booth Tarkington, 1902.

Paleologos, Faith, housekeeper to Bonnyfeather. *Anthony Adverse,* Hervey Allen, 1934.

Paley, architect.
Christine, his wife.
The Feast, Margaret Kennedy, 1950.

Paley, law student. *Pendennis,* W. M. Thackeray, 1848–50.

Palfrey, maid to the Stonors. *Before Lunch,* Angela Thirkell, 1939.

Palfrey, Farmer.
His wife.
Letita and **Penelope,** their daughters.
Brother Jacob, George Eliot, 1864.

Palfrey, Florence, of the Angel Hotel.
John, her invalid husband.
Sorrell and Son, W. Deeping, 1925.

Palfrey, Jane, actress (originally Price), central character, m. Marquess of Babraham, her cousin. *Antigua Penny Puce,* R. Graves, 1936.

Palfreyman, ornithologist, member of Voss's expedition. *Voss,* Patrick White, 1957.

Pallant, M.P. 'The Village that Voted the Earth was Flat' (s.s.), *A Diversity of Creatures,* R. Kipling, 1917.

Pallant, Ina, American T.V. executive. *The Tremor of Forgery,* Patricia Highsmith, 1969.

Pallet, Layman, painter, Parisian acquaintance of Peregrine. *Peregrine Pickle,* T. Smollett, 1751.

Palliser, Admiral.
His wife.
Jane, their daughter, m. Francis Gresham.
Frank, their son. *See also* DUKE OF OMNIUM.
The *Barsetshire* series, Angela Thirkell, 1933 onwards.

Palliser, Constance, aunt of Garret Hamil, m. James Wayward. *The Firing Line,* R. W. Chambers, 1908.

Palliser, Plantagenet, politician.
Lady Glencora, his wife.
Phineas Finn, 1869, and elsewhere, A. Trollope.

Palmer, of the Special Intelligence Department. *But Soft—We Are Observed!,* H. Belloc, 1928.

Palmer, The, alias of Wilfred, Knight of Ivanhoe. *Ivanhoe,* W. Scott, 1820.

Palmer, Mrs Charlotte, daughter of Mrs Jennings. *Sense and Sensibility,* Jane Austen, 1811.

Palmer, Emily, m. Richard Whitelaw. *Roots,* Naomi Jacob, 1931.

Palmer, Zachary, village carpenter, friend of Micah Clarke. *Micah Clarke,* A. Conan Doyle, 1889.

Palmieri, Giuseppe, gondolier, m. Tessa.
Marco, his brother, gondolier, m. Gianetta.
The Gondoliers (comic opera), Gilbert & Sullivan, 1889.

Palmley, Mrs, poor widow.
Harriet, her niece.
Her son.
'The Winters and the Palmleys,' *Life's Little Ironies,* T. Hardy, 1894.

Palsworthy, Lady, widow, social leader. *Ann Veronica,* H. G. Wells, 1909.

Pam, Colonel, inveterate card-player. *Sketches and Travels,* 1847–50, and elsewhere, W. M. Thackeray.

Pambé Serang. 'The Limitations of Pambé Serang' (s.s.), *Life's Handicap,* R. Kipling, 1891.

Pambo, Abbot. *Hypatia,* C. Kingsley, 1853.

Pamphilius. *The Apple Cart* (play), G. B. Shaw, 1929.

Panama Pete. *The Sport of Kings* (play), Ian Hay, 1924.

Pancks, agent for Christopher Casby. *Little Dorrit,* C. Dickens, 1857.

Panda, Zulu king.
Nandie, his daughter, m. Saduko.
Child of Storm, H. Rider Haggard, 1913.

Pandarus, uncle of Cressida. *Troilus and Cressida* (play), W. Shakespeare.

Pandolfo, Sir Victor, K.B.E., financier and inventor, central character, m. (1) Emily, (2) Nesta de Bréville, (3) Paula Field.
Angelo, his father.
Susan, his mother.
The Great Pandolfo, W. J. Locke, 1915.

Pangloss, Dr, tutor to Dick Dowlas. *The Heir at Law* (play), G. Colman the Younger, 1797.

Pangloss, Mrs, housekeeper and mistress of Walter Herries. *The Fortress*, Hugh Walpole, 1932.

Panin, Nikolai Andrievitch, Russian archaeologist. *The Labyrinth Makers*, Anthony Price, 1970.

Pankerton, Miss. *Diary of a Provincial Lady*, E. M. Delafield, 1930.

Panniford, Molly, central character, in love with Garry Anson.
  Sir William, her father.
  Wenda, his wife.
The Calendar, E. Wallace.

Pansa, an aedile. *The Last Days of Pompeii*, Lord Lytton, 1834.

Pansay, Theobald Jack. 'The Phantom Rickshaw' (s.s.), *Wee Willie Winkie*, R. Kipling, 1888.

Pantaleon, 'Don Panta,' Indian friend of Guevez Abel. *Green Mansions*, W. H. Hudson, 1904.

Panteus, friend of King Kleomenes III of Sparta. *The Corn King and The Spring Queen*, Naomi Mitchison, 1931.

Panthea, daughter of Arane. *A King and No King* (play), Beaumont & Fletcher, 1611.

Panther, Great Big Little, redskin. *Peter Pan* (play), J. M. Barrie, 1904.

Panthino, servant to Antonio. *Two Gentlemen of Verona* (play), W. Shakespeare.

Panzoust, de, Lady Parvula, an eccentric old woman. *Valmouth*, Ronald Firbank, 1919.

Paolo. *See* MALATESTA.

Papadakis, Nick, an hotel proprietor.
  Cora, his young wife.
The Postman Always Rings Twice, James M. Cain, 1934.

Pape, Mrs de Bray. *Last Post*, Ford Madox Ford, 1928.

Papkov, Serezha, valet, masquerading as Prince Golubchik. *The Weak and the Strong*, G. Kersh, 1945.

Papworth, Sir Miles, 'a fast-handed Whig.' *The Ordeal of Richard Feverel*, G. Meredith, 1859.

Paradine, Marmaduke ('Uncle Duke'), fraudulent financier, father-in-law of Paul Bultitude. *Vice Versa*, F. Anstey, 1882.

Paramor, Mr, family lawyer. *The Country House*, John Galsworthy, 1907.

Paramore, Dr. *The Philanderer* (play), G. B. Shaw, 1893.

Paramour, Viscount. 'Shameless Behaviour of a Lord' (s.s.), *These Charming People*, M. Arlen, 1920.

Parboil, Jessie, employee of Grope. *Albert Grope*, F. O. Mann, 1931.

Pardiggle, O. A., F.R.S., friend of Mrs Jellyby.
  His wife.
  Francis, one of their children.
Bleak House, C. Dickens, 1853.

Pardriff, Paul, of *The Ripton Gazette*.
  Alice, his wife.
Mr Crewe's Career, W. Churchill, 1908.

Pargeter, Wilfred. *See* LORD BLACKWATER.

Pargiter, Colonel Abel.
  His daughters:
    Eleanor.
    Delia.
    Milly.
    Rose.
  His sons:
    Edward.
    Morris.
    Martin.
      Celia, Morris's wife.
        North and **Peggy,** their children.
  Sir Digby, Abel's brother.
    Eugenie, his wife.
      Maggie and **Sara,** their daughters.
        Renny, Maggie's husband.
The Years, Virginia Woolf, 1937.

Paridel, a libertine knight. *The Faërie Queene* (poem), E. Spenser, 1590.

Paris, young nobleman. *Romeo and Juliet* (play), W. Shakespeare.

Paris, son of Priam. *Troilus and Cressida* (play), W. Shakespeare.

Paris, Judith, *née* Herries, central character.
  Georges, her husband.
  Adam, her illegitimate son by Warren Forster, m. Margaret Kraft.
    Vanessa, their daughter, m. Ellis Herries.
      Sally, her illegitimate daughter by Benjamin Herries.
Judith Paris, 1931, *The Fortress*,

1932, and *Vanessa*, 1933, Hugh Walpole.

Paris, Count Robert of (semi-hist.).
  Brenhilda, his wife.
Count Robert of Paris, W. Scott, 1832.

Parish, Christopher, tea merchant's employee, m. Polly Sparkes. *The Town Traveller*, G. Gissing, 1898.

Parker, Lord Windermere's butler. *Lady Windermere's Fan* (play), O. Wilde, 1892.

Parker, maid engaged to cope with the Sea Lady. *The Sea Lady*, H. G. Wells, 1902.

Parker, 'Ma.' 'Life of Ma Parker' (s.s.), *The Garden Party*, Katherine Mansfield, 1922.

Parker, Mrs. *The Letter* (play), W. S. Maugham, 1927.

Parker, Chief Inspector Charles, close friend of Lord Peter Wimsey, m. Lady Mary Wimsey. *Strong Poison*, 1930, and many others, Dorothy L. Sayers.

Parker, Freddy, Financial Commission, Nicaragua.
  Lola, his stepsister and mentor.
South Wind, N. Douglas, 1917.

Parker, Miss Lettice. *A New Departure* (s.s.), R. S. Hichens.

Parker, Stan, Australian pioneer.
  Amy, his wife.
    Ray, their son.
    Thelma, their daughter.
The Tree of Man, Patrick White, 1955.

Parkin, secretary, Handlers' Union. *Put Yourself in his Place*, C. Reade, 1870.

Parkington, Susie.
  Augustus, her husband.
  Their children:
    Alice, m. (1) Duc de Brantés, (2) Sanderson.
    William.
    Herbert.
    Eddie.
Mrs Parkington, L. Bromfield, 1944.

Parkins, Professor of Ontography. 'Oh Whistle and I'll Come to You, my Lad' (s.s.), *Ghost Stories of an Antiquary*, M. R. James, 1910.

Parkins, Rose, chambermaid. *Holy Deadlock*, A. P. Herbert, 1934.

Parkinson, Montagu, news correspondent. *A Burnt-Out Case*, Graham Greene, 1961.

Parkinson, Robert ('Parky'), private secretary to Victor Joyce. *Flamingo*, Mary Borden, 1927.

Parkinson, Rev. Theodore.
  Mavis, his wife.
  Harold, their son.
Happy Returns, Angela Thirkell, 1952.

Parkis, Alfred, private detective.
  Lance, his young son.
The End of the Affair, Graham Greene, 1951.

Parkoe, Dora, maid to Mrs Bramson. *Night Must Fall* (play), Emlyn Williams, 1935.

Parkson, Lancashire Quaker, fellow student of Lewisham. *Love and Mr Lewisham*, H. G. Wells, 1900.

Parkyn, parish clerk. *The Silver King* (play), H. A. Jones, 1882.

Parnesius, Roman soldier. 'A Centurion of the Thirtieth,' 'On the Great Wall' and others, *Puck of Pook's Hill*, R. Kipling, 1906.

Parolles, follower of Bertram. *All's Well That Ends Well* (play), W. Shakespeare.

Parracombe, William, renegade sailor turned Indian. *Westward Ho!*, C. Kingsley, 1855.

Parratt, Miss Charlotte. *Quality Street* (play), J. M. Barrie, 1902.

Parravicin, Sir Paul, bravo and bully. *Old St Paul's*, W. H. Ainsworth, 1841.

Parrenness, Duncan. 'The Dream of Duncan Parrenness' (s.s.), *Life's Handicap*, R. Kipling, 1891.

Parris, Miss, sewing-woman. *Mr Ingleside*, E. V. Lucas, 1910.

Parrish, Lizzie, central character, m. Jim Brown.
  Her father.
  Gertie and **Susan,** her sisters.
  Bert, her brother.
They Wanted to Live, Cecil Roberts, 1939.

Parrot, Farmer.
  His wife.
  Bessie, their daughter.
'Mr Gilfil's Love Story,' *Scenes of Clerical Life*, George Eliot, 1857.

Parrott, Imogen, actress. *Trelawny of the Wells* (play), A. W. Pinero, 1898.

Parry, Mr.
  Helena, his sister.

Mrs Dalloway, Virginia Woolf, 1925.

Parry, Ronald. *Caesar's Wife* (play), W. S. Maugham, 1919.

Parry-Lewis, Mary Millicent, insane inmate of asylum.
James, her father.
All in a Month, A. Raine, 1908.

Parsell, ethnologist. *Gallions Reach*, H. M. Tomlinson, 1927.

Parsimonious, the gathering bee. *Parliament of Bees* (play), J. Day, 1641.

Parsloe, George. *The Heart of a Goof*, P. G. Wodehouse, 1926.

Parsons, fellow apprentice of Polly at the Port Burdock Bazaar. *The History of Mr Polly*, H. G. Wells, 1910.

Parsons, Father, Jesuit priest. *Westward Ho!*, C. Kingsley, 1855.

Parsons, Miss, matron of Kiplington High School. *South Riding*, Winifred Holtby, 1936.

Parsons, Fred, one-time rival of William Latch for Esther. *Esther Waters*, G. Moore, 1894.

Parsons, Gabriel, sugar broker. *Sketches by Boz*, C. Dickens, 1836.

Parsons, Tom.
His wife. Neighbours of Winston Smith.
Their seven-year-old daughter, who betrays her father.
1984, G. Orwell, 1949.

Partlet, Mrs.
Constance, her daughter, m. Dr Daly.
The Sorcerer (comic opera), Gilbert & Sullivan, 1877.

Partlit, Lady, m. Jerry Jerningham. *The Good Companions*, J. B. Priestley, 1929.

Parton, Bob and **Billy.** *Rambles of a Rat*, A.L.O.E., 1854.

Partridge, Mrs, housekeeper to the Heaths. *Alice-for-Short*, W. de Morgan, 1907.

Partridge, Mrs, elderly housekeeper. *The Boys and I*, Mrs Molesworth.

Partridge, Benjamin, schoolmaster.
His wife.
Tom Jones, H. Fielding, 1749.

Partridge, Oswald, Royalist. *The Children of the New Forest*, Captain Marryat, 1847.

Pascoe, Dr. *The Great Adventure* (play), Arnold Bennett, 1913.

Pascoe, Farmer. 'Farmer on the Fairway' (s.s.), *Sun on the Water*, L. A. G. Strong, 1940.

Pascoe, Rev. Hubert, vicar.
His wife.
Mary and **Belinda,** their daughters.
My Cousin Rachel, Daphne du Maurier, 1951.

Pash, watchmaker, member of the Philosophers' Club. *Daniel Deronda*, George Eliot, 1876.

Pasquale, Laura, posing as Jonah Dermott's wife. *At Mrs Beam's* (play), C. K. Munro, 1923.

Passavente, Amilcare. 'The Duchess of Nono' (s.s.), *Little Novels of Italy*, M. Hewlett, 1899.

Passepoil, Norman swashbuckler. *The Duke's Motto*, J. H. McCarthy, 1908.

Passmore, Lucy, 'white witch,' victim of the Inquisition. *Westward Ho!*, C. Kingsley, 1855.

Pastereau, Athanasius, French refugee and silk weaver.
His 2nd wife.
George, his son.
Henry Esmond, W. M. Thackeray, 1852.

Pastmaster, Earl of. *See* BESTE-CHETWYNDE.

Paston, minister of Church in Lantern Yard. *Silas Marner*, George Eliot, 1861.

Paston, Elizabeth, m. George Winterbourne. *Death of a Hero*, R. Aldington, 1929.

Paston, Placida, widow. *The Tower of London*, W. H. Ainsworth, 1840.

Patalamon. *See* KERICK BOOTERIN.

Patch, Anthony Comstock, young American.
Gloria, his wife, *née* Gilbert.
Adam, his grandfather, millionaire known as 'Cross Patch.'
The Beautiful and the Damned, F. Scott Fitzgerald, 1922.

Pate-in-Peril. *See* MAXWELL OF SUMMERTREES.

Paterson, manager to local rice mill, central character. *The Jacaranda Tree*, H. E. Bates, 1949.

Patience, a dairymaid, m. Archibald Grosvenor. *Patience* (comic opera), Gilbert & Sullivan, 1881.

Paton, Mr H., schoolmaster. *St Winifred's*, F. W. Farrar, 1862.

Patroclus, Grecian commander. *Troilus and Cressida* (play), W. Shakespeare.

Patsie, the Commissioner's child. 'His Majesty the King' (s.s.), *Wee Willie Winkie,* R. Kipling, 1888.

Patten, Mrs, rich and elderly tenant of Cross Farm. 'The Rev. Amos Barton,' *Scenes of Clerical Life,* George Eliot, 1857.

Patterne, Sir Willoughby, m. Laetitia Dale.
Captain Patterne, of Marines, his cousin.
Crossjay, Captain Patterne's son, protégé of Vernon Whitford.
The Egoist, G. Meredith, 1879.

Patterson, Editor, *The Courier. Master Jim Probity,* F. Swinnerton, 1952.

Patterson, Alice, sister of Mrs Sykes, companion of Lady Elizabeth Carn. *The Case for the Defence,* Mary Fitt, 1958.

Patty, Miss Throssel's maid. *Quality Street* (play), J. M. Barrie, 1902.

Pau Amma, a crab. 'The Crab that Played with the Sea,' *Just So Stories,* R. Kipling, 1902.

Paul, central character.
Joan, his mother.
The Rocking Horse Winner (s.s.), D. H. Lawrence.

Paul, Father. *The Duenna* (play), R. B. Sheridan, 1775.

Paul, John, bald, solemn serving man. *The Master of Ballantrae,* R. L. Stevenson, 1889.

Paulina, wife of Antigonus. *A Winter's Tale* (play), W. Shakespeare.

Pauline, cook at Joseph Sedley's Brussels lodgings. *Vanity Fair,* W. M. Thackeray, 1847–8.

Paull, Christine, one-time fiancée of David Herries. *Rogue Herries,* Hugh Walpole, 1930.

Paulle, Lady Queenie. *The Pretty Lady,* Arnold Bennett, 1918.

Pauloff, Colonel, Russian spy. *Trumpeter, Sound!,* D. L. Murray, 1933.

Paulvitch, Alexis (alias Michael Sabrov). *Tarzan of the Apes,* etc., E. R. Burroughs, 1912–32.

Paunceford, Squire, *nouveau riche. Humphry Clinker,* T. Smollett, 1771.

Pavia, Julius, retired East India merchant. *The Power House,* J. Buchan, 1916.

Pavillon, Hermann, of Liège.
Mabel, his wife.
Gertrude, his daughter.
Quentin Durward, W. Scott, 1823.

Pavloussi, Hero, mistress of Hurtle Duffield.
Cosmas, her husband, Greek shipping magnate.
The Vivisector, Patrick White, 1970.

Pavlovitch Shuvarov, Prince Nicholas. 'A Cavalier of the Streets' (s.s.), *These Charming People,* M. Arlen, 1920.

Pawkie, James, draper, later Provost.
Sarah, his wife.
Jenny, their daughter, m. Mr Caption.
The Provost, J. Galt, 1822.

Pawkins, Major, American swindler. *Martin Chuzzlewit,* C. Dickens, 1844.

Pawle, Olive, m. James Hardcome. 'The History of the Hardcomes,' *Life's Little Ironies,* T. Hardy, 1894.

Paxton, Gilbert. *Our Betters* (play), W. S. Maugham, 1923.

Payne, maid to Amelia Sedley. *Vanity Fair,* W. M. Thackeray, 1847–8.

Payne, Damaris, actress. *Wandering Stars,* Clemence Dane, 1924.

Pazzini, La, fruit seller in Milan. 'Mr Gilfil's Love Story,' *Scenes of Clerical Life,* George Eliot, 1857.

Peabody, Mrs Fay, mystery-story writer who tries to commit a murder. *The Judgment of Paris,* Gore Vidal, 1952.

Peace, Rachel, Quaker actress, m. Lord Mandeville. *Incomparable Bellairs,* A. & E. Castle, 1904.

Peach, Walter Herries's agent. *The Fortress,* Hugh Walpole, 1932.

Peach, Ralph, m. Mab Sewell. *A Sort of Traitors,* N. Balchin, 1949.

Peachum.
His wife.
Polly, their daughter, m. Macheath.
The Beggar's Opera, 1728, and *Polly,* 1729 (comic operas), J. Gay.

Peacock, Alec, m. Violet Antrim. *The Well of Loneliness,* Radclyffe Hall, 1928.

Peak, manservant to Sir John Chester. *Barnaby Rudge,* C. Dickens, 1841.

Peake, Adrian, m. Princess von and zu Dwornitzchek. *Summer Moonshine,* P. G. Wodehouse, 1938.

Peake, Enoch. *Clayhanger,* Arnold Bennett, 1910.

Peake, Selina, m. de Jong.
Simeon, her father.
Sarah and **Abbie,** her aunts.
So Big, Edna Ferber, 1924.

Pearce, shop assistant at Shalford's. *Kipps,* H. G. Wells, 1905.

Pearce, Mrs. *Pygmalion* (play), G. B. Shaw, 1914.

Pearce, Mrs, seaside landlady. *Jacob's Room,* Virginia Woolf, 1922.

Pearce, Joe.
Elsie, his wife, sister of Eddie Cator.
A Way through the Wood, N. Balchin, 1951.

Pearce, Johnny, godson of Lord Ickenham. *Cocktail Time,* P. G. Wodehouse, 1958.

Pearman, Mrs.
Jim, her husband, miller.
Joseph and his Brethren, H. W. Freeman, 1928.

Pearson, Roger, cricketer, m. Patience Piercey. *The Cuckoo in the Nest,* Mrs Oliphant, 1894.

Pearson, Tom, uncle of Stanley Brooke. *On the Irrawaddy,* G. A. Henty, 1897.

Peartree, Abel. *These Twain,* Arnold Bennett, 1916.

Peasemarch, Albert, butler to Sir Raymond Bastable, m. Phoebe Wisdom. *Cocktail Time,* P. G. Wodehouse, 1958.

Peberdy. *Tracy's Tiger,* W. Saroyan, 1951.

Peck, Rev. George, vicar. *Brat Farrar,* Josephine Tey, 1949.

Peckover, Rev. Milward, Rector of Kiplington. *South Riding,* Winifred Holtby, 1936.

Pecksniff, Seth, architect and arch-hypocrite.
His daughters:
Charity.
Mercy, m. Jonas Chuzzlewit.
Martin Chuzzlewit, C. Dickens, 1844.

Peden, Ralph, central character, m. Winsome Charteris.
Gilbert, his father.
The Lilac Sunbonnet, S. R. Crockett, 1894.

Pedr. 'A Just Man in Sodom' (s.s.), *My People,* Caradoc Evans, 1915.

Pedringano, servant of Bellimperia. *The Spanish Tragedy* (play), T. Kyd, 1594.

Pedro, servant of Hieronimo. *The Spanish Tragedy* (play), T. Kyd, 1594.

Pedro, Don, Prince of Arragon *Much Ado about Nothing* (play), W. Shakespeare.

Peebles, Peter, notorious litigant. *See* Paul Plainstanes. *Redgauntlet,* W. Scott, 1824.

Peel, Margaret, university lecturer, Jim Dixon's 'girl.' *Lucky Jim,* K. Amis, 1953.

Peel, Oliver. *Dangerous Corner* (play), J. B. Priestley, 1932.

Peel, 'Statesman.'
His sons.
Rogue Herries, Hugh Walpole, 1930.

Peel-Swynnerton, Matthew, friend of Cyril Povey. *The Old Wives' Tale,* Arnold Bennett, 1908.

Peep-bo, ward of Ko-ko. *The Mikado* (comic opera), Gilbert & Sullivan, 1885.

Peeper, Peggy. *Polly* (comic opera), J. Gay, 1729.

Peetoot, Eskimo fur-hunter. *Ungava,* R. M. Ballantyne, 1857.

Peeve, Editor, *The Liberal. Men Like Gods,* H. G. Wells, 1923.

Peggotty, Clara, nurse to David Copperfield, m. Barkis.
Daniel, her brother.
Little Em'ly, his niece.
Ham, his nephew, intended husband of Em'ly.
David Copperfield, C. Dickens, 1850.

Peile, Hester.
Harry, her husband.
'The Lover,' *Wandering Stars,* Clemence Dane, 1924.

Peink, chauffeur to Cecil Burleigh. *Men Like Gods,* H. G. Wells, 1923.

Pelagia. *Hypatia,* C. Kingsley, 1853.

Pelet, François, schoolmaster, m. Zoraide Reuter. *The Professor,* Charlotte Brontë, 1857.

Pelham, Herbert, m. Monica Ingram. *Thank Heaven Fasting,* E. M. Delafield, 1932.

Pelham, Sir John, magistrate. 'Hal o' the Draft,' *Puck of Pook's Hill,* R. Kipling, 1906.

Pell, Solomon, attorney. *Pickwick Papers,* C. Dickens, 1857.

Pellagrin, Roy, Julia Springster's 1st husband. *The Judge's Story,* C. Morgan, 1947.

Pellatt, war correspondent of *The Day.* 'Two or Three Witnesses' (s.s.). *Fiery Particles,* C. E. Montague, 1923.

Pelleas of the Isles, Sir. 'Pelleas and Ettarre' (poem), *Idylls of the King,* Lord Tennyson, 1859.

Pellegrini, Mrs Rosa. 'The Angel and the Sweep' (s.s.), *Adam and Eve and Pinch Me,* A. E. Coppard, 1921.

Pelly, college friend of Caryl Bramsley. *C.,* M. Baring, 1924.

Pelton, Squire. *Daniel Deronda,* George Eliot, 1876.

Pelumpton, Mrs. *Angel Pavement,* J. B. Priestley, 1930.

Pember, Detective Inspector. *Ten Minute Alibi* (play), A. Armstrong, 1933.

Pemberton, Lady Honoria. *Cecilia,* Fanny Burney, 1782.

Pemberton, Joyce, actress.
Her mother.
In Cotton Wool, W. B. Maxwell, 1912.

Pemberton, Richard. *The Heart of the Matter,* Graham Greene, 1948.

Pembroke, Earl of (hist.) (William Marshall). *King John* (play), W. Shakespeare.

Pembroke, Agnes, m. Frederick (Rickie) Elliot.
Herbert, her brother, housemaster at public school.
The Longest Journey, E. M. Forster, 1907.

Pembroke, Mary.
Julian, her husband.
The End of the House of Alard, Sheila Kaye-Smith, 1923.

Pembury, Anthony. *The Fifth Form at St Dominic's,* T. Baines Reed, 1887.

Pemming, Mrs, Sir Reuben Levy's cook. *Whose Body?,* Dorothy L. Sayers, 1923.

Penaluna, 'Melia. *The Delectable Duchy,* A. Quiller-Couch, 1893.

Pendant, sycophant of Count Frederick. *A Woman is a Weathercock* (play), N. Field, 1612.

Pendennis, Arthur ('Pen'), central character of *Pendennis,* narrator of *The Newcomes* and *The Adventures of Philip,* m. Helen Laura Bell (Laura), adopted daughter of his mother.
Their children:
Arthur ('Arty').
Tom.
Helen.
Laura.
Florence.
Helen, Pen's mother.
Major Arthur, Pen's uncle and guardian.
The Doctor, headmaster of Greyfriars School, blustering and kindly.
W. M. Thackeray, 1848–62.

Pender.
His wife.
A Psychical Invasion' (s.s.), *John Silence,* A. Blackwood, 1908.

Pender, Ablard, inventor of the monster, m. Alicia Maidston. *The Last Revolution,* Lord Dunsany, 1951.

Penderton, Captain Weldon.
Leonora, his wife, mistress of Major Langdon.
Reflections in a Golden Eye, Carson McCullers, 1940.

Pendexter, Misses Mary and **Grace.** *The Fortress,* Hugh Walpole, 1932.

Pendleton, Colonel Henry, guardian of Yerba Buena. *A Ward of the Golden Gate,* Bret Harte.

Pendleton, Jervis (alias Mr Smith, alias Daddy-Long-Legs), trustee and philanthropist, m. Jerusha Abbott. *Daddy-Long-Legs,* Jean Webster, 1912.

Pendragon, Admiral. 'The Perishing of the Pendragons,' *The Wisdom of Father Brown,* G. K. Chesterton, 1914.

Pendragon, Charles, brother of Lady Vandeleur. 'The Rajah's Diamond,' *New Arabian Nights,* R. L. Stevenson, 1882.

Pendrell, banker.
His wife.
Felix Holt, George Eliot, 1866.

Pendril, Andrew Vanstone's lawyer. *No Name,* W. Collins, 1862.

Pendyce, George, heir to Worsted Skeynes.
 Horace, his father.
 Margery, his mother.
 The Country House, John Galsworthy, 1907.

Penelope. *The Gamester* (play), J. Shirley, 1637.

Penelosa, Miss, hypnotist. *The Parasite,* A. Conan Doyle, 1894.

Penfeather, Lady Penelope, chief patroness of the Well. *St Ronan's Well,* W. Scott, 1824.

Penfentenyou, Hon. A. M., Minister of Ways and Woodsides. 'The Puzzler' (s.s.), *Actions and Reactions,* 1909, and 'The Vortex' (s.s.), *A Diversity of Creatures,* 1917, R. Kipling.

Penfold, Mrs, friend of Agnes Twysden.
 Her husband.
 The Adventures of Philip, W. M. Thackeray, 1861–2.

Penhale, William, miner, friend of Basil.
 Mary, his wife.
 Susan, their daughter.
 Basil, W. Collins, 1852.

Peniston, Mrs, widow, *née* Bart, aunt of Lily Bart. *The House of Mirth,* Edith Wharton, 1905.

Penius, Roman commander. *Bonduca* (play), Beaumont & Fletcher, 1614.

Penkethman, Nancy, friend of Lord Watlington. *Imperial Palace,* Arnold Bennett, 1930.

Pennett, Mr, George Sherston's trustee. *Memoirs of a Fox-Hunting Man,* Siegfried Sassoon, 1929.

Penniman, Lavinia, widowed elder sister of Dr Sloper, and his housekeeper. *Washington Square,* H. James, 1880.

Penninck, banker.
 His wife.
 The Fountain, C. Morgan, 1932.

Pennington, Sarah, close friend of Steve Monk, once in love with his father. *The World in the Evening,* C. Isherwood, 1954.

Pennington, Vanessa.
 John, her husband.
 Cross Currents (s.s.), 'Saki' (H. H. Munro).

Pennock, Sam, boyhood friend of George Webber. *You Can't Go Home Again,* T. Wolfe, 1947.

Pennsylvania. *See* Jacob Boller.

Penny, Miss, journalist. 'Nuns at Luncheon' (s.s.), *Mortal Coils,* A. Huxley, 1922.

Penny, Christopher (The Coward). *The Passing of the Third Floor Back* (play), J. K. Jerome, 1910.

Penny, Robert, shoemaker. *Under the Greenwood Tree,* T. Hardy, 1872.

Pennybet, Archibald.
 His mother.
 Tell England, E. Raymond, 1922.

Pennycuik, John. 'The Comprehension of Private Copper' (s.s.), *Traffics and Discoveries,* R. Kipling, 1904.

Pennyfeather, Paul, central character. *Decline and Fall.* E. Waugh, 1928.

Penriddocke. Family name of the Earl of St Wythiol.

Penrose, Captain, of the *Terrible. True Blue,* W. H. G. Kingston.

Penrose, Joan, secretary to Lady Swanney, m. Jack Treloar.
 Rachel, her mother, *née* Tresinney.
 Grace, her stepmother.
 The Winds of Chance, S. K. Hocking.

Penrose, Robert, of Tregony. *Frenchman's Creek,* Daphne du Maurier, 1941.

Penrose, Ted.
 Delia, his wife.
 Eva and **Trevellan,** their children.
 The Second Mrs Conford, Beatrice K. Seymour, 1951.

Pentland, Bascom, uncle of Eugene Gant, central character. *Of Time and the River,* T. Wolfe, 1935.

Pentland, Major Thomas.
 Eliza, his daughter, 2nd wife of Oliver Gant.
 Henry, William, Jim, Thaddeus, Elmer and **Greeley,** his sons.
 Look Homeward, Angel, T. Wolfe, 1929.

Pentreath, Lord.
 His wife.
 Clementina, their daughter.
 Daniel Deronda, George Eliot, 1876.

Pentreath, Sir Gordon.
 His wife.
 Maurice, their son, Kit Sorrell's college friend.

Molly, their daughter, m. Kit Sorrell.
Sorrell and Son, W. Deeping, 1925.

Pentstemon, Uncle, 'an aged rather than venerable figure.' *The History of Mr Polly,* H. G. Wells, 1910.

Penwarden, Mr and Mrs. 'Tea at Mrs Armsby's' (s.s.), *The Owl in the Attic,* J. Thurber, 1931.

Pepe el Matador, Spanish swashbuckler. *The Duke's Motto,* J. H. McCarthy, 1908.

Pepin, hack writer. *Theophrastus Such,* George Eliot, 1879.

Pepino. *The Small Miracle,* P. Gallico, 1951.

Pepita. *The Bridge of San Luis Rey,* T. Wilder, 1927.

Pepper, Edward ('Long Ned'), thief. *Paul Clifford,* Lord Lytton, 1830.

Pepper, George, and his wife **Lily,** a vaudeville couple. *Red Peppers* (play), Noël Coward, 1936.

Pepper, Hetty, New York shop girl. 'The Third Ingredient' (s.s.), *Options,* O. Henry, 1909.

Peps, Dr Parker, attending Mrs Dombey. *Dombey and Son,* C. Dickens, 1848.

Peralta, Don, mad landowner.
Demetria, his daughter.
The Purple Land, W. H. Hudson, 1885.

Peran-Wisa, Tartar general *Sohrab and Rustum* (poem), M. Arnold, 1853.

Perceval, Sybil Fuller, m. Joey Thorpe.
Their son.
Joseph Vance, W. de Morgan, 1906.

Perch, messenger at Dombey and Son. *Dombey and Son,* C. Dickens, 1848.

Perch, Mrs.
Freddy, her son.
If Winter Comes, A. S. M. Hutchinson, 1920.

Percival, Clementine's butler. *The Onion Eaters,* J. P. Donleavy, 1971.

Percival, Mr, schoolmaster. *St Winifred's,* F. W. Farrar, 1862.

Percivale, ex-knight. 'The Holy Grail' (poem), *Idylls of the King,* Lord Tennyson, 1859.

Percy, Lady, Hotspur's wife (hist.). *Henry the Fourth* (play), W. Shakespeare.

Percy, Henry, son of Northumberland (hist.). *Richard the Second* (play), W. Shakespeare.

Percy, Ralph, central character and narrator, m. Lady Jocelyn Leigh. *By Order of the Company,* Mary Johnston, 1900.

Perdicone, m. Lise. *How Lise Loved the King* (poem), George Eliot, 1869.

Perdita, daughter of Leontes, m. Camillo. *A Winter's Tale* (play), W. Shakespeare.

Perelli, Tony. *On the Spot* (play), E. Wallace, 1930.

Perichole, Camila, famous actress, mistress of Don Andres de Ribera. *The Bridge of San Luis Rey,* T. Wilder, 1927.

Pericles, Prince of Tyre. *Pericles* (play), W. Shakespeare.

Perigot. *The Faithful Shepherdess* (play), Beaumont & Fletcher, 1609.

Perion de la Forêt. *Jurgen,* J. B. Cabell, 1921.

Perissa, stepsister of Elissa. *The Faërie Queene* (poem), E. Spenser, 1590.

Periwinkle, Princess. *The Grateful Fair* (play), C. Smart, 1747.

Perker, Pickwick's lawyer, and election agent. *Pickwick Papers,* C. Dickens, 1837.

Perkin, fellow clerk of Eliza's husband. *Eliza,* 1900, and others, Barry Pain.

Perkins, stockbroker.
His wife.
Thomas, their son.
Mrs Perkins's Ball, The Book of Snobs, 1846–7, and elsewhere, W. M. Thackeray.

Perkins, a deacon. *David Harum,* E. Noyes Westcott, 1898.

Perkins, Miss, stenographer in John Fane's publishing firm. *Going their own Ways,* A. Waugh, 1938.

Perkins, Emma Jane, school friend of Rebecca Randall. *Rebecca of Sunnybrook Farm,* Kate D. Wiggin, 1903.

Perkins, Jerry. *Riceyman Steps,* Arnold Bennett, 1923.

Perkins, John, barrister. *The Bedford Row Conspiracy,* W. M. Thackeray, 1840.

Perkins, Rev. Tom, headmaster. *Of Human Bondage,* W. S. Maugham, 1915.

Perkiss, Monty, in love with Doreen Smyth. *London Belongs to Me,* N. Collins, 1945.

Perkupp, principal at Pooter's office. *The Diary of a Nobody,* G. & W. Grossmith, 1892.

Perkyn, one of 'Moggy' Fyfe's band. *The Story of Ragged Robyn,* O. Onions, 1945.

Perne, the Misses Deborah, Jenny and **Haddie,** schoolmistresses. *Pilgrimage,* Dorothy M. Richardson, 1915–38.

Peroo, a lascar. 'The Bridge Builders' (s.s.), *The Day's Work,* R. Kipling, 1898.

Perowne, a prefect. 'An Unsavoury Interlude,' *Stalky & Co.,* R. Kipling, 1899.

Perrault, Father (hist.), surviving as the High Lama. *Lost Horizon,* J. Hilton, 1933.

Perriam, head of firm of oriental importers. *Gallions Reach,* H. M. Tomlinson, 1927.

Perrichet, *sergent de ville. At the Villa Rose,* A. E. W. Mason, 1910.

Perrin, Rev. Theodore.
His children:
Doris, Tom Florey's first love.
Clara ('Clare').
Olive.
Jimmie.
Madeline.
Tom Tiddler's Ground, E. Shanks, 1934.

Perrin, Vincent, schoolmaster. *Mr Perrin and Mr Traill,* Hugh Walpole, 1911.

Perrot, farmer.
His wife.
Gladys, their daughter.
'Mala' (s.s.), *Here and Hereafter,* Barry Pain, 1911.

Perry, apothecary, 'intelligent, gentlemanly-like.' *Emma,* Jane Austen, 1816.

Perry, Dr and Mrs. The *Barsetshire* series, Angela Thirkell, 1933 onwards.

Perry, Rev. Clarence.
His wife.
My Brother Jonathan, F. Brett Young, 1928.

Perry, Frances, rich aunt of Violet Comper. *For Us in the Dark,* Naomi Royde-Smith, 1937.

Perseus, Mr, narrator. 'The House Surgeon' (s.s.), *Actions and Reactions,* R. Kipling, 1909.

Pertinax, centurion. 'On the Great Wall' and elsewhere, *Puck of Pook's Hill,* R. Kipling, 1906.

Pervaneh. *Hassan* (play), J. E. Flecker, 1923.

Pesca, Professor. *The Woman in White,* W. Collins, 1860.

Pescud, John A., plate-glass agent, m. Jessie Allyn. 'Best Seller' (s.s.), *Options,* O. Henry, 1909.

Peshkov, Madame. 'The Quiet Woman' (s.s.), *Adam and Eve and Pinch Me,* A. E. Coppard, 1921.

Pestler, apothecary.
His wife.
Vanity Fair, W. M. Thackeray, 1847–8.

Pestorijee Bomonjee, a Parsee. 'How the Rhinoceros got his Skin,' *Just So Stories,* R. Kipling, 1902.

Petchworth, Lady, friend of Philip Pope. *Marriage,* H. G. Wells, 1912.

Peter, 'the tall reader.' *Hypatia,* C. Kingsley, 1853.

Peter, successor to Ben. 'Little Foxes' (s.s.), *Actions and Reactions,* R. Kipling, 1909.

Peter, friend of Porgy. *Porgy,* Du Bose Heyward, 1925.

Peter Pan. *Peter Pan* (play), J. M. Barrie, 1904.

Peter Rabbit.
His mother.
Her other children:
Flopsy.
Mopsy.
Cottontail.
The Tale of Peter Rabbit, 1902, and elsewhere, Beatrix Potter.

Peter the First, boy king of the Isisi. *Sanders of the River,* E. Wallace, 1911.

Peterby, personal servant of Barnabas Barty. *The Amateur Gentleman,* J. Farnol, 1913.

Peters, Sir Harrison, K.B.E. *The Laughing Lady* (play), A. Sutro, 1922.

Peters, Ivy, shady lawyer. *A Lost Lady,* Willa Cather, 1923.

Peters, Jeff, m. Mame Dugan. 'Cupid à la Carte' (s.s.), *Heart of the West,* O. Henry, 1907.

Peters, Madge, m. Tyson. *Starvecrow Farm,* Stanley Weyman, 1905.

Peters, Stanley, part owner of the local garage. *The Franchise Affair,* Josephine Tey, 1948.

Peters, William, central character, known as The King's Own, as an orphan, parents unknown, entered on ship's books as William Seymour, midshipman; in love with Emily Rainscourt. *See also* ADAMS.
  Edward, his father, actually de Courcy, executed for mutiny.
  Ellen, his mother.
The King's Own, Captain Marryat, 1830.

Petersen, Captain, of the *Olaf. The Vultures,* H. Seton Merriman, 1902.

Petersen, Harald, m. Kay Strong. *The Group,* Mary McCarthy, 1963.

Petersen Sahib. 'Toomai of the Elephants' (s.s.), *The Jungle Book,* R. Kipling, 1894.

Peterson, Carl.
  Irma, his daughter.
Bulldog Drummond, 'Sapper' (H. C. McNeile), 1920.

Pethel, James. *Seven Men,* Max Beerbohm, 1919.

Petherwin, Ethelberta, *née* Chickerell, widow, central character, m. Lord Mountclere.
  Lady Petherwin, her mother-in-law, widow of Sir Ralph Petherwin.
The Hand of Ethelberta, T. Hardy, 1876.

Petit-Andrée, assistant to Tristan l'Hermite. *Quentin Durward,* W. Scott, 1823.

Petkoff, Major Paul.
  Catherine, his wife.
  Raina, their daughter.
Arms and the Man (play), G. B. Shaw, 1894.

Petruchio, m. Katharina. *The Taming of the Shrew* (play), W. Shakespeare.

Pettican, Mrs, cook to Norman Urquhart. *Strong Poison,* Dorothy L. Sayers, 1930.

Pettican, Charles, cousin of Mrs Sharland.
  Admonition, his wife.
Mehalah, S. Baring-Gould, 1880.

Pettifer, Mrs, friend of Janet Dempster. 'Janet's Repentance,' *Scenes of Clerical Life,* George Eliot, 1857.

Pettigrew, journalist. *My Lady Nicotine,* J. M. Barrie, 1890.

Pettigrew, Mrs, housekeeper. *The Would-be-Goods,* E. Nesbit, 1901.

Pettigrew, Lady Anne.
  Her children:
    Tom,
    Kate, eng. to Peter Standish.
    Helen, central character, loved by Peter Standish.
Berkeley Square (play), J. L. Balderston, 1926.

Pettigrew, Mrs Mabel, nurse. *Memento Mori,* Muriel Spark, 1959.

Pettinger, Miss, headmistress, Barchester High School. The *Barsetshire* series, Angela Thirkell, 1933 onwards.

Pettipois, Hon. and **Rev. Lionel.** *The Book of Snobs,* W. M. Thackeray, 1846–7.

Pettitoes, Aunt, aunt of Pigling Bland. *The Tale of Pigling Bland,* Beatrix Potter, 1913.

Pettitt, maid to Lady Betty Cochrane. *Sophia,* Stanley Weyman, 1900.

Petulant, follower of Mrs Millamant. *The Way of the World* (play), W. Congreve, 1700.

Petulengro, Jasper, gipsy friend of Lavengro. *Lavengro,* George Borrow, 1851.

Peveril, Julian, central character.
  Sir Geoffrey, his father, head of the family.
  Margaret, his mother, *née* Stanley.
Peveril of the Peak, W. Scott, 1822.

Pew, David, blind beggar. *Treasure Island,* 1883, and *Admiral Guinea* (play), 1892, R. L. Stevenson.

Pew, Sherman, a young Negro with blue eyes; amanuensis of Judge Fox Clane. *Clock Without Hands,* Carson McCullers, 1961.

Pewter, Mr, skittle player. *The Water Gipsies,* A. P. Herbert, 1930.

Peyrolles, Monsieur de, factotum of Louis de Gonzague. *The Duke's Motto,* J. H. McCarthy, 1908.

Peythroppe. 'Kidnapped' (s.s.), *Plain Tales from the Hills,* R. Kipling, 1888.

Peyton, Mrs, Clyde Griffiths's landlady. *An American Tragedy,* T. Dreiser, 1925.

Peyton, Laura, m. Charles Leicester. *Lewis Arundel,* F. E. Smedley, 1852.

Pfaff, Fräulein Lily. *Pilgrimage,* Dorothy M. Richardson, 1915–38.

Pfyfe, Lander. *The Benson Murder Case,* S. S. van Dine, 1926.

Phao, a wolf, leader of the pack. 'Red Dog,' *The Second Jungle Book,* R. Kipling, 1895.

Pharamond, Prince of Spain. *Philaster* (play), Beaumont & Fletcher, 1611.

Pharaoh. *Absalom and Achitophel* (poem), J. Dryden, 1681.

Pharmacopolis, the Quacksalving Bee. *Parliament of Bees* (play), J. Day, 1641.

Phebe, a shepherdess. *As You Like It* (play), W. Shakespeare.

Phelan, Mrs Rosie, widowed cousin of the Considines, m. Tom Barry. *Without My Cloak,* Kate O'Brien, 1931.

Phenyl, Dick, barrister. *Sweet Lavender* (play), A. W. Pinero, 1888.

Pheroras, brother of Herod. *Herod* (play), S. Phillips, 1900.

Phi-oo, moon guardian, with Tsi-Puff, of Cavor. *The First Men in the Moon,* H. G. Wells, 1901.

'Phil.' 'Aunt Ellen' (s.s.), *Limits and Renewals,* R. Kipling, 1932.

Phil, Master, friend of Griselda.
  His mother.
The Cuckoo Clock, Mrs Molesworth, 1877.

Philammon, a monk. *Hypatia,* C. Kingsley, 1853.

Philander, counsellor to Porrex. *Gorboduc* (play), T. Sackville & T. Norton, 1562.

Philario, friend of Posthumous. *Cymbeline* (play), W. Shakespeare.

Philaster, heir to the crown of Sicily. *Philaster* (play), Beaumont & Fletcher, 1611.

Philbrick, school butler, impostor. *Decline and Fall,* E. Waugh, 1928.

Philby, schoolmaster.
  His wife.
Dance of the Years, Margery Allingham, 1943.

Philemus, a messenger. *Tamburlaine* (play), C. Marlowe, 1587.

Philip, King of France (hist.). *King John* (play), W. Shakespeare.

Philip. *The Bothie of Tober-na-Vuolich* (poem), A. H. Clough, 1848.

Philip, a servant. *A King and No King* (play), Beaumont & Fletcher, 1611.

Philip, Father, sacristan at St Mary's. *The Monastery,* W. Scott, 1820.

Philipot, Henri, poet and rebel. *The Comedians,* Graham Greene, 1966.

Philippa, Jim Manning's mistress. *A Way through the Wood,* N. Balchin, 1951.

Philips, Madeleine, actress, with 'the sweetest eyes,' eng. to Captain Douglas. *Bealby,* H. G. Wells, 1915.

Philipson, Arthur.
  Seignor Philipson (name assumed by the exiled Earl of Oxford), his father.
Anne of Geierstein, W. Scott, 1829.

Phillada. *Phillada Flouts Me* (poem), Anon.

Phillibrand, Maureen, m. Tim Cornwell. *The Widow,* Francis King, 1957.

Phillida. *Galathea* (play), J. Lyly, 1592.

Phillipe, Sancho, landlord, le Lapin d'Or.
  Lucia, his wife.
  Ricco, his son.
'Three Ladies' (s.s.), *Last Recollections of My Uncle Charles,* N. Balchin, 1954.

Phillips, once called Jim, a Sleepee who becomes a Texec in a world of the future. Central character. *Earthjacket,* Jon Hartridge, 1970.

Phillips, Mrs, sister of Mrs Bennet. *Pride and Prejudice,* Jane Austen, 1813.

Phillips, Guy, bone specialist.
  Elizabeth, his wife.
  Terence, their son.
Thursday Afternoons, Monica Dickens, 1945.

Phillips, Mervyn, school friend of Huw Morgan.
  Ceinwen, his sister.
How Green Was My Valley, R. Llewellyn, 1939.

Phillips, Sam, stonemason. *Adam Bede,* George Eliot, 1859.

Phillips, Sydney, m. Pearl Rakonitz. *Mosaic,* G. B. Stern, 1930.

Phillips, Sir Watkin, Bt, of Jesus College, Oxford, friend of Jeremy Melford. *Humphry Clinker,* T. Smollett, 1771.

Phillis, a servant. *The Conscious Lovers* (play), R. Steele, 1722.

Phillotson, Richard, m. Sue Bridehead. *Jude the Obscure,* T. Hardy, 1896.

Philo the Jew. *Hypatia,* C. Kingsley, 1853.

Philologus. *The Conflict of Conscience* (play), N. Woodes, 1581.

Philpot, geographer. *Crotchet Castle,* T. L. Peacock, 1831.

Philpotts, Stephen. *Where their Fire is not Quenched* (s.s.), May Sinclair.

Philylla, Spartan girl. *The Corn King and The Spring Queen,* Naomi Mitchison, 1931.

Phippard, Joanna, m. Captain Joliffe.
Her mother.
'To Please his Wife,' *Life's Little Ironies,* T. Hardy, 1894.

Phipps, Lord Goring's servant. *An Ideal Husband* (play), O. Wilde, 1895.

Phipps, 'a callow youth,' devoted to Mrs Hetty Milton. *The Wheels of Chance,* H. G. Wells, 1896.

Phipps, of the *Daily Intelligence. The Adventures of Philip,* W. M. Thackeray, 1861–2.

Phipps, Miss. *The Queen was in the Parlour* (play), N. Coward, 1926.

Phipps, Denis. *South Wind,* N. Douglas, 1917.

Phoebe. *Colin and Phoebe* (poem), J. Byrom.

Phoebus, an artist. *Lothair,* B. Disraeli, 1870.

Phoenix (Geronimo Trujillo), Mrs Witt's half-breed Arizonan groom. *St Mawr,* D. H. Lawrence, 1925.

Phoenix, Francis, friend of Thorold Progers. *Albert Grope,* F. O. Mann, 1931.

Phra, central character and narrator. *Phra the Phoenician,* E. Lester Arnold.

Phroso (Euphrosyne). *Phroso,* A. Hope, 1897.

Phrynia, mistress of Alcibiades. *Timon of Athens* (play), W. Shakespeare.

Phunky, junior barrister for Pickwick. *Pickwick Papers,* C. Dickens, 1837.

Phuong, Indo-Chinese mistress of Thomas Fowler, later of Alben Pyle.
Hei, her sister.
The Quiet American, Graham Greene, 1955.

Phyllis, Arcadian shepherdess, m. Strephon. *Iolanthe* (comic opera), Gilbert & Sullivan, 1882.

Pibble, Detective Inspector James.
Mary, his wife.
A Pride of Heroes, 1969, and others, Peter Dickinson.

Pichot, Captain Amédée. *Tom Burke of Ours,* C. Lever, 1843.

Pickerbaugh, Dr Almus, of McGurk Institute. *Martin Arrowsmith,* Sinclair Lewis, 1925.

Pickering, Colonel. *Pygmalion* (play), G. B. Shaw, 1914.

Picklan, Provost. *The Provost,* J. Galt, 1822.

Pickle, Peregrine, adopted by Commodore Trunnion; central character.
Gamaliel, his father.
Sally, his mother, *née* Appleby.
Gamaliel, his younger brother.
Sally, his sister, m. Charles Clover.
Grizzle, his aunt, m. Commodore Trunnion.
Peregrine Pickle, T. Smollett, 1751.

Pickthank. *See* Envy.

Pickwick, Samuel, founder of the Pickwick Club, central character. Also a member of Master Humphrey's Club. *Pickwick Papers,* 1837, and *Master Humphrey's Clock,* 1841, C. Dickens.

Piddingquirk, William. 'The Jilting of Jane' (s.s.), *The Plattner Story,* H. G. Wells, 1897.

Pidge, Misses E, F and Z, schoolteachers. *The Professor,* W. M. Thackeray, 1837.

Pidgeon, attendant at Pendennis's and Warrington's chambers. *Pendennis,* 1848–50, and *The Newcomes,* 1853–5, W. M. Thackeray.

Pidgeon, Miss, governess to Steven Hingston. *Portrait of Clare,* F. Brett Young, 1927.

Pie, Sir Omicron, physician. *Barchester Towers,* A. Trollope, 1857.

Pierce, Robin, close friend of Rupert Carey. *The Woman with the Fan,* R. S. Hichens, 1904.

Piercey, Gervase, 'softy,' m. Patience Hewitt.
Sir Giles, his father.
His mother.
Francis, distant cousin, heir to the baronetcy.

Gerald, his son, m. Meg Osborne.
Meg, niece of Sir Giles, m. (1) Captain Osborne, (2) Gerald Piercey.
The Cuckoo in the Nest, Mrs Oliphant, 1894.
Pierpoint, Mrs.
Ethel, her daughter.
Mid-Channel (play), A. W. Pinero, 1909.
Pierre, butler to Stephen Gordon.
Pauline, his wife.
Adèle, their daughter, m. Jean.
The Well of Loneliness, Radclyffe Hall, 1928.
Pierson, Esther, nurse to the Gower children. *The Boys and I,* Mrs Molesworth.
Pierston, Isaac, m. Ann Avice Caro. *The Well Beloved,* T. Hardy, 1897.
Pierston, Jocelyn, sculptor, m. Marcia Bencombe. *The Well Beloved,* T. Hardy, 1897.
Pietosa de Bréauté, Isoult, La Desirous (La Désirée), Countess of Hauterive, m. Prosper le Gai. *The Forest Lovers,* M. Hewlett, 1898.
Piety. *See* PRUDENCE.
Piffingcap, Elmer, barber, of Bagwood. 'Piffingcap' (s.s.), *Adam and Eve and Pinch Me,* A. E. Coppard, 1921.
Pig-Baby, The. *Alice in Wonderland,* L. Carroll, 1865.
Pigeon, Frederick, gullible young gambler. *Vanity Fair,* 1847–8, and elsewhere, W. M. Thackeray.
Pigeoncote, Sir Wilfrid, Bt.
Wilfrid, his cousin.
Peter, his cousin.
Peter's wife.
The Seven Cream Jugs (s.s.), 'Saki' (H. H. Munro).
Pigg, James, huntsman and stable manager. *Handley Cross,* R. S. Surtees, 1843.
Piggot, Jesse. *The Oriel Window,* Mrs Molesworth, 1896.
Piggott, medical student. *Whose Body?,* Dorothy L. Sayers, 1923.
Piggott, Mrs. *A Sister for Susan,* Dale Collins.
Piglet, Henry Pootel, a small pig. *Winnie the Pooh,* 1926, and elsewhere, A. A. Milne.
Pignatelli, James Knox Polk ('Dandy'), m. Henrietta Thatcher.
Their two daughters.
Anita, his sister.
Jay, his illegitimate son by Kathryn Isham, m. Lulie Harrington.
Chosen Country, J. dos Passos, 1951.
Pigwiggin, an elf. *Nymphidia* (poem), M. Drayton, 1627.
Pike, editor. *If Winter Comes,* A. S. M. Hutchinson, 1920.
Pike, Private. 'Gentle Counsels' (s.s.), *Last Recollections of My Uncle Charles,* N. Balchin, 1954.
Pike, Arthur, 'lab man.' *A Sort of Traitors,* N. Balchin, 1949.
Pilar, wife of Pablo. *For Whom the Bell Tolls,* E. Hemingway, 1940.
Pilgrim, Dr, Milby. 'Janet's Repentance,' *Scenes of Clerical Life,* George Eliot, 1857.
Pilgrim, Mr, minister. *Miss Mole,* E. H. Young, 1930.
Pilia Porsa, a bully. *The Jew of Malta* (play), C. Marlowe, 1633.
Pilkington, Lord. *See* PERCY POTTER.
Pilkington, Mrs, housekeeper, Gauntly Hall. *Vanity Fair,* W. M. Thackeray, 1847–8.
Pilkins, Dr, family practitioner of the Dombeys. *Dombey and Son,* C. Dickens, 1848.
Pillans, Alexander. *The Thinking Reed,* Rebecca West, 1936.
Pillin, Joseph.
Robert, his son, in love with Phyllis Larne.
A Stoic, J. Galsworthy, 1918.
Pillson, Georgie.
Hermione and **Ursula,** his sisters.
Queen Lucia, E. F. Benson, 1920.
Pilward, Ted, m. Heather Adams. The *Barsetshire* series, Angela Thirkell, 1933 onwards.
Pim, Carraway. *Mr Pim Passes By* (play), A. A. Milne, 1920.
Pimm, Mr, imaginary friend of James Sampson. *The Distant Horns of Summer,* H. E. Bates, 1967.
Pinch, Tom, employee of Pecksniff.
Ruth, his sister, governess to a rich brassfounder, m. John Westlock.
Martin Chuzzlewit, C. Dickens, 1844.
Pinchwife, Jack, jealous husband.
Mrs Pinchwife, his dissatisfied wife.
Alithea, his sister, society woman.

The Country Wife (play), William Wycherley, 1673.

Pincini, Andreas, tattooist.
His wife.
The Background (s.s.), 'Saki' (H. H. Munro).

Pinckney, Leila J., writer of popular 'squashily sentimental' novels; aunt of James Rodman. *Meet Mr Mulliner,* P. G. Wodehouse, 1927.

Pincot, maid to Rachel, Lady Castlewood. *Henry Esmond,* W. M. Thackeray, 1852.

Pincot, Mrs Eliza. *The Virginians* W. M. Thackeray, 1857–9.

Pine, surgeon on convict ship. *For the Term of his Natural Life,* M. Clarke, 1874.

Pine-Avon, Mrs Nichola, m. Alfred Somers. *The Well Beloved,* T. Hardy, 1897.

Pinecoffin. 'Pig' (s.s.)., *Plain Tales from the Hills,* R. Kipling, 1888.

Pineda, Martha, Brown's mistress.
Luis, her husband, South American ambassador in Haiti.
Angel, their son.
The Comedians, Graham Greene, 1966.

Pinfold, Gilbert, middle-aged writer and country squire who hears voices.
His wife.
The Ordeal of Gilbert Pinfold, Evelyn Waugh, 1957.

Ping Siang, cruel and extortionate mandarin. *The Wallet of Kai Lung,* E. Bramah, 1900.

Pingitzen. *Tracy's Tiger,* W. Saroyan, 1951.

Pinhorn, Hester, cook to Count Fosco. *The Woman in White,* W. Collins, 1860.

Pinhorn, Mary, children's maid, m. Dick Bedford, the butler. *Lovel the Widower,* W. M. Thackeray, 1860.

Pink, saddler, Treby Magna. *Felix Holt,* George Eliot, 1866.

Pinkbell, butler who never appears but makes his presence felt. *The Chalk Garden* (play), Enid Bagnold, 1955.

Pinkerton, Miss Barbara, head of Pinkerton's Seminary for Young Ladies.
Jemima, her sister.
Vanity Fair, 1847–8, *The Newcomes,* 1853–5, and elsewhere, W. M. Thackeray.

Pinkie, gang leader, m. Rose Wilson. *Brighton Rock,* Graham Greene, 1938.

Pinkle Purr.
Tattoo, his mother.
Now We Are Six, A. A. Milne, 1926.

Pinkney.
His sisters:
Mabel, m. Kenneth Eliot.
Honor.
'Death of a Dog' (s.s.), *Louise,* Viola Meynell, 1954.

Pinnegar, Miss, manageress of James Houghton's drapery. *The Lost Girl,* D. H. Lawrence, 1920.

Pinner, Josephine and **Constantia.** 'The Daughters of the late Colonel' (s.s.), *The Garden Party,* Katherine Mansfield, 1922.

Pinsent, Miss, dressmaker. *The Lie* (play), H. A. Jones, 1923.

Pinsent, Cordely, widow.
William, her son.
The Delectable Duchy, A. Quiller-Couch, 1893.

Pinsent, Iris, once eng. to Henry Chandler. *Bachelors* (s.s.), Hugh Walpole.

Pintle, John, shop assistant to Bartley. *Both of this Parish,* J. S. Fletcher.

Pinto, Biscayan swashbuckler. *The Duke's Motto,* J. H. McCarthy, 1908.

Piny, apple-woman. *Winterset* (play), Maxwell Anderson, 1935.

Pio, Uncle, factotum to Camila Perichole. *The Bridge of San Luis Rey,* T. Wilder, 1927.

Pioche, cuirassier of the guard. *Tom Burke of Ours,* C. Lever, 1844.

Pipchin, Mrs, keeper of a children's boarding-house. *Dombey and Son,* C. Dickens, 1848.

Piper, Miss, companion, m. Harrison. *Heartsease,* Charlotte M. Yonge, 1854.

Piper, Colonel the Hon. Gerald.
Charles, his brother. Brothers of the late Lord Monchensey.
The Family Reunion (play), T. S. Eliot, 1939.

Pipes, servant of Hawser Trunnion. *Peregrine Pickle,* T. Smollett, 1751.

Pipkin, Hannibal. *The Clever Ones* (play), A. Sutro, 1914.

Pipkin, Nathaniel, parish clerk. *Pickwick Papers,* C. Dickens, 1837.

Pippa, child worker at Gaddi's silk mills. *Pippa Passes* (poem), R. Browning, 1841.

Pir Khan, John Holden's servant. 'Without Benefit of Clergy' (s.s.), *Life's Handicap,* R. Kipling, 1891.

Piranha, Donna Emilia, *née* de Leyva.
Rosa, her daughter.
Odtaa, J. Masefield, 1926.

Pirate King, The. *The Pirates of Penzance* (comic opera), Gilbert & Sullivan, 1880.

Pirolo, Victor, of the Aerial Board of Control. 'As Easy as A B C' (s.s.), *A Diversity of Creatures,* R. Kipling, 1917.

Pirrip, Philip ('Pip'), orphan, central character, loves Estella.
His sister, Joe Gargery.
Great Expectations, C. Dickens, 1861.

Pisanio, servant of Posthumus. *Cymbeline* (play), W. Shakespeare.

Pish-Tush, a noble lord. *The Mikado* (comic opera), Gilbert & Sullivan, 1885.

Pistol, follower of Falstaff, later a soldier. *The Merry Wives of Windsor, Henry the Fourth* and *Henry the Fifth* (plays), W. Shakespeare.

Pitman, William Dent, artist and ne'er-do-well. *The Wrong Box,* R. L. Stevenson & L. Osbourne, 1889.

Pitsner, Mr, of a music publishing firm. *The Good Companions,* J. B. Priestley, 1929.

Pitt, Jeremiah. *Captain Blood,* R. Sabatini, 1922.

Pitt, Jimmy, central character, m. Molly McEachern. *A Gentleman of Leisure,* P. G. Wodehouse, 1910.

Pitt-Heron, Charles.
His wife.
The Power House, J. Buchan, 1916.

Pitti-Sing, ward of Ko-ko. *The Mikado* (comic opera), Gilbert & Sullivan, 1885.

Pittle, Rev. Mr. *The Provost,* J. Galt, 1822.

Pittman, Milby lawyer, partner of Robert Dempster.
His four daughters.
'Janet's Repentance,' *Scenes of Clerical Life,* George Eliot, 1857.

Pivart, farmer at Ripple, enemy of Edward Tulliver. *The Mill on the Floss,* George Eliot, 1860.

Pizarro (hist.). *Pizarro* (play), R. B. Sheridan, 1799.

Placide, housekeeper to the Baronne d'Archeville. *The Spanish Farm,* R. H. Mottram, 1924.

Plagiary, Sir Fretful. *The Critic* (play), R. B. Sheridan, 1779.

Plaice, publisher's reader. *The Dream,* H. G. Wells, 1924.

Plainstanes, Paul, defendant in old lawsuit against Sir Peter Peebles. *Redgauntlet,* W. Scott, 1824.

Planger, Oriana, of the Church of Ancient Truth. *Albert Grope,* F. O. Mann, 1931.

Planquet, Maître, master cook at the hotel. *Imperial Palace,* Arnold Bennett, 1930.

Plant, advertising agent. 'The Man with no Face,' *Lord Peter Views the Body,* Dorothy L. Sayers, 1928.

Plant, C., shoemaker friend of Gulley Jimson. *The Horse's Mouth,* Joyce Cary, 1944.

Plantagenet, Richard (hist.) (later Duke of York). *Henry the Sixth* (play), W. Shakespeare.

Platt, fellow apprentice with Polly at the Port Burdock Bazaar. *The History of Mr Polly,* H. G. Wells, 1910.

Platt, John, partner in dry goods emporium, m. Helen Asher. 'The Buyer from Cactus City' (s.s.), *The Trimmed Lamp,* O. Henry, 1907.

Platt, Tom, sailor on the *We're Here. Captains Courageous,* R. Kipling, 1897.

Platte, subaltern. 'Watches of the Night' (s.s.), *Plain Tales from the Hills,* R. Kipling, 1888.

Plattner, Gottfried, language master at the Sussexville School. *The Plattner Story,* 1897, and elsewhere, H. G. Wells.

Platz, Mrs, housekeeper. *The Benson Murder Case,* S. S. van Dine, 1926.

Plaugastel, Comtesse Thérèse. *Scaramouche,* R. Sabatini, 1921.

Playgate, Hamilton.
Caroline, his wife.
The Laughing Lady, A. Sutro, 1922.

Plaza Toro, Duke of.
His wife.
Casilda, their daughter, m. Luiz.

The Gondoliers (comic opera), Gilbert & Sullivan, 1889.

Plessington, Hubert, ex-Oxford don.
'Aunt Plessington,' his wife.
Marriage, H. G. Wells, 1912.

Plessy, Lord. *Middlemarch*, George Eliot, 1871–2.

Plethern, Charles, central character, m. Viola Marvell.
'King,' his father.
Rowena, his mother, *née* Walsingham.
James, his twin brother.
Rosalind, his wife.
Corinne, their daughter.
Chris, their son.
Desolate Splendour, M. Sadleir, 1923.

Pleydell, Berry, central character.
Daphne, his wife.
His cousins:
Vandy.
Emma.
May.
Berry and Co., D. Yates, 1920.

Pleydell, Paulus, Edinburgh advocate. *Guy Mannering*, W. Scott, 1815.

Pleydon, Dodge, artist and sculptor, in love with Linda Condon. *Linda Condon*, J. Hergesheimer, 1918.

Pliable, neighbour of Christian. *See* OBSTINATE. *Pilgrim's Progress*, J. Bunyan, 1678, 1684.

Pliant, Sir Paul. *The Double Dealer* (play), W. Congreve, 1693.

Plimsing, house detective at the Hotel. *Imperial Palace*, Arnold Bennett, 1930.

Plinlimmon, Marquess of, eldest son of the Duke of St David's, varsity friend of Pendennis. *Pendennis*, W. M. Thackeray, 1848–50.

Plomacy, steward to Wilfred Thorne. *Barchester Towers*, A. Trollope, 1857.

Plomer, Count. *See* HAWKESWORTH.

Plornish, Thomas, plasterer.
His wife, *née* Nandy.
Little Dorrit, C. Dickens, 1857.

Ploss, Philip, murdered poet. *The Secret Vanguard*, M. Innes, 1940.

Plougastel, Comtesse de. *See* ANDRÉ-LOUIS MOREAU.

Pluche, Jeames de la, really James Plush, ex-footman who makes a fortune and loses it; m. Mary Ann Hoggins.
James Angelo, Angelina and **Mary Anne,** their children.
Jeames's Diary, 1846, and elsewhere, W. M. Thackeray.

Pluffles, a subaltern. 'The Rescue of Pluffles' (s.s.), *Plain Tales from the Hills*, R. Kipling, 1888.

Plum, Colonel. *Put Out More Flags*, E. Waugh, 1942.

Plume, Sir. *The Rape of the Lock* (poem), A. Pope.

Plumer, Mrs.
George, her husband, university professor.
Jacob's Room, Virginia Woolf, 1922.

Plumer, Sherrard, penniless artist. 'A Madison Square Arabian Night' (s.s.), *The Trimmed Lamp*, O. Henry, 1907.

Plummer, Caleb, toy-maker.
Edward, his son, m. May Fielding.
Bertha, his daughter, blind.
The Cricket on the Hearth, C. Dickens, 1846.

Plummer, Edwin, in love with Lady Maud Marsh.
Millie, his sister.
A Damsel in Distress, P. G. Wodehouse, 1919.

Plumtre, Lady, witness for the defence of Martella Baring. *Enter Sir John*, Clemence Dane & Helen Simpson, 1929.

Plush, James. *See* JEAMES DE LA PLUCHE.

Plyem, Sir Peter, Parliamentary candidate for five boroughs. *The Heart of Midlothian*, W. Scott, 1818.

Plymdale, wealthy manufacturer.
Selina, his wife.
Edward, their son, m. Sophy Toller.
Middlemarch, Geo. Eliot, 1871–2.

Plymdale, Lady (Laura). *Lady Windermere's Fan* (play), O. Wilde, 1892.

Pocket, Matthew, cousin of Miss Havisham.
His wife.
Herbert, their son.
Sarah, a relative.
Great Expectations, C. Dickens, 1862.

Pocklington, Sir Thomas Gibbs.
His wife.
Our Street, W. M. Thackeray, 1848.

Pocock, Mrs, sister of Chadwick Newsome.
Mamie, her sister-in-law.
The Ambassadors, Henry James, 1903.

Podger, Mr, undertaker. *The History of Mr Polly,* H. G. Wells, 1910.

Podger, Uncle.
Maria, his wife.
Three Men in a Boat, J. K. Jerome, 1889.

Podgers, Lady Southdown's Brighton doctor. *Vanity Fair,* W. M. Thackeray, 1847–8.

Podgers, Dr. *Hawbuck Grange,* R. S. Surtees, 1847.

Podgers, John, widower. *Master Humphrey's Clock,* C. Dickens, 1840–1.

Podgers, Septimus R., chiromantist. *Lord Arthur Savile's Crime,* O. Wilde, 1891.

Podmarsh, Rollo, m. Mary Kent.
His mother.
'The Awakening of Podmarsh' (s.s.), *The Heart of a Goof,* P. G. Wodehouse, 1926.

Podsnap, Mr, marine insurance agent.
His wife.
Georgiana, their daughter.
Our Mutual Friend, C. Dickens, 1865.

Poe, attorney. *Vanity Fair,* W. M. Thackeray, 1847–8.

Poetaster, the Poetical Bee. *Parliament of Bees* (play), J. Day, 1641.

Poges, Cyril, pompous English businessman.
Souhaun, his mistress.
Purple Dust (play), Sean O'Casey, 1940.

Pogram, Elijah, member of Congress. *Martin Chuzzlewit,* C. Dickens, 1844.

Pogson, Sam, English traveller fleeced in Paris.
His aunt.
Paris Sketch Book, W. M. Thackeray, 1840.

Pohetohee. *Polly* (comic opera), J. Gay, 1729.

Poiccart, one of the Four. *See* Gonsalez. *The Four Just Men,* E. Wallace, 1905.

Poins. *Henry the Fourth* (play), W. Shakespeare.

Point, Jack, strolling jester. *The Yeomen of the Guard* (comic opera), Gilbert & Sullivan, 1888.

Pointdextre, Sir Marmaduke, m. Lady Sangazure.
Alexis, his son, m. Aline Sangazure.
The Sorcerer (comic opera), Gilbert & Sullivan, 1877.

Pointing, Arthur, friend of Charles Heywood. *Judgment in Suspense,* G. Bullett, 1946.

Poirot, Hercule, Belgian detective. *The Mysterious Affair at Styles,* 1920, and many others, Agatha Christie.

Pok, Belial. *Sunrise in the West,* Bechofer Roberts, 1945.

Pokorny, Manfred, composer. *The Troubled Air,* Irwin Shaw, 1951.

Pole, Miss. *Cranford,* Mrs Gaskell, 1853.

Pole, Millicent, protégée of Fleur Forsyte. *Swan Song,* 1928, and elsewhere, J. Galsworthy.

Polixenes, King of Bohemia.
Florizel, his son.
A Winter's Tale (play), W. Shakespeare.

Polk-Faraday, Alex, publisher-writer.
Hittie, his wife.
A Suspension of Mercy, Patricia Highsmith, 1965.

Pollen, Venice. *The Green Hat,* M. Arlen, 1924.

Pollexfen, Sir Hargrave, Bt, villain. *Sir Charles Grandison,* S. Richardson, 1754.

Pollitt, Frank (Valma, professional pianist). *The Gay Lord Quex* (play), A. W. Pinero, 1899.

Pollock, assistant to Sierra Leone trader. 'Pollock and the Porrah Man,' *The Plattner Story,* 1897, and elsewhere, H. G. Wells.

Pollock, Major. *Separate Tables* (play), T. Rattigan, 1955.

'Polly, Aunt,' Tom's guardian. *Tom Sawyer,* Mark Twain, 1876.

Polly, Alfred, draper, and eventually jack-of-all-trades at the Potwell Inn; central character, m. Miriam Larkins, his cousin.
Lizzie, his mother.
The History of Mr Polly, H. G. Wells, 1910.

Polonia, Prince, wealthy Italian banker.
His wife.
His grandfather.

Vanity Fair, 1847–8, and elsewhere, W. M. Thackeray.

Polonius, fashionable jeweller. *The Great Hoggarty Diamond*, 1841, and *Vanity Fair*, 1847–8, W. M. Thackeray.

Polonius, Lord Chamberlain, father of Ophelia and Laertes. *Hamlet* (play), W. Shakespeare.

Polperro, 2nd Baron (Family name Trefoyle).
The 3rd Baron, his eldest son.
Hon. Adela, his daughter, m. Lucian Gildersleeve.
The 4th Baron.
The Town Traveller, G. Gissing, 1898.

Polpette, Monsieur, of the Pension Bourgeoise, *The Pottleton Legacy*, Albert Smith, 1849.

Polteed, private detective. The *Forsyte* series, J. Galsworthy, 1906–1933.

Polter, Bob, navvy. 'Bob Polter' (poem), *Bab Ballads*, W. S. Gilbert, 1869.

Pomander, Sir Charles, 'gentleman of pleasure,' friend of Ernest Vane. *Peg Woffington*, C. Reade, 1853.

Pomeroy, Avisa, of Vixen Tor Farm, widow, m. Arthur Brown.
Ives, her son by 1st husband, m. Ruth Rendle.
Lizzie, her daughter.
The Mother, E. Phillpotts, 1908.

Pomeroy-Nelson, Eric Vivian ('Rick'), playwright, close friend of Lanny Budd.
Nina, his wife.
Alfig, their son.
Dragon's Teeth, Upton Sinclair, 1942.

Pomfret, undergraduate. *Gaudy Night*, Dorothy L. Sayers, 1935.

Pomfret, lady's maid at Donnithorne Chase. *Adam Bede*, George Eliot, 1859.

Pomfret, Eleanor, m. George Hingston.
Her cousin, vicar.
Portrait of Clare, F. Brett Young, 1927.

Pomfret, Lord (Gillie) (Family name Foster).
Sally, his wife, *née* Wicklow.
Their children:
Lord Mellings (Ludo), m. Lavinia Merton.
Emily.
Giles.
The *Barsetshire* series, Angela Thirkell, 1933 onwards.

Pomfret-Walpole, a schoolboy. *Mr Perrin and Mr Traill*, Hugh Walpole, 1911.

Pomjalovsky, Nicholas, friend of Eleanor Pargiter. *The Years*, Virginia Woolf, 1937.

Pommeroy, Judge. *A Lost Lady*, Willa Cather, 1923.

Pommier, Noël, shoemaker. *Shadows on the Rock*, Willa Cather, 1932.

Pompey, Negro slave of Beatrix Esmond. *Henry Esmond*, W. M. Thackeray, 1852.

Pompey (Sextus Pompeius). *Antony and Cleopatra* (play), W. Shakespeare.

Pompey, Sir. 'The Matchmaker' (s.s.), *Sir Pompey and Madame Juno*, M. Armstrong, 1927.

Pompiona, daughter of the King of Moldavia. *The Knight of the Burning Pestle* (play), Beaumont & Fletcher, 1609.

Ponder, Mrs, servant of Jennifer Herries. *Judith Paris*, Hugh Walpole, 1931.

Ponder, Miss Edna Earl, hotel proprietor.
Daniel, her uncle.
Bonnie Dee Peacock, Uncle Daniel's 'trial' wife.
The Ponder Heart, Eudora Welty, 1953.

Ponderevo, George, central character and narrator, m. Marion Ramboat.
Edward, his uncle and employer, unsuccessful chemist, later inventor of Tono Bungay and spectacularly successful financier.
Susan, Edward's wife.
Tono Bungay, H. G. Wells, 1909.

Pons, Monsieur, French master. *Mr Perrin and Mr Traill*, Hugh Walpole, 1911.

Ponsonby, Inspector, in charge of search for Pru Tuke. *Miss Gomez and The Brethren*, W. Trevor, 1971.

Ponsonby, Miss. *Another Year*, R. C. Sherriff, 1948.

Ponsonby, The Misses. *Catherine Furze*, M. Rutherford, 1893.

Ponsonby, Loelia, James Bond's secretary. *Thunderball*, 1961, and others, Ian Fleming.

Pontiac, treacherous Indian chief.

Settlers in Canada, Captain Marryat, 1844.

Pontifex, Theobald.
 Christina, his wife, *née* Allaby.
 Their children:
  Ernest, bigamously m. Ellen.
  Joseph.
  Charlotte.
 George, his father.
 Eliza, Mary and **Alethea,** his sisters.
 John, his brother.
 The Way of all Flesh, S. Butler, 1903.

Ponto, Major.
 His wife.
 Their children:
  Lieutenant Wellesley.
  Emily.
  Maria.
 The Book of Snobs, 1846–7, and *Vanity Fair*, 1847–8, W. M. Thackeray.

Ponts, Captain. *A Woman is a Weathercock* (play), N. Field, 1612.

Pontus, Prince of Paphlagonia.
 Leonatus, his son.
 The Story of the Unkind King (s.s.), Philip Sidney.

Pontypool, Lord.
 His wife.
 Dowager Lady Pontypool, his mother.
 Pendennis, W. M. Thackeray, 1848–1850.

Pooh. *See* WINNIE-THE-POOH.

Pooh-Bah, Lord High Everything Else. *The Mikado* (comic opera), Gilbert & Sullivan, 1885.

Pool, Klaas, farmer.
 m. (1) **Maartje.**
  Roelf, Geertje and **Jozina,** their children.
 (2) **Widow Paarlenberg.**
 So Big, Edna Ferber, 1924.

Poole, crippled spy. *The Ministry of Fear*, Graham Greene, 1943.

Poole, manservant of Dr Jekyll. *Dr Jekyll and Mr Hyde*, R. L. Stevenson, 1886.

Poole, Grace, Mrs Rochester's keeper. *Jane Eyre*, Charlotte Brontë, 1847.

Poole, Stanley. *Angel Pavement*, J. B. Priestley, 1930.

Poorgrass, Joseph, farm-hand. *Far from the Madding Crowd*, T. Hardy, 1874.

Pooter, Charles, central character and narrator.
 Carrie, his wife.
 Lupin (William), their son, once eng. to Daisy Mutlar, m. Lilian Posh.
 The Diary of a Nobody, G. & W. Grossmith, 1892.

Poots, apothecary and miser.
 Amine, his daughter, m. Philip Vanderdecken.
 The Phantom Ship, Captain Marryat, 1839.

Pope, Philip, coach-builder.
 His wife.
 Their children:
  Daphne, m. Will Magnet.
  Marjorie, m. Richard Trafford.
  Romola.
  Sydney.
  Theodore.
 Marriage, H. G. Wells, 1912.

Pope, Wilberforce. 'The Dragon's Head,' *Lord Peter Views the Body*, Dorothy L. Sayers, 1928.

Popinjay, Lady. *The Newcomes*, W. M. Thackeray, 1853–5.

Popjoy, Hon. Percy. *Pendennis*, W. M. Thackeray, 1848–50.

Poppets, Mrs, landlady. *Three Men in a Boat*, J. K. Jerome, 1889.

Poppi, Antonio, Venetian servant. *The Notorious Mrs Ebbsmith* (play), A. W. Pinero, 1895.

Poppins, Mary, nurse and good fairy who 'flies' in and out of the Banks family's lives. The *Mary Poppins* series, 1934 onwards, P. L. Travers.

Poppleby, Mr, proprietor of dining-rooms. *The Good Companions*, J. B. Priestley, 1929.

Poppleworth, chief clerk. *Sons and Lovers*, D. H. Lawrence, 1913.

Popworth and family. *Eliza*, 1900, and others, Barry Pain.

Porgy, Negro crippled beggar, central character. *Porgy*, Du Bose Heyward, 1925.

Pork, Negro valet-butler to the O'Haras. *Gone with the Wind*, Margaret Mitchell, 1936.

Porlet, Lady. *Poet's Pub*, E. Linklater, 1929.

Porlock, Lord. *See* COUNTESS DE COURCY.

Pornic, Morrowbie Jukes's horse. 'The Strange Ride of Morrowbie

Jukes' (s.s.), *Wee Willie Winkie*, R. Kipling, 1888.

Pornick, Sid, boyhood friend of Kipps.
Fanny, his wife.
Ann, his sister, m. Kipps.
Old Pornick, his father.
Kipps, H. G. Wells, 1905.

Porphyria. *Porphyria's Lover* (poem), R. Browning.

Porphyro, m. Madeline. 'The Eve of St Agnes,' *Lamia and other Poems*, J. Keats, 1820.

Porrex, son of Gorboduc. *Gorboduc* (play), T. Sackville & T. Norton, 1562.

Porringer, Win-Grace, 'Muggletonian' transported to Virginia. *The Old Dominion*, Mary Johnston, 1899.

Porson, Ronald, embittered failure, in love with Ann March. *The Conscience of the Rich*, 1958, part of the *Strangers and Brothers* sequence, C. P. Snow.

Porteous, Rev. Robert, curate, St Peter's, Winstonbury, tutor to Kit Sorrell. *Sorrell and Son*, W. Deeping, 1925.

Porter, Rev. Hopley. 'The Rival Curates' (poem), *Bab Ballads*, W. S. Gilbert, 1869.

Porter, Jimmy.
Alison, his wife, *née* Redfern.
Look Back in Anger (play), J. Osborne, 1956.

Porter, Rt Hon. Sir Joseph, K.C.B., First Lord of the Admiralty.
Hebe, his cousin.
H.M.S. Pinafore (comic opera), Gilbert & Sullivan, 1878.

Portia (alias Balthasar), heiress, m. Bassanio. *The Merchant of Venice* (play), W. Shakespeare.

Portia, wife of Brutus. *Julius Caesar* (play), W. Shakespeare.

Portico, Sir Blennerhasset, K.C.B. 'The Mystic Selvagee' (poem), *Bab Ballads*, W. S. Gilbert, 1869.

Portlaw, William van Beuren, m. Alida Ascott. *The Firing Line*, R. W. Chambers, 1908.

Portman, assistant manager, rice mill.
His wife.
The Jacaranda Tree, H. E. Bates, 1949.

Portman, Dr, master of Brazenface College. *The Adventures of Mr Verdant Green*, C. Bede, 1853.

Portman, Rev. Mr, Vicar of Clavering St Mary.
His wife and daughter.
Pendennis, W. M. Thackeray, 1848–50.

Portnoy, Alexander, native of Newark, New Jersey, representative man of his age.
Sophie, his mother (*née* Ginsky).
Jack, his father.
Hannah, his sister.
Portnoy's Complaint, Philip Roth, 1969.

Portson, R.N.V.R., peace-time stockbroker. 'Sea Constables' (s.s.), *Debits and Credits*, R. Kipling, 1926.

Portway, Elvira, Robin Middleton's mistress.
Lilian, her grandmother, ex-actress.
Anglo-Saxon Attitudes, Angus Wilson, 1956.

Posh, Murray, hat manufacturer, m. Daisy Mutlar.
Lilian, his sister, m. Lupin Pooter.
The Diary of a Nobody, G. & W. Grossmith, 1892.

Posky, Captain, m. Glorvina O'Dowd. *Vanity Fair*, W. M. Thackeray, 1847–8.

Post, Edward, one-time fiancé of Maggie Campion. *The Perennial Bachelor*, Anne Parrish, 1925.

Post, Jacob, servant to Scarve. *The Miser's Daughter*, W. H. Ainsworth, 1842.

Poste, Flora, central character, m. Charles Fairford. *Cold Comfort Farm*, Stella Gibbons, 1932.

Postgate, Mary, a companion. 'Mary Postgate' (s.s.), *A Diversity of Creatures*, R. Kipling, 1917.

Posthumus, Leonatus, husband of Imogen. *Cymbeline* (play), W. Shakespeare.

Postlethwaite, 'able and vigilant' barmaid of the Anglers' Rest. *Meet Mr Mulliner*, P. G. Wodehouse, 1927.

Pot, Gilbert, grandson of Gunnora Braose. *The Tower of London*, W. H. Ainsworth, 1840.

'Potatoes,' waterman and fireman at Murdstone & Grinby.
Mealy, his son.
David Copperfield, C. Dickens, 1850.

Pothinus. *Caesar and Cleopatra* (play), G. B. Shaw, 1900.

Potion, Roger, apothecary and one-time friend of Lieutenant Bowling. *Roderick Random,* T. Smollett, 1748.

Pott, editor, *Eatanswill Gazette.*
Minerva, his wife.
His daughters.
Pickwick Papers, C. Dickens, 1837.

Potter, house physician.
His father and mother.
Marjory, his sister.
Thursday Afternoons, Monica Dickens, 1945.

Potter, Rev. Dr, Rector, Rosebury.
His wife.
Tom, their son.
Their daughters.
The Newcomes, W. M. Thackeray, 1853–5.

Potter, Joseph (Jo-Jo), chairman of commercial development group.
Laura, his wife.
Christopher Potter, his father. (*See* BAUM.)
Mervyn Rose, his cousin.
The Long Time Growing Up, John Pudney, 1971.

Potter, Mamie, soubrette of Good Companions concert party. *The Good Companions,* J. B. Priestley, 1929.

Potter, Muff, accused of murdering Dr Robinson. *Tom Sawyer,* Mark 1876.

Potter, Natty, Robert Rogers's secretary.
Ann, his daughter, m. Langdon Towne.
Northwest Passage, Kenneth Roberts, 1938.

Potter, Percy, later Lord Pilkington.
His wife, novelist 'Leila Yorke.'
Their children:
Rev. Frank.
Peggy, his wife.
Clare.
Johnny.
Jane, Johnny's twin, eng. to Arthur Gideon, m. Oliver Hobart.
Potterism, Rose Macaulay, 1920.

Pottery, Bill, Captain of the *Godsend. The Splendid Spur,* A. Quiller-Couch, 1889.

Potticary, Albert. *Brat Farrar,* Josephine Tey, 1949.

Pottle, Gaffer. *The Silver King* (play), H. A. Jones, 1882.

Potton, Private. *The Snow Goose,* P. Gallico, 1941.

Potts, former tutor of Guy Morville. *The Heir of Redclyffe,* Charlotte M. Yonge, 1853.

Potts, Captain. *The Moon in the Yellow River* (play), D. Johnston, 1932.

Potts, Mrs, guest-house manager. *No News from Helen,* L. Golding, 1943.

Potts, Arthur, friend of Paul Pennyfeather. *Decline and Fall,* E. Waugh, 1928.

Potts, Joe ('Ginger'), boy in Pym's Publicity. *Murder Must Advertise,* Dorothy L. Sayers, 1933.

Potts, Tom, reporter and editor, *Newcome Independent. The Newcomes,* W. M. Thackeray, 1853–5.

Potzdoff, Captain de. *Barry Lyndon,* W. M. Thackeray, 1844.

Pouldour, Madame.
Yannik, her grand-daughter.
The Face of Clay, H. A. Vachell, 1906.

Poulengey, Bertrand de. *Saint Joan* (play), G. B. Shaw, 1924.

Pouliski, Maria. *On the Spot* (play), E. Wallace, 1930.

Poulter, old soldier turned schoolmaster, Kingslorton. *The Mill on the Floss,* George Eliot, 1860.

Pounce, Captain Peter. *Joseph Andrews,* H. Fielding, 1742.

Poundtext, Peter, Presbyterian minister. *Old Mortality,* W. Scott, 1816.

Poupon, Monsieur. 'The Shoelace' (s.s.), *The Little Dog Laughed,* L. Merrick, 1930.

Pourauges, Marquis of, Brigadier-General. The *Hornblower* series, C. S. Forester, 1937 onwards.

Pourville, Philip de ('Peter Poop'). *Housemaster* (play), Ian Hay, 1936.

Povey, Samuel, highly trusted shop assistant at Baines's, m. Constance Baines.
Cyril, their son.
Daniel, his father, hanged for murdering his wife.
Dick, his nephew, m. Lily Holl.
The Old Wives' Tale, Arnold Bennett, 1908.

Powderell, retired ironmonger.
His wife.
Middlemarch, Geo. Eliot, 1871–2.

Powell, drinking friend of Willy Carmichael. *Time, Gentlemen! Time!*, Norah Hoult, 1930.

Powell, Jotham. *Ethan Frome,* Edith Wharton, 1911.

Powell, Leonard. *Mr Billingham, the Marquis and Madelon,* E. P. Oppenheim.

Powell, Marcus.
  Colonel Powell, his uncle.
  No Son of Mine, G. B. Stern, 1948.

Powell, Olwen, an heiress, m. Noah Watts.
  Her parents.
  The Black Venus, Rhys Davies, 1944.

Power, Captain Frederick, inseparable companion of Charles O'Malley, m. Inez Emanuel. *Charles O'Malley,* C. Lever, 1841.

Power, Hannah. 'The Mystery of Hannah Power' (s.s.), *Old Patch's Medley,* Marjorie Bowen, 1930.

Power, Paula, m. George Somerset.
  John, her dead father.
  Abner, her uncle.
  A Laodicean, T. Hardy, 1881.

Power, Reginald, a schoolboy.
  Sir Lawrence Power, his father.
  Lady Power, his mother.
  St Winifred's, F. W. Farrar, 1862.

Power, Valentine, cousin of Tony Rakonitz, m. Stephen Greenways.
  Haidée, her mother, *née* Czelovar.
  Francis, her father.
  Tents of Israel and others, 1924 onwards, G. B. Stern.

Powheid, Lazarus, sexton. *Castle Dangerous,* W. Scott, 1832.

Powler, Violet, housekeeper, m. Evelyn Orcham. *Imperial Palace,* Arnold Bennett, 1930.

Pownceby, Mr, solicitor. *The Cuckoo in the Nest,* Mrs Oliphant, 1894.

Powys, Leonora, m. Edward Ashburnham. *The Good Soldier,* Ford Madox Ford, 1915.

Poynings, Lord George, younger son of Lord Tiptoff. *Barry Lyndon,* W. M. Thackeray, 1844.

Poynter. *The Glory of Clementina Wing,* W. J. Locke, 1911.

Poyser, Mrs Malkah.
  Isrol, her husband.
    Becky, Jack and **Harry,** their children.
  Magnolia Street, L. Golding, 1932.

Poyser, Martin, tenant of Hall Farm, uncle of Hester Sorrel.
  Rachel, his wife.
    Marty, Thomas and **Charlotte,** their children.
  'Old Martin,' his father.
  Adam Bede, George Eliot, 1859.

Pozzo. *Waiting for Godot,* S. Beckett, 1952.

Praed. *Mrs Warren's Profession* (play), G. B. Shaw, 1902.

Prance, Dr, 'a little medical lady.' *The Bostonians,* H. James, 1886.

Prang, student of advanced English. *The Purple Plain,* H. E. Bates, 1947.

Pratt, Milby doctor.
  Eliza, his daughter.
  His sister and housekeeper.
  'Janet's Repentance,' *Scenes of Clerical Life,* George Eliot, 1857.

Pratt, Anastasia (Chalkline Annie), delinquent girl who introduces Joe Buck to sex. *Midnight Cowboy,* James Leo Herlihy, 1966.

Pratt, Helen, Berlin correspondent. *Mr Norris Changes Trains,* C. Isherwood, 1935.

Pratt, Richard, trainer. *Not So Bad after All,* Nat Gould.

Pratt, Sam, milk-lorry driver. *Fed Up,* G. A. Birmingham, 1931.

Preciosa, m. Victorian. *The Spanish Student* (poem), H. W. Longfellow, 1858.

Preece, Arthur. *Milestones* (play), Arnold Bennett & E. Knoblock, 1912.

Preemby, Albert Edward, house-agent's clerk, m. Chrissie Hossett.
  Christina Alberta, central character, nominally his daughter. *See* HOSSETT.
  Christina Alberta's Father, H. G. Wells, 1925.

Preen, William.
  Emily, his wife.
  Shall We Join the Ladies? (play), J. M. Barrie, 1921.

Prendergast, ex-clergyman, schoolmaster. *Decline and Fall,* E. Waugh, 1928.

Prendergast, Hon. and **Rev.,** non-resident rector, Milby. 'Janet's Repentance,' *Scenes of Clerical Life,* George Eliot, 1857.

Prendergast, E. P., aircraft industry. *No Highway,* N. Shute, 1948.

Prendergast, Sidney (Snap), chum of

Joby Weston. *Joby,* Stan Barstow, 1964.

Prendergast, William. *Dr Nikola,* G. Boothby, 1896.

Prendick, Edward, biologist, central character and narrator. *The Island of Dr Moreau,* H. G. Wells, 1896.

Prentice, secret service. *The Ministry of Fear,* Graham Greene, 1943.

Prentice, General. *The Metropolis,* Upton Sinclair, 1908.

Presbury, Miss. *Monsieur Beaucaire* (play), Booth Tarkington, 1902.

Prescott, Dr.
  Lawrence, his son, m. Elmira Edwards.
  Jerome, Mary E. Wilkins, 1897.

Prescott, Dick, friend of Lord Saxby. *Sinister Street,* C. Mackenzie, 1913.

Press, Alice, mistress of Francis Herries, 'sold' to Rosen for 40s. *Rogue Herries,* Hugh Walpole, 1930.

Presset, Paul Arthur, central character, schoolmaster. *See also* MYRA BAWNE.
  Elinor, his wife.
  Aubrey, his father.
  Jane, his mother.
  Winnie, his sister.
  We the Accused, E. Raymond, 1935.

Preston. *The Vortex* (play), N. Coward, 1924.

Preston, Mr, Lord Cumnor's agent. *Wives and Daughters,* Mrs Gaskell, 1866.

Preston, Rt Hon. Edmund.
  Lady Jane, his wife.
  The Great Hoggarty Diamond, W. M. Thackeray, 1841.

Preston, Sally, m. Tom Kitchener. 'Something to Worry About' (s.s.), *The Man Upstairs,* P. G. Wodehouse, 1914.

Presumption. *See* SIMPLE.

Pretty, Bob. 'A Tiger's Skin' (s.s.) and elsewhere, *The Lady of the Barge,* W. W. Jacobs, 1902.

Prettyman, Major. 'Farmer on the Fairway' (s.s.), *Sun on the Water,* L. A. G. Strong, 1940.

Prettyman, Prince. *The Rehearsal* (play), George, Duke of Buckingham, 1671.

Preysing, Herr, general-direktor.
  Mulle, his wife.
  Popsy and **Babs,** their daughters.
  Grand Hotel, Vicki Baum, 1931.

Priam, King of Troy. *Troilus and Cressida* (play), W. Shakespeare.

Price, Anabel ('Billy'), famous athlete. *The Metropolis,* Upton Sinclair, 1908.

Price, Sir Bulkeley. *The Miser's Daughter,* W. H. Ainsworth, 1842.

Price, Eiluned, friend of Harriet Vane. *Strong Poison,* Dorothy L. Sayers, 1930.

Price, Elias, lay preacher. *Abraham Lincoln* (play), J. Drinkwater, 1918.

Price, Fanny, art student.
  Albert, her brother.
  Of Human Bondage, W. S. Maugham, 1915.

Price, Mrs Frances, *née* Ward, sister of Lady Bertram.
  Lieutenant Price, her husband.
  Their children:
    Fanny, m. Edmund Bertram.
    William.
    Susan, and others.
  Mansfield Park, Jane Austen, 1814.

Price, Julia.
  Herbert, her brother.
  The Ghost Train (play), A. Ridley, 1925.

Price, Myfanwy, in love with Mog Edwards. *Under Milk Wood* (play), Dylan Thomas, 1954.

Price, Oliver.
  m. (1) Edith Whitebillet.
    Reginald, their son.
    Sarah, their daughter.
  (2) Edna Smith, *née* Whitebillet.
  Jane, his sister. *See* PALFREY.
  His father and mother.
  Antigua Penny Puce, R. Graves, 1936.

Price, Snobby. *Major Barbara* (play), G. B. Shaw, 1905.

Price, 'Tilda, m. John Browdie. *Nicholas Nickleby,* C. Dickens, 1839.

Price, Willie, in love with Anna Tellwright. *Anna of the Five Towns,* Arnold Bennett, 1902.

Price-Stables, Mrs.
  Her husband.
  Peter, Lucy, Rosalind and **Christopher,** their children, charges of Simpson.
  Simpson, E. Sackville-West, 1931.

Prickshaft, Sir Adam, suitor of Mistress Miniver. *Satiromastix* (play), Thomas Dekker, 1601.

Priddle, Retty, dairymaid. *Tess of the D'Urbervilles*, T. Hardy, 1891.

Pridham, Sir Edmund. The *Barsetshire* series, Angela Thirkell, 1933 onwards.

Priest, Judge. 'Boys will be Boys' (s.s.), *From Place to Place*, Irvin S. Cobb, 1920.

Priest, Roger, dentist. *H. M Pulham, Esq.*, J. P. Marquand, 1941.

Priestley, Schofield, m. Sophia Ormerod. West Riding Love Story' (s.s.), *Love and Money*, Phyllis Bentley, 1957.

Prig, a knavish beggar. *The Beggar's Bush* (play), Beaumont & Fletcher, 1622.

Prime, Mrs Bridget, friend of the Joyces. *Flamingo*, Mary Borden, 1927.

Primrose, Dr Charles, Vicar of Wakefield, central character and narrator.
  Deborah, his wife.
  Their children:
    George, m. Arabella Wilmot.
    Moses, m. Miss Flamborough.
    Olivia, m. Squire Thornhill.
    Sophia, m. Sir William Thornhill.
The Vicar of Wakefield, O. Goldsmith, 1766.

Primrose, Dulcie. *The Sport of Kings* (play), Ian Hay, 1924.

Primrose, Mark, who runs an enterprise to reorientate missing persons.
  Julia, his wife.
Thin Air, John Pudney, 1961.

Prince, security investigator. *A Sort of Traitors*, N. Balchin, 1949.

Prince, Dick, employee of Frank Morton. *Ungava*, R. M. Ballantyne, 1857.

Princhester, Bishop of. *See* EDWARD SCROPE.

Prindle, Si.
  Julie, his eldest daughter, m. Armstrong.
    Hugh, her illegitimate son.
The Woodcarver of 'Lympus, Mary E. Waller, 1909.

Pringle, Caryl Bramsley's housemaster at Eton. *C.*, M. Baring, 1924.

Pringle, Miss Agnes. *The Land of Promise* (play), W. S. Maugham, 1914.

Pringle, Guy, lecturer in English department of the University of Bucharest.
  Harriet, his wife.
The Great Fortune, Olivia Manning, 1960, and others.

Pringle, Mary-Ann, aspiring young actress. *Myra Breckinridge*, Gore Vidal, 1968.

Prinsloo, Lisbet, m. John Grafton.
  Barend, her brother.
The City of Gold, F. Brett Young, 1939.

Prior, Captain Montagu, late of the Militia.
  His wife.
  Elizabeth (*see* BESSIE BELLENDEN), their eldest daughter, m. as 2nd wife Adolphus Frederick Lovel.
Lovel the Widower, W. M. Thackeray, 1860.

Prior, Tom. *Outward Bound* (play), S. Vane, 1923.

Priscilla, m. John Alden. *The Courtship of Miles Standish* (poem), H. W. Longfellow.

Priscilla, maid to Mrs Jellyby. *Bleak House*, C. Dickens, 1853.

Prism, Miss Laetitia, governess to Cecily Cardew, originally nurse to John Worthing, m. Canon Chasuble. *The Importance of Being Earnest* (play), O. Wilde, 1895.

Prissy. *See* DILCEY.

Pritchard, Mrs Ogmore-Pritchard's 2nd husband. *Under Milk Wood* (play), Dylan Thomas, 1954.

Pritchard, Sergeant. 'Mrs Bathurst' (s.s.), *Traffics and Discoveries*, R. Kipling, 1904.

Pritchard, Cynlais.
  His wife.
  Dilys, their daughter, murdered by Idris Atkinson.
How Green Was My Valley, R. Llewellyn, 1939.

Pritchard, Henry.
  His wife.
Caesar's Wife (play), W. S. Maugham, 1919.

Privett, Sue, kitchenmaid at Sir Edmund Roundelay's.
  Her grandmother.
A Footman for the Peacock, Rachel Ferguson, 1940.

Privett, William.
  Betty, his wife.
  'The Superstitious Man's Story' (s.s.), *Life's Little Ironies,* T. Hardy, 1894.

Privilege, Lord, rascally uncle of Peter Simple.
  Hawkins, his illegitimate son.
  Peter Simple, Captain Marryat, 1834.

Probe, a surgeon. *A Trip to Scarborough* (play), R. B. Sheridan, 1777.

Probert, Gareth, poet. *That Uncertain Feeling,* Kingsley Amis, 1955.

Probert, Rosie. *Under Milk Wood* (play), Dylan Thomas, 1954.

Probity, James, m. Olga Pryde.
  Jack, their son.
  James, his father.
  Master Jim Probity, F. Swinnerton, 1952.

Proctor, printer, stationer, and librarian. 'Janet's Repentance,' *Scenes of Clerical Life,* George Eliot, 1857.

Proctor, Pog, name assumed by James Morton when he wishes to disappear. *Thin Air,* John Pudney, 1961.

Procurio, Edward, 'groom of the Chambers.' *The Young Visiters,* Daisy Ashford, 1919.

Prodger, Walter. *The Dove's Nest,* Katherine Mansfield, 1923.

Profond, Monsieur Prosper. The *Forsyte* series, J. Galsworthy, 1906–33.

Progers, Thorold, Grope's first friend, m. Rosalind Malley. *Albert Grope,* F. O. Mann, 1931.

Prosper Le Gai, central character, m. Isoult Pietosa de Brèauté. *The Forest Lovers,* M. Hewlett, 1898.

Prospero, rightful Duke of Milan. *The Tempest* (play), W. Shakespeare.

Prospero, Prince. *The Masque of the Red Death* (s.s.), E. A. Poe.

Pross, Miss, nurse and attendant of Lucie Manette.
  Solomon (alias John Barsad), her degraded brother.
  A Tale of Two Cities, C. Dickens, 1859.

Prosser, Mrs Sally (*née* Gray), political virago. 'The Speech' (s.s.), *Blind Love,* V. S. Pritchett, 1969.

Proteus, gentleman of Verona. *Two Gentlemen of Verona* (play), W. Shakespeare.

Prothero, Mary (Pokey), graduate of Vassar. *The Group,* Mary McCarthy, 1963.

Prothero, William, school and college friend of William Benham. *The Research Magnificent,* H. G. Wells, 1915.

Protheroe, a doctor. *Middlemarch,* George Eliot, 1871–2.

Protheroe, Annie. 'Annie Protheroe' (poem). *Bab Ballads,* W. S. Gilbert, 1869.

Protheroe, Lydia. *See* ALICE JENNINGS.

Proudfute, Oliver, bonnet-maker.
  Maudie, his wife.
  The Fair Maid of Perth, W. Scott, 1828.

Proudhammer, Leo, an American Negro actor.
  Caleb, his brother, a preacher.
  Tell Me How Long The Train's Been Gone, James Baldwin, 1968.

Proudie, Dr, Bishop of Barchester.
  His wife.
  Olivia, their daughter, m. Rev. Tobias Tickler.
  Framley Parsonage, 1861, and others, A. Trollope.

Prout, Mr ('Heffy'), Stalky's housemaster. *Stalky & Co.,* 1899, and 'The United Idolaters' (s.s.), *Debits and Credits,* R. Kipling, 1926.

Provis. *See* ABEL MAGWITCH.

Prowd, Treby watchmaker. *Felix Holt,* George Eliot, 1866.

Prowde, Mrs, aunt of Hazel Woodus.
  Albert, her son.
  Gone to Earth, Mary Webb, 1917.

Prowse, Tom. 'Communion' (s.s.), *Adam and Eve and Pinch Me,* A. E. Coppard, 1921.

Prudence, Piety and **Charity** of the Palace Beautiful. *Pilgrim's Progress,* J. Bunyan, 1678 and 1684.

Prufrock, J. Alfred. *The Love Song of J. Alfred Prufrock* (poem), T. S. Eliot, 1915.

Prune, Elizabeth, object of Dr Arnold-Browne's passion. *They Winter Abroad,* T. H. White, 1932.

Pryar, Matthew, a snob. *The Unspeakable Skipton,* Pamela Hansford Johnson, 1959.

Pryce, David.
  Winifred, his wife.
  'Look at the Clock' (poem), *The Ingoldsby Legends,* R. H. Barham, 1837.

Pryde, Olga, m. James Probity. *Master Jim Probity,* F. Swinnerton, 1952.

Pryde, Lady Sarah, m. Stephen Fortis.
The Earl of Thanet, her father.
'The Mystery of Hannah Power,' *Old Patch's Medley,* Marjorie Bowen, 1930.

Pryer, Rev. Mr, fellow curate with Ernest Pontifex. *The Way of all Flesh,* S. Butler, 1903.

Pryke, Dame Eleanor.
Derek, her son, father of Sweetie by Margaret Hart.
Children of the Archbishop, N. Collins, 1951.

Prynne, Amanda, ex-wife of Elyot Chase.
Victor, her husband.
Private Lives (play), N. Coward, 1930.

Prynne, Dorothea, m. Jeff Jerrythought.
Her sister, water-colour artist.
Alice-for-Short, W. de Morgan, 1907.

Prynne, Hester, 'scarlet woman.'
Pearl, her daughter.
The Scarlet Letter, N. Hawthorne, 1850.

Prynne, Ruth, actress. *Manhattan Transfer,* J. dos Passos, 1925.

Pryor, Mrs, former governess to Caroline Helstone. *Shirley,* Charlotte Brontë, 1849.

Psyche, Lady, Professor of Humanities, sister of Florian, m. Cyril. *The Princess* (poem), Lord Tennyson, 1847. *Princess Ida* (comic opera), Gilbert & Sullivan, 1884.

Ptolemy, Dionysius, King of Egypt. *Caesar and Cleopatra* (play), G. B. Shaw, 1900.

Ptthmllnsprts, Professor. *The Water Babies,* C. Kingsley, 1863.

Publius, son of Marcus. *Titus Andronicus* (play), W. Shakespeare.

Pubsey & Co. *See* FLEDGEBY.

Puck (Robin Goodfellow), a fairy. *A Midsummer Night's Dream* (play), W. Shakespeare. Also central character, *Puck of Pook's Hill,* etc., R. Kipling, 1906–10.

Pucken, Tom, farm-hand at Laverings.
Sarah, his wife, ex-kitchen-maid.
Lucasta, their youngest daughter.
Before Lunch, Angela Thirkell, 1939.

Puddleduck, Jemima. *The Tale of Jemima Puddleduck,* Beatrix Potter, 1908.

Puddleton, Miss ('Puddle'), governess and faithful friend of Stephen Gordon. *The Well of Loneliness,* Radclyffe Hall, 1928.

Puddy, Mr, neighbour of the Jossers. *London Belongs to Me,* N. Collins, 1945.

Puff. *The Critic* (play), R. B. Sheridan, 1779.

Puff, Partenopex. *Vivian Grey,* B. Disraeli, 1826–7.

Puffington, a sportsman. *Mr Sponge's Sporting Tour,* R. S. Surtees, 1853.

Pufford, Miss, schoolmistress. 'Tom Tiddler's Ground,' *Christmas Stories,* C. Dickens, 1861.

Pug. *The Devil Is an Ass* (play), B. Jonson, 1616.

Pugh, Miss, Miss Guthrie's rival. 'Neighbours' (s.s.), *A Beginning,* W. de la Mare, 1955.

Pugh, Mr.
His wife.
Under Milk Wood (play), Dylan Thomas, 1954.

Pugh, Mrs. *The Trial,* Charlotte M. Yonge, 1864.

Pugh, Sir Bartlemy. *The Constant Nymph,* Margaret Kennedy, 1924.

Pugh, Lizzie, a malicious hunchback. *The Black Venus,* Rhys Davies, 1944.

Pugh, Sarah. *The Corn is Green* (play), Emlyn Williams, 1938.

Pugwash, Isaac.
Sally, his wife.
Their three children.
The Tragedy of the Till (s.s.), D. Jerrold.

Pulci, drug-seller.
Tessa, his daughter.
Paolo and Francesca, Stephen Phillips, 1900.

Pulham, butler to Sir R. Foxfield. *Let the People Sing,* J. B. Priestley, 1939.

Pulham, Henry Moulton, Investment Counsel, central character and narrator, m. Cornelia Motford (Kay).
George and **Gladys,** their children.
John, his father.

Mary, his mother, *née* Knowles.
Mary, his sister.
Jim, his brother.
H. M. Pulham, Esq., J. P. Marquand, 1941.

Pullen, Archie, bank manager. 'Death of a Dog' (s.s.), *Louise*, Viola Meynell, 1954.

Pullet, gentleman farmer.
Sophy, his wife, *née* Dodson.
The Mill on the Floss, George Eliot, 1860.

Pulleyn. Family name of EARL OF DORKING.

Pullford, Roman Catholic Bishop of. *The Three Taps*, R. A. Knox, 1927.

Pulteney, Edward. *The Three Taps*, R. A. Knox, 1927.

Pumblechook, corn-chandler, uncle of Joe Gargery. *Great Expectations*, C. Dickens, 1861.

Pummel, valet to Theophrastus Such. *Theophrastus Such*, George Eliot, 1879.

Pumphrey, Professor. *Babbitt*, Sinclair Lewis, 1923.

Pumphrey, Kit, in love with Sydney Fairfield.
Rev. Christopher, his father.
A Bill of Divorcement (play), Clemence Dane, 1921.

Pumphrey, Maggo, cook, and Lord Trehick's mistress.
Asa, her brother.
For Us in the Dark, Naomi Royde-Smith, 1937.

Pumphrey, Robert, schoolmaster, later brigadier.
His wife.
Tom Tiddler's Ground, E. Shanks, 1934.

Punch, a small boy. 'Baa Baa Black Sheep' (s.s.), *Wee Willie Winkie*, R. Kipling, 1888.

Puncheon, Hector, journalist and drug trafficker. *Murder Must Advertise*, Dorothy L. Sayers, 1933.

Punt, Mrs May, friend of Mrs Johnson. *The History of Mr Polly*, H. G. Wells, 1910.

Punter, Count, of Hanover, gambler. *The Newcomes*, 1853-5, and elsewhere, W. M. Thackeray.

Pupillary, John, rather unpleasant young hero. *They Winter Abroad*, T. H. White, 1932.

Purcell, Tom, employer of David Grieve.
Lucy, his daughter, m. David Grieve.
The History of David Grieve, Mrs Humphry Ward, 1892.

Purdie, Amos, M.P.
His wife.
Joe, their son.
Katie, their daughter.
The Sport of Kings (play), Ian Hay, 1924.

Purdie, John.
Mabel, his wife.
Dear Brutus (play), J. M. Barrie, 1917.

Purdue, Angela, m. Wilfred Mulliner. *Meet Mr Mulliner*, P. G. Wodehouse, 1927.

Pure, Simon. *A Bold Stroke for a Wife* (play), Mrs Susanna Centlivre, 1718.

Purfoy, Sarah, maid to Mrs Vickers, in love with John Rex. *For the Term of his Natural Life*, M. Clarke, 1874.

Purkin, Cyril, laundry manager. *Imperial Palace*, Arnold Bennett, 1930.

Purkins, a policeman. *The Last Revolution*, Lord Dunsany, 1951.

Purlitt, Miss. *Monsieur Beaucaire* (play), Booth Tarkington, 1902.

Purnell, Captain Timothy. 'With the Night Mail' (s.s.), *Actions and Reactions*, R. Kipling, 1909.

Pursewarden, Percy, an ironical English writer.
Liza, his blind sister.
The Alexandria Quartet, 1957-61, Lawrence Durrell.

Purun Dass, Sir Dewar, K.C.I.E. (Purun Bhagat). 'The Miracle of Purun Bhagat' (s.s.), *The Second Jungle Book*, R. Kipling, 1895.

Purves, Stanley, second lieutenant. *Peter Jackson, Cigar Merchant*, G. Frankau, 1919.

Purvis, Captain, head of Military Police. *A Bell for Adano*, John Hersey, 1944.

Purvis, Mrs Daisy, cockney charwoman. *You Can't Go Home Again*, T. Wolfe, 1947.

'Pussy Abanazar,' a prefect. 'Slaves of the Lamp,' *Stalky & Co.*, 1899, and 'The United Idolaters,' *Debits and Credits*, 1926, R. Kipling.

Putley, painter and decorator. *The Diary of a Nobody,* G. & W. Grossmith, 1892.

Puttick, Mrs, school matron. *The Hill,* H. A. Vachell, 1905.

Putty, James, election agent. *Felix Holt,* George Eliot, 1866.

Pybus, Mrs, gossip. *Pendennis,* W. M. Thackeray, 1848–50.

Pybus, Mrs, sister of Unwin. *Joan and Peter,* H. G. Wells, 1918.

Pycroft, Emanuel, petty officer. 'The Bonds of Discipline,' 'Steam Tactics' (s.ss.), *Traffics and Discoveries,* 1904, and others, R. Kipling.

Pycroft, Hall. 'The Stockbroker's Clerk,' *Memoirs of Sherlock Holmes,* A. Conan Doyle, 1894.

Pye, Rev. John, Headmaster, Helstonleigh Choir School. *The Channings,* Mrs Henry Wood, 1862.

Pye, Mrs P. J. (Belinda), m. Frank Bailey.
  Daffodil, her daughter by 1st husband.
We're Here, D. Mackail, 1947.

Pyke, Dame Johanna, prioress of the Benedictine convent at Oby (1360–1368). *The Corner That Held Them,* Sylvia Townsend Warner, 1948.

Pyle, Alben, 'quiet American.' *The Quiet American,* Graham Greene, 1955.

Pym, chairman of Pym's Publicity. *Murder Must Advertise,* Dorothy L. Sayers, 1933.

Pym, Dr Cyrus. *Manalive,* G. K. Chesterton, 1912.

Pym, Miss Laetitia, psychologist. *Miss Pym Disposes,* Josephine Tey, 1946.

Pym, Ned, later Lord Monkhurst.
  His wife.
  Muriel, their daughter.
Milestones (play), Arnold Bennett & E. Knoblock, 1912.

Pyncheon, Colonel, enemy of Matthew Maule, found dead as Maule prophesied.
  Gervaise, his grandson.
  Hephzibah, aged descendant, shopkeeper.
  Clifford, Hephzibah's brother.
  Phoebe, cousin of Hephzibah, m. Holgrave.
  Arthur, Phoebe's father.
  Jaffrey, Judge, cousin of Hephzibah.
The House of the Seven Gables, N. Hawthorne, 1851.

Pynsent, George, ambitious, aristocratic.
  Lady Diana, his wife.
Pendennis, W. M. Thackeray, 1848–50.

Q

Quabil, Sidonian port inspector. 'The Manner of Men' (s.s.), *Limits and Renewals*, R. Kipling, 1932.

Quackenboss, fashionable doctor. *The Newcomes*, W. M. Thackeray, 1853–5.

Quackleben, Dr Quentin, 'man of medicine.' *St Ronan's Well*, W. Scott, 1824.

Quadrant, Captain, R.N. *Born to be a Sailor*, G. Stables.

Quale, friend of Mrs Jellyby. *Bleak House*, C. Dickens, 1853.

Quallon, banker, of Wanchester. *Daniel Deronda*, George Eliot, 1876.

Quantock, Mrs Daisy.
 Robert, her husband.
Queen Lucia, E. F. Benson, 1920.

Quarles, Philip, novelist, m. Elinor Bidlake.
 Philip, their son.
 Sidney, Philip's father.
 Rachel, his mother.
Point Counter Point, Aldous Huxley, 1928.

Quarmby, Hugh de. 'Revenge upon Revenge' (s.s.), *Love and Money*, Phyllis Bentley, 1957.

Quatermain, Allan (native name Macumazahn); big-game hunter and one of the three explorers with Good and Curtis; narrator. *King Solomon's Mines*, 1885, and others, H. Rider Haggard.

Quayle, Glory. *The Christian*, Hall Caine, 1897.

Quayne, Portia, aged sixteen, central character.
 Thomas, her half-brother, an advertising agent.
 Anna, his wife.
The Death of the Heart, Elizabeth Bowen, 1938.

Queen, Ellery, American detective.
 Inspector Richard Queen of New York Homicide Squad, his father.
The Chinese Orange Mystery, 1934, and many others, Ellery Queen.

Queen, Else, maid at Kinraddie Manse. *A Scots Quair* trilogy, 1932–4, Lewis Grassic Gibbon.

Queequeg, Indian harpooner. *Moby Dick*, H. Melville, 1851.

Quelch, Mr, Remove master at Greyfriars. The *Billy Bunter* series, Frank Richards.

Quen-ki-Tong, 'the charitable.' *The Wallet of Kai Lung*, E. Bramah, 1900.

Quentin, Pauncefort. *The Vortex* (play), N. Coward, 1924.

Querini, Count Flavio, Venetian with singing ambitions. *The Unspeakable Skipton*, Pamela Hansford Johnson, 1959.

Querry, man of arid heart. *A Burnt-Out Case*, Graham Greene, 1961.

Quesnel, Monsieur. brother of Mme St Aubert.
 His wife, Italian heiress.
The Mysteries of Udolpho, Mrs Radcliffe, 1794.

Quest, Martha, daughter of British farmer settled in South Africa, central character.
 Alfred and **May,** her parents.
 Douglas Knowell, her husband, civil servant.
 Caroline, her daughter.
Children of Violence series, Doris Lessing, 1952–69.

Quested, Adela. *A Passage to India*, E. M. Forster, 1924.

Quex, Marquess of. *The Gay Lord Quex* (play), A. W. Pinero, 1899.

Quickly, Dame, a landlady. *Rosalind* (play), J. M. Barrie, 1912.

Quickly, Mrs, servant of Dr Caius, and hostess. *The Merry Wives of Windsor, Henry the Fourth* and *Henry the Fifth* (plays), W. Shakespeare.

Quickshott, John, m. Dorothy Sinnier. *The Porch*, 1937, and *The Stronghold*, 1939, R. Church.

Quiggin, J. G., left-wing critic. *A Question of Upbringing*, 1951, and others in *The Music of Time* series, Anthony Powell.

Quigley, Miss, governess. *The Newcomes,* W. M. Thackeray, 1853–5.

Quigley, Doll, neighbour of the Parker family.
Bub, her feebleminded brother.
The Tree of Man, Patrick White, 1955.

Quigley, Failey, Cabinet Minister, brother-in-law of Phil Doyle. 'Hymeneal' (s.s.), *The Talking Trees,* Sean O'Faolain, 1971.

Quigley, Dr Peter, crooked alienist. *The Judas Window,* C. Dickson, 1938.

Quilp, Daniel, evil deformed dwarf.
His wife.
The Old Curiosity Shop, C. Dickens, 1841.

Quilpe, Peter. *The Cocktail Party* (play), T. S. Eliot, 1950.

Quimsby, Harold, ordinary seaman, *Artemis. The Ship,* C. S. Forester, 1943.

Quin, dramatic critic, *The Liberal. The Street of Adventure,* P. Gibbs, 1909.

Quin, Captain, m. Honoria Brady. *Barry Lyndon,* W. M. Thackeray, 1844.

Quin, Widow. *The Playboy of the Western World* (play), J. M. Synge, 1907.

Quin, Agnes, prostitute. *Mrs Eckdorf in O'Neill's Hotel,* William Trevor, 1969.

Quin, Auberon, 'King Auberon.' *The Napoleon of Notting Hill,* G. K. Chesterton, 1904.

Quin, James, 'a real voluptuary,' friend of Jeremy Melford. *Humphry Clinker,* T. Smollett, 1771.

Quinbus, Flestrin (man mountain), Gulliver's name in Lilliput. *Gulliver's Travels,* J. Swift, 1726.

Quince, a carpenter. *A Midsummer Night's Dream* (play), W. Shakespeare.

Quince, Mary, 'somewhat ancient' maid to Maud Ruthyn. *Uncle Silas,* Sheridan le Fanu, 1864.

Quinion, manager of Murdstone & Grinby. *David Copperfield,* C. Dickens, 1850.

Quinlan, Julie, daughter of Ella, Baroness van Leyden, by 1st husband, m. Rupert von Narwitz. *The Fountain,* C. Morgan, 1932.

Quinn, Harrison.
Alice, his wife.
The Thin Man, D. Hammett, 1934.

Quinney, Joseph, antique dealer, central character.
Susan, his wife, *née* Biddlecombe.
Josephine ('Posy'), their daughter.
Quinneys', H. A. Vachell, 1914.

Quinquart, famous French comedian, m. Suzanne Brouette. 'The Judgment of Paris' (s.s.), *All the World Wondered,* L. Merrick, 1911.

Quint, Peter, the late; valet, malignant ghost at Bly. *The Turn of the Screw,* H. James, 1898.

Quinton, Barbara.
Lord Quinton, her father.
Simon Dale, A. Hope, 1898.

Quintus, son of Titus Andronicus. *Titus Andronicus* (play), W. Shakespeare.

Quirk, Thady, friend and servant of the family, narrator.
Jason, his son.
Castle Rackrent, Maria Edgeworth, 1800.

Quisara. *The Island Princess* (play), J. Fletcher, 1647.

Quiverful, Rev. Mr, Rector of Puddingdale. *Barchester Towers,* A. Trollope, 1857.

Quixtus, Dr Ephraim, solicitor and antiquarian, m. Clementina Wing. *The Glory of Clementina Wing.* W. J. Locke, 1911.

Quodling, Mrs.
Francis, her illegitimate son.
The Town Traveller, G. Gissing, 1898.

Quong, narrator and commentator. *The Hands of Mr Ottermole* (s.s.), and elsewhere, T. Burke.

Quong Yan Miun. *Dr Nikola,* G. Boothby, 1896.

Quorlen, Tory printer, Treby Magna. *Felix Holt,* George Eliot, 1866.

R

Raa, Lord, dissolute fortune hunter, m. (1) Mary O'Neill, his cousin. *The Woman Thou Gavest Me*, Hall Caine, 1913.

Rabbit (and his friends and relations). *Winnie the Pooh*, 1926, and others, A. A. Milne.

Rabbit, The White. *Alice in Wonderland*, L. Carroll, 1865.

Rabbit, 'Brer.' *Uncle Remus*, J. C. Harris, 1880–95.

Rabbit, Rev. Edward.
His wife.
Mehalah, S. Baring-Gould, 1880.

Rabbit, Mary Anne, m. Tony Hynes.
James, her grandfather.
Famine, L. O'Flaherty, 1937.

Rabbits, butler to Lady Drew. *Tono Bungay*, H. G. Wells, 1909.

'Rabbit's Eggs,' local carrier. 'Slaves of the Lamp,' *Stalky & Co.*, R. Kipling, 1899.

Raby, Aurora. *Don Juan* (poem), Lord Byron, 1819–24.

Raby, Guy, 'antique Tory squire,' m. Jael Dence.
Edith, his sister, m. James Little.
Put Yourself in his Place, C. Reade, 1870.

Race, James, of the *Chicago Sentinel*. *Trial by Terror*, P. Gallico, 1952.

Rackham, John, Sir Oliver Raydon's groom, m. Susan Trant. *An Affair of Dishonour*, W. de Morgan, 1910.

Rackrent (originally O'Shaughlin).
Sir Patrick and **Sir Murtagh,** his sons.
Sir Kit, his brother.
His wife.
Sir Condy, distant relative, m. Isabelle Moneygawl.
Castle Rackrent, Maria Edgeworth, 1800.

Rackstraw, The Ladies Hermengilde and **Yseult,** twin beauties. *The Newcomes*, W. M. Thackeray, 1853–1855.

Rackstraw, Ralph, able seaman, m. Josephine Corcoran. *H.M.S. Pinafore* (comic opera), Gilbert & Sullivan, 1878.

Rackstraw, Roger, tutor to John Herries and Adam Paris. *The Fortress*, Hugh Walpole, 1932.

Radcliffe, Leonard, last product of a once-aristocratic family.
John, his father.
Stella, his mother.
Elizabeth, his sister.
Radcliffe, David Storey, 1963.

Raddle, Mr and Mrs. *Pickwick Papers*, C. Dickens, 1837.

Radeff, Redbeard, Communist interrogator. *A Bargain with the Kremlin* (s.s.), P. Gibbs.

Radford, Mrs.
Clara, her daughter, m. Baxter Dawes.
Sons and Lovers, D. H. Lawrence, 1913.

Radlett. Family name of LORD ALCONLEIGH.

Radley, junior housemaster. *Tell England*, E. Raymond, 1922.

Radnytz, Dr, in love with Medwin Blair. *The Prodigal Heart*, Susan Ertz, 1950.

Radulescu, Countess, friend of Mr Fosdick. *The Prodigal Heart*, Susan Ertz, 1950.

Raeburn, nurseryman. 'The Rajah's Diamond' (s.s.), *New Arabian Nights*, R. L. Stevenson, 1882.

Raeburn, Aldous, later Lord Maxwell, m. Marcella Boyce.
His aunt.
Marcella, Mrs Humphry Ward, 1894.

Raff, Captain, of doubtful reputation.
His wife.
The Book of Snobs, W. M. Thackeray, 1846–7.

Raffles, dissipated bully, stepfather of Joshua Rigg. See PETER FEATHERSTONE. *Middlemarch*, George Eliot, 1871–2.

Raffles, A. J., amateur cracksman, central character. *Raffles* series, 1899 onwards, E. W. Hornung.

Rafi, King of the Beggars. *Hassan* (play), J. E. Fletcher, 1923.

Raftery, Patrick, blind harper, aristocrat, central character.
Hilaria, his Spanish-born wife.
Blind Raftery, Donn Byrne, 1924.

Rag, Captain, snob and swindler. *The Book of Snobs,* W. M. Thackeray, 1846–7.

Ragamoffski, Prince Gregory, m. Miss Hulker. *Vanity Fair,* 1847–8, and *Pendennis,* 1848–50, W. M. Thackeray.

Raggles, one-time butler turned grocer, finally ruined.
His wife, formerly a cook.
Vanity Fair, W. M. Thackeray, 1847–8.

Raikes, Sub-Lieutenant, *Saltash. The Cruel Sea,* N. Monsarrat, 1951.

Raikes, Jack, m. Polly Wheedle. *Evan Harrington,* G. Meredith, 1861.

Railton-Bell, Mrs.
Sybil, her daughter.
Separate Tables (play), T. Rattigan, 1955.

Raine, Roger, drunken tapster, the Peveril Arms.
His wife.
Peveril of the Peak, W. Scott, 1822.

Raines, Sergeant. 'Love o' Women' (s.s.), *Many Inventions,* R. Kipling, 1893.

Rainey, Mrs.
John, her husband.
Tom and **Hugh,** their sons.
Mixed Marriage (play), St John Ervine, 1911.

Rainey, Mrs Fate, town gossip.
Virgie, her daughter.
The Golden Apples, Eudora Welty, 1949.

Rainier, Charles (alias Smith), central character.
Helen, his wife, formerly Paula Ridgeway (alias Helen Hanslett).
Kitty, her stepdaughter.
His brothers and sisters:
Jill.
Chetwynd.
Lydia, his wife.
George.
Vera, his wife.
Julia, m. Dick Fontwell.
Julian.
Bridget.
Random Harvest, J. Hilton, 1941.

Rainscourt, cousin, supposed heir, of Admiral de Courcy; murderer and suicide.
Emily and **Norah,** his daughters.
The King's Own, Captain Marryat, 1830.

Rais, Gilles de (Bluebeard). *Saint Joan* (play), G. B. Shaw, 1924.

Rake, soldier-servant to Bertie Cecil. *Under Two Flags,* Ouida, 1867.

Rakell, Mr. *Monsieur Beaucaire,* Booth Tarkington, 1902.

Rakes, Lady Fanny, m. Earl of Tiptoff. *The Great Hoggarty Diamond,* W. M. Thackeray, 1841.

Rakonitz, Anastasia (The Matriarch), widow of Paul Rakonitz.
Sigismund, her father, son of Simon and Babette Rakonitz.
Her children:
Bertrand, m. Susan Lake.
Antoinette ('Toni'), their daughter, m. Giles Goddard.
Gerald, their son.
Truda, m. Benno Silber, later Silver.
Ludovic.
Blaise.
Sophie, m. Oliver Maitland.
Simone, her sister, m. Karl Czelovar.
Her brothers:
Felix.
Dietrich.
Maximilian.
Louis, her half-brother.
Wanda, her half-sister.
Elsa, *née* Czelovar, widow of her Uncle Albrecht.
Her 'good daughters':
Melanie.
Freda.
Gisela.
Pearl, m. Sydney Phillips.
Tents of Israel and others in the series, G. B. Stern, 1924 onwards.

Raleigh, school Captain. *The Fifth Form at St Dominic's,* T. Baines Reed, 1887.

Raleigh, James, second lieutenant. *Journey's End* (play), R. C. Sherriff, 1928.

Ralph. *Doctor Faustus* (play), C. Marlowe, 1604.

Ralph, citizen's apprentice. *The Knight of the Burning Pestle* (play), Beaumont & Fletcher, 1609.

Ralph, Brian's man. *The Merry Devil of Edmonton* (play), Anon.

Ralph of Tenber.
Melise, his daughter.

Unending Crusade, R. E. Sherwood, 1932.

Ralston, Brookfield headmaster. *Goodbye, Mr Chips,* J. Hilton, 1934.

Ram, second-hand bookseller. *Daniel Deronda,* George Eliot, 1876.

Rama, the herd-bull. 'Tiger Tiger,' *The Jungle Book,* R. Kipling, 1894.

Ramage, stockbroker and newspaper proprietor, friend of Ann Stanley's father. *Ann Veronica,* H. G. Wells, 1909.

Ramboat, Marion, tea-gown designer, m. (1) George Ponderevo, (2) Wachorn.
Her mother.
Her aunt.
Tono Bungay, H. G. Wells, 1909.

Ramdez, Joe, 'the Agent', Arab mixed up in many shady deals in Jordan.
Abdul, his son, who teaches Arabic to Freddy Hamilton.
Suzi, his daughter.
The Mandelbaum Gate, Muriel Spark, 1965.

Ramer, Viscount, artist friend of Mr Ingleside. *Mr Ingleside,* E. V. Lucas, 1910.

Ramgolan, Hindu sailor. *Hard Cash,* C. Reade, 1863.

Ramirez, Don. 'The Striped Chest' (s.s.), *Tales of Pirates and Blue Water,* A. Conan Doyle.

Ramkin, John. *Tom Tiddler's Ground,* E. Shanks, 1934.

Ramon. *The Power and the Glory,* Graham Greene, 1940.

Ramon, Sir Philip, Foreign Secretary, enemy of the Just Men. *The Four Just Men,* E. Wallace, 1905.

Ramorny, Sir John, Master of the House to the Duke of Rothesay. *The Fair Maid of Perth,* W. Scott, 1828.

Ramper, Leonie.
Her father and mother.
Juan in America, E. Linklater, 1931.

Ramsay, Lieutenant-Commander, Captain of *Sorrel.* *The Cruel Sea,* N. Monsarrat, 1951.

Ramsay, David, watchmaker and clock constructor to James I.
Margaret, his daughter, m. Nigel Olifaunt.
The Fortunes of Nigel, W. Scott, 1822.

Ramsay, James, professor of philosophy.
His wife.
James, their son.
Camilla, their daughter.
To The Lighthouse, Virginia Woolf, 1927.

Ramsbottom, Olga. *Shabby Tiger,* H. Spring, 1934.

Ramsdell, Louis, interned in Holland. *The Fountain,* C. Morgan, 1932.

Ramsden, private investigator. *The Franchise Affair,* Josephine Tey, 1948.

Ramsden, Rev. Mr, vicar. *The Daisy Chain,* Charlotte M. Yonge, 1856.

Ramsden, J. St Rollo, headmaster, St Jerome's College. *Before the Bombardment,* O. Sitwell, 1926.

Ramsden, Roebuck.
Susan, his sister.
Man and Superman (play), G. B. Shaw, 1903.

Ramshall, Mr, m. Charlotte Clare. *Still She Wished for Company,* Margaret Irwin, 1924.

Ramshorn, Dr, head of boys' school. *Vanity Fair,* 1847–8, and *Pendennis,* 1848–50, W. M. Thackeray,

Rance, Albert. *The Grapes of Wrath,* J. Steinbeck, 1939.

Randall, Captain, Royal Marines. *The Middle Watch* (play), Ian Hay & S. King-Hall, 1929.

Randall, Mrs Aurelia, *née* Sawyer, widow of Lorenzo de Medici Randall, music master.
Her children:
Hannah Lucy.
Rebecca, central character.
Five others.
Rebecca of Sunnybrook Farm, Kate D. Wiggin, 1903.

Randall, Lady Elizabeth. *See* AYR AND STIRLING.

Randall, Captain William T., drunkard and general bad hat. 'The Beach of Falesa' (s.s.), *Island Nights' Entertainments,* R. L. Stevenson, 1893.

Randolph, Mr. 'A Naval Mutiny' (s.s.), *Limits and Renewals,* R. Kipling, 1932.

Randolph, Charles.
Dora, his wife.
Their children:
Hilda.
Margery.

Cynthia.
Nicholas.
Their grandchildren:
Hugh.
Laurel, Hugh's wife.
Edna, Hugh's mother.
Bill.
Flouncy.
Scrap.
Dear Octopus (play), Dodie Smith, 1939.

Random, Roderick, central character and narrator, m. Narcissa Topehall.
Don Rodrigo, his father.
Charlotte, his mother.
Roderick Random, T. Smollett, 1748.

Rangely, Herbert. 'The Burglar' (s.s.), *Cops 'n' Robbers,* J. Russell.

Ranger. *Love in a Wood* (play), W. Wycherley, 1672.

Rank, Father, Roman Catholic priest. *The Heart of the Matter,* Graham Greene, 1948.

Ranken, Robert, m. Jenny Jimson. *The Horse's Mouth,* Joyce Cary, 1944.

Rankin, a missionary. *Captain Brassbound's Conversion* (play), G. B. Shaw, 1900.

Rann, the kite. 'Kaa's Hunting,' *The Jungle Book,* R. Kipling, 1894.

Rann, Joshua, shoemaker and parish clerk, Hayslope. *Adam Bede,* George Eliot, 1859.

Rannock, the lover. *The King of Elfland's Daughter,* Lord Dunsany, 1924.

Ransom, detective. 'Vanity and some Sables' (s.s.), *The Trimmed Lamp,* O. Henry, 1907.

Ransom, Basil, cousin of the Chancellors, m. Verena Tarrant. *The Bostonians,* H. James, 1886.

Ransome, cabin-boy, the *Covenant,* murdered by Shuan. *Kidnapped,* R. L. Stevenson, 1886.

Ransome, John, m. Marvin Myles. *H. M. Pulham, Esq.,* J. P. Marquand, 1941.

Ransome, John. *Put Yourself in his Place,* C. Reade, 1870.

Ransome, John R. F., central character, m. Vi Usher.
Fulleylove, his father.
Emma, his mother, *née* Randall.
The Combined Maze, May Sinclair, 1913.

Ransome, Julian, one-time fiancé of Ariadne Ferne. *No Other Tiger,* A. E. W. Mason, 1927.

Raoul, Duquette, Parisian. *Je ne parle pas Français* (s.s.), Katherine Mansfield.

Raphael, chemist. *The Mystery of a Hansom Cab,* F. Hume, 1886.

Raphaelson, Kermit, midget, a painter.
Laureen, his wife.
Malcolm, James Purdy, 1959.

Rapkin, Mrs, Horace Ventimore's landlady.
Her husband, a waiter.
The Brass Bottle, F. Anstey, 1900.

Rappaccini, Giacomo, famous doctor.
Beatrice, his daughter.
Rappaccini's Daughter (s.s.), N. Hawthorne, 1844.

Rappit, hairdresser, St Oggs. *The Mill on the Floss,* George Eliot, 1860.

Rashleigh, Captain, of the *Merry Fortune.* *Frenchman's Creek,* Daphne du Maurier, 1941.

Rasle, Maria. *See* TWIDDIE.

Rassendyll, Rudolf, central character.
The Earl and **Countess,** his brother and sister-in-law.
The Prisoner of Zenda and *Rupert of Hentzau,* A. Hope, 1894–8.

Raste, Dr.
Milly, his wife.
Eva, his daughter.
Riceyman Steps, 1923, and *Elsie and the Child,* 1924, Arnold Bennett.

Rastignac. *Beau Geste,* P. C. Wren, 1924.

Rastle, Mr, schoolmaster. *The Fifth Form at St Dominic's,* T. Baines Reed, 1887.

Rat, Dr, curate. *Gammer Gurton's Needle* (play), Anonymous, 1575.

Ratcliffe, servant of Mardyke, later of Lisle. *The Sin of David* (play), S. Phillips, 1914.

Ratcliffe, Inspector. *See* MARQUIS DE ST EUSTACHE.

Ratcliffe, Amos, angelic youth. *Eustace Chisholm and the Works,* James Purdy, 1968.

Ratcliffe, Hubert, humble friend and benefactor of Sir Edward Mauley. *The Black Dwarf,* W. Scott, 1816.

Ratcliffe, James, ex-thief turned

turnkey. *The Heart of Midlothian,* W. Scott, 1818.

Ratcliffe, Nick, central character, m. Muriel Roscoe.
Dr Jim, his brother.
Olga, his daughter.
The Way of an Eagle, Ethel M. Dell, 1912.

Rathbone, Caspar, illegitimate half-caste cousin of Sophia Willoughby. *Summer Will Show,* Sylvia Townsend Warner, 1936.

Ratler, M.P., Liberal whip. *Phineas Finn,* 1869, and elsewhere, A. Trollope.

Ratliff, V. K., sewing machine agent. *The Snopes* trilogy, William Faulkner, 1940–59.

Ratterer, Thomas, a bell-hop.
Louise, his sister.
An American Tragedy, T. Dreiser, 1925.

Rattler, Martin, central character. *Martin Rattler,* R. M. Ballantyne, 1858.

Ratto, central character.
Oddity, his brother.
Rambles of a Rat, A.L.O.E., 1854.

Rattray, a prefect. 'An Unsavoury Interlude,' *Stalky & Co.,* R. Kipling, 1899.

Rattray, Colonel. *If Winter Comes,* A. S. M. Hutchinson, 1920.

Raunce, Charley, a butler. *Loving,* Henry Green, 1945.

Raunham, Rev. John, 'solitary bachelor.' *Desperate Remedies,* T. Hardy, 1871.

Raven, butler to Christopher Glowry. *Nightmare Abbey,* T. L. Peacock, 1818.

Raven, Mrs Margaret.
John, her husband.
Margaret, their daughter.
Tom, their son.
The Water Gipsies, A. P. Herbert, 1930.

Ravenal, Magnolia (*née* Hawks), famous actress.
Gaylord Ravenal, her husband, gambler and actor.
Kim, their daughter, famous actress, m. Kenneth Cameron.
Show Boat, Edna Ferber, 1926.

Ravenel. Family name of EARL OF LUXMORE.

Ravenel, Paul, central character, m. Marguerite Lambert. *The Winding Stair,* A. E. W. Mason, 1923.

Ravenshoe, Charles, central character.
Ellen, his sister.
Denzil, his father.
Ravenshoe, H. Kingsley, 1861.

Ravenstock, Sir Everard.
Rowena, his daughter, m. Max Tryte.
Portrait of a Playboy, W. Deeping, 1947.

Ravenswing, The, stage name of Mrs Howard Walker, *née* Crump. 'The Ravenswing,' *Men's Wives,* W. M. Thackeray, 1843.

Ravenswood, Master of (Edgar).
Allan, Lord Ravenswood, his father.
Auld Ravenswood, his grandfather.
The Bride of Lammermoor, W. Scott, 1819.

Rawkins, eccentric apothecary-surgeon. *The Adventures of Mr Ledbury,* Albert Smith, 1844.

Rawkins, Rev. Simeon, assistant at Lady Whittlesea's chapel. *The Newcomes,* W. M. Thackeray, 1853–1855.

Rawlings, Hubert, later Sir, m. Violet Baynet. *Peter Jackson, Cigar Merchant,* G. Frankau, 1919.

Rawlins, Sal, daughter of Mark Frettleby, half-sister and servant of Madge Frettleby. *The Mystery of a Hansom Cab,* F. Hume, 1886.

Rawson, Lieutenant, of Barry Lyndon's regiment. *Barry Lyndon,* W. M. Thackeray, 1844.

Ray, Philip, m. Annie Arden, believed widowed. *Enoch Arden* (poem), Lord Tennyson.

Ray, Rupert, narrator.
His mother.
The Colonel, his grandfather.
Tell England, E. Raymond, 1922.

Rayber, George F., uncle of Francis Tarwater.
Bernice, his wife.
Bishop, their idiot son.
The Violent Bear It Away, Flannery O'Connor, 1960.

Raybrook, Alf, a fisherman, and his family. 'A Message from the Sea,' *Christmas Stories,* C. Dickens, 1860.

Raydon, Sir Oliver, Bt, m. Lucinda

Mauleverer. *An Affair of Dishonour,* W. de Morgan, 1910.

Raye, Charles Bradford, barrister, m. Anna, a maid. 'On the Western Circuit,' *Life's Little Ironies,* T. Hardy, 1894.

Raye, Lady Jane, eng. to Mr Jennings. *Shall We Join the Ladies?* (play), J. M. Barrie, 1921.

Rayley, Paul, in love with Minta Doyle. *To The Lighthouse,* Virginia Woolf, 1927.

Raymond, Captain. *Caleb Williams,* W. Godwin, 1794.

Raymond, Dr. *The Great God Pan,* A. Machen, 1894.

Raymond, Geoffrey (alias Spencer Gray).
Wilbur, his uncle.
A Damsel in Distress, P. G. Wodehouse, 1919.

Raymond, Ichabod de, of the Papal Guard. *The Eternal City,* Hall Caine, 1901.

Raymond, Tim, nephew of Mrs Marlene Cooper. *The Bachelors,* Muriel Spark, 1961.

Raynald, Robert, decd.
Natalie, his widow, *née* Morrow.
Sarah, his mother.
Requiem for Robert, Mary Fitt, 1942.

Rayne, Herbert, actor manager. *The Actor Manager,* L. Merrick, 1898.

Rayner, Derek, lieutenant, friend of the Mablethorpes. *A Knight on Wheels,* Ian Hay, 1916.

Raynor, Mrs, milliner, mother of Janet Dempster. 'Janet's Repentance,' *Scenes of Clerical Life,* George Eliot, 1857.

Razumov, Kirylo Sidorovitch, student in St Petersburg, central character. *Under Western Eyes,* Joseph Conrad, 1911.

Read, Jack.
Lois, his wife.
'Mrs Sludge' (s.s.), *Last Recollections of My Uncle Charles.* N. Balchin, 1954.

Reade, Rickenbach. *You Can't Go Home Again,* T. Wolfe, 1947.

Ready, Masterman, old seaman, the *Pacific,* central character. *Masterman Ready,* F. Marryat, 1841–2.

Rebecca. *See* MAX DE WINTER.

Rebecca, daughter of Isaac of York, championed by Ivanhoe. *Ivanhoe,* W. Scott, 1820.

Rebecca, maid to the Bowen family. *Tomorrow To Fresh Woods,* Rhys Davies, 1941.

Rebecca of Sunnybrook Farm. *See* RANDALL.

Rebow, Elijah, m. Mehalah Sharland.
His mad brother.
Mehalah, S. Baring-Gould, 1880.

Rebura, Don.
Donna Clara, his wife.
Donna Agnes, his daughter.
Philip and **Martin,** his sons.
Mr Midshipman Easy, Captain Marryat, 1836.

Red, shanghaied American sailor on Pacific island. 'Red' (s.s.), *The Trembling of a Leaf,* W. S. Maugham, 1921.

Red, Guy Theodore, anarchist, tenant of Lord Manton. *The Search Party,* G. A. Birmingham, 1913.

Red-haired Girl, The, friend of Maisie. *The Light that Failed,* R. Kipling, 1890.

Red Jacket, American Indian. 'Brother Square Toes' and elsewhere, *Rewards and Fairies,* R. Kipling, 1910.

Red King, Queen and Knight. *Alice Through the Looking-glass,* L. Carroll, 1872.

Red Reiver. *See* WILLIE OF WESTBURNFLAT.

Redbrook. *Captain Brassbound's Conversion* (play), G. B. Shaw, 1900.

Redbrook, James, 'member from Mercer.' *Mr Crewe's Career,* W. Churchill, 1908.

Redburn, Jack, librarian, Master Humphrey's Club. *Master Humphrey's Clock,* C. Dickens, 1840–1841.

Redburn, Wellingborough, young man on his first voyage. *Redburn,* Herman Melville, 1849.

Redcar, Lord, coal-owner. *In the Days of the Comet,* H. G. Wells, 1906.

Reddin, John, seducer of Hazel Marston. *Gone to Earth,* Mary Webb, 1917.

Redding, Rosamund, school friend of Katy Carr. *What Katy Did at School,* Susan Coolidge, 1873.

Redfern, Colonel, father of Alison

Porter. *Look Back in Anger* (play), J. Osborne, 1956.

Redgauntlet, Sir Arthur Darsie, brought up as Darsie Latimer.
Sir Henry, his father.
His mother.
Lilias, his sister.
Redgauntlet, W. Scott, 1824.

Redherring, Rabbi Remorse. *The King of Schnorrers,* I. Zangwill, 1894.

Redington, Keith. *Nocturne,* F. Swinnerton, 1917.

Redland, Squire.
His wife and two daughters.
Judith Paris, Hugh Walpole, 1931.

Redlaw. *The Haunted Man,* C. Dickens, 1848.

Redmayne, Luke.
Annie-Laurie, his wife. *See also* JIM MALONY.
The Herb of Grace, Elizabeth Goudge, 1948.

Redmaynes of Lionsden, neighbours of the Castlewoods. *The Virginians,* W. M. Thackeray, 1857–9.

Redmond, Benjamin J., lawyer and ex-partner of Colonel John Sartoris. *The Unvanquished,* William Faulkner, 1938.

Redmond, Molly.
Her father and mother.
The Land of Spices, Kate O'Brien, 1941.

Redmond, Rosie. *The Plough and the Stars* (play), S. O'Casey, 1926.

Redpenny, medical student. *The Doctor's Dilemma* (play), G. B. Shaw, 1906.

Redruth, Tom, of the *Hispaniola. Treasure Island,* R. L. Stevenson, 1883.

Redshields, Norman, film director. *Fergus,* Brian Moore, 1971.

Redvers, Henry, manservant of Sir Ferris Clayton. *Cricket in Heaven,* G. Bullett, 1949.

Redwood, Professor, scientist colleague of Bensington.
His son, a giant.
The Food of the Gods, H. G. Wells, 1904.

Redworth, Thomas, admirer of Diana Warwick. *Diana of the Crossways,* George Meredith, 1885.

Reece, Captain, of the *Mantelpiece.* 'Captain Reece' (poem), *Bab Ballads,* W. S. Gilbert, 1869.

Reece, Mrs, Mrs Halliburton's lodger. *Mrs Halliburton's Troubles* Mrs Henry Wood, 1862.

Reed, Dr, m. Alice Barton. *A Drama in Muslin,* G. Moore, 1886.

Reed, Mrs, aunt and guardian of Jane Eyre.
John, her son.
Eliza and **Georgina,** her daughters.
Jane Eyre, Charlotte Brontë, 1847.

Reed, Alma, m. Gerald Dryden. *In Cotton Wool,* W. B. Maxwell, 1912.

Reed, Mary Jane, girl friend of Alexander Portnoy. *Portnoy's Complaint,* Philip Roth, 1969.

Reefy, Dr. *Winesburg, Ohio,* Sherwood Anderson, 1919.

Rees, Aneurin, bank manager, m. Blodwen Page. *The Citadel,* A. J. Cronin, 1937.

Rees, P. C. Attila. *Under Milk Wood* (play), Dylan Thomas, 1954.

Rees, Sir Vaughan Ap, suitor of Mistress Miniver. *Satiromastix* (play), Thomas Dekker, 1601.

Reeves, Anna, m. William Leadford as 2nd wife. *In the Days of the Comet,* H. G. Wells, 1906.

Reeves, Archibald.
His wife. Cousins of Harriet Byron.
Sir Charles Grandison, S. Richardson, 1754.

Reffold, Wilfrid, consumptive.
Winifred, his wife.
Ships that Pass in the Night, Beatrice Harraden, 1893.

Regan, daughter of King Lear. *King Lear* (play), W. Shakespeare.

Regula Baddun, racehorse called after Mrs Reiver. 'The Broken Link Handicap' (s.s.), *Plain Tales from the Hills,* R. Kipling, 1888.

Reid, Peter, landlord and benefactor of the Jardines. *Penny Plain,* O. Douglas, 1920.

Reignier, Duke of Anjou (hist.). *Henry the Sixth* (play), W. Shakespeare.

Reilley, Weary, friend of Studs Lonigan. *Studs Lonigan,* a trilogy, James T. Farrell, 1935.

Reilly, Jocelyn Chadwick's groom. *Famine,* L. O'Flaherty, 1937.

Reilly, Agnes, Dobelle's cook.
Willie, her son, gunman.

The Moon in the Yellow River (play), D. Johnston, 1932.

Reilly, Harry, wealthy man. *Appointment in Samarra,* John O'Hara, 1935.

Reilly, Nora. *John Bull's Other Island* (play), G. B. Shaw, 1904.

Reingelder. 'Reingelder and the German Flag' (s.s.), *Life's Handicap,* R. Kipling, 1891.

Reinhart, Hetty, Peter Stubland's artist girl-friend. *Joan and Peter,* H. G. Wells, 1918.

Reiver, Mrs, fast, heartless and unscrupulous Anglo-Indian. 'The Rescue of Pluffles' (s.s.) and elsewhere, *Plain Tales from the Hills,* R. Kipling, 1888.

Reldresal, state secretary, Lilliput. *Gulliver's Travels,* J. Swift, 1726.

Rellerton, Lady.
Lucy, her daughter.
Monsieur Beaucaire, Booth Tarkington, 1902.

Remington, Richard, central character and narrator.
Arthur, his father, science master.
His mother.
The New Machiavelli, H. G. Wells, 1911.

Remsen, Ellsworth, millionaire, close friend of O'Roon. 'The Badge of Policeman O'Roon' (s.s.), *The Trimmed Lamp,* O. Henry, 1907.

Remus, Uncle, Negro ex-slave, narrator.
Aunt Tempy, his sister.
Uncle Remus series, J. C. Harris, 1880–95.

Renard, French doctor. *The Man who was Thursday,* G. K. Chesterton, 1908.

Renard, Simon, French courtier. *The Tower of London,* W. H. Ainsworth, 1840.

Renart, Philippe.
Lady Virginia ('Poots'), his wife.
The Thinking Reed, Rebecca West, 1936.

Renata, the Contessa loved by Col. Richard Cantrell. *Across the River and Into the Trees,* Ernest Hemingway, 1950.

Renato, barber, friend of Paolo di Leo. *The Roman Spring of Mrs Stone,* Tennessee Williams, 1950.

Renauld, Paul, formerly Georges Conneau.
Eloise, his wife.
Jack, their son, m. Bella Duveen.
Murder on the Links, Agatha Christie, 1923.

Renault. *Venice Preserved* (play), T. Otway, 1682.

Rendal, Joe, m. Mary Hill. 'Three from Dunsterville' (s.s.), *The Man Upstairs,* P. G. Wodehouse, 1914.

Rendezvous, Colonel, friend of Britling. *Mr Britling Sees It Through,* H. G. Wells, 1916.

Rendle, Ruth, barmaid, The Jolly Huntsman, m. Ives Pomeroy. *The Mother,* E. Phillpotts, 1908.

Rendle, Timothy ('Theophilus'), m. school friend of Philip Meldrum.
Lady Rendle, his mother.
A Knight on Wheels, Ian Hay, 1916.

Renée, mistress of Basil Fane. *Going their own Ways,* A. Waugh, 1938.

Renfield, R.M. *Dracula,* B. Stoker, 1897.

Renfrew, Dottie, graduate of Vassar. *The Group,* Mary McCarthy, 1963.

Renfrew, Malcolm, of Ard Daraich. *No Son of Mine,* G. B. Stern, 1948.

Renier, wealthy farmer. *Unending Crusade,* R. E. Sherwood, 1932.

Renisenb, widow of Khay, m. Hori. *Death Comes as the End,* Agatha Christie, 1945.

Renling, Mrs, who wants to adopt Augie. *The Adventures of Augie March,* Saul Bellow, 1953.

Rennit, Mr, private detective. *The Ministry of Fear,* Graham Greene, 1943.

Resker, Agnes. *Tobermory* (s.s.), 'Saki' (H. H. Munro).

Resmond, Sir John. 'Isabella, Isabella' (s.s.), *Love and Money,* Phyllis Bentley, 1957.

Reston, Hon. Pamela, Lord Bidborough's sister, m. Lewis Elliot. *Penny Plain,* O. Douglas, 1920.

Retarrier, Canon Paul, brother of Lord Trehick.
Gerald, their illegitimate half-brother, father of Francie Trehick's child.
For Us in the Dark. Naomi Royde-Smith, 1937.

Retlow (alias Muhlen), 1st husband of Mrs Meadows. *South Wind,* N. Douglas, 1917.

Reuben, Israelite attendant on Isaac and Rebecca. *Ivanhoe,* W. Scott, 1820.

Reuter, Zoraide, m. François Pelet.
Her mother.
The Professor, Charlotte Brontë, 1857.

Revel, friend of the Walsinghams. *Kipps,* H. G. Wells, 1905.

Rex, John, lover of Sarah Purfoy. *For the Term of his Natural Life,* M. Clarke, 1874.

Rexall, Jack, friend of Bert Holm. *Other Gods,* Pearl Buck, 1940.

Reyer, Anglo-French night manager. *Imperial Palace,* Arnold Bennett, 1930.

Reynolds (supposed **Nugent**), **Grace.** *The Absentee,* Maria Edgeworth, 1812.

Rhayader, Philip. *The Snow Goose,* P. Gallico, 1941.

Rhead, John (later **Sir**).
Rose, his wife, *née* Sibley.
Gertrude, his sister.
His mother.
Milestones (play), Arnold Bennett & E. Knoblock, 1912.

Rheims, Archbishop of (hist.). *Saint Joan* (play), G. B. Shaw, 1924.

Rhiw, Evan. 'Lamentations' (s.s.), *My People,* Caradoc Evans, 1915.

Rhys, Mr.
Eleanor, his wife.
The Old Helmet, Elizabeth Wetherell, 1863.

Riach, second officer, *Covenant. Kidnapped,* R. L. Stevenson, 1886.

'Riah, benevolent old Jew employed by Fledgeby. *Our Mutual Friend,* C. Dickens, 1865.

Ribston, Mrs ('Ribby'), cat, cousin of Tabitha Twitchit. *The Tale of Samuel Whiskers,* Beatrix Potter.

Ribstone, Sir Pepin.
His wife.
Their son.
Pendennis, W. M. Thackeray, 1848–1850.

Rica, Don Petro.
His daughters:
Maritana.
Mary, m. Roland Cashel *See also* LEICESTER.
Roland Cashel, C. Lever, 1850.

Ricardo, Julius, dilettante, 'Watson' to Hanaud. *At the Villa Rose,* 1910, and others, A. E. W. Mason.

Riccabocca, Dr. *My Novel,* Lord Lytton, 1853.

Rice. *See* CRUTTENDEN.

Rice, Bessie, m. Dude Lester. *Tobacco Road,* E. Caldwell, 1948.

Rice, Perry C. *See* LEMMY CAUTION.

Rice, Sammy, back-room boy, central character and narrator.
Susan, a typist, his mistress.
The Small Back Room, N. Balchin, 1943.

Rice, Trenny, legal adviser to Sir John Saumarez. *Enter Sir John,* Clemence Dane & Helen Simpson, 1929.

Riceyman, T. T., decd, uncle of Henry Earlforward. *Riceyman Steps,* Arnold Bennett, 1923.

Rich, Lieutenant Brackenbury. 'The Suicide Club' (s.s.), *New Arabian Nights,* R. L. Stevenson, 1882.

Richard, Duke of Normandy ('The Fearless') (hist.). *The Little Duke,* Charlotte M. Yonge, 1854.

Richardetto, phoney physician.
Hippolita, his wife.
'Tis Pity She's A Whore (play), John Ford, *c.* 1624.

Richards ('Fatty'), house servant. 'An Unsavoury Interlude,' *Stalky & Co.,* R. Kipling, 1899.

Richards, Dr. *How Green Was My Valley,* R. Llewellyn, 1939.

Richards, Mr. *South Wind,* N. Douglas, 1917.

Richards, Effie, m. Howard Conford as 1st wife. *The Second Mrs Conford,* Beatrice K. Seymour, 1951.

Richards, Max, m. Mariette Lepage. *If Sinners Entice Thee,* W. le Queux, 1898.

Richards, Milly, m. Tony Kytes. 'Tony Kytes, the Arch-Deceiver,' *Life's Little Ironies,* T. Hardy, 1894.

Richardson, young servant. *Alice Sit-by-the-Fire* (play), J. M. Barrie, 1905.

Richelieu, Cardinal (hist.). *Richelieu* (play), Lord Lytton, 1839.

Richie, close friend of Helen Michel. *The World My Wilderness,* Rose Macaulay, 1950.

Richland, Miss, m. Honeywood. *The Good Natured Man* (play), O. Goldsmith, 1768.

Richmond, Mr and Mrs.
Martin, their son, who co-exists

as a child with the grown-up George Granvile.
Eileen ('Bunny'), their daughter, who dies and whose ghost haunts the house.
Thunder on the Left, C. Morley, 1925.

Richmond, Augustus F. G. Roy, m. Marian Beltham.
Harry, their son, central character and narrator, m. Janet Ilchester.
Anastasia, Augustus's mother, *née* Dewsbury.
The Adventures of Harry Richmond G. Meredith, 1871.

Richmond, R., Cruden's solicitor. *Reginald Cruden*, T. Baines Reed, 1894.

Rickards, Mrs, widowed landlady, m. Swan.
Martha, her daughter.
Savoir Faire (s.s.), W. Pett Ridge.

Rickets, Mabel, aged Northumbrian nurse. *Rob Roy*, W. Scott, 1818.

Ricketts, schoolboy. *The Fifth Form at St Dominic's*, T. Baines Reed. 1887.

Ridd, John (later **Sir**), central character and narrator, m. Lorna Doone.
Sarah, his mother.
Annie, his sister.
Lorna Doone, R. D. Blackmore, 1869.

Ridden, Highworth Foliat ('Hi'), central character.
Bill, his father.
Sarah, his mother.
Bell, his sister.
Odtaa, J. Masefield, 1926.

Ridding, Mr and Mrs. *Miss Mole*, E. H. Young, 1930.

Rideout, Sampson, central character, m. Delia Falkirk, widow. *Sampson Rideout, Quaker*, Una Silberrad, 1911.

Riderhood, Roger ('Rogue'), Thames night-bird and scoundrel.
Pleasant, his daughter, pawnbroker, m. Venus.
Our Mutual Friend, C. Dickens, 1865.

Ridgeley, Sir Daniel.
His wife.
Their children:
Pryce.
Geraldine.
Annabel Mary, dead 1st wife of Filmer Jesson.
His House in Order (play), A. W. Pinero, 1906.

Ridgeon, Sir Colenso, a doctor. *The Doctor's Dilemma* (play), G. B. Shaw, 1906.

Ridgeway, Paula. *See* RAINIER.

Ridler, Seton.
Sir Marmaduke Ridler, his father.
Lady Ridler, his mother.
No. 5 John Street, R. Whiteing, 1902.

Ridley, Lord Barralonga's chauffeur. *Men Like Gods*, H. G. Wells, 1923.

Ridley, Miss, headmistress. *Mr Ingleside*, E. V. Lucas, 1910.

Ridley, Barbara, Evelina Foster's maid. *Beau Austin* (play), W. E. Henley & R. L. Stevenson, 1897.

Ridley, John James ('J.J.'), celebrated R.A., friend of the Newcomes.
Samuel, his father, butler and valet to Lord Todmorden.
His mother, ex-housekeeper.
The Newcomes, W. M. Thackeray, 1853–5.

Ridvers, Charlie, cinema proprietor. *The Good Companions*, J. B. Priestley, 1929.

Riesling, Paul.
Zilla, his wife.
Babbitt, Sinclair Lewis, 1923.

Riga, Captain, master of the *Highlander*. *Redburn*, Herman Melville, 1849.

Rigaud, Monsieur, imprisoned abroad for wife-murder, but escapes to England. *Little Dorrit*, C. Dickens, 1857.

Rigby, King's Proctor, detective. *Holy Deadlock*, A. P. Herbert, 1934.

Rigby, John, M.P. for Tippleton. *Barry Lyndon*, W. M. Thackeray, 1844.

Rigby, Right Hon. Nicholas, Lord Monmouth's political factotum. *Coningsby*, B. Disraeli, 1844.

Rigg, Joshua. *See* PETER FEATHERSTONE.

Rigget, Peter, accountant, Barnabas Ltd. *Flowers for the Judge*, Margery Allingham, 1936.

Rijar, Jacques, m. Adrienne de Vriaac. *The Marquise* (play), N. Coward, 1927.

Rikki Tikki Tavi, a mongoose. 'Rikki Tikki Tavi,' *The Jungle Book*, R. Kipling, 1894.

Riley, auctioneer and valuer. *The Mill on the Floss*, George Eliot, 1860.

Riley, Kitty, m. (1) Flanagan, (2) Tom Durfy. *Handy Andy*, S. Lover, 1842.

Riley, S., accountant. 'A Bank Fraud' (s.s.), *Plain Tales from the Hills*, R. Kipling, 1888.

Riley, Rabbit, alias of Brer Rabbit. *Uncle Remus*, J. C. Harris, 1880–1895.

Rima (Riolama), child-heroine. *Green Mansions*, W. H. Hudson, 1904.

Rimanez, Prince Lucio. *The Sorrows of Satan*, Marie Corelli, 1895.

Rimmer, Kay, sister of Milly Drover. *It's a Battlefield*, Graham Greene, 1935.

Rinaldi, lieutenant and surgeon. *A Farewell to Arms*, E. Hemingway, 1929.

Rindskopf, Goldie. *Counsellor-at-Law* (play), Elmer Rice, 1931.

Riney, Peter, old servant of John Gourlay. *The House with the Green Shutters*, G. Douglas, 1901.

Ringert. *Tracy's Tiger*, W. Saroyan, 1951.

Ringgan, Fleda. *Queechy*, Elizabeth Wetherell, 1852.

Ringling, a young Sherpa. *The Rose of Tibet*, Lionel Davidson, 1962.

Ringwood, Dr. *And Now Goodbye*, J. Hilton, 1931.

Ringwood, Earl.
His sons:
Lord Cinqbars.
Hon. Thomas, his son.
Hon. Frederick.
Sir John, of Appleshaw.
His wife.
Their children:
A daughter.
Philip and **Franklin.**
Sir Francis, his brother.
Colonel Philip, father of Mrs G. B. Firmin and Mrs Troysden.
The Adventures of Philip, W. M. Thackeray, 1861–2.

Rink, Effie, typist in Ponderevo's office, and for a time his mistress. *Tono Bungay*, H. G. Wells, 1909.

Rintoul, Earl of. *The Little Minister*, J. M. Barrie, 1891.

Rintoul, Jimmy, central character. *The Killing Bottle* (s.s.), L. P. Hartley.

Riotor, Marie Leonie, m. Sir Mark Tietjens. *Last Post*, Ford Madox Ford, 1928.

Ripley, Samantha Ann, Avilda Cummin's servant, m. Dave Milliken. *Timothy's Quest*, Kate D. Wiggin, 1892.

Rippenger, headmaster.
Julia, his wife.
The Adventures of Harry Richmond, G. Meredith, 1871.

Risingham, Earl. *The Black Arrow*, R. L. Stevenson, 1888.

Rita, Dona, heiress of Henry Allegre, central character. *The Arrow of Gold*, J. Conrad, 1919.

Ritchie, Peter.
Kate, his wife.
Magnolia Street, L. Golding, 1932.

Ritchie-Hook, Brigadier Ben, Company Commander. *Men at Arms*, Evelyn Waugh, 1952.

Ritornello, Pasticcio.
His three daughters.
The Critic (play), R. B. Sheridan, 1779.

Ritson, Robert, and family. *Judith Paris*, Hugh Walpole, 1931.

Ritter, Sidney, a postman. 'The Astral Body of a U.S. Mail Truck' (s.s.), *A Story That Ends With A Scream*, James Leo Herlihy, 1968.

Ritz, John Brogan's mistress. *The Weak and the Strong*, G. Kersh, 1945.

Rivers, Captain, highwayman. *Deacon Brodie* (play), W. E. Henley & R. L. Stevenson, 1892.

Rivers, Earl, brother of Queen Elizabeth (hist.). *Richard the Third* (play), W. Shakespeare.

Rivers, Connie, m. Rosasharn Joad. *The Grapes of Wrath*, J. Steinbeck, 1939.

Rivers, Isabel, assistant editor, the *Blue Weekly*.
Sir Graham, her father.
The New Machiavelli, H. G. Wells, 1911.

Rivers, Isobel and **Claudia.** *Beau Geste*, P. C. Wren, 1924.

Rivers, Margaret ('Meta'), m. Rev. Norman May.
George, her brother, m. Flora May.
Their father.
Lady Leonora, their aunt.

The Daisy Chain, 1856, and elsewhere, Charlotte M. Yonge.

Rivers, Paul, central character.
Margaret, his sister, m. Richard Messenger.
The Education of Uncle Paul, A. Blackwood, 1909.

Rivers, St John, cousin of Jane Eyre.
Diana and **Mary,** his sisters.
Jane Eyre, Charlotte Brontë, 1847.

Riverton, Cambridge graduate, in love with Eleanor Scrope. *The Soul of a Bishop,* H. G. Wells, 1917.

Rizzo, Enrico (Ratso), cripple from the Bronx. *Midnight Cowboy,* James Leo Herlihy, 1966.

Roach, convict, murderer, friend of Trail. *The Old Dominion,* Mary Johnston, 1899.

Roanoke, Lucinda, niece of Jane Carbuncle, eng. to Sir Griffin Tewitt. *The Eustace Diamonds,* A. Trollope, 1873.

Roantree, Liza.
Jesse, her father.
'On Greenhow Hill' (s.s.), *Life's Handicap,* R. Kipling, 1891.

Robarts, Rev. Mark, Rector of Framley.
Fanny, his wife, *née* Monsell.
His father and mother.
Lucy, his sister, m. Lord Lufton.
Framley Parsonage, A. Trollope, 1861.

Robbins, Captain, of the *John. Afloat and Ashore,* J. Fenimore Cooper, 1844.

Robbins, Lieutenant-Colonel Willie, war hero, central character. 'The Moment of Victory' (s.s.), *Options,* O. Henry, 1909.

Robert, Count. See PARIS.

Roberta, farmer's daughter. *Heaven's My Destination,* Thornton Wilder, 1935.

Roberts, Lieutenant Benjamin.
His Indian wife.
Northwest Passage, Kenneth Roberts, 1938.

Roberts, John, steersman on the *Jumping Jenny. Redgauntlet,* W. Scott, 1824.

Roberts, Judson, ex-football star. *Elmer Gantry,* Sinclair Lewis, 1927.

Roberts, Robbart. *The Corn is Green* (play), Emlyn Williams, 1938.

Robertson, Mr, housemaster. *St Winifred's,* F. W. Farrar, 1862.

Robertson, George. *See* GEORGE STAUNTON.

Robichon, famous French comedian. 'The Judgment of Paris' (s.s.), *All the World Wondered,* L. Merrick, 1911.

Robie, gardener to Miss Gilchrist. *St Ives,* R. L. Stevenson, 1897.

Robin. *Doctor Faustus* (play), C. Marlowe, 1604.

Robin, Fanny, servant betrayed by Sergeant Troy. *Far from the Madding Crowd,* T. Hardy, 1874.

Robin, James (alias James Braund), criminal.
Anna, his wife.
Mr Billingham, the Marquis and Madelon, E. P. Oppenheim.

Robinson, bank manager. *The Heart of the Matter,* Graham Greene, 1948.

Robinson ('Holy Terror'), Chester's partner. *Lord Jim,* J. Conrad, 1900.

Robinson, Dr, body-snatcher. *The Adventures of Tom Sawyer,* Mark Twain, 1876.

Robinson, Arthur (alias Wilson), 'bad hat,' m. Charlotte Anne Clark. *Gaudy Night,* Dorothy L. Sayers, 1935.

Robinson, Ben, store-keeper. *A Lamp for Nightfall,* E. Caldwell, 1952.

Robinson, Chris, politician. *The New Machiavelli,* H. G. Wells, 1911.

Robinson, Octavius.
Violet, his sister, m. Hector Malone.
Man and Superman (play), G. B. Shaw, 1903.

Robinson, Paul. *An Englishman's Home* (play), Guy du Maurier, 1909.

Robinson, 'Red,' formerly foreman, dye works.
Nancy, his cousin.
A Glastonbury Romance, J. C. Powys, 1932.

Robinson, Tom, convict and gold prospector. *It Is Never Too Late to Mend,* C. Reade, 1856.

Robolski, Prince Michael (Michael Brown). *To Have the Honour* (play), A. A. Milne, 1924.

Robotham, Marie, m. Charles Crane as 2nd wife.
Her mother.
Harry, her brother.

The Case for the Defence, Mary Fitt, 1958.

Robsart, Amy (hist.), m. the Earl of Leicester.

Sir Hugh, her father.

Kenilworth, W. Scott, 1821.

Robson, brother of Mrs Bloomfield. *Agnes Grey,* Anne Brontë, 1847.

Robson, Sylvia, m. Philip Hepburn, her cousin.

David, her father.

Bella, her mother, *née* Hepburn.

Sylvia's Lovers, Mrs Gaskell, 1863.

Roby, Dr. *Tancred,* B. Disraeli, 1847.

Roby, Thomas, M.P., Tory whip. *Phineas Finn,* 1869, and elsewhere, A. Trollope.

Roche, Father, priest. *Rogue Herries,* Hugh Walpole, 1930.

Roche, Father, priest. *Famine,* L. O'Flaherty, 1937.

Roche, Alban, assistant in pet-shop, in love with Prudence Tuke. *Miss Gomez and The Brethren,* William Trevor, 1971.

Roche, Charles, 'Eton, Oxford, etc.' *Rosalind* (play), J. M. Barrie, 1912.

Roche, Christina, illegitimate farm-hand, loved by Denis Considine, m. Emil Pahren. *Without My Cloak,* Kate O'Brien, 1931.

Rochecliffe, Dr Joseph Albany, antiquarian and alleged discoverer of subject-matter of the book. *See also* JOSEPH ALBANY. *Woodstock,* W. Scott, 1826.

Rochefidele, Count.

His wife.

The American, H. James, 1877.

Rochester, Edward Fairfax, guardian of Adele Varens, employer of Jane Eyre, whom he marries as 2nd wife.

Bertha, his 1st wife, *née* Mason.

Jane Eyre, Charlotte Brontë, 1847.

Rochester, Phyllis, sister of Barney Newmark.

Clarence, her husband.

Vanessa, Hugh Walpole, 1933.

Rockage, Lord (Ernest) (Family name Bligh).

Maria, his wife.

Carey, their son.

Phyllis, their daughter, m. Stephen Newmark.

Rogue Herries, etc., Hugh Walpole, 1930–3.

Rockarvon, Earl of. *Desolate Splendour.* M. Sadleir, 1923.

Rockingham, Marquess of ('The Seraph'), son of the Duke of Lyonesse. *Under Two Flags,* Ouida, 1867.

Rockminster, Countess of, 'centre of fashion.'

The Dowager Countess.

Pendennis, W. M. Thackeray, 1848–50.

Rod, Genevieve, friend of John Andrews. *Three Soldiers,* John dos Passos, 1921.

Rodd, Miss. *The Voice from the Minaret* (play), R. S. Hichens, 1919.

Rodd, Martha, 'prim snippet of a maid.' 'The Almond Tree' (s.s.), *The Riddle,* W. de la Mare, 1923.

Roddice, Hermione, owner of an estate. *Women in Love,* D. H. Lawrence, 1921.

Roden, Mr and Mrs, uncle and aunt of Caryl Bramsley. *C.,* M. Baring, 1924.

Roderick, Veronica, rich company director's mistress. *Hurry on Down,* John Wain, 1953.

Roderigo, Venetian gentleman. *Othello* (play), W. Shakespeare.

Rodman, James, distant cousin of Mr Mulliner, author of sensational mystery stories. *Meet Mr Mulliner,* P. G. Wodehouse, 1927.

Rodney, Jim, mole-catcher and poacher. *Silas Marner,* George Eliot, 1861.

Rodney, Stella, attractive widow.

Roderick, her soldier son.

The Heat of the Day, Elizabeth Bowen, 1949.

Rodrigo, Don. *See* RODERICK RANDOM.

Roe, travelling preacher of Treddleston. *Adam Bede,* George Eliot, 1859.

Roebel, Dr Albrecht.

Frau Maia, his wife.

Enzoi, their son.

Siegmund, Albrecht's son by 1st wife.

Tom Tiddler's Ground, E. Shanks, 1934.

Roederer, 'licentiate' and author. *Prince Otto,* R. L. Stevenson, 1885.

Roehampton, Lord. *Cautionary Tales,* H. Belloc.

Roger, Saxon knight. *Unending Crusade,* R. E. Sherwood, 1932.

Roger, Father, mentally deranged

clergyman. *The World My Wilderness*, Rose Macaulay, 1950.

Roger of Salerno. 'The Eye of Allah' (s.s.), *Debits and Credits*, R. Kipling, 1926.

Rogers, landlord, Blue Boar. *Badger's Green* (play), R. C. Sherriff, 1930.

Rogers, Captain (alias Mullet). 'Captain Rogers' (s.s.), *The Lady of the Barge*, W. W. Jacobs, 1902.

Rogers, Lieutenant-Commander, R. N. *French without Tears* (play), T. Rattigan, 1936.

Rogers, Mr, friend of the Dons. *A Well-remembered Voice* (play), J. M. Barrie, 1918.

Rogers, Ben. *The Adventures of Tom Sawyer*, Mark Twain, 1876.

Rogers, Sir Jasper, Chief Justice, Calcutta. *Pendennis*, W. M. Thackeray, 1848–50.

Rogers, Jim. 'The Master' (s.s.), *Last Recollections of My Uncle Charles*, N. Balchin, 1954.

Rogers, Mildred (alias Mrs Miller). *Of Human Bondage*, W. S. Maugham, 1915.

Rogers, Milton K., partner of Lapham. *The Rise of Silas Lapham*, W. D. Howells, 1885.

Rogers, Major Robert (hist.), m. Elizabeth Broune.
James, his brother.
Northwest Passage, Kenneth Roberts, 1938.

Roget, Marie. *The Mystery of Marie Roget* (s.s.), E. A. Poe, 1842.

Rohan, Lord Archibald.
His wife. Uncle and aunt of Barty Josselin, and his guardians.
The Martian, George du Maurier, 1897.

Rohn, Johannes ('Hansi'), Jewish musician.
Bessie, his wife, *née* Budd.
Freddi, their son.
His wife.
Dragon's Teeth, Upton Sinclair, 1942.

Rohna, Count, head reception clerk. *Grand Hotel*, Vicki Baum, 1931.

Roister Doister, Ralph, central character. *Ralph Roister Doister* (play), N. Udall, 1551.

Rojas, General, Vice-President, Olancho. *Soldiers of Fortune*, R. H. Davis, 1897.

Rokesmith, John. *See* John Harmon.

Rokoff, Nicholas, Russian 'arch-fiend.' The *Tarzan* series, E. R. Burroughs, 1912–32.

Roland, Stephen, father of Becky Warder. *The Truth* (play), Clyde Fitch, 1907.

Roland, Thomas, musician, owner of the Pelican Hotel, Winstonbury. *Sorrell and Son*, W. Deeping, 1925.

Roldan, a juggler.
Pablo, his son.
The Spanish Gypsy (poem), George Eliot, 1868.

Rolewicz, Josef, Polish soldier, 1st husband of Bessie Hipkiss. *Jezebel's Dust*, Fred Urquhart, 1951.

Rolfe, John.
Lady Rebekah, his dead wife, an Indian princess.
By Order of the Company, Mary Johnston, 1900.

Rolla. *Pizarro* (play), R. B. Sheridan, 1799.

Rollencourt, Armand de, French lieutenant.
General Rollencourt, his father.
Lucile, his sister.
Through the Storm, P. Gibbs, 1945.

Rolles, Gregory, student at Cambridge. *The Saliva Tree*, Brian W. Aldiss, 1966.

Rolles, Rev. Simon, lodger of Raeburn, nurseryman. 'The Rajah's Diamonds,' *New Arabian Nights*, R. L. Stevenson, 1882.

Rolleston, valet. *The Admirable Crichton* (play), J. M. Barrie, 1902.

Rolleston, Felix. *The Mystery of a Hansom Cab*, F. Hume, 1886.

Rollison, Hon. Richard, an amateur detective, known as 'The Toff'. Hero of series of novels by John Creasey, 1938 on.

Rolliver, Mrs, landlady. *Tess of the D'Urbervilles*, T. Hardy, 1891.

Rolliver, James J., m. Indiana Frusk. *The Custom of the Country*, Edith Wharton, 1913.

Rollo, Stephen. *Alice Sit-by-the-Fire* (play), J. M. Barrie, 1905.

Rolt, Helen, castaway, mistress of Henry Scobie. *The Heart of the Matter*, Graham Greene, 1948.

Rolt, Ruth, housekeeper and laundress.
Lavender, her daughter.

Sweet Lavender (play), A. W. Pinero, 1888.

Romagna, Bartolomio ('Mio'). *Winterset* (play), Maxwell Anderson, 1935.

Romaine, Daniel, solicitor to the Count de St Yves. *St Ives,* R. L. Stevenson, 1898.

Romanova, Tatiana, Corporal of State Security. *From Russia, With Love,* Ian Fleming, 1957.

Rome, Aurora, actress. 'The Man in the Passage,' *The Wisdom of Father Brown,* G. K. Chesterton, 1914.

Romeo, son of Montague; lover of Juliet. *Romeo and Juliet* (play), W. Shakespeare.

Romero, Pedro, Spanish bull-fighter. *The Sun Also Rises* (or *Fiesta*), Ernest Hemingway, 1926.

Romford, Facey, selfmade M.F.H., central character. *Mr Facey Romford's Hounds,* R. S. Surtees, 1865.

Romiaux, Lady. *See* BLANCHE MORGAN.

Romilayu, native guide. *Henderson The Rain King,* Saul Bellow, 1959.

Ronald, Lord. *Lady Clara Vere de Vere* (poem), Lord Tennyson.

Rondabale, princess affianced to Alasi. *Vathek,* W. Beckford, 1786.

Ronder, Rev. Frederick, Canon of Polchester.

Alice, his aunt.

The Cathedral, Hugh Walpole, 1922.

Rony, Louis, Communist. *The Second Confession,* Rex Stout, 1950.

Rook, Captain Tom, crook and general blackguard.

Rev. Athanasius, his father.

Harriet, his sister.

'Captain Rook,' *Character Sketches,* W. M. Thackeray, 1841.

Rooney, Andy, later Lord Scatterbrain, central character, m. Oonah, his cousin.

Lord Scatterbrain, his father (alias Rooney).

Hon. Sackville, his brother.

Handy Andy, S. Lover, 1842.

Rooney, Paul, attorney.

His wife.

Jack Hinton, C. Lever, 1843.

Roos, Lily, Bert Holm's first wife. *Other Gods,* Pearl Buck, 1940.

Rooster, Viscount. *See* EARL OF DORKING.

Rooter, Sir Alfred and Lady. *C.,* M. Baring, 1924.

Roothing, Bobby, London journalist in love with Christina Alberta. *Christina Alberta's Father,* H. G. Wells, 1925.

Rore, Mr, Principal, Colham Grammar School. *The Beautiful Years,* H. Williamson, 1921.

Rosa. *Good Night, Good Night* (poem), T. Moore.

Rosa, Gian-luca Boselli's foster-mother.

Geppe and **Berta,** her children.

Adam's Breed, Radclyffe Hall, 1926.

Rosalba, rightful queen of Crim Tartary, m. Prince Giglio. *The Rose and the Ring,* W. M. Thackeray, 1855.

Rosaleen. *Dark Rosaleen* (poem), J. C. Mangan.

Rosalind (alias Ganymede), daughter of the banished duke, m. Orlando. *As You Like It* (play), W. Shakespeare.

Rosaline, attending on princess. *Love's Labour's Lost* (play), W. Shakespeare.

Roscoe, Nurse, at Bolt House.

Dot, her sister.

Joy and Josephine, Monica Dickens, 1948.

Roscoe, Muriel, central character, m. Nick Ratcliffe.

Brigadier-General Roscoe, her father.

The Way of an Eagle, Ethel M. Dell, 1912.

Rose, a neurotic woman who kills her stepmother. *Nobody Answered the Bell,* Rhys Davies, 1971.

Rose, signalman, *Compass Rose. The Cruel Sea,* N. Monsarrat, 1951.

Rose of Rathgar, a nymphomaniac with an appetite for food. *The Onion Eaters,* J. P. Donleavy, 1971.

Rose, Mr, form master. *Eric, or Little by Little,* F. W. Farrar, 1858.

Rose, Rev. Mr, independent minister. 'Janet's Repentance,' *Scenes of Clerical Life,* George Eliot, 1857.

Rose, Sergeant-Major. *The Small Back Room,* N. Balchin, 1943.

Rose, George Arthur, Englishman who becomes Pope. *Hadrian the Seventh,* Baron Corvo (F. W. Rolfe), 1904.

Rose, Gregory Nazianzen.
Jemima, his sister.
The Story of an African Farm, Olive Schreiner, 1883.

Rose, Hester, shop assistant at the Fosters'.
Alice, her mother.
Sylvia's Lovers, Mrs Gaskell, 1863.

Rose, Mervyn, hero. *The Long Time Growing Up,* John Pudney, 1971.

Rose, Rev. Otto, head of Richmond Preparatory School.
His wife and son.
The Book of Snobs, W. M. Thackeray, 1846–7.

Rose, Timothy, gentleman farmer, Leek Malton. *Felix Holt,* George Eliot, 1866.

Rose Cottage, Mrs.
Mae, her eldest.
Under Milk Wood (play), Dylan Thomas, 1954.

Rosedale, Simon, *nouveau riche. The House of Mirth,* Edith Wharton, 1905.

Roseley, Sir Jackson and Lady. *Evan Harrington,* G. Meredith, 1861.

Roselli, Dr Joseph. *See* VOLONNA.

Rosen, Mr, of Kendal, 'buys' Alice Press from Francis Herries for 40s. *Rogue Herries,* Hugh Walpole, 1930.

Rosen, Countess von (Anna). *Prince Otto,* R. L. Stevenson, 1885.

Rosen, Waldo. *Mr Fortune Finds a Pig,* H. C. Bailey, 1943.

Rosenbaum, Mr. *The Treasure Seekers,* E. Nesbit, 1899.

Rosencrantz, a courtier. *Hamlet* (play), W. Shakespeare.

Rosenfeld, Mrs Joanna, 'guide' to Halcyon Day.
Miriam, her sister-in-law.
Little Red Horses, G. B. Stern, 1932.

Rosenfelt, Hannah, Max Gollantz's secretary. *Young Emmanuel,* Naomi Jacob, 1932.

Rosenstein, Nathan, brother of Mrs Carcow. *The One Before,* Barry Pain, 1902.

Rosenthall, Reuben, illicit diamond buyer. *Raffles,* E. W. Hornung, 1899–1901.

Rosetree, Harry (born Haim Rosenbaum), factory owner. *Riders in the Chariot,* Patrick White, 1961.

Rosewater, Victor. *The Thin Man,* D. Hammett, 1934.

Rosherville, Earl of.
Lady Ann Milton, his daughter, m. Rev. Mr Hobson.
Pendennis, W. M. Thackeray, 1848–50.

Rosie, the Freemans' parlourmaid. *The Fanatics* (play), M. Malleson, 1924.

Rosina.
Her sister.
The Story of Rosina (poem), A. Dobson, 1895.

Rosing, Jacob ('Holy Mo'), bookmaker's clerk.
Rachel, his sister.
Shabby Tiger, H. Spring, 1934.

Roskill, Squadron Leader Hugh, Audley's assistant. *The Labyrinth Makers,* Anthony Price, 1970.

Ross, Colonel, owner of Silver Blaze. 'Silver Blaze,' *Memoirs of Sherlock Holmes,* A. Conan Doyle, 1894.

Ross, Miss, Anglican missionary turned Buddhist. *The Jacaranda Tree,* H. E. Bates, 1949.

Ross, Barbara, Jerome Warren's stepniece. 'Schools and Schools' (s.s.), *Options,* O. Henry, 1909.

Ross, Duncan, confederate of John Clay. 'The Red-headed League,' *The Adventures of Sherlock Holmes,* 1892.

Ross, Ferdinand, central character.
Walter, his father.
Leila, his mother.
Chrissie, his sister.
The Oriel Window, Mrs Molesworth, 1896.

Ross, Captain Kenneth, uncle of Alan Merivale, m. Maud Carthew. *Sinister Street,* C. Mackenzie, 1913.

Ross, Philip, later Sir.
Emily, his wife.
The Will (play), J. M. Barrie, 1913.

Ross, Sandie, saw-miller. *Born to be a Sailor,* W. G. Stables, 1896.

Rosse, a nobleman of Scotland. *Macbeth* (play), W. Shakespeare.

Rosse, Jenny.
Billy, her husband.
'A Dead Cert' (s.s.), *The Talking Trees,* Sean O'Faolain, 1971.

Rossi, David (known in London as David Leone), deputy and revolutionary idealist, central character, m. Roma Volonna. *The Eternal City,* Hall Caine, 1901.

Rossignol, Adèle. *At the Villa Rose,* A. E. W. Mason, 1910.

Rossiter, Jim, m. Pipette Wilmot. *Pip,* Ian Hay, 1907.

Rossiter, Mrs Primrose, *née* Cumberland, m. Justin le Faber. *The Five Sons of Le Faber,* E. Raymond, 1945.

Rosy, Dr. *St Patrick's Day* (play), R. B. Sheridan, 1775.

Roth, Johann.
 Amelie, his wife, formerly von Rohn.
 Freya, their daughter, in love with Hans Breitner.
 Her child by him.
 Rudi, their son.
 The Mortal Storm, Phyllis Bottome, 1937.

Rotherham, Sir Henry, guardian of Anne Marton. *I Live Under a Black Sun,* Edith Sitwell, 1937.

Rothschild, Father, a Jesuit. *Vile Bodies,* Evelyn Waugh, 1930.

Rothwell, Ingrid, a typist, m. Vic Brown.
 Her parents.
 A Kind of Loving, Stan Barstow, 1960.

Rotti, *hôtelier.* *The Weak and the Strong,* G. Kersh, 1945.

Rouberry, Miss. *The Corn is Green* (play), Emlyn Williams, 1938.

Roubier, Father, Catholic priest. *The Garden of Allah,* R. S. Hichens, 1904.

Rougedragon, Lady Rachel, 'a meagre old Scotch lady.' *Redgauntlet,* W. Scott, 1824.

Rougeron, Colonel.
 His wife and daughter.
 The Pied Piper, N. Shute, 1942.

Rougierre, Madame de la, governess to Maud Ruthyn. *Uncle Silas,* Sheridan le Fanu, 1864.

Rouncewell, Mrs, housekeeper to Sir Leicester Dedlock. *Bleak House,* C. Dickens, 1853.

Rouncy, Miss, actress friend of Miss Fotheringay. *Pendennis,* W. M. Thackeray, 1848–50.

Roundbegg, Jonathan, botanist. *The Great Pandolfo,* W. J. Locke, 1925.

Roundelay, Sir Edmund, of Delaye.
 Evelyn, his wife.
 Margaret, their daughter.
 Frances, his grandmother.
 Her daughters:
 Emerald, m. B. Cloudesley.
 Crystal, m. Maxwell Dunston.
 Amethyst.
 Saphire.
 Jacynth.
 A Footman for the Peacock, Rachel Ferguson, 1940.

Roundhand, secretary, *West Diddlesex Independent.*
 Ann Milly, his vulgar wife.
 The Great Hoggarty Diamond, W. M. Thackeray, 1841.

Rouse, Barbara, student at Leys College. *Miss Pym Disposes,* Josephine Tey, 1946.

Rousillon, Countess of, mother of Bertram. *All's Well That Ends Well* (play), W. Shakespeare.

Roussencq, Hospel, escaped convict, ally of Clutter. *No Other Tiger,* A. E. W. Mason, 1927.

Routh, butler (alias Tuke).
 His brother, a down-and-out.
 The Power House, J. Buchan, 1916.

Routh, Joanna.
 Fargie, her husband.
 Farewell, Miss Julie Logan, J. M. Barrie, 1932.

Rover, The Red. *See* THOMAS DE LONGUEVILLE.

Rowan, Laura, young girl, granddaughter of Count Nikolai Diakonov.
 Tania and **Edward Rowan,** her parents.
 The Birds Fall Down, Rebecca West, 1966.

Rowan, Richard, Irish writer.
 Bertha, his common law wife.
 Archie, their small son.
 Exiles (play), James Joyce, 1918.

Rowbotham, Editor, the *Wire.* *When a Man's Single,* J. M. Barrie, 1888.

Rowdy, John, banker, of Stumpy Rowdy & Co.
 Arthur, his son and partner.
 Lady Cleopatra, Arthur's wife, *née* Stonehenge.
 Sketches and Travels, W. M. Thackeray, 1847–50.

Rowe, Arthur (alias Digby), central character, m. Anna Hilfe. *The Ministry of Fear,* Graham Greene, 1943.

Rowena, Lady, of Hargottstandstede, descendant of Alfred, m. Ivanhoe. *Ivanhoe,* W. Scott, 1820.

Rowens, Mrs Marilla, widow. *Elsie Venner*, O. W. Holmes, 1861.

Rowland, Sergeant, Sir Barnes Newcome's counsel. *The Newcomes*, W. M. Thackeray, 1853–5.

Rowlands, Dr, head of Roslyn School. *Eric, or Little by Little*, F. W. Farrar, 1858.

Rowlands, Moesen, a Welsh squire. *The Black Venus*, Rhys Davies, 1944.

Rowlatt, W. W., architect.
Cyrus, R. A., his brother.
The Fortunate Youth, W. J. Locke, 1914.

Rowley, steward to Sir Oliver Surface. *The School for Scandal* (play), R. B. Sheridan, 1777.

Rowley, valet to the Count de St Yves. *St Ives*, R. L. Stevenson, 1897.

Rowley, Sir Marmaduke, colonial governor.
His eight daughters.
He Knew He Was Right, A. Trollope, 1869.

Rowlinson, Basil. *See Naples and Die* (play), Elmer Rice, 1932.

Rowse, Mrs, charwoman to John Grey.
Lizzie and **Maud,** her daughters.
The City of Beautiful Nonsense, E. T. Thurston, 1909.

Roxton, Lord John, explorer. *The Lost World*, 1912, and *The Poison Belt*, 1913, A. Conan Doyle.

Roy, Mrs, newsagent, Cleg Kelly's employer. *Cleg Kelly*, S. R. Crockett, 1896.

Royallieu, Viscount. *See* BERTIE CECIL.

Royce, A. L. *The Truth about Blayds* (play), A. A. Milne, 1921.

Royce, Lady Jane.
Julia, her daughter.
The Martian, George du Maurier, 1897.

Royce, Vernon, Master of a Cambridge college.
Lady Muriel, his wife.
Joan, their daughter.
The Masters, 1951, part of the *Strangers and Brothers* sequence, C. P. Snow.

Roylance, Sir Archibald, Bt. *Huntingtower*, J. Buchan, 1922.

Roylott, Dr Grimesby. 'The Speckled Band,' *The Adventures of Sherlock Holmes*, A. Conan Doyle, 1892.

Ruark.
Rukrooth, his mother.
The Shaving of Shagpat, G. Meredith, 1856.

Rubelle, Madame.
Her husband.
The Woman in White, W. Collins, 1860.

Rubrick, Rev. Mr, non-juring clergyman.
His four daughters.
Waverley, W. Scott, 1814.

Rucastle, Jephro.
His wife.
Alice, their daughter.
'The Copper Beeches,' *The Adventures of Sherlock Holmes*, A. Conan Doyle, 1892.

Rudd, schoolboy at Fernhurst. *The Loom of Youth*, A. Waugh, 1917.

Rudd, Jason (Jinks), film producer, 5th husband of Marina Gregg. *The Mirror Crack'd from Side to Side*, Agatha Christie, 1962.

Ruddie, Mrs. *Mr Ingleside*, E. V. Lucas, 1910.

Ruddiman, assistant master. 'The Pig and Whistle' (s.s.), *The House of Cobwebs*, G. Gissing, 1906.

Ruddle, Mrs, housekeeper. *Busman's Honeymoon*, Dorothy L. Sayers, 1937.

Rudge, Rye grocer and smuggler.
Sukey, his daughter.
Denis Duval, W. M. Thackeray, 1864.

Rudge, Barnaby, half-witted red-haired youth, whose closest friend is Grip, a raven; central character.
His late father, steward and murderer of Reuben Haredale.
Mary, his mother.
Barnaby Rudge, C. Dickens, 1841.

Rudge, Mrs Thyrza, housekeeper to Dr Weir. *Portrait of Clare*, F. Brett Young, 1927.

Rudolf the Fifth, King of Ruritania (Red Elphberg). *The Prisoner of Zenda*, A. Hope, 1894.

Ruff, Harry Warrington's landlord.
His wife.
The Virginians, W. M. Thackeray, 1857–9.

Ruff, Major-General Theophilus. *Cleg Kelly*, S. R. Crockett, 1896.

Rufford, Nancy, ward of Leonora Ashburnham, in love with Edward Ashburnham. *The Good Soldier*, Ford Madox Ford, 1915.

Rufio. *Caesar and Cleopatra* (play), G. B. Shaw, 1900.

Rugg, general agent, landlord of Pancks.
Anastasia, his daughter.
Little Dorrit, C. Dickens, 1857.

Ruggles, 'Chicken,' hobo, formerly Black Eagle, Texas bandit. 'The Passing of Black Eagle' (s.s.), *Roads of Destiny*, O. Henry, 1909.

Ruggles, Ruby, m. John Crumb.
Daniel, her grandfather, of Sheeps Acre Farm.
The Way We Live Now, A. Trollope, 1875.

Rugnah. *The Green Goddess* (play), W. Archer, 1921.

Ruiz, Mme Camilla, a wealthy, influential hostess.
Vittorio, her son, who seduces Edna Mouth.
Prancing Nigger, Ronald Firbank, 1924.

Rukh, Rajah of. *The Green Goddess* (play), W. Archer, 1921.

Rum Tum Tugger, The. *Old Possum's Book of Practical Cats* (poems), T. S. Eliot, 1939.

Rumbold, Fishbourne china dealer, neighbour of Polly.
His wife and mother-in-law.
The History of Mr Polly, H. G. Wells, 1910.

Rumbold, George, artist.
Clara, his pretty sister.
Our Street, W. M. Thackeray, 1848.

Rumford, Purdy.
Lydia, his wife, *née* Waring.
Chosen Country, J. dos Passos, 1951.

Rummyng, Elynour, old Tudor 'ale wife' or tavern-keeper. *The Tunnying of Elynour Rummyng*, John Skelton, *c.* 1517.

Rumpelteazer. *See* MUNGOJERRIE.

Runcible, Agatha, bright young thing. *Vile Bodies*, Evelyn Waugh, 1930.

Rundle, Dr and Mrs. *The Farmer's Wife* (play), E. Phillpotts, 1924.

Runi, South American Indian chief. *Green Mansions*, W. H. Hudson, 1904.

Runnington, Mr, Charles Aubrey's solicitor. *Ten Thousand a Year*, S. Warren, 1839.

Runswick, Lord, father of Barty Josselin. *The Martian*, George du Maurier, 1897.

Runt, Rev. Mr, chaplain to Lady Lyndon. *Barry Lyndon*, W. M. Thackeray, 1844.

Rushworth, Maria, *née* Bertram.
James, her husband.
Mansfield Park, Jane Austen, 1814.

Rushworth, Miles, friend of the Lextons. *The Story of Ivy*, Mrs Belloc Lowndes, 1927.

Rusk, Mrs, aged housekeeper to Austin Ruthyn. *Uncle Silas*, Sheridan le Fanu, 1864.

Rusk, Hubert, tutor to Denis Bracknel. *The Bracknels*, Forrest Reid, 1911.

Rusper, ironmonger, Fishbourne, neighbour of Polly.
His wife.
The History of Mr Polly, H. G. Wells, 1910.

Russell, Lady, close friend of Sir W. Elliot. *Persuasion*, Jane Austen, 1818.

Russell, Rev. Mr, introducer of cricket among girls. *Comin' Through the Rye*, Helen Mathers, 1875.

Russell, Edwin, school friend of Eric Williams. *Eric, or Little by Little*, F. W. Farrar, 1858.

Russet, Peter. *Captains All* (s.s.), and elsewhere, W. W. Jacobs.

Rust, Ezekiel.
Isabella, his wife.
Odtaa, J. Masefield, 1926.

Rustum, Persian general, father of Sohrab. *Sohrab and Rustum* (poem), M. Arnold, 1853.

Rustum Beg. 'A Legend of the Foreign Office' (poem), *Departmental Ditties*, R. Kipling, 1886.

Ruth, pirate maid-of-all-work. *The Pirates of Penzance* (comic opera), Gilbert & Sullivan, 1880.

Ruth, a professional bridesmaid. *Ruddigore* (comic opera), Gilbert & Sullivan, 1887.

Ruth, Dusky. 'Dusky Ruth' (s.s.), *Adam and Eve and Pinch Me*, A. E. Coppard, 1921.

Rutherford, friend of Hugh Conway. *Lost Horizon*, J. Hilton, 1933.

Ruthven, school friend of Frank Hargate.
Sir James, his father.
His mother.
By Sheer Pluck, G. A. Henty, 1883.

Ruthyn, Maud, central character and narrator.
Austin, her father.
Silas, her uncle.
Milly, his daughter.
Dudley, his son, m. Sarah Mangles.
Uncle Silas, Sheridan le Fanu, 1864.

Ruttledge, Job, smuggler and friend of Alan Fairford. *Redgauntlet,* W. Scott, 1824.

Ruy Dias, lover of Quisara. *The Island Princess* (play), J. Fletcher, 1647.

Ruyslaender, Mrs. 'The Practical Joker,' *Lord Peter Views the Body,* Dorothy L. Sayers, 1928.

Ryan, patrolman. *On the Spot* (play), E. Wallace, 1930.

Ryan, Eddie, a Chicago student who works in a garage.
Mrs Dunne, his grandmother (*née* Grace Hogan).
Joseph Dunne, his dead grandfather.
The Silence of History, James T. Farrell, 1963.

Rycker, André, manager of a palm-oil factory.
Marie, his wife.
A Burnt-Out Case, Graham Greene, 1961.

Ryde, Rev. Mr, Rector of Broxton. *Adam Bede,* George Eliot, 1859.

Ryde, Dr Hillingdon, D.D.
Jenny, his wife.
Adam of Dublin, C. O'Riordan, 1920.

Ryder, Charles, narrator, m. Lady Celia, sister of Lord Mulcaster.
John, their son.
Caroline, their daughter.
His father.
Jasper, his cousin.
Brideshead Revisited, E. Waugh, 1945.

Ryder, James, head attendant at Hotel Cosmopolitan. 'The Blue Carbuncle,' *The Adventures of Sherlock Holmes,* A. Conan Doyle, 1892.

Ryder, Samson, 'a hard, cold man.' *Black Beauty,* Anna Sewell, 1877.

Ryder, Violet. *Poor Women,* Norah Hoult, 1929.

Ryle, Precentor, Polchester Cathedral.
Charlotte, his wife.
The Cathedral, Hugh Walpole, 1922.

Rylett, Alf. *Nocturne,* F. Swinnerton, 1917.

Rysing, David.
Jan, his son.
Liz, Jan's wife, *née* Sturgis.
If Four Walls Told, E. Percy, 1922.

S

Sabien, lover of Nadya. *The Queen was in the Parlour* (play), N. Coward, 1926.

Sabina, Lily, maid to Antrobus family in New Jersey. *The Skin of Our Teeth* (play), Thornton Wilder, 1942.

Sabre, Mark, author, idealist, central character.
Mabel, his wife.
If Winter Comes, A. S. M. Hutchinson, 1920.

Sabrina. *Comus* (poem), J. Milton.

Sabrov, Michael. *See* ALEXIS PAULVITCH.

Sacharissa, girl graduate. *Princess Ida* (comic opera), Gilbert & Sullivan, 1884.

Sackbut, curate and tutor. *Peregrine Pickle,* T. Smollett, 1751.

Sackett, a District Attorney. *The Postman Always Rings Twice,* James M. Cain, 1934.

Saddletree, Bartoline, harness-maker.
His wife.
The Heart of Midlothian, W. Scott, 1818.

Sadgrove, Denny, 1st wife of Nat Grimshaw.
Her father.
Farewell to Youth, Storm Jameson, 1928.

Sadik Pacha, the Moufettish. 'At the Mercy of Tiberius,' *Donovan Pasha,* Gilbert Parker, 1902.

Sadis-Lausitz, H.S.H. Princess Marie Ottilie. *The Pride of Jennico,* A. & E. Castle, 1898.

Sadrach, of Danyrefail.
Achsah, his wife.
Their eight children.
'A Father in Sion' (s.s.), *My People,* Caradoc Evans, 1915.

Saduko, Zulu chief, m. (1) Mameena, (2) Nandie.
Matiwane, his father.
Bangu and **Tshoza,** his brothers.
Child of Storm, H. Rider Haggard, 1913.

Sady, George Esmond's Negro servant. *The Virginians,* W. M. Thackeray, 1857–9.

Safford, drunken captain of the *Happy Return.* *Tom Fool,* F. Tennyson Jesse, 1926.

Saffyn, Dion, a pierrot.
Mary, his imaginary wife, *née* Arbuthnot, 'above his class.'
Ennis and **Pauline,** their imaginary daughters.
The Brontës went to Woolworth's, Rachel Ferguson, 1931.

Safie, Arabian refugee, in love with Felix de Lacey. *Frankenstein,* Mary W. Shelley, 1818.

Sagacity. *Pilgrim's Progress,* J. Bunyan, 1678, 1684.

Sagely, Mrs, friend of Random. *Roderick Random,* T. Smollett, 1748.

Sahi, the porcupine. 'Letting in the Jungle,' *The Second Jungle Book,* R. Kipling, 1895.

Saïd, central character.
Hasneh, his wife. *See also* FERIDEH.
Saïd the Fisherman, M. Pickthall, 1903.

Sailors, Sinbad, in love with Gossamer Beynon.
Mary Ann, his grandmother.
Under Milk Wood (play), Dylan Thomas, 1954.

Saint, Jacob (*né* Simes), uncle of Arthur Surbonadier. *Enter a Murderer,* Ngaio Marsh, 1935.

'Saint, The.' *See* TEMPLAR.

St Aldegonde, Lord Bertram, heir to a dukedom. *Lothair,* B. Disraeli, 1870.

St Amour, Madame de, keeper of Parisian *pension.* *Vanity Fair,* W. M. Thackeray, 1847–8.

St André. *Beau Geste,* P. C. Wren, 1924.

St Aubert.
Mona, his wife.
Emily, their daughter.
The Mysteries of Udolpho, Mrs Radcliffe, 1790.

St Aubin, Lucy, loved by William Waverley. *Waverley,* W. Scott, 1814.

St Aubyn, Sir P. Borlase, Bt.
  Patricia ('Paddy'), his daughter, m. Ivor Warwick.
  Ruth, his aunt.
The Young Men Are Coming, M. P. Shiel, 1937.

St Aumerle, Duc de. *Still She Wished for Company,* Margaret Irwin, 1924.

St Bungay, Duke of. *Phineas Finn,* 1869, and elsewhere, A. Trollope.

St Clair, Agnes, m. Charles Aubrey. *Ten Thousand a Year,* S. Warren, 1839.

St Clair, Mollie.
  George, her father, circus proprietor.
A Voyage to Purilia, Elmer Rice, 1930.

St Clair, Neville.
  His wife.
'The Man with the Twisted Lip,' *The Adventures of Sherlock Holmes,* A. Conan Doyle, 1892.

St Clare, French Jesuit priest. *John Inglesant,* J. H. Shorthouse, 1881.

St Clare, General. 'The Sign of the Broken Sword,' *The Innocence of Father Brown,* G. K. Chesterton, 1911.

St Clare, Augustine, son of wealthy Louisiana planter, purchaser of Uncle Tom.
  Marie, his wife.
    Evangeline (Little Eva), their daughter.
  Alfred, his twin brother.
    Henrique, Alfred's son.
Uncle Tom's Cabin, Harriet B. Stowe, 1852.

St Cleeve, Swithin, central character, m. bigamously Viviette, Lady Constantine.
  Rev. M., his father.
  Dr Jocelyn, his uncle.
Two on a Tower, T. Hardy, 1882.

St Colomb, Sir Harry.
  Dona, his wife.
    Henrietta, their daughter.
    James, their son.
Frenchman's Creek, Daphne du Maurier, 1941.

St Duthac, Abbot of Aberbrothock. *Waverley,* W. Scott, 1814.

St Erme, Lord. *Heartsease,* Charlotte M. Yonge, 1854.

St Erth, Lord. *Loyalties* (play), J. Galsworthy, 1922.

St Eustache, Marquis de (Wednesday) (Inspector Ratcliffe). *The Man who was Thursday,* G. K. Chesterton, 1908.

St Evremonde, Marquis de, uncle of Charles Darnay.
  The Marquise, Darnay's mother.
A Tale of Two Cities, C. Dickens, 1859.

St George, Viscount. *See* DUKE OF DENVER.

St George, Shirley, sister of Lord Tarlyon, eng. to Major Hugo Cypress. 'Major Cypress Goes Off the Deep End' (s.s.), *These Charming People,* M. Arlen, 1920.

St Jean, servant to de Florac. *The Newcomes,* W. M. Thackeray, 1853–1855.

St Jerome, Lord and Lady. *Lothair,* B. Disraeli, 1870.

St Just, Armand, brother of Lady Blakeney. *The Scarlet Pimpernel,* Baroness Orczy, 1905.

St Leath, Lord (John). *The Cathedral,* Hugh Walpole, 1922.

St Leon.
  Marguerite, his wife.
  Charles, their son.
St Leon, W. Godwin, 1799.

St Lys, Rev. Aubrey, Vicar of Mowbray. *Sybil,* B. Disraeli, 1845.

St Marys, Lady Barbara, daughter of the Earl of Bungay. *A Little Dinner at Timmins,* W. M. Thackeray, 1848.

St Maugham, Mrs, old lady, keen gardener.
  Laurel, her grand-daughter.
    Olivia, Laurel's mother.
The Chalk Garden (play), Enid Bagnold, 1955.

St Mawr, Lou Witt's stallion. *St Mawr,* D. H. Lawrence, 1925.

St Olpherts, Duke of, uncle by marriage of Lucas Cleeve. *The Notorious Mrs Ebbsmith* (play), A. W. Pinero, 1895.

St Simon, Lord Robert. 'The Noble Bachelor,' *The Adventures of Sherlock Holmes,* A. Conan Doyle, 1892.

St Wythiol, Earl of (Family name Penriddocke).
  His wife.
  Lord Penriddocke, their son, m. Marie-Gilberte de Vernier.
  Gilberte, their daughter, eng. to Jan Norrington.
  Laura, his sister.

For Us in the Dark, Naomi Royde-Smith, 1937.

St Yves, Viscount Anne de Kéroual de, French prisoner of war, central character and narrator, m. Flora Gilchrist.
Alain, his rascally cousin and spy.
Count de Kéroual de St Yves, his great-uncle (alias Champdivers and Edward Ducie).
St Ives, R. L. Stevenson, 1897.

Sait, Jack, prize-fighter. *The Sailor's Return*, David Garnett, 1925.

Sakers, Miss. *Eliza*, 1900, and elsewhere, Barry Pain.

Sal, Cherokee, 'dissolute and irreclaimable.'
Tommy, her son.
The Luck of Roaring Camp, Bret Harte, 1868.

Salanio, friend of Antonio. *The Merchant of Venice* (play), W. Shakespeare.

Salarino, friend of Antonio. *The Merchant of Venice* (play), W. Shakespeare.

Saldagno, Portuguese swashbuckler. *The Duke's Motto*, J. H. McCarthy, 1908.

Salisbury, Earl of (William Longsword) (hist.). *King John* (play), W. Shakespeare.

Salisbury, Earl of (hist.). *Henry the Sixth* (play), W. Shakespeare.

Sallafranque, Marc, m. Isabella Tarry.
His mother.
Natalie and **Yolande,** his sisters.
The Thinking Reed, Rebecca West, 1936.

Sallet, Unity. 'Tony Kytes, the Arch-Deceiver,' *Life's Little Ironies*, T. Hardy, 1894.

Sally. *Sally in our Alley* (poem), H. Carey.

Sally, servant to Miss Honeyman. *The Newcomes*, W. M. Thackeray, 1853–5.

Sally, Old, nurse at the workhouse where Oliver was born. *Oliver Twist*, C. Dickens, 1838.

Salmon, Patrico, hero of a 'great fight with gipsies.' *Guy Mannering*, W. Scott, 1815.

Salt, wool-factor. *Felix Holt*, George Eliot, 1866.

Salt, Jim ('Sandy Jim'), carpenter.
Elizabeth, his wife ('Timothy's Bess').
Adam Bede, George Eliot, 1859.

Salteena, Alfred, 'an elderly man of forty-two.' *The Young Visiters*, Daisy Ashford, 1919.

Salterne, Rose ('The Rose of Torridge'), victim of the Inquisition.
William, her father, merchant.
Westward Ho!, C. Kingsley, 1855.

Salters, Uncle, of the crew of the *We're Here*. *Captains Courageous*, R. Kipling, 1897.

Saltiera, Rudy, criminal. *Poison Ivy*, P. Cheyney, 1937.

Saltire, Lord. *Ravenshoe*, H. Kingsley, 1861.

Saltire, Lord. *The Book of Snobs*, W. M. Thackeray, 1846–7.

Saltonstone, Lacy, friend of the Ammidons. *Java Head*, J. Hergesheimer, 1919.

Salusbury, Sir Norfolk. *The Miser's Daughter*, W. H. Ainsworth, 1842.

Sam, deck-hand on the *Seamew*. *The Skipper's Wooing*, W. W. Jacobs, 1897.

Sambo, the Ethiopian who changed his skin. 'How the Leopard got his Spots,' *Just So Stories*, R. Kipling, 1902.

Samela. *Samela* (poem), Robert Greene.

Samgrass, history don. *Brideshead Revisited*, E. Waugh, 1945.

Samoa, native friend of Taji, the narrator. *Mardi*, Herman Melville, 1849.

Sampson, Dean of Polchester. *The Cathedral*, Hugh Walpole, 1922.

Sampson, chaplain to Lord Castlewood.
Patty, his sister.
The Virginians, W. M. Thackeray, 1857–9.

Sampson, Mr, surgeon. *Of Human Bondage*, W. S. Maugham, 1915.

Sampson, Mrs. *The Mystery of a Hansom Cab*, F. Hume, 1886.

Sampson, Dominie Abel, librarian to Colonel Mannering. *Guy Mannering*, W. Scott, 1815.

Sampson, George, friend of the Wilfers and fiancé of Lavinia. *Our Mutual Friend*, C. Dickens, 1865.

Sampson, James, small boy with imagination. *The Distant Horns of Summer*, H. E. Bates, 1967.

Samson, 'Wardie,' crook blacksmith. *Flowers for the Judge,* Margery Allingham, 1936.

Samson, Captain Valentine, R.N., retd. *Portrait of a Playboy,* W. Deeping, 1947.

Samuel, Pirate King's lieutenant. *The Pirates of Penzance* (comic opera), Gilbert & Sullivan, 1880.

Samuel Whiskers, a rat.
  Anna Maria, his wife.
The Tale of Samuel Whiskers, Beatrix Potter.

Samuels, Jake (The Rogue). *The Passing of the Third Floor Back* (play), J. K. Jerome, 1910.

Samuelson, coloured U.S. soldier, father of Letty Brickett. 'The Tinfield Mascot' (s.s.), *Last Recollections of My Uncle Charles,* N. Balchin, 1954.

Samuelson, Captain, aircraft pilot. *No Highway,* N. Shute, 1948.

San Martino, Duchess of (self-styled). *South Wind,* N. Douglas, 1917.

Sancho y Moraima, Donna Concepcion. *The Four Armourers,* F. Beeding, 1930.

Sand, Silver, smuggler. *The Raiders,* S. R. Crockett, 1894.

Sandbeck, Oscar. *The Dark Horse,* Nat Gould.

Sandbourne, Phil, architect. *Manhattan Transfer,* J. dos Passos, 1925.

Sanders ('Sandi'), commissioner, 'the Little Butcher Bird,' alias Imgani, outcast man. *Sanders of the River,* E. Wallace, 1911.

Sanders, friend of Richard Dick.
  His wife. Prisoners of Guy Red.
The Search Party, G. A. Birmingham, 1913.

Sanders, Leslie. *The Young in Heart,* I. A. R. Wylie, 1939.

Sanderson, 2nd husband of Alice, Duchesse de Brantes, *née* Parkinton. *Mrs Parkington,* L. Bromfield, 1944.

Sandford, Harry, farmer's son. *Sandford and Merton,* T. Day, 1783–9.

Sandhills, Lord. *The Choice* (play), A. Sutro, 1919.

Sandler, Arthur. *Counsellor-at-Law* (play), Elmer Rice, 1931.

Sandler, Robert, radio sponsor. *The Troubled Air,* Irwin Shaw, 1951.

Sandomir, Alix, central character, in love with Basil Doye.
  Daphne, her mother.
  Paul and **Nicholas,** her brothers.
Non-Combatants and Others, Rose Macaulay, 1916.

Sands, Lord. *Henry the Eighth* (play), W. Shakespeare.

Sands, Bedwin, Eastern traveller. *Pendennis,* 1848–50, and *Vanity Fair,* 1847–8, W. M. Thackeray.

Sands, Bernard, novelist.
  Ella, his wife.
    Elizabeth, their daughter, journalist.
    James, their son, barrister.
      Sonia, James's wife.
Hemlock and After, Angus Wilson, 1952.

Sandys, Diana. *Hamlet, Revenge!,* M. Innes, 1937.

Sandys, Sir Edwyn.
  George, his brother.
By Order of the Company, Mary Johnston, 1900.

Sandys, John.
  Heather, his wife, *née* North.
  David, their son.
  Susan, their daughter.
The Happy Prisoner, Monica Dickens, 1946.

Sandys, Norman, schoolmaster. *We the Accused,* E. Raymond, 1935.

Sandys, Tommy, central character.
  Jean, his mother, *née* Myles.
  Elspeth, his sister.
Sentimental Tommy, J. M. Barrie, 1896.

Sang, Captain of the *Rose.* *Catriona,* R. L. Stevenson, 1893.

Sang, Tam, coach-driver of the Royal Charlotte. *The Antiquary,* W. Scott, 1816.

Sangaletti, Count Cosimo, 1st husband of Rachel Coryn. *My Cousin Rachel,* Daphne du Maurier, 1951.

Sangazure, Lady, m. Sir Marmaduke Pointdextre.
  Aline, her daughter, m. Alexis Pointdextre.
The Sorcerer (comic opera), Gilbert & Sullivan, 1877.

Sanger, Teresa ('Tessa'), central character.
  Her father.
  Her sisters:
    Kate.
    Paulina.
    Antonia, m. Jacob Birnbaum.

The Constant Nymph, Margaret Kennedy, 1924.

Sangree, Peter, in love with Joan Maloney. 'The Camp of the Dog' (s.s.), *John Silence*, A. Blackwood, 1908.

Sannie, 'Tant,' a Boer, m. as 3rd husband Piet van der Walt. *The Story of an African Farm*, Olive Schreiner, 1883.

Sans, general merchant. *Highland River*, N. M. Gunn, 1937.

Sansom, Edward, father of Joel Harrison Knox. *Other Voices, Other Rooms*, Truman Capote, 1948.

Sans-Pareille, Dame, owner of a ship. *The Bowge of Court*, John Skelton, 1498.

Sant, Comrade Jeremiah, Socialist who murders Pope Hadrian. *Hadrian the Seventh*, Baron Corvo (F. W. Rolfe), 1904.

Santaguano, El Duco (Esteban).
  Miguel, his son by Elvise de Kestournel.
The Marquise (play), N. Coward, 1927.

Santiago, old Cuban fisherman. *The Old Man and The Sea*, Ernest Hemingway, 1952.

Saphir, Lady, a rapturous maiden, m. Colonel Calverley. *Patience* (comic opera), Gilbert & Sullivan, 1881.

Sapphire, Helen, musician. *Pending Heaven*, William Gerhardie, 1930.

Sappleton, Mrs.
  Vera, her niece.
The Open Window (s.s.), 'Saki' (H. H. Munro).

Sapsea, Thomas, auctioneer, Mayor of Cloisterham. *Edwin Drood*, C. Dickens, 1870.

Sapt, Colonel. *The Prisoner of Zenda*, etc., A. Hope, 1894–8.

Saradine, Prince. 'The Sins of Prince Saradine,' *The Innocence of Father Brown*, G. K. Chesterton, 1911.

Sarah, maid of the Pooters. *The Diary of a Nobody*, G. & W. Grossmith, 1892.

Saranoff, Major Sergius, eng. to Raina Petkoff. *Arms and the Man* (play), G. B. Shaw, 1894.

Sardanapalus, King of Nineveh and Assyria.
  Zarina, his queen.
Sardanapalus (play), Lord Byron, 1821.

Sargent, Dr, D.D., Master of Boniface. *Lovel the Widower*, W. M. Thackeray, 1860.

Sargent, Frank, in love with Sarah Burling Ward. *Angle of Repose*, Wallace Stegner, 1971.

Sargent, Netty, m. Jasper Cliff. 'Netty Sargent's Copyhold,' *Life's Little Ironies*, T. Hardy, 1894.

Sargent, Wilton, wealthy American. 'An Error in the Fourth Dimension' (s.s.), *The Day's Work*, R. Kipling, 1898.

Sark, Lord and Lady, neighbours of the Castlewoods. *Henry Esmond*, W. M. Thackeray, 1852.

Sarn, Prudence, central character, m. Kester Woodseaves.
  Gideon, her brother.
Precious Bane, Mary Webb, 1924.

Sarnac, physiologist. *The Dream*, H. G. Wells, 1924.

Sarrett, Mrs Molly, George Severidge's sister. *The Judge's Story*, C. Morgan, 1947.

Sarti, Caterina ('Tina'), Italian singer, daughter of a broken-down Milanese musician, adopted by the Cheverels; m. Maynard Gilfil. 'Mr Gilfil's Love Story,' *Scenes of Clerical Life*, George Eliot, 1857.

Sartoris, Bayard, young American who served with R.A.F. in 1914–18 war.
  Bayard, his grandfather, m. Narcissa Benbow.
  Colonel John Sartoris, his great-grandfather.
    Aunt Jenny (Virginia Du Pre), sister of Colonel John Sartoris.
Sartoris, William Faulkner, 1929.

Sartoris, Marengo ('Ringo'), Bayard's Negro playmate and servant. *The Unvanquished*, William Faulkner, 1938.

Sartorius.
  Blanche, his daughter.
Widowers' Houses (play), G. B. Shaw, 1892.

Sarum, Mr Justice, judge trying Roderick Strood. *The Jury*, G. Bullett, 1935.

Sasha, Russian princess loved by Orlando. *Orlando*, Virginia Woolf, 1928.

Saskia, Princess.
  Eugenie, her cousin.
Huntingtower, J. Buchan, 1922.

Satchel, aged bailiff to Squire Donnithorne.
His wife.
Adam Bede, George Eliot, 1859.

Satchel, Andrew, m. Jane Vallens.
His brother and sister-in-law.
'Andrey Satchel and the Parson and Clerk,' *Life's Little Ironies,* T. Hardy, 1894.

Satchell, Stella Summersley, companion to Lady Mary Justin. *The Passionate Friends,* 1913, and elsewhere, H. G. Wells.

Satin. *The Devil Is an Ass* (play), B. Jonson, 1616.

Satipy, wife of Yahmose, by whom she is murdered. *Death Comes as the End,* Agatha Christie, 1945.

Saturninus, late Emperor of Rome. *Titus Andronicus* (play), W. Shakespeare.

Saul. *Absalom and Achitophel* (poem), J. Dryden, 1681.

Saumarez. 'False Dawn' (s.s.), *Plain Tales from the Hills,* R. Kipling, 1888.

Saumarez, Sir John, actor manager, central character. *Enter Sir John,* Clemence Dane & Helen Simpson, 1929.

Saunders, Mr, chief character, 'best doctor in the Far East.' *The Narrow Corner,* W. S. Maugham, 1932.

Saunders, Mrs, mother of Esther Waters.
Her brutal husband.
Esther Waters, G. Moore, 1894.

Saunders, Elizabeth. *Our Betters* (play), W. S. Maugham, 1923.

Saunders, Jane.
Jerry, her brother.
Tex of Bar-20, C. E. Mulford, 1922.

Saunter, Mr. *Lolly Willowes,* Sylvia Townsend Warner, 1926.

Sauron, the Dark Lord of Mordor. *The Lord of the Rings* trilogy, 1954–5, J. R. R. Tolkien.

Sauveterre, Duc de (Fabrice), lover of Linda Talbot, *née* Radlett.
Fabrice, their illegitimate son.
The Pursuit of Love, 1945, and elsewhere, Nancy Mitford.

Savary, Colonel, of the Gendarmerie Élite. *Tom Burke of Ours,* C. Lever, 1844.

Savage, Eleanor, last love of Amory Blaine. *This Side of Paradise,* F. Scott Fitzgerald, 1920.

Savage, Rampion, gentle, peace-loving antiquary who becomes a private detective, chief character.
Deirdre, his sister.
The Frontiers of Death, 1957 and others, James Turner.

Savage, Richard Ellworth, assistant to J. Ward Moorehouse. *U.S.A.* trilogy, John dos Passos, 1930–6.

Savelli, Paul. *See* SILAS FINN.

Saverne, Comte de, the elder.
Francis Stanislas, his son, Vicomte de Barr, later Count.
Clarisse, his wife, *née* Viomesnil.
Agnes, their daughter, m. Denis Duval.
Francis's unmarried sisters.
Denis Duval, W. M. Thackeray, 1864.

Savile, Lord Arthur, central character, m. Sybil Merton. *Lord Arthur Savile's Crime,* O. Wilde, 1891.

Savile, Lucy. 'Fellow Townsmen,' *Wessex Tales,* T. Hardy, 1888.

Savill, George, school friend of Nathaniel Grimshaw. *Farewell to Youth,* Storm Jameson, 1928.

Saville, Clara, m. Frank Fairlegh.
Lady Saville, her mother, *née* Elliot.
Frank Fairlegh, F. E. Smedley, 1850.

Saville, Helen, friend of the Lancasters. *The Vortex* (play), N. Coward, 1924.

Saville, Mrs Margaret, sister of Richard Walton. *Frankenstein,* Mary W. Shelley, 1818.

Savio, King of Paflagonia. *The Rose and the Ring,* W. M. Thackeray, 1855.

Saviola, Vincentio, celebrated fencing instructor. *The Monastery,* W. Scott, 1820.

Savonarola (hist.). *Romola,* George Eliot, 1863.

Savott, Sir Henry, Bt.
Grace, his daughter.
Imperial Palace, Arnold Bennett, 1930.

Savoyard, Cecil. *Fanny's First Play* (play), G. B. Shaw, 1905.

Sawbridge, Lieutenant, H.M.S. *Harpy.* *Mr Midshipman Easy,* Captain Marryat, 1836.

Sawbridge, Ellen, m. Sir Isaac Harman. *The Wife of Sir Isaac Harman,* H. G. Wells, 1914.

Sawdon, Tom, publican.
 Lily, his wife.
 South Riding, Winifred Holtby, 1936.

Sawkins, owner of coster barrow. *Sorrell and Son,* W. Deeping, 1925.

Sawle, Sam, boatman. *My Son, My Son,* H. Spring, 1938.

Sawyer, Bob, medical student, close friend of Ben Allen. *Pickwick Papers,* C. Dickens, 1837.

Sawyer, John Standish, country gentleman, fox-hunter. *Market Harborough,* G. Whyte-Melville, 1861.

Sawyer, Mr Justice C. *The Newcomes,* W. M. Thackeray, 1853–5.

Sawyer, Miranda and **Jane,** aunts of Rebecca Randall.
 Aurelia, their sister, m. Lorenzo Randall.
 Rebecca of Sunnybrook Farm, Kate D. Wiggin, 1903.

Sawyer, Rosa, m. Billy Wakeling. *A Town like Alice,* N. Shute, 1950.

Sawyer, Tom, central character.
 Sid, his half-brother.
 The Adventures of Tom Sawyer, 1876; also *Huckleberry Finn,* 1884, Mark Twain.

Saxby, Lord (Charles), lover of Mrs Fane and father of Michael and Stella. *Sinister Street,* C. Mackenzie, 1913.

Saxby, Howard, literary agent. *Cocktail Time,* P. G. Wodehouse, 1958.

Saxe, central character. *The Crystal Hunters,* G. Manville Fenn.

Saxenden, Lord ('Snubby'). *Maid in Waiting,* J. Galsworthy, 1931.

Saxingham, Earl of, friend of Lord Vargrave. *Alice,* Lord Lytton, 1838.

Saxon, Decimus, part-owner of *The Providence.* *Micah Clarke,* A. Conan Doyle, 1889.

Saxton, George, m. Meg of The Ramme.
 Emily, Mollie, Tom and **Arthur,** his sisters and brothers.
 The White Peacock, D. H. Lawrence, 1911.

Sayer, Rose. *The African Queen,* C. S. Forester, 1935.

Sayes, Lord, undergraduate. *Zuleika Dobson,* Max Beerbohm, 1911.

Sayle, John, later Lord of Appeal.
 His wife.
 For Us in the Dark, Naomi Royde-Smith, 1937.

Saywell, Rev. Arthur, country parson.
 Cynthia, his erring wife.
 Cissie, his sister.
 Granny, or **the Mater,** his mother.
 Lucille, his daughter.
 Yvette, his daughter, in love with Joe Boswell, the gipsy.
 The Virgin and The Gipsy, D. H. Lawrence, 1930.

Scadder, Zephaniah, swindling agent for the Eden Settlement. *Martin Chuzzlewit,* C. Dickens, 1844.

Scaddon, Henry. *See* MAURICE CHRISTIAN.

Scadgers, Lady, great-aunt of Mrs Sparsit. *Hard Times,* C. Dickens, 1854.

Scaife, servant to McGillivray. *The Thirty-nine Steps,* 1915, and *The Power House,* 1916, J. Buchan.

Scaife, Reginald ('Demon'), friend of John Verney. *The Hill,* H. A. Vachell, 1905.

Scales, house steward and head butler to Sir Maximus Debarry. *Felix Holt,* George Eliot, 1866.

Scales, Buck, American robber and murderer.
 Magdalena, his wife.
 Death Comes for the Archbishop, Willa Cather, 1927.

Scales, Gerald, commercial traveller, m. Sophia Baines. *The Old Wives' Tale,* Arnold Bennett, 1908.

Scaley, bailiff. *Nicholas Nickleby,* C. Dickens, 1839.

Scally, Sarah, Irish nursemaid. *Laura's Bishop,* G. A. Birmingham, 1949.

Scanlon, Lucy, loved by Studs Lonigan. *Studs Lonigan,* a trilogy, James T. Farrell, 1935.

Scantlebury, assessor of dilapidations.
 Obadiah, his brother, asylum proprietor.
 His wife.
 In the Roar of the Sea, S. Baring-Gould, 1892.

Scape, honest man ruined by roguery.
 Fanny, Florence and **Walter,** his children.
 Vanity Fair, W. M. Thackeray, 1847–8.

Scapethrift, Bailey's servant. *Gammer Gurton's Needle* (play), Anonymous, 1575.

Scaramouche. *See* ANDRÉ-LOUIS MOREAU.

Scarlett, American in French secret service, central character and narrator, m. Eline, Countess de Vassart. *The Maids of Paradise,* R. W. Chambers, 1903.

Scarlett, Sylvia, m. Philip Iredale. *Sinister Street,* 1913, etc., C. Mackenzie.

Scarpa, Giovanna Vanna, wife of Baldassare. 'Madonna of the Peach Tree' (s.s.), *Little Novels of Italy,* M. Hewlett, 1899.

Scarsdale, Captain, 'a poor brother' at Grey Friars. *The Newcomes,* W. M. Thackeray, 1853–5.

Scarthe, Black Will. *Holmby House,* G. Whyte-Melville, 1860.

Scarve ('Starve'), miser.
Hilda, his daughter.
The Miser's Daughter, W. H. Ainsworth, 1842.

Scatcherd, Roger, later Sir Roger, Bt, stonemason and contractor.
His wife.
Louis Philippe, their son, 2nd baronet.
Mary, their daughter. *See also* MARY THORNE
Doctor Thorne, A. Trollope, 1858.

Scatter, Dr. *Tracy's Tiger,* W. Saroyan, 1951.

Scatterbrain, Lord. *See* ANDY ROONEY.

Schatzweiler, Americanized German Jew, partner of Chris Tietjens. *Last Post,* Ford Madox Ford, 1928.

Schedoni, a monk. *The Italian,* Mrs Radcliffe, 1797.

Schiavone, Giorgio, Tiber waterman. *The Duke of Gandia* (play), A. C. Swinburne, 1908.

Schiller, Richard F., m. Dolores (Lolita) Haze. *Lolita,* Vladimir Nabokov, 1955.

Schinderhausen, Olearius, professor at Leyden. *The Abbot,* W. Scott, 1820.

Schindler, Frau Hedwig, widow of armaments king. *The Four Armourers,* F. Beeding, 1930.

Schlangenbad, Contesse de. *The Newcomes,* 1852–3, and elsewhere, W. M. Thackeray.

Schlangenwald, Wolfgang von.
Hierom, his cousin.
The Dove in the Eagle's Nest, Charlotte M. Yonge, 1866.

Schlegel, Helen and **Margaret.**
Tibby, their brother.
Ernst, their German father.
Frieda, their cousin.
Howard's End, E. M. Forster, 1910.

Schlemmer, Gordon, film producer. *The Prodigal Heart,* Susan Ertz, 1950.

Schlesinger, Mrs, widow. *The Tragedy of the Korosko,* A. Conan Doyle, 1898.

Schlessinger, Belle, sister-in-law of Charles and Dora Randolph. *Dear Octopus* (play), Dodie Smith, 1939.

Schley, Miss Pimpernel, American actress.
Her father and mother.
The Woman with the Fan, R. S. Hichens, 1904.

Schmalz, Herr Max, m. Lili Meininger. *Tom Tiddler's Ground,* E. Shanks, 1934.

Schmidt, servant, blackmailer of Norris. *Mr Norris Changes Trains,* C. Isherwood, 1935.

Schmidt, waiter at the Capo di Monte. *Adam's Breed,* Radclyffe Hall, 1926.

Schminck, Frau, dance hostess. *Sunrise in the West,* Bechofer Roberts, 1945.

Schmitt, Rose, school-teacher.
Berta, her sister.
The Heart of a Child, Phyllis Bottome, 1940.

Schneider, Baron Charles von, munitions king. *Dragon Harvest,* Upton Sinclair, 1946.

Schofield, Harry.
Milner, his brother. Strike leaders.
Isaiah, their father.
Their mother.
A Modern Tragedy, Phyllis Bentley, 1934.

Schofield, Leo, piano-tuner, owner of music shop.
Lois, his wife.
The Sleepless Moon, H. E. Bates, 1956.

Scholey, Laurence, servant attending Magnus Troil. *The Pirate,* W. Scott, 1822.

Schomberg, hotel owner. *Victory,* Joseph Conrad, 1915.

Schoning, Maria Eleonora. *Maria Schoning* (s.s.), S. T. Coleridge.

Schouler, Marcus, one-time close friend of McTeague. *McTeague,* F. Norris, 1899.

Schreckenwald, Hal, faithful but vicious steward of Count Albert of Geierstein. *Anne of Geierstein,* W. Scott, 1829.

Schreiber, Mits, Aintree steward. *National Velvet,* Enid Bagnold, 1935.

Schreiderling, Colonel.
His wife.
'The Other Man' (s.s.), *Plain Tales from the Hills,* R. Kipling, 1888.

Schreiner, Philip, K.C., counsel for Oliver Price. *Antigua Penny Puce,* R. Graves, 1936.

Schriften, pilot of *The Ter Schilling. The Phantom Ship,* Captain Marryat, 1839.

Schroeder, Fräulein Lina, landlady. *Mr Norris Changes Trains,* 1935, and *Goodbye to Berlin,* 1939, Christopher Isherwood.

Schultz, Mrs. *Mrs Wiggs of the Cabbage Patch,* Alice H. Rice, 1901.

Schultz, Hermann, captain (retd), public prosecutor. *Sunrise in the West,* Bechofer Roberts, 1945.

Schumann, ship's doctor. *Ship of Fools,* Katherine Anne Porter, 1962.

Schutz, Trudi, art teacher, m. Bernhardt Monck. *Dragon's Teeth,* 1942, and elsewhere, Upton Sinclair.

Schutzmacher, Dr. *The Doctor's Dilemma* (play), G. B. Shaw, 1906.

Schwartz. *Beau Geste,* P. C. Wren, 1924.

Schwengauer, Mattie, college girl. *So Big,* Edna Ferber, 1924.

Scindia. 'With Scindia to Delhi' (poem), *Barrack-room Ballads,* R. Kipling, 1892.

Scintilla, pleasure-loving wife of Mixtus. *Theophrastus Such,* George Eliot, 1879.

Scobie, Henry, Deputy Commissioner of Police, central character.
Louise, his wife.
Catherine, their dead daughter.
The Heart of the Matter, Graham Greene, 1948.

Scobie, Joshua, English homosexual employed by the Egyptian police. *The Alexandria Quartet,* 1957–61, Lawrence Durrell.

Score, Mrs, landlady of the Bugle. *Catherine,* W. M. Thackeray, 1839–1840.

Scott, of the Irrigation Department, m. William Martyn. 'William the Conqueror' (s.s.), *The Day's Work,* R. Kipling, 1898.

Scott, David, young American painter.
Jenny Brown, his mistress.
Ship of Fools, Katherine Anne Porter, 1962.

Scott, Dr Dennis, 'boffin'; narrator.
Shirley, his wife.
No Highway, N. Shute, 1948.

Scott, Duncan, film-star.
Ethel, his wife, *née* Frobisher.
Sorrell and Son, W. Deeping, 1925.

Scott, Captain Mat, half-owner of the *Aunty Mine.* 'The Iliad of Sandy Bar' (s.s.), *The Luck of Roaring Camp,* Bret Harte, 1868.

Scott, Roberta, American girl vegetarian. *Birds of America,* Mary McCarthy, 1971.

Scott, Thomas, farmer, central character. *Hawbuck Grange,* R. S. Surtees, 1847.

Scott, Tom, errand-boy to Quilp. *The Old Curiosity Shop,* C. Dickens, 1841.

Scott, William, soldier. *Abraham Lincoln* (play), J. Drinkwater, 1918.

Scott-Brown, Surgeon-Lieutenant, of *Saltash. The Cruel Sea,* N. Monsarrat, 1951.

Scougal, Andie, captain of the *Thistle. Catriona,* R. L. Stevenson, 1893.

Scouler, Dr. 'God and the Machine' (s.s.), *Last Recollections of My Uncle Charles,* N. Balchin, 1954.

Scout, lawyer to Lady Booby. *Joseph Andrews,* H. Fielding, 1742.

Scoutbush, Lord, absentee Irish peer. *Two Years Ago,* C. Kingsley, 1857.

Scrabster, Angela, painter. *Poet's Pub,* E. Linklater, 1929.

Scragga, son of Twala, paramount chief. *King Solomon's Mines,* H. Rider Haggard, 1885.

Scraper, Lady Susan, daughter of the Earl of Bagwig.
Scraper Buckram and **Sydney,** her sons.
Two daughters.
The Book of Snobs, W. M. Thackeray, 1846–7.

Screwby, servant to Sir Miles Warrington. *The Virginians,* W. M. Thackeray, 1857–9.

Scriven, Sir John.
Toby, his son.
Shabby Tiger, H. Spring, 1934.

Scrivener. *Ralph Roister Doister,* N. Udall, 1551.

Scrooge, Ebenezer, central character. *A Christmas Carol,* C. Dickens, 1843.

Scroop, Sir Stephen, *Richard the Second* and *Richard the Third* (plays), W. Shakespeare.

Scroop, Titus. *See* ALFRED TITUS CHALLIS.

Scrope, Edward, Bishop of Princhester.
Ella, his wife, daughter of Lord Birkenholme.
Eleanor, eldest of their five daughters.
The Soul of a Bishop, H. G. Wells, 1917.

Scrope, Jane, the sparrow's mistress. *The Boke of Phyllyp Sparowe,* John Skelton, *c.* 1508.

Scrub, Squire Sullen's servant. *The Beaux' Stratagem* (play), G. Farquhar, 1707.

Scrubby, ship's steward. *Outward Bound,* S. Vane, 1923.

Scrymgeour, artist and man of means. *My Lady Nicotine,* J. M. Barrie, 1890.

Scrymgeour, Francis, Edinburgh bank clerk. 'The Rajah's Diamond' (s.s.), *New Arabian Nights,* R. L. Stevenson, 1882.

Scuddamore, Silas Q., wealthy American. 'The Suicide Club' (s.s.), *New Arabian Nights,* R. L. Stevenson, 1882.

Scudder. *The Thirty-nine Steps,* J. Buchan, 1915.

Scudder, Alec, young gamekeeper in love with Maurice Hall. *Maurice,* E. M. Forster, 1971.

Scudmore, in love with Bellafront Worldly. *A Woman is a Weathercock* (play), N. Field, 1612.

Scully, Violet, school friend of the Bartons, m. Lord Kilcarney.
Fred, her brother.
Their mother, ex-shop girl.
A Drama in Muslin, G. Moore, 1886.

Scully, William Pitt, Liberal M.P. for Oldborough.
Sally, his sister.
The Bedford Row Conspiracy, W. M. Thackeray, 1840.

Sea Catch, a seal.
Matkah, his wife.
Kotick, their son.
'The White Seal,' *The Jungle Book,* R. Kipling, 1894.

Sea Cow. 'The White Seal,' *The Jungle Book,* R. Kipling, 1894.

Sea Rat. *The Wind in the Willows,* K. Grahame, 1908.

Sea Vitch, a walrus. 'The White Seal,' *The Jungle Book,* R. Kipling, 1894.

Seacombe, Hon. John, uncle of William Crimsworth. *The Professor,* Charlotte Brontë, 1857.

Seaforth, Lieutenant Charles, m. Caroline Ingoldsby. 'The Spectre of Tappington' (s.s.), *The Ingoldsby Legends,* R. H. Barham, 1837.

Seagrave, William.
His wife.
William, Thomas, Caroline, and **Albert,** their children.
Masterman Ready, Captain Marryat, 1841–2.

Seagrim, Molly.
George, her father, a gamekeeper.
Tom Jones, H. Fielding, 1749.

Seal, Basil, central character, m. Angela Lyne.
Cynthia, Lady Seal, his mother.
Barbara, his sister, m. Freddy Sothill.
Put Out More Flags, 1942, and elsewhere, E. Waugh.

Seal, Martin, of the B.B.C. *Holy Deadlock,* A. P. Herbert, 1934.

Searing, Jerome, Confederate private. 'One of the Missing' (s.s.), *In the Midst of Life,* A. Bierce, 1898.

Searle, the Calcrafts' family doctor. *In Cotton Wool,* W. B. Maxwell, 1912.

Seaton, Arthur.
His aunt.
'Seaton's Aunt' (s.s.), *The Riddle,* W. de la Mare, 1923.

Seaway, Anne, dupe of Aeneas Manston. *Desperate Remedies,* T. Hardy, 1871.

Sebastes of Mitylene, sentinel at the Golden Gate, ex-pirate and robber. *Count Robert of Paris,* W. Scott, 1832.

Sebastian, brother of Alonso. *The Tempest* (play), W. Shakespeare.

Sebastian, brother of Viola. *Twelfth Night* (play), W. Shakespeare.

Sebastian, Antoine, ex-French aristocrat, fiddler and dancing master.
His daughters:
Mathilde, in love with de Casimir.
Désirée, m. Charles Darragon.
Barlasch of the Guard, H. Seton Merriman, 1903.

Sebastian, Luiz, convict. *The Old Dominion,* Mary Johnston, 1899.

Secret, messenger to summon Christiana. *Pilgrim's Progress,* J. Bunyan, 1678, 1684.

Seddon, Mrs, Paul Finn's landlady.
Jane, her daughter.
The Fortunate Youth, W. J. Locke, 1914.

Seddon, Rev. Gerald, friend of Father Bott. *The Feast,* Margaret Kennedy, 1950.

Seddon, Margaret. *The New Machiavelli,* H. G. Wells, 1911.

Sedgemoor, Susan, m. Greaves Oakley. *Sir Lancelot Greaves,* T. Smollett, 1762.

Sedgett, Nic, bigamist and general bad character. *Rhoda Fleming,* G. Meredith, 1865.

Sedgmire, Lord, Robert Carne's father-in-law. *South Riding,* Winifred Holtby, 1936.

Sedley, Amelia.
m. (1) George Osborne.
Georgy, their son.
(2) Major William Dobbin.
John, her father.
Her mother.
Joseph, her brother.
Vanity Fair, W. M. Thackeray, 1847–8.

Sedley, Joanna (alias John Matcham), m. Sir Richard Shelton. *The Black Arrow,* R. L. Stevenson, 1888.

Seebach, Martha, maid to Mme de Saverne. *Denis Duval,* W. M. Thackeray, 1864.

Seecombe, servant of Ambrose Ashley. *My Cousin Rachel,* Daphne du Maurier, 1951.

Seegrave, Superintendent, of the Frizinghall Police. *The Moonstone,* W. Collins, 1868.

Seelencooper, one-eyed captain, governor of Ryde Hospital. *The Surgeon's Daughter,* W. Scott, 1827.

Seeley, Andrew, nephew of Mrs Caroline Faraday. *Police at the Funeral,* Margery Allingham, 1931.

Sefton, a bully. 'The Moral Reformers,' *Stalky & Co.,* R. Kipling, 1899.

Sefton, Lady Sophia, of Camborne (alias Charmian Brown), m. Sir Peter Vibart. *The Broad Highway,* J. Farnol, 1910.

Ségouin, Hungarian pianist. 'After the Race' (s.s.), *The Dubliners,* James Joyce, 1914.

Seipel, Mrs Hannah.
Reuben, her husband, cabinet-maker.
Janey, Sam, Eli and **Berel,** their children.
Magnolia Street, L. Golding, 1932.

Selamlek Pasha.
Mustapha Bey, his son.
'A Treaty of Peace,' *Donovan Pasha,* Gilbert Parker, 1902.

Selby, George.
Marianna, his wife. Uncle and aunt of Harriet Byron.
Lucy, their daughter.
Sir Charles Grandison S. Richardson, 1754.

Selby, Guy, racehorse owner, central character, m. Myra Winchemore, widow.
Madeline, his sister, m. William Symington.
Not so Bad after All, Nat Gould.

Selby, Solomon. 'A Tradition of 1804,' *Life's Little Ironies,* T. Hardy, 1894.

Selden, escaped convict, brother of Mrs Barrymore. *The Hound of the Baskervilles,* A. Conan Doyle, 1902.

Selden, Mrs, cook. *Manservant and Maidservant,* Ivy Compton-Burnett, 1947.

Selden, Jim.
His mother. Slaves escaping with George and Eliza.
Uncle Tom's Cabin, Harriet B. Stowe, 1851.

Selden, Lawrence. *The House of Mirth,* Edith Wharton, 1905.

Seldom, Lady Jessica, m. Robin le Faber. *The Five Sons of Le Faber,* E. Raymond, 1945.

Seldon, Mrs Matilda, owner of the Wattle Tree Inn, m. Ben Middleton. *The Dark Horse,* Nat Gould.

Selenites, moon inhabitants. *The First Men in the Moon,* H. G. Wells, 1901.

Selim, Turkish negotiator. *The Capsina,* E. F. Benson, 1899.

Selim, Saïd's servant.
 Musa, his son.
 Saïd the Fisherman, M. Pickthall, 1903.

Selim. *Hassan* (play), J. E. Flecker, 1923.

Sellabach, Klaus, great-grandson of Simon Rakonitz. *Tents of Israel,* 1924, and others, G. B. Stern.

Sellars, Poppy. *Angel Pavement,* J. B. Priestley, 1930.

Sellers, Reginald, fifth-rate artist. *The Man Upstairs,* P. G. Wodehouse, 1914.

Selston, Mrs, caretaker. *My Adventure in Norfolk* (s.s.), A. J. Alan.

Selvaggia. 'Messer Cino and the Live Coal' (s.s.), *Little Novels of Italy,* M. Hewlett, 1899.

Selwyn, Frank. *The Silver King* (play), H. A. Jones, 1882.

Semmering, Lady Gertrude. *See* COUNTESS OF CASTERLEY.

Semper, dresser at the Metropolitan Opera House. *Grand Opera,* Vicki Baum, 1942.

Semphill, Rev. George, who becomes a cardinal. *Hadrian the Seventh,* Baron Corvo (F. W. Rolfe), 1904.

Sempronius, a lord. *Timon of Athens* (play), W. Shakespeare.

Sempronius. *The Apple Cart* (play), G. B. Shaw, 1929.

Sen Heng. *The Wallet of Kai Lung,* E. Bramah, 1900.

Senf, hall porter. *Grand Hotel,* Vicki Baum, 1931.

Senior, Rev. Dr Thomas, headmaster.
 Tom, his son.
 The Fifth Form at St Dominic's, T. Baines Reed, 1887.

Sennet, Robert Devizes's clerk. *The Will* (play), J. M. Barrie, 1913.

Sentiment, Mr Popular, novelist. *The Warden,* A. Trollope, 1855.

Sentry, Captain, 'of invincible modesty.' Essay in *The Spectator,* J. Addison, 1711–14.

Sephardo, Salomo, Jewish astrologer. *The Spanish Gypsy* (poem), George Eliot, 1868.

Septimus, friend of Alcander. *The Bee,* O. Goldsmith, 1759–60.

Serafimov, Russian exile. *The Seven Who Fled,* Frederic Prokosch, 1937.

Sereda, Mother. *Jurgen,* J. B. Cabell, 1921.

Sergeant, The. *Quality Street* (play), J. M. Barrie, 1902.

Sergison, Rudd, central character, m. Helen Brooke.
 Tom, his father.
 His mother.
 Ben, his uncle.
 Landmarks, E. V. Lucas, 1914.

Sermay, Jenny, daughter of a Wing Commander.
 Raymond, her brother, junior reporter.
 Thin Air, John Pudney, 1961.

Service, stipendiary magistrate. *But Soft—We Are Observed!,* H. Belloc, 1928.

Setabhai, Queen of the Maharajah of Gokral Seetaren. *The Naulakha,* R. Kipling and W. Balestier, 1892.

Seth, attendant of Isaac and Rebecca. *Ivanhoe,* W. Scott, 1820.

Seti, Mahommed, ex-murderer, central character. 'The Price of the Grindstone and the Drum,' *Donovan Pasha,* Gilbert Parker, 1902.

Seton, Rev. James.
 His children:
 Alan.
 Walter.
 David Stuart ('Buff').
 Elizabeth, eng. to Arthur Townshend.
 The Setons, O. Douglas, 1917.

Seton, Patrick, spiritualist medium accused of fraud. *The Bachelors,* Muriel Spark, 1961.

Seton, Sally, later Lady Rosseter. *Mrs Dalloway,* Virginia Woolf, 1925.

Settle, Athene. *The Clever Ones* (play), A. Sutro, 1914.

Seumas Beg.
 Brigid, his sister. Children who meet the leprechaun.
 The Crock of Gold, J. Stephens, 1912.

Severidge, George, false friend of Judge Gaskony; brother of Molly Sarrett. *The Judge's Story,* C. Morgan, 1947.

Sevilla, Philip, central character. *Ten Minute Alibi* (play), A. Armstrong, 1933.

Seward, Dr. *Dracula*, Bram Stoker, 1897.

Seward, William, Secretary of State (hist.). *Abraham Lincoln* (play), J. Drinkwater, 1918.

Sewell, Frances, eng. to John Freeman. *The Fanatics* (play), M. Malleson, 1924.

Sewell, Professor Lucas, head of Haughton Laboratory.
Rose, his wife.
Mab, their daughter, m. Ralph Peach.
A Sort of Traitors, N. Balchin, 1949.

Sewis, Old, half-caste butler to Squire Beltham. *The Adventures of Harry Richmond,* G. Meredith, 1871.

Sexton.
His wife.
Tivvyriah, their daughter.
Sammy, their son.
Precious Bane, Mary Webb, 1924.

Seyfang, Otto. *Tracy's Tiger,* W. Saroyan, 1951.

Seymore, Clive (Andrew), father of Fanny Hooper.
Lady Alicia, his wife.
Sir Everard, his father.
Fanny by Gaslight, M. Sadleir, 1940.

Seymour, Humphrey, editor of Communist scandal sheet. *The Conscience of the Rich,* 1958, part of the *Strangers and Brothers* sequence, C. P. Snow.

Seymour, Valerie. *The Well of Loneliness,* Radclyffe Hall, 1928.

Seymour, William. *See* WILLIAM PETERS.

Seymour, Sir Wilson. 'The Man in the Passage,' *The Wisdom of Father Brown,* G. K. Chesterton, 1914.

Seysen, Father, parish priest. *The Phantom Ship,* Captain Marryat, 1839.

Shaban, chief eunuch. *Vathek,* W. Beckford, 1786.

Shabata, Frank, neighbour of the Bergsons. *O Pioneers!,* Willa Cather, 1913.

Shackles, a racehorse. 'The Broken Link Handicap' (s.s.), *Plain Tales from the Hills,* R. Kipling, 1888.

Shadbolt, Wilfred, head jailer and assistant tormentor, m. Phoebe Meryll. *The Yeomen of the Guard* (comic opera), Gilbert & Sullivan, 1888.

Shadd, Dinah, m. Terence Mulvaney.
Sergeant Shadd, her father.
Her mother.
'The Courtship of Dinah Shadd' (s.s.), *Life's Handicap,* 1891, 'The Big Drunk Draf' (s.s.), *Soldiers Three,* 1888, and others, R. Kipling.

Shade, John, an American poet.
Sybil, his wife.
Hazel, their daughter.
Pale Fire, Vladimir Nabokov, 1962.

Shadrach, money-lender. *Digby Grand,* G. Whyte-Melville, 1853.

Shafiz Ullah Khan. 'One View of the Question' (s.s.), *Many Inventions,* R. Kipling, 1893.

Shafton, Sir Piercie, 'witty and accomplished courtier.'
Shafton of Wilverton, his father.
The Monastery, W. Scott, 1820.

Shafton, Walter, music-hall artist. *Let the People Sing,* J. B. Priestley, 1939.

Shagpat, clothier.
Kadza, his wife.
The Shaving of Shagpat, G. Meredith, 1856.

Shale, Sir Robert, Bt.
Elinor and **Lucy,** his granddaughters.
The Lie (play), H. A. Jones, 1923.

Shales, humpbacked tailor.
His wife.
Aylwin, T. Watts-Dunton, 1899.

Shalford, Edwin, proprietor, Folkestone Drapery Bazaar, employer of Kipps. *Kipps,* H. G. Wells, 1905.

Shallard, Frank, minister, Elmer Gantry's chief antagonist. *Elmer Gantry,* Sinclair Lewis, 1927.

Shallow, country justice. *The Merry Wives of Windsor* (play), W. Shakespeare.

Shallum, Mrs, 'Parisianized figure.'
Harvey, her husband.
The Custom of the Country, Edith Wharton, 1913.

Shaloony, Irish patriot. *The Newcomes,* W. M. Thackeray, 1853–5.

Shame. *See* DISCONTENT.

Shamlegh, The Woman of. *Kim,* R. Kipling, 1901.

Shand, John, m. Maggie Wylie. *What Every Woman Knows* (play), J. M. Barrie, 1908.

Shandon, Captain Charles, kind-hearted, ne'er-do-well Irish journalist.
His wife, m. (2) Jack Finucane.
Mary, their daughter.
Pendennis, 1848–50, and elsewhere, W. M. Thackeray.

Shandy, Tristram, central character, narrator.
Walter, his father, retired turkey merchant.
Elizabeth, his mother.
Bobby, his elder brother.
Captain Toby, his uncle.
Dinah, Toby's wife.
Tristram Shandy, L. Sterne, 1767.

Shangois, travelling notary. *The Pomp of the Lavilettes,* Gilbert Parker, 1897.

Shankland, Mrs Ann, ex-wife of John Malcolm. *Separate Tables* (play), T. Rattigan, 1955.

Shannon, Miss Betsy, actress. *Mr Facey Romford's Hounds,* R. S. Surtees, 1865.

Sharker, ship's captain. *The Fortunes of Nigel,* W. Scott, 1822.

Sharkey, Captain, a pirate. 'Captain Sharkey' (s.s.), *Tales of Pirates and Blue Water,* A. Conan Doyle.

Sharland, Mehalah (Glory), central character, m. Elijah Rebow.
Lydia, her mother.
Mehalah, S. Baring-Gould, 1880.

Sharp, senior master at Salem House. *David Copperfield,* C. Dickens, 1850.

Sharp, Mr. *Money* (play), Lord Lytton, 1840.

Sharp, Mr and Mrs. *The Land of Promise* (play), W. S. Maugham, 1914.

Sharp, Mrs, maid to Lady Cheverel. 'Mr Gilfil's Love Story,' *Scenes of Clerical Life,* George Eliot, 1857.

Sharp, Rebecca ('Becky'), central character, charming and utterly unscrupulous; m. Rawdon Crawley.
Her father, an artist.
Her mother, a French opera dancer.
Vanity Fair, W. M. Thackeray, 1847–8.

Sharpe, first mate. *Hard Cash,* C. Reade, 1863.

Sharpe, Mrs, landlady (The Cheat). *The Passing of the Third Floor Back* (play), J. K. Jerome, 1910.

Sharpe, Marion, defendant on trial for kidnapping and assault, m. Robert Blair.
Her mother.
The Franchise Affair, Josephine Tey, 1948.

Sharpitlaw, Gideon, Procurator Fiscal. *The Heart of Midlothian,* W. Scott, 1818.

Sharpless, Edward, villain. *By Order of the Company,* Mary Johnston, 1900.

Shaughnessy, Major Galahad, m. Pauline d'Hemecourt. 'Café des Exiles' (s.s.), *Old Creole Days,* G. W. Cable, 1879.

Shaugodaya, a coward. *The Song of Hiawatha* (poem), H. W. Longfellow, 1855.

Shaw, Edith, cousin of Margaret Hale, m. Captain Lennox.
Her mother.
North and South, Mrs Gaskell, 1855.

Shaw, Linn. *Comrade, O Comrade,* Ethel Mannin, 1946.

Shaw, Ronald, homosexual film star. *The City and The Pillar,* Gore Vidal, 1948.

Shawel, head huntsman.
Hugh, his son.
Unending Crusade, R. E. Sherwood, 1932.

Shawn, Albert.
His wife.
John James, his brother.
The Great Adventure (play), Arnold Bennett, 1913.

Shaynor, John, chemist. 'Wireless' (s.s.), *Traffics and Discoveries,* R. Kipling, 1904.

Shear, Tony, friend of Paul Hathaway. *A Ward of the Golden Gate* (s.s.), Bret Harte.

Shearwater, James.
Rosie, his wife.
Antic Hay, A. Huxley, 1923.

Sheehy, Judy.
Her mother.
'The Courtship of Dinah Shadd' (s.s.), *Life's Handicap,* R. Kipling, 1891.

Sheehy, Norah, m. Larry Lanaghan. *Comrade, O Comrade,* Ethel Mannin, 1946.

Sheen Nic Leoid. *See* NIC LEOID.

Sheepshanks. Family name of the EARL OF SOUTHDOWN.

Sheepshanks, Mr. *Wives and Daughters*, Mrs Gaskell, 1866.

Shelby, Arthur, original owner of Uncle Tom.
Emily, his wife.
'Mas'r George,' their son.
Uncle Tom's Cabin, Harriet B. Stowe, 1851.

Sheldon, the Rainiers' butler. *Random Harvest*, J. Hilton, 1941.

Shelmerdine. *These Charming People*, M. Arlen, 1920.

Shelmerdine, Marmaduke Bonthrop, Orlando's husband. *Orlando*, Virginia Woolf, 1928.

Shelter, Lady, super-tactless hostess. *A Footman for the Peacock*, Rachel Ferguson, 1940.

Shelton, Lady. *Gentlemen Prefer Blondes*, Anita Loos, 1925.

Shelton, Richard, later Sir, central character, m. Joanna Sedley.
Sir Harry, his father.
The Black Arrow, R. L. Stevenson, 1888.

Shend. 'The Dog Hervey' (s.s.), *A Diversity of Creatures*, R. Kipling, 1917.

Shenley, Mrs Olive, div. wife of Richard Adscombe. *Judgment in Suspense*, G. Bullett, 1946.

Shepard, Sarah, foster mother of Hugh McVey. *Poor White*, Sherwood Anderson, 1920.

Shepherd, John, 'civil, cautious,' legal adviser to Sir Walter Elliot.
His daughter, m. Clay.
Persuasion, Jane Austen, 1818.

Shepherdsons, enemies feuding with the Grangerfords. *Huckleberry Finn*, Mark Twain, 1884.

Sheppard, Jack, housebreaker and jailbreaker.
Joan, his mother.
Jack Sheppard, W. H. Ainsworth, 1839.

Sheppard, Dr Steven, consultant, central character.
Ruth, his wife.
Carol, their dead daughter.
Thursday Afternoons, Monica Dickens, 1945.

Shepperson, Miss. 'A Charming Family' (s.s.), *The House of Cobwebs*, G. Gissing, 1906.

Shepperton, Randy.
Margaret, his sister.
You Can't Go Home Again, T. Wolfe, 1947.

Sherburn, Colonel *Huckleberry Finn*, Mark Twain, 1884.

Shere Khan ('Lungri'), the Tiger. 'Mowgli's Brothers' and others, *The Jungle Books*, R. Kipling, 1894–1895.

Shergold, Dr.
Emma, his wife.
'A Lodger in Maze Pond' (s.s.), *The House of Cobwebs*, G. Gissing, 1906.

Sheridan, 1st husband of Audrey Blake. *The Little Nugget*, P. G. Wodehouse, 1913.

Sheridan, Laura.
Laurie, her brother.
Their mother.
'The Garden Party' (s.s.), *The Garden Party*, Katherine Mansfield, 1922.

Sheridan, Sir Thomas. *Rogue Herries*, Hugh Walpole, 1930.

Sheriff, Kate. *The Naulakha*, R. Kipling & W. Balestier, 1892.

Sherlock, Rev. Theodore, curate, Treby Magna. *Felix Holt*, George Eliot, 1866.

Sherrard ('The Ganger').
Margaret, his wife.
The Pottleton Legacy, Albert Smith, 1849.

Sherrick, wine merchant and moneylender, kindly, vulgar.
His wife, formerly an opera singer.
Julia, his daughter, m. Charles Honeyman.
The Newcomes, W. M. Thackeray, 1853–5.

Sherston, George, central character.
Evelyn, his aunt.
Memoirs of a Fox-Hunting Man, 1929, and *Memoirs of an Infantry Officer*, 1930, Siegfried Sassoon.

Sherwin, Margaret, m. Basil.
Her father, a draper; a small tyrant.
Her mother.
Basil, W. Collins, 1852.

Sheva. *Absalom and Achitophel* (poem), J. Dryden, 1681.

Shillitoe, tailor, Bursley. *The Card*, Arnold Bennett, 1911.

Shimerda, Antonia, Bohemian peasant girl in Nebraska. *My Antonia*, Willa Cather, 1918.

Shiner, Fred, farmer-churchwarden.

Under the Greenwood Tree, T. Hardy, 1872.

Shingfu, aged Chinese philosopher. *A Citizen of the World*, O. Goldsmith, 1762.

Shingle, Corporal Vincent. 'The Woman in his Life' (s.s.), *Limits and Renewals*, R. Kipling, 1932.

'Shiny William,' deputy hostler, Bull Inn, Rochester. *Pickwick Papers*, C. Dickens, 1837.

Shinza, Edward, an African politician. *A Guest of Honour*, Nadine Gordimer, 1971.

Shipley, Hagar Currie, 90-year-old narrator, chief character. Daughter of a storekeeper in Canadian prairie town.
- **Brampton Shipley,** her husband, farmer.
  - **Marvin,** their son.
    - **Doris,** his wife.
  - **John,** 2nd son of Hagar and Brampton.

The Stone Angel, Margaret Laurence, 1964.

'Shipton, Mother.' 'The Outcasts of Poker Flat' (s.s.), *The Luck of Roaring Camp*, Bret Harte, 1868.

Shirley, Peter. *Major Barbara* (play), G. B. Shaw, 1905.

Shoats, Hoover, a religious racketeer. *Wise Blood*, Flannery O'Connor, 1952.

Shobbes, friend of George Winterbourne. *Death of a Hero*, R. Aldington, 1929.

Shoe, Miss. *At Mrs Beam's* (play), C. K. Munro, 1923.

Shoesmith, friend of Remington; founder, *Blue Weekly*. *The New Machiavelli*, H. G. Wells, 1911.

Shoesmith, Tom. 'The Dymchurch Flit,' *Puck of Pook's Hill*, R. Kipling, 1906.

Shole, Dr, scientist. *A Sort of Traitors*, N. Balchin, 1949.

Sholto, Major John.
- **Thadeus** and **Bartholomew,** his sons.

The Sign of Four, A. Conan Doyle, 1890.

Shorne, Mrs Julie.
- Her husband.

Evan Harrington, G. Meredith, 1861.

'Shorty.' *The Virginian*, O. Wister, 1902.

Shotover, Captain. *Heartbreak House* (play), G. B. Shaw, 1917.

Shotover, Lord. *See* FALLOWFIELD.

Shott, Annie, mother of Kim O'Hara. *Kim*, R. Kipling, 1901.

Shovel.
- **'Ameliar,'** his sister.

Sentimental Tommy, J. M. Barrie, 1896.

Shreve, fellow student of Quentin Compson. *The Sound and the Fury*, W. Faulkner, 1931.

Shropshire, Marquess of, grandfather of Marjorie Ferrar. *The Silver Spoon*, J. Galsworthy, 1926.

Shropton, Sir William, m. Lady Agatha Caradoc.
- **Ann,** their daughter.

The Patrician, J. Galsworthy, 1911.

Shrubfield, Mrs, county *grande dame*. *Before the Bombardment*, O. Sitwell, 1926.

Shuan, brutal mate of the *Covenant*. *Kidnapped*, R. L. Stevenson, 1886.

Shuckleford, Mrs, widow.
- **Sam,** her son.
- **Jemima,** her daughter.

Reginald Cruden, T. Baines Reed, 1894.

Shulman, Rabbi.
- His wife.
- Their children: **Rachel, Sally, Benjamin, Yossel, Yankel, Issy, Mick** and **Abey.**

Magnolia Street, L. Golding, 1932.

Shuman, Zella. *An American Tragedy*, T. Dreiser, 1925.

Shushions, Mr. *Clayhanger*, Arnold Bennett, 1910.

Shute, Bernard.
- **Cecilia,** his sister.

Some Experiences of an Irish R.M., Œ. Somerville & Martin Ross, 1899.

Shuter, Sergeant. *The Amazons* (play), A. W. Pinero, 1893.

Shuttlethwaite, Mrs Julia. *The Cocktail Party* (play), T. S. Eliot, 1950.

Shuttleworth, Lady.
- **Sir Augustus,** her son, in love with Princess Priscilla.

Princess Priscilla's Fortnight, Countess von Arnim, 1905.

Shuttleworth, George.
- **Olga Bracely,** his wife, prima donna.

Queen Lucia, E. F. Benson, 1920.

Shuttleworthy. *Thou Art the Man* (s.s.), E. A. Poe.

Shylock, a Jew.
Jessica, his daughter, m. Lorenzo.
The Merchant of Venice (play), W. Shakespeare.

Sibley, Samuel.
Nancy, his wife.
Richard, their son.
Rose, his sister, m. John Rhead.
Milestones (play), Arnold Bennett & E. Knoblock, 1912.

Sibwright, Percy, neighbour of Pendennis in Lamb Court. *The Newcomes,* 1853–5, and elsewhere, W. M. Thackeray.

Sichcliffe, Moira. 'The Dog Hervey' (s.s.), *A Diversity of Creatures,* R. Kipling, 1917.

Sicinius, Velutus, tribune. *Coriolanus* (play), W. Shakespeare.

Siddal, Dick.
Barbara, his wife. Hotel-keepers.
Gerry, Duff and **Robin,** their children.
The Feast, Margaret Kennedy, 1950.

Sidi el Assif, a woman sheik. *Captain Brassbound's Conversion* (play), G. B. Shaw, 1900.

Sidney, Mr, farmer.
His unmarried 'wife.'
'My Son's Wife' (s.s.), *A Diversity of Creatures,* R. Kipling, 1917.

Sidonia, a Spanish Jew. *Coningsby,* 1844, and *Tancred,* 1847, B. Disraeli.

Sieppe, Mr and Mrs, uncle and aunt of Marcus Schouler.
Trina, their daughter, m. McTeague.
McTeague, F. Norris, 1899.

Sievewright, blacksmith in Castlewood.
Nancy, his daughter.
Henry Esmond, W. M. Thackeray, 1852.

Sigglesthwaite, Agnes, high school mistress.
Her mother.
Edie, her sister.
South Riding, Winifred Holtby, 1936.

Sikauli ('Scowl'), Kaffir servant of Quatermain. *Child of Storm,* H. Rider Haggard, 1913.

Sikes, Bill, burglar and murderer. *Oliver Twist,* C. Dickens, 1838.

Silas, Great-Uncle, bawdy country character.
Abel, his only son.
Georgina, Abel's wife.
Uncle Cosmo, Silas's foreign-travelling brother.
My Uncle Silas stories, H. E. Bates, 1939.

Silber, Benno.
Truda, his wife, *née* Rakonitz.
Maxine, Derek and **Iris** (later Silver), their children.
Tents of Israel and others, G. B. Stern, 1924 onwards.

Silcot, Aubrey.
Emily, his wife.
'An Anniversary' (s.s.), *A Beginning,* W. de la Mare, 1955.

Silence, John, 'the Psychic Doctor,' central character and sometimes narrator in a series of stories. *John Silence,* A. Blackwood, 1908.

Silenus, 'Professor' Otto, architect. *Decline and Fall,* E. Waugh, 1928.

Silk, Ambrose. *Put Out More Flags,* E. Waugh, 1942.

Silla, m. Rev. Andrew Flood.
Her mother.
God's Stepchildren, Sarah G. Millin, 1924.

Sillabub, Marquis of. See LOLLIPOP.

Silton, Ben. *The Man of Feeling,* H. Mackenzie, 1771.

Silva, Dr, Dean of Medical School. *Martin Arrowsmith,* Sinclair Lewis, 1925.

Silva, Duke, betrothed to Fedalma. *The Spanish Gypsy* (poem), George Eliot, 1868.

Silva, Joe. *Mourning becomes Electra* (play), E. O'Neill, 1931.

Silver, Long John. *Treasure Island,* R. L. Stevenson, 1883.

Silver, Louise. See LOUISE EUGÉNIE D'ARGENT.

Silver, Mattie, cousin of Zeena Frome. *Ethan Frome,* Edith Wharton, 1911.

Silver Man, The. 'The Mark of the Beast' (s.s.), *Life's Handicap,* R. Kipling, 1891.

Silverbridge, Lord. See DUKE OF OMNIUM.

Silvercross, Julian, m. Ida Fynes.
Adam, his father, banker.
His mother, *née* Derwent.
Muriel and **Harriet,** his sisters.
The Old Bank, W. Westall, 1902.

Silvertop, Captain George Granby, m. Lady Angela Thistlewood, his cousin. *Jeames's Diary,* W. M. Thackeray, 1846.

Silvestre, Dom José da, Portuguese possessor of chart to the mines. *King Solomon's Mines,* H. Rider Haggard, 1885.

Silvia, daughter of the Duke of Milan. *Two Gentlemen of Verona* (play), W. Shakespeare.

Silvius, a shepherd. *As You Like It* (play), W. Shakespeare.

Simcoe, incumbent of Clavering St Mary.
  Hon. Mrs Simcoe, his wife.
Pendennis, W. M. Thackeray, 1848–50.

Simkin, lawyer to the Aintree stewards. *National Velvet,* Enid Bagnold, 1935.

Simmonds, nephew of Jephthah Mottram. *The Three Taps,* R. A. Knox, 1927.

Simmons, parish beadle. *Sketches by Boz,* C. Dickens, 1836.

Simmons, commissionaire at *The Courier. Master Jim Probity,* F. Swinnerton, 1952.

Simmons, Miss, Lady Catherine Lasenby's maid. *The Admirable Crichton* (play), J. M. Barrie, 1902.

Simmons, Mr, housemaster.
  Laura, his wife.
Young Woodley (play), J. van Druten, 1928.

Simmons, Private. 'In the Matter of a Private' (s.s.), *Soldiers Three,* R. Kipling, 1888.

Simmons, Ned, enemy of Henry Little. *Put Yourself in his Place,* C. Reade, 1870.

Simmons, Verena, malicious gossip. *Holy Deadlock,* A. P. Herbert, 1934.

Simmons, William, van driver. *Martin Chuzzlewit,* C. Dickens, 1844.

Simms, Bill, a schoolboy. *The Channings,* Mrs Henry Wood, 1862.

Simms, Noble, friend of Rob Angus. *When a Man's Single,* J. M. Barrie, 1888.

Simnel, Lambert (hist.). *Perkin Warbeck* (play), John Ford, 1634

Simon, George, central character.
  Cora, Lena and **David.**
Counsellor-at-Law (play), Elmer Rice, 1931.

Simon, Paul, Parisian Jew, musician, m. Olga. *Through the Storm,* P. Gibbs, 1945.

Simon, Rachel, cousin of the Vinneys. *Non-Combatants and Others,* Rose Macaulay, 1916.

Simon of Penrhos.
  Beca, his wife.
'The Way of the Earth' (s.s.), *My People,* Caradoc Evans, 1915.

Simonides, King of Pentapolis.
  Thaisa, his daughter.
Pericles (play), W. Shakespeare.

Simonides, a merchant.
  Rachel, his dead wife.
  Esther, his daughter, m. Judah Hur.
Ben Hur, L. Wallace, 1880.

Simpkin, a cat. *The Tailor of Gloucester,* Beatrix Potter, 1903.

Simpkins, a cyclist. 'The Cat in the Bag,' *Lord Peter Views the Body,* Dorothy L. Sayers, 1928.

Simpkins, Colby, clerk to Sir Claude Mulhammer; son of Mrs Guzzard. *The Confidential Clerk* (play), T. S. Eliot, 1954.

Simple, Peter, naval officer.
  Ellen, his sister.
  Lord Privilege, their uncle.
Peter Simple, Captain Marryat, 1834.

Simple, Sloth and **Presumption,** encountered by Christian. *Pilgrim's Progress,* J. Bunyan, 1678 and 1684.

Simpson, page to Rawdon Crawley. *Vanity Fair,* W. M. Thackeray, 1847–8.

Simpson, Abner, village 'bad hat.'
  His wife and family.
Rebecca of Sunnybrook Farm, Kate D. Wiggin, 1903.

Simpson, George, general manager of theatre. *Enter a Murderer,* Ngaio Marsh, 1935.

Simpson, John, senior midshipman and bully, *Justinian.* The *Hornblower* series, C. S. Forester, 1937 onwards.

Simpson, Polly. *Love Among the Artists,* G. B. Shaw, 1900.

Simpson, Ruth, children's nurse, central character.
  Robert, her father.
  Her brothers and sisters:
    Joe.

Harry.
Bob.
Rose, m. Fred Meres.
Will.
Dorothy.
Simpson, E. Sackville-West, 1931.

Simpson, Tom, partner of Peter Jackson. *Peter Jackson, Cigar Merchant,* G. Frankau, 1919.

Sims, a pilot. *A Shabby Genteel Story,* W. M. Thackeray, 1840.

Sims, Sir Harry.
Emmy, his wife.
Kate, his ex-wife, typist.
The Twelve Pound Look (play), J. M. Barrie, 1910.

Sims, Sowerby, defending counsel for Martella Baring. *Enter Sir John,* Clemence Dane & Helen Simpson, 1929.

Simson, Tom, elopes with Piney Woods. 'The Outcasts of Poker Flat' (s.s.), *The Luck of Roaring Camp,* Bret Harte, 1868.

Sincere. *See* KNOWLEDGE.

Sinclair, central character and narrator. *No. 5 John Street,* R. Whiteing, 1902.

Sinclair, eminent solicitor. *The Protégé* (s.s.), W. B. Maxwell.

Sinclair, chief officer, *Altair. Gallions Reach,* H. M. Tomlinson, 1927.

Sinclair, Highland chief.
His daughter, m. Magnus Troil.
The Pirate, W. Scott, 1822.

Sinclair, Captain. *Settlers in Canada,* Captain Marryat, 1844.

Sinclair, Mrs, accomplice of Lovelace in kidnapping Clarissa. *Clarissa Harlowe,* S. Richardson, 1748.

Sinclair, Rev. Mr. *The Ministry of Fear,* Graham Greene, 1943.

Sinclair, Captain Aurelius, of the *Mohock. The Good Ship 'Mohock,'* W. Clark Russell, 1894.

Sinclair, Danielle (Dani), girl living with Fergus.
Mrs Dusty Sinclair, her mother, an ageing starlet.
Fergus, Brian Moore, 1971.

Sinclair, Esther, loved by Ewan Gray. *My Mortal Enemy,* Willa Cather, 1928.

Sinclair, Colonel Tom.
Mildred, his wife, *née* Frenton.
Lighten Our Darkness, R. Keable, 1927.

Sinding, Mrs, employer of Susan Daw. *I Live Under a Black Sun,* Edith Sitwell, 1937.

Singer, John, a dumb man. *The Heart is a Lonely Hunter,* Carson McCullers, 1940.

Singh, Hurree Jamset Ram, one of the Famous Five at Greyfriars. The *Billy Bunter* series, Frank Richards.

Singh, Rutton.
Attar, his brother.
'In the Presence' (s.s.), *A Diversity of Creatures,* R. Kipling, 1917.

Singleton, Adrian, friend of Dorian Gray. *The Picture of Dorian Gray,* O. Wilde, 1891.

Singleton, Mrs Anthea.
Harvey, her husband.
A Pride of Heroes, Peter Dickinson, 1969.

Singleton, Captain Harry. 'The Man who Lost his Likeness' (s.s.), *Short Stories,* Morley Roberts, 1928.

Singleton, Captain Robert, pirate, central character and narrator, m. Miss Walters. *Captain Singleton,* D. Defoe, 1720.

Singleton, Sam, painter. *Roderick Hudson,* H. James, 1875.

Sinico, Mrs.
Captain Sinico, her husband.
Mary, their daughter.
'A Painful Case' (s.s.), *The Dubliners,* James Joyce, 1914.

Sinker, Q.C. *Daniel Deronda,* George Eliot, 1876.

Sinnatus, a tetrarch. *The Cup* (play), Lord Tennyson, 1881.

Sinnier, Mary, m. Robin Finch.
Dorothy, her sister, m. John Quickshott.
The Porch, 1937, and *The Stronghold,* 1939, R. Church.

Sinnott, Mrs, old deaf and dumb owner of a Dublin hotel.
Eugene, her son.
Philomena, his wife.
Timothy John, their son.
Enid Mary Sinnott, daughter, m. Desmond Gregan.
Mrs Eckdorf in O'Neill's Hotel, William Trevor, 1969.

Sinquier, Sarah, an actress, daughter of a canon. *Caprice,* Ronald Firbank, 1917.

Sir Oliver, an old brown hunter. *Black Beauty,* Anna Sewell, 1877.

Sirena. *Sirena* (poem), M. Drayton.

Sitwell, Sir Jasper.
His wife.
'Mr Gilfil's Love Story,' *Scenes of Clerical Life*, George Eliot, 1857.

Sixsmith, Mrs Serephine, a scheming woman. *Caprice*, Ronald Firbank, 1917.

Skallagrim, Lambstail, ex-enemy, later Eric's henchman. *Eric Brighteyes*, H. Rider Haggard, 1891.

Skeggs, keeper of the slave depot in which Uncle Tom is sold. *Uncle Tom's Cabin*, Harriet B. Stowe, 1851.

Skellorn, Mr, rent collector.
Enoch, his son.
His daughter, m. Grant.
Hilda Lessways, Arnold Bennett, 1911.

Skelmersdale, village shopkeeper. 'Mr Skelmersdale in Fairyland' (s.s.), *Tales of the Unexpected*, 1923, and elsewhere, H. G. Wells.

Skene, Lieutenant Geoffrey.
His uncle.
The Spanish Farm trilogy, R. H. Mottram, 1924–7.

Skewton, Hon. Mrs, friend of Dombey, mother of Edith Granger. *Dombey and Son*, C. Dickens, 1848.

Skiffins, Miss.
Her brother.
Great Expectations, C. Dickens, 1861.

Skiggins, butcher, Grope's first employer. *Albert Grope*, F. O. Mann, 1931.

Skill, 'ancient and well-approved physician.' *Pilgrim's Progress*, J. Bunyan, 1678 and 1684.

Skimbleshanks, railway cat. *Old Possum's Book of Practical Cats* (poems), T. S. Eliot, 1939.

Skimlit, Mrs, elderly perennial visitor in Italian hotel. *They Winter Abroad*, T. H. White, 1932.

Skimmerhorn, rascally judge. *High Tor* (play), Maxwell Anderson, 1937.

Skimpole, Harold, dilettante and sponger.
His wife.
Arethusa, Kitty and **Laura,** their daughters.
Bleak House, C. Dickens, 1853.

Skinner, clerk at Hardie's Bank. *Hard Cash*, C. Reade, 1863.

Skinner, Dr, headmaster of Ernest Pontifex's school.
His daughter.
The Way of all Flesh, S. Butler, 1903.

Skinner, Mr and Mrs, in charge of Bensington's and Redwood's experimental farm, grandparents of Albert Caddles. *The Food of the Gods*, H. G. Wells, 1904.

Skinner, Captain Herbert ('The Spider'). *The Silver King* (play), H. A. Jones, 1882.

Skinner, Nicholas, cab-owner. *Black Beauty*, Anna Sewell, 1877.

Skionar, 'transcendental poet,' friend of MacCrotchet. *Crotchet Castle*, T. L. Peacock, 1831.

Skipps, Matthew, rag-and-bone man said to have been turned into a dog by Jennet Jourdemayne, the witch. *The Lady's Not For Burning* (play), Christopher Fry, 1948.

Skipton, Daniel, a writer, Knight of the Most Noble Order of SS. Cyril and Methodius. *The Unspeakable Skipton*, Pamela Hansford Johnson, 1959.

Skirving, Walter, 'bonnet laird.'
Ailie, his wife, *née* Gordon. Grandparents of Winifred Charteris.
The Lilac Sunbonnet, S. R. Crockett, 1894.

Skittles, Sir Barnet.
His son, pupil of Dr Blimber.
Dombey and Son, C. Dickens, 1848.

Skratch, violinist, protégé of Mrs Beelbrow. 'Mrs Beelbrow's Lions' (s.s.), *Miss Bracegirdle and Others*, Stacy Aumonier, 1923.

Skrebensky, Anton, son of exiled Polish baron, lover of Ursula Brangwen. *The Rainbow*, D. H. Lawrence, 1915.

Skreigh, clerk and precentor. *Guy Mannering*, W. Scott, 1815.

Skulany, General Jan. *See Naples and Die* (play), Elmer Rice, 1932.

Skully, Amy, m. Edward Sansom.
Randolph, her cousin.
Other Voices, Other Rooms, Truman Capote, 1948.

Skurliewhitter, Andrew, smooth-tongued villain employed by Lord Dalgarno. *The Fortunes of Nigel*, W. Scott, 1822.

Skylark, Mr, red-haired boatman. *David Copperfield,* C. Dickens, 1850.

Skylights, a pirate. *Peter Pan* (play), J. M. Barrie, 1904.

Skyresh, Bogolam, councillor, bitter enemy of Gulliver. *Gulliver's Travels,* J. Swift, 1726.

Skyrme, Robyn ('Ragged Robyn,' alias Eccles and Waygood), central character.
  Ned, his father.
  John and **Margaret,** his uncle and aunt, and his adoptive parents.
The Story of Ragged Robyn, O. Onions, 1945.

Slammekin, Mrs. *Polly* (comic opera), J. Gay, 1729.

Slammer, Dr, surgeon at Chatham Barracks. *Pickwick Papers,* C. Dickens, 1837.

Slane, Corporal, m. Jhansi McKenna. 'A Daughter of the Regiment' (s.s.), 1888, and elsewhere, *Plain Tales from the Hills,* R. Kipling.

Slane, Lady (Deborah), widow of Henry, Lord Slane (Family name Holland).
  Her children:
    Herbert.
      Mabel, his wife.
      Deborah, their grand-daughter.
      Richard, their grandson.
    Carrie.
      Roland, her husband.
    Charles.
    William.
      Lavinia, his wife.
    Kay.
    Edith.
All Passion Spent, V. Sackville-West, 1931.

Slaney, Mr, Lincoln's secretary (hist.). *Abraham Lincoln* (play), J. Drinkwater, 1918.

Slaney, Abe. 'The Dancing Men,' *The Return of Sherlock Holmes,* A. Conan Doyle, 1905.

Slang, Adolphus, theatrical manager. 'The Ravenswing,' *Men's Wives,* W. M. Thackeray, 1843.

Slattery, Emmie, and her family, poor whites; later m. Jonas Wilkerson. *Gone with the Wind,* Margaret Mitchell, 1936.

Sleaford, Lord, former husband of Lady Molly Jeavons. *A Question of Upbringing,* 1951 and others in *The Music of Time* series, Anthony Powell.

Sleary. 'The Post that Fitted' (poem), *Departmental Ditties,* R. Kipling, 1886.

Sleary, circus owner.
  Josephine, his daughter.
Hard Times, C. Dickens, 1854.

Slender, cousin of Shallow. *The Merry Wives of Windsor* (play), W. Shakespeare.

Slick, Hugo, coach-driver. *The Dark Horse,* Nat Gould.

Slickum, Negro servant of Bakharoff. *Grand Opera,* Vicki Baum, 1942.

Slide, Quintus, editor, the *People's Banner. Phineas Finn,* 1869, and elsewhere, A. Trollope.

Slightly, a member of Peter's band. *Peter Pan* (play), J. M. Barrie, 1904.

Slingsby, village schoolmaster. *Bracebridge Hall,* W. Irving, 1823.

Slingstone, Countess of. *Vanity Fair,* W. M. Thackeray, 1847–8.

Slinkton, Julius, murderer. *Hunted Down,* C. Dickens, 1860.

Slipper. *Some Experiences of an Irish R.M.,* Œ. Somerville & Martin Ross, 1899.

Slipslop, Mrs, waiting-woman. *Joseph Andrews,* H. Fielding, 1742.

Sloane, smooth-skinned young man, chief character. *Entertaining Mr Sloane* (play), Joe Orton, 1964.

Sloane, Mrs, meddling woman.
  Arthur, her husband, Liverpool docker.
Ebb and Flood, James Hanley, 1932.

Slocum, Jabez, odd-job man. *Timothy's Quest,* Kate D. Wiggin, 1896.

Slop, Dr, 'man-midwife.' *Tristram Shandy,* L. Sterne, 1767.

Slope, Rev. Obadiah, chaplain to Bishop Proudie. *Barchester Towers,* A. Trollope, 1857.

Sloper, Dr Austin, widower.
  Catherine, his daughter, eng. to Morris Townsend. *See also* LAVINIA PENNIMAN.
Washington Square, H. James, 1880.

'Sloppy,' workhouse child, assistant to Betty Higden. *Our Mutual Friend,* C. Dickens, 1865.

Sloth. *See* SIMPLE.

Slow-Solid, the tortoise. 'The Beginning of the Armadillos,' *Just So Stories,* R. Kipling, 1902.

Slowcoach, Verdant Green's tutor. *The Adventures of Mr Verdant Green,* C. Bede, 1853.

Sludge. *Mr Sludge the Medium* (poem), R. Browning.

Sludge, Dickie, 'queer, shambling, ill-made urchin,' guide to Edmund Tressilian.
His mother.
Kenilworth, W. Scott, 1821.

Slumkey, Hon. Samuel, 'Blue' Party candidate for Eatanswill. *Pickwick Papers,* C. Dickens, 1837.

Slurk, Editor, *Eatanswill Independent. Pickwick Papers,* C. Dickens, 1837.

Slush, Barnaby, novelist. *Death of a Hero,* R. Aldington, 1929.

Sly, Christopher, drunken tinker. *The Taming of the Shrew* (play), W. Shakespeare.

Slyme, Chevy, kinsman of old Martin Chuzzlewit. *Martin Chuzzlewit,* C. Dickens, 1844.

Smain, Arab servant of Count Anteoni.*The Garden of Allah,* R. S. Hichens, 1904.

Small, Mrs. *The Clever Ones* (play), A. Sutro, 1914.

Small, Abner. *Mourning becomes Electra* (play), E. O'Neill, 1931.

Small, Professor Beverly F., Peter Levi's adviser. *Birds of America,* Mary McCarthy, 1971.

Small, Jonathan, one of the Four. *See* ABDULLAH KHAN. *The Sign of Four,* A. Conan Doyle, 1890.

Small, Sam. *Captains All* (s.s.), and elsewhere, W. W. Jacobs.

Small, Sam.
His wife.
Judy, their daughter.
A Town like Alice, N. Shute, 1950.

Small, Septimus, m. Julia Forsyte. The *Forsyte* series, J. Galsworthy, 1906–33.

Small Porgies, a large animal. 'The Butterfly that Stamped,' *Just So Stories,* R. Kipling, 1902.

Smallbury, Jacob.
Billy, his son, both farm-hands.
Liddy, Billy's youngest daughter, servant-companion to Bathsheba Everdene.
Jacob's father, the maltster.
Far from the Madding Crowd, T. Hardy, 1874.

Smalls, Lily, Mrs Beynon's 'treasure.' *Under Milk Wood* (play), Dylan Thomas, 1954.

Smallsole, Master, H.M.S. *Harpy. Mr Midshipman Easy,* Captain Marryat, 1836.

Smallways, Bert, jack-of-all-trades, central character, m. Edna Bunthorne.
Tom, his brother, greengrocer.
Jessica, his wife.
Old Tom, their father.
War in the Air, H. G. Wells, 1908.

Smallweed, Joshua ('Grandfather'), blackmailer.
His wife.
Bartholomew, their grandson.
Judy, their grand-daughter.
Bleak House, C. Dickens, 1853.

Smatch, Sam, one-legged Negro fiddler. *True Blue,* W. H. G. Kingston.

Smeddum, tobacconist. *The Provost,* J. Galt, 1822.

Smee, pirate boatswain. *Peter Pan* (play), J. M. Barrie, 1904.

Smee, Andrew, portrait-painter. *The Newcomes,* 1853–5, and elsewhere, W. M. Thackeray.

Smeeth, Mr.
His wife.
Edna, their daughter.
George, their son.
Angel Pavement, J. B. Priestley, 1930.

Smerdon, George, Sarah, Sophie and **Teddy.** *The Farmer's Wife* (play), E. Phillpotts, 1924.

Smid, armourer. *Hypatia,* C. Kingsley, 1853.

Smiggers, Joseph, Perpetual Vice-President, Pickwick Club. *Pickwick Papers,* C. Dickens, 1837.

Smike, pupil of Squeers, son of Ralph Nickleby. *Nicholas Nickleby,* C. Dickens, 1839.

Smiler, the whale. 'How the Whale got his Throat,' *Just So Stories,* R. Kipling, 1902.

Smiling, Mrs Mary, friend of Flora Poste. *Cold Comfort Farm,* Stella Gibbons, 1932.

Smirke, curate and tutor.
Belinda, his wife.
Pendennis, W. M. Thackeray, 1848–50.

Smith. *The One Hundred Dollar Bill* (s.s.), Booth Tarkington, 1923.

Smith, half-pay lieutenant. *The*

Great Hoggarty Diamond, W. M. Thackeray, 1841.

Smith, Peter Burns's valet. *The Little Nugget*, P. G. Wodehouse, 1913.

Smith, Mrs, cousin of John Willoughby. *Sense and Sensibility*, Jane Austen, 1811.

Smith, Mrs, guardian of Clarissa in captivity.
Her husband.
Clarissa Harlowe, S. Richardson, 1748.

Smith, Mrs, one-time governess of Anne Elliot. *Persuasion*, Jane Austen, 1818.

Smith, Rev. Mr, 'Independent' minister, Milby. 'Janet's Repentance,' *Scenes of Clerical Life*, George Eliot, 1857.

Smith, Angela, Toby Barnard's secretary. *A Net for Venus*, David Garnett, 1959.

Smith, Bildad. 'The Sad Horn Blowers' (s.s.), *Horses and Men*, Sherwood Anderson, 1924.

Smith, 'Blackberry,' son of Shulie Galantry by her 2nd husband, half-brother to James Galantry. *Dance of the Years*, Margery Allingham, 1943.

Smith, Bob, Margate draper. *A Shabby Genteel Story*, W. M. Thackeray, 1840.

Smith, Bobette, air hostess. *The Long Time Growing Up*, John Pudney, 1971.

Smith, Caleb, of Lincoln's cabinet (hist.). *Abraham Lincoln* (play), J. Drinkwater, 1918.

Smith, Concepcion. *The Pretty Lady*, Arnold Bennett, 1918.

Smith, Culverton, 'The Dying Detective,' *His Last Bow*, A. Conan Doyle, 1917.

Smith, Rev. Cyril. *Magic* (play), G. K. Chesterton, 1913.

Smith, Freddy, m. Edna Whitebillet. *Antigua Penny Puce*, R. Graves, 1936.

Smith, Geoffrey. *An Englishman's Home* (play), Guy du Maurier, 1909.

Smith, George, robber. *Deacon Brodie* (play), W. E. Henley & R. L. Stevenson, 1892.

Smith, George, a rich, lonely man. *A Singular Man*, J. P. Donleavy, 1964.

Smith, Harold, ex-politician.
Harriet, his wife, *née* Sowerby.
Framley Parsonage, A. Trollope, 1861.

Smith, Harriet, protégée of Emma Woodhouse, m. Robert Martin. *Emma*, Jane Austen, 1816.

Smith, Harry (the 'I' of Sarnac's dream), m. (1) Hetty Marcus, (2) Milly Kimpton.
Fanny, his sister, elopes with Richard Newberry.
Ernest, his brother.
Mortimer, his father.
The Dream, H. G. Wells, 1924.

Smith, Innocent. *Manalive*, G. K. Chesterton, 1912.

Smith, Iseult, Eva's schoolteacher, m. Eric Arble. *Eva Trout*, Elizabeth Bowen, 1969.

Smith, Kitty. 'Moon of Other Days' (poem), *Departmental Ditties*, R. Kipling, 1886.

Smith, Lena, maid to the Lindsells, m. Kleinhans. *God's Stepchildren.* Sarah G. Millin, 1924.

Smith, Mary, central character and diarist.
Robert, her husband, agent to Lady Boxe.
Vicky, their daughter.
Robin, their son.
Diary of a Provincial Lady, E. M. Delafield, 1930.

Smith, Melissa (M'liss), central character. 'M'liss' (s.s.), *The Luck of Roaring Camp*, Bret Harte, 1868.

Smith, Mordecai, boat-owner. *The Sign of Four*, A. Conan Doyle, 1890.

Smith, Purdy, m. Tilly Ocock, *née* Beamish.
Aurelia, his daughter.
The Fortunes of Richard Mahony, H. H. Richardson, 1917–30.

Smith, Sam, the host. *Shall We Join the Ladies?* (play), J. M. Barrie, 1921.

Smith, Septimus Warren.
Lucrezia, his wife.
Mrs Dalloway, Virginia Woolf, 1925.

Smith, Stephen Fitzmaurice, eng. to Elfride Swancourt.
John, his father.
Jane, his mother.
A Pair of Blue Eyes, T. Hardy, 1873.

Smith, Violet. 'The Solitary Cyclist,' *The Return of Sherlock Holmes*, A. Conan Doyle, 1905.

Smith, Wayland, Edmund Tressilian's confidential servant and old playfellow of Dickie Sludge. *Kenilworth,* W. Scott, 1821.

Smith, William Abel, American presidential candidate visiting Haiti.
His wife, vegetarian and idealist.
The Comedians, Graham Greene, 1966.

Smith, Winston, central character.
Katharine, his wife.
1984, G. Orwell, 1949.

Smithers, fellow student at South Kensington with Lewisham. *Love and Mr Lewisham,* H. G. Wells, 1900.

Smithers. *Sinister Street,* C. Mackenzie, 1913.

Smithers, solicitor. *The Great Hoggarty Diamond,* W. M. Thackeray, 1841.

Smithie, Persian robe designer and maker, cousin and employer of Marion Ramboat. *Tono Bungay,* H. G. Wells, 1909.

Smoit, King, a ghost. *Jurgen,* J. B. Cabell, 1921.

Smoke, hunter on *Ghost. The Sea Wolf,* Jack London, 1904.

Smolensk, Baronne, Parisian boarding-house keeper. *The Adventures of Philip,* W. M. Thackeray, 1861–1862.

Smollett, Captain. *Treasure Island,* R. L. Stevenson, 1882.

Smollett, Dr Fabian.
Florence, his wife.
A House and its Head, Ivy Compton-Burnett, 1935.

Smooth, Captain Dudley. *Money* (play), Lord Lytton, 1840.

Smorltork, Count, 'literary man.' *Pickwick Papers,* C. Dickens, 1837.

Smotherwell, Stephen, executioner. *The Fair Maid of Perth,* W. Scott, 1828.

Smug, a smith of Edmonton. *The Merry Devil of Edmonton* (play), Anon.

Smyth, Doreen, friend of Doris Josser.
Her mother.
London Belongs to Me, N. Collins, 1945.

Smyth, Sir Japhet, throat specialist. *The Face of Clay,* H. A. Vachell, 1906.

Smythe, Carvell. *The One Before,* Barry Pain, 1902.

Smythe, Miss 'Chiffon,' friend of Vera Fanshawe. *Act of God,* F. Tennyson Jesse, 1936.

Smythe, Isadore. 'The Invisible Man,' *The Innocence of Father Brown,* G. K. Chesterton, 1911.

Smythe, Richard, a Rationalist. *The End of the Affair,* Graham Greene, 1951.

Snaffle, a livery-stable keeper. 'The Ravenswing,' *Men's Wives,* W. M. Thackeray, 1843.

Snagsby, law stationer. *Bleak House,* C. Dickens, 1853.

Snaith, Alderman Anthony, rich business man. *South Riding,* Winifred Holtby, 1936.

Snake. *The School for Scandal* (play), R. B. Sheridan, 1777.

Snap, Laetitia, pickpocket, wife of Jonathan Wild. *Jonathan Wild,* Henry Fielding, 1793.

Snarleyow, an artillery horse. 'Snarleyow' (poem), *Barrack-room Ballads,* R. Kipling, 1892.

Snawley, stepfather of two boys left with Squeers. *Nicholas Nickleby,* C. Dickens, 1839.

Sneer. *The Critic* (play), R. B. Sheridan, 1779.

Sneerwell, Lady. *The School for Scandal* (play), R. B. Sheridan, 1777.

Sneezum, Hartley.
His wife.
Alicia, their daughter, m. Sydney Bartleby.
A Suspension of Mercy, Patricia Highsmith, 1965.

Snell, bosun's mate, *Terrible. True Blue,* W. H. G. Kingston.

Snell, John, landlord of the Rainbow. *Silas Marner,* George Eliot, 1861.

Snell, Samuel, disreputable old lawyer and indigo smuggler. *Pendennis,* W. M. Thackeray, 1848–1850.

Snellaby, Sir Joseph, alchemist. *Micah Clarke,* A. Conan Doyle, 1889.

Snevellici, Miss, leading lady in Crummles's theatrical company. *Nicholas Nickleby,* C. Dickens, 1839.

Snobb, The Hon., friend of Ralph Nickleby. *Nicholas Nickleby,* C. Dickens, 1839.

Snodgrass, Augustus, member of the

Pickwick Club, m. Emily Wardle. *Pickwick Papers*, C. Dickens, 1837.

Snopes, Flem, president of bank in Jefferson, Mississippi, m. Eula Varner.

Linda Snopes Kohl, Eula's daughter.

Mink Snopes, murderer, Flem's cousin.

Montgomery Ward Snopes, pornographer.

The Snopes trilogy, William Faulkner, 1940–59.

Snopes, Byron, writer of indecent love letters.

Sartoris, William Faulkner, 1929.

Snopes, Ab, horse trader.

The Unvanquished, William Faulkner, 1938.

Snout, a tinker. *A Midsummer Night's Dream* (play), W. Shakespeare.

Snow (alias Henty), lorry driver. *The Loss of the 'Jane Vosper,'* F. Wills Crofts, 1936.

Snow, Mrs, chronic invalid and grumbler.

Milly, her daughter.

Pollyanna, Eleanor H. Porter, 1913.

Snow, Henry (alias Scarlett), friend of Sylvia Scarlett.

Juliette, his wife.

His six stepdaughters.

Sylvia Scarlett, C. Mackenzie, 1918.

Snowe, Lucy, companion to Paulina Home, central character and narrator. *Villette*, Charlotte Brontë, 1853.

Snowe, Nicholas, farmer.

Faith, his daughter.

Lorna Doone, R. D. Blackmore, 1869.

Snubbin, Sergeant, barrister briefed for Mrs Bardell. *Pickwick Papers*, C. Dickens, 1837.

Snug, a joiner. *A Midsummer Night's Dream* (play), W. Shakespeare.

Soames, Enoch, an unsuccessful poet. *Seven Men*, Max Beerbohm, 1919.

Soames, Quentin. *Landscape with Figures*, R. Fraser, 1925

Sobek, m. Kait, murdered by Yahmose. *Death Comes as the End*, Agatha Christie, 1945.

Sobieska, Princess Clementina, daughter of the King of Poland (hist.). *Clementina*, A. E. W. Mason, 1901.

Softly, Rev. Knox, m. Olivia Kennyfeck. *Roland Cashel*, C. Lever, 1850.

Sohemus. *Herod* (play), S. Phillips, 1900.

Sohrab. Tartar warrior, son of Rustum. *Sohrab and Rustum* (poem), M. Arnold, 1853.

Soldesby, Dr Istvan, Hungarian torturer. *Trial by Terror*, P. Gallico, 1952.

Sole, ex-public schoolboy. *The Old Boys*, William Trevor, 1964.

Solent, Wolf, history master.

Gerda, his wife, *née* Torp.

Ann Solent, his mother.

Wolf Solent, J. C. Powys, 1929.

Solinus, Duke of Ephesus. *A Comedy of Errors* (play), W. Shakespeare.

Solmes, Lord Etherington's confidential servant and a villainous traitor. *St Ronan's Well*, W. Scott, 1824.

Solmes, Roger, suitor of Clarissa. *Clarissa Harlowe*, S. Richardson, 1748.

Soltyk, Louis, a Polish artist in Paris. *Tarr*, Wyndham Lewis, 1918.

Sombremere, Lord.

Amy, his wife.

Lychnis, their daughter, m. Ambrose Herbert.

Landscape with Figures, R. Fraser, 1925.

Somerford, Harry, lover of Fanny Hooper and father of her daughter Evelyn.

His mother.

Kate, his sister.

Fanny by Gaslight, M. Sadleir, 1940.

Somers, head of the school. *St Winifred's*, F. W. Farrar, 1862.

Somers, Mrs. 'interested in bees.' *Diary of a Provincial Lady*, E. M. Delafield, 1930.

Somers, Alfred, painter, m. Mrs Pine-Avon. *The Well Beloved*, T. Hardy, 1897.

Somers, Etty, cousin of the Curtises. *Invitation to the Waltz*, Rosamond Lehmann, 1932.

Somers, Richard Lovat, English poet visiting Australia.

Harriet, his wife.

Kangaroo, D. H. Lawrence, 1923.

Somers, Willie. *Spring Cleaning* (play), F. Lonsdale, 1925.

Somerset, Earl of (hist.). *Henry the Sixth* (play), W. Shakespeare.

Somerset, George, m. Paula Power.
His father.
A Laodicean, T. Hardy, 1881.

Somerton, Mr. 'The Treasure of Abbot Thomas' (s.s.), *Ghost Stories of an Antiquary*, M. R. James, 1910.

Somerville, Miss, cousin and companion of Lady Drew. *Tono Bungay*, H. G. Wells, 1909.

Sommerville, Mr, advocate. *The Highland Widow*, W. Scott, 1827.

Sone, Captain, General Mead's aide-de-camp. *Abraham Lincoln* (play), J. Drinkwater, 1918.

Sonnaz, Duchesse de (Jeanne), mistress of Sergius Zouroff.
Paul, her husband.
Their children.
Moths, Ouida, 1880.

Sonntag. 'The Luck Piece' (s.s.), *From Place to Place*, Irvin S. Cobb, 1920.

Sophy, Great-Aunt, *née* Channing, wife of Great-uncle Peter, yeoman farmer. 'The County Wench' (s.s.), *Last Recollections of My Uncle Charles*, N. Balchin, 1954.

Soranzo, nobleman.
Vasques, his servant.
'Tis Pity She's A Whore (play), John Ford, *c.* 1624.

Sordo. *For Whom the Bell Tolls*, E. Hemingway, 1940.

Sorel, Gottfried.
Johanna, his wife.
Hugh, his brother.
Christina, Hugh's daughter, central character, m. Gottfried Adlerstein.
The Dove in the Eagle's Nest, Charlotte M. Yonge, 1866.

Sorgan, Mr. *Tom Tiddler's Ground*, E. Shanks, 1934.

Sorrel, Hester ('Hetty'), betrayed by Arthur Donnithorne. *Adam Bede*, George Eliot, 1859.

Sorrell, Christopher ('Kit'), central character, m. Molly Pentreath.
Captain Stephen, his father, odd-man, the Angel Hotel, later manager of the Pelican, m. (2) Fanny Garland.
Dora, his div. mother. *See* DUGGAN.
Sorrell and Son, W. Deeping, 1925.

Sosia, a slave. *The Last Days of Pompeii*, Lord Lytton, 1834.

Sotheby, Emmanuel, village grocer.
His wife.
Rachel, their daughter.
Richard, their son, an artist in Paris.
Go She Must!, David Garnett, 1927.

Sothill, Mrs Barbara, sister of Basil Seal.
Freddy, her husband.
Put Out More Flags, E. Waugh, 1942.

Sotomayor de Soto, Don Guzman, prisoner of Amyas Leigh, lover and betrayer of Rose Salterne. *Westward Ho!*, C. Kingsley, 1855.

Soulis, Rev. Murdoch, Minister of Balweary. 'Thrawn Janet' (s.s.), *The Merry Men*, R. L. Stevenson, 1887.

Souss, Richard.
Margaret, his wife.
Spring Cleaning (play), F. Lonsdale, 1925.

South, Dr. *Of Human Bondage*, W. S. Maugham, 1915.

South, John, villager.
Marty, his daughter.
The Woodlanders, T. Hardy, 1887.

Southam, Paul. *Saint's Day*, J. Whiting, 1951.

Southby, Allen, Ph.D. *Wickford Point*, J. P. Marquand, 1939.

Southdown, Earl of (Clement William) (Family name Sheepshanks).
His daughters:
Emily, m. Rev. Silas Hornblower.
Jane, m. Pitt Crawley.
Matilda, dowager countess, his mother.
Vanity Fair, W. M. Thackeray, 1847–8.

Southwark, Duke of (Tim), one-time friend of Christina. *The Fortunes of Christina McNab*, S. Macnaughtan, 1901.

Southwold, James, Royalist traitor. *Children of the New Forest*, Captain Marryat, 1847.

Sowerberry, parochial undertaker to whom Oliver is apprenticed. *Oliver Twist*, C. Dickens, 1838.

Sowerby, Nathaniel, M.P., spendthrift friend of Mark Robarts.
Harriet, his sister, m. Harold Smith.
Framley Parsonage, A. Trollope, 1861.

Sowerby, Lieutenant William. 'A Treaty of Peace,' *Donovan Pasha*, Gilbert Parker, 1902.

Sownds, beadle. *Dombey and Son*, C. Dickens, 1848.

Spaconia, daughter of Lygones. *A King and No King* (play), Beaumont & Fletcher, 1611.

Spade, Sam, detective. *The Maltese Falcon*, Dashiell Hammett, 1930.

Spain, King of. *The Spanish Tragedy* (play), T. Kyd, 1594.

Spalding, American Minister at Florence, visiting London.
 Carry and **Livvy,** his daughters.
He Knew He Was Right, A. Trollope, 1869.

Spandrell, critic. *Point Counter Point*, Aldous Huxley, 1928.

Spangler, manager, telegraph office. *The Human Comedy*, W. Saroyan, 1943.

Spank, an 'approver.' *Lorna Doone*, R. D. Blackmore, 1869.

Spanner, Agnes, lifelong friend of Rosamund Fraser. *Chatterton Square*, E. H. Young, 1947.

Spark, Timothy, cousin of Mrs Pettican. *Mehalah*, S. Baring-Gould, 1880.

Sparkes, Polly, programme seller, niece of Mrs Clover, m. Chris Parish.
 Ebenezer, her father, waiter.
The Town Traveller, G. Gissing, 1898.

Sparkler, Edmund, son of Mrs Merdle by her 1st husband, m. Fanny Dorrit. *Little Dorrit*, C. Dickens, 1857.

Sparks, London jeweller. *The Virginians*, W. M. Thackeray, 1857–9.

Sparling, Madeleine, headmistress, Hosiers' School, m. Sidney Carton. The *Barsetshire* series, Angela Thirkell, 1933 onwards.

Sparowe, Phyllyp, bird slain at Carowe. *The Boke of Phyllyp Sparowe*, John Skelton, *c.* 1508.

Sparrow, Jeremy, preacher. *By Order of the Company*, Mary Johnston, 1900.

Sparser, friend of Clyde Griffiths. *An American Tragedy*, T. Dreiser, 1925.

Sparsit, Mrs, housekeeper to Bounderby. *Hard Times*, C. Dickens, 1854.

Spaulding, Vincent. *See* John Clay.

Spaur, Father, priest to Countess Luxstein. *The Courtship of Morrice Buckler*, A. E. W. Mason, 1896.

Spavin, friend of Foker. *Pendennis*, W. M. Thackeray, 1848–50.

Spear, Dave.
 Persephone, his wife.
A Glastonbury Romance, J. C. Powys, 1932.

Spearing, Dame Elaine. *The Tale of a Trumpet* (poem), T. Hood.

Spearman, Rosanna, second housemaid to Lady Verinder. *The Moonstone*, W. Collins, 1868.

Speed, a clownish servant. *Two Gentlemen of Verona* (play), W. Shakespeare.

Speed, James, Imperial Military Police. *The Maids of Paradise*, R. W. Chambers, 1903.

Speers, agent of Sir Brian Newcome. *The Newcomes*, W. M. Thackeray, 1853–5.

Spelman, Mrs Rose, aunt of Jill Watson. *The Herb of Grace*, Eliza beth Goudge, 1948.

Spence, Corporal Colin, central character. *The Immortal Sergeant*, J. Brophy, 1942.

Spence, Miss Janet. 'The Gioconda Smile' (s.s.), *Mortal Coils*, A. Huxley, 1922.

Spencer, legal friend of George Warrington. *The Virginians*, W. M. Thackeray, 1857–9.

Spencer, Dr. *The Daisy Chain*, 1856, and elsewhere, Charlotte M. Yonge.

Spencer, Janey ('Grizzle'), m. Joseph Vance.
 Randall, her father.
 Her mother.
 Sarita, her sister, m. Alison Farquharson.
Joseph Vance, W. de Morgan, 1906.

Spencer, Sir John.
 Sybil, his wife.
 Rollo, their son.
 Marigold, their daughter.
Invitation to the Waltz, Rosamond Lehmann, 1932.

Spencer, Tom, Digby's friend. *Digby Grand*, G. Whyte-Melville, 1853.

Spenlow, Dora, m. David Copperfield.
 Her father, attorney.
 Her aunts.
David Copperfield, C. Dickens, 1850.

Spenser-Smith, Mrs Lilla, cousin of Hannah Mole.
Ernest, her husband.
Miss Mole, E. H. Young, 1930.

Sperling, James U., mining magnate.
His children:
James U. jnr.
Madeline, in love with Archie Goodwin.
Gwenn.
The Second Confession, R. Stout, 1950.

Sperrit, Connie, m. Frankwell Midmore.
Her father, lawyer.
'My Son's Wife' (s.s.), *A Diversity of Creatures,* R. Kipling, 1917.

Spettigue, Stephen, solicitor.
Amy, his niece.
Charley's Aunt (play), Brandon Thomas, 1892.

Sphaeros of Borysthenes, stoic philosopher, tutor of King Kleomenes III of Sparta. *The Corn King and The Spring Queen,* Naomi Mitchison, 1931.

Spicer, member of Pinkie's gang. *Brighton Rock,* Graham Greene, 1938.

Spicer, Captain. *Incomparable Bellairs,* A. & E. Castle, 1904.

Spicer, Captain, card-sharper and swindler. *Frank Fairlegh,* F. E. Smedley, 1850.

Spicer, Lieutenant. *Quality Street* (play), J. M. Barrie, 1902.

Spidel, enemy of Princess Saskia. *Huntingtower,* J. Buchan, 1922.

Spiel, Karl, central character, eldest child; brother of **Marta, Elsa, Fritz, Peter, Berta, Gretchen, Hans.**
Their father and mother.
The Heart of a Child, Phyllis Bottome, 1940.

Spilkins, landlord of the Cross Keys, Treby Magna. *Felix Holt,* George Eliot, 1866.

Spinachi, Lord.
His sons and daughters.
The Rose and the Ring, W. M. Thackeray, 1855.

Spinfield, Kezia. *Melloney Holtspur* (play), J. Masefield, 1922.

Spink, Captain A. S. 'The One and Only Spink' (s.s.), *Short Stories,* Morley Roberts, 1928.

Spinks, Elias. *Under the Greenwood Tree,* T. Hardy, 1872.

Spiridion, Lord of Goltres, scholar. *The Forest Lovers,* M. Hewlett, 1898.

Splint, shipbuilder. *Barry Lyndon,* W. M. Thackeray, 1844.

Splinter, First Lieutenant, *Breeze. Tom Cringle's Log,* M. Scott, 1836.

Splinters, Negro boy. *The Iron Pirate,* M. Pemberton, 1893.

Spode, a journalist. 'The Tillotson Banquet' (s.s.), *Mortal Coils,* A. Huxley, 1922.

Spoffard, Henry. *Gentlemen Prefer Blondes,* Anita Loos, 1925.

Spong, Dominic, friend of Ernest Bellamy, m. Camilla Christy as 3rd husband. *Men and Wives,* Ivy Compton-Burnett, 1931.

Sponge, Soapey, cockney sportsman, m. Lucy Glitters, actress. *Mr Sponge's Sporting Tour,* R. S. Surtees, 1853.

Spooner, H. Tidd, rich young 'Oxford man.' *The Pottleton Legacy,* Albert Smith, 1849.

Spots, the leopard. 'How the Leopard got his Spots,' *Just So Stories,* R. Kipling, 1902.

Spottletoes, Mrs, niece of Martin Chuzzlewit.
Her husband.
Martin Chuzzlewit, C. Dickens, 1844.

Spragg, Undine, central character, m. (1) Elmer Moffat, (2) Ralph Marvell, (3) Marquis of Chelles, (4) Elmer Moffat.
Her mother.
The Custom of the Country, Edith Wharton, 1913.

Sprague, Dr, senior physician. *Middlemarch,* George Eliot, 1871–2.

Spratt, universally hated manager of Spraxton Colliery. *Felix Holt,* George Eliot, 1866.

Spray, 'independent' minister, St Oggs. *The Mill on the Floss,* George Eliot, 1860.

Sprent, Solomon, old sailor. *Micah Clarke,* A. Conan Doyle, 1889.

Sprickett, Elsie, charwoman, later maid to the Earlforwards, m. Joe. *Riceyman Steps,* 1923, and *Elsie and the Child,* 1924, Arnold Bennett.

Sprigge, Algernon. *The Sport of Kings* (play), Ian Hay, 1924.

Spring, Sam, 'betting man.' *Jor-*

rocks's Jaunts and Jollities, R. S. Surtees, 1838.

Springett, Ralph. 'The Wrong Thing,' *Rewards and Fairies*, R. Kipling, 1910.

Springrove, Edward, m. Cytherea Graye.
 John, his father.
 His mother.
 Desperate Remedies, T. Hardy, 1871.

Springster, Julia, early lover of Judge Gaskony, m. (1) Roy Pellagrin, (2) Phil Brown. *The Judge's Story*, C. Morgan, 1947.

Sprot, George. *Landscape with Figures*, R. Fraser, 1925.

Sprowle, Colonel and Mrs. *Elsie Venner*, O. W. Holmes, 1861.

Spurrier, Major-General Sir Ralph, Commander-in-Chief, Madras. *The Newcomes*, W. M. Thackeray, 1853–5.

Spurstow, a doctor. 'At the End of the Passage' (s.s.), *Life's Handicap*, R. Kipling, 1891.

Squales, Henry, m. Mrs Jan Byl. *London Belongs to Me*, N. Collins, 1945.

Squallop, Mrs, Tittlebat Titmouse's landlady. *Ten Thousand a Year*, S. Warren, 1839.

Square, Thomas. *Tom Jones*, H. Fielding, 1749.

Squeers, Wackford, schoolmaster, of Dotheboys Hall.
 His wife.
 Fanny, their daughter.
 Young Wackford, their son.
 Nicholas Nickleby, C. Dickens, 1839.

Squercum, Longstaffe, attorney. *The Way We Live Now*, A. Trollope, 1875.

Squilling, Rev. Mr, minister of Chapel of Ancient Truth.
 Georgina and **Martha,** his daughters.
 Albert Grope, F. O. Mann, 1931.

Squint, Lawyer. *A Citizen of the World*, O. Goldsmith, 1762.

Squintum, Dr. *The Minor* (play), S. Foote, 1760.

Squire, Bob.
 Dora, his wife, formerly mistress of Juan Motley.
 Juan in America, E. Linklater, 1931.

Squires, captain of bell-hops. *An American Tragedy*, T. Dreiser, 1925.

Squod, Phil, employed by Mr George. *Bleak House*, C. Dickens, 1853.

Stack, Virginian minister. *The Virginians*, W. M. Thackeray, 1857–9.

Stack, Henry, Wilfrid Desert's confidential servant. *Flowering Wilderness*, J. Galsworthy, 1932.

Stackard, Tom, friend of Sylvester Clayton. *Cricket in Heaven*, G. Bullett, 1949.

Stackpole, Henrietta, American newspaper correspondent. *The Portrait of a Lady*, Henry James, 1881.

Stadger, Captain, a sadist. *Eustace Chisholm and the Works*, James Purdy, 1968.

Staffeln, Melchior, Alpine guide. *The Crystal Hunters*, G. Manville Fenn.

Stafford, M.P. *Diary of a Late Physician*, S. Warren, 1832.

Stafford, Tom, suitor of Kitty Bellairs. *Incomparable Bellairs*, A. & E. Castle, 1904.

Stagg, owner of cellar near Barbican. *Barnaby Rudge*, C. Dickens, 1841.

Stagg, Bill, tobacco smuggler. *The Hole in the Wall*, A. Morrison, 1902.

Stahr, Monroe, 'wonder boy' head of great film studio. *The Last Tycoon*, F. Scott Fitzgerald, 1941.

Stainer, Mark, publisher. *Thursday Afternoons*, Monica Dickens, 1945.

Stainford, Aubrey, a forger. *Swan Song*, J. Galsworthy, 1928.

Stalkenberg, Baron von.
 Count Otto, his brother.
 East Lynne, Mrs Henry Wood, 1861.

Stalky. *See* ARTHUR CORKRAN.

Staminer, Dr, friend of Mr Ingleside. *Mr Ingleside*, E. V. Lucas, 1910.

Stanbury, Hugh, close friend of Louis Trevelyan.
 His mother.
 Priscilla and **Dorothy,** his sisters.
 Jemima, his aunt, of the county set, who discards him.
 He Knew He Was Right, A. Trollope, 1869.

Standing, Sir Miles. *Ten Minute Alibi* (play), A. Armstrong, 1933.

Standish, lawyer. *Middlemarch*, George Eliot, 1871–2.

Standish, Lady. *A Bath Comedy*, 1899, and *Incomparable Bellairs*, 1904, A. & E. Castle.

Standish, Lady Laura, Lord Brentford's daughter, m. Robert Kennedy.
Charles, her cousin.
Phineas Finn, 1869, and elsewhere, A. Trollope.

Standish, Captain Miles, middle-aged widower.
Rose, his late wife.
The Courtship of Miles Standish (poem), H. W. Longfellow.

Standish, Peter, eng. to Marjorie Frant, and in the past to Kate Pettigrew; loves Helen Pettigrew. *Berkeley Square* (play), J. L. Balderston, 1926.

Stane, Mr, undesirable friend of George Paris, murdered by him. *Judith Paris,* Hugh Walpole, 1931.

Stanforth, Colonel Edward. *The Heir,* V. Sackville-West, 1922.

Stangerson, Joseph. *A Study in Scarlet,* A. Conan Doyle, 1887.

Stangrave, American, m. Marie le Cordifiamma. *Two Years Ago,* C. Kingsley, 1857.

Stanhope, Dennis, Company Commander, central character. *Journey's End* (play), R. C. Sherriff, 1928.

Stanhope, Rev. Vesey, D.D., Prebendary, Barchester.
His children:
Ethelbert.
Charlotte.
Madeline, m. Neroni.
Barchester Towers, A. Trollope, 1857.

Staniforth, Hugh, Olive Paxton's leading man. *The Flower Girls,* Clemence Dane, 1952.

Stanley, head of the school. *Tell England,* E. Raymond, 1922.

Stanley, Lord. *Richard the Third* (play), W. Shakespeare.

Stanley, Major-General.
His daughters:
Mabel, m. Frederic.
Kate.
Isabel, and many others.
The Pirates of Penzance (comic opera), Gilbert & Sullivan, 1880.

Stanley, Ann Veronica, central character, m. Godwin Capes.
Peter, her father.
Jim, Roddy, Alice and **Gwen,** her brothers and sisters.
Mollie, her aunt.
Ann Veronica, H. G. Wells, 1909.

Stanley, Elsa.
Frank, her husband, shoemaker.
Arthur ('Otto') and **Charles,** their sons.
Magnolia Street, L. Golding, 1932.

Stanley, George, fur-trader.
His wife.
Edith, their daughter.
Ungava, R. M. Ballantyne, 1857.

Stanley, Rose, schoolgirl, member of 'the Brodie set.' *The Prime of Miss Jean Brodie,* Muriel Spark, 1961.

Stanley, Sir William, Lord Chamberlain. *Perkin Warbeck* (play), John Ford, 1634.

Stanly, Glen, Pierre Glendinning's cousin. *Pierre,* Herman Melville, 1852.

Stanner, Sergeant. *The Trumpet Major,* T. Hardy, 1880.

Stannidge, landlord.
His wife.
The Mayor of Casterbridge, T. Hardy, 1886.

Stant, Charlotte, friend of Maggie Verver, who marries Maggie's father, Adam. *The Golden Bowl,* Henry James, 1904.

Stanton, Adam, famous surgeon.
Anne, his sister, social worker.
All The King's Men, Robert Penn Warren, 1946.

Stanton, Charles. *Dangerous Corner* (play), J. B. Priestley, 1932.

Stanton, Edwin, of Lincoln's Cabinet (hist.). *Abraham Lincoln* (play), J. Drinkwater, 1918.

Staples, Lawrence, chief warder, Kenilworth Castle. *Kenilworth,* W. Scott, 1821.

Stapleton (real name Baskerville).
His wife, passing as his sister.
The Hound of the Baskervilles, A. Conan Doyle, 1902.

Starbottle, Colonel, 'gentleman of the old school,' m. Clara Tretherick. 'An Episode of Fiddletown' (s.s.), 1868, and elsewhere, *The Luck of Roaring Camp,* Bret Harte.

Starbuck, chief mate of the *Pequod.* *Moby Dick,* H. Melville, 1851.

Stareleigh, Justice, judge in Bardell v. Pickwick. *Pickwick Papers,* C. Dickens, 1837.

Stark, Arabella. *An American Tragedy,* T. Dreiser, 1925.

Stark, Cecil, of Vermont, m. Grace Malherb. *The American Prisoner,* E. Phillpotts, 1904.

Stark, Colonel Douglas, later Brigadier-General.
Alice, his wife.
Peter Jackson, Cigar Merchant, G. Frankau, 1919.

Stark, Colonel Lysander. 'The Engineer's Thumb,' *The Adventures of Sherlock Holmes,* A. Conan Doyle, 1892.

Stark, Willie, Governor of an American state.
Lucy, his wife, an ex-schoolteacher.
All The King's Men, Robert Penn Warren, 1946.

Starkadder, Judith.
Amos, her husband.
Their children:
Reuben.
Seth.
Elfine, m. Richard Hawk-Monitor.
Old Mrs Starkadder (Aunt Ada Doom).
Other relatives: **Micah, Urk, Ezra, Caraway, Harkaway, Luke, Mark** and their wives.
Rennett, m. Mybug.
Cold Comfort Farm, Stella Gibbons, 1932.

Starke, Sir Philip, wealthy recluse. *By The Pricking of My Thumbs,* Agatha Christie, 1968.

Starkey, Gentleman, a pirate. *Peter Pan* (play), J. M. Barrie, 1904.

Starkey, Miss. *The Title* (play), Arnold Bennett, 1918.

Starlight, cattle thief. *Robbery under Arms,* R. Boldrewood, 1888.

'Starlight Tom,' head of poaching gang. *Bracebridge Hall,* W. Irving, 1823.

Starr, Mirabell, m. Francis Herries as 2nd wife.
Jane, her mother.
Harry, her lover, killed by Anthony Thawn.
Rogue Herries, Hugh Walpole, 1930.

Starter, Miss Juliana, lady in waiting to royalty. *Before Lunch,* Angela Thirkell, 1939.

Startop, friend of Philip Pirrip. *Great Expectations,* C. Dickens, 1861.

Starveling, a tailor. *A Midsummer Night's Dream* (play), W. Shakespeare.

Starwick, Francis, friend of Eugene Gant. *Of Time and the River,* T. Wolfe, 1935.

Stasia, a slavey (The Slut). *The Passing of the Third Floor Back* (play), J. K. Jerome, 1910.

Staunas of a thousand faces, Pole who assumes many identities, including that of George Oliphant. *Thin Air,* John Pudney, 1961.

Staunton, George (alias Robertson), later Sir George, accomplice of Andrew Wilson, m. Effie Deans.
'The Whistler,' their son.
Rev. Robert, his father.
The Heart of Midlothian, W. Scott, 1818.

Staupitz, German swashbuckler. *The Duke's Motto,* J. H. McCarthy, 1908.

Staveley, Mr and Mrs, friend of the Gracedieus. *The Legacy of Cain,* W. Collins, 1889.

Staveley, Dick.
Sir John Staveley, his father.
Lady Staveley, his mother.
The Shrimp and the Anemone, L. P. Hartley, 1944.

Stedge, Nurse, later Matron, children's home. *Children of the Archbishop,* N. Collins, 1951.

Stedman, Ruth, Quaker friend of the Hallidays. *Uncle Tom's Cabin,* Harriet B. Stowe, 1851.

Steele, Anne.
Lucy, her sister, m. Robert Ferrars.
Sense and Sensibility, Jane Austen, 1811.

Steele, Charles, artist. *Jacob's Room,* Virginia Woolf, 1922.

Steele, Christie, landlady, the Treddles Arms. *The Highland Widow,* W. Scott, 1827.

Steele, Ernest. *Spring Cleaning* (play), F. Lonsdale, 1925.

Steeltrap, Sir Simon, J.P., M.P for Crouching Curtown. *Crotchet Castle,* T. L. Peacock, 1831.

Steene, veterinary surgeon, Grimworth.
His wife.
Brother Jacob, George Eliot, 1864.

Steenson, Steenie, servant and friend of Sir Henry Redgauntlet, grandfather of Wandering Willie. *Redgauntlet,* W. Scott, 1824.

Steer, Eva.
Dora, her sister.
Their father.
The Promise of May (play), Lord Tennyson, 1882.

Steerforth, Captain. *The Ordeal of Gilbert Pinfold*, Evelyn Waugh, 1957.

Steerforth, James, head boy at Dr Creakle's, friend of David, and seducer of Em'ly Peggotty.
His mother.
David Copperfield, C. Dickens 1850.

Steerforth, John Adair, a dead R.A.F. Flight Lieutenant.
Faith, his daughter, who now calls herself Jones.
The Labyrinth Makers, Anthony Price, 1970.

Stefanopoulos, Constantine. *Phroso*, A. Hope, 1897.

Steighton, Timothy, clerk to Edward Crimsworth. *The Professor*, Charlotte Brontë, 1857.

Steinfeldt, Baroness, suspected of poisoning the Baron von Arnheim. *Anne of Geierstein*, W. Scott, 1829.

Steinhart, Frau.
Catherine, Lize, Fritz and **Trudchen,** her children.
Ships that Pass in the Night, Beatrice Harraden, 1893.

Steinmetz, Karl. *The Sowers*, H. Seton Merriman, 1896.

Stella, Lady. *Men Like Gods*, H. G. Wells, 1923.

Stelling, Rev. Walter, curate, Kings Lorton, and schoolmaster.
Louisa, his wife.
Laura, their daughter.
The Mill on the Floss, George Eliot, 1860.

Stepanoff, Alexis, Foreign History tutor, Drayton College, Oxford, m. Patricia O'Neill. *The Dark Tide*, Vera Brittain, 1923.

Stephano, a drunken butler. *The Tempest* (play), W. Shakespeare.

Stephano, manager, The Honour Bound. 'Mine Host' (s.s.), *Last Recollections of My Uncle Charles*, N. Balchin, 1954.

Stephanos, the Wrestler. *Count Robert of Paris*, W. Scott, 1832.

Stephen de Sautre, abbot of St Illod's.
Anne of Norton, his wife.
'The Eye of Allah' (s.s.), *Debits and Credits*, R. Kipling, 1926.

Stephens, Mr, m. Chloe Fraser. *Chatterton Square*, E. H. Young, 1947.

Stephens, James. *The Tragedy of the Korosko*, A. Conan Doyle, 1898.

Stepney, Grace.
Jack, her husband.
The House of Mirth, Edith Wharton, 1905.

Steptoe, Bob, drunken cobbler, m. an aunt of Lizarann Coupland. *It Never Can Happen Again*, W. de Morgan, 1909.

Steptoe, Gerald and **Nancy,** friends of the Cherrington children.
Major Steptoe, their father.
Bet, their mother.
The Shrimp and the Anemone, etc., L. P. Hartley, 1944.

Sterling.
His daughters:
Betty.
Fanny, m. Lovewell.
Miss Sterling, his sister.
The Clandestine Marriage (play), G. Colman the Elder, 1766.

Sterling, John. *The Ghost Train* (play), A. Ridley, 1925.

Stern, Ben, Christian missionary. *Magnolia Street*, L. Golding, 1932.

Stern, Gregory, publisher, m. Isobel Turbot. *The Rich Pay Late*, 1964, and others in the *Alms for Oblivion* sequence, Simon Raven.

Stern, Mike, understudy to Bhakaroff, eng. to Olga Kalish. *Grand Opera*, Vicki Baum, 1942.

Sterndale, Dr Leon. 'The Devil's Foot,' *His Last Bow*, A. Conan Doyle, 1917.

Sternersen, Captain.
Moran, his daughter.
Shanghaied, F. Norris, 1904.

Sterroll, Julie.
Frederick, her husband.
Fallen Angels (play), N. Coward, 1925.

Stettson Major, a day boy. 'A Little Prep,' *Stalky & Co.*, R. Kipling, 1899.

Steuben, Paul. *Ming Yellow*, J. P. Marquand, 1935.

Stevens, Basil Arthur Gerald ('Bags'), artist, m. Florrie (*see* WINIGLE). *Master Jim Probity*, F. Swinnerton, 1952.

Stevens, Gavin, lawyer, m. Melisandre Harriss Backus. *The Snopes* trilogy, 1940–59, and *Requiem for a Nun*, 1950, William Faulkner.

Stevens, Gowan, m. Temple Drake. *Sanctuary*, 1931 and *Requiem For A Nun*, 1950, William Faulkner.

Stevenson, Stewart, artist.
His father, 'a simple soul.'
His mother.
The Setons, O. Douglas, 1917.

Stewart, history tutor. *The Babe, B.A.*, E. F. Benson, 1897.

Stewart, journalist and playwright, cousin of Judy Corder. *Four Frightened People*, E. Arnot Robertson, 1931.

Stewart, Alan. *See* William Walterson.

Stewart, Charles, writer to the Signet. *Catriona*, R. L. Stevenson, 1893.

Stewart, Ollie, city dandy. *The Shepherd of the Hills*, H. B. Wright, 1907.

Steyne, Marquess of (George Augustus) (Family name Gaunt)
Lady Mary, his wife, *née* Caerlyon.
Their children:
Lord Gaunt, m. Lady Blanche Thistleweed.
George.
His wife, *née* Johnes.
Plantagenet, their son, an idiot, heir presumptive.
Vanity Fair, 1847–8, and elsewhere, W. M. Thackeray.

Steynlin, Madame. *South Wind*, N. Douglas, 1917.

Stickles, Jeremy, apparitor of the King's Bench. *Lorna Doone*, R. D. Blackmore, 1869.

Stickly-Prickly, a hedgehog. 'The Beginning of the Armadillos,' *Just So Stories*, R. Kipling, 1902.

Stiggins, hypocritical and ranting pastor. *Pickwick Papers*, C. Dickens, 1837.

Stikkersee, a weasel. *Tarka the Otter*, H. Williamson, 1927.

Stiles, Miss Ellen, friend of the Ronders. *The Cathedral*, Hugh Walpole, 1922.

Stilham, Amory. *See also* Esther Hobson.
Helen, his wife, grand-daughter of Mrs Parkington.
Jack, their son.
Janie, their daughter, m. Ned Talbot.
Mrs Parkington, L. Bromfield, 1944.

Stillbrook, friend of Cummings. *The Diary of a Nobody*, G. & W. Grossmith, 1892.

Stillbrook, Stephen, detective sergeant. *Robbery under Arms*, R. Boldrewood, 1888.

Stilton, Dowager Duchess of. *Vanity Fair*, W. M. Thackeray, 1847–8.

Stimson, Simon, director of choir. *Our Town* (play), Thornton Wilder, 1938.

Stingo, Jacob, a brewer. The *Sailor's Return*, David Garnett, 1925.

Stoat, Donald. *You Can't Go Home Again*, T. Wolfe, 1947.

Stoat of Stitchley, Lady (Adine), friend of Dolly Vanderdecken.
Gwen, her daughter.
Moths, Ouida, 1880.

Stobbs, Charley, m. Belinda Jorrocks.
His father, a gentleman farmer.
His sister.
Handley Cross, R. S. Surtees, 1843.

Stock, Simon, civil servant. *Sunrise in the West*, Bechofer Roberts, 1945.

Stockdale, Richard, m. Lizzy Newberry. 'The Distracted Preacher,' *Wessex Tales*, T. Hardy, 1888.

Stockman, Carl, business tycoon. 'Among Friends' (s.s.), *Last Recollections of My Uncle Charles*, N. Balchin, 1954.

Stockton, John. *See* Bruce Dudley.

Stockwool, Mrs Ruth, companion to Ann Avice Caro. *The Well Beloved*, T. Hardy, 1897.

Stoddard, Eleanor, interior decorator. *U.S.A.* trilogy, John dos Passos, 1930–6.

Stoddard, Mabel, m. Bushrod Page.
Her father.
Steamboat Gothic, Frances Parkinson Keyes, 1952.

Stoddart, Corporal, of the Wiltshires. *The Plough and the Stars* (play), S. O'Casey, 1926.

Stogumber, Chaplain de. *Saint Joan* (play), G. B Shaw, 1924.

Stohwaeser, Herr, German master at Dr Grimstone's. *Vice Versa*, F. Anstey, 1882.

Stoke. *See* D'Urberville.

Stoke, Basil, colleague of Cyril Poges.
Avril, his mistress.

Purple Dust (play), Sean O'Casey, 1940.

Stoke, Lord (Tom), brother of Lady Bond. The *Barsetshire* series, Angela Thirkell, 1933 onwards.

Stoker, Mrs Morland's maid. The *Barsetshire* series, Angela Thirkell, 1933 onwards.

Stoker, G. Paul, wealthy business man.
Jinny, his wife.
'The Bars of the Cage' (s.s.), *Last Recollections of My Uncle Charles,* N. Balchin, 1954.

Stoker, J. Washburn.
Dwight, his son.
Pauline, his daughter, m. Lord Chuffnell.
Thank You, Jeeves, P. G. Wodehouse, 1934.

Stokes, Captain. *Pendennis,* W. M. Thackeray, 1848–50.

Stokes, Mrs, Titmarsh's landlady.
Bob, her son.
Selina, her daughter.
The Great Hoggarty Diamond, W. M. Thackeray, 1841.

Stokes, Leland, lover of Rosa Emerson. *A Lamp for Nightfall,* E. Caldwell, 1952.

Stone, sailor in the torpedoed *Aurora. The Ocean,* J. Hanley, 1946.

Stone, Major, murdered by Forester. *Ministry of Fear,* Graham Greene, 1943.

Stone, Mr, neighbour of Lincoln. *Abraham Lincoln* (play), J. Drinkwater, 1918.

Stone, Denis, young poet. *Crome Yellow,* Aldous Huxley, 1922.

Stone, Mrs Dolly. *At Mrs Beam's,* C. K. Munro, 1923.

Stone, Mrs Ethel. *Poor Women,* Norah Hoult, 1929.

Stone, Mrs Karen, famous actress.
Tom, her dead husband.
The Roman Spring of Mrs Stone, Tennessee Williams, 1950.

Stone, Nettie, m. (1) Stanley de Lyndesay, (2) Anthony Dixon. *Crump Folk Going Home,* Constance Holme, 1913.

Stone, Rodney, central character and narrator.
Lieutenant Anson Stone, his father.
Mary, his mother, *née* Tregellis.
Rodney Stone, A. Conan Doyle, 1896.

Stone, Mrs Sarah. *Adam Bede,* George Eliot, 1859.

Stoner, Helen, stepdaughter of Dr Roylott.
Julia, her dead twin sister.
'The Speckled Band,' *The Adventures of Sherlock Holmes,* A. Conan Doyle, 1892.

Stonor, Gabriel, Paul Renauld's secretary. *Murder on the Links,* Agatha Christie, 1923.

Stonor, Mrs Lilian, widowed sister of John Middleton, m. Alister Cameron.
Denis, her stepson.
Daphne, her stepdaughter, m. Hon. Cedric Bond.
The *Barsetshire* series, Angela Thirkell, 1933 onwards.

Stoopid, servant to H. Foker. *Pendennis,* W. M. Thackeray, 1848–50.

Stopley, Canon, friend of the Arrowpoints. *Daniel Deronda,* George Eliot, 1876.

Stopley, Lord. *Laura's Bishop,* G. A. Birmingham, 1949.

Storefield, George.
Grace, his sister, m. Dick Marston.
His mother and father.
Robbery under Arms, R. Boldrewood, 1888.

Storey, Beth, friend of Louise. *Louise,* Viola Meynell, 1954.

Storey, Philip, murderer. 'The Cat in the Bag,' *Lord Peter Views the Body,* Dorothy L. Sayers, 1928.

Storm, Rev. John. *The Christian,* Hall Caine, 1897.

Storm, Theodore, m. Paula Arnold. *So Big,* Edna Ferber, 1924.

Stornway, Milton.
Ethel, his daughter.
A Penniless Millionaire, D. Christie Murray, 1907.

Storr, Bob.
Eva, his wife.
Room at the Top, J. Braine, 1957.

Stortford, Bishop of. *Meet Mr Mulliner,* P. G. Wodehouse, 1927.

Stossen, Mrs.
Her daughter.
The Boar Pig (s.s.), 'Saki' (H. H. Munro).

Stott, George ('Ginger'), cricketer.
Ellen Mary, his wife.
Victor (The Wonder), their son.

The Hampdenshire Wonder, J. D. Beresford, 1911.

Stout. *Money* (play), Lord Lytton, 1840.

Stowe, Joe, m. Bella Brill. *Wickford Point*, J. P. Marquand, 1939.

Strachan, portrait-painter and illustrator, secretary of golf club.
His wife.
The Five Red Herrings, Dorothy L. Sayers, 1931.

Strachan, Chae, farmer in the Howe o' the Mearns.
Kirsty, his wife.
A Scots Quair trilogy, 1932–4, Lewis Grassic Gibbon.

Strachan, Harry, m. Euphemia Throndson. 'Why Billy Went Back' (s.s.), *All the World Wondered*, L. Merrick, 1911.

Strachan, Noel, solicitor, narrator. *A Town like Alice*, N. Shute, 1950.

Stradlater, Holden Caulfield's room-mate at Pencey. *The Catcher in the Rye*, J. D. Salinger, 1951.

Strafe, young schoolmaster. *Desirable Villa* (s.s.), T. Burke.

Straight, Samson. *The Title* (play), Arnold Bennett, 1918.

Strakencz, Marshal. *The Prisoner of Zenda*, A. Hope, 1894.

Straker, rising young barrister. *Miss Tarrant's Temperament* (s.s.), May Sinclair.

Straker, Henry, John Tanner's chauffeur. *Man and Superman* (play), G. B. Shaw, 1903.

Straker, John. 'Silver Blaze,' *Memoirs of Sherlock Holmes*, A. Conan Doyle, 1894.

Straker, Lavinia, artist's model and singer, 1st wife of Charles Heath. *Alice-for-Short*, W. de Morgan, 1907.

Strang, Nick, Editor-in-chief, *Chicago Sentinel*, Paris office. *Trial by Terror*, P. Gallico, 1952.

Strang, Ronald, gamekeeper and factor, m. Wilhelmina Douglas-Stuart.
Maggie, his sister.
Rev. Andrew, his brother.
James, Alexandra, Rosina and **Esther,** his children.
White Heather, W. Black, 1885.

Strange, Master, merchant, in love with Katherine Worldly. *A Woman is a Weathercock* (play), N. Field, 1612.

Strange, Brian, in love with Dinah Marden. *Mr Pim Passes By* (play), A. A. Milne, 1920.

Stranger, The, central character. *The Passing of the Third Floor Back* (play), J. K. Jerome, 1910.

Stranger, Sandy, schoolgirl, member of 'the Brodie set,' who becomes Sister Helena of the Transfiguration. *The Prime of Miss Jean Brodie*, Muriel Spark, 1961.

Strangeways, Nigel, m. Clare Massinger, chief character in *The Widow's Cruise*, 1959 and others, Nicholas Blake.

Strangways, Phyllis.
Roger, her brother.
The Accident (s.s.), Ann Bridge.

Strangwick, Brother C. 'Madonna of the Trenches' (s.s.), *Debits and Credits*, R. Kipling, 1926.

Strap, Hugh, school friend of Roderick Random. *Roderick Random*, T. Smollett, 1748.

Stratfield, George Basil, younger son, m. Liane Brooker.
Sir John, Bt, his father.
John (alias Charles Holroyde), his elder brother.
If Sinners Entice Thee, W. le Queux, 1898.

Strato. *The Maid's Tragedy* (play), Beaumont & Fletcher, 1611.

Stratton, Mr.
His wife.
Separate Tables (play), T. Rattigan, 1955.

Stratton, Ewyas, A.B. and bad hat, *Blackgauntlet*. *The Bird of Dawning*, J. Masefield, 1933.

Stratton, Stephen, central character and narrator. *The Passionate Friends*, H. G. Wells, 1913.

Strauchan, armour-bearer. *The Talisman*, W. Scott, 1825.

Street, Della, confidential secretary of Perry Mason.
Aunt Mae, her aunt.
The Case of the Blonde Bonanza, 1962, and others, Erle Stanley Gardener.

Street, Jeremy, lecturer on Greek subjects. *The Widow's Cruise*, Nicholas Blake, 1959.

Strephon, an Arcadian shepherd, son of Iolanthe and the Lord

Chancellor, m. Phyllis. *Iolanthe* (comic opera), Gilbert & Sullivan, 1882.

Strether, Lambert, friend of Chadwick Newsome. *The Ambassadors,* Henry James, 1903.

Strether, Wulfstan, great novelist hiding under name of Buckmaster in Portugal. *I Like It Here,* Kingsley Amis, 1958.

Strett, Sir Luke, eminent doctor. *The Wings of the Dove,* Henry James, 1902.

Stretton, Joy, surreptitiously adopted on death of Josephine by Mrs Abinger, and renamed Josephine Abinger. *Joy and Josephine,* Monica Dickens, 1948.

Strickland, Charles, artist who goes to Tahiti.
Amy, his English wife.
Ata, his Tahitian wife.
The Moon and Sixpence, W. S. Maugham, 1919.

Strickland, E., of the Indian police.
Agnes, his wife, *née* Youghal.
Adam, their son.
'Miss Youghal's Sais' (s.s.), *Plain Tales from the Hills,* 1888, 'A Deal in Cotton' (s.s.), *Actions and Reactions,* 1909, and others, R. Kipling.

Strickland, Lieutenant-Colonel John, late Coldstream Guards, m. Lady Ariadne Ferne. *No Other Tiger,* A. E. W. Mason, 1927.

Strijdom, Carel, m. Maria Grafton.
Suzanna, his sister, m. Adrian Grafton.
The City of Gold, F. Brett Young, 1939.

Strike, Major, m. Caroline Harrington. *Evan Harrington,* G. Meredith, 1861.

Striker, Barnaby, attorney.
His wife.
Petronilla, their daughter.
Roderick Hudson, H. James, 1875.

Strines, Alexander.
Mary, his artist wife.
The World in the Evening, C. Isherwood, 1954.

Stringham, Mrs, friend of Milly Theale. *The Wings of the Dove,* Henry James, 1902.

Stringham, Arlington.
Eleanor, his wife.
The Jesting of Arlington Stringham (s.s.), 'Saki' (H. H. Munro).

Stringham, Charles. *A Question of Upbringing,* 1951, and others in *The Music of Time* series, Anthony Powell.

Stripes, servant to Major Ponto. *The Book of Snobs,* W. M. Thackeray, 1846–7.

Stroeve, Dirk, friend of Charles Strickland.
Blanche, his wife.
The Moon and Sixpence, W. S. Maugham, 1919.

Strofzin, Anton von. *Rupert of Hentzau,* A. Hope, 1898.

Strong, Dr, schoolmaster.
His young wife.
David Copperfield, C. Dickens, 1850.

Strong, Captain Edward ('The Chevalier Strong'), friend of Sir Francis Clavering. *Pendennis,* W. M. Thackeray, 1848–50.

Strong, Kay Leiland, graduate of Vassar, m. Harald Petersen. *The Group,* Mary McCarthy, 1963.

Strong, Mark, narrator.
Roderick and **Mary,** his close friends.
The Iron Pirate, M. Pemberton, 1893.

Strongitharm, Lord.
Hon. Lenox, his son.
The Adventures of Philip, W. M. Thackeray, 1861–2.

Strood, Duchess of. *The Gay Lord Quex* (play), A. W. Pinero, 1899.

Strood, Roderick, charged with the murder of his wife, Daphne. *The Jury,* G. Bullett, 1935.

Strorks, a rhinoceros. 'How the Rhinoceros got his Skin,' *Just So Stories,* R. Kipling, 1902.

Strother, Simon, old Negro coachman, retainer of Sartoris family. *Sartoris,* William Faulkner, 1929.

Strumpfer, Nick, a 'square-made dwarf.' *The Pirate,* W. Scott, 1822.

Struthers, Rev. Mr. *The House with the Green Shutters,* G. Douglas, 1901.

Stryver, C. J., counsel for Charles Darnay.
His wife.
A Tale of Two Cities, C. Dickens, 1859.

Stuart, Captain, ex-Gordon Highlanders, commanding the President's bodyguard. *Soldiers of Fortune*, R. H. Davis, 1897.

Stuart, Rev. John. *The Tragedy of the Korosko*, A. Conan Doyle, 1898.

Stuart, Nettie, elopes with and m. Edward Verral.
Her father, head gardener to Mrs Verral.
In the Days of the Comet, H. G. Wells, 1906.

Stubb, second mate, the *Pequod*. *Moby Dick*, H. Melville, 1851.

Stubbins, Mr. *Mrs Wiggs of the Cabbage Patch*, Alice H. Rice, 1901.

Stubble, Ensign. *Vanity Fair*, W. M. Thackeray, 1847–8.

Stubbs, English undergraduate in Paris. 'Providence and the Guitar' (s.s.), *New Arabian Nights*, R. L. Stevenson, 1882.

Stubbs, Yorkshire friend of Jorrocks. *Jorrocks's Jaunts and Jollities*, R. S. Surtees, 1838.

Stubbs, manservant to Sinclair. *No. 5 John Street*, R. Whiteing, 1902.

Stubbs, Robert.
Eliza and **Lucy,** his sisters.
Thomas, his father.
Susan, his mother.
The Fatal Boots, W. M. Thackeray, 1839.

Stubland, Peter, central character, m. Joan Debenham, his cousin.
Arthur, his father. *See* MISS BLEND.
Dolly, his mother, *née* Sydenham.
Joan and Peter, H. G. Wells, 1918.

Studdard, Colonel and Mrs.
Their daughters:
Laurel, m. Edward Tilney.
Janet, m. Rodney Meggatt.
Friends and Relations, Elizabeth Bowen, 1931.

Stuffle, lieutenant in Major Gahagan's regiment. *The Adventures of Major Gahagan*, W. M. Thackeray, 1838–1839.

Stulpnagel, Peter, expert electrician. 'The Los Amigos Fiasco' (s.s.), *Round the Red Lamp*, A. Conan Doyle, 1894.

Stultz, tailors. *The Newcomes*, 1853–1855, and elsewhere, W. M. Thackeray.

Sturgis, Mrs.
Her children:
Benjy.
Clare.
Liz, m. Jan Rysing.
If Four Walls Told (play), E. Percy, 1922.

Sturmer, Mrs Lucy, *née* Targett.
Her husband.
The Sailor's Return, David Garnett, 1925.

Sturmthal, Melchior, banner-bearer of Berne. *Anne of Geierstein*, W. Scott, 1829.

'Stute Fish, The. 'How the Whale got his Throat,' *Just So Stories*, R. Kipling, 1902.

Stutfield, Lady. *Lady Windermere's Fan* (play), O. Wilde, 1892.

Subtle. *The Alchemist* (play), B. Jonson, 1610.

Such, Theophrastus, central character and narrator.
Rev. Theophrastus, his father.
Theophrastus Such, George Eliot, 1879.

Such-a-One, Chinese steward. *Landscape with Figures*, R. Fraser, 1925.

Suckling, Bob, man of fashion. *Vanity Fair*, 1847–8, and *Pendennis*, 1848–50, W. M. Thackeray.

Suddhoo. 'In the House of Suddhoo' (s.s.), *Plain Tales from the Hills*, R. Kipling, 1888.

Suddlechop, Benjamin, 'most renowned barber in Fleet Street.'
Dame Ursula, his wife.
The Fortunes of Nigel, W. Scott, 1822.

Sue, artist friend of Joanna. 'The Last Leaf' (s.s.), *The Trimmed Lamp*, O. Henry, 1907.

Suetonius (hist.), Roman general. *Bonduca* (play), Beaumont & Fletcher, 1614.

Suffolk, Duke of (hist.). *Henry the Eighth* (play), W. Shakespeare.

Suffolk, Earl of (hist.). *Henry the Sixth* (play), W. Shakespeare.

Sugamo, Captain, Japanese officer in Malaya. *A Town like Alice*, N. Shute, 1950.

Sugden, Mrs, neighbour of the Oakroyds. *The Good Companions*, J. B. Priestley, 1929.

Sugden, William. *Eden End* (play), J. B. Priestley, 1935.

Sugg, Inspector, of Scotland Yard. *Whose Body?*, 1923, and others, Dorothy L. Sayers.

Suket, Singh. 'Through the Fire'

(s.s.), *Life's Handicap*, R. Kipling, 1891.

Suleiman-im-Daoud (Solomon). 'The Butterfly that Stamped,' *Just So Stories*, R. Kipling, 1902.

Sulinor ('Mango'), guard-boat captain. 'The Manner of Men' (s.s.), *Limits and Renewals*, R. Kipling, 1932.

Sullen, Squire, country blockhead, son of Lady Bountiful.
His wife.
The Beaux' Stratagem (play), G. Farquhar, 1707.

Sullivan, Mrs, *née* Cooper.
William, her son, m. Gertrude Amory.
The Lamplighter, Maria S. Cummins, 1854.

Sullivan, David, lawyer in love with Hazel Carter. *The Glass Cell*, Patricia Highsmith, 1965.

Sullivan, Big Mike (self-styled Count Fernando Mazzini). 'The Count and the Wedding Guest' (s.s.), *The Trimmed Lamp*, O. Henry, 1907.

Sullivan, Patrick, m. Eily Driscoll. 'The Whistling Thief' (s.s.), *Countrymen All*, Katherine Tynan, 1915.

Sullivan, Paul, bisexual novelist. *The City and The Pillar*, Gore Vidal, 1948.

Sumfit, Mrs, cook to the Flemings. *Rhoda Fleming*, G. Meredith, 1865.

Summerlee, Professor, explorer. *The Lost World*, 1912, and *The Poison Belt*, 1913, A. Conan Doyle.

Summers, Felicity, actress. *A City of Bells*, Elizabeth Goudge, 1936.

Summers, Isabel, mistress of Stephen Birch, m. Tom Florey. *Tom Tiddler's Ground*, E. Shanks, 1934.

Summers, Timothy, clockmaker. 'The Three Strangers,' *Wessex Tales*, T. Hardy, 1888.

Summerson, Esther ('Dame Durden'), orphan niece of Miss Barbary, illegitimate daughter of Captain Hawdon and Lady Dedlock (before her marriage); central character and narrator, m. Allan Woodcourt. *Bleak House*, C. Dickens, 1853.

Sumner, Mr ('Señor Zoumna'). *Shining and Free*, G. B. Stern, 1935.

Sumner, Fred, soldier; seducer of Hetty Smith and father of her son, later her husband. *The Dream*, H. G. Wells, 1924.

'Sunday,' President, Anarchist Council of European Dynamiters. *The Man who was Thursday*, G. K. Chesterton, 1908.

Sunderbund, Lady (Agatha), rich American widow. *The Soul of a Bishop*, H. G. Wells, 1917.

Sung, Herr, Chinese, elopes with Cacalie Forster. *Of Human Bondage*, W. S. Maugham, 1915.

Sunray, lover of Sarnac. *Men Like Gods*, H. G. Wells, 1923.

Sunwood, Rev. Gordon, m. Deborah Herries.
Their sons:
Reuben, itinerant preacher.
Humphrey.
Rogue Herries, Hugh Walpole, 1930.

Super, Martin, Canadian trapper. *Settlers in Canada*, Captain Marryat, 1844.

Superstition. *See* ENVY.

Supple, Rev. Mr, curate. *Tom Jones*, H. Fielding, 1749.

Supplehouse, of the *Jupiter*. *Framley Parsonage*, A. Trollope, 1861.

Surbiton, Lord, brother of Lord Arthur Savile. *Lord Arthur Savile's Crime*, O. Wilde, 1891.

Surbonadier, Arthur (*né* Simes), actor. *Enter a Murderer*, Ngaio Marsh, 1935.

Surennes, Duchesse de. *Our Betters* (play), W. S. Maugham, 1923.

Suresby, Sym, servant to Gawyn Goodluck. *Ralph Roister Doister*, N. Udall, 1551.

Surface, Sir Oliver.
Joseph and **Charles,** his nephews.
The School for Scandal (play), R. B. Sheridan, 1777.

Surget, Mrs Amy. *Steamboat Gothic*, Frances Parkinson Keyes, 1952.

Surrey, Earl of (hist.). *Henry the Eighth* (play), W. Shakespeare.

Surrey, Earl of (hist.). *Perkin Warbeck* (play), John Ford, 1634.

Surrogate, Mr, a Communist. *It's a Battlefield*, Graham Greene, 1935.

Surtees, Mr Devizes's clerk. *The Will* (play), J. M. Barrie, 1913.

Susan. *Black-eyed Susan* (poem), J. Gay.

Susan, a mulatto slave.
Emmeline, her daughter.

Uncle Tom's Cabin, Harriet B. Stowe, 1851.

Susan (Gentleman Susan), travelling pedlar. *The Romantic Age* (play), A. A. Milne, 1920.

Susskind, Henry. *Counsellor-at-Law* (play), Elmer Rice, 1931.

Sutherland, Mr.
Mary.
Love Among the Artists, G. B. Shaw, 1900.

Sutherland, Mary. 'A Case of Identity,' *The Adventures of Sherlock Holmes,* A. Conan Doyle, 1892.

Suthurst, Mrs Annie, faithful servant of the O'Riordens. *My Son, My Son,* H. Spring, 1938.

Sutton, private detective acting for insurance company.
His wife.
The Loss of the 'Jane Vosper,' F. Wills Crofts, 1936.

Sutton, Dame Alice, nun who sings too loudly at the convent of Oby. *The Corner That Held Them,* Sylvia Townsend Warner, 1948.

Sutton, Beatrice, friend of Anna Tellwright. *Anna of the Five Towns,* Arnold Bennett, 1902.

Suvretta, famous musician. *Gallions Reach,* H. M. Tomlinson, 1927.

Suydam, Virginia, relative of Garret Hamil. *The Firing Line,* R. W. Chambers, 1908.

Svengali, musician, and evil genius. *Trilby,* George du Maurier, 1894.

Svoboda, Tilly, old nurse of the Landons. *The Ballad and the Source,* Rosamond Lehmann, 1944.

Swabber, Lieutenant-General. *A Shabby Genteel Story,* W. M. Thackeray, 1840.

Swaffer, a farmer.
His daughter.
'Amy Foster' (s.s.), *Typhoon,* J. Conrad, 1903.

Swain, Patty.
Henry, her father.
Richard Carvel, W. Churchill, 1899.

Swallowtail, Colonel. *Pendennis,* W. M. Thackeray, 1848–50.

Swan, porter, m. Mrs Rickards. *Savoir Faire* (s.s.), W. Pett Ridge.

Swan, Eric, schoolboy 'who looks at masters through his spectacles,' later schoolmaster, m. Justinia Lufton. The *Barsetshire* series, Angela Thirkell, 1933 onwards.

Swancourt, Elfride, m. Lord Luxellian.
Rev. Christopher, her father, m. (2) Mrs Charlotte Troyton.
A Pair of Blue Eyes, T. Hardy, 1873.

Swang, Captain, of the Indian Army. *The Adventures of Philip,* W. M. Thackeray, 1861–2.

Swann, Madeleine, grand-daughter of Mrs Parkington.
The Colonel, her 4th husband.
Mrs Parkington, L. Bromfield, 1944.

Swanney, Sir William.
Janet, his wife.
The Winds of Chance, S. K. Hocking.

Swanson, Eddie, car agent.
Louetta, his wife.
Babbitt, Sinclair Lewis, 1923.

Swanson, Hugh, employer and suitor of Lulie Harrington. *Chosen Country,* J. dos Passos, 1951.

Swartz, Rhoda, wealthy mulatto, m. James McMull. *Vanity Fair,* W. M. Thackeray, 1847–8.

Sweatley, Tranter.
Barbree, his wife. *See also* TIM TANKENS.
'The Fire at Tranter Sweatley's,' *Wessex Poems,* T. Hardy, 1898.

Sweedlepipe, Paul, barber and bird-fancier, landlord of Mrs Gamp. *Martin Chuzzlewit,* C. Dickens, 1844.

Sweeney, custom house officer, and rogue. *Afloat and Ashore,* J. Fenimore Cooper, 1844.

Sweeney, Mrs, laundress, bad character. *The Uncommercial Traveller,* C. Dickens, 1860.

Sweet William, travelling showman. *The Old Curiosity Shop,* C. Dickens, 1841.

Sweetie. *See* MARGARET HART.

Sweeting, Rev. David, curate of Nunnely. *Shirley,* Charlotte Brontë, 1849.

Sweetland, Samuel.
Sibley and **Petronnel.**
The Farmer's Wife (play), E. Phillpotts, 1924.

Sweetwinter, Mabel, miller's daughter.
Bob, her brother.
The Adventures of Harry Richmond, G. Meredith, 1871.

Swertha, aged and avaricious housekeeper of Mertoun. *The Pirate,* W. Scott, 1822.

Swift, Kate, former schoolteacher of George Willard. *Winesburg, Ohio,* Sherwood Anderson, 1919.

Swigby, Joseph.
Linda, his wife, *née* Wellesley.
A Shabby Genteel Story, W. M. Thackeray, 1840.

Swindon, Major. *The Devil's Disciple* (play), G. B. Shaw, 1899.

Swingler, Thomas, private detective. *The Old Boys,* William Trevor, 1964.

Swinney, Zeke. *David Harum,* E. Noyes Westcott, 1898.

Swint, Pluto. *God's Little Acre,* E. Caldwell, 1933.

Swinton, Denny, cousin of Lord Wheatley. *Phroso,* A. Hope, 1897.

Swishtail, Dr, headmaster. *Vanity Fair,* 1847–8, and elsewhere, W. M. Thackeray.

Swithin, Mrs Lucy, widowed sister of Bartholomew Oliver. *Between The Acts,* Virginia Woolf, 1941.

Swiveller, Richard, friend of the Trents and clerk to Brass, m. The Marchioness. *The Old Curiosity Shop,* C. Dickens, 1841.

Swizzle, Roger, red-faced apothecary.
His wife.
Handley Cross, R. S. Surtees, 1843.

Swyndle, Rev. Ernest, curate, Dormer, m. Ruby Darke.
Ernest jnr, their son.
The House in Dormer Forest, Mary Webb, 1920.

Sycamore, family solicitor of the Stublands. *Joan and Peter,* H. G. Wells, 1918.

Sydenham, Oswald, V.C., ex-midshipman, cousin of Dolly Stubland, with whom he is in love.
Will, Dolly's brother. *See* JOAN DEBENHAM.
Lady Charlotte, Oswald's aunt.
Joan and Peter, H. G. Wells, 1918.

Sydney, Henry. *See* DUKE OF CLUMBER.

Sykes, Christopher.
Dora and **Harriet,** his daughters.
Shirley, Charlotte Brontë, 1849.

Sykes, Janie, m. John Crane.
Her father and mother.
The Case for the Defence, Mary Fitt, 1958.

Syllabub, Timothy, hack writer. *A Citizen of the World,* O. Goldsmith, 1762.

Sylvester, Raymond, tutor, of St Giles, Oxford, m. Daphne Lethbridge. *See also* LUCIA FARRETTI. *The Dark Tide,* Vera Brittain, 1923.

Sylvestre, an acolyte.
Simone, his sister.
Act of God, F. Tennyson Jesse, 1936.

Sylvestre, Mrs Agnes. *Through One Administration,* Frances H. Burnett, 1881.

Syme, philologist, friend of Winston Smith. *1984,* G. Orwell, 1948.

Syme, Gabriel (Thursday), poet and detective. *The Man who was Thursday,* G. K. Chesterton, 1908.

Symington, William, m. Madeline Selby. *Not so Bad after All,* Nat Gould.

Symmes, Farmer, rescuer of Eliza and her child. *Uncle Tom's Cabin,* Harriet B. Stowe, 1851.

Sympson, Mr, and family. *Shirley,* Charlotte Brontë, 1849.

Synesius, Bishop of Cyrene. *Hypatia,* C. Kingsley, 1853.

Synorix, ex-tetrarch. *The Cup* (play), Lord Tennyson, 1881.

Syntax, a schoolmaster. *Roderick Random,* T. Smollett, 1748.

T

Taafe, Martin, barber. *The Bay,* L. A. G. Strong, 1941.

Tabaqui, the jackal. 'Mowgli's Brothers' and elsewhere, *The Jungle Books,* R. Kipling, 1894.

Tacco, Paduan doctor. *Romola,* George Eliot, 1863.

Tacker, chief assistant to Mould. *Martin Chuzzlewit.* C. Dickens, 1844.

Tackle, Hon. George.
His father, proprietor, *Courier and Echo.*
Sanders of the River, E. Wallace, 1911.

Tackleton, of Gruff & Tackleton. *The Cricket on the Hearth,* C. Dickens, 1845.

Tadman, grocer.
His wife.
Cissie, their daughter.
South Riding, Winifred Holtby, 1936.

Tadpole, political opportunist. *Coningsby,* B. Disraeli, 1844.

Taffimai Metallumai ('Taffy'), little girl, daughter of Tegumai. 'How the First Letter was Written' and elsewhere, *Just So Stories,* R. Kipling, 1902.

Taffy. *See* TALBOT WYNNE.

Taft, Jacob, Hayslope patriarch. *Adam Bede,* George Eliot, 1859.

Tag-Rag, Mr, Titmouse's employer.
Dolly, his wife.
Tabitha, their daughter.
Ten Thousand a Year, S. Warren, 1839.

Tait, Rev. Francis.
His wife.
Their children:
Jane, m. Edgar Halliburton.
Rev. Francis.
Robert.
Margaret.
Mrs Halliburton's Troubles, Mrs Henry Wood, 1862.

Taji, young American sailor, narrator. *Mardi,* Herman Melville, 1849.

Takahira, of the Aerial Board of Control. 'As Easy as A B C' (s.s.), *A Diversity of Creatures,* R. Kipling, 1917.

Talacryn, Dr Francis, Bishop of Carleon, later a Cardinal. *Hadrian the Seventh,* Baron Corvo (F. W. Rolfe), 1904.

Talakku, an Assyrian captain 'The King of the World' (s.s.), *Adam and Eve and Pinch Me,* A. E. Coppard, 1921.

Talbot, Colonel. *Waverley,* W. Scott, 1814.

Talbot, Lord, later Earl of Shrewsbury (hist.). *Henry the Sixth* (play), W. Shakespeare.

Talbot, Christian, m. Linda Radlett.
Fabrice, Linda's son. *See* SAUVETERRE.
The Pursuit of Love, Nancy Mitford, 1945.

Talbot, Mary.
Tom, her husband.
Cannery Row, J. Steinbeck, 1945.

Talbot, Ned, m. Janie Stilham. *Mrs Parkington,* L. Bromfield. 1944.

Talboys, George, legal husband of Lady Audley.
Harcourt, his father.
Clara, his sister.
Lady Audley's Secret, Mary E. Braddon, 1862.

Talkapace, Tibet, maid to Dame Custance. *Ralph Roister Doister* (play), N. Udall, 1551.

Talkative. *Pilgrim's Progress,* J. Bunyan, 1678 and 1684.

Tall, Laban, farm-hand.
His wife.
Far from the Madding Crowd, T. Hardy, 1874.

Tallant, Kit, m. Bert Holm.
Robert, her father.
Dottie, her mother.
Gail, her sister, m. Harvey Crane.
Other Gods, Pearl Buck, 1940.

Tallantire, Dick. 'The Head of the District' (s.s.), *Life's Handicap,* R. Kipling, 1891.

Tallboy, group manager, Pym's Publicity. *Murder Must Advertise,* Dorothy L. Sayers, 1933.

Tallboys, gunner, H.M.S. *Harpy. Mr Midshipman Easy,* Captain Marryat, 1836.

Tallentyre, Nina, m. Jim Carthew. *A Safety Match*, Ian Hay, 1911.

Tallow, Petty Officer Bob, coxswain of *Compass Rose*. *The Cruel Sea*, N. Monsarrat, 1951.

Tallyman, Charles, suitor of Ruth Simpson. *Simpson*, E. Sackville-West, 1931.

Talmadge, Captain, of General Braddock's army. *The Virginians*, W. M. Thackeray, 1857–9.

Talmouth, Superintendent C. W. *The Four Just Men*, E. Wallace, 1905.

Talvace, Harry, master-mason who builds a church for Ralf Isambard.
- **Gilleis Otley,** his wife.
  - **Harry,** their son, who seeks revenge on Ralf Isambard for his father's death.

The Heaven Tree trilogy, Edith Pargeter, 1961–3.

Tam o' Shanter. *Tam o' Shanter* (poem), R. Burns.

Tamaroo, Miss, employee of Mrs Todgers. *Martin Chuzzlewit*, C. Dickens, 1844.

Tamb' Itam, personal guardian of Jim in Patu San. *Lord Jim*, J. Conrad, 1900.

Tamburlaine, a Scythian shepherd. *Tamburlaine* (play), C. Marlowe, 1587.

Tamerlane. *Tamerlane* (play), N. Rowe, 1702.

Tamlowrie, Laird of. *The Antiquary*, W. Scott, 1816.

Tamlyn, Mr and Mrs, servants of Ambrose Ashley. *My Cousin Rachel*, Daphne du Maurier, 1951.

Tamora, Queen of the Goths, *Titus Andronicus* (play), W. Shakespeare.

Tamson, Samuel.
- **Eppie,** his wife.

The Raiders, S. R. Crockett, 1894.

Tancred. *See* DUKE OF BELLAMONT.

Tancred, Mrs. *Juno and the Paycock* (play), S. O'Casey, 1925.

Tandy, Mr and Mrs.
- Their two daughters.

Tom Fool, F. Tennyson Jesse, 1926.

Tangs, Timothy (the Elder), top sawyer.
- **Timothy** (the Younger), bottom sawyer, m. Suke Damson.

The Woodlanders, T. Hardy, 1887.

Tania, mistress of N. A. Giles. *Going their own Ways*, A. Waugh, 1938.

Tankens, Tim, lover of Barbree Sweatley, later her 2nd husband. 'The Fire at Tranter Sweatley's,' *Wessex Poems*, T. Hardy, 1898.

Tanner, John. *Man and Superman* (play), G. B. Shaw, 1903.

Tanpinar, Halidë, Turkish woman doctor. *The Towers of Trebizond*, Rose Macaulay, 1956.

Tanqueray, Aubrey, central character.
- **Paula,** his 2nd wife.
- **Ellean,** his daughter by 1st wife.

The Second Mrs Tanqueray (play), A. W. Pinero, 1893.

Tansey, Sara. *The Playboy of the Western World* (play), J. M. Synge, 1907.

Tansley, Charles, friend of Mr Ramsay. *To The Lighthouse*, Virginia Woolf, 1927.

Tantamount, Lucy, girl with whom Walter Bidlake is infatuated. *Point Counter Point*, Aldous Huxley, 1928.

Taper, political opportunist. *Coningsby*, B. Disraeli, 1844.

Tapewell, Barry Lyndon's agent. *Barry Lyndon*, W. M. Thackeray, 1844.

Tapley, Mark, hostler at the Blue Dragon, later servant of Martin, m. Mrs Lupin. *Martin Chuzzlewit*, C. Dickens, 1843.

Tapling, Mr, of the Diplomatic service. *Mr Midshipman Hornblower*, C. S. Forester, 1950.

Taplow, a schoolboy. *The Browning Version* (play), T. Rattigan, 1948.

Tapper, Thirza. *The Farmer's Wife* (play), E. Phillpotts, 1924.

Tappercoom, Justice. *The Lady's Not For Burning* (play), Christopher Fry, 1948.

Tappertit, Simon, apprentice to Gabriel Varden. *Barnaby Rudge*, C. Dickens, 1841.

Tardew, agent to Lord Scoutbush. *Two Years Ago*, C. Kingsley, 1857.

Targett, William, sailor, central character.
- **Tulip (Gunderney),** his wife, daughter of King Gaze-oh of Dahomey.
  - **Sambo** and **Sheba,** their children.

His brothers and sisters:
John.
His wife.
Harry.
Francis.
Lucy, m. Sturmey.
Dolly, m. Stevie Barnes.
The Sailor's Return, David Garnett, 1925.

Tarka, an otter, central character. *Tarka the Otter,* H. Williamson, 1927.

Tarlenheim, Fritz von. *The Prisoner of Zenda,* etc., A. Hope, 1894–8.

Tarleton, a white missionary. 'The Beach of Falesa' (s.s.), *Island Nights' Entertainments,* R. L. Stevenson, 1893.

Tarleton, second lieutenant, a Creole. *In Greek Waters,* G. A. Henty, 1892.

Tarleton, Stuart and **Brent,** twins.
Jim, their father.
Beatrice, their mother.
Tom and **Boyd,** their brothers.
Four sisters.
Gone with the Wind, Margaret Mitchell, 1936.

Tarlton, Marguerite, widow of Howard Tarlton.
Lee, her daughter.
American Wives and English Husbands, Gertrude Atherton, 1898.

Tarlyon, Lord (George). 'The Man with the Broken Nose' (s.s.), *These Charming People,* M. Arlen, 1920.

Tarn.
Mala, his wife.
'Mala' (s.s.), *Here and Hereafter,* Barry Pain, 1911.

Tarne, Captain Robert, m. Lady Arabella Ware. 'The Mystery of Lady Arabella Ware' (s.s.), *Old Patch's Medley,* Marjorie Bowen, 1930.

Tarquol, son of **Tarka.** *Tarka the Otter,* H. Williamson, 1927.

Tarr, Frederick, an English artist. *Tarr,* Wyndham Lewis, 1918.

Tarrant, 'Fluffy,' 'with the eyes of a young leopardess.' *Sorrell and Son,* W. Deeping, 1925.

Tarrant, Miss Philippa. *Miss Tarrant's Temperament* (s.s.), May Sinclair.

Tarrant, Verena, m. Basil Ransom.
Dr Tarrant, her father, 'mesmeric healer.'
Selah, her mother.
The Bostonians, H. James, 1886.

Tarrik, chief of Marob, the Corn King.
Erif Der, the Spring Queen, his wife.
The Corn King and The Spring Queen, Naomi Mitchison, 1931.

Tarrion, an officer. 'Consequences' (s.s.), *Plain Tales from the Hills,* R. Kipling, 1888.

Tarry, Isabella, m. Marc Sallafranque.
Roy, her daughter by 1st husband.
The Thinking Reed, Rebecca West, 1936.

Tartan, Lucy, Pierre Glendinning's fiancée. *Pierre,* Herman Melville, 1852.

Tartar, naval lieutenant, retd. *Edwin Drood,* C. Dickens, 1870.

Tartar, Captain, of H.M.S. *Aurora. Mr Midshipman Easy,* Captain Marryat, 1836.

Tarver, manservant of Nathaniel Brookes. *The One Before,* Barry Pain, 1902.

Tarvin, James, headmaster, employer of Inigo Jollifant.
His wife.
The Good Companions, J. B. Priestley, 1929.

Tarvin, Nicholas, in love with Kate Sheriff. *The Naulakha,* R. Kipling & W. Balestier, 1892.

Tarvrille, Lord, cousin of Lady Mary Christian.
His wife.
The Passionate Friends, 1913, and elsewhere, H. G. Wells.

Tarwater, Francis Marion, boy trained to be a prophet.
Mason, his great-uncle, a religious fanatic.
The Violent Bear It Away, Flannery O'Connor, 1960.

Tarworth, Mr, American realtor. 'The Prophet and the Country' (s.s.), *Debits and Credits,* R. Kipling, 1926.

Tarzan of the Apes. *See* LORD GREYSTOKE.

Tasbrugh, Jean, m. Hubert Charwell.
Alan, her brother, in love with Dinny Charwell.
Their father, the Rector.
Maid in Waiting, etc., J. Galsworthy, 1931–3.

Tascher, army comrade of Tom Burke. *Tom Burke of Ours,* C. Lever, 1844.

Tasker, Joseph, Captain Bowers's man, eng. to Selina Vickers. *Dialstone Lane,* W. W. Jacobs, 1904.

Tasker, Leonard, fraudulent mill-owner.
  Marian, his wife.
A Modern Tragedy, Phyllis Bentley, 1934.

Tasky, James, Russian jockey whose name and papers Velvet Brown uses. *National Velvet,* Enid Bagnold, 1935.

Tate, Phineas. *Simon Dale,* A. Hope, 1898.

Tatt, Eric, M.D., D.Sc., Nazi agent. *Mr Fortune Finds a Pig,* H. C. Bailey, 1943.

Tattycoram (Harriet Beadle), foundling, maid to Miss Meagles, *Little Dorrit,* C. Dickens, 1857.

Taube, Mrs Laurette, m. Albert Grope. *Albert Grope,* F. O. Mann, 1931.

Taunton, Mrs, widow. *Sketches by Boz,* C. Dickens, 1836.

Taunton, Gervase ('Mhor'), adopted by Jean Jardine.
  His dead mother, formerly wife of Francis Jardine.
Penny Plain, O. Douglas, 1920.

Tausch, Herr. *The Moon in the Yellow River* (play), D. Johnston, 1932.

Tavendale, Ewan, 1st husband of Chris Guthrie.
  Ewan, their son, a revolutionary.
A Scots Quair trilogy, 1932–4, Lewis Grassic Gibbon.

Tavistock, ex-lover of Mrs White's daughter.
  His wife.
Shining and Free, G. B. Stern, 1935.

Tawnie, Steve, innkeeper.
  Maggie, his wife.
  Nellie, their daughter, m. Andy Dexter.
Magnolia Street, L. Golding, 1932.

Taylor, Corporal, fuse specialist. *The Small Back Room,* N. Balchin, 1943.

Taylor, Miss. *See* Mrs Weston.

Taylor, Frank, central character, m. Norah Marsh. *The Land of Promise* (play), W. S. Maugham, 1914.

Taylor, Jean, religious octogenarian, former companion of Charmian Colston. *Memento Mori,* Muriel Spark, 1959.

Taylor, Mi, ex-boxer and odd-job man.
  Dan, his father, trainer of Araminty Brown.
National Velvet, Enid Bagnold, 1935.

Taylor, Shirley, schoolgirl who loves Graham Wier and gets him into trouble.
  Mrs Doris Taylor, her mother.
Term of Trial, James Barlow, 1961.

Teach, pirate captain of the *Sarah. The Master of Ballantrae,* R. L. Stevenson, 1889.

Tearsheet, Doll. *Henry the Fourth* (play), W. Shakespeare.

Teasdale, Monica, ageing film actress. *No Highway,* N. Shute, 1948.

Teazle, Sir Peter.
  His wife.
The School for Scandal (play), R. B. Sheridan, 1777.

Tebben, Gilbert.
  His wife.
  Richard, their son, m. Susan Dean.
  Margaret, their daughter, m. Laurence Dean.
The *Barsetshire* series, Angela Thirkell, 1933 onwards.

Tebrick, Richard, English gentleman.
  Silvia, his wife (*née* Fox), who turns into a vixen.
Lady into Fox, David Garnett, 1923.

Techelles, follower of Tamburlaine. *Tamburlaine* (play), C. Marlowe, 1587.

Ted, mate, the *Arabella*; brother-in-law of Captain John Gibbs, eng. to Miss Harris. *The Lady of the Barge,* W. W. Jacobs, 1902.

Teddy, secretary to Britling.
  Letty, his wife, *née* Corner.
Mr Britling Sees It Through, H. G. Wells, 1916.

Teddy, a small boy, owner of Rikki-tikki-tavi.
  His father and mother.
'Rikki Tikki Tavi' (s.s.), *The Jungle Book,* R. Kipling, 1894.

Tedesco, John P. *Counsellor-at-Law* (play), Elmer Rice, 1931.

Teez Negah, conjuror. *Hajji Baba and the Stolen Money* (s.s.), J. Morier, 1824.

Tegeus-Chromis. *A Phoenix Too Frequent* (play), Christopher Fry, 1946.

Tegg, Lieutenant, R.N.V.R. 'Sea

Constables' (s.s.), *Debits and Credits*, R. Kipling, 1926.

Tegumai Bopsulai, a caveman, father of Taffy.

Teshumai Tewindrow, his wife. 'How the First Letter was Written' and elsewhere, *Just So Stories*, R. Kipling, 1902.

Teioa.

His wife.

Mr Fortune's Maggot, Sylvia Townsend Warner, 1927.

Telfair, Colonel Aquila. 'The Rose of Dixie' (s.s.), *Options*, O. Henry, 1909.

Telfer, James.

His wife. Of Bagnigge Wells Theatre.

Trelawny of the Wells (play), A. W. Pinero, 1898.

Telfer, Sigismund.

Jacquetta, his wife.

Poet's Pub, E. Linklater, 1929.

Tellwright, Ephraim, miser.

Anna, his oldest daughter.

Agnes, his youngest daughter.

Anna of the Five Towns, Arnold Bennett, 1902.

Temperley, Jack, close friend of William Maddison.

His father and mother.

Doris and **Margaret,** his sisters.

The Beautiful Years, H. Williamson, 1921.

Tempest, Geoffrey. *The Sorrows of Satan*, Marie Corelli, 1895.

Tempest, Leslie, m. Lettice Beardsall. *The White Peacock*, D. H. Lawrence, 1911.

Templar, Simon, gentleman-adventurer fighting crime by criminal methods. Known as 'The Saint'. Chief character in *The Saint in New York*, 1935, and others, Leslie Charteris.

Temple, Miss, headmistress of Lowood. *Jane Eyre*, Charlotte Brontë, 1847.

Temple, Claire, an old literary figure. *There Were No Windows*, Norah Hoult, 1944.

Temple, Edward. *The Fortress*, Hugh Walpole, 1932.

Temple, Gus, school friend of Harry Richmond. *The Adventures of Harry Richmond*, G. Meredith, 1871.

Temple, Pump.

Fanny, his wife, *née* Figtree.

The Book of Snobs, W. M. Thackeray, 1846–7.

Templer, Peter, friend of Nicholas Jenkins.

Mona, his wife.

Jean, his sister, one-time mistress of Nicholas Jenkins.

Bob Duport, Jean's ex-husband.

A Question of Upbringing, 1951, and others in *The Music of Time* series, Anthony Powell.

Templeton, Julia, m. Guy Bracebridge. *Bracebridge Hall*, W. Irving, 1823.

Tempy, Aunt, sister of Uncle Remus. *Uncle Remus*, J. C. Harris 1880–1895.

Tenbruggen, Dutch merchant, m. Elizabeth Chance. *The Legacy of Cain*, W. Collins, 1889.

Tench. *The Power and the Glory*, Graham Greene, 1940.

Tender, Lady (Margot).

Lord Tender, her husband.

Master Jim Probity, F. Swinnerton, 1952.

Tennant, Mrs, owner of a great mansion.

Mrs Jack Tennant, her daughter-in-law.

Loving, Henry Green, 1945.

Tennant, Cecilia, m. Donald Iverach.

Robert, her father.

Cleg Kelly, S. R. Crockett, 1896.

Tennant, Charles, lover of Lady Alicia Seymore. *Fanny by Gaslight*, M. Sadleir, 1940.

Tenois, Rose.

Her aunt.

The Pied Piper, N. Shute, 1942.

Tenterden, Lady Sybil. *What Every Woman Knows* (play), J. M. Barrie, 1908.

Teppich, Chancellor of Ruritania.

His wife.

Franz, his brother.

The Prisoner of Zenda, A. Hope, 1894.

Terence, Mrs, Mrs Bramson's cook. *Night Must Fall* (play), Emlyn Williams, 1935.

Tergiversation, Duke of. *Hawbuck Grange*, R. S. Surtees, 1847.

Terrill, Sir Walter, a courtier of William Rufus.

Caelistine, his bride.

Sir Quintilian Shorthose, her father.

Satiromastix (play), Thomas Dekker, 1601.

Tertius ('Emperor of China'). 'Slaves of the Lamp,' *Stalky & Co.*, 1899, and 'The United Idolaters' (s.s.), *Debits and Credits*, 1926, R. Kipling.

Teshoo Lama, abbot of Suchzen. *Kim*, R. Kipling, 1901.

Teshumai Tewindrow. *See* TEGUMAI.

Tessa, *contadina*, mistress of Tito Melema. *Romola*, George Eliot, 1862.

Tessa, *contadina*, m. Giuseppe Palmieri. *The Gondoliers* (comic opera), Gilbert & Sullivan, 1889.

Tester, a schoolboy at Fernhurst. *The Loom of Youth*, A. Waugh, 1917.

Tester, Mrs, 'bedmaker' to Verdant Green. *The Adventures of Mr Verdant Green*, C. Bede, 1853.

Tetley, a rancher.
Gerald, his son.
The Ox-Bow Incident, Walter Van Tilburg Clark, 1940.

Tetraides, a gladiator. *The Last Days of Pompeii*, Lord Lytton, 1834.

Tetterby, newsvendor.
His wife and family.
The Haunted Man, C. Dickens, 1848.

Tewarri, Subadar Prag. 'The Grave of the Hundred Dead' (poem), *Departmental Ditties*, R. Kipling, 1886.

Tewitt, Sir Griffin, fiancé of Lucinda Roanoke. *The Eustace Diamonds*, A. Trollope, 1873.

Teylesmore, Lord. *The High Road* (play), F. Lonsdale, 1927.

Tha, first of the elephants. 'How Fear Came,' *The Second Jungle Book*, R. Kipling, 1895.

Thacker, U.S. Consul at Buenas Tierras. 'A Double Dyed Deceiver' (s.s.), *Roads of Destiny*, O. Henry, 1909.

Thacker, T. T., journalist. 'The Rose of Dixie' (s.s.), *Options*, O. Henry, 1909.

Thaisa, daughter of Simonides. *Pericles* (play), W. Shakespeare.

Thaliard, a lord of Antioch. *Pericles* (play), W. Shakespeare.

Thane, Mary. *Comrade, O Comrade*, Ethel Mannin, 1946.

Thatcher, Becky, Tom's sweetheart.
Judge Thatcher, her father.
His wife.
The Adventures of Tom Sawyer, Mark Twain, 1876.

Thatcher, Ed.
Susie, his wife.
Manhattan Transfer, J. dos Passos, 1925.

Thatcher, General Lucius.
Henrietta, his niece, m. Jim Pignatelli.
Chosen Country, J. dos Passos, 1951.

Thawn, Anthony. *Rogue Herries*, Hugh Walpole, 1930.

Thaxter, Katherine, m. Douglas Blackstock. *No Man's Land*, L. J. Vance, 1910.

Theale, Milly, rich American girl. *The Wings of the Dove*, Henry James, 1902.

Thenot. *The Faithful Shepherdess* (play), Beaumont & Fletcher, 1609.

Theodore, peasant labourer, later discovered to be rightful Prince of Otranto; m. Isabella of Vicenza. *The Castle of Otranto*, Horace Walpole, 1765.

Theodotus. *Caesar and Cleopatra* (play), G. B. Shaw, 1900.

Theridamas, a Persian lord. *Tamburlaine* (play), C. Marlowe, 1587.

Thersites, deformed and scurrilous Grecian. *Troilus and Cressida* (play), W. Shakespeare.

Thery (alias Saimont), criminal, one of the Four. *See* GONSALEZ. *The Four Just Men*, E. Wallace, 1905.

Theseus, Duke of Athens. *A Midsummer Night's Dream* (play), W. Shakespeare.

Thesiger, Rev. Edward, Rector of St Peter's, Middlemarch.
His wife.
Middlemarch, Geo. Eliot, 1871–2.

Thibault of Montigni, 'the kindest soul alive.' *Quentin Durward*, W. Scott, 1823.

Thicket, Sir Timothy.
His sister.
Roderick Random, T. Smollett, 1748.

Thiele, Captain, an autocrat. *Ship of Fools*, Katherine Anne Porter, 1962.

Thing, Miss Jane (Cinderella), a cleaner, *A Kiss for Cinderella* (play), J. M. Barrie, 1916.

Thipps, Alfred, architect, in whose bath the body was found.
Georgiana, his mother.
Whose Body?, Dorothy L. Sayers, 1923.

Thirdly, Parson. *Far from the Madding Crowd*, T. Hardy, 1874.

Thirdman, Alex and **Willa.**
Theodora, their daughter.
Friends and Relations, Elizabeth Bowen, 1931.

Thistlewood. Family name of EARL OF BAREACRES.

Tholer, Thomas ('Tom Saft'), half-witted farm-hand. *Adam Bede*, George Eliot, 1859.

Tholoway, Ben, farm labourer. *Adam Bede*, George Eliot, 1859.

Thomas, a friar. *Measure for Measure* (play), W. Shakespeare.

Thomas, Lord Loam's first footman. *The Admirable Crichton* (play), J. M. Barrie, 1902.

Thomas, servant to Sir Anthony Absolute. *The Rivals* (play), R. B. Sheridan, 1775.

Thomas ('Long Thomas'). *Sixty-four, Ninety-four*, R. H. Mottram, 1925.

Thomas, Brother, infirmarian at St Illod's. 'The Eye of Allah' (s.s.), *Debits and Credits*, R. Kipling, 1926.

Thomas, Father, credulous monk. *A Burnt-Out Case*, Graham Greene, 1961.

Thomas, Mr, a servant. *The Conscious Lovers* (play), R. Steele, 1722.

Thomas, True, a song-maker. 'The Last Rhyme of True Thomas' (poem), *The Seven Seas*, R. Kipling, 1896.

Thomas, Glyn. *The Corn is Green* (play), Emlyn Williams, 1938.

Thomas, Nancibel, housemaid.
Her mother.
The Feast, Margaret Kennedy, 1950.

Thomas the Good, Sir.
Lady Jane the Fair, his wife.
'The Knight and the Lady' (poem), *The Ingoldsby Legends*, R. H. Barham, 1837.

Thomé, Mademoiselle, governess to Derek Jesson. *His House in Order* (play), A. W. Pinero, 1906.

Thompkins, Idabel, a wild girl.
Florabel, her twin, a prissy girl.
Other Voices, Other Rooms, Truman Capote, 1948.

Thompson, friend of Random, believed drowned. *Roderick Random*, T. Smollett, 1748.

Thompson, Henry T., father-in-law of George Babbitt.
His wife.
Babbitt, Sinclair Lewis, 1923.

Thompson, Jean, attorney.
His wife, *née* Lemaitre.
'Madame Delphine' (s.s.), *Old Creole Days*, G. W. Cable, 1879.

Thompson, Mrs Joan, Joe Lampton's landlady.
Cedric, her husband.
Room at the Top, J. Braine, 1957.

Thompson, Lily, farmer's daughter, m. Luke Bishop. *The Poacher*, H. E. Bates, 1935.

Thompson, Millicent, expert fitter at Toni's. *A Deputy was King*, G. B. Stern, 1926.

Thompson, Pip, an R.A.F. recruit. *Chips With Everything* (play), Arnold Wesker, 1962.

Thompson, Ripton, school friend of Richard. *The Ordeal of Richard Feverel*, G. Meredith, 1859.

Thompson, Sadie, prostitute at Pago Pago. 'Miss Thompson' (s.s.), *The Trembling of a Leaf*, W. S. Maugham, 1921, also *Rain* (play).

Thompson, Will, m. Rosamund Walden. *God's Little Acre*, E. Caldwell, 1933.

Thomson, alias assumed by Alan Breck to help Balfour. *Kidnapped*, R. L. Stevenson, 1886.

Thomson, Rev. Frank. *Outward Bound* (play), S. Vane, 1923.

Thomson, Mrs Ianthe, daughter of Mrs Jardine by 1st husband.
Her husband.
Maisie, Malcolm and **Cherry,** their children.
The Ballad and the Source, Rosamond Lehmann, 1944.

Thomson, John.
Jeanie, his wife.
Robert, Alick and **Jessie,** their children.
The Setons, O. Douglas, 1917.

Thomson, Olivia (Livvy), friend of Lois Farquar. *The Last September*, Elizabeth Bowen, 1929.

Thong, Miss, dressmaker to the 'Good Companions.' *The Good Companions*, J. B. Priestley, 1929.

Thopas, Sir. 'The Tale of Sir

Thopas' (poem), *The Canterbury Tales*, G. Chaucer, 1373 onwards.

Thord the Northman. *Ben Hur*, L. Wallace, 1880.

Thorgrimur, of the Iron Toe, wealthy yeoman, father of Eric. *Eric Brighteyes*, H. Rider Haggard, 1891.

Thorn, Frederick. *East Lynne*, Mrs Henry Wood, 1861.

Thornberry, Job. *John Bull* (play), G. Colman the Younger, 1805.

Thorndale, Lord.
 James, his son, friend of Guy Morville.
 The Heir of Redclyffe, Charlotte M. Yonge, 1853.

Thorne, Captain, Divisional Superintendent of Police, Mogok. *No Other Tiger*, A. E. W. Mason, 1927.

Thorne, Roland, once fiancé of Clementina Wing. *The Glory of Clementina Wing*, W. J. Locke, 1911.

Thorne, Dr Thomas.
 Rev. Prebendary, D.D., his father.
 Henry, his profligate brother.
  Mary, Henry's illegitimate daughter, adopted by Dr Thorne, m. Frank Gresham.
 Thorne of Ullathorne.
  Monica, his sister.
 Doctor Thorne, 1858, and elsewhere, A. Trollope.

Thornhill, Sir William (alias Burchell), m. Sophia Primrose.
 His son, dissipated man-about-town, m. Olivia Primrose.
 The Vicar of Wakefield, O. Goldsmith, 1766.

Thornicroft, Lady Clementina, m. Marquis of Lossie. *The Marquis of Lossie*, G. MacDonald, 1877.

Thornton, Captain. *Rob Roy*, W. Scott, 1818.

Thornton, Judge.
 His wife.
 Elsie Venner, O. W. Holmes, 1861.

Thornton, Frederic Bas.
 His wife.
 John, Emily, Edward, Rachel and **Laura,** their children.
 High Wind in Jamaica, R. Hughes, 1929.

Thornton, John, m. Margaret Hale.
 His mother.
 Fanny, his sister.
 North and South, Mrs Gaskell, 1855.

Thornycroft, Emma, friend of Agatha Bowen.
 James, her husband.
 Agatha's Husband, Mrs Craik, 1853.

Thorod of Greenfell, uncle of Eric.
 Unna, his daughter, m. as 2nd wife Asmundson Asmund.
 Eric Brighteyes H. Rider Haggard, 1891.

Thoroughfare, Captain Dick, a romantic hero.
 Mrs Elizabeth Thoroughfare, his mother.
 Niri-Esther, his black wife, niece of Mrs Yajnavalkya.
 Valmouth, Ronald Firbank, 1919.

Thorpe, Dr.
 His children:
  Lucilla ('Lossie'), m. General Sir Hugh Desprez.
  Violet ('Vicey'), m. Lord Towerstairs.
  Oliver, m. Maisie Maxey.
  Joey, m. Sybil Percival.
 Joseph Vance, W. de Morgan, 1906.

Thorpe, Mrs.
 Her children:
  Isabella, close friend of Catherine Morland.
  John.
  Edward.
  William.
 Northanger Abbey, Jane Austen, 1818.

Thorpe, Mrs Gertrude, widow, sister of Amos Winterfield. *The Notorious Mrs Ebbsmith* (play), A. W. Pinero, 1895.

Thorpe, Samuel, schoolmate of James Galantry.
 Phoebe, his illegitimate half-sister, mistress of James Galantry, m. Sir Robin Carver.
 Dance of the Years, Margery Allingham, 1943.

Thrace, Henry, friend of Mr Ingleside. *Mr Ingleside*, E. V. Lucas, 1910.

Thragnar. *Jurgen*, J. B. Cabell, 1921.

Thrasiline. *Philaster* (play), Beaumont & Fletcher, 1611.

Thraso, or Polypragmus, the Plush Bee, *Parliament of Bees* (play), J. Day, 1641.

Thrawn, Mrs, fortune-teller. *The Story of Ivy*, Mrs Belloc Lowndes, 1927.

Threegan, Minnie, friend of Emma Deercourt, m. Captain Gadsby. *Story of the Gadsbys*, Kipling, 1888.

Threl. *The King of Elfland's Daughter*, Lord Dunsany, 1924.

Thriepneuk, Professor Habakkuk, uncle of Ralph Peden.
His daughters:
Jemima.
Kezia.
Keren-Happuch.
The Lilac Sunbonnet, S. R. Crockett, 1894.

Thrift, Viscount, M.P. *Phineas Finn*, A. Trollope, 1869.

Thriplow, Mary, ex-governess.
Jim, her late husband.
Those Barren Leaves, A. Huxley, 1925.

Throgmorton, Rev. Constantine, Vicar of Duke's Denver.
His wife.
Whose Body?, Dorothy L. Sayers, 1923.

Throndson, Euphemia, authoress, m. Harry Strachan. 'Why Billy Went Back' (s.s.), *All the World Wondered*, L. Merrick, 1911.

Throssel, Phoebe, m. Valentine Brown.
Susan, her elder sister.
Quality Street (play), J. M. Barrie, 1902.

Throstle, Mr. *Berkeley Square* (play), J. L. Balderston, 1926.

Thrum, Sir George.
His wife.
'The Ravenswing,' *Men's Wives*, W. M. Thackeray, 1843.

Thumb, Tom, a mouse.
Hunca Munca, his wife.
The Tale of Two Bad Mice, Beatrix Potter, 1904.

Thurbon, Victor, a novelist. *Pending Heaven*, William Gerhardie, 1930.

Thurio, rival to Valentine. *Two Gentlemen of Verona* (play), W. Shakespeare.

Thurnall, Tom, wanderer and jack-of-all-trades, central character.
Dr Thurnall, his father.
Two Years Ago, C. Kingsley, 1857.

Thursby, Floyd, murdered accomplice of Brigid O'Shaughnessy. *The Maltese Falcon*, Dashiell Hammett, 1930.

Thursley, Captain. *We're Here*, D. Mackail, 1947.

Thurstan, Richard, central character, ex-priest, lover of Ann, Lady Carew. *Lighten Our Darkness*, R. Keable, 1927.

Thurston, student and opium addict. *The Ivory God* (s.s.), J. S. Fletcher.

Thurston, Hope, m. Joyce Fane. *Going their own Ways*, A. Waugh, 1938.

Thurston, Lady May, m. Henry Franklin. *The Osbornes*, E. F. Benson, 1910.

Thwacker, quartermaster. *Redgauntlet*, W. Scott, 1824.

Thwackum, Rev. Mr, tutor to Tom Jones. *Tom Jones*, H. Fielding, 1749.

Thwaites. *The Little Minister*, J. M. Barrie, 1891.

Thwaites, Miss. *Gaslight* (play), Patrick Hamilton, 1939.

Thye, dreamer of songs. *The King of Elfland's Daughter*, Lord Dunsany, 1924.

Ti Hung, an idol maker.
Ning, his daughter, m. Yung Chang.
The Wallet of Kai Lung, E. Bramah, 1900.

Tib, Gammer Gurton's maid. *Gammer Gurton's Needle* (play), Anonymous, 1575.

Tibbets, John ('Ready-money Jack').
Jack, his son, m. Phoebe Wilkins.
Bracebridge Hall, W. Irving, 1823.

Tibbett, Mrs. *If Four Walls Told* (play), E. Percy, 1922.

Tibbitt, Dr, m. Minetta Bunker. 'Zenobia's Infidelity' (s.s.), *Short Sixes*, H. C. Bunner, 1890.

Tibbitts, Darrell, m. May Lindsell. *God's Stepchildren*, Sarah G. Millin, 1924.

Tibbs, hack writer.
His wife.
A Citizen of the World, O. Goldsmith, 1762.

Tibbs, Mrs, lodging-house keeper.
Her husband.
Sketches by Boz, C. Dickens, 1836.

Tiburce, brother of Valerian. 'The Second Nun's Tale,' *Canterbury Tales*, G. Chaucer, 1373 onwards.

Ticehurst, Will, a mason. 'Hal o' the Draft,' *Puck of Pook's Hill*, R. Kipling, 1906.

Tickeridge, Colonel. *Men at Arms*, Evelyn Waugh, 1952.

Tickler, Rev. Tobias, m. Olivia Proudie, *Framley Parsonage,* 1861, and elsewhere, A. Trollope.

Tiddler, Tom, twin of Tom Fiddler. *Adam's Opera* (play), Clemence Dane, 1928.

Tiddler, Det.-Sergeant William (Tom), *The Mirror Crack'd from Side to Side,* Agatha Christie, 1962.

Tidmarsh, Sir Timothy, Bt.
His wife.
Their six sons.
Evelyn, their daughter.
Before the Bombardment, O. Sitwell, 1926.

Tiernan, Jerry ('Hangover'), reporter and criminal. *Poison Ivy,* P. Cheyney, 1937.

Tiernay, Dr. *Roland Cashel,* C. Lever, 1850.

Tietjens, Strickland's dog. 'The Return of Imray' (s.s.), *Life's Handicap,* R. Kipling, 1891.

Tietjens, Sir Mark, Bt, m. Marie Leonie Riotor.
Christopher, his younger brother, antique furniture dealer.
Sylvia, his wife.
Mark, their son.
Last Post, F. M. Ford, 1928.

Tigellinus, evil genius of the book. *The Sign of the Cross,* W. Barrett, 1896.

Tiger Lily, a redskin. *Peter Pan* (play), J. M. Barrie, 1904.

Tigg, Montague, shabby swindler, friend of Chevy Slyme. *Martin Chuzzlewit,* C. Dickens, 1844.

Tiggy-Winkle, Mrs, a hedgehog. *The Tale of Mrs Tiggy-Winkle,* Beatrix Potter, 1905.

Tighe, Hamilton.
His wife.
'The Legend of Hamilton Tighe' (poem), *The Ingoldsby Legends,* R. H. Barham, 1837.

Tighe, Larry. 'Love o' Women' (s.s.), *Many Inventions,* R. Kipling, 1893.

Tigili, King of the N'Gombi. *Sanders of the River,* E. Wallace, 1911.

Tigner, Jimmy. 'Fairy-Kist' (s.s.), *Limits and Renewals,* R. Kipling, 1932.

Tigranes, King of Armenia. *A King and No King* (play), Beaumont & Fletcher, 1611.

Tilbury, Edward, young lawyer, lover of Alicia Bartleby. *A Suspension of Mercy,* Patricia Highsmith, 1965.

'Tilda, a flower girl. *No. 5 John Street,* R. Whiteing, 1902.

'Tildy, Negro house-girl. *Uncle Remus,* J. C. Harris, 1880–95.

Tiliot, wealthy spirit merchant.
Mary, his wife.
Felix Holt, George Eliot, 1866.

Tillotson, friend of Glover. *The Skipper's Wooing,* W. W. Jacobs, 1897.

Tillotson, Comrade, of Records Department. *1984,* G. Orwell, 1949.

Tillotson, Walter, nonogenarian artist. 'The Tillotson Banquet' (s.s.), *Mortal Coils,* A. Huxley, 1922.

Tilney, Edward, m. Laurel Studdard.
Anna, their daughter.
Simon, their son.
Lady Elfrida, divorcee, Edward's mother.
Friends and Relations, Elizabeth Bowen, 1931.

Tilney, Henry, m. Catherine Morland.
General Tilney, his father.
Captain Fred, his brother.
Eleanor, his sister.
Northanger Abbey, Jane Austen, 1818.

Tilsit, aunt of Betty Kane. *The Franchise Affair,* Josephine Tey, 1948.

Tiltwood, Dick, army friend of George Sherston. *Memoirs of a Fox-Hunting Man,* Siegfried Sassoon, 1929.

Timandra, mistress of Alcibiades. *Timon of Athens* (play), W. Shakespeare.

Timberlake, Asa.
Lavinia, his wife, *née* Fitzroy.
Their children:
Andrew.
Maggie, his wife.
Roy, m. Peter Kingsmill.
Stanley.
In this our Life, Ellen Glasgow, 1942.

Timberlake, Sir Horace, *The Masters,* 1951, part of the *Strangers and Brothers* sequence, C. P. Snow.

Timbs. *See* MRS BOODY.

Timlin, Father Tom, P.P., pilgrim to Lourdes. 'Feed My Lambs' (s.s.), *The Talking Trees,* Sean O'Faolain, 1971.

Timmins, Miss, maid to Mrs Dunscombe. *The Wide, Wide World,* Elizabeth Wetherell, 1850.

Timon, a noble Athenian. *Timon of Athens* (play), W. Shakespeare.

Timorous and **Mistrust,** neighbours of Christian, who turned back. *Pilgrim's Progress,* J. Bunyan, 1678 and 1684.

Timothy Tim. *Now We Are Six* (poem), A. A. Milne, 1927.

Timpany, 'second resurrectionist.' *The Good Companions,* J. B. Priestley, 1929.

Timpany, Dr, schoolmaster. *The Newcomes,* W. M. Thackeray, 1853–1855.

Timson, Alfred.
His wife.
William, their son.
Elizabeth, their daughter, m. James Galantry. *See also* FRANK CASTOR.
Other children.
Dance of the Years, Margery Allingham, 1943.

Tina, Matthaus. 'The Melancholy Hussar,' *Life's Little Ironies,* T. Hardy, 1894.

Tingcourt, Hannibal, steward to Sir Deakin Killigrew. *The Splendid Spur,* A. Quiller-Couch, 1889.

Tinker Bell, a fairy. *Peter Pan* (play), J. M. Barrie, 1904.

Tinkerton, Grace, Lady Wutherwood's maid. *Surfeit of Lampreys,* Ngaio Marsh, 1941.

Tinkler, housemaster at Dr Grimstone's. *Vice Versa,* F. Anstey, 1882.

Tinley, Sergeant, of the Wiltshires. *The Plough and the Stars* (play), S. O'Casey, 1926.

Tinman, The Flaming, a bully of the roads. *Lavengro,* George Borrow, 1851.

Tinto, Dick, artist, later celebrated. *The Bride of Lammermoor,* 1819, and elsewhere, W. Scott.

Tinwell, Minnie, bigamously married to Dubedat. *The Doctor's Dilemma* (play), G. B. Shaw, 1906.

Tiny Tim. *See* CRATCHIT.

Tippin, Lady, friend of the Veneerings. *Our Mutual Friend,* C. Dickens, 1865.

'Tippytilly,' Negro turned dervish. *The Tragedy of the Korosko,* A. Conan Doyle, 1898.

Tipstead, Eric.
His wife.
The Good Companions, J. B. Priestley, 1929.

Tiptoff, Earl of.
Lady Fanny, his wife, *née* Rakes.
The Great Hoggarty Diamond, W. M. Thackeray, 1841.

Tiptoff, Marquess of. *See* LORD GEORGE POYNINGS.
His wife.
Barry Lyndon, W. M. Thackeray, 1844.

Tiptop, Crasher's groom. *Market Harborough,* G. Whyte-Melville, 1861.

Tirlsneck, Johnnie, beadle. *St Ronan's Well,* W. Scott, 1824.

Tisher, Mrs, widow. *Edwin Drood,* C. Dickens, 1870.

Tisisthenes, son of Kallikrates and Amenartas. *She,* H. Rider Haggard, 1887.

Titania, Queen of the Fairies. *A Midsummer Night's Dream* (play), W. Shakespeare.

'Titania' ('Tita'), wife of the anonymous narrator.
Tom and **Jack,** their sons.
The Strange Adventures of a Phaeton, W. Black, 1872.

'Tite Poulette, m. Kristian Koppig. ''Tite Poulette' (s.s.), *Old Creole Days,* G. W. Cable, 1879.

Titmarsh, Samuel, central character and narrator.
Mary, his wife, *née* Smith.
His mother and nine sisters.
The Great Hoggarty Diamond, W. M. Thackeray, 1841.

Titmouse, Tittlebat, shopman, Tag-rag & Co., m. Lady Cecilia Dredlington. *Ten Thousand a Year,* S. Warren, 1839.

Tittlemouse, Mrs Thomasina. *The Tale of Mrs Tittlemouse,* 1910, and elsewhere, Beatrix Potter.

Titus Andronicus, a noble Roman general. *Titus Andronicus* (play), W. Shakespeare.

Titus Fulvius, Roman senator.
His father.
The Wonderful History of Titus and Gisippus (s.s.), T. Elyot, *c.* 1540.

Tiverton, Timmy, 'eccentric' music-hall comedian, central character, m. Daisy Barley. *Let the People Sing,* J. B. Priestley, 1939.

Toad, Mr, central character. *The Wind in the Willows,* K. Grahame, 1908.

Toberman, Basil, 'the other side' of Eustace Kinnit's business. *The China Governess,* Margery Allingham, 1963.

Tobermory, Lady Blemley's cat who talks. *Tobermory* (s.s.), 'Saki' (H. H. Munro), 1911.

Tobias, Tony, ex-paratrooper, Reg Mills's partner in crime. *The Patriots,* James Barlow, 1960.

Tobrah, a small boy. 'Little Tobrah' (s.s.), *Life's Handicap,* R. Kipling, 1891.

Tod, a self-confessed thief. *The Life and Death of Mr Badman,* J. Bunyan, 1680.

Tod, Mrs, landlady of John Halifax and Phineas Fletcher. *John Halifax, Gentleman,* Mrs Craik, 1856.

Todd, half-caste trader who loves Dickens. *A Handful of Dust,* Evelyn Waugh, 1934.

Todd, Captain, civil war veteran.
 Benton, his son.
 Night Rider, Robert Penn Warren, 1939.

Todd, Anne, Mrs Morland's secretary. The *Barsetshire* series, Angela Thirkell, 1933 onwards.

Todd, Ireton ('Last-trick Todd'). 'The Mistake of the Machine,' *The Wisdom of Father Brown,* G. K. Chesterton, 1914.

Toddington, Sir Herbert, judge.
 Mildred, his wife.
 The Brontës went to Woolworth's, Rachel Ferguson, 1931.

Toddle, Sandy. *The House with the Green Shutters,* G. Douglas, 1901.

Todgers, Mrs, boarding-house keeper. *Martin Chuzzlewit,* C. Dickens, 1844.

Todhunter, Rev. Mr, ex-vicar of St Peter's, Woodbank. *Another Year,* R. C. Sherriff, 1948.

Todhunter, John, m. Clare Doria. *The Ordeal of Richard Feverel,* G. Meredith, 1859.

Tods. 'Tods' Amendment' (s.s.), *Plain Tales from the Hills,* R. Kipling, 1888.

'Toinette, hotel servant, Paris. 'The Amours of Mr Deuceace,' *The Yellowplush Papers,* W. M. Thackeray, 1852.

Tolefree, Rev. Richard.
 Lucy, his niece, m. John Aquila.
 'A Case of Conscience,' *Love and Money,* Phyllis Bentley, 1957.

Tolland, Isobel, m. Nicholas Jenkins.
 Alfred, Earl of Warminster, her brother.
 Priscilla, her sister, m. Chips Lovell.
 A Question of Upbringing, 1951, and others in *The Music of Time* series, Anthony Powell.

Tollemache, Jack. *Sampson Rideout, Quaker,* Una Silberrad, 1911.

Toller, Middlemarch doctor. *Middlemarch,* George Eliot, 1871–2.

Toller, Mr and Mrs, servants to Jephro Rucastle. 'The Copper Beeches,' *The Adventures of Sherlock Holmes,* A. Conan Doyle, 1892.

Toller, Harry, brewer.
 Sophy, his daughter, m. Edward Plymdale.
 Middlemarch, Geo. Eliot, 1871–2.

Tolliver, Senator, leader of local affairs. *Night Rider,* Robert Penn Warren, 1939.

Tolloller, Earl. *Iolanthe* (comic opera), Gilbert & Sullivan, 1882.

Tolman, a lawyer. 'One Thousand Dollars' (s.s.), *The Voice of the City,* O. Henry, 1908.

Tolson, Victor, mate and lover of Leonard Radcliffe.
 Audrey, his wife.
 Radcliffe, David Storey, 1963.

Tom, a chimney sweep, later water baby, central character. *The Water Babies,* C. Kingsley, 1863.

Tom, 'Uncle,' Negro slave, central character.
 'Aunt Chloe,' his wife.
 Uncle Tom's Cabin, Harriet B. Stowe, 1851.

Tom, Sir Thomas. *Now We Are Six,* A. A. Milne, 1927.

Tom the Toff. *The Yellow Scarf* (s.s.), T. Burke.

Tomato, Salvatore (Sally), a Mafia leader imprisoned in Sing-Sing. *Breakfast at Tiffany's,* Truman Capote, 1958.

Tombases, President, Hydra's revolutionists. *The Capsina,* E. F. Benson, 1899.

Tombes, Sir Harry Sims's butler. *The Twelve Pound Look* (play), J. M. Barrie, 1910.

Tomes, Ramsey. *It Never Can Happen Again,* W. de Morgan, 1909.

Tomkins, Joseph ('Honest Joe,' 'Fibbet,' etc.), clerk to Colonel Desborough. *Woodstock*, W. Scott, 1826.

Tomlin, Sam, brother-in-law of Joseph Quinney. *Quinneys'*, H. A. Vachell, 1914.

Tomling, Sir Christopher, engineer. 'The Puzzler' (s.s.), *Actions and Reactions*, R. Kipling, 1909.

Tomlinson, rich, uneducated miller of Milby. 'Janet's Repentance,' *Scenes of Clerical Life*, George Eliot, 1857.

Tomlinson, a dilettante, accepted neither in Heaven nor Hell. 'Tomlinson' (poem), *Barrack-room Ballads*, R. Kipling, 1892.

Tomlinson, Augustus, journalist, and tutor to Paul. *Paul Clifford*, Lord Lytton, 1830.

Tomos. 'A Heifer without Blemish' (s.s.), *My People*, Caradoc Evans, 1915.

Tompkins, Major ('The Bully').
His wife ('The Shrew').
Vivian, their daughter ('The Hussy').
The Passing of the Third Floor Back (play), J. K. Jerome, 1910.

Tompsett, a coachman. *The Admirable Crichton* (play), J. M. Barrie, 1902.

Tompson, valet to Paul Verdayne. *Three Weeks*, Elinor Glyn, 1907.

Tomson, Arthur Wellesley, a small boy. *Quality Street* (play), J. M. Barrie, 1902.

Tomson, Elias, Julius Ricardo's servant. *No Other Tiger*, A. E. W. Mason, 1927.

Tomson, Sally, George Smith's secretary. *A Singular Man*. J. P. Donleavy, 1964.

Toobad, dearest friend of Chris. Glowry.
Celinda (alias Stella), his daughter, m. Flosky.
Nightmare Abbey, T. L. Peacock, 1818.

Toodle, a stoker.
His wife.
Dombey and Son, C. Dickens, 1848.

Toogood, a 'co-operationist.' *Crotchet Castle*, T. L. Peacock, 1831.

Toogood, Parson Billy. 'Andrey Satchel and the Parson and Clerk,' *Life's Little Ironies*, T. Hardy, 1894.

Took, Peregrin (Pippin), cousin of Frodo Baggins. *The Lord of the Rings* trilogy, 1954–5, J. R. R. Tolkien.

Tooke, Granny, almost a centenarian.
Thetis, her grand-daughter.
David, her grandson, young dairyman.
Valmouth, Ronald Firbank, 1919.

Tookey, deputy parish clerk, Raveloe. *Silas Marner*, George Eliot, 1861.

Toole, Owney, 'Owney' (s.s.), *Countrymen All*, Katherine Tynan, 1915.

Toomai, Little.
Big Toomai, his father.
'Toomai of the Elephants,' *The Jungle Book*, R. Kipling, 1894.

Toomer, Horace, friend of George Brumley, a leader of the Fabian Society. *The Wife of Sir Isaac Harman*, 1914, and elsewhere, H. G. Wells.

Toomey, Dan, m. Nappa Kilmartin. *Famine*, L. O'Flaherty, 1937.

Toop, Joel, farmer.
Peter, his brother, barman, the Jolly Huntsman, m. Rachel Bolt.
The Mother, E. Phillpotts, 1908.

Toothill, Sir Reginald, Bt. *The Sport of Kings* (play), Ian Hay, 1924.

Tootles, a member of Peter's band. *Peter Pan* (play), J. M. Barrie, 1904.

Toots, P., head boy at Dr Blimber's, m. Susan Nipper.
Their children.
Dombey and Son, C. Dickens, 1848.

Topaz, Sir. *A Fairy Tale* (poem), T. Parnell.

Topehall, Narcissa, m. Roderick Random.
Orson, her brother.
Her aunt.
Roderick Random, T. Smollett, 1748.

Topham, Lord, British Ambassador. *The Prisoner of Zenda*, A. Hope, 1894.

Topham, Barbara, aunt of Lady Castlewood. *Henry Esmond*, W. M. Thackeray, 1852.

Topsy, Negro child slave, protégée of Eva St Clare. *Uncle Tom's Cabin*, Harriet B. Stowe, 1851.

Torkingham, Rev. Mr. *Two on a Tower*, T. Hardy, 1882.

Torp, Gerda, m. Wolf Solent.
Her father, a stonecutter.
Lob, her brother.
Wolf Solent, J. C. Powys, 1929.

Torpenhow, Gilbert Belling, close friend of Dick Heldar. *The Light that Failed,* R. Kipling, 1890.

Torquil of the Oak, aged forester and father of eight sons. *The Fair Maid of Perth,* W. Scott, 1828.

Torrance, John.
Ellen, his wife.
Roger and **Emma,** their children.
The New Word (play), Barrie, 1915.

Torrent, Lady.
Sir James, her husband.
Ariadne, Nigel, Helen and **Denzil,** their children, all four charges of Simpson.
Simpson, E. Sackville-West, 1931.

Torrigiano, an Italian builder. 'The Wrong Thing,' *Rewards and Fairies,* R. Kipling, 1910.

Torrington, Captain, friend of Henleigh Grandcourt.
His wife.
Daniel Deronda, George Eliot, 1876.

Tortillion, Lord. Family name de Travers).
His son and daughter-in-law.
Their children:
Anne, m. Henry Melville.
Fanny.
Bluebeard's Keys, Anne Thackeray, 1874.

Tortoise, Mr Alderman Ptolemy. *The Tale of Jeremy Fisher,* Beatrix Potter, 1906.

Tosh, Silva. *The Little Minister,* J. M. Barrie, 1891.

Tott, Laura, governess. *Holy Deadlock,* A. P. Herbert, 1934.

Tottenham, Lord. *The Treasure Seekers,* E. Nesbit, 1899.

Tottle, Watkins. *Sketches by Boz,* C. Dickens, 1836.

Touchandgo, Miss, daughter of financial swindler; intended fiancée of MacCrotchet jnr. *Crotchet Castle,* T. L. Peacock, 1831.

Touchett, Ralph, cousin of Isabel Archer. *The Portrait of a Lady,* Henry James, 1881.

Touchstone, a clown, m. Audrey. *As You Like It* (play), W. Shakespeare.

Touchwood. *Theophrastus Such,* George Eliot, 1879.

Touchy, Tom, confirmed litigant. Essay in *The Spectator,* J. Addison, 1711–14.

Tough, Mr Defts, counsel in Peebles v. Plainstanes. *Redgauntlet,* W. Scott, 1824.

Toulouse, Dr, Robert.
Julie, his wife.
The Weak and the Strong, G. Kersh, 1945.

Tovesky, Marie, neighbour of the Bergsons. *O Pioneers!,* Willa Cather, 1913.

Towers, Dowager Duchess of (Family name Harcourt).
Her children:
The present **Duke.**
Franklin, his American wife.
Their children
Lady Gwendolen, m. Caleb Oriel.
Lady Elaine.
The Rev. Lord William, m. Edith Graham.
Gwendolen Sally, their daughter.
Love at All Ages, 1959 and elsewhere, The *Barsetshire* series, Angela Thirkell.

Towers, Tom, of the *Jupiter. The Warden,* A. Trollope, 1855.

Towerstairs, Lord (Dick), m. Violet Thorpe. *Joseph Vance,* W. de Morgan, 1906.

Towler, servant to Sir F. Clavering. *Pendennis,* W. M. Thackeray, 1848–50.

Towler, Dick, an ostler. *Black Beauty,* Anna Sewell, 1877.

Townbrake, Lord. *Monsieur Beaucaire* (play), Booth Tarkington, 1902.

Towne, Langdon, central character and narrator, m. Ann Potter.
Humphrey, his father.
Eden, Richard, Nathan, Enoch and **Odiorne,** his brothers.
Rebecca, Sarah and **Mary,** his sisters.
Northwest Passage, Kenneth Roberts, 1938.

Towneley, college friend of Ernest Pontifex. *The Way of All Flesh,* S. Butler, 1903.

Towneley, Lord and Lady. *The Provok'd Husband* (play), J. Vanbrugh & C. Cibber, 1728.

Townley, Captain. *Trumpeter, Sound!*, D. L. Murray, 1933.

Townley, Colonel, J.P. *Adam Bede*, George Eliot, 1859.

Townley, Miss, schoolmistress, Milby. 'Janet's Repentance,' *Scenes of Clerical Life*, George Eliot, 1857.

Townly, Colonel. *A Trip to Scarborough* (play), R. B. Sheridan, 1777.

Townsend, theatrical agent. *The Actor Manager*, L. Merrick, 1898.

Townsend, Arthur, eng. to Marian Almond.
  Morris, his cousin, eng. to Catherine Sloper.
Washington Square, H. James, 1880.

Townsend, Pixie, m. Anthony Kroesig. *The Pursuit of Love*, Nancy Mitford, 1945.

Townshend, Bow Street runner. *Lost Sir Massingberd*, James Payn, 1864.

Townshend, Arthur, fiancé of Elizabeth Seton. *The Setons*, O. Douglas, 1917.

Townshend, Hilary. *The Green Hat*, M. Arlen, 1924.

Towrowski, Count, eloped with Miss Bagg. *The Book of Snobs*, W. M. Thackeray, 1846–7.

Tow-Wouse, Mr and Mrs, innkeepers. *Joseph Andrews*, H. Fielding, 1742.

Tox, Miss, close friend of Mrs Chick. *Dombey and Son*, C. Dickens, 1848.

Tozer, Leora, m. Martin Arrowsmith as 1st wife.
  Her father and mother.
  Albert, her brother.
Martin Arrowsmith, Sinclair Lewis, 1925.

Trabb, a tailor.
  Trabb's Boy, his errand-boy.
Great Expectations, C. Dickens, 1861.

Trabbit, Mrs, aunt of Jim Cartledge.
  Euphemia, her daughter.
Both of this Parish, J. S. Fletcher.

Tracey, 'Colonel.'
  Leonora, his wife, masquerading as his daughter.
'Patience' (s.s.), *Last Recollections of My Uncle Charles*, N. Balchin, 1954.

Tracy. *Tracy's Tiger*, W. Saroyan, 1951.

Tracy, Lady, *née* Betty Marston. *The Courtship of Morrice Buckler*, A. E. W. Mason, 1896.

Tracy, Howard, a schoolboy. *St Winifred's*, F. W. Farrar, 1862.

Traddles, Tom, schoolfellow and close friend of David Copperfield, m. Sophy Crewler, 'the dearest girl in the world.' *David Copperfield*, C. Dickens, 1850.

Trafford, Richard Andrew, brilliant scientist, m. Marjorie Pope.
  Margharita, Godwin, Rachel and **Edward,** their children.
  Richard's mother.
Marriage, H. G. Wells, 1912.

Traherne, Dr Basil. *The Green Goddess* (play), W. Archer, 1921.

Traherne, Caroline, daughter of Selwyn Faramond. *The Gates of Summer* (play), John Whiting, 1956.

Trail, convict and murderer. *The Old Dominion*, Mary Johnston, 1899.

Trail, Rt Rev., Bishop of Ealing.
  His wife and son.
Vanity Fair, W. M. Thackeray, 1847–8.

Traill, Archie, schoolmaster, m. Isabel Desart. *Mr Perrin and Mr Traill*, Hugh Walpole, 1911.

Traill, Mary. *Captain Blood*, R. Sabatini, 1922.

Trampas, 'bad man.' *The Virginian*, O. Wister, 1902.

Tranfield, Grace, *née* Cuthbertson. *The Philanderer* (play), G. B. Shaw, 1893.

Transom, Captain the Hon., H.M.S. *Firebrand*. *Tom Cringle's Log*, M. Scott, 1836.

Transome, temporary alias of Prince Otto. *Prince Otto*, R. L. Stevenson, 1885.

Transome, Mr, of Transome Court.
  Arabella, his wife.
  Durfey, their semi-imbecile son.
  Harold, Arabella's son by Matthew Jermyn.
Felix Holt, George Eliot, 1866.

Trant, Sergeant. *Trumpeter, Sound!*, D. L. Murray, 1933.

Trant, Elizabeth, financier and benefactor of the Good Companions, m. Hugh McFarlane.
  Hilary, her nephew.
The Good Companions, J. B. Priestley, 1929.

Trant, Susan, widow of farmer Trant, ex-mistress of Oliver Raydon, m. John Rackham. *An Affair of Dishonour,* W. de Morgan, 1910.

Tranter, John. *The White Company,* A. Conan Doyle, 1891.

Trapbois, 'Golden,' money-lender.
Martha, his daughter.
The Fortunes of Nigel, W. Scott, 1822.

Trapes, Diana. *The Beggar's Opera,* 1728, and *Polly,* 1729 (comic operas), J. Gay.

Trapnel, X., impecunious and eccentric author. *Books Do Furnish A Room,* 1971, and others in *The Music of Time* series, Anthony Powell.

Trask, Adam, a settler.
Cathy, his wife, *née* Ames, who changes her name to Kate, prostitute and murderess.
Caleb and **Aron,** their twin sons.
Charles Trask, Adam's half-brother.
East of Eden, John Steinbeck, 1952.

Travers. *Housemaster* (play), Ian Hay, 1936.

Travers, Hiram G. *Bulldog Drummond,* 'Sapper' (H. C. McNeile), 1920.

Travers, Muriel, Luke Mangan's 1st wife.
Her father and mother.
Lance, her brother.
The Bay, L. A. G. Strong, 1941.

Traverse. *The Clandestine Marriage* (play), G. Colman the Elder, 1766.

Trawler, Rutherford (Rusty), a millionaire. *Breakfast at Tiffany's,* Truman Capote, 1958.

Treadwell, Mary, a divorcée. *Ship of Fools,* Katherine Anne Porter, 1962.

Trebell, Miss Henry. *Waste* (play), H. Granville-Barker, 1907.

Trebonius, conspirator against Caesar. *Julius Caesar* (play), W. Shakespeare.

Tredennis, Colonel Philip. *Through One Administration,* Francis H. Burnett, 1881.

Tredgold, Clay.
Clara, his wife.
Martin Arrowsmith, Sinclair Lewis, 1925.

Tredgold, Edward.
His father. Estate agents.
Dialstone Lane, W. W. Jacobs, 1904.

Trefoyle. Family name of LORD POLPERRO.

Trefusis, Samuel, ne'er-do-well artist, brother of Mrs Cole. *Jeremy,* Hugh Walpole, 1919.

Tregannon, Dr, crooked alienist. *The Judas Window,* C. Dickson, 1938.

Tregarvan, Sir John, Bt, M.P.
His wife.
The Adventures of Philip, W. M. Thackeray, 1861–2.

Tregellis, Sir Charles, uncle and patron of Rodney. *Rodney Stone,* A. Conan Doyle, 1896.

Treginnis, Brenda.
Her brothers:
Owen.
George.
Mortimer.
'The Devil's Foot,' *His Last Bow,* A. Conan Doyle, 1917.

Tregoning, Hope. *If Four Walls Told* (play), E. Percy, 1922.

Tregunter, Miss, 'old maid.' *Magnolia Street,* L. Golding, 1932.

Treherne, Rev. John. *The Admirable Crichton* (play), J. M. Barrie, 1902.

Trehick, Lord, m. Francie Comper.
His mother. *See also* RETARRIER.
For Us in the Dark, Naomi Royde-Smith, 1937.

Trehune, Cass, lady with a poodle. *Midnight Cowboy,* James Leo Herlihy, 1966.

Trejago, Christopher. 'Beyond the Pale' (s.s.), *Plain Tales from the Hills,* R. Kipling, 1888.

Trelawney, Squire. *Treasure Island,* R. L. Stevenson, 1883.

Trelawny, Rose, central character. *Trelawny of the Wells* (play), A. W. Pinero, 1898.

Trellick, Tom, a farmer, m. Mary Lynton. *The Second Mrs Conford,* Beatrice K. Seymour, 1951.

Treloar, Jack, m. Joan Penrose.
Milly, his sister, m. Roderick Nancarrow.
The Winds of Chance, S. K. Hocking.

Tremayne, Belinda.
Jack, her husband.
Delia, their daughter.
Belinda (play), A. A. Milne, 1918.

Tremlett, William, a villager. *The Trumpet Major,* T. Hardy, 1880.

Tremouille, La, Chamberlain.
The Duchesse.
Saint Joan (play), G. B. Shaw, 1924.

Trenail, Second Lieutenant, of the *Breeze. Tom Cringle's Log,* M. Scott, 1836.

Trench, Lord.
His wife.
The High Road (play), F. Lonsdale, 1927.

Trench, Dr Harry. *Widowers' Houses* (play), G. B. Shaw, 1892.

Trench, Isabelle. *Caroline* (play), W. S. Maugham, 1916.

Trenchard, Sir Rowland. *Jack Sheppard,* W. H. Ainsworth, 1839.

Trencher. 'The Luck Piece' (s.s.), *From Place to Place,* Irvin S. Cobb, 1920.

Trennery, an innkeeper. *For Us in the Dark,* Naomi Royde-Smith, 1937.

Trenor, George Augustus.
Judy, his wife.
Hilda and **Muriel,** their daughters.
The House of Mirth, Edith Wharton, 1905.

Trent, Mrs Gwennie, wardrobe mistress. *Antigua Penny Puce,* R. Graves, 1936.

Trent, Nellie ('Little Nell'), central character.
Frederick, her worthless brother.
Her grandfather.
The Old Curiosity Shop, C. Dickens, 1841.

Trent, Paul, solicitor and philosophical anarchist. *A Glastonbury Romance,* J. C. Powys, 1932.

Trent, Philip, artist, newspaper reporter and investigator, central character. *Trent's Last Case,* E. C. Bentley, 1912.

Trent, Rosamund, friend of Alayne Whiteoak. *Finch's Fortune,* Mazo de la Roche, 1931.

Trent, Sonia, friend of Dodo Baker. *Britannia Mews,* Margery Sharp, 1946.

Tresham, sleeping partner in Osbaldistone & Tresham.
Will, his son.
Rob Roy, W. Scott, 1818.

Tresham, Richard (alias General Witherington), m. Zilia de Moncada.
Richard Middlemas, their son before marriage.
The Surgeon's Daughter, W. Scott, 1827.

Tresham, Earl Thorold.
Mildred, his sister.
Austin, his brother.
Guendolen, his cousin, betrothed to Austin.
A Blot in the 'Scutcheon (play), Robert Browning, 1843.

Tresinney, Abel, fraudulent claimant. *The Winds of Chance,* S. K. Hocking.

Tressilian, Edmund, suitor of Amy Robsart. *Kenilworth,* W. Scott, 1821.

Tressilvain, Lord, m. Helen Wayward as 2nd husband. *The Firing Line,* R. W. Chambers, 1908.

Tretherick, Clara, poetess.
Her 2nd (bigamous) husband.
Caroline, his daughter.
m. (3) Colonel Starbottle.
'An Episode of Fiddletown,' *The Luck of Roaring Camp,* Bret Harte, 1868.

Trevanion, largest officer in the English Army. *Harry Lorrequer,* C. Lever, 1839.

Trevedian, Peter.
Max, his half-brother.
Luke, their dead father.
Campbell's Kingdom, H. Innes, 1952.

Trevelyan, Bunk, poor tobacco farmer. *Night Rider,* Robert Penn Warren, 1939.

Trevelyan, Laura, niece of Mrs Bonner. *Voss,* Patrick White, 1957.

Trevelyan, Louis.
Emily, his wife, daughter of Sir Marmaduke Rowley.
He Knew He Was Right, A. Trollope, 1869.

Trevelyan, Dr Percy. 'The Resident Patient,' *Memoirs of Sherlock Holmes,* A. Conan Doyle, 1894.

Trevi, Maddalena, m. Gian-luca Boselli. *Adam's Breed,* Radclyffe Hall, 1926.

Trevignac, de, French officer. *The Garden of Allah,* R. S. Hichens, 1904.

Treville, Julian, lover of Laura Delacourt. *The Duenna,* Mrs Belloc Lowndes.

Trevis, crippled young friend of Howat Freemantle.
His father.
And Now Goodbye, J. Hilton, 1931.

Trevisa, Judith, m. Captain Curll Coppinger.
Rev. Peter, Rector, St Enodoc, her father.
James, her twin brother.
Dionysius, her aunt.
In the Roar of the Sea, S. Baring-Gould, 1892.

Trevor, a duellist. *Diary of a Late Physician,* S. Warren, 1832.

Trevor, Mrs, aunt of Eric Williams.
Fanny, her daughter.
Eric, or Little by Little, F. W. Farrar, 1858.

Trevor, Angus, red-haired reporter, *The Flame. No Other Tiger,* A. E. W. Mason, 1927.

Trevor, Martin, squire's son engaged to Joanna Godden, but dies. *Joanna Godden,* Sheila Kaye-Smith, 1921.

Trevor, Victor, college friend of Sherlock Holmes. 'The Gloria Scott,' *Memoirs of Sherlock Holmes,* A. Conan Doyle, 1894.

Trewe, Robert, poet. 'An Imaginative Woman,' *Wessex Tales,* T. Hardy, 1888.

Trewhella, William James (Jaz), coal and wood merchant.
Rose, his wife.
Kangaroo, D. H. Lawrence, 1923.

Trewsbury, Captain Cyril ('Cruiser'), central character. *The Bird of Dawning,* J. Masefield, 1933.

Tric-Trac, French criminal. *The Maids of Paradise,* R. W. Chambers, 1903.

Trig, Lord Benira. 'The Three Musketeers' (s.s.), *Plain Tales from the Hills,* R. Kipling, 1888.

Trigorin, Kiril. *The Constant Nymph,* Margaret Kennedy, 1924.

Trilby. *See* TRILBY O'FERRALL.

Trim, Corporal, servant to Toby Shandy. *Tristram Shandy,* L. Sterne, 1767.

Trim, Lord, governor of the Sago Islands. *The Adventures of Philip,* W. M. Thackeray, 1861–2.

Trimingham, 9th Viscount (Hugh Francis Winlove), m. Marian Maudsley. *The Go-Between,* L. P. Hartley, 1953.

Trimmer, Mr. *Sketches by Boz,* C. Dickens, 1836.

Trimmins, George, fiancé of Nora Hopper.
His mother.
'The Face' (s.s.), *A Beginning,* W. de la Mare, 1955.

Trinculo, a jester. *The Tempest* (play), W. Shakespeare.

Trindle, Miss, governess to the Newmark children. *The Fortress,* Hugh Walpole, 1932.

Tring, Exeter Battleby. 'Public Waste' (poem), *Departmental Ditties,* R. Kipling, 1886.

Tringham, Parson. *Tess of the D'Urbervilles,* T. Hardy, 1891.

Trink, Stephen. *The Bloomsbury Wonder* (s.s.), T. Burke.

Trip. *The School for Scandal* (play), R. B. Sheridan, 1777.

Triplet, James, tenth-rate dramatist-actor and scene-painter.
Jane, his wife.
Lucy, Lysimacus and **Roxalana,** their children.
Peg Woffington, C. Reade, 1853.

Triplex, Julia, friend of Georgiana Longestaff, m. Sir Damask Monogram. *The Way We Live Now,* A. Trollope, 1875.

Trippet, Tom. *Catherine,* W. M. Thackeray, 1839–40.

Tristan L'Hermite, provost marshal of Louis's household. *Quentin Durward,* W. Scott, 1823.

Tristram, in love with Isolt, slain by Mark. 'The Last Tournament' (poem), *Idylls of the King,* Lord Tennyson, 1859.

Tristram, Mr.
His wife.
The American, H. James, 1877.

Triton, Lord, philanthropist. *Middlemarch,* George Eliot, 1871–2.

Trivett, Bobby, a subaltern. 'The Honours of War' (s.s.), *A Diversity of Creatures,* R. Kipling, 1917.

Troil, Ulla ('Norma of the Fitful Head').
Erland, her father.
Olave, her uncle.
Magnus, his son.
His wife, *née* Sinclair.
Minna and **Brenda,** their daughters.
See also CAPTAIN CLEMENT CLEVELAND and BASIL MERTOUN.
The Pirate, W. Scott, 1822.

Troilus, son of Priam. *Troilus and Cressida* (play), W. Shakespeare.

Troop, a prefect at Peter Stubland's school. *Joan and Peter,* H. G. Wells, 1918.

Troop, Disko, captain of the *We're Here.*
Dan, his son, friend of Harvey Cheyne jnr.
His wife.
Captains Courageous, R. Kipling, 1897.

Trotman, John, landlord of the Cat and Fiddle. *Sybil,* B. Disraeli, 1845.

Trott, Alexander. *Sketches by Boz,* C. Dickens, 1836.

Trotter, 'opulent oilman.'
His wife and daughters.
The Sketch Book, W. Irving, 1820.

Trotter. *Fanny's First Play* (play), G. B. Shaw, 1905.

Trotter, Second Lieutenant. *Journey's End* (play), R. C. Sherriff, 1928.

Trotter, Benjamin. *The Land of Promise* (play), W. S. Maugham, 1914.

Trotter, Emma, m. Lord Methusaleh.
Her mother.
Mrs Perkins's Ball, W. M. Thackeray, 1847.

Trotter, Job, servant of Jingle. *Pickwick Papers,* C. Dickens, 1837.

Trotter, Nellie, fishwife. *St Ronan's Well,* W. Scott, 1824.

Trotwood, Betsey, great-aunt of David Copperfield.
Her good-for-nothing husband.
David Copperfield, C. Dickens, 1850.

Troughton-Harrington-Yorke, Captain the Hon. Miles ('Methy') of *Artemis. The Ship,* C. S. Forester, 1943.

Trounce, Sergeant. *St Patrick's Day* (play), R. B. Sheridan, 1775.

Trout, Eva, heiress.
Jeremy, her small son (illegitimate).
Willy, her dead father.
Eva Trout, Elizabeth Bowen, 1969.

Trout, Joanna. *Dear Brutus* (play), J. M. Barrie, 1917.

Trowse, Meriel, owner of riding school. *Twelve Horses and the Hangman's Noose,* Gladys Mitchell, 1956.

Troy, Agatha, sculptress, m. Roderick Alleyn. *Ngaio Marsh*'s series of detective stories, 1934 onwards.

Troy, Sergeant Francis, m. Bathsheba Everdene.
His mother.
Far from the Madding Crowd, T. Hardy, 1874.

Troyton, Mrs Charlotte, m. Rev. Christopher Swancourt. *A Pair of Blue Eyes,* T. Hardy, 1873.

Trubody, Faith, a neurotic teenager.
Peter, her twin brother.
The Widow's Cruise, Nicholas Blake, 1959.

Truffigny, Monsieur de, attaché at French Embassy. *Vanity Fair,* W. M. Thackeray, 1847–8.

Trufoot, Harriet Vane's publisher. *Strong Poison,* Dorothy L. Sayers, 1930.

Trull, Dolly. *Polly,* J. Gay, 1729.

Trumbull, Borthrop, auctioneer. *Middlemarch,* George Eliot, 1871.

Trumbull, Douglas, friend of Clyde Griffiths.
Jill, Gertrude and **Tracy,** his children.
An American Tragedy, T. Dreiser, 1925.

Trumbull, Tom ('Tom Turnpenny'). *Redgauntlet,* W. Scott, 1824.

Trump, Dr, m. Felicity Warple. *Children of the Archbishop,* N. Collins, 1951.

Trumper, Tom.
His wife.
Hawbuck Grange, R. S. Surtees, 1847.

Trumpington, Captain. 'The Ravenswing,' *Men's Wives,* 1843, and elsewhere, W. M. Thackeray.

Trumpington, Lady. *The Virginians,* W. M. Thackeray, 1857–9.

Trumpington, Sir Alastair Digby Vane.
Sonia, his wife.
Decline and Fall, 1928, and elsewhere, E. Waugh.

Trundle, m. Isabella Wardle. *Pickwick Papers,* C. Dickens, 1837.

Trunnion, Commodore Hawser, commanding local garrison.
Grizzle, his wife, *née* Pickle.
Peregrine Pickle, T. Smollett, 1751.

Truog, Maria, a servant, m. Warli. *Ships that Pass in the Night,* Beatrice Harraden, 1893.

Trupenie, Tom, servant to Dame Custance. *Ralph Roister Doister,* N. Udall, 1551.

Trusbut, Cicely, supposed daughter of **Peter,** and **Potentia,** his wife, later revealed as Angela, daughter of Sir Almeric Mountjoy. *The Tower of London,* W. H. Ainsworth, 1840.

Truscott, Inspector Jim, crooked

policeman. *Loot* (play), Joe Orton, 1966.

Trustie, Tristram, friend of Goodluck. *Ralph Roister Doister,* N. Udall, 1551.

Trusty, Mrs. *The Clandestine Marriage* (play), G. Colman the Elder, 1766.

Truthful James, of Table Mountain. *The Society upon the Stanislaus* (poem), and elsewhere, Bret Harte.

Tryan, Rev. Edgar, curate at Paddiford Common, Milby.
His sister.
'Janet's Repentance,' *Scenes of Clerical Life,* George Eliot, 1857.

Tryte, John Maxwell ('Max'), author, artist and playboy, m. Rowena Ravenstock. *Portrait of a Playboy,* W. Deeping, 1947.

Tsi-Puff, moon guardian of Cavor. *The First Men in the Moon,* H. G. Wells, 1901.

Tubal, a Jew, friend of Shylock. *The Merchant of Venice* (play), W. Shakespeare.

Tubbe, Waldo, friend of George Winterbourne. *Death of a Hero,* R. Aldington, 1929.

Tubbs, Mrs, landlady. *The Actor Manager,* L. Merrick, 1898.

Tucca, Captain, a roisterer. *Satiromastix* (play), Thomas Dekker, 1601.

Tuck, Mrs Angela, adventuress. *The Rich Pay Late,* 1964, and others in the *Alms for Oblivion* sequence, Simon Raven.

Tuck, Thomas ('Tyburn Tom'), footpad. *The Heart of Midlothian,* W. Scott, 1818.

Tucker, curate to Edward Casaubon. *Middlemarch,* Geo. Eliot, 1871–2.

Tucker, Dan. *Put Yourself in his Place,* C. Reade, 1870.

Tucker, Kate and **Evie,** daughters of Emily Frampton by 1st husband. *Non-Combatants and Others,* Rose Macaulay, 1916.

Tucker, Mildred A., housekeeper to Mrs Strood. *The Jury,* G. Bullett, 1935.

Tucker, Sarah, upper housemaid to the Barfields. *Esther Waters,* G. Moore, 1894.

Tucker, William, merchant. *Abraham Lincoln* (play), J. Drinkwater, 1918.

Tucket, Mrs. *September Tide,* Daphne du Maurier, 1948.

Tudge, Job, protégé of Felix Holt. *Felix Holt,* George Eliot, 1866.

Tudor, Father, teacher at Belvedere Preparatory School. *Adam of Dublin,* C. O'Riordan, 1920.

Tudor, Rev. Septimus.
Hon. Mrs, his wife.
The Farmer's Wife (play), E. Phillpotts, 1924.

Tuesday, Paterson's Burmese 'boy.'
Nadia, his elder sister, Paterson's mistress.
The Jacaranda Tree, H. E. Bates, 1949.

Tufthunt. *See* Rev. Thomas Tufton Hunt.

Tufto, Lieutenant-General Sir George Granby.
His wife.
Tom, his grandson.
Vanity Fair, 1847–8, and elsewhere, W. M. Thackeray.

Tuggridge, Albert, friend of Leonard Oakroyd. *The Good Companions,* J. B. Priestley, 1929.

Tuggs, Joseph, grocer.
His wife.
Simon, their son.
Charlotte, their daughter.
Sketches by Boz, C. Dickens, 1836.

Tugtail, Anthony. *Hawbuck Grange,* R. S. Surtees, 1847.

Tuke. *See* Routh.

Tuke, Mrs Beryl, landlady of public house awaiting demolition.
Her husband.
Prudence, her daughter, in love with Alban Roche.
Miss Gomez and The Brethren, William Trevor, 1971.

Tulke, a prefect. 'The Last Term,' *Stalky & Co.,* R. Kipling, 1899.

Tulkinghorn, family lawyer of Sir Leicester Dedlock. *Bleak House,* C. Dickens, 1853.

Tull, Mormon elder and scoundrel. *Riders of the Purple Sage,* Zane Grey, 1912.

Tulla, Earl of, brother of George Morris. *Phineas Finn,* A. Trollope, 1869.

Tullidge, Corporal. *The Trumpet Major,* T. Hardy, 1880.

Tulliver, Edward, miller.
Elizabeth, his wife, *née* Dodson.
Tom, their son.

Maggie, their daughter.
'Gritty,' his sister, m. Moss.
The Mill on the Floss, George Eliot, 1860.

Tulse, Mr, of the Church of Ancient Truth. *Albert Grope,* F. O. Mann, 1931.

Tung Fel, goat keeper, seeker of jade. *The Wallet of Kai Lung,* E. Bramah, 1900.

Tunmarsh, Lord, chairman of Aintree stewards. *National Velvet,* Enid Bagnold, 1935.

Tunstall, Frank, 'sharp-witted, active apprentice' of David Ramsay. *The Fortunes of Nigel,* W. Scott, 1822.

Tupman, Gwendoline, sister of Mabel Hemworth. *Distinguished Villa* (play), Kate O'Brien, 1926.

Tupman, Tracy, member of the Pickwick Club. *Pickwick Papers,* C. Dickens, 1857.

Tupper, George, friend of Corcoran and Ukridge. *Ukridge,* 1924, and elsewhere, P. G. Wodehouse.

Tupple, clerk at Somerset House. *Sketches by Boz,* C. Dickens, 1836.

Turbot, Isobel, m. Gregory Stern.
Patricia, her sister, m. Tom Llewyllyn.
The Rich Pay Late, 1964, and others in the *Alms for Oblivion* sequence, Simon Raven.

Turgis. *Angel Pavement,* J. B. Priestley, 1930.

Turk, Johnnie. *A Sister for Susan,* Dale Collins.

Turkovitch, Ivan, cigar salesman. *Peter Jackson, Cigar Merchant,* G. Frankau, 1919.

Turnbull. *The Thirty-nine Steps,* J. Buchan, 1915.

Turnbull, schoolmaster. *Twelve Horses and the Hangman's Noose,* Gladys Mitchell, 1956.

Turnbull, Radical M.P.
His wife and children.
Phineas Finn, 1869, and elsewhere, A. Trollope.

Turnbull, Dr. *The Mill on the Floss,* George Eliot, 1860.

Turnbull, Alfred M., of Chicago. *Magnolia Street,* L. Golding, 1932.

Turnbull, Miss Henrietta. *Quality Street* (play), J. M. Barrie, 1902.

Turnbull, Michael, bold borderer. *Castle Dangerous,* W. Scott, 1832.

Turner, Mrs, Sherlock Holmes's landlady. *A Study in Scarlet,* A. Conan Doyle, 1887.

Turner, Bill, hooligan. *The Oriel Window,* Mrs Molesworth, 1896.

Turner, Jim ('Captain Flint'), houseboat owner. *Swallows and Amazons,* A. Ransome, 1931.

Turner, John.
His daughter.
'The Boscombe Valley Mystery,' *Adventures of Sherlock Holmes,* A. Conan Doyle, 1892.

Turner, Melford, grocer, mayor of small town who loves hunting.
Constance, his wife.
The Sleepless Moon, H. E. Bates, 1956.

Turner, Roland, one-time fiancé of Kitty (*see* Rainier). *Random Harvest,* J. Hilton, 1941.

Turner, Tom.
Delph, Rube, Sintha and **Melissa,** his children.
Old Joel, his father.
The Little Shepherd of Kingdom Come, J. Fox, Jnr, 1903.

Turnham, Polly, m. Richard Mahony.
Her brothers:
John.
m. (1) Emma.
Johnny, their son.
Emma, their daughter.
(2) Jinny Beamish.
(3) Lizzie Timms Kelly.
Ned.
Jerry.
Sarah, her sister, m. Hempel.
Lisby, her mother.
The Fortunes of Richard Mahony, H. H. Richardson, 1917–30.

Turnpenny, Tim. *A Sister for Susan,* Dale Collins.

Turrell, Miss Helen.
Michael, her nephew or son.
'The Gardener' (s.s.), *Debits and Credits,* R. Kipling, 1926.

Turtle, James, ex-public schoolboy. *The Old Boys,* William Trevor, 1964.

Turton, collector.
Mary, his wife.
A Passage to India, E. M. Forster 1924.

Turvey, valet to Sir Hugo Mallinger. *Daniel Deronda,* George Eliot, 1876.

Turveydrop, Prince, m. Caddy Jellyby.

His father, living on his reputation for deportment.
His son.
Bleak House, C. Dickens, 1853.

Tusher, Dr Robert, Vicar of Castlewood.
His wife.
Thomas, their son, a bishop, m. Beatrix Esmond.
Henry Esmond, W. M. Thackeray, 1852.

Tusk, Abel. *Brat Farrar*, Josephine Tey, 1949.

Twala, usurping chief of the Kukuana tribe, killed in combat with Sir Henry Curtis. *King Solomon's Mines*, H. Rider Haggard, 1885.

Tweedledee and **Tweedledum.** *Alice Through the Looking-glass*, L. Carroll, 1872.

Tweedy, Marion (Molly), m. Leopold Bloom. *Ulysses*, James Joyce, 1922.

Tweenwayes, Earl of (Alfred). *The Amazons* (play), A. W. Pinero, 1893.

Tweeny, a kitchenmaid. *The Admirable Crichton* (play), J. M. Barrie, 1902.

Tweetyman, m. Marian Forsyte.
One child.
The *Forsyte* series, J. Galsworthy, 1906–33.

Twelvetree, Agnes, solicitor's daughter with a malicious tongue. *The Sleepless Moon*, H. E. Bates, 1956.

Twelvetree, Anthea, farmer's daughter, in love with David Mortimer.
Prunella, her sister.
The Fallow Land, H. E. Bates, 1932.

Twiddie (Theodora), illegitimate daughter of Philip Vanever and Maria Rasle. *See also* 'SHIM' LEWIS. *The Woodcarver of 'Lympus*, Mary E. Waller, 1909.

Twigg, Mr. *Badger's Green* (play), R. C. Sherriff, 1930.

Twin I and **Twin II,** boys in Peter's band. *Peter Pan* (play), J. M. Barrie, 1904.

Twinch, Septimus, lawyer.
Letitia and **Martha,** his daughters.
The Pottleton Legacy, Albert Smith, 1849.

Twinkleton, Miss, boarding-school proprietress, *Edwin Drood*, C. Dickens, 1870.

Twisden, Jacob. *Loyalties* (play), J. Galsworthy, 1922.

Twist, Bonnie Birdie, music-hall artist, m. Herbert Duckie. *Over Bemerton's*, E. V. Lucas, 1908.

Twist, Oliver, workhouse boy, son of Agnes Fleming; central character. *Oliver Twist*, C. Dickens, 1838.

Twistleton. Family name of EARL OF ICKENHAM.

Twitchit, Mrs Tabitha.
Her children:
Tom Kitten.
Moppet.
Mittens.
The Tale of Tom Kitten, 1907, and elsewhere, Beatrix Potter.

Twitterton, Agnes, secretly eng. to Frank Crutchley. *Busman's Honeymoon*, Dorothy L. Sayers, 1937.

Two Tails, the elephant. 'Her Majesty's Servants,' *The Jungle Book*, R. Kipling, 1894.

Twycott, Rev. Mr, m. Sophy, a servant.
Randolph, their son.
'The Son's Veto,' *Life's Little Ironies*, T. Hardy, 1894.

Twymley, Mrs Amelia, a charwoman. *The Old Lady Shows Her Medals* (play), J. M. Barrie, 1917.

Twyning, 'Old,' of Sabre & Twyning.
'Young' Twyning, his son.
If Winter Comes, A. S. M. Hutchinson, 1920.

Twysden, Talbot.
His wife, *née* Ringwood.
Their children:
Ringwood.
Blanche.
Agnes, m. Grenville Woolcomb.
The Adventures of Philip, W. M. Thackeray, 1861–2.

Tybach, Twm.
Madlin, his wife.
'The Glory that was Sion's,' *My People*, Caradoc Evans, 1915.

Tybalt, nephew to Lady Capulet. *Romeo and Juliet* (play), W. Shakespeare.

Tybar, Lord (Tony).
Nona, his wife.
If Winter Comes, A. S. M. Hutchinson, 1920.

Tyke, Rev. Walter, curate, Middlemarch. *Middlemarch*, George Eliot, 1871–2.

Tymowski, Colonel, Polish officer.

The Adventures of Philip, W. M. Thackeray, 1861–2.

Tyndar, a parasite. *Gorboduc* (play), T. Sackville & T. Norton, 1562.

Tyrell, Dr. *Of Human Bondage*, W. S. Maugham, 1915.

Tyrell, Sir James, killer of the Princes (hist.), *Richard the Third* (play), W. Shakespeare.

Tyrell, Sandy. *Hay Fever* (play), N. Coward, 1925.

Tyrrel. Family name of EARL OF ETHERINGTON.

Tyrrell, Thornton, philosopher. *Memoirs of an Infantry Officer*, Siegfried Sassoon, 1930.

Tyrwhitt, Sir Thomas, Kt, friend of Maurice Malherb. *The American Prisoner*, E. Phillpotts, 1904.

Tyson, a flashy apothecary.

Madge, his wife, *née* Peters.

Starvecrow Farm, Stanley Weyman, 1905.

Tyson, Hebble, Mayor of Cool Clary, a market town.

Margaret Devize, his sister.

The Lady's Not For Burning (play), Christopher Fry, 1948.

U

Udai Chand. 'The Last Suttee' (poem), *Barrack-room Ballads*, R. Kipling, 1892.

Udeschini, Cardinal Egidio Maria. *The Cardinal's Snuff-box*, H. Harland, 1900.

Udney, Henry, English consul at Livorno.
  Florence, his daughter.
  Anthony Adverse, Hervey Allen, 1934.

Ugh-Lomi, central character.
  Eudena, his mate.
  'A Story of the Stone Age' (s.s.), *Tales of Space and Time*, H. G. Wells, 1899.

Uglow, Gregory, Victor Pandolfo's secretary.
  Sir Ponsonby, his uncle.
  The Great Pandolfo, W. J. Locke, 1925.

Ukridge, Stanley Featherstonehaugh, central character.
  Millie, his wife.
  Julia, his aunt.
  Love Among the Chickens, 1906, *Ukridge*, 1924, and elsewhere, P. G. Wodehouse.

Ulad, poet king. 'The Melancholy of Ulad' (s.s.), *Spiritual Tales*, Fiona MacLeod, 1903.

Ulford, Sir Donald.
  Leo, his son.
  The Woman with the Fan, R. S. Hichens, 1904.

Ulver, Delly, a farm girl. *Pierre*, Herman Melville, 1852.

Ulysses, Grecian commander. *Troilus and Cressida* (play), W. Shakespeare.

Uma, native wife of Wiltshire. 'The Beach of Falesa' (s.s.), *Island Nights' Entertainments*, R. L. Stevenson, 1893.

Umney, Mrs, housekeeper at Canterville Chase. *The Canterville Ghost* (s.s.), O. Wilde, 1887.

Umpopa, native servant of Sir Henry Curtis, later revealed as Ignosi, rightful chief of the Kukuanas. *King Solomon's Mines*, H. Rider Haggard, 1885.

Umr Singh, a native trooper. 'A Sahib's War' (s.s.), *Traffics and Discoveries*, R. Kipling, 1904.

Una, sister of Dan, central character with him. *Puck of Pook's Hill*, 1906, and *Rewards and Fairies*, 1910, R. Kipling.

Uncas, young Mohican Indian. *The Last of the Mohicans*, J. Fenimore Cooper, 1826.

Uncleharri.
  Harry, his son.
  'Baa Baa Black Sheep' (s.s.), *Wee Willie Winkie*, R. Kipling, 1888.

Unda. *See* Janki Meah.

Underhay, Charles, foreman of the jury. *The Jury*, G. Bullett, 1935.

Underhill, Ed, 'hot-gospeller.' *The Tower of London*, W. H. Ainsworth, 1840.

Undershaft, Andrew.
  Lady Britomart, his wife.
  Their children:
    Stephen.
    Barbara (central character).
    Sarah.
  Major Barbara (play), G. B. Shaw, 1905.

Ung, a maker of pictures. 'The Story of Ung' (poem), *The Seven Seas*, R. Kipling, 1896.

Unity, servant at Endelstow Vicarage, m. Martin Cannister. *A Pair of Blue Eyes*, T. Hardy, 1873.

Unna, daughter of Thorod, 2nd wife of Asmund. *Eric Brighteyes*, H. Rider Haggard, 1891.

Unwin, 'abject' confidential maid of Lady Charlotte Sydenham. *Joan and Peter*, H. G. Wells, 1918.

Updike, Mrs.
  Her husband and two daughters.
  The *Barsetshire* series, Angela Thirkell, 1933 onwards.

Upjohn, Frank, painter. *Death of a Hero*, R. Aldington, 1929.

Upjohn, John, journeyman. *The Woodlanders*, T. Hardy, 1887.

Uploft, George, squire. *Evan Harrington*, G. Meredith, 1861.

Ure, Lord Robert.
His wife.
The Christian, Hall Caine, 1897.

Urique, Don Santos.
His wife.
Don Francisco, his son, impersonated by the Llano Kid.
'A Double-dyed Deceiver' (s.s.), *Roads of Destiny*, O. Henry, 1909.

Urquhart, Norman, solicitor; poisoner of Philip Boyes. *Strong Poison*, Dorothy L. Sayers, 1930.

Urquhart, Squire, wealthy historian. *Wolf Solent*, J. C. Powys, 1929.

Ursini, Paulo Giordano, Duke of Brachiano.
Isabella, his wife.
Giovanni, their son.
The White Devil (play), John Webster, *c.* 1612.

Ursula, apostate nun at the convent of Oby.
Jackie, her illegitimate son, known later as Jackie Pad or Jack the Latiner, a thief.
The Corner That Held Them, Sylvia Townsend Warner, 1948.

Urswick, chaplain to the King. *Perkin Warbeck* (play), John Ford, 1634.

Usher, Violet, m. John Ransome.
Her father and mother.
The Combined Maze, May Sinclair, 1913.

Ustane, a native girl. *She*, H. Rider Haggard, 1887.

Ustis, ex-Captain Ronald.
Violet, his twin sister, a medium.
A New Departure (s.s.), R. S. Hichens.

Usumcasane, follower of Tamburlaine. *Tamburlaine* (play), C. Marlowe, 1587.

Utterson, solicitor to and friend of Dr Jekyll. *Dr Jekyll and Mr Hyde*, R. L. Stevenson, 1886.

Utterword, Lady Randall. *Heartbreak House* (play), G. B. Shaw, 1917.

V

Vaile, Mr.
Miss Bella, his sister.
Shall We Join the Ladies? (play), J. M. Barrie, 1921.

Vaillant, Father Joseph, Vicar General at Albuquerque, and assistant to Jean Marie Latour. *Death Comes for the Archbishop,* Willa Cather, 1927.

Valancourt, Chevalier, lover of Emily St Aubert. *The Mysteries of Udolpho,* Mrs Radcliffe, 1794.

Valdes, friend of Faustus. *Doctor Faustus* (play), C. Marlowe, 1604.

Valdez, Diego, Spanish Admiral (hist.). 'The Song of Diego Valdez' (poem), *The Five Nations,* R. Kipling, 1903.

Valens, a Roman general. *The Briton* (play), A. Philips, 1722.

Valens, a Roman soldier.
Lucius Sergius, his uncle, Prefect of Police.
'The Church that was at Antioch' (s.s.), *Limits and Renewals,* R. Kipling, 1932.

Valentin, Aristide, Chief of Police. 'The Secret Garden,' *The Innocence of Father Brown,* G. K. Chesterton, 1911.

Valentine, a gentleman of Verona. *Two Gentlemen of Verona* (play), W. Shakespeare.

Valentine, a dentist. *You Never Can Tell* (play), G. B. Shaw, 1895.

Valentine, Miss, friend of Elizabeth Firminger. *The Story of Ragged Robyn,* O. Onions, 1945.

Valentine, Jimmy, a safe-breaker (alias Ralph D. Spencer). 'A Retrieved Reformation' (s.s.), *Roads of Destiny,* O. Henry, 1909.

Valentini, Dr. *A Farewell to Arms,* E. Hemingway, 1929.

Valentino, officer of Paolo's company. *Paolo and Francesca* (play), S. Phillips, 1900.

Valentinois. *See* MADAME CORNICHON.

Valeria, friend of Virgilia. *Coriolanus* (play), W. Shakespeare.

Valerian, brother of Tiburce.
Cecile, his wife.
'The Second Nun's Tale' (poem), *The Canterbury Tales,* G. Chaucer, 1373 onwards.

Valery, Anne. *Agatha's Husband,* Mrs Craik, 1853.

Valiant-for-Truth. *Pilgrim's Progress,* J. Bunyan, 1678, 1684.

Vallens, Jane, m. Andrew Satchel. 'Andrey Satchel and the Parson and Clerk,' *Life's Little Ironies,* T. Hardy, 1874.

Valleys, Earl of (Geoffrey) (Family name Caradoc).
Lady Gertrude, his wife, *née* Semmering.
Their children:
Lord Miltoun.
Hon. Hubert.
Lady Agatha, m. Sir William Shropton.
Lady Barbara, m. Lord Harbinger.
The Patrician, J. Galsworthy, 1911.

Valliscourt, Lionel, central character.
John, his father.
The Mighty Atom, Marie Corelli, 1896.

Valora. *Tracy's Tiger,* W. Saroyan, 1951.

Valoroso, King of Paflagonia. *The Rose and the Ring,* W. M. Thackeray, 1855.

Valverde, servant to Pizarro. *Pizarro* (play), R. B. Sheridan, 1799.

Valvona, Miss Doreen, believer in astrology. *Memento Mori,* Muriel Spark, 1959.

Van Adam, elderly American. *The Buick Saloon* (s.s.), Ann Bridge.

Van Allen, Letitia, Hollywood agent. *Myra Breckinridge,* Gore Vidal, 1968.

Van Brennen, Philip Vanderdecken's uncle. *The Phantom Ship,* Captain Marryat, 1839.

Van Brunt, Abraham, m. Fortune Emerson. *The Wide, Wide World,* Elizabeth Wetherell, 1850.

Van Brunt, Abraham, known as Brom Bones. *The Legend of Sleepy Hollow,* Washington Irving, 1819–1820.

Van Buren, Theodore. *Poet's Pub*, E. Linklater, 1929.

Vance, Joseph, central character and narrator, m. Janey Spencer.
Christoforo, his adopted son.
Christopher, his father, m. (2) Seraphina Dowdeswell.
Joseph Vance, W. de Morgan, 1906.

Vance, Philo, dilettante detective, central character. *The Benson Murder Case*, 1926, and many others, S. S. van Dine.

Van Cheele.
His sister.
Gabriel Ernest (s.s.), 'Saki' (H. H. Munro).

Van Degen, Peter, m. Clare Dagonet.
Thurber, his father, wealthy banker.
The Custom of the Country, Edith Wharton, 1913.

Vandeleur, Major-General Sir Thomas.
Clara, his wife, *née* Pendragon.
John, his brother.
'The Rajah's Diamond' (s.s.), *New Arabian Nights*, R. L. Stevenson, 1882.

Van den Bosch, Dutch settler in Albany.
Lydia, his grand-daughter, m. 2nd Earl Castlewood.
The Virginians, W. M. Thackeray, 1857–9.

Vandenhuten, Victor.
Jean Baptiste, his son.
The Professor, Charlotte Brontë, 1857.

Vanderbluff. *Polly* (comic opera), J. Gay, 1729.

Vanderbrook, Jack, a millionaire. *A Voyage to Purilia*, Elmer Rice, 1930.

Vanderdecken, Lady Dolly, m. (1) Vere Herbert, (2) Vanderdecken. *See* VERE HERBERT. *Moths*, Ouida, 1880.

Vanderdecken, Philip, central character, m. Amine Poots.
William, his father.
Catherine, his mother.
The Phantom Ship, Captain Marryat, 1839.

Vanderfelt, Colonel, fellow officer of Paul Ravenel's father.
Phyllis, his daughter.
The Winding Stair, A. E. W. Mason, 1923.

Vanderflint, Emmanuel, a Belgian officer.
Teresa Diabologh, his wife.
Sylvia Ninon Therese Anastathia, their daughter.
The Polyglots, William Gerhardie, 1925.

Vanderlynden, Madeleine, central character, loves Georges d'Archeville.
Jerome, her father, tenant of Spanish Farm.
Sylvie, her dead mother.
Marie, her elder sister.
Marcel, her brother.
The *Spanish Farm* trilogy, R. H. Mottram, 1924–6.

Vandermeer, friend of Ephraim Quixtus. *The Glory of Clementina Wing*, W. J. Locke, 1911.

Vandernoodt, American of Dutch descent. *Daniel Deronda*, George Eliot, 1876.

Vanderwoort, Dutch ship's captain, murdered by Emily Thornton. *High Wind in Jamaica*, R. Hughes, 1929.

Van Diver, Charlie, old friend of Mrs Parkington. *Mrs Parkington*, L. Bromfield, 1944.

Vandiver, Robert, press agent, m. Annie Ashton. 'Rus in Urbe' (s.s.), *Options*, O. Henry, 1909.

Van Dorn, Van, owner of High Tor, m. Judith. *High Tor* (play), Maxwell Anderson, 1937.

Van Duren, Prof. Augustus S. F. X., 'the Thinking Machine,' central character. *The Professor in the Case* (series), J. Futrelle.

Vane, Austen, central character, m. Victoria Flint.
Hon. Hilary, his father.
Sarah, his mother, *née* Austen.
Mr Crewe's Career, W. Churchill, 1908.

Vane, Ernest, wealthy Shropshire squire.
Mabel, his wife.
Peg Woffington, C. Reade, 1853.

Vane, Harriet, authoress, accused of murder, m. Lord Peter Wimsey. *Strong Poison*, 1930, and many others, Dorothy L. Sayers.

Vane, Lady Isabel, daughter of Lord Mount Severn, m. Archibald Carlyle.
Raymond, her brother, later Lord Mount Severn.
Emma, his wife, grand-daughter of Mrs Levison.

East Lynne, Mrs Henry Wood, 1861.

Vane, Sybil, jilted by Dorian Gray.
Her mother.
James, her brother.
The Picture of Dorian Gray, O. Wilde, 1891.

Vanelden, Mrs.
Her daughters:
Esther, in love with Jonathan Hare.
Mollie.
I Live Under a Black Sun, Edith Sitwell, 1937.

Vanever, Philip, friend and patron of Hugh Armstrong, m. Madeline Cope. *See also* TWIDDIE. *The Woodcarver of 'Lympus*, Mary E. Waller, 1909.

Van Eyck, Margaret.
Peter, her father, friend of Gerard Eliasson.
The Cloister and the Hearth, C. Reade, 1861.

Van Gilbert, Colonel, corporation lawyer. *The Iron Heel*, Jack London, 1908.

Vanholt, Duke of.
His wife.
Doctor Faustus (play), C. Marlowe, 1604.

Van Hopper, Mrs, employer of the anonymous heroine. *Rebecca*, Daphne du Maurier, 1938.

Van Huyten, Mr, owner of a music shop. *A Kind of Loving*, Stan Barstow, 1960.

Van Jaarsweld, police captain. *Cry, the Beloved Country*, A. Paton, 1948.

Van Kerrel, Jan, Boer farmer, in love with Deborah Krillet. *The Shulamite*, A. & C. Askew, 1904.

Van Koppen, Cornelius, a millionaire. *South Wind*, N. Douglas, 1917.

Vannucci, Signora. *Romance* (play), E. Sheldon, 1914.

Vanor, a British prince. *The Briton* (play), A. Philips, 1722.

Van Osburgh, Mrs Eva.
Gwen, her daughter.
The House of Mirth, Edith Wharton, 1905.

Vanringham, Tubby, m. Prudence Whittaker.
Joe, his brother, m. Jane Abbott.
Summer Moonshine, P. G. Wodehouse, 1938.

Van Rosenbom, Burgomaster of Flushing. *Jorrocks's Jaunts and Jollities*, R. S. Surtees, 1838.

Vanstone, Andrew, m. (2) Mrs Wragge, widow.
Their daughters, born prior to marriage:
Norah.
Magdalen, m. (1) Noel Vanstone, (2) Captain Kirke.
Michael, Andrew's elderly and vindictive brother.
Noel, his miserly son, m. Magdalen Vanstone.
Selina, his daughter.
No Name, W. Collins, 1862.

Vansuythen, Mrs.
Major Vansuythen, her husband.
'A Wayside Comedy' (s.s.), *Wee Willie Winkie*, R. Kipling, 1888.

Van Swieten, Ghysbrecht, Burgomaster of Tergon, miser and villain. *The Cloister and the Hearth*, C. Reade, 1861.

Van Tassel, Katrina, daughter of a rich farmer. *The Legend of Sleepy Hollow*, Washington Irving, 1819–1820.

Van Trompe, John, friend of Senator Bird. *Uncle Tom's Cabin*, Harriet B. Stowe, 1851.

Van Tuyl, 'High Lord of Devil-may-Care.' *No Man's Land*, L. J. Vance, 1910.

Van Tuyl, Cornelius.
Susan, his niece.
Romance (play), E. Sheldon, 1914.

Vanucle, Pietro, artist, friend of Gerard Eliasson. *The Cloister and the Hearth*, C. Reade, 1861.

Van Weyden, Humphrey, narrator, m. Maud Brewster. *The Sea Wolf*, Jack London, 1904.

Van Winkle, Rip, henpecked husband in the Kaatskill Mountains who sleeps for twenty years.
Dame Van Winkle, his wife.
Judith, their daughter.
Rip Van Winkle, Washington Irving, 1819–20.

Van Zyl, Adrian, commando. 'The Captive' (s.s.), *Traffics and Discoveries*, R. Kipling, 1904.

Vapid. *The Dramatist* (play), F. Reynolds, 1789.

Varden, Dolly, m. Joe Willet.
Gabriel, her father, locksmith.
Her mother.
Barnaby Rudge, C. Dickens, 1841.

Varens, Adèle, daughter of Celine, Rochester's mistress; his ward, and pupil of Jane Eyre. *Jane Eyre,* Charlotte Brontë, 1847.

Varese, Mario, waiter at the Capo di Monte. *Adam's Breed,* Radclyffe Hall, 1926.

Vargrave, Lord (Lumley).
  The Dowager Lady, his mother, *née* Alice Darvil, early lover of Ernest Maltravers.
  Evelyn (Cameron), her supposed daughter, m. George Legard.
Alice, Lord Lytton, 1838.

Varick, Katherine, friend of Jane Potter. *Potterism,* Rose Macaulay, 1920.

Varnish, Tom, of the Middle Temple. *Tom Varnish,* R. Steele, *c.* 1709.

Varnum, Lawyer.
  Ruth, his daughter, m. Ned Hale.
Ethan Frome, Edith Wharton, 1911.

Varolyas, Professor, Communist psychiatrist. *Trial by Terror,* P. Gallico, 1952.

Varrillat, Dr Evariste.
  His wife.
'Madame Delphine' (s.s.), *Old Creole Days,* G. W. Cable, 1879.

Varwell, Richard, Arthur, Joe, Jennifer and **Mary.** *Yellow Sands* (play), E. & A. Phillpotts, 1926.

Vasek, Anastasya, a Russian exile in Paris. *Tarr,* Wyndham Lewis, 1918.

Vasili, servant of Mme Zalenska. *Three Weeks,* Elinor Glyn, 1907.

Vassili. *The Sowers* H. Seton Merriman, 1896.

Vassiloff, Orlo, fiancé of Jeanne-Marie de Jong.
  The Count, his father.
A Deputy was King, G. B. Stern, 1926.

Vathek, Caliph. *Vathek,* W. Beckford, 1786.

Vaucaire, Hélène, m. Charles Whitelaw. *Roots,* Naomi Jacob, 1931.

Vaughan. *Fanny's First Play* (play), G. B. Shaw, 1905.

Vaughan ('Taffy'), a surgeon. 'Unprofessional' (s.s.), *Limits and Renewals,* R. Kipling, 1932.

Vaughan, Barbara, Roman Catholic half-Jewish schoolteacher who disappears on a pilgrimage in Jordan. *The Mandelbaum Gate,* Muriel Spark, 1965.

Vaughan, Helen (also Beaumont and other aliases), *femme fatale.*
  Mary, her mother.
The Great God Pan, A. Machen, 1894.

Vaughan, Mary, m. George Callender. 'Deep Waters' (s.s.), *The Man Upstairs,* P. G. Wodehouse, 1914.

Vaughan, Maurice, m. Meg Whiteoak.
  Patience, their daughter.
  Pheasant, his illegitimate daughter, m. Piers Whiteoak.
The Whiteoak Chronicles, Mazo de la Roche, 1927 onwards.

Vaughan, Ryland, friend of Philip Boyes. *Strong Poison,* Dorothy L. Sayers, 1930.

Vaughan, Stephanie, leading actress. *Enter a Murderer,* Ngaio Marsh, 1935.

Vauquier, Hélène, maid to Mme Dauvray. *At the Villa Rose,* A. E. W. Mason, 1910.

Vaux, Lord, kinsman of Mary Cave. *Holmby House,* G. Whyte-Melville, 1860.

Vaux, Sir Nicholas. *Henry the Eighth* (play), W. Shakespeare.

Vauxhall, Lord. 'The Ravenswing,' *Men's Wives,* W. M. Thackeray, 1843.

Vavasour, Elsley, poet (*né* John Briggs).
  Lucia, his wife, sister of Lord Scoutbush.
Two Years Ago, Charles Kingsley, 1857.

Vavasour, Lorraine, money-lender. *The Search Party,* G. A. Birmingham, 1913.

Vaynol, Livia, in love with Oliver Essex and his father. *My Son, My Son,* H. Spring. 1938.

Veal, Mrs, close friend of Mrs Bargrave.
  Her brother.
The Apparition of Mrs Veal (s.s.), D. Defoe.

Veal, Rev. Laurence.
  His wife.
Vanity Fair, W. M. Thackeray, 1847–8.

Veck, Toby, porter, central character. *The Chimes,* Charles Dickens, 1844.

Veilchen, Annette, in attendance on Anne. *Anne of Geierstein,* W. Scott, 1829.

Veitch, Mrs.
Maggie and **Kate,** her daughters.
The Setons, O. Douglas, 1917.

Velie, Sergeant Thomas, of New York Homicide Squad. *The Chinese Orange Mystery*, 1934, and many others, Ellery Queen.

Velindre, Rachel, m. Solomon Darke. Her mother-in-law.
Catherine, distant cousin.
The House in Dormer Forest, Mary Webb, 1920.

Venables, Hon. Charles. *What Every Woman Knows* (play), J. M. Barrie, 1908.

Venables, John, steward of the junior common room. *Sinister Street*, C. Mackenzie, 1913.

Venasalvatica, Marchesa della, *née* Lady Daphne Page. *Adam of Dublin*, C. O'Riordan, 1920.

Veneering, Hamilton, owner of Chicksey, Veneering & Stobbles.
Anastasia, his wife.
Our Mutual Friend, C. Dickens, 1865.

Venice, Duke of. *The Merchant of Venice* (play), W. Shakespeare.

Venice, Duke of. *Othello* (play), W. Shakespeare.

Venn, Diggory, travelling reddleman, m. as 2nd husband Thomasin Yeobright. *The Return of the Native*, T. Hardy, 1878.

Venner, 'Uncle.' *The House of the Seven Gables*, N. Hawthorne, 1851.

Venner, Elsie, central character.
Dudley, her father.
Richard, her cousin.
Elsie Venner, O. W. Holmes, 1861.

Venner, Tillie. 'Wressley of the Foreign Office' (s.s.), *Plain Tales from the Hills*, R. Kipling, 1888.

Venters, Bern, 'gentile' befriended by Jane Withersteen; m. Bess Erne. *Riders of the Purple Sage*, Zane Grey, 1912.

Ventidius, false friend of Timon. *Timon of Athens* (play), W. Shakespeare.

Ventidius, friend of Antony. *Antony and Cleopatra* (play), W. Shakespeare.

Ventimore, Horace, architect, central character, m. Sylvia Futvoye. *The Brass Bottle*, F. Anstey, 1900.

Ventnor, Charles, solicitor. *A Stoic*, J. Galsworthy, 1918.

Venturewell, a merchant.
Luce, his daughter.
The Knight of the Burning Pestle (play), Beaumont & Fletcher, 1609.

Ventvogel, Hottentot servant. *King Solomon's Mines*. H. Rider Haggard, 1885.

Venus, Mr, taxidermist, friend of Silas Wegg, m. Pleasant Riderhood. *Our Mutual Friend*, C. Dickens, 1865.

Venus Annodomini (Kitty). 'Venus Annodomini' (s.s.), *Plain Tales from the Hills*, R. Kipling, 1888.

Verd, Cyrus. 'Some Notes on Cyrus Verd' (s.s.), *Here and Hereafter*, Barry Pain, 1911.

Verdant, Miss Virginia, cousin of Mr Green. *The Adventures of Mr Verdant Green*, C. Bede, 1853.

Verdayne, Paul, central character.
Sir Charles, his father.
Lady Henrietta, his mother.
Three Weeks, Elinor Glyn, 1907.

Verdew, Rollo.
Vera, his wife.
Randolph, his brother.
The Killing Bottle (s.s.), L. P. Hartley.

Verdley, Mrs Lydia, sister of Stephen Leuknor. *The Old Bank*, W. Westall, 1902.

Verdun, Kitty, ward of Stephen Spettigue. *Charley's Aunt* (play), Brandon Thomas, 1892.

Vere, Captain, commanding officer of H.M.S. *Indomitable*. *Billy Budd*, Herman Melville, 1924.

Vere, Isabel, m. Patrick Earnscliff.
Richard, Laird of Ellieslaw, his father.
Letitia, his mother.
The Black Dwarf, W. Scott, 1816.

Vere de Vere, Lady Clara. *Lady Clara Vere de Vere* (poem), Lord Tennyson.

Vereker, Rev. Brian.
His children:
Daphne, m. Sir Johnson Carr.
Aloysius ('Ally').
Cecilia ('Cilly'), m. Rev. Godfrey Blunt.
Stephen ('Stiffy').
Veronica ('Nicky').
Anthony.
A Safety Match, Ian Hay, 1911.

Veresy, Christopher, father of Paula Field.
Myrtilla, his elder daughter.

The Great Pandolfo, W. J. Locke, 1925.

Verges, a foolish officer. *Much Ado about Nothing* (play), W. Shakespeare.

Vergil, Winter ('Daddy'). 'A Naval Mutiny' (s.s.), *Limits and Renewals*, R. Kipling, 1932.

Verily, Judge Fox Clane's Negress cook.
Grown Boy, her nephew.
Clock Without Hands, Carson McCullers, 1961.

Verinder, General Sir George, V.C. *In Cotton Wool*, W. B. Maxwell, 1912.

Verinder, Lady (Julia), *née* Herncastle, widow of Sir John.
Rachel, her daughter, m. Franklin Blake.
The Moonstone, W. Collins, 1868.

Verisopht, Lord Frederick, killed in a duel with Sir Mulberry Hawk. *Nicholas Nickleby*, C. Dickens, 1839.

Verity, Azure, actress. *Over Bemerton's*, E. V. Lucas, 1908.

Verity, John, farmer.
Kate, his wife.
Their daughters:
Patty.
Rachel.
Nellie, m. Richard Morton.
High Meadows, Alison Uttley, 1938.

Verlaine, Maria, friend of Jim Willard. *The City and The Pillar*, Gore Vidal, 1948.

Verloc, Mr (Adolf), foreign spy who runs shady shop in Soho.
Winnie, his English wife.
Stevie, Winnie's weak-minded brother.
The Secret Agent, Joseph Conrad, 1907.

Vermilye, Gerard, ruined man-about-town, defeated candidate at Kingswell election. *John Halifax, Gentleman*, Mrs Craik, 1856.

Vermont, Ophelia ('Miss Ophelia'), unmarried cousin of St Clare. *Uncle Tom's Cabin*, Harriet B. Stowe, 1851.

Vernet, Claudine, French friend of Margaret Roundelay. *A Footman for the Peacock*, Rachel Ferguson, 1940.

Verney, Lord. *The Bath Comedy*, 1899, and *Incomparable Bellairs*, 1904, A. & E. Castle.

Verney, John, central character.
John, his father.
The Hill, 1905, and elsewhere, H. A. Vachell.

Verney, Patricia.
Colonel Verney, her father.
Lettice, her aunt.
The Old Dominion, Mary Johnston, 1899.

Vernoe, unprincipled guardian of Clara Saville. *Frank Fairlegh*, F. E. Smedley, 1850.

Vernon, Diana, niece of Lady Osbaldistone, m. Frank Osbaldistone.
Sir Frederick, her father.
Rob Roy, W. Scott, 1818.

Vernon, Laurence. *The Thinking Reed*, Rebecca West, 1936.

Vernon, Paddy, a sub-prefect. 'Regulus' (a 'Stalky' story), *A Diversity of Creatures*, R. Kipling, 1917.

Vernon, Virginia, newspaper woman, a lesbian. *Lovey Childs*, John O'Hara, 1969.

Vernon-Smith, Herbert, the Bounder of Greyfriars. The *Billy Bunter* series, Frank Richards.

Verona, Duke of, Della Scala Mastino, m. Isotta d'Este. *The Viper of Milan*, Marjorie Bowen, 1905.

Verral, Edward, wealthy landowner, m. Nettie Stuart.
His mother.
In the Days of the Comet, H. G. Wells, 1906.

Verrinder, aged art student.
His wife.
Alice-for-Short, W. de Morgan, 1907.

Verver, Maggie, central character, m. Prince Amerigo.
Adam, her father, American millionaire, m. Charlotte Stant.
The Golden Bowl, Henry James, 1904.

Vesey, reporter, *The Enterprise*. 'Calloway's Code' (s.s.), *Whirligigs*. O. Henry, 1910.

Vesey, Mrs, former governess of Marian Fairlie. *The Woman in White*, W. Collins, 1860.

Vesey, Sir John, Bt.
Georgina, his daughter.
Money (play), Lord Lytton, 1840.

Vespasian, Negro sailor on the *Agra*. *Hard Cash*, C. Reade, 1863.

Vesson, Andrew, John Reddin's servant. *Gone to Earth,* Mary Webb, 1917.

Vezin, Arthur, central character. 'Ancient Sorceries,' *John Silence,* A. Blackwood, 1908.

Vezzis, Miss. 'His Chance in Life' (s.s.), *Plain Tales from the Hills,* R. Kipling, 1888.

Vholes, solicitor to Richard Carstone. *Bleak House,* C. Dickens, 1853.

Viaino, Maestro, unprincipled mountebank. *Romola,* George Eliot, 1863.

Vian, Vivian, a transvestite.
  Elvira Vian Cookson, his/her mother, also known as Madge Baum.
The Long Time Growing Up, John Pudney, 1971.

Vibart, Peter, central character and narrator.
  Sir George, his uncle.
  Sir Maurice ('Buck'), his cousin.
The Broad Highway, J. Farnol, 1910.

Vicary, news editor, *The Liberal. The Street of Adventure,* P. Gibbs, 1909.

Vicentio, Duke of Vienna. *Measure for Measure* (play), W. Shakespeare.

Vicenza, Isabella of, m. Theodore.
  Frederic, Marquis of Vicenza, her father.
The Castle of Otranto, Horace Walpole, 1765.

Vickers, Selina, fiancée of Joseph Tasker. *Dialstone Lane,* W. W. Jacobs, 1904.

Vickers, Sylvia, m. Maurice Frere.
  Captain Vickers, her father.
  Her mother.
For the Term of his Natural Life, M. Clarke, 1874.

Vickery, Lieutenant. The *Hornblower* series, C. S. Forester, 1937 onwards.

Vickery, Mr ('Click'). 'Mrs Bathurst' (s.s.), *Traffics and Discoveries,* R. Kipling, 1904.

Victor, of *The Courier. Master Jim Probity,* F. Swinnerton, 1952.

Victor, Brother. 'The Record of Badalia Herodsfoot' (s.s.), *Many Inventions,* R. Kipling, 1893.

Victor, Father, a priest. *Kim,* R. Kipling, 1901.

Victor, Felix, reporter. *Trial by Terror,* P. Gallico, 1952.

Victoria, Prefect's daughter. *Hypatia,* C. Kingsley, 1853.

Victorian, student, of Alcala, m. Preciosa. *The Spanish Student* (poem), H. W. Longfellow, 1858.

Vidalis, Nicholas, revolutionary. *The Capsina,* E. F. Benson, 1899.

Vidler, apothecary.
  His daughter.
The Newcomes, W. M. Thackeray, 1853–5.

Viedima, General Cipriano, m. Kate Leslie. *The Plumed Serpent,* D. H. Lawrence, 1926.

Viel, master ploughman. *The King of Elfland's Daughter,* Lord Dunsany, 1924.

Vigil, Dr Arturo Diaz, Geoffrey Firmin's doctor. *Under the Volcano,* Malcolm Lowry, 1947.

Vigil, Gregory, Helen Bellew's guardian. *The Country House,* John Galsworthy, 1907.

Vigors, bully of midshipmen's berth. *Mr Midshipman Easy,* Captain Marryat, 1836.

Vigors, Bert, ex-soldier and market gardener. 'A Friend of the Family' (s.s.), *Debits and Credits,* R. Kipling, 1926.

Vigot, Chief of Police. *The Quiet American,* Graham Greene, 1955.

Vilbert, itinerant quack doctor. *Jude the Obscure,* T. Hardy, 1896.

Vile, Lord Henry, Aintree steward. *National Velvet,* Enid Bagnold, 1935.

Villamarti, a matador. 'The Bull that Thought' (s.s.), *Debits and Credits,* R. Kipling, 1926.

Villars, Rev. Arthur. *Evelina,* Fanny Burney, 1778.

Villebecque, steward of Lord Monmouth.
  Flora, his supposed stepdaughter, daughter of Lord Monmouth.
Coningsby, B. Disraeli, 1844.

Villeblanche, Conte de la, m. Lucy Hawthorn. *The Perennial Bachelor,* Anne Parrish, 1925.

Villiers, friend of Charles Herbert. *The Great God Pan,* A. Machen, 1894.

Villiers, Beau. *The Miser's Daughter,* W. H. Ainsworth, 1842.

Villiers, Miss Judith, aunt of the Beverley children. *The Children* *of the New Forest*, Captain Marryat, 1847.

Vincent, Father, English priest. *Cry, the Beloved Country,* A. Paton, 1948.

Vincent, Armande, friend of Cary Page, m. Pierre de Chanet.
Savoie, her brother, m. Cary Page.
Larry, their son.
Lamartine, her father.
Aureline, her mother.
Steamboat Gothic, Frances Parkinson Keyes, 1952.

Vincent, Jenkin ('Jin Vin'), apprentice. *The Fortunes of Nigel,* W. Scott, 1822.

Vincent, Suzette, m. Alan Carew.
General Vincent, her father.
Molly, her aunt, m. Mornington.
Sons of Fire, Mary E. Braddon, 1896.

Vincey, Leo, reincarnation of Kallikrates, his ancestor, ward of Ludwig Holly. *She,* H. Rider Haggard, 1887.

Vincitata, Marquis de.
Maria, his wife, daughter of a Scottish merchant.
Anthony Adverse, her son by Denis Moore, attached Royal Horse Guards, killed in a duel.
Anthony Adverse, Hervey Allen, 1934.

Vinck, Mrs.
Emma, her daughter.
Almayer's Folly, J. Conrad, 1895.

Vincott, Joseph, Sir Julian Harnwood's attorney. *The Courtship of Morrice Buckler,* A. E. W. Mason, 1896.

Vincy, Walter, Mayor of Middlemarch.
Lucy, his wife.
Their children:
Fred, m. Mary Garth.
Bob.
Rosamond, m. Tertius Lydgate.
Louise.
Middlemarch, Geo. Eliot, 1871–2.

Vine, Walter, foreman, m. Lizzie Bishop. *The Poacher,* H. E. Bates, 1935.

Viner, Father. *Sinister Street,* C. Mackenzie, 1913.

Viney, ex-shipowner. *The Hole in the Wall,* A. Morrison, 1902.

Vining, house prefect. *Young Woodley* (play), J. van Druten, 1928.

Vinney, Vincent.
Floss, his wife.
Sid, his brother.
Non-Combatants and Others, Rose Macaulay, 1916.

Viola (alias Cesario), m. Orsino. *Twelfth Night* (play), W. Shakespeare.

Violante. *My Novel,* Lord Lytton, 1853.

Violet. *Caesar's Wife* (play), W. S. Maugham, 1919.

Violet, maid to the Winslows. *The Winslow Boy* (play), T. Rattigan, 1946.

Violetta, Pepino's donkey. *The Small Miracle,* P. Gallico, 1951.

Viomesnil, Clarisse de, m. Francis Saverne. *Denis Duval,* W. M. Thackeray, 1864.

Virgilia, wife of Coriolanus. *Coriolanus* (play), W. Shakespeare.

Virginia, companion to Agnes de Medina, m. Don Lorenzo de Medina. *The Monk,* M. G. Lewis, 1796.

Virginian, The, anonymous central character. *The Virginian,* O. Wister, 1902.

Virolet.
Juliana, his wife.
The Double Marriage (play), J. Fletcher, 1647.

Visconti, Gian Galeazzo Maria, Duke of Milan ('The Viper').
Tisio, his brother.
Valentine, his sister.
The Viper of Milan, Marjorie Bowen, 1905.

Vitali, Dominetta, actress, mistress of Emilio Largo. (Real name Petacchi.)
Giuseppe Petacchi, her brother, air pilot.
Thunderball, Ian Fleming, 1961.

Vitelli, Popeye, psychopathic gangster executed for murder. *Sanctuary,* 1931, and *Requiem for a Nun,* 1950, William Faulkner.

Vittoria, a *contadina*. *The Gondoliers* (comic opera), Gilbert & Sullivan, 1889.

Viveash, Myra. *Antic Hay,* A. Huxley, 1923.

Viveash, Mrs Nora. *Miss Tarrant's Temperament* (s.s.), May Sinclair.

Vivian, Sir Walter.
Walter, his son.
Lilia, his daughter.
Elizabeth, his sister.
The Princess (poem), Lord Tennyson, 1847.

Vivien, 'the wily.' 'Merlin and Vivien' (poem), *Idylls of the King*, Lord Tennyson, 1859.

Vixen, the author's dog. 'My Lord the Elephant,' *Many Inventions*, 1893, 'Garm—a Hostage,' *Actions and Reactions*, 1909, and elsewhere, R. Kipling.

Vixen, Mrs. *Polly* (comic opera), J. Gay, 1729.

Vizzard, Mrs Kitty, landlady. *London Belongs to Me*, N. Collins, 1945.

Vlacho, innkeeper. *Phroso*, A. Hope, 1897.

Vladimir. *Waiting for Godot*, S. Beckett, 1952.

Vladimir, Mr, First Secretary of unnamed embassy. *The Secret Agent*, Joseph Conrad, 1907.

Voaden, dramatist.
Sheila, his drunken wife.
Landmarks, E. V. Lucas, 1914.

Voiron, Monsieur André. 'The Bull that Thought' (s.s.), *Debits and Credits*, R. Kipling, 1926.

Voler, Theodoric. *The Mouse* (s.s.), 'Saki' (H. H. Munro).

Volkov, Katherine, Australian pianist, child-love and inspiration of Hurtle Duffield in old age. *The Vivisector*, Patrick White, 1970.

Vollar, Nettie. *Java Head*, J. Hergesheimer, 1919.

Volonna, Donna Roma (alias Rossi), sculptor; social beauty in Rome; mistress of Baron Bonelli; m. David Rossi.
Her father (alias Joseph Roselli).
The Eternal City, Hall Caine, 1901.

Volpone, a wealthy sensualist. *Volpone, or the Fox* (play), B. Jonson, 1605.

Volumnia, mother of Coriolanus. *Coriolanus* (play), W. Shakespeare.

Von Ahlen, Count Otto. *Clementina*, A. E. W. Mason, 1901.

Von Arting, Helmuth, dwarf, nephew of Frau Schindler. *The Four Armourers*, F. Beeding, 1930.

Von Bodicke, Helmuth, German captain on *Legnano*. *The Ship*, C. S. Forester, 1943.

Von Bork. 'His Last Bow,' *His Last Bow*, A. Conan Doyle, 1917.

Von Bruning, Commander of German gunboat, *Blitz*. *The Riddle of the Sands*, E. Childers, 1903.

Von Galen, Colonel Paul, m. Anna von Leyde.
Heinrich, their son.
The Other Side, Storm Jameson, 1946.

Von Herling, Baron. 'His Last Bow,' *His Last Bow*, A. Conan Doyle, 1917.

Von Koeldwethout.
His wife.
Nicholas Nickleby, C. Dickens, 1839.

Von Kohler, Frau Else. *You Can't Go Home Again*, T. Wolfe, 1947.

Von Langen, German baron.
His wife.
Daniel Deronda, George Eliot, 1876.

Von Leyde, Baroness Bertha, widow.
Anna, her daughter, m. Paul von Galen.
Johann, their son, m. Marie Jouvenet.
Lotte, sister of Anna, m. Richard Gauss.
The Other Side, Storm Jameson, 1946.

Von Leyden. *See* LEYDEN.

Von Lichtenberg, Baron.
Carl, his son.
Drums of War, H. de Vere Stacpoole, 1910.

Von Narwitz. *See* NARWITZ.

Von Pregnitz, Baron Kuno. *Mr Norris Changes Trains*, C. Isherwood, 1935.

Von Rohn, Amelie, widow of **Rudolf.**
Their sons:
Olaf, m. Sophia Maberg.
Emil.
m. (2) Johann Roth.
The Mortal Storm, Phyllis Bottome, 1937.

Von Rosen, Count Oswald, lieutenant of cavalry, m. 'Bell.' *The Strange Adventures of a Phaeton*, W. Black, 1872.

Von Schulembourg, Count Conrad, lover of Valentine Visconti. *The Viper of Milan*, Marjorie Bowen, 1905.

Von Stalhein, Erich, arch-enemy of 'Biggles' (Air-Detective Inspector Bigglesworth). 'Biggles' books, Captain W. E. Johns.

Von Stroom, supercargo. *The Phantom Ship,* Captain Marryat, 1839.

Von Wald, Joachim, Austrian geologist. *The Seven Who Fled,* Frederic Prokosch, 1937.

Vorticella, authoress of a guide-book. *Theophrastus Such,* George Eliot, 1879.

Vosier (Vawse), Nancy.
Her grandmother.
The Wide, Wide World, Elizabeth Wetherell, 1850.

Vosper, a butler. 'Keeping in with Vosper' (s.s.), and elsewhere, *The Heart of a Goof,* P. G. Wodehouse, 1926.

Vosper, Jane, procuress.
John, her husband.
Mr Weston's Good Wine, T. F. Powys, 1927.

Vosper, Samuel, 'odd fish,' friend of Rudd Sergison. *Landmarks,* E. V. Lucas, 1914.

Voss, Johann Ulrich, German explorer in Australia, 1845. *Voss,* Patrick White, 1957.

Voules, licensed victualler, uncle of Miriam Larkins.
His wife.
The History of Mr Polly, H. G. Wells, 1910.

Voules, Police Sergeant, uncle of Constable Dobson. *Thank You, Jeeves,* P. G. Wodehouse, 1934.

Vouvray, Claudine, mistress of Adrian Levine.
Marion and **Adrienne,** their daughters.
Angele, Claudine's daughter by her husband.
Mosaic, G. B. Stern, 1930.

Vowle, Sandy. 'The Lang Men o' Larut' (s.s.), *Life's Handicap,* R. Kipling, 1891.

Vox, Valentine, ventriloquist, central character. *Valentine Vox,* H. Cockton, 1840.

Vrinoff, Nellie, third victim of the Strangling Horrors. *The Hands of Mr Ottermole* (s.s.), T. Burke.

Vuffin, a travelling showman. *The Old Curiosity Shop,* C. Dickens, 1841.

Vulliamy, Mrs. *Trumpeter, Sound!,* D. L. Murray, 1933.

Vulliamy, Ernest, solicitor and trustee of Francie Comper's estate. *For Us in the Dark,* Naomi Royde-Smith, 1937.

Vulmea, Private Tim. 'Black Jack' (s.s.), *Soldiers Three,* R. Kipling, 1888.

Vye, Eustacia, central character, m. Clym Yeobright.
Captain Vye, her grandfather.
The Return of the Native, T. Hardy, 1878.

Vyse, Cecil, one-time fiancé of Lucy Honeychurch.
His mother.
A Room with a View, E. M. Forster, 1908.

W

Wabstow, Jenny. 'The Record of Badalia Herodsfoot' (s.s.), *Many Inventions*, R. Kipling, 1893.

Wachorn, 2nd husband of Marion Ramboat. *Tono Bungay*, H. G. Wells, 1909.

Wackerbart, head of a Herne Bay academy. *A Shabby Genteel Story*, W. M. Thackeray, 1840.

Wackerbath, Squirrel, Horace Ventimore's wealthy patron. *The Brass Bottle*, F. Anstey, 1900.

Wackles, Mrs, of the ladies' seminary.
Her daughters:
Melissa.
Sophie m. Alick Cheggs.
Jane.
The Old Curiosity Shop, C. Dickens, 1841.

Wad, Emir Ibrahim. *The Tragedy of the Korosko*, A. Conan Doyle, 1898.

Waddington, Miss. *Before the Bombardment*, O. Sitwell, 1926.

Waddle, Henry N. M., a folk-dance fanatic. *They Wanted to Live*, Cecil Roberts, 1939.

Waddy, father of Arthur Kipps.
His father, who leaves Kipps a fortune.
Kipps, H. G. Wells, 1905.

Waddy, Mary, widow, landlady. *The Adventures of Harry Richmond*, G. Meredith, 1871.

Wade, Miss. *Little Dorrit*, C. Dickens, 1857.

Wade, Eleanor, m. Sir Richard Devine. *For the Term of his Natural Life*, M. Clarke, 1874.

Wade, George, chairman of a rugby club. *This Sporting Life*, David Storey, 1960.

Wade, Lord Julian, King's Envoy. *Captain Blood*, R. Sabatini, 1922.

Wade, Oscar, lover of Harriott Leigh. *Where their Fire is not Quenched* (s.s.), May Sinclair.

Wadman, Widow, loved by Captain Shandy. *Tristram Shandy*, L. Sterne, 1767.

Waffle, Sir Henry, K.C. *Obiter Dicta*, H. Belloc.

Wafty, Bessie. *The Corn is Green* (play), Emlyn Williams, 1938.

Wagg, author, wit and snob. *Pendennis*, 1848–50, and elsewhere, W. M. Thackeray.

Waghorn, Carrie, refreshment-room attendant, m. Nibby. *The Town Traveller*, G. Gissing, 1898.

Wagner, servant of Faustus. *Doctor Faustus* (play), C. Marlowe, 1604.

Wagstaff, Mrs. *We're Here*, D. Mackail, 1947.

Wagstaff, Mrs, Edgar Tryan's landlady. 'Janet's Repentance,' *Scenes of Clerical Life*, George Eliot, 1857.

Wagstaff, Ruth, Bemerton's niece. *Over Bemerton's*, E. V. Lucas, 1908.

Wagstaffe, Michael, pseudo-American assassin. 'The Man with the Broken Nose' (s.s.), etc. *These Charming People*, M. Arlen, 1920.

Wagtail, Mistress, gentlewoman to Lady Ninny. *A Woman is a Weathercock* (play), N. Field, 1612.

Wahrfield, J. Churchill, defaulting banker.
Isabel, his daughter, m. Frank Goodwin.
Cabbages and Kings, O. Henry, 1905.

Wainsworth, Joe, harness-maker. *Poor White*, Sherwood Anderson, 1920.

Wainwright, Mr, a surgeon. *East Lynne*, Mrs Henry Wood, 1861.

Wait, James, central character, *The Nigger of the 'Narcissus'*, J. Conrad, 1898.

Waite, Felix.
His wife.
Thomas, their son.
'Salute the Cavalier' (s.s.), *These Charming People*, M. Arlen, 1920.

Waitwell, servant of Mirabell. *The Way of the World* (play), W. Congreve, 1700.

Wake, Muriel, m. 'young' Roger Forsyte. The *Forsyte* series, J. Galsworthy, 1906–33.

Wakefield, Vicar of. *See* DR CHARLES PRIMROSE.

Wakefield, Harry, one of the drovers. *The Two Drovers,* W. Scott, 1827.

Wakefield, Mary, m. Philip Whiteoak. *The Whiteoak Chronicles,* Mazo de la Roche, 1927 onwards.

Wakeling, Billy, m. Rosa Sawyer. *A Town like Alice,* N. Shute, 1950.

Wakem, lawyer at St Oggs.
Philip, his son, a crippled artist, in love with Maggie Tulliver.
The Mill on the Floss, George Eliot, 1860.

Walden, Ty Ty.
His children:
Jim Leslie.
Gussie, his wife.
Shaw.
Buck.
Griselda, his wife.
Rosamund, m. Will Thompson.
Jill ('Darling Jill').
God's Little Acre, E. Caldwell, 1933.

Waldman, lecturer on chemistry. *Frankenstein,* Mary W. Shelley, 1818.

Waldo, son of Otto, an overseer. *The Story of an African Farm,* Olive Schreiner, 1883.

Waldo, Mr.
Blodwen, his wife.
Their son.
Under Milk Wood (play), Dylan Thomas, 1954.

Waldon, an Oxford scholar. *Sir Charles Grandison,* S. Richardson, 1754.

Waldort, Franz, geologist. *The Woodcarver of 'Lympus,* Mary E. Waller, 1909.

Walen, Burton, editor. 'The Edge of the Evening' (s.s.), *A Diversity of Creatures,* R. Kipling, 1917.

Waler, Mr, an American visitor. *Mr Ingleside,* E. V. Lucas, 1910.

Wales, Jack, in love with Susan Brown. *Room at the Top,* J. Braine, 1957.

Walford, Colonel, C.B., Assistant Commissioner of Police. *The Ringer* (play), E. Wallace, 1926.

Walham, Lady, mother of Lord Kew. *The Newcomes,* W. M. Thackeray, 1853–5.

Wali Dad. 'On the City Wall' (s.s.), *Soldiers Three,* R. Kipling, 1888.

Walker, administrator of Talua, island in the Samoan group. 'Mackintosh' (s.s.), *The Trembling of a Leaf,* W. S. Maugham, 1921.

Walker, Dr. *The Circular Staircase,* Mary R. Rinehart, 1908.

Walker, Mr, a miner. *A Safety Match,* Ian Hay, 1911.

Walker, Mr, a solicitor. *London Wall* (play), J. van Druten, 1931.

Walker, Mrs, a hospital nurse. *A Farewell to Arms,* E. Hemingway, 1929.

Walker, Rev. Mr, Sub-Precentor. 'For Conscience' Sake,' *Life's Little Ironies,* T. Hardy, 1894.

Walker, Bill. *Major Barbara* (play), G. B. Shaw, 1905.

Walker, Captain Howard.
His wife, *née* Crump, 'The Ravenswing.'
Howard Woolney, their son.
'The Ravenswing,' *Men's Wives,* W. M. Thackeray, 1843.

Walker, John, Susan, Titty, Roger and **Vicky.**
Their father and mother.
Swallows and Amazons, A. Ransome, 1930.

Walker, Mick, a boy at Murdstone & Grinby. *David Copperfield,* C. Dickens, 1850.

Walker, Peter, a pedlar. *The Heart of Midlothian,* W. Scott, 1818.

Walker, Ruth, a canal girl.
Henry, her father.
The Water Gipsies, A. P. Herbert, 1930.

Walkin, Hiram J. *The Young Idea* (play), N. Coward, 1923.

Walkinghame, Sir Henry. *The Daisy Chain,* Charlotte M. Yonge, 1856.

Wallace, Mrs. *The Green Hat,* M. Arlen, 1924.

Wallace, Lionel, brilliant politician obsessed by a visionary door. 'The Door in the Wall' (s.s.), *The Country of the Blind,* H. G. Wells, 1911.

Wallace, Timothy.
Wilkie, his son.
The Grapes of Wrath, J. Steinbeck, 1939.

Wallenrode, Earl, Hungarian warrior. *The Talisman,* W. Scott, 1825.

Wallenstein, Mr and Mrs.
Wally, their son.
May, his wife.
Lummox, Fannie Hurst, 1924.

Waller, Jack, army friend of Lorrequer. *Harry Lorrequer,* C. Lever, 1839.

Wailing, Robert, 1st husband of Mrs Alden. *The Metropolis,* Upton Sinclair, 1908.

Wallinger, Sir Joseph.
His wife.
Coningsby, B. Disraeli, 1844.

Wallingford, Miles, central character and narrator, in love with Lucy Hardinge.
Grace, his sister.
Afloat and Ashore, J. Fenimore Cooper, 1844.

Walmsley, Mabel, mistress of John Fane, later his 2nd wife.
Edward, her 1st husband, who divorces her.
Going their own Ways, A. Waugh, 1938.

Walpole, shipping agent. *Captain Kettle* series, C. J. Cutcliffe Hyne, 1898–1932.

Walpole, Cutler. *The Doctor's Dilemma* (play), G. B. Shaw, 1906.

Walpurgo, Fräulein, cousin of Armgart. *Armgart* (poem), George Eliot, 1871.

Walsh, Peter, old suitor of Mrs Dalloway. *Mrs Dalloway,* Virginia Woolf, 1925.

Walsingham, Helen, one-time fiancée of Kipps.
Her mother.
Her brother, a defaulting solicitor.
Kipps, H. G. Wells, 1905.

Walt, Piet van der, m. 'Tant' Sannie. *The Story of an African Farm,* Olive Schreiner, 1883.

Walter, Mademoiselle, the Bramsleys' governess. *C.,* M. Baring, 1924.

Walter, Sir James.
Colonel Valentine, his brother.
'The Bruce-Partington Plans,' *His Last Bow,* A. Conan Doyle, 1917.

Walters, a cyclist. 'The Cat in the Bag,' *Lord Peter Views the Body,* Dorothy L. Sayers, 1928.

Walters, school superintendent. *The Adventures of Tom Sawyer,* Mark Twain, 1876.

Walters, a seaman, m. Ann Dunn. *The Bay,* L. A. G. Strong, 1941.

Walters, William, Quaker surgeon.
His sister, m. Captain Singleton.
Captain Singleton, D. Defoe, 1720.

Walterson, William, the Younger (alias Alan Stewart, alias Malins). *Starvecrow Farm,* Stanley Weyman, 1905.

Walton, Miss, an heiress. *The Man of Feeling,* H. Mackenzie, 1771.

Walton, Lady Jane. *Spring Cleaning* (play), F. Lonsdale, 1925.

Walton, Captain Richard, seaman, part narrator. *Frankenstein,* Mary W. Shelley, 1818.

Wamba, Cedric's jester. *Ivanhoe,* W. Scott, 1820.

Wan Lee, Chinese conjuror's child. 'Wan Lee the Pagan,' *The Luck of Roaring Camp,* Bret Harte, 1868.

Wan Nan, one-time wife of Deotlan. *Four Frightened People,* E. Arnot Robertson, 1931.

Wanderwide, Peter. *The Death and Last Confession of Wandering Peter* (poem), H. Belloc.

Wandl, Kunegunde. *See Naples and Die* (play), Elmer Rice, 1932.

Wandle, Lord, godfather of Aldous Raeburn. *Marcella,* Mrs Humphry Ward, 1894.

Wang, Axel Heyst's servant. *Victory,* Joseph Conrad, 1915.

Wang Li.
Hsiao, his son.
Yuan, his great-grandson. Chinese sages.
Landscape with Figures, R. Fraser, 1925.

Wang Yu, carping critic of Kai Lung's stories. *The Wallet of Kai Lung,* E. Bramah, 1900.

Wannop, Valentine, suffragette, mistress of Christopher Tietjens. *Last Post,* Ford Madox Ford, 1928.

Wansborough, 'Old' and 'Young,' parish clerks. *The Woman in White,* W. Collins, 1860.

Wapshot, Sir Giles.
His wife and daughters.
Vanity Fair, W. M. Thackeray, 1847–8.

Wapshot, Rev. Grimes, m. Mrs Susan Hoggarty. *The Great Hoggarty Diamond,* W. M. Thackeray, 1841.

Wapshot, Leander, a philosopher and sea captain.
Sarah Coverly Wapshot, his wife.
Their sons:
Coverly, a Public Relations man.
Moses, an alcoholic.

Betsey, Coverly's wife.
Melissa, Moses's wife.
Honora Wapshot, wealthy cousin and family matriarch.
The Wapshot Chronicle, 1957, and *The Wapshot Scandal,* 1963, John Cheever.

Warbeck, Captain Davey, m. Emily, aunt of Fanny and sister of Lady Alconleigh. *The Pursuit of Love,* Nancy Mitford, 1945.

Warbeck, Gerald, publisher of Fanny's Life. *Fanny by Gaslight,* M. Sadleir, 1940.

Warbeck, Perkin (hist.). *Perkin Warbeck* (play), John Ford, 1634.

Warbuckle, Bessie, m. Reg Aythorne. *South Riding,* Winifred Holtby, 1936.

Warburton, Dr. *The Family Reunion* (play), T. S. Eliot, 1939.

Warburton, Lord, English suitor of Isabel Archer, American heiress. *The Portrait of a Lady,* Henry James, 1881.

Ward ('Mr Swindles'), head groom to Arthur Barfield. *Esther Waters,* G. Moore, 1894.

Ward, Mr and Mrs.
Their children:
Henry.
Leonard.
Averil, m. Tom May.
Ella.
Minna.
The Trial, Charlotte M. Yonge, 1864.

Ward, Captain Bill, dead aircraft pilot. *No Highway,* N. Shute, 1948.

Ward, Billy, an 'innocent.' *Little Men,* 1871, and *Jo's Boys,* 1886, Louisa M. Alcott.

Ward, Marcolina, American-Irish night-club singer. *Destiny Bay,* Donn Byrne, 1928.

Ward, Oliver, engineer, inventor and dam constructor.
Sarah Burling Ward, his wife, artist and novelist.
Their children:
Oliver.
Betsy.
Agnes.
Lyman, their grandson, Oliver's son, narrator, m. Ellen Hammond.
Rodman, son of Lyman and Ellen.
Angle of Repose, Wallace Stegner, 1971.

Warden, Henry (also known as Henry Wellwood). *The Monastery* and *The Abbot,* W. Scott, 1820.

Warden, Michael, m. Marion Jeddler. *The Battle of Life,* C. Dickens, 1846.

Warder, Tom.
Becky, his wife, *née* Roland.
The Truth (play), Clyde Fitch, 1907.

Wardlaw, Mr, a schoolmaster. *Prester John,* J. Buchan, 1910.

Wardle, Mr.
His mother.
His daughters:
Emily, m. Augustus Snodgrass.
Isabella, m. Trundle.
Rachel, his sister.
Pickwick Papers, C. Dickens, 1837.

Wardour, Isabella. m. Mr Lovel.
Sir Arthur, Bt, her father.
Sir Anthony, her grandfather.
Captain Reginald, her brother.
The Antiquary, W. Scott, 1816.

Wardrop, Mr, chief engineer of the *Haliotis.* 'The Devil and the Deep Sea' (s.s.), *The Day's Work,* 1898, and elsewhere, R. Kipling.

Ware, Lady Arabella, m. Captain Robert Tarne. 'The Mystery of Lady Arabella Ware,' *Old Patch's Medley,* Marjorie Bowen, 1930.

Ware, Geoffrey. *The Silver King* (play), H. A. Jones, 1882.

Ware, Minny.
Roma, her illegitimate daughter by Eden Whiteoak.
The Whiteoak Chronicles, Mazo de la Roche, 1927 onwards.

Waring, Grandmother.
Her daughters:
Lydia, m. Purdy Rumford.
Lucy, m. Ezekiel Harrington.
Chosen Country, J. dos Passos, 1951.

Waring, George, naval lieutenant. *Where their Fire is not Quenched* (s.s.), May Sinclair.

Waring, Sir Harry.
His wife.
Cecil, his nephew and heir, commander, R.N., m. Lady Cora Palliser.
Leslie, his niece, m. Philip Winter.
The *Barsetshire* series, Angela Thirkell, 1933 onwards.

Waring, Isabella, one-time fiancée of

Paul Verdayne. *Three Weeks,* Elinor Glyn, 1907.

Waring, Major Percy, in love with Margaret Lovell. *Rhoda Fleming,* G. Meredith, 1865.

Waring, Robert, English overseer, m. Joan Desborough. *The Shulamite,* A. & C. Askew, 1904.

Waring, Robert, at school with Sammy Rice. *The Small Back Room,* N. Balchin, 1943.

Warkworth, Dilly, distant cousin of the Whiteoaks. *Whiteoak Brothers,* Mazo de la Roche, 1952.

Warli, a hunchback postman, m. Maria Truog. *Ships that Pass in the Night,* Beatrice Harraden, 1893.

Warming, E., cousin of Graham, the sleeper. *When the Sleeper Awakes,* H. G. Wells, 1899.

Warminster, Alfred, Earl of, an eccentric left-wing peer.
His sisters:
Isobel Tolland, m. Nicholas Jenkins.
Priscilla Tolland, m. Chips Lovell.
A Question of Upbringing, 1951, and others in *The Music of Time* series, Anthony Powell.

Warner, Dr. *Manalive,* G. K. Chesterton, 1912.

Warner, Adam, inventor.
Sibyll, his daughter.
The Last of the Barons, Lord Lytton, 1843.

Warner, Dr Alec. *Memento Mori,* Muriel Spark, 1959.

Warner, Duncan, condemned desperado. 'The Los Amigos Fiasco' (s.s.), *Round the Red Lamp,* A. Conan Doyle, 1894.

Warner, Georgie.
Doc, his father.
His mother.
Chosen Country, J. dos Passos, 1951.

Warnham, Ernest, solicitor. *The Old Bank,* W. Westall, 1902.

Warple, Bishop.
His wife.
Felicity, their daughter, m. Dr Trump.
Children of the Archbishop, N. Collins, 1951.

Warren, Jerome.
Gilbert, his adopted son.
Dick, his brother.
Nevada, his daughter.
'Schools and Schools' (s.s.), *Options,* O. Henry, 1909.

Warren, Keith, farmer. *The Labyrinth Makers,* Anthony Price, 1970.

Warren, Mrs Kitty, *née* Vavasour.
Vivie, her daughter.
Mrs Warren's Profession (play), G. B. Shaw, 1902.

Warren, Philip, young American, central character. *The Judgment of Paris,* Gore Vidal, 1952.

Warrener, Amy, close friend of Violet North.
Sarah, her mother.
Madcap Violet, W. Black, 1876.

Warrigal, a half-caste boy. *Robbery under Arms,* R. Boldrewood, 1888.

Warrington, Duke of. *The High Road* (play), F. Lonsdale, 1927.

Warrington, George.
Rachel, his wife, *née* Esmond (she reverted to the name of Esmond after his death).
Their twin sons:
George Esmond, m. Theodosia Lambert.
Their children:
Captain Miles.
Theodosia, m. Joseph Blake.
Hester, m. Captain Handyman.
Mary.
Henry Esmond, m. Fanny Mountain.
Sir Miles, Bt, uncle of the twins.
His wife.
Their children:
Miles.
Flora, m. Tom Claypole.
Dora, m. Rev. Mr Juffles.
The Virginians, W. M. Thackeray, 1857–9.

Warwick, last of the Barons.
His wife.
Lady Anne, their daughter.
The Last of the Barons, Lord Lytton, 1843.

Warwick, Earl of (hist.). *Henry the Sixth* (play), W. Shakespeare.

Warwick, Earl of, Richard de Beauchamp. *Saint Joan* (play), G. B. Shaw, 1924.

Warwick, Diana, central character.
Augustus, her husband.
Diana of the Crossways, George Meredith, 1885.

Warwick, Dr Oscar, F.R.S.
Dame Felicia, his wife.
Ivor Oscar, their son, chief engineer, Bermondsey power-station, m. Patricia St Aubyn.
The Young Men Are Coming, M. P. Shiel, 1937.

Washford, Joseph. 'Jerry Jarvis's Wig' (s.s.), *The Ingoldsby Legends,* R. H. Barham, 1837.

Washington, 'Smiler', R.A.F. recruit. *Chips With Everything* (play), Arnold Wesker, 1962.

Wastle, Willie.
His wife.
Sic a Wife as Willie Had (poem), R. Burns.

Wat the Devil, Northumbrian free-booter. *Rob Roy,* W. Scott, 1818.

Watchett, Mrs, the Time-Traveller's landlady. *The Time Machine,* H. G. Wells, 1895.

Watchett, Ted, friend of Hubert Lapell.
His father.
Phoebe, his cousin.
'Hubert and Minnie' (s.s.), *The Little Mexican,* A. Huxley, 1924.

Watchful. *See* KNOWLEDGE.

Water Rat, 'Ratty.' *The Wind in the Willows,* K. Grahame, 1908.

Waterbrook, agent of Wickfield.
His wife.
David Copperfield, C. Dickens, 1850.

Waterhall, Dr. *We the Accused,* E. Raymond, 1935.

Waterhouse, Canon, English chaplain at Fraxinet. *Act of God,* F. Tennyson Jesse, 1936.

Waterhouse, Colonel.
His wife.
Diana, their daughter.
Poet's Pub, E. Linklater, 1929.

Waterman, Dan, 'colossus of finance.' *The Metropolis,* Upton Sinclair, 1908.

Waters, Mrs (Jenny Jones), supposed to be wife of Captain Waters and mother of Tom Jones. *Tom Jones,* H. Fielding, 1749.

Waters, Barbara, loved by Francis Chelifer. *Those Barren Leaves,* A. Huxley, 1925.

Waters, Esther, kitchenmaid, central character, m. William Latch.
Her illegitimate child.
Her mother, m. Saunders as 2nd husband.
Esther Waters, G. Moore, 1894.

Waters, Michael, artist. *The Five Red Herrings,* Dorothy L. Sayers, 1931.

Watherstone, John, one-time fiancé of Catherine Winslow. *The Winslow Boy* (play), T. Rattigan, 1946.

Watkins, valet to the Rajah of Rukh. *The Green Goddess* (play), W. Archer, 1921.

Watkins, godfather of Kate Nickleby. *Nicholas Nickleby,* C. Dickens, 1839.

Watkins, Mr, owner of Dalberry Lees.
His wife.
Cassandra Cleopatra, their daughter.
Mr Facey Romford's Hounds, R. S. Surtees, 1865.

Watkins, Idris, miner who marries the Bowens's maid Rebecca. *Tomorrow To Fresh Woods,* Rhys Davies, 1941.

Watkins, Sally, nurse to Phineas Fletcher. *John Halifax, Gentleman,* Mrs Craik, 1856.

Watkins, Sim, 'chucker-out' to Steve Tawnie. *Magnolia Street,* L. Golding, 1932.

Watkins, Utah.
His wife.
Under Milk Wood (play), Dylan Thomas, 1954.

Watling, Belle, mistress of Rhett Butler; keeper of a brothel. *Gone with the Wind,* Margaret Mitchell, 1936.

Watlington, Lord, enormously wealthy. *Imperial Palace,* Arnold Bennett, 1930.

Watson, Miss, sister of Widow Douglas. *The Adventures of Tom Sawyer,* 1876, and *Huckleberry Finn,* 1884, Mark Twain.

Watson, Charlie. *Judith Paris,* Hugh Walpole, 1931.

Watson, Jill, nurse to the Eliot children.
Alf, her dead husband.
The Herb of Grace. Elizabeth Goudge, 1948.

Watson, Dr John (? James), intimate friend of Sherlock Holmes and recorder of his adventures, m. Mary Morstan. *A Study in Scarlet,*

1887, and succeeding volumes, A. Conan Doyle.

Watson, Lettice, widow of Roger Watson, daughter of William Marling; m (2) Tom Barclay.

Diana.

Clare. Her daughters by 1st husband.

The *Barsetshire* series, Angela Thirkell, 1933 onwards.

Watt, Jean, Brodie's mistress. *Deacon Brodie* (play), W. E. Henley & R. L. Stevenson, 1892.

Watters, Dr Irving. *Martin Arrowsmith*, Sinclair Lewis, 1925.

Wattey, Corporal, a fen-man. *The Story of Ragged Robyn*, O. Onions, 1945.

Wattle, Weasel. *Uncle Remus*, J. C. Harris, 1880–95.

Watts, Jim, chief E.R.A., *Compass Rose*, eng. to Gladys Bell. *The Cruel Sea*, N. Monsarrat, 1951.

Watts, Mrs Leora, prostitute. *Wise Blood*, Flannery O'Connor, 1952.

Watts, Noah, a minister, m. Olwen Powell. *The Black Venus*, Rhys Davies, 1944.

Watty, bankrupt client of Perker. *Pickwick Papers*, C. Dickens, 1837.

Watty, Mrs. *The Corn is Green* (play), Emlyn Williams, 1938.

Waugh, Mr, an actor playing the butler in a stately home. *A Pride of Heroes*, Peter Dickinson, 1969.

Waule, Jane, *née* Featherstone, rich and greedy widow.

Her children:

John.

Eliza.

Joanna.

Rebecca.

Middlemarch, Geo. Eliot, 1871–2.

Waverley, Edward, central character.

Sir Richard, his father.

Sir Giles, his grandfather.

Sir Nigel, his great-grandfather.

Sir Everard, his uncle.

Rachel, his aunt.

William, his brother, in love with Lucy St Aubin.

Waverley, W. Scott, 1814.

Waxy, solicitor. *Vanity Fair*, W. M. Thackeray, 1847–8.

Wayburn, Irene ('Raney') heroine, in love with Stewart O'Murry.

Nelson Darby Wayburn, her father, newsagent, Plymouth Brother.

Her mother.

A Georgian Love Story, Ernest Raymond, 1971.

Wayland-Leigh, Lieutenant-General. *The General*, C. S. Forester, 1936.

Wayland Smith. *See* WELAND.

Wayne, Provost of Notting Hill. *The Napoleon of Notting Hill*, G. K. Chesterton, 1904.

Wayne, Chance, unsuccessful Hollywood beach-boy. *Sweet Bird of Youth* (play), Tennessee Williams, 1959.

Waynflete, Lady Cicely, sister-in-law of Sir Howard Hallam. *Captain Brassbound's Conversion* (play), G. B. Shaw, 1900.

Wayward, James, m. (1) Helen Malcourt, (2) Constance Palliser. *The Firing Line*, R. W. Chambers, 1908.

Weare, Dr. *Strong Poison*, Dorothy L. Sayers, 1930.

Weatherby, Twink. *The Yearling*, Marjorie K. Rawlings, 1928.

Weathers, Connie, a flighty nurse. *Other Gods*, Pearl Buck, 1940.

Weaver, Charles, rich industrialist interested in rugby football.

Diane, his wife, interested in rugby players.

This Sporting Life, David Storey, 1960.

Weaver, Robert, friend of Eugene Gant. *Of Time and the River*, Thomas Wolfe, 1935.

Weazel, Captain. *Roderick Random*, T. Smollett, 1748.

Weazeling, Lord, Lord Chancellor. *Phineas Finn*, 1869, and elsewhere, A. Trollope.

Webb, Mr, newspaper editor.

His wife.

Wally, their son.

Emily, their daughter, m. George Gibbs.

Our Town (play), Thornton Wilder, 1938.

Webb, Brigadier, a beefy, red-faced infantryman. *The General*, C. S. Forester.

Webber, Frank, practical joker. *Charles O'Malley*, C. Lever, 1841.

Webber, George, author, central character.

John, his father.

Amelia, his mother, *née* Joyner.

You Can't Go Home Again, T. Wolfe, 1947.

Webberley, Alec. *Distinguished Villa* (play), Kate O'Brien, 1926.

Weber, Alexander Petrovitch ('Sasha'). *Tobit Transplanted*, Stella Benson, 1931.

Webley, Everard, murdered by Spandrell. *Point Counter Point*, Aldous Huxley, 1928.

Webster, 'Fatty.' *Sonia*, S. McKenna, 1917.

Webster, George, pillar of the establishment responsible for Reg Mills's imprisonment. *The Patriots*, James Barlow, 1960.

Webster, Nanny. *The Little Minister*, J. M. Barrie, 1891.

Wedderburn, C. St C., college friend of Michael Fane. *Sinister Street*, C. Mackenzie, 1913.

Wedderburn, Geoffrey, banker. *See also* CLEMENT HALE. *Sweet Lavender* (play), A. W. Pinero, 1888.

Wedgecroft, Gilbert. *Waste* (play), H. Granville-Barker, 1907.

Wedgwood, Michael, cousin of the Barnabases, m. as 2nd husband Gina Brande. *Flowers for the Judge*, Margery Allingham, 1936.

Wee Willie Winkie. *See* PERCIVAL WILLIAM WILLIAMS.

Weedle, Nancy.
  Jim, her father.
'The Superstitious Man's Story,' *Life's Little Ironies*, T. Hardy, 1894.

Weedon, Miss Tuffy, guardian of Charles Stringham during his dipsomania. *A Question of Upbringing*, 1951, and others in *The Music of Time* series, Anthony Powell.

Weeks, a schoolmaster. *Elsie Venner* O. W. Holmes, 1861.

Weeks, Mrs. *Gentlemen Prefer Blondes*, Anita Loos, 1925.

Weena, one of the Eloi; devoted to the Traveller. *The Time Machine*, H. G. Wells, 1895.

Wegg, Silas, owner of fruit and sweet stall, friend of Venus; hired by Boffin. *Our Mutual Friend*, C. Dickens, 1865.

Weigall, school friend of Caryl Bramsley. *C.*, M. Baring, 1924.

Weinberg, Hubert Howard. *Counsellor-at-Law* (play), Elmer Rice, 1931.

Weir, Dr.
  His daughters:
    Catherine.
    Sylvia, m. Ambrose Lydiatt.
Portrait of Clare, F. Brett Young, 1927.

Weir, Adam, Lord of Hermiston, Lord Chief Justice's clerk.
  Jean, his wife.
  Archibald ('Erchie'), their son.
Weir of Hermiston, R. L. Stevenson, 1896.

Weir, Morgan.
  Loo, his wife.
A Way through the Wood, N. Balchin, 1951.

Weland (Weyland Smith), smith to the Gods. 'Weland's Sword' and elsewhere, *Puck of Pook's Hill*, R. Kipling, 1906.

Welbore, Welbore, M.P. *Pendennis*, W. M. Thackeray, 1848–50.

Welch, Edward ('Neddy'), Professor of History.
  His wife.
  Bertrand, their son.
Lucky Jim, K. Amis, 1953.

Welch, Philip.
  Ann, his wife.
The Deep Blue Sea (play), T. Rattigan, 1952.

Weldon, Ernest.
  Grace, his wife.
'Too Bad' (s.s.), *Here Lies*, Dorothy Parker, 1939.

Welford, Fanny, mistress of George Winterbourne. *Death of a Hero*, R. Aldington, 1929.

Wellburn, Tommie, m. Fanny Elsing. *Gone with the Wind*, Margaret Mitchell, 1936.

Weller, Alice, actress. *The Troubled Air*, Irwin Shaw, 1951.

Weller, Sam, boots at an inn, later friend and servant of Pickwick, m. Mary, Pickwick's housekeeper.
  Tony, his father, a coachman.
  His stepmother, formerly Mrs Clarke, landlady of the Marquis of Granby.
Pickwick Papers, 1837, and *Master Humphrey's Clock*, 1841, C. Dickens.

Welles, Gideon, of Lincoln's cabinet (hist.). *Abraham Lincoln* (play), J. Drinkwater, 1918.

Wellesley, Lady Barbara, m. (1) Admiral Sir Percy Leighton, (2)

Horatio Hornblower. The *Hornblower* series, C. S. Forester, 1937 onwards.

Wells, Archie. *Spring Cleaning* (play), F. Lonsdale, 1925.

Wells, Hannah Elizabeth.
Robert, her father.
Sampson Rideout, Quaker, Una Silberrad, 1911.

Wells, John Wellington, of J. W. Wells & Co., family sorcerers. *The Sorcerer* (comic opera), Gilbert & Sullivan, 1877.

Wellwood, Henry. *See* HENRY WARDEN.

Wellwood, Sophia, m. Guy Mannering. *Guy Mannering,* W. Scott, 1815.

Welsh, Allan, minister of the Marrow Kirk, Dullarg. *The Lilac Sunbonnet,* S. R. Crockett, 1894.

Welsh, Anne Comfort.
Waldo, her husband.
Chosen Country, J. dos Passos, 1951.

Welter, Lord. *Ravenshoe,* H. Kingsley, 1861.

Wembury, Divisional Detective Inspector. *The Ringer* (play), E. Wallace, 1926.

Wemmick, clerk to Jaggers.
His father, 'the Aged.'
Great Expectations, C. Dickens, 1861.

Wendigee, Julius, Dutch electrician. *The First Men in the Moon,* H. G. Wells, 1901.

Wenham, writer and M.P., confidential servant of Lord Steyne. *Vanity Fair,* 1847–8, and elsewhere, W. M. Thackeray.

Wennerberg, Annie, lodging-house landlady. *Lummox,* Fannie Hurst, 1924.

Wenonah, mother of Hiawatha. *The Song of Hiawatha* (poem), H. W. Longfellow, 1855.

Wentworth, Colonel.
His wife, *née* Feverel.
Austin, their son.
The Ordeal of Richard Feverel, G. Meredith, 1859.

Wentworth, Captain Frederick, R.N., m. Anne Elliot.
His brother, former curate of Monkford.
His sister, m. Admiral Croft.
Persuasion, Jane Austen, 1818.

Wentworth-Williams, Mrs Sandra. *Jacob's Room,* Virginia Woolf, 1922.

Wentz, Hjalmar, settler in an African state.
Margot, his wife.
Emmanuelle, their daughter.
Stephen, their son.
A Guest of Honour, Nadine Gordimer, 1971.

Werneth, history don. *Random Harvest,* J. Hilton, 1941.

Wertheim, Count de.
Clotilda, his daughter, m. as his 1st wife Francis, 1st Earl Castlewood.
Henry Esmond, W. M. Thackeray, 1852.

Wesendonck (Donkey), schoolboy, friend of Tony Morland. *High Rising,* Angela Thirkell, 1933.

Weser Dreiburg, Princess of, giantess who falls in love with young Redwood. *The Food of the Gods,* H. G. Wells, 1904.

Wessels, Mrs Emily, aunt of Laura Dearborn. *The Pit,* F. Norris, 1903.

Wessen, Lucy.
Wilbur, her brother.
'I'm a Fool' (s.s.), *Horses and Men,* Sherwood Anderson, 1924.

Wessner, a scoundrel. *Freckles,* Gene S. Porter, 1905.

Wesson, Aesop R., pseudo book collector. *Poet's Pub,* E. Linklater, 1929.

West, Arthur Cadogan. 'The Bruce-Partington Plans,' *His Last Bow,* A. Conan Doyle, 1917.

West, Rev. C. M. V., friend of Nicholas Sandomir. *Non-Combatants and Others,* Rose Macaulay, 1916.

West, Dora, m. Tommy Bangs. *Little Men,* 1871, and *Jo's Boys,* 1886, Louisa M. Alcott.

West, Lady Dora. *See* DOWAGER COUNTESS OF AUSTELL.

West, Jane. *The Fourth Wall* (play), A. A. Milne, 1928.

West, John Henry, boy aged six, Frankie Addams's cousin. *The Member of the Wedding,* Carson McCullers, 1946.

West, Molly, close friend of Joan Penrose, m. Hugh Drummond.
Her father and mother.
The Winds of Chance, S. K. Hocking.

West, Raymond, author, Miss Marple's nephew.
Joan, his wife.
Various novels featuring Miss Marple, Agatha Christie.

Westbrook, Harold (Schultzy), actor, m. Elly Chipley. *Show Boat,* Edna Ferber, 1926.

Westbury, Captain Jack. *Henry Esmond,* W. M. Thackeray, 1852.

Western, Squire.
Sophia, his daughter, m. Tom Jones.
Mrs Western, his sister.
Tom Jones, H. Fielding, 1749.

Western, Jasper ('Eau-Douce'), m. Mabel Dunham. *The Pathfinder,* J. Fenimore Cooper, 1840.

Western, Roger, an Indian, m. Evelyn Childs. *A Lamp for Nightfall,* E. Caldwell, 1952.

Westfall, James.
His wife.
The Virginian, O. Wister, 1902.

Westlock, Hannah, maid to Norman Urquhart. *Strong Poison.* Dorothy L. Sayers, 1930.

Westlock, John, pupil of Pecksniff, m. Ruth Pinch. *Martin Chuzzlewit,* C. Dickens, 1844.

Westmore, Bessy, mill owner, *née* Langhope, m. John Amherst.
Mr Langhope, her father.
The Fruit of the Tree, Edith Wharton, 1907.

Westmorland, Earl of. *Henry the Fourth* and *Henry the Fifth* (plays), W. Shakespeare.

Weston, Mr. *Mr Weston's Good Wine,* T. F. Powys, 1927.

Weston, Mrs, m. Colonel Boucher. *Queen Lucia,* E. F. Benson, 1920.

Weston, Mrs, *née* Taylor, close friend and one-time governess of Emma Woodhouse.
Her husband. *See also* FRANK CHURCHILL.
Emma, Jane Austen, 1816.

Weston, Rev. Edward, m. Agnes Grey.
Edward, Agnes and **May,** their children.
Agnes Grey, Anne Brontë, 1847.

Weston, Joseph Barry (Joby), a small boy, central character.
Reg, his father.
Norah, his mother.
Daisy, his aunt.
Ted, his uncle.
Mona, his cousin.
Joby, Stan Barstow, 1964.

Weston, Muriel. *Call it a Day* (play), Dodie Smith, 1935.

Westrupp, Hephzibah, guardian of Jane Coventry. *Sampson Rideout, Quaker,* Una Silberrad, 1911.

Wetheral, Bruce Campbell, late captain, R.A.C., central character and narrator, m. Jean Lucas.
John Henry, his father.
Eleanor, his mother, *née* Campbell.
Campbell's Kingdom, H. Innes, 1952.

Wetherby, Brookfield headmaster. *Goodbye, Mr Chips,* J. Hilton, 1934.

Wetherby, Captain. *Trumpeter, Sound!,* D. L. Murray, 1933.

Wetherby, Dr.
His wife.
Dickie, their son.
Badger's Green, R. C. Sherriff, 1930.

Wetherell, Hon. Sylvester, Colonial Secretary, N.S.W. *Dr Nikola,* G. Boothby, 1896.

Wethermill, Henry, murderer of Mme Dauvray. *At the Villa Rose,* A. E. W. Mason, 1910.

Weycock, Mordred, Manager, United Sugar Co.
Roger, his nephew.
Odtaa, J. Masefield, 1926.

Whacker, Dr. *Captain Blood,* R. Sabatini, 1922.

Whamond, Peter.
Old Peter, his father.
Sentimental Tommy, J. M. Barrie, 1896.

Whamond, Thomas. *The Little Minister,* J. M. Barrie, 1891.

Whang, the miller. *A Citizen of the World,* O. Goldsmith, 1762.

Wharfedale, pseudo **Duchess of** (Kitty Cobham, actress). The *Hornblower* series, C. S. Forester, 1937 onwards.

Wharton, Harry, one of the Famous Five at Greyfriars. The *Billy Bunter* series, Frank Richards.

Wharton, Henry S., M.P. *Marcella,* Mrs Humphry Ward, 1894.

Wheather, an officer. *Sixty-four, Ninety-four,* R. H. Mottram, 1925.

Wheatley, Lord (Charles), central

character and narrator. *Phroso*, A. Hope, 1897.

Wheedle, Mrs. *Polly* (comic opera), J. Gay, 1729.

Wheedle, Polly, a maid, m. Jack Raikes.
Susan, her sister.
Evan Harrington, G. Meredith, 1861.

Wheeler, Lem. *The Shepherd of the Hills*, H. B. Wright, 1907.

Wheeler, Sarah, nurse-housekeeper to the Beltons. The *Barsetshire* series, Angela Thirkell, 1933 onwards.

Whelby, Sir Reginald. *The High Road* (play), F. Lonsdale, 1927.

Whichehalse, Baron Hugh de.
Marwood, his son.
Lorna Doone, R. D. Blackmore, 1869.

Whipple, Albert, ordinary seaman, *Artemis*. *The Ship*, C. S. Forester, 1943.

Whiskerandos, 'hero' rat. *Rambles of a Rat*, A.L.O.E., 1854.

Whiskers, Samuel. *See* SAMUEL.

Whistler, The, 'a young savage,' Effie Deans's child. *The Heart of Midlothian*, W. Scott, 1818.

Whitbread, Hugh.
Evelyn, his wife.
Mrs Dalloway, Virginia Woolf, 1925.

White, a schoolmaster. *Mr Perrin and Mr Traill*, Hugh Walpole, 1911.

White, rationalist journalist, friend of Benham. *The Research Magnificent*, H. G. Wells, 1915.

White, Mr and Mrs.
Herbert, their son.
'The Monkey's Paw' (s.s.), *The Lady of the Barge*, W. W. Jacobs, 1902.

White, Mrs. *Carrots*, Mrs Molesworth, 1876.

White, Mrs, protégée of the Matriarch.
Her daughter.
Shining and Free, G. B. Stern, 1935.

White, Arthur. *A Lamp for Nightfall*, E. Caldwell, 1952.

White, Charlie ('Piggy'), bookmaker. *Shabby Tiger*, H. Spring, 1934.

White, Helen, friend of George Willard. *Winesburg, Ohio*, Sherwood Anderson, 1919.

White, Johnson. *Abraham Lincoln* (play), J. Drinkwater, 1918.

White, Lucy. *The Professor's Love Story* (play), J. M. Barrie, 1894.

White, Moll, a witch. Essays in *The Spectator*, J. Addison, 1711–14.

White, R. ('Moles'). *Tell England*, E. Raymond, 1922.

White, Wylie, screenwriter. *The Last Tycoon*, F. Scott Fitzgerald, 1941.

White Cobra, The (Thuu). 'The King's Ankus,' *The Second Jungle Book*, R. Kipling, 1895.

White-Jacket, sailor on board U.S.S. *Neversink*. *White-Jacket*, Herman Melville, 1850.

White King, Queen and **Knave, The.** *Alice Through the Looking-glass*, L. Carroll, 1872.

Whitebillet, Edith, m. Oliver Price.
Edna, her twin, m. (1) Freddy Smith, (2) Oliver Price as 2nd wife.
Sir Reginald, their father.
Antigua Penny Puce, R. Graves, 1936.

Whitecraft, John, landlord of the Cat and Fiddle, Altringham. *Peveril of the Peak*, W. Scott, 1822.

Whitefield, Mrs. *Tom Jones*, H. Fielding, 1749.

Whitefield, Ann.
Her mother.
Man and Superman (play), G. B. Shaw, 1903.

Whitehead, Harry. 'I'm a Fool' (s.s.), and elsewhere, *Horses and Men*, Sherwood Anderson, 1924.

Whitehouse, Betty.
Gordon, her husband.
Freda, his sister, m. Robert Caplan.
Dangerous Corner (play), J. B. Priestley, 1932.

Whitelaw, Martin.
m. (1) Julia Makepeace.
Their sons:
Charles, m. Helene Vaucaire.
Their children:
Helen. *See* HERBERT WILSON.
Rudolph, m. Maria Lousada.
Charles, m. Joan Crowther.
Richard, their son.
Richard Martin, m. Emily Palmer.
(2) Sarah Brockett.
Roots, Naomi Jacob, 1932.

Whitelegg, George Henry, dead climber. *The Accident* (s.s.), Ann Bridge.

Whiteoak, Renny, m. Alayne Archer. *See also* MOLLY GRIFFITH.
Their children: **Adeline.**
Archer.
His grandparents **Captain Philip** and **Adeline,** *née* Court (old Mrs Whiteoak).
His parents **Philip,** and **Margaret,** *née* Ramsay.
Philip's 2nd wife, **Mary Wakefield.**
His uncles and aunts:
Augusta, Lady Buckley.
Nicholas (divorced).
Ernest.
Meg, his sister, m. Maurice Vaughan.
His half-brothers:
Eden, 1st husband of Alayne Archer. *See also* MINNY WARE.
Piers, m. Pheasant Vaughan. Their sons:
Maurice ('Mooey').
Finch.
Philip.
Finch, m. Sarah Leigh, *née* Court, as 2nd husband.
Wakefield.
The Whiteoak Chronicles, Mazo de la Roche, 1927 onwards.

White-tip, a female otter. *Tarka the Otter,* Henry Williamson, 1927.

Whitford, Vernon, m. Clara Middleton. *The Egoist,* G. Meredith, 1879.

Whitgift, Widow.
Her two sons.
'The Dymchurch Flit,' *Puck of Pook's Hill,* R. Kipling, 1906.

Whitman.
His wife.
Their two daughters.
Robbery under Arms, R. Boldrewood, 1888.

Whitney, Isa, an opium addict.
Kate, his wife.
'The Man with the Twisted Lip,' *Adventures of Sherlock Holmes,* A. Conan Doyle, 1892.

Whitstable, George, m. Sophia Longestaffe. *The Way We Live Now,* A. Trollope, 1875.

Whittaker, an Admiralty official. *The Thirty-nine Steps,* J. Buchan, 1915.

Whittaker, Betty. *All Our Yesterdays,* H. M. Tomlinson, 1930.

Whittaker, Prudence, secretary to Sir Buckstone Abbott, m. Tubby Vanringham. *Summer Moonshine,* P. G. Wodehouse, 1938.

Whittier, Pollyanna, central character. *Pollyanna,* Eleanor H. Porter, 1913.

Whittington, Henry. *Clementina,* A. E. W. Mason, 1901.

Whittington, Hugh, who disappears in Tibet. Half-brother of Charles Houston. *The Rose of Tibet,* Lionel Davidson, 1962.

Whittle, Abel. *The Mayor of Casterbridge,* T. Hardy, 1886.

Whybarne, a countryman. 'A Habitation Enforced' (s.s.), *Actions and Reactions,* R. Kipling, 1909.

Whybrow, Mr and Mrs, first victims of the Strangling Horrors. *The Hands of Mr Ottermole* (s.s.), T. Burke.

Whyte, Oliver. *The Mystery of a Hansom Cab,* F. Hume, 1886.

Wibird, Olive, friend of the Ammidons. *Java Head,* J. Hergesheimer, 1919.

Wick, Second Lieutenant Robert Hanna. 'Only a Subaltern' (s.s.), *Wee Willie Winkie,* R. Kipling, 1888.

Wickenden, Jim.
His mother.
Mary, his adopted daughter.
'Friendly Brook' (s.s.), *A Diversity of Creatures,* R. Kipling, 1917.

Wickett, Mrs, Mr Chips's landlady. *Goodbye, Mr Chips,* J. Hilton, 1934.

Wickett, Jill, m. Rupert Johnson. *The Mother,* E. Phillpotts, 1908.

Wickett, Dr Terry. *Martin Arrowsmith,* Sinclair Lewis, 1925.

Wickfield, Mr, lawyer.
Agnes, his daughter, m. as 2nd wife David Copperfield.
David Copperfield, C. Dickens, 1850.

Wickham, Noel Merton's agent. The *Barsetshire* series, Angela Thirkell, 1933 onwards.

Wickham, friend of Michael Finsbury. *The Wrong Box* (s.s.), R. L. Stevenson & Lloyd Osbourne, 1889.

Wickham, Mrs, nurse to Paul Dombey. *Dombey and Son,* C. Dickens, 1848.

Wickham, George, m. Lydia Bennet. *Pride and Prejudice,* Jane Austen, 1813.

Wickham, James.
Dorothy, his wife.
The Land of Promise (play), W. S. Maugham, 1914.

Wickham, Lady Mary, in love with Anton Balakireff. *A Bargain with the Kremlin* (s.s.), P. Gibbs.

Wicklow, Roddy, agent and brother-in-law of Lord Pomfret, m. Alice Barton. The *Barsetshire* series, Angela Thirkell, 1933 onwards.

Wicks, bank cashier. *Fed Up,* G. A. Birmingham, 1931.

Wickson, Philip, a convert to socialism. *The Iron Heel,* Jack London, 1908.

Wickstead, murdered by Griffin. *The Invisible Man,* H. G. Wells, 1897.

Wickthorpe, Earl of ('Ceddy'), friend of Lanny Budd. *Dragon Harvest,* Upton Sinclair, 1946.

Widdows, Mrs, Hannah Mole's employer. *Miss Mole,* E. H. Young, 1930.

Widdowson, John, senior partner of Barnabas, publishers, cousin of the Barnabases. *Flowers for the Judge,* Margery Allingham, 1936.

Widdup, Mrs, m. Coulson. 'The Merry Month of May' (s.s.), *Whirligigs,* O. Henry, 1910.

Widgery, Douglas, friend of Mrs Milton. *The Wheels of Chance,* H. G. Wells, 1896.

Widgetts, The, neighbours of Peter Stanley. *Ann Veronica,* H. G. Wells, 1909.

Widmerpool, Kenneth, financier and Labour Member of Parliament, m. Pamela Flitton. *A Question of Upbringing,* 1951, and others in *The Music of Time* series, Anthony Powell.

Widow of Florence, A. *All's Well That Ends Well* (play), W. Shakespeare.

Wiener, jeweller at Leubronn. *Daniel Deronda,* George Eliot, 1876.

Wier, Graham, schoolteacher charged with indecent assault of girl pupil.
Freda, his wife.
Term of Trial, James Barlow, 1961.

Wigemwell, Captain, of *The Breeze. Tom Cringle's Log,* M. Scott, 1836.

Wiggle, Desborough. *The Book of Snobs,* W. M. Thackeray, 1846–7.

Wiggs, Mrs.
Billy, her husband.
Mrs Wiggs of the Cabbage Patch, Alice H. Rice, 1901.

Wilberforce, Miss Amy, drunkard. *South Wind,* N. Douglas, 1917.

Wilbur, Amy, m. Maurice Garden. *Told by an Idiot,* R. Macaulay, 1923.

Wilbur, Ross, central character. *Shanghaied,* F. Norris, 1904.

Wilburn, Dudley, solicitor.
m. (1) Edith.
Joyce and **Evelyn,** their daughters.
(2) Clare Hingston (her 2nd husband.)
Portrait of Clare, 1927, and *My Brother Jonathan,* 1928, F. Brett Young.

Wilcher, Thomas Loftus, bachelor, solicitor, owner of Tolbrook Manor.
Edward, his brother, politician.
Ann, Edward's daughter, m. cousin Robert Brown.
Major Bill Wilcher, another brother.
John, son of Bill, m. Gladys.
Lucy, sister, m. Puggy Brown.
Robert, their son.
To Be A Pilgrim (1942) and others, Joyce Cary.

Wilcocks, Thomas, captain of ship that rescued Gulliver. *Gulliver's Travels,* J. Swift, 1726.

Wilcox, Henry, friend of Arthur Rowe.
Doris, his wife.
The Ministry of Fear, Graham Greene, 1943.

Wilcox, Miss Semiramis. *The Quest of the Golden Girl,* R. le Gallienne, 1896.

Wild, Jim. *Jim* (poem), Bret Harte.

Wild, Jonathan, rogue.
Laetitia Snap, his wife.
Jonathan Wild, Henry Fielding, 1743, and *Jack Sheppard,* W. H. Ainsworth, 1839.

Wildblood, Miss, book-keeper at 'Toni's.' *A Deputy was King,* G. B. Stern, 1926.

Wildenbruch, Hugo, German geologist. *The Seven Who Fled,* Frederic Prokosch, 1937.

Wilder, Mrs, friend of Stanley Timberlake. *In this our Life,* Ellen Glasgow, 1942.

Wilderspin, a Bohemian painter. *Aylwin,* T. Watts-Dunton, 1899.

Wilderspin, friend of Bailey. *Through a Window* (s.s.), H. G. Wells, 1894.

Wildeve, Damon, m. Thomasin Yeobright; lover of Eustacia Yeobright. *The Return of the Native,* T. Hardy, 1878.

Wildfire, Madge. *See* MADGE MURDOCKSON.

Wilding.
His wife.
The Gamester (play), J. Shirley, 1637.

Wilding, Charlotte. *Jacob's Room,* Virginia Woolf, 1922.

Wildney, Charles, one of the school's 'bad boys.' *Eric, or Little by Little,* F. W. Farrar, 1858.

Wildrake, Roger, college friend of Markham Everard. *Woodstock,* W. Scott, 1826.

Wilfer, Bella, central character, m. John Harmon.
Reginald, her father.
Her mother.
Lavinia, her sister, eng. to George Sampson.
Our Mutual Friend, C. Dickens, 1865.

Wilford, Stephen, society rake. *Frank Fairlegh,* F. E. Smedley, 1850.

Wilfred. *See* IVANHOE.

Wilkerson, Jonas, overseer to the O'Haras, m. Emmie Slattery. *Gone with the Wind,* Margaret Mitchell, 1936.

Wilkes, Ashley, m. Melanie Hamilton, his cousin.
Beau, their son.
John, his father.
Honey and **India,** his sisters.
Gone with the Wind, Margaret Mitchell, 1936.

Wilkett, C. R., bacteriologist. 'Tender Achilles' (s.s.), *Limits and Renewals,* R. Kipling, 1932.

Wilkin, divorce detective. *Holy Deadlock,* A. P. Herbert, 1934.

Wilkins, groom to Lord Dorincourt. *Little Lord Fauntleroy,* Frances H. Burnett, 1886.

Wilkins, Mr. *A Laodicean,* T. Hardy, 1881.

Wilkins, Cassandra. *Manhattan Transfer,* J. dos Passos, 1925.

Wilkins, Mrs Deborah, Squire Allworthy's servant. *Tom Jones,* H. Fielding, 1749.

Wilkins, Edgar, novelist. *The New Machiavelli,* 1911, and elsewhere, H. G. Wells.

Wilkins, Major Frank, friend of Mrs Delacroix. *The Little Girls,* Elizabeth Bowen, 1964.

Wilkins, Mrs Lotty.
Mellersh, her husband.
The Enchanted April, Countess von Arnim, 1922.

Wilkins, Phoebe, companion to Julia Templeton, m. Jack Tibbets. *Bracebridge Hall,* W. Irving, 1823.

Wilkinson, Charles Plethern's agent. *Desolate Splendour,* M. Sadleir, 1923.

Wilkinson, Dr Adam, a specialist. 'A False Start' (s.s.), *Round the Red Lamp,* A. Conan Doyle, 1894.

Wilkinson, Miss Emily. *Of Human Bondage,* W. S. Maugham, 1915.

Wilkinson, Dr Horace. 'A False Start' (s.s.), *Round the Red Lamp,* A. Conan Doyle, 1894.

Wilkinson, Maureen, friend of Middleton. *The Restoration of Arnold Middleton* (play), David Storey, 1967.

Wilkinson, Peter, neurotic young Englishman, lover of Otto Nowak. *Goodbye to Berlin,* Christopher Isherwood, 1939.

Wilks, actor (alias Professor de Worms). *The Man who was Thursday,* G. K. Chesterton, 1908.

Wilks, Nurse, aged and tyrannical ex-nanny of Frederick Mulliner. *Meet Mr Mulliner,* P. G. Wodehouse, 1927.

Will, 'master and tutor in wickedness.' *Colonel Jack,* Defoe, 1722.

Willan, friend of Cyril Burnage, in love with Clare Browell. *Right Off the Map,* C. E. Montague, 1927.

Willard, George, young reporter.
Elizabeth, his mother.
Tom, his father, owner of local hotel.
Winesburg, Ohio, Sherwood Anderson, 1919.

Willard, Jim, young Virginian, central character. *The City and The Pillar,* Gore Vidal, 1948.

Willard, Hildegarde.
Hortense, her sister.
Chosen Country, J. dos Passos, 1951.

Willatale, queen of the Arnewi tribe. *Henderson The Rain King,* Saul Bellow, 1959.

Willcox, Henry, occupant of Howards End.
His children:
Charles.
Dorothea, his wife.
Paul and **Eve.**
Howards End, E. M. Forster, 1910.

Willems, Peter, central character, *An Outcast of the Islands,* J. Conrad, 1896.

Willersley, varsity friend of Remington. *The New Machiavelli,* H. G. Wells, 1911.

Willesden, Miss, an old lady. *London Wall* (play), J. van Druten, 1931.

Willet, John, landlord of the Maypole.
Joe, his son, m. Dolly Varden.
Barnaby Rudge, C. Dickens, 1841.

Willett, Ted, 2nd husband of Nancy Geaiter. *Joseph and his Brethren,* H. W. Freeman, 1928.

Willi. *The Dark Is Light Enough* (play), Christopher Fry, 1954.

William, old servant and confidant of Dona St Colomb. *Frenchman's Creek,* Daphne du Maurier, 1941.

William (Walter Boon), waiter. *You Never Can Tell* (play), G. B. Shaw, 1895.

William, son of a jail doctor. 'The Debt' (s.s.), *Limits and Renewals* R. Kipling, 1932.

William, Prince of Greck. *The Queen's Husband* (play), R. E. Sherwood, 1928.

William the Conqueror. *See* WILLIAM MARTYN.

Williams, friend of Olaf Henderson. *The Benefactor,* J. D. Beresford.

Williams, chairman of visiting justices, Hawes's Jail. *It Is Never Too Late to Mend,* C. Reade, 1856.

Williams. *Dr Nikola,* G. Boothby, 1896.

Williams, driver of milk lorry. *My Adventure in Norfolk* (s.s.), A. J. Alan.

Williams, Farmer, suitor of Olivia Primrose. *The Vicar of Wakefield,* O. Goldsmith, 1766.

Williams, Mr. 'The Mezzotint' (s.s.), *Ghost Stories of an Antiquary,* M. R. James, 1910.

Williams, Nurse, nurse to Sir Victor Pandolfo. *The Great Pandolfo,* W. J. Locke, 1925.

Williams, Nurse, attendant on Philip Boyes. *Strong Poison,* Dorothy L. Sayers, 1930.

Williams, Sergeant, assistant to Alan Grant. *A Daughter of Time,* 1951, and elsewhere, Josephine Tey.

Williams, Rev. Arthur. *Pamela,* S. Richardson, 1740.

Williams, Lady Betty, widow. *Sir Charles Grandison,* S. Richardson, 1754.

Williams, Bobby. *Spring Cleaning* (play), F. Lonsdale, 1925.

Williams, Caleb, central character. *Caleb Williams,* W. Godwin, 1794.

Williams, Clinton, a boy reaching out for life.
Ralph Williams, his father.
Annabel Williams, his mother.
Berry-Berry, his elder brother.
All Fall Down, James Leo Herlihy, 1960.

Williams, Eliza, daughter of Colonel Brandon's dead love; betrayed by John Willoughby. *Sense and Sensibility,* Jane Austen, 1811.

Williams, Private Ellgee, a silent innocent young soldier. *Reflections in a Golden Eye,* Carson McCullers, 1940.

Williams, Eric, central character.
His father and mother.
Vernon, his brother.
Eric, or Little by Little, F. W. Farrar, 1858.

Williams, Fred, m. Violet North. *The Happy Prisoner,* Monica Dickens, 1946.

Williams, Grafton, lawyer. *Lovey Childs,* John O'Hara, 1969.

Williams, Gus.
Henry, his nephew, sneak and coward.
Tex of Bar-20, C. E. Mulford, 1922.

Williams, Janey, private secretary.
Joe, her brother.
U.S.A. trilogy, John dos Passos, 1930–6.

Williams, Percival William ('Wee Willie Winkie').
Colonel Williams, his father.
'Wee Willie Winkie' (s.s.), *Wee Willie Winkie,* R. Kipling, 1888.

Williams, Peter, an evangelist.
Winifred, his wife.
Lavengro, George Borrow, 1851.

Williams, 'Slogger,' Tom's opponent in the big fight. *Tom Brown's Schooldays,* T. Hughes, 1857.

Williams, William, walking out with Gladys Horrocks. *Whose Body?*, Dorothy L. Sayers, 1923.

Willie, 'Holy.' *Holy Willie's Prayer and Epitaph* (poem), R. Burns.

Willie of Westburnflat ('Red Reiver'). *The Black Dwarf*, W. Scott, 1816.

Willing, Mr, George Apley's biographer. *The Late George Apley*, J. P. Marquand, 1937.

Willings, Rev. Mr. *The Old Lady Shows Her Medals* (play), J. M. Barrie, 1917.

Willis, copywriter, Pym's Publicity. *Murder Must Advertise*, Dorothy L. Sayers, 1933.

Willis, Captain. *Two Years Ago*, C. Kingsley, 1857.

Willis, Mr and Mrs.
Lilian, their daughter.
Edward, Willis's son by 1st wife.
My Brother Jonathan, F. Brett Young, 1928.

Willis, Private, Grenadier Guards, m. Queen of the Fairies. *Iolanthe* (comic opera), Gilbert & Sullivan, 1882.

Willon, villainous head groom. *Under Two Flags*, Ouida, 1867.

Willoughby, Mrs, passenger on the cargo ship *Oroya*. *Captain Bottell*, James Hanley, 1933.

Willoughby, Lord. *Now We Are Six* (poems), A. A. Milne, 1927.

Willoughby, Sir Clement. *Evelina*, Fanny Burney, 1778.

Willoughby, Flora. *Comrade, O Comrade*, Ethel Mannin, 1946.

Willoughby, John. *Sense and Sensibility*, Jane Austen, 1811.

Willoughby, Miss Mary.
Miss Fanny, her sister.
Quality Street (play), J. M. Barrie, 1902.

Willoughby, Sophia, *née* Aspen, wealthy owner of Blandamer House, Dorset, central character.
Frederick, her husband.
Augusta and **Damien,** their children who die of smallpox.
Summer Will Show, Sylvia Townsend Warner, 1936.

Willow, Kate, 'witty and mischievous.' Essays in *The Spectator*, J. Addison, 1711–14.

Willowes, Laura ('Lolly'), central character.
Everard, her father.
Henry, her brother.
Caroline, his wife.
James, her brother.
Sibyl, his wife.
Titus, their son.
Lolly Willowes, Sylvia Townsend Warner, 1926.

Wills, Marjorie, niece and ward of Marcus Chesney, m. George Harding. *The Black Spectacles*, J. Dickson Carr, 1948.

Wills, Colonel Nathan P., U.S.A.
His wife
The Good Ship 'Mohock,' W. Clark Russell, 1894.

Willum, Big, foreman to Temperley. *The Beautiful Years*, H. Williamson, 1921.

Willy Nilly, postman.
His wife.
Under Milk Wood (play), Dylan Thomas, 1954.

Willys, Briggs, fat American with the death wish. *The Judgment of Paris*, Gore Vidal, 1952.

Wilmarth, nurse to Mrs Cruger. 'Horsie' (s.s.), *Here Lies*, Dorothy Parker, 1939.

Wilmer, Casper Gutman's bodyguard. *The Maltese Falcon*, Dashiell Hammett, 1930.

Wilming, Dolly, protégée of Louis Malcourt, stage aspirant. *The Firing Line*, R. W. Chambers, 1908.

Wilmington, school friend of Joan and Peter. *Joan and Peter*, H. G. Wells, 1918.

Wilmot.
His wife.
The Fatal Curiosity (play), G. Lillo, 1736.

Wilmot, Captain, admiral of pirate fleet. *Captain Singleton*, D. Defoe, 1720.

Wilmot, Rev. Mr.
Arabella, his daughter, m. George Primrose.
The Vicar of Wakefield, O. Goldsmith, 1766.

Wilmot, Annabella, m. Lord Lowborough.
Her uncle.
The Tenant of Wildfell Hall, Anne Brontë, 1848.

Wilmot, Anne, m. Jon Forsyte.
Francis, her brother.

The *Forsyte* series, J. Galsworthy, 1906–33.

Wilmot, Rev. Edward, tutor.
His father and mother.
The Daisy Chain, Charlotte M. Yonge, 1856.

Wilmot, Philip ('Pip'), central character, m. Elsie Innes.
Dorothea ('Pipette'), his sister, m. Jim Rossiter.
Philip, their father.
Pip, Ian Hay, 1907.

Wilshire, Jane, 'aunt' (actually cousin) of the Britlings. *Mr Britling Sees It Through,* H. G. Wells, 1916.

Wilson, maid to the Hares, later to Lady Isabel Carlyle. *East Lynne,* Mrs Henry Wood, 1861.

Wilson, servant of Sir Charles Grandison. *Sir Charles Grandison,* S. Richardson, 1754.

Wilson, a veteran soldier. *The Red Badge of Courage,* Stephen Crane, 1895.

Wilson, actor. *See* CHARLES DENNISON.

Wilson, elderly manufacturer, former acquaintance of Uncle Tom. *Uncle Tom's Cabin,* Harriet B. Stowe, 1851.

Wilson, Captain, the *London Merchant. Settlers in Canada,* Captain Marryat, 1844.

Wilson, Captain, H.M.S. *Harpy. Mr Midshipman Easy,* Captain Marryat, 1836.

Wilson, Captain and owner of *Seamew. The Skipper's Wooing,* W. W. Jacobs, 1897.

Wilson, Colonel. 'Oh Whistle and I'll Come to You, my Lad' (s.s.), *Ghost Stories of an Antiquary,* M. R. James, 1910.

Wilson, Doc. *The Yearling,* Marjorie K. Rawlings, 1938.

Wilson, 'General,' Provost of Bayswater. *The Napoleon of Notting Hill,* G. K. Chesterton, 1904.

Wilson, Mrs, farmer's widow.
Jane, Robert and **Richard,** her children.
The Tenant of Wildfell Hall, Anne Brontë, 1848.

Wilson, Mrs, housekeeper to Francis Herries; a witch, later drowned. *Rogue Herries,* Hugh Walpole, 1930.

Wilson, Andrew ('Handie Dandie'), smuggler. *The Heart of Midlothian,* W. Scott, 1818.

Wilson, Davy ('Snuffy Davy'). *The Antiquary,* W. Scott, 1816.

Wilson, Edgar. 'The Man's Story' (s.s.), *Horses and Men,* Sherwood Anderson, 1924.

Wilson, Edward, in love with Louise Scobie. *The Heart of the Matter,* Graham Greene, 1948.

Wilson, George.
Alice, his wife.
Their children:
Jane.
Jem, m. Mary Barton.
Will, sailor, m. Margaret.
Mary Barton, Mrs Gaskell, 1848.

Wilson, George ('Spike'), sailor.
George, his father.
Grace, his mother, *née* Gillespie.
Time Will Knit, Fred Urquhart, 1938.

Wilson, Henry, white settler in Jim Valley. 'Drifting Crane' (s.s.), *Prairie Folks,* H. Garland, 1892.

Wilson, Herbert, seducer of Helen Whitelaw. *Roots,* Naomi Jacob, 1931.

Wilson, Ivy.
'Sairy,' his wife.
The Grapes of Wrath, J. Steinbeck, 1939.

Wilson, Jabez, pawnbroker. 'The Red-headed League,' *Adventures of Sherlock Holmes,* A. Conan Doyle, 1892.

Wilson, James, grocer and ironmonger.
His wife.
The House with the Green Shutters, G. Douglas, 1901.

Wilson, Rev. John, oldest clergyman in Boston. *The Scarlet Letter,* N. Hawthorne, 1850.

Wilson, Myrtle, mistress of Tom Buchanan.
George, her husband.
Catherine, her sister.
The Great Gatsby, F. Scott Fitzgerald, 1925.

Wilson, Pete, friend of Tex. *Tex of Bar-20,* C. E. Mulford, 1922.

Wilson, Rose, waitress, m. Pinkie.
Her father and mother.
Brighton Rock, Graham Greene, 1938.

Wilson, William, narrator. *William Wilson* (s.s.), E. A. Poe.

Wilton ('Raven'), a schoolboy. *St Winifred's*, F. W. Farrar, 1862.

Wilton, Miss Erna, a rich old maid.
Miss Dolores, her sister.
'The Day of the Seventh Fire' (s.s.), *A Story That Ends With A Scream*, James Leo Herlihy, 1968.

Wiltshire, John, central character and narrator, m. Uma. 'The Beach of Falesa,' (s.s.), *Island Nights' Entertainments*, R. L. Stevenson, 1893.

Wimble, Will. Essays in *The Spectator*, J. Addison, 1711–14.

Wimbush, Henry, owner of Crome.
Anne, his niece.
Crome Yellow, Aldous Huxley, 1922.

Wimsey, Lord Peter Death Bredon (alias Death Bredon), philanthropist and amateur sleuth; younger son of the Dowager Duchess of Denver and brother of the present peer; central character, m. Harriet Vane. *Whose Body?*, 1923, and a long series of detective novels
Lady Mary, his sister, m. Chief Inspector Parker.
Dorothy L. Sayers.

Winberg, Bella.
Julius, her father.
Eric, her brother.
Dora, her sister (later Fedora).
Magnolia Street, L. Golding, 1932.

Winbrooke, Sir George. *The Man of Feeling*, H. Mackenzie, 1771.

Winch, Mr, tutor to Francis Herries's children. *Judith Paris*, Hugh Walpole, 1931.

Winch, Tom, agitator. *A Safety Match*, Ian Hay, 1911.

Wincham, Alfred, m. Fanny Logan.
Their children.
The Pursuit of Love, 1945, and elsewhere, Nancy Mitford.

Winchcombe, Rev. Basil, curate. *A Footman for the Peacock*, Rachel Ferguson, 1940.

Winchell, Sergeant. *The Family Reunion* (play), T. S. Eliot, 1939.

Winchelsea, Miss, high school mistress. 'Miss Winchelsea's Heart' (s.s.), *Tales of Life and Adventure*, 1913, and elsewhere, H. G. Wells.

Winchemore, Mrs Myra, m. Guy Selby. *Not so Bad after All*, Nat Gould.

Winchester, Bishop of (Henry Beaufort). *Henry the Sixth* (play), W. Shakespeare.

Winchester, Hon. Francis, emigrant sheepfarmer and speculator. *It Is Never Too Late to Mend*, C. Reade, 1856.

Winchmore, Lieutenant, R.N.V.R. 'Sea Constables' (s.s.), *Debits and Credits*, R. Kipling, 1926.

Wincott, Eveline, m. Robert Day.
Her father.
Earle and **Leicester,** her brothers.
Little Red Horses, G. B. Stern, 1932.

Windeatt, Louisa. *The Farmer's Wife* (play), E. Phillpotts, 1924.

Windermere, Lord (Arthur).
Margaret, his wife.
Lady Windermere's Fan (play), O. Wilde, 1892.

Windibank, traveller in wines, masquerading as Hosmer Angel. 'A Case of Identity,' *Adventures of Sherlock Holmes*, A. Conan Doyle, 1892.

Wing, Clementina, artist, central character, m. Dr Ephraim Quixtus. *The Glory of Clementina Wing*, W. J. Locke, 1911.

Wingate, Mrs, air-raid warden. *No News from Helen*, L. Golding, 1943.

Wingate, Charles, ambitious young member of the R.A.F. *Chips With Everything* (play), Arnold Wesker, 1962.

Wingfield, curate. *Heartsease*, Charlotte M. Yonge, 1854.

Wingfield, Amanda.
Laura, her daughter.
Tom, her son.
The Glass Menagerie (play), Tennessee Williams, 1948.

Wingrove, big-game hunter. *No Other Tiger*, A. E. W. Mason, 1927.

Winigle, Mrs Bess, aunt of Jim Probity.
Perce, her husband.
Her dead daughter's children:
Harold.
Florrie, m. Basil Stevens.
Master Jim Probity, F. Swinnerton, 1952.

Winkle, Nathaniel, member of the Pickwick Club, m. Arabella Allen. *Pickwick Papers*, C. Dickens, 1837.

Winkles, Stephen, F.R.S., etc., pupil of Redwood. *The Food of the Gods*, H. G. Wells, 1904.

Winlove, family name of Viscount Trimingham. *The Go-Between*, L. P. Hartley, 1953.

Winnick, Louis, oil consultant and crook. *Campbell's Kingdom*, H. Innes, 1952.

Winnie the Pooh (alias Edward Bear), a bear of very little brain. *Winnie the Pooh*, 1926, and elsewhere, A. A. Milne.

Winslow, Ronnie, ex-cadet, Osborne, expelled for stealing, later vindicated.
 Arthur, his father.
 Grace, his mother.
 Catherine, his sister.
 Dickie, his brother.
The Winslow Boy (play), T. Rattigan, 1946.

Winsor, Charles.
 Lady Adela, his wife.
Loyalties (play), J. Galsworthy, 1922.

Winter. 'The Unseen Power' (s.s.), *Here and Hereafter*, Barry Pain, 1911.

Winter, Miss, governess to the Mays. *The Daisy Chain*, Charlotte M. Yonge, 1856.

Winter, Dr Adam. *Martin Arrowsmith*, Sinclair Lewis, 1925.

Winter, Allan. *Odtaa*, J. Masefield, 1926.

Winter, Jack.
 His mother.
'The Winters and the Palmleys,' *Life's Little Ironies*, T. Hardy, 1894.

Winter, Josiah, tutor to Robert Raynald. *Requiem for Robert*, Mary Fitt, 1942.

Winter, Leah, a prostitute. *Magnolia Street*, L. Golding, 1932.

Winter, Philip, schoolmaster, m. Leslie Waring. The *Barsetshire* series, Angela Thirkell, 1933 onwards.

Winter, Sherman, theatrical producer. *Hemlock and After*, Angus Wilson, 1952.

Winter-Willoughby, Lady Emily Gertrude Maud, daughter of the Duke of Bude, m. General Curzon.
 Lord George, her uncle.
  Lady Constance, his wife.
   Captain Horatio, their son.
The General, C. S. Forester, 1936.

Winterbaum, Philip, friend of Joan and Peter. *Joan and Peter*, H. G. Wells, 1918.

Winterblossom, Philip, 'the Man of Taste.' *St Ronan's Well*, W. Scott, 1824.

Winterbottom, Inspector. 'The Man with no Face,' *Lord Peter Views the Body*, Dorothy L. Sayers, 1928.

Winterbourne, young American expatriate in Italy. *Daisy Miller*, Henry James, 1878.

Winterbourne, Lady, sister of Lord Maxwell. *Marcella*, Mrs Humphry Ward, 1894.

Winterbourne, George, central character.
 Elizabeth, his wife, *née* Paston.
 George, his father.
 Isabel, his mother.
 His grandparents.
Death of a Hero, R. Aldington, 1929.

Winterbourne, Giles, in love with Grace Melbury.
 John, his father.
The Woodlanders, T. Hardy, 1887.

Winterbury, Bishop of. *Robert's Wife* (play), St John Ervine, 1937.

Winterfeld, Graf von, secretary to Prince Karl Albert. *War in the Air*, H. G. Wells, 1908.

Winterfield, Rev. Mr, father of Anthea Clayton. *Cricket in Heaven*, G. Bullett, 1949.

Winterfield, Rev. Amos, brother of Gertrude Thorpe. *The Notorious Mrs Ebbsmith* (play), A. W. Pinero, 1895.

Winterset, Duke of. *Monsieur Beaucaire*, Booth Tarkington, 1902.

Wintersloan, illustrator of Will Magnet's work. *Marriage*, H. G. Wells, 1912.

Winthrop, Ben, wheelwright.
 Dolly, his wife.
 Aaron, his son, gardener, m. Eppie Cass.
Silas Marner, George Eliot, 1861.

Winthrop, Richard.
 Elsie, his wife.
The Ghost Train (play), A. Ridley, 1925.

Winton, 'Pater,' schoolboy. 'Regulus' (a 'Stalky' story), *A Diversity of Creatures*, R. Kipling, 1917.

Winwike, Gervaise, senior warden. *The Tower of London*, W. H. Ainsworth, 1840.

Winwood, Ursula.
Colonel Winwood, her brother.
The Fortunate Youth, W. J. Locke, 1914.

Wirk, family blacksmith. *If Winter Comes,* A. S. M. Hutchinson, 1920.

Wirt, Miss, an elderly governess. *The Book of Snobs,* 1846–7, and elsewhere, W. M. Thackeray.

Wisdom, Mrs Phoebe, sister of Sir Raymond Bastable, m. Albert Peasemarsh.
Cosmo, her son by 1st husband.
Cocktail Time, P. G. Wodehouse, 1958.

Wiseman, Mr, narrator. *The Life and Death of Mr Badman,* J. Bunyan, 1680.

Wishaw, Mrs. *Evan Harrington,* G. Meredith, 1861.

Wishfort, Lady.
Her daughter, m. Fainall.
The Way of the World (play), W. Congreve, 1700.

Wislack, Mrs. *On Approval* (play), F. Lonsdale, 1927.

Wissenheit, Father, priest. *The Heart of a Child,* Phyllis Bottome, 1940.

Wister, a detective. *Justice* (play), J. Galsworthy, 1910.

Wistons, Rev. Mr. *The Cathedral,* Hugh Walpole, 1922.

Witches, Three. *Macbeth* (play), W. Shakespeare.

Witham, Arthur, plumber.
Albert, his brother, an Oxford man.
The Lost Girl, D. H. Lawrence, 1920.

Witherden, Mr, notary. *The Old Curiosity Shop,* C. Dickens, 1841.

Withering, Squire, m. Deborah Herries. *Judith Paris,* Hugh Walpole, 1931.

Witherington, General. *See* RICHARD TRESHAM.

'Withernsea,' Queen of.
'Duke of Spurn,' her son.
Her daughter, later queen. Titles assumed by the Fyfe family, fen ruffians.
The Story of Ragged Robyn, O. Onions, 1945.

Withers, page to Mrs Skewton. *Dombey and Son,* C. Dickens, 1848.

Withers, friend of Arthur Seaton; narrator. 'Seaton's Aunt' (s.s.), *The Riddle,* W. de la Mare, 1923.

Withers, John. *The Letter* (play), W. S. Maugham, 1927.

Withers, Patsy. *Miss Mole,* E. H. Young, 1930.

Witherspoon, Miss, landlady. 'Sea View' (s.s.), *Sir Pompey and Madame Juno,* M. Armstrong, 1927.

Witherspoon, Jordan.
Martin, his son, an albino.
Simpson, E. Sackville-West, 1931.

Withersteen, Jane, ranch owner, m. Lassiter. *See also* FAY LARKIN. *Riders of the Purple Sage,* Zane Grey, 1912.

Wititterly, Julia, employer of Kate Nickleby.
Her husband.
Nicholas Nickleby, C. Dickens, 1839.

Witla, Eugene, artist, central character, m. Angela Blue.
Thomas, his father, sewing-machine agent.
Sylvia and **Myrtle,** his sisters.
The Genius, Theodore Dreiser, 1915.

Witt, Lou, rich American, m. Sir Henry (Rico) Carrington.
Her mother.
St Mawr, D. H. Lawrence, 1925.

Witta, Danish sea captain. 'The Knights of the Joyous Venture,' *Puck of Pook's Hill,* R. Kipling, 1906.

Wittenhagen, Martin. *The Cloister and the Hearth,* C. Reade, 1861.

Witwoud, follower of Mrs Millamant.
Sir Wilfull, his half-brother.
The Way of the World (play), W. Congreve, 1700.

Wix, Captain. *Judith Paris,* Hugh Walpole, 1931.

Woburn, librarian to Charles Rainier. *Random Harvest,* J. Hilton, 1941.

Woffington, Peg (hist.). *Peg Woffington,* C. Reade, 1853.

Wogan, Sir Charles (alias the Chevalier Warner), Irish emissary of the Pope, central character. *Clementina,* A. E. W. Mason, 1901.

Wolf, Rip Van Winkle's dog. *Rip Van Winkle,* Washington Irving, 1819–20.

Wolf, 'Brer.' *Uncle Remus,* J. C. Harris, 1880–95.

Wolf, Julia, ex-mistress and secretary of Clyde Wynant. *The Thin Man,* D. Hammett, 1934.

Wolfe, Mr and Mrs, owners of dress house, employers of Toni Rakonitz, *Tents of Israel,* G. B. Stern, 1924.

Wolfe, Nero, private investigator. *The Second Confession,* 1950, and elsewhere, Rex Stout.

Wolfram, Abbot, of St Edmund's. *Ivanhoe,* W. Scott, 1820.

Wolfsheim, Meyer, friend and patron of Gatsby. *The Great Gatsby,* F. Scott Fitzgerald, 1925.

Wolfstein, Amalia.
Her husband. Jewish *nouveaux riches.*
The Woman with the Fan, R. S. Hichens, 1904.

Wollenhope, William.
Eliza, his wife. Lodging-house keepers.
Sophia, Stanley Weyman, 1900.

Wollin, Henry. 'Fairy-Kist' (s.s.), *Limits and Renewals,* R. Kipling, 1932.

Wolsey, Cardinal (hist.). *Henry the Eighth* (play), W. Shakespeare.

Wolsey, Hester, housekeeper. *Mother and Son,* Ivy Compton-Burnett, 1954.

Wolstenholme, Sir Charles, late Attorney-General. *Ten Thousand a Year,* S. Warren, 1839.

Wolverbury, Lord. *See* Sir Joseph Hingston.

Wonder, John Fennil, Viceroy's secretary. 'The Germ Destroyer' (s.s.), *Plain Tales from the Hills,* R. Kipling, 1888.

Wong, Chinese trader. *Ming Yellow,* J. P. Marquand, 1935.

Wonham, Stephen, half-brother of Rickie Elliot. *The Longest Journey,* E. M. Forster, 1907.

Wonnacott, of the Archaeological Society. *The Glory of Clementina Wing,* W. J. Locke, 1911.

Wontner, a subaltern. 'The Honours of War' (s.s.), *A Diversity of Creatures,* R. Kipling, 1917.

Won-Toller, a lone wolf. 'Red Dog,' *The Second Jungle Book,* R. Kipling, 1895.

Wood, Bob.
Luke, his father.
Esther, his mother.
The World in the Evening, C. Isherwood, 1954.

Wood, Marjorie, protégée of the Matriarch. *Shining and Free,* G. B. Stern, 1935.

Wood, Mary Stark, school-teacher, m. The Virginian.
Her mother.
The Virginian, O. Wister, 1902.

Wood, Owen, carpenter.
Winifred, his daughter.
Jack Sheppard, W. H. Ainsworth, 1839.

Woodbury, Miss. 'I'm a Fool' (s.s.), *Horses and Men,* Sherwood Anderson, 1924.

Woodcock, Adam, Falconer of Avenel. *The Abbot,* W. Scott, 1820.

Woodcourt, Allan, physician to Miss Flite, m. Esther Summerson.
His mother.
Bleak House, C. Dickens, 1853.

Woodhouse, newspaper man. 'The Village that Voted the Earth was Flat' (s.s.), *A Diversity of Creatures,* R. Kipling, 1917.

Woodhouse, Emma, central character, m. George Knightley.
Her father.
Isabella, her sister, m. John Knightley.
Emma, Jane Austen, 1816.

Woodley, house prefect.
His father.
Young Woodley (play), J. van Druten, 1928.

Woodley, John. 'The Solitary Cyclist,' *The Return of Sherlock Holmes,* A. Conan Doyle, 1905.

Woodrofe, Mark, illegitimate son of Lord Blackwater, m Fancy Fawkes.
His mother.
Trumpeter, Sound!, D. L. Murray, 1933.

Woodrow, George Garden, proprietor of Kipps's 'superior' school. *Kipps,* H. G. Wells, 1905.

Woods, Detective Barney. 'The Clarion Call' (s.s.), *The Voice of the City,* O. Henry, 1908.

Woods, Ginger, orphan, m. Sweetie Hart. *Children of the Archbishop,* N. Collins, 1951.

Woods, Milly, friend of Yerba Buena.
Her father and mother.
A Ward of the Golden Gate (s.s.), Bret Harte.

Woods, Piney, elopes with Tom Simson. 'The Outcasts of Poker Flat' (s.s.), *The Luck of Roaring Camp,* Bret Harte, 1868.

Woodseaves, Kester, m. Prudence Sarn. *Precious Bane,* Mary Webb, 1924.

Woodson, Colonel Verney's overseer. *The Old Dominion,* Mary Johnston, 1899.

Woodus, Hazel, central character, m. Edward Marston.
 Abel, her father.
 Gone to Earth, Mary Webb, 1917.

Woodville, Lieutenant of the Tower. *Henry the Sixth* (play), W. Shakespeare.

Woodville, Anthony, Lord Scales. *The Last of the Barons,* Lord Lytton, 1843.

Woodville, Lord (Frank), of Woodville Castle. *The Tapestried Chamber,* W. Scott, 1828.

Woodward, Bella, actress, m. Arthur Marsden.
 Tom, her father.
 All the World Wondered, L. Merrick, 1911.

Woodwell, Rev. Mr, Baptist minister. *A Laodicean,* T. Hardy, 1881.

Wool, Mrs. *The Mill on the Floss,* George Eliot, 1860.

Woolcomb, Grenville, rich mulatto officer in the Life Guards Green, m. Agnes Twysden. *The Adventures of Philip,* W. M. Thackeray, 1861–2.

Woolley, Hon. Ernest. *The Admirable Crichton* (play), J. M. Barrie, 1902.

Woollie, (Hildegarde Blank), ex-opera singer, prompter. *Grand Opera,* Vicki Baum, 1942.

Woolsey, of Linsey Woolsey, tailors. *Vanity Fair,* 1847–8, and elsewhere, W. M. Thackeray.

Wooster, Bertie. *Thank You, Jeeves,* 1934, and others, P. G. Wodehouse.

Wopsle, parish clerk, friend of Mrs Gargery. *Great Expectations,* C. Dickens, 1861.

Worcester, Earl of (Thomas Percy). *Henry the Fourth* (play), W. Shakespeare.

Worksop, dentist.
 His wife.
 We the Accused, E. Raymond, 1935.

Worldly, Sir John.
 His daughters:
  Bellafront.
  Katherine.
  Lucida.
 A Woman is a Weathercock (play), N. Field, 1612.

Worldly-Wiseman, of the town of Carnal-Policy. *Pilgrim's Progress,* J. Bunyan, 1678 and 1684.

Worm, William, factotum of Mr Swancourt.
 His wife.
 A Pair of Blue Eyes, T. Hardy, 1873.

Wornock, Geoffrey, Indian cavalry.
 His mother.
 Sons of Fire, Mary E. Braddon, 1896.

Worrett, Mrs, friend of the Carrs. *What Katy Did at School,* Susan Coolidge, 1873.

Worsley, Gladys and **Enid,** twins.
 Lennie, their father.
 Victoria, their mother.
 Sylvia Scarlett, C. Mackenzie, 1918.

Worthing, John, J.P. (Ernest), m. Gwendolin Fairfax. *The Importance of Being Earnest* (play), O. Wilde, 1895.

Worthington, Lieutenant, central character. *The Poor Gentleman* (play), G. Colman the Younger, 1802.

Wotherspoon, Miss, companion to Kirsty Gilmour. *Pink Sugar,* O. Douglas, 1924.

Wotton, Helen, Ostrog's niece. *When the Sleeper Awakes,* H. G. Wells, 1899.

Wotton, Lord Henry, evil genius of Dorian Gray.
 His wife.
 Lady Gwendolyn, his sister.
 The Picture of Dorian Gray, O. Wilde, 1891.

Wracketts, Mr and Mrs, socialites. *The Pottleton Legacy,* Albert Smith, 1849.

Wragg, Doreen, mistress at Leys College. *Miss Pym Disposes,* Josephine Tey, 1946.

Wragge, Mr ('Rags') **and Mrs,** faithful servants of the Whiteoak family. *The Whiteoak Chronicles,* Mazo de la Roche, 1926 onwards.

Wragge, Mrs (alias Bygrave), widow of Dr Wragge, m. (2) Andrew Vanstone.
 'Captain' Wragge, her son.
  Joyce, his wife.
 No Name, W. Collins, 1862.

Wragge, Colonel Horace.
 His sister.

'The Nemesis of Fire,' *John Silence*, A. Blackwood, 1908.

Wrathie, Sir Joseph.
His wife.
Shall We Join the Ladies? (play), J. M. Barrie, 1921.

Wraxall, Mr. 'Count Magnus' (s.s.), *Ghost Stories of an Antiquary*, M. R. James, 1910.

Wraxall, Triptolemus, of 'Universal Security.' *It Never Can Happen Again*, W. de Morgan, 1909.

Wraxton, Canon.
Evangeline, his daughter.
The Feast, Margaret Kennedy, 1956.

Wray, trainer for Garry Anson. *The Calendar*, E. Wallace.

Wrayburn, Mrs (stage name Cremona Garden), aged and senile great-aunt of Philip Boyes and Norman Urquhart. *Strong Poison*, Dorothy L. Sayers, 1930.

Wrayburn, Eugene, schoolmaster, friend of Mortimer Lightwood, m. Lizzie Hexam. *Our Mutual Friend*, C. Dickens, 1865.

Wraysford, Horace. *The Fifth Form at St Dominic's*, T. Baines Reed, 1887.

Wrench, Tom, of Bagnigge Wells Theatre. *Trelawny of the Wells* (play), A. W. Pinero, 1898.

Wressley. 'Wressley of the Foreign Office' (s.s.), *Plain Tales from the Hills*, R. Kipling, 1888.

Wright, Clothilde, formerly widow of Hugh Brill.
Archie, her 2nd husband.
Wickford Point, J. P. Marquand, 1939.

Wright, Jessie, widow, elopes with Benny Edelman.
Tommy, her son.
Magnolia Street, L. Golding, 1932.

Wright, Joey K. (The Satyr). *The Passing of the Third Floor Back* (play), J. K. Jerome, 1910.

Wright, Walter, friend and biographer of Caryl Bramsley. *C.*, M. Baring, 1924.

Wrigley, A. P., jeweller. 'The Sad Horn Blowers' (s.s.), *Horses and Men*, Sherwood Anderson, 1924.

Wrigley, Ron, homosexual cockney youth. *Hemlock and After*, Angus Wilson, 1952.

Wrydale, Elizabeth, m. Stephen Monk. *The World in the Evening*, C. Isherwood, 1954.

Wu, Chinese servant. *East of Suez* (play), W. S. Maugham, 1922.

Wu, General. *Ming Yellow*, J. P. Marquand, 1935.

Wulf. *Hypatia*, C. Kingsley, 1853.

Wunsch, Professor, music teacher. *The Song of the Lark*, Willa Cather, 1915.

Wutherwood and Rune, Marquis of (Gabriel), elder brother of Lord Charles Lamprey.
Violet, his wife.
Surfeit of Lampreys, Ngaio Marsh, 1941.

Wyant, Dr. *The Fruit of the Tree*, Edith Wharton, 1907.

Wyat, Lucy, housekeeper to Silas Ruthlyn. *Uncle Silas*, Sheridan le Fanu, 1864.

Wyatt, Constance, 'the Dean's daughter,' m. Raoul Czelovar. *Tents of Israel*, 1924, and others, G. B. Stern.

Wyatt, Sir Francis, governor of Virginia.
Margaret, his wife.
By Order of the Company, Mary Johnston, 1900.

Wyborn, Sarah, *née* Fletcher, children's nurse. *Mr Ingleside*, E. V. Lucas, 1910.

Wybrow, Captain Anthony, nephew and heir of Sir Christopher Cheverel, eng. to Beatrice Assher. 'Mr Gilfil's Love Story,' *Scenes of Clerical Life*, George Eliot, 1857.

Wycherley, Mr. *Miss Esperance and Mr Wycherley*, 1908, and elsewhere, L. Allen Harker.

Wycherley, Captain Fred, elopes with Rose Ormerod. *Vanessa*, Hugh Walpole, 1933.

Wycherly, maid to Anastasia Rakonitz. *Shining and Free*, G. B. Stern, 1935.

Wychwood, Lord. The *Hornblower* series, C. S. Forester, 1937 onwards.

Wykeham, Charles, undergraduate. *Charley's Aunt* (play) Brandon Thomas, 1892.

Wylie, Maggie, central character, m. John Shand.
Alick, her father.
David and **James,** her brothers.
What Every Woman Knows (play), J. M. Barrie, 1908.

Wylie, Thomas ('Tam'). *The House with the Green Shutters*, G. Douglas, 1901.

Wyman, Millie, m. Rudi Czelovar. *Mosaic,* G. B. Stern, 1930.

Wynant, Dorothy.
Clyde, her div. father, inventor. *See also* JULIA WOLF.
Mimi, her mother, m. (2) Christian Jorgensen.
Gilbert, her brother.
Alice, her aunt.
The Thin Man, D. Hammett, 1934.

Wyndham, Bimbashi. 'The Man at the Wheel,' *Donovan Pasha,* Gilbert Parker, 1902.

Wyndham, Major Paul, in love with Honor Meredith. *Captain Desmond, V.C.,* Maud Diver, 1906.

Wynn, Mr and Mrs, uncle and aunt and guardians of Elizabeth Kane.
Leslie, their son.
The Franchise Affair, Josephine Tey, 1948.

Wynne, Alderley, K.C.
His wife, stepsister of Kent Falconer.
Their children:
Naomi, m. Kent Falconer.
Drusilla, m. a doctor.
Frank, journalist.
His wife and children.
Lionel.
His mother.
Over Bemerton's, E. V. Lucas, 1908.

Wynne, Clement, solicitor. *The Land of Promise* (play), W. S. Maugham, 1914.

Wynne, Sam, a magistrate.
His wife and family.
Shirley, Charlotte Brontë, 1849.

Wynne, Talbot ('Taffy'), art student. *See also* MCALLISTER. *Trilby,* George du Maurier, 1894.

Wynne, Winifred, m. Henry Aylwin.
Tom, her father, organist and ne'er-do-well.
Aylwin, T. Watts-Dunton, 1899.

Wynne-Jones, Gwladys, central character and narrator.
Her father, Vicar of Llanwialen.
Gwen, her sister.
All in a Month, Allen Raine, 1908.

Wynton, Lily, actress. 'Glory in the Daytime' (s.s.), *Here Lies,* Dorothy Parker, 1939.

Wynton, Hon. Willie.
His wife.
The Last of Mrs Cheyney (play), F. Lonsdale, 1925.

Wyvern, Lord.
His wife.
Felix Holt, George Eliot, 1866.

Wyvern, William, journalist, m. Margaret Marrapit.
Professor Wyvern, his father.
Once Aboard the Lugger, A. S. M. Hutchinson, 1908.

Wyvil, Maurice, really the Earl of Rochester. *Old St Paul's,* W. H. Ainsworth, 1841.

Wyvill, Ebenezer, customs officer. *In the Roar of the Sea,* S. Baring-Gould, 1892.

X

Xavier, Father, convent confessor. *Anthony Adverse,* Hervey Allen, 1934.

Xit, dwarf at the Tower, later knighted as Sir Narcissus le Grand. *The Tower of London,* W. H. Ainsworth, 1840.

Xury, ship's boy. *Robinson Crusoe,* D. Defoe, 1719.

Y

Yacob, 'a kindly man,' friend of Medina Saroté. *The Country of the Blind* (s.s.), with other stories, H. G. Wells, 1911.

Yahmose, mass murderer, eldest son of Imhotep.
Satipy, his wife.
Death Comes as the End, Agatha Christie, 1945.

Yakimov, Prince, a White Russian remittance-man in Bucharest. *The Great Fortune,* Olivia Manning, 1960.

Yajnavalkya, Mrs, a masseuse of Afro-Asian stock. *Valmouth,* Ronald Firbank, 1919.

Yar Khan. 'Ballad of the King's Mercy' (poem), *Barrack-room Ballads,* R. Kipling, 1892.

Yardley-Orde. 'The Head of the District' (s.s.), *Life's Handicap,* R. Kipling, 1891.

Yarlett, James ('Big James'), a compositor. *Clayhanger,* Arnold Bennett, 1910.

Yasmin. *Hassan* (play), J. E. Flecker, 1923.

Yates, Miss. *Britannia Mews,* Margery Sharp, 1946.

Yates, Blanche, friend of Isabella Sallafranque. *The Thinking Reed,* Rebecca West, 1936.

Yates, Hon. John, m. Julia Bertram. *Mansfield Park,* Jane Austen, 1814.

Yawkins, a smuggler, in league with the Maxwells; captain of the *Van Hoorn. The Raiders,* S. R. Crockett, 1894.

Yeardley, Sir George, Governor of Virginia. *By Order of the Company,* Mary Johnston, 1900.

Yeates, Sinclair, resident magistrate.
Philippa, his wife.
Some Experiences of an Irish R.M., Œ. Somerville & Martin Ross, 1899.

Yeere, Otis. 'The Education of Otis Yeere' (s.s.), *Wee Willie Winkie,* R. Kipling, 1888.

Yeld, Mrs, wife of the Bishop of Elmham. *The Way We Live Now,* A. Trollope, 1875.

Yellowless, Dr. *The Professor's Love Story* (play), J. M. Barrie, 1894.

Yellowless, Henry, clerk in lesser orders, custos of the convent at Oby. *The Corner That Held Them,* Sylvia Townsend Warner, 1948.

Yellowley, Triptolemus, factor of the High Chamberlain, Orkney and Shetland.
Jasper, his father.
The Pirate, W. Scott, 1822.

Yenadizze, dandy and idler. *The Song of Hiawatha* (poem), H. W. Longfellow, 1855.

Yeo, Chief Detective-Inspector. *Dancers in Mourning,* 1937, and others, Margery Allingham.

Yeo, Mrs.
Mary, her daughter.
'The Last Term,' *Stalky & Co.,* R. Kipling, 1899.

Yeo, Salvation, veteran mariner. *Westward Ho!,* C. Kingsley, 1855.

Yeobright, Clym, m. Eustacia Vye.
Thomasin, his cousin, m (1) Damon Wildeve, (2) Diggory Venn.
His mother.
The Return of the Native, T. Hardy, 1878

Yestreen, Rev. Adam, narrator. *Farewell, Miss Julie Logan,* J. M. Barrie, 1932.

Yillah, blonde Polynesian symbolizing Good. *Mardi,* Herman Melville, 1849.

Yitzchok, Yankele Ben, m. Deborah da Costa. *The King of Schnorrers,* I. Zangwill, 1894.

Yniol, Earl of, father of Enid. *Idylls of the King* (poem), Lord Tennyson, 1859.

Yoland, Prince. *An Englishman's Home* (play), Guy du Maurier, 1909.

Yolland, Mrs, friend of Rosanna Spearman. *The Moonstone,* W. Collins, 1868.

Yorick, dead jester. *Hamlet* (play), W. Shakespeare.

Yorick, Rev. Mr. *Tristram Shandy,* L. Sterne, 1767.

York, Duke of (Edmund de Langley) (hist.). *Richard the Second* (play), W. Shakespeare.

York, Duke of, cousin to the King (hist.). *Henry the Fifth* (play), W. Shakespeare.

York, Duke of (later Richard III).
Duchess of York, mother of Edward IV.
Richard the Third (play), W. Shakespeare.

York, Henry J., half-owner of the Amity Mine. 'The Iliad of Sandy Bar' (s.s.), *The Luck of Roaring Camp*, Bret Harte, 1868.

York, Rowland, fencing master. *Westward Ho!*, C. Kingsley, 1855.

Yorke, 'Yorkshire gentleman *par excellence*.'
His wife.
Matthew, Mark, Martin, Rose and **Jessy,** their children.
Shirley, Charlotte Brontë, 1849.

Yorke, Lady Augusta, widow of Rev. Theodore.
George, Roland, Gerald, Theodora, Caroline and **Fanny,** her children.
Two other boys.
Rev. William, distant relative, m. Constance Channing.
The Channings, Mrs Henry Wood, 1862.

Yorke, Leila. *See* PERCY POTTER.

Youghal, Miss, m. Strickland.
Her father and mother.
'Miss Youghal's Sais' (s.s.), *Plain Tales from the Hills*, 1888, and elsewhere, R. Kipling.

Youghal, Courtney, young Member of Parliament. *The Unbearable Bassington*, 'Saki' (H. H. Munro), 1912.

Young, Bertha.
Harry, her husband.
Her baby daughter.
Bliss (s.s.), Katherine Mansfield, 1920.

Young, Mildred, Christian Scientist. *Antigua Penny Puce*, R. Graves, 1936.

Young, Ronald, junior counsel for the defence. *The Jury*, G. Bullett, 1935.

Younge, Mrs, former governess of Georgiana Darcy. *Pride and Prejudice*, Jane Austen, 1813.

Yownie, Thomas, of the Gorbals Diehards. *Huntingtower*, J. Buchan, 1922.

Yram, jailer's daughter. *Erewhon*, S. Butler, 1872.

Yuen, Taou, Manchu wife of Gerrit Ammidon. *Java Head*, J. Hergesheimer, 1919.

Yule, Alfred, literary hack.
Marian, his daughter.
Amy, his niece, m. Edwin Reardon.
The New Grub Street, George Gissing, 1891.

Yule, Telford. *Flowering Wilderness*, J. Galsworthy, 1932.

Yum-Yum, ward of Ko-Ko, m. Nanki-poo. *The Mikado* (comic opera), Gilbert & Sullivan, 1885.

Yundt, Karl, delegate of International Red Committee. *The Secret Agent*, Joseph Conrad, 1907.

Yung, Chang, m. Ning, daughter of Ti Hung. *The Wallet of Kai Lung*, E. Bramah, 1900.

Yunkum, Sahib. 'At Howli Thana' (s.s.), *Soldiers Three*, R. Kipling, 1888.

Yusef, blackmailer and usurer. *The Heart of the Matter*, Graham Greene, 1948.

Yvonne, daughter of Earl Dorm, m. Sir Agravaine. 'Sir Agravaine' (s.s.), *The Man Upstairs*, P. G. Wodehouse, 1914.

Z

Zabina. *See* BAJAZETH.

Zadoc. *Absalom and Achitophel* (poem), J. Dryden, 1681.

Zaimes, Greek servant of Herbert Beveridge. *In Greek Waters,* G. A. Henty, 1892.

Zal, father of Rustum. *Sohrab and Rustum* (poem), M. Arnold, 1853.

Zalenska, Madame, pseudonym of a queen. *Three Weeks,* Elinor Glyn, 1907.

Zambra, dauntless lion-tamer, m. Valentine Dutripon, *née* Bompard. 'The Vengeance of Monsieur Dutripon' (s.s.), *The Little Dog Laughed,* L. Merrick, 1930.

Zamor, Negro servant of Barry Lyndon. *Barry Lyndon,* W. M. Thackeray, 1844.

Zana, maid to Nadya. *The Queen was in the Parlour* (play), N. Coward, 1926.

Zarca, gypsy chief, father of Fedalma. *The Spanish Gypsy* (poem), George Eliot, 1868.

Zarin, Count. *They Wanted to Live,* Cecil Roberts, 1939.

Zeck, Arnold. *The Second Confession,* Rex Stout, 1950.

Zeenut, Maihl, concubine of Mogul King. *On the Face of the Waters,* F. A. Steel, 1896.

Zeggi, chief of police, Yanrin. *Aissa Saved,* Joyce Cary, 1932.

Zend ('Moonstruck'). *The King of Elfland's Daughter,* Lord Dunsany, 1924.

Zenocrate, daughter of the Soldan of Egypt. *Tamburlaine* (play), C. Marlowe, 1587.

Zephyrine, Madame. 'The Suicide Club' (s.s.), *New Arabian Nights,* R. L. Stevenson, 1882.

Zerkow, a junk dealer, m. Maria Macapa. *McTeague,* F. Norris, 1899.

Zichy, Count Peter, 2nd husband of Gelda Rosmarin. *The Dark Is Light Enough* (play), Christopher Fry, 1954.

Zigler, Laughton O., inventor.
 Tommy, his wife.
'The Captive' (s.s.), *Traffics and Discoveries,* 1904, and 'The Edge of the Evening' (s.s.), *A Diversity of Creatures,* 1917, R. Kipling.

Zikali, dwarf witch-doctor, foster-father of Saduko. *Child of Storm,* H. Rider Haggard, 1913.

Zillah, Heathcliff's servant. *Wuthering Heights,* Emily Brontë, 1847.

Zimmerman, headmaster of school. *The Centaur,* John Updike, 1963.

Zimri. *Absalom and Achitophel* (poem), J. Dryden, 1681.

Zind, gypsy nurse to Fedalma. *The Spanish Gypsy* (poem), George Eliot, 1868.

Zirconderel, the witch. *The King of Elfland's Daughter,* Lord Dunsany, 1924.

Ziska, Princess (alias Charmazel). *Ziska,* Marie Corelli, 1897.

Zizzbaum, wholesale costumier. 'The Buyer from Cactus City' (s.s.), *The Trimmed Lamp,* O. Henry, 1907.

Zobraska, H.H. Princess Sophia, m. Paul Finn. *The Fortunate Youth,* W. J. Locke, 1914.

Zorah, a professional bridesmaid. *Ruddigore* (comic opera), Gilbert & Sullivan, 1887.

Zoumna, Señor. *See* SUMNER.

Zouroff, Prince Sergius, m. Vere Herbert. *Moths,* Ouida, 1880.

Zoyland, Will, illegitimate son of Lord P.
 Nell, his wife.
 Lady Rachel, daughter of Lord P.
A Glastonbury Romance, J. C. Powys, 1932.

Zubiaga, Lopez, President of Santa Barbara, dictator.
 Don José, his son.
Odtaa, J. Masefield, 1926.

Zuleika. *Zuleika* (poem), A. O'Shaughnessy.

Zuleika, Mrs. 'The Brushwood Boy'

(s.s.), *The Day's Work*, R. Kipling, 1898.

Zurvan, son of the emir. *The Shaving of Shagpat*, G. Meredith, 1856.

Zuyland, a journalist. 'A Matter of Fact' (s.s.), *Many Inventions*, R. Kipling, 1893.

Zu-zu, a *demi-mondaine*. *Under Two Flags*, Ouida, 1867.

·007, a locomotive engine. '·007' (s.s.), *The Day's Work*, R. Kipling, 1898.

007, James Bond's secret service number. Novels by Ian Fleming.

INDEX OF AUTHORS

A

B

C

10126 Dict. Fict. Char. 2--12-8 6

D

E

F

G

H

I

J

K

L

M

N

O

P

Q

R

S

T

U

V

W

Y

Z

INDEX OF TITLES

The Index is in strictly alphabetical form, neglecting any preliminary definite or indefinite articles. Numerals in titles, such as '1984', are treated as if written in letters, e.g. '1984' is indexed under letter 'N'.

A

Amir's Homily, The, R. Kipling
Among Friends, N. Balchin
Amours de Voyage, A. H. Clough
Amours of Mr Deuceace, The, W. M. Thackeray
Amy Foster, J. Conrad
Ancient Sorceries, A. Blackwood
And Now Goodbye, J. Hilton
Andrey Satchel and the Parson and Clerk, T. Hardy
Angel, Elizabeth Taylor
Angel and the Sweep, The, A. E. Coppard
Angel Pavement, J. B. Priestley
Angle of Repose, Wallace Stegner
Anglo-Saxon Attitudes, A. Wilson
Ann Veronica, H. G. Wells
Anna Christie, E. O'Neill
Anna of the Five Towns, Arnold Bennett
Annabel Lee, E. A. Poe
Annals of the Parish, J. Galt
Anne of Geierstein, Sir W. Scott
Annie Laurie, Douglass
Annie Protheroe, W. S. Gilbert
Anniversary, An, W. de la Mare
Another Temple Gone, C. E. Montague
Another Year, R. C. Sherriff
Anthony Adverse, Hervey Allen
Antic Hay, A. Huxley
Antigua Penny Puce, R. Graves
Antiquary, The, Sir W. Scott
Antonio and Mellida, John Marston
Antony and Cleopatra, W. Shakespeare
Apparition of Mrs Veal, The, D. Defoe
Apple, The, H. G. Wells
Apple Cart, The, G. B. Shaw
Apple Tree, The, J. Galsworthy
Appointment in Samarra, John O'Hara
Arcadia, Sir P. Sidney
archy and mehitabel, Don Marquis
Argallo and Ledgett, Max Beerbohm
Argonauts of the Air, H. G. Wells
Armgart, George Eliot
Arms and the Man, G. B. Shaw
Army Headquarters, R. Kipling
Army of a Dream, The, R. Kipling
Arrest of Lieutenant Golightly, The, R. Kipling
Arrow of Gold, The, J. Conrad
Arthur in Avalon, N. Balchin
Article in Question, The, Dorothy L. Sayers
As Easy as A B C, R. Kipling
As it is Written, Caradoc Evans
As You Like It, W. Shakespeare
Ash-tree, The, M. R. James
Aspiring Miss De Laine, The, Bret Harte
Astral Body of a U.S. Mail Truck, The, James Leo Herlihy
At Casterbridge Fair, T. Hardy
At Howli Thana, R. Kipling
At Lady Molly's, A. Powell
At Mrs Beam's, C. K. Munro
At the End of the Passage, R. Kipling
At the Mercy of Tiberius, Gilbert Parker
At the Villa Rose, A. E. W. Mason
At Twenty-two, R. Kipling
Auld Robin Gray, Lady Anne Lyndsay
Aunt Ellen, R. Kipling
Aunt Hetty, M. Armstrong
Aurora Leigh, Elizabeth B. Browning
Awakening of Podmarsh, The, P. G. Wodehouse
Ayesha, J. J. Morier
Aylmer's Field, Lord Tennyson
Aylwin, T. Watts-Dunton

B

Baa Baa Black Sheep, R. Kipling
Bab Ballads, W. S. Gilbert
Babbitt, Sinclair Lewis
Babe, B.A., The, E. F. Benson
Bachelor's Dream, The, T. Hood
Bachelors, Hugh Walpole
Bachelors, The, Muriel Spark
Background, The, 'Saki'
Bad Sir Brian Botany, A. A. Milne
Badge of Policeman O'Roon, The, O. Henry
Badger's Green, R. C. Sherriff
Baines Carew, Gentleman, W. S. Gilbert
Balder, S. Dobell
Balder Dead, M. Arnold
Balin and Balan, Lord Tennyson
Ballad and the Source, The, Rosamond Lehmann
Ballad of Boh da Thone, The, R. Kipling
Ballad of East and West, A, R. Kipling

Ballad of Oriana, The, Lord Tennyson
Ballad of the King's Mercy, R. Kipling
Bank Fraud, A, R. Kipling
Barbara's Wedding, J. M. Barrie
Barbe of Grand Bayou, J. Oxenham
Barber Cox, W. M. Thackeray
Barchester Towers, A. Trollope
Barefoot in the Head, Brian W. Aldiss
Bargain with the Kremlin, A, P. Gibbs
Barlasch of the Guard, H. Seton Merriman
Barnaby Rudge, C. Dickens
Barrack Room Ballads, R. Kipling
Barry Lyndon, W. M. Thackeray
Bars of the Cage, The, N. Balchin
Barsetshire series, The, Angela Thirkell
Bartholomew Fair, B. Jonson
Baseless Fabric, The, Helen Simpson
Basil, W. Collins
Bath Comedy, The, A. & E. Castle
Battle of Alcazar, The, G. Peele
Battle of Life, The, C. Dickens
Bay, The, L. A. G. Strong
Be this her Memorial, Caradoc Evans
Beach of Falesa, The, R. L. Stevenson
Bealby, H. G. Wells
Beau Austin, W. E. Henley & R. L. Stevenson
Beau Geste, P. C. Wren
Beautiful and the Damned, The, F. Scott Fitzgerald
Beautiful Years, The, H. Williamson
Beauty Spots, R. Kipling
Beaux' Stratagem, The, G. Farquhar
Beckoning Lady, The, Margery Allingham
Bedford Row Conspiracy, The, W. M. Thackeray
Bee, The, O. Goldsmith
Before Lunch, Angela Thirkell
Before the Bombardment, O. Sitwell
Beggar's Bush, The, Beaumont & Fletcher
Beggar's Opera, The, J. Gay
Beginning, A, W. de la Mare
Beginning of the Armadillos, The, R. Kipling
Belinda, Maria Edgeworth
Belinda, A. A. Milne
Bell, The, Iris Murdoch
Bell for Adano, A, J. Hersey
Bella Donna, R. S. Hichens
Belle's Stratagem, The, Mrs Hannah Cowley
Belles Demoiselles Plantation, G. W. Cable
Ben Hur, L. Wallace
Benefactor, The, J. D. Beresford
Benson Murder Case, The, S. S. van Dine
Berkeley Square, J. L. Balderston
Berry and Co., Dornford Yates
Bertran and Bimi, R. Kipling
Beryl Coronet, The, A. Conan Doyle
Beside the Bonnie Brier Bush, I. Maclaren
Best Seller, O. Henry
Betrothed, The, Sir W. Scott
Between The Acts, Virginia Woolf
Beyond the Pale, R. Kipling
Beyond This Place, A. J. Cronin
Bibliomania, T. F. Dibdin
Big Blonde, Dorothy Parker
Big Drunk Draf, The, R. Kipling
Big Sleep, The, R. Chandler
Biggles Books, The, Captain W. E. Johns
Bill of Divorcement, A, Clemence Dane
Bill's Paper Chase, W. W. Jacobs
Billy Budd, H. Melville
Billy Bunter series, The, Frank Richards
Bird of Dawning, The, J. Masefield
Birds Fall Down, The, Rebecca West
Birds of America, Mary McCarthy
Bisara of Pooree, The, R. Kipling
Black Arrow, The, R. L. Stevenson
Black Beauty, Anna Sewell
Black Dwarf, The, Sir W. Scott
Black-eyed Susan, J. Gay
Black Jack, R. Kipling
Black Mosquetaire, The, R. H. Barham
Black Spectacles, The, J. Dickson Carr
Black Venus, The, Rhys Davies
Bleak House, C. Dickens
Blind Love, V. S. Pritchett
Blind Man's Holiday, O. Henry
Blind Raftery, Donn Byrne
Bliss, Katherine Mansfield
Blithe Spirit, N. Coward
Bloomsbury Wonder, The, T. Burke
Blot in the 'Scutcheon, A, R. Browning
Blue Carbuncle, The, A. Conan Doyle
Blue Lagoon, The, H. de Vere Stacpoole
Bluebeard's Keys, Anne Thackeray
Boar Pig, The, 'Saki'
Boarding-house, The, James Joyce
Bob Polter, W. S. Gilbert

Body Snatcher, The, R. L. Stevenson & L. Osbourne
Boke of Phyllyp Sparowe, The, John Skelton
Bold Stroke for a Wife, A, Mrs Susanna Centlivre
Bonds of Discipline, The, R. Kipling
Bonduca, Beaumont & Fletcher
Bone of Contention, The, Dorothy L. Sayers
Bonnie Lesley, R. Burns
Book of Snobs, The, W. M. Thackeray
Books Do Furnish A Room, A. Powell
Boon, H. G. Wells
Born to be a Sailor, G. Stables
Borough, The, G. Crabbe
Boscombe Valley Mystery, The, A. Conan Doyle
Boss, The, H. G. Wells
Bostonians, The, H. James
Both of this Parish, J. S. Fletcher
Bothie of Tober-na-Vuolich, The, A. H. Clough
Bottle Imp, The, R. L. Stevenson
Bowge of Court, The, John Skelton
Box and Cox, J. M. Morton
Boys and I, The, Mrs Molesworth
Boys will be Boys, Irvin S. Cobb
Bracebridge Hall, W. Irving
Bracknels, The, Forrest Reid
Brass Bottle, The, F. Anstey
Brat Farrar, Josephine Tey
Brave New World, A. Huxley
Bravo of Venice, The, M. G. Lewis
Bread upon the Waters, R. Kipling
Breakfast at Tiffany's, Truman Capote
Bride of Abydos, The, Lord Byron
Bride of Lammermoor, The, Sir W. Scott
Bride's Tragedy, The, T. L. Beddoes
Brideshead Revisited, E. Waugh
Bridge Builders, The, R. Kipling
Bridge of San Luis Rey, The, T. Wilder
Brief Encounter, N. Coward
Brighton Rock, Graham Greene
Britannia Mews, Margery Sharp
Briton, The, A. Philips
Broad Highway, The, J. Farnol
Broken Link Handicap, The, R. Kipling
Bronckhorst Divorce Case, The, R. Kipling
Brontës went to Woolworth's, The, Rachel Ferguson
Brother Jacob, George Eliot
Brother Square Toes, R. Kipling
Brothers, The, R. Cumberland
Brothers, The, L. A. G. Strong
Brown of Calaveras, Bret Harte
Brown Wallet, The, Stacy Aumonier
Browning Version, The, T. Rattigan
Brownings, The, Viola Meynell
Bruce-Partington Plans, The, A. Conan Doyle
Brugglesmith, R. Kipling
Brushwood Boy, The, R. Kipling
Buckingham Palace, A. A. Milne
Buick Saloon, The, Ann Bridge
Bull that Thought, The, R. Kipling
Bulldog Drummond, H. C. McNeile ('Sapper')
Burglar, The, J. Russell
Buried Treasure, O. Henry
Burnt-out Case, A, Graham Greene
Busman's Honeymoon, Dorothy L. Sayers
But Soft—We Are Observed!, H. Belloc
Butterfly that Stamped, The, R. Kipling
Buyer from Cactus City, The, O. Henry
By Order of the Company, Mary Johnston
By Sheer Pluck, G. A. Henty
By the Pricking of My Thumbs, Agatha Christie
By Word of Mouth, R. Kipling

C

C., M. Baring
Cabbages and Kings, O. Henry
Caesar and Cleopatra, G. B. Shaw
Caesar's Wife, W. S. Maugham
Café des Exiles, G. W. Cable
Cakes and Ale, W. S. Maugham
Caleb Williams, W. Godwin
Calendar, The, E. Wallace
Call it a Day, Dodie Smith
Calloway's Code, O. Henry
Camp of the Dog, The, A. Blackwood
Campbell's Kingdom, Hammond Innes
Canaries Sometimes Sing, F. Lonsdale
Candida, G. B. Shaw
Cannery Row, J. Steinbeck

Canon Alberic's Scrapbook, M. R. James
Canterbury Tales, G. Chaucer
Canterville Ghost, The, O. Wilde
Capitalist, A, G. Gissing
Caprice, R. Firbank
Capsina, The, E. F. Benson
Captain Blood, R. Sabatini
Captain Bottell, J. Hanley
Captain Brassbound's Conversion, G. B. Shaw
Captain Desmond, V.C., Maud Diver
Captain Kettle series, J. Cutcliffe Hyne
Captain of the 'Polestar', The, A. Conan Doyle
Captain Reece, W. S. Gilbert
Captain Rogers, W. W. Jacobs
Captain Rook, W. M. Thackeray
Captain Sharkey, A. Conan Doyle
Captain Singleton, D. Defoe
Captains All, W. W. Jacobs
Captains Courageous, R. Kipling
Captive, The, R. Kipling
Card, The, Arnold Bennett
Cardboard Box, The, A. Conan Doyle
Cardinal's Snuffbox, The, H. Harland
Cards for the Colonel, N. Balchin
Careless Husband, The, C. Cibber
Caretaker, The, H. Pinter
Caroline, W. S. Maugham
Carrots, Mrs Molesworth
Cartouche, The, W. de la Mare
Case, The, T. Burke
Case for the Defence, The, Mary Fitt
Case of Conscience, A, Phyllis Bentley
Case of Have To, A, Morley Roberts
Case of Identity, A, A. Conan Doyle
Case of the Blonde Bonanza, The, Erle Stanley Gardner
Cask of Amontillado, The, E. A. Poe
Castle Dangerous, Sir W. Scott
Castle of Otranto, The, Horace Walpole
Castle Rackrent, Maria Edgeworth
Cat in the Bag, The, Dorothy L. Sayers
Cat on a Hot Tin Roof, Tennessee Williams
Catcher in the Rye, The, J. D. Salinger
Cathedral, The, Hugh Walpole
Catherine, W. M. Thackeray
Catherine Furze, M. Rutherford
Cato, J. Addison
Catriona, R. L. Stevenson
Cautionary Tales, H. Belloc
Cavalier of the Streets, A, M. Arlen
Cecilia, Fanny Burney
Cenci, The, P. B. Shelley
Centaur, The, J. Updike
Centurion of the Thirtieth, A, R. Kipling
Certain Personal Matters, H. G. Wells
Chalk Garden, The, Enid Bagnold
Channings, The, Mrs Henry Wood
Character Sketches, W. M. Thackeray
Charles O'Malley, C. Lever
Charley's Aunt, Brandon Thomas
Charming Family, A, G. Gissing
Chatterton Square, E. H. Young
Chester Forgets Himself, P. G. Wodehouse
Child of Storm, H. Rider Haggard
Childe Harold's Pilgrimage, Lord Byron
Childe Waters, Bishop Thomas Percy
Children of the Archbishop, N. Collins
Children of the Ghetto, I. Zangwill
Children of the New Forest, The, Captain Marryat
Children of the Tempest, N. Munro
Children of Violence series, Doris Lessing
Chimes, The, C. Dickens
China Governess, The, Margery Allingham
Chinese Orange Mystery, The, Ellery Queen
Chink and the Child, The, T. Burke
Chips With Everything, A. Wesker
Choice, The, A. Sutro
Chosen Country, J. dos Passos
Christabel, S. T. Coleridge
Christian, The, Hall Caine
Christina Alberta's Father, H. G. Wells
Christmas Carol, A, C. Dickens
Christmas Party, The, V. Sackville-West
Christmas Stories, C. Dickens
Christopherson, G. Gissing
Chronicles of the Canongate, Sir W. Scott
Chrononhotonthologos, H. Carey
Church that was at Antioch, The, R. Kipling
Circular Staircase, The, Mary R. Rinehart
Citadel, The, A. J. Cronin
Citizen of the World, A, O. Goldsmith
City and The Pillar, The, Gore Vidal
City of Beautiful Nonsense, The, E. T. Thurston
City of Bells, A, Elizabeth Goudge
City of Gold, The, F. Brett Young
Clandestine Marriage, The, G. Colman the Elder

Clarion Call, The, O. Henry
Clarissa Harlowe, S. Richardson
Clayhanger trilogy, The, Arnold Bennett
Cleg Kelly, S. R. Crockett
Clementina, A. E. W. Mason
Clerk's Quest, The, G. Moore
Clever Ones, The, A. Sutro
Clock Without Hands, Carson McCullers
Cloister and the Hearth, The, C. Reade
Cocktail Party, The, T. S. Eliot
Cocktail Time, P. G. Wodehouse
Code of Morals, A, R. Kipling
Cold Comfort Farm, Stella Gibbons
Colin and Lucy, T. Tickell
Colin and Phoebe, J. Byrom
Colin Clout, John Skelton
Colin Clout's Come Home Again, E. Spenser
Collected Poems, J. Betjeman
Colonel Jack, D. Defoe
Combined Maze, The, May Sinclair
Comedians, The, Graham Greene
Comedy of Errors, A, W. Shakespeare
Comin' Through the Rye, Helen Mathers
Coming of Arthur, The, Lord Tennyson
Communion, A. E. Coppard
Comprehension of Private Copper, The, R. Kipling
Comrade, O Comrade, Ethel Mannin
Comus, J. Milton
Confederacy, The, J. Vanbrugh
Conference of the Powers, A, R. Kipling
Confidential Clerk, The, T. S. Eliot
Conflict of Conscience, The, N. Woodes
Coningsby, B. Disraeli
Conquered, The, Naomi Mitchison
Conquest of Granada, The, J. Dryden
Conscience of the Rich, The, C. P. Snow
Conscious Lovers, The, R. Steele
Consequences, R. Kipling
Constant Nymph, The, Margaret Kennedy
Contessa, The, M. Armstrong
Conversion of Aurelian McGoggin, The, R. Kipling
Conversion of St Wilfred, The, R. Kipling
Convict's Return, The, C. Dickens
Copper Beeches, The, A. Conan Doyle
Cops 'n' Robbers, J. Russell
Corinna's Gone A-maying, R. Herrick
Coriolanus, W. Shakespeare
Cormorant Crag, G. Manville Fenn
Corn is Green, The, Emlyn Williams
Corn King and the Spring Queen, The, Naomi Mitchison
Corner That Held Them, The, Sylvia Townsend Warner
Cornet of Horse, The, G. A. Henty
Corsair, The, Lord Byron
Cotillon, The, L. P. Hartley
Counsellor-at-Law, Elmer Rice
Count and the Wedding Guest, The, O. Henry
Count Magnus, M. R. James
Count Robert of Paris, Sir W. Scott
Count's Courtship, The, W. de la Mare
Country House, The, J. Galsworthy
Country of the Blind, The, H. G. Wells
Country Wife, The, W. Wycherley
Countrymen All, Katherine Tynan
County Wench, The, N. Balchin
Courtship of Dinah Shadd, The, R. Kipling
Courtship of Miles Standish, The, H. W. Longfellow
Courtship of Morrice Buckler, The, A. E. W. Mason
Cousin Phillis, Mrs Gaskell
Crab that Played with the Sea, The, R. Kipling
Cranford, Mrs Gaskell
Crewe Train, Rose Macaulay
Cricket in Heaven, G. Bullett
Cricket on the Hearth, The, C. Dickens
Crime at Vanderlyndens, The, R. H. Mottram
Crime of Olga Jibinsky, The, L. Merrick
Critic, The, R. B. Sheridan
Crock of Gold, The, J. Stephens
Crome Yellow, A. Huxley
Crooked Man, The, A. Conan Doyle
Cross Currents, 'Saki'
Crotchet Castle, T. L. Peacock
Cruel Sea, The, N. Monsarrat
Crump Folk Going Home, Constance Holme
Cry, the Beloved Country, A. Paton
Crystal Hunters, The, G. Manville Fenn
Cuckoo Clock, The, Mrs Molesworth
Cuckoo in the Nest, The, Mrs Oliphant
Cue, The, T. Burke
Cup, The, Lord Tennyson
Cupboard Love, W. W. Jacobs
Cupid à la Carte, O. Henry
Cupid's Arrows, R. Kipling

Curious Story, A, Helen Simpson
Custard Heart, The, Dorothy Parker
Custom of the Country, The, Edith Wharton
Cutter of Colman Street, A. Cowley
Cymbeline, W. Shakespeare
Cynara, E. Dowson

D

Daddy-Long-Legs, Jean Webster
Daisy, The, Katherine Tynan
Daisy Chain, The, Charlotte M. Yonge
Daisy Miller, H. James
Damsel in Distress, A, P. G. Wodehouse
Dance of the Years, Margery Allingham
Dancers in Mourning, Margery Allingham
Dancing Druids, The, Gladys Mitchell
Dancing Men, The, A. Conan Doyle
Dangerous Corner, J. B. Priestley
Daniel Deronda, George Eliot
Danny Deever, R. Kipling
D'Archville, a Portrait, R. H. Mottram
Dark Horse, The, Nat Gould
Dark is Light Enough, The, Christopher Fry
Dark Laughter, Sherwood Anderson
Dark Rosaleen, J. C. Mangan
Dark Tide, The, Vera Brittain
Darling Buds of May, The, H. E. Bates
Daughter of the Regiment, A, R. Kipling
Daughter of Time, A, Josephine Tey
Daughters of the late Colonel, The, Katherine Mansfield
Daughters of the Vicar, D. H. Lawrence
David Copperfield, C. Dickens
David Harum, E. Noyes Westcott
Day of the Seventh Fire, The, James Leo Herlihy
Day's Work, The, R. Kipling
Dayspring Mishandled, R. Kipling
Deacon Brodie, W. E. Henley & R. L. Stevenson
Dead, The, James Joyce
Dead Drummer, The, R. H. Barham
Dead Hand, The, W. Collins
Dead Quire, The, T. Hardy
Deal in Cotton, A, R. Kipling
Dear Brutus, J. M. Barrie
Dear Octopus, Dodie Smith
Death and Last Confession of Wandering Peter, The, H. Belloc
Death Comes as the End, Agatha Christie
Death Comes for the Archbishop, Willa Cather
Death of a Dog, Viola Meynell
Death of a Hero, R. Aldington
Death of a Salesman, Arthur Miller
Death of the Heart, The, Elizabeth Bowen
Debits and Credits, R. Kipling
Debt, The, R. Kipling
Decline and Fall, E. Waugh
Deep Blue Sea, The, T. Rattigan
Deep Waters, P. G. Wodehouse
Deerslayer, The, J. Fenimore Cooper
Delectable Duchy, The, Sir A. Quiller-Couch
Delilah, R. Kipling
Delina Delaney, Amanda Ros
Delta Wedding, Eudora Welty
Denis Duval, W. M. Thackeray
Departmental Ditties, R. Kipling
Deputy was King, A, G. B. Stern
Desirable Villa, T. Burke
Desire Under the Elms, E. O'Neill
Desolate Splendour, M. Sadleir
Desperate Remedies, T. Hardy
Destiny Bay, Donn Byrne
Detective Stories, Dorothy L. Sayers
Devil and the Deep Sea, The, R. Kipling
Devil in Eden, The, Caradoc Evans
Devil Is an Ass, The, B. Jonson
Devil's Disciple, The, G. B. Shaw
Devil's Foot, The, A. Conan Doyle
Devils, The, J. Whiting
Dialstone Lane, W. W. Jacobs
Diana of the Crossways, G. Meredith
Diary of a Late Physician, S. Warren
Diary of a Nobody, The, G. & W. Grossmith
Diary of a Provincial Lady, E. M. Delafield
Diary of Henry Brocken, The, W. de la Mare
Digby Grand, G. Whyte-Melville
Disappearance of Lady Frances Carfax, The, A. Conan Doyle

Disobedience, A. A. Milne
Distant Horns of Summer, The, H. E. Bates
Distinguished Villa, Kate O'Brien
Distracted Preacher, The, T. Hardy
Disturber of Traffic, A, R. Kipling
Disturbing Experience of an Elderly Lady, Helen Simpson
Diversity of Creatures, A, R. Kipling
Doctor Angelus, J. Bridie
Doctor Faustus, C. Marlowe
Dr Jekyll and Mr Hyde, R. L. Stevenson
Dr Marigold's Prescription, C. Dickens
Dr Nikola, G. Boothby
Dr No, I. Fleming
Doctor of Medicine, A, R. Kipling
Doctor Thorne, A. Trollope
Doctor's Dilemma, The, G. B. Shaw
Dodsworth, Sinclair Lewis
Dog Hervey, The, R. Kipling
Doll in the Pink Silk Dress, The, L. Merrick
Dombey and Son, C. Dickens
Don Juan, Lord Byron
Don Sebastian, J. Dryden
Donovan Pasha, Gilbert Parker
Door in the Wall, The, H. G. Wells
Double Dealer, The, W. Congreve
Double-dyed Deceiver, A, O. Henry
Double Gallant, The, C. Cibber
Double Marriage, The, J. Fletcher
Dove in the Eagle's Nest, The, Charlotte M. Yonge
Dove's Nest, The, Katherine Mansfield
Dover Road, The, A. A. Milne
Dow's Flat, Bret Harte
Dracula, Bram Stoker
Dragon Harvest, Upton Sinclair
Dragon Seed, Pearl Buck
Dragon's Head, The, Dorothy L. Sayers
Dragon's Teeth, Upton Sinclair
Drama in Muslin, A, G. Moore
Dramatist, The, F. Reynolds
Dray Wara Yow Dee, R. Kipling
Dream, The, H. G. Wells
Dream of Duncan Parranness, The, R. Kipling
Dream of Eugene Aram, The, T. Hood
Drifting Crane, H. Garland
Drums of the Fore and Aft, The, R. Kipling
Drums of War, H. de Vere Stacpoole
Dubliners, The, James Joyce
Duchess of Malfi, The, John Webster
Duchess of Nono, The, M. Hewlett
Duel of Doctor Hirsch, The, G. K. Chesterton
Duenna, The, Mrs Belloc Lowndes
Duenna, The, R. B. Sheridan
Duke of Gandia, The, A. C. Swinburne
Duke of Milan, The, P. Massinger
Duke's Motto, The, J. H. McCarthy
Dunstone's Dear Lady, H. G. Wells
Dusky Ruth, A. E. Coppard
Dying Detective, The, A. Conan Doyle
Dymchurch Flit, The, R. Kipling

E

Earthjacket, Jon Hartridge
East Lynne, Mrs Henry Wood
East of Eden, J. Steinbeck
East of Suez, W. S. Maugham
Ebb and Flood, J. Hanley
Echoing Grove, The, Rosamond Lehmann
Eden End, J. B. Priestley
Edge of the Evening, The, R. Kipling
Education of Otis Yeere, The, R. Kipling
Education of Uncle Paul, The, A. Blackwood
Edward Gray, Lord Tennyson
Edwin Drood, C. Dickens
Egoist, The, G. Meredith
Elder Statesman, The, T. S. Eliot
Elephant's Child, The, R. Kipling
Elevation of Lulu, The, L. Merrick
Eliza, Barry Pain
Eliza's Husband, Barry Pain
Ellen Brine of Allenburn, W. Barnes
Ellen Irwin, W. Wordsworth
Elmer Gantry, Sinclair Lewis
Elsie and the Child, Arnold Bennett
Elsie Venner, O. W. Holmes
Emma, Jane Austen
Empty House, The, A. Conan Doyle
Enchanted April, The, Countess von Arnim
Enchanted Profile, The, O. Henry
End of the Affair, The, Graham Greene
End of the House of Alard, The, Sheila Kaye-Smith

Engineer's Thumb, The, A. Conan Doyle
England Made Me, Graham Greene
Englishman's Home, An, Guy du Maurier
Enoch Arden, Lord Tennyson
Enoch Soames, Max Beerbohm
Entail, The, J. Galt
Enter a Murderer, Ngaio Marsh
Enter Sir John, Clemence Dane & Helen Simpson
Entertaining Mr Sloane, Joe Orton
Enthusiast, The, N. Balchin
Epicene, B. Jonson
Episode of Fiddletown, An, Bret Harte
Erewhon, S. Butler
Erewhon Revisited, S. Butler
Eric, or Little by Little, F. W. Farrar
Eric Brighteyes, H. Rider Haggard
Ernest Maltravers, Lord Lytton
Error in the Fourth Dimension, An, R. Kipling
Esmé, 'Saki'
Essays of Elia, C. Lamb
Esther Waters, G. Moore
Eternal City, The, Hall Caine
Ethan Frome, Edith Wharton
Ethel Churchill, L. E. Landon
Eugene Aram, Lord Lytton
Eustace Chisholm and the Works, J. Purdy
Eustace Diamonds, The, A. Trollope
Eva Trout, Elizabeth Bowen
Evan Harrington, G. Meredith
Evangeline, H. W. Longfellow
Evarra and his Gods, R. Kipling
Eve of St Agnes, The, J. Keats
Evelina, Fanny Burney
Eveline, James Joyce
Everyman in his Humour, B. Jonson
Everyman out of his Humour, B. Jonson
Exiles, James Joyce
Exploits of Brigadier Gerard, The, A. Conan Doyle
Eye of Allah, The, R. Kipling
Eye of Apollo, The, G. K. Chesterton
Eye of the Needle, The, Gilbert Parker
Eyeless in Gaza, A. Huxley

F

Face, The, W. de la Mare
Face of Clay, The, H. A. Vachell
Faërie Queene, The, E. Spenser
Fair Ines, T. Hood
Fair Maid of Perth, The, Sir W. Scott
Fair Penitent, The, N. Rowe
Fairy-Kist, R. Kipling
Fairy Tale, A, T. Parnell
Faithful Sally Brown, T. Hood
Faithful Shepherdess, The, Beaumont & Fletcher
Faithless Nelly Gray, T. Hood
Falcon, The, Lord Tennyson
Fall of Jack Gillespie, The, R. Kipling
Fallen Angels, N. Coward
Fallow Land, The, H. E. Bates
False Dawn, R. Kipling
False Start, A, A. Conan Doyle
Family Reunion, The, T. S. Eliot
Famine, L. O'Flaherty
Fanatics, The, M. Malleson
Fanny by Gaslight, M. Sadleir
Fanny's First Play, G. B. Shaw
Far from the Madding Crowd, T. Hardy
Fardarougha the Miser, W. Carleton
Farewell, Miss Julie Logan, J. M. Barrie
Farewell to Arms, A, E. Hemingway
Farewell to Youth, Storm Jameson
Farewell Victoria, T. H. White
Farmer on the Fairway, L. A. G. Strong
Farmer's Boy, The, R. Bloomfield
Farmer's Wife, The, E. Phillpotts
Fatal Boots, The, W. M. Thackeray
Fatal Curiosity, The, G. Lillo
Fatal Dowry, The, P. Massinger
Fatal Marriage, The, T. Southerne
Father in Sion, A, Caradoc Evans
Feast, The, Margaret Kennedy
Feast and the Reckoning, The, Barry Pain
Fed Up, G. A. Birmingham
Felix Holt, George Eliot
Fellow Townsman, T. Hardy
Fergus, Brian Moore
Fiddler of the Reels, The, T. Hardy
Fielding had an Orderly, Gilbert Parker
Fiery Particles, C. E. Montague
Fifth Form at St Dominic's, The, T. Baines Reed
Filmer, H. G. Wells
Final Problem, The, A. Conan Doyle

Finances of the Gods, The, R. Kipling
Financier, The, T. Dreiser
Finch's Fortune, Mazo de la Roche
Finest Story in the World, The, R. Kipling
Finnegans Wake, James Joyce
Fire at Tranter Sweatley's, The, T. Hardy
Fire-Dwellers, The, Margaret Laurence
Firing Line, The, R. W. Chambers
Firmilian, W. E. Aytoun
First Men in the Moon, The, H. G. Wells
First Mrs Fraser, The, St John Ervine
Fisher of Men, The, Fiona Macleod
Fisherman, The, M. Armstrong
Fitz-Boodle Papers, The, W. M. Thackeray
Five Nations, The, R. Kipling
Five Orange Pips, The, A. Conan Doyle
Five Red Herrings, The, Dorothy L. Sayers
Five Sons of Le Faber, The, E. Raymond
Flag of their Country, The, R. Kipling
Flamingo, Mary Borden
Flower Girls, The, Clemence Dane
Flowering Wilderness, J. Galsworthy
Flowers for the Judge, Margery Allingham
Fog in Santone, A, O. Henry
Folly of Brown, The, W. S. Gilbert
Food of the Gods, The, H. G. Wells
Footman for the Peacock, A, Rachel Ferguson
Footsteps that Ran, The, Dorothy L. Sayers
For Conscience' Sake, T. Hardy
For the Term of his Natural Life, M. Clarke
For Us in the Dark, Naomi Royde-Smith
For Whom the Bell Tolls, E. Hemingway
Forest Lovers, The, M. Hewlett
Forge, The, Katherine Tynan
Forsaken Merman, The, M. Arnold
Forsyte Saga, The, J. Galsworthy
Forsyte series, The, J. Galsworthy
Fortress, The, Hugh Walpole
Fortunate Youth, The, W. J. Locke
Fortunes of Christina McNab, The, S. Macnaughtan
Fortunes of Nigel, The, Sir W. Scott
Fortunes of Richard Mahoney, The, H. H. Richardson
Fountain, The, C. Morgan
Four Armourers, The, F. Beeding
Four Frightened People, E. Arnot Robertson
Four Just Men, The, E. Wallace
Fourth Wall, The, A. A. Milne
Fox Hunter, The, Katherine Tynan
Framley Parsonage, A. Trollope
Franchise Affair, The, Josephine Tey
Frank Fairlegh, F. E. Smedley
Frankenstein, Mary W. Shelley
Franny and Zooey, J. D. Salinger
Freckles, Gene S. Porter
French Lieutenant, The, R. Church
French without Tears, T. Rattigan
Frenchman's Creek, Daphne du Maurier
Friend of the Family, A, R. Kipling
Friend's Friend, A, R. Kipling
Friendly Brook, R. Kipling
Friends and Relations, Elizabeth Bowen
Friends in San Rosario, O. Henry
From Place to Place, Irvin S. Cobb
From Russia With Love, I. Fleming
Frontiers of Death, The, J. Turner
Fruit of the Tree, The, Edith Wharton

G

Gabriel, Ernest, 'Saki'
Galathea, J. Lyly
Gallions Reach, H. M. Tomlinson
Gallowsmith, The, Irvin S. Cobb
Gamester, The, E. Moore
Gamester, The, J. Shirley
Gammer Gurton's Needle, Anon.
Garden of Allah, The, R. S. Hichens
Garden Party, The, Katherine Mansfield
Gardener, The, R. Kipling
Gardener, The, Barry Pain
Garm—a Hostage, R. Kipling
Gaslight, P. Hamilton
Gate of a Hundred Sorrows, The, R. Kipling
Gates of Summer, The, J. Whiting
Gaudy Night, Dorothy L. Sayers
Gay Lord Quex, The, A. W. Pinero
Gemini, R. Kipling

General, The, C. S. Forester
General Burton's Ghost, Katherine Tynan
Genius, The, T. Dreiser
Gentle Counsels, N. Balchin
Gentle Craft, The, T. Deloney
Gentleman of Leisure, A, P. G. Wodehouse
Gentlemen Prefer Blondes, Anita Loos
George Barnwell, G. Lillo
Georgian Love Story, A, E. Raymond
Georgie Porgie, R. Kipling
Geraint and Enid, Lord Tennyson
Germ Destroyer, A., R. Kipling
Ghost Stories of an Antiquary, M. R. James
Ghost Train, The, A. Ridley
Giffen's Debt, R. Kipling
Gioconda Smile, The, A. Huxley
Girls in Their Married Bliss, Edna O'Brien
Glass Cell, The, Patricia Highsmith
Glass Key, The, D. Hammett
Glass Menagerie, The, Tennessee Williams
Glastonbury Romance, A, J. C. Powys
Gloria Scott, The, A. Conan Doyle
Gloriana, R. Kipling
Glory in the Daytime, Dorothy Parker
Glory of Clementina Wing, The, W. J. Locke
Glory that was Sion's, The, Caradoc Evans
Go She Must !, D. Garnett
Go Tell It On The Mountain, James Baldwin
Go-Between, The, L. P. Hartley
God and the Machine, N. Balchin
God's Little Acre, E. Caldwell
God's Prisoner, J. Oxenham
God's Stepchildren, Sarah G. Millin
Going their own Ways, A. Waugh
Gold Bug, The, E. A. Poe
Golden Apples, The, Eudora Welty
Golden Bowl, The, H. James
Golden Boy, Clifford Odets
Golden Legend, The, H. W. Longfellow
Goldfinger, I. Fleming
Gondoliers, The, Gilbert & Sullivan
Gone to Earth, Mary Webb
Gone with the Wind, Margaret Mitchell
Good Companions, The, J. B. Priestley
Good Earth, The, Pearl Buck
Good Natured Man, The, O. Goldsmith
Good Night, Good Night, T. Moore
Good Ship ' Mohock ', The, W. Clark Russell
Good Soldier, The, Ford Madox Ford
Goodbye, Mr Chips, J. Hilton
Goodbye to Berlin, C. Isherwood
Gorboduc, T. Sackville & T. Norton
Grace, James Joyce
Gracie Goodnight, T. Burke
Grand Hotel, Vicki Baum
Grand Opera, Vicki Baum
Grapes of Wrath, The, J. Steinbeck
Grateful Fair, The, C. Smart
Grave of the Hundred Dead, The, R. Kipling
Great Adventure, The, Arnold Bennett
Great Expectations, C. Dickens
Great Fortune, The, Olivia Manning
Great Gatsby, The, F. Scott Fitzgerald
Great God Pan, The, A. Machen
Great Hoggarty Diamond, The, W. M. Thackeray
Great Pandolfo, The, W. J. Locke
Green Goddess, The, W. Archer
Green Hat, The, M. Arlen
Green Mansions, W. H. Hudson
Green Tea, Sheridan Le Fanu
Grey Sand and White Sand, Helen Simpson
Group, The, Mary McCarthy
Growing Up, Angela Thirkell
Gryll Grange, T. L. Peacock
Guest of Honour, A, Nadine Gordimer
Gulliver's Travels, J. Swift
Gunga Din, R. Kipling
Gunroom, The, C. Morgan
Guy Mannering, Sir W. Scott

H

Habitation Enforced, A, R. Kipling
Hadrian the Seventh, Baron Corvo (F. W. Rolfe)
Hajji Baba, J. J. Morier
Hal o' the Draft, R. Kipling
Hamlet, W. Shakespeare
Hamlet, Revenge !, M. Innes
Hammer of God, The, G. K. Chesterton

Hampdenshire Wonder, The, J. D. Beresford
Hand of Ethelberta, The, T. Hardy
Handful of Dust, A, E. Waugh
Handley Cross, R. S. Surtees
Hands of Mr Ottermole, The, T. Burke
Handy Andy, S. Lover
Hangman's House, Donn Byrne
Happy Prisoner, The, Monica Dickens
Happy Returns, Angela Thirkell
Hard Cash, C. Reade
Hard Times, C. Dickens
Harlem Tragedy, A, O. Henry
Harry Lorrequer, C. Lever
Harvester, The, Gene S. Porter
Hassan, J. E. Flecker
Hatter's Castle, A. J. Cronin
Haughty Actor, The, W. S. Gilbert
Haunted House, The, C. Dickens
Haunted Man, The, C. Dickens
Haunted Ships, The, Allan Cunningham
Hawbuck Grange, R. S. Surtees
Hay Fever, N. Coward
He Knew He Was Right, A. Trollope
Head of Caesar, The, G. K. Chesterton
Head of the District, The, R. Kipling
Head to Toe, Joe Orton
Heart is a Lonely Hunter, The, Carson McCullers
Heart of a Child, The, Phyllis Bottome
Heart of a Goof, The, P. G. Wodehouse
Heart of Darkness, J. Conrad
Heart of Midlothian, The, Sir W. Scott
Heart of the Matter, The, Graham Greene
Heart of the West, O. Henry
Heartbreak House, G. B. Shaw
Heartsease, Charlotte M. Yonge
Heat of the Day, The, Elizabeth Bowen
Heaven and Earth, Lord Byron
Heaven Tree, The, trilogy, Edith Pargeter
Heaven's My Destination, T. Wilder
Hedge School, The, W. Carleton
Heifer without Blemish, A, Caradoc Evans
Heir, The, V. Sackville-West
Heir at Law, The, G. Colman the Younger
Heir of Redclyffe, The, Charlotte M. Yonge
Helen's Babies, J. Habberton
Hemlock and After, A. Wilson
Henderson The Rain King, Saul Bellow
Henry Esmond, W. M. Thackeray
Henry the Eighth, W. Shakespeare
Henry the Fifth, W. Shakespeare
Henry the Fourth, W. Shakespeare
Henry the Sixth, W. Shakespeare
Her Majesty's Servants, R. Kipling
Her Son, V. Sackville-West
Herb of Grace, The, Elizabeth Goudge
Here and Hereafter, Barry Pain
Here Lies, Dorothy Parker
Heritage of Hatcher Ide, The, Booth Tarkington
Herod, S. Phillips
Herries Chronicles, The, Hugh Walpole
Herself Surprised, Joyce Cary
High Meadows, Alison Uttley
High Rising, Angela Thirkell
High Road, The, F. Lonsdale
High Stakes, P. G. Wodehouse
High Tor, Maxwell Anderson
High Wind in Jamaica, R. Hughes
Highland River, N. M. Gunn
Highland Widow, The, Sir W. Scott
Hilda Lessways, Arnold Bennett
Hill, The, H. A. Vachell
His Chance in Life, R. Kipling
His House in Order, A. W. Pinero
His Last Bow, A. Conan Doyle
His Majesty the King, R. Kipling
His Private Honour, R. Kipling
His Wedded Wife, R. Kipling
History of David Grieve, The, Mrs Humphry Ward
History of Mr Polly, The, H. G. Wells
History of the Fairchild Family, The, Mrs Sherwood
History of the Hardcomes, The, T. Hardy
H. M. Pulham, Esq., J. P. Marquand
H.M.S. Pinafore, Gilbert & Sullivan
Hole in the Wall, The, A. Morrison
Holiday Task, A, 'Saki'
Hollow Man, The, T. Burke
Holmby House, G. Whyte-Melville
Holy Deadlock, A. P. Herbert
Holy Grail, The, Lord Tennyson
Holy Willie's Prayer and Epitaph, R. Burns
Honours Easy, C. E. Montague
Honours of War, The, R. Kipling
Hoodwinked, Irvin S. Cobb
Hornblower series, The, C. S. Forester
Horse Marines, The, R. Kipling
Horse's Mouth, The, Joyce Cary
Horses and Men, Sherwood Anderson
Horsie, Dorothy Parker
Hound of the Baskervilles, The, A. Conan Doyle

House and its Head, A, Ivy Compton-Burnett
House in Dormer Forest, The, Mary Webb
House in Paris, The, Elizabeth Bowen
House of Children, A, Joyce Cary
House of Cobwebs, The, G. Gissing
House of Mirth, The, Edith Wharton
House of the Seven Gables, The, N. Hawthorne
House Surgeon, The, R. Kipling
House with the Green Shutters, The, G. Douglas
Housemaster, Ian Hay
How Fear Came, R. Kipling
How Green Was My Valley, R. Llewellyn
How Lisa Loved the King, George Eliot
How the Camel got his Hump, R. Kipling
How the First Letter was Written, R. Kipling
How the Leopard got his Spots, R. Kipling
How the Rhinoceros got his Skin, R. Kipling
How the Whale got his Throat, R. Kipling
Howard's End, E. M. Forster
Hubert and Minnie, A. Huxley
Huckleberry Finn. *See* Adventures of Huckleberry Finn, The
Hue and Cry after Fair Amoret, A, W. Congreve
Human Comedy, The, W. Saroyan
Humphry Clinker, T. Smollett
Humplebee, G. Gissing
Hunchback, The, J. S. Knowles
Hunted Down, C. Dickens
Hunter after Wild Beasts, The, M. Arlen
Huntingtower, J. Buchan
Hurry on Down, J. Wain
Hypatia, C. Kingsley
Hypocrite, The, I. Bickerstaffe

I

I Like It Here, K. Amis
I Live Under a Black Sun, Edith Sitwell
I Will Repay, Baroness Orczy
I'm a Fool, Sherwood Anderson
Ideal Husband, An, O. Wilde
Idyll of Red Gulch, The, Bret Harte
Idylls of the King, Lord Tennyson
If Four Walls Told, E. Percy
If Sinners Entice Thee, W. le Queux
If Winter Comes, A. S. M. Hutchinson
Iliad of Sandy Bar, The, Bret Harte
Imaginative Woman, An, T. Hardy
Immortal Sergeant, The, J. Brophy
Imperial Palace, Arnold Bennett
Importance of Being Earnest, The, O. Wilde
Impressionists, The, R. Kipling
In Ambush, R. Kipling
In Chancery, J. Galsworthy
In Cotton Wool, W. B. Maxwell
In Error, R. Kipling
In Flood Time, R. Kipling
In Greek Waters, G. A. Henty
In the Days of the Comet, H. G. Wells
In the House of Suddhoo, R. Kipling
In the Interests of the Brethren, R. Kipling
In the Library, W. W. Jacobs
In the Matter of a Private, R. Kipling
In the Midst of Life, A. Bierce
In the Presence, R. Kipling
In the Pride of his Youth, R. Kipling
In the Roar of the Sea, S. Baring-Gould
In the Rukh, R. Kipling
In the Same Boat, R. Kipling
In the Tunnel, Bret Harte
In this our Life, Ellen Glasgow
Incarnation of Krishna Mulvaney, The, R. Kipling
Incident in the Life of Mr George Crookhill, An, T. Hardy
Incomparable Bellairs, A. & E. Castle
Inconstant, The, G. Farquhar
Informer, The, L. O'Flaherty
Ingoldsby Legends, The, R. H. Barham
Ingoldsby Penance, The, R. H. Barham
Innocence of Father Brown, The, G. K. Chesterton
Interlopers at the Knap, T. Hardy
Invisible Man, The, G. K. Chesterton
Invisible Man, The, H. G. Wells
Invitation to the Waltz, Rosamond Lehmann
Iolanthe, Gilbert & Sullivan

Ion, T. N. Talfourd
Ippolita in the Hills, M. Hewlett
Iron and Smoke, Sheila Kaye-Smith
Iron Heel, The, Jack London
Iron Pirate, The, M. Pemberton
Isaac Comnenus, H. Taylor
Isabella, Isabella, Phyllis Bentley
Island Nights' Entertainments, R. L. Stevenson
Island of Dr Moreau, The, H. G. Wells
Island Princess, The, J. Fletcher
Isle of Voices, The, R. L. Stevenson
It Is Never Too Late to Mend, C. Reade
It Never Can Happen Again, W. de Morgan
It's a Battlefield, Graham Greene
Italian, The, Mrs Radcliffe
Ivanhoe, Sir W. Scott
Ivory God, The, J. S. Fletcher

J

Jacaranda Tree, The, H. E. Bates
Jack Hinton, C. Lever
Jack Sheppard, W. H. Ainsworth
Jackanapes, Juliana H. Ewing
Jackdaw of Rheims, The, R. H. Barham
Jacob's Room, Virginia Woolf
Jane Clegg, St John Ervine
Jane Eyre, Charlotte Brontë
Janeites, The, R. Kipling
Janet's Repentance, George Eliot
Java Head, J. Hergesheimer
Je ne parle pas Français, Katherine Mansfield
Jeames's Diary, W. M. Thackeray
Jemmy Dawson, W. Shenstone
Jennie Gerhardt, T. Dreiser
Jeremy, Hugh Walpole
Jerome, Mary E. Wilkins
Jerry Jarvis's Wig, R. H. Barham
Jest of God, A, Margaret Laurence
Jesting of Arlington Stringham, The, 'Saki'
Jew of Malta, The, C. Marlowe
Jews in Shushan, R. Kipling
Jezebel's Dust, F. Urquhart
Jilting of Jane, The, H. G. Wells
Jim, Bret Harte
Jim Bludso, John Hay
Jo's Boys, Louisa M. Alcott
Joan and Peter, H. G. Wells
Joanna Godden, Sheila Kaye-Smith
Joby, Stan Barstow
John Anderson, My Jo John, R. Burns
John Bull, G. Colman the Younger
John Bull's Other Island, G. B. Shaw
John Chilcote, M.P., Katherine C. Thurston
John Gilpin, W. Cowper
John Gladwyn Says—, O. Onions
John Halifax, Gentleman, Mrs Craik
John Inglesant, J. H. Shorthouse
John O' Dreams, Katherine Tynan
John Silence, A. Blackwood
Jonathan Wild, H. Fielding
Jorrocks's Jaunts and Jollities, R. S. Surtees
Joseph and his Brethren, H. W. Freeman
Joseph Andrews, H. Fielding
Joseph Vance, W. de Morgan
Journey's End, R. C. Sherriff
Joy and Josephine, Monica Dickens
Juan in America, E. Linklater
Judas Window, The, C. Dickson
Jude the Obscure, T. Hardy
Judge's Story, The, C. Morgan
Judgment in Suspense, G. Bullett
Judgment of Borso, The, M. Hewlett
Judgment of Dungara, The, R. Kipling
Judgment of Paris, The, L. Merrick
Judgment of Paris, The, Gore Vidal
Judith Paris, Hugh Walpole
Judson and the Empire, R. Kipling
Julius Caesar, W. Shakespeare
Jungle Books, The, R. Kipling
Juno and the Paycock, S. O'Casey
Jurgen, J. B. Cabell
Jury, The, G. Bullett
Just Man in Sodom, A, Caradoc Evans
Just So Stories, R. Kipling
Justice, J. Galsworthy
Justine, L. Durrell

K

Kaa's Hunting, R. Kipling
Kangaroo, D. H. Lawrence
Kathleen ni Houlihan, W. B. Yeats
Keeping in with Vosper, P. G. Wodehouse
Kenilworth, Sir W. Scott
Kickleburys on the Rhine, The, W. M. Thackeray
Kidnapped, R. Kipling
Kidnapped, R. L. Stevenson
Killing Bottle, The, L. P. Hartley
Kilmeny, J. Hogg
Kim, R. Kipling
Kind of Loving, A, Stan Barstow
King and No King, A, Beaumont & Fletcher
King John, W. Shakespeare
King Lear, W. Shakespeare
King of Elfland's Daughter, The, Lord Dunsany
King of Schnorrers, The, I. Zangwill
King of the World, The, A. E. Coppard
King Solomon's Mines, H. Rider Haggard
King's Ankus, The, R. Kipling
King's Own, The, Captain Marryat
Kipps, H. G. Wells
Kismet, E. Knoblock
Kiss for Cinderella, A, J. M. Barrie
Knife and Naked Chalk, The, R. Kipling
Knight and the Lady, The, R. H. Barham
Knight of the Burning Pestle, The, Beaumont & Fletcher
Knight on Wheels, A, Ian Hay
Knights of the Joyous Venture, The, R. Kipling

L

La Mère Bauche, A. Trollope
Labyrinth Makers, The, A. Price
Lady Audley's Secret, Mary E. Braddon
Lady Chatterley's Lover, D. H. Lawrence
Lady Clara Vere de Vere, Lord Tennyson
Lady Frederick, W. S. Maugham
Lady into Fox, D. Garnett
Lady of Lyons, The, Lord Lytton
Lady of Pleasure, The, J. Shirley
Lady of the Barge, The, W. W. Jacobs
Lady Windermere's Fan, O. Wilde
Lady's Not For Burning, The, Christopher Fry
Lalla Rookh, T. Moore
Lamentations, Caradoc Evans
Lamia and other Poems, J. Keats
Lamp for Nightfall, A, E. Caldwell
Lamplighter, The, Maria S. Cummins
Lancelot and Elaine, Lord Tennyson
Land of Promise, The, W. S. Maugham
Land of Spices, The, Kate O'Brien
Landmarks, E. V. Lucas
Landscape with Figures, R. Fraser
Lang Men o' Larut, The, R. Kipling
Laodician, A, T. Hardy
Last and the First, The, Ivy Compton-Burnett
Last Days of Pompeii, The, Lord Lytton
Last Leaf, The, O. Henry
Last of Mrs Cheyney, The, F. Lonsdale
Last of Summer, The, Kate O'Brien
Last of the Barons, The, Lord Lytton
Last of the Mohicans, The, J. Fenimore Cooper
Last Post, Ford Madox Ford
Last Recollections of My Uncle Charles, N. Balchin
Last Revolution, The, Lord Dunsany
Last Rhyme of True Thomas, The, R. Kipling
Last September, The, Elizabeth Bowen
Last Suttee, The, R. Kipling
Last Term, The, R. Kipling
Last Tournament, The, Lord Tennyson
Last Tycoon, The, F. Scott Fitzgerald
Late George Apley, The, J. P. Marquand
Late in the Afternoon, Lettice Cooper
Laughing Lady, The, A. Sutro
Laura, T. Campion
Laura's Bishop, G. A. Birmingham
Lavengro, George Borrow

Leatherstocking Tales, J. Fenimore Cooper
Legacy of Cain, The, W. Collins
Legend of Hamilton Tighe, The, R. H. Barham
Legend of Jubal, The, George Eliot
Legend of Montrose, The, Sir W. Scott
Legend of Sleepy Hollow, The, W. Irving
Legend of the Foreign Office, A, R. Kipling
Legend of the Rhine, A, W. M. Thackeray
Leipzig, T. Hardy
Let the People Sing, J. B. Priestley
Letter, The, W. S. Maugham
Letters from a Self-made Merchant to his Son, G. H. Lorimer
Letting in the Jungle, R. Kipling
Lewis Arundel, F. E. Smedley
Lie, The, H. A. Jones
Lieutenant-Colonel Flare, W. S. Gilbert
Life and Death of Mr Badman, The, J. Bunyan
Life in London, Pierce Egan
Life of Ma Parker, Katherine Mansfield
Life's Handicap, R. Kipling
Life's Little Ironies, T. Hardy
Lifted Veil, The, George Eliot
Light in August, W. Faulkner
Light that Failed, The, R. Kipling
Lighten our Darkness, R. Keable
Lilac Sunbonnet, The, S. R. Crockett
Limitations of Pambé Serang, The, R. Kipling
Limits and Renewals, R. Kipling
Linda Condon, J. Hergesheimer
Lionel and Clarissa, I. Bickerstaffe
Lise Lillywhite, Margery Sharp
Lispeth, R. Kipling
Little Cloud, A, James Joyce
Little Dinner at Timmins, A, W. M. Thackeray
Little Dog Laughed, The, L. Merrick
Little Dorrit, C. Dickens
Little Duke, The, Charlotte M. Yonge
Little Foxes, The, Lillian Hellman
Little Foxes, R. Kipling
Little Girls, The, Elizabeth Bowen
Little Lord Fauntleroy, Frances H. Burnett
Little Men, Louisa M. Alcott
Little Mexican, The, A. Huxley
Little Minister, The, J. M. Barrie
Little Novels of Italy, M. Hewlett
Little Nugget, The, P. G. Wodehouse
Little Prep, A, R. Kipling
Little Red Horses, G. B. Stern
Little Shepherd of Kingdom Come, The, J. Fox junr
Little Tobrah, R. Kipling
Little Women, Louisa M. Alcott
Liza of Lambeth, W. S. Maugham
Locksley Hall, Lord Tennyson
Lodger in Maze Pond, A., G. Gissing
Lodging for the Night, A, R. L. Stevenson
Lolita, Vladimir Nabokov
Lolly Willowes, Sylvia Townsend Warner
London Belongs to Me, N. Collins
London Wall, J. van Druten
Long Time Growing Up, The, J. Pudney
Longest Journey, The, E. M. Forster
Look at the Clock, R. H. Barham
Look Back in Anger, J. Osborne
Look Homeward, Angel, T. Wolfe
Loom of Youth, The, A. Waugh
Loot, Joe Orton
Lord Arthur Savile's Crime, O. Wilde
Lord Jim, J. Conrad
Lord of the Dynamos, H. G. Wells
Lord of the Rings trilogy, The, J. R. R. Tolkien
Lord Peter Stories, The, Dorothy L. Sayers
Lord Peter Views the Body, Dorothy L. Sayers
Lorna Doone, R. D. Blackmore
Los Amigos Fiasco, The, A. Conan Doyle
Loss of the 'Jane Vosper', The, F. Wills Crofts
Lost Blend, The, O Henry
Lost Endeavour, J. Masefield
Lost Generation, The, M. Arlen
Lost Girl, The, D. H. Lawrence
Lost God, The, John Russell
Lost Hearts, M. R. James
Lost Horizon, J. Hilton
Lost Lady, A, Willa Cather
Lost Legion, The, R. Kipling
Lost Mr Blake, W. S. Gilbert
Lost Sir Massingberd, James Payn
Lost Weekend, The, C. Jackson
Lost World, The, A. Conan Doyle
Lothair, B. Disraeli
Louise, Viola Meynell
Love à la Mode, C. Macklin
Love Among the Artists, G. B. Shaw
Love Among the Chickens, P. G. Wodehouse
Love and Money, Phyllis Bentley

Love and Mr Lewisham, H. G. Wells
Love at All Ages, Angela Thirkell
Love for Love, W. Congreve
Love in a Cold Climate, Nancy Mitford
Love in a Wood, W. Wycherley
Love o' Women, R. Kipling
Love on the Dole, W. Greenwood
Love Song of J. Alfred Prufrock, The, T. S. Eliot
Love's Labour's Lost, W. Shakespeare
Love's Last Shift, C. Cibber
Lovel the Widower, W. M. Thackeray
Lovey Childs, John O'Hara
Loving, H. Green
Loving Eye, The, W. Sansom
Loyalties, J. Galsworthy
Luck of Roaring Camp, The, Bret Harte
Luck Piece, The, Irvin S. Cobb
Lucky Boy, Viola Meynell
Lucky Jim, K. Amis
Lucy Gray, W. Wordsworth
Lummox, Fanny Hurst

M

McAndrew's Hymn, R. Kipling
Macbeth, W. Shakespeare
McTeague, F. Norris
Madame Delphine, G. W. Cable
Madcap Violet, W. Black
Madison Square Arabian Night, A, O. Henry
Madonna of the Peach Tree, M. Hewlett
Madonna of the Trenches, A, R. Kipling
Magic, G. K. Chesterton
Magnolia Street, L. Golding
Maid in Waiting, J. Galsworthy
Maid's Tragedy, The, Beaumont & Fletcher
Maiden and Married Life of Mary Powell, The, Anne Manning
Maids of Paradise, The, R. W. Chambers
Major Barbara, G. B. Shaw
Major Cypress goes off the Deep End, M. Arlen
Mala, Barry Pain
Malcolm, J. Purdy
Maltby and Braxton, Max Beerbohm
Maltese Cat, The, R. Kipling
Maltese Falcon, The, D. Hammett
Man and Superman, G. B. Shaw
Man and the Snake, The, A. Bierce
Man at the Wheel, The, Gilbert Parker
Man in the Passage, The, G. K. Chesterton
Man of Feeling, The, H. Mackenzie
Man of Mode, The, Sir G. Etherege
Man of the World, The, C. Macklin
Man Upstairs, The, P. G. Wodehouse
Man Who Became a Woman, The, Sherwood Anderson
Man who could Write, The, R. Kipling
Man who Lost his Likeness, The, Morley Roberts
Man Who Was, The, R. Kipling
Man who was Thursday, The, G. K. Chesterton
Man who would be King, The, R. Kipling
Man with Copper Fingers, The, Dorothy L. Sayers
Man with no Face, The, Dorothy L. Sayers
Man with the Broken Nose, The, M. Arlen
Man with the Twisted Lip, The, A. Conan Doyle
Man's Story, The, Sherwood Anderson
Manalive, G. K. Chesterton
Mandelbaum Gate, The, Muriel Spark
Manfred, Lord Byron
Manhattan Transfer, J. dos Passos
Manner of Men, The, R. Kipling
Manservant and Maidservant, Ivy Compton-Burnett
Mansfield Park, Jane Austen
Many Inventions, R. Kipling
Marcella, Mrs Humphry Ward
Marching Song, J. Whiting
Marching to Zion, A. E. Coppard
Mardi, H. Melville
Mare's Nest, The, R. Kipling
Maria Schoning, S. T. Coleridge
Marian, Mrs S. C. Hall
Mariana, Lord Tennyson
Marino Faliero, Lord Byron
Mark of the Beast, The, R. Kipling
Market Harborough, G. Whyte-Melville
Marklake Witches, R. Kipling
Marquis and Miss Sally, The, O. Henry
Marquis of Lossie, The, G. MacDonald

Marquise, The, N. Coward
Marriage, H. G. Wells
Marriage à la Mode, J. Dryden
Martian, The, George du Maurier
Martin Arrowsmith, Sinclair Lewis
Martin Chuzzlewit, C. Dickens
Martin Lightfoot's Song, C. Kingsley
Martin Rattler, R. M. Ballantyne
Mary Barton, Mrs Gaskell
Mary Gloster, The, R. Kipling
Mary Poppins Books, The, P. L. Travers
Mary Postgate, R. Kipling
Mary Rose, J. M. Barrie
Masque of the Red Death, The, E. A. Poe
Master, The, N. Balchin
Master Humphrey's Clock, C. Dickens
Master Jim Probity, F. Swinnerton
Master of Ballantrae, The, R. L. Stevenson
Masterman Ready, Captain Marryat
Masters, The, C. P. Snow
Matchmaker, The, M. Armstrong
Matter of Fact, A, R. Kipling
Matter of Taste, A, Dorothy L. Sayers
Maurice, E. M. Forster
Mayor of Casterbridge, The, T. Hardy
Measure for Measure, W. Shakespeare
Meet Mr Mulliner, P. G. Wodehouse
Mehalah, S. Baring-Gould
Melancholy Hussar, The, T. Hardy
Melancholy of Ulad, The, Fiona Macleod
Melincourt, T. L. Peacock
Melloney Holtspur, J. Masefield
Melmoth the Wanderer, Charles Robert Maturin
Member of the Wedding, The, Carson McCullers
Memento Mori, Muriel Spark
Memoirs of a Fox-Hunting Man, S. Sassoon
Memoirs of an Infantry Officer, S. Sassoon
Memoirs of Sherlock Holmes, A. Conan Doyle
Men and Wives, Ivy Compton-Burnett
Men at Arms, E. Waugh
Men Like Gods, H. G. Wells
Men's Wives, W. M. Thackeray
Merchant of Venice, The, W. Shakespeare
Merlin and Vivien, Lord Tennyson
Merry Devil of Edmonton, The, Anon.
Merry Men, The, R. L. Stevenson
Merry Month of May, The, O. Henry
Merry Wives of Windsor, The, W. Shakespeare
Message from the Sea, A, C. Dickens
Messer Cino and the Live Coal, M. Hewlett
Metropolis, The, Upton Sinclair
Mezzotint, The, M. R. James
M.F., Anthony Burgess
Miasma, The, P. G. Wodehouse
Micah Clarke, A. Conan Doyle
Mid-Channel, A. W. Pinero
Middle Watch, The, Ian Hay & S. King-Hall
Middlemarch, George Eliot
Midnight Cowboy, James Leo Herlihy
Midsummer Night's Dream, A, W. Shakespeare
Miggles, Bret Harte
Mighty Atom, The, Marie Corelli
Mikado, The, Gilbert & Sullivan
Milestones, Arnold Bennett & E. Knoblock
Mill on the Floss, The, George Eliot
Mine Host, N. Balchin
Ming Yellow, J. P. Marquand
Ministry of Fear, The, Graham Greene
Minor, The, S. Foote
Miracle of Purun Bhagat, The, R. Kipling
Miracle of St Jubanus, The, R. Kipling
Mirror Crack'd from Side to Side, The, Agatha Christie
Miser's Daughter, The, W. H. Ainsworth
Miss Bracegirdle and Others, Stacy Aumonier
Miss Bracegirdle does her Duty, Stacy Aumonier
Miss Bunting, Angela Thirkell
Miss Esperance and Mr Wycherley, L. Allen Harker
Miss Gomez and The Brethren, W. Trevor
Miss in her Teens, D. Garrick
Miss Mole, E. H. Young
Miss Pym Disposes, Josephine Tey
Miss Tarrant's Temperament, May Sinclair
Miss Winchelsea's Heart, H. G. Wells
Miss Youghal's Sais, R. Kipling
Mistake of the Machine, The, G. K. Chesterton
Misunderstood, Florence Montgomery
Mixed Marriage, St John Ervine
M'liss, Bret Harte
Moby Dick, H. Melville
Modern Tragedy, A, Phyllis Bentley

Moll Flanders, D. Defoe
Moment of Victory, The, O. Henry
Monastery, The, Sir W. Scott
Money, Phyllis Bentley
Money, Lord Lytton
Monk, The, M. G. Lewis
Monkey's Paw, The, W. W. Jacobs
Monsieur Beaucaire, Booth Tarkington
Moon and Sixpence, The, W. S. Maugham
Moon in the Yellow River, The, D. Johnston
Moon of Other Days, R. Kipling
Moonstone, The, W. Collins
Moorland Cottage, The, Mrs Gaskell
Moral Reformers, The, R. Kipling
Morning Tide, N. M. Gunn
Mortal Coils, A. Huxley
Mortal Storm, The, Phyllis Bottome
Mosaic, G. B. Stern
Mother, A, James Joyce
Mother, The, E. Phillpotts
Mother, The, Katherine Tynan
Mother and Son, Ivy Compton-Burnett
Mother Hive, The, R. Kipling
Moths, Ouida
Moti Guj—Mutineer, R. Kipling
Mourning becomes Electra, E. O'Neill
Mourning Bride, The, W. Congreve
Mouse, The, 'Saki'
Mowgli's Brothers, R. Kipling
Mr and Mrs Monroe, J. Thurber
Mr Billingham, the Marquis and Madelon, E. P. Oppenheim
Mr Bolfry, J. Bridie
Mr Brisher's Treasure, H. G. Wells
Mr Britling Sees It Through, H. G. Wells
Mr Crewe's Career, W. Churchill
Mr Durant, Dorothy Parker
Mr Facey Romford's Hounds, R. S. Surtees
Mr Fortune (series), H. C. Bailey
Mr Fortune Finds a Pig, H. C. Bailey
Mr Fortune's Maggot, Sylvia Townsend Warner
Mr Gilfil's Love Story, George Eliot
Mr H., C. Lamb
Mr Ingleside, E. V. Lucas
Mr Kerrigan and the Tinkers, L. A. G. Strong
Mr Ledbetter's Vacation, H. G. Wells
Mr Midshipman Easy, Captain Marryat
Mr Midshipman Hornblower, C. S. Forester
Mr Norris Changes Trains, C. Isherwood
Mr Perrin and Mr Traill, Hugh Walpole
Mr Pim Passes By, A. A. Milne
Mr Rowl, D. K. Broster
Mr Skelmersdale in Fairyland, H. G. Wells
Mr Sludge the Medium, R. Browning
Mr Sponge's Sporting Tour, R. S. Surtees
Mr Weston's Good Wine, T. F. Powys
Mrs Bathurst, R. Kipling
Mrs Beelbrow's Lions, Stacy Aumonier
Mrs Bradley Detective Stories, The, Gladys Mitchell
Mrs Brown in Paris, A. Sketchley
Mrs Dalloway, Virginia Woolf
Mrs Eckdorf in O'Neill's Hotel, W. Trevor
Mrs Galer's Business, W. Pett Ridge
Mrs Halliburton's Troubles, Mrs Henry Wood
Mrs Lirriper's Lodgings, C. Dickens
Mrs McWilliams and the Lightning, Mark Twain
Mrs Miniver, Jan Struther
Mrs Parkington, L. Bromfield
Mrs Perkins's Ball, W. M. Thackeray
Mrs Sludge, N. Balchin
Mrs Warren's Profession, G. B. Shaw
Mrs Wiggs of the Cabbage Patch, Alice H. Rice
Much Ado About Nothing, W. Shakespeare
Mulholland's Contract, R. Kipling
Municipal Report, A, O. Henry
Murder Must Advertise, Dorothy L. Sayers
Murder on the Links, Agatha Christie
Murders in the Rue Morgue, The, E. A. Poe
Musgrave Ritual, The, A. Conan Doyle
Music, W. de la Mare
Music of Time series, The, A. Powell
Mutiny of the Mavericks, The, R. Kipling
My Adventure in Norfolk, A. J. Alan
My Antonia, Willa Cather
My Aunt Margaret's Mirror, Sir W. Scott
My Brother Jonathan, F. Brett Young
My Cousin Rachel, Daphne du Maurier
My Lady Nicotine, J. M. Barrie
My Lord the Elephant, R. Kipling
My Mortal Enemy, Willa Cather

N

O

Of Time and the River, T. Wolfe
Oh Whistle and I'll Come to You, my Lad, M. R. James
Ohio Pagan, An, Sherwood Anderson
Old Ancient Ship, The, Morley Roberts
Old Audrey's Experience, T. Hardy
Old Bachelor, The, W. Congreve
Old Bank, The, W. Westall
Old Boys, The, W. Trevor
Old Creole Days, G. W. Cable
Old Curiosity Shop, The, C. Dickens
Old Dominion, The, Mary Johnston
Old Helmet, The, Elizabeth Wetherell
Old Lady Shows Her Medals, The, J. M. Barrie
Old Man and the Sea, The, E. Hemingway
Old Men at Pevensey, R. Kipling
Old Mortality, Sir W. Scott
Old Patch's Medley, Marjorie Bowen
Old Possum's Book of Practical Cats, T. S. Eliot
Old St Paul's, W. H. Ainsworth
Old Times, H. Pinter
Old Wives' Tale, The, Arnold Bennett
Oliver Twist, C. Dickens
O'Malley Comes Home, An, Katherine Tynan
On Approval, F. Lonsdale
On Greenhow Hill, R. Kipling
On Patrol, M. Armstrong
On the City Wall, R. Kipling
On the Face of the Waters, Flora A. Steel
On the Great Wall, R. Kipling
On the Irrawaddy, G. A. Henty
On the Spot, E. Wallace
On the Strength of a Likeness, R. Kipling
On the Western Circuit, T. Hardy
Once Aboard the Lugger, A. S. M. Hutchinson
One and Only Spink, The, Morley Roberts
One Before, The, Barry Pain
One Day in the Shires, G. Frankau
One Dollar's Worth, O. Henry
One Hundred Dollar Bill, The, Booth Tarkington
One of the Missing, A. Bierce
One Thousand Dollars, O. Henry
One View of the Question, R. Kipling
Onion Eaters, The, J. P. Donleavy
Only a Subaltern, R. Kipling
Open Window, The, 'Saki'
Options, O. Henry
Ordeal of Gilbert Pinfold, The, E. Waugh
Ordeal of Richard Feverel, The, G. Meredith
Orford Mystery, The, Marjorie Bowen
Oriel Window, The, Mrs Molesworth
Orlando, Virginia Woolf
Oroonoko, Mrs Aphra Behn
Orphan, The, T. Otway
Osbornes, The, E. F. Benson
Othello, W. Shakespeare
Other Gods, Pearl Buck
Other Man, The, R. Kipling
Other Side, The, Storm Jameson
Other Voices, Other Rooms, Truman Capote
Our Betters, W. S. Maugham
Our Mutual Friend, C. Dickens
Our Street, W. M. Thackeray
Our Town, T. Wilder
Outcast of the Islands, An, J. Conrad
Outcasts of Poker Flat, Bret Harte
Outward Bound, S. Vane
Over Bemerton's, E. V. Lucas
Over the River, J. Galsworthy
Owl in the Attic, The, J. Thurber
Owney, Katherine Tynan
Ox-Bow Incident, The, Walter Van Tilburg Clark

P

Pagett, M.P., R. Kipling
Painful Case, A, James Joyce
Pair of Blue Eyes, A, T. Hardy
Pale Fire, Vladimir Nabokov
Pamela, S. Richardson
Pandosto, Robert Greene
Paolo and Francesca, S. Phillips
Paradise Lost, J. Milton
Paradise of Thieves, The, G. K. Chesterton
Parasite, The, M. Armstrong
Parasite, The, A. Conan Doyle
Paris Sketch Book, W. M. Thackeray
Parliament of Bees, J. Day
Passage to India, A, E. M. Forster
Passing of Arthur, The, Lord Tennyson

Passing of Black Eagle, The, O. Henry
Passing of the Third Floor Back, The, J. K. Jerome
Passionate Friends, The, H. G. Wells
Pastors and Masters, Ivy Compton-Burnett
Pastyme of Pleasure, The, S. Hawes
Pathfinder, The, J. Fenimore Cooper
Patience, N. Balchin
Patience, Gilbert & Sullivan
Patrician, The, J. Galsworthy
Patriots, The, James Barlow
Paul Clifford, Lord Lytton
Pavilion on the Links, The, R. L. Stevenson
Peasant's Confession, The, T. Hardy
Peg Woffington, C. Reade
Pelleas and Ettarre, Lord Tennyson
Pendennis, W. M. Thackeray
Pending Heaven, W. Gerhardie
Penniless Millionaire, A, D. Christie Murray
Penny Plain, O. Douglas
Percy's Reliques, Bishop Thomas Percy
Peregrine Pickle, T. Smollett
Perennial Bachelor, The, Anne Parrish
Pericles, W. Shakespeare
Perishing of the Pendragons, The, G. K. Chesterton
Perkin Warbeck, John Ford
Persuasion, Jane Austen
Peter Bell, W. Wordsworth
Peter Jackson, Cigar Merchant, G. Frankau
Peter Pan, J. M. Barrie
Peter Simple, Captain Marryat
Peter the Wag, W. S. Gilbert
Peveril of the Peak, Sir W. Scott
Phantom Rickshaw, The, R. Kipling
Phantom Ship, The, Captain Marryat
Philanderer, The, G. B. Shaw
Philaster, Beaumont & Fletcher
Philip van Artevelde, H. Taylor
Phillada Flouts Me, Anon.
Phineas Finn, A. Trollope
Phoenix too Frequent, A, Christopher Fry
Phra the Phoenician, E. Lester Arnold
Phroso, A. Hope
Pickwick Papers, C. Dickens
Picture of Dorian Gray, The, O. Wilde
Pie and the Patty Pan, The, Beatrix Potter
Pied Piper, The, N. Shute
Pierre, H. Melville
Piffingcap, A. E. Coppard
Pig, R. Kipling
Pig and Whistle, The, G. Gissing
Pilgrim's Progress, J. Bunyan
Pilgrimage, Dorothy M. Richardson
Pink Sugar, O. Douglas
Pip, Ian Hay
Pippa Passes, R. Browning
Pirate, The, Sir W. Scott
Pirate of the Land, A, A. Conan Doyle
Pirates of Penzance, The, Gilbert & Sullivan
Pit, The, F. Norris
Pizarro, R. B. Sheridan
Plain Dealer, The, W. Wycherley
Plain Language from Truthful James, Bret Harte
Plain Tales from the Hills, R. Kipling
Plattner Story, The, H. G. Wells
Playboy of the Western World, The, J. M. Synge
Pledge, The, Helen Simpson
Plough and the Stars, The, S. O'Casey
Plumed Serpent, The, D. H. Lawrence
Poacher, The, H. E. Bates
Poet's Pub, E. Linklater
Point Counter Point, A. Huxley
Poison Belt, The, A. Conan Doyle
Poison Ivy, P. Cheyney
Police at the Funeral, Margery Allingham
Pollock and the Porrah Man, H. G. Wells
Polly, J. Gay
Pollyanna, Eleanor H. Porter
Polyglots, The, W. Gerhardie
Pomp of the Lavilettes, The, Gilbert Parker
Ponder Heart, The, Eudora Welty
Poor Gentleman, The, G. Colman the Younger
Poor White, Sherwood Anderson
Poor Women, Norah Hoult
Poorhouse Fair, The, J. Updike
Porch, The, R. Church
Porgy, Du Bose Heyward
Porphyria's Lover, R. Browning
Portnoy's Complaint, P. Roth
Portrait of a Gentleman, M. Arlen
Portrait of a Lady, The, H. James
Portrait of a Playboy, W. Deeping
Portrait of Clare, F. Brett Young
Post that Fitted, The, R. Kipling
Postman Always Rings Twice, The, James M. Cain
Postmistress of Laurel Run, The, Bret Harte
Potterism, Rose Macaulay
Pottleton Legacy, The, Albert Smith
Power and the Glory, The, Graham Greene

Power House, The, J. Buchan
Practical Joker, The, Dorothy L. Sayers
Prairie Folk, H. Garland
Prancing Nigger, R. Firbank
Precious Bane, Mary Webb
Prelude, Katherine Mansfield
Prescription, The, Marjorie Bowen
Prester John, J. Buchan
Pretty Lady, The, Arnold Bennett
Price of the Grindstone and the Drum, The, Gilbert Parker
Pride and Prejudice, Jane Austen
Pride of Heroes, A, P. Dickinson
Pride of Jennico, The, A. & E. Castle
Prime of Miss Jean Brodie, The, Muriel Spark
Prince and the Pauper, The, Mark Twain
Prince Otto, R. L. Stevenson
Princess, The, Lord Tennyson
Princess Ida, Gilbert & Sullivan
Princess of Kingdom Gone, The, A. E. Coppard
Priscilla's Fortnight, Countess von Arnim
Prisoner of Grace, Joyce Cary
Prisoner of Zenda, The, A. Hope
Private Learoyd's Story, R. Kipling
Private Life of Henry Maitland, The, Morley Roberts
Private Life of Mr Bidwell, The, J. Thurber
Private Lives, N. Coward
Private Wound, The, Nicholas Blake
Prodigal Heart, The, Susan Ertz
Professor, The, Charlotte Brontë
Professor, The, W. M. Thackeray
Professor in the Case, The, J. Futrelle
Professor's Love Story, The, J. M. Barrie
Progress of Private Lilyworth, The, Russell Braddon
Promise of May, The, Lord Tennyson
Propagation of Knowledge, The, R. Kipling
Prophet and the Country, The, R. Kipling
Protégé, The, W. B. Maxwell
Proud Maisie, Sir W. Scott
Providence and the Guitar, R. L. Stevenson
Provok'd Husband, The, J. Vanbrugh & C. Cibber
Provok'd Wife, The, J. Vanbrugh
Provost, The, J. Galt
Psychical Invasion, A, A. Blackwood
Public Waste, R. Kipling
Puck of Pook's Hill, R. Kipling
Purple Dust, S. O'Casey
Purple Land, The, W. H. Hudson
Purple Plain, The, H. E. Bates
Purple Wig, The, G. K. Chesterton
Pursuit of Love, The, Nancy Mitford
Put Out More Flags, E. Waugh
Put Yourself in his Place, C. Reade
Puzzler, The, R. Kipling
Pygmalion, G. B. Shaw

Q

Quality Folk, Irvin S. Cobb
Quality Street, J. M. Barrie
Queechy, Elizabeth Wetherell
Queen Lucia, E. F. Benson
Queen was in the Parlour, The, N. Coward
Queen's Husband, The, R. E. Sherwood
Quentin Durward, Sir W. Scott
Quest, The, 'Saki'
Quest of the Golden Girl, The, R. Le Gallienne
Question of Upbringing, A, A. Powell
Question to Lisetta, The, M. Prior
Quiet American, The, Graham Greene
Quiet Woman, The, A. E. Coppard
Quinneys', H. A. Vachell
Quiquern, R. Kipling

R

Rabbit, Run, J. Updike
Radcliffe, D. Storey
Raffles, E. W. Hornung
Raiders, The, S. R. Crockett
Rainbow, The, D. H. Lawrence
Raising the Wind, J. Kenney

Rajah's Diamond, The, R. L. Stevenson
Ralph Roister Doister, N. Udall
Rambles of a Rat, A.L.O.E.
Random Harvest, J. Hilton
Ransom of Red Chief, The, O. Henry
Rape of the Lock, The, A. Pope
Rappaccini's Daughter, N. Hawthorne
Rash Bride, The, T. Hardy
Ravenshoe, H. Kingsley
Ravenswing, The, W. M. Thackeray
Rebecca, Daphne du Maurier
Rebecca of Sunnybrook Farm, Kate D. Wiggin
Record of Badalia Herodsfoot, The, R. Kipling
Recruiting Officer, The, G. Farquhar
Red Badge of Courage, The, Stephen Crane
Red Circle, The, A. Conan Doyle
Red Dog, R. Kipling
Red House Mystery, The, A. A. Milne
Red Peppers, N. Coward
Redburn, H. Melville
Redgauntlet, Sir W. Scott
Red-headed League, The, A. Conan Doyle
Reflections in a Golden Eye, Carson McCullers
Reginald Cruden, T. Baines Reed
Regulus, R. Kipling
Rehearsal, The, George, Duke of Buckingham
Reingelder and the German Flag, R. Kipling
Relapse, The, J. Vanbrugh
Relative Values, N. Coward
Requiem for a Nun, W. Faulkner
Requiem for Robert, Mary Fitt
Research Magnificent, The, H. G. Wells
Rescue of Pluffles, The, R. Kipling
Resident Patient, The, A. Conan Doyle
Restoration of Arnold Middleton, The, D. Storey
Return, The, W. de la Mare
Return of Imray, The, R. Kipling
Return of Sherlock Holmes, The, A. Conan Doyle
Return of the Native, The, T. Hardy
Return of the Soldier, The, Rebecca West
Rev. Amos Barton, The, George Eliot
Revenge upon Revenge, Phyllis Bentley
Revisitation, The, T. Hardy
Rewards and Fairies, R. Kipling
Rhoda Fleming, G. Meredith
Rhyme of the Three Sealers, The, R. Kipling
Rice Pudding, A. A. Milne
Riceyman Steps, Arnold Bennett
Rich Man, Poor Man, I. Shaw
Rich Pay Late, The, S. Raven
Richard Carvel, W. Churchill
Richard the Second, W. Shakespeare
Richard the Third, W. Shakespeare
Richelieu, Lord Lytton
Riddle, The, W. de la Mare
Riddle of the Sands, The, E. Childers
Riders in the Chariot, P. White
Riders of the Purple Sage, Zane Grey
Right off the Map, C. E. Montague
Right Royal, J. Masefield
Rikki Tikki Tavi, R. Kipling
Ring and the Book, The, R. Browning
Ringer, The, E. Wallace
Rip Van Winkle, W. Irving
Rise of Silas Lapham, The, W. D. Howells
Rival Curates, The, W. S. Gilbert
Rivals, The, R. B. Sheridan
Roads of Destiny, O. Henry
Roaring Girle, The, T. Dekker & T. Middleton
Rob Roy, Sir W. Scott
Robbery under Arms, R. Boldrewood
Robert's Wife, St John Ervine
Robinson Crusoe, D. Defoe
Rocking Horse Winner, The, D. H. Lawrence
Roderick Hudson, H. James
Roderick Random, T. Smollett
Rodney Fails to Qualify, P. G. Wodehouse
Rodney Stone, A. Conan Doyle
Rogue Herries, Hugh Walpole
Roland Cashel, C. Lever
Rolling Stones, O. Henry
Roman Spring of Mrs Stone, The, Tennessee Williams
Romance, E. Sheldon
Romancers, The, 'Saki'
Romantic Age, The, A. A. Milne
Romany Rye, George Borrow
Romeo and Juliet, W. Shakespeare
Romola, George Eliot
Room at the Top, J. Braine
Room with a View, A, E. M. Forster
Roots, Naomi Jacob
Rosalind, J. M. Barrie
Rosary, The, Florence Barclay
Rose and the Ring, The, W. M. Thackeray

Rose Aylmer, W. S. Landor
Rose of Dixie, The, O. Henry
Rose of Tibet, The, Lionel Davidson
Rough-hew them how we Will, P. G. Wodehouse
Round the Red Lamp, A. Conan Doyle
Rout of the White Hussars, The, R. Kipling
Rovers, The, G. Canning
Rubaiyat of a Scotch Highball, The, O. Henry
Ruddigore, Gilbert & Sullivan
Rupert of Hentzau, A. Hope
Rus in Urbe, O. Henry

S

Sacrifice of Er-Heb, The, R. Kipling
Sad Horn Blowers, The, Sherwood Anderson
Safety Match, A, Ian Hay
Sahib's War, A, R. Kipling
Said the Fisherman, M. Pickthall
Sailor's Return, The, D. Garnett
St Bride of the Isles, Fiona Macleod
St Clement's Eve, H. Taylor
Saint in New York, The, L. Charteris
St Ives, R. L. Stevenson
Saint Joan, G. B. Shaw
St Leon, W. Godwin
St Mawr, D. H. Lawrence
St Patrick's Day, R. B. Sheridan
St Ronan's Well, Sir W. Scott
St Winifred's, F. W. Farrar
Saint's Day, J. Whiting
Saint's Tragedy, The, C. Kingsley
Salad of Colonel Cray, The, G. K. Chesterton
Saliva Tree, The, Brian W. Aldiss
Sally in our Alley, H. Carey
Salute the Cavalier, M. Arlen
Samela, Robert Greene
Sampson Rideout, Quaker, Una Silberrad
Sanctuary, W. Faulkner
Sanders of the River, E. Wallace
Sandford and Merton, T. Day
Sardanapalus, Lord Byron
Sartoris, W. Faulkner
Satiromastix, T. Dekker
Saving Grace, The, C. Haddon Chambers
Savoir Faire, W. Pett Ridge
Savonarola Brown, Max Beerbohm
Scandal in Bohemia, A, A. Conan Doyle
Scaramouche, R. Sabatini
Scarlet Letter, The, N. Hawthorne
Scarlet Pimpernel, The, Baroness Orczy
Scenes of Clerical Life, George Eliot
School for Scandal, The, R. B. Sheridan
Schools and Schools, O. Henry
Scots Quair, A, Lewis Grassic Gibbon
Sea Constables, R. Kipling
Sea Lady, The, H. G. Wells
Sea View, M. Armstrong
Sea Wolf, The, Jack London
Search Party, The, G. A. Birmingham
Seasons, The, J. Thomson
Seaton's Aunt, W. de la Mare
Second Confession, The, R. Stout
Second Jungle Book, The, R. Kipling
Second Mrs Conford, The, Beatrice K. Seymour
Second Mrs Tanqueray, The, A. W. Pinero
Second Nun's Tale, The, G. Chaucer
Second-rate Woman, A, R. Kipling
Second Stain, The, A. Conan Doyle
Secret Agent, The, J. Conrad
Secret Garden, The, G. K. Chesterton
Secret Life of Walter Mitty, The, J. Thurber
Secret Places of the Heart, The, H. G. Wells
Secret Vanguard, The, M. Innes
Secret Worship, A. Blackwood
Secrets, R. Besier & May Edginton
See Naples and Die, Elmer Rice
Select Conversations with an Uncle, H. G. Wells
Self-Control, Mrs Brunton
Sending of Dana Da, The, R. Kipling
Sense and Sensibility, Jane Austen
Sentimental Tommy, J. M. Barrie
Separate Tables, T. Rattigan
September Tide, Daphne du Maurier
Setons, The, O. Douglas
Settlers in Canada, Captain Marryat
Seven Cream Jugs, The, 'Saki'
Seven Men, Max Beerbohm
Seven Poor Travellers, C. Dickens
Seven Seas, The, R. Kipling

Seven Who Fled, The, F. Prokosch
Severed Head, A, Iris Murdoch
Shabby Genteel Story, A, W. M. Thackeray
Shabby Tiger, H. Spring
Shadow of the Glen, J. M. Synge
Shadows on the Rock, Willa Cather
Shall We Join the Ladies?, J. M. Barrie
Shameless Behaviour of a Lord, M. Arlen
Shanghaied, F. Norris
Shaving of Shagpat, The, G. Meredith
She, H. Rider Haggard
She Stoops to Conquer, O. Goldsmith
She Wolf, The, 'Saki'
Shepherd of the Hills, The, H. B. Wright
Shillin' a Day, R. Kipling
Shining and Free, G. B. Stern
Ship, The, C. S. Forester
Ship of Fools, Katherine Anne Porter
Ship that Found Herself, The, R. Kipling
Ships that Pass in the Night, Beatrice Harraden
Shirley, Charlotte Brontë
Shoelace, The, L. Merrick
Shoemaker's Holiday, The, T. Dekker
Short Sixes, H. C. Bunner
Show Boat, Edna Ferber
Shrimp and the Anemone, The, L. P. Hartley
Shulamite, The, A. & C. Askew
Sic a Wife as Willie Had, R. Burns
Siege of Corinth, The, Lord Byron
Sign of Four, The, A. Conan Doyle
Sign of the Broken Sword, The, G. K. Chesterton
Sign of the Cross, The, W. Barrett
Silas Marner, George Eliot
Silence of History, The, James T. Farrell
Silver Blaze, A. Conan Doyle
Silver King, The, H. A. Jones
Silver Spoon, The, J. Galsworthy
Silver Trumpets, Viola Meynell
Simon Dale, A. Hope
Simple Simon, R. Kipling
Simpson, E. Sackville-West
Sin of David, The, S. Phillips
Singing Lesson, The, Katherine Mansfield
Sing-song of Old Man Kangaroo, The, R. Kipling
Singular Man, A, J. P. Donleavy
Sinister Street, Compton Mackenzie
Sins of Prince Saradine, The, G. K. Chesterton
Sir Agravaine, P. G. Wodehouse
Sir Aldingar, Bishop Thomas Percy
Sir Charles Grandison, S. Richardson
Sir Lancelot Greaves, T. Smollett
Sir Nigel, A. Conan Doyle
Sir Patient Fancy, Mrs Aphra Behn
Sir Pompey and Madame Juno, M. Armstrong
Sire de Malétroit's Door, The, R. L. Stevenson
Sirena, M. Drayton
Sister Carrie, T. Dreiser
Sister for Susan, A, Dale Collins
Sisters, The, James Joyce
Sixty-four, Ninety-four, R. H. Mottram
Sketch Book, The, W. Irving
Sketches and Travels, W. M. Thackeray
Sketches by Boz, C. Dickens
Sketches of Young Gentlemen, C. Dickens
Skin Game, The, J. Galsworthy
Skin of Our Teeth, The, T. Wilder
Skipper's Wooing, The, W. W. Jacobs
Sky Pilot, The, R. Connor
Slaves of the Lamp, R. Kipling
Sleep of Prisoners, A, Christopher Fry
Sleepless Moon, The, H. E. Bates
Small Back Room, The, N. Balchin
Small Miracle, The, P. Gallico
Smile of Karen, The, O. Onions
Smith's Gazelle, Lionel Davidson
Snarleyow, R. Kipling
Snopes trilogy, The, W. Faulkner
Snow Goose, The, P. Gallico
So Big, Edna Ferber
Society upon the Stanislaus, The, Bret Harte
Sohrab and Rustum, M. Arnold
Soldier's Fortune, The, T. Otway
Soldier's Song, The, L. A. G. Strong
Soldiers of Fortune, R. H. Davis
Soldiers Three, R. Kipling
Solid Muldoon, The, R. Kipling
Solitary Cyclist, The, A. Conan Doyle
Some Experiences of an Irish R.M., Œ. Somerville & Martin Ross
Some Notes on Cyrus Verd, Barry Pain
Something to Worry About, P. G. Wodehouse
Son's Veto, The, T. Hardy
Song of Diego Valdez, The, R. Kipling
Song of Hiawatha, The, H. W. Longfellow
Song of the Lark, The, Willa Cather
Sonia, S. McKenna
Sons and Lovers, D. H. Lawrence

Sons of Fire, Mary E. Braddon
Sophia, S. Weyman
Sorcerer, The, Gilbert & Sullivan
Sorrell and Son, W. Deeping
Sorrows of Satan, The, Marie Corelli
Sort of Traitors, A, N. Balchin
Soul of a Bishop, The, H. G. Wells
Sound and the Fury, The, W. Faulkner
South Riding, Winifred Holtby
South Wind, N. Douglas
Sowers, The, H. Seton Merriman
Spanish Farm trilogy, The, R. H. Mottram
Spanish Gypsy, The, George Eliot
Spanish Student, The, H. W. Longfellow
Spanish Tragedy, The, T. Kyd
Spears Against Us, Cecil Roberts
Speckled Band, The, A. Conan Doyle
Spectator (Essays in), The, J. Addison
Spectre of Tappington, The, R. H. Barham
Speed the Plough, T. Morton
Sphinx without a Secret, The, O. Wilde
Spiritual Tales, Fiona Macleod
Splendid Spur, The, Sir A. Quiller-Couch
Sport of Kings, The, Ian Hay
Spring Cleaning, F. Lonsdale
Stalky and Co., R. Kipling
Starvecrow Farm, S. Weyman
Steam Tactics, R. Kipling
Steamboat Gothic, Frances Parkinson Keyes
Still She Wished for Company, Margaret Irwin
Stockbroker's Clerk, The, A. Conan Doyle
Stoic, A, J. Galsworthy
Stolen White Elephant, The, Mark Twain
Stone Angel, The, Margaret Laurence
Story of a Short Life, The, Juliana H. Ewing
Story of an African Farm, The, Olive Schreiner
Story of Ivy, The, Mrs Belloc Lowndes
Story of Muhammed Din, The, R. Kipling
Story of Ragged Robyn, The, O. Onions
Story of Rosina, The, A. Dobson
Story of the Days to Come, H. G. Wells
Story of the Gadsbys, The, R. Kipling
Story of the Stone Age, H. G. Wells
Story of the Unkind King, The, Philip Sidney
Story of Ung, The, R. Kipling
Story of Uriah, The, R. Kipling
Story That Ends With A Scream, A, James Leo Herlihy
Straggler of '15, A, A. Conan Doyle
Strange Adventures of a Phaeton, The, W. Black
Strange Interlude, E. O'Neill
Strange Ride of Morrowbie Jukes, The, R. Kipling
Stranger, The, Katherine Mansfield
Strangers and Brothers sequence, C. P. Snow
Street of Adventure, The, P. Gibbs
Streetcar Named Desire, A, Tennessee Williams
Strictly Business, O. Henry
Strike the Father Dead, J. Wain
Striped Chest, The, A. Conan Doyle
Stroke of Business, A, L. A. G. Strong
Strong Poison, Dorothy L. Sayers
Stronghold, The, R. Church
Studs Lonigan trilogy, James T. Farrell
Study in Scarlet, A, A. Conan Doyle
Study of an Elevation in Indian Ink, R. Kipling
Subaltern's Love Song, A, J. Betjeman
Suicide Club, The, R. L. Stevenson
Summer Half, Angela Thirkell
Summer Moonshine, P. G. Wodehouse
Summer Will Show, Sylvia Townsend Warner
Sun Also Rises, The, E. Hemingway
Sun on the Water, L. A. G. Strong
Sunrise in the West, Bechofer Roberts
Superstitious Man's Story, The, T. Hardy
Surfeit of Lampreys, Ngaio Marsh
Surgeon's Daughter, The, Sir W. Scott
Suspension of Mercy, A, Patricia Highsmith
Swallows and Amazons, A. Ransome
Swan Song, J. Galsworthy
Sweet Bird of Youth, Tennessee Williams
Sweet Lavender, A. W. Pinero
Swept and Garnished, R. Kipling
Sybil, B. Disraeli
Sylvia Scarlett, Compton Mackenzie
Sylvia's Lovers, Mrs Gaskell

T

Tailor of Gloucester, The, Beatrix Potter
Taking of Lungtungpen, The, R. Kipling
Tale of a Trumpet, The, T. Hood
Tale of Benjamin Bunny, The, Beatrix Potter
Tale of Jemima Puddleduck, The, Beatrix Potter
Tale of Jeremy Fisher, The, Beatrix Potter
Tale of Meliboeus, The, G. Chaucer
Tale of Mrs Tiggy-Winkle, The, Beatrix Potter
Tale of Mrs Tittlemouse, The, Beatrix Potter
Tale of Peter Rabbit, The, Beatrix Potter
Tale of Pigling Bland, The, Beatrix Potter
Tale of Samuel Whiskers, The, Beatrix Potter
Tale of Sir Thopas, The, G. Chaucer
Tale of Squirrel Nutkin, The, Beatrix Potter
Tale of the Flopsy Bunnies, The, Beatrix Potter
Tale of the Ragged Mountains, A, E. A. Poe
Tale of Tom Kitten, The, Beatrix Potter
Tale of Two Bad Mice, The, Beatrix Potter
Tale of Two Cities, A, C. Dickens
Talent Thou Gavest, The, Caradoc Evans
Tales of Life and Adventure, H. G. Wells
Tales of my Landlord, Sir W. Scott
Tales of Pirates and Blue Water, A. Conan Doyle
Tales of Space and Time, H. G. Wells
Tales of the Unexpected, H. G. Wells
Talisman, The, Sir W. Scott
Talking Trees, The, Sean O'Faolain
Tam o' Shanter, R. Burns
Tamburlaine, C. Marlowe
Tamerlane, N. Rowe
Taming of the Shrew, The, W. Shakespeare
Tancred, B. Disraeli
Tapestried Chamber, The, Sir W. Scott
Tarantella, H. Belloc
Tarka the Otter, H. Williamson
Tarr, Wyndham Lewis
Tarzan series, E. R. Burroughs
Tea at Mrs Armsby's, J. Thurber
Teigne, Helen Simpson
Telemachus, Friend, O. Henry
Tell England, E. Raymond
Tell Me How Long The Train's Been Gone, James Baldwin
Tempest, The, W. Shakespeare
Ten Minute Alibi, A. Armstrong
Ten North Frederick, John O'Hara
Ten Thousand a Year, S. Warren
Tenant of Wildfell Hall, The, Anne Brontë
Tender Achilles, R. Kipling
Tender is the Night, F. Scott Fitzgerald
Tents of Israel, G. B. Stern
Term of Trial, James Barlow
Tess of the D'Urbervilles, T. Hardy
Tex of Bar-20, C. E. Mulford
Thank Heaven Fasting, E. M. Delafield
Thank You, Jeeves, P. G. Wodehouse
That Uncertain Feeling, K. Amis
Their Lawful Occasions, R. Kipling
Theophrastus Such, George Eliot
There Were No Windows, Norah Hoult
These Charming People, M. Arlen
These Twain, Arnold Bennett
They, R. Kipling
They Wanted to Live, Cecil Roberts
They Winter Abroad, T. H. White
Thin Air, J. Pudney
Thin Man, The, D. Hammett
Thing in the Hall, The, E. F. Benson
Things which Belong, The, Constance Holme
Thinking Reed, The, Rebecca West
Third Ingredient, The, O. Henry
Thirty-nine Steps, The, J. Buchan
This Side of Paradise, F. Scott Fitzgerald
This Sporting Life, D. Storey
Thomas Winterbottom Hance, W. S. Gilbert
Those Barren Leaves, A. Huxley
Thou Art the Man, E. A. Poe
Thrawn Janet, R. L. Stevenson
Three and an Extra, R. Kipling
Three from Dunsterville, P. G. Wodehouse

Three Ladies, N. Balchin
Three Men in a Boat, J. K. Jerome
Three Musketeers, The, R. Kipling
Three Soldiers, J. dos Passos
Three Strangers, The, T. Hardy
Three Taps, The, R. A. Knox
Three Weeks, Elinor Glyn
Through a Window, H. G. Wells
Through One Administration, Frances H. Burnett
Through the Fire, R. Kipling
Through the Storm, P. Gibbs
Thrown Away, R. Kipling
Thunder on the Left, C. Morley
Thunderball, I. Fleming
Thunders of Silence, The, Irvin S. Cobb
Thursday Afternoons, Monica Dickens
Tie, The, R. Kipling
Tiger Tiger, R. Kipling
Tiger's Skin, A, W. W. Jacobs
Tillotson Banquet, The, A. Huxley
Time, Gentlemen! Time!, Norah Hoult
Time Machine, The, H. G. Wells
Time of Hope, C. P. Snow
Time Will Knit, F. Urquhart
Time's Laughing Stocks, T. Hardy
Timon of Athens, W. Shakespeare
Timothy's Quest, Kate D. Wiggin
Tinfield Mascot, The, N. Balchin
Tinker's Wedding, The, J. M. Synge
'Tis Pity She's a Whore, John Ford
'Tite Poulette, G. W. Cable
Title, The, Arnold Bennett
Titus Andronicus, W. Shakespeare
To Amarantha, R. Lovelace
To Anthea, R. Herrick
To Be A Pilgrim, Joyce Cary
To be Filed for Reference, R. Kipling
To Clarinda, R. Burns
To Have the Honour, A. A. Milne
To Please his Wife, T. Hardy
To the Lighthouse, Virginia Woolf
Tobacco Road, E. Caldwell
Tobermory, 'Saki'
Tobit Transplanted, Stella Benson
Tod's Amendment, R. Kipling
Toff series, The, John Creasey
Told by an Idiot, Rose Macaulay
Tom Bowling, C. Dibdin
Tom Brown's Schooldays, T. Hughes
Tom Burke of Ours, C. Lever
Tom Cringle's Log, M. Scott
Tom Fool, F. Tennyson Jesse
Tom Jones, H. Fielding
Tom Sawyer. *See* Adventures of Tom Sawyer, The
Tom Tiddler's Ground, C. Dickens
Tom Tiddler's Ground, E. Shanks
Tom Varnish, R. Steele
Tomb of his Ancestors, The, R. Kipling
Tomlinson, R. Kipling
Tomorrow To Fresh Woods, Rhys Davies
Tono Bungay, H. G. Wells
Tony Kytes, the Arch-Deceiver, T. Hardy
Too Bad, Dorothy Parker
Toomai of the Elephants, R. Kipling
Top of the Stairs, The, T. Burke
Torrents of Spring, The, E. Hemingway
Tower of London, The, W. H. Ainsworth
Towers of Trebizond, The, Rose Macaulay
Town Like Alice, A, N. Shute
Town Traveller, The, G. Gissing
Tracy's Tiger, W. Saroyan
Tradition of 1804, The, T. Hardy
Traffics and Discoveries, R. Kipling
Tragedy of the Korosko, The, A. Conan Doyle
Tragedy of the Till, The, D. Jerrold
Tragedy of Two Ambitions, A, T. Hardy
Travelling Grave, The, L. P. Hartley
Travelling Woman, A, J. Wain
Treasure and the Law, The, R. Kipling
Treasure Island, R. L. Stevenson
Treasure of Abbot Thomas, The, M. R. James
Treasure of Franchard, The, R. L. Stevenson
Treasure Seekers, The, E. Nesbit
Treaty of Peace, A, Gilbert Parker
Tree of Man, The, P. White
Trelawny of the Wells, A. W. Pinero
Trembling of a Leaf, The, W. S. Maugham
Tremor of Forgery, The, Patricia Highsmith
Trent's Last Case, E. C. Bentley
Trial, The, Charlotte M. Yonge
Trial by Terror, P. Gallico
Trilby, George du Maurier
Trimmed Lamp, The, O. Henry
Trip to Scarborough, A, R. B. Sheridan
Tristram Shandy, L. Sterne
Troilus and Cressida, W. Shakespeare
Troubled Air, The, I. Shaw
Truce of the Bear, The, R. Kipling
True Blue, W. H. G. Kingston
Trumpet Major, The, T. Hardy

Trumpeter, Sound!, D. L. Murray
Truth, The, C. Fitch
Truth about Blayds, The, A. A. Milne
Tunnying of Elynour Rummyng, The, John Skelton
Turkish Mahomet, The, G. Peele
Turn of the Screw, The, H. James
Twelfth Night, W. Shakespeare
Twelve Horses and the Hangman's Noose, Gladys Mitchell
Twelve Pound Look, The, J. M. Barrie
Twelve Stories and a Dream, H. G. Wells
Two Drovers, The, Sir W. Scott
Two Gallants, James Joyce
Two Gentlemen of Verona, W. Shakespeare
Two on a Tower, T. Hardy
Two or Three Witnesses, C. E. Montague
Two Years Ago, C. Kingsley
Typhoon, J. Conrad
Tyrant and a Lady, A, Gilbert Parker

U

Ukridge, P. G. Wodehouse
Ulysses, James Joyce
Unbearable Bassington, The, 'Saki'
Uncle Bernac, A. Conan Doyle
Uncle Meleager's Will, Dorothy L. Sayers
Uncle Remus, J. C. Harris
Uncle Silas, Sheridan Le Fanu
Uncle Tom's Cabin, Harriet B. Stowe
Uncommercial Traveller, The, C. Dickens
Under Milk Wood, Dylan Thomas
Under the Greenwood Tree, T. Hardy
Under the Red Robe, S. Weyman
Under the Volcano, Malcolm Lowry
Under Two Flags, Ouida
Under Western Eyes, J. Conrad
Undertakers, The, R. Kipling
Undying Fire, The, H. G. Wells
Unending Crusade, R. E. Sherwood
Ungava, R. M. Ballantyne
United Idolators, The, R. Kipling
Unprofessional, R. Kipling
Unrest Cure, The, 'Saki'
Unsavoury Interlude, The, R. Kipling
Unseen Power, The, Barry Pain
Unspeakable Skipton, The, Pamela Hansford Johnson
Untilled Field, The, G. Moore
Unvanquished, The, W. Faulkner
U.S.A. trilogy, J. dos Passos
Utility Baby, Dale Collins
Utopia, Sir Thomas More

V

Valentine Vox, H. Cockton
Valmouth, R. Firbank
Vanessa, Hugh Walpole
Vanity and some Sables, O. Henry
Vanity Fair, W. M. Thackeray
Vathek, W. Beckford
Vengeance of Monsieur Dutripon, The, L. Merrick
Venice Preserved, T. Otway
Venus Annodomini, R. Kipling
Vicar of Wakefield, The, O. Goldsmith
Vice Versa, F. Anstey
Victim, The, Saul Bellow
Victory, J. Conrad
Vile Bodies, E. Waugh
Villa Désirée, The, May Sinclair
Village that Voted the Earth was Flat, The, R. Kipling
Villette, Charlotte Brontë
Violent Bear It Away, The, Flannery O'Connor
Viper of Milan, The, Marjorie Bowen
Virgin and the Gipsy, The, D. H. Lawrence
Virginian, The, O. Wister
Virginians, The, W. M. Thackeray
Vivian Grey, B. Disraeli
Vivisector, The, P. White
Voice from the Minaret, The, R. S. Hichens
Voice of the City, The, O. Henry
Voice of the Turtle, The, J. van Druten

Volpone, or the Fox, B. Jonson
Vortex, The, N. Coward
Vortex, The, R. Kipling
Voss, P. White
Voyage to Purilia, A, Elmer Rice
Vultures, The, H. Seton Merriman

W

Waiting for Godot, S. Beckett
Wakefield's Course, Mazo de la Roche
Walking Delegate, A, R. Kipling
Wallet of Kai Lung, The, E. Bramah
Wan Lee the Pagan, Bret Harte
Wanderer, The, Fanny Burney
Wandering Jew, The, R. Kipling
Wandering Stars, Clemence Dane
Wapshot Chronicle, The, J. Cheever
Wapshot Scandal, The, J. Cheever
War in the Air, H. G. Wells
War of the Worlds, The, H. G. Wells
Ward of the Golden Gate, A, Bret Harte
Warden, The, A. Trollope
Washington Square, H. James
Waste, H. Granville-Barker
Watches of the Night, R. Kipling
Water Babies, The, C. Kingsley
Water Gipsies, The, A. P. Herbert
Waverley, Sir W. Scott
Way of All Flesh, The, S. Butler
Way of an Eagle, The, Ethel M. Dell
Way of the Earth, The, Caradoc Evans
Way of the World, The, W. Congreve
Way through the Wood, A, N. Balchin
Way We Live Now, The, A. Trollope
Wayside Comedy, A, R. Kipling
We the Accused, E. Raymond
Weak and the Strong, The, G. Kersh
Wedding Group, The, Elizabeth Taylor
Wee Willie Winkie, R. Kipling
Weir of Hermiston, R. L. Stevenson
Weland's Sword, R. Kipling
Well, The, W. W. Jacobs
Well-Beloved, The, T. Hardy
Well of Loneliness, The, Radclyffe Hall
Well-remembered Voice, A, J. M. Barrie
We're Here, D. Mackail
Wessex Poems, T. Hardy
Wessex Tales, T. Hardy
West Riding Love Story, Phyllis Bentley
Westward Ho!, C. Kingsley
What Every Woman Knows, J. M. Barrie
What Happened, R. Kipling
What Katy Did at School, Susan Coolidge
Wheels of Chance, The, H. G. Wells
When a Man's Single, J. M. Barrie
When First I Dared, W. Mason
When the Nightingale Sang in Berkeley Square, M. Arlen
When the Sleeper Awakes, H. G. Wells
When We Become Men, Naomi Mitchison
When We Were Very Young, A. A. Milne
Where Angels Fear to Tread, E. M. Forster
Where their Fire is not Quenched, May Sinclair
While the Sun Shines, T. Rattigan
Whirligigs, O. Henry
Whistling Chambermaid, The, Naomi Royde-Smith
Whistling Thief, The, Katherine Tynan
White Cliffs, The, Alice D. Miller
White Company, The, A. Conan Doyle
White Devil, The, John Webster
White-headed Boy, The, L. Robinson
White Heather, W. Black
White-Jacket, H. Melville
White Monkey, The, J. Galsworthy
White Peacock, The, D. H. Lawrence
White Seal, The, R. Kipling
Whiteoak Brothers, Mazo de la Roche
Whiteoak Chronicles, The, Mazo de la Roche
Whose Body?, Dorothy L. Sayers
Why Billy Went Back, L. Merrick
Wickford Point, J. P. Marquand
Wide Sargasso Sea, Jean Rhys
Wide, Wide World, The, Elizabeth Wetherell
Widow, The, Francis King
Widow's Cruise, The, Nicholas Blake
Widowers' Houses, G. B. Shaw
Wife of Sir Isaac Harman, The, H. G. Wells
Will, The, J. M. Barrie

Will ye go to the Hielands?, R. Burns
William the Conqueror, R. Kipling
William Wilson, E. A. Poe
Wind in the Willows, The, K. Grahame
Winding Stair, The, A. E. W. Mason
Window in Thrums, A, J. M. Barrie
Winds of Chance, The, S. K. Hocking
Windsor Castle, W. H. Ainsworth
Winesburg, Ohio, Sherwood Anderson
Winged Hats, The, R. Kipling
Wings of the Dove, The, H. James
Winner, The, R. H. Mottram
Winnie the Pooh, A. A. Milne
Winslow Boy, The, T. Rattigan
Winter's Tale, A, W. Shakespeare
Winters and the Palmleys, The, T. Hardy
Winterset, Maxwell Anderson
Wireless, R. Kipling
Wisdom of Father Brown, The, G. K. Chesterton
Wise Blood, Flannery O'Connor
Wish House, The, R. Kipling
Wisteria Lodge, A. Conan Doyle
With Edged Tools, H. Seton Merriman
With Scindia to Delhi, R. Kipling
With the Main Guard, R. Kipling
With the Night Mail, R. Kipling
Withered Arm, The, T. Hardy
Without Benefit of Clergy, R. Kipling
Without My Cloak, Kate O'Brien
Wives and Daughters, Mrs Gaskell
Wolf Solent, J. C. Powys
Wolves and the Lamb, The, W. M. Thackeray
Woman in his Life, The, R. Kipling
Woman in White, The, W. Collins
Woman is a Weathercock, A, N. Field
Woman Thou Gavest Me, The, Hall Caine
Woman Who Did, The, Grant Allen
Woman who Sowed Iniquity, The, Caradoc Evans
Woman with the Fan, The, R. S. Hichens
Women in Love, D. H. Lawrence
Wonder, The, Mrs Susanna Centlivre
Wonderful History of Titus and Gisippus, The, Sir T. Elyot
Wonderful Visit, The, H. G. Wells
Woodcarver of 'Lympus, The, Mary E. Waller
Woodlanders, The, T. Hardy
Woodstock, Sir W. Scott
World Enough and Time, R. P. Warren
World in the Evening, The, C. Isherwood
World My Wilderness, The, Rose Macaulay
World Set Free, The, H. G. Wells
Would-be-Goods, The, E. Nesbit
Wressley of the Foreign Office, R. Kipling
Wrong Box, The, R. L. Stevenson & L. Osbourne
Wrong Thing, The, R. Kipling
Wuthering Heights, Emily Brontë

Y

Yearling, The, Marjorie K. Rawlings
Years, The, Virginia Woolf
Yellow Face, The, A. Conan Doyle
Yellow Sands, E. & A. Phillpotts
Yellow Scarf, The, T. Burke
Yellowplush Papers, W. M. Thackeray
Yeomen of the Guard, The, Gilbert & Sullivan
Yoked with an Unbeliever, R. Kipling
You Can't Go Home Again, T. Wolfe
You Never Can Tell, G. B. Shaw
You See—, Phyllis Bentley
Young Emmanuel, Naomi Jacob
Young Idea, The, N. Coward
Young in Heart, The, I. A. R. Wylie
Young Men are Coming, The, M. P. Shiel
Young Men at the Manor, R. Kipling
Young Visiters, The, Daisy Ashford
Young Woodley, J. van Druten

Z

Zanoni, Lord Lytton
Zenobia's Infidelity, H. C. Bunner
Ziska, Marie Corelli
Zuleika, A. O'Shaughnessy
Zuleika Dobson, Max Beerbohm

·007, R. Kipling